D1621358

Enlightened Planning

Strategy, risk management and project management are often considered separately by those applying their principles – but at their most effective, all are dependent on each other for success. *Enlightened Planning* teaches this holistic perspective and demonstrates how a synthesis of these approaches yields far greater opportunities. A strategic, calculated risk, for example, can be less inherently risky than chronic risk aversion over time.

Here, a respected specialist and teacher demonstrates how to become an 'enlightened planner', one who is aware of project, strategy and risk concerns and their potential interplay. Following the core principle of Keep It Simple Systematically, he shows how organised, systematic thought processes can demystify the complexities of decision-making when considering a huge variety of concerns at once.

Supported throughout with real-life cases from the author's considerable experience with commercial organisations, it is also supported by a website containing even more cases and learning and teaching materials. This book is essential reading for any practitioner specialising in risk management, project management or strategy; as well as those teachers or participants in executive programmes.

Chris Chapman is an experienced consultant, the basis of his research as Professor of Management Science at Southampton University. He has published widely on uncertainty, opportunity, and risk management for projects, operations and corporate management. He is a past President of the Operational Research Society.

Enlightened Planning

Using Systematic Simplicity to Clarify
Opportunity, Risk and Uncertainty for
Much Better Management Decision Making

Chris Chapman

Routledge
Taylor & Francis Group

LONDON AND NEW YORK

First published 2020
by Routledge
2 Park Square, Milton Park, Abingdon, Oxon OX14 4RN

and by Routledge
52 Vanderbilt Avenue, New York, NY 10017

Routledge is an imprint of the Taylor & Francis Group, an informa business

British Library Cataloguing-in-Publication Data
A catalogue record for this book is available from the British Library

Library of Congress Cataloging-in-Publication Data
A catalog record for this book has been requested

ISBN: 978-1-138-35352-7 (hbk)
ISBN: 978-0-429-42539-4 (ebk)

Typeset in Galliard
by Apex CoVantage, LLC

MIX
Paper from
responsible sources
FSC www.fsc.org   FSC™ C013985

Printed in the United Kingdom
by Henry Ling Limited

To Jean

Contents

PART 3
Further synthesising and reflecting   579

Foreword by Stephen Ward

We all engage in planning. As individuals much of our planning is of a tacit, informal nature, but for managers there is an expectation, even a requirement, that planning will be a more formalised process, with clear rationale and objectives requiring the cooperation of various other parties. However, this clarity can be difficult to achieve, not least because complexity, uncertainty, and risk must be confronted, whatever the context. Appreciating and planning appropriately for the implications of complexity, uncertainty, and risk associated with different possible courses of action are major challenges.

Whatever the enterprise, some degree of planning is necessary to achieve desired outcomes, and large projects require a great deal of planning. But common experience shows that plans frequently require major modification, become thwarted, or fall short of achieving desired outcomes, usually because of factors that were not considered sufficiently during the process of planning.

In this book, Chris Chapman explains how we can do much better by adopting an 'enlightened planning' approach that systematically addresses complexity, uncertainty and risk that really matters, together with a creative search for opportunities. The concept of 'enlightened planning' involves a coherent synthesis of a rich variety of concepts and analytical tools that can be used directly in a wide range of contexts.

As a practical matter, all planning and attendant decision making must make simplifying assumptions about reality. Unfortunately, managers, particularly hard-pressed ones, often seem to be attracted to simplistic approaches that limit the scope of analysis and result in important features of a planning context being ignored.

A very common example is a preference for estimates of key contextual variables that consist of unrealistically narrow ranges of possible values, or even just single value (point) estimates. Simplistic estimates of this kind can seriously compromise the credibility and usefulness of plans.

Another example is the common practice of using probability-impact grids to characterise sources of risk, with attendant simplistic assumptions that all sources of risk are derived only from a set of events that may or may not occur and that events are assumed to be independent of one another. This practice severely restricts recognition of important aspects of uncertainty that drive risk, including knock-on effects of one event on another.

How to keep things appropriately simple in any planning process requires careful thought. Rather than uncritical use of simplistic approaches, enlightened planning calls for intelligent and critical use of simplifying assumptions in scoping planning effort that facilitates the exploration of key issues and related uncertainty that really matters. What are these key issues? They include deciding what factors to take into account, the potential for dynamic interactions among factors, understanding the goals of all relevant stakeholders, the ambiguous nature of some goals, potential trade-offs between goals, how far ahead to plan, and how much detail to go into. Uncertainty and risk are associated not only with such features of the planning context but also with the planning process itself.

A particularly valuable feature of this book is its focus on practice, employing detailed case studies (tales), derived from Professor Chapman's extensive consulting experience in a wide range of planning contexts. Each of the tales in Part 2 illustrates aspects of enlightened planning, describing how recognition and understanding of key issues and what to do about them develops as protagonists progress their analysis and thinking. Each of these tales is set in a particular context, but the approaches described are readily transferrable to other organisation contexts. All the issues addressed are of strategic importance to operations management, project management, and corporate management. Most ought to be of concern at board level to ensure effective governance of planning processes, and leadership of enlightened planning.

This book is the culmination of decades of reflection about what best practice planning and decision making under uncertainty should look like. Potential readers should on no account be deterred by the length of this book, or of individual chapters. For, make no mistake, this book represents a major opportunity for all managers, and their advisors, to substantially enhance organisational performance through enlightened planning.

Stephen Ward is Emeritus Professor in Management,
Southampton Business School, University of Southampton

Comments by other colleagues

Matthew Leitch is a consultant, author, business school educator and risk standards committee member whose website is www.WorkingInUncertainty.co.uk

Enlightened Planning is not just a book about how to manage risk on projects or in business planning, but if you need a book on those topics then this is an excellent choice. It does two things that are important steps forward. First, it includes a management process explicitly designed to incorporate a wide range of appropriate methods. This is not just a process which boils down to a list of risks and a procedure for doing things with them. Instead, it encourages consideration of a much wider range of techniques from operations research modelling down to quick estimates. This kind of flexibility is a frequent aspiration for risk management publications, but in this book, Chapman successfully achieves it. Second, the book focuses on how to choose the right management technique at the right time to get the best combination of clarity and economy. It explicitly tackles something most busy managers can feel all the time, which is a drive to know and understand more, frustrated by a lack of time and an opportunity to do so.

The book is extensively illustrated with detailed practical examples from real life, including calculations and charts. The rich conceptual content and practical detail mean this is not a book you can read over a weekend. But tackled patiently, a section at a time, over a period, it will make most intelligent managers into better managers.

Paul Thornton was a founder and Managing Partner at The French Thornton Partnership. He is past President of the Management Consultancies Association and the Operational Research Society.

French Thornton was a programme management consultancy that led numerous well-known initiatives in the financial, transport, and retail logistics sectors, and my earlier management consultancy career involved a wide range of clients. As a lifelong management consultant, I focused on helping organisations to achieve lasting, beneficial change. Because I came from an operational research background, my instincts were to adopt a modelling approach to whatever problems we were confronted with. If standard models didn't adequately represent the real-life complexities of the situation, then develop and extend them until they did was the basic idea. This approach risked getting bogged down in endless cycles of model development and redevelopment. However, the main alternative (and the one often favoured by macho managers) was to assert that the problem was really a simple one and to solve that problem irrespective of how much genuine complexity was being brushed under the carpet.

I first became aware of Chris Chapman's work in the 1980s, and we got to know each other in the early 1990s when he succeeded me as president of the Operational Research

Society. Chris was providing long-term support to major corporations and utilities on projects that flew under the 'risk management' banner, many of them concerned with huge capital investment programmes. Drawing on these multiyear consulting engagements, and his extensive research work, Chris has now codified significant subsequent evolution of his approach, which is set out fully for the first time in this new 'enlightened planning' book.

A key aspect of this new book's approach is that much of the real-world complexity is addressed by thoughtfully tailoring the overall planning process to accommodate the cultural stresses and strains within the enterprise. This frequently facilitates the use of very simple conceptual and operational tools that build on sophisticated underlying conceptual and operational tools. 'Systematic simplicity' is an excellent description for this approach. For example, as discussed in Chapter 6, simple but effective quantitative probabilistic analysis can be used when assessing competitor behaviour in a bidding context based on work Chris did with IBM UK and earlier work with BP International, but qualitative cultural issues also need attention, like a corporate understanding of the difference between good luck and good management, bad luck and bad management, and why people taking more risk and knowing what they are doing can be crucial to organisational survival, explored in detail in Chapter 3.

I also like the 'systematic simplicity' approaches to cultural concerns, including sound ethics. For example, Figure 11.1 in the last chapter uses a 'red face test' notion Chris attributes to me, but what I particularly like is the way this simple ethical test is linked to more general 'frowns test' and 'smiles test' variants, driven by a systematic approach to important concerns which are not amenable to simple metrics but need simple systematic attention. Examples used earlier in the book in the IBM based bidding example in Chapter 6 include staff being needed if the bid is won who are already heavily committed to other crucial contracts (a 'frown') and a bid in a new area of business the company doing the bidding wants to develop expertise for with a view to future business (a 'smile'). Railway safety as addressed in Chapter 9 raises more complex ethical issues involving trade-offs among monetary costs, avoided fatalities, and avoided injuries, and these ethical issues are crucial and current in a wide range of important contexts.

Professor Jeffrey K. Pinto, Black Chair in Technology Management, Penn State University, USA.

Creating and managing knowledge as it applies to project management has, at times, taken on the nature of a Sisyphean labour. At an age when project-based work has grown ever more common and projects of the broadest array – infrastructure, information systems, new technology and services development – represent real opportunities to advance the human condition, our understanding of how best to manage them for maximum value often remains mired in misapplication, flawed thinking, and a variety of personal and organisational biases. In short, the dichotomy is real and it is growing: between, on one hand, the increased need for organisational undertakings best supported by projects and project management and, on the other, the seemingly intractable challenges in advancing our knowledge base sufficiently to gain best use from our efforts. The data support this contradiction: the Project Management Institute reports that for every billion US dollars invested in projects, some 125 million USD is classified 'at risk', a figure that is actually growing at double digits year-on year on year. Failure rates in information technology projects are high and have remained depressingly stable for well over a decade. The data are clear: the need for projects is at an all-time high while the manner in which practitioners and academics alike deliver on this promise remains mired.

It is against this backdrop: a time for projects that is both highly exciting in its possibilities and rather sterner in its realisation, that Professor Chris Chapman's book is so welcome. The underlying premise of his work (and it is a message that is born out again and again in projects great and small alike) focuses on the nature of project front-end planning and offers a deceptively simple message regarding what we keep getting wrong with these processes – we continue to make the simple difficult while making the difficult seem seductively simple. Professor Chapman has been one of the leading theorists and original, holistic thinkers in the project management discipline for several decades now. In *Enlightened Planning*, he brings his considerable talents to bear in a work that is compelling and powerful. It offers a new way of viewing the project planning process: one that directly considers the ways in which our organisations, culture, and processes can interact to get planning done the right way. Equally welcome is the manner in which Professor Chapman illustrates these ideas, through a series of compelling case examples that show in practice the principles he espouses. I have a strong admiration for this book. Terms like 'strategic clarity', 'enlightened planning', and 'systematic simplicity' are certain to become more than talking points; they offer the means to reorient our thinking. They cut right to the heart of what we need to be doing to put into practice effective project planning approaches. The framework provided also links this thinking directly to planning for operations management and corporate strategy formation concerns which are directly interrelated in important ways. The final result is a thought-provoking and important work for practitioners and scholars alike.

Professor Terry Williams *is Director of the Risk Institute, University of Hull, UK.*

As Professor and Head of the Management Science Department at Strathclyde University and Professor and then Director of the Management School of the University of Southampton before coming to Hull, I have been aware of the work Chris was doing for many years. I invited him to be a key speaker at a NATO Science Programme conference in Kiev in 1996, used *Project Risk Management* (Chapman and Ward, 1997) in my book *Modelling Complex Projects* (Williams, 2002), which shares his (and my) 'practitioner who is also an academic' perspective, and invited him to contribute a chapter to my book *Project Governance: Getting Investment Right* (Williams and Samset, 2012). His new *Enlightened Planning* book provides a reflective synthesis of his earlier work plus a comprehensive set of important new conceptual and operational tools with significant implications.

An irony of the risk management field is that it has become prone to the risk of standardised ways of considering and quantifying risk. The paper 'Organising Risk: Discourse, Power, and "Riskification"' (Hardy and Macquire, 2016) in the *Academy of Management Review* has shown how organisations and 'experts' in risk have developed a dominant discourse which limits the way we think about risk. What the field urgently needs is thinking that takes us to the basics of what risk and uncertainty are, and looks at them in a fresh way. This book is indeed such thinking, introducing important new fundamental concepts such as 'clarity efficiency' and the 'estimation-efficiency spectrum' (although keeping some well-used ideas from previous books such as the 'seven Ws'). Pleasingly, it aims to provide good estimates rather than the simple assumption of bias and the application of standardised contingency factors, often done following Flyvbjerg's work. Having edited a couple of books about planning projects with scant information, this book would have given us a really useful structure on which to consider the ideas with which we had to grapple, and I hope its ideas are taken up by practitioners, academics, and the various bodies of knowledge.

***Stephen Cresswell** practices as Into Risk Ltd, London UK, www.intorisk.com.*

I have been an independent consultant for a decade, building on an earlier decade of experience, initially in business development in the IT and Telecoms industry, then as a project management consultant with Bombardier Transportation and the Sweett Group. My growing interest in risk and uncertainty led me to Chris's publications in the early 2000s, and I took part in his 2006 International Project Management Association 'Managing Project Risk & Uncertainty in New Ways' Advanced Training Course in Copenhagen. This course and subsequent reading of his publications have been a key influence in my development as a 'reflective practitioner' – with many of the methodologies and approaches being applied, with success and benefit, in my client assignments. Particularly important was an appreciation of how to get beyond seeing 'risk' in terms of independent events, treat interdependencies effectively, and meet the challenges involved in persuading clients' personnel conditioned by simplistic approaches to change their approaches.

The 'enlightened planning' perspective explored in this new book involves deep thinking about strategy, uncertainty, complexity, and implementation, with considerable attention to perspective and some philosophical aspects. However, this new book is also rich in simple tools and practical concepts and mantras that help with the 'how to do it' and 'craftsmanship' associated with planning and analysis in new ways. I fully anticipate using all aspects when faced with challenging problems. My favourite new concept is 'closure with completeness'. The basic underlying ideas have always been there in the approaches Chris has advocated, but they are now brought together, made explicit, and named. Closure with completeness gives a very concise plain English label and rationale for the inclusion of items such as an 'allowance for unidentified risk' in a project cost estimate. It also naturally prompts people to question whether the analysis addresses everything relevant.

This new book builds on a consolidation of an extensive research and consulting career, drawing on both successful applications of new ideas and some lessons learned the hard way. Reading this book from beginning to end was a serious challenge, but I expect to get large return on the time invested.

***Mike Annon**, PMP, is Owner of I&C Engineering Associates, Waterford CT, USA.*

My 45 years of experience with more than 50 nuclear energy and fossil-fuelled power plant facilities in managerial and management consulting roles has convinced me that most organisations believe they know how to plan. However, too frequently they need to 'rescue' their plans at considerable cost, with serious associated delays, because their initial planning efforts were incomplete. Since the 1980s I have published, led workshops and managed projects with a focus on the processes, other tools, and teamwork needed to 'get started on the right foot' and to rescue projects which failed to do so.

After I attended a 2009 professional training course in Chicago led by Chris based on the second edition of his book *Project Risk Management* (Chapman and Ward, 2003), I started to embed many of his ideas about new ways of looking at 'uncertainty', 'risk' and 'opportunity' in my work with clients. Contributing feedback comments on his book *How to Manage Project Opportunity and Risk* (Chapman and Ward, 2011) helped me to extend and update these ideas. His new *Enlightened Planning* book has a wide range of further new ideas which will be incorporated into my planning efforts with future clients. I particularly like his new book's approach to visualising what I would term 'beginning with the end in mind', explicitly linking the assumed project lifecycle framework plus the 'seven Ws' framework and a 'goals–plans framework' to the project planning phase structure framework which integrates these four key frameworks. It helps with the front end of project management, and with integrating operations management and corporate management team concerns, to facilitate delivering what both the project owners and the project's ultimate 'customer' actually want by asking them the right questions at the right time and engaging in the right kind of dialogue.

Rodney Turner is now retired. Most recently he was Professor of Project Management at SKEMA Business School, in Lille, France, where he was Scientific Director for the PhD in Project and Program Management. Rodney is Vice President, Honorary Fellow and former Chairman of the UK's Association for Project Management, and Honorary Fellow and former President and Chairman of the International Project Management Association.

Consider a trio of quotations:

> *No battle plan ever survives first contact with the enemy.*
> – Field Marshal Helmuth von Moltke

> *In preparing for battle I have always found that plans are useless, but planning is indispensable.*
> – General Dwight D. Eisenhower

> *The perfect is the enemy of the good. By this I mean that a good plan violently executed now is better than a perfect plan next week. War is a very simple thing, and the determining characteristics are self-confidence, speed, and audacity. None of these things can ever be perfect, but they can be good.*
> – General George S. Patton

The quotation by Field Marshal von Moltke can suggest there is no point planning because the plans will be wrong. But President Eisenhower, while agreeing that the battle will not evolve as the plans envisage, suggests that the process of planning is essential because it creates a strategy for the battle, and though the battle will not evolve as the plan envisages, having done the planning, we can understand what the likely scenarios are and respond to the scenarios that occur. General Patton takes a slightly different approach. He starts by quoting Voltaire and says we should not aim for the perfect plan because we will already have lost the battle. But we should aim for a good plan, one of the defining characteristics of what Chris Chapman refers to as 'systematic simplicity'.

Henry Simon, in his concept of bounded rationality, agrees with these sentiments with ideas also supportive of a systematic-simplicity approach. We can never make a perfect decision, because we do not have all the information we need, we cannot perfectly analyse all the information we do have, and most important of all, we cannot foretell the future, so we do not know precisely how things will evolve. Therefore, we need to make good decisions, ones that satisfice, and not strive for perfect decisions.

Chris Chapman, in this unique book, explores how we can plan effectively in this uncertain environment. In Chapter 2 he introduces a universal planning and complexity management process that outlines how we can be better able to respond as plans unfold. This process is based on 'systematic simplicity' with the aim of providing good plans based on a sound interpretation of the data plus wider possibilities. In Chapter 3 he introduces a range of approaches to uncertainty using this process – the plan will not evolve precisely as envisaged, and we can't predict the future, but we can make forecasts within sensible ranges and plan effectively for likely scenarios. Chapters 4 to 7 further explain the use of these systematic simplicity ideas in project management areas where Chris has an established international reputation and related operations management areas. Chapter 8 addresses strategy formation and corporate planning, and Chapter 9 expands further when low probability but very high impact scenarios may be involved when planning for the likely and unlikely scenarios, understanding the possible range of outcomes, and developing robust plans that are appropriately prudent.

This book will be invaluable to anyone involved in strategic planning or corporate decision making as well as those interested in project planning.

Martin Hopkinson is a project risk professional and author based in Winchester, UK.

With the advent of computerised tools, our business and project planning processes have evolved to demand ever increasing levels of breakdown and detail. This book identifies why this approach has become less enlightened than we might think. For example, projects often maintain schedules with thousands of activities, employing a team of planners to keep abreast of the myriad of changes as they occur. Chris Chapman describes how these projects could improve their estimates, make better decisions and foster a progressive planning culture by limiting the number of activities to 75 or fewer. His approach involves understanding activities, interdependencies and the implications of uncertainty in greater depth. It is underpinned by a welcomed clarity about the assumptions that we make when planning, often without noticing.

The book is illustrated with practical examples drawn from the author's long experience of working with businesses and government departments in wide range of different industries and countries. If you deploy only some of the tools and techniques that are described, it is difficult to see how your planning process cannot become more enlightened.

Jesper Schreiner, Managing Director, Danish Project Management Association.

I attended the Copenhagen IPMA (International Project Management Association) advanced training programme on Project Risk Management provided by Chris in 2012, subsequently used his ideas as a practitioner and as a teaching consultant, and contributed a two hour session to his 2017 IPMA programme as a Visiting Speaker, discussing my experience putting his ideas into practice with clients, so I was familiar with his overall approach when reading his new 'enlightened planning' book.

What I particularly like about this new book is the way Chapter 1 clarifies key basic concepts like the relationship between opportunity, risk, uncertainty and underlying complexity, and Chapter 3 then clarifies the relationship between all the components of his 'opportunity efficiency' concept, using practical examples based on his work with BP, IBM UK, the UK Ministry of Defense and other clients.

I also like the Chapter 7 ideas which are new to me – in particular, breaking down the current practice silos within project management among risk management, estimating and other aspects of planning.

I find the new *Enlightened Planning* book – and the embedded mindset of systematic simplicity – a very useful contemporary contribution to a better understanding of the fundamental complexity often encountered in the handling and the clarifying of risk and opportunities for better management decision making.

Dr Dale F Cooper, Director, Broadleaf Capital International, www.Broadleaf.com.au

Chris Chapman has written an important but challenging book. It is important because it addresses matters central to most organisations: how to make important decisions when confronted by significant uncertainty. I shall return to the challenges later.

This book describes two journeys. The first is the one we readers are invited to join, an intellectual exploration as concepts are developed from relatively simple matters through to ideas that seem deceptively simple at first but are embedded in a subtle matrix of nuance that requires profound understanding and interpretation. The second is Chris Chapman's own journey along roughly the same route but with many of the bumps and wrinkles smoothed out to make the lives of his readers easier. This second journey, interwoven through the first, provides the justification for the steps along the way. It explains the practical circumstances in which the main concepts were developed, with case studies from some of Chris's large clients emphasising the significant practical value and the substantial benefits that can be obtained for modest investments of time and effort.

Here I must declare an interest. I joined Chris at the University of Southampton in 1978. With a background in operational research and mathematical modelling, an understanding of psychology and a fascination with decision-making, I was drawn quickly into risk management with Chris. Our first work together was with Acres, examining the reliability of an LNG facility proposed for the high Arctic, using software Chris had developed with BP and adapted by us for the specific reliability context, combined with semi-Markov analysis that seemed innovative at the time. We went on to work together on other large projects: hydroelectric developments in Alaska and northern Alberta, upstream oil and gas off Newfoundland and oil and gas pipeline transport in Alaska, some of which are described in this book. Although our paths have diverged geographically since then, and we often use slightly different words to describe similar things, the approaches I learned from Chris, and those we developed together, are still central to my own international risk management practice.

In particular, my risk management work has always had a strong focus on practical value, on how risk management can be used to support better decisions, with a clear recognition that analysis by itself is not sufficient. This is echoed strongly in this book: uncertainty must be analysed but only so far as is necessary to add value and make a sound decision, one that can be explained and justified clearly to stakeholders. Enlightened planning, as described by Chris in this book, provides a window into how this might be achieved.

Some of the core concepts in this book that I still use regularly (albeit sometimes using different words) are risk efficiency and opportunity efficiency, diagrams like histogram and activity trees that explore and explain important uncertainties and their interrelationships, graphs that demonstrate key sensitivities and their practical implications, and illustrations of the differences between options so decision makers can evaluate outcomes outside the constraints of simplistic one-dimensional metrics.

Another important concept that resonates strongly with me and my colleagues at Broadleaf is that developing an understanding of the structure of uncertainty is an unequivocally necessary precursor to quantification. We have seen far too many examples of quantitative models where understanding was clearly lacking and the outcomes were at best misleading, often technically incorrect and at worst fatally flawed.

A core concept that Chris develops is clarity efficiency. This reflects the notion that there should be a balance between the amount of effort that is devoted to exploring important decisions (with the context and uncertainty that surrounds them) and the understanding that is generated for those who must make those decisions. Making such trade-offs is a critical part of enlightened planning, just as it is of risk management as we practise it.

This brings me back to the challenging aspect of this book – you need to read it carefully and with close attention to detail to form the necessary understanding and to get the most from it. There is no 'magic formula' that you can extract and apply in a few minutes. The answer does not leap off the page but must be absorbed as concepts are developed along the path described here. You must follow the path, without shortcuts, to gain the enlightenment that Chris offers. Your understanding will almost certainly be different in detail from Chris's or mine, but the effort you apply will be well worthwhile.

Michael Pidd *is Professor Emeritus of Management Science in the Lancaster University Management School. He is Past President of the Operational Research Society, Fellow of the British Academy of Management, and Fellow of the Academy of Social Sciences.*

Systematic simplicity, via enlightened planning, is the main theme of this welcome book from Chris Chapman. Why is it welcome? Stories of large projects that exceed their initial cost estimates or fail altogether are easy to find in the media. It's easy to criticise, but much harder to show all relevant parties how things could be done better. Introducing significant change in an organisation is never easy. Why is it never easy? Because any major corporate change requires a response that links and integrates operations management, project management and corporate management. Successfully managing such changes is particularly difficult.

Chris addresses this complex challenge using a very broadly grounded 'enlightened planning' approach based on many years as a professor and international consultant. The scope of the material covered, the broad intended audience, and the demonstration of important nuances involved in practice are discussed using case studies, which explore qualitative as well as qualitative concerns.

As Chris Chapman puts it, 'there are no silver bullets, but some approaches are much better than others'. Operational Research and Management Science are sometimes defined as 'the science of better'. This fits well the book's advocacy of a 'systematic simplicity' approach based on rigorous analysis and practical insights.

Preface

'Enlightened planning' provides an operational basis for an effective and efficient approach to developing a shared understanding of all relevant uncertainty and underlying complexity in order to grasp the key opportunities and avoid inappropriate risk when addressing all aspects of an organisation's management decision making in a holistic manner. *Much better* management decision making than most current 'good practice' is the overall goal, a step-change improvement. Even if 'very good practice' is the current norm, demonstrating that this is the case is a planned by-product of an enlightened planning approach and a good reason for organisations formally embracing a variant of the approach explored in this book.

Enlightened planning in an 'operations management' context may include bottom-up corporate strategic planning driven by operations management concerns. Enlightened planning in a 'project management' context may include bottom-up corporate strategic plan ning driven by project management and interdependent operations management concerns. Enlightened planning in a 'corporate management' context should include top-down corporate strategic planning, its integration with bottom-up corporate strategic planning, corporate governance, and planning for all other corporate tasks which are not seen as part of operations management or project management.

In all contexts using an enlightened planning approach implies some uncertainty usually needs immediate attention in strategic terms, and ongoing attention to strategy and tactics as operations, project and corporate plans evolve will raise new management decision-making concerns. Interdependencies between operations, project and corporate planning are often important. The underlying goals of all relevant parties are always central, and the ambiguous nature of some goals plus the need to consider important trade-offs between goals which may be complex can be crucial issues.

The focus of this book is 'commercial organisations' broadly defined, but both the scope of the key tools and the origins of many of the underlying concepts are much wider.

A paper by Warren Black (Black, 2017), with the title *Originals: How Non-conformists Will Ultimately Disrupt the World of Risk Management*, inspired by Adam Grant's 2016 *New York Times* best-selling book *Originals, How Non-conformists Move the World*, argues that my work with Stephen Ward on 'uncertainty management' makes us 'risk originals' who will disrupt the world of 'risk management'. Black's paper places us in the same category as the behavioural economist Daniel Kahneman, a Nobel Prize winner and the best-selling author of *Thinking, Fast and Slow* (Kahneman, 2012). Black's flattering assessment of my work with Stephen Ward involves a focus on features which we would not emphasise as much as alternative features because our agenda is much wider than mainstream 'risk management', and any comparison of this kind cannot be taken too far. However, there are features of our 'enlightened planning' approach to uncertainty management which have links to Black's paper worth exploring briefly in this Preface and the following Overview as part of the process of explaining what this book is about and how its approach is different, with a view to tempting you to read it whatever your background, perspective, and concerns.

Subjective biases are central to Kahneman's work, a psychologist by background who is widely viewed as one of the leading founders of behavioural economics. The acronym 'KISS' is an illustration of a common bias towards ideas which are 'simplistic' in a pejorative sense when it is associated with the common interpretation 'keep it simple, stupid'. This common interpretation of KISS implies that how to keep it simple is obvious, even if you are stupid, requiring very little systematic and intelligent thought, demonstrably not the case. Overcoming this common bias towards simplistic approaches to all an organisation's management decision making is a central goal of this book. A very different reinterpretation of KISS, 'keep it simple systematically', is a core mantra of the enlightened planning approach. The key aspirations are facilitating opportunities to simplify in the 'right way' while avoiding risks associated with simplifying in the 'wrong way', using systematic processes which are well founded and make good use of intelligence and creativity to deliver effective and efficient management decision making. Associated goals are seeking approximately correct answers to the right questions in the right timeframe, which all those involved can trust, based upon appropriately shared clarity about the rationale. Associated concerns are avoiding precise answers to the wrong questions, answers that take too long, or answers which generate a lack of trust. Seeking simplicity in this enlightened manner, avoiding simplistic approaches which simplify in the wrong way, is a basic characteristic of all the approaches discussed in this book.

Addressing all relevant planning concerns from the perspective of this enlightened planning approach is challenging. One reason is the framing assumptions must be as broad as possible, by design, with clarity about the implications of *all* working assumptions. There are no 'silver bullets' – and no 'golden' or 'magic' variants. However, some conceptual frameworks plus closely coupled operational toolsets are *much better* than others, and the implications of using the best available approaches drawing on a synthesis of 'best practice' from all relevant management practice and underlying useful theory can be 'game-changing', not just a marginal improvement.

Successful enlightened planning depends on the capability and culture of those involved. At the heart of success is a nuanced and well-founded corporate understanding of 'what needs to be done' in all relevant contexts – 'strategic clarity'. Organisations that have strategic clarity and can deploy dependable teams that have the tactical clarity to know which tools to use and how to use them with an effective understanding of the interdependencies between operations, project and corporate management decisions enjoy an important corporate capability. In a competitive context this capability is a crucial competitive advantage.

The gist of what this book is about is enhancing your personal understanding of 'what needs to be done' for organisations to achieve strategic clarity. However, to understand what needs to be done, some aspects of 'how to do it' require an overview understanding. The central core of this book is using illustrations drawn from practice to illustrate what needs to be done *plus* the requisite overview understanding of how to do it in selected example contexts. Strategic clarity plus the requisite tactical clarity in these example contexts will provide you with a basis for facilitating ongoing development of operational forms of strategic and tactical clarity for all the contexts of interest to you.

A key foundation level tool this book explores is clarity about the most general set of framing assumptions and habitual working assumptions to employ to achieve clarity about the best full set of working assumptions for any given context. You can integrate the understanding this provides with your current understanding and build on it in the long-term. But an immediate pay-off also provided is a closely coupled toolset of conceptual and operational tools which can be used directly and immediately.

'Systematic simplicity' is the term adopted by this book to characterise all variants of an enlightened planning approach which involve different people and different organisations adopting their own particular versions of enlightened planning conceptual and operational tools to best suit their context. The only constraint is a comparable set of shared basic foundation framing assumptions which ensure that effective and efficient communication is feasible. Terminology is an important component of all framing assumption sets, because the way basic concepts and operational tools are perceived depends upon communication.

Enlightened planning is my current understanding of what systematic simplicity ought to involve, described using terminology which provides a basis for communication which is as simple and unambiguous but usefully nuanced as I could make it. The term 'systematic simplicity' will be used sparingly in this book, and it can be viewed as a complex composite concept which is not formally defined until the end of Chapter 1. However, a key characteristic of enlightened planning is the form of adaptability highlighted by the basic nature and purpose of the systematic simplicity concept as just explained. That is the rationale for using the term 'systematic simplicity' in the subtitle of this book and explaining its basic role in this Preface.

Target readers at an overview level share several important common attributes, but the key one is most of them already are, or they would like to become, effective 'reflective practitioners' who are interested in systematic approaches to keeping planning and associated management decision making simple, and even the exceptions would like more clarity about what being an effective reflective practitioner and using systematic approaches to keeping it simple ought to imply. Management decision making which is effective and efficient in a 'best practice' sense depends on effective reflective practitioners, and this book is about best practice in a sense experienced 'reflective practitioners' should be comfortable with.

A closely coupled key characteristic of the target audience is a broad range of backgrounds in terms of education and experience – this book makes no specialist knowledge assumptions, and it makes minimal general background knowledge assumptions. This was deemed essential because providing an understanding of planning which is as broadly accessible as possible is an essential feature of an enlightened planning approach.

Background knowledge in specialist areas is not required, and general background assumptions are minimal, but what is required is a significant interest in sustained exploration of new perspectives, toolsets and mindsets, plus a tolerance for some very carefully pruned but still extensive how to do it material which needs broad understanding in order to appreciate what needs to be done with strategic clarity.

This book assumes that some target readers will have no mathematical or statistical background beyond their secondary education and a limited interest in mathematically based concepts, other target readers will be highly mathematically inclined and have a very strong formal training in mathematics and statistics, but most will occupy the middle ground. All target readers need an overview understanding of some mathematical and statistical concepts in what needs to be done terms. This common overview understanding is provided using two frameworks via strategies introduced in Part 1 using an approach all target readers should be comfortable with and find useful.

A central challenge which writing this book had to confront directly was avoiding unhelpful detail while systematically clarifying key how to do it concepts in sufficient depth for all target readers. As part of meeting this challenge, for some purposes target readers were characterised in four groups: directors, experts, students and other target readers. The purpose of this decomposition was keeping it simple when considering the key implications of different perspectives and concerns. The next few pages provide initial advice for each specific target reader group. The focus is directly relevant advice for that group which should also be of interest to all other target reader groups. You may be in more than one group.

Directors means all those in executive and non-executive director roles in private sector commercial organisations plus their equivalents in public sector organisations. 'Commercial organisations' in this book means 'providing services or products to customers at a price'. This involves a very broad interpretation of 'commercial' if we explicitly assume that a service receiver need not be the party paying for the service. Examples used extensively in this book include international oil and gas energy–sector companies, an international computer systems company, a national railway company, a provincial electricity utility, a regional water and sewage utility, and a family-owned company manufacturing lawnmowers. But the relevant spectrum is much broader, with debatable boundaries.

If you associate yourself with directors of commercial organisations in this broad sense, and your experience base includes a reasonably broad exposure to disciplines addressing the sciences, arts and crafts of planning and management more generally, you will already have your own well-developed variant of the 'enlightened planning' frameworks developed in this book. In some respects, your version may be significantly more enlightened than mine, as well as being wider and deeper in the areas of relevance to you. However, this book's approach will probably challenge some reasonably fundamental aspects of your current views in a useful manner. Meeting this challenge should help you to enhance your current 'toolset' of concepts and operational techniques for planning.

A key challenge associated with maintaining your interest is persuading you to tolerate how to do it detail in areas which may not be of direct interest to you in order to clarify what needs to be done. By the end of Chapter 1 you should be starting to see where this book is taking you and why the journey may be useful, but ongoing patience is needed. The rest of Part 1 provides much more clarity. Part 2 tales in Chapters 7, 8 and 9 are all set at board level for major organisations, but Chapter 6 is at marketing manager level for regional sales by an international organisation, Chapter 5 begins with what appears to be a very tactical inventory management issue for a small family-owned manufacturing organisation, and Part 1 needs reading first. I am very aware of good practical reasons why most board level managers are reluctant to read long books, but I hope you will be persuaded by the rest of this Preface, the following Overview, and the earlier comments by my colleagues, to treat this book as an exception.

To develop the holistic what needs to be done framework and the associated strategic clarity which is central to my version of enlightened planning, this book uses an approach involving reasonably close attention to selected aspects of relevant detail which is layered, section by section, and chapter by chapter. In some areas the approaches advocated depart from conventional frameworks in basic ways for reasons which need understanding by anyone with your level of corporate decision-making and governance responsibilities. However, the reasons are not easily explained in advance, and clarity about the implications requires how to do it understanding at an overview level in some key areas.

To begin to encourage you to read further, consider one illustrative example. Risk management of many different kinds has been receiving growing attention in most organisations over many decades. However, there are many popular approaches to risk management which do not address all relevant risk, fail to integrate the management of risk with opportunities, and do not link either to *all* relevant underlying objectives, uncertainty and complexity in an operationally effective manner. These shortcomings mean they are fundamentally flawed and require radical reframing. Some key risk management concepts and operational tools promoted by many 'experts' need to be scrapped. You need to be aware of the key issues, the nature of associated controversy, and what needs to be done about it, with sufficient clarity to deal with experts who disagree. Some of these experts may report to you, and some may serve on the same board or report to other directors. In some cases, widely advocated approaches are doing more harm than good. In some cases, counterproductive approaches are being promoted by professional organisations which need to be directly challenged in an open and public manner which, so far, they have escaped or simply failed to respond to. Chapter 7 addresses why in the context of 'project risk management' in terms all board members need to understand. Preceding chapters prepare some of the ground. Chapter 8 generalises to address some very fundamental board level 'enterprise risk management' (ERM) issues of general concern which are frequently not part of an ERM perspective. Chapter 9 uses a broadly defined ERM perspective to consider approaches to 'safety and security management' which can cope with very low probability but very high-impact incidents, as well as a full range of less serious variants, considering an operations management context with crucial board level corporate strategic planning implications. There are further implications for regulators and governments, and related implications in a wide range of different contexts.

To operate effectively at a director level in governance terms you need an overall understanding of how to do it for opportunity, risk and uncertainty management issues which risk management experts in your organisation applying common practice may have seriously misjudged. If experts have misjudged important risk management issues in your organisation, you need to be aware of what needs to be done about it, even if 'getting it done' is not your responsibility.

There are further organisation-wide how to do it issues which you need to understand at an overview level for strategic clarity about what needs to be done. One example is an answer to the questions, 'What discount rate is appropriate for capital investment decisions, and why?' explained at a level everybody who should be interested in the questions can understand and trust. You need to understand why an 'opportunity cost' or a 'risk premium' component of the discount rate is often a driver of myopic thinking, leading to a focus on high risk 'quick-buck' developments, and the neglect of 'sure-thing' opportunities, the antithesis of what is needed. You may not even need to know 'who to ask who knows how to do it', because that may be the responsibility of another director who will respond to your concerns using his or her access to relevant expertise. However, you need to understand important impacts of inappropriate discount rates in your areas of direct responsibility, as well as the key concepts associated with what needs to be done by others, in order to play the effective overall corporate decision-making and governance roles your position requires.

Throughout this book the treatment of how to do it issues emphasises strategic clarity about what needs to be done using conceptual and operational tools which make framing and working assumptions as easy to clarify and test as possible. The development of this toolset was partly driven by a need to use and explain new decision-making tools at board level when the common practice alternatives had proved unsatisfactory.

You and your fellow directors are key target readers. Without your support everyone else within your organisation is likely to experience ongoing problems trying to implement key features of an enlightened planning approach, unless your organisation experiences an obvious crisis and those reporting to you are able to 'lead from the middle' or replace you. Effective leadership from the top and from the front is always desirable, often crucial.

If you want to apply some of the enlightened planning ideas developed in this book in your organisation, you may need early support from at least one other board level colleague. You may want internal or external short courses to ensure that everyone involved in any necessary corporate change processes understands how to move in the same direction. You may need consultancy support to help make some features operational. A crucial issue before proceeding too far will be ensuring that your organisation has a collaborative team which covers all relevant areas of expertise with the collective skill set and mindset to lead the required change management. This team will have to collectively understand how to get it done in practice as well as what needs to be done and how to do it in principle, including understanding how to 'learn by experience' as progress is made. Initial clarity needs to be 'fit for the purpose', not fully enlightened in terms of long-term aspirational goals.

Experts include directors who are experts, but the focus of the next page or so is those not yet at board level who are experienced managers with line management responsibilities in areas like marketing, supply chain management, production management, project management, safety and security management, corporate strategic management and risk management, plus experienced supporting staff with expertise in any of these areas. This includes consultants, who may be external or internal. You will have your own well-developed views about a variant of my enlightened planning approach which may be significantly better than mine in some areas, as well as being broader and deeper in areas of particular interest to you. However, this book can probably challenge some of your core beliefs in a useful manner, to help you enhance your current toolset and mindset for planning, even if the primary focus of your concerns is not addressed in a direct manner in this book.

Within your areas of expertise the nature of your current planning frameworks may be much richer than most of those with director level concerns. But outside your areas of expertise your planning skills may be much less developed than those with director level concerns. Furthermore, both your perspective and your concerns may be *very* different.

One key difference is that you will find the treatment of your area of expertise lacks some of the how to do it detail you need to 'get it done'. You will need further reading and discussions with colleagues to put some of the principles and operational tools developed in this book into practice in your areas of expertise. Chapter 11 addresses some of these how to do it concerns on an expert area of focus basis but only at a level of detail which is of possible relevance to experts in other areas and other target readers.

The second key difference is that you will encounter many areas of application which may seem well beyond the scope of your current concerns, exacerbating the lack of detail you would like in your areas of focus, and you will lack the overall corporate governance concerns of directors to motivate your interest in these areas. However, you are encouraged to view this potential problem as an opportunity in several important senses. You may be seriously surprised by the usefulness of the widely applicable holistic corporate toolset of 'clarity efficient' approaches and operational tools which involve very little effort and cost in a very wide range of appropriate contexts, including your own. You may also be surprised by the impact on your mindset of an enhanced understanding of the importance of all experts having a shared toolset, plus your potential role in collaborative approaches working across traditional planning silos with other experts in different areas with different professional perspectives.

Consider one example concern which is relevant to all an organisation's experts, plus all directors, students and other target readers – the need for a corporate-wide shared understanding of the nature of uncertainty, including the role of subjective probabilities and underlying complexity. Understanding uncertainty is a much broader concern than understanding risk. For example, the creation and use of all estimates of cost, duration, or other performance measures are directly dependent upon understanding uncertainty. Understanding uncertainty is directly relevant to all experts, and it is also directly relevant to everyone else they interact with. All experts who do not have an effective and well-founded practical understanding of uncertainty need to be challenged by everyone else who does understand uncertainty appropriately, and *nobody* can afford to fail to understand what needs to be done to provide unbiased estimates with an appropriate level of clarity.

Furthermore, the low to high clarity range of approaches explored in 'estimation-efficiency spectrum' terms in Chapter 3 can be generalised to consider a low to high clarity range of both processes and embedded models relevant to any area of expertise, as demonstrated in Part 2. The overall treatment of these concerns in Parts 1, 2, and 3 should provide you with an effective holistic framework for addressing your particular interests and areas of expertise using the systematic approach to simplicity demonstrated by the examples.

A central assumption underlying this book's approach is that you are prepared to work effectively with other experts plus other key parties in a collaborative manner, whatever your area of focus as an expert. To do this you and all those you communicate with need compatible overall conceptual frameworks and a number of common very flexible and portable operational tools. Jointly you can use these shared approaches and tools to move your organisation towards a more coherent enlightened planning perspective. Most organisations need experts who strongly promote coordination and collaboration which involves 'big teams' at several levels. These big teams should not be constrained by traditional professional perspectives, traditional corporate silos, or corporate boundaries. Holistic changes which cannot be limited to your current spheres of interest may be big opportunities for you and your organisation. If you are interested in the nature of the integration and interfaces needing attention, and key aspects of what is sometimes characterised as 'the big picture', you will find the challenges are significant, but successfully meeting them is a very rewarding experience.

You are a key target reader, and you are perhaps the most likely point of entry for enlightened planning approaches in your organisation. Even if the director level managers you report to are highly supportive of an enlightened approach to planning, perhaps because you have initiated and then encouraged the development of your interests jointly, to get things done you will have to 'lead from the middle'. A management team which is led from the top, the middle, and the bottom as and when appropriate, with everyone moving in the same direction, is usually the best way forward.

Students, as a target reader group, includes students on university courses and participants on professional courses, but it also includes all those on an independent learning path of their own design who see themselves as 'a student of systematic approaches to planning and associated management decision making'. All these students are key target readers. For any student, it is important to appreciate that this is not a textbook in the usual sense. However, it can serve as a core text, and it can also complement conventional textbooks. This book can help you to construct an enlightened planning framework of your own design, to build on for the rest of your career. If your exposure to the sciences, arts, and crafts of planning and management more generally is still in a formative stage, a crucial early acquisition is a framework to help you integrate your understanding as you test the validity of conflicting views in the literature and other inconsistent advice against actual outcomes. A coherent framework for acquiring practical experience and testing your accumulating expertise is essential for any effective reflective practitioner, along with a habit of critical reflection on what has been learned so far via a synthesis of different experiences. You need an ongoing interest in addressing the gaps in your understanding which might be filled, with priorities dependent upon current and longer-term responsibilities and interests.

Avoid skimming material in a way which leads to a very superficial understanding of issues that matter in terms of your acquisition of strategic clarity, and do not try dipping into topics out of sequence. Conventional textbooks are often designed to facilitate this approach, but the likelihood of misunderstanding this book is very high if this approach is taken, even by experts or directors. The reason is the layered approach to accumulating understanding because of the interdependencies involved, a key characteristic of this book which you and all other readers need to appreciate to use it effectively.

Assume you will need to read more and work with experts before this book's framework becomes a fully functioning toolset. In an ideal world you would gain experience working with enlightened experts in an organisation led by enlightened directors, but this is not an ideal world. You will have to learn to accommodate the implications as best you can.

You are the experts and directors of the future, if you are not already one or both, and experts and directors are encouraged to see themselves as 'lifelong students', if this is not already the case. 'Reflective managers' who are successful directors and experts are usually lifelong students.

Other target readers as a group includes all those who are not comfortable within at least one of the director, expert and student characterisations just considered, plus anyone else who may be interested in how planning might be enlightened or unenlightened. For example, you might be particularly interested in some of the implications for regulation and associated government policy developed in later chapters, or 'third sector' organisations like charitable trusts, or you might be interested in planning as an aspect of management from an academic perspective which is much less practice-driven and more focused on specific aspects of theory than mine.

You will need to interpret as you see fit when a limited number of suggestions for particular categories of reader are made. No doubt you would have done so without me suggesting this, but I did not want you to feel neglected by a simplistic three group characterisation of target readers.

Overview

In this book 'telling tales' means using examples which are case-based stories which have been retold in a way which makes understanding key messages easier and more memorable.

Tales facilitate understanding by providing practical illustrations of a wide range of broadly applicable complex concepts, like 'risk efficiency'. Broadly applicable concepts like risk efficiency and specific tools like the 'decision diagrams' used to achieve risk efficiency are 'portable' in the sense that they can be used in many very different contexts. However, context always shapes the way conceptual and operational tools are used and the nuances of their interpretation. A practical approach to planning has to accommodate 'context' issues. This book uses 'tales' to deal with a number of context dependency issues.

Part 1 uses a series of short tales. Part 2 use one longer tale per chapter. The rationale is context always needs to be understood when making decisions, and once we get beyond the introductory overviews in Part 1, tales which are chapter-sized stories are the most effective way to convey context related concerns.

Each tale is based on personal practical experience, shaped into a tale to develop key conceptual and operational planning tools in an accessible order. Discussing the credibility of the tales in Part 2 is an integral feature of the approach adopted.

Drawing on practical experience is crucial in this book, but gives rise to potential problems of several kinds. This book's strategy for avoiding or mitigating these problems has several strands.

In Part 1 some of the relatively short tales directly linked to real organisations are just slightly fictionalised to keep the examples simple and bring the intended messages up to date.

Each of the chapter-length tales in Part 2 is a story which mixes experience from more than one organisation. Four of the five tales were directly shaped by consulting relationships with one or more named organisations, but none of these tales is just a simple 'disguised variant' of work within named organisations at some point in the past. These Part 2 tales do not describe any real organisation in a direct way, and they are not dated by the time period of the tale. They employ a synthesis of organisational features and broader contextual issues appropriate to communicating messages relevant to a post-2020 world which is changing at an accelerating rate.

None of the organisations mentioned have any reason not already in the public domain to be embarrassed by association with the tales, and in most cases they can be very proud of their contribution to what has become widely acknowledged as best practice. For the most part the work with clients this book draws on was a very positive experience, and when approaches I recommended were not accepted, or some aspects of their implementation did not work as effectively as intended, I am happy to take my share of any blame and concentrate on positive lessons learned. I have avoided being coy if there are useful lessons to convey, but used problems positively without dwelling on them.

A chapter by chapter overview 'road map' follows – provided as a preliminary to beginning Part 1 which I hope all target readers will find useful.

Chapter 1 explores why formal planning is usually vital but often difficult and frequently inept. As part of this exploration the meaning of key words like 'opportunity', 'risk', and 'uncertainty' are treated as examples of framing assumptions. This approach means that the definitions used must be as general (unrestrictive) as possible, supported by working assumptions which simplify in the 'right way', to clarify what best practice ought to involve in any given context. Chapter 1 also provides an overview of the other basic framing assumptions and some related working assumptions the rest of the book builds on.

Chapter 2 introduces a '*universal* planning and complexity management *process*' concept, contracted to 'universal process' or 'UP'. This concept is the basis for all process concerns addressed throughout this book. It is grounded on traditional and 'soft' OR (Operational Research or Operations Research) and broader Management Sciences ideas with the explicit use of other additional ideas I have found useful plus a provision for any further process ideas its users may be aware of. This comprehensive and explicitly open nature provides a systematic basis for thinking about all process choices. Its discussion assumes readers may have never previously encountered OR, Management Science, or the basis of other key contributing components, providing an overview of all any reader needs to know about the historical basis of a conceptual and operational tool which draws on some very different perspectives and disciplines.

The direct use of this UP concept in practice as a default process is explored in Chapter 5. It is used to design and develop a 'specific process' (SP) in Chapter 6. It is used to adapt what is commonly referred to as a 'generic process' in Chapter 7. It also has an identifiable role in Chapters 8 and 9. It provides a toolset for 'keeping it simple systematically' in terms of processes.

A core feature of the UP is a 'capability-culture' concept. The capability-culture concept explicitly links the capability and culture assets an organisation has and wants to use during the development and implementation of plans to the nature of its formal and informal planning processes. It also addresses associated liabilities – missing or defective assets. Example assets are requisite skills and information. Example liabilities are untrained or badly motivated staff and incorrect information.

Chapter 2 begins with an overview of the seven phase structure of the advocated form of the UP concept and the role of the associated capability-culture concept. The origins and evolution of this UP concept are then explored so that you understand its provenance and the scope for modifying its basis while adjusting its nature to meet your personal concerns and the needs of your organisation.

Chapter 3 is a central aspect of Part 1. It is practice-based, but it has been built on a synthesis of theoretical advances by acknowledged leaders in relevant areas, a characteristic of this book as a whole. It is worth exploring in much more detail than any other chapter in this Overview because the three efficiency concepts it develops are central to the enlightened planning approach as a whole and the way enlightened planning departs from a lot of common practice.

Chapter 3 addresses achieving unbiased estimates of basic attributes like project duration or cost, using examples which allow exploration of 'low clarity' to 'high clarity' approaches while exploring the 'estimation-efficiency spectrum'. Making use of work by Kahneman and others on unconscious behavioural estimation biases is part of 'what has to be done' to overcome all relevant bias effectively and efficiently, as part of the broader clarity efficiency concept central to this chapter. 'Clarity' in a clarity efficiency context implies understanding that can be communicated to all relevant people. Clarity efficiency is about achieving any given level of clarity at the lowest feasible level of cost/effort by systematically using the right kind of simplicity, avoiding the 'wrong kind' of simplicity.

Chapter 3 begins with a 'minimum clarity' approach designed to size expected outcomes and the uncertainty range of actual outcomes at the lowest acceptable level of clarity for a minimum level of cost/effort. The 1990s context used to provide a simple numerical and graphical example involves a UK Ministry of Defence (MoD) warship programme manager asking his team to estimate the duration of a single activity. The tale then explores small but significant increases in clarity for very modest levels of additional effort. The focus is on illustrating key issues at the low clarity end of a low to high clarity spectrum. One set of issues involves understanding why the common practice of using single value estimates is usually inappropriate and should be scrapped for most purposes, and why range-based interval estimates are usually essential. Another involves the need to distinguish and clarify aspirational targets, commitment targets and intermediate balanced targets that may be expected outcomes (the basic ABCs of targets). A third involves the role of inescapable basic assumptions which all estimates depend on and *everyone* involved in both *producing* and *using* estimates should understand.

The discussion then moves on to the high clarity end of the range of approaches of interest. 'Risk efficiency' is explored in the context of a tale about the approach to contingency planning which I developed for BP International for their North Sea offshore oil and gas projects over an eight year period beginning in 1976. This approach was used by BP on a worldwide basis for about a decade before they moved on to simpler approaches. These simpler approaches failed them in 2010 in the Gulf of Mexico, with fairly disastrous consequences. 'Risk efficiency' means a minimum level of risk for any given level of expected reward. Risk efficiency is a concept Harry Markowitz won a Nobel Prize for in 1990, embraced internationally by economists in a portfolio theory context by the 1960s, but still not understood or used effectively by many practitioners and theorists in many risk management contexts. An effective aggressive pursuit of risk efficiency using the conceptual and operational tools which I developed working with BP provided increased expected reward via lower expected cost *plus* less risk (an increase in risk efficiency) while *simultaneously* providing duration and cost estimates which were unbiased. This meant that projects could be delivered with *both* lower expected costs *and* less risk, usually within budgets and on time, despite some significant surprises. By the early 1980s what needed to be done and how to do it was understood at board level as well as by everyone engaged in project management roles. And early confidence in this approach was verified by a decade of experience and empirical evidence. The BP operational processes and other tools were designed to cope with what we labelled 'unknown unknowns', as well as 'known unknowns' which had been identified but treated qualitatively as 'conditions' and 'known knowns' which had been quantified in probabilistic terms.

By the early 1990s a senior MoD colleague responsible for key aspects of MoD procurement processes was arguing that every £1 spent on this kind of approach by the MoD should save about £100, a massive return on investment in a risk efficiency driven approach which produced unbiased estimates as a by-product of much more effective and efficient planning.

This kind of risk efficiency driven approach is usefully perceived as an opportunity which should be seized by all organisations not currently using it, failure to do so because its benefits and nature are not understood constituting the realisation of a serious corporate capability risk. My senior MoD colleague had mixed success getting the MoD as a whole to use it for reasons relevant to central concerns addressed by this book. Many MoD experts bought into my BP-based risk efficiency driven approach, which was the basis of MoD internal courses run for several years and widely acknowledged MoD best practice over several decades. However, from the outset, some MoD 'experts' maintained a preference for simplistic, less effective approaches, still a crucial issue in need of resolution within and beyond the defence context worldwide. Some of the reasons for this, and appropriate responses, are addressed directly in all Part 2 chapters.

Chapter 3 then employs the risk efficiency framework developed for BP and the BP examples in a manner used for IBM UK in the 1990s to promote taking *more* risk in a risk efficient manner at a local decision-making level in a context like bidding for a £20 million contract. The goal in this context was increasing overall profitability while decreasing overall corporate risk, understanding the difference between good management and good luck, bad management and bad luck. This discussion explores what IBM and subsequent clients liked to call 'enlightened caution' as well as 'enlightened gambles'. This use of the term 'enlightened' was the origin of the enlightened planning label and other related uses of 'enlightened' in this book. Identifying enlightened caution involves using a high clarity 'decision diagram' tool initially developed for BP to identify risk efficient choices. It uses what is usually referred to as a 'stochastic dominance' generalisation of a Markowitz approach. Enlightened caution is an issue when one option is a potentially deceptive risk inefficient 'unenlightened gamble' – it involves a higher most likely reward but a lower expected reward as well as a higher level of risk because a highly asymmetric distribution with one very long tail is involved. 'Enlightened caution' facilitates avoiding 'unenlightened gambles' which involve more risk and less expected reward when it is easy to make errors of judgement if unenlightened intuition is relied on. Without high clarity decision diagrams, unenlightened gambles may seem to be the obvious preferred choices, but high clarity decision diagrams make it clear that being capable of identifying the opportunity to avoid unenlightened gambles is crucial. 'Enlightened gambles' involve risk efficient gambles worth taking for the additional reward. Once these issues are understood, a linked corporate culture change can then be engineered. Once people get used to working with the new toolset, simpler diagrams or simple verbal comments with no diagrams are often all that is needed for most management decision-making practice.

These ideas and their behavioural implications are explained in Chapter 3 using graphs in a way most people find clear and convincing whatever their background and interests, as part of explaining, at an overview level, the concept of 'opportunity efficiency'.

'Opportunity efficiency' is a composite concept which is explored in 'what needs to be done' overview terms towards the end of Chapter 3. Opportunity efficiency involves selecting the most appropriate level of risk–reward trade-off for all relevant attributes. This requires the exercise of enlightened prudence when relevant, reducing expected reward to avoid inappropriate risk. Opportunity efficiency also involves making appropriate trade-offs among all relevant attributes, plus choosing suitable trade-offs between clarity and the cost of clarity. Opportunity efficiency is an operational definition of 'best practice'.

My work with IBM UK was central to a culture change programme for all senior and middle managers based on IBM's two day Forum 2 programme, run about 40 times in the early 1990s. The IBM chief executive officer opened the morning of the first day by outlining the strategic changes IBM had to make and explaining why the concepts to be covered by my contribution were central to those changes. I then outlined the key concepts they needed to understand until lunchtime. After lunch, I used a case study exercise designed with an

IBM senior executive to put the general conceptual ideas into an IBM context they could associate with directly and give them feedback on the nature of some of the changes they had to make in operational terms with cultural implications. The second day they discussed how they would implement related changes in their areas of operation. This programme was a significant success, leading to IBM corporate process and culture changes. Several follow-on consulting assignments were triggered. In addition to its role in Chapter 3, this work for IBM is central to Chapter 6.

The low to high clarity estimation-efficiency spectrum explored by Chapter 3 provides a conceptual and operational framework which is central to an enlightened planning approach. Chapter 3 synthesises and clarifies a core portion of all my earlier work, plus more recent work with a wide range of colleagues, Stephen Ward's contributions over the last 20 years being of particular importance. It builds on earlier work by others like Kahneman, Markowitz, and those behind stochastic dominance. It treats unbiased estimates and the pursuit of opportunity efficiency defined by component risk efficiency and clarity efficiency as nonseparable concepts at a framing assumption level.

Chapter 3 builds on the understanding of a very general approach set out in Chapters 1 and 2, but it uses important explicit simplifying assumptions to avoid difficult complexities, and it skips over several challenging complexities which need addressing at a foundation level.

Chapter 4 addresses the challenging complexities which need confronting within the holistic framework this book's approach has provided thus far. Its starting point is directly useful operational tools skipped over in Chapter 3, like a high clarity form of 'sensitivity diagram'. Sensitivity diagrams were initially developed for BP to understand the relative importance of different sources of uncertainty in a complex model from the outset of analysis, helping analysts to build their understanding from the bottom up. Selective use at board level in a top-down mode for somewhat different purposes is amongst the ideas explored. The basic ideas are relevant in a wide range of contexts. Effective use of sensitivity analysis is a core best practice analysis capability for most of the people involved in almost any context – including planners and supporting analysts, their managers at all levels, and the organisation's suppliers or customers, as illustrated in Part 2 chapters. A midpoint Chapter 4 topic is low clarity decision diagrams, used as simple operational tools to address risk efficiency in terms of a basic primary attribute like cost when trade-offs involving non-measurable attributes or attributes not worth measuring need consideration and may be crucial. Again the core capabilities demonstrated are widely applicable. Towards the end of this chapter the focus shifts to high clarity operational tools and conceptual frameworks for addressing multiple attributes which may involve complex ethical choices. Chapter 4 closes by exploring the limitations of formal analysis.

Part 1 as a whole explores a wide range of foundation level framing assumptions and associated working assumptions as part of beginning to explain why some of the difficulty encountered in practical decision-making contexts has been generated by both academic and practitioner 'experts' who are unable to distinguish between the right kind of simplicity and the wrong kind of simplicity. This is a difficulty which needs to be addressed by *everybody* affected – *it cannot just be 'left to the experts'*.

Part 2 illustrates the use of the conceptual and operational toolset outlined in Part 1, including key operational links between corporate planning, operations planning and project planning. These links include the roles of operations and project planning in the generation of bottom-up corporate strategic planning considerations which are driven by new operational requirements and their strategic relevance for the organisation as a whole. 'Project planning' is viewed as the management of change in a very general sense whenever this is useful. So far as I am aware these interdependences have never been addressed in terms of a holistic and collaborative framework for a wide range of target readers in the way this book does. This book explicitly acknowledges that planning in different areas can be usefully assumed to be 'separable' for some purposes, but interdependencies that always matter need constant direct attention, and interdependencies that may matter need routine testing for relevance and responding to when necessary. What is meant by 'separable' here and in many other contexts has important practical operational implications, explored throughout the book.

Chapter 5 uses a very simple supply side operations management context to illustrate the use of the universal process (UP) developed in outline in Chapter 2. In the context of Chapter 5 the UP concept is used in a default process mode – in any context if it is not clear what process should be used, a UP is the default choice. Chapter 5 assumes readers may have no supply side operations management knowledge and no previous OR, Management Science, or cognate discipline knowledge, along with perhaps a limited interest in acquiring new knowledge of any of these areas. This UP concept is a new synthesis of what I have always understood as a practical view of the classical textbook 'OR process or method' and the more recent 'soft OR' ideas, plus further key ideas involving a capability-culture concept suggested by authors in best-selling recent books whose perspectives are very different – Gawande (2011) and Kennedy (2014) in particular. It also integrates this basis with process phase ideas in my 'uncertainty management' work with Stephen Ward in a project planning context. Chapter 5 sets the scene for Part 2 in an initially very simple practical context, keeping the details of the examples as simple as possible, but explaining inherently complex issues like the role of key assumptions, the crucial role of collaboration between organisations for mutual benefit, and the difference between simple models used to understand key trade-offs and plans which go well beyond simple model capabilities.

This focus of Chapter 5 is using a UP concept in bottom-up mode with 'the top' at a very low level initially but successively moving the starting position upwards and gradually becoming more strategic. It demonstrates the importance of teamwork which is not constrained by organisational silos or professional perspectives and the way an effective universal process can generate 'propositions' of strategic importance to the organisation, potentially leading to transformational changes when integrated with top-down corporate strategic planning.

As with all other chapters, the focus is what needs to be done, not how to do it. The simplicity of the context helps to keep the requisite how to do it discussion simple. If you are a director or an expert with extensive experience, your initial impression may be the issues and tools addressed by this tale are seriously lacking in sophistication and strategic implications. However, there are some important nuances you are likely to find useful in the context of the overall approach, and these nuances are further developed when addressing the inherently complex concerns confronted by the rest of the book.

Chapter 6 explores how a sales manager for the regional office of an international organisation might develop a bidding process, building on ideas developed during the IBM UK culture change programme discussed in Chapter 3. It demonstrates how a capable sales manager who understood some of the concepts developed in earlier chapters, plus a team with complementary skills, might address bidding and broader organisational issues when the context focus is demand-side driven. One of the key roles of this chapter is illustrating the use of the *universal* process (UP) concept to design a *specific* process (SP) for bidding. This approach generalises the use of generic models usually employed by OR processes as illustrated in Chapter 5, moving part of the way towards working with 'generic processes' as addressed in Chapter 7.

Subtle concerns of importance to an underlying corporate culture change management programme and a broad capability transformation programme are addressed along the way. They include identifying when some people are biasing cost estimates to accommodate strategic concerns not previously considered explicitly, which actually need simple but explicit qualitative consideration, as well as numerical adjustments to estimates used for decision making in some cases. They also include using marginal costs rather than standard internal transfer prices when the difference matters and maintaining a level playing field for internal staff groups that are competing with external organisations which are crucial strategic partners. Furthermore, they include effective quantitative analysis of likely bid pricing behaviour by competitors coupled to non-quantifiable 'value added' features which potential customers might be provided with in order to win bids.

This discussion emphasises the importance of non-price concerns for both customers and vendors and the role of trust when vendors look after their customers' interests effectively without overlooking their own best interests. It also emphasises when taking more risk at the level addressed is essential to reduce the risk of corporate failure, and the operational implications of this kind of mindset and skill set change. No marketing or other demand-side management knowledge as assumed.

By the end of this chapter you should see why some of the key ideas explored will need further reflection in terms of the overall enlightened planning (EP) approach even if the technical bidding process issues are not a direct interest. The chapter ends with a section indicating some areas for further reflection as the book progresses to get you started.

Chapter 7 addresses project planning in the context of a water and sewage utility. It considers planning projects like the construction of new water supply pipelines and sewage treatment plants. It provides a what needs to be done level of understanding of the how to do it ideas in the book *How to Manage Project Opportunity and Risk* (Chapman and Ward, 2011). I believe all members of any board ought to understand these ideas at a what needs to be done level for a wide range of reasons. One is being capable of exercising their overall board level governance role when judging the competence of project directors and *all* project managers reporting to themselves and to other directors. I believe everybody else in all organisations who might be tempted to read this book will also find it valuable to acquire the basic what needs to be done level of strategic clarity about change management provided by Chapter 7, some also requiring significant further how to do it tactical clarity. Chapter 7 continues to build on all earlier chapters, following the layered approach of the book as a whole. It does not assume any prior project management knowledge.

Chapter 8 provides a what needs to be done level of understanding of corporate planning driven by top-down corporate strategic planning integrated with all other planning. It uses an electricity utility context, initially considering the corporate strategic planning concerns that I was asked to address as an expert witness for a Province of Ontario government enquiry into Ontario Hydro's strategic plans at the beginning of the 1990s. Ontario Hydro wanted to build 10 new nuclear power stations over a 25 year period. I was hired by an 'official intervenor' to object on their behalf, funded by Ontario Hydro under Ontario government rules. My published report explored in outline what Ontario Hydro should have done in the process of explaining why their corporate strategic planning approach was inappropriate and their conclusions were unsound. Ontario Hydro withdrew their plans a week or so before I was due to present oral evidence, for reasons anticipated and addressed by my report.

Initially, a radical corporate strategic change, including culture changes, is not discussed. The focus is given current knowledge about feasible futures in technical terms at a long-term planning horizon 20 years hence and current understanding of the significant uncertainty about future costs and prices, what should the utility be aiming for in terms of a portfolio of power station types, and what commitments should be made for new projects which need to be started as soon as possible.

After a framework for this kind of corporate strategic planning has been developed, more radical change is explored. Corporate goals and feasible futures are reassessed in terms of corporate capability-culture issues as well as potential new technology physical facility issues. What has been termed 'designing desirable futures' is taken as the basis for a much broader perspective – where organisations ought to start in practice if they want to address what really matters in an iterative manner driven by goals which may not be feasible, dealing effectively with priority and precedence relationships.

This chapter also addresses capability-culture concerns which have since driven Ontario Hydro towards the kind of privatisation visited upon the UK Central Electricity Generating Board in the 1980s. By the end of this chapter it should be clear why all organisations need a suitable variant of the kind of corporate planning discussed in this chapter, fully integrated with the kinds of planning discussed earlier, adapted to the context the organisation has to deal with.

No background knowledge of corporate strategic planning or ERM (Enterprise Risk Management) is assumed.

Chapter 9 extends the corporate planning framework and integrated operations and project planning frameworks provided earlier to very high impact but very low probability incidents plus a full range of less serious incident variants. It builds on a review of Railtrack's approach to a strategic planning framework for UK railway safety management which I undertook for their head of safety in the 1990s. It also builds on a new framework derived from a review for the UK MoD over a three year period from 2010 until 2013. My understanding is this MoD work has subsequently received attention at a NATO level. The MoD consultancy addressed justifying high levels of expenditure on a portfolio of preventative and responsive contingency plans for protecting troops from non-conventional weapon attacks.

Railtrack did not take my advice, but they went bankrupt a couple of years later. My 1990s work for them would have been significantly enhanced by my 2010–13 MoD framework's approach as generalised in this book, perhaps leading to Railtrack accepting an enhanced version of my 1990s recommendations. The reasons for Railtrack's corporate failure were multiple and debatable, but two very serious accidents within a short period were certainly crucial. Anticipation of this kind of possible scenario, or an even more serious scenario, coupled with effective planning to prevent or deal with such circumstances, was central to my recommendations.

The tale of this chapter integrates railway accident and malicious incident concerns, addressing potential terrorist attacks as well as accidents for a European railway system. It explains important practical reasons for this integrated approach, *including crucial simplifications* of the right kind. The key new issues relative to earlier chapter discussions are driven by the role of trade-offs between money and attributes like 'lives' (people killed who might not have been killed if more money had been spent or spent more effectively). It also addresses associated 'injuries' (over a range of levels of seriousness).

Keeping it simple but dealing with very serious levels of complexity that really matters in a formal planning framework is the central concern of this chapter.

A key aspect of the strategy is a focus on a small set of scenarios which deal with correlated metrics for attributes associated with different objectives, like levels of fatalities, levels of injuries, levels of operational disruption to the railway system, and all associated cost and lost revenue concerns, including reputational risk implications. If all the interested parties can agree what level of expenditure is appropriate to reduce the severity or probability of each scenario in this limited set of scenarios, with an initial focus on a 'worst case' outcome, the different parties do not need to agree in detail about their relative priorities for each component metric. This is a crucial simplification in a very complex situation, and it provides a significant opportunity which common practice overlooks.

Furthermore, there is no need to assume that common practice metrics like 'the value of an avoided fatality' have to be constant for any number of fatalities, or that such metrics need to be based on cost–benefit analysis concepts which are at best debatable, and at their worst lacking a moral compass and failing any ethically driven political acceptability test. These are crucial complications which really matter, and addressing them effectively is facilitated by the linked simplifications.

Concluding discussions in this chapter explore other even more difficult trade-offs in the sense of further analytical complexities and complications, generalising the railway context approach to deal with further relevant metrics like environmental damage. One example briefly considered is the 2010 Gulf of Mexico Macondo (Deepwater Horizon) incident which has cost BP about $60 billion to date, largely driven by environmental damage consequences, although everybody on the rig involved died as well. No background knowledge of safety or security analysis and management is assumed.

Part 2 as a whole might be summed up as follows: Chapter 7 is about delivering change which meets or surpasses the expectations of all the key stakeholders in that change whenever possible. Chapter 8 is about deciding what to change, and the resources needed, including addressing capability-culture asset and liability concerns. Chapters 5 and 6 deal with ongoing operations management issues which interface with the concerns addressed in later chapters, but they are considered first because they provide basic tools needed to understand the approaches developed in later chapters. Chapters 5 to 8 are all relevant to all organisations. Chapter 9 deals with special case issues which are crucially important whenever they are relevant, and if we generalise very serious accidents or terrorist attacks to include moderately serious environmental, cybersecurity, fraud, or loss of corporate reputation issues of any other kind deserving moderately serious attention, most organisations need to think very carefully about addressing potential concerns of this kind.

Part 3 provides further synthesis and reflection in two relatively short chapters.

Chapter 10 provides further synthesis and reflection at an overview level to clarify what needs to be done concerns in terms of addressing immediate and later priorities. Chapter 10 makes it clear that some of the ideas developed in Chapters 8 and 9 need attention as a first priority in practice, moving on to less urgent concerns *after* dealing with starting point concerns like overall corporate goals. By the end of this chapter you should have a consolidated understanding of the strategic clarity all organisations need.

Chapter 10 also reflects in more detail on public/private ownership issues which surface earlier. Some *private* sector organisations need effective planning which addresses regulatory issues and pressures. This may include the need to address the way their competitive advantage depends on regulator or government interventions which they may be able to influence. As a special case, 'nationalisation risk' may be relevant. Some *public* sector organisations need to understand the pressures driving them towards privatisation and respond effectively to 'privatisation risk' considering all relevant interests.

There is an upside and a downside to both private and public sector status from a variety of perspectives. How both are implemented determines the best choices for all the interested parties, whose interests may not coincide, with the context being crucial in a number of ways. You should understand some of the basic issues in a new framework by the end of this chapter, along with other ideas relevant to all organisations in both sectors. This framework might be used by readers with different agendas in very different ways.

You may have heard the mantra 'what cannot be measured cannot be managed', often cited by those in both private and public sector organisations. After reading Chapter 10 it should be clear why those advocating this mantra do not understand what decision making in most practical planning contexts ought to involve, or they are being deliberately misleading to serve their own agendas, or both.

By the time you have finished Chapter 10 you should also understand some of the advantages and limitations of:

1   metrics for relevant objectives,
2   quantification in appropriate probabilistic terms,
3   the role of qualitative models which structure and support formal planning,
4   the crucial way informal planning has to support all formal planning approaches,
5   the way corporate capability-culture concerns have to serve as part of the foundation for the whole edifice, and
6   key limitations of approaches to decision making which do not address these concerns in an enlightened manner.

Chapter 11 begins with a focus on teamwork and wider collaboration, unbiased decision making, and contingency planning aspects of ongoing enhancement of strategic clarity and tactical clarity. Broad planning areas, approaches, perspectives, concerns and issues requiring ongoing strategic and tactical clarity enhancement are then addressed, finishing with a brief discussion of a diagram which has evolved over many years which portrays the corporate benefits of an enlightened planning approach in terms of more 'smiles' linked to more 'pleasure' and less 'pain'. Reward, usually centred on profit metrics, is a primary concern, but capability-culture concerns which are crucial need focused attention, and this diagram is a useful final summary of what is involved in delivering the goals of enlightened planning.

Parts 1 through 3 as a whole are about why some aspects of planning usually need to be sophisticated, subtle and creative, and why simplistic, inflexible approaches do not work as a general rule, but appropriate simplifications are essential and can be very powerful. Generally we all need *approximately correct answers to the right questions within the right timeframe which everyone involved can trust*. We do not want *precise answers to the wrong questions or answers which are too late or answers which cannot be received with well-founded trust*. The difference matters greatly, and understanding what the difference involves is what this book is about.

Regulation, politics and ethics sometimes have to be addressed, with examples in four of the five Part 2 tales. Using a broad interpretation of what regulation might involve can be very important, including ensuring that all valuable players in a marketplace enjoy 'a level playing field'. The complexities involved in planning undertaken by regulators and their political masters are not addressed in detail, but some key concerns are clarified, and some of the concepts and tools developed are directly relevant to regulatory concerns. One UK regulator already moving in the suggested direction is discussed briefly in Chapter 11, and there is increasing evidence of significant international movement of this kind involving a very wide range of regulation which needs to be encouraged and facilitated. But it would be naïve to think that some very serious concerns needing attention are going to be straightforward to resolve.

Politics in the most general sense can only rarely be ignored, and ethics are almost always relevant. Although political decision making is well beyond the scope of this book, as are appropriate ethics, both are relevant to *any* enlightened planning perspective. I specifically avoid political dogma and moral imperatives. For example, when 'good' and 'bad' are discussed in ethical, political, economic, or any other sense, the boundaries are always assumed to be debatable. However, this does not mean the issues involved do not matter. It means we need to be particularly careful about our assumptions and deal with important uncertainty associated with ambiguity. It also means we need to cope in a practical manner with interdependencies among political, legal, regulatory, and ethical issues which may be inherently extremely complex and controversial.

The need to clarify a generalisation of the 'uncertainty management' ideas underlying the book *How to Manage Project Opportunity and Risk : Why Uncertainty Management Can Be a Much Better Approach than Risk Management*, (Chapman and Ward, 2011) has been the focus of my efforts on successive drafts of this book for several years. The need to do so in a carefully considered manner which would be accessible to a very broadly defined target audience has become increasingly clear each year for several decades. During this period, Stephen Ward and I have been aware that our evolving uncertainty management approach was critically acclaimed as helping to define the leading edge of international best practice by a significant number of people. But we were also aware that many people preferred to support common practice that they perhaps saw as good practice which was simpler without understanding the implications of the nature of the simplicity employed. And we were concerned that many others had never come across the basic ideas we believe to be crucial. What is meant by 'bad' practice, 'best' practice, and a range of intermediate 'good' practices remains ambiguous and controversial – issues this book confronts directly, to allow you to judge for yourself, and shape your own future version of best practice.

Much of the bad, good, and best practice controversy is deeply rooted in the difficulties that we all have when adjusting the framing assumptions and habitual working assumptions which define our view of a best practice approach to management decision making plus underlying planning and analysis in any context. Testing and adjusting assumptions that we have trusted for some time but may need to change is never easy. But it is a core competency for reflective managers, and it is a central concern and explicit focus throughout this book. The emphasis on this explicit focus is new relative to Chapman and Ward (2011) and my earlier publications. Chapter 1 makes a point of explaining some example shifts in my own framing assumptions, and comparable working assumptions, during the writing of later drafts of this book, in part to encourage you to think about shifting some of your routine assumptions throughout. A key message for you to take away from this book is the importance of the issues you can uncover by an explicit focus on the set of framing assumptions and comparable working assumptions which define your perspective. They really matter.

My goals when writing this book included providing you with an operational best practice toolset for all management decision making which you can put to immediate use, plus an underlying set of conceptual frameworks you can use immediately and then build on. I hope you will find this book of immediate value and useful as a stimulus for generalising your toolset, skill set and mindset along some of the lines explored.

About the author

The approach to planning advocated by this book was synthesised from a career based on pursuing a practice–research–teaching–practice cycle for about 50 years. Improving practice was always a central goal in this iterative process. Understanding the way my pursuit of this goal evolved in relation to the content of this book with a kind of detail most authors do not provide may help you to better understand what this book is about and why it takes the form employed – the rationale for the approach taken to the next few pages. It should also help to underpin the candid conversational style used throughout this book, a style which seemed essential given the nature of some of the intended messages.

I was born and brought up in Toronto. A University of Toronto BASc in Industrial Engineering (1962) and a University of Birmingham MSc in Operational Research (1964) provided my initial academic grounding. An Athlone Fellowship funded by the UK Board of Trade gave me the opportunity to spend 1962 through 1964 in the UK.

I spent 1964–5 as an IBM computer sales trainee in Toronto. This built on my computer systems experience working for IBM in Toronto for three summers during my undergraduate degree, plus a year working in a project planning systems development role with Ferranti in London as the first part of the Athlone Fellowship. Working for IBM Canada initially, and then seeing where that led, was the 'career plan A' adopted while still an undergraduate.

In 1965 I accepted an offer of a lectureship (assistant professorship) in econometrics from Gordon Fisher – the opportunity was unanticipated but too good to miss. Gordon had taught one of my University of Birmingham MSc programme econometrics options, and the following year he founded the Econometrics Department at the University of Southampton as its first Professor of Econometrics. For nine years, my career focus was managing a new MSc programme in Economics, Econometrics and Operational Research (OR), designing and teaching the OR content, and completing a PhD in consumer behaviour theory as a staff candidate supervised by the economist Professor Ivor Pearce. The PhD shaped my view of 'separability' and several closely coupled concepts which underlie the foundations of this book as a whole, building on Pearce (1964). It also provided a deep understanding of the foundations of risk management central to this book, building on Markowitz (1959). During this period, I developed a passion for research into the issues exposed by practice, initially centred on the development of consumer behaviour theory to support marketing decision making for the UK Milk Marketing Board. I also started to acquire a passion for consulting. One key client relevant to this book was Buckinghamshire County Council. On Gordon Fisher's recommendation they hired me as an expert witness to help stop a 'Third London Airport' being built at Cublington. The economists David Pearce and John Wise were recruited to help, working as a fully integrated partnership. The Cublington recommendation was scrapped. We obviously cannot take full credit, but I believe we were on the right side of a complex cost–benefit analysis argument, and some of the issues and approaches are directly related to those addressed in Chapter 9. During this period I became a senior lecturer (associate professor) and served as the assistant dean of my faculty (Social Sciences). Taken as a whole, this period was a central part of an extensive apprenticeship which significantly shaped my career and perspective. I had not seriously considered an academic career or living in England until Gordon's offer but never regretted my 1965 largely intuitive change of mind, despite ongoing uncertainty about the permanence of these decisions for 20 years.

For 15 months during 1974–5 I worked full-time with Acres Consulting Services in Canada. This opportunity was initiated by a three month consultancy assignment invitation from Oskar Sigvaldason. Oskar was then head of Acres Special Services Department, later president of Acres. I learned a lot about consulting, including key team-working and client management concerns. One key study relevant to this book was leading the risk and uncertainty analysis of a proposal to reduce by one year the construction duration of a pipeline to bring high Arctic gas to US markets. Another was a comparison of Canadian and US design regulations for nuclear power stations in relation to seismic (earthquake) risk. I built a lasting relationship with Acres. However, I declined the offer of a permanent full-time role with Acres in Canada. I returned to the Department of Economics at the University of Southampton, which had absorbed Econometrics while I was away. Working for Acres was immensely stimulating, and my wife, Jean, and I and our two young sons greatly enjoyed living in Niagara-on the Lake. However, with a young family I was not prepared to accommodate commuting to clients in Calgary, Edmonton, Ottawa, and similar locations for a week at a time for a significant proportion of the year, and for a complex set of reasons on balance, an academic career based in the UK seemed the best feasible choice.

For the next decade one focal area of my career was consulting to help clients build processes and embedded model sets which addressed problem areas with no available 'off-the-shelf' approaches. Through Robin Charlwood, an Acres colleague, I established an eight year relationship with BP International in London. I helped BP to develop planning and costing approaches for their North Sea operations, adopted by BP for worldwide use on all large or sensitive projects for more than a decade. In this period BP projects using the approaches I helped to develop were generally within time and cost commitments, with no surprises which could not be accommodated. Through Oskar Sigvaldason, Robin Charlwood, Gavin Warnock, and several other Acres colleagues I also worked with Acres teams for other clients in Canada and the US, building on the BP work, with any lengthy assignments scheduled so that my family could accompany me. Illustrative key clients included Gulf Canada (Beaufort Sea and Grand Banks oil and gas project design studies, including the Hibernia oil production platform project off the east coast of Canada, where icebergs were a key concern, and platform cost uncertainty coupled to oil reserve volume uncertainty plus oil price uncertainty proved critical), Petro-Canada (a design strategy study for a pilot liquefied natural gas project on Melville Island in the high Arctic), Fluor Engineers and Contractors Inc (a design study addressing how best to get a proposed 48 inch gas pipeline across the Yukon River in close proximity to an existing 48 inch oil line, with a wide range of relevant threats and interested parties), and Potomac Electric Power Company and the US Department of Energy (comparison of energy storage via pumped hydro or compressed air in deep mines). Research driven by my consulting interests was published, and I became a reader in Management Science. The other focal area of my career during this period was helping Professor Ken Hilton develop the Department of Accounting and Management Science, which he extracted from the Department of Economics with my support. As well as teaching, I managed new MSc programmes and undertook various other academic roles. This period put into practice the maturing practice–research–teaching–practice basis of this book, initiating and shaping some of the basic ideas.

For nearly a decade the focus of my career then shifted significantly. I had become a Professor of Management Science with a personal chair, and Head of the Department of Accounting and Management Science. I now made a full commitment to maintaining an academic career base. Ken Hilton had increased the size of our department by 50%. I increased it by a further 100%, adding two new groups with professorial leadership: Finance & Banking and Information Systems. My consultancy became more UK-focused. I started accepting invitations to work through UK based consultants, including work with Sir William Halcrow and Partners of direct relevance to Chapter 9. Some consultancy was undertaken through the university. Examples central to this book include several studies helping National Power to develop BP type approaches to building electricity generation stations, and a series of studies over the period from 1993 to 1995 helping UK Nirex to plan a repository for nuclear waste disposal and deal with Department of the Environment (DoE) arguments about deferring the project. The DoE adopted a Her Majesty's (HM's) Treasury mandated real discount rate of 6% when 3% would have been more appropriate in terms of my arguments at the time. HM Treasury's own post-2003 advice is consistent with my 3%, for directly related but different reasons. These issues are important in private as well as public sector contexts, and the reasons are explored in Chapter 7. I pursued research conventionally funded by research councils and professional bodies as well as the MoD and other organisations, some directly relevant to this book. Involvement with professional bodies began, including accepting an invitation to act as founding chair for the Association for Project Management (APM) Specific Interest Group on Project Risk Management. I started to spend more time teaching experienced managers, including a significant culture change programme for IBM UK, its 'Forum 2' programme. This was a two day in-house event run about 40 times, introduced by their CEO on each occasion, built around my input, central to Chapters 3 and 6. This wider set of activities and concerns reduced the time available for consultancy, but it did not weaken the practice–research–teaching–practice basis of my career, and prototype variants of many of the key ideas in this book matured during this period.

A five year break from university management roles then involved a different slight shift in focus, centred around two years as president of the Operational Research Society.

My three years as director of the Southampton University Management School (SUMS) then involved a new university management role. I was appointed director with a transformation mandate by a new vice-chancellor. While I had been head of the Department of Accounting and Management Science the University had established SUMS as a separate Management School to provide MBAs and other post-experience courses. My advice to avoid making these activities separate was rejected, but SUMS had my support once that decision had been made. The new vice-chancellor wanted SUMS fully integrated with the university, located on campus, made profitable, and made reputable in research terms. These objectives were achieved in the planning horizon which I eventually set myself. My successful exit strategy from my role as director involved recommending that the current the head of the Department of Accounting and Management Science take over as director of a new Management School created by a full merger of SUMS plus the department, with me in supporting roles to help complete the transition. Outcomes included doubling MSc and MBA student numbers, an RAE (Research Assessment Exercise) rating of five (the top rating on the scale used for UK research assessment at that time) for the new Management School, and strengthened relationships with the faculties of Engineering and Mathematics. The latter was facilitated by founding the Centre for Operational Research, Management Science and Information Systems (CORMSIS), with the director's post alternating every two years between Management and Mathematics, initially held by the professor of OR in Mathematics, Paul Williams. The new School of Management has continued to evolve, becoming the Southampton Business School (SBS) in 2014. CORMSIS has thrived with a series of directors focused on collaboration within and beyond the university, the sustained joint efforts of Sally Brailsford (Management/SBS) and Chris Potts (Mathematics) being particularly important. A separate but overlapping Centre for Risk Research (CRR), founded in 1990 by Johnnie Johnson (Management/SBS), which he led with great success until retiring at the end of 2018, also thrives and continues to evolve. Both centres embrace an emphasis on practice and a broadly defined perspective.

From 1991 until 1993 I served as an expert witness providing a critical review of Ontario Hydro's strategic plans for the next 25 years, central to Chapter 8.

In 1992 and 1996 I served as a Business and Management Studies panel member for the RAE. The judgements of these panels determined the distribution of the research funding component of the UK government's university funding for business and management for two four year periods. At the invitation of the panel's chair as his 'quantitative analysis expert' I unobtrusively but explicitly confronted the management and governance implications of different people arguing for different weightings when using quantitative measures of attributes which do not lend themselves to simple metrics plus important non-measurable concerns when important decisions have to be made by a group of people with very different perspectives and agendas, and the need to use available measures coherently as far as possible, issues which are central to this book as a whole.

In 1999 I was elected an Honorary Fellow of the Institute of Actuaries. My work on its joint working parties with the Institution of Civil Engineers on risk management guides addressing projects, then whole enterprises, then operations, shaped the three component separability structure for all management decision making adopted by this book.

From 1997 to 2003 I served as a non-executive director of Southern Water, with three different chairmen of the board and three different ownership structures, useful in terms of background for Chapter 7 and direct governance experience relevant to Chapters 7 to 9.

There are a number of relevant differences between advising other organisations and taking your own advice when directly engaged in management and governance functions. My operations, project and corporate management experience as a head of an academic department, my change management experience as a management school director, a variety of other academic and professional roles, and my board level governance experience as a Southern Water non-executive director, all reinforced my consultancy experience in a manner relevant to the overall 'practice basis' for this book. They were all modest roles in corporate terms, and you may not see universities as 'commercial organisations', but each helped shape and let me directly test some of the concepts and other tools discussed in this book, and they all influenced my views on requisite skill sets and mindsets in ways directly relevant to this book. They were an integral part of the education and practical experience basis that underlies my current perspective. That is the primary reason for mentioning them here, as part of explaining 'where I am coming from' before you start Chapter 1, to help you see where this book might take you. One secondary reason is encouraging you to see 'commercial organisations' through a broader lens than you might be used to, with a wide range of objectives. A defining characteristic of this book is encouraging a broader view than you may be used to of most concepts involved.

In 2004 I retired from my full-time academic post, became an emeritus professor on a part-time contract and accepted an invitation from Mike Nichols to become a senior associate of the Nichols Group. Three subsequent consultancy studies are directly relevant to this book.

In 2005 I worked in Venice with Gavin Warnock and Robin Charlwood, renewing our Acres connections begun in 1974. Both had been Acres vice-presidents but now had their own consultancy companies, Gavin based in Edinburgh and Robin in Seattle. We worked through Gavin's Monitor (International) Ltd. Our client was Consorzio Venezia Nuova, the contractor for the MOSE flood protection scheme for Venice. We were successful in persuading the government that the cost estimates had to be significantly increased because earlier risk provisions based on conventional 'received wisdom' estimation methodologies were biased on the optimistic side. The MOSE project proceeded, with construction due to complete in 2018. This study helped to shape Chapters 3 and 7.

In 2006 and 2007 I worked with Mike Nichols and a small team to help him write a report for the secretary of state for transport which explained why UK Highways Agency cost estimates were consistently optimistically biased, despite following HM Treasury guidelines on these issues and what to do about it. I then supported a team of Nichols consultants help the Highways Agency start to implement our recommendations, initially revising all current cost estimates in a manner approved and supported by HM Treasury. At that time Mike Nichols was chairman of the Association for Project Management. We met when he chaired the joint working party of the Institution of Civil Engineers and the Institute and Faculty of Actuaries that I served on which produced the *RAMP Risk Analysis and Management of Projects* (1998 and 2005) guides. These Highways Agency studies and the RAMP guides also helped to shape Chapters 3 and 7.

From 2010 until 2013 I provided advice to the UK Ministry of Defence (MoD) on appropriate frameworks for justifying high levels of expenditure on preventative and mitigating measures for low probability non-conventional weapon attacks on troops, a form of analysis also relevant to terrorist activities. A generalisation of the framework developed underpins Chapter 9, along with earlier work on strategic approaches to safety for Railtrack.

The book *How to Manage Project Opportunity and Risk: Why Uncertainty Management Can Be a Much Better Approach than Risk Management* (Chapman and Ward, 2011) was the extensively rewritten and retitled third edition of *Project Risk Management: Processes, Techniques and Insights* (Chapman and Ward, 1997, 2003). The 1997 first edition was a critically acclaimed modest best seller, with roughly a third of its sales in Europe, a third in North America, and a third in the rest of the world, with Chinese and Greek language versions. A significant evolution in perspective was involved in the 2003 and 2011 editions.

This book's Chapter 7 continues the evolution outlined by Chapman and Ward (2011), developing it from a broader perspective. The rest of this book continues the same evolution and clarification in terms of a scope which has been further broadened to include all aspects of planning needing effective integrated treatment within private and public sector commercial organisations. Its focus is on practice in a rapidly changing post-2020 world. Its evolution has been the focus of my professional activities over the last few years.

Promoting the use of enlightened planning ideas in any systematic simplicity form its users find appropriate in whatever ways I can is central to my future professional goals.

Acknowledgements

Dale Cooper reviewed the first draft of this book, and many useful detailed changes throughout this current draft, plus several significant changes in the approach to framing and presenting key concepts flowed directly from his comments. Particularly valuable was clarification of areas where there were important differences of opinion, forcing me to test and develop my understanding, resulting in important new insights in addition to significantly better explanations. Dale and I worked together as consultants as well as joint authors in the same academic department for many years in the 1980s and 1990s, before Dale returned to Australia and founded Broadleaf, his consultancy company. Working with Dale was always a very enlightening and enjoyable experience, and we have kept in touch as good friends.

Stephen Ward reviewed the second draft, which incorporated revisions to respond to Dale's suggestions. Because Stephen and I have continued to work together on joint and individual publications since the 1980s, and remained close academic colleagues as well as good friends, our ongoing differences of opinion on key issues are minimal. However, Stephen has always brought a highly constructive and candid critical perspective to bear on anything I write which he has co-authored or reviewed, and many of the ideas used or developed in this book were initiated by Stephen. One simple illustrative example is the redefined KISS mantra (keep it simple systematically). But many of the sophisticated underlying concepts which are central to the whole of this book are also Stephen's creations. The third draft was completely different from the second. It involved a much more coherent and productive structure, plus other significant changes in approach, as a direct result of Stephen's feedback on the second draft.

Stephen then provided further crucial feedback on the third draft. The key changes this time were focused on making the ideas more accessible for the diverse set of target readers. However, the changes were significant, including further restructuring, and further insights were also important, a spinoff from the focus on communicating ideas.

Paul Thornton also provided very helpful overview comments on the third draft, followed by insightful detailed comments which further shaped the current draft to a significant extent. Paul was a founding partner of French Thornton, and his broad experience as a management consultant operating at the board level was of immense value in terms of sharpening the focus on what matters most for both 'directors' and 'experts' in a broad range of organisations and areas of analysis. Our friendship was initially triggered by Paul being my mentor in the early 1990s, when I became president-elect of the Operational Research Society (ORS). The ORS had a tradition of 'practitioners' alternated with 'academics' as presidents, with two years as a president preceded by a year as president-elect, followed by a year as immediate past president, and Paul was my practitioner mentor within this cycle. He revisited a different version of the practitioner mentor role to great effect for this book.

A number of the more than a thousand participants on the IBM Forum 2 programme provided insights used directly in Chapter 6. For more than 20 years I have been teaching a course at the University of Southampton on Project Risk Management which now attracts more than a hundred students per year from more than ten MSc programmes. In the last few years several students provided ideas in their assessment essays which were incorporated directly in this book by the completion of the fourth draft. Post-experience in-house and public course participants, as well as university students, have helped to shape my thinking since I started teaching, acquiring new insights from 'students' with practical experience being one of the many positive features of teaching which I particularly enjoy. International Project Management Association (IPMA) advanced training 'master classes' in Milan and Copenhagen are part of the 'plot' of two Part 2 tales, and my IPMA course at the end of 2017 in Copenhagen was one of the most stimulating to date.

Colleagues, friends and family have commented on the fourth draft and contributed to this final fifth draft in a number of ways, including the thoughtful gift or loan of books which proved useful. My younger son Andy and our joint friend Stephen Cresswell need specific acknowledgement for early support of various kinds. Stephen Ward was yet again enormously helpful, with insightful 'less is more' pruning, material re-sequencing and other editorial suggestions.

All colleagues providing contributions to the 'Comments by other colleagues' section need a special thank you for their feedback and encouragement as well as helping to persuade you to rise to the challenge of reading this book.

Many of the colleagues I have worked with employed by client organisations as well as consulting organisations have played a crucial role in the ongoing evolution of the toolset for planning discussed in this book. Some are mentioned, but all sources of assistance not identified directly are gratefully acknowledged. Only the misconceptions and mistakes are entirely mine.

Amy Laurens, my senior editor at Routledge, provided important feedback which shaped this book's final form, and both Amy and her senior editorial assistant Alex Atkinson made the process of completing the book as painless as possible. Their support was greatly appreciated.

I am very grateful for permission from John Wiley and Sons to use figures and tables from *How to Manage Project Opportunity and Risk* (Chapman and Ward, 2011), some directly and some with various degrees of adaptation and development.

This book is dedicated to my wife, Jean. Jean died in 2015, after living more than two years as fully as she could whilst coping with palliative treatment for cancer. For 50 years Jean was the centre of my universe. She is still the star that I steer by. Jean set her own agendas with clarity and pursued them with determination, but she always instinctively understood what really mattered to other people and responded with empathy and kindness. Jean's serious passions included our sons, daughters-in-law, and grandchildren; her many friends; medical practice and medical education; music; art; and archaeology, but management in a management sciences sense was never even a remote interest. Asking Jean to read a draft of this book or discuss technical content issues was never considered. But she had a deep understanding of what motivated this book, and she inspired and supported its evolution in crucial ways, as well as playing a central role in shaping the perspective which underlies it.

Part 1

Foundations

Chapters 1 to 4 contents indicating sections within chapters

1 Why planning is usually vital but often difficult and frequently inept

This chapter begins the process of clarifying why planning is usually vital but often difficult and frequently inept. Several further goals are also pursued throughout this chapter. The central further goal is providing an overview of key foundation level concepts, using a layered approach, with each layer building on earlier discussion. Another important related goal is beginning to clarify why some significant departures from common practice planning are needed, including aspects of common practice which are widely believed to be good practice.

The next two sections outline what 'planning' means in this book. A third section explores key implications of 'enlightened planning' (EP) at an overview level. This is followed by a series of sections introducing specific defining features of enlightened planning. The final section provides a summary with linked inferences. By the close of this chapter you should have an overview understanding of why planning is usually vital but often difficult and frequently inept, what is implied by enlightened planning terms like 'strategic clarity', and why it may be worthwhile investing the time to read the rest of this book if you already are, or you would like to become, an effective 'reflective practitioner' with an interest in approaches to planning and associated management decision making which keep it simple systematically.

Formal planning and related informal planning

'Plans' sometimes begin as very simple descriptions of a concept or intent. Plans may evolve into explicit base plans (like an aspirational target 'plan A' – what an organisation would like to do assuming there are no new significant opportunities or big problems) plus contingency plans ('plan B', 'plan C', and so on – a set of alternative plans to be used if circumstances arise which make 'plan A' inappropriate). Base plans plus contingency plans usually need to include ways to capitalise on possible good luck as well as possible bad luck. Contingency plans frequently have to address ambiguous scenarios involving 'unknown unknowns' of the 'any other unspecified major opportunity or problem' variety. 'Plan A' may need refinement, relabelling it as A1, and then replacing A1 with A2 followed by A3 to incorporate proactive adjustment of the base plan to better cope with uncertainty prior to plan implementation. One or more contingent 'exit plans' may be prudent, as well as prior plan B and plan C contingency planning.

Sometimes plans are usefully described as 'policy', in the sense that plans are broadly defined strategies for making specific kinds of decisions rather than plans for use on a single occasion. Sometimes plans are usefully described as 'process', in the sense that plans are a flexible process for implementing policy. Sometimes plans are usefully defined as 'procedures' or 'protocols', in the sense that plans are sets of rules for implementing policy with minimal room for creative interpretation normally assumed. Plans may address activities, resources, designs, operating policies, strategies, operational rules, formal contracts and informal relationships.

The basic role of all the planning addressed by this book is effective and efficient approaches to management decision making in 'commercial organisations'. Commercial organisations are broadly defined to include all product and service providers who charge a price for what they provide. The example organisations considered in Part 2 span a wide range of examples, but a much wider range of application areas and planning concerns is within the scope of the approaches explored in this book.

Planning may involve significant amounts of underlying analysis. In some contexts, you and many others may regard 'analysts' as a more appropriate term than 'planners' for those doing the work referred to as planning in this book. Furthermore, many of the people involved in planning whom this book addresses as key target readers may prefer to see themselves as 'managers', not 'planners' or 'analysts', with planners and analysts reporting to them.

Target readers may serve their organisations in a wide variety of roles, as project managers, marketing managers, corporate strategy managers, or managing directors, for example. A key premise this book is based on is all target readers need to be able to communicate effectively and efficiently about planning, using a shared common language and shared key assumptions about other important concerns.

You can interpret the word 'planning' in plain English terms, along with most other words used in this book. However, to 'keep it simple' this book's default interpretation of planning is *formal* planning, including all associated formal analysis.

The roles of formality when planning include ensuring that all the people involved in creating and shaping the plans make explicit what they have in mind. Associated purposes include testing assumptions and conveying information to other people who need to understand the implications of the plans in various ways. These other people may need to understand the plans because of the need for mutual support when 'component teams' of a 'big team' adjust their component plans and actions to the plans of other component teams. This is a key contingency planning issue within a broader concern for coordination and collaboration as part of effective and efficient teamwork. Other specific reasons for shared understanding relevant to some players may include their role in helping to execute the plans, their role in helping to test the plans, and their role in approving the plans. Controlling the relationship between what planners had in mind initially and evolving development and realisation of the plans may also be a crucial role for formality. Ongoing learning from experience and more general corporate knowledge capture may be further reasons of considerable importance for employing formal planning rather than relying on informal planning.

Assumed 'non-players' may become relevant players if they are not prepared to tolerate the plans – a potentially serious risk. But those initially assumed to be in opposition to or indifferent to plans may become important allies if mutual opportunities are identified – a potentially important opportunity.

Making specific aspects of planning formal involves crucially important implications for associated informal planning. Sometimes these implications are just mentioned in this book, sometimes they are developed immediately, and sometimes they are developed later at a more convenient point in the overall dialogue.

All relevant planning concerns must be dealt with via one of three options:

1   formal planning,
2   informal planning, and
3   being ignored.

Clarity about which of these three options is being used to deal with each category and area of planning, as well as ensuring appropriate option choices, is a central aspect of the 'strategic clarity' concerns which formal planning has to address.

Sometimes informal planning of some aspects is more appropriate than formal planning, and where the line is drawn between formal and informal treatment is often crucial. Usually effective understanding of informal planning using more sophisticated structures and more detail is a crucial basis for effective formal planning. All formal planning certainly needs underpinning by background informal planning. Almost invariably effectively implementing formal plans involves further detailed informal planning plus creative leaps and real-time responses to unfolding events. 'Constructive insubordination' can be crucial – departing from prescribed formal plans which are inappropriate, even in military or emergency service contexts, where disobeying orders or protocols is generally discouraged in fairly harsh terms.

Any holistic formal planning process has to integrate formal and informal components and anticipate how best to encourage creative implementation in addition to creativity at the outset and creativity throughout the planning process. Deciding whether formal or informal treatment is the most appropriate option raises complex concerns, and simply ignoring planning issues raises quite different concerns which also have complex implications. The core issues include 'capability-culture' considerations involving the capabilities provided by the relevant players and systems and the culture these capabilities are embedded in.

Two 'modes' of planning are distinguished: 'top down' and 'bottom up'. In the top-down mode 'goals' at the current decision-making level are the starting point, asking questions like 'What are we trying to achieve, and what matters most?' In the bottom-up model the starting point is decomposing what we *think* needs to be done to get to where we *think* we want to go, asking questions like 'How are we going to do it, how long is it going to take, and how much is it going to cost?' The use of 'we *think*' implies we may change our mind.

Sometimes 'the top' needs moving up or 'the bottom' needs moving down in terms of the organisational hierarchy or scope of analysis, as part of considered revisions to the planned approach through an iterative process.

Multiple iterations are a central process feature of many of the most effective and efficient formal approaches to planning. Planned iterations can be a cost-effective feature of immense importance, built into processes with this in mind. But unplanned iterations may prove essential because of earlier errors of judgement. Unplanned iterations may be very costly.

This kind of planned plus unplanned iterative process is often inherently complex. It is always important to keep planning processes as simple as possible for all those involved. However, oversimplification in the 'wrong way' can have seriously dysfunctional implications, and how to simplify in the 'right way' may not be obvious unless the approach to simplicity employed is well informed and systematic.

Planning application areas

To keep this book's discussion as simple as possible all relevant planning is decomposed into three very broad application areas:

1   operations management,
2   project management,
3   corporate management.

These three application areas need separable treatment because significant differences in approach need attention, but they are interdependent in important ways.

Each of these three application areas can be further decomposed, and often this is important in practice. However, the greater the level of decomposition, the more difficult and crucial treating interdependency issues becomes, and the importance of commonalities may be lost.

'Operations management' is sometimes interpreted as the day-to-day management of ongoing operations with a focus on short-term planning for the physical systems used by an organisation plus input supply chains. However, in this book operations management and all embedded 'operations planning' also addresses the ongoing operation of all other systems and resources, including output marketing chains. Furthermore, generating corporate strategy propositions to address future operations concerns is a crucial aspect of the interdependence between operations and corporate planning. Using this broad interpretation of operations planning, all Part 2 chapters involve a central concern for different kinds and levels of operations planning, with key roles for a traditional 'Operations Director' in Chapters 7, 8 and 9.

'Corporate management' effort and associated 'corporate planning' may be focused on formulating corporate strategy in a top-down planning mode in some organisations. For some people, this kind of strategic planning is the focus of all corporate planning. But in this book corporate management and all embedded corporate planning includes five aspects:

1   Top-down corporate planning, which starts by clarifying the corporate mission or vision in terms of goals and then moves on to strategic planning top-down to achieve those goals effectively and efficiently.
2   Corporate planning, which involves the strategic scope of operations and project planning intersecting with the rest of corporate planning.
3   Planning for all corporate resources and capabilities needing attention which may not be covered fully, if at all, by operations planning or project planning, including corporate information systems, corporate finance and human resources functions.
4   Dealing with all relevant interdependency concerns not picked up elsewhere.
5   Effective corporate governance addressing everything that matters, including all relevant capability-culture concerns.

Consideration of corporate planning in a top-down sense and its integration with other corporate planning is deferred until Chapter 8 so that we can build on the earlier discussion of component concerns. But corporate governance, as well as lower levels of governance, is directly relevant to all Part 2 chapters, as are interdependencies.

'Project management' in this book can be interpreted as the management of change in a very general sense. 'Project planning' led by a 'Projects Director' and all comparable project planning requiring effective integration with both operations and corporate management is addressed explicitly in detail for the first time in Chapter 7. But the approach developed in Chapter 7 underlies all the other chapters. Chapters 3 and 4 use examples primarily drawn from project planning contexts, and the core ideas they illustrate are central to this book as a whole. An immediate consequence is project planning is usefully explored in a little more detail now.

Project planning is often given a relatively narrow interpretation which is focused on delivering 'assets' which are physical systems. This is a convenient focus for the contexts addressed directly in Chapter 7 and most Chapter 3 and 4 examples. However, this discussion requires an interpretation in terms of a much broader scope for project planning, a scope which embraces delivering any kind of change, with a linked very broad view of the assets a project may deliver. For example, the asset delivered may be a change in corporate understanding resulting from a new planning process which helps to drive associated corporate culture changes, illustrated in Chapter 6.

Sometimes it is very useful to distinguish 'programmes' and 'portfolios' (of projects or programmes) from simpler 'project' concepts. This book assumes this will be done when relevant. But it sticks to a simple 'project planning' label most of the time, with a broad interpretation of projects which includes all programme and project portfolio concepts.

Project planning as discussed in Chapter 7 involves four key frameworks which this book refers to as 'the four Fs':

1   a project (asset) lifecycle framework,
2   a seven Ws framework,
3   a goals–plans relationships framework, and
4   a process framework.

The four Fs terminology provides a useful label or 'handle' for a key conceptual structure, a handy contraction of '*four* key conceptual and operational *frameworks*'.

Each of these four frameworks is a 'gateway concept', and the way the complete set of four frameworks which make up the four Fs work together in an integrated manner is an example of a higher level form of composite gateway concept. In the language of 'learning and teaching' a gateway concept is a portal facilitating entry into a way of thinking about an important set of lower level basic concepts and operational tools which helps to structure our overall understanding and make that understanding operational (Biggs and Tang, 2011). In this particular case the four Fs concept is a portal for understanding key aspects of project planning as an integrated interdependent coherent whole in the sense that it is central to understanding how to approach all aspects of project planning. Each of the four component frameworks is itself a portal for understanding a range of concepts and issues with key interdependencies.

Project lifecycle frameworks are usefully defined in terms of the asset provided by the change involved, including use of the asset until disposal by the project owners. However, as an illustration of the practical complications needing effective resolution, everyone involved has to accommodate the implications of contractors often favouring a different view of project lifecycles than their clients. A 'conceptualisation' stage followed by three more stages is a simple common practice portrayal for both clients and contractors. The other three stages viewed from a client's perspective are usually 'planning', 'execution and delivery', and 'utilisation'. But contractors often use planning, execution, and delivery, dropping the utilisation stage if this does not involve them and decomposing 'execution and delivery' because interfacing with different groups of people with different objectives is involved.

These common practice four stage project lifecycle portrayals are significantly elaborated for two basic reasons. One reason is recognising the crucial role of governance and capturing corporate learning at 'gateway stages', a further lower level 'gateway concept' in several senses. The other reason is recognising the crucial significance of different people with different concerns being involved as the initial concept evolves into a planned and delivered functioning asset and that asset is then employed.

The seven Ws framework is a generalisation of Rudyard Kipling's 'six honest serving men'. It begins with the 'who' (the parties involved), the 'why' (the objectives of all relevant parties) and the 'what' (the design of the asset being created). All the 'seven Ws' are formally developed and linked via an influence diagram to different kinds of plans, building on the lifecycle framework.

A goals–plans relationships framework has to be built on the project lifecycle and the seven Ws frameworks. Its purpose is to develop clarity about the relationships between the very broad top-level corporate goals being pursued by an organisation and the project plans being used to achieve selected aspects of those goals. For example, the national railway company central to Chapter 9 is associated with a corporate mission statement like 'The best railway travelling experience in Europe, delivered to our passengers by railway staff who understand and care about what good service means, including comfort, safety, punctuality and convenience at a cost which is fair and good value'. 'The best railway travelling experience in Europe' might be interpreted as its central composite corporate goal, with everything that follows viewed as interdependent component central goals which need a balanced approach bearing in mind the different preferences of different parties. These central goals might be associated with a list of attributes like travelling comfort, punctuality, safety and reasonable fares. A central set of criteria associated with overall costs might aggregate overall expected annual costs and associated cost risk involving high-side variations from expected values, assuming that realised costs drive fares and corporate profits. All the other goals might have various metrics. Assumptions about the central 'goals', their component 'attributes', and the bottom level 'criteria' relationships with plans collectively define the overall goals–plans relationships of interest for project plans.

Goals, attributes and criteria can all be referred to as 'objectives' in a hierarchy involving crucial and complex interdependencies. You may prefer alternative terminology, but all those involved in any given organisation need clarity about well-defined relationships between the plans of interest, relevant top level central goals, all associated attributes, and component criteria. This book assumes that a framework for 'goals–plans relationships' covers the whole range and all relevant interdependencies, with the goals, attributes and criteria hierarchy distinctions just made used as convenient working assumptions.

To deliver formal project planning as a fully integrated approach, a project planning process framework is the final component of the four Fs. This process framework has to use an iterative phase structure which builds on the frameworks provided by the project lifecycle stages, the seven Ws, and the goals–plans relationships. This fourth framework and its interactions with the first three are the central concern of Chapter 7, with implications for all Part 2 chapters.

Currently you may not think about project planning as the management of change in terms of explicitly using this four Fs concept. But by the end of this book, the case for explicit corporate recognition of some variant of this perspective and the four Fs framework should be clear. Any organisation not using one common explicit four Fs concept is using one or more implicit variants, and incompatibilities associated with different versions and missing key features may be the cause of important planning failures.

Corporate and operations planning contexts need variants of the project planning four Fs concept which is both broadly comparable and compatible. Compatibility is required to address interdependencies among corporate, operations and project planning. Variants of the planning horizon aspects of the project lifecycle, the seven Ws and the goals–plans relationships framework concepts are used throughout Part 2, within a common overall approach to decision-making processes. By the end of this book the case for explicit corporate recognition of this role for the four Fs beyond project planning should be clear.

If you now perceive planning for the purposes of this book from the perspective outlined so far, it should be reasonably clear already why some aspects of planning in a formal, structured manner are usually vital, and why a comprehensive understanding of 'what needs to be done' is not always obvious to all those responsible for planning approach choices or perceived in the same way by everybody involved. You may also see why a very broadly defined approach to planning is a useful perspective on all associated management decision making.

The rest of this book builds on this overview of planning to clarify inherent planning difficulties and to lay the foundations for exploring effective practical ways to resolve these difficulties.

What enlightened planning (EP) means at an overview level

The approach to planning advocated in this book is referred to as 'enlightened planning', contracted to 'EP'.

The scope of EP includes creating, enhancing, shaping, testing, interpreting and implementing all relevant plans from operations, project and corporate management perspectives using management decision-making frameworks which include process management components building upon variants of the four Fs.

'Enlightened' is used in a plain English sense. But for the purposes of this book the term 'enlightened planning' involves an effective, efficient, robust, flexible and creative approach to a long list of interrelated planning concerns. These concerns include:

1 obtaining a shared understanding of *all* relevant uncertainty to the extent this is both possible and useful, with *no* significant blind spots;
2 obtaining a shared understanding of underlying complexity to the extent this is useful, with a well-founded overview appreciation of what is not understood;
3 creating a rich set of opportunities and seizing all appropriate opportunities;
4 taking appropriate risk but avoiding imprudent or unnecessary risk;
5 making appropriate trade-offs between all relevant competing objectives;
6 integrating an organisation's operations, project, and corporate planning roles;
7 collaborating with other organisations whenever this is valuable;
8 making all assumptions as explicit, internally coherent and consistent as possible;
9 ensuring an appropriately shared common understanding of all assumptions that really matter; and
10 facilitating clarity about which parties are responsible if key assumptions do not hold.

This list implies EP has very ambitious goals, but if any goals of importance to you or organisations of interest to you have been missed, they can be added to help you shape any organisation's own variant of EP. The EP concept has a flexible design to facilitate variant development in different ways for organisations with different concerns.

The term 'enlightened planning' and its contraction to EP are useful for a number of reasons. Your immediate and very reasonable response to this assertion might be 'this particular choice of label is too pretentious or too ambitious'. To dampen this concern, *enlightened* planning was chosen to characterise a plausible but deliberately ambitious 'aspirational target' which is worth seeking. Plausible aspirational targets can be very useful if an opportunity management emphasis is important, and this feature of the EP approach seems worth emphasis to me. By the end of this book the value of planning to meet ambitious aspirational targets as well as making decisions based on realistic expectations with appropriate contingencies defining commitments and suitable contingency plans ready to meet crisis and disaster should be clear. However, if you are not convinced by the choice of enlightened planning as a label for any reason, change it to something you prefer once you are confident you understand what EP as I currently see it is about, and how your version might usefully emphasise different concerns. There are certainly very good reasons for using different labels in some contexts. The 'enhanced planning' alternative label preserving the EP contraction used in Chapter 7 is just one example of a number of suitable options.

The 'tools' in the 'toolset' for enlightened planning provided by this book range from broad principles and general processes to specific graphical formats, from conceptual devices to operational techniques, covering most aspects of formal planning. The associated requisite 'skill set' includes supporting craft skills, which can be crucial. The 'mindset' issues which EP has to address have a very broad nature. The toolset issues are the focus of this book, but skill set and mindset concerns will be touched on and sometimes developed when relevant.

EP uses a planning perspective and the terminology of planning to address concerns often considered using other terminology and different conceptual frameworks, such as decision making, decision analysis, decision theory, decision support, portfolio theory, risk management, uncertainty management, problem solving (or resolving or dissolving), and the use of various approaches to 'messes' (used in both the plain English sense and the technical sense of 'systems of interconnected problems') via various forms of systems analysis.

A basic feature of any formal planning is the nature of the assumptions employed in the planning process. An enlightened approach to planning formally distinguishes two basic types of assumptions: framing assumptions and working assumptions.

This distinction helps to clarify the process of testing assumptions, which is important because the 'right kind' of simplifying assumption is an opportunity and the 'wrong kind' of simplifying assumption is a risk.

From an EP perspective,

> *'Framing assumptions' define our perspective.*
> *'Working assumptions' are assumptions of convenience,*
> *selected to make a complex reality tractable*
> *in an effective and efficient manner.*

Framing assumptions for EP purposes include *habitual* working assumptions which we do not test because, for all practical purposes, any working assumptions which have an effect comparable to framing assumptions which are defined in more fundamental terms are indistinguishable in their effect.

One example of a framing assumption from an EP perspective is 'all organisations need explicit specific forms for each component of the four Fs concept, defined by suitable working assumptions'. This is not likely to prove contentious.

Another example of an EP framing assumption is 'uncertainty' is appropriately defined simply as a 'lack of certainty' in 'nominal definition' terms. This example is contentious for some people. It will be explored shortly, to couple this simple nominal definition to an underlying elaborated definition which provides greater clarity at a framing assumption level. Associated working assumptions will also be explored to further enhance overall clarity about the meaning of the word 'uncertainty'.

One example of a working assumption is any particular operational form developed by any specific organisation for the general project lifecycle concept which was explored briefly in the last section as part of the four Fs concept for project planning. Many other examples will be developed in every chapter.

The EP framing assumption concept and its relationship with working assumptions are explored throughout this chapter and further developed later. The core role of framing assumptions is the facilitation of an enlightened approach to choosing working assumptions, including a robust basis for effectively testing both virtually permanent ongoing working assumptions and very provisional initial working assumptions at the start of an analysis.

At a conceptual level there may sometimes be a case for distinguishing framing assumptions which define fundamental beliefs from working assumptions we habitually use without testing them. We may habitually use assumptions we know are not strictly true without testing them because we trust them, because we do not know how to test them, or because it has never occurred to us there was any need to test them. To 'keep it simple systematically' the EP framing assumption concept explicitly avoids exploring these distinctions, but if they are of interest to you whatever complexity is deemed useful can be added, as for all EP framing assumptions.

In Part 1 the focus is framing assumptions which shape basic conceptual, process and other operational toolset choices. Part 2 tales also explore the implications of organisations using inappropriate framing assumptions in a much broader sense, involving mindset assumptions as well as toolset assumptions. For example, the general manager of the organisation which Chapter 5 is centred on begins with the simple long-standing personal mindset assumption that he is running a family-owned manufacturing company as well as very simple toolset assumptions, but when he is stimulated into beginning to adopt a less restrictive mindset and toolset framing assumption perspective, he and the rest of his management team start to explore significant organisational transformation possibilities. Chapters 8 and 9 address radically rethinking the nature of both mindset and toolset framing assumptions which are comparatively complex. Other Part 2 chapters also address what might be viewed as habitual untested working assumptions which include mindset and toolset assumptions with inappropriate framing assumption implications.

EP involves a new way of looking at a rich variety of mainstream approaches, but the basis of EP is not new – its considerable ambitions would not be credible if it were. From the outset, this book acknowledges key contributions to the basis of EP when this is useful for most readers or particularly helpful for some readers with directly relevant background.

Features of EP explored in this book which are new include significantly enhanced visibility of:

1 controversial framing assumptions about concepts, processes, and other toolset components which need clear understanding for any variant of EP or any coherent alternative to EP which you or any organisations of interest to you may subscribe to,
2 interconnected fundamental problems with some features of 'received wisdom' (conventional thinking and common practice) which need rejecting by any EP variant,
3 useful relationships between decision support processes for managing all relevant uncertainty (framed in terms of associated opportunity and risk plus underlying complexity) which are 'universal' (very general) and other decision support processes which are 'specific' (to an organisation or approach or other context features to various degrees),
4 the role of teamwork and broader collaboration considerations as an integral part of the overall framework for approaches to planning, and
5 the role of capability and culture considerations as part of the relevant context concerns plus further context issues.

Seeing your current toolset for planning from an EP perspective provides a basis for reflecting on your current approaches as well as enhancing your mindset and skill set. Seeing other people's approaches from an EP perspective will inform well-founded critiques of received wisdom and effective synthesis across different 'schools of thought'. Serving both these purposes are central missions for this book, and understanding some key areas of contention may be very important for you. The nature of the cases against particular approaches which are currently entrenched in your world view may need particular clarification. Assistance with your critique of received wisdom where its failures are a serious concern for you may also be important. For all target readers these concerns are addressed as directly as possible. In some areas this means confronting concepts you may initially see as beyond your usual comfort zone in terms of 'how to do it' detail. However, you should see the point reasonably quickly, and as far as possible what any target readers could reasonably see as unnecessary detail has been minimised.

Dealing with process design choices

A general planning difficulty is 'How do we choose or design and develop the most appropriate process for planning in any given context?' At all levels of decision making in all organisations these process choice concerns require attention, and a systematic approach which clarifies the issues associated with keeping it simple in the right way can make the process choices both more effective and easier. These choices are crucial to an organisation's success, they are not easy, and there is a lot of scope for errors of judgement if a clear and coherent framework for making them is not available to everyone involved.

These choices are also highly controversial, with many different competing claims about both what needs to be done and how to do it. Dealing with the considerable difficulties involved in these important and controversial process design choices is a central EP concern.

Three closely coupled EP framing assumptions are the following:

> *All but the simplest of planning should be based on systematic exploratory processes.*
> *All planning processes should use a systematic toolset to clarify uncertainty and complexity, building suitable variants of this toolset into the resulting plans as and when this is useful.*
> *Opportunity is always a central concern, but risk is often important and sometimes crucial.*

These framing assumptions underlie the most general approach to choosing or designing and developing a suitable planning process which I have found useful in practice, including testing the validity of alternative process options as part of the process. It is outlined and its provenance briefly explored in Chapter 2. It is referred to as a '*universal* planning uncertainty and complexity management *process*', usually contracted to 'universal process' or 'UP'. All following chapters build on this UP concept, a key EP tool with both conceptual and operational roles.

One key role for the UP concept is providing a default planning process if it is not clear what other approach might be appropriate, illustrated by the tale of Chapter 5. A second key role is providing a process for building a planning process for a specific context, referred to as a '*specific* planning uncertainty and complexity management *process*', contracted to 'specific process' or 'SP'. This second role is initially illustrated by the tale of Chapter 6. A third key role is providing a process for adapting what is now commonly called a 'generic process' (a process developed for general use). This third role is illustrated by the tale of Chapter 7. Building on all these roles, a UP can be used as a basis for making comparisons between potentially suitable alternative planning processes and component models, testing relative effectiveness and efficiency, as illustrated throughout Part 2. In a related but further additional role, Chapter 8 uses a UP indirectly to define an appropriate overall framework for corporate planning. Chapter 9 then extends this Chapter 8 role to consider dealing with low-probability high-impact incident scenarios plus a related set of less serious incident scenarios within an appropriate corporate planning framework.

As an aside or footnote on a minor point of detail just in case you wondered, using 'a UP' implies saying 'UP' using two words ('u' and 'p'), for consistency with SP and EP. Should you prefer one word and 'an UP', that alternative is obviously an option. You may prefer alternatives for any of my EP terminology choices for good reasons, and what concepts are called is not an important issue unless the label significantly colours the meaning or common uses of the concept in ways that really matter.

The simplicity dilemma and the enlightened simplicity response

'Enlightened simplicity' is at the heart of a UP and enlightened planning in general – my current view of what Stephen Ward labelled 'constructive simplicity' (Ward, 1989) plus systematic approaches to using constructive simplicity which we have jointly pursued since the 1990s and others have pursued for many years using various labels. Whatever you chose to call it, the enlightened simplicity concept has been developed to address a widely understood and crucial 'simplicity dilemma'. Stated simply, the simplicity dilemma is the following:

> *Everybody obviously wants simplicity when making decisions in planning processes,*
> *but the issues may be very uncertain and inherently extremely complex,*
> *so how do we choose the right kind of simplicity and avoid the wrong kind of simplicity?*

The essence of an enlightened response to this simplicity dilemma involves seven key aspects:

1   It depends on a common joint understanding of all the relevant issues in points 2 through 7 at an appropriate level by all the parties involved, although some people may need to understand some issues in much greater depth than others.
2   It is crucially dependent on the context.
3   It requires an explicit understanding of the working assumptions employed to reduce complexity.
4   It involves explicitly testing all working assumptions and revising them when appropriate to improve robustness whenever working assumptions may be crucial to important choices, including decision-making process choices.
5   It requires an explicit understanding of framing assumptions which define an overall perspective, including the approach taken to testing working assumptions for robustness.
6   It requires effective and efficient integration of operations, project, and corporate planning roles.
7   It requires knowledge and craft skills from all relevant disciplines which have been integrated into a coherent and unified whole.

You may decide to add to or rearrange these seven key aspects by the time you finish this book, but they are a useful starting position to work with in the meantime.

Three key concerns follow from this seven-aspect view of enlightened simplicity – again you may wish to extend or modify this list later:

1　If any organisation does not have a common understanding of the limitations of its framing assumptions, it will fail to understand the limitations of its collective knowledge and skills.
2　If those leading decision making use knowledge and skills from relevant disciplines which employ incompatible framing assumptions without dealing with the implications, an organisation's collective perspective will lack coherence.
3　If those involved do not understand the dissonance involved in an incoherent perspective, or its implications in terms of lack of robustness, or the limitations of the collective knowledge and skills employed, they will be surprised by the mistakes that are made, and they will keep making the same or similar mistakes.

This book is about using enlightened simplicity for decision making in formal planning frameworks and related informal planning frameworks so we can integrate relevant knowledge and craft skills from all relevant disciplines and perspectives and learn from our experience. It is about hanging our learning and experience on a framework which is as general, flexible, and robust as possible.

The framing assumptions mantra

A popular quote known as Occam's razor, attributed to William of Occam (1285–1349), is often cited in a form like this:

> *No more things should be presumed to exist than are necessary.*

The basis of both EP and enlightened simplicity is a version of Occam's razor in the form of 'the framing assumptions mantra':

> *Keep your framing assumptions as general as possible,*
> *because you cannot routinely test framing assumptions for robustness,*
> *as you can and should for all working assumptions.*

A mantra used in this way is a framing assumption, and the framing assumption mantra is a defining feature of enlightened planning.

As pointed out earlier, working assumptions are assumptions of convenience. Working assumptions are simplifications to make a complex reality tractable and easier to deal with in an effective and efficient way. Working assumptions should be explicit, and they should be routinely tested during EP processes to ensure that they are not misleading, with a clear understanding that this is *much* easier said than done.

As also pointed out earlier, framing assumptions define our overall perspective. We can test framing assumptions by hypothesising more general framing assumptions as part of a process of reflective review of past experience, testing these hypotheses in the future. But in most operational decision-making contexts it is not practical to propose and test suitable new framing assumptions in the middle of any given planning exercise.

Deliberately pre-planned development exercises for planning processes may allow extensive testing of framing assumptions, and sometimes this can be a very useful approach, with several examples provided later. But in most circumstances, we need to do our operational planning using a framing assumption perspective we are comfortable with, and it is often convenient to also use explicit working assumption option sets that we are familiar with.

Because testing framing assumptions is inherently difficult, and routine testing of framing assumptions in the middle of decision-making processes is not practical, it follows that all EP framing assumptions should be as general and unrestrictive as we can make them by design. Furthermore, the greater the generality achieved, the broader the scope for appropriate working assumption choices, enhancing the scope for choosing the right kind of simplicity while avoiding the wrong kind of simplicity.

While drafting this book I have hypothesised more general framing assumptions than those used earlier in a number of areas to see if this might be useful, and continued this process until further tests did not seem likely to prove productive. The extent to which framing assumptions and related key working assumptions have or have not been tested empirically has been clearly identified, to help you judge the validity of any advocated framing assumptions which differ from those you currently subscribe to. You, and organisations of interest to you, might wish to continue this process in some contexts. But testing framing assumptions is not something anyone will have the time or inclination to do routinely when trying to make operational decisions in practice – the time pressures will normally prevent it.

'Doing better next time' based on past failures is a common and essential basis for testing alternative framing assumptions plus key associated working assumptions. Both individuals and organisation taking a reflective approach to learning from experience routinely test and evolve their framing and working assumptions based on earlier misjudgements. Part of the cost of learning by experience in this way is the pain caused by the earlier mistakes, usefully viewed as lost opportunities to have done better. Reading books and papers or attending courses which challenge beliefs and discussing concerns with mentors and other colleagues can play a similar but much less painful role.

One of this book's goals is to help you learn what you need to know to take an enlightened approach to planning with as little pain as possible. However, to make effective use of reading this book you will need to test the EP framing assumptions and associated working assumptions used by this book against your own current framing and working assumptions as your reading progresses, not always a straightforward or painless task. You will then need to further test your resulting framing and working assumptions in practice, confirming the replacement of your own earlier framing assumptions with better (more general) ones and related working assumptions with better (more effective and efficient ones) whenever you establish a case for doing so.

To put this in more enticing light, the ultimate goal is 'more reward' plus 'more smiles' in the 'more pleasure' and 'less pain' sense discussed using Figure 11.1 in Chapter 11, a portrayal of systematically searching for opportunities while avoiding risks which reflects capability and culture concerns in a holistic manner using an EP approach.

Stealth assumptions which matter

If colleagues or any other relevant players in a joint decision-making process are using framing assumptions or dependent working assumptions which are seriously dysfunctional because they are restrictive in inappropriate ways, something needs to be done about it as soon as possible. The same issue arises if we discover that we are using inappropriate framing assumptions or dependent working assumptions ourselves.

'Stealth assumptions' which matter are defined as framing or associated working assumptions which we or other people seem to be using with seriously dysfunctional implications when adopting any approach which does not make sense from the broadest feasible EP perspective. These stealth assumptions may be explicit, consciously adopted because of a failure to recognise the implications of bad advice, which may be based on conventional wisdom which is unwise. But stealth assumptions may be tacit, the result of following other peoples' bad practice without questioning its basis. Stealth assumptions *which matter* are viewed as important sources of concern in this book, serious sources of risk which need to be avoided.

It is generally very difficult to understand some of our own deeply seated stealth assumptions, but we can sometimes identify them when we generalise our perspective via new insights. This happened to me a lot when writing this book, because I was particularly focused on generalising my framing assumptions in order to develop a coherent and holistic framework which would help you to generalise yours. However, seeking the most general perspective feasible has been a conscious goal for many years, and the insights sometimes revealed are one of the 'pleasant surprises' life has to offer.

We cannot know what other people are actually thinking, but we can usually surmise or hypothesise an explanation for other peoples' behaviour in the form of stealth assumptions. Sometimes this is very useful.

Confronting the terminological quagmire

All key words used as technical terms, and some key multiple-word technical terms, are conceptually important in any planning framework. From an EP perspective, all words given an important technical terminology role are usefully seen as very basic and important tools, with interconnected operational as well as conceptual implications.

Some key words are as fundamental to EP as the UP concept and the four Fs. This is because specific meanings for crucial words which are restrictive can limit perspectives as much as processes or models or any other conceptual or operational tools which lack generality. Key words which are conceptually limiting are a form of seriously dysfunctional framing assumption, stealth assumptions which really matter.

Over several decades the importance of avoiding restrictive technical definitions for key words has become more and more obvious to me and many colleagues. However, many other people, including some close colleagues and friends, have strongly defended restrictive views. In a few of these cases, the definitions involved are not restrictive in obvious ways, and assuming the differences do not matter may seem reasonable. But in some cases, the definitions adopted are so highly restrictive their numerous critics have argued vigorously for decades that they should be abandoned.

Some people defending demonstrably inappropriate definitions insist that their restrictive views must be appropriate because they are endorsed (or seem to be endorsed) by published guides and standards, some of these guides and standards being seen as highly reputable and beyond reproach. Some of the most vigorous arguments I have been involved in have taken place on working parties for reputable guides and standards, but none of these guides or standards reveal this controversy, and some attempt to embrace a range of views with a serious and regrettable level of ambiguity and inconsistency. This is also true of other guides and standards I am aware of, although comparable controversy has been involved in all the many cases I have discussed with contributing authors. This makes the nature and purpose of all guides and standards controversial and contentious in ways which are not generally understood. This section explores some of the immediately relevant implications for planning processes. You will find it useful to understand these implications now, whether or not guides and standards and the technical issues they address are of any direct ongoing interest.

The terms 'uncertainty', 'opportunity', 'risk' and 'complexity' are a core quartet, particularly in need of clarity. From an EP perspective, what is meant by these four key words is a very good example of why being clear about framing assumptions matters, why the way framing assumptions relate to associated working assumptions matters, and why understanding these issues helps to clarify the nature of the stealth assumptions which matter associated with common practice you need to avoid.

This section explains how we can escape the terminological quagmire which common practice is bogged down in, and why doing so is essential. Relying on guides and standards and textbooks or papers by authors whose opinions are based on guides and standards is not a viable route to safe ground.

The EP approach developed in this section may initially seem unnecessarily pedantic – but the concern is keeping it as simple as possible with the flexibility and nuanced clarity which all planners and decision makers need in practice. It is an example of the more general concern for keeping it simple in the 'right way', avoiding keeping it simple in the 'wrong way'. It illustrates the value of an initial investment in capability to achieve massive ongoing payoffs in terms of more clarity for less effort.

Uncertainty

Uncertainty is inherent in all aspects of planning and associated management. You need a clear understanding of how to perceive and deal with uncertainty, and organisations need a clear shared understanding. Consider the closely coupled pair of simple nominal definitions:

'Uncertainty' means 'lack of certainty', and 'uncertain' means 'not certain'.

When discussing any aspects of 'uncertainty', the 'lack of certainty' definition has been the simple plain English interpretation of preference for me and a number of colleagues for many years. We have not explicitly used 'uncertain' means 'not certain' quite so much, but its usage was always implicit because they are just two ways to define the same concept.

Over the past decade, several colleagues have explicitly rejected these 'one-part' lack of certainty or underlying not certain definitions for the purpose of defining professional guidelines on working parties I have served on. Their grounds for doing so have been that this kind of simple definition is circular. My strenuous objections have been overruled. There were no hard feelings about it, but I remained unconvinced and unrepentant, without really understanding the nature of the underlying issues driving our differences in opinion.

From an EP perspective the underlying problems are now clear to me, confirming that my intuitive concerns were valid. This EP perspective did not emerge until the fourth draft of this book, and understanding the nature of the clarification process should help you to understand the rationale of the EP perspective now advocated.

The starting point for this clarification was linking the one-part, very simple nominal definitions provided earlier to an elaboration definition developed using dictionary definitions as well as technical definitions, testing to see what this elaboration definition might reveal.

Standard dictionary definitions (using several recent editions of the *Concise Oxford Diction-ary* to get started) suggested three quite different meanings for *uncertain*:

1   not certainly known or knowing;
2   unreliable;
3   changeable or erratic.

Circularity is clearly involved in the one-part nominal definitions provided earlier – there is no disagreement on this issue. However, that is also the case for the 'not certainly known or knowing' dictionary meaning of 'uncertain'. Amongst the colleagues rejecting 'lack of certainty' or 'not certain', the common preference for 'unknown' or 'not known' misses the extremely important nuance 'may be partially known' interjected by 'not certainly' in the first dictionary meaning, as well as completely missing the second two dictionary meanings. These omissions matter.

The EP position now advocated is using the one-part *nominal* definitions 'lack of cer-tainty' or 'not certain' as usefully simple summary components of the *'overall* definition', but explicitly interpreting these one-part nominal definitions using a 'three-part' *'elabo-ration* definition' which involves all three dictionary definitions for 'uncertain' *so that no important dictionary meanings or nuances are lost.* This makes the EP 'overall definitions' approach (nominal plus elaboration definitions) as general as possible.

Having established the generality of this overall definition approach for EP framing assumption purposes, briefly consider what lies behind some alternative common restric-tive definitions which everyone needs to avoid. There are technical definitions of 'uncer-tainty' and 'uncertain' which insist that probabilities cannot be associated with uncertainty. For about 50 years this idea has been explicitly rejected as inappropriately restrictive by most well-informed experts, and an EP approach follows suit. However, a dysfunctional link between uncertainty and a lack of 'probabilities' lingers in the sense that many people still regard a lack of objective probabilities and uncertainty as closely coupled if not synonymous, and a lot of inept planning is the direct result.

The reasons most well-informed experts now reject this connection may be clear to you already. If not they should be clear by the end of Chapter 3. But it may be helpful for you to understand now that arguing probabilities cannot be associated with uncertainty is usually grounded on a classical decision analysis perspective rejected by modern decision analysis in the 1960s, when subjective probabilities became accepted as proper probabilities which should embed objective probabilities as a component part if relevant data was available and worth using, but a lack of data should not preclude using probabilities defined as statements of belief, following acknowledged experts like Howard Raiffa (1968). The economist Frank Knight (1921) is often blamed for the initial confusion, but the classical decision analysis framing assumptions are probably a fairer target, if blame is an issue.

From an EP perspective, decision makers can always use subjective probabilities to describe uncertainty whenever that is helpful, but sometimes not doing so is preferable, for reasons outlined in Chapter 3.

It is often extremely useful – arguably crucial – to use working assumptions which build on this comprehensive overall definition of 'uncertainty' and 'uncertain' to clarify what is involved. These working assumptions provide valuable conceptual tools with important operational implications.

During the 1970s and 1980s I used working assumptions involving what I now see as three explicitly envisaged 'portrayals' of uncertainty, and for about two decades prior to the fourth draft of this book, four portrayals of uncertainty seemed useful. I am now convinced that adding a fifth portrayal is very important.

The EP perspective advocated in this book uses the *framing assumption* that multiple portrayals of uncertainty are crucial. For present *working assumption* purposes, five portrayals of uncertainty can be operationally useful:

1 'event uncertainty',
2 'variability uncertainty',
3 'ambiguity uncertainty',
4 'capability-culture uncertainty', and
5 'systemic uncertainty'.

The most recent addition is number four, a need for number three emerging in the 1980s. The ordering of the list was designed to simplify the explanations to follow.

Event uncertainty is inherent in some contexts, in the sense that 'a machine failing or not' may be seen as a form of uncertainty associated with a simple event happening or not. However, event uncertainty may also be associated with a scenario representing a complex range of outcomes involving many attributes which is treated as a discrete event on an outcome branch of a decision tree. For example, Chapter 9 considers a 'catastrophic incident scenario' associated with a railway involving a conditional expectation of 350 fatalities (associated with a range from 200 to 1,200+), plus an associated conditional expectation of injuries with degrees of seriousness on many scales, plus a further associated conditional expectation of physical damage to the railway system with ongoing operational cost and lost revenue implications, plus reputational damage and the implications of lawsuits and fines which may lead to bankruptcy of the railway company. This incident will be treated *for some purposes* as a discrete event which may result from earlier decisions, but that is a working assumption, a convenient portrayal of extremely complex circumstances, not an inherent event concept. Chapter 3 develops a range of much simpler 'scenario' examples of event uncertainty using a 'histogram and tree' (HAT) framework to provide coherent framing and working assumptions for an approach based on an 'event uncertainty' portrayal which links it to all the other portrayals of uncertainty.

Variability uncertainty may be inherent in the sense that uncertainty about 'good or bad weather' in terms of a lay-barge being able to lay an oil or gas pipeline in the North Sea during a one month period may be viewed on a continuous variable scale over the range 0 to 31 'lay' (working) days. However, variability uncertainty may also be a very useful way of portraying uncertainty about the total cost of an offshore project – which is a mixture of inherent variability uncertainty, event uncertainty, ambiguity uncertainty, capability-culture uncertainty and systemic uncertainty.

Ambiguity uncertainty can be a particularly useful portrayal of uncertainty associated with knowledge we would like to have which could be acquired at a low cost relative to the expected cost of carrying on without this knowledge. However, it can also be an important way to look at some uncertainty which will be partially reduced as a result of ongoing planning processes, the implementation of plans and the passage of time. Ambiguity uncertainty is a generalisation of what some decision analysis literature approaches address via 'the value of information' in 'perfect information' and 'imperfect information' forms.

Capability-culture uncertainty encompasses the uncertainty underlying all relevant 'human error' issues, interpreted to include the underlying basis of all associated lack of capability and behavioural risk concerns plus relevant supporting systems concerns. Gawande

(2011) provides an example discussed in more detail in Chapter 2 which links human capability issues to associated systems – Boeing's approach to supporting aircrew faced with very serious low probability incidents which uses an on-board computer-based information system. A well-trained co-pilot can use the system to access the best advice available in a very short period to prevent an accident. A system of this nature can cover a huge range of issues most pilots will never encounter, and it can be kept updated from a wide range of sources. All four of the alternative portrayals of uncertainty may be viewed within or overlap this portrayal. This way of looking at uncertainty draws on all three of the dictionary meanings, incorporating associated nuances as well.

Systemic uncertainty may be reasonably straightforward or exceedingly difficult to characterise. At the relatively straightforward end of the spectrum, systemic uncertainty may underlie the sum of the uncertainty associated with a sequence of activities in a project in the sense that if one activity is delayed, a second following activity may be more likely to be delayed, and knock-on effects including cascade effects may make the delay worse. Two somewhat different types of dependence may be involved, one associated with the chance of initiating conditions, the other associated with consequences and responses to consequences. Both might be addressed in statistical dependence terms or in causal dependence terms. While early responses to specific problems and general responses to sets of accumulating problems may dampen accumulating delays, consequential positive and negative feedback loops can be complex and difficult to disentangle. The relationships involved can become very complex very quickly if we keep digging, even in a relatively straightforward project planning context limited to how long a sequence of activities might take. Much more complex situations can be associated with contexts involving concerns like macroeconomics and geopolitics.

All five portrayals of uncertainty may be involved, with important interdependencies which systemic uncertainty might portray. Concepts involving uncertainty which may be beyond the bounds of conventional analysis, like 'black swans' (Taleb, 2007), 'exceptional uncertainty' (Marshall, 2015) and 'radical uncertainty' (King, 2016), need to be associated with all five when relevant, sometimes as components of what this book calls 'unknown unknowns'.

Unknown unknowns is a term which I initially used in 1970s work with BP, in a way discussed in Chapter 3. I now see 'unknown unknowns' as a useful EP term for uncertainty which may be unknowable but might be knowable if we were more capable or had more time and *often* is simply not worth understanding any better in the current context at this particular time. This unknown unknowns kind of uncertainty might be associated with any of the five portrayals just outlined and linked to uncertainty beyond the bounds of conventional analysis. For example, 'black swans' is now a well-known term for uncertainty missed by conventional thinking in a financial analysis area (Taleb, 2007), with wider implications. 'Radical uncertainty' is a term formally defined to go beyond conventional economic thinking in a book on global economics including underlying geopolitical issues by Mervyn King (King, 2016), a distinguished economist who was governor of the Bank of England from 2003 to 2013. There are many ways of looking at unknown unknown concepts, and you may have your own preferred terminology, but it is convenient to have one unifying concept which serves all the purposes of the unknown unknowns EP concept. Forms of systemic uncertainty which may be extremely difficult to clarify include links between capability-culture uncertainty and ambiguity uncertainty – like an unknown ability to deal with non-predictable initiating events which can turn a potential crisis into a catastrophe very quickly, the role of feedback loops between parties to a project whose objectives are not aligned which can lead to a complete breakdown in relationships which means everybody is in serious trouble, and economic or geopolitical issues. Forms of uncertainty which simply may not be worth resolving at present include the events which might disrupt the detailed plans for executing a project which we have not yet decided to undertake and may reject if better opportunities are identified. Dealing with some of the relatively straightforward kinds of unknown unknown is not that difficult if we understand what needs to be done and how to do it, but the capability required to do so effectively is not currently as widely available as it might be.

Risk/uncertainty distinctions are important in this book, with uncertainty underlying risk. For example, 'systemic uncertainty' is an uncertainty management term for the uncertainty underlying what some people call 'systemic risk'. From an EP perspective, risk and uncertainty should not be confused, for reasons we will start to explore shortly. Systemic risk, risk associated with variability and risk associated with events are all well-known risk management concerns, although they are not always considered in the same framework by all risk management experts. Risk associated with human factors and related systems failures are also well-developed areas by those who focus on these areas. Risk associated with ambiguity is often implicit, but addressing ambiguity explicitly is not a new idea. Explicitly addressing all five of the portrayals of sources of uncertainty which this book assumes may underlie risk, and linking this to a broad EP interpretation of unknown unknowns, may be novel – I have not encountered it before. But others have used variants of the same basic ideas, and what really matters is that everyone who needs to explicitly employ these five portrayals of uncertainty, plus an effective and efficient overlapping unknown unknowns concept, can whenever this is useful, avoiding any relevant blind spots. Ways of doing so are demonstrated later.

Four general observations about key words are worth brief reflection before moving on.

First, we all want simple definitions, but useful simple definitions with an element of circularity may be in need of elaboration. One kind of elaboration is illustrated by the explicit referral to all three dictionary definitions for 'uncertain' discussed earlier. More generally, an elaboration definition approach to the 'overall definition' for EP framing assumption purposes *may* be a useful approach.

Second, this kind of simple nominal definition is nominal in two senses: it needs a closely coupled elaboration definition, and even the elaboration definition is nominal in the sense that if you prefer a slightly different dictionary definition this is not a problem.

Third, as we will see shortly, some nominal definitions may need to deal directly with multiple meanings because there is no useful simple one-part definition, circular or otherwise.

Fourth, having obtained the framing assumption generality that we need in terms of the simplest feasible overall definition, we may also need elaboration in terms of specific identified working assumptions – like five portrayals of uncertainty – to provide operational ways of looking at the general concepts delivered by unrestrictive framing assumptions.

A general concern addressed by this EP approach to definitions is the need to avoid a 'Red Queen syndrome'. In *Alice in Wonderland* (Carroll, 1865), the Red Queen declares that 'words mean exactly what I want them to mean' (because I am the Queen, and anyone who disagrees will lose their head). None of us are Red Queens, even when serving as the authors of standards and guides, and we do not live in Wonderland.

Opportunity

Recognising and exploiting all feasible opportunities to improve plans is a key aspect of all enlightened planning. Consider direct use of the three-part nominal definition:

1   *'Opportunity' means 'a favourable situation'; or*
2   *'a situation with a good chance of a favourable outcome'; or*
3   *'a potential favourable outcome'.*

The first two meanings are key dictionary meanings which are clearly different, while the third is arguably a very special case of the first, and there is no simple one-part definition in a circular form or any other form.

Not until the fourth draft of this book was underway did it become clear to me that none of these meanings on its own is a suitable overall definition in the sense an EP approach requires; there is no simple definition that captures all three of these meanings with requisite clarity, circular or otherwise, *and* all three meanings are actually crucially important aspects of what we all mean by 'opportunity' in different contexts. All three meanings are worth including separately in the direct three-part approach to the *nominal* definition used earlier, further enhanced by any alternative variants you think are important.

Along with *some* colleagues I have subscribed to the third definition as a technical definition of 'opportunity' for *some* purposes for many years. But it is now clear that we were *implicitly* using a more general interpretation which included the first two parts of this three-part definition for other purposes, and this inconsistency was unhelpful. We did not have a simple one-part circular equivalent to the uncertain and uncertainty definitions, and we do not need one. What we do need is a three-part (or more) approach to a nominal definition concept for opportunity.

My colleague Matthew Leitch has in effect been telling me this for some time. For example, when providing feedback on a draft of Chapman and Ward (2011) he argued that he saw opportunities as 'a set of circumstances which made it relatively easy to do what you wanted to do' – a very useful illustration of a variant of the first dictionary meaning in an 'opportunity efficiency' context which is ignored by the third meaning. It took Stephen Ward's suggestion to carefully study dictionary definitions linked to also reappraising useful technical definitions for 'the penny to drop' – I have been a slow learner on this issue. However, I have not been as slow as those in the risk management 'experts' community who have continued to insist that 'opportunities' are 'favourable events' in an 'upside risk event' sense or continued to promote tools which imply this perspective without careful and explicit health warnings.

Limiting 'opportunities' to 'favourable events' is obviously too restrictive. It results in a focus on event uncertainty which ignores variability uncertainty, ambiguity uncertainty, capability-culture uncertainty, and all forms of systemic uncertainty. Indeed, what actually prompted my formal 'favourable potential outcome' interpretation was an attempt to explicitly avoid a 'favourable event' interpretation when its promoters became vocal and strident in the 1990s, keeping it simple in a comparable manner. But a one-part definition restriction involved a serious mistake. I had fallen into the common trap of being simplistic because of a well-intentioned wish to keep it simple, avoiding simplifying in one wrong way, but still simplifying in another 'wrong way'. Explicitly embracing the first two definitions as well as the third helps to clarify some of the very important more complex roles and nuances of 'opportunity efficiency', addressed in outline shortly, in more detail in Chapter 3 and all following chapters. This clarification is very useful, and a three-part nominal definition which needs no elaboration definition is the simplest feasible way to achieve the needed generality of 'opportunity' from an EP perspective.

Risk

Recognising and deciding what to do about risk is an important part of all management activity, and risk should be a key concern in all planning processes. Risk is not just the province of specialist risk management experts.

Consider the two part nominal definition:

1   *'Risk' is 'the possibility of unfavourable outcomes'; or*
2   *'a person or thing that could cause unfavourable outcomes'.*

Until the need for the definitions of uncertainty and opportunity just discussed became clear, my focus was on the first part of this two part nominal definition of 'risk'. But both these two quite different meanings for 'risk' are well worth making explicit.

The second part of this definition is particularly rich in implications when coupled to recognising the crucial role of 'capability-culture uncertainty'. For example, a 'risk' may be a thing or a person which is an inherent source of risk, 'an accident waiting to happen' in common parlance, a 'hazard' in some peoples' terms. One key associated uncertainty may be how long it will take to happen, but all five portrayals of uncertainty may be relevant, not just events. For example, if a person is unreliable, badly trained, poorly motivated, or not suitably supported by the systems they work with, in plain English we can say they are a risk or a source of risk, even if nothing has happened yet, and we have no real idea what sort of misfortunes might be forthcoming.

From an EP perspective there is no need for an underlying elaboration definition, but working assumptions which build on this two part nominal definition of 'risk' to provide additional clarity are very important. One aspect of desirable clarity is developing an effective understanding of the issues involved in 'risk appetite' concerns. These concerns can be fairly simple or very complex. A suitably general framework for thinking about risk appetite in terms of an attribute like profit or loss with a monetary metric requires recognition that as the probability or size of a potential loss increases, the appetite for more risk may change. Furthermore, different relevant parties may have very different risk–reward preferences. Explicitly accommodating these issues effectively may be important. Relatively simple practical ways of implementing this general framework are available in some contexts, but others require more sophistication.

From an EP perspective, a lot of common practice is based on definitions of 'risk' which are far too narrow. For example, briefly consider the definition 'risk = probability × impact'. This is the most unacceptably narrow technical definition of 'risk' available. It is what many 'risk experts' meant by risk 50 years ago, and some still do. The directly linked definition of 'opportunity' is an 'upside risk event' variant of the 'downside risk event' definition. Joint use of these definitions implies risk and opportunity necessarily involve events (or conditions) which either happen or do not happen. That is, risk and opportunity are limited to 'event uncertainty' from an EP perspective, which involves unacceptable stealth assumptions which matter greatly. Variability uncertainty, ambiguity uncertainty, capability-culture uncertainty, and systemic uncertainty concepts may overlap, but they collectively cover *much more* than just 'event uncertainty'. Sometimes fundamental changes in the nature of the issues which need addressing become very clear if we replace an event uncertainty basis for risk with an EP nominal definition, in addition to the order of magnitude increases in the scale and the importance of the potential uncertainty involved.

If you understand the operational implications of the five portrayals of uncertainty, it will be obvious that a focus on risk associated with event uncertainty is seriously myopic because it excludes the other four kinds of uncertainty. Basic problems remain even if advice linked to using an event-based risk concept urges concern for causes. Skilled users of event-based approaches may address causal uncertainty structures in great detail, but they may be blind to other crucial aspects of uncertainty. All risk management approaches which use framing assumptions limiting 'risk' to event uncertainty need to be reframed, and some associated tools need to be scrapped.

Furthermore, 'risk = probability × impact' implies that 'risk' can be measured by the expected outcomes of possible events as defined by this equation, completely ignoring the variability uncertainty associated with events, never mind the variability uncertainty incorporating correlation (systemic uncertainty) and embedded ambiguity which the mean-variance formulation of relevant risk developed by Harry Markowitz (1959) captures via variance and underlying covariance, and alternative working assumptions can address in other frameworks. Completely ignoring variability in the sense of possible departures from expected outcomes when defining 'risk' should *never* be tolerated – it is almost beyond belief that anyone currently claiming to be a 'risk expert' could seriously support such an approach. Surprisingly, many risk experts still seem to believe this is an appropriate starting position for considering risk, even in contexts where the variability aspects of risk matter enormously. Chapter 9 provides one key example.

Some risk management experts think that an event-based definition of risk requires a linked restrictive definition of 'issues', whenever a probability of one is involved. Some also think that an event-based definition of risk implies that *objective* probabilities of the events occurring are required – otherwise, we are talking about uncertainties with unknown or unreliable subjective probabilities. Those who subscribe to this latter view see risks and uncertainties as mutually exclusive, although some others see the terms 'risk' and 'uncertainty' as interchangeable equivalents.

This kind of limiting and confusing thinking about risk, opportunity, and uncertainty is clearly interconnected in complex ways, linked to underlying assumptions about what is meant by other key concepts – like probability.

The confusion which widespread support for these restrictive framing assumption positions adds to an already difficult set of planning concerns is demonstrably unhelpful. The inevitable result is unnecessarily inept treatment of risk, uncertainty, and opportunities, usually adding to, compounding, and confusing the nature of further reasons for widespread planning difficulties. Illustrative examples will be explored to clarify what is involved later.

Complexity

Effective and efficient planning requires a 'fit-for the purpose' level and form of understanding of complexity associated with both the planning context and the planning process being used. Consider the very simple one-part nominal definition:

> *'Complexity' means 'lack of simplicity'.*

This definition is clearly circular in the same sense as 'uncertainty' defined as 'lack of certainty' is circular. Dictionary definitions of complexity mention 'component parts' and 'complicated'. Experts with a focus on complexity often make distinctions between situations which are 'complex' and situations which are just 'complicated'. For example, Gawande (2011) illustrates the difference using 'putting someone on the moon is complicated', but 'bringing up children is complex'. These are just different kinds of complexity for present purposes, related to the number of relevant factors and the extent of their interactions. There is no reason why you should not make these distinctions using multiple part elaboration definitions or working assumptions if and when doing so is useful. But for the purposes of this book, there are no obvious disadvantages to limiting the 'overall definition' of 'complexity' to a simple one-part nominal definition, with a provision for further working assumptions where this is useful.

Complexity is assumed to underlie uncertainty when we do not fully understand complexity, and complexity is viewed as pervasive and not easily characterised or separated from uncertainty. Uncertainty is assumed to underlie opportunity and risk.

Some further nominal definitions

Having explored the meanings for three of the four crucial key words in considerable detail, followed by a relatively light-touch approach to the fourth, we can now use a relatively light-touch approach to generalise this nominal definition concept for six further key terms which need nominal definitions to clarify the discussion to follow.

Each of these further nominal definitions began as a simple plain English definition, used to capture associated technical definition concerns for many years. But each has now been carefully tested against dictionary definitions and common technical interpretations, to maintain as much simplicity as possible without being restrictive or excluding any useful nuances. The six further nominal definitions are

1   'probability' means 'a subjective measure of likelihood which may embed data-based objective measures',
2   'robustness' incorporates 'resilience' and comparable concepts when they do not need separate treatment,
3   'scenarios' are qualitative or quantitative analysis constructs,
4   'separable' means 'able to be separated',
5   'synthesis' incorporates 'synergistic synthesis' in the usual sense of going beyond a simple sum of the parts plus going beyond the current scope of analysis in an imaginative and creative manner whenever this is appropriate, and
6   'analysis' incorporates 'synthesis' in the broad sense just defined and includes understanding all key aspects of interconnectedness and context.

Restrictive technical definitions for any of these words should be avoided. You may prefer to view some of these further nominal definitions as explicit working assumptions, not definitions in the framing assumption sense associated with the four nominal definitions considered first. For example, I see the 'probability' definition given earlier as a crucially important framing assumption but the 'robustness' definition as a convenient working assumption. You or your organisation may want to add to these six.

It was convenient to provide these nominal definitions in the order used, but it is convenient to provide brief clarification of each working from the bottom up.

Analysis explicitly avoids precluding any specific approaches or separating analysis from linked synthesis in terms of the broad interpretation of synthesis just defined. Sometimes it will be useful to use the word 'synthesis' separately or in conjunction with analysis for emphasis, usually implying a broad interpretation of synthesis without being tedious by repeatedly saying so.

Synthesis in the broad sense defined earlier is usefully illustrated with a simple example. You might arrange an afternoon business meeting of importance several weeks in advance in a city some distance away which you do not know. When you come to plan the trip to get there, you might discover your initial base plan for travelling during the morning of the meeting day involves unanticipated complications which could lead to you being late for the meeting. Train or airplane leg 'A' followed by a connection to 'B' and then 'C' might involve a significant chance of a failed connection, for example. Standard analysis approaches to contingency planning might involve making plans to tackle leg C differently depending on the outcome of legs A and B. But contingency planning approaches using analysis incorporating a broad view of synthesis might suggest going a day early, perhaps spending time doing some work that could be particularly productive while you have no other distractions, or perhaps going several days early and making a mini-holiday of the extra time in an unfamiliar city or nearby countryside, possibly taking someone with you so you can both enjoy the opportunity. An imaginative creative leap well beyond the initial analysis is triggered by a problem initially addressed via conventional analysis and synthesis. This approach to synthesis is a core characteristic of EP in all contexts. Chapter 5 provides more extensive examples, as do Chapters 6 to 10.

Separable adopts the basic dictionary plain English interpretation 'able to be separated', but it also facilitates explicit use of a much broader technical definition than usual, of the form 'a working assumption implying a sequential treatment selected to make interdependence assumptions which are as appropriate as possible'. For example, if an iterative process has sequential component phases 1, . . . , n, phase separability implies that the phase partitions are useful because different kinds of issues are conveniently separated in this decomposition structure, and it also implies that the ordering reflects useful precedence relationship assumptions. The first pass through the process assumes that phase 1 can be addressed without knowing the outcomes from phases 2, . . . , n, the first pass through phase 2 can be addressed knowing the outcome of phase 1 but not the outcome of phases 3, . . . , n, the first pass through phase 3 can be addressed knowing the outcome of phases 1 and 2 but not the outcome of phases 4, . . . , n, and so on. A second complete pass can readdress phase 1 knowing the first pass outcomes for all n phases, in some circumstances in effect just addressing marginal changes. Provided an iterative process converges to a stable overall assessment, full interdependence between all the issues addressed in all the phases is a viable framing assumption. Separability is just a working assumption, which employs a structure chosen for effectiveness and efficiency. The underlying basis of this interpretation is a form of pairwise separability used throughout this book. A what needs to be done intuitive understanding developed via examples will be provided for all readers as needed as this book progresses. For those interested in more how to do it detail, the initial exploration in Chapman (1974, 1975), based on Pearce (1964), is further developed and updated in Chapman and Ward (2002).

Scenarios are usefully visualised using a wide range of approaches, some involving 'quantitative' interpretations (probability-based) and some involving purely 'qualitative' interpretations (no probabilities), as advocated by authors like MacNulty (1977), Becker (1983), Schoemaker (1992, 1995), and van der Heijden (1996).

Robustness is defined in general terms to include 'resilience', and comparable concepts like 'redundancy', whenever it is useful to do so for simplicity and comprehensiveness. A concern for robustness in a very broad sense is central to an EP approach, as a key aspect of a 'keep it simple' perspective. Distinguishing concepts like resilience and robustness or using several words when one will do is not helpful much of the time, but sometimes helpful distinctions can be made. For example, there are times when it is useful to associate 'robustness' with effective testing of prior planning analysis in a general sense, to not only tease out any working assumptions which are not appropriate, including assumptions driving a lack of resilience, but also associate 'resilience' with plans which embody a post-implementation ability to respond to circumstances which could not have been anticipated. This may help to clarify how resilience will be used as part of an overall strategy to achieve robustness.

Probability is a tool for quantifying *some* uncertainty *when this is useful*, using a modern decision analysis view of subjective probabilities for framing assumption purposes which embeds an objective probability basis when this is appropriate. It is important to recognise there is no such thing as an objective probability for making decisions if anything other than the data is relevant and any of the statistical analysis assumptions may not be strictly true. For example, the future may not replicate the past associated with the available data. Using an objective data-based probability involves a statement of belief, whether or not decision makers and their analysts care to recognise this is the case. It is also important to recognise that no data may be available, if data are available its quality may be debatable, and it may not be cost-effective or feasible to use data in the time available. While some people like a 0–1scale for probabilities all of the time, others find a percentage scale or a '1 in x chance' or a 'return period of y years' useful some of the time, and whatever approach is judged most appropriate for the context is the working assumption adopted by this book.

Nominal definitions as a whole

The high level of clarity sought when addressing these ten general (unrestrictive) nominal definitions usefully clarifies the use of these words in the rest of this book. But this does not mean that the use of these words cannot be given alternative interpretations using clearly articulated assumptions whenever this is helpful. Provided the differences do not lead to different decisions they do not matter. However, if they do lead to different decisions you need to test the implications, looking for stealth assumptions that really matter. What *always* matters is framing assumptions which are as general as possible, plus working assumptions which are fit for purpose, with clarity about the role and implications of all relevant assumptions.

Risk efficiency, clarity efficiency and opportunity efficiency

Three interdependent 'efficiency' concepts frame an EP approach to overall planning efficiency and effectiveness. Because routine repetition of 'efficiency and effectiveness' would be tedious, this book follows the convention established by the Markowitz 'risk efficiency' term, explicitly embedding 'effectiveness' as well as efficiency concerns in each of the three EP terms:

1   'risk efficiency',
2   'clarity efficiency', and
3   'opportunity efficiency'.

Consider 'risk efficiency' first, because in the context of this section risk efficiency is the simplest place to start to understand all three EP efficiency concepts.

Risk efficiency

As explained in the Overview when discussing Chapter 3, the use by BP of an approach to planning North Sea projects based on risk efficiency delivered lower expected costs, *plus* less risk, *plus* reliable estimates of project cost and duration, *simultaneously*. Risk efficiency is also the basis of many other planning benefits explored in Chapter 3 in relation to IBM UK and the UK MoD, elaborated in Chapter 4 and all Part 2 chapters.

From an EP perspective,

'Risk efficiency' means a minimum level of risk
for any given level of expected reward.

The term 'risk efficiency' is usually associated with Markowitz and a mean–variance interpretation of risk, but EP requires a much more general interpretation.

To begin to appreciate what risk efficiency means in generalised EP terms, it can be useful to start with the common simplifying working assumptions in a Markowitz portfolio analysis context:

1   only one attribute is of interest, referred to as 'reward';
2   reward is measured by total profit;
3   we can estimate probability distributions for all the components of expected profit and associated risk; and
4   all these probability distributions are Normal (Gaussian) and unconditional.

Given these working assumptions, 'expected reward' is a 'best estimate' of what should happen on average, formally defined as the first moment about the origin of the associated probability distribution. Overall portfolio expected reward can be expressed as a linear function of component investment values multiplied by their expected rewards per monetary unit invested. 'Variance' associated with expected reward is a suitable surrogate measure for risk associated with any given expected reward, because Normal distributions are fully defined by their mean (expected value) plus their variance (a measure of spread relative to the mean, formally defined as the second moment about the mean). That is, as the variance gets bigger, the probability of any given downside departure from the expected value increases, so risk in terms of the EP nominal definition unambiguously gets bigger. Overall portfolio variance involves a quadratic functional form for combining all component variance and covariance terms.

Chapter 3 explores approaches which are simpler *and* less restrictive assuming that one measurable reward attribute is relevant, maintaining only the first of these four working assumptions. Chapter 4 starts to explore the more difficult situations when multiple attributes are involved. All further chapters build on this basis, with some particularly complex and contentious multiple attribute concerns addressed in Chapters 8 and 9.

Clarity efficiency

Now consider the second aspect of EP efficiency – 'clarity efficiency', a focal point for an EP implementation of enlightened simplicity:

'Clarity efficiency' means a minimum level of planning cost/effort
for any given level of relevant clarity.

The word 'clarity' in this book can be given a plain English meaning if the context is a general discussion, but if the context is the role of clarity efficiency or the 'strategic clarity' and 'tactical clarity' concepts discussed shortly, an associated working assumption is that 'clarity' means 'relevant insight which can be shared'.

If relevant understanding of key issues of concern which require a degree of common understanding cannot be communicated effectively to all those who need to understand, we do not have 'clarity' in a clarity efficiency sense.

Achieving a higher level of clarity while simultaneously expending less planning cost/ effort and then making sure that the trade-offs between clarity achieved and the marginal planning cost/effort of more clarity is appropriate is what enlightened simplicity is about, a central feature of an EP approach.

The practical issues requiring confrontation include the following:

1   clarity is not a single attribute,
2   most of the relevant multiple attributes are not measurable, and
3   what 'relevant clarity' implies is complex in a dynamic sense.

Chapters 3 and 4 deal with these difficulties by carefully ordering the issues addressed to keep the discussion as simple as possible. Part 2 confronts the practical implications of these difficulties in a range of contexts, systematically exploring how non-measurable multiple attributes and other aspects of the complexity involved can be accommodated with a minimal level of planning cost/effort, tailoring the approach to the contexts involved.

The dynamic nature of the complexity associated with relevant clarity arises because the clarity which is relevant depends upon what our planning process is trying to achieve, and our understanding of our planning goals may evolve as the planning process proceeds in a manner which is partially but not wholly predictable. For example, in the concept stage of a project we need initial clarity about the robustness of the business case for proceeding with a project concept, and we can predict approximately how that robustness will grow if there are no really big surprises as project definition proceeds. However, big surprises are both frequent and inherently unpredictable. Chapters 3 and 4 explore some predictable aspects in a preliminary way, further developed in all later chapters. Chapter 5 will initiate exploration of some unpredictable aspects which the rest of Part 2 builds on.

Opportunity efficiency

The third aspect of EP efficiency, 'opportunity efficiency', is formally defined in terms of three key component assumptions.

> *'Opportunity efficiency' requires*
> *risk efficiency with respect to all relevant attributes,*
> *plus appropriate trade-offs between risk and reward for each attribute,*
> *plus appropriate trade-offs between all attributes.*

Opportunity efficiency is clearly a very complex composite concept. But it would be unacceptably naïve not to face this complexity and deal with all aspects of it to the best of our ability.

One aspect of this complexity is clarified and amplified if we recognise that clarity efficiency attributes are directly relevant, and we also insist on the explicit working assumption:

> *Both 'relevant attributes' and 'appropriate trade-offs'*
> *should be judged by all parties with legitimate concerns.*

Opportunity efficiency builds on both the risk efficiency and the clarity efficiency concepts, neither of which is simple and straightforward. Opportunity efficiency can be seen as the basis of effectiveness as well as efficiency, in the sense that achieving both effectiveness and efficiency in an appropriately balanced manner with a balance that may vary over time is the same thing as achieving opportunity efficiency. Opportunity efficiency can also be seen as a crucial way of viewing 'best practice', in the sense that opportunity efficiency is an operational definition of what best practice *ought* to mean from an EP perspective.

It would be surprising if you did not have an initial intuitive feel for most aspects of what opportunity efficiency involves. If you are mathematically inclined, intuitively it is a kind of 'universal optimality' concept, going beyond conventional 'global optimality' concepts used by mathematicians in the sense that it considers trade-offs between the cost of seeking optimality and the virtues of 'satisficing' behaviour and the use of 'coping strategies' in a stochastic framework which goes beyond the limitations of probability distribution representation of uncertainty in a quantified form. If you are not mathematically inclined, you may find the rejection of conventional 'global optimisation' in favour of a practical emphasise driven by clarity efficiency usefully encouraging, and the decomposition structure intuitively attractive.

However, it would also be surprising if you were not concerned about the multi-faceted nature of opportunity efficiency, and the operational implications of the implied approaches to seeking opportunity efficiency in practice. These concerns will be addressed – that is what this book is about. But there is no easy direct route to resolving your concerns – they will have to be addressed gradually as this book progresses.

The essence of what this book is about is using opportunity efficiency as an operational approach to achieving best practice, with a view to avoiding the common ambiguity if not outright confusion about what best practice and good practice actually mean. We all know very bad practice when we see it, if it is bad enough. Most of us know very good practice when we see it, if it is good enough. What is much more difficult is deciding what best practice *ought* to mean in advance in the context of a particular organisation, and then getting a group of people to agree to pursue it with a common vision and shared conceptual and operational tools, with effective leadership from the top, the middle, and the bottom as appropriate.

To reinforce your initial intuitions, to outline in broad terms where we are going, and to indicate why getting there matters, consider a one-paragraph overview of a few clues.

Clarity about what is meant by 'risk appetite' in terms of all relevant attributes can be an important part of opportunity efficiency. Relevant concerns include everyone in an organisation understanding why an aggressive approach to financial risk up to a limit determined by each individual's role may be both sound and essential practice, but an aggressive approach to reputation risk will not be tolerated. In terms of key trade-offs between attributes, important concerns may include issues like appropriate trade-offs between expected levels of environmental security, expected levels of safety in terms of fatalities and injuries, expected levels of cost or profit, and all associated potential departures from expectations. At simpler levels, opportunity efficiency addresses trade-off questions like 'How much is it worth to finish a project earlier than currently expected, perhaps by increasing the cost, or perhaps by reducing the functionality of what is being delivered?' At the simplest level, the concern may be 'if all we want is an unbiased estimate of an activity's duration to plan the rest of a project, what does a minimum-clarity approach to estimation involve, and what kinds of additional clarity might be worthwhile if they were available for a modest level of additional effort?'

This very simple overview of what opportunity efficiency addresses is not going to resolve all your concerns, and there is no simple way to do so because opportunity efficiency is an

inherently complex concept. However, Chapters 3 and 4 explore some basic aspects successfully addressed by organisations like BP International and IBM UK in the 1970s, 1980s,
and 1990s, successfully employed by many other organisations during that period and since,
along with some key complexities, all further developed in later chapters. *Achieving* opportunity efficiency and *achieving* enlightened planning are synonymous, involving the same
goals viewed through a different lens. Both need understanding developed in a layered manner. The rest of this book will gradually build your understanding of opportunity efficiency,
layer by layer, as an integral part of building your understanding of EP.

You may find it helpful to see opportunity efficiency as another composite gateway concept, at a higher level of composition than the four Fs discussed at the outset of this chapter.
Risk efficiency and clarity efficiency are component gateway concepts.

Framing multiple objective trade-off approaches

One section in Chapter 4 briefly outlines the nature of 'goal programming' as a general *conceptual* basis for framing all multiple objective planning approaches. Goal programming uses
a mathematical programming approach to providing a consistent basis for assessing alternative operational procedures for achieving opportunity efficiency trade-offs using 'shadow
price' and 'shadow cost' concepts. Mathematical programming tools are never used directly
in this book, and those who are not mathematically inclined should be comfortable with the
Chapter 4 treatment of this issue and the way it is used throughout this book. However,
shadow price and cost concepts are crucial components of an EP understanding of both
simple and complex trade-offs in opportunity efficiency terms, another important gateway
concept or portal which provides a very general conceptual basis for simple operational tools
which all target readers need to understand.

Risk efficiency in Markowitz mean–variance terms can be interpreted in terms of a goal
programming perspective to address the trade-offs between the criteria expected reward and
reward risk when reward involves a single attribute like profit – two criteria associated with a
single attribute. But more general multiple attribute contexts can also be addressed.

One important example of the role of this goal-programming perspective is the EP
approach to discounted cash flow assessments outlined in Chapter 7. Common practice
approaches to discounted cash flow analysis are usually based on *framing* assumptions that
imply a single 'hurdle rate' test associated with the discount rate is appropriate. In Chapter 7
a case is made for a multiple 'hurdle rate' test approach within a simple iterative procedure
which uses a discount rate based on the expected cost of capital and avoids embedding
consideration of any other criteria in the discount rate. It argues that it is a serious error to
embed the implications of risk premiums or opportunity costs associated with other possible
uses for the capital in the discount rate. Multiple hurdle rate tests in an iterative process
are required for all concerns beyond an expected return which covers the expected cost of
capital. A single hurdle rate discounting test is often seriously misleading, even if return on
capital is the only concern. For example, including an inappropriate 'risk premium' in the
discount rate can drive organisations away from key opportunities involving very low risk
long pay-off profile projects towards very high risk 'quick-buck' projects, the exact opposite
of what is intended and needed.

HM Treasury (2003a) explicitly recognised the multiple hurdle rate test requirement
in a public sector context, the first publication to do so that I am aware of. Chapman,
Ward and Klein (2006) clarifies the goal programming perspective underlying the 2003
HM Treasury position in a public sector context, using disposal of nuclear waste by UK

Nirex as the example context, and Chapman and Ward (2011) extends the approach to private sector decisions in the way it is used for a private sector water and sewage utility in Chapter 7.

Chapter 9 employs the same underlying goal programming conceptual framework approach, plus a 'revealed preference' interpretation of trade-offs, leading to a more complex but still practical operational approach, the most complex level of generalisation of this framework used in this book.

Most Part 2 chapters use simpler interpretations within the same overall conceptual framework, beginning with simple conventional opportunity cost approaches in Chapter 5. Shadow price and cost concepts are a generalisation of 'opportunity cost' concepts in common widespread use long before the mathematical programming basis of goal programming was developed in the 1950s.

This very general framing of all multiple objective approaches provides EP with a coherent framework for assessing different operational procedures in different contexts, to achieve clarity efficiency as well as risk efficiency and overall opportunity efficiency. This avoids a range of common practice pitfalls. The discounting issues in Chapter 7 and the trade-offs among money, lives and injuries in Chapter 9 are the most obvious examples of common practice pitfalls discussed in this book, but there are further less obvious implications.

Stochastic modelling framework choices

Chapter 3 introduces the use of a very simple 'histogram and tree' (HAT) framework for understanding all the individual sources of uncertainty which are modelled in quantitative (probabilistic) terms for stochastic modelling purposes in this book. The HAT framework facilitates thinking about uncertainty in continuous variable histogram forms or discrete variable probability tree forms, using graphs or tables or both in ways most people can follow fairly easily even if they are not numerically inclined. It makes the use of parametrically defined specific probability distribution choices an option when this is clarity efficient, but it avoids ever making them a required framing assumption.

Chapter 4 uses a single section to explain how this framework can deal with multiple sources of uncertainty involving a range of dependence structures using discrete probability arithmetic approaches. These approaches facilitate understanding stochastic modelling using numerical examples portrayed by graphs and linked tables which are kept as simple as possible in Part 2. This section also briefly explains how standard Monte Carlo simulation procedures can be employed to produce comparable results and the role of other computational approaches and related conceptual frameworks.

This HAT conceptual and operational framework is another EP tool which contributes to the opportunity efficiency of the approach as a whole, helping to overcome common practice shortfalls like ineffective treatment of dependence and weak treatment of sensitivity analysis by both analysts and the managers using their analysis. Without a HAT framework many people are confused about how to choose between alternative approaches to stochastic modelling, with competing claims from advocates of components of a HAT approach which can seem incompatible alternatives, like decision trees, methods based on moments, and Monte Carlo simulation. All target readers need a basic common understanding of clarity efficient and opportunity efficient option choices, even if they are senior managers who are users of analysis provided by others and they are usually not interested in analysis details.

Risk management failures as part of a very complex mess

Understanding what opportunity efficiency involves, why it matters, and how to achieve it, is not easy. However, ignoring the implications is not a good idea, and although failing to achieve opportunity efficiency is frequent, this need not be the case.

To illustrate why the pursuit of opportunity in an opportunity efficiency sense is worth the effort, whatever your role and organisational context, consider the nature of the case against a common-practice risk management view of 'risk' which goes well beyond specific risk management technical problems in areas like the Chapter 9 safety concerns, taking a much wider and deeper view.

Components of this generalised perspective are developed in *every* Part 2 chapter. For example, the generalisation of risk efficiency in this book goes well beyond the reasonably obvious generalisations of a traditional mean–variance approach like the use of 'stochastic dominance'. It includes the need for a clear view of *all* appropriate objectives in multiple attribute terms in all contexts. It also includes addressing objectives which cannot be measured in any direct sense or are not worth trying to measure. Furthermore, it includes recognising that sometimes making decisions with a focus on expected cost, revenue, or profit values, *explicitly ignoring all associated variability and risk*, may be opportunity efficient, *any* effort devoted to risk management in these circumstances wasting time and money as well as distracting people from what really matters.

Chapter 5 reflects this perspective using a simple risk management perspective which does not even employ the term 'risk management' – it is simply not relevant. Chapter 6 uses a more sophisticated risk management perspective, but the term 'risk management' is still not relevant. Chapter 7 addresses dissolving an existing 'project risk management' department to formally integrate a transformed version of what its members currently do into the toolset, skill set, and mindset of a single fully integrated Projects Group team. This integrated team treats 'estimating', 'risk management' and 'planning driven by a search for opportunities' as inseparable because the problems needing confrontation involve a mess of interconnections which are too complex to address successfully in any other way. The associated 'mess' becomes more complex in Chapter 8, well beyond the scope of most Enterprise Risk Management (ERM), still more complex in terms of some particular issues in Chapter 9.

Those insisting on using *framing* assumptions for risk management which are too narrow should be *much more* vigorously publicly criticised than is currently the case, with *all* the relevant people whose concerns are impacted understanding why risk management is an issue which cannot be left to the risk management experts in specific areas. But the mess involving risk management is by no means attributable to risk management experts on their own – it is also attributable to everyone else who has failed to see that risk management issues are part of a much bigger mess, the tip of a proverbial iceberg. The volume of ice underwater represents the extent of further more general concerns which go well beyond a collective view of all common-practice risk management concerns, as illustrated in all Part 2 chapters.

The good or bad behaviours and practices mantra

An EP approach uses the general notion that 'bad practices and behaviours can drive out good practices and behaviours unless good practices and behaviours are promoted and protected and bad practices and behaviours are contested and constrained'.

As a simple example, an organisation setting up a bidding process to deal with contractors providing or modifying a corporate asset needs to ensure that the 'good' potential contractors have a level playing field, and the bidding process does not favour 'bad' potential contractors lacking expertise or ethics. This is part of a broader concern for good client–contractor relationships from a client perspective. If the least competent and biggest liar wins, that is in part a consequence of bad planning by the client.

The interpretation of this notion as illustrated by this simple example can be generalised, and its implications extended in several ways. For example, if good contractors keep losing, good contractors may need to take collective action to create a level playing field or do much more to help their potential clients become more enlightened or both. In some cases, good contractors and good clients may need to take collective political action, to ensure that marketplaces are not permanently damaged by unscrupulous players who a majority of the population would be better off without. In some contexts, this kind of response by the suppliers or customers of goods or services may drive important regulatory and legal changes. In general, markets which involve a level playing field are not a simple matter. An EP approach can help address the complexity in a clarity efficient and opportunity efficient manner, explored briefly in later chapters.

Generalising this notion means encouraging good behaviours and practices in any one of a diverse variety of ways which are central to the EP concept as a whole – including making effective and efficient use of good teamwork, appropriate collaboration, and corporate understanding of the difference between good management and good luck, bad management and bad luck. The role of this form of generalisation is important enough to state the general notion as an explicit EP mantra. For simplicity we can contract 'good behaviours and practices' to 'the good', with a comparable interpretation of 'the bad'. The 'good or bad behaviours and practices mantra' can then be stated simply and concisely as

> *Promote and protect the good, contest and constrain the bad.*

What is good and bad is, of course, debatable, but this does not make the issues unimportant; it just increases the difficulties involved which makes the need for an effective approach more important.

A mantra of this kind can be viewed as a framing assumption. It is a framing assumption which is well worth keeping in mind in a world with an uncomfortably high level of bad behaviours and practices. It is also worth bearing in mind that a less obvious but sizable proportion of the players at both individual and corporate levels are very open to being motivated to deliver good behaviours and practices, and very willing to respond positively to effective promotion and protection of the good, provided the bad are effectively contested and constrained.

Two further enlightened planning mantras

'KISS' is commonly interpreted as 'keep it simple, stupid'. A mantra which is central to EP is 'the redefined KISS mantra':

> *Keep it simple systematically.*

This redefinition was Stephen Ward's idea to capture systematic use of his 'constructive simplicity' concept as it was evolving towards the EP concepts of enlightened simplicity and opportunity efficiency embracing risk efficiency and clarity efficiency in our early work together. Our joint project risk management publications have used it for many years. It is central to the clarity efficiency concept and the opportunity efficiency concept as a whole.

We all have a natural desire to keep it as simple as possible, which induces a natural bias to oversimplify *even if* we avoid a simplistic 'keep it simple, stupid' approach and 'keep it simple systematically' in a clarity efficiency sense. To emphasise the role of opportunity efficiency, another very useful mantra is 'the second-mile mantra' in the following form:

> *Always go the second mile in terms of erring on the side of more clarity*
> *when making decisions with important implications,*
> *making a point of avoiding the wrong level of simplicity*
> *as an inherent aspect of avoiding the wrong kind of simplicity*
> *when misjudgements may have serious consequences.*

Part of the rationale is a practical need to deal with the asymmetric implications of too little versus too much clarity when trying to assess an appropriate trade-off between further clarity and the associated cost/effort. Viewing the wrong level of simplicity as an inherent aspect of the wrong kind of simplicity is a useful general reminder we need opportunity efficiency as well as clarity efficiency as part of the 'right kind' of simplicity.

Strategic clarity and tactical clarity

Now consider two very high level composite concepts relevant to operations, project and corporate planning contexts from two closely coupled but quite different perspectives.

The two concepts are strategic clarity and tactical clarity. These two concepts have an inherent complexity driven by their composite nature. Like opportunity efficiency, they require gradual clarification as this book progresses. But they need understanding in terms of overview definitions before the end of this opening chapter.

The two perspectives are your personal perspective and the perspective of your organisation, using 'your organisation' as a convenient contraction of 'any organisation of interest to you, now or in the future, with a focus on one you are currently embedded in if this is relevant':

> *Strategic clarity from the perspective of your organisation means 'everyone in the organisation has appropriate clarity (shared understanding) about "what needs to be done" by themselves and by those they interact with in all relevant teams to achieve all relevant corporate goals in EP terms'.*
>
> *Tactical clarity from the perspective of your organisation means 'everyone in the organisation has appropriate clarity (shared understanding) about "how to do it" for all the common ground EP tasks which have to be understood for strategic clarity plus further "how to do it" toolsets, skill sets and mindsets for all the tasks they have to take responsibility for or assist with'.*
>
> *Strategic clarity from your perspective means 'as a target reader you have appropriate strategic clarity about "what needs to be done" including key common ground "how to do it" concerns relevant to all your roles in your organisation'.*
>
> *Tactical clarity from your perspective means 'as a target reader you have appropriate clarity about "how to do it" for all the common-ground EP tasks which have to be understood for strategic clarity plus further "how to do it" toolsets, skill sets, and mindsets for all the tasks you have to take responsibility for or assist with'.*

These terms are bound to seem even more ambiguous than opportunity efficiency at this stage, in part because they are even higher order gateway concepts than opportunity efficiency. But by the time you finish Part 1 they should be starting to become useful shorthand labels or 'handles' for what this book aims to provide.

Strategic clarity is explored in this book in terms of key what needs to be done issues which need a holistic perspective appropriately shared by all members of an organisation. Each organisation will have to address its own complete set of what needs to be done concerns to achieve overall strategic clarity, drawing on their current strengths and confronting their most pressing weaknesses. Very different organisations will need perspectives which may have novel and unique features. One vision of strategic clarity will not fit all organisations, and your personal vision of strategic clarity will have to depend on your roles within an organisation as well as your experience and knowledge to date and your career plans for the future. The focus of this book is providing a strategic clarity concept which facilitates adaptation to the context as needed.

Tactical clarity, as explored in this book, is about key how to do it issues which need a holistic perspective in order to understand relevant strategic clarity concerns. Strategic and tactical clarity concerns are not separable – they involve complex overlaps and interdependences. If people do not have an overview understanding of what is involved in how to do it terms in some key areas they will not understand what needs to be done. But each of the key how to do it areas explored in this book involves many further issues which experts in these areas will have to address.

Put slightly differently, this book's approach to strategic clarity is as comprehensive as possible, while its focus on tactical clarity is limited to the common ground essential to strategic clarity, avoiding tactical clarity detail which target readers do not need to understand for strategic clarity.

As an illustrative example of what the rest of Part 1 aims to achieve in these terms, Chapter 3 begins with a very simple 'low clarity' approach to unbiased clarity efficient estimates of how long a project activity might take, gradually adding more clarity for a minimal increase in cost/effort. It then begins to explore interdependent 'efficiency' issues, involving risk efficiency, clarity efficiency, and opportunity efficiency concerns. This 'estimation-efficiency spectrum' is explored throughout Chapter 3 maintaining working assumptions which keep the discussion as simple as possible. Chapter 4 addresses relaxing some of these assumptions. By the conclusion of Chapter 4 you should understand the basis of strategic clarity, including requisite tactical clarity. The focus of Chapters 3 and 4 is estimating and closely coupled efficiency concerns which everyone involved in providing estimates or using estimates ought to have in any organisation aspiring to strategic and tactical clarity. This Part 1 focus is relevant to all target readers, and each chapter in Part 2 enriches this understanding in different ways for very different contexts and kinds of organisations.

Your perspective and your organisation's perspective on strategic and tactical clarity are gateway concepts at a very high level of composition. If you have strategic clarity you have an operational understanding of all the gateway concepts like opportunity efficiency and the four Fs which are needed to make a significant contribution to your organisation in EP terms, but you may need a lot more tactical clarity in particular areas of responsibility.

Your organisation's needs are much more complex than your needs because they involve capability-culture issues for the organisation as a whole.

For some readers who usually associate 'strategy' exclusively with corporate planning there may be a risk of possible confusion because strategic clarity plus tactical clarity concepts are being used in project and operations planning contexts as well as corporate strategy contexts. However, we have to think both strategically as well as tactically in *all* planning areas, so we cannot avoid confronting this complication. Indeed, organisations need both strategic and tactical clarity about the key interdependencies between corporate, project, and operations planning to make an enlightened planning approach fully operational. In part this is demonstrated by the need to address bottom-up strategic planning in operations and project planning contexts, but it is also demonstrated in other ways throughout this book. You may find it useful to regularly remind yourself that strategic clarity is about what needs to be done, whereas tactical clarity is about how to do it.

Systematic simplicity as a composite concept

Systematic simplicity is the basis of strategic clarity plus tactical clarity as you see it, as your organisation sees it, and as others see it, assuming that an appropriate variant of an enlightened approach to all operations, project and corporate planning incorporating a systematic approach to keeping it simple has been adopted. Enlightened planning including enlightened simplicity is my particular variant of the systematic simplicity concept. You and your organisation may need your own versions of some of the conceptual and operational frameworks, including alternative terminology, adapting my advocated enlightened planning approach to better suit your context.

A 'common ground' term for the composite concept which defines what we are seeking from different but closely coupled perspectives is useful for several purposes. One key purpose is to emphasise that you and your organisation should feel free to tailor both conceptual and operational tools as well as their terminology to best suit your own context. Assuming this is done, we need a label for the implied common ground, and 'systematic simplicity' is my suggestion, because 'keeping it simple systematically' is at the core of any best practice systematic approach to planning.

Further purposes are explored later via the website discussed briefly at the end of this book, accessed via 'enlightenedplanning.uk'. These further purposes will involve ongoing adaptation and development of EP concepts using a shared view of the need to 'keep it simple systematically' as the starting point.

A summary with linked inferences

A summary of why planning is usually vital but often difficult and frequently inept concludes this chapter, along with linked inferences about how EP can help to ease the difficulties and reduce the level of inept planning to more acceptable levels.

Why planning is usually vital

For reasons initially explored in the opening two sections on what this book means by the word 'planning' and the role of planning in different areas, it should be reasonably clear why some aspects of planning in formal terms are usually vital, as is related informal planning.

Consolidating these reasons with those touched on in later sections suggests the following:

1   Plans need common understanding by a significant number of people for a range of different reasons.
2   A lot of planning is done in different 'silos' for very good efficiency-driven reasons, but corporate effectiveness means interdependences need special care in terms of communication between components of formal planning process structures, as in the need to coordinate operations, corporate, and project planning.

3   Governance and control as plans evolve and then get implemented is crucial, usually at several levels: project managers, boards, and regulators, for example.
4   Organisational learning and knowledge capture as experience is gained is essential, usually at several different levels, with crucial common ground.

Why planning is often difficult

You may have begun this book thinking that what needs to be done and why it is often difficult are reasonably obvious. But some new concerns may have surfaced already, and both new and familiar concerns involve difficulties that you may be able to address in new ways based on this book's conceptual and operational tools.

Consolidating key issues raised in this chapter, reasons why planning is often difficult include the following:

1   Different people need a common understanding of plans, but their information needs and their perspectives and conceptual frameworks can vary significantly, depending on their role. Ensuring that plans address the right questions on behalf of all the relevant players, and provide approximately correct unbiased answers in a suitable timeframe, is rarely straightforward.
2   People who work in silos can become acclimatised to working in separate bubbles with minimal communication between groups. Making sure that they collaborate effectively is crucial. All relevant people need to understand the full range of outcomes associated with sources of uncertainty others face which they may be able to help to manage for better overall corporate performance. This is usually easier said than done. However, the pay-offs from doing so are huge, and there is no excuse for ignoring this or any of the other difficulties planning practice has to confront.
3   Testing working assumptions effectively while plans are being evolved by planners as well as during governance gateway stages prior to the implementation of plans is rarely straightforward, and effective and efficient contingency planning to deal with working assumptions which may not hold is almost never straightforward.
4   Correctly inferring *exactly* what needs learning from experience, and capturing the knowledge that really matters, is inherently difficult.
5   Even if an organisation has a fully developed enlightened planning capability and culture, the collective implications of inherent difficulties can be very daunting.
6   Confusion caused by the multitude of conflicting and restrictive concepts and tools promoted by different interest groups involved in decision making and associated planning makes an inherently difficult situation significantly worse, and the resolution of this self-inflicted set of difficulties in the near future is unlikely. Confusion about what risk management ought to mean is just the tip of a very big iceberg, with all sorts of associated 'growlers' (little icebergs), like how can organisations distinguish between good luck and good management, bad luck and bad management.

Why planning is frequently inept

Meeting all the vital planning needs for organisations in a way which overcomes all the important difficulties in a clarity efficient manner with the most appropriate trade-off levels between different clarity attributes and the effort/cost involved is demanding.

If *everybody* involved is not clear about what needs to be done in broad 'big picture' terms, plus their role in doing it and how to execute their role, inept planning is frequently the almost inevitable result. Only one weak link in a chain will cause a chain to fail, but multiple people not having clarity in terms of this basic requirement will have a cumulative effect.

Some of the people involved have to ensure that appropriate risk–reward trade-offs are made using suitable decision-making tools effectively and efficiently, coping with both good luck and bad luck positively within a culture which understands and pursues opportunity efficiency in an effective manner. If any key players providing these toolsets, skill sets, and mindsets do not understand what needs to be done and how to play their role effectively, inept planning will be the consequence.

Achieving opportunity efficiency may be difficult, but it can be reasonably simple in some contexts. We have to seek simplicity systematically and confront complexity when it really matters. This is at the heart of what 'best practice' ought to be about in effective operational terms. *If we pretend the issues facing us are simpler than they really are, this does not make them simpler. It just confuses people and makes overcoming the results of this confusion an additional set of problems and concerns which could have been avoided.*

Some people are routinely hampered and confused by best or good practice standards based on assumptions which are inappropriately restrictive, seriously aggravating what are already inherently difficult planning concerns. In principle this problem is not necessary, but in practice, until it is resolved you will have to confront the implications as best you can.

Key inferences from this section and earlier aspects of this chapter

If your organisation is already highly effective and efficient, exploring the scope for your organisation finding further opportunity efficiency improvements via an EP approach may provide only marginal benefits. But the reassurance that a fresh perspective on your organisation's approach confirms that best practice is already in place may still prove extremely useful. In particular, it may help to clarify what your organisation means by best practice and its ability to maintain its current high levels of performance when circumstances change, including coping with a run of bad luck. Simply assuming your organisation does not need to test its capability and culture in this way may be very risky.

If your organisation is well short of opportunity efficiency, the scope for improvement will mean the effort involved in developing an effective opportunity efficiency driven EP approach more than pays for itself.

EP is not a 'silver bullet'. But it offers a fresh perspective, based on synthesising many tried-and-true perspectives. In particular, it offers a way forward which will resolve some of the unnecessary difficulties and easily avoidable sources of inept decision making for those prepared to invest the effort. If key players in an organisation make a collective effort to understand the overall EP agenda, they can begin implementing the key ideas that matter the most for their context with a view to what is easiest and most productive first. However, before they even make preliminary implementation plans, they need an understanding of the available possibilities. You may be able to help your organisation with this.

One way to look at this overall goal is you achieving strategic clarity in order to assist your organisation to achieve strategic clarity. You and everyone else will also need to acquire the further tactical clarity needed to play your roles, but strategic clarity needs to lead tactical clarity, so starting with a focus on strategic clarity is appropriate.

There are 'no free lunches'. A significant investment in time and effort may be required to significantly enhance EP competence by individuals and organisations. But the pay-offs can involve a massive return on the investment, with no significant risk. The risk associated with a failure to seek feasible competence enhancements may be very high, and it will not be understood if the issues are not addressed.

This chapter has laid part of the foundations for Parts 2 and 3, by introducing key concepts which frame the recommended approach to planning at an overview level as a first step in explaining what enlightened planning addresses and involves.

This chapter has also provided brief initial outline answers to the question, 'Why is planning usually vital but often difficult and frequently inept?' You might reasonably see these initial answers as little more than the source of a set of further questions which need much more developed answers. But the complex interdependency of the issues to be considered in a layered manner in the following chapters makes this inevitable.

One aspirational target for this chapter was encouraging you to pursue more developed answers to the new questions raised by reading the rest of this book. Even if you are 'daunted easily', it is important to avoid being too daunted by the scope of the issues which need to be addressed, the complex interdependencies involved, and the combined length of the remaining ten chapters. You will find it useful to develop a full understanding of the what needs to be done aspects of strategic clarity. Difficulties understood and overcome are transformed into opportunities, and the processes involved can be very satisfying. Difficulties misunderstood or ignored do not go away. They simply become chronic liabilities and threats, ongoing sources of anxiety, possibly leading to disaster.

2   A 'universal planning uncertainty and complexity management process' (UP)

Planning processes with a very wide range of forms, purposes and provenances are a defining feature of 'common practice' planning. A closely coupled feature is the use of assumptions which involve potentially important restrictions without trade-offs between the benefits and costs of limitations imposed by these restrictions being clear.

One set of resulting challenges is dealing with the questions 'Could this planning process and the resulting outcomes be significantly improved by using a different approach based on different assumptions, and if so, how?' The basis for answering these questions from an EP perspective is addressed in this chapter, starting with the more general question 'what general process should we use to plan a way forward if we do not have a specific process which is clearly appropriate for the issues needing attention?' An intermediate question is 'What process should we use to develop a specific process for repeated use in a particular context?'

Two basic planning process types are key tools for 'keeping it simple systematically'. One is as general as possible, by definition and design, the focus of this chapter and Chapter 5. All other planning processes are specific, by definition and design, the focus of Chapters 6 and 7.

The general form addressed in this chapter is a '*universal* planning uncertainty and complexity management *process*', usually contracted to 'universal process' or 'UP'. The purpose of the full name is a clear description of its role, but contraction is more convenient for routine usage.

The next section provides an overview of the UP recommended by this book. Several following sections outline key components and concepts. A penultimate section briefly describes the origins and evolution of the recommended UP. The concluding section further clarifies key aspects of what a UP is and what a UP is not from an EP perspective.

This book assumes that you may not be familiar with Operational Research or Operations Research (OR), Management Science (MS) or cognate disciplines. This chapter explains all that you need to know about the basis of their contributions to the UP concept to follow the discussion in the rest of this book.

A UP overview

'*Universal* process' signifies a general nature in more than one sense. For example, a UP can be used on its own, inserted in other processes, draw on other processes which might serve as useful components, and be employed to design or test other processes.

The UP concept advocated in this book has been designed for maximum generality (flexibility due to lack of limiting restrictions) and power (effectiveness and efficiency) in any relevant context. A key design criterion was clarity about *all* the key working assumptions used by the UP, including clarity about the relationships between working assumptions and the objectives of each component of the UP portrayed by Figure 2.1.

The flow chart of Figure 2.1 provides an overview of the recommended universal process depicted as a set of seven sequential phases with an iterative structure providing maximum flexibility plus supporting capability-culture assets and capability-culture liabilities which require attention.

The basis of Figure 2.1 is my current synthesis of all the relevant planning and decision support processes that I am aware of which have proved useful in practice with an explicit provision for further processes which you and your organisation might find useful. If you start with the UP of Figure 2.1, the basis of any tentative modifications can be tested within this framework.

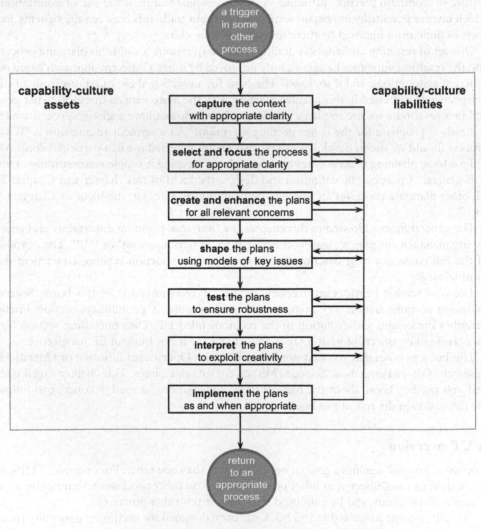

Figure 2.1 A universal planning uncertainty and complexity management process, contracted to 'universal process' or 'UP'.

One key contention underlying this book is that all organisations without an explicit corporate UP variant have an implicit set of different UP variants, independently defined by different individuals and groups of people making an organisation's decisions. One related contention is these implicit UP variants are probably incompatible in some areas. Another is some of them are probably not as effective or efficient as the UP concept advocated by this book. An important follow-on implication is some decision makers are probably making inappropriate 'stealth assumptions', and careful examination of these stealth assumptions would reveal why a more effective and efficient explicit UP would be preferable.

Recall from Chapter 1 that 'stealth assumptions' which matter are framing assumptions which by definition are unhelpful because they are restrictive in seriously inappropriate ways, and they are invisible or inappropriately understood. The result of a set of stealth assumptions which matter in the context of the UP concept used by an organisation is an inept mix of incompatible approaches to making decisions with defects which may be 'off the radar'. They may be affecting all current management decision-making processes in all planning areas – an operations, project, and corporate management concern for everyone involved.

By implication, one single agreed-on UP concept which is as general, flexible, effective and efficient as possible ought to provide an opportunity for improvement. How much that opportunity matters will depend on the diversity, effectiveness and efficiency of the current processes consolidated in a single explicit UP.

The 'universal' nature of this UP concept does not mean that other processes are not required. UPs need to work alongside SPs (specific processes) as well as drawing upon other processes as part of the UP 'select and focus the process' phase, and UPs need to be used to routinely test the effectiveness and efficiency of all SPs as they evolve with changing circumstances.

Using a UP requires explicit leadership or coordination of all the phases by one or more of the people involved. There are good reasons why the first three phases might be led by different people in some contexts, but joint management requires coordination. All the following phases involve the possibility of leadership and management by further new players, but an ongoing need for coordination. An overall facilitator/coordinator role might be useful, but everyone involved needs to know how to play their role effectively and efficiently, and teamwork is usually a crucial success factor.

Process initiation and termination

As indicated by the circle at the top of Figure 2.1, a UP can be entered from any other process, initiated by a 'trigger' like recognising an issue which needs to be addressed is beyond the scope of the current planning process. As indicated by the circle at the bottom, completing a UP can involve returning to the original process or moving on to some other appropriate process. For example, a problem associated with implementing a current plan might be recognised, triggering a decision to address the problem using a UP, returning to the implementation of the revised plan when the UP intervention is complete.

Process phase structure

As may be self-evident from the diagram, phase separations signal changes in the nature and purpose of process components worth explicit recognition in terms of a separate phase. This section considers each phase in sequence.

Phase 1: capture the context with appropriate clarity

Sometimes 'capture the context with appropriate clarity' is usefully contracted to 'capture the context' or just 'capture' if the meaning is still clear. A comparable approach to contractions will be used for all phase descriptors, although sometimes a suitable single word contraction is not feasible.

'Context' is used in a plain English sense, with a scope which is wide enough to address everything of relevance. Everybody directly involved in a UP needs a common understanding of the circumstances which define the context at a level of detail appropriate to their role and concerns. The capture the context phase involves making explicit a common understanding of working assumptions which appropriately capture the relevant key aspects of the context. These working assumptions are assumptions of convenience to reduce complexity.

All working assumptions in this and later phases should be made explicit for two reasons. First, they need to be formally identified and then clarified for everyone involved who needs to understand them to interpret the plans for a wide range of purposes as and when appropriate. Second, they need to be tested for robustness, immediately and later in the process. It is important to appreciate that identifying, communicating, and testing working assumptions is *much* easier said than done. The reasons are worth understanding, and they are explored in some detail in Chapter 5. All following Part 2 chapters build on this foundation.

Working assumptions identified in the capture the context phase and the associated shared understanding of the context will need to evolve as the process proceeds, one reason ongoing testing of assumptions is necessary.

If more than one person is involved, one or more of the people involved must coordinate or lead the process of identifying, clarifying, and sharing information about the working assumptions which capture the context during this first phase.

Phase 2: select and focus the process for appropriate clarity

The 'select and focus the process for appropriate clarity' phase chooses between different types of available processes and then tailors the way the selected process operates within a UP based on the context as captured by the preceding phase and further working assumptions.

This select and focus the process phase is a higher order 'planning the planning' component of the UP concept. It is central to managing a UP as an integrated whole but usefully separated because it involves higher order planning with a different kind and level of complexity. The UP concept is effective when it is not clear what working assumptions about process choices would be appropriate at the outset of the capture the context phase because of its generality, but the cost of this generality is a lack of efficiency. Preliminary working assumptions about a suitable process selection and focus are needed almost immediately, using restrictive assumptions to increase efficiency. These assumptions need immediate and later ongoing routine testing for robustness, with different concerns as an analysis matures.

The process approaches which might be selected and then focused must lend themselves to clarity efficiency – this is the only constraint. That is, the initial process choice and its subsequent focus during its ongoing use must facilitate maximising the level of appropriate insight which can be captured and communicated for any given level of effort/cost associated with acquiring that clarity.

Using a UP requires explicit leadership of process choices and ongoing tailoring of the process selected by someone who understands the feasible options. At this point you may have no idea what options involving standard planning tools of various kinds or more specialist planning tools drawing on disciplines like OR might imply, and limited interest in what might be involved. However, in 'what needs to be done' terms you need to appreciate that someone who understands the feasible option choices needs to be involved during the select and focus phase of a UP for this universal planning process concept to work effectively.

To illustrate one possible option, the context as captured in the first phase may suggest that a simple 'project' is involved, requiring a simple process for planning a sequence of tasks. There may be a simple 'off the shelf' project planning process that could be used effectively, associated with a suitable family of widely used project planning models, the focus aspect further narrowing the model set proposed.

Alternatively, the context may suggest a traditional OR process, and a particular family of associated OR models may seem to suit 'the problem', defining 'the problem' as 'specific concerns requiring decisions when the most appropriate choices are not obvious but relevant generic tools are available'.

However, a very general 'soft OR' situation structuring process for exploring 'messes' might be more appropriate, defining 'messes' as 'interconnected systems of problems'. This soft OR approach might be used as a front-end analysis stage process choice to be followed later by further stages making use of other processes, but the need for a soft OR stage might not become evident until a simpler approach is tried first.

A series of evolutionary steps which underlie the UP of Figure 2.1 are worth understanding in outline, provided later. The key thing to grasp at this point is the Figure 2.1 UP concept is a flexible process framework by design, the power of that flexibility depending upon the skills of the people making the process choices. A direct implication you need to bear in mind is there are 'no free lunches' in this context as in many others – general and powerful processes require skilful process choices which require well-informed and skilful people. Pretending this is not a concern simply means crude and ineffective choices become the norm – a potential stealth assumption of crucial importance.

Adjusting select and focus phase process choices may be triggered as the overall or partial process iterations identify unexpected issues – the select and focus phase involves working assumptions about the most appropriate process which may need adjusting many times as the overall process unfolds. These changes may affect the approach taken to the preceding capture phase as well as later phases. Part of the rationale for the feedback structure of Figure 2.1 is meeting this need for possible adjustments to earlier phases as the process unfolds in a flexible manner, without waiting until the end of the current pass and making a complete further pass through the process. In practice the approach to early phases may approximate proceeding in parallel because of very frequent partial iterations.

Adjusting the nature of a UP as the context becomes clearer may involve more or less emphasis on top-down thinking relative to bottom-up thinking, more or less concern for problems versus messes, more or less focus on overall strategy versus specific tactics, and so on.

Phase 3: create and enhance the plans for all relevant concerns

The central concern of initial plan creation may be formulating tentative first thoughts on goals to be achieved and how to proceed. The plans created initially will be tailored by current understanding provided by the capture the context phase plus the select and focus the process phase. Initial plans may be an aspirational target, a robust safe option, or an appropriate intermediate option.

In some situations, initial plans may be focused on learning more about the context, using an exploratory approach explicitly driven by this concern. In other situations, a very specific initial plan may be assumed.

Proactively seeking inspiration and the use of imagination can be crucial when identifying and choosing between initial plan options. What some people see as craft-based understanding of an ends–means synthesis may be crucial – knowing how to get from where we are to where we want to be. To some extent relevant practical experience is usually important to synthesise what works and what doesn't work.

The people best suited to lead plan creation and enhancement may not be the same as those best suited to lead earlier or later phases, and the issues involved may include complications like a problem 'owner' who identifies a need to resolve concerns directly having an impact on his or her areas of responsibility may wish to continue to exercise control over what is done, even when it becomes clear other people's areas of responsibility are also affected.

Once plans have been created in an initial form, enhancing plans includes enriching the plans using a broader scope or providing more detail. For example, the initial planning of what needs to be done might be followed by considering what resources are needed and how these resources might be obtained and deployed, this kind of detail enhancing the planner's understanding of what the plans imply.

'Enhancement' to address wider concerns and new issues at any stage in the process is crucially dependent on creativity, building on and complementing the creativity of the initial planning in a supportive manner.

Revisiting the create and enhance the plans phase until all relevant concerns have been addressed as part of the iterative nature of a UP may lead to adjustment and further enhancement of any of the initial plans – planning on a different basis or dealing with a wider set of concerns or specific issues not addressed earlier.

The create and enhance the plans phase involves a third set of working assumptions, building on the working assumptions developed in the first two phases. This time the working assumptions are about the nature of the plans and how the plans relate to the context. These plans and associated working assumptions should reflect anticipated issues as well as current concerns. Sharing appropriate associated information between the parties involved to the extent that this is useful is part of the create and enhance the plans phase, as for all other phases. But in this phase using structured documentation linking some of the key outputs of successive phases can begin to become crucial. A process facilitator may be involved to help with the sharing and documentation, but plan creators and enhancers have to play a central role. Training to help everyone work as a team can be invaluable. Everyone involved becoming fully engaged in 'learning by doing' may be the key, as illustrated in Chapter 5.

During this phase, addressing resilience may be worth explicit initial treatment. Building resilience into the plans themselves addresses issues like creating imaginative contingency plans to facilitate recovering from situations which may be inherently unpredictable.

Simply providing 'slack' in the system is a basic approach to providing one form of resilience. Systems which are highly optimised in a deterministic sense with no slack are inherently fragile. 'Organisational slack' is a useful more general form of this idea, implying people can find the time, energy, and other resources to deal with disruptive unpredictable opportunities, crises and disasters. These kinds of distinctions can become even more relevant in the next phase if specific explicit approaches to resilience are modelled.

Phase 4: shape the plans using models of key issues

'Shape the plans using models of key issues' usually involves developing explicit formal 'models' of some selected core issues which have been partially or fully identified during plan creation and enhancement. Generally, it is not sensible to even contemplate trying to model all relevant concerns. Examples of simple common 'generic' planning models include the discounted cash flow models used by financial planners for business case plans, the bar charts used by project planners, the checklists used by airline pilots to ensure that no crucial steps are overlooked, and the 'to do' lists most of us employ. These models may have mathematical, graphical or verbal forms. A joint mathematical and graphical form can be useful – an approach strongly promoted by most of the OR community. However, some particularly useful qualitative structuring models with no quantitative meaning also have OR roots, like the seven Ws model explored in Chapter 7. Furthermore, some very simple purely qualitative models which have no OR roots and are common practice in many contexts can also be useful, as illustrated by a red to green to blue traffic light model in Chapter 6. These 'models' are all abstractions designed to simplify some aspects of a complex reality in formal ways which facilitate communication and may allow useful manipulation. For example, activities in a bar chart can have their durations or precedence relationships changed to see what effect this has on project duration, the numbers used in a discounted cash flow model can be adjusted to see how this affects a business case, and tasks in a to-do list can be reordered to consider the implications of alternative priorities.

'Plans' are invariably more comprehensive and sophisticated than the models used to formally address selected key aspects of the plans. The associated informal planning content may be crucial. For example, an experienced project planner using a bar chart showing activity timing as the only formal model employed will intuitively address key resource availability assumptions which may underlie some activity timing and precedence relationship assumptions, and a simple 'to do' list may imply what needs to be done and how to do it plans which have been developed without using formal models.

Not all key issues lend themselves to effective and efficient modelling, but it can be important to understand when important exclusions are involved. For example, if those responsible for business case plans are not clear about *all* their objectives, including 'soft' and 'qualitative' concerns, trying to get them to articulate and possibly quantify objectives may be a useful modelling exercise. But if they refuse or are unable to agree on a coordinated approach to all the objectives of actual concern, perhaps because some objectives involve concealed agendas and hidden motives, then modelling is not going to resolve one of the most crucial and fundamental of all planning issues.

Modellers are often associated with a facilitator role, but all the people involved in a planning exercise must share a common understanding of what they are doing. A facilitator to ensure that everyone involved understands all working assumptions appropriately may be useful, but the individuals involved need to consciously seek a common understanding.

Shaping the plans using models in this fourth phase involves a fourth set of working assumptions, building on earlier assumptions in the preceding three phases. This fourth set of working assumptions must reflect the implications of key aspects of the plans which are not modelled as well as the directly modelled aspects. What is not modelled does not go away, and failing to understand the implications can be serious.

Phase 5: test the plans to ensure robustness

This phase involves testing *all four sets* of working assumptions made in the four preceding phases to ensure robustness in holistic terms. It must trigger looping back to modify working assumptions if tests suggest a lack of robustness which implies the emerging analysis and synthesis conclusions might be misleading. In some circumstances, a loop back to explore the implications of alternative working assumptions may be the best test of current assumptions which look suspect. In the 'test' phase, *all the working assumptions* must be understood in terms of an underlying set of more general *framing assumptions*. This is always easier said than done, and someone involved in a UP needs to have the capability and inclination to ensure that this happens.

As pointed out earlier, framing assumptions shape the way we look at the complexities of reality. Framing assumptions which lack generality limit and impair the way we look at the robustness of working assumptions, limiting and impairing the way we look at reality. A popular saying which reflects this idea is 'if the only tool in your toolkit is a hammer, every problem looks like a nail'.

As also pointed out earlier, the recommended UP concept and all the other key EP tools are as general as possible by definition and design – the EP toolset is as unrestrictive as possible. An implication is the *team* involved in using a UP must have the collective skill set and mindset needed to take full advantage of the flexibility and power of the available collective toolset. Different team members may contribute very different component toolsets, skill sets, and mindsets, but they need a common basis for mutual understanding.

Phase 6: interpret the plans to exploit creativity

This phase involves drawing on the analysis and synthesis just undertaken and further synthesising it with all other relevant understanding. A broad form of synthesis which exploits all available creativity and inspiration is essential. The 'interpret' phase has to be linked as far as possible to everything that matters, possibly drawing on new people with fresh perspectives. Looping back to earlier phases to revisit understanding of the context or any intermediate aspect of the process from a perspective enhanced by new contributors to the process can be a crucial option in this phase.

At this point in the process those involved need to keep looping back to earlier phases on a selective basis or using complete further passes of the whole process until they believe the process should be terminated. Iteration control involves a final testing of the complete set of relevant assumptions before terminating iterations and moving on to implementation.

Iteration control is *one* of the key functions of the interpret phase, a final version of earlier iteration control in the test phase. However, the basic purpose of the interpret phase is making sense of all previous process activity, using what has been learned to make further creative leaps, and then assessing what else may need to be done.

All relevant players in the process need to contribute in an appropriate manner at an appropriate time. The scope of this interpret the plans phase means members of decision-making teams who may not have contributed earlier might make highly significant contributions now. One example is a senior manager approving earlier analysis by his or her team with modest-looking but important amendments before their analysis goes beyond that team. Another example is board level decision makers, whose primary role might be seen as governance, suggesting that board approval must be conditional on key modifications being incorporated in the plans submitted to the board.

Phase 7: implement the plans as and when this is appropriate

This final phase involves making use of UP analysis and synthesis when implementation becomes appropriate assuming no further iterations are called for at present. The option to loop back from the implement the plans phase in Figure 2.1 allows for adjustments to the plans when implementation is underway. This is a central component of ongoing control and respond functions which are needed until the planning process is terminated or replaced.

Capability-culture concepts

Using a UP involves making working assumptions in a direct manner during each of the first four phases, plus further working assumptions in the following three phases. It also requires making use of other analysis skill sets and mindsets in all seven phases. The complete set of all relevant skill set and mindset working assumptions involves organisational capability and culture issues which may not align with individual phases. This means that considering a 'capability-culture' concept separately is useful.

Approaching some of the full set of all working assumptions requiring identification and clarification using separate 'capability-culture assets' and 'capability-culture liabilities' components of this overall capability-culture concept can help to clarify what is involved while 'keeping it simple' in a systematic and robust manner.

The capability-culture 'assets' are all the 'good' capability-culture 'elements' embedded in the organisation which planning assumptions reflect, like 'immediately available requisite knowledge and skills required for immediate use'.

A key working assumption is that those involved in using a UP know about these assets when constructing plans and will plan to make the best possible use of these assets during the whole of the universal planning process, including the creation, shaping, testing, and implementation of the plans.

If those using a UP do not have assets which would be useful, liabilities are generated. If assets are available but they are defective in important ways, liabilities are generated. If none of those involved knows about the missing assets which would be useful if they were available, or the asset defects, they generate unknown liabilities – unknown variants of the missing and defective asset liabilities.

Somewhat different 'liabilities' may be associated with all the 'bad' capability-culture elements embedded in the organisation which may or may not be known – like employees who are wilfully dishonest or computer-based systems which are seriously full of 'bugs' or any other systems which are dysfunctional for many other reasons.

All known capability-culture liabilities are problems which may need resolution involving risks which may need managing. All unknown capability-culture liabilities are potentially important capability-culture uncertainty sources which may give rise to risk with an unknown unknown character which needs attention.

Capability-culture liabilities may require 'accommodations' – a clearly defined means of managing the implications of these liabilities. As an illustration, the Projects Director who is the focus of Chapter 7 believed that the required number of in-house planning staff to deal with detailed planning was not a cost-effective proposition, and he fully supported the policy his predecessor adopted to outsource all detailed planning work to their contractors, a form of accommodation for the absence of in-house capability. Only liabilities that an organisation is aware of and understands can be addressed via accommodations, but sometimes robust accommodations for ill-defined liabilities may be feasible.

Four example *capability* aspects of the capability-culture *asset* set are:

1   immediately available knowledge and skills required for immediate use,
2   pathways for drawing upon and integrating all requisite knowledge and skills,
3   pathways for feeding back and systematically accumulating requisite learning, and
4   pathways for all other relevant communication.

The matching capability-culture *liabilities* include knowledge and skills which an organisation knows are not available although they are needed immediately, and so on. Liabilities also include those generated by 'knowledge' which is assumed to be correct but is false and misleading, skills assumed to be in place which are substandard, pathways which are substandard, and so on. As an example, if in the create and enhance plans phase a business plan model is addressed in the early stages of planning a project, an organisation may know that some key knowledge is not available at present, but it will be at a later stage in the planning process, and other key knowledge will not be available until the project has been completed. These two different types of unavailable knowledge may require different kinds of accommodations, but both might be addressed as ambiguity uncertainty for some estimation purposes.

Four example *culture* aspects of the capability-culture *asset* set are:

1   routine encouragement and empathetic governance initiated when appropriate from the top downwards and from the bottom upwards,
2   fully developed teamwork and cooperation at all times and at all levels,
3   a spirit of continuous improvement at all levels, and
4   encouragement of innovative leaps at all levels.

The matching capability-culture *liabilities* include those generated by lack of routine encouragement and empathetic governance initiated from the top downwards, and so on, whether or not they are seen as missing assets. It also includes those generated by related 'bad' capability-culture characteristics, like self-serving, inflexible, or unsympathetic governance from the top downwards which goes beyond indifference to become dysfunctional to an untenable degree. For example, if during the shape the plans phase one member of the planning team identifies a major misconception in the assumptions underlying the current strategy and a way to deal with it effectively which some higher level managers want to ignore for inappropriate reasons, effective accommodations may not be possible short of more senior managers dealing with the managers who are being dysfunctional. If this is not done everyone associated with the implications may suffer: members of the board, employees, customers, subcontractors, shareholders, the public and the regulators who are supposed to be looking after the best interests of some of these other parties.

Two *middle ground* illustrative example aspects of the capability-culture *asset* set are:

1   corporate mechanisms which encourage positive behaviours for all relevant parties, and
2   corporate mechanisms which discourage negative behaviours for all relevant parties.

The first category of examples are mechanisms which encourage positive behaviours like being fully engaged in teamwork, supporting colleagues who need help, and delivering on promises. The second are corporate mechanisms which discourage negative behaviours like being unhelpful and dishonest.

Elaborating briefly on the role of these two middle ground elements, the most general way to frame *some* of the relevant behavioural, political, and ethical planning concerns which I find useful in practice is adopting the 'good or bad behaviours and practices' mantra, discussed briefly in Chapter 1 and stated as

Promote and protect the good, contest and constrain the bad.

Looking for effective corporate mechanisms to make this mantra operational within the use of UP based corporate processes (payment systems and rules defining required corporate behaviour for example) as an integral part of all enlightened planning processes is a central EP concern. However, a key associated framing assumption is leaving what is meant by 'good' and 'bad' open for discussion. Different people involved in any decision-making process will inevitably see the boundaries between good and bad in different places. But if they are going to work together in an effective manner, they may have to negotiate a working definition of 'good' and 'bad' to enable implementation of this mantra in proactive terms. Not addressing these concerns is a source of obvious problems, rarely an effective solution.

'Contest and constrain' has to address a complete spectrum from gentle but effective proactive discouragement to whatever limits are allowed by the politics and ethics of key players. There may be legal implications. This range has to include all feasible disincentives and sanctions, going well beyond simple financial remedies.

'Promote and protect' has to address a similarly broad and exhaustive spectrum of incentives, encouragements and facilitation, with further potential political, ethical, and legal implications.

'Carrots and sticks' in the usual sense may be part of this. Carrots (positive incentives) are widely held to be more effective and efficient than sticks (negative incentives), but both may be needed, and it is the effectiveness and efficiency of the joint effect that matter.

The ten elements identified above might be thought of as my current 'top ten' partially separable elements, worth separate identification for emphasis and focus, referred to as 'elements one to ten'. You or your organisation may find it useful to modify these choices.

'Element 11' of the asset set is a residual element formally defined as a generalisation of what some people call the 'right stuff', including a synthesis of whatever 'top ten' individual elements your organisation may prefer plus any missed out. Using my top ten elements the missing element concepts might include:

1 professionalism in an appropriate form at all levels for all the people executing the organisation's responsibilities;
2 loyalty and trust in appropriate forms;
3 character, creativity, and courage as needed;
4 effective accommodations for *all* capability-culture liabilities;
5 an explicit residual involving *all* other relevant elements;
6 plus all eleven elements put together in a creative manner.

Element 11 of the liability set is a matching set of any missing element eleven assets. For example, an organisation which lacks appropriate leadership and professional standards clearly has a 'wrong stuff' variant of the 'right stuff'.

Table 2.1 provides a summary of the eleven elements of the capability-culture concept described as assets which might serve as a useful checklist.

Table 2.1 The 11 elements of capability-culture assets.

1   immediately available knowledge and skills required for immediate use
2   pathways for drawing on and integrating all requisite knowledge and skills
3   pathways for feeding back and systematically accumulating requisite learning
4   pathways for all other relevant communication
5   routine encouragement and empathetic governance initiated top-down and bottom-up
6   fully developed teamwork and cooperation at all times and at all levels
7   a spirit of continuous improvement when appropriate at all levels
8   encouragement of and valuation of innovative leaps at all levels
9   corporate mechanisms which encourage positive behaviours for all relevant parties
10 corporate mechanisms which discourage negative behaviours for all relevant parties
11 the 'right stuff' as a synthesis of all the above plus any other relevant element concepts

This 11 element capability-culture concept can be seen as a way of separating issues which are largely generic to an organisation's competence and culture from issues which are specific to each particular application of a UP, further distinguishing between competence in 'capability' and 'culture' terms in an individual 'assets' and 'liabilities' framework. However, this separability involves useful working assumptions, not framing assumptions. Key element 11 issues usually need attention, including overlaps, omissions and synergy concerns.

This capability-culture concept approach can also be viewed as a variant of the traditional idea of 'corporate strengths and weaknesses'. When doing so it may be important to understand that some 'corporate characteristics' in a strengths and weaknesses framework may be both strengths and weaknesses (assets and liabilities), and they might be framed in a way which is not quite the same as the elements concept used here. Furthermore, the distinction between 'capabilities' and 'culture' is not always clear-cut in any framework.

You or your organisation may well find additional capability-culture example elements useful or alternative groupings preferable. However, the addition of the element 11 concept to some broadly equivalent grouping of your top ten elements is crucial – an element defined as an explicit comprehensive 'everything else' composite using synthesis in its broadest sense for effective holistic approaches to dealing with what we know is important but cannot easily define – the right stuff in common parlance. Furthermore, a failure to ensure the 'right stuff' is in place may imply the 'wrong stuff'.

The generality of the capability-culture concept and the way this feature of the Figure 2.1 portrayal of the UP concept contributes are important. However, the generality of this capability-culture concept's nature and the limited degree of definition provided means it will need specific examples to clarify its use and roles, and tailoring it to your concerns in particular contexts may be crucial.

The roles this capability-culture concept can play might be decomposed in several ways. However, the basis is being clear about assumptions made about the capabilities available and the culture shaping their use when creating plans, when implementing plans, and all the intermediate aspects of planning, including dealing effectively with missing assets which may or may not be known about.

Underlying this capability-culture concept are influences and values generated by 'organisational structure' characteristics, which include 'ownership structure' (e.g. various forms of private and public sector ownership as explored in later Part 2 chapters and Chapter 10), 'employee structure' (e.g. various levels of outsourcing and insourcing using related variants of 'strategic partnership' approaches, as explored in Chapter 6), 'integration structure' (e.g. various forms of horizontal and vertical integration as explored in Chapter 5), and 'diversification structure' (e.g. to facilitate various kinds of opportunities as well as managing risk via various forms of self-insurance as explored in Chapter 8). Why this is the case needs clarification via examples in later chapters in conjunction with clarifying the roles of the capability-culture concept itself.

When looking at a UP in overview terms, some uncertainty can be usefully interpreted as 'incomplete knowledge or skills which could be acquired by drawing on what is known about decision making in general and this kind of decision-making context in particular'. Relevant knowledge and skills include tacit knowledge and craft skills, and practical understanding about what works and what does not work based on experience as well as information.

Often organisations need to feedback and capture what has been learned for future use. An explicit UP should operate as a learning process, and to some extent a UP may involve investing in future decision-making capability as well as making immediate decisions. Even if learning from feedback and structured accumulation of knowledge is not relevant, gathering relevant knowledge from different people and other sources is usually essential, and doing so effectively and efficiently using appropriate facilitation capability is invariably crucial.

Effective communication is central to drawing on and using knowledge held by different people and organisations and to feeding back learning. But effective communication also has wider roles, which include keeping everyone who needs to be informed up to date, for governance purposes or public relations purposes for example.

As more than one person is usually involved in the use of a UP, the implications of more than one point of view usually have to be addressed. Simply assuming that a fully informed collaborative joint effort will be involved throughout is usually inappropriate and often dangerous. Even if only one person is involved, unconscious sources of bias may be crucial. In addition, organisations also have to be prepared to deal with 'gaming behaviour', including parties prepared to wilfully manipulate the rules of engagement and behave in a criminal manner. Organisations can exploit relevant 'game theory', 'market behaviour knowledge', 'agency theory', and more general behavioural knowledge. Furthermore, they can use their experience and skills to develop appropriate internal and external contracts, as well as other rules or laws, to constrain behaviour. But organisations may have to make explicit adjustments and provisions for behaviour which could go beyond current knowledge and models, to cope with the realities of all relevant behaviour. Further still, all other gaps in knowledge and skills have to be coped with. Ensuring all these concerns are addressed effectively may require explicit monitoring and review, perhaps separate governance processes. Assuming otherwise as working assumptions without testing the robustness of these assumptions may be very unwise, in some cases negligent in a legal sense. Unanticipated market failures, political crises, or frauds of direct relevance are examples of some of the extremes which may be involved.

You and your organisation do not want to exclude anything from the uncertainty and complexity concepts employed without making a conscious working assumption which can be tested for robustness *when appropriate*, and achieving this in practice is never easy.

The 'closure with completeness' concept

The element 11 aspect of the capability-culture concept illustrates a general approach to decomposition/composition which is usefully clarified and given a contraction label at this point in the development of EP foundation concepts.

If n separable components 1, . . . , n are used in a decomposition/composition process for working assumption purposes, whenever doing so is appropriate component n can be defined to provide '*closure* of the decomposition/composition process using an "everything else" interpretation which includes a holistic approach to synergy to ensure *completeness*' – contracted to a 'closure with completeness' component or concept. In the capability-culture context element n = 11 serves as a closure with completeness component.

This closure with completeness concept will be used in a variety of ways in what follows. The capability-culture element n = 11 context provides a usefully simple initial illustration in the sense that my working assumption that a top 10 separable set of elements might have been a top 5 or a top 20, and other choices within the top 10 might have been made, but the right stuff element n which completes any alternative choices that you or your organisation may prefer should still provide closure with completeness.

UP generality in principle and in practice

As indicated earlier, one way to use a UP is as a default choice for planning in novel contexts, illustrated in Chapter 5. Chapter 5 illustrates the details of formally and explicitly using a UP with a focus on a bottom-up mode of use. This starts to make Figure 2.1 an operational concept in terms of its phase structure and the capability-culture concept. It does so using simple, traditional generic models of manufacturing process inventories as a starting point. Part of the purpose of Chapter 5 is to demonstrate the creative aspects of a UP, the potential strategic flavour of a UP even when we start with simple tactical concerns, the top-down implications of a UP even when a bottom-up starting position is involved, the corporate collaboration it can help to generate, the need for teamwork in process terms across all levels of management, and the value of cooperation with other organisations.

Further ways of using a UP and top-down modes of operation are illustrated by all the other Part 2 chapters. The range of UP uses and the range of organisations which can use a UP demonstrated by Part 2 is very wide. Part 2 limits itself to 'commercial organisations', but much broader bounds could be explored. In principle there are no real limits that I am aware of with regard to the core concepts, in the sense that they have a very broad provenance based on ideas which have a track history of portability, including extensive use for military planning, police service planning, health service planning and other government planning.

The provenance of the UP concept

This section explains how various prototype variants of the UP of Figure 2.1 and its Table 2.1 capability-culture components have been used in practice in the past, its empirical basis.

The primary aim is an overview of the provenance of the recommended universal process for those who may have never heard of the disciplines associated with its starting point and evolution and may have limited interest in learning more. A closely coupled and important secondary purpose is clarifying the EP perspective on aspects where different people have different views.

Operational Research (commonly contracted to OR) can be viewed as the starting point contributor to the UP concept of Figure 2.1, the perspective adopted in this section. The evolution from this starting point involved contributions from a group of cognate disciplines centred on 'Operations Research' (also contracted to OR) and MS. A common joint contraction is MS/OR (or OR/MS). This book associates the MS/OR label with the broadest possible interpretation of an MS/OR perspective, but relevant cognate disciplines which can overlap but are usually viewed as separate disciples with their own decomposition structures include engineering, mathematics, statistics, economics, and all the behavioural and social sciences, to mention just a few key ones.

All target readers need an overview understanding of the provenance of the Figure 2.1 universal process to begin to clarify the nature of the roles a UP can play at this point. Later all readers will need a richer understanding of the range of roles a UP can play and what these roles involve in 'what needs to be done' terms, addressed in the rest of this book. Some readers may want to develop still further understanding of selected subsets of these issues, going into 'how to do it' territory beyond the scope of this book.

Those who already have a deep understanding of MS/OR may find this section useful in terms of reinforcing shared views and testing views where we differ. However, exploring the implications of alternative views or perspectives is a matter for another time and place.

Eight 'contributors' (contributing schools of thought or perspectives) which embrace *some* of the sciences, arts and crafts relevant to an EP interpretation of a UP are outlined in this section in eight separate subsections. A ninth 'contributor' makes an explicit provision for anything not covered in the first eight plus a synthesis of all contributions, another closure with completeness concept. Many of the later contributions have only limited connections with MS/OR, however broadly this term is interpreted.

Contributor 1: 1930s/40s OR

A British creation in the 1930s and 1940s, OR was widely acknowledged as an important contributor to the victory of the Allied Forces in World War II. As war approached in the late 1930s, OR groups making use of British scientists from a range of backgrounds started to address pressing military planning problems. The success of early efforts led to a significant expansion of OR activity when war began.

Some of the planning problems addressed were very big and very complex – like given radar was technically operational, how should radar be deployed effectively as part of a command and control system designed to get British fighter aircraft into the air at the best time and in the best place to meet incoming enemy aircraft? What became known as 'the Battle of Britain' depended on this system, and assisting with its development was an important early OR contribution to British military planning. According to Patrick Rivett (1994), the first OR scientists were the physicists who had invented and developed radar who were then given the task of introducing the radar sets to the army units who would use them. In doing so they were drawn into planning the operational use of radar. This activity was initially called 'radar operational research', later generalised and contracted to 'operational research (OR)'. It was estimated at the time that radar doubled the effectiveness of the Royal Air Force fighter squadrons in the Battle of Britain, and that OR doubled it again.

Other planning problems were relatively simply stated but still big and complex – like given a limited number of anti-aircraft guns were available as 'the Battle of the Atlantic' began, should merchant ships be given significant priority or should priority be given to shore-based batteries. This relatively simply stated planning problem can be used to briefly illustrate the spirit of one approach sometimes taken, as described by one of my University of Toronto professors when I was first introduced to OR at the beginning of the 1960s.

Statistical analysis comparing the proportion of enemy aircraft destroyed when a ship or shore-based anti-aircraft gun opens fire on incoming enemy aircraft confirmed the anticipated 'productivity' superiority (in terms of enemy aircraft damaged or destroyed) of shore-based guns and measured its extent. Common sense had suggested that a stable shore base would make hitting enemy aircraft easier, but by how much was uncertain.

Common sense had also suggested that aircraft attempting to bomb a merchant ship are more likely to drop their bombs at a greater distance and miss if they are being vigorously shot at by effective anti-aircraft guns on the ship being attacked, and the morale of those serving on the ships would be greatly enhanced if they could defend themselves effectively. Further statistical analysis comparing the proportion of ships sunk by attacking enemy aircraft when they were or were not equipped with anti-aircraft guns confirmed and measured the extent to which attacking aircraft were more likely to miss when they were being fired at. Morale was recognised as important but not measurable.

Because winning the Battle of the Atlantic was essential to avoid losing the war, the merchant ships were given significant priority. What could be usefully measured in the time available was measured, but the politics and ethics of different competing objectives were managed by senior military commanders interpreting the results with a clear understanding of both the power and the limitations of the quantitative analysis. Senior military commanders made the choices and considered non-measurable issues like morale on the ships and related operational effectiveness as well as the ethical implications of important consequences for those targets not protected by anti-aircraft guns. OR support staff provided systematic statistical analysis and complementary non-quantitative analysis and synthesis where this was feasible and useful.

These early British OR groups were so successful they were soon followed by similar groups supporting military planning in all Allied Forces. In the US and some other countries, OR was referred to as Operations Research rather than Operational Research because of differences in military terminology, preserving the common OR contraction.

At the end of the war many of those involved in British OR went back to doing what they had been doing before the war. For example PMS Blackett, the Admiralty's chief of OR who led a group referred to as 'Blackett's Circus', went back to an academic life at the University of Cambridge, although he championed ongoing OR use and had political interests and ambitions. Blackett is a useful example because he won a Nobel Prize in Physics, which clearly illustrates the quality of the thinking involved, undoubtedly of significant importance. Many others involved in British wartime OR groups were instrumental in setting up OR groups in industry after the war, especially in the newly nationalised industries like coal, steel and railways. Patrick Rivett (Rivett, 1994) first applied OR to armaments, but became the head of OR at the National Coal Board and then the manager of OR at Arthur Anderson before becoming the first UK professor of OR at Lancaster University in 1962. Industrially based OR also started in other counties.

A key characteristic of OR in this period was a highly successful practice-driven development which drew on people with backgrounds often lacking mainstream management or military expertise but strong on systematic analysis and synthesis working in highly motivated collaborative teams with people who had the military technical knowledge and the military management experience to jointly create successful plans.

Some civilian scientists and military decision makers did not mix easily. When the zoologist Solly Zuckerman produced an OR report recommending bombing nodal points on the continental railway network to slow down German reinforcements after D-Day, his recommendation was famously ridiculed by Arthur 'Bomber' Harris as 'a panacea by a civilian professor whose forte is the sexual aberrations of apes' (Kennedy, 2014). But history confirms that Zuckerman was clearly right, and Harris was demonstrably wrong as well as being ridiculously rude.

To make sense of *all* corporate processes from an EP perspective, you do not need a deep or detailed understanding of OR, but you do need a broad understanding of the issues which can be addressed by OR broadly defined plus all cognate disciplines in the kind of synthesis provided by the UP concept.

Contributor 2: 1950s/60s OR

A key feature of 1950s/60s OR was the attempts to capture what the 1930s/40s OR groups had been doing in terms of process – usually referred to as the 'OR method' or the 'OR process'. A central feature of these 1950s/60s OR process models in terms of their textbook portrayal was a synthesis with a limited selection of earlier relevant generic models for making decisions, like the inventory models explored in Chapter 5. Early OR textbooks, largely a creation of academics and practitioners based in the US, presented OR as a practical approach to decision making using this new OR process plus previously developed relevant generic models. This led to significant further developments in OR theory, new areas of OR practice based on this new OR theory, and the first university courses teaching OR theory and practice from a range of perspectives.

To help put this book's approach into context and clarify my perspective, issues illustrated using some of my background may be helpful.

My BASc in Industrial Engineering at the University of Toronto (1962) was redesigned just before I started it. It was the first undergraduate programme in North America with a significant and central OR content. Part of its new core was based on these 1950s/60s OR developments, linked to current developments in MS from a North American Industrial Engineering perspective. By the 1980s many people saw the term *Management Science* as synonymous with OR, but in the context of my BASc, 'Management Science' was broadly defined to include earlier Industrial Engineering and Scientific Management ideas, plus Industrial Psychology (how individuals behave in an organisational context) and Sociology (how groups of people behave in an organisational context). At that time the term *Management Science* was replacing earlier use of the label 'Scientific Management' as a behavioural science critique of Scientific Management was developed. The term *Scientific Management* had been introduced by innovators like Frederick Taylor and Henry Gantt, in books like *The Principles of Scientific Management* (Taylor, 1911). Although the basis of some of their work was rejected, some early contributions by both Taylor and Gantt were still relevant in the 1960s, and some will remain relevant in the 2020s and beyond. Much of the existing core of this BASc was basic engineering sciences. A course in economics was taken by all University of Toronto engineering students, and in my case a very charismatic economics professor stimulated a transformative interest in economics.

My MSc in OR at the University of Birmingham (1964) was the first postgraduate course in the UK centred on OR. This course was already well established when I took it, with a very relevant option in Economics and Econometrics. Taking this MSc enriched my understanding of OR in the 1950s/60s OR sense from a British perspective, and it provided an important set of different perspectives from economics and econometrics.

My first academic post, starting in 1965 as a lecturer (assistant professor) in Econometrics, involved managing an MSc in Economics, Econometrics and OR and developing and teaching the OR content.

The starting position for my understanding of a UP was the OR processes described in 1950s/60s OR textbooks like *Operations Research: Methods and Problems* (Sasieni, Yaspan and Friedman, 1959). Table 2.2 is a common form of a brief summary of this OR process.

Table 2.2 A five phase portrayal of the OR process.

1 **describe** the problem,
2 **formulate** a model of the problem,
3 **solve** the model,
4 **test** the solution for robustness, and
5 **implement** the solution.

Comparing the five phase structure of Table 2.2 with Figure 2.1 assuming a comparable iterative structure, there are fairly obvious similarities and some very important differences.

By the end of the 1960s, I was aware that some practitioners who were pioneers of early British OR practice, like Patrick Rivett, had serious reservations about the oversimplicity of this textbook portrayal. Rereading parts of *The Craft of Decision Modelling* (Rivett, 1994) recently has helped to clarify why. Patrick and I never had a conversation about this topic, and I can no longer discuss his views at the convivial lunch discussions he used to chair in London at Blackett Club meetings he instituted, but I would like to think Patrick and earlier pioneers like Blackett and Zuckerman would prefer the UP of Figure 2.1 to the basic five phase OR process of Table 2.2. I think they would prefer the *formal planning* process focus instead of a *problem modelling and solving* process focus, the UP's front end which flows from its formal planning process focus, and other changes which flow from this revised front end. Furthermore, I believe they would appreciate the role of the capability-culture concept. I also think the senior decision makers and all the other people they worked with would be much more comfortable with the Figure 2.1 portrayal of what was involved.

Using the anti-aircraft guns example, the Figure 2.1 front-end formal planning process emphasises the importance of the plans as a whole in a broad view of the context, with the statistical modelling employed focused on a subset of the relevant issues which are suitable for this kind of quantitative modelling and in urgent need of immediate attention as part of a much broader overall planning approach. This avoids overplaying the role of quantitative modelling, and it paints a more realistic picture of how formal analysis using quantitative analysis can assist senior decision makers plus everyone else involved. It was of crucial importance to see 'the overall planning concern' as winning the Battle of the Atlantic in the context of not losing the Second World War. Any attempt to see this overall concern in terms of the quantitative OR models used would have seriously oversimplified and inevitably failed, because not losing the Second World War was in both plain English and technical language terms a huge 'mess' – a very complex set of interconnected issues and associated problems which were certainly well beyond the direct modelling capabilities of OR at that time, arguably still well beyond MS/OR capabilities.

However, for many years I had no serious reservations about simple OR process portrayals like Table 2.2 as the direct equivalent for my implicit UP. With hindsight I may have been implicitly presuming that other people would see formal quantitative modelling in the broader perspective of some prototype variant of Figure 2.1 without really exploring or properly understanding the implications of my assumptions – a personal stealth assumption I failed to identify and test. Whatever the explanation, I now believe explicitly exploring and clarifying the implications of Figure 2.1 instead of just using a textbook OR method perspective is useful. In the process of writing this book I have uncovered other significant stealth assumptions in my own earlier thinking, now resolved via generalisation of a range of concepts as a direct consequence of applying a UP perspective shaped by Figure 2.1.

Another key feature of 1950s/60s OR was that *different people saw it very differently* – an issue which may be less obvious now, but it persists, with important ongoing implications. For example, OR practitioners who were managers or consultants with an OR background and perspective tended to see OR as drawing on many disciplines, including all those in their own background which they found useful plus all those in the background of their colleagues which they found useful. However, academics tended to claim what they saw as the useful aspects of OR as part of their own academic discipline domain, sometimes underplaying or ignoring the rest, for what might be interpreted as academic group cultural reasons driven by territorial concerns.

For example, Gordon Fisher, the Foundation Professor of Econometrics and the head of the Department of Econometrics at Southampton University, who taught one of my econometrics courses at the University of Birmingham and gave me my first academic job in his new Department of Econometrics, saw OR as a subset of econometrics. He referred to this view as 'the Dutch perspective' because he shared it with several Dutch econometrician colleagues. My PhD supervisor, Ivor Pearce, professor of Economics and later the head of the Department of Economics at Southampton, saw OR and econometrics as separate subsets of economics. The Mathematics Department at Southampton saw OR as a subset of applied mathematics and created a separate OR group with a professor of OR to lead it and develop this perspective. My MSc from the University of Birmingham implied economics and econometrics were a subset of OR which was a subset of engineering. My Industrial Engineering professors at the University of Toronto probably saw OR as a subset of what is now commonly referred to as MS/OR plus a broader view of MS and the integration of this very broadly defined MS/OR concept as a subset of engineering.

A perspective you might find attractive, especially if you are an engineer, is using my favourite definition of 'engineering' – *creative synthesis of ends and means* – and defining a UP as a universal process for 'engineering planning' (EP) in any context requiring 'opportunity engineering'. This provides an 'engineering flavour' to the EP perspective and the UP without changing the contraction labels. Opportunity engineering generalises the 'risk engineering' term Dale Cooper suggested which we used for joint publications in the 1980s, and it may appeal to people who do not see themselves as engineers in the usual sense.

More generally, you can develop your own flavour, and you can embed an EP perspective in whatever disciplines shape your own outlook and approach to the UP concept.

My 1960s prototype UP accepted the limitations of the OR process description. But it explicitly embraced the notion that all the sciences, arts and crafts which were relevant to planning in the widest sense used in this book needed to be drawn upon so far as possible.

A key feature of the UP of Figure 2.1 is drawing on all relevant disciplines, without competing for territory, in a practical planning tradition incorporating problem solving and mess resolution which predates OR, MS and cognate disciplines.

Contributor 3: Ackoff's creativity and strategic vision critiques of OR

Russell Ackoff was one of the pioneers of 1950s/60s OR based in the US. He co-authored one of the first international textbooks on the subject, *Introduction to Operations Research* (Churchman, Ackoff and Arnoff, 1957). His book *Fundamentals of Operations Research* (Ackoff and Sasieni, 1968) became a standard international text. *A Manager's Guide to Operational Research* (Rivett and Ackoff, 1967) was an early transatlantic book.

Ackoff was also one of the most perceptive critics of mainstream 1970s OR. *Redesigning the Future* (Ackoff, 1974) develops a number of ideas that the UP concept and associated

SPs attempt to capture – in particular, the idea that top-down strategic planning ought to start by being clear about goals and formally address designing the future we want, as developed in Chapter 8 of this book.

Ackoff also emphasised the role of creativity, adopted as a fundamental feature of most phases of a UP or derivative SP. The create and enhance plans phase of Figure 2.1 and the creative aspects of other phases reflect in part my long-standing view that creativity is crucial. Creativity is crucial in the models used for quantitative analysis, but creativity is even more crucial in the much broader plans themselves and in the way the analysis plus the broader plans are interpreted. Good planners have relevant creative craft skill sets as well as effective and efficient toolsets. Ackoff stimulated the clarification and development of those views.

Ackoff's creative design ideas (he was an architect by initial training) are of central importance to a UP concept, as are his concerns for promoting a strategic vision which embraces 'designing a desirable future'. He was an American who had a deep understanding of OR developments on both sides of the Atlantic and had a profound worldwide impact.

Contributor 4: Soft Systems, soft OR and related process concerns

Qualitative (soft) factors, as well as quantitative (hard) factors, are essential aspects of an EP perspective.

'Soft Systems' was the creation of Peter Checkland, who was concerned about the practical limitations of traditional 'hard systems' approaches. *Systems Thinking, Systems Practice* (Checkland, 1981) is a seminal text, and Checkland and Scholes (1990) is a useful companion volume.

Checkland found a particularly appreciative audience amongst those who saw his approach as a very general form of 'soft OR' process, often viewing soft OR as an important alternative to a 'traditional', or 'hard, OR' approach.

Rational Analysis for a Problematic World (Rosenhead, 1989) is a seminal text on soft OR, addressing Checkland's approach plus a range of other soft OR alternatives, and Rosenhead and Mingers (2001) is a useful update. In part, the critique soft OR applied to mainstream 1970s/80s OR was the need to address complex messes – interconnected systems of problems as distinct from problems suitable for independent treatment. I would argue that 1930s/40s OR often took an integrated hard and soft systems view of messes, but 1970s/80s OR seemed to have forsaken a systems perspective as those advocating soft approaches saw it. In part, the critique soft approaches applied was the need to avoid a 'reductionist' form of analysis – to always see the big picture and the interconnections – to explore the interconnectivity of messes rather than to solve problems. In part the critique it applied was the need to maintain an interest in concerns which could not be quantified, including ethical issues.

My personal use of soft OR tools in practice has been limited, probably because my formal training did not include them. But I have used some simple soft OR tools myself and with colleagues successfully (the seven Ws structure in Chapter 7 initially created by Stephen Ward using a technique developed by Colin Eden is an example – see Eden [1988] for an overview). And I have suggested clients should bring in experts with requisite soft OR experience when sophisticated use of soft OR tools looked promising, advice followed very successfully by one client (Bombardier – who subsequently built an ongoing relationship with Colin Eden and his colleagues at Strathclyde University). Soft OR processes and tools should be an optional choice in the select and focus the process phase at any stage in an analysis if they are relevant to an organisation's concerns.

It is useful to interpret all soft approaches as systematic *qualitative* approaches which are not immediately concerned with *quantitative* analysis, as part of a broader set of *qualitative* analysis approaches which may or may not be concerned with eventual *quantitative* analysis.

It is also useful to be very clear that there is no such thing as a quantitative model which does not need *very* careful qualitative structuring and interpretation, and this was a universal truth long before any kind of MS/OR/Soft Systems approaches.

Put slightly differently, quantitative and qualitative analysis are not separable concepts in the sense that we can have qualitative analysis without quantitative analysis, but we cannot have quantitative analysis without associated qualitative analysis.

Contributor 5: behavioural, political and ethical concerns relevant to planning

As noted earlier, behavioural science critiques of 'Scientific Management' led to 'Management Science', defined to include the development of Industrial Psychology and Sociology. My Industrial Engineering BASc had a significate behavioural science emphasis which addressed Management Science in this sense. However, the OR process in its 1950s/60s form and subsequent variants do not usually embed any behavioural or cultural content in a direct and explicit form. They certainly do not emphasise political and ethical content or concerns. This is an oversight which any UP concept needs to avoid.

Some authors associated with soft OR and underlying systems ideas, like Rosenhead and Churchman, have been very explicit about the need to address behavioural, political, and ethical concerns, and Churchman was the lead author of the 1957 OR text cited earlier which shaped the foundations of textbook OR. I am not suggesting there is anything fundamentally new about addressing these concerns in a UP concept. However, those who want to keep such issues out of planning are potentially distorting an effective interpretation of analysis in a way which needs general understanding by all potential users of their analysis. Part of the role of the capability-culture concept is helping to frame planning in a manner which may offer some fresh insights about the pertinence of behavioural, political and ethical matters, and how to approach them in practice.

The mantra 'promote and protect the good, contest and constrain the bad' was associated with the basis of the two 'middle ground' example elements of the Table 2.1 capability-culture concept. This mantra can be applied to planning to accommodate behaviour as simple and ubiquitous as conscious (deliberate) bias when estimating parameters. As an example, *Megaprojects and Risk – an Anatomy of Ambition* (Flyvbjerg, Bruzelius and Rothengatter, 2003) uses the euphemism 'strategic misrepresentation' to avoid directly accusing people of lying, arguably very useful to encourage discussion but potentially dangerous if it encourages rather than discourages deliberate bias. What is crucial is encouraging open discussion of conscious bias and explicitly discouraging tolerance of dishonesty which can shade into fraud which should not be tolerated.

The mantra 'promote and protect the good, contest and constrain the bad' can also be applied to avoiding the implications of behaviour which is more complex. Elaborating on the Chapter 1 example, it may be important to help a project owner planning a bidding process to avoid a situation which results in the winning bidder being the tenderer who least understands the task being bid for (the most incompetent) or is most prepared to set up their contracts in a way which lets them add costs as the work progresses ('claims engineering') or is simply the one prepared to tell the biggest and boldest lies (the biggest crook). In this case, the immediate issue is protecting a given client, but an underlying problem may be honest and competent bidders will go out of business unless the bad is contested and constrained. Dishonest and incompetent bidders need to be dealt with effectively by the combined efforts of clients planning bidding processes and other interested parties – otherwise, they will ruin the marketplace for everyone else. Honest and competent bidders may have to take the lead with prospective clients, trade associations, the press, government regulators, and public prosecutors. The line between honest and dishonest is wilfully made fuzzy and ambiguous by those who believe sharp practice is just acceptable business practice, but there is no fundamental reason why everyone else should not prevent them from getting away with unacceptable practice.

Furthermore, this mantra applies to dealing with the implications of important political and ethical issues which can be very complex and highly controversial, like should an organisation providing a basic utility service like water supply or electrical power supply be private sector, public sector, or some combination. What is bad and what is good involves ethical concerns at personal, organisational, and political levels.

The mantra 'promote and protect the good, contest and constrain the bad' may involve consciously adapting processes to cope effectively with some people pursuing self-interest in a straightforward way, other people pursuing the interests of others in genuine altruistic terms, and a range of intermediate positions, including what some people see as 'enlightened self-interest'. However, and this is crucial, there may be no need to seek agreement between those involved about some key decision-making issues *beyond what is necessary*, provided an enlightened structuring of components of the supporting analysis is deployed. Chapter 9 addresses this aspect of decision making explicitly when it is especially important, but it is central to EP as a whole. Society has grave difficulties attempting to agree about what should be legal or illegal, and what is moral or immoral is much more complex. But this does not mean we can give up addressing related concerns, which can be crucial. When it matters, we have to try very hard to agree what we mean by 'good' and 'bad' and how we are going to promote and protect the good and contest and constrain the bad *to the extent that it matters*. If we fail to agree, we still have to confront the need for working assumptions addressing effective and efficient accommodations to cope with our ongoing failure to agree. The issues do not go away if they are not dealt with because they are 'too difficult'.

Associating requisite agreement about appropriate decisions with the capability-culture asset set and any linked failures needing accommodations with the capability-culture liability concept of Figure 2.1 serves several purposes. One important role is acting as a reminder to deal effectively with relevant behavioural, political, and ethical concerns by testing crucial assumptions and taking appropriate proactive action when necessary. Another is ensuring any failures are recognised and treated via effective accommodations.

Contributor 6: Paul Kennedy's and Atul Gawande's approaches to capability-culture

A useful reminder of the importance of culture to making plans work is one of the important roles for the capability-culture concept. Including the capability-culture asset examples like 'encouragement and empathetic governance top-down and bottom-up' and 'a spirit of continuous improvement when appropriate at all levels' was used earlier to illustrate what was involved. I have been conscious of the need to consider these issues for most of my career, but the incentive to do so in this particular way was triggered by reading the final chapter of *Engineers of Victory: The Problem Solvers Who Turned the Tide in the Second World War* (Kennedy, 2014). The starting point for the structuring of the capability-culture concept of

Table 2.1 was the discussion starting on page 365 of what Paul Kennedy terms the 'culture of encouragement' or the 'culture of innovation' and related capability and culture issues associated with why the Allies won the Second World War.

Paul Kennedy is an influential and bestselling military historian based at Yale, with strong British links. His 2014 book argues from a very broad perspective the importance of the collective role of the 'forgotten' scientists, designers, engineers, technicians, test pilots, military and civilian planners, businessmen, and others who helped to deliver victory via all three services in all theatres of the Second World War. He mentions OR (and Blackett) but just in passing. Some of his more developed examples include

1   the PhD students who initially developed a prototype magnetron in Britain at the University of Birmingham and the chain of people who ensured that it was taken to Massachusetts Institute of Technology (MIT) to be further developed and then produced in the US as the basis of all compact radar systems used on aircraft and ships by the Allies;

2   the British test pilot who first suggested that the American P51 Mustang's original engine (US designed and built) made it an indifferent performer but that with a Merlin engine as used in the Spitfire, the Mustang would be a world-class long-range fighter (with a much longer range than the Spitfire) and the chain of people who ensured that Packard-built US Merlin engines were used;

3   the American tank designer whose ideas became the basis of the Russian T34 tank and the chain of people who ensured it progressed through initial and in-service development in Russia;

4   the 'Seabees' (US Navy Construction Battalions) who were crucial to all the US campaigns against the Japanese; and

5   the planners who made D-Day work as perhaps the best example of highly successful planning in the whole war.

Having borrowed from Kennedy's ideas to recraft earlier prototype versions of the Table 2.1 capability-culture concept during the third draft of this book and tried them out, redrafting the tales developed in later chapters, it now seems obvious to me that the revised structure of the capability-culture concept greatly improved the usefulness of the UP concept as a whole, and the basic idea of a capability-culture concept of some kind embedded in a UP is crucial. Ongoing further testing and development are clearly needed, but the basic nature and the role of a capability-culture concept are clear and robust.

The Checklist Manifesto: How to Get Things Right (Gawande, 2011) was another important contributor to shaping the capability-culture concept underlying the UP concept. It has been coupled to Kennedy's contribution because it was encountered at the same time as well as addressing directly related issues.

Atul Gawande is a US based surgeon, an advisor to the World Health Organization, plus many other bodies, and a best-selling author. He came to my attention when he was invited to give the 2014 Reith Lectures on the BBC. He treats checklist concepts borrowed from aircraft safety, construction industry planning, and other contexts as planning and communication tools in a medical context, addressing capability-culture issues in surgical teams, plus some other contexts, with very wide implications for planning in all contexts.

Gawande uses the word 'checklist' when I would use 'plan', with checklists as a special case of plans in some cases and with checklists as procedures for testing the robustness of plans in other cases. His checklist concept is arguably overstretched in a way which confuses some of his messages by making them seem less general in their applicability than they actually are. However, this is a minor presentational quibble, 'checklist manifesto' has a much better ring about it than 'plan manifesto', and his key messages are very important. Many of his key messages chime with those taken from Kennedy, and they helped to shape the emerging structure of the capability-culture concept. For example, Gawande explains why it is important for members of a surgical team to know each other's names, spend a minute or two discussing what they are planning to do and key sources of uncertainty before starting, and for nurses and junior doctors to feel able to point out potential procedural errors by a senior surgeon which are anticipated because of prior actions *before* the errors are made – the essence of good communication pathways, teamwork, and enlightened governance.

As another example, Gawande explains in considerable detail how the knowledge needed by the aircrew of an airplane to deal with a low-probability potentially catastrophic fault was updated in weeks for *all* aircrew flying Boeing aircraft after one incident demonstrated the need to change the advice and accessed when it was needed soon after the update in a way which probably saved many lives. This example illustrates the essence of good pathways to feedback learning, to accumulate knowledge in a structured manner, and to access key knowledge about detailed contingency plans when needed, as well as a procedure to test plans being put in place to deal with an emergency.

As a further example, Gawande indicates the kind and degree of 'professionalism' we expect of aviators includes a concern for 'discipline' (following a prudent procedure in functioning with others) which is currently not expected of surgeons and some other professions society depends upon. He argues this kind of discipline should be not only expected; it should also be demanded. This is linked to the need to deal with complexity which requires a team effort to an extent which challenges conventional wisdom about the autonomy required or simply desired by some players in a team, discussed explicitly in terms of a change in what society should mean by the right stuff, a term made popular by Tom Wolfe's 1979 best-selling book *The Right Stuff* about the history of the Mercury space programme and the early development of NASA.

The focus of this book is planning in private and public sector commercial organisations, but the starting place for the UP phase structure and the current form of the capability-culture concept are both attributed to ideas drawn from warfare. This may raise concerns for you about the transfer of warfare-based ideas into the contexts of direct interest. Furthermore, the surgical team emphasis of Gawande's work may also seem remote from a common interpretation of the focus of this book. This may raise more general concerns about the relevance of some sources of UP concepts. However, this kind of transferability or portability of concepts is a characteristic of MS/OR grounded ideas. The generality of the UP concept is one of its defining characteristics, with significant earlier precedents in terms of all 'contributors' and all associated application areas. Portability is simply an aspect of the generality of the UP concept in the MS/OR tradition.

Contributor 7: the SP for projects perspective of the first four UP phases

The structure, function and labels of the first four phases of the UP were derived by generalising the front-end phases of the SP for projects discussed in Chapter 7, following a suggestion by Stephen Ward. This suggestion was important for several reasons, and the project management provenance involved has useful implications.

First, it helps to clarify the interpretation of the front end of the UP at an overall what needs to be done level simply because it facilitates effective integration of all the concerns outlined earlier in this section.

Second, when we come to considering the specific process for projects which is developed in Chapter 7 at a what needs to be done level, the common structure is an important basis for understanding the relationship between the universal process concept and specific processes in a general sense as well as understanding the specific process addressed in Chapter 7.

Third, when we come to use the UP in practice in any context it has significant how to do it implications with directly related and very important what needs to be done implications. This is because there is a rich experience base associated with the front end of the specific process for projects of Chapter 7 which is directly relevant to making operational use of the UP concept.

Fourth, by decomposing the process of making working assumptions into four phases the UP concept clarifies four significantly different kinds of working assumptions which are required as the process progresses, orders their consideration in a useful manner, and reminds us to address all four sets in relation to a very unrestrictive set of framing assumptions.

Finally, separating the four sets of working assumptions associated with the first four phases helped to trigger the recognition that we need to explicitly consider a further separate set of working assumptions associated with all the capability-culture concerns plus their overall role in the UP portrayed by Figure 2.1. In retrospect, this explicit recognition is clearly needed. This further set of working assumptions is usefully seen as applying to the way all seven phases work with the capability-culture concept to give the recommended UP concept an operational form which might be adapted by you or your organisation.

The UP concept is explicitly associated with the key framing assumption:

Some explicit operational UP concept is essential to avoid implicitly accepting a situation where more than one UP variant is probably in use and they are likely to be incompatible.

Consider what this implies in terms of each of the first four phases of the UP, the UP's capability-culture concept, and the UP concept as a whole.

'Capture the context with appropriate clarity' is a generalisation of an extensively tested 'define the project' phase. This generalised capture the context phase is about forming a strategic vision of the context in 'big picture' terms. This vision must include key concerns and their interconnectedness while the process is as general as possible. There must be a clear focus on what seems to really matter. When any important limiting assumptions about the context are detected via testing later in the process, the key defining features of this strategic view of the context need to be adjusted and elaborated as necessary as the process evolves. Even in a relatively limited project planning context the equivalent phase involves consideration of all seven Ws, starting with the *who*, the key players. It addresses all objectives of all the key players explicitly, as well as all the other important seven Ws concerns. The reason the 'who' and the 'why' are the starting points is that they jointly drive what it is that has to be done and how it needs to be done. Misaligned or misunderstood objectives are crucial. These and other related ideas are developed in more detail with a focus on projects in Chapter 7, with extensive backup in Chapman and Ward (2011). Of central importance in this subsection, these ideas can be built on in any context, as demonstrated throughout Part 2.

'Select and focus the process for appropriate clarity' is about making conscious and explicit planning the planning decisions to start gaining efficiency with a minimal loss of effectiveness. This must begin as soon as the key context issues have been captured in a way which allows the key planning issues to begin emerging. The select and focus the process phase addresses a big picture view of all potentially useful processes, a very different set of concerns and working assumptions to those considered in the capture the context phase. When crucial working assumptions about process choices look debatable during robustness testing later in the process, revisiting the process assumptions used to gain efficiency is crucial, as is adapting the process as a result whenever this is appropriate. There is no one best way to proceed, and initial working assumptions may need revising. As a generalisation of an extensively tested focus the process phase in a project planning context, the select and focus the process phase in the UP opens a portal to *all* useful processes. This includes the whole range of soft and hard OR methodologies. But of crucial importance, it also includes any other methodologies which may be useful. A rich range of methodologies associated with planning in particular areas offers a whole universe of particularly attractive and relevant options. Some of these planning process option choices may have some MS/OR in their background DNA, the CPM (Critical Path Method) process for example, but others may be entirely different in their origins. Drawing on process ideas entirely unrelated to mainstream MS/OR is potentially very important, and an unrestrictive portal into process choices from anywhere is an important feature of the select and focus the process phase which can be attributed to contributor 7. Using very different methodologies on different passes may prove crucial, and the ideas developed in Chapter 7 and Chapman and Ward (2011) can be generalised and built on in any UP application context, as demonstrated in Part 2 chapters.

'Create and enhance plans for all relevant concerns' then uses the context and process assumptions made in the first two phases to make further dependent plan creation and enhancement assumptions. Separating this phase opens an additional unrestricted portal, this time to *all* plan creation and portrayal tools relevant to the aspects and areas of planning being addressed. This create and enhance the plans phase is a central concern of the UP, it is well beyond the bounds of mainstream MS/OR processes by design, and it takes us beyond Chapman and Ward (2011) in some important respects which are explained in Chapter 7 and illustrated in all Part 2 chapters.

'Shape the plans using models of some key issues' leaves until the fourth phase the introduction of modelling which the basic 1950s/60s OR process addressed in the second phase of the Table 2.2 portrayal. This delayed introduction of modelling facilitates a less restrictive and more powerful perspective overall than the Table 2.2 approach because of the enhanced clarity provided by the earlier Figure 2.1 phases. Again, the portal involved is by design not restricted to MS/OR models. By this point we may be using a process which is very different from a traditional OR process, drawing on a different vision of 'plans' and a different vision of associated model sets. For example, in Chapters 8 and 9 you may find it useful to visualise the planning involved using a range of conventional strategic planning or safety and security planning tools within a partially structured mess, the partial structuring of the mess being the result of earlier use of the UP concept in comparable situations with very limited obvious direct links to traditional MS/OR visions of what an OR process is about.

The further set of working assumptions associated with capability-culture concerns will influence all seven phases of the process, with implications which can obviously have an impact on and interact in specific ways with the four sets of working assumptions just considered plus those associated with phases 5, 6, and 7. For example, if someone leading the application of a UP approach does not understand soft OR processes, they are not going to be part of the toolset which might be applied, with similar observations applying to more basic planning tools like basic project planning techniques or cash flow models.

A 'closure with completeness' concept which includes the proposed specific operational form of the UP can be associated with the capability-culture set of working assumptions.

Contributor 8: a 'learning organisation' as an explicit corporate goal

The Fifth Discipline: The Art and Practice of the Learning Organisation (Senge, 1990) is a popular book in the field of organisations and their management which is focused on achieving 'a learning organisation' using a systems dynamics perspective. Rethinking the Fifth Discipline (Flood, 1999) takes a systems overview of 'the learning organisation' which generalises the systems dynamics basis of Senge's approach to embrace further systems ideas originated by Ackoff, Beer, Bertalanaffy, Checkland, and Churchman. Flood is using systems ideas from authors I have drawn on earlier in this section in a different way to do something rather different, but there are overlaps, and the idea that a learning organisation ought to be an explicit corporate goal is widely accepted as a sensible proposition for many people working in a wide range of organisations. An organisation which explicitly promotes 'reflective practice about systematic approaches to planning' as part of the best practice being sought is the EP aspect of direct interest.

A 'learning organisation' in the particular sense developed by Senge and Flood, pursued using variants of their approach, is not a central part of the EP agenda. However, pursuing a learning organisation corporate goal in a manner suited to the organisation being considered using the capability-culture concept as an explicit tool for promoting 'reflective practice about systematic approaches to planning' is part of the UP agenda. This idea is developed in all Part 2 tales. It is not given a lot of attention, but it is a good example of a UP feature which might be much further developed if it is relevant to your organisation.

Teaching for Quality Learning at University: What the Student Does (Biggs and Tang, 2011) provides a conceptual framework for teaching referred to as 'constructive alignment'. This involves starting with the intended learning outcomes for different kinds of students with different levels of motivation to achieve different goals, and given these intended learning outcomes for the parties directly affected, seeks to align course design, delivery, and assessment. This approach is consistent with an EP approach to all planning, and generalising some of their ideas to address corporate learning processes might prove useful in some organisations. Their notion of gateway concepts has already been drawn on as a characterisation of concepts like strategic and tactical clarity, opportunity efficiency, and the four Fs for project planning.

Contributor 9: all other relevant concerns, plus a broad synthesis

A formal provision for further contributors which you or your organisation may find useful plus a broad synthesis of all contribution sources is the final 'contributor' category in my list, a further 'closure with completeness' concept in the same spirit as element 11 of the capability-culture concept. The role of contributors unrelated to MS/OR may build significantly on portals of the kind opened by contributors 6 and 7.

You may wish to alter the UP in terms of structure or detail as a consequence of past experience or as new experience is gained and lessons are learned from other sources. The UP concept of Figure 2.1 is flexible by design. However, don't rush to change the Figure 2.1 and Table 2.1 portrayals and interpretations too quickly, and develop some feel for how the UP concept of Figure 2.1 works before you commit to any changes which are not tested routinely. And think about proposed changes as alternative working assumptions in relation to all the working assumption sets discussed in this chapter.

Further clarifying what a UP is and is not from an EP perspective

At an OR Society Annual Conference in the 1990s an intriguing demonstration of soft OR was a central attraction. It involved extended parallel sessions in a number of rooms which delegates could wander in and out of. The session in each room employed one of about four different soft OR approaches to address the questions, 'Should OR be rebranded, and if so, what should it be called?'

It was an extremely interesting live demonstration of different soft OR approaches at work. It did not resolve the OR branding controversy, but it is probable that no approach could, then or now. Most members of the OR community agreed a long time ago that the OR label is seriously unhelpful from a marketing perspective, but they still cannot agree on what to change it to, because of the wide range of perspectives on what it is about. 'Decision Analytics', 'Business Analytics', and just 'Analytics' are one illustrative set of current propositions, but none of these options enjoys unanimous support. Management Science and the composite *MS/OR* term are alternatives with different but related brand-label problems.

The spirit of 1930s/40s' OR is deeply embedded in the UP of Figure 2.1, and this specific operational form of the more general UP concept has been shaped by all following OR developments. The UP concept and the EP concept more generally also embed the spirits of early-1900s Scientific Management, later Management Science critiques, Soft Systems, and soft OR critiques. One description of OR promoted by the OR Society which many members endorse and find useful is 'the science of better', and the UP concept and EP more generally reflect this spirit. The MS/OR roots of the UP and EP concepts are important and useful to understand, even if you have no further interest in what they involve.

However, within the scope of the planning focus which underlies this book it is also important to appreciate that the UP and EP concepts have provenance, scope and ambitions which go well beyond MS/OR as these areas are usually interpreted, and well beyond the individual contributions of the many obvious and not so obvious related adjunct subject and discipline contributions.

All disciplines and professions contributing toolsets, skill sets and mindsets which are relevant to your planning concerns can be drawn upon, and these disciplines and professions can, in turn, freely draw on an EP perspective, including the UP concept.

Equally important is appreciating that the planning focus which underlies this book involves a significant narrowing in focus relative to many of the ambitions of MS/OR and the numerous other disciplines and professions drawn on within the UP.

To make the central issues of concern in this section as clear as possible,

> *The UP concept is emphatically not a 'rebranded' OR process*
> *and EP is emphatically not 'rebranded' MS/OR,*
> *because they draw upon and are relevant to a wide spectrum of approaches to*
> *management decision making in planning contexts requiring*
> *both formal and informal approaches,*
> *with crucial supporting craft and team-working skills.*

The UP of Figure 2.1 and OR processes are very closely related, but from an EP perspective they are also quite different concepts in several crucial respects. Comparable differences apply to the broader EP and MS/OR concepts, arguably driving the UP and OR process differences.

Relative to the whole spectrum of ambitions addressed by MS/OR approaches and other related disciplines and professions, the UP of Figure 2.1 and the EP concept as a whole as explored in this book have a very restricted focus – planning in formal terms plus underpinning informal planning within commercial organisations, bearing in mind the crucial importance of informal planning and capability-culture concerns. However, within this restricted focus a very wide range of ideas are relevant – by definition and design there are no limits. The front-end structuring of the UP of Figure 2.1 facilitates both the efficiency gains flowing from the heightened focus and the effectiveness gains flowing from the generalisation of the areas drawn on within the planning focus. Furthermore, aspects of the capability-culture concept change both the emphasis and the basic foundation level framing assumptions.

Some people might want to ignore this degree of difference and suggest that EP is just marginally narrower in some senses and marginally wider in other senses than MS/OR, or 'modestly narrower but deeper', to simplify the differences. But in my view, this is too simplistic. From an EP perspective there are too many kinds of subtle and not-so-subtle differences that matter to use this kind of analogy. The underlying features of EP which drive all these differences as I see it is the lack of exclusive ownership or parentage of the EP concept by any of the contributing disciplines. EP has multiple parents and guardians with many different perspectives to draw upon, and it is worth being explicit about this characteristic, recognising its importance.

To begin to clarify why, when discussing the deep and important two-way relationships between empire building and science in the early days of empire building by European powers in the best-selling book *Sapiens: A Brief History of Humankind*, Yurval Harari (2014) points out that 'setting up a scientific discipline was an imperial project'. There are still very strong echoes of this imperial project flavour in most science and discipline areas. In the 1990s during an OR Society Annual Conference public discussion, I suggested to the soft OR advocate giving a paper on his brand of soft OR that he was misrepresenting what traditional OR was about, and my view of the traditional OR process (a prototype UP in my mind, but not his) could and should absorb his view of soft OR in its front end (in the implicit select and focus the process phase of my prototype UP). He immediately accused me of 'intellectual imperialism', deeply annoyed by the implications. He saw traditional OR as a back-end process option for a set of framing assumptions which made soft OR of his particular brand the basic framework. He was, in effect, promoting a new and competing empire himself, an imperial enterprise playing by his rules. This illustrates the nature of territorial issues which remain powerful forces within both academic disciplines and professional societies. Some of the latter are empire builders on an epic scale, with very limited interest in collaboration across the boundaries of professional societies, although this is not true of MS/OR related societies I am familiar with, the OR Society perhaps being the least territorial of all the societies I have come across.

If you are interested in the implications of these territorial issues in an academic context, Lewis (2017) provides some interesting observations about the social sciences, psychology, and economics in particular, in addition to a very useful background for understanding decision-making bias and related planning failures.

One key foundation level framing assumption feature of the UP concept and EP more generally is they belong to all disciplines and all professions and all professional societies and all individuals who choose to use them – by definition and design. You and your organisation can adopt whatever features seem relevant and adapt both the UP and EP to background and context considerations regardless of the disciplines or professional perspectives involved. The UP and EP concepts are an intellectual free-trade zone, explicitly not a basis for a new empire and not a territory for imperial occupation by any existing empires on a basis which excludes free access by others.

Four particular features of the UP and EP concepts may be worth noting to help clarify why they are conceptually different from the OR process and MS/OR perspectives.

First, the full range of arts and crafts, as well as sciences relevant to planning and associated management, needs to be drawn on, without inhibition, well beyond the range of any discipline or profession, and this is an essential operational feature, not a marketing ploy.

Second, the role of imagination and creative aspects of planning is crucial, and imagination and creativity are clearly not the exclusive territory of any single profession, discipline, or other grouping.

Third, making teams and wider collectives work effectively involves some team members having important social skills plus a genuine interest in other people which again is beyond the bounds of any professional or academic grouping.

Fourth, the capability-culture concept is a foundation level component, and the right stuff is a key component of the capability-culture concept. This yet again takes the UP and EP concepts beyond the reach of any single group, because no group can claim exclusive ownership of a concept like the right stuff, and different people are free to interpret what it means with some very different nuances.

Those with extensive MS/OR backgrounds are very much part of the target audience, but they are not catered to in a direct way as a special group in this or following chapters beyond helping them to see some key links which may be of limited interest to other target readers. On the website discussed briefly at the end of this book, they will be addressed directly as one of the groups who may be interested in using this book in specific planning areas and what might be called 'enlightened process planning', building on this chapter is currently the assumed focus.

Whatever your background and interests, I hope this chapter has provided the grounding you need to make use of the UP concept and all the other EP tools explored in this book at a strategic clarity level even if you have had very limited previous exposure to MS/OR. It was written with you in mind. If you use specific EP tools at an operational level, what you call them should be judged in your own best interests according to the context, working from whatever professional perspective you are comfortable with. Their presentation in this book has been framed for anyone interested in using them.

3 Low to high clarity approaches and the 'estimation-efficiency spectrum'

A key component of most plans is estimates of the parameters which define the anticipated outcome values of all relevant performance measures. Examples of relevant performance measures include levels of future corporate revenues and costs, associated sales levels and prices, the reliability, safety, and security of future operations, the cost of capital, the durations and costs of projects. Key parameters defining these values include expected outcomes and outcome range measures.

Corporate goals in terms of overall performance estimates need to be linked to component performance parameter estimates and plans via a goals–plans relationships framework, and goals–plans relationships usually need an understanding which has been developed bottom up as well as top down. For example, starting at the bottom, how long project activities will take and the cost per unit of time of associated resources will define part of the associated direct cost. Other aspects of the cost of project activities which also need consideration include the cost of the materials used, associated equipment purchases, and indirect costs. Corporate and operations management examples involve comparable goals–plans relationships.

In all planning areas common practice often involves the use of 'point' (single-value) estimates for performance parameters at a component level and at aggregate levels. Often, the component estimates are combined via 'deterministic' planning models (models which do not use probabilities) to yield overall performance estimates. This usually means clarity about the implications of underlying uncertainty is negligible.

Competence in EP terms means that *all* performance parameter estimates at *all* levels of component aggregation in *all* plans *must meet or exceed* a minimum acceptable level of clarity. Furthermore, they *must be framed* by a process which can provide additional clarity as and when it may be needed in a clarity efficient manner.

Even the mandated minimum level of clarity requires a coherent view of uncertainty and underlying complexity in terms of five key issues:

1   expected outcomes and possible associated estimation bias;
2   outcome range measures and possible associated estimation bias;
3   appropriate 'aspirational targets', if relevant;
4   robust associated 'commitment targets', if relevant; and
5   associated 'balanced targets', by default for a minimum clarity approach assumed equal to expected values.

The basic 'ABCs of targets' embedded in the working assumptions used for issues 3 to 5 in a minimum clarity estimate approach might be as follows, within the framing assumption that all working assumption choices should suit the context.

'Aspirational targets' might be associated with a 'plan A' intended to aggressively exploit any good luck that might occur.

'Balanced targets' might be associated with a 'plan B' intended to portray a plausible mid-range outcome, assumed to be the expected outcome for convenience and simplicity in a minimum clarity context.

'Commitment targets' might be associated with a 'plan C' intended to cope with bad luck, including all the reasonably plausible knock-on implications of this bad luck possibility, based on a plausible preliminary view of what a bad luck scenario might look like.

To begin to illustrate how an appropriate minimum clarity approach might compare to common practice in a project planning context, a basic common practice Critical Path Method (CPM) approach (Moder and Philips, 1970) often begins with direct point estimates for the duration of each component activity. These estimates are then used in a deterministic CPM algorithm based on a network model of activity precedence relationships to compute a point estimate of the project duration. This defines what some people may see as an appropriate point estimate of the project duration, perhaps assumed to be a balanced target outcome equal to the expected outcome. However, these component activity and overall project duration parameter estimates may be regarded by other people as commitment targets, although aspirational targets may have actually been the initial intention of those preparing the estimates. At the very least everybody involved needs a common basis for interpreting whether point value estimates are suitable balanced targets, different unbiased expectations, reasonable aspirational targets, reliable commitment targets, or 'none of the above'. If 'most likely' estimates are used as point estimates at the activity level, adding component most likely estimates which are not additive results in a very muddled overall estimate which is one common example of none of the above. Very often further clarity for very little extra effort is both possible and invaluable – a 'quick win' which can be captured with minimal effort by an enlightened approach.

These CPM based examples involve a project management context, the illustrative context used throughout this chapter. But all the concepts developed in this chapter also apply to operations and corporate planning contexts, and examples building on this chapter's ideas involving operations and corporate planning contexts, as well as project planning, are illustrated in Part 2. For example, Chapter 5 looks at probabilistic modelling of uncertainty about how long it might take to restock an inventory for 'safety stock' purposes, employing a simple approach in a very simple operations management example context. Chapter 5 also considers an even simpler treatment of unbiased expected value estimates for deterministic optimal order quantity models when probability distributions are of limited interest. Chapter 9 looks at the implications of the large number of people who might be killed in a catastrophic railway incident caused by an accident or malicious terrorist attack, with correlated injury levels, physical damage to the system and other knock-on implications, a relatively complex operations management example with direct corporate strategic management implications. Intermediate levels of complexity are illustrated in Chapters 6 to 8.

In all contexts we want to be 'clarity efficient' – defining *clarity* as insight which can be shared, we want to achieve a maximum level of appropriate clarity for any given level of effort/cost associated with acquiring clarity.

All clarity efficient approaches may provide more clarity for less effort than some common practice approaches for more than one reason, and high clarity approaches can offer a very rich bundle of advantages. To some extent seeking more clarity of one kind tends to generate more clarity of other kinds, and which kind of clarity should be seen as the primary objective may be debatable. If half a dozen different clarity enhancement objectives are all achieved concurrently, which is the primary objective and which are the secondary objectives does not really matter in some ways, although motivation, presentation or storytelling concerns may be important. Everybody can work in a coherent manner towards the common goals even if their priorities are not the same, and this unity of purpose despite the possibility of different individual priorities can be a crucial aspect of teamwork and broader collaboration.

In some contexts, we need as much clarity as we can get of all available kinds. Most of the time a modest level of clarity will suffice, provided we are clear about what clarity characteristics matter in this particular context. On the first pass of an iterative planning process, when it is not clear which project aspects may be important, a minimum clarity approach to estimation is usually appropriate. On later passes, once it is clear what matters and why it matters, much more clarity of specific kinds may be essential.

To explore the whole 'estimation-efficiency spectrum' addressed within the focus of this chapter, the next section considers a minimum clarity approach to estimating the duration of one activity in a project. The following few sections explore options which provide modest but useful amounts of further clarity at a relatively low cost. More following sections gradually add further aspects of clarity by addressing the underlying complexity which may be worthwhile, eventually considering the role of clarity efficiency, risk efficiency, and then opportunity efficiency. This takes us well beyond just effective and efficient unbiased 'estimation' plus recognising the role of the ABCs of targets as deliverables of clarity efficient estimation processes. Indeed, once risk efficiency is clearly understood, it usually becomes a central goal for most people in most organisations, with unbiased estimates plus the ABCs of targets usefully seen as by products or component aspects of an approach designed to seek opportunity efficiency, including component risk efficiency and clarity efficiency. However, a need for unbiased estimates of expected outcomes and associated ranges motivated most of the organisations involved in this chapter's tales, so starting from an estimation perspective with a focus on the five key concerns about estimation noted earlier is a useful way to begin. This gives us a clear basis for all relevant estimation bias concerns plus an understanding of the aspirational, balanced, and commitment target distinctions involved in the basic ABCs of targets at the outset. We can then gradually add further interdependent considerations.

This approach is a useful way to begin to explore the complex relationships between unbiased estimates, clarity efficiency, risk efficiency and opportunity efficiency. EP requires strategic clarity about these relationships. Risk efficiency and opportunity efficiency become the obvious central or driving concerns at the upper end of the clarity range, but they are actually underlying concerns at all levels of clarity, including providing an underpinning conceptual basis for a minimum clarity approach.

An important simplifying assumption is maintained throughout this chapter – we are dealing with a single attribute at any one time, like duration or cost. Whenever multiple attributes need consideration, this chapter assumes that *either* of the following:

1   All relevant attributes can be expressed in terms of a single attribute without difficulties needing explicit attention. For example, converting uncertainty about project duration into a suitable component of overall project cost is straightforward.
2   The pursuit of the primary attribute on its own will deliver an aligned optimality in terms of all other attributes, so there is no need to worry about attribute trade-offs.

Problems associated with managing trade-offs between multiple attributes which are not straightforward will be considered later, starting in Chapter 4.

The next section introduces the histogram and tree (HAT) approach to stochastic (proba-bilistic) modelling at a minimum clarity level. A single source of uncertainty is portrayed by a histogram with an underlying probability tree interpretation using the simplest feasible probability distribution. This approach is gradually made more sophisticated in subsequent sections. The HAT approach is a central EP conceptual and operational tool. It is a synthesis of several approaches often viewed as alternatives. Its more complex relationships with these alternatives are outlined later in this chapter in a separate section which addresses the nature of the synthesis defining the HAT approach in a reasonably comprehensive overview manner.

The span of applications of the HAT approach discussed in this chapter ranges from very simple examples at the outset to quite complex examples towards the end. The more com-plex examples draw on my experience with BP North Sea project planning over an eight year period beginning in 1976. During this period BP developed computer software to imple-ment a HAT based approach using a probability arithmetic basis for combining probability distributions. Most organisations now using HAT based approaches use off the shelf Monte Carlo simulation software. The simple examples considered early in this chapter draw on a 2001 UK Ministry of Defence (MoD) consulting contract which made use of a range of developments in the intervening decades. Some of the early discussion draws on BP practice linked to their use of HAT based software and comparable use of simulation-based software when this is helpful.

A minimum clarity approach to estimation

To illustrate the discussion in the first few sections of this chapter, consider a revised and embellished version of a conversation I had with 'William' (not his real name) in 2001. I was undertaking a review of UK MoD project risk management processes. My MoD con-tract manager, who initiated the review, was responsible for some of the processes used to approve new MoD projects and budget amendments. At his request the review was in part based on conversations with senior MoD personnel, including the air vice-marshall respon-sible for the MoD's procurement budget, who we will return to later. William was the pro-gramme manager for a major weapon programme – think of his project as a next-generation warship – with 'Warship William' as a reminder of his role.

Our discussion began by William suggesting that we use an example of immediate rel-evance to him. Say he wanted members of his warship programme team to provide an unbi-ased estimate of how long it would take to get approval for an unanticipated design change which had significant financial implications. Say the need for the change had just emerged. Say he wanted this estimate in order to get his team to re plan other aspects of his warship programme. What was the best way for his team to proceed? I responded 'start with a mini-mum clarity estimate', which I would illustrate by producing one with him, where:

> *by definition and design a 'minimum clarity estimate'*
> *provides a clarity efficient estimate*
> *at the minimum acceptable level of clarity*
> *given current working assumptions.*

My first question was 'What was a plausible maximum duration, using an approximate P90 (90th percentile) value as a default approach unless some alternative percentile value (like a P95) was preferred with good reason?' A P90 has a 90% chance of not being exceeded. William's response was a P90 estimate of 18 weeks.

My second question was 'What was a plausible minimum duration, using an approximate P10 (tenth percentile) value as a default approach or an alternative consistent with the plausible maximum?' William's response was a P10 of 2 weeks.

These two questions are a 'clarity efficient question set' for an initial minimum clarity estimate. They use a minimum level of effort to extract the information needed in the most appropriate form and order given current working assumptions.

Figure 3.1 portrays the recommended 'minimum clarity estimation model' based on William's answers to my clarity efficient question set.

The model used by Figure 3.1 assumes a uniform probability density function, a key working assumption used for all minimum clarity estimates. This implies a linear cumulative probability distribution.

Figure 3.1 portrays William's 18 week plausible maximum as a P90 and his two week plausible minimum estimate as a P10. The corresponding absolute minimum and maximum values for the model are 0 and 20 weeks, and these values make it clear that there was an assumed 10% chance of a value below 2 weeks and an assumed 10% chance of a value above 18 weeks.

Further key working assumptions that a minimum clarity estimation approach is based on in all contexts which need emphasis now include those preparing the estimate may not know at this stage in the process whether or not potential variability matters, but an unbiased view of both the expected outcome and potential variability might matter, aspirational target and commitment target distinctions might matter, and data might or might not be available.

The minimum clarity approach assumes that the balanced target is equal to the expected outcome and defined as the plausible minimum plus the plausible maximum divided by 2,

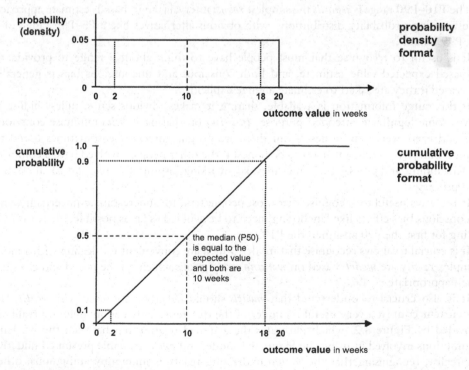

Figure 3.1 A minimum clarity estimation model with the P10 = 2 weeks and the P90 = 18 weeks.

in this case $(2 + 18)/2 = 10$ weeks. Assuming any alternative plausible maximum and minimum bounds were consistent and departed from the P10 and P90 in a symmetric manner, any plausible range estimate would yield the same result. Given the uniform density function assumption, the expected value is always equal to the P50.

There was no need to plot Figure 3.1 to determine the expected outcome and make direct use of a minimum clarity approach, but Figure 3.1 is the conceptual and operational model which underlies the use of a minimum clarity approach. If William wanted his team members to start planning with a simple deterministic CPM model, they could immediately use the expected value of 10 weeks as the design change approval estimated duration parameter for a CPM model. However, William should reveal the 2–18 weeks plausible range used to estimate the 10 weeks expected value to anyone who would find this information useful, unless there were good reasons for not doing so. Indeed, a usefully simple and practical approach for communication between all parties involved would be describing this minimum clarity estimate as 10+/−8 weeks, with a P10–P90 interpretation of the range and an explicit acknowledgement that both the expected value and the range are approximate with an underlying Figure 3.1 interpretation.

The expected value definition and the distribution shapes used in Figure 3.1 are the simplest available. The uniform density function means that expected values are midpoints in all relevant minimum clarity range estimates. The uniform density function also means that the cumulative function is linear, useful when minimum clarity estimates are used for a 'minimum clarity option choice model' as discussed in Chapters 4 and 6.

It is always important to avoid estimating ranges in terms of absolute maximum or minimum values unless there is an identifiable appropriate physical minimum or maximum value – the P0–P100 range should normally be avoided for estimate elicitation purposes.

The P10–P90 range is *usually* the simplest *robust* interval (range-based) estimate approach to estimating probability distributions, with obvious alternatives like a P5–P95 range or a P1–P99 range.

It is useful to recognise that most people have to think about a range to provide an unbiased expected value estimate, and both conscious and unconscious bias is generally decreased if they are asked to estimate a range explicitly.

If this range information is available, sharing it makes obvious sense, unless hiding it serves some legitimate intended purpose. *Insisting* on sharing it *helps* minimise conscious bias and keep everybody honest – but there are no guarantees. It is sometimes useful to remind ourselves that it only pays to be honest if the other people involved have a common understanding and play by the same rules, key working assumptions relevant to all estimation processes.

It is always useful to recognise that most people tend to underestimate uncertainty, and unconscious bias effects like 'anchoring' need to be avoided as far as possible, the reason for asking for first the P90 and then the P10.

It is crucial to always recognise that models which are convenient for dealing with a more complex reality are *models* based on *working* assumptions which can be tested and changed when appropriate.

It is also crucial to understand that *models* should never be confused with *reality*. In the current context a very useful reminder of the difference between models and reality is provided by Figure 3.2, which illustrates the assumed relationship between the working assumptions involved in using the Figure 3.1 model and *one* reasonable presumed underlying reality, recognising that the *actual* underlying reality is inherently ambiguous, other presumptions are possible, and different perceptions may be plausible and relevant.

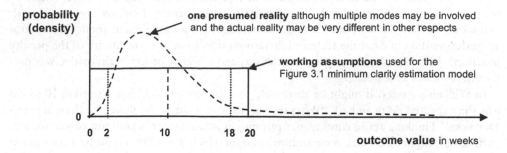

Figure 3.2 One presumed reality underlying the approximation involved in Figure 3.1.

It is important *everybody* involved in using minimum clarity estimates – *or any comparable simple estimates* – understands the kind of approximation relationship Figure 3.2 portrays. The fact that different people may all have slightly different presumed realities is not a concern so long as the model being used is a reasonable approximation to all relevant presumed realities and everybody understands the implications. The particularly simple nature of the minimum clarity model clarifies and emphasises this issue, often lost sight of if more sophisticated alternatives are used.

A minimum clarity estimate uses a very simple and crude model which should get the expected value and the P10–P90 range about right on average, but there should be no illusions about the very different reality being approximated and the ambiguity associated with the exact nature of that reality. Furthermore, there should be no illusions about the limited value of a more refined smooth curve like that of Figure 3.2 if different people think it should be in very different places, some people think two or more modes might be relevant, and differences in opinion that matter are not explicitly addressed and resolved.

Sometimes a useful secondary interpretation of the P10 is a default value for an 'aspirational target'. If William wanted his team to be ready to get on with activities delayed while approval was being sought, an 'aspirational target' might matter. A reasonable working assumption for an 'aspirational target' in this case would be a 'no problems' target to aim for to exploit good luck if it occurs, assuming that his team can control the plans post-approval but not the duration of the approvals process. If the duration of the activity being addressed was within their control, a no problems interpretation might be given a 'stretch target' label and emphasis to encourage everyone to work as hard as possible in the smartest possible manner to achieve the best performance feasible. This kind of motivation might be important as well as understanding the assumed no problems nature of what was being considered. If a higher or lower alternative aspirational target was preferred, it should be stipulated if targets are relevant. In William's context it might be very important for him to avoid just assuming that 10 weeks was the expected delay and explicitly ask 'What could his team plan to do about the delay if it was just 2 weeks?' At the very least, his team members need to address some contingency planning because of the delay their warship project was facing and think about contingency planning if a good luck or no problems scenario occurred might be valuable.

Sometimes a useful secondary interpretation of the P90 is a default 'commitment target'. A commitment target is what is promised, or 'counted on', in some other sense, as distinct from what is aspired to or expected. A commitment target can be important to manage possible bad luck. An assumed 90% chance of this commitment being achieved might be reasonable, given common levels of asymmetry in the 'penalty function' associated with being early or late. But 80% or 95% might be better. Making a judgement about this requires an understanding of what the technical literature refers to as 'the asymmetry of the penalty function'. If a commitment target was relevant, and a higher or lower alternative was preferred, it should be stipulated.

In William's context it might be absolutely vital for him to avoid just assuming 10 weeks was the expected delay and ask, 'What should his team plan to do about the delay if it was 18 weeks?' Thinking about contingency planning if a bad luck or 'significant problems' scenario arises might be crucial. A commitment target which was a P90 might be a convenient bad luck outcome to be prepared for, in conjunction with a P10 good luck outcome of 2 weeks plus a mid-range average luck outcome of 10 weeks.

Planners *should* manage both good and bad luck, and *everyone* interpreting plans *should* understand the implications if planners do or do not do so effectively. A failure to manage bad luck may be particularly visible. A failure to manage good luck may be less visible but even more important. If all the good luck in a series of activities is lost because its possible use is not planned for, and following activities cannot be started early whenever starting early is feasible, then all the bad luck will accumulate without good luck offsets. This will ratchet out the delay. Good luck will be wasted. There will be no 'swings and roundabouts' effect, cancelling out the good and bad luck variability. What some people may choose to interpret as overall bad luck may actually be an inept accumulation of individual sources of variability which fails to capture the good luck – a capability-culture liability which is common, directly driven by a failure to understand very basic 'uncertainty management' in terms of knowing how to manage both good and bad luck effectively.

A 'balanced target' is what planners should aim for when balancing the aspirational and commitment targets for some mid-range estimation purposes. Assuming the balanced target is equal to the expected value implies a 'symmetric penalty function'. In William's case a directly calculated expected outcome assumed equal to a P50 mid-range value might be sensible for some quite sophisticated reasons considered later – a minimum clarity estimate of 10+/−8 weeks is actually much more sophisticated than the analysis thus far may suggest. More complex examples when balanced targets need to reflect 'asymmetric penalty functions' are illustrated in Chapter 8.

It is always crucial to understand the potential differences between 'expected' values and the 'target' values of all three kinds – the ABCs of targets. A lot of common dysfunctional organisational behaviour is a direct result of a failure to recognise these distinctions, for a number of reasons, all grounded on a failure to understand basic uncertainty management. Some involve inappropriate decisions because the expected values which ought to be used are biased; others involve communication failures and loss of trust concerns because aspirations, expectations and commitments are confused; and both are frequently part of a complex muddle. Part 2 considers a number of examples, usually involving a mix of issues.

A very important implication of the aspirational and commitment target and expected value distinction of relevance in many contexts is that the expected value minus the aspirational target defines what is usually referred to as a 'provision' – in this case time over and above the aspirational target which *will be needed on average* if expected value estimates are unbiased.

Another very important closely coupled implication is that the commitment target minus the expected value defines what is usually referred to as a 'contingency' – in this case time over and above the expected value which *will NOT be needed on average* if expected value estimates are unbiased, but will be needed to meet the commitment target with the assumed level of probability.

Cost provisions and contingencies are usually crucial, and from an EP perspective, a point (single-value) estimate of *any* performance measure attribute like duration or cost is only appropriate if the P10 and P90 are equal and the assumption that this information is correct is shared as appropriate, even in a minimum clarity estimate context. Even if all that decision makers want is a single value for a deterministic model, they need a range-based estimation approach to avoid expected value bias, and the ranges used are useful information which should *always* be shared unless there are legitimate reasons for not doing so.

The minimum clarity estimation model is useful for getting an expected value estimate in about the right place relative to the expected value for a more sophisticated model closer to the underlying reality. Usually a minimum clarity estimate significantly reduces expected value estimation bias relative to any other simple estimation approach, almost invariability outperforming any point estimation approach. The minimum clarity estimation model is also useful for getting the P10 and P90 in about the right place, providing a crude but reasonably unbiased estimate of potential variability. Furthermore, these P10 and P90 values provide reasonable default aspirational and commitment target values for contingency planning.

A minimum clarity estimate communicates sufficient understanding of uncertainty *if*:

1 *everyone involved understands it is a minimum clarity estimate, and what that means;*
2 *it is obvious that there is no need to waste time thinking about the more complex underlying reality or the need for more sophisticated target and commitment values on the current process pass.*

A minimum clarity estimate involves a very simple and particularly convenient portrayal of uncertainty in terms of variability for a 'first pass' approach to providing an estimate in a multiple pass process. A key role for a minimum clarity approach is its use on a first pass when it is not clear which performance measure components in the goals–plans relationships structure may be important. Assuming estimation takes place within a UP or a related iterative specific process, a first pass approach implies more effort may be appropriate on later passes, with the level of additional clarity sought depending on the importance of the uncertainty identified on earlier passes.

It was convenient to begin the discussion in this chapter with William using a minimum clarity approach given considerable attention, but in my actual discussion with William it was soon obvious he needed more clarity. William was shown Figures 3.1 and 3.2, but he was not actually given all the information just discussed because much of it was not immediately relevant. Furthermore, William actually asked a slightly different question and provided some data (about to be revealed) using numbers which have been modestly modified to keep the example discussed as simple as possible. A 'tale' has just been told, and continuing the tale involving William in this spirit will be useful.

When I finished my explanation, William then revealed that his estimates of 2 and 18 weeks were the two extremes of five actual observations or 'data points' he was aware of, based on his knowledge of the time actually taken for comparable design change approvals in the past. He indicated the other three data points were three, four, and six weeks. Furthermore, he indicated two weeks was the current 'corporate guideline' for the duration of a design change approval of this kind. He asked if this information ought to change the minimum clarity estimate approach.

My reply took several parts. First, using the minimum of the five data points to define the P10 and the maximum to define the P90 was entirely appropriate. Second, if a much larger number of observations were used to define a percentile range via the minimum and maximum observed values, a P5–P95 range basis might be more appropriate. Third, the corporate guideline of two weeks seemed to be based on the assumption that a guideline ought to be a no problems target – which might be explicit, but I suspected it was a 'stealth assumption'. Some people might be confused and think a guideline was an expectation or a commitment, and in practice it was extremely important to make the nature of *all* guideline values *very* clear. Fourth, the potential 'outlier' nature of the 18 week data point suggested that using a two scenario approach might be a worthwhile way to acquire additional clarity.

A two scenario HAT example

This section considers a 'two scenario' HAT approach, building on the last section's 'single scenario' minimum clarity HAT approach. This section still addresses a single source of uncertainty within a single component (activity) of the goals–plans relationships structure, assumptions maintained for the whole of the tale associated with William.

William's data suggested that a two scenario generalisation of the minimum clarity estimation model would add useful clarity for a minimal level of additional effort. The four observations of two, three, four, and six weeks could be associated with one scenario, a 'usual range outcome' scenario. The relatively isolated single observation of 18 weeks could be associated with a second somewhat different 'high outcome' scenario. Some people might see and refer to 18 weeks as an outlier observation because it looks so different relative to 2, 3, 4 and 6. This involves assumptions which William should avoid making unless he has clear evidence.

William was asked to consider the 'usual range outcome' scenario first. A minimum clarity approach to this scenario associated a plausible minimum with a P10 of 2 weeks, a plausible maximum with a P90 of 6 weeks, and a $(2 + 6)/2 = 4$ weeks midpoint expected value estimate.

The four of five data points involved suggested that the probability of the 'usual range outcome' scenario was $4/5 = 0.8$, and $0.8 +/- 0.1$ provided an illustrative nominal range for the expected value given the sample size of only five observations. Using $0.8 +/- 0.1$ implied that $0.2 +/- 0.1$ was the probability of a high outcome scenario.

Using $+/- 0.15$ instead of $+/- 0.1$ would have had no significant implications, but $+/- 0.3$ was clearly too big, and $+/- 0.0$ was clearly too small. It would not have been clarity efficient to waste time and effort worrying about a more refined approach to estimating a range for the 0.8 and 0.2 expected values of these probabilities. But it was worth being clear that the probability estimates were themselves uncertain, as were the ranges associated with the 0.8 and 0.2 expected values.

William was then asked to consider the 'high outcome' scenario. A minimum clarity approach could obviously associate the single data point of 18 weeks with the midpoint expected value estimate. Someone obsessed with data-based probabilities might optimistically assume that 18 weeks was the only data-based estimate of both a minimum and a maximum. They might then use $(18 + 18)/2 = 18$. But common sense and normal statistical practice suggest 18 weeks with an unknown variability which could be significant in the absence of reasons to believe otherwise.

A crucial generalisation of this point is that even if William and his team had some data, they always needed to think beyond the data, in this instance in terms of realistic P10 and

P90 values associated with the 18 weeks expected value estimate for the high outcome scenario.

An estimate of 18+/–4 weeks in P10 to P90 range terms for an 18 weeks expected value *might* have been reasonable, implying an absolute range of 18+/–5 weeks, but a bigger or smaller range might be more appropriate.

If it had been worth exploring this range, William and his team might have asked the questions 'Do we know why the case with an observed outcome of 18 weeks took this long, and what other reasons for comparable high outcome value delays might be relevant?' For example was this project known to be in trouble? Was making the design change request a good excuse for a review? Was it a summer vacation period? Was the end of the financial year looming? And what other reasons of this kind might be relevant?

Now assume that William decided to assume 18+/–8 weeks in P10–P90 terms, implying an absolute range of 18+/–10, so he could use Figure 3.3, once I had explained the implications.

Using 18+/–4 weeks in P10–P90 terms in the context of a revised version of Figure 3.3 would imply a bimodal probability distribution. A bimodal distribution assumption raises questions about the possibility of further modes because of very different kinds of sources of uncertainty underlying the different modes. To avoid expending time and effort on these questions, a simple default working assumption was a single mode distribution in terms of the current two scenario HAT structure, implying that 18 weeks was not an outlier. This

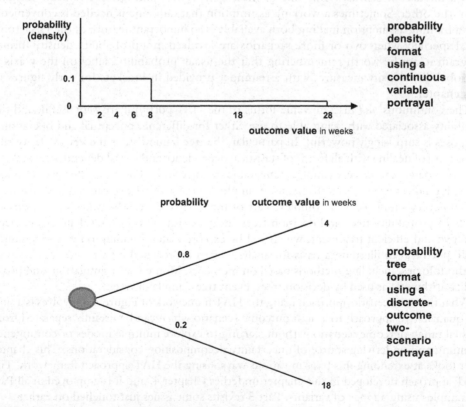

Figure 3.3 A two scenario model with a HAT portrayal.

useful assumption implied an absolute range of 18+/−10 weeks for the high outcome scenario, 18+/−8 weeks in P10–P90 terms, as illustrated in Figure 3.3. It was sensible for William to prefer this approach when he understood the implications.

The density format of the top half of Figure 3.3 treats the outcome value (in weeks) in continuous variable terms which are consistent with the single-mode assumption of Figure 3.2 and the data points, a useful basic way to interpret the available information. The alternative bottom-half probability tree format that treats the outcomes as discrete values can also be *very* useful. The joint use of both involves a HAT interpretation of Figure 3.3. This HAT interpretation implies that a default assumption associated with the tree portrayal is discrete values are conditional expectations for an underlying continuous variable distribution, rectangular in form for portrayal simplicity in density format. That is, 4 weeks was a conditional expectation given a value in the range from 0 to 8 weeks, and 18 weeks was a conditional expectation given a value in the range from 8 to 28 weeks.

Figure 3.1 can now be interpreted as a one scenario special case of the HAT portrayal illustrated in Figure 3.3. The underlying tree aspect of Figure 3.1 was not of immediate use, but it was in place from the outset, and it might prove useful later if multiple sources of uncertainty were being modelled.

The dual discrete *and* continuous variable interpretation of Figure 3.3 explicitly gives it a *dual nature* which avoids a framing assumption or a working assumption that only one of these two modelling approaches applied, common practice often locking people into a mindset which uses only one of these perspectives and ignores valuable insights from the other. Sometimes a working assumption that only one is needed is convenient, but a framing assumption making both available is an important feature of the HAT toolset. Especially when two or more scenarios are involved in a probability density format diagram it can be worth remembering that the usual 'probability' label on the y-axis is a probability density measure, with a reminder provided in brackets for early figures in this chapter.

The continuous *and* discrete value forms of the HAT portrayal are *both* useful, and the flexibility associated with being able to use either for different conceptual and operational purposes is surprisingly powerful. In particular, the tree framework is the key to clarity efficient ways of dealing with all forms of statistical dependence and causal dependence. Statistical dependence can be very simple, comparable to correlation, but it may be very complex, involving non-linear cascade effects, for example. Causal dependence can require treatment which is very simple or very complex. Part of the complexity can be portrayed by various kinds of probability trees and decision trees. Both statistical and causal dependence need effective and efficient treatment, which will be explored later, building on this very simple HAT portrayal to illustrate a basis for analysis often approached by a range of alternative methodologies, including methods based on moments, Monte Carlo simulation, and probability arithmetic as used by decision trees, event trees, and fault trees.

What the two scenario approach using the HAT framework of Figure 3.3 involves is a simple quantitative approach to a high outcome scenario which can be usefully separated from a usual range outcome scenario without starting to explore multiple modes or contingency planning and underlying source of uncertainty decomposition considerations. This chapter later looks at extending this basis in various ways, using the HAT approach framework. The HAT approach developed in this chapter underlies Chapter 4, and it is employed in all Part 2 examples using a range of variants. Part 3 revisits some issues just touched on earlier.

Whatever range or model structure is associated with the 18 weeks 'high outcome' scenario, the overall expected outcome using the two scenario structure is computed via

$$(4 \times 0.8) + (18 \times 0.2) = 3.2 + 3.6 = 6.8.$$

This computation just weights the conditional expectations of 4 weeks and 18 weeks by their probabilities, estimating the probabilities for each scenario using the associated data points. It clearly demonstrates that the clustering of the four 'usual outcome range' data points in the range of 2 to 6 weeks means that they collectively make a smaller contribution to the expected value than the single high outcome data point of 18 weeks.

Perhaps less obvious, this clustering example also demonstrates these data points make a smaller contribution than data points uniformly distributed in the range of 2 to 18 weeks.

The increase in clarity provided by two scenarios includes a significant reduction in the expected value – from 10 weeks to 6.8 weeks. This is a direct consequence of recognising and modelling the low-end clustering, consistent with, although not quite the same as, using the five individual data points to calculate the expected outcome via

$$(2 + 3 + 4 + 6 + 18) / 5 = 6.6.$$

A two scenario approach makes more use of the complete data set than does a one scenario approach, formally recognising the asymmetry involved, which is clearly sensible. More clarity about the high outcome value tail is also important.

Thinking about reasons for variability around the observed 18 weeks in terms of both what actually happened in the past in the case of the one available data point and what might happen in the future with comparable impact is valuable for better estimation. But it also has other benefits if the approach we are discussing is going to be used to think about contingency planning, especially if it is used earlier in the project lifecycle. Used earlier it might lead to revising a base plan, to pre-plan likely design revision requests so that they avoid the end of the financial year or holiday period requests if feasible, for example. Even if for formal quantitative analysis purposes decision makers limit themselves to simple planning models which do not consider this kind of contingency planning issue in formal terms, understanding the underlying reasons for variability provides additional qualitative information of considerable value. Discussion of alternative reasons why a high outcome scenario like 18 weeks might occur has direct value in terms of enhanced clarity.

The 'additional clarity' provided by a two scenario approach involved a model-based formal representation which was closer to the presumed reality – that is part of what we mean by more clarity. But the potential importance of the 18 week outcome and associated sources identified and used informally was also part of the increased clarity because the insight it provided can be communicated without ambiguity by an analyst to everyone using the analysis in an informed manner.

Also important was the very modest increase in required effort, whether or not data were available, and whether reasons for high outcome scenario variability were worth exploring.

Given these data, it was obvious that the suggested two scenario approach provides an unequivocal improvement in clarity for modest additional effort. But even if these data had not been available, if the presumed reality involved significant skew as shown in Figure 3.2, then the two scenario model might be a very worthwhile clarity efficient refinement.

If William's focus of interest was what he should do in this particular case, he might find the *simplification* inherent in contingency planning based on a two scenario approach useful and the *focus* on associated sources of uncertainty that matter most particularly helpful. He could stop worrying about separate contingency plans for 2, 10 and 18 weeks based on his single scenario model. He could focus on a base plan associated with a usual range outcome scenario expected value of 4 weeks plus contingency plans for a high outcome scenario expected value of 18 weeks, perhaps with more time spent on the 18 weeks scenario, including starting to think about contingency responses based on what might have led to this outcome. If contingency planning was relevant this simplification might be very worthwhile.

If a fairly symmetric distribution was anticipated, a two scenario model might not provide much benefit for the additional effort. The scope for more insight is driven by working assumptions about the presumed probability distribution shape for the uncertain underlying reality. The relevance of more insight will also be driven by the way the estimate will be used, so those involved in preparing estimates and those involved in using estimates should have a common understanding of these concerns.

More than two scenarios to 'refine' an estimate

The two scenario approach just outlined provided a useful starting point for beginning to generalise the minimum clarity HAT approach into a conceptual and operational toolset with very broad EP roles and capabilities.

The next step is considering more than two scenarios to 'refine' an estimate when 'refinement' implies portraying a single source of uncertainty with a probability distribution shape closer to a presumed reality, as suggested by the Figure 3.2 illustrative example.

If an n = 1 or n = 2 choice is judged not refined enough, then n = 5 as a default value in a range like 3 to 10 is an approach relevant to William's situation. To put this in context, when BP developed HAT based software they provided for n = 1 to 20, but rarely used more than 10 for a direct specification, and 3 to 10 was the usual range. Given that William had five data points, n = 5 is a convenient choice for illustrative purposes.

Often it is convenient to use a simple rectangular density form for the histogram whatever value of n is being used, equating the expected outcomes for each interval to the 'class marks' (central values) for the histogram intervals. Sometimes it is also convenient to assume a common interval for this histogram over part of its range or all its range. The HAT approach to refining estimates explored in this section uses a rectangular histogram with the expected values for each of the n = 5 histogram intervals as scenario values to define the probability tree.

William now provided an opening for starting to explain the basis of this section's generalisation of the HAT approach by asking, 'How could the approach of Figures 3.1 through 3.3 capture more fully the information content of all five of his data points?'

I responded by suggesting that we consider the probability tree in tabular form of Table 3.1 plus the associated rectangular histogram of Figure 3.4. This would provide a five scenario example of the generalisation of the HAT approach which made maximum use of the information content of his five data points.

Consider the working assumptions used to construct the probability tree portrayed in tabular form by Table 3.1 plus the directly dependent Figure 3.4 rectangular histogram density function portrayal and its piecewise linear cumulative equivalent.

Table 3.1 The HAT probability tree portrayal underlying Figure 3.4 using a 2-week common interval basis.

Delay scenario S (nominal range, span)	Probability P and components 0.2 per data point	Probability density P/span	Contribution to expected delay D S × P (expressed as a %)
1 (0–2, 2)	0.2 / 2 = 0.1	0.1 / 2 = 0.05	1 × 0.1 = 0.1 (2%)
3 (2–4, 2)	0.1 + 0.2 + 0.1 = 0.4	0.4 / 2 = 0.20	3 × 0.4 = 1.2 (18%)
5 (4–6, 2)	0.1 + 0.1 = 0.2	0.2 / 2 = 0.10	5 × 0.2 = 1.0 (15%)
7 (6–8, 2)	0.1	0.1 / 2 = 0.05	7 × 0.1 = 0.7 (11%)
18 (8–28, 20)	0.2	0.2 / 20 = 0.01	18 × 0.2 = 3.6 (54%)
			D = 6.6 (100%)

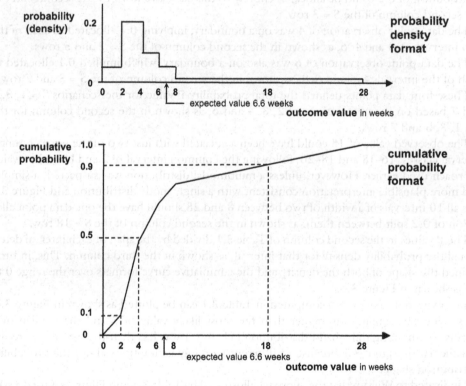

Figure 3.4 A five scenario HAT model with the P10 = 2 weeks and the P90 = 18 weeks.

The first involved assuming that because five data points were involved, each contributed a probability of 1/5 = 0.2, as indicated in the second column of Table 3.1 in the third line of the heading.

The next involved assuming that a two week 'common interval structure' beginning at zero was an appropriate basis for portraying the lowest four data points. The rationale for this choice was William had four data points in the range 2 to 6 (2, 3, 4 and 6), so the most effective and plausible simple histogram portrayal of the uncertainty associated with these four data points involved a common interval class width of two over the range from 0 to 8, with classes representing the intervals 0 to 2, 2 to 4, 4 to 6, and 6 to 8, using midpoint class marks defining scenario S values at 1, 3, 5 and 7.

This was linked to the assumptions that data points in the middle of any of these interval ranges (3 in this example) should have their probability fully assigned to that range, but data points on boundaries (2, 4 and 6 in this example) should have their probabilities split between the two classes adjacent to the boundary.

Working through this example one data point at a time, the data point observation of 2 was on a boundary, which implied a probability component of $0.2/2 = 0.1$ allocated to each of the two intervals 0 to 2 and 2 to 4. This was shown in Table 3.1 by the only entry in the second column of the S = 1 row and by the first entry in the second column of the S = 3 row.

The data point observation of 3 was in the middle of the interval 2–4, so its probability contribution of 0.2 could be allocated entirely to this class, as shown by the second entry in the second column of the S = 3 row.

The data point observation of 4 was on a boundary, implying 0.1 allocated to each of the two intervals 2–4 and 4–6, as shown in the second column of the S = 3 and 5 rows.

The data point observation of 6 was also on a boundary, which implied 0.1 allocated to each of the intervals 4–6 and 6–8, as shown in the second column of the S = 5 and 7 rows.

These four data points defined the total probability P value for the scenarios S = 1, 3, 5 and 7 based on the observations of 2, 3, 4 and 6, as shown in the second column for the S = 1, 3, 5 and 7 rows.

The observed value of 18 could have been associated with just two of the same common interval classes, 16–18 and 18–20, following the common interval of 2 and boundary-value approach used earlier. However, unless a multimodal distribution was suspected, a simpler and more plausible interpretation consistent with a single mode distribution and Figure 3.3 was all 10 intervals of a width of two between 8 and 28 should have the one data point allocation of 0.2 split between them, as shown in the second column of the S = 18 row.

The P values in the second column of Table 3.1 divided by the span of each interval determined the probability density for that interval, as shown in the third column. This, in turn, defined the shape of both the density and the cumulative curve formats over the range 0 to 28 as shown in Figure 3.4.

The expected value of 6.6 computed in Table 3.1 can be plotted as shown in Figure 3.4. This value was significantly bigger than the most likely value of 3 and the median of 4 because of the long right-hand distribution tail. But it was less than the 6.8 of Figure 3.3 and the 10 of Figure 3.1 because of different working assumptions about the probability distribution shape.

I indicated to William that the approach illustrated by Table 3.1 and Figure 3.4 used a synthesis of a standard basic textbook approach to histograms plus a common sense approach to avoiding multiple mode portrayals which were not intended. It extracted the maximum information content from the set of five data points which aligned the resulting histogram with a simple probability tree interpretation. Its treatment as a histogram in Figure 3.4 was directly equivalent to the simple five branch probability tree of Table 3.1, where the discrete branch outcome values correspond to the five class mark S values of 1, 3, 5, 7, and 18, with probabilities 0.1, 0.4, 0.2, 0.1, and 0.2. The expected value of 6.6 was exactly the same as the sum of the data point observations divided by five used to compute the expected value earlier.

However, William and his team members were free to modify the Table 3.1 and Figure 3.4 portrayal if they believed that a multimodal distribution was appropriate, restricting the range associated with the observation of 18 weeks. Furthermore, they could use a probability tree based on the observed data values if they were more comfortable with this. Table 3.1 plus Figure 3.4 was a more refined model than the Figure 3.1 minimum clarity model or the Figure 3.3 model, but it was still a model, open to alternative working assumptions and further refinement, including making use of any information not yet considered.

Although this example has been designed to demonstrate using n scenarios to capture the full information content of more than two data points, William and his team did not need any data points to make use of the representation of uncertainty provided by Table 3.1 plus Figure 3.4 if it portrayed their subjective view of what was involved. That is, if no data were available, they could drop the second column computations of Table 3.1 and estimate the probabilities associated with an appropriate set of S values directly in subjective probability terms.

The approach adopted by BP usually assumed no readily available data. The first step was estimating a maximum plausible S value. The second step was estimating a minimum plausible S value. The third step was rounding both onto a suitable scale to yield enough intermediate values to provide the level of refinement deemed appropriate given the anticipated probability distribution shape, usually involving n scenarios in the range 1 to 10. The fourth step, assuming an n of 3 or more, was estimating the probability of the least attractive outcome, then the most attractive outcome, followed by allocating the residual probability to all the other possible outcomes, ensuring that the overall distribution shape was consistent with what those present with relevant experience believed was an unbiased judgement. Obvious simplifications apply for n = 1 or 2, which are clearly special cases. The fifth and final step was checking the outcome with those not present who might have a useful contribution to make. This approach has been recommended since for all users of a HAT approach.

In practice, *if* good data is readily available, *and* it is important to make immediate effective use of it, then 10 to 100 data points is the norm, and 1 to 10 classes will usually provide a clarity efficient portrayal of what the data is saying. The most effective portrayal of the data will depend on the shape of the underlying probability distribution, sometimes usefully visualised initially using a scatter diagram. But in practice good data is rarely readily available, and even if it is obtainable, acquiring and analysing it may involve significant cost, and it will take time which may not be available. Most of the time a purely subjective first pass estimate based on the best readily available judgement is a clarity efficient approach, with whatever level of refinement seems to best suit the context. Further passes can address a possible need for data, more refinement and clarification via decomposition, which will be discussed shortly.

We can now see this section's HAT approach to any number of scenarios worth quantitative treatment as a general approach, with n = 1 to 10 the usual range whether or not data are available, the approaches of Figures 3.1 through 3.3 as special cases for n = 1 and 2, and Figure 3.4 a special case example for n = 5.

One or more 'condition' scenarios

I then suggested to William that *even if he and his team members had data readily at hand, they should ALWAYS be prepared to go beyond the available data, how much depending on the quantity and quality of the data and the assumed gap between the data and the aspects of reality that really mattered.*

To begin to address this issue, building on the approaches of Figures 3.1 through 3.4, William was asked the question, 'What was the chance of a '*very* high outcome' scenario, like 52 weeks, well beyond his data set?' The rationale behind this question was that William's five data points were clearly a very small sample. It might well be the case that serious problems with this project or overall MoD budget constraints and pressing reasons for spending money differently might put this project on hold for an extended period if an expensive design change request was made, a delay of the order of a year being a representative scenario approximation to all possible outcomes involving more than the range associated with their data set.

William replied that 'there was a probability of about 0.02+/-0.01 of a 52 weeks delay', roughly a 1 in 50 chance. Using this estimate to illustrate the implications, assuming the 0.02 probability was subtracted from the 0.2 probability of a high outcome scenario to keep the arithmetic simple, the overall expected outcome was

$$(4 \times 0.8) + (18 \times (0.2 - 0.02)) + (52 \times 0.02) = 3.16 + 3.42 + 1.04 = 7.48.$$

This was 13% more than the 6.6 expected value suggested by the full data set using a simple mean or the HAT approach of Table 3.1 and Figure 3.4, a significant increase. It clearly demonstrated that an estimate which does not go beyond the full data set might be systematically biased because it involved an important stealth assumption – *observations beyond the range indicated by the data set are not going to happen.*

This stealth assumption clearly mattered, and it demonstrated that we should always explicitly address this potential bias by considering a suitable 'very high outcome' scenario, and if relevant, a suitable 'very low outcome' scenario. Doing so involves two approach options.

One option is usually referred to as a 'conditional' estimate approach. It involves formally recognising one or more conditions – such as 'this estimate assumes no possibility of an outcome beyond x weeks, where x is defined by the assumed plausible maximum scenario'.

A second option is usually referred to as an 'unconditional' estimate approach. It involves formally estimating conditional outcomes should these scenarios beyond the data set occur plus their probability of occurrence, avoiding the bias built into the first option because conditions are only addressed in qualitative analysis terms. For the 'unconditional' label to be appropriate in a strict sense an unconditional approach must *justifiably* assume that *all* the relevant conditions have been identified and can be treated in this way.

If the first option is chosen, it is clearly important to understand the implied bias relative to an unconditional estimate, and the unconditional/conditional estimate distinction. If the second option is chosen, it is clearly important to be justifiably confident that all relevant scenario possibilities like a 52-week delay scenario have been identified and treated appropriately.

Furthermore, whichever of these two options is selected, arguably a key insight which flows from understanding the possibility of a 52-week scenario was clarity about the significant impact on the project of a possible one year delay *if it happened* – perhaps with knock-on effects leading to the cancellation of the project. William soon realised that he might be well advised to put some effort into addressing the risk of this possibility in terms of proactive (preventative) as well as reactive contingency planning without unduly worrying about the exact probability of it happening or attempting to precisely measure its impact on the expected outcome. Responding to a possible delay scenario of the order of 52 weeks involved very different issues compared to those associated with 18 weeks.

The obvious follow-on question was, 'What was the chance of a "project cancelled" scenario, an infinite delay?' The whole project concept might be overtaken by changes in circumstances which render it redundant, and the design change request might or might not be the trigger for this being recognised.

William responded that 'there was about a 0.01 chance of the project being cancelled', clearly revealing a further earlier stealth assumption – *'there was NO chance of a cancelled project'*.

It soon became clear that it might be very useful for the project team as a whole to be aware of the possible cancellation of the project as an explicit formal planning issue.

At a more general level, it soon became clear that it was important to appreciate that the duration estimate and all other aspects of their planning were now explicitly based on the assumption or condition 'project cancellation *does not* occur'. This kind of condition can be of crucial importance when relevant. Together with the very-high outcome scenario condition it can provide a starting point for generalising to an extensive list of further conditions worth specific individual attention plus the notion of a 'no quibbles' provision concerned with a comprehensive set of further conditions.

It is of course important to avoid attempting to include a possible 'infinite delay' in the expected value in a manner which makes the expected value infinite, rendering it useless. This meant that ongoing treatment of the project cancelled scenario not occurring as a condition was a sensible working assumption option. Indeed, it is often important to recognise that 'unconditional estimates' are not really an appropriate aspiration. The key underlying issue is a clear understanding of the extent to which identified or unidentified conditions are relevant.

The expected value of 10 weeks associated with the minimum clarity approach can now be interpreted as less naïve than it might have seemed earlier in terms of a plausible provision for a very high outcome possibility *if* a highly asymmetric distribution is involved. A possible very long list of other conditions associated with a no quibbles provision is discussed later in this chapter and related Chapter 8 concerns extend and enhance this argument.

Going beyond the data as illustrated by these two further scenario examples, and recognising the implications of associated conditions, provides an obvious and unequivocal improvement in clarity for minimal additional effort. Furthermore, even if no data had been available as a starting point to go beyond, these possible extreme outcome concepts can clearly be a very worthwhile enhancement of an EP perspective.

Whether or not data are available, *starting* by considering the chance of a cancelled project, or a very big delay, could be very useful if these possibilities were suspected to help minimise unconscious bias, further generalising the five-step approach outlined in the previous section.

Some variant of the generalisation of Table 3.1 and Figure 3.4 provided by the last section, plus making effective use of the conditions concept, with or without data, was the way William and his team should plan to use this HAT approach in practice most of the time. This would include the routine use of a first pass minimum clarity alternative when a very simple first pass approach looked useful, seeing the approaches in Figures 3.1 and 3.3 as special cases.

Use of these HAT variants has been a practical operational approach in a wide variety of contexts for a wide range of organisations for many decades, and they remain a recommended tool in the EP estimation toolset for both conceptual and operational purposes.

Of considerable importance is a clear understanding that in the light of these two further scenario concepts and associated conditions, plus the general tendency of most people to be overly optimistic, the minimum clarity approach in Figure 3.1 is actually not naïve all – it is a sophisticated low effort but robust first pass approach designed to neutralise optimistic bias not worth attention if it might not matter too much.

Also of importance is a clear understanding that William and his team needed to appreciate that if they had the data and the refined portrayal of Table 3.1 plus Figure 3.4 but failed to think about it in the way the usual range outcome, high outcome, very high outcome, and project cancelled scenarios suggested, *they might actually have less insight for more effort than using a minimum clarity single scenario model aware of the implications of a full range of possible outcome scenarios.* This would be clarity inefficient.

William could have his team use a one week class interval to provide even more precision if doing so looked likely to be useful in the sense of a smoother curve looking more like the presumed underlying curve in Figure 3.2. Any desired level of precision was available. However, William and his team members should not confuse smoother looking curves with more clarity, although they could have both smooth curves *and* the clarity of multiple scenario models *if they clearly understood what they were looking for.*

It is useful to see histogram definition of quantified uncertainty using rectangular density functions plus identification of associated conditions plus associated probability trees as discussed so far as a starting point for further generalisation of the HAT approach. These HAT generalisations allow a flexible approach to precision whether or not data are available.

Both scenario and histogram approaches are inherently flexible, as are associated probability tree approaches, perhaps linked to lower or higher level decision tree branches. None of these approaches are restrictive in a framing assumption sense, provided they are seen as special cases in a more general HAT approach framework. However, there are important trade-offs in terms of clarity and effort/cost of analysis which need to be addressed in terms of appropriate working assumptions for particular applications.

Any HAT approach involving a *nominal* common interval basis for conceptual simplicity (like using 2 for S = 1, 3, 5 and 7 scenarios) can be generalised using wider classes (like using a class width of 20 for the S = 18 weeks scenario). Another approach to generalising is replacing linear scales by logarithmic scales if this is useful, as illustrated in Chapter 9.

Generalising the minimum clarity approach of Figure 3.1 using all the HAT approaches discussed so far is usefully thought of as employing 'refinement options'. All these *refinement options* stick to one source of uncertainty within the goals–plans relationships component of interest in terms of formal modelling, which distinguishes them from 'decomposition options'. Decomposition options involve multiple sources of uncertainty, formally separated with a view to possible quantification, to be considered shortly.

Parametrically defined probability distribution special cases

Before moving on to decomposition options, briefly consider refinement options in terms of an important potential option *within* the HAT framework which many people see as an *alternative* approach to defining probability distributions.

William provided an opening for considering parametrically defined probability distributions by asking 'What if some of my team wanted to use common practice probability distributions like a Normal distribution?'

Using a probability distribution function formally defined in terms of parameters, like a Normal (Gaussian) distribution, can sometimes prove very useful. The Normal probability distribution is defined by just two parameters, its mean and its variance, making this approach very economical with data. Being economical in terms of data requirements is one of several reasons parametrically defined probability distribution approaches are dearly loved by many people with a significant knowledge of statistical methodology. Sometimes this love affair is well founded, but sometimes it is misjudged, and likely to end in tears.

From an EP perspective it is crucial to see the use of parametrically defined probability distribution function approaches as potentially useful special cases within a general EP approach to probability distributions based on a HAT perspective. This allows us to test the robustness of any parameter defined probability distribution approach within the HAT framework. Crucially, it avoids making assumptions which are difficult to test unless we have an unrestrictive HAT framework to fall back on. *Our framing assumptions should never REQUIRE a parametrically defined approach, but parametrically defined approaches should be seen as potentially useful options within a framework which facilitates testing their working assumptions and overriding inappropriate implications.*

For example, I suggested to William that after exposure to the generalisation of Figure 3.4, he should see very clearly that if anyone on his team suggested that the best practice approach to using his five data points involved employing a Normal distribution, dropping the 18 week data point as an outlier because it was associated with a project in trouble and their project would not get into trouble, they should be enlightened or found another job as quickly as possible. This was just a simple and reasonably obvious example of how someone unduly attached to a simple Normal distribution approach might try to get away with a seriously inappropriate parametric probability distribution approach assumption, but it was a parody of real people routinely encountered.

That said, BP computer software to implement a HAT based approach allowed users the option of specifying a Normal distribution defined by P10 and P90 values or other comparable plausible maximum and minimum values, with the software converting this into an n = 20 variant of Table 3.1. What proved more popular were a log-Normal equivalent and a beta distribution equivalent, the latter allowing a hybrid with asymmetric probability distribution tails outside the P10 and P90 maximum and minimums used along with the most likely value to provide the three defining parameters for a beta distribution.

One more complex and subtle example which I have encountered involved dealing with all the implications of 10,000 year return period design specification assumptions for seismic events leading to core meltdown of nuclear power stations with only a 100 years or so of reliable data plus debatable underlying assumptions about where epicentres might occur. Another involved missing data plus limited numbers of observations when making use of a negative exponential distribution assumption for 100 year return period estimates of deep ice-scour damage to proposed oil pipelines buried in deep trenches in the Beaufort Sea (Chapman, 1988). In both these cases, extrapolating on the basis of a very limited data set is probably the only reasonable starting point for a hybrid approach which also has to address plausible information about extreme events from any available sources, plus relaxing naïve assumptions like 'provided an event is within the design specification the facility will survive an extreme event, but as soon as an event is outside the design specification event it will fail'. HAT frameworks provided a useful perspective for thinking about and synthesising *all* relevant information about *both* the past and the future in both these cases.

You may sometimes find it useful to see the distribution shape assumed, via a parametrically defined special case or a histogram structure special case, as one of the conditions associated with expected outcome and range estimates. They are certainly working assumptions which condition estimates, and they sometimes matter.

This book will usually avoid discussing the details of 'how to do it' choices associated with these sorts of issues. They are only mentioned very selectively or developed in outline. In this case, the rationale is to make clear that all the issues just explored are comfortably within the scope of what can be addressed via the HAT framework component of an EP perspective, to overview the scope of the generality which can be provided whenever it is worthwhile, and to clarify the rationale for using relevant data with great care to deal with a future which may not resemble the past for reasons which may not be readily identifiable.

The synthesis underlying a HAT approach

This section provides an overview of key linkages between the very simple HAT models used earlier in this chapter, all subsequent discussion of modelling using a generalised HAT approach in this book, and the application of these approaches in contexts of interest to you.

It is useful to see a generalised HAT approach as a synthesis of six categories of approach which has been designed to deliver the advantages of all six without any of the disadvantages associated with narrower combinations:

1   probability trees with embedded decision trees using probability arithmetic,
2   continuous variable histograms,
3   probability distribution functional integration,
4   methods based on moments,
5   all other useful approaches which do not involve sampling, and
6   all useful simulation approaches employing sampling as a computation option.

Consider each in turn.

Probability trees with embedded decision trees using probability arithmetic provide the skeleton and primary muscular structure which supports the generalised HAT approach. The basic decision tree and probability tree graphical forms and the probability arithmetic are as used by decision analysis (decision theory) as approached by authors such as Raiffa (1968) and Goodwin and Wright (2014). They are also central to safety modelling using various specialist forms of probability trees like 'event trees' and 'fault trees' – see NUREG (1975) for example. A HAT framework assumes that the discrete outcome and probability values employed are associated with scenarios. These outcomes and probabilities are conditional expectations for associated continuous variables. Usually these conditional expectations are assumed to be central class mark values associated with rectangular histograms. The probability arithmetic treatment of illustrative numerical examples assuming discrete values in Part 2 have all used this approach. It keeps the examples as simple as possible while building the basis of the nuanced understanding of strategic clarity which all target readers need.

Continuous variable histograms provide an explicit generalised interpretation of probability trees plus embedded decision trees in continuous variable terms, analogous to the skin and secondary muscularity which completes the shape and form of the HAT framework, as illustrated in very simple basic terms earlier in this chapter. This continuous variable interpretation of a discrete value underlying structure is usually implicit in conventional decision and probability tree usage, whether or not point estimates of outcomes and probabilities are associated with ranges. The HAT approach makes a dual discrete and continuous variable interpretation explicit and mandatory because both discrete and continuous variable interpretations may matter, and the ability to test whether they matter is an important feature of the general framework which an EP approach provides.

Probability distribution functional integration becomes a useful component HAT tool when combining two or more sources of uncertainty. For example, if two sequential activities both had duration distributions defined by Figure 3.1, and we wanted to determine the probability distribution for the sum of these two activity durations assuming *independence*, functional integration theory tells us the resulting density function will be *triangular*, with a minimum of 0 + 0 = 0 weeks, a maximum of 20 + 20 = 40 weeks, a mode at 10 + 10 = 20 weeks, and a median and expected value of 20 weeks. If we assumed a *perfect positive correlation*, the minimum, the maximum, the median, and the expected value would be the same, but the density function would be *uniform*, with no discernible mode. If we assumed *perfect negative correlation*, the minimum, the maximum, and central values would all be 20 weeks, with *no residual uncertainty*. This is a useful simple demonstration of the role of dependence.

The insight provided by this functional integration approach can also be usefully employed to recognise the computational error implicit in *any* discrete probability approach to probability and decision tree portrayals when an underlying continuous variable distribution is being approximated and correct it appropriately whenever doing so is worth the effort. For example, if two sequential activities both had their duration distributions defined by Figure 3.4, and we added them assuming independence, the kind of probability arithmetic approach explored in Part 2 could use the class mark values 1, 3, 5, . . . and assign the resulting probability products to joint distribution class mark values at 2, 4, 6, . . . with the same interval of 2 weeks used over all the distribution ranges. It could associate a joint duration of 1 + 1 = 2 with one possible route to this outcome and a probability of 0.1 × 0.1 = 0.01, a joint duration of 4 with two possible routes to this outcome involving 1 + 3 and 3 + 1 = 4 with a probability obtained by 0.1 × 0.4 + 0.4 × 0.1 = 0.08, a joint duration of 6 with 1 + 5 and 3 + 3 and 5 + 1 with a probability involving three possible routes, and so on. This probability arithmetic result would be precise and computation error-free if we could assume that the variables were truly discrete. But if we recognise that a duration of 1 week means 0–2 weeks, assumed to have a uniform within class distribution, and we associate the whole of the 0.1 × 0.1 = 0.01 product with 2 weeks interpreted as 1–3 weeks, an error is clearly involved, with a similar error associated with all other probability product allocations. Assuming independence, the triangular distribution actually associated with 0–4 weeks instead of 1–3 weeks implies one-eighth of the probability ought to be assigned to the half interval 0–1 weeks, another one-eighth to the bottom half of the interval 3–5 weeks associated with a class mark value of 4 weeks, with comparable corrections needed for all other probability products.

As explored in Cooper and Chapman (1987), a HAT approach can build on this insight to show that assuming independence within classes the overall error can be corrected by moving one-eighth of the difference between adjacent class probabilities outwards from modal values in the joint distribution. This correction approach used in conjunction with more classes can virtually eliminate computation error and provide smooth shapes for the resulting distributions.

In this book, numerical examples in Part 2 do not bother to make these corrections or provide smooth curves to keep discussion of the examples as simple as possible. The errors needing correction are demonstrably small, getting smaller as the number of classes is increased, and the basic shape and form of the distributions computed ignoring these 'computation error' corrections are not affected. But in practice correction is feasible if doing so is worthwhile, and several possible approaches can be employed, including using commercially available Monte Carlo simulation software as an alternative computational approach.

An approach to correcting this computation error directly based on a version of the adjustments to a basic probability arithmetic approach just illustrated was embedded in the HAT based software BP developed early in its evolution of the approaches discussed in the next section. Later evaluation showed that the same level of precision using Monte Carlo simulation approaches (subject to a comparable 'sampling error') involved about 1,000 times more computational effort. The drawbacks of this BP software approach are twofold: the need for an investment in specialist computer software and the need for a 'reducible' sequence of combinations. Most current users of an EP approach avoid both of these problems by using readily available Monte Carlo simulation computer software within a HAT framework, discussed briefly for those who are interested in Chapter 11.

The role of probability distribution functional integration in the HAT framework is a contributing tool which makes the integration of the first two categories of approach more powerful. It extends the role provided by histograms earlier in this chapter to multiple sources of uncertainty contexts. It means that a probability arithmetic framework can control a measurable computation error to a virtually error-free level if this is worthwhile, the computation error being part of any discrete value probability approach approximating a continuous variable reality, whether or not this is appreciated. This verifies the conceptual model role of a HAT approach, whether or not discrete probability arithmetic is used operationally. Simulation provides an alternative and complementary tool to be discussed shortly. The next three categories of approach are also useful tools in a similar spirit for somewhat different reasons.

Methods based on moments (sometimes just called 'methods of moments') are the general category of approaches that a mean–variance approach falls into. Using a HAT approach to estimating unbiased expected values and then testing dependence assumptions, followed by using a deterministic modelling approach, can be interpreted as a very useful special case methods based on moments approach. It is relevant when only the first moment about the origin (expected value) matters, because variability is just noise and systemic uncertainty issues are not a concern. This is often an extremely valuable approach because of its simplicity. It can be useful to see it as drawn from the set of approaches based on methods of moments developed by Markowitz (1959), using a Markowitz mean–variance framework at a conceptual level to explore why systemic variability may pose problems for any deterministic approach and when a simple deterministic model is a sound choice.

It is also sometimes convenient to see mean–variance models as a way of thinking about the implications of well-behaved correlation and separability assumptions in terms of a Markowitz (1959) approach to portfolio analysis or early Program Evaluation and Review Technique (PERT) model usage (Moder and Philips, 1970). However, variance-based approaches and the use of further higher moments to measure 'peakedness' and 'kurtosis' have no direct operational role in the HAT approach as it is used by this book because methods that use them are too restricted or clarity inefficient in the contexts considered. If you wish to use them, they can be formally included within the HAT framework in the sense that associated approximation error can be tested in a more general framework.

All other useful approaches which do not involve sampling form a broad residual category which includes all the parametric specifications of probability distributions discussed in the previous section. This residual category also includes approaches based on understanding that a random arrivals process implies a Poisson distribution of arrivals over any given time period and a negative exponential distribution of times between arrivals, drawn on in Chapter 9. Furthermore, it includes the use of Normal probability distributions based on the Central Limit Theorem which holds approximately even for small numbers of added sources of uncertainty provided they are independent, plus other useful statistical ideas not developed in this book. Basic statistics texts cover a wide range of these kinds of ideas, and more specialist texts addressing subjects like queuing theory and safety theory cover further comparable ideas.

All useful simulation approaches using sampling as a computation option for combining multiple sources of uncertainty form another broad category which is usefully seen as part of the generalised HAT framework. Simulation using sampling in a basic Monte Carlo simulation sense adapted to the context modelled (e.g. see Hertz, 1964, or Grey, 1995) is essential in some very complex 'non-reducible' contexts as a way of *combining* sources of uncertainty which have been *specified* using a HAT approach or any other comparable component distribution approach. These simulation approaches are also a clarity efficient optional approach to computation associated with all the HAT models discussed in this book if software is needed, specialist HAT software based on probability arithmetic is not available, and developing this kind of specialist software is not clarity efficient.

All post-1980s clients of mine who did not have access to BP discrete probability arithmetic based software used HAT based approaches like those discussed in this book in conjunction with readily available commercial simulation packages like '@ Risk' for the probabilistic modelling aspects of analysis requiring computer software support. My post-1980s publications with a range of colleagues have always assumed that those using prototype EP approaches would take the same route. Your organisation should also take this route when software is needed unless a lot of HAT based modelling computation becomes the norm.

The key basic drawback of a simulation approach based on sampling is 'sampling error', which can be controlled by just using bigger samples, or by various sampling stratification assumption approaches. For example, to use Monte Carlo simulation to compute the total duration distribution for two sequential activities with individual independent duration probability distributions defined by Table 3.1 and Figure 3.4, each 'sample' involves extensive computational effort. A pseudorandom number generator routine has to be used to generate a random (uniform distribution) number over the range 0–1. This random number is entered on the *y*-axis of the cumulative form of Figure 3.4 to read off a sample duration result. Separate samples for each component to be combined are required, with the results of these samples then combined to yield one sample observation of the overall result. Repeating this for 1,000 to 10,000 sets of samples yields a reasonably error-free overall result, the precision required depending on the extent to which the low probability regions of the overall probability curve matter.

The obvious advantage of using a readily available commercial package like @ Risk is low cost software. Users of EP approaches who are not interested in the technical how to do it issues need not concern themselves with the difference if a sampling approach is used rather than a probability arithmetic approach *provided the analysts in charge of computation know what they are doing in terms of both dealing with dependence and dealing with sensitivity analysis concerns.* Some of these issues are briefly discussed near the beginning of Chapter 4 and are revisited towards the end of Chapter 11.

Simulation in a more general sense as explored by books like *Tools for Thinking* (Pidd, 1996) involve more general process and modelling philosophy ideas in addition to computational options. Some of these ideas can be seen as valuable additions to the set of process styles to be considered during the select and focus the process phase of a UP. Simulation in this broader sense might not make use of a HAT approach, but it could do so, and simulation in this broader sense has a wide variety of application areas and exploratory roles beyond the scope of this book.

The overall rationale for the adoption of a HAT approach as a core conceptual and operational framework for this book includes five important arguments:

1   it does not require any restrictive framing assumptions when specifying probability distributions;
2   it maximises the flexibility of approaches to all forms of statistical and causal dependence, including embedding decision trees;
3   using a generalised probability arithmetic approach to combining multiple sources of uncertainty as illustrated by the numerical examples in Part 2 clarifies what is being assumed for all relevant parties – the model builders working 'at the sharp end', the 'directors' and 'experts' who have to approve or make all the key decisions, and everybody else who needs to take part in the decision making or just understand the rationale underlying decisions beyond their immediate control;
4   clarity efficient special cases of all other useful other approaches can be embedded, be they simple shortcuts like limiting modelling to deterministic analysis using unbiased expected values or Poisson process modelling assumptions for more modelling power or the use of readily available commercial simulation software when this is expedient; and
5   all working assumptions which have been deemed appropriate for the context are visible and can be tested, including the use of a specific parametrically defined distribution like a Normal (Gaussian) when this working assumption is judged useful.

HAT approaches adapted to specific contexts within an EP perspective should explicitly aim for the support of decision-making approaches which are opportunity efficient in an overall sense – considering decision-error costs as well as decision-making costs. HAT approaches are a key component of the overall EP toolset which influences the EP mindset.

Any alternative to a fully generalised HAT approach which limits itself to a smaller subset of the six categories of approaches just outlined is potentially less clarity efficient, with opportunity-inefficiency implications. This is because it gives up generality which may be useful conceptually or operationally. A key loss may be clarity about the use of sensitivity analysis tools like those first explored at the beginning of Chapter 4 and then used throughout that chapter and Part 2. Any loss of clarity associated with failing to undertake this kind of effective sensitivity analysis is potentially a very serious issue.

Systematic decomposition of multiple sources of uncertainty

An important source of insight for William when the two scenario approach was introduced was qualitative consideration of the particular source of uncertainty responsible for the data point observation of an 18 week delay plus other potential sources of comparable delays for his project. This *qualitative* analysis on an *informal* basis allowed William to start thinking systematically about contingency planning, including dealing with a 52 weeks scenario and a project cancelled possibility.

We now need to develop this idea further on a *formal* planning basis, addressing systematic formal *quantitative* analysis as well as associated supportive formal *qualitative* analysis. We also need to address doing so in the context of all the components of interest in a goals–plans relationship structure – for example all the activities requiring completion to define overall project duration and cost when planning a project. In project, operations and overall corporate management contexts we need to embrace a multiple sources of uncertainty perspective with a view of the role of contingency planning which is as general, powerful and flexible as possible.

To illustrate part of what this involves, continuing in a project planning illustrative context, consider another tale. This tale is a revised and embellished version of a conversation I had with a small group of BP International offshore North Sea oil and gas programme managers in London in 1976. I was making a sales pitch for BP hiring me as a consultant via Acres International Management Services at the beginning of a consultancy relationship with BP which was very close over a period of eight years. The BP programme managers were responsible for projects involving the construction of offshore platforms, float-out and installation of the platforms in the North Sea, buying the pipe and arranging for the pipe sections to be coated with concrete, laying pipelines between the platforms and their terminals on the shore, and the fabrication and installation of all the 'modules' which packaged the oil and gas production facilities and accommodation facilities on the platforms, plus all associated hook-up and integration operations.

One programme manager I will call Peter started and led the discussion on behalf of his colleagues. He indicated that BP's current planning approaches were not letting them deliver these projects on-time or within budget. They were under great pressure from their board to achieve both. His wish to resolve this pressure was the reason for our conversation. They all knew cost was heavily time-driven, but they did not know how to effectively capture the complexity this involved. They were particularly interested in understanding how they could do better with estimating the duration and cost of laying an offshore oil pipeline. They wanted to begin by discussing estimating how long it would take to lay a pipeline given various assumptions about when to start and what wave height capability lay-barge to use, computing an unbiased expected value of the duration of the pipe-laying activity. They then wanted to use this analysis approach as a basis for an approach to obtaining an unbiased estimate of all other activity durations plus the expected costs associated with all activities. What was the best way to proceed?

I began by indicating that the common practice PERT probabilistic models developed in the late 1950s which they were familiar with had been acknowledged by a growing number of practitioners as a significant improvement on similar CPM deterministic models (Moder and Philips, 1970). One key reason was less bias associated with activity expected duration estimates because an explicit range-based interval estimate was used for the duration of each activity. However, PERT model estimates of overall project duration were usually far too optimistically biased to have any credibility, and associated cost estimates were generally even more optimistically biased. One key reason was a PERT model assumed that the probability distribution defining the duration of each activity was independent of all other activity durations. In practice, dependence was significant and crucial, and two quite different aspects of dependence needed careful attention.

One aspect involved dependence in terms of the sources of uncertainty encountered by base plans plus direct knock-on effects. PERT models assumed that if activity X was followed by activity Y, the probabilities that activity Y will experience no problems or a lot of problems were independent of the probabilities that activity X would experience no problems or a lot of problems. In practice, there were usually common reasons for many of the problems arising in different activities, like the same initial planner or contractor with the same level of competence. In addition, in practice there were usually important knock-on effects that implied a further significant positive correlation. These knock-on effects might include exceedingly complex forms of positive dependence sometimes referred to as cascade effects. Sometimes it might be convenient and practical to treat this dependence in statistical dependence terms via fairly simple correlation assumptions. But sometimes an in-depth understanding of the causal dependence relationships generating this kind of dependence was crucial. Intermediate cases best served by probability tree specification of complex statistical dependence could also be relevant.

The other aspect involved recognising the crucial importance of causal dependence associated with reacting to delays to base plans via contingency plans. PERT models assumed that the plan for executing activity Y after X had been completed was always created and assessed without considering how long X might actually take. But in practice, if activity X took significantly more or less time than expected, the plan for a following activity Y might be altered, whether or not prepared contingency plans were in place in advance. Furthermore, in practice planning and control *should* be closely coupled with this important response possibility in mind, and in practice some degree of prior contingency planning *should* be part of most planning, associated with 'proactive responses' which alter base plans plus 'reactive responses' which respond after the fact but may need set up in advance. PERT models ignored consideration of prior contingency planning and unplanned later responses to delay or earlier-than-expected completion. With or without prior contingency planning, after-the-fact contingency responses usually reduced the duration of Y when X was delayed, inducing negative correlation in terms of activity durations to keep the overall project duration within the original estimate if possible. But this increased the cost, amplifying the positive dependence between cost components because of common market forces, introducing a key causal interdependency between duration and cost which was driven by contingency plans.

'Generalised PERT' had been developed in the early 1960s to consider prior contingency planning. These generalised PERT models embedded decision trees at the beginning of each activity. If prior activities were late, a contingency plan could be triggered. For example, if activity X was on time, base plan Y1 could be used, but if activity X was late, contingency plan Y2 could be triggered, and if activity X was early, contingency plan Y3 could be used. BP needed models with this prior contingency planning capability, in addition to an approach to correlation forms of dependency plus conditional treatment of more complex statistical dependencies which was general and flexible. The HAT framework basis for the Generalised PERT approach, which was explained in outline in terms of prototype variants, would provide much more realistic estimates of expected duration and cost outcomes because it could address both statistical and causal dependence, base plans and contingency plans.

I then suggested that BP also needed a generalised Markov process structure (dealing with semi-Markov processes for those who want to get technical, with time-dependent transition distributions), further extending the HAT approach within a Generalised PERT framework. BP planners could begin with a textbook GERT (Graphical Evaluation and Review Technique) model. Moder and Philips (1970) discussed GERT as well as more basic CPM/PERT models, but at that time GERT had limited applications outside the US aerospace industry to illustrate the approach. These models could decompose the uncertainty about the answer to the question, 'How long would it take to lay the pipe?' into 'How much pipe could be laid in each successive month?' A generalised Markov process structure was ideal for dealing with weather windows. I explained how I had used these GERT models successfully on an Acres Consulting Services study a year earlier of a major Canadian Arctic oil pipeline project, when a somewhat different but equally important weather window was involved. North Sea pipe-laying was not feasible in the winter; summer was ideal. Spring and autumn shoulder seasons were difficult and risky but could be crucial. A generalised Markov process structure would allow consideration of different weather expectations in each month using appropriate weather data and reactive responses geared to progress each month, in addition to the Generalised PERT responses at the end of each month of the pipe-laying activity. This approach would give BP project planners the ability to test the implications of different lay-barge capabilities and different assumed start dates making good use of available weather data.

But in order to separate weather effects from other sources of uncertainty, and use weather data directly in an effective way, BP planners also needed a further feature, a further extension of the HAT approach within a GERT framework – later called the SCERT (Synergistic Contingency Evaluation and Response Technique) approach (Chapman, 1979).

The basis for the SCERT approach had occurred to me when reviewing what had been learned from the Acres Arctic pipeline study. One analysis problem associated with using the basic GERT approach arose every time we addressed the question, 'If we experience delays in month X, what should we do to speed things up in the following month Y?' The preferred answer was almost invariably dependent on what went wrong. But the basic GERT model does not consider that question.

Insightful analysis yielding high levels of clarity has to focus on *all* the questions that really matter. If questions that really matter are not being asked, something effective and efficient needs to be done about it.

This review coincided with a separate review considering lessons learned during a separate Acres study of the best way to approach seismic risk associated with the location and design of nuclear power stations. I had reviewed US standards with several Acres colleagues with a view to contributing to the drafting of Canadian standards, which Acres wanted to address as a marketing investment.

The key to SCERT was borrowing fault tree and event tree ideas from the common approaches to nuclear safety issues, plus basic decision tree approaches to model specific sources of uncertainty which could be addressed by responses specific to those sources and embedding these additional model features in GERT models without losing the general response features of a GERT approach.

I had not yet tried out this prototype SCERT idea, but the approach looked promising. It would involve breaking down the quantified uncertainty associated with progress in each month for an activity like pipe-laying into multiple sources of uncertainty, drawing on the fault tree and event tree ideas used for US nuclear power station seismic risk studies (NUREG, 1975), plus basic decision tree ideas. Using this approach within the GERT model structure, the focus for a key activity like pipe-laying might be a small number of 'specific responses' for very important specific sources of uncertainty, but 'general responses' to deal with the residual after all the specific responses for each successive month would also be involved. Maintaining the general response concept would facilitate dealing with all threats and opportunities not fully dealt with via specific responses, including any 'unknown unknowns'.

The first key source requiring separate quantitative treatment for the pipe-laying activity was 'weather' – more specifically wave height. One reason for the separate treatment of weather was the significant impact of this source of uncertainty. Closely coupled further reasons were the wave height capability specification of the chosen lay-barge was a key prior decision, good wave height weather data was available, and given the obvious importance of weather, it would be sensible to make effective use of the available wave height data.

Wave height data for the sea areas in question could be used to assess a probability distribution for the number of working days in each month during the working season given the wave height capability of the assumed lay-barge. If 'productivity variations' implied 1 to

5 km of pipe laid per 'lay-day' when the waves were below the assumed lay-barge capability limit, with a mean of 3 km/day, then an expected value of 3 km/day could be used to transform wave height distributions into rate of progress distributions. The initial working assumption would be that 'productivity variations' due to all sources of uncertainty other than weather cancelled out, and no further specific sources of uncertainty other than weather were involved. Markov process runs could assume a given lay-barge wave height capability and start date and compute the probability of completion within the planned single season, plus the chance of further seasons, with a cumulative probability distribution for completion within each month in the feasible completion date range. BP planners could experiment with different start dates or lay-barge wave height capabilities and get a feel for what 'weather' on its own might do to their plans. They could understand the implications of good luck, bad luck, and everything in between in terms of weather on its own. They could then start to address any other sources of uncertainty deemed important enough to warrant separate treatment.

The next separate source of uncertainty on this agenda might be 'wet buckles' – the smooth S shape of the pipeline section from the lay-barge to the ocean bed develops a kink which fractures the steel in the pipeline, letting in water. The pipeline then becomes too heavy for the barge to hold, ripping itself off the barge unless it is released very quickly, sinking to the ocean floor. The basic response is 'repair' – send down divers to cut the damaged pipe away and 'cap the pipe' (sealing the end with steel cap), 'dewater the pipe' by sending a 'pig' (a torpedo-shaped object which just fits the pipe) through it under air pressure (valves in the cap let the water out as the pig progresses), and then pick up the dewatered pipeline and carry on. However, a rich range of alternative responses could be explored – like a bigger lay-barge which is less prone to buckles (and faster because it can lay pipe in worse weather).

Furthermore, secondary sources of uncertainty could be explored – like repairing a pipe buckle might lead to the pig sent through the pipe getting stuck because of debris in the pipe, with more than one relevant secondary response, both involving the possible loss of a significant amount of coated pipe which might be difficult to replace without a significant delay. Divers could be sent down to cut off the pipe behind a stuck pig and fit a new cap, then another pig could be used to dewater the shortened pipe. Alternatively, the air pressure could be turned up to try to pop the pig through the debris, with a possibility of this response resulting in structural damage to the pipe involving even more lost pipe than cutting off the pipe behind the stuck pig.

Further still, the loss of pipe involved as a consequence of a stuck pig should trigger consideration of dependence with both earlier and later decisions. For example, should extra pipe be ordered and coated for this project in advance? If it was not needed for this project because no buckles occurred, should it be suitable for subsequent projects? And does this imply a pipeline design strategy common to all offshore projects?

Dependence between decomposed sources of uncertainty because of common underlying problems could be modelled directly in various ways *if it mattered*. For example, the common interval rectangular histogram probability density function approach could be used in a HAT framework to define anticipated lay-days and rate of progress distributions for each month of the year when pipe-laying might be attempted. Using this starting point, progress for each month and overall progress by the end of each month could be considered in terms of a probability tree using class mark values. In this framework different risks of a wet buckle could be associated with very good weather, very bad weather, and intermediate situations, recognising that the highest risk might involve the intermediate situations. This is because in very bad weather no pipe-laying would be attempted, and in very good weather no problems are likely, but in the mid-range problems were highly likely.

Other important decomposed separate sources to follow might be major equipment failures (perhaps also weather dependent), a late start because an earlier contract involving the barge contracted for was delayed, coated pipe supplies delay, and so on.

A 'dry buckle', when a buckle occurred but the pipeline steel did not fracture, could be resolved fairly quickly. In effect, the lay-barge could just back up and recover the damaged pipeline, then carry on. This was a useful example of a relatively minor problem not requiring separate treatment. Dry buckles were an identified example of the 'productivity variations' source of uncertainty, along with a list of other identified minor problem not worth separate planning attention at this stage, plus all unidentified minor problems.

I argued that if this approach was used, along with significantly simplified versions for other activities which might not need a Markov framework, BP planners could develop what was later labelled the SCERT approach (Chapman, 1979). It should provide an unbiased approach to activity duration estimation and associated cost estimation, because it would address the identified flaws in current common practice approaches which gave rise to observed bias.

Once the BP planners understood the duration of a central activity like pipe-laying in these terms, they could build a dependent cost estimate on this framework. For example, the cost of a lay-barge per working (lay) day and per idle (weather) day during the period the barge was on hire could be estimated in probability distribution terms, and the cost of the pipe, coating it and transporting it, could also be considered. Once the duration and cost of pipe laying were understood, earlier and later activities could be addressed, building a model which considered dependencies between activities, including the knock-on effects of delays to or partial incompletion of earlier activities on following activities. For example, if delayed completion of module construction onshore threatened a missed weather window for their installation, offshore completion of the modules could be considered, trading off the different extra costs of the available options.

The modelling involved would address a causal understanding of some key sources of uncertainty with a view to managing it more effectively as well as estimating its implications, managing it more effectively ultimately proving even more valuable than unbiased estimates, and the prime motivator for the SCERT approach.

This conversation with Peter and his colleagues, just recounted as a tale, is a modified version of the actual conversation. In particular, it uses some ideas I did not understand until later, and it omits a discussion of risk efficiency, part of my original sales pitch. However, as a result of the actual conversation the BP programme managers were persuaded to try out my suggested approach.

The SCERT label indicates a further generalisation in the tradition of PERT, Generalised PERT and GERT, treating all these earlier approaches as special cases of SCERT, and emphasising the broadly defined form of synthesis essential when analysis involves a formal decomposition process of this kind. BP referred to SCERT as Probabilistic Project Planning (PPP), but this book sticks to the SCERT label.

SCERT was the first sophisticated high clarity prototype of the specific process (SP) for projects concept explored in Chapter 7. The SCERT approach was developed with significant input from a number of BP staff. It was mandated by the BP board for worldwide use for all large and sensitive projects. SCERT was used by BP for about a decade. As I understand it, simpler approaches were introduced after a decade on the assumption that BP planners now understood the issues very much better, as did their contractors, and both felt they did not need the high clarity analysis SCERT provided. This was closely coupled to a policy shift in terms of contracting lay-barge operators on what amounted to a fixed price basis instead of the time-and-materials basis used earlier as part of a broader shift to outsourcing the management of uncertainty. The eventual implications of these policy changes will be touched on shortly and are further considered briefly in Part 2.

The first step in developing SCERT was trying out the modelling ideas and an associated specific process using a 'passive project'. I revisited a project recently completed by BP with a senior BP planning engineer who had been directly involved. We asked the question, 'If BP were doing this project again, using a prototype of the new SCERT process and associated models, how should the planning team proceed?'

The next step was trying out the ideas just developed on a 'live project' – the Magnus Field project, which came in on schedule and within budget despite some surprises.

Later statistical analysis of offshore North Sea BP projects which was undertaken to assess bias associated with using the SCERT approach showed that projects delivered on time and within budget was an appropriate expectation, but it was crucial to acknowledge that all underlying assumptions ought to be understood by all the parties involved and treated as conditions, with some nuances we had not fully anticipated in advance.

Understanding the assumptions underlying any approach to estimation is an important clarity issue. When reviewing the outcomes for BP projects which had been planned using SCERT to assess bias issues, we found that it was useful to discuss an explicit formal decomposition of all relevant uncertainty into three components:

1   the 'known knowns' – sources of uncertainty which were 'quantified' (in the sense that they were modelled probabilistically and understood appropriately in conjunction with associated response structures using decision trees as well as statistical dependence structures using probability trees),
2   the 'known unknowns' – sources of uncertainty which were identified but 'not quantified' (in the sense that they were treated as assumptions underlying the quantitative analysis – usually referred to as conditions), and
3   the 'unknown unknowns' – sources of uncertainty which were either not identified or misconceived.

The expected values and associated aspirational and commitment target values embodying identified 'provisions' and 'contingency' obtained via the SCERT models addressed all the known knowns in quantified analysis terms involving the well-founded causal and statistical understanding of uncertainty modelled probabilistically. They also highlighted the conditions these estimates assumed would hold, defined by the known unknowns. This had been understood by everyone involved from the outset.

The BP board chose a P80 confidence level for budget determination from the outset, and everyone involved saw the uplift from the expected outcome to the budget in terms of a contingency which on average should not be needed. The P80 value rather than a P70 or a P90 was a board level judgement to deal with the asymmetric implications of cost overruns and under-runs from a board perspective.

The known unknowns were seen from the outset as identified conditions which the probabilistic analysis depended up. In addition to decomposing sources of uncertainty associated with PERT models of duration and linked quantitative analysis of cost estimates, SCERT also decomposed sources of uncertainty which were not quantified, developing a reasonably rich understanding of conditions. Examples are 'analysis assumes no more than 10 km of pipe in excess of the planned pipeline length will be ordered and coated' and 'no major equipment failures or fires'. When assessing bias by analysing completed projects we had to recognise the implications of these assumptions for all the identified conditions which were not met. Several assumed conditions failing to hold were common, usually without serious implications.

The unknown unknowns were seen from the outset as significant surprises that we might have anticipated but did not. We were surprised by each but not by the fact there would be surprises. Their overall impact was limited and well within the contingency associated with defining the budget in P80 terms. However, when assessing bias we had to accept that the contingency provision used earlier was not actually set at the P80 level with the explicit consideration of realising unknown unknowns in mind, and we really should have made an explicit provision for the expected total impact of surprises. It is now self-evident this might be a crucially important issue in some circumstances. It is clearly *very* difficult to assess the unknown unknowns because, by definition, we do not know what is involved. However, a reasonable expectation about their collective impact is obviously greater than zero, so zero is obviously an optimistically biased estimate.

This is a useful example of a very difficult issue which does not go away if you just put it into a 'too difficult' box and forget it. *From an enlightened planning perspective, those involved in planning should never be allowed to use a 'too difficult box' to ignore difficult issues needing explicit attention.* Explicit working assumptions which may be wrong are always a preferred alternative to a 'too difficult box' which is ignored.

As a useful illustrative example, in retrospect we understood that it was clearly worth making a provision for all the known unknowns that could be interpreted as 'fine print quibbles' which those involved were not going to want to discuss, which together with a possible provision for the unknown unknowns might be called a 'no quibbles provision'. This could be viewed as an updated and enlightened version of the traditional 'plus 10% (or more) for errors or omissions' added to a deterministic estimate for centuries, perhaps millennia, by most practical engineers and other cost estimators. It could also be viewed as another illustration of using a closure with completeness component. In this case its purpose was to avoid bias associated with concerns not identified and addressed individually on a decomposed basis – because some potential concerns are simply 'unknowable' and some are 'knowable' in principle, but in practice it may not feasible to consider them on a decomposed basis, and some are just not worth the trouble of even considering for decomposed treatment.

Dealing with both the known unknowns and the unknown unknowns was an issue identified as needing further sophisticated attention in each high clarity analysis context, also needing further attention to address simple but robust approaches for all low clarity analysis contexts.

Approaches to no quibbles provisions in all contexts remains a work in progress of importance, with no general best strategy that I am aware of. Approaches to very serious extreme events is a separate area of ongoing concern. Approaches which are appropriate to any given context may warrant great care or just very simple rules or something in between.

An important general implication is that what we mean by 'unbiased estimation' requires clarity about the treatment of a no quibbles provision and any other relevant unknown unknowns. It also requires clarity about who is accountable when what may have seemed like sensible identified conditions (assumptions) do not hold.

One reason the BP project planning staff I worked with used the PPP label instead of the 'Project Risk Management' (PRM) label then in early adopter usage was the term 'risk', interpreted in the safety sense, was another BP group's responsibility. Risk in a safety sense was a rather special kind of known unknown from the perspective of the planners I was working with, and they did not want to challenge the safety function's ownership of the 'risk management' label or stray into the territory the safety department operated in. The project planners assumed their treatment of safety and that of their contractors was reduced to ensuring that they jointly planned to meet all standards and restrictions imposed on them by the safety department.

The board had to look to a separate source of advice on safety. An implication I did not consider at the time is the board also needed a separate source of advice on the linked environmental risk issues raised by the 2010 Deepwater Horizon Gulf of Mexico disaster, plus the complex relationships between contractual approaches and both safety and environmental concerns, both considered briefly in terms of a coordinated approach in Chapter 9.

Higher or lower levels of clarity when appropriate

Acres used the experience base our early success with BP provided with a wide range of other clients in Canada and the US. BP collaboration with Acres included letting Acres use the SCERT software systems which I helped BP develop for other Acres client studies in Canada and the US, extensively adapted by my colleague Dale Cooper in some cases, as discussed in Cooper and Chapman (1987). This HAT based software used a probability arithmetic approach incorporating a first order arithmetic correction for the calculation error involved of the kind discussed earlier in this chapter. Standard commercially available Monte Carlo simulation packages which can do the same job in some circumstances became available later, now the usual approach to implementing a HAT framework. Some of these Canadian and US studies used lower levels of clarity, but some used very high levels of clarity for specific decisions, like the study discussed in Chapman, Cooper, Debelius, and Pecora (1985).

Soon other UK based clients also followed, like National Power. National Power wanted a simplified variant of SCERT as developed for BP, adapted to suit planning the construction of electricity generation power stations at a comparable stage in the project lifecycle to that addressed by BP – the 'execution and delivery strategy progress stage' in the language of Chapter 7. This stage followed an earlier 'concept strategy progress stage' and then a 'design, operation and termination strategy progress stage'. Most of the Canadian and US Acres studies addressed the earlier stages in project lifecycles, looking at project concept strategy decision-making concerns.

The National Power approach was the result of the board member responsible for all engineering projects approaching me after a public seminar on SCERT approaches. He initiated discussions which led to a combined cycle gas-fired power station being planned and then built as a 'demonstration project'. The demonstration project was carefully selected as a learning context. The planning was led by a National Power planning engineer, with my support, after internal training courses for everyone involved so they all understood in broad terms what we were trying to achieve. The National Power variant of SCERT did not use Markov processes, but it did use 1 to 10 separate sources of uncertainty per activity, general as well as specific responses, and most other BP variants of SCERT characteristics. It can be characterised as a medium clarity approach, midway between the simple low clarity approaches discussed with William and the much more sophisticated high clarity approaches to offshore pipe-laying discussed with Peter.

One defining characteristic of a HAT framework, as we move from the simplest of the low clarity variants discussed with William towards the high clarity variants used by Peter and his BP colleagues in a SCERT model, is the additional understanding of sources of uncertainty. This involves causal understanding of uncertainty as well as sophisticated statistical understanding of uncertainty. It involves being very clear about the known knowns. It also involves very valuable insights into the known unknowns and the unknown unknowns.

While BP used some very sophisticated high clarity SCERT approaches for pipe-laying, they also employed much simpler low clarity variants for activities which were less complex and less crucial. When National Power introduced a simplified version of BP's approach, it used a portfolio of simpler approaches, depending on the complexity and importance of each project and each activity within each project, as did other SCERT users. It soon became clear that all organisations using SCERT variants needed a toolset of approaches which ranged from the minimum clarity approach discussed at the beginning of the conversation with William to the high clarity approach discussed with Peter or beyond.

Furthermore, even if they never found the level of complexity involved in the BP pipe-laying approach directly applicable to their project's activities, most SCERT users found the high clarity conceptual framework employed by BP useful. It was useful as an underlying conceptual framework for thinking about the simplifications needed for their approaches. It was directly comparable to what some people refer to as 'useful theory'. But it was not *theory*. It was *high clarity best practice*, and the difference is subtle but important.

A key goal for this book is providing you with an understanding of high clarity best practice approaches to underpin your understanding of strategic clarity to help you to understand how lower clarity approaches can be selected to best suit particular contexts that you and your organisation have to deal with.

The defining characteristics of an EP approach to estimation include understanding in broad terms the structure of the ambiguity uncertainty which underlies very simple minimum clarity portrayals like Figure 3.1 which could be given a high clarity analysis. It is important to understand from the outset when using a very simple approach that some selected aspects of the underlying complexity may be worth more detailed understanding later using suitable high clarity approaches. If the earlier simpler approach suggests that particular details matter enough to make the extra effort worthwhile, being able to apply further effort *where and how it will pay the biggest dividends* is a key aspect of clarity efficiency.

More generally, an EP approach is concerned about always using the simplest portrayal of relevant uncertainty which is suitable for the immediate task, but doing so with a clear understanding of the nature and implications of underlying simplifying assumptions to facilitate testing overall understanding and looping back to develop more clarity whenever it looks as if that might be worthwhile.

Strategic clarity when choosing low clarity approaches requires an understanding of what high clarity approaches can provide and the associated costs of additional clarity of various kinds. The high clarity BP framework can be used as a high clarity conceptual tool to facilitate always asking the right questions with a view to simplifying systematically, exploiting opportunities to simplify in the right way, avoiding risks associated with simplifying in the wrong way.

Clarity efficient boundary concepts

This section interprets the 'efficient frontier' portrayal of clarity and the cost of acquiring clarity portrayed by Figure 3.5 in terms of clarity efficient approaches to estimating as discussed so far in this chapter, retaining a focus on project management contexts. Later sections of this chapter and Chapter 4 broaden the scope of the clarity concerns addressed

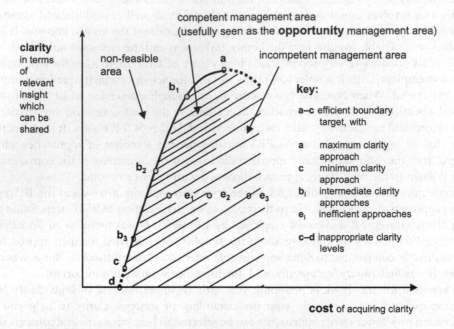

Figure 3.5 Clarity and the cost of acquiring clarity in an efficient-frontier portrayal.

and consider corporate and operations management contexts. The rest of this book builds on this foundation.

An efficient frontier interpretation of the clarity efficiency concept is a key conceptual tool in the EP toolset. It is not an operational tool in a direct sense. However, understanding the concepts which Figure 3.5 portrays makes practice much more effective.

Consider the framework of the portrayal of clarity efficiency of Figure 3.5 first and then its interpretation.

The *x*-axis is not cost in £ or $ or some other currency because 'cost' has to be given a more general effort/cost interpretation which incorporates not only the cost of immediate effort but also earlier investments in learning processes and formal training to develop competence plus softer concerns like distinguishing between effort which is disagreeable and effort which is satisfying. Effort which is disagreeable or awkward carries a higher opportunity cost than effort which is satisfying and straightforward, recognising that different people may hold different views on the direct and indirect implications.

The *y*-axis is 'clarity' in the sense of 'relevant insight which can be shared'. This is not a simple metric like 'probability' on the y-axis of earlier probability distributions diagrams. In this chapter, 'relevant clarity' has been kept as simple as possible thus far by a focus on unbiased estimation as the current dominant goal, but more than one kind of clarity is almost always relevant – clarity is inherently a complex, multiple-attribute concept.

The minimum clarity estimate approach outlined for William is represented by the clarity efficient point 'c' – less clarity is not appropriate, and using more cost (effort or time) to acquire the same level of clarity is inefficient.

A high clarity approach like that associated with BP's SCERT approach to pipe-laying might be associated with point b_1.

A maximum level of clarity, represented by the clarity efficient point 'a', can be assumed to exist, but our usual concern is the intermediate clarity efficient approaches to points like b_1, b_2, and b_3 along with the minimum clarity point c approach.

The tale associated with William started with point 'c' but then explored additional clarity associated with the clarity efficient boundary between points 'c' and b_3. The focus of the quantitative analysis was unbiased estimation with an appropriate understanding of associated uncertainty, but qualitative understanding of issues relevant to contingency planning was also touched on, as were higher clarity understanding of aspirational target and commitment target plus expected value and balanced target issues. This discussion addressed what might be called 'additional clarity without decomposition' or 'refinement without restructuring', with a concern for clarity efficient estimation of activity duration treating all quantified uncertainty as a single source of uncertainty. This single source within a single activity was first estimated in terms of a very simple minimum clarity approach, later in terms of multiple scenario approaches, including the n scenario (or classes) generalisation of the HAT approach of Table 3.1 and Figure 3.4, plus conditions associated with extreme outcomes not embedded in the probabilistic analysis. Both simpler and more sophisticated variants of Figure 3.4 could have been used, employing as many scenarios or classes as necessary to capture the shape of the single source of uncertainty appropriately. In this sense, the HAT approach as a whole as developed for William provided a flexible toolset for dealing with a single source of uncertainty representation which generalised a PERT approach to each activity, recommended as both a conceptual basis and as an operational starting point.

William's tale also touched on additional clarity if the relevance of understanding how to manage the underlying causes of the more extreme delay possibilities is a possible concern.

The discrete scenario interpretations explored in the HAT framework with William enrich our interpretation of a continuous variable single source of uncertainty model. They also hint at linked multiple source of uncertainty probability and decision tree quantitative modelling approaches without developing these ideas.

The tale associated with Peter explores an example of seeking a point like b_1 in a somewhat different and much more complex context, employing a significantly generalised variant of the HAT approach. It addresses multiple sources of uncertainty within each activity plus multiple activities directly. The Markov process approach also breaks activity duration into progress each month plus total progress achieved to date before decomposing sources of uncertainty like weather and buckles. There are direct implications for contingency planning based on a comprehensive understanding of key cause–effect relationships. Decomposing activity durations into rate of progress distributions for successive months was crucial for offshore pipe-laying, but so was decomposing separate sources of uncertainty within the monthly progress distributions. The focus of this discussion was still unbiased estimation, but effective formal contingency planning with project implementation benefits was also involved.

National Power's expectations, which were met and exceeded, were analogous to seeking overall clarity for key project activities at a point like b_2, with an understanding of how to use most of the b_1–b_3 range as needed for specific projects. Indeed, BP needed the whole range, as did the MoD, recognising that warships, offshore oil projects, and electric power generation projects are all very different, as are individual components within each project in any context.

Whether any given organisation is currently in the competent management region at points like e_1, in the incompetent management region at points like e_3, or on the boundary between competent and incompetent management at a point like e_2, is clearly a sensitive and potentially contentious issue. However, all organisations need to assess where they are in relation to the competence/incompetence boundary, in terms of all relevant aspects of clarity efficiency. This assessment needs to be understood at the level of those designing processes, at the level of those using processes, and at the level of those responsible for associated governance. If significantly different views amongst these players are involved, a lack of corporate competence is probably a reasonable default assumption.

Getting onto the clarity efficient boundary involves more insight for less effort, which can be seen as an opportunity which needs to be identified and captured. But it also means more reward for less risk, a form of opportunity with significant potential tangible rewards explored further in the following sections of this chapter. More generally, an important issue to be developed later is seeing the competent management area as an opportunity management area.

The focus of EP as a whole is opportunity management – being in the opportunity management area of Figure 3.5. This implies a constant search for clarity efficiency at the most appropriate level of clarity. It involves understanding both the benefits and the costs of more clarity in unbiased expected value and range terms. It also involves understanding the consequences of misjudging what is needed, as a part of the more general understanding of the consequences of incompetence.

In practice any organisation may want to use approaches over most of the c–b_1 range, perhaps even approaching point 'a', with choices depending on the circumstances. To do so effectively they need to understand all the available options.

Being able to think about uncertainty over the whole of this range in flexible discrete or continuous variable forms within a HAT framework is a useful capability, part of the capability-culture concept an EP approach is concerned with developing to ensure organisations can operate in the opportunity management area of Figure 3.5. A HAT based approach is clarity efficient when simple approaches are needed, and it can become crucial if complex dependencies are involved.

Being able to think about uncertainty at various levels of decomposition, and choose appropriate levels within appropriate structures, is also crucial. So is pursuing contingency planning and option planning more generally, within whatever source of uncertainty structure best suits the context.

Clarity can be increased as appropriate via well-founded causal understanding of all important sources of uncertainty whenever this is feasible and worthwhile. Within both causal and statistical dependency approaches it is important to have appropriate clarity about ambiguity uncertainty as well as variability uncertainty, event uncertainty, capability-culture uncertainty and systemic uncertainty.

Having at least one person on any management decision-making team and in every associated planning team who knows how best to add clarity within this complex mix is a key EP corporate capability, central to corporate strategic clarity.

Board level managers do not need to know how to engineer clarity efficiency – but they do need to know enough about how it works to detect when it is missing, and they do need to know what needs to be done about it. Others will also need to know how to do it or who to speak to who knows how to do it.

Even if an organisation's only concern when choosing an appropriate level of clarity for estimation purposes is an unbiased estimate of a performance measure attribute like the duration or cost of a project to be on the clarity efficient boundary, for this purpose alone it is crucial to appreciate that the estimation process involves underlying plans. In a project management context uncertainty about duration or cost is driven by uncertainty about the underlying plans, and the assumptions those plans are based on, as well as what might or might not happen if the plans are pursued.

Given this understanding, it should be clear that *all* uncertainty about the plans is relevant. This includes uncertainty about important strategic issues which are not yet fully understood. It also includes uncertainty about detailed planning concerns to be addressed later in the project lifecycle. Furthermore, it includes capability-culture issues including capability-culture uncertainty often not addressed directly until things go wrong. To be in the competent management area of Figure 3.5 requires a competent understanding of *all* potentially relevant uncertainty. Being very near the clarity efficient boundary requires a very high degree of competence.

If we look at all uncertainty in terms of the high clarity SCERT approach developed for BP, it should be clear that a 'source of uncertainty' in the EP sense illustrated by this context may involve:

1   event uncertainty (a buckle may or may not happen), but it also involves
2   variability uncertainty (weather and its wave height metric are matters of degree), plus
3   systemic uncertainty (dependence of various kinds), plus
4   ambiguity uncertainty (what we do not understand about 1 through 3 above, as well as all the unknown unknowns), plus
5   capability-culture uncertainty (including assumptions about all relevant capability and culture concerns involving contractors and their subcontractors).

By 1980 the BP North Sea project planners I worked with were systematically looking at the first three and beginning to develop a comprehensive understanding of the fourth. We did not address the fifth, in the sense that contractors were paid on a time and materials basis to follow BP developed plans created by those I was working with within operating standards and rules specified by other BP players, and questioning the capability of other BP players was not part of the agenda. With hindsight this was a potentially important weakness in the analysis approach, but at that time the implicit capability-culture stealth assumptions were well founded and held – problems associated with stealth assumptions not holding did not arise.

If we now look at all uncertainty in terms of a low clarity approach like a basic PERT model of a pipe-laying activity and an associated cost estimate, it should be clear that duration and cost estimates treated as single sources of uncertainty at the activity component level also involve all five of the uncertainty types listed earlier, but we are treating them collectively as if they were a single source of variability uncertainty for each activity. Furthermore, we are omitting consideration of any kind of uncertainty about relationships between activities and associated cost estimates (systemic uncertainty), including that associated with potential contingency planning of the SCERT variety. In a PERT framework our 'quantitative' understanding of uncertainty is largely a 'statistical understanding' of uncertainty which is very limited in scope and capability, with little in the way of competent 'causal understanding' of uncertainty beyond the role of simple precedence relationships. The same is true of PERT models of simpler contexts, although the inherent underlying complexity may be less.

Even if a simple minimum clarity approach is used for a single activity, as discussed with William, the single source of uncertainty addressed has to embrace all of these kinds of uncertainty.

There is a good case for arguing that with hindsight the basic 1960s PERT models embraced a broad view of uncertainty comparable in many ways to a minimum clarity approach extended to address multiple plan components and that was the most sensible place to start. However, the minimum clarity model nature was implicit, the 1960s PERT model did not lend itself to generalising in an obvious way, and it did not draw attention to the limited scope and competence of the quantification of uncertainty. What the clarity efficient set of approaches to unbiased expected outcomes illustrated in this chapter does is generalise PERT, via Generalised PERT, GERT, and then SCERT. This clarifies the severe limitations of the basic 1960s PERT approach, without implying that all or some of its simplifications relative to SCERT should not be used whenever this is appropriate.

In a project planning context, classic illustrations of organisations in the incompetent management area of Figure 3.5 are those organisations which fail to consider *any* uncertainty explicitly, sticking to a CPM approach based on point estimates and comparable deterministic costing approaches. For example, they might decompose the current plan for a large project into 500 or even 5,000 or more activities and carefully plan and cost each individually in point estimate terms, but omit to systematically consider any uncertainty. What BP demonstrated convincingly in the 1970s and 1980s was that using just 20 to 50 activities, but extensively decomposing the sources of uncertainty and contingency responses to those sources, plus secondary sources when appropriate, is usually a *much better* approach.

More contemporary illustrations of organisations in the incompetent management area of Figure 3.5 are all those organisations that subscribe to project risk management approaches which involve a focus on an event or condition view of 'risks' that may or may not happen, using long 'risk lists' or 'risk logs' and 'probability impact grids' (matrices). This is a very widespread current practice, and a serious source of concern, addressed briefly in what needs to be done terms in Chapter 7.

Moving beyond project planning, in numerous very important decision-making areas far too many organisations are in this 'incompetent management' area. There is a tendency to use too much of the wrong kind of detail to ask the wrong kind of questions, and a failure to understand that the right questions addressed in a clarity efficient manner will provide more insight for less effort.

Even minimum clarity estimates can deliver much more than unbiased estimates for a minimal level of effort. The SCERT approach developed for BP provided the unbiased approach to estimation being sought, and the spinoff benefit of target value, expected value, and commitment value distinctions. But the decomposition of sources of uncertainty and associated contingency planning also involved a very different approach to the underlying complexity than the minimum clarity approach outlined for William, and part of the pay-off was risk efficiency plus opportunity efficiency, not yet considered but of central importance.

More generally, clarity efficiency in terms of 'appropriate clarity' can involve issues which are not limited to unbiased estimates and delivering projects on time and within cost. We can add *much more* clarity in a *rich variety of ways for a rich variety of reasons*.

We now need to start to explore how and why by addressing further issues. The first of these additional issues is seeking risk efficiency with a view to avoiding 'risk inefficiency'.

Risk efficiency – with avoiding risk inefficiency as the focus

Formal contingency planning implies that choices between decision options are relevant in direct and explicit formal terms. *As soon as any choices between decision options become an explicit issue, in ANY context, 'risk efficiency' should become a central concern needing explicit attention, whether or not formal contingency planning gives rise to the choices.* This attention requires a clear understanding of what risk efficiency means in both conceptual and operational terms, why risk inefficiency should be avoided, and how systematically seeking risk efficiency should be approached in both formal and informal terms.

'Risk efficiency' means '*a minimum level of risk for any given level of expected reward*'. Another way of saying the same thing is 'a maximum level of expected reward for any given level of risk'. However, the former is operationally more useful. This is because direct metrics for expected reward are often feasible, but measuring risk is usually *much* more difficult.

'Risk inefficiency' involves taking more risk for less expected reward than necessary, arguably a very serious form of incompetence if significant risk inefficiency is involved. It is usually easily avoided by those who are competent in EP terms, but it is often an unknown-unknown risk, endemic in organisations that do not understand what risk efficiency implies or how to deal with it in a clarity efficient manner.

To discuss making use of the risk efficiency concept in practice, it is often convenient to replace 'reward' by 'revenue', assuming costs are fixed, or by 'cost', assuming revenue is fixed. In both cases, assuming that a simple metric correlated with 'profit' is a suitable financial measure of reward is implied. For example, in the BP offshore project planning context, oil and gas revenue was assumed to be independent of what the BP planners I was working with were concerned about most of the time, apart from opportunity costs associated with any delays to first oil or gas availability, which had to be estimated and used to address unproductive capital and lost revenue issues. In this context, 'cost risk' becomes a way of looking at 'reward risk' without addressing revenue beyond opportunity cost implications.

This section assumes that project contingency planning using a cost metric was being undertaken, and the focus of concern was risk efficiency in terms of avoiding cost risk inefficiency.

Risk efficiency is a concept misunderstood and overlooked by many 'experts' in the risk management field. Whether or not you are interested in risk management at a technical level, understanding risk efficiency in general terms and what risk inefficiency implies is absolutely essential. You also need to understand 'enlightened caution', 'enlightened gambles', and 'enlightened prudence', concepts closely linked to an understanding of risk efficiency. This set of concepts has important behavioural implications for those organisations which understand the difference between good management and good luck, bad management and bad luck, and for those organisations which do not. 'Risk appetite' is another important concern which also needs understanding in a framework centred on risk efficiency.

Risk efficiency is a concept with origins usually associated with Harry Markowitz, who received a Nobel Prize in Economic Sciences in 1990 for his work developing the risk efficiency concept in the context of efficient diversification of a portfolio of financial investments. Risk efficiency as discussed by Markowitz in his seminal 1959 book, and embedded in much of economics since, uses 'variance' as a surrogate measure of risk. Variance is a basic statistical measure of spread or range. Much of the power of Markowitz's approach is associated with the way he deals with statistical dependence in covariance or correlation terms. The EP approach to risk efficiency is much more general, addressing various forms of causal dependence as well as statistical dependence. Furthermore, an EP approach explicitly avoids the assumption that risk can be measured via variance. It uses a 'decision diagram' concept for each relevant attribute to avoid *any* surrogate measures of risk, and it offers scope for various ways of approaching complex multiple attribute trade-offs. You do not need to understand the full details of why this EP approach is much more powerful than a Markowitz framework if the details are not of interest, but you do need to understand the details with sufficient depth to grasp the implications explored in this chapter and the rest of this book, starting with the rest of this section. Risk efficiency is a core gateway concept for any viable version of EP.

When the first BP project to use the SCERT process, the Magnus project, sought board approval and release of funds to begin construction, SCERT analysis had been undertaken using extensive decomposition of sources of uncertainty as described earlier, in part to give the board confidence in the plans and associated cost estimates.

By this time BP had appointed an internal leader for the development of SCERT use within BP, who I supported. He and all the project staff involved understood that our primary goal was seeking risk efficiency via contingency planning using SCERT. Unbiased estimates were usefully seen as by-products of an effective approach to seeking risk efficiency and avoiding risk inefficiency. The central issue was risk efficiency. Obtaining an unbiased estimate of the expected cost was just part of the process of seeking risk efficiency.

Demonstrating risk efficiency within the project management team meant demonstrating that the team could not find a lower expected cost approach which did not involve more risk or a lower risk approach which did not involve a higher expected cost. To seek risk efficiency, the project team had to understand what might happen and why, and what could be done to reduce risk or expected cost or both. This might involve after the fact reactive mitigating contingency planning responses, which might require prior actions to make these response options available. It might also require up-front proactive responses, which might initially be conceived as preventative contingency planning responses for specific problems, with the later realisation that they actually delivered even more beneficial changes in the base plans for other reasons. Specific sources of uncertainty might be catered for directly in an extensive manner, but general responses dealing with the cumulative effect of sets of sources of uncertainty net of specific responses plus unknown unknowns might be absolutely crucial.

At the core of what we were doing was engaging in a search for opportunities to reduce expected cost and risk at the same time – improving risk efficiency and avoiding risk inefficiency. This can be seen as a core component and crucial driver of opportunity management – a central part of the process of seeking opportunity efficiency. We were all interested in all available opportunities to improve risk efficiency. As a consultant I was especially interested in opportunities for big improvements which might have been missed if I had not been employed to demonstrate the value of my role. However, the project manager and all the members of his team shared this objective and understood what was required.

One activity involved a 'hook-up' operation – connecting the pipeline between the shore and the production platform to the platform. It had a target date in August. In the base plan, a 1.6-metre barge was specified, equipment which could work in waves up to a nominal 1.6-m height. Analysis demonstrated that August was an appropriate aspirational target date and that the use of a 1.6-m barge was appropriate in August. However, this analysis also demonstrated there was a significant chance that the hook-up would have to be attempted much later, in November or December for example, because the hook-up operation was late in the overall project sequence, and there was considerable scope for an accumulation of delays to preceding activities. Using a 1.6-m barge in winter months would be time-consuming and might mean that the hook-up could not be completed until the following spring, with severe opportunity cost implications associated with deferred revenue after significant investment in the project assets.

An alternative option was available – a 3-m wave-height-capability barge. A 3-m barge would cost more than twice as much per working day and per idle (weather) day as the 1.6-m barge, and a 3-m barge would have to be contracted in advance, before BP knew whether preceding activities were delayed. A revised analysis assuming the use of the more capable 3-m barge virtually eliminated the risk of going into the next season and the associated risk of a significant cost overrun, a 'lost season scenario' with an expected cost of the order of £100 million. But crucial to this example, *choosing the 3-m barge also reduced the expected cost of hook-up* by about £5 million. Despite the significantly higher cost per unit of time because of the additional capability, the expected cost was lower because a much shorter duration could be expected and the opportunity costs associated with a lost season were very high.

The decision diagram used to make this decision is illustrated in Figure 3.6.

The cumulative probability distribution curves for the two barge choice options crossed above the P50 (50 percentile value). This indicated that the 1.6-m barge was more likely to be the cheaper option than the 3-m barge. However, the 3-m barge distribution curve was much steeper because the outcome was less uncertain. And crucially, the 1.6-m barge distribution had a much longer tail on the top right-hand side because of the relatively low probability, but high cost, of a lost season. The much flatter 1.6-m barge curve *in combination* with the significant skew underlying the long tail to the right dragged the expected cost of the 1.6-m barge option to the right of the expected cost for the 3-m barge option. And *the combination* of the lower expected cost of the 3-m barge *plus* the lower risk was what really mattered. The analysis portrayed by Figure 3.6 indicated that the 1.6-m barge had a better than 50:50 chance of being cheaper, but the expected cost of using the 3-m barge was less than the expected cost of using the 1.6-m barge by about £5 million, in addition to the 3-m barge avoiding the risk of a lost season with an additional cost expectation of about £100 million.

Even if the long right-hand tail of the 1.6-m choice actually involved multiple modes as a consequence of possible lost seasons, which might have been estimated and portrayed, this graphic portrayal made it visually clear what was involved. We did not need to work within the limitations of a mean–variance model. All probability distribution moments were portrayed by Figure 3.6, not just variance. 'Clarified dominance' was involved, a form of 'stochastic dominance' interpretation. We were using what might be called a 'mean plus full cumulative distribution comparison graph' approach with a background understanding of 'stochastic dominance' and visibility of all percentile values from P0, P1, . . ., P100 instead of a mean–variance approach.

BP and other later users of variants of this decision diagram portrayal liked the term 'enlightened caution' associated with the 3-m barge choice in this example, because despite

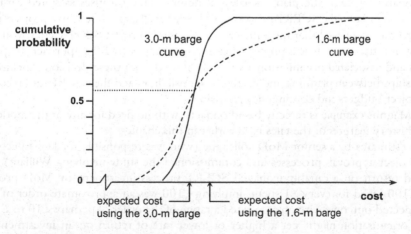

Figure 3.6 Decision diagram: one risk efficient choice example.

the obvious fact that the 1.6-m barge looked like a better choice most of the time, its expected cost was higher, *and* it was also riskier in the sense it might cost a great deal more than its expected cost. The 3-m barge was actually *the only risk efficient choice*, and choosing the 3-m barge involved a subtle kind of clarified stochastic dominance referred to as enlightened caution.

The term 'enlightened caution' is useful for several reasons. One of immediate concern is emphasising that a reasonably high level of clarity is sometimes needed to identify and then communicate the implications of a complex situation so that everybody can understand what is involved.

Based on the discussion of Figure 3.6 the base plan was changed at the project team level. Much later, when the project manager took his fully developed plans and budget request to the board for release-of-funds approval for the project, he used Figure 3.6 to persuade the board that this change was appropriate. In addition, he used Figure 3.6 to persuade the board that this one change paid for the entire SCERT study many times over – *and this change would not have been identified if they had not used the SCERT approach and* Figure 3.6 *format decision diagrams.* The SCERT process being used could be expected to provide a massive return on the analysis investment involved. Indeed, the systematic search for opportunities to both lower expected cost *and* reduce risk *simultaneously* via effective contingency planning should be seen as the central reason for the SCERT approach. Unbiased estimates were best seen as a useful by-product component part of risk efficiency.

The BP team planning the Magnus project used decision diagrams like Figure 3.6 to make many risk efficient plan changes, shaping the plans to deliver less expected cost and less risk. Once it was clear to everybody what was involved, sometimes it wasn't even necessary to produce a diagram to make a convincing case. Effective pursuit of risk efficiency using the SCERT contingency planning process saved money on average, as well as reducing risk in the sense of costs above what was expected, and that was best seen as its core role. SCERT analysis was not an overhead cost to give the board comfort, although it also delivered strategic plans the board could trust, and budget requests the board could understand and approve with confidence. The overall impact was a step change reduction in both expected costs and associated risk – an increase in risk efficiency – plus a significant increase in trust based on much more clarity than the earlier approaches had provided and a number of further by-product benefits.

The board approved the plan – successful despite some surprises as noted earlier. The board also mandated the SCERT process worldwide for all large or sensitive projects because the board was convinced that the anticipated increases in project risk efficiency would more than pay for the costs of the process. Significant changes to BP's approach to planning projects and associated organisational structure flowed from these decisions, including the relationships between planning and costing responsibilities and the way BP set up corporate level project budgets and contingency provisions.

This Magnus example is directly based on facts, with no need for any of the modest revision of history features of the tales used earlier in this chapter.

Later estimates by a senior MoD colleague (who was responsible for key aspects of the MoD project approvals processes and commissioned the study involving William) put the expected return on a capably managed SCERT process investment by MoD projects at about £100 saved for every £1 spent, implying £100 was an approximate order of magnitude expected outcome with an associated a range of the order of perhaps £10 to £1000.

Your organisation might get a higher or lower rate of return on an investment in EP capability which included always delivering risk efficiency *just in terms of the direct benefits of avoiding risk inefficiency*, with unbiased estimates plus further benefits to be discussed in later sections of this chapter viewed as very important indirect second order benefits which are not included in the £100 per £1 invested return because they are very difficult to measure. The exact rate of return obtained will always be uncertain, but this uncertainty is of secondary importance. What is crucial is seeing EP capability which delivers risk efficiency and avoids risk inefficiency as a very sound investment, delivering a secure high yield direct return plus important further benefits, not an overhead cost to provide comfort about unbiased estimates. Unbiased estimates can be viewed as a by-product of risk efficiency provided at no cost, just the first of a set of further spinoff benefits still to be explored.

Risk efficiency – with enlightened caution as the focus

Figure 3.6 illustrates risk efficiency in clarified dominance terms when the performance improvement is significant if the best choice is made but the better of the two options available is a fairly close call. In a complex situation like that captured by Figure 3.6, a high clarity approach may be needed to clarify what is involved. If the 3-m barge curve had been much farther to the left, perhaps entirely clear of the 1.6-m barge curve, it would have been obvious that the 3-m barge was the only appropriate choice. Clarified dominance is the general feature distinguishing a risk efficient choice from a risk inefficient choice. Enlightened caution is a special case when it is a close call and a high clarity decision diagram is needed to clarify what is involved *for all relevant players prior to making a decision.*

In the event, the Magnus project hook-up was actually completed in October in good weather conditions. It was evident *after the event that* BP could have got away with using a 1.6-m barge. However, the prior use of Figure 3.6 demonstrated clearly to everyone involved that the project manager had done a good job as well as making the right barge choice and that BP had been lucky with the weather. Making the right barge choice had involved enlightened caution, avoiding an 'unenlightened gamble' with the 1.6-m barge which was not risk efficient.

Enlightened caution in this case involved a willingness to commit to a plan option which involved highly likely additional expenditure which might not be needed because in expected value terms (on average) it would be cost-effective to commit to this option, *and* this choice also involves less risk.

Had problems in the earlier parts of the Magnus project caused the hook-up to take place in November or December, with seasonably bad weather, the change to a 3-m barge would have been clearly justified. The wisdom of enlightened caution associated with the choice of barge would have been verified empirically. However, given that the hook-up actually took place in October in good weather, it was very important to be able to explain why deploying the more expensive 3-m barge was still the most appropriate decision. *It was important to clarify that both good luck plus good management were involved, and to neutralise any potential negative interpretations of what had happened.*

If an effective prototype EP approach using Figure 3.6 had not been followed, and the decision to use a 3-m barge had been made on informal intuitive grounds by the project manager, his career might have looked much less promising when it became clear he could have got away with a 1.6-m barge. That is, the Figure 3.6 decision diagram was an EP tool for *formal* planning which helped to make the best choice in advance (before the event). But it also made it very clear later (*after the event*) that the project manager had made the only risk efficient barge capability choice; *plus* the project manager and his team had done well to achieve hook-up by October, *and* BP had been lucky with the weather. If the project manager had decided to opt for the 3-m barge without the Figure 3.6 analysis output, the project manager would have been exposed to being accused of wasting money on the more expensive barge, overlooking completely both his more enlightened choice and his good management of the project (getting to the hook-up by October). This might have seriously blighted his career because his enlightenment was misunderstood. A worldly wise project manager might explicitly recognise this possibility and might opt for the 1.6-m barge in the absence of a decision diagram with these features. This would involve deliberately making a bad management decision from a corporate perspective because good luck with the weather would subsequently be confused with good management and bad luck with the weather would subsequently just be interpreted as plain bad luck.

If an organisation cannot distinguish between good luck and good management, bad luck and bad management, individuals will manage risk and opportunity accordingly. Without EP support to demonstrate the rationale for their decisions, astute managers who are naturally and reasonably cautious with respect to their own careers may regard risk efficient decisions comparable to choosing the 3-m barge in Figure 3.6 as unwise, potentially dangerous to their careers, seeming to demonstrate a 'wimpish', uncalled-for caution whenever they actually manage the preceding work effectively. Very astute managers may avoid even looking for opportunities to increase risk efficiency in this way to avoid the moral hazard of the obvious conflict of interests, and perhaps consider looking for a more enlightened employer.

More generally, if good luck and good management or bad luck and bad management cannot be distinguished, enlightened caution opportunities like that illustrated by Figure 3.6 will not be looked for, and there will be a tendency to pass over this kind of opportunity if they are stumbled upon.

If everyone involved understands the after the event implications of examples like that illustrated by Figure 3.6, the organisational culture can change. This change can be driven by everyone looking for and choosing planning options which increase risk efficiency when enlightened caution is involved, in addition to looking for increases in risk efficiency which are obvious even in a simplified low clarity framework employing clarified dominance. This means that sometimes most people will spend money on some options involving capabilities that are not subsequently needed, even when there was a high probability they would not be needed, because on average this will save money. Any organisation which does not always spend some money on capabilities which may not be needed but on average will be needed is habitually taking unenlightened risk. This is comparable to gambling in a casino where you will always lose on average.

Enlightened caution needs to be both facilitated and demonstrated. The documentation and making common knowledge of instances when the wisdom of enlightened caution was not empirically verified is of particular importance.

Facilitating risk efficiency to reduce expected cost and risk simultaneously *and demonstrating this was being done* was soon seen as the primary goal of the SCERT approach by BP and all its other users. In the same spirit an *appropriately demonstrated* risk efficiency approach embracing a clarified dominance view of enlightened caution is a primary goal for any EP approach to formal planning.

This section has been about seeking a reasonably deep understanding of enlightened caution in after the event corporate culture terms as an important addition to understanding the broader clarified dominance basis of risk efficiency. Risk efficiency achieved in a clarity efficient manner within the EP framework can deliver the culture change insights of enlightened caution as well as freedom from risk inefficiency and unbiased estimates. They come as a package – in marketing terms a 'bundled product'. However, it is not '*buy* one and get the whole bunch'; it is 'invest in one and in addition to a big return on your investment you will get a valuable package of further benefits', because the achievement of risk efficiency is self-financing with a significant return on the cost and effort invested.

We have now looked at a clarity efficiency and risk efficiency as a bundle with multiple benefits, beginning to explore the implications of opportunity efficiency as an overall gateway concept. But we have not yet considered further opportunity efficiency aspects which are key parts of the full package, all provided in one EP bundled product. Opportunity efficiency can provide much more than has been revealed so far, and some of the other aspects of opportunity efficiency need attention now.

Opportunity efficiency – with enlightened gambles as the focus

The next step towards an understanding of opportunity efficiency in strategic clarity terms involves considering risk–reward trade-offs when taking *more* risk in a risk efficient manner when only one key attribute is involved. The focus of this section is an important additional by-product of the risk efficiency basis of an EP approach – encouraging and facilitating 'enlightened gambles'. Enlightened gambles are arguably an even more important component of the overall cultural change EP can deliver than 'enlightened caution'.

'Enlightened gambles' are defined as the selection of a potentially high return option from a set of risk efficient options when the additional risk that comes with the high return is considered both bearable and worthwhile by all relevant parties.

Figure 3.7 is a fabricated alternative to Figure 3.6, derived from Figure 3.6. It was initially developed for use in conjunction with Figure 3.6 and a version of the discussion in the last few sections using the BP examples in a culture change programme referred to by IBM UK as their Forum 2 programme. IBM ran this two day programme at an IBM training site in Hampshire in the early 1990s about 40 times and included all senior and middle level IBM UK managers. The responsibilities of these managers included corporate, operations and project management.

The opening session on the first day was an introduction by their Chief Executive Officer (CEO), who explained in overview terms why IBM UK needed to take more risk in a risk efficient manner to stay in business. For the rest of the morning I provided an overview of

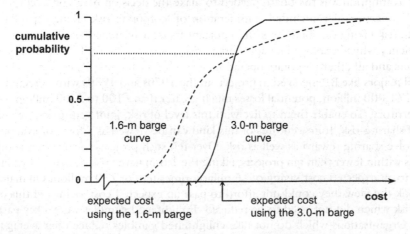

Figure 3.7 Decision diagram: two risk efficient choices example.

'what needed to be done' to achieve the CEO's goals. After lunch, all the participants spent about an hour working on a bidding case study in groups of about eight people to try out some of the key conceptual and operational tools which I had introduced. Then presentations were made by each group of 'their bid', and its rationale, to all the other groups. My follow-up presentation summarised current thinking as displayed by the individual group presentations and explored how current thinking needed to change. General discussion then completed the first day. The second day involved those taking part in the Forum 2 event discussing how they might help IBM UK to implement what had been learned from the first day.

Figure 3.6 was the basis for Figure 3.7, but the cumulative probability distribution for the 3-m barge in Figure 3.7 was shifted to the right so that the £5 million expected cost advantage associated with the 3-m barge of Figure 3.6 became a £5 million disadvantage in Figure 3.7. This was a fabricated example. It was obtained by simply moving the Figure 3.6 curve for the 3-m barge to the right, but if the numbers in the real example had been different, this result might have been obtained, as explained to the Forum 2 participants.

The point where the curves cross now suggested that the 1.6-m barge had about an 80% chance of being cheaper, an increase from about 60% for Figure 3.6. However, the significant change that really mattered was the ordering of the expected outcomes was reversed – *the expected cost of the 3-m barge was now about £5 million more than the expected cost of the 1.6-m barge.* In terms of the expected value criteria, the 1.6-m barge was now preferable. This raised a conflict between the maximising expected reward criteria and the minimising risk criteria. There was no longer a single risk efficient choice. The long tail for the 1.6-m barge still implied much more risk, associated with a lost season scenario which was assumed, for illustrative purposes, to be comparable to a 10% chance of an extra £100 million in costs. But the expected cost of the 1.6-m barge option was now £5 million less than the 3-m barge option.

The first key question was 'Should this extra risk be taken by BP?'

Assuming these two options were the only risk efficient options available, the choice of barge was now a 'risk appetite' concern – a matter of decision-maker preference because both options were risk efficient. The 3-m barge option involved less risk but a higher expected cost, while the 1.6-m barge involved more risk but a lower expected cost.

This raised a second key question, 'Who should be the decision maker?' A useful initial working assumption was the board needed to make the decision based on a 'corporate risk appetite' concept which included consideration of 'corporate risk taking capability'. This corporate risk taking capability was an important issue, determined via a corporate view of risk efficiency which employed an appropriate risk–reward trade-off for the BP portfolio of all projects and all other corporate operations.

For oil majors like BP involved in projects in the 1970s and 1980s with expected costs in excess of £1,000 million, potential losses much greater than £100 to £200 million were part of the territory. To enable them to live with this level of risk, joint ventures were common, a way of sharing risk. Joint ventures of this kind can be viewed as a form of insurance, but they involve sharing reward as well as risk. Over ten such projects, or over ten comparable decisions within fewer than ten projects, taking the 1.6-m barge risk described by Figure 3.7 equates to an expected cost saving of £5 million times ten, or £50 million. Oil majors generally took the view they could not afford to pass up expected cost savings of this order to reduce risk which did not need to be reduced. Enlightened gambles were a key part of the culture. Organisations which do not take enlightened gambles reduce their average profitability and may eventually go out of business as a direct result. A formal UP or linked SP like the SCERT approach can facilitate, demonstrate and encourage enlightened gambles as a basis for a direct increase in expected profit *plus* an important basis for engineering associated organisational culture changes with linked indirect benefits.

In the context of a choice like that portrayed in Figure 3.7, if the gamble paid off, the wisdom of the enlightened gamble would be verified empirically. However, the occasional visible failure of such gambles can be extremely important because they demonstrate that good decision makers who take risk efficient gambles are sometimes unlucky. If no quantified uncertainty analysis were undertaken to demonstrate an expected cost savings associated with an enlightened gamble like that of Figure 3.7, this message would be lost, whatever the outcome. In the absence of a demonstrated expected cost benefit plus an organisational culture which promotes enlightened gambles, astute managers might not take such gambles, and very astute managers may not even look for them. This was another aspect of the need for an organisational capability to distinguish between good luck and good management, bad luck and bad management.

Further key questions which needed addressing included: when should the board want to make this kind of decision, when should the board leave this kind of decision to project managers, and if the board leaves this kind of decision to project managers, how should the board ensure that the project manager's risk appetite is aligned with the board's preferences? For illustrative purposes in the IBM context it was useful to continue to assume a 10% chance of an extra £100 million in costs if the enlightened gamble was lost, and we can carry on in the same way.

If an additional £100 million was going to mean the project's budget was breached, and if the board would prefer the £100 million × 0.1 – £10 million provision for the enlightened gamble was not in the budget to be spent on other things if the 1.6-m barge gamble works, the enlightened thing for the board to do was make the decision to use the 1.6-m barge and take the risk at board level – making a £10 million board level provision against a possible £100 million call on BP self-insurance. To give the risk to the project manager along with a £10 million provision in this context would involve a 'lose–lose' situation for the board, because if the extra £100 million was needed the budget would be breached and the board would have to be involved in dealing with it, but if the extra £100 million was not needed the project manager might spend the £10 million provision on something else which might not be really needed. If the board made the decision and held the contingency, the project manager would be responsible for managing the risk but not for taking it financially within his or her budget. All very high impact and low probability risks warrant this treatment, with the board deciding when the impact was too high for the gamble to be enlightened given the expected cost and risk of an alternative 'enlightened prudence' option. The level of contingency in the budget should be directly geared to the level of impact triggering board responsibility.

If an additional £100 million would not breach the project's budget because the board trusts the project manager with provisions plus a contingency big enough to handle problems of this order on a swings and roundabouts basis, the enlightened thing for the board to do was leave the project manager to make the choice.

In either case, the board has to trust the project manager and vice versa, motivating all project managers to perform by judging how well they pursue corporate best interests. Whether or not they are lucky should not be confused with whether or not they are good managers. At the time these interconnected capability-culture issues centred on trust and other enlightened planning issues did not seem to be a problem for BP – the corporate ethos meant that project manager relationships with the board were exemplary as far as I was able to judge – amongst the very best I have ever encountered.

The key culture-change message for IBM UK staff was to recognise the corporate advantages of everybody in IBM UK collectively looking for enlightened gambles, taking more risk whenever this was appropriate within a well-understood risk efficiency framework, and recognising that they were currently not taking many important potential enlightened gambles because they were not seeing them as opportunities. This was linked to also using enlightened caution and more obvious clarified dominance, but at the level of decision making being addressed, a crucial additional focus of IBM UK risk management should be taking *more* risk, fully understanding what was involved, not less risk.

It was important for IBM staff to understand that BP, had they been faced with Figure 3.7 instead of Figure 3.6, would probably have opted for the enlightened gamble choice, and at the IBM decision-making level being addressed, all staff involved needed to emulate this behaviour to increase expected return for IBM, in addition to making risk efficient decisions comparable to that illustrated by Figure 3.6. But IBM staff did not necessarily need high clarity decision diagrams like Figures 3.6 and 3.7 to identify enlightened caution or enlightened gambles – they could often get by with simple low clarity decision diagrams, illustrated later in Chapters 4 and 6. The tale of Chapter 6 is based on this IBM culture-change programme and demonstrates in more detail why opportunity associated with taking more risk in a risk efficient manner can be crucial. Chapter 6 also demonstrates how all the estimation-efficiency spectrum ideas demonstrated in a project management context in this chapter can be applied in an operations management context.

At the level of decision making being addressed, in all operations, corporate and project management contexts, IBM needed to achieve risk efficiency *and take enlightened gambles* that were not currently seen as opportunities. Often this was just a matter of maximising expected return – viewing the 'risk' that currently worried people inappropriately as just 'noise' which should be embraced via a culture change which was based on a corporate understanding of directly relevant corporate risk appetite concerns plus the difference between good luck and good management, bad luck and bad management. More sophisticated risk appetite and related corporate capability issues will need further attention.

The key message of this section is what is involved when looking for risk efficiency *plus taking more risk when appropriate* is an important aspect of 'opportunity management', a kind of 'treasure hunt', where the treasure is opportunity efficient choices which deliver both risk efficiency *and* the additional expected return of enlightened gambles whenever gambles are appropriate. As well as the direct impact on performance, the wider implications of the culture change involved can be crucial, including the impact of everyone knowing they are working for an organisation which understands the difference between good luck and good management, bad luck and bad management, will tolerate bad luck but not bad management, and encourages appropriate enlightened gambles as well as enlightened caution.

Opportunity efficiency – with enlightened prudence as the focus

Taking enlightened gambles needs to be coupled to and constrained by encouraging and facilitating enlightened prudence.

'Enlightened prudence' is defined as the selection of a risk efficient option which reduces return relative to a higher risk and return option because the additional risk is judged not bearable or not worthwhile for one of the parties, and a prudent decision-making process suggests not taking the additional risk.

Enlightened prudence means avoiding taking a gamble which is beyond the risk appetite of *any* of the parties with a legitimate interest in the outcomes. Enlightened prudence was not a serious concern for IBM *at the level of decision making being addressed*, because IBM was big enough to self-insure the risks involved at this level. But whenever enlightened prudence does need attention, it is a complex concern which requires capable treatment in an appropriately general (unrestricted) conceptual framework using viable working assumptions.

There are two key risk appetite reasons why enlightened prudence may need to constrain gambles with a view to avoiding unenlightened gambles. Both need to be clearly understood by all relevant people.

Most important, the additional risk may not be bearable by one or more of the parties involved. A consensus involving *all* relevant parties may be crucial to avoid this kind of unenlightened gamble, and reaching a consensus may involve negotiating a change in the risk–reward distributions involved. Usually enlightened management decision makers will be very aware of the need to consider all relevant concerns, but some decision makers may ignore the legitimate interests of other parties through ignorance or self-seeking behaviour if governance is inadequate.

Also very important, but secondary, the additional risk may not be worthwhile in terms of the operational cost implications of disrupted financial plans – suddenly having to find an extra £100 million may involve abnormal costs even for an organisation like BP, and for very small expected cost savings even a risk which is bearable may not be worthwhile.

All decision makers need to be clear about what is involved when either of these issues arises, one or the other is often a concern, neither lends itself to simple rules in all potentially relevant circumstances, and simplistic treatment can be counterproductive. Governance needs to address all these concerns.

For example, if very serious potential problems associated with the 1.6-m barge might cost BP an extra £100 billion, the risk involved might be judged unbearable and certainly not worthwhile for an expected benefit of just £5 million. Assuming the £100 billion possibility is understood, deciding to avoid this level of risk might be straightforward and obvious, needing very little effort. But even if the additional maximum cost was just £100 million and the £5 million expected savings might make it worth the enlightened gamble, a £0.05 million expected savings would probably not be enough to justify the risk of an extra £100 million, and this might also be the case for an expected saving of £0.5 million. For a significant risk when the gamble is within the bearable range, *exactly* where the flip point expected cost saving is may be unclear, but it is not £0 million, and it clearly ought to vary with the maximum amount at risk.

In effect, *whenever the risk is significant* the flip from enlightened gamble to enlightened prudence does not occur as the difference between riskier and safer choice passes a zero expected cost difference point, £100 million being assumed to be bearable but significant in this example context.

If any additional significant risk is bearable and it is avoidable, the trade-off between additional expected reward and additional risk needs careful attention – risk appetite involves trade-offs which are a function of *both* the risk *and* the reward involved. Clarity is crucial, and a high clarity decision diagram like Figure 3.7 can be an invaluable decision-making tool.

If any additional significant risk is not bearable and it is avoidable, it should not be taken. When this situation arises, clarity is also crucial. High clarity decision diagrams like Figure 3.7 can be an invaluable decision-making tool whenever a close call is involved.

Whenever the risk is not significant, there is obviously no need to consider risk appetite concerns – simply maximising expected reward is the preferred sound and simple clarity efficient strategy. Enlightened gambles are the default option, with no need to test for the possible need for enlightened prudence.

Insurance and other forms of partial or full risk transfer may complicate matters by introducing further new options, but the complications this raises will be deferred until later, along with additional clarity to deal with complex enlightened prudence concerns involving multiple attributes and multiple parties whose concerns may be very different.

Chapters 8 and 9 address contexts in which enlightened prudence requires formal planning model consideration with strategic corporate management implications. Chapters 5 and 6 emphasise a focus on maximising expected reward for most purposes. All Part 2 chapters employ the same EP toolset, building on both the toolset and mindset issues addressed in this chapter.

Interim consolidation of the opportunity efficiency concept

Decision diagrams like Figures 3.6 and 3.7 are key tools for all EP contexts, to portray option choices which are relevant to operations planning and corporate planning as well as project planning. So are simpler linear versions, which are illustrated later. Decision diagrams are the basis for opportunity efficient choices to achieve clarified dominance including enlightened caution, plus making appropriate trade-offs when clarified trade-offs involve distinguishing between enlightened prudence and enlightened gambles.

Figure 3.8 is a useful basis for consolidating the ideas explored in the last few sections, for linking this consolidation to further discussion of risk appetite issues, and for building on during the rest of this book as further complications are addressed.

The 'efficient frontier' view of risk efficiency provided by Figure 3.8 is a conceptual tool which you need to understand as clearly as possible as part of the foundations of strategic clarity. It can only be used directly as an operational tool if very strong working assumptions are employed, considered shortly, but it is a very general conceptual tool which needs

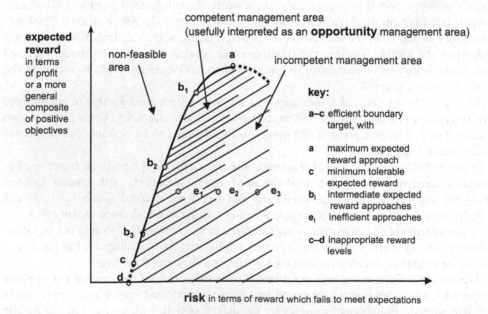

Figure 3.8 Expected reward and associated risk in an efficient frontier portrayal.

to be understood in conjunction with Figure 3.5 to help you to interpret what the last few sections have been about as a basis for understanding what the rest of this book is about.

Figure 3.8 is a variant of the 'efficient frontier diagram' which *Portfolio Selection: Efficient Diversification of Investments* (Markowitz, 1959) uses to discuss risk efficiency employing a mean–variance framework. Economists routinely use comparable efficient frontier diagrams to discuss efficient choices and associated trade-offs between any two criteria. Figure 3.5 was based on Figure 3.8, using a common format to simplify joint understanding. Figure 3.8 has been central to my understanding of risk and uncertainty since first encountering Markowitz and embedding his concepts in my PhD research around 1970.

Start by considering Figure 3.8 in the context of a portfolio of securities in mean–variance terms. Markowitz could use Figure 3.8 as an operational model as well as a conceptual framework, because he assumed variance was a suitable surrogate measure for risk.

The securities investment portfolio plans being considered by Markowitz in a mean–variance framework were defined by the amounts of money invested in each of the possible securities, the X_i values, with $i = 1, \ldots, n$ for n securities. These X_i variable values had to be associated with estimates of a complete set of E_i parameter values which measured the expected return per \$ or £ or other relevant currency unit invested in security i. A complete set of V_{ij}^2 parameter values for $j = 1, \ldots, n$ as well as $i = 1, \ldots, n$, which measured all the associated variances and co-variances also required estimation, with $V_{ij}^2 = V_i^2$ when $i = j$.

The y-axis was expected reward, expected return on the portfolio as a whole measured by E, equal by definition to the sum of all the $E_i X_i$ over $i = 1, \ldots, n$.

The x-axis was risk associated with reward that fails to meet expectations as measured by V^2, the variance of the probability distribution defining E, a quadratic function of $V_{ij}^2 X_i X_j$ terms summed for both i and j over $1, \ldots, n$.

Point 'a' was defined when the objective function $E - k V^2$ was maximised for $k = 0$ (risk was ignored – given zero weight). Graphically a horizontal line (slope zero) was pushed up as far as it would go to still provide a feasible solution to locate point 'a', maximising E. As the value of k increased the same optimisation meant that b_1 was reached, then b_2, then b_3, and then c. Graphically the line defined by $E - k V^2$ with slope k was pushed as far as it would go upwards and to the left to still provide a feasible solution at the point of tangency with the boundary. The c–d region involved too little reward to be of interest. A quadratic programming approach to this model allowed the identification of a suitable selection of portfolios on the boundary from point a to point c.

The decision maker could then select the preferred portfolio, indirectly choosing a value for k. The value of k at the chosen optimal solution point defined the trade-off between expected reward as measured by E and risk as measured by V^2 at the optimal solution – a special case of what is now commonly referred to as risk appetite, defined in terms of what is now commonly known as a shadow price. In this case the shadow price could be defined as the increase in expected reward which could be obtained if the constraint on risk were relaxed by one unit at the currently chosen optimal solution.

The relationships between the X_i values defining the plans and the two relevant criteria (E and V^2) are the goals–plans relationships. These criteria are linear in the case of E and quadratic in the case of V^2. The model provides crucial understanding of the role of dependence between different sources of uncertainty associated with plans as a central part of the goals–plans relationships framework.

Point 'a' involves investing all available money in the single highest expected value outcome security available – a classic 'putting all your eggs in one basket' plan. Moving down the efficient frontier is about efficient diversification, changing the plan by adding more securities to the portfolio in an optimal manner. This involves choosing to add those securities which per unit of expected return foregone have a maximum level of independence or, ideally, a negative dependence 'hedging' effect, to provide a maximum reduction in risk for any given reduction in expected return. A minimum sacrifice of expected return for a maximum decrease in risk is what is being sought, over the whole of the boundary from point a to point c.

Now consider Figure 3.8 in the context of the Magnus project BP example. When BP adopted a 3-m barge as discussed in the context of Figure 3.6, BP moved from a point like e_1 to a point like b_2, involving less risk and more expected reward (less expected cost). BP was in what we judged (from a prototype EP perspective) as a 'competent management area', usefully treated as an opportunity management area, looking for better ways to shape their project plans for execution and delivery at a strategic level. The goals–plans relationships structure associated with a causal understanding of uncertainty was more complex than the security portfolio example in some ways, simpler in others. It was certainly different. But it was manageable by skilled planners because activity-based plans and contingency plans with associated duration uncertainty and linked resource choices drove overall cost uncertainty in a way which could be defined and understood by those involved. The BP board members could not be sure that the BP project planners had reached the efficient boundary for this particular decision because only two points identified by their planners had been explained using Figure 3.6. However, the board members could be *very* sure their planners knew what to look for, their planners had looked at other options, and they had moved their plans in the right direction as far as they could. All the other proactive and reactive contingency planning done by the BP planning staff was part of the shaping of base and contingency plans to move closer to the risk efficient boundary.

A choice like that discussed with IBM UK staff as portrayed by Figure 3.7 is like a choice between b_2 and b_1. The additional risk levels involved in the higher risk options were bearable, and the complication of enlightened prudence was not seen as a concern worth emphasising at the level of decision making being addressed. To 'keep it simple' the IBM culture change programme was about everybody in the organisation understanding risk efficiency with sufficient strategic clarity to be prepared to use this enhanced understanding to both seek risk efficiency *and* take more risk – not less risk. Most of the time this just meant using a highest expected profit approach, not even bothering to consider risk which could be accommodated, making the working assumption they could focus on achieving point 'a' in Figure 3.8 terms. However, the underlying concern was using clarified dominance to achieve enlightened caution plus enlightened trade-offs, including enlightened gambles most of the time and enlightened prudence when relevant. The key was moving all organisational decision making into the opportunity management area, whether or not formal analysis was used to make particular decisions. Understanding the relationship between uncertainty, opportunity and risk at a corporate level was the key to a significant corporate culture change.

More generally, whether or not a choice like b_1 or a should be taken instead of a choice like b_2 or b_3 ought to depend on whether or not risk at the level being considered is just noise or significant. If it is significant then the issue is whether it is both bearable (the absolute level of risk and its full implications) and worthwhile (the slope of the risk efficient boundary defining the trade-offs between risk and reward). Risk appetite in EP terms is about prudence in terms of both the risk–reward trade-offs and the absolute levels of risk involved. If the risk level involved is not significant, a focus on point 'a' choices without wasting any time on risk may be sensible and clarity efficient. If the risk level involved is significant, then proportionately more effort will be worthwhile to ensure appropriate choices are made.

Risk appetite in the context of the many organisations which do not understand what this chapter is about may be very different. Some organisations use risk appetite concepts which from an EP perspective are a serious corporate-capability liability.

Chapter 5 elaborates on the use of expected value decision making when risk associated with quantified uncertainty is assumed to be tolerable and not worth avoiding or even taking the trouble to think about in some cases. It does this assuming that bias in the usual sense is not an issue provided there is a full understanding of underlying working assumptions, linked to several approaches to addressing risk associated with unquantified uncertainty that matters. Chapter 6 explores the idea of taking more risk knowing what you are doing in the spirit of the IBM UK culture change programme, using a tale which is, in part, based on the IBM culture change programme and associated follow-on consultancy. Chapter 7 explores the mixture of clarified dominance and trade-off issues usually encountered in projects in more detail, using a water and sewage utility example. Chapter 8 develops some further risk–reward trade-off concerns in a corporate planning context using an electricity utility example. Chapter 9 considers a railway safety example when both enlightened caution and enlightened prudence involving multiple attribute issues becomes a key concern, raising complexities resolved in a framework which generalises the interpretation of what Figures 3.5 through 3.8 involve.

Of immediate interest, from an EP perspective some organisations are clearly in the incompetent management area, at points like e_3, because they do not even understand the concepts of risk efficiency or opportunity efficiency. If people do not know what they should be looking for, they are very unlikely to find it or recognise its value when they stumble on it by accident.

People who think risk management is primarily about managing risks in the uncertain event sense generally take this view because they do not understand risk efficiency in the sense of Figures 3.5 through 3.8. This means that from an EP perspective people employing a common practice approach based on an uncertain event interpretation of risks and associated overall risk are generally in the incompetent management area for at least three reasons which have been addressed in this section and previous sections in this chapter:

1   they are not providing unbiased estimates of outcomes in a manner which facilitates delivering projects on time and within cost and making other comparable operations and corporate management decisions which are based on unbiased parameter estimates,
2   they are not delivering opportunity management by finding risk efficient choices,
3   they are not ensuring appropriate risk–reward trade-offs or judging prudent choices in terms of absolute risk levels on a sound basis, because they are using an inappropriately restricted risk appetite concept.

They may also be in the incompetent management region for a significant number of further reasons, one addressed in the next section, others addressed in later chapters.

The importance of seeking both specific and general responses

When decision trees were embedded in PERT project planning models, and this Generalised PERT model was further extended to incorporate Markov processes in the GERT approach, 'general' responses became a standard generic feature of these planning models. When I first used the GERT approach for a practical application working with Acres in 1975 on an Arctic pipeline project, a key lesson was the power of general responses to an accumulation of problems. If part way through any activity an accumulation of problems meant that a project was falling behind schedule, a general response can sometimes deal with the effect of all these problems, including unknown unknowns as well as an accumulation of known unknowns and known knowns, net of responses both specific and general in earlier activities. *Sometimes* proactive responses could provide this generality in advance. This involves building in resilience and flexibility.

A linked but separate key lesson was the need for prior contingency planning addressing specific responses to specific concerns *in addition* to general responses, a key new feature of the SCERT approach developed for BP during the late 1970s. Specific sources of uncertainty and responses were not part of GERT.

The focus of much of the effort when SCERT was first used by BP was specific sources of uncertainty and responses. For example, if a wet buckle occurs, an immediate repair was required, unless the pipeline laid so far was abandoned, and the lay-barge went back to the beginning to start again (because not much pipe has been laid and it was cheaper to start again). This focus on specific responses was in part because these specific responses were very important, in part because specific responses were a new feature of SCERT relative to GERT. However, we soon realised that identifying key general responses remained a crucial concern. Furthermore, we also learned that thinking about specific responses was sometimes the catalyst for identifying very important general responses which needed to be recognised and fully exploited as general responses. For example, when exploring how to deal with the impact of more than one wet buckle when laying an offshore pipeline, one of the planning engineers suggested a second lay-barge working from the other end with a submarine connection when the two ends of the pipeline met. This suggestion was immediately welcomed by everyone involved. It was soon realised that the cost of taking an option on a second barge, probably necessary if this response was potentially important, would be too high to justify if more than one buckle was the only relevant issue. However, it might be worthwhile paying for an option on a second barge given this response could also deal with any combination of problems leading to pipe-laying running late, including coated pipe being delivered late, the first barge arriving late or proving unreliable, the weather being unusually bad, and so on. That is, a second lay-barge was initially identified as a 'specific response' to a 'specific source of risk', but we quickly realised that it was, in fact, a particularly powerful general response which we would not have thought about if it had not been initially identified in a systematic search for specific responses. This prompted the development of a systematic search for general responses within all the sets of specific responses, as a design feature of the SCERT process methodology. The desirability of a contractual option to use two or three shift operations of the pipe-coating facility if needed, negotiated before the contract was agreed, was identified as a direct consequence, one example of the generalised search for general responses using specific responses in another context as a starting point.

When National Power introduced a simplified variant of the BP SCERT approach using a combined cycle gas turbine electricity generation power station as a demonstration project, we spent a lot of time looking for general responses to deal with potential delays, including systematically reviewing specific responses for ideas which might have wider relevance. We could not find any initially, and two sources of uncertainty were particularly worrying to the planning team.

One of these sources of uncertainty was the potential cost of the power station being ready to use gas later than anticipated. The owners of the gas supply had agreed to build a pipeline from their gas field to the power station with first gas availability at a contracted date to be specified by National Power, with heavy penalties for the gas supplier if it was late completing the pipeline. However, National Power would have to pay for the gas from that date, whether it used it or not. This was a 'take-or-pay' contract, specified by the gas supplier to avoid getting no revenue from a completed pipeline.

The second of these sources of uncertainty was a series of permissions required from regulators for environmental concerns like warm cooling water being put into a river – issues involving more uncertainty than might usually be the case because this was the first power station of this kind to be built by a newly privatised UK electricity utility, and nobody had a clear idea about the implications of privatisation for regulatory issues. Although some suspected tougher regulation was likely, others had a converse view.

The planning team eventually identified a general response strategy which proved central to the whole plan. Initially the key general response idea was 'start the whole project several months early, leaving the first gas contract date in August as initially planned, to build a contingency cushion'. Key further ideas building on this starting point included 'contract for a separate gas supply from the national grid gas supplier so that if the power station is available early the opportunity can be used to do all the testing early'. Gas provided by the national grid supplier could not be used to run the power station at full power for a sustained period, but it could be used for test purposes. It was soon realised that the gas characteristics were different, which meant that a more flexible specification of the gas to be burnt needed to be part of the turbine contract, initially viewed as a problem and then viewed as another potential opportunity. A more flexible gas specification for the turbines would make the power station less dependent on the main gas supplier, potentially a significant asset later.

The National Power engineering function soon became absolutely delighted with the combined effect of these changes and the very high probability of being able to go to full power if needed as soon as the main gas supply became available – it sold them on making the SCERT model approach the new standard National Power practice.

The National Power finance function then became involved. It recommended that all the general response ideas developed thus far should be retained, but the whole project, *including the first gas availability date*, should now be delayed so that the first full power capability could be exploited in November to give National Power a better cash flow for the project.

The National Power board was delighted by this joint engineering and finance functions collaboration, a very high-profile example of resolving potential risk associated with sources of uncertainty and finding a whole series of opportunities by unravelling the key complexities that really mattered. Its basis was a general response quite different and unrelated to any responses identified earlier. It was identified by a search for general responses which was creative as well as systematic, exploiting collaboration across as well as within functions like engineering and finance.

The analysis was synergistic in the broad sense that it went well beyond the bounds of the sources of uncertainty originally identified as a problem, to deal with much more fundamental concerns. The opportunity that really mattered was a very complex set of relationships which had been disentangled by a creative team of planners working across the usual organisational silo boundaries.

The general EP idea that these BP and National Power examples illustrate in an activity planning context is that responses to a single specific source of uncertainty in one activity can be crucial, but so can general responses within an activity to all sources of uncertainty to date, and so can overall project level responses, with crucial prior proactive measures involved as well as post-event reactive contingency responses which may need prior actions. At its simplest, what safety and reliability engineers called fault trees and event trees deal with specific sources. At an intermediate level, decision trees involving both specific and general responses are embedded in network diagrams or Markov processes. At a maximum level of complexity, underlying decision trees dealing with what some decision analysis experts refer to as a 'bushy mess' may need carefully picking apart because the multiple stage tangled mess matters, and sometimes it can be tamed if those involved know what to look for and how to deal with it, using a well-designed systematic and creative interactive process.

The broad ideas go beyond activity structures, as explored later. While contingency planning in a project planning context is a convenient illustrative framework for building on an unbiased approach to estimation starting point for this chapter, *any* option choice generation and selection context gives rise to the same issues, in whatever goals–plans relationship framework is appropriate to the context, whether or not a formal approach to planning which addresses the associated opportunities is used.

More interim consolidation of the opportunity efficiency concept

After the risk efficient frontier portrayed by Figure 3.8 was introduced and basic risk efficiency issues consolidated, this chapter addressed opportunity efficiency in terms of risk–reward trade-offs involving a single attribute like cost or profit. This built on earlier consolidation of clarity efficiency in terms of Figure 3.5. Before ending this chapter, we need to consolidate the meaning of opportunity efficiency within the single attribute limitations of this chapter's focus by briefly but formally linking opportunity efficiency to underlying risk efficiency and clarity efficiency. Later chapters will continue to develop the nature of opportunity efficiency in broader terms.

Figures 3.5 and 3.8 both have a competent management area just below the efficient frontiers which define clarity and risk efficient approaches, also labelled as an opportunity management area. Further examination of what this implies in terms of a synthesis of the risk, clarity and opportunity efficiency trio is the concern of this section.

Risk efficiency in Markowitz's mean–variance terms is a useful starting point. Given only one measurable attribute is of interest (profit, revenue, or cost), a specific known mean value for all components which have a known additive relationship, and an assumption that all variability about these mean values for all components is well behaved and Normally distributed, then variance is a suitable surrogate measure for risk.

If the working assumption that a single measurable attribute is maintained, but all the other working assumptions just noted are abandoned, then decision diagrams using the format of Figures 3.6 and 3.7 can cope provided we assume that all the available options can be considered two at a time in sequence. We can generalise this to cope with up to about half a dozen options on a single diagram variant of Figures 3.6 and 3.7, but two at a time in sequence is often easier. We can also define the 'options' as proportions, allowing us to address optimal portfolios of securities or other forms of investment – for example in Chapter 8 alternative sources of electric power (like nuclear, thermal of various kinds, hydro, and other renewables) for electricity utility planning are addressed in this way. What we cannot do is draw upon mathematical programming techniques, like the quadratic programming tools developed for Markowitz mean–variance models, to make a variant of Figure 3.8 with risk measured by variance an operational tool.

A generalised variant of the moment-based approach Markowitz adopted could add measures of skew and kurtosis (peakedness) to accommodate asymmetric distributions, but this would not cope with the complex badly behaved dependence which a HAT approach can deal with. Nor would it avoid eliminating a quadratic programming approach. An approach based on Figures 3.6 and 3.7 can accommodate any dependence structures or distribution shapes that the very general HAT based portrayal of uncertainty might lead to.

There is a price for this generality, in addition to not being able to use mathematical programming. Within the contexts they are concerned about, the decision makers have to be capable of making suitable judgements about enlightened gambles, enlightened prudence, and enlightened caution in the framework of high clarity decision diagrams like Figures 3.6 and 3.7 or comparable variants, visualising the implications of the whole of the relevant probability distributions as well as identified means (expected outcomes), and they have to consider options in pairs or small groups, understanding the working assumptions implied by the grouping structures chosen. Someone in the team involved has to have the skills and knowledge to manage the process this involves. From the perspective of an EP framework this is generally a price worth paying. It requires an investment in corporate capability, but that investment will provide a significant return.

One aspect of the opportunity efficiency this involves is appropriate risk–reward trade-offs for all relevant attributes. Assuming only one attribute, in terms of Figure 3.8 this means choosing appropriately from among points like a, b_1, b_2, and b_3, as addressed earlier.

A second aspect of the opportunity efficiency involved is to need to achieve risk efficiency in the first place – getting onto or near the risk efficient boundary. BP planners understood this was the primary goal of the SCERT approach to contingency planning – a search for decision options which, if identified and taken, reduced expected cost and risk simultaneously. Indeed, for the BP planners I worked with in the 1970s and 1980s, the treasure hunt for opportunities to reduce expected cost and risk simultaneously was the central purpose of the whole project planning exercise – once they understood what the rich contingency planning approach SCERT provided was about. That is why the competent management area of Figure 3.8 which they were already in was referred to as the opportunity management area. Figure 3.8 was used to explain SCERT to all planning staff, and it went to the main board so that all levels of management had the same understanding of what they were collectively doing. All those involved in the National Power use of simplified SCERT variants to plan new electricity power stations also understood this, as did those involved in the IBM UK culture change programme, and most of the other clients I have worked with since. Indeed, the hope has always been that all those reading *How to Manage Project Opportunity and Risk* (Chapman and Ward, 2011), and all earlier publications developing these ideas since the late 1970s, understood these concepts too. However, some people have put these ideas into a too difficult box or contested them for other reasons, some addressed later.

A third aspect of the opportunity efficiency involved is the need to get on or near the clarity efficient boundary with a suitable clarity and cost of clarity trade-off while pursuing risk efficiency and appropriate risk–reward trade-offs plus absolute levels of risk for all relevant attributes. The approach adopted has to reflect the particulars of the context to achieve this clarity efficiency concern. That is part of the reason why the clarity efficient boundary portrayal of Figure 3.5 also has a competent management (opportunity management) area. This was not a problem for Peter and his colleagues, because it was clear that the SCERT approach was delivering a significant return on the analysis investment, in addition to delivering unbiased estimates the board could trust. Peter, his project manager colleagues, all their project management teams, and the BP board, quickly developed an understanding of when more detailed decomposition of sources of uncertainty might or might not prove worthwhile, and they were all convinced that a better overall framework for thinking about all these concerns was not available. They were buying into a 'bundled product', but they could vary the effort and cost associated with buying more or less clarity of particular kinds in an efficient manner, achieving clarity efficiency in a quite sophisticated way without actually calling it that at the time.

William and Peter both had an initial interest in estimates of expected performance parameter estimates and associated variability estimates which were free of bias, so they could deliver projects within time and cost commitments. What they realised, and all those who followed their example realised, is they could use a SCERT approach to achieve the unbiased estimates they wanted as a spinoff from a search for opportunities to reduce expected cost and cost risk simultaneously. And this process as a whole would more than pay for itself – providing a big return on the investment, perhaps £100 in project cost savings for every £1 spent on clarity efficient analysis. Risk efficiency achieved in a clarity efficient manner provided a big return on the effort invested, as well as reliable estimates. Furthermore, the search for risk efficiency coupled to its clarity efficient pursuit was at the centre of what opportunity management and opportunity efficiency were about, understood at that time in slightly different terms.

The minimum to high clarity estimation-efficiency spectrum examples explored in this chapter are centred on a project context when a single attribute was the focus because multiple attributes like duration and cost could be integrated via goals–plans relationships which were understood. The early emphasis with William was unbiased estimation, understanding the distinction between what was quantified in probabilistic terms and associated conditions, plus the crucial differences between aspirational targets, commitments, and expected outcomes. The value of understanding associated scenarios in terms of underlying sources of uncertainty for contingency planning purposes was introduced but not modelled formally. The discussion with Peter developed the role of formal contingency planning to identify the options whose existence defined the need for risk efficiency – because if we have choices in terms of the plans we are making, some choices are better than others, and the risk efficiency aspects matter. The discussions with William and Peter also begin to explore the complexity associated with achieving clarity efficiency – because we have choices when we choose how to do the planning. Some choices about how we do the planning are better than others – so clarity efficiency matters. Furthermore, the discussion with Peter begins to explore the complexity associated with achieving clarity and opportunity efficiency when duration and cost are interdependent and their relationship needs to be understood.

One key message to take away from this chapter is a minimum clarity approach to estimation involves a relatively simple but subtle set of aspirations associated with unbiased expected value estimates, plus a clear understanding of the associated range, also estimated without bias and interpreted in relation to the ABCs of targets when relevant.

Building on this, adding clarity may involve more refined estimates, but the key is further clarity attributes or dimensions driven by contingency planning which increases expected reward, including taking more risk which is bearable and worthwhile but avoiding any risk which is not bearable, not worthwhile, or not necessary because risk inefficiency is involved.

These ideas are associated with clarity efficiency, risk efficiency and opportunity efficiency, the last a composite concept embedding the first two.

One manifestation of corporate understanding of these concepts is a corporate understanding of the role of clarified dominance, enlightened caution, enlightened gambles, enlightened prudence, and the foundations of what corporate risk appetite ought to address. Another is a corporate understanding of the difference between good luck and good management, bad luck and bad management, and the foundations of what EP corporate culture changes might deliver. Yet another is a corporate understanding of the need to see choosing a suitable level of clarity on the estimation-efficiency spectrum for any given component of an analysis based on opportunity efficiency.

The benefits of full corporate understanding of these issues include culture changes which will affect informal planning and may change deep cultural issues like ethics as well as formal planning, with widespread implications.

However, multiple attributes which are not reducible to a single attribute like cost have not yet been addressed, and clarity itself is clearly a multiple dimension concept which is not directly measurable in any dimension. This chapter's initial focus on estimation, then moving into efficiency (clarity, risk and opportunity), maintaining a focus on just one directly relevant attribute at any given time, meant that we did not have to confront a potential conflict between more clarity in terms of contingency planning versus less clarity about unbiased estimation or priorities which might change over time. For example, at the concept creation stage of a project's lifecycle *some* contingency planning is not relevant until we are committed to the concept strategy, but an unbiased estimate of the pay-off from the strategy is crucial. Furthermore, this chapter has not confronted plans which themselves involve multiple attributes which matter when there is no obvious well-founded way to consider the implications.

EP, as explored in the rest of this book, is about further generalising these ideas. Chapter 4 will start by confronting some of the central challenges which were ignored or navigated around in this chapter, to complete the foundation level conceptual toolset needed for Part 2.

4 Confronting challenging complexities usually needing more clarity

To keep the discussion as simple as possible, a number of challenging complexities were avoided in Chapters 1 through 3. Those usually needing confrontation in a systematic manner using the basic EP conceptual framework require overview attention now, along with some key EP toolset components not yet discussed.

The next three sections consider challenges that Peter and his colleagues had to confront and overcome to identify and capture the opportunities they were facing in their North Sea projects which have direct implications for challenges needing confrontation in all Part 2 chapters. As in Chapter 3, these three sections focus on contexts when a reasonable working assumption is we are dealing with formal planning in terms of a single measurable attribute in the sense that multiple attributes like cost and duration can be reduced to a single metric without difficulty.

A general view of issues associated with unbiased estimates is then considered, drawing further on the discussions involving William as well as Peter.

A watershed following section introduces a general framework which facilitates addressing multiple objectives involving difficulties which need explicit attention before Part 1 finishes.

This watershed section is followed by two sections addressing planning when multiple objectives involving multiple attributes require effective explicit attention but reasonably straightforward formal approaches may be viable, one section emphasising an important warning against excessive focus on what can be measured, a section considering 'planning the planning' in terms of key implications for some of the more difficult challenges associated with complex multiple objective concerns addressed in Part 2 chapters, and a section on a key strategy for dealing with multiple objectives.

The penultimate section briefly reflects on the need to understand that any issues not addressed formally *always* require informal treatment if they are not going to be simply ignored without understanding the implications. Informal treatment which is as effective as possible is obviously preferable to just ignoring issues that matter, and insightful informal treatment should be informed by our understanding of both what a more sophisticated formal approach might achieve and the limitations of formal planning approaches.

A final section concludes with a 'menu view' of what EP decision-making processes based on a UP can provide, with inferences about how the UP concept can be tailored to broad context issues as illustrated in Part 2.

Sensitivity diagrams as portals to further opportunities

Sensitivity diagrams of many different kinds are key EP tools. Sensitivity diagrams of one particular kind initially developed in a high clarity form for use in the SCERT process by BP planners are considered in this section. These sensitivity diagrams portray the way several lower level sources of uncertainty have been combined to define a higher level composite source of uncertainty, incorporating dependence in an underlying composition structure. An example is the sensitivity diagram illustrated in Figure 4.1.

When using a UP or any associated SP, it is always crucial to begin the test phase by understanding the sensitivity of results to working assumptions about contributing components. Different forms of analysis using different kinds of component structures often require very different approaches to different kinds of sensitivity analysis. If the analysis involves quantitative (probabilistic) treatment of multiple sources of uncertainty, then sensitivity diagrams like Figure 4.1 are central to an EP approach to the test phase and related interpret phase concerns. They have been used in various forms for a wide range of applications involving EP prototypes ever since their first use by BP. In the BP context their importance extended to use in the interpret phase to explain what really mattered to the main board. In later studies they played a similar role in most cases.

In the context of BP introducing a SCERT approach, it soon became very clear that it was important everybody involved in using sensitivity diagrams understood how they were used by the planners to evolve the plans, what messages the sensitivity diagrams could convey, and what assumptions they made. This included board members. It required a widespread

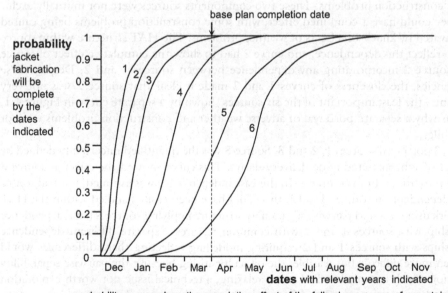

probability curves show the cumulative effect of the following sources of uncertainty:

1. yard not available or mobilisation delays
2. construction problems/adverse weather
3. subcontracted nodes delivery delays
4. material delivery delays
5. industrial disputes
6. delayed award of fabrication contract

notes:
1. the curves assume a minimum fabrication period of 20 months
2. no work is transferred offsite to improve progress
3. no major fire, explosion, or other damage

Figure 4.1 Sensitivity diagram: North Sea oil project platform jacket fabrication example.

'what needs to be done' level of understanding grounded upon key aspects of 'how to do it' understanding.

Figure 4.1 portrayed the uncertainty associated with fabricating the platform 'jacket' for an offshore oil production project. The jacket was the steel structure fabricated in a 'yard' (dry-dock facility) which was then floated out to the location of the production well, upended and pinned to the ocean floor, fitted with all necessary modules (production facilities and accommodation), and connected to the pipeline taking the oil to shore.

Curve 1 portrayed 'source of uncertainty 1', a quantified source (known known) defined at a composite level by the possible effects of two underlying sources of uncertainty associated with starting this activity – the yard might not be available on the contracted date because another jacket being constructed in the yard had been delayed and could not be moved out until it was completed, or the yard might not have been used for some time and it might take time to hire and train some of the staff required. These were mutually exclusive component sources of uncertainty – one might occur but not both. Combining them was useful because of this mutual exclusivity. As indicated by the upper end of curve 1, a delay of more than two months was possible, although a delay of less than one month was likely. All these curves are cumulative format portrayals to show the probability of completion by the date indicated.

Curve 2 portrayed source 1 plus source 2. The gap between curves 1 and 2 was defined by the cumulative effect of source 2. Source 2 was the quantified uncertainty defined by the combined effect of two further component sources – possible adverse weather and possible construction problems. These two components sources were not mutually exclusive. They could have a combined effect, with some construction problems being caused or aggravated by knock-on effects of weather problems. The HAT structure within source 2 had to reflect this dependence, and curve 2 had to show the cumulative effect of source 1 plus source 2 incorporating any dependence between sources 1 and 2. Despite these dependencies, the closeness of curves 1 and 2 made it clear that source 2 was not very important – the least important of the six sources shown by a separate curve in Figure 4.1. That was why a separate portrayal of adverse weather and construction problems was not worthwhile.

Curve 3 portrayed sources 1, 2 and 3. Source 3 was the quantified uncertainty defined by the effect of subcontracted node delivery delays. This curve showed the effect as source 3 was added to source 1 plus source 2. In this case independence was assumed, but had source 3 been dependent on sources 1 and 2, this could have been easily handled within the HAT framework using a nested pairwise separability structure implying source 3 has a dependence relationship with sources 1 and 2 with common features. Separate different dependence relationships with sources 1 and 2 requiring modelling reflecting these differences would have been more difficult but feasible, the difficulty arising because the pairwise separability assumption which is easily handled needs relaxing, a technical issue not worth exploration here. The closeness of curves 2 and 3 made it clear that the source 3 uncertainty about subcontracted nodes was not a particularly big source of concern, although it was marginally bigger than source 2.

Curve 4 relative to curve 3 portrayed the effect of source 4, quantified uncertainty defined by the effect of material delivery delays. Again, curve 4 shows the cumulative effect. And again, dependence among sources 1, 2, 3 and 4 would be simple to deal with using a pairwise separability assumption, separate different dependency relationships requiring modelling involving more difficulty. The bigger spread between curves 3 and 4 makes it clear that material delivery delays are much more important than sources 1, 2 or 3.

Curves 5 and 6 continued in the same way. They showed the largest source was 'industrial disputes' (source 5). But 'delayed award of fabrication contract' (source 6) was also significant.

The notes identified sources of uncertainty treated as known unknowns – quantification was conditional on these assumptions.

One purpose for Figure 4.1 was explaining to the managers responsible for letting the fabrication contract why it was important there was no unnecessary delay. That was why 'delayed award of fabrication contract' was positioned last in the sequence of six sources. Curve 6 showed that current analysis assumptions suggested a 0.15 probability of achieving the base plan completion date at the end of March, but this increased to 0.45 if the possible fabrication contract delay portrayed by curve 6 could be eliminated. This was part of a case for 'getting on with letting the contract'.

A very important outcome from early use of Figure 4.1 was triggering an extensive data review to test the assumptions made by the planners who assessed source 5 (industrial disputes). Because this source clearly mattered, it became a focus of attention. Source 5 had been initially quantified by the planners on a purely subjective basis, drawing on their general knowledge of offshore industry issues. What a detailed analysis of recent industrial disputes data for all potential yards in Europe showed was the planners had sized source 5 correctly, but they had misunderstood what was driving the potential problems and what might be done to reduce them. None of the disputes which were explored using available data had occurred in the first 90% of the contract duration – they were all concentrated at the end of contracts. And they had only occurred when no more work was scheduled to come into the yard on completion of this contract. The current assumptions that tight contract conditions and penalties would contain the problems were not well founded. But if Figure 4.1 went to the board, recommending collaboration with other oil majors to get a smoother flow of work to the yards they were all using, the board might initiate a very effective and efficient form of collaboration which could reduce exposure to industrial disputes *and* get better prices for *all* the oil majors by avoiding the current 'feast or famine' situation for the yards and their employees. This could be good for all the oil majors using the yards, the yard owners, and the yard employees. What was involved was a very useful potential win–win–win opportunity identified by a creative planner who could see the bigger picture when he used Figure 4.1 to trigger deeper analysis addressing data which he chose to chase because sensitivity analysis made it clear that understanding this data might matter.

The board needed to understand what sensitivity diagrams like Figure 4.1 were saying at various points in the analysis cycle to understand this sort of discussion. The board found sensitivity diagrams in this format particularly useful when employed in a top-down manner to portray the four or five key sources of overall uncertainty in the proposed budget cost, with the option of also looking at lower level curves to further decompose these components. A comparable breakdown of project completion date uncertainty was also useful at the board level.

The Figure 4.1 example was memorably useful, but use of up to about half a dozen sensitivity diagrams of this kind for board level top-down presentations became routine, drawn from a comprehensive set of sensitivity diagrams which had become a key operational tool when building the analysis from the bottom up.

Figure 4.1 is an activity level sensitivity diagram for one activity in terms of duration. Higher and lower level diagrams were also used in terms of duration, and cost was addressed in a comparable nested structure. The analysis as a whole involved several hundred cost sources of uncertainty components, including associated duration source of uncertainty components, but the board was only presented with a limited set of sensitivity diagrams highlighting key issues from a top-down perspective.

The planners needed to present their results from the top down, using a very selective small set of key diagrams. But the planners had to build an extensive nested sensitivity diagram structure from the bottom up as a central aspect of managing the iterative SCERT process and understanding interdependencies. For example, the planners needed separate the analysis of the two components of source 1 before combining them and the interdependent analysis of the two sources underlying source 2.

Developing the nested sensitivity diagram structure and understanding the associated interdependence relationships was strongly encouraged and directly facilitated by the BP software because of its discrete probability arithmetic basis, but the same results could have been obtained using commercially available Monte Carlo simulation software. Later users of this approach usually used simulation-based software. The key was encouraging the analysts to use the same underlying HAT models, understanding what was involved when making these modelling decisions, and using the models to engage with their boards or other senior decision makers in the same way. For example, at a modelling level to produce Figure 4.1 they would have to set up the simulation so that the sum of sources 1 and 2 was captured to plot curve 2; the sum of sources 1, 2, and 3 was captured to plot the source 3 curve; and so on.

Within BP and later users of related processes, the overall analysis process often involved 'moving the bottom down' when it became clear that more detailed understanding of a critical area would be useful. For example, while reasonably low clarity subjective probability analysis on a first pass minimised time wasted on sources which were relatively unimportant, the planners had to go back to important sources, like source 5, and seek more clarity using all their skills and creativity. That was what opportunity management in an 'opportunity efficient' manner which included underlying clarity efficiency was about.

The board and other senior decision makers did not need to know how the planners did this in detail, but they did need to understand in overview terms what was being done and the quality of the thinking that lay behind the summary top level portrayals of direct interest.

All contexts require their own forms of sensitivity analysis, tailored to the context. In some cases, quite different forms of sensitivity diagrams or tables may be best suited to the sensitivity analysis issues addressed. But everyone involved needs to understand sensitivity analysis issues at an appropriate level in a useful manner. Figure 4.1 is just a high clarity example when multiple sources of uncertainty assessed within a HAT structure are involved. However, the Figure 4.1 format has some particularly useful implications with relevance to many contexts.

An aspect of an organisation's capability-culture assets which matters is having planners who know how to structure the initial decomposition of analysis components (in this case, activities, sources of uncertainty, and responses) estimate associated key parameters and uncertainty, synthesise and interpret the results using sensitivity diagrams, and then revise and refine their analysis where doing so will pay dividends – increasing clarity efficiency. Acquiring and using these skills are dependent on understanding the full set of potential roles for sensitivity diagrams within all aspects of the decision-making process as a whole in all relevant contexts.

Another aspect of an organisation's capability-culture assets which matters is having board level managers who know how to use planners with these skills to best effect, encouraging and facilitating the right stuff.

Sensitivity diagrams like Figure 4.1 are another gateway concept in several senses, an aspect of tactical clarity which needs overview understanding for strategic clarity.

Sensitivity diagrams have roles in the same or comparable forms in all Part 2 chapters, in corporate and operations management contexts, as well as project management contexts.

Source-response diagrams as portals for further clarity

Some BP board members wanted to understand Figure 4.1 in terms of what underlay it in more depth. This was often the case for senior managers using Figure 4.1 variants in many other contexts.

BP board members found Figure 4.2 a useful portrayal of the uncertainty underlying source 1 in Figure 4.1, clarifying the source 1 uncertainty by decomposing it in a structured manner. Figure 4.2 provides a useful example of the deeper understanding of complexity which an EP approach can facilitate for all those who need it, using 'source-response' diagrams in this particular context.

What Figure 4.2 portrayed was the preferred response if the yard was not available (because another jacket under construction in the yard had not been completed) was 'mobilise and accept a short delay' (ship steel to an adjacent site, for example). This might not work because of a secondary source associated with the assumed primary response (accepting a short delay might not work because a long delay was inevitable). The next preference primary response was 'find an alternative yard' (breaking the original contract). This might

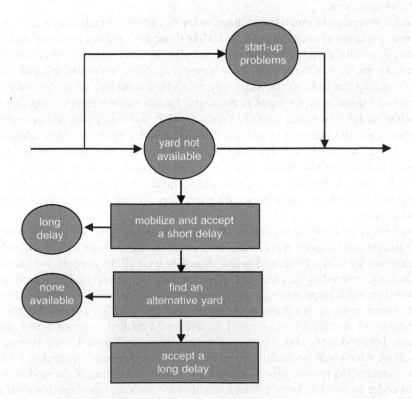

Figure 4.2 Source-response diagram: source 1 in Figure 4.1.

not work either (because an alternative yard might not be available). Accepting a long delay was then the only response available.

Figure 4.2 also implicitly indicated that 'start-up' problems (associated with a yard which had not been used for some time) had not been associated with any response option choices involving BP actions – because it was assumed these problems would and should be dealt with reasonably effectively by the yard and intervention by BP would not be appropriate. This rationale might have been made explicit on the diagram.

Figure 4.2 is useful as a portal to the kind of 'what needs to be done' and associated requisite 'how to do it' level of understanding of the contingency planning underlying the earlier discussion.

The project manager and his team members needed the additional clarity provided by complete sets of source-response diagrams addressing all sources of uncertainty developed with extensive team discussion to test their understanding of the structure of uncertainty *prior to quantifying uncertainty*. They could not have built the sophisticated quantitative HAT models used without this qualitative understanding because of the complexities they had to deal with.

The board needed to understand that this was what the planners had done, with sufficient exposure to a few examples of interest to understand broadly how it was done, but not the details of all the diagrams used by the planning team.

This is an example of explicitly using formal qualitative analysis to facilitate bottom-up quantitative analysis and then using the resulting quantitative and qualitative analysis diagrams to explain results on a top-down basis which is focused on what really matters to the senior decision makers.

Figure 4.2 was part of a much larger diagram for this activity, which portrayed all the identified primary sources of uncertainty as circles like those for 'yard not available' and 'start-up problems', in parallel if they were mutually exclusive, in series if they were cumulative. The third primary source was at the end of the arrow from 'yard not available', and the others further moved to the right in the same way, to show a complete set of 'primary sources' for this activity using as many pages as necessary. *Specific reactive* response options were in boxes below, ordered to reflect preferred choices, with 'secondary sources' as circles to the left as shown for the first two responses. *Specific proactive* responses were identified and noted separately when relevant. Proactive responses involve a new base plan A2 to replace the original base plan A now known as plan A1, while reactive responses involve a fall-back plan B or C, perhaps dependent on prior arrangements being put in place. Diagrams for successive activities with potential knock-on effects were linked, and other interdependences were also shown.

The net effect of all primary sources and their specific responses was associated with a 'residual uncertainty' source, represented by a circle on the extreme right-hand side of the overall diagram for each activity, and below this circle were all the *general reactive* responses for this activity, ordered in the preferred sequence and showing secondary risks if appropriate. *General proactive* responses were listed separately with the specific proactive responses.

These source-response diagrams were drawn and discussed to ensure that the project team understood the relevant uncertainty in structured qualitative terms *before* quantification began. Identifying the conditions portrayed as 'notes' in Figure 4.1 was part of the discussion about what could be usefully quantified and what was better treated as a condition.

Other contexts may require other forms of qualitative structuring of the underlying complexity in order to build a clarity efficient quantitative analysis, but those involved need to understand the issues at an appropriate level for their role in the planning process, using approaches designed to meet their needs in an effective and efficient manner. This is just a high clarity example when multiple sources of uncertainty are involved in a reasonably sophisticated HAT structure.

Chapman and Ward (2011) discuss the use of Figures 4.1 and 4.2 in a generalised version of the SCERT process as a whole in more detail, and Chapter 7 in this book updates this at a strategic clarity 'what needs to be done' level of understanding. All you need to understand at present is this kind of complexity can be successfully confronted when it is relevant if analysts who know how to do it are involved. It can be very relevant when opportunity efficiency and underlying risk efficiency plus clarity efficiency are pursued using sensitivity diagrams like Figure 4.1 in conjunction with decision diagrams like Figures 3.6 and 3.7.

More generally, an enlightened approach to structuring the way uncertainty sources and associated responses are related is essential. Those shaping the analysis approach need to understand the toolset at their disposal. They also need the skill set and mindset to use these tools effectively, including explaining the basis of recommended plans to others. Those involved at the board level need to understand the quality of the underlying analysis as a whole, as well as the rationale of the approach and the results of specific interest. Furthermore, if tools like the sensitivity diagram of Figure 4.1 are never employed, board level managers need to understand their role well enough to question why, with a view to testing the competence of those leading the planning.

Consolidating unbiased parameter estimation issues

Chapter 3 began with a focus on unbiased estimates of performance measures like activity duration to initiate an exploration of clarity efficiency with a focus on bias before linking clarity efficiency, risk efficiency and opportunity efficiency. Five key bias issues were considered during the discussions involving William and Peter. These five issues are briefly structured and summarised now, followed by a brief exploration of a sixth issue.

The consolidated view of these six issues outlined in this section provides a 'what needs to be done' EP framework for managing all unbiased parameter estimation concerns in a coordinated manner. This helps to unify Part 2 discussions involving parameter estimation bias and biased decision making in broader terms. It also confronts an important concern avoided earlier.

Issue 1 – working assumptions about sources of uncertainty treated qualitatively

In the discussion with William, it was made clear that if feasible scenarios beyond the scope of past experience are not quantified, biased estimates will result. Furthermore, any feasible outcome scenarios treated qualitatively as conditions need to be understood when addressing bias. These ideas were later considered in various ways, including the concept of a no quibbles provision briefly explored in Chapter 3 and the conditions illustrated by notes addressing known unknowns in Figure 4.1.

Issue 2 – working assumptions about parametrically defined probability distributions

Parametrically defined probability distributions are common practice and often useful, but as working assumptions they need testing for bias. Furthermore, they are never suitable framing assumptions because they always need testing. The HAT approach facilitates a flexible approach to testing the robustness of parametrically defined probability distributions, and its open 'synthesis of all relevant approaches' nature means that it will deal with all of the issues which I have had to confront. Most readers do not need deep knowledge in this area, but their organisations do need requisite capability when it matters, and all senior managers need to understand in broad terms what this involves and why parametrically defined probability distributions can be a source of serious risk if the associated assumptions are not well founded.

Issue 3 – working assumptions about the role of dependence

The HAT approach facilitates a general approach to both statistical and causal dependence, which is essential to avoid very serious bias. A failure to deal with important interdependences, including complex knock-on and feedback effects, is a common problem. Often it renders formal quantitative (probabilistic) analysis dangerous – well beyond useless to the extent that an organisation would be much better off if they just trusted reasonably well-grounded informal intuition and either retrained or got rid of all 'experts' who cannot deal with dependence effectively. Some of these 'experts' hide behind textbooks, standards and guides which fail to clarify the implications of ineffective treatment of issues like interdependences or provide adequate guidance for effectively dealing with these issues.

Issue 4 – working assumptions about minimising unconscious behavioural bias

Unconscious behavioural bias associated with estimating probabilities directly or eliciting them from others was mentioned when discussing a minimum clarity approach and its generalisations for William in Chapter 3, and dealing effectively and efficiently with issues like 'anchoring' always matters. There is a large literature on unconscious behavioural bias, with some entry points indicated in Chapter 11. Behavioural bias always needs to be understood by all those engaged directly in estimation processes, and responsible senior managers need to be able to judge associated competence levels. Misunderstanding the limitations of data as well as misinterpreting data can be viewed as part of this issue. Misunderstanding the nature of subjective probabilities and their relationship with component objective estimates can also be viewed as a very important part of this issue.

Issue 5 – working assumptions about 'strategic misrepresentation'

The working assumptions addressing the first four issues all involve 'competence' concerns addressed in Chapter 3. A fifth issue mentioned earlier but not explored is deliberate bias in the 'strategic misrepresentation' sense (Flyvbjerg, Bruzelius, and Rothengatter, 2003). *Strategic misrepresentation* is usually used as a euphemism for lying – comparable to the phrase 'being economical with the truth'. This takes us into broader capability-culture concerns and decision-making bias which arguably goes beyond biased parameter estimates. Whenever it is relevant strategic misrepresentation needs insight and care, because it matters a great deal. It can have roots which go well beyond simple lying for personal and corporate gain, and it may have complex roots linked to both important ethical concerns and incentive issues. It is an important concern which is widely cited and addressed, but how best to respond to its implications is not a simple matter. Significant controversy about implications overlooked by many common practice responses to strategic misrepresentation which simplify in the 'wrong way' is arguably just adding fuel to the fire and making matters worse.

Issue 6 – all other relevant working assumptions including a 'conspiracy of optimism'

It is useful to have a residual category to synthesise all the earlier categories, make sure that overlaps are not double-counted, and pick up any issues that were missed earlier. This is another area which requires an approach involving a 'closure with completeness' component.

One set of issues only partially covered earlier needs further attention now.

At the beginning of my discussion with the air vice-marshall responsible for the Ministry of Defence (MoD) procurement budget during the study involving William discussed in Chapter 3, my opening question was 'What did he think was the main problem with the MoD approach to project risk management?' His immediate answer, with a smile on his face and a glint in his eyes, was a very blunt 'everybody lies to me'.

Having captured my very close attention, he then rephrased his answer in a form that might be used for my report, saying that the MoD suffered from what he liked to refer to as a 'conspiracy of optimism'. He then went on to explain in some detail what this implied.

The 'conspiracy of optimism' euphemism is arguably much richer than strategic misrepresentation, although there are important overlaps. A conspiracy of optimism is still cited in MoD circles; it is discussed in my earlier books with Stephen Ward, and I sometimes hear it in other contexts. It immediately became and remains one of my all-time favourite euphemisms. Writing this book further clarified for me the considerable understanding it can portray if explored in detail.

One key concern which a conspiracy of optimism portrays is that MoD people are very loyal to their teams, which is a crucial corporate culture characteristic of armed forces personnel, and 'a very good thing' in most contexts, a capability-culture asset. However, if this loyalty leads to conscious bias (strategic misrepresentation) in their contributions to duration or cost or other performance estimates, the associated optimism bias needs to be accommodated when producing a corporate estimate. Corporate clarity about aspirational targets which are 'stretch' targets and their relationships with expected outcomes and commitment targets can help facilitate dealing with this kind of conscious bias, but this may not be the only response needed.

Another key concern which a conspiracy of optimism portrays is that MoD people have a corporate culture 'can do' attitude linked to thinking positively which needs to be encouraged and preserved, up to a point, another capability-culture asset. However, this natural and desirable positive trait also needs to be accommodated when they contribute to performance estimates leading to expenditure commitments which are difficult to revise when bias becomes evident, in the sense that if and when overconfidence which is misplaced is involved, it needs to be neutralised. Corporate clarity about aspirational targets and their relationships with expected outcomes and commitment targets can also help facilitate dealing with this kind of unconscious bias. But dealing with it effectively may be difficult, and again this may not be enough. 'Commitment targets' may involve commitments by the MoD procurement functions to the serving forces, to politicians, and to the public, with various shades of complex implications. Furthermore, MoD procurement function commitments invariably involve interdependent commitments to the MoD from contractors who may have serious misconceptions about what is required or agendas which are not aligned with MoD goals, perhaps because of inappropriate contract structures.

Both these concerns were understood by the MoD people I worked with directly by the beginning of the 1990s. So were some aspects which had no positive implications. For example, most people do not like to reveal a lack of understanding about something they are supposed to have deep expert knowledge about, even to themselves, and part of the conspiracy of optimism may be attributed to deliberately hiding a lack of understanding or overconfidence associated with an unconscious equivalent. Furthermore, a lack of competence of other kinds may be an issue needing attention.

Some conspiracy of optimism concerns overlap, at least in part, the five issues addressed earlier in this section, but some new 'culture' issues are also involved. Once it is clear that bias is a capability-culture asset and liability concern of considerable complexity, recognising the role of accommodations for capability-culture assets and liabilities presents itself as a potentially useful tool.

For example, Chapter 6 explores the idea that a senior manager may accommodate concerns about key staff being involved in a potential new contract who are already heavily committed to other important contracts by deliberately introducing a form of bias designed to 'correct for' what they might reasonably see as 'corporate oversights' if there is no other way of avoiding unwise overcommitments. Providing them with a much more effective direct way of ensuring that their concerns are effectively addressed is demonstrably better than this kind of informal 'accommodation' using bias. In some cases, these 'correction accommodations' needing attention may take a 'conspiracy of pessimism' form, generalising the conspiracy of optimism concept, as illustrated in the tale of Chapter 6. 'Strategic misrepresentation' in the usual sense is not involved, although that term could be used if you prefer it, and the corporate competence issues being corrected for are not one of the issues identified above. The choice of label is optional, but dealing with these kinds of issues effectively is not an option if unbiased estimates as part of a broader concern for unbiased decision making is the goal.

As an example of a quite different kind of bias which clearly goes beyond the preceding five, using an inappropriate discount rate for Net Present Values (NPV) calculations as discussed in Chapter 7 can be construed as an issue 6 source of bias associated with biased estimates of parameters. This example may stretch your view of what parameter estimation bias covers too far, and you may prefer to see it as a different and separate form of biased decision making, a more fundamental kind of decision-making error. However, it needs dealing with however it is perceived, and in some contexts, viewing it as a particularly pernicious and significant form of parameter estimation bias can be useful.

The six issue framework as a comprehensive EP toolset component

All Part 2 chapters deal with biased parameter estimation issues of various forms in the context of seeking unbiased decision making, and the six issue framework for bias just outlined may help you to see the links. It may also serve as a useful checklist of sources of bias you need to be aware of for all estimation tasks your organisation has to confront. Strategic clarity about bias issues is essential for any director or expert and all supporting staff within any organisation. At a how to do it level managing bias requires a range of tools used in a competent manner by all those who need to know how to use them and interpret the results.

As a final comment in this section, the competent management area of Figures 3.5 and 3.8 may be usefully thought of as an opportunity management area for a number of reasons. One foundation level reason is a key feature of competent management is always seeking better ways to understand and communicate what most needs to be understood. As part of this, understanding why biased estimates of key parameters which decision making depends on are so endemic and what needs to be done to eliminate bias effectively and efficiently is a crucial opportunity.

A general *conceptual* framework for multiple objectives

Often the focus of decision making is one attribute (like cost) which is measurable in terms of one criterion (like expected cost). Sometimes when one attribute (like cost) is the focus other metrics like lost time or revenue can be addressed via 'opportunity cost' concepts that allow transformations into a single metric using simple common practice approaches without any particularly difficult challenges. For example, project duration delay is often converted into cost by considering overhead costs and lost revenue opportunity costs which can be estimated without serious conceptual or practical difficulties.

But frequently the effective pursuit of all relevant goals means that more than one objective is actually extremely important, and it is not straightforward to deal with multiple objectives involving multiple attributes as well as multiple criteria for each attribute. While suitable metrics for some of these objectives may be readily available, other objectives may not be measurable without additional effort or cost, which may not be worthwhile, and it may not be feasible to measure some important objectives in any useful sense.

We need a conceptual framework to understand all the potentially relevant issues in all contexts which is as general as possible, used to design specific practical approaches which best suit the frameworks used to address goals–plans relationships in any particular circumstances. That is what this section is about.

The focus of this section is an appropriate *conceptual* framework for considering all the measurable or indirectly/partially measurable multiple objectives issues underlying an organisation's goals–plans framework for decision making. The approach taken is a core gateway concept.

This book associates the goals–plans framework with a goals–attributes–criteria hierarchy of objectives, implying criteria are the lowest level 'objectives' within attributes, and attributes are an intermediate level of objectives within goals, as indicated earlier. The concern in this section is multiple objectives at a criteria level for all relevant attributes and goals.

'Mathematical programming' is not used directly in operational terms anywhere in this book, but a 'goal programming' variant of mathematical programming is of importance as a central conceptual tool. This conceptual tool has direct operational implications in several chapters, and a goal programming perspective provides a useful 'what needs to be done' framework for this book as a whole. Even if you have never heard of mathematical programming, and you have very little inclination to confront mathematical approaches, the basic ideas needed for strategic clarity considered briefly in this section should make reasonable intuitive sense at an overview level.

Mathematical programming was developed initially from the input–output economic analysis used to replan the US economy for the 1940s war effort in a linear programming form. Linear programming evolved rapidly as computer capability increased into a well-developed set of planning tools used worldwide by the end of the 1960s. Quadratic and other non-linear forms soon followed.

One key idea which has been central to the use of any form of mathematical programming models in practice since the 1950s is the shadow price or shadow cost concept. Understanding the implications of this shadow price/cost concept is crucial.

Mathematical programming involves optimising a single 'objective function' subject to a set of 'constraints'. If the objective function measures 'expected reward' (e.g. expected profit) and it is being maximised, at the optimal solution each constraint has a 'shadow price' which defines the amount by which expected reward could be further increased if this constraint could be relaxed by one unit. If the objective function measures 'expected cost' and it is being minimised, at the optimal solution each constraint has a 'shadow cost' which defines the amount by which expected cost could be further reduced if this constraint could be relaxed by one unit. Some constraints are usefully seen as 'hard' because of physical reasons or because they operate as definitions that cannot be relaxed. Other constraints are usefully seen as 'soft' because they can be adjusted at a cost which is beyond the bounds of considerations embedded in the model. An immediate implication of practical importance is the relaxation of all soft constraints needs consideration post-optimisation, as a crucial form of sensitivity analysis. In practice, whether or not mathematical programming is employed, it is always important to analyse the relationship between the shadow price/cost and an assumed actual cost of relaxing all the soft constraints, adjusting constraints appropriately, as a form of sensitivity analysis comparable in some respects to the use of Figure 4.1 in a rather different framework for analysis.

The quadratic programming approach developed to deal with a mean–variance Markowitz portfolio management framework makes use of these ideas, the basis of the parameter k defining the optimal risk–return trade-off between E and V^2, discussed earlier in terms of maximising $E - kV^2$. In practice minimising V^2 is usually treated as the quadratic objective function, minimising V^2 subject to a constraint on E, using a set of assumed minimum values for E to define a set of optimal portfolios in mean-variance terms, each associated with a shadow price k. A classic, basic mean–variance Markowitz model involves one attribute decomposed into two criteria, expected outcome E and variance V^2.

Goal programming builds on this idea by providing a powerful general approach to multiple objective decision making. If there are n objectives, one objective is treated as the 'primary objective' and used to define the objective function, the choice being a matter of convenience. The other n − 1 objectives are treated as 'secondary objectives' and used to define constraints. In an iterative process, an initial 'best guess' is made of a suitable constraint level for each soft constraint associated with a secondary objective.

At the optimal solution the shadow price/cost associated with each secondary objective defines the trade-off between that objective and the primary objective. Each constraint defined by a secondary objective can be relaxed if this trade-off value seems too high and tightened if it seems too low. Sometimes even non-measurable objectives can be incorporated as constraints in this structure – simply constraining an option's feasibility if it violates an ethical objective for example. Furthermore, an iterative adjustment process can be initiated and then continued until convergence is achieved with a set of shadow price/cost values which the decision makers believe represent appropriate trade-offs between all criteria. Further still, 'too high' or 'too low' or 'about right' are ultimately a 'revealed preference' statement of appropriate trade-offs by the decision makers. Crucially:

1   *Whether or not goal programming is used explicitly, this framework can be associated with multiple objective decision making, and whether or not those making choices acknowledge the existence of this underlying goal programming framework and all the associated revealed preference trade-offs, they may be directly relevant. If it is not practical to use goal programming directly, which is usually the case, decision makers need a reasonably simple practical process for systematically seeking an appropriate approximation to the*

optimal trade-offs between all objectives visualised in shadow price or shadow cost terms, understanding what trade-off values are implied by the solution chosen and the relevant implications.

2   *Ignorance of the existence of this underlying framework and a failure to address a suitable approximate approach does not mean that a full set of shadow prices/costs addressing trade-offs between all relevant constraints does not exist. It means that those making the decisions do not know what the trade-offs are, and they are probably using inconsistent trade-offs for successive decisions, which implies inconsistent decision making. This may be seriously inept, and it should be seen as incompetent and avoided in all circumstances where the consistent use of appropriate trade-offs really matters.*

For example, in the safety and security context of Chapter 9 we know that all interested parties want to minimise fatalities on a railway system, but they also want to minimise costs. This implies revealed preference trade-offs between fatalities and cost generally referred to as 'the value of an avoided fatality' or 'the value of a prevented fatality'. A value of an avoided fatality concept based on a shadow cost and revealed preference interpretation should never be confused with a direct attempt to put a monetary value on a life in the way attempted by some early approaches to cost–benefit analysis. A failure to explicitly update the traditional cost–benefit analysis interpretations of the 'value of an avoidable fatality' concept using a shadow cost basis plus a revealed preference perspective is inept. Arguably it is also unethical, with ignorance not being an acceptable defence in a legal context or an acceptable excuse in a more general sense. The reasons are explored in Chapter 9.

As another example, in a discounted cash-flow context using NPV, if multiple objectives are involved, almost always the case, a goal programming perspective is imperative, for reasons explored in Chapter 7.

Traditional opportunity costs, which were in widespread common use well before mathematical programming was developed, can be viewed as a special case of shadow prices or costs, a useful way to embed opportunity costs in a single comprehensive framework for all relevant multiple objective trade-offs. Before the development of shadow price/cost concepts, opportunity costs were sometimes explicitly associated with constraints in a calculus framework, implying a comparable mathematical foundation. This kind of simple traditional opportunity cost plays a key role in Chapter 5, and variants of this general goal programming framework at various levels of sophistication between those of Chapters 5 and 9 are used in Chapters 6, 7 and 8.

This book will not use a goal programming approach in terms of direct operational use of mathematical programming algorithms, but it will use a goal programming perspective in a mathematical programming conceptual framework in conjunction with a revealed preference interpretation of shadow prices or costs at a conceptual level with operational implications. This is an extremely valuable conceptual framework, even if some important objectives are not measurable. It is the most general and powerful *conceptual* framework for thinking about and framing *operational* approaches to multiple objectives decision making which keep it simple systematically that I am aware of. That is the reason it is a foundation level EP conceptual tool and a key component of the EP toolset. If you are not familiar with mathematical programming and would like an introduction which relates mathematical programming to separability concepts without getting too technical, see *Management for Engineers* (Chapman, Cooper and Page, 1987), an introductory level textbook which includes an annotated list of references to many of the key classical mathematical programming texts. For an overview of goal programming, see Tamiz, Jones and Romero (1998).

Whenever the term 'revealed preferences' is used in this book, usually in a shadow price or cost context, a plain English interpretation will suffice, and the implications of more technical interpretations will be illustrated when relevant using numerical examples. However, you may find an understanding of the nature of the underlying concerns addressed by technical meanings useful. Economists who use 'preference' functions (also called 'utility' functions) to provide a theoretical basis for the 'demand equations' which are used to predict consumer behaviour sometimes use the term '*revealed* preferences'. They do so to formally acknowledge that the preferences of consumers (purchasers) revealed by marketplace responses to price and income changes reflect the collective behaviour of a set of people whose individual preference functions cannot be combined mathematically in any meaningful way, as demonstrated by Arrow's 'impossibility theorem'. Chapman (1975) discusses some of this literature, and the use of revealed preferences for decision making in the context of a pairwise separability approach to demand analysis. When an organisation's board members sanction any decision involving trade-offs, they always reveal *collective* preferences (whether or not they are prepared to acknowledge this fact) which cannot be seen as a simple combination of individual preferences, and operational management of the implications involves practical issues of importance in some contexts. For example, in Chapter 9 the shadow costs revealed by the decisions sanctioned by the board are the board's *collective* revealed preferences, in the sense that the board has collectively agreed to the implied trade-offs between attributes like money and avoided fatalities plus avoided injuries, but this does not mean a simple average of individual preferences is involved, with very useful implications which are developed in Chapter 9. You may also find it useful to understand that all preference or utility functions employed by economists in contexts like demand theory are very different from the utility functions used in decision analysis texts like Raiffa (1968) and Keeney and Raiffa (1976), and some of the implications are explored in Chapman and Ward (2002).

Seeking effective low clarity views of trade-offs

The high clarity provided by the decision diagrams illustrated by Figures 3.6 and 3.7 is often very useful. But if risk–reward criteria trade-offs in terms of attributes like cost are not the only concern, and it may be important to consider further attributes at low levels of clarity, using a lower clarity decision diagram like Figure 4.3 may be a more opportunity efficient tool.

Figure 4.3 was initially developed in the mid-1980s to explain how such situations might be approached for public seminar purposes – courses provided by commercial professional training organisations which I gave in London initially, internationally later. They were then used for follow-on in-house courses for client organisations. For example, IBM made extensive use of variants of Figure 4.3 in the bidding context used for its Forum 2 programme case studies and subsequent bidding process development, and examples based on these uses are employed in Chapter 6. Low clarity decision diagrams comparable to Figure 4.3 are now a widely used component of the EP toolset.

When Figure 4.3 was first used, the illustrative example employed involved replacing a photocopier. In the mid-1980s, as a newly appointed head of a university academic department, replacing the department's photocopier was one of the first departmental decisions to be made; the need for simple decision diagrams using the format of Figure 4.3 arose at about the same time, and 'the photocopier problem' seemed a useful story to illustrate the low clarity decision diagram concept.

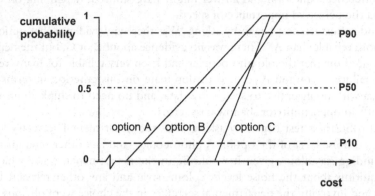

Figure 4.3 Decision diagram: comparison of options A, B, and C.

The photocopier story will be told as a tale – in reality, my approach was less clarity efficient and more time-consuming. The version of the tale provided here builds on a version used for *The Wiley Encyclopaedia of Operations Research and Management Science* (Chapman and Harwood, 2011) to provide a requested definition of 'optimal risk taking and risk-mitigation'.

The tale begins when my department's only photocopier failed terminally. The service engineer delivering the bad news explained that a new photocopier with appropriate features from his firm could probably be delivered within a few days on a new five year contract. This would involve a rental cost of £x per month plus a servicing charge of £y per copy.

The departmental secretary provided records showing copy numbers by months for recent years. This historical record was projected forward for five years, as the basis for an approximate P10–P90 range estimate for a nominal five year planning horizon defined by the contract duration. The Figure 4.3 axes were constructed, with the cost scale indicating total cost over the five year contract period. The P10–P90 values were then used along with the service engineer's £x per month and £y per copy contract explanation to obtain the 'option A' line shown in Figure 4.3. Telephoning two alternative photocopier suppliers revealed identical contract structures for photocopiers with comparable features. But the alternative suppliers had higher £x rates and lower £y rates. These rates were used to plot the 'option B' and 'option C' lines in Figure 4.3.

Contract cost was assumed to be the only concern as an initial working assumption, so option A was the only risk efficient choice, by a significant margin. This was clearly illustrated in stochastic dominance terms in Figure 4.3, because the line portraying option A was well to the left of the lines for options B and C. However, testing the robustness of the working assumption that cost as currently measured was the only relevant objective was obviously essential.

The premise that copying speed might matter was tested first. This robustness test began by asking, 'Was the copying speed of option A faster than that of options B and C?' It was faster than both – so option A dominated on this criterion too. No more effort was required in terms of the initial working assumption that speed did not matter. Had option A been significantly slower than B or C, then the cost of the additional lost time might have been estimated in opportunity cost terms, but a simple 'Was the contract cost difference worth the speed difference?' question and answer might have sufficed, depending on the figures involved and the perceived importance of speed.

The second robustness test began by asking 'Was there any evidence that options B or C might be more reliable than A?' There was no evidence about B or C, but the departmental secretary assured me that the old photocopier had been very reliable for many years before its terminal failure, so option A seemed to dominate on this criterion in terms of readily available data with no incentive to seek more data, and no need to think about reliability–cost trade-offs in opportunity or shadow cost terms.

The third robustness test began by asking 'Was the departmental secretary happy with the anticipated noise level of the option A photocopier, and any other relevant features or aspects, including its colour, given it would be in the departmental office which was her office?' Enquiring about the noise levels, colour, style and any other relevant features of the options and involving the departmental secretary in the choice were obvious matters of courtesy. It suits the flow of the tale to introduce these issues now, but in fact, this would have been the best place to start, including asking her at the outset if there were any issues other than those considered earlier which she thought ought to be explored. She was better placed to see some relevant forthcoming technology and organisational changes than I was. She was also the most directly interested party, and her views were crucial. If colour or style or noise or some combination of these issues mattered, Figure 4.3 was still relevant, but the attributes of interest to the departmental secretary would need very careful explicit attention, and if they were important enough they might prove the dominant concerns in shadow cost terms. She liked the option A features on all counts, so it remained the obvious choice, without the need to make extensive comparisons with B and C.

The fourth robustness test began by asking 'Could the supplier of option A actually deliver a new photocopier in a few days?' If several months might be involved, and option A was now viewed as non-feasible, the choice might move to B or C. Both were risk efficient assuming A was not available – B involved a lower expected outcome cost than C but a higher level of risk, indicated by the curves crossing above the expected values (associated with a lower £x rate but a higher £y rate, so the outcome was more variable). However, the additional cost 'risk' associated with option B relative to C was really just 'noise' – it was not worth worrying about.

With new supplier reliability now recognised as a potentially important issue, a valuable new option required identification – the option A supplier making an interim machine available until the ordered one could be delivered. More generally, we are always free to think about new options if the current set of options seems unsatisfactory, an important fall-back contingency planning option to always keep in mind. It may help you to remember the availability of this option if you always include a residual 'any other options we have not yet considered' possibility, another closure with completeness concept.

One key point this tale should make clear in Figure 4.3 is a simple low clarity decision diagram version of Figures 3.6 and 3.7, but it provides all the clarity needed in this relatively simple context. Another important closely coupled message from this tale is if you are used to using the low clarity decision diagram approach of Figure 4.3 and visualising range estimates associated with P50 expected values, you do not even need to draw Figure 4.3 to visualise the expected cost and cost risk trade-offs involved. A related key issue this tale should clarify is if risk is just noise for some attributes, then just using expected values is a very important shortcut. Knowing that this is the case in advance improves clarity efficiency and improves opportunity efficiency by capturing an important opportunity to achieve more insight for less effort/cost.

A further key learning point for you to take from this tale is that variability and risk should *never* be confused – option A involves significantly *greater* contract cost variability than B or C but much *less* risk. This is clearly demonstrated in Figure 4.3 by the different slopes but the large gap between the curves for options A and B or C, because the low £x rate for option A more than neutralises the cost variability driven by the higher £y rate for option A. This addresses a complication with Markowitz's mean–variance approach which he understood very clearly, but many people using his approach do not. Variance is *never* an appropriate direct measure of risk. A closely coupled issue is variance is only an appropriate *surrogate* measure of risk *given* a particular assumed expected outcome and *given* probability distributions with the same shape can be assumed.

Yet another key point is the potentially crucial importance of non-measurable issues, like the implications of the photocopier's colour or style. They need consideration in relation to what can be measured, with questions like 'If option B is the preferred choice in terms of a set of non-measurable advantages and disadvantages concisely expressed in verbal terms, is the contract cost difference between options A and B worth it?' If the choice is a close call, this may suggest further effort and care would be worthwhile. The choice made reveals preferences, a very simple example of a revealed preference interpretation involving a shadow price/cost associated with insisting on the preferred colour by constraining the option choice.

All the key learning points developed in this section were central to the IBM culture change programme discussed in Chapter 3 which underlies the tale of Chapter 6. They also underlie all the other Part 2 chapters. More generally, what is crucial is:

1 starting with a simple approach which can address more complexity whenever doing so looks worthwhile;
2 comprehensive, effective and efficient assessment of robustness for the simple approach employed initially, testing all relevant working assumptions to decide whether more clarity is worthwhile;
3 seeking more clarity of the kind needed when and where it is needed; and
4 a possible expansion of the option set, with creativity an essential capability.

The starting point for any particular analysis will always be context specific, but the conceptual framework drawn on should be general. Chapter 6 illustrates the use of very similar variants of the Figure 4.3 approach. Chapter 7 draws in Figures 3.6 and 3.7, the high clarity versions. Chapters 8 and 9 build on both.

A generalisation of the clarified-dominance concept introduced in Chapter 3 involves robustness testing of the kind just discussed *before* asserting that 'clarified dominance' *in terms of all relevant objectives* is involved.

Simple but effective strategies for dealing with multiple objectives

The last section used one simple example to illustrate several general strategies for seeking clarity efficient approaches to multiple objectives. In practice, those leading an EP approach need a simple but effective operational how to do it toolset of such strategies, and at a what needs to be done level you may find an initial feel for the nature of these strategies useful now, to provide a base to build on in Part 2. For example, one useful strategy involves starting by assuming that an analysis based on the primary objective will provide a solution which dominates in terms of all secondary objectives. Testing the robustness of this assumption for each relevant secondary objective has to follow, ensuring that no objectives that matter are overlooked, even if they are difficult to measure or completely impossible to measure.

A central concern when seeking opportunity efficiency is always testing the robustness of a clarified dominance hypothesis by asking the question, 'Is it worth trying to measure anything else before we consider making a decision, bearing in mind the costs and benefits of more measurement, and are there any concerns which need qualitative attention whether or not they are measurable?'

If any potentially important further objective is not measurable (like photocopier colour or style as perceived by the departmental secretary), the only choice may be to look at the difference in cost and ask, 'Is the difference worth it?' in consultation with all relevant parties, employing a consultation process that all relevant parties will trust.

If any potentially important further objective is measurable, it can be important to assess whether doing so is worthwhile. An opportunity cost might be estimated (like the value of the time wasted because of a slower photocopier) to extend what the primary objective measures. But it may be simpler and more effective to just look at the difference (in cost and speed/time in the photocopier case) and make a judgement without expending effort decomposing the associated uncertainty.

We always need to make sensible judgements based on what has been measured and what has not been measured but might be important.

This is a very short section, but the issues addressed are important, and you can build on the examples provided during the rest of this book and via your own experience.

For those interested in the more technical concerns, applying this approach in a complex context is central to a journal paper (Chapman, Cooper, Debelius, and Pecora, 1985) which discusses extensive analysis of a single very important decision for the Fluor Corporation by a team of about 30 Acres consultants over a period of several months.

A very dangerous myth and a closely coupled bias

This book is about systematic *qualitative* analysis and systematic *quantitative* analysis, predominantly in terms of their joint use. Quantitative analysis starts gently in Chapter 5, but it becomes reasonably sophisticated halfway through Chapter 6. Chapter 7 is focused on qualitative analysis issues, but the discussion builds on the quantitative analysis discussions of Chapters 3 and 4. Chapter 8 is more quantitative than most corporate strategic planning before a strong emphasis on qualitative analysis issues. Chapter 9 pushes quantitative analysis about as far as it can go in a safety context at a what needs to be done level. The discussion throughout Part 2 is focused on what needs to be done, not tactical quantitative analysis details that you do not need for strategic clarity. However, the value of useful quantitative analysis underpinned by appropriate qualitative analysis is championed by this book, while rationing the discussion of how to do it tactics to the minimum needed for strategic clarity.

From an EP perspective it is very important to appreciate that whatever the level of sophistication of the quantitative and qualitative analysis being used, there are important limitations on both what can be measured in quantitative analysis terms and what can even be considered in purely qualitative terms in a systematic formal manner.

At a strategic clarity level, it is crucial that *everybody* in any organisation you care about understands that the mantra 'what cannot be measured cannot be managed' is a *very* dangerous myth with a closely coupled bias towards making decisions in terms of objectives limited to easily measured criteria. Those who subscribe to any variant of this mantra are using a framing assumption which should not be tolerated. If they hold positions of power and influence, they may be seriously dangerous. If it is not feasible to enlighten them, they should be contested and their influence constrained in an effective manner before they do too much damage, if this is feasible. They are *not* pushing a well-founded practical mantra, they are pushing a very dangerous myth, and the difference matters greatly. Arguably this should be self-evident in most circumstances that really matter. But many powerful and influential people seem to buy into the myth, some because it suits hidden agendas which they want to keep hidden, some because they genuinely seem to have been seduced by numbers, and some because they seem to implicitly assume that no really serious damage will be done by what they see as a helpful focus on measurable attributes and quantitative evidence without fully understanding the implications or the alternatives.

Such people can be an important capability-culture risk to the best interests of everyone else. Responding to the risks they create may require enlightened planning and management to avoid serious organisational misjudgements.

'What cannot be measured cannot be managed' is often promoted and sometimes even mandated as part of a bundle of notions using the acronym SMART as a contraction of underlying definitions like 'Specific, Measurable, Achievable, Relevant, and Time-framed'. There is clearly *potential* merit in an *initial* focus on SMART concerns in this sense, but at the very least there is also a clear need to recognise that *any* focus on measurable separate components demands a 'closure with completeness' component involving a synthesis of what has been addressed within a SMART framework *plus everything else which really matters*. If this is not done *in a way which includes non-measurable concerns* there will be an obvious bias towards attributes which are measurable. This is likely to involve immediate errors of judgement. Arguably even more serious, people or organisations whose performance is judged based on a limited set of easily measurable attributes will be encouraged to change their behaviour, ignoring attributes which cannot be measured or are just difficult to measure. There is an endemic and seriously damaging bias towards the use of attributes which are easily measurable even when people are well aware they do not tell the whole story and would not even consider mandating a SMART approach.

The primary reason for raising these issues now is explicitly and emphatically avoiding the impression that EP means quantification is essential or central. Often quantification is not worthwhile if a qualitative analysis is convincing. Frequently further quantification is not worthwhile if partial quantification plus appropriate further qualitative analysis is convincing. Crucially, whatever the level of formal quantitative analysis, management decision making almost always also needs further qualitative analysis plus sound well-grounded intuition and informal planning.

The photocopier example used to explain Figure 4.3 emphasised objectives which could not be measured as well as objectives which it was not worth measuring in a simple context. The last section generalised these approaches.

Looking back to Chapter 2, the role in the UP of the capability-culture concept is focused on concerns which include *non-measurable or difficult to measure* issues like team-working skills plus the right stuff.

Judged from an EP perspective, anyone who seriously argues 'what cannot be measured cannot be managed' is using an unacceptable framing assumption because *'what cannot be measured directly but matters actually needs VERY special care and attention to ensure effective treatment'*. Capability-culture issues are obvious illustrative example concerns, but there are many others.

A multiple objectives approach to planning the planning

The last four sections have addressed formal consideration of multiple objectives going beyond a single primary attribute of interest. From the beginning of any planning process, clarity about multiple criteria associated with a primary attribute plus further clarity about more than one attribute is almost always needed. Sometimes these multiple attributes are associated with very different kinds of goals, sometimes key goals have priorities for different players which are radically different, and sometimes one player's gains in terms of a key goal are another player's loss. The general issue is 'For each relevant multiple attribute, should we attempt *formal* consideration as part of the planning process, or are informal planning judgements, perhaps coupled to formal or informal negotiations, more likely to prove appropriate?'

The need for formality when addressing important issues is a concern requiring explicit planning attention. It is one of several non-measurable aspects of an extensive set of higher-order 'planning the planning' concerns which need explicit care and attention.

The select and focus phase of the UP of Figure 2.1 involves separation of the formal plus informal planning the planning phases from all the other UP phases. It provides a basis for treating the overall management of a UP as a project which needs planning in its own right. This project planning framework for planning the planning is used for all Part 2 chapters, with some tailoring to specific contexts. A brief overview of some implications is useful now. It provides a conceptual background for Part 2 to be put to work from the outset of Chapter 5.

Consider Figure 4.4, a bar chart (Gantt chart) portraying how the first complete pass through the UP of Figure 2.1 might be visualised and planned.

Figure 4.4 portrays precedence and timing relationships in a way many project planners would have understood a century ago, following the promotion of this bar chart format by Henry Gantt as part of the Scientific Management movement associated with Frederick Taylor (1911).

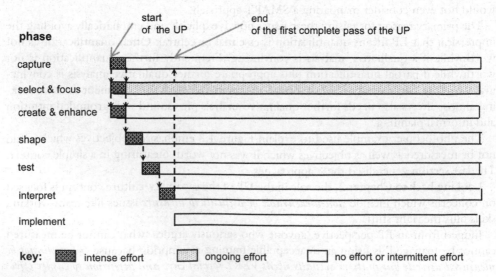

Figure 4.4 An example bar chart (Gantt chart) for planning the first pass of the UP shown in Figure 2.1.

Figure 4.4 includes the current practice option of 'linked bar chart' dotted arrows used to clarify precedence relationships, usually implicit a century ago. Precedence relationships define what activities must follow or precede other activities and what can proceed in parallel. For example, as suggested in Chapter 2 in slightly different terms, Figure 4.4 used as a supplement to Figure 2.1 implies:

1　the select and focus (the process) phase cannot start until the capture (the context) phase has started, but the first pass through the capture phase does not need to be completed before moving on to start the select and focus phase;

2　the create and enhance (the plans) phase cannot start until the select and focus (the process) phase has been started, but the first pass through the select and focus phase does not need completing before moving on to start the create and enhance phase;

3　it is generally useful to take a flexible approach to proceeding with the first three phases, employing frequent jumps among these phases and unplanned partial iterations until initial plans have been created and enhanced, pursuing these three phases in parallel in formal planning terms as assumed in the portrayal of Figure 4.4;

4　before starting to shape the plans, finishing a first complete pass through the capture, select and focus, and create and enhance phases as an integrated trio is a sound practical strategy;

5　testing the plans in the formal terms portrayed in Figure 4.4 has to follow shaping the plans, although informal testing within each phase with potential loops back as a result is clearly sensible;

6　interpreting the plans plus the test phase analysis of all relevant assumptions has to be completed before looping back for a second pass through the process as a whole; and

7　it is usually useful to *plan* to treat the fourth, fifth, and sixth phases in series, although exceptionally using loops back prior to the first complete pass may be convenient.

The 'start-to-start' and 'finish-to-finish' precedence relationships which Figure 4.4 uses for the first three phases assume that these phases are pursued in parallel for formal planning purposes, but in practice, an informal unplanned iterative structure within these three phases is anticipated, as indicated less explicitly when discussing Figure 2.1 in Chapter 2. The 'finish-to-start' precedence relationships for the following phases imply a somewhat different approach, also indicated when discussing Figure 2.1. Joint use of these different precedence relationships as portrayed in Figure 4.4 is a very useful portrayal of the subtle nature of the way the first pass of the process might be pursued which Figure 2.1 facilitates but does not emphasise. Further passes are anticipated in Figure 4.4, building on earlier results, but only the first pass has been formally planned.

It is very useful to see managing a UP or any SP developed via a UP based approach as a form of project management. The seven phases of the UP of Figures 2.1 and 4.4 can be visualised as project activities, and we can manage the UP phases as a project. If we see all other processes in a comparable framework, as is the case in Chapters 6 and 7, we can generalise this idea. Indeed, the select and focus the process phase of the UP of Figure 2.1 was a generalisation of the focus the process phase explored in Chapter 7.

Furthermore, it is useful to see all project management tools *which have been explicitly geared to contexts involving significant uncertainty* as directly relevant to process management, which means everything addressed in Chapter 7 of this book can be applied to managing the UP associated with Chapter 2 in all its Part 2 roles.

One important implication of this is the seven Ws concept which is central to the Chapter 7 process means we need to start the select and focus phase by asking questions about who is involved in the analysis process, as well as who is involved in the context being addressed, and what objectives are relevant from the point of view of all the key parties in both groups. This has to define and shape the deliverables of the 'project' associated with using a UP. Multiple objectives for a UP are inevitable, and aligning the objectives of multiple parties in both groups is crucial.

As an illustration of the subtle implications of the different interests of the team managing the planning process and the much broader set of interests of all people involved in a planning context, if I am hired as a consultant by a project manager to help him or her deal with a project and their board, my mandate is clear, provided they are not engaged in strategic misrepresentation. But this situation is different from being hired by a project manager's board to deal with the same project and its project manager, especially if the project manager is engaged in strategic misrepresentation. And both may be very different from being hired by a regulator or another third party concerned about what the organisation is planning to do via this particular project. These kinds of differences may not matter in some contexts, but they can be crucial.

More generally, at the outset of the use of any UP driven process, a key issue is what are the objectives of all the players involved in shaping the planning exercise, the wider set of all the players involved in context of what is being analysed, and how can we best begin and then evolve the analysis process to reflect all relevant goals with appropriate trade-offs at all levels in all of the goals–plans relationship frameworks needing attention.

A key strategy for dealing with multiple objectives

A key strategy for dealing with multiple objectives is seeking an alignment of objectives for all the interested parties which will avoid the need to address trade-offs in formal planning terms. This avoids having to deal with trade-offs which are difficult to manage, and it may also help to avoid failures of trust, gaming behaviour and serious breakdowns in relationships.

This might be seen as 'resolving' or 'dissolving' potential problems instead of 'solving' them, a useful aspect of some soft systems strategies. But a more helpful perspective is avoiding creating problems in the first place. Seeking alignment of objectives at the outset involves prevention instead of cure. Furthermore, it can be even more useful to see the potential problems arising from a failure to align objectives as just the symptoms of a deeper mess associated with a need for collaborative approaches as a very general aspect of seeking opportunity efficiency.

Put simply, if crudely, if the broad basis of how a cake will be shared equitably can be agreed on in advance, and everyone then concentrates on making the cake as big as possible, with no 'free riders', quibbling about the portions served later should less of an issue. For this strategy to work, well-founded trust has to be an explicit early central goal, pursued effectively throughout to achieve ongoing alignment of all the other goals. Variants of this strategy are involved in all Part 2 tales.

Informal treatment of all objectives not addressed formally

Before finishing Part 1 and moving on to Part 2, it is worth briefly reflecting upon and emphasising a particularly important implication of the EP framework noted earlier:

> *If any aspects of planning are not addressed in formal terms,*
> *they will need effective informal treatment;*

otherwise, they will be overlooked,
with no understanding of the implications;
they will not go away,
and if they are important this will matter.

One key role of the capability-culture concept is considering and dealing with the implications. Looking back to the last two sections, the way the UP of Figures 2.1 and 4.4 or comparable equivalents are used clearly involves a lot of informal planning, and the quality of that informal planning matters a great deal. That quality will depend on the capability and culture of all the people involved in the process, not just those leading the process, although the leadership provided is crucial.

Looking back to the photocopier tale, sometimes very simple formal treatment of what can be easily structured, with some components measured, facilitates consideration of complexity which matters even though that complexity is not worth measuring (like the relative photocopier speed issue), or it is simply impossible to measure (like the photocopier style and colour issue).

At a more general level, looking back to the multiple objectives discussion in a goal programming framework, dealing with multiple objectives which need formal treatment can clearly be very complex and exceedingly difficult. However, if the issues involved are not treated formally in a planning framework that all interested parties understand and trust, they are going to have to be treated informally by all the decision makers responsible for both recommending and approving the choices. They are not going to go away because they are 'too difficult'. If they are not treated explicitly in formal or informal terms, they are being ignored.

The nature of the 'expertise' required in many important decision-making areas includes tactic knowledge and implicit decision-making skills which can be virtually impossible to assess or test directly. However, if key issues are 'left to the experts', it may be very dangerous to assume that these experts have all the necessary expertise *and* their objectives are fully aligned with all other relevant parties. These assumptions certainly need testing as and when this is feasible in whatever ways are feasible.

A 'menu view' of decision-making process goals

A menu view of decision-making process goals when using any process based on the UP of Figures 2.1 and 4.4 is the concern of this final section in Chapter 4. Its role is a form of synthesis of all of the EP foundation concepts developed in Part 1 which you may find useful as a basis for starting Part 2.

The 1980s public seminars which I provided of the kind the director of engineering of National Power attended to learn about SCERT based approaches concluded with a slide which listed key 'benefits' if this kind of approach to planning was used. By the mid-1990s, based on the evolving thinking behind the first edition of *Project Risk Management* (Chapman and Ward, 1997), this list of benefits was reframed as a much richer list of 'potential objectives'. The 'menu of potential goals' approach used in this section further generalises in the EP framework of this book.

Using an EP goals–plans relationship structure as a useful starting point framework, the potential goals of any organisation need interpretation as a menu in the sense that if an organisation adopts the SP for projects of Chapter 7 or any of the other applications of the UP illustrated in Part 2, it is important to consciously choose to emphasise or not the benefits which the particular context requires on each application occasion, treating the benefits of particular interest as explicit key goals. The achievement of all other goals should be treated as useful spin-offs to the extent that they come at no extra cost (they have a zero shadow cost). They are part of the bundled product which as a whole suits the organisation in this context. They may need to become important goals to be explicitly pursued on later passes, but they are not an explicit priority on the early passes of an analysis of what changes need to be made to how the organisation operates.

This is in part a multiple goals perspective on what the 'focus phase' prototype of the more general UP select and focus the process phase has always been about, but greater clarity and a wider scope have emerged over time.

The key potential goals for all variants of decision-making processes grounded on a UP are:

1   clarity, risk and opportunity efficiency in the sense is developed so far;
2   associated and additional culture changes are geared to the context;
3   the ABCs of targets and expectations are clarified and extended;
4   communication in overall terms is emphasised in ways which suit the context;
5   bottom-up communication is encouraged and facilitated when appropriate;
6   creativity and satisfaction (fun) are used as effective objectives;
7   corporate learning and knowledge are made explicit;
8   better linkages exist among operations, project, and corporate management; and
9   an opportunity management appetite is stimulated via opportunity efficiency.

All Part 2 chapters involve building on the point 1 concepts outlined so far, plus all issues associated with points 2 through 9, further enhanced by an accumulated understanding of all aspects of opportunity efficiency.

Before we conclude Part 1, looking at points 2 through 9 on a point-by-point basis may enhance your understanding of where this book is going.

Associated and additional culture changes are geared to the context

Moving a corporate culture towards taking more risk when that is appropriate as discussed in Chapter 3 in terms of the IBM Forum 2 programme is a key issue addressed in Chapter 6. But many other culture changes are addressed in Chapter 6, and all other Part 2 chapters illustrate further corporate culture changes which may be relevant to your organisation. For example, the culture in the organisation involved in Chapter 5 was grounded on the premise 'we are a small manufacturing business in a particular sector'. Collective use of a UP concept by all relevant managers tested the implicit working assumptions involved, and began to create a new culture which generated plans based on much broader premises, like 'we might become a marketing organisation in a bigger sector, manufacturing only some of what we sell, although that might involve increasing current production capacity as well as marketing a wider range of products with some products manufactured by other organisations'.

The ABCs of targets and expectations are clarified and extended

In Chapter 3 William was encouraged to understand why it was important to understand the basic ABCs of targets and distinguish between aspirational targets, balanced targets equal to expected values, and commitment targets. Expected values that might or might not be conditional were also explored. Some of these ideas were further developed in the discussion with Peter, in particular, relating them to the implications of formal as well as informal contingency planning.

Feedback from BP project managers I worked with in the 1970s and 1980s, and many other client groups since, suggests that in all comparable contexts the implications can be of enormous importance, because of the improvement in clarity of communication plus well-founded trust between people charged with doing work at various levels. The implications include changes in governance processes at all relevant levels built on the resulting mutual understanding and trust. These lessons are directly embedded in the tale of Chapter 7 and indirectly in all the other Part 2 chapters.

In Chapter 8 the balanced target and expected value distinction is explored, in terms of when to plan to have a new electricity generation capability available if the 'penalty function' associated with being early or late is asymmetric. The ideas involved are often useful even in very simple contexts, sometimes involving purely informal planning, like adding half an hour or more to the expected time to get to an airport to catch a flight you do not want to miss.

Clarity about the ABCs of targets and expectations can be simple in other contexts in different ways, or much more complex, and dealing effectively with both can be very important. For example, if someone you report to asks how much something will cost and you know that a simple one value estimate is all they will listen to, adding an appropriate level of contingency to the expected value to define a commitment target is the only sensible response. But in the very different and complex safety and security assessment context of Chapter 9 a more sophisticated approach is required. Everyone involved in safety and security management contexts involving potential low probability but high impact incidents needs to understand that zero fatalities are always an appropriate aspirational target, the actual level of fatalities in any given year should *usually* be well below the expected level of fatalities because of the asymmetric distributions involved, and the commitments made to customers, the public, and regulators need to be very carefully thought through and presented. Simply adding a contingency allowance to the expected outcome as a published 'commitment target' for safety in this kind of context is not a sensible idea, failing to be honest or looking inept can be extremely serious, and muddled thinking about this issue can be directly instrumental in corporate failure.

Communication in overall terms is emphasised in ways which suit the context

Communication has a crucial role in all planning, and fully developing all relevant aspects of communication is an important EP concern which has to be at least partially driven by the context. Communication between project managers and the board within BP was clearly enhanced significantly by the use of tools like Figures 3.5 through 3.8, 4.1 and 4.2. Communication facilitated by EP tools in this way will be emphasised in all Part 2 tales. Often other organisations are involved. Usually what needs communication is reasonably straightforward to deal with if a complete EP toolset is available, with tools discussed in Part 1 playing a central role. But issues driven by capability-culture concerns which are complex and somewhat different need particular attention in the later portions of the tale of Chapter 8. Communication by the electricity utility involved with customers, contractors, and potential collaborators aimed at transforming the fundamentals of the business model become central. Communication about ethical issues becomes central in Chapter 9. When communication beyond the usual bounds of corporate communication is an issue it may be exceptionally important, in extreme cases a corporate survival issue.

Bottom-up communication is encouraged and facilitated when appropriate

In the 1980s, one Acres consultancy assignment for Gulf Canada involved being contracted to provide advice on an appropriate process for estimating the cost of the Hibernia project. This project involved a planned offshore 'gravity' platform for the production of oil off the east coast of Canada, in a sea area frequented by icebergs. In the process of sizing the uncertainty sources in prototype minimum clarity terms to think about how a more detailed cost estimation process might work, I explored broader context issues by talking to a range of Gulf personnel on an informal basis as part of a more general exploration of the context. My conversations with oil reservoir engineers and oil market experts led me to the view that given what all the relevant Gulf staff knew at that time about oil volume uncertainty, plus oil price uncertainty when the oil came to market, plus cost uncertainty for the gravity structure, Gulf really ought to look more closely at a 'ship-shape' alternative to the gravity platform, or drill more exploratory wells before proceeding.

The gravity structure approach involved relatively high capital cost coupled to low operating cost, high safety, and high oil production output levels. It also needed East Coast Canadian labour to construct it (with coupled political and other benefits). These were key reasons why it was preferred. The ship-shape approach might use an existing oil tanker to provide a floating oil production facility over a subsea well. Icebergs would be avoided by removing the ship-shape, interrupting production, with revenue effects involving contractual implications for prices as well as oil production volume impacts. Icebergs would be managed via high-powered tugs when needed if the gravity structure was used, having designed the gravity structure to cope with most of the icebergs anticipated.

The problem with proceeding with the gravity structure without drilling more exploratory wells was a scenario involving a plausible minimum oil volume *plus* a plausible minimum oil price when the oil came to market *plus* a plausible maximum capital cost for the gravity structure. Current plan assumptions meant that the financial implications of this scenario involving three concurrent downside variability aspects needed explicit attention, and prudence was likely to suggest reducing the risk associated with this scenario.

This was not the advice contracted for, and it was not what the senior Gulf managers I reported to wanted to hear. But they acted on it, and their actions proved important. The advice provided was based on letting the members of senior management know what their own staff knew in a structured form they could act on, a form of bottom-up communication which can be invaluable. In principle, organisations should not need consultants to tell them what they already know, although in practice they often do, sometimes simply because communication structures linking different concerns addressed by different people are not in place.

The key message to take away from this story is organisations need to both encourage and facilitate structured bottom-up communication which may not take place unless a systematic approach to this issue is an explicit part of the agenda, a capability-culture concern with various degrees of importance in each Part 2 chapter. Its importance, and the need to address it explicitly, was a key message I took away from many of my Acres projects.

Creativity and satisfaction (fun) are used as effective objectives

One of the reasons I greatly enjoyed working with Acres in Canada and the US was the ethos of creativity and 'fun' in the sense of working with interesting people doing interesting things that mattered. It was a conscious and explicit part of the Acres 'business model', explicitly articulated by Oskar Sigvaldason, my head of department while I worked with Acres. Its purpose was attracting and keeping good people who would help to generate and deliver high quality work. The explicit belief was this would generate immediate profit plus more interesting work, which, in turn, would attract more good people and interesting work, an explicit use of the notion of seeking 'virtuous circles' and avoiding 'vicious circles'.

If your organisation wants to use this approach it needs to be designed into the approaches employed. An important agenda item for all those engaged in designing decision-making processes, or managing the 'select and focus the process' phase equivalent, is keeping the processes challenging and interesting to attract and keep good people who are capable of doing a good job.

The quality of the people attracted and retained may matter much more than anything else which is within the control of the organisation's management decision makers. This idea is in the background, not up front or explicit, in all Part 2 chapters, but it matters greatly. At a what needs to be done level it is almost always important, and strategic clarity about the basis of how to do it effectively is a crucial senior management capability.

Corporate learning and knowledge capture are made explicit

The first live SCERT application for a BP project took about six months, with a full-time BP facilitator/modeller, my help about half time, plus significant input from the project team, and this built upon an extensive earlier process development stage revisiting an earlier project. Within about two years, comparable studies were taking about 6 weeks, with no direct involvement from me.

Part of this change was going down a learning curve in terms of process development and embedding process implementation skills. BP recognised the importance of this by promoting the facilitator/modeller and keeping him in this role with managerial responsibility for a growing team servicing a rapidly growing portfolio of projects and then restructuring his team plus the estimating and planning groups as a whole.

Another part of this change was all the staff involved benefitting from the way corporate knowledge about offshore oil and gas projects was captured. As one of the BP programme managers put it, they did not have to 'keep reinventing the wheel'. This, too, was recognised by BP on a widespread basis and enhanced by standards associated with the documentation of work in progress as well as reviews. For example, when a major offshore project was decomposed into about 30 activities, like 'laying the pipeline', 'building the platform', and so on, each activity was numbered and concisely documented so everyone involved could refer to a common understanding of what was included and what was excluded. Each specific source of uncertainty treated separately was numbered within the activity, as in 3.2 for the second source in the third activity, and associated with a paragraph or more concisely indicating what was included and excluded. Each response to these primary sources was numbered within this structure, as in 3.2.1 for the first specific response to the second source within the third activity. Secondary sources of uncertainty and responses continued this numbering system hierarchy. This word-processed text form of information was kept updated and accessible. Together with the graphical associated information using Figure 4.2 source-response diagram formats, plus later graphical sensitivity diagrams and decision diagrams, it provided an effective audit trail of how and why decisions were made. All this information also provided a valuable knowledge capture facility, useful for new staff joining an ongoing project as well as staff beginning a new project with some common features.

Expertise and learning are very valuable assets for organisations, an important part of their capability-culture asset set. Opportunity efficiency includes capturing this knowledge and making ongoing use of it in the most effective and efficient manner possible.

Better linkages exist among operations, project and corporate management

Better linkages among operations management concerns, project management concerns and corporate strategy concerns ought to be a clear and explicit goal for all aspects of enlightened planning, a core aspect of the opportunity efficiency concept which opportunity management seeks. All Part 2 chapters demonstrate in outline what this implies.

An opportunity management appetite is stimulated via opportunity efficiency

The ultimate goal of this book as a whole is an enhanced appetite for effective and efficient opportunity management. This should include aspects like encouraging creativity and the use of all feasible approaches to a better capability-culture. Its achievement should involve seeking opportunity efficiency in the broadest sense as a basis for best practice as a corporate goal, defining this goal with as much clarity as possible. Each Part 2 chapter indicates in outline what this might involve in the context of the tale being told, building on the Part 1 foundations. Opportunity efficiency is an operation form or statement of best practice, and while opportunity efficiency may be seen as an ambiguous concept which is only slowly beginning to acquire clarity as this book finishes Part 1, best practice without this kind of opportunity efficiency basis is much more ambiguous and much too limited in ambition.

Part 2

Employing planning tools in practice – five illustrative tales

Chapters 5 to 9 contents indicating sections within chapters

Using risk efficiency as a basis for option choices
Enlightened prudence and the board's leadership role
Sensitivity diagram portrayal of option costs
A process for clarifying NER revealed preferences
The core revealed preference issues for NER
Communication and capability issues for NER
Enlightened regulation and risk sharing
Ambiguity which may be resolvable at least in part
Sophie's closing remarks
Biases, blind spots and bounds on formal analysis
Earlier examples of related safety and security analysis
Sophie's views on politics and personal ethics
Public/private sector issues with regulator implications
Integration of safety planning and other corporate planning
Applications in other contexts when well-founded trust matters

5   Using a UP – an initially simple supply chain management example

This chapter's tale begins by addressing what looks like a simple economic order quantity analysis of a particular input component for a manufacturing process. But the initial analysis soon evolves into the exploration of integrated supply chain management involving collaborative contracts with other organisations, setting up new organisations, and then considering integrated demand chain management and further broad corporate strategy issues. Exploring complexity in a clarity efficient manner from a simple starting point can be an effective route into complex strategic thinking, as illustrated in this chapter.

This chapter's tale is set in a firm which manufactures lawnmowers – The Lawnmower Company, contracted to TLC. The central characters were

George, general manager;
Nicola, a niece of George's who had just started work at TLC;
Pete, production manager;
Ajit, accountant;
Bob, buyer;
Surinder, sales manager; and
Dave, driver of a TLC van.

Your perspective may lead you to identify with one or two particular characters more than the others. This is not a problem, but a crucial feature of the capability culture of TLC was the way all these individuals worked together as a team.

The historical setting is the 1980s. However, all the discussion is relevant for the 2020s and beyond. Why this is the case is addressed towards the chapter's end.

George initiated a simple planning process in an operations planning context by asking Nicola to analyse the order quantity for an input component for the manufacturing process. Nicola used a textbook variant of the OR process, but TLC's evolving understanding of the way this process could be used will be considered from a UP perspective throughout.

You may not be interested in manufacturing companies, or the inventory order quantity model initiating discussion, or direct use of a UP from an analyst's perspective. Inventories are examples of a much more general buffer concept which most target readers need to understand at an overview 'how to do it' level for strategic clarity. However, the key reason you need to follow the general flow of the approach to analysis employed as this chapter's tale unfolds is to acquire strategic clarity about the way the UP concept can be used as a basic component of an EP approach in any context.

This chapter's tale provides a useful basis for developing aspects of tactical clarity which need to be understood to achieve strategic clarity in all decision-making areas for all commercial organisations. There are several reasons which are worth understanding at the outset.

First, it is a conveniently simple context for beginning to explore the UP concept from an EP perspective, illustrating features of the EP perspective as well as the UP. You need a broad appreciation of what can be achieved and what is involved in successful very basic applications of the UP concept from an EP perspective to understand what this book is about.

Second, the way the tale develops provides an illustration of some key features of the UP concept which apply to its use in more sophisticated forms as illustrated in all subsequent chapters. In particular, it illustrates defining characteristics of the process as a whole, the central role of its iterative nature, the role of models as formal abstractions of a more complex reality, the need to understand broader plans which go beyond the limitations of associated models, the need to understand and test key context assumptions, the importance of shared understanding of goals–plans relationships, the implications of a very broad and systematic approach to all robustness testing, the way generalising working assumptions can be used to test robustness and create new insights, the importance of creative thinking, an overview of UP process differences relative to more limited textbook interpretations of OR processes, and some basic operational aspects of the nature of the relationships among clarity efficiency, risk efficiency, and opportunity efficiency.

Third, the tale demonstrates the way simple common practice generic models can help us to formalise and develop plans, and how using a UP to make these simple models more sophisticated in a clarity efficient manner can deepen our understanding by reducing the ambiguity uncertainty associated with assumptions, including unknown unknowns.

Fourth, the iteration issues explored include using successive passes through a UP to seek a progressively wider or deeper perspective, depending on which is most relevant at that point in the analysis. This 'looking wider or deeper' when managing the iteration process, sometimes usefully characterised as 'expansive strategic exploration of complexity or deeper tactical exploration of complexity', involves an important change in direction. Recognising when analysis priorities change in a way requiring a change in analysis direction can be crucial.

Early sections of this chapter follow the multiple pass iteration structure of the UP outlined in Chapters 2 and revisited in Chapter 4 using Figures 2.1 and 4.4. Initiating the first pass of the process is discussed in the next section, which covers concerns addressed by the first three phases in an indirect manner. The fourth phase, the 'shape the plans' phase, is addressed in the following section. 'Test the plans' and 'interpret the plans' resulting from this initial first pass analysis suggest a need to refine the analysis by generalising key assumptions, leading to a second pass. This second pass then prompts a third pass, which further redefines some of the initial modelling assumptions in a significant manner. Creative interpretation of the implications, followed by a fourth pass, then leads to a much broader view of the plans involved. Subsequent sections extend the discussion to consider wider perspectives before drawing together what all readers should find useful about this chapter's tale.

The crucial working assumptions which must hold for this chapter's tale to work as intended include your finding it credible that an organisation like TLC could have the requisite relevant capabilities for effective use of UP variants after Nicola's arrival without it having occurred to anyone to identify the potential opportunities explored by this tale prior to Nicola's arrival; that Nicola was capable enough to transform her understanding of textbook concepts into a practical approach and lucky enough for a good fit between the theory she happens to be aware of and the practice requirements of the context; that Bob,

George, Surinder, and Pete were all individually capable enough to use Nicola's explanation of her first three passes to make immediate use of the UP concept in a manner appropriate to their TLC roles; and Ajit was capable enough to understand what he needed to know about a UP from Nicola's explanation of her first three passes to make immediate use of it in terms of somewhat different top-down thinking about corporate planning in a way which complemented the focus of the others. If these working assumptions stretch your credibility you are simply being reasonable and realistic. However, this stretch is in a good cause because it maximises the scope to communicate what effective use of a UP can achieve. Please approach the credibility of the tale with this in mind. The closing sections discuss plausibility issues and the future relevance of this chapter's ideas in other organisations.

For clarity the language of EP developed in Part 1 is used whenever this is helpful in this and all other Part 2 tales, translating from the language usage you might expect in the actual context of the tales as well as during asides linking back to Part 1 discussion. The past tense is used for describing the evolving scene for all the tales and observations by the characters within the context of the tales, with the present tense used to distinguish asides and interjections related to wider implications and applications in other contexts.

Pass 1 – initiating the process

Nicola was a central character in this chapter's tale. Nicola completed a degree in mechanical engineering in the 1980s. She undertook a year of travel between university and beginning her career to see the world while she still had the freedom from responsibilities. She was not lacking in ambition or talent, but she was uncertain about her career plans and wanted to think about them carefully after her year of travelling. When Nicola returned home, she took her mother's long-standing advice and asked her uncle George for a job, making her current career indecision clear to George to avoid misleading him.

Nicola's uncle George was the general manager of TLC, a traditional family business of modest size and success which manufactured a limited range of lawnmowers in the UK's industrial Midlands, in Birmingham. George had run TLC since his father retired, having previously worked in various roles in TLC and in other similar manufacturing companies. George hired Nicola because she was his niece and his sister was a silent partner in the business. During the first three days, Nicola worked for George without a clearly defined role, 'learning the ropes' and doing odd jobs.

On day four of her new job, Nicola was accompanying her uncle as he walked around the premises. George was observing what was going on and discussing issues which people wanted to raise. George was approached by Dave, who appeared somewhat agitated. Dave used a large van to pick up input components for the production process from local suppliers. Dave also made some of the local deliveries of finished lawnmowers. Most finished lawnmowers were shipped to customers via a range of delivery services, according to order size and destination location. Inputs which were bulky, or came from a distance, were delivered by the supplier.

Dave was a valued TLC employee for several good reasons, but he was not very socially adept. About a month before Nicola's arrival, Dave had offended the dispatch staff of the supplier of engine speed controls which were used for all the firm's lawnmowers by complaining about the quality of the tea and biscuits they offered him. Their response when Dave returned for another order about the time of Nicola's arrival was to stop giving him any refreshment. After brooding about this, Dave resolved to try to persuade George that less frequent trips to the engine speed control supplier would be a good idea.

With Nicola listening in, Dave suggested to George that it was silly for him to pick up the standard order of 2,000 controls about once a month. His van could cope with about 12,000 every six months. The cost each trip incurred in terms of his time plus wear and tear on the van and fuel could be reduced if he only went once every six months, and some of the time saved might be used to deliver more of the finished lawnmowers, saving external delivery service charges which were expensive compared to the cost of sending him.

George was aware that Pete, his production manager, had determined the order size of 2,000 in consultation with Bob. Bob was his 'buyer', responsible for the supply of all production components, along with other duties. George was also aware that Pete would probably not mind larger orders of these relatively small components, and could probably find space for them. However, George knew that Ajit, his accountant, would object to the extra funds tied up in larger inventories unless it could be demonstrated that overall costs would be reduced, with good reason from George's perspective. George explained these concerns to Dave and Nicola and suggested that it might be useful if Nicola undertook an analysis to test Dave's suggestion. Dave had made an issue of the order size which needed resolution. Although George's intuition suggested that 2,000 was about right, and he knew Dave well enough to suspect the kind of ulterior motives that lay behind Dave's suggestion; his approach to all TLC employees meant that if he did not take Dave's advice he wanted Dave to understand why. He also thought this might be an interesting challenge for Nicola. He knew she had studied some management as part of her engineering degree, and he wanted to test her capabilities. He also wanted to stretch her and give her an opportunity to feel she might be a useful contributor to TLC.

At this stage nobody questioned the assumption 'the plan we are interested in is an optimal order quantity', and there was no obvious need to involve Ajit, Bob or Pete beyond letting them know what Nicola had been asked to do, indicating they would be involved if anything interesting emerged, and asking them to help Nicola if called upon. This can be interpreted as an implicit treatment of all three front-end UP phases in terms of accepting the status quo, assumptions questioned later but not initially.

As part of her engineering degree Nicola had taken an introductory management course. The material covered by this course later led to the textbook *Management for Engineers* (Chapman, Cooper and Page, 1987), which provides a broad coverage of a range of topics, including an introduction to uncertainty and complexity management processes using basic inventory generic models and a textbook 1980s OR process variant of the UP concept. Nicola was aware that these common practice generic inventory models were deliberate abstractions of reality which could be used to capture the core issues of the relevant decisions in a useful manner, analogous to a map being useful to plan a walk or a car journey. She also understood the role of OR processes comparable to a UP at the 'hard tactical analysis' end of the spectrum of possible UP approaches in an operations planning tactical decision-making context. But she had never used this kind of model or process, she had no understanding of alternatives, and she had a very limited understanding of the more strategic aspects of using bottom-up or top-down approaches to planning.

Nicola spent several days talking with people, observing what went on, and developing her ideas about modelling the issues associated with an optimal order quantity model. This confirmed the desirability of a multiple pass iterative analysis which would consider the costs associated with reordering and holding inventory given different order levels, starting with the simplest available model and adding more complexity in the process of testing earlier working assumptions by exploring alternatives.

Nicola then prepared a presentation for George which is described in the following sections. She made the presentation in a manner which reflected the iterative nature of her deliberations, as if she were going through the process with George, eliminating the unproductive blind alleys she had explored along the way and glossing over the incidentals but incorporating educational initial oversimplifications. She acknowledged her management course sources, but she presented the analysis as 'her creation shared with George'.

Pass 1 – creating the initial model to begin shaping the plan

Nicola's chosen formal modelling approach started with the simplest inventory control model she was aware of, the most basic form of the Economic Order Quantity (EOQ) model, with closely linked Periodic Review variants, described in most management textbooks that deal with modelling inventory issues.

Constructing her model began by identifying a variable which would be used to define her first pass 'base plan', referred to as a 'decision variable' in the language of this kind of OR modelling. A 'primary decision variable' was the OR modelling terminology for what had to be decided in a direct manner, the 'order quantity' Q_o. In EP terms, Q_o can be viewed as a core component of a very simple goals–plans relationships framework which TLC needed to explore to determine the base plan defined by Q_o^*, the 'optimal value of the order quantity'.

Nicola was aware that looking for Q_o^* involved an important basic working assumption – it was reasonable to assume that asking 'What should the optimal order quantity be?' was a sensible question to begin with. However, she could see no reason not to start on this basis. George had asked her to question the size of the current fixed order quantity of 2,000 controls, but not the fixed order quantity assumption itself.

Key parameters that would influence the optimal order quantity were identified next. One obviously important parameter was the 'demand rate' for controls, R_d. As a simplifying working assumption, R_d was assumed to be a constant, implying a stable monthly total output of lawnmowers of all types (they all used the same control). Nicola estimated R_d at about 2,000 controls per month, as indicated by Dave and confirmed by Pete.

The decision of direct interest was the optimal order quantity, but given a constant demand rate assumption, a Q_o value implied indirect determination of an 'order interval' T_o value, a 'secondary decision variable' which had an implied optimal value linked to Q_o^*. T_o was defined in terms of R_o and Q_o by the 'identity' constraint

$$T_o = Q_o / R_d.$$

Nicola then focused on the identification of an 'objective function'. The objective function had to define what was to be maximised or minimised in terms of the decision variables and associated parameters subject to any relevant constraints. To start to identify a suitable objective function, Nicola defined the 'order cost' parameter C_o as 'all costs which are incurred on a per order basis'.

C_o posed problems in terms of measurement precision. When Nicola consulted Ajit he suggested that C_o could be as low as £20 during the mid-winter period: about £15 for Dave's time, vehicle wear and tear plus fuel, and a further £5 to cover the cost of processing the associated invoice. During the winter Dave and his van had periods of idle time, staff processing the associated invoices also had spare time, and only basic salary and marginal vehicle operating costs needed consideration. But C_o could be as much as £40 in the spring when significant opportunity costs or overtime/extra staff costs were involved, say, an extra

£18 opportunity cost for Dave and his van, plus an extra £2 to cover the cost of processing the associated invoice using agency staff. In the spring the upturn in demand for gardening equipment meant Dave working overtime and TLC still having to use expensive external delivery services for low volume local deliveries which Dave could deal with given more available hours. In addition, the spring rush of orders meant inexperienced agency accounting staff had to be taken on and managed carefully to avoid mistakes.

For her first-pass analysis Nicola decided to use $(£20 + £40)/2 = £30$, an average value C_o estimate. Ajit's £20 and £40 estimates were treated as plausible minimum and maximum values and a mid-range £30 was equated to a Figure 3.1 minimum clarity estimate of the expected value. However, systemic uncertainty associated with an annual cycle was clearly involved in addition to other variability uncertainty which might not be systematic. This systematic uncertainty had implications which might be exploited by a more sophisticated analysis. Nicola planned to return to the implications of this systematic uncertainty and associated extremes later, if these variations seemed relevant, and she pointed this out to George when explaining her thinking. The seasonal variations underlying the $C_o = £30$ value were a form of variability uncertainty which was largely predictable, but that predictability was not being addressed by TLC's current fixed order quantity approach, and it was not addressed by Nicola's pass 1 model. Its presence suggested that any optimal order quantity should perhaps be a function of the time of year, with bigger orders in the spring and smaller orders in the winter. This kind of policy would clearly introduce a significant complication involving complexity which Nicola prudently wanted to avoid for the time being, but it was important to be aware of the issue.

Nicola next defined the 'holding cost' parameter C_h as 'all costs per control (item of inventory) per unit time (using months)'. Ajit had suggested C_h was about £0.06 per control per month, involving two components. Assuming a value per control of about £3 and an average cost of capital of about 20% per annum, £0.05 per control per month was the approximate cost of capital component. Assuming other holding costs of the order of £0.01 per control per month (an allowance for space, security, insurance, and pilfering) seemed about right to Ajit. Pete had confirmed that space was not a problem, and he could think of no other holding costs. Nicola indicated that C_h was subject to the cost of capital variations which Ajit associated with pressure on working capital in the spring when lawnmower inventories peaked and at other times of the year if new equipment had to be purchased. They were less important than seasonal variations associated with C_o because they were smaller and less systematic, so she had relied on Ajit's 20% estimate basis for C_h and not bothered to use a range-based approach to estimating the cost of capital component.

Having explained these variables and parameters, Nicola then showed George Figure 5.1.

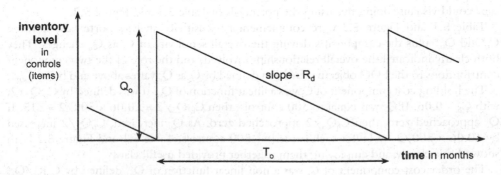

Figure 5.1 Order cycle relationships.

Nicola explained that Figure 5.1 was a simple graphical portrayal of a typical order cycle. Figure 5.1 indicated working assumptions already noted, like a constant demand rate R_d, and further working assumptions, like no planned shortages.

In addition to assuming no *planned* shortages, she was currently assuming no *unplanned* shortages, both assumptions she would return to later. Pete had indicated that Dave usually responded to an order for more speed controls the next day, and never took more than three days, so Pete used a 'safety stock' of three days of production, ordering more controls three days before he ran out of stock. This safety stock was not part of her pass 1 model, but it was part of Pete's plan, and it made the 'no unplanned stock-outs' assumptions reasonably robust.

Nicola then defined the composite parameter C_c as the 'joint cost per order cycle', where

$$C_c = C_o + C_h T_o Q_o / 2,$$

and used Figure 5.1 to explain the obvious C_o term (one order cost per order cycle) and the less obvious C_h term. C_h was the cost per control per month. C_h had to be multiplied by the area of the triangle (the base times the height divided by 2), because this area defined the number of 'control months' (one engine speed control held in stock for one month = one control month).

Nicola explained that the joint cost per *cycle* defined by C_c was a convenient place to start looking at joint order cost and inventory holding cost because it related clearly to the cycle portrayed by Figure 5.1 as just explained. However, of more interest was C_t, the 'joint cost per unit *time* (month)', defined by dividing her expression for C_c by T_o to obtain

$$C_t = C_o / T_o + C_h Q_o / 2.$$

To reduce the two interdependent decision variables to one independent decision variable, Nicola then substituted the identity defining T_o into the C_t expression to obtain the form of the C_t expression used as an objective function to define the EOQ model,

$$C_t = C_o R_d / Q_o + C_h Q_o / 2.$$

The Periodic Review variant of the EOQ model uses T_o instead of Q_o as the primary decision variable, reversing the substitution. In either case the only constraint is employed to transform the objective function into a function of only one variable, facilitating a direct and simple approach to optimisation using a table, graph or calculus.

Nicola then explained that the EOQ model assumed they wanted to minimise C_t, and they could visualise doing this using the portrayals of Table 5.1 and Figure 5.2.

Table 5.1 and Figure 5.2 were complementary sensitivity analysis portrayals, showing C_t^* and Q_0^* plus the components driving the overall sensitivity of C_t as Q_o changes. They both clearly indicated the overall relationships involved, and the role of the two component contributions to the EOQ objective function defined by C_t as Q_o varies above and below Q_0^*.

The holding cost component of C_t was a linear function of Q_o. It was defined by $C_h Q_o / 2$, with $C_h = 0.06$. If Q_o was equal to 500 controls, then $C_h Q_o / 2 = £0.06 \times 500 / 2 = £15$. If Q_o approached zero, then $C_h Q_o / 2$ approached zero. As Q_o increased, $C_h Q_o / 2$ increased by $£0.06 \times 500 / 2 = £15$ for each successive 500 controls. Table 5.1 and Figure 5.2 both showed this clearly, and employing them together provided useful clarity.

The order cost component of C_t was a non-linear function of Q_o, defined by $C_o R_d / Q_o$, with $C_o = 30$ and $R_d = 2000$. Each time Q_o was doubled, the order cost component was

Table 5.1 Joint cost per month and its components as the order quantity changes.

Order quantity Q_o	500	1000	1500	2000	2500	3000
Order cost component $C_o R_d/Q_o$	120	60	40	30	24	20
Holding cost component $C_h Q_o/2$	15	30	45	60	75	90
Joint cost per month C_t	135	90	85	90	99	110

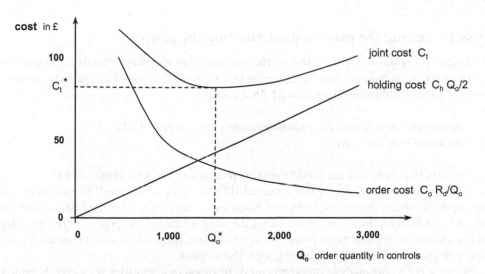

Figure 5.2 Joint cost per month and its components as the order quantity changes.

halved, and each time Q_o was halved, the order cost component was doubled. Table 5.1 and Figure 5.2 both showed this clearly.

In addition, Table 5.1 and Figure 5.2 showed why C_t had an optimal value, C_t^* in the region of £85 per month, associated with an optimal order quantity, Q_o^* in the region of 1,500 controls (shown in bold in Table 5.1).

Table 5.1 and Figure 5.2 showed C_t^* was not very sensitive to rounding Q_o^*. For example, rounding Q_o^* from 1,500 to 1,000 or 2,000 (plus or minus 500) increased C_t by 90 – 85 = £5 per month. However, they also showed that sensitivity associated with rounding errors was not symmetric: increasing Q_o from 1,500 to 2,500 (plus 1,000) increased C_t by 99 – 85 = £14, while decreasing Q_o from 1,500 to 500 (minus 1,000) increased C_t by 135 – 85 = £50. This asymmetry suggested 'round up the order quantity when in doubt about the robustness of the assumptions used'. This can be viewed as a very simple example of using an understanding of an asymmetric 'penalty function' to choose a 'balanced target'.

The optimal values C_t^* and Q_o^* were defined by the point of zero slope of the C_t curve portrayed by Figure 5.2, in turn defined by the point where the negative slope of the order cost component curve became equal in absolute terms to the positive slope of the holding cost component curve. Calculus could be used to determine the classic EOQ formula for Q_o^*:

$$Q_o^* = \left(2 R_d C_o / C_h\right)^{1/2},$$

also known as the economic lot size or Wilson formula (after one of its earliest [1920s] proponents). The square root nature of this formula also led to a 'square root rule' terminology some people preferred, and it was a notable feature of the relationship because it dampened the sensitivity of the optimal order quantity to parameter estimate errors.

In this case setting $R_d = 2000$, $C_o = £30$, and $C_h = £0.06$ implied $Q_0{}^* = 1414$, but it was convenient and sensible to round this up to 1,500, to avoid implying spurious precision. Because the sensitivity in $C_t{}^*$ terms was low, this rounding involved an increase of only £1.56 per month.

Pass 1 – testing the plans and interpreting the plans

To begin to explain the idea of testing the robustness of the plans, Nicola developed the spurious precision issue further. She began by pointing out that rounding the order quantity from 1414 to 1500 involved an extra £1.56 *assuming*:

1   *that all the current model parameter estimates were correct, AND*
2   *the model itself was correct.*

'Correct' in the context of the model being correct meant 'the joint effect of all the assumptions involved reflect the reality being modelled in an unbiased manner'. The second set of assumptions, about the model itself, was much more important than the first because the second set of assumptions were about asking the right questions, as opposed to the precision of the answers to the questions posed. A clarity efficient approach at an appropriate level of clarity requires everyone understanding what this implies.

At this stage in her analysis the 'correctness' of this simple model was inherently limited and highly uncertain in all aspects of its assessments because its relationship with the full complexities of reality was highly uncertain. One simple implication was they might consider more significant rounding to reflect the relative sensitivity of rounding up or down in relation to gaps between the model and the reality of interest. For example, rounding the answer to 2,000 might be appropriate. As Table 5.1 showed, C_t increased by £5 if Q_o was increased from 1,500 to 2,000, but an important merit of 2,000 was that it confirmed the status quo. This confirmed Pete's judgement in choosing 2,000 some time ago, and it avoided making matters worse for Dave. It *might* be very important to avoid challenging the status quo for potential cost improvements which were both uncertain and small, especially if doing so could make matters worse for other reasons. What was very clear was the way Table 5.1 and Figure 5.2 jointly illustrated the lack of sensitivity to this kind of adjustment. This sensitivity analysis was a very useful feature of the model for its creators and users. Nicola emphasised that it was *much* more important to understand the asymmetry driven by the non-linearity of one component this sensitivity analysis portrayed than the calculus-derived optimum.

Developing this sensitivity analysis issue further, Nicola explained that uncertainty associated with estimates of C_o, C_h, and R_d could be explored in the same framework. For example, as the EOQ formula suggested, overestimating the value of C_o would involve overestimating the value of $Q_o{}^*$, which would involve a lower cost penalty than underestimating C_o. However, errors in both directions had an impact on cost which was relatively small because of the square root relationship involved. For example, assuming C_o was £45 when, in fact, it was £30, a +50% error, could be shown to involve a 2% increase in cost, while assuming C_o was £15 when in fact it was £30, a –50% error, involved a 6% increase. This demonstrated a remarkable robustness to parameter errors which was a very useful feature of EOQ models. It also demonstrated the advantages of erring on the high side when estimating C_o and R_d but erring on the low side when estimating C_h.

Nicola went on to point out that sensitivity analysis was an important component of robustness analysis, and arguably it was a useful place to start because it was the simplest aspect of robustness analysis. However, she made it very clear to George that robustness testing should *never* be limited to sensitivity testing. It was *much* more important to understand the implications of inappropriate assumptions which shaped the form of the models being used plus more fundamental assumptions about the underlying plans and context, arguably starting with the most vulnerable looking assumptions. This was most easily explained and explored by looking at less restrictive working assumptions while exploring linked possibilities for more refined analysis using a sequence which starts with the relatively simple changes.

Put slightly differently, Nicola had to assess all relevant assumptions for robustness, and in order to develop some feel for which assumptions mattered the most, she needed to explore their implications by pursuing generalisations which relaxed them in a sequence suitable for building her understanding and George's. The second and further passes explained now are the explorations of generalisations built on earlier hunches about the need to relax specific earlier assumptions which proved well-founded, ordered to achieve a systematic building of understanding.

Pass 2 – refining the analysis by considering stock-outs

Nicola indicated that she had started pass 2 by exploring the implications of possible *planned* stock-outs, but her main concern was building on this to consider *unplanned* stock-outs.

Planned stock-outs (shortages) in the context of the optimal order size component of the plan were equivalent to deliberately planning to run out of the controls needed to produce lawnmowers for finished goods inventory, implying putting lawnmowers into 'finished' goods inventory without controls fitted. Planned stock-outs could be visualised in terms of a variant of Figure 5.1 as a negative inventory of controls which equated to a positive inventory of lawnmowers without controls fitted, requiring post-production rectification. Nicola suggested that the cost of a controls stock-out per unit of inventory per unit time might be about 100 times the cost of holding controls inventory per unit of inventory per unit time, because a lawnmower without a control ties up about 50 times as much capital, and it would probably be worth at least doubling this figure to reflect the inconvenience for Pete and his production staff. She had assumed a factor of 100 for illustrative purposes, but Pete would have to confirm or revise this before her analysis results were used, if the analysis suggested changes. Extending the model to allow for planned shortages this way, the new optimal order quantity was 1,428 (compared with 1,414), with a 'planned shortage' of 14. Taking the model literally, it was worth being out of controls for about $(14/1,428) \times 100 = 1\%$ of the time production takes place, about 2 hours each month, to avoid carrying the extra 14 controls for the rest of the cycle.

Nicola emphasised that it would be silly to take this pass 2 extended model too literally, and both versions provided an answer which needed rounding to $Q_o{}^* = 1500$. However, the idea that limited *planned* stock outage was not a disaster and might be viewed as an opportunity rather than a problem was a useful insight, and even more useful was the implications in terms of a starting point for modelling the possibility of *unplanned* stock-outs.

For those who are interested in the modelling details, the equivalent of Figure 5.1 involves two degrees of freedom instead of one (the maximum stock-out as well as Q_o), so the mathematics becomes marginally more complex, as explored by Chapman, Cooper, and Page (1987). Nicola shrewdly avoided troubling George with this.

Nicola then used this planned stock-out model discussion as a basis to consider *unplanned* stock-outs, suggesting that it would prove much more useful to refine this part of their pass 1 plan assumptions.

During her investigations Nicola observed that Pete kept a 'safety stock' as noted earlier, a second part of his overall plan. Pete's 'plan part 1' was order 2,000 at a time. His 'plan part 2' was a form of pre-emptive contingency plan for delivery which might not be immediate. It used a safety stock of 300 controls, placing an order for another 2,000 when there were still about 300 left. Pete's rationale for 300 was that most of the time, Dave delivered an order almost immediately (the same day), but sometimes other jobs took priority and it took a day; occasionally it took two or three days. TCL produced lawnmowers for about 20 'production' (working) days a month, about 100 lawnmowers per production day, so Pete's safety stock equated to about three days of production. Pete currently used a 'two bin' safety stock system, initiating an order when the main bin was empty, but he was planning to move to a computer-based equivalent shortly.

Nicola suggested that the chances associated with Dave taking zero to three days to replenish the stock could be defined using Table 5.2, which treats 'days' as a discrete variable.

She had estimated the P(n) probability values herself, based on a conversation with Pete, and she had not yet confirmed them with Pete, but she believed they were the right order of magnitude. She had then calculated the CP(n) cumulative probability values, which define the probability of n days or more, convenient for the next step.

Nicola then used Table 5.2 in conjunction with the assumption that a mower without a control held in inventory cost about 100 times as much as a control held in inventory to produce the analysis of four discrete alternative policies portrayed by Table 5.3.

Pete's current policy of 'a safety stock of 300 controls' (three days of production) was selected by Nicola as the 'base case' for policy 1 of Pete's plan part 2, with three obvious alternatives working to the nearest 100 controls. For those familiar with decision analysis, Table 5.3 is a decision tree in tabular form. For all readers, this is a very simple and convenient HAT (histogram and tree) approach.

All the costs addressed by this safety stock model were over and above the EOQ model costs, which ignored safety stock costs and the cost of stock-outs.

To appreciate the modelling choice Nicola made with her approach based on Tables 5.2 and 5.3, you need to know there are alternative common practice 'prescriptive models' which, like the EOQ model, provide optimal solutions. The 'descriptive model' HAT approach in Tables 5.2 and 5.3 was used by Nicola's textbook because it is more general (less restrictive) and more insightful. The approach used in Tables 5.2 and 5.3 is characterised as a 'descriptive model' because it describes the implications of alternative options without

Table 5.2 Days to replenish stock: probability and cumulative probability distributions.

n, number of days	3	2	1	0
P(n), probability	0.01	0.04	0.15	0.80
CP(n), cumulative probability	0.01	0.05	0.20	1.00

Table 5.3 Safety stock policy – analysis of four alternative policy options for Pete's 'plan part 2'.

Policy 1: Pete's current policy as a base case
- Safety stock of 300, 3 days production.
- No chance of a stock-out, no stock-out costs.
- Total safety stock cost per month = extra holding cost per month = $300 \times C_h = £18$.
- *Total rounded cost £18.*

Policy 2: modest reduction in safety stock
- Safety stock of 200, 2 days production.
- Probability of a stock-out of 100 for 1 day = 0.01.
- Expected cost of stock-outs per month = $0.01 \times 100\ C_h \times 100/30 = £0.20$
  (the probability $P(n)$ times $100\ C_h$ times the 100 controls times $1/30$ of a month).
- Extra holding costs per month = $200 \times C_h = £12$.
- Total expected safety stock cost per month = $£0.20 + £12 = £12.20$.
- *Total rounded cost £12.*

Policy 3: aggressive reduction in safety stock
- Safety stock of 100, 1 day of production.
- Probability of a stock-out of 100 for 1 day = 0.05,
  200 for 1 day = 0.01.
- Expect cost of stock-outs per month =
  $(0.05 \times 100\ C_h \times 100/30) + (0.01 \times 100\ C_h \times 100/30) = 1 + 0.40 = £1.40$.
- Extra holding cost per month = $100 \times C_h = £6$.
- Total expected safety stock cost per month = $£1.40 + £6 = £7.40$.
- *Total rounded cost £7.*

Policy 4: elimination of safety stock
- Zero safety stock – reorder when stock-out occurs.
- Probability of a stock-out of 100 for 1 day = 0.20,
  200 for 1 day = 0.05,
  300 for 1 day = 0.01.
- Expected cost of stock-outs per month
  = $(0.20 \times 100\ C_h \times 100/30) + (0.05 \times 100\ C_h \times 100/30) + (0.01 \times 100\ C_h \times 100/30)$
  = $£4 + £2 + £0.6 = £6.60$.
- Extra holding cost per month = zero.
- Total expected safety stock cost per month = $£6.60$.
- *Total rounded cost £7.*

---

using calculus or any other direct form of optimisation to choose an option in the manner of a 'prescriptive model' like the EOQ approach, but it clearly provides relevant information for making choices, including sensitivity analysis. George did not need to know this, but understanding the need to make modelling choices like this is part of strategic clarity.

George was taken through this analysis of the four policies fairly quickly. He wanted to understand the analysis implications in broad 'what needs to be done' terms, but not the modelling choices or the calculation details. His focus was the final line for each policy in Table 5.3, rounded to the nearest pound as a reminder to avoid attributing spurious accuracy to the results. It was the £18 to £12 to £7 and then another £7 that really interested George.

Nicola might have prepared a decision tree equivalent to Table 5.3 and used it to explain the arithmetic. She did not bother because the implications which concerned George were clear from the table, and it would not have been clarity efficient to expend her effort or George's time in this way.

Furthermore, Nicola might have produced a decision diagram comparable to Figure 4.3 or Figures 3.6 and 3.7 to relate the expected outcomes of Table 5.3 to potential variability to help make the case for risk efficient choices which did not accept more cost to reduce risk. It is useful to understand this possibility is available, *but it would not be clarity efficient for anyone to expend their effort in this way in this context.*

It was important for Nicola to acknowledge that stock-outs have an important nuisance value for Pete and his staff which might go significantly beyond the stock-out penalty cost factor of 100 relative to C_h which this model assumes. Pete would have to be consulted before using this analysis, and even if the factor of 100 and all the other parameters were acceptable to Pete, a zero safety stock would probably not be a good idea, despite its apparent slight advantage prior to rounding. She provisionally recommended a safety stock of 100, policy 3, most of the year, noting the special problems during the spring rush might deserve a special spring policy, like a safety stock of 300 plus bigger orders, a point to be revisited later.

Nicola suggested that given her current assumptions, from a corporate perspective Pete might be adopting a slightly cautious 'zero risk of stock-outs' policy that might not be a good idea from a broad TLC perspective *except* when the spring rush was involved, although it made obvious sense from Pete's perspective all year round. Policy 3 involved 0.01 probability of a two-day stock-out and 0.04 probability of a one-day stock-out. This might sound (and feel) significant to Pete in the context of a stock-out cost 100 times C_h. But in the context of a monthly order of 2,000, a safety stock of 200 involved 100 controls which were only needed for one day every $1/0.01 = 100$ months and another 100 which were only needed for one day every $1/0.05 = 20$ months, on average. The consequences of a stock-out were irritating for Pete and potentially serious for TLC during the spring rush but not catastrophic for either. In addition, effective routine communication between Pete and Dave about priorities could make the recommended safety stock of 100 fairly free of hassle as well as cost-effective, provided Nicola's ongoing concerns about seasonal swings were addressed and her factor of 100 assumption was confirmed.

Given her current assumptions Pete's current policy was probably costing TLC about £10 per month more than a safety stock of 100 = one days production policy, which she characterised as 'an aggressive reduction in safety stock' policy. Adjusting Q_o from 1,500 to 2,000 might increase C_t by about £5 per month, which might (or might not) be overlooked because of other considerations. However, regardless of whether the order quantity was 1,500 or 2,000, adjusting the safety stock reorder rule from three days production to one days production might save about £10 per month (£18 − 7.40 = £10.60 rounded).

Nicola finished this part of her presentation by indicating that if both changes suggested by her pass 1 and 2 analysis were implemented, a Q_o of 1,500 and a one-day reorder rule, about £15 per month could be saved *given her current assumptions.* This would involve an EOQ based monthly order and holding cost of about £85, plus a safety stock holding and storage cost component of about £10, a total cost of about £95 per month. The major saving would be associated with a more aggressive approach to shortages with a modest downside which would be minimalised by Pete simply letting Dave know when more controls were needed.

Pass 3 – reconsidering all relevant influences on holding costs

By this stage George was seriously impressed by Nicola's presentation. He could see clearly that the issues raised went beyond controls and savings of £15 per month. Nicola then explained to George that she had needed the first two passes at modelling the decision context to gain experience and confidence, but she also needed to take George on the same learning curve she had travelled because they both needed a shared basis for understanding what was to follow. Building on George's growing confidence and respect, Nicola suggested they needed to further refine the plans portrayed by her pass 2 models to incorporate additional aspects of the decision context and a broader approach to TLC plans.

During her investigations, Nicola had observed that invoices for controls orders take about 25 days to arrive, payment falls due in 30 days, and there were usually payment transfer delays of about 5 days. This implied a 'free credit period', T_c, of about two months. She pointed out that during this period C_h was *actually* only £0.01, not the £0.06 *assumed* earlier, because the £0.05 cost of capital component did not apply. Furthermore, Nicola observed that inflation on components like controls was currently running at about 16% per annum, implying an inflation-driven 'capital appreciation' on inventory holdings, C_a, of about £0.04 per control per month.

Nicola explained that the EOQ models used earlier assumed that inventory holding costs applied from the moment inventory arrived, and inflation-driven price increases she associated with 'appreciation' on inventory holdings was not relevant – both important assumptions to test for robustness. Indeed, her university 'management for engineers' course had addressed how the basic EOQ model could be further extended to consider the impact of both the inflation-driven capital appreciation and the free credit period. The mathematics of this model were considerably more complex than that used earlier, but the basic approach was the same, and all George needed to understand was Figure 5.3, Table 5.4, and Figure 5.4, which she now showed him and explained.

Nicola first explained that Figure 5.3 was a generalisation of Figure 5.1, with T_c defining the free credit period previously assumed to be zero. That is, Figure 5.1 was just a special case of Figure 5.3 which assumed no free credit period and ignored inflation, both *stealth* assumptions of importance if economic lot size formula users are not aware of them. The area of the shape *abcd* could be associated with the £0.01 holding cost component less inflation-driven appreciation of £0.04 but no cost of capital. This involved a negative cost (positive appreciation net of holding cost) of £0.01 – £0.04 = -£0.03. The rest of the usual holding cost triangle could be associated with £0.06 holding cost component less appreciation of £0.04, implying a £0.06 – £0.04 = £0.02 positive cost.

Helping George to interpret Table 5.4 and the associated Figure 5.4, Nicola explained that what was involved was a generalisation of Table 5.1 and Figure 5.2, with the same special case relationship just considered. The order cost component of Table 5.4 was the same as that in Table 5.1. A more complex expression was needed to derive the holding cost component, with negative costs (net appreciation savings) which reached a minimum between $Q_o = 6,000$ and 7,000, when the rate of growth of further appreciation costs was overtaken by the rate of growth of further holding costs. This effect together with the continually declining order cost component as Q_o increased meant that the joint cost per month, C_t, reached its minimum of about –£64 per month at a Q_o of about 7,000, highlighted in Table 5.4 for easy identification. In terms of this generalised model, a Q_o of 2,000 implied a C_t of zero, and a Q_o of 1,500 implied a C_t of a little more than +£20 per month – her pass 3 result was about £64 per month cheaper than the current situation and about £85 per month cheaper than her pass 1 suggestion because of crucial changes in her working assumptions.

Helping George understand why the order quantity was so much bigger, Nicola explained that two systematic effects were working together, both missed completely by her earlier models. Inflation-driven appreciation meant a lower holding cost, in general,

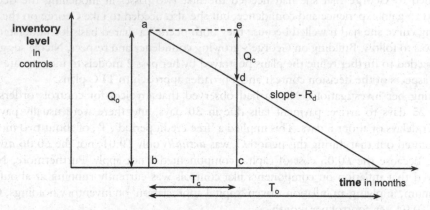

Figure 5.3 Order cycle relationships: credit period allowed.

Table 5.4 Joint cost per month and its components as the order quantity changes: two months free credit period.

Order quantity Q_o	1000	2000	3000	4000	5000	6000	7000	8000
Order cost component	60	30	20	15	12	10	9	8
Holding cost component	−15	−30	−45	−60	−70	−73	−73	−70
Joint cost C_t	45	0	−25	−45	−58	−63	−64	−63

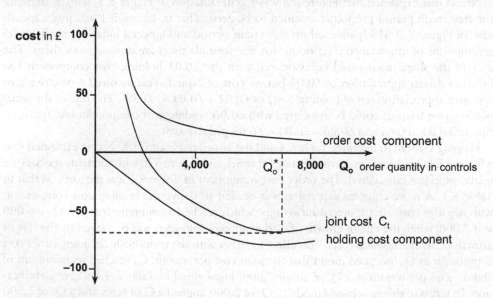

Figure 5.4 Joint cost per month and its components as the order quantity changes: two months free credit period.

potentially a negative holding cost (positive return on investment). Furthermore, appreciation in conjunction with somebody else's money being used as working capital meant a profit on somebody else's money – 'gearing' or 'leverage' in financial parlance. She had pointed out earlier that the optimal order quantity was more sensitive to overestimating

C_h than it was to underestimating, and ignoring both appreciation driven by inflation and a free credit period was a form of very serious overestimation of C_h which went beyond biased parameter estimation in the usual sense because it was the pass 2 decision-making model that was biased.

In part to make George more comfortable with the subtle but massive implications of this new pass 3 model, she pointed out that many people using EOQ models were not aware that 'no appreciation and immediate payment for stock on arrival' were underlying assumptions, although the details were developed in her course materials (the basis of Chapman, Cooper and Page [1987] chapter 12).

As an aside addressing a point Nicola did not make, I did not realise the importance of the 'cash on delivery' and 'no inflation' assumptions implicit in basic EOQ models until the early 1980s, 50 years after these models were first used and 20 years after studying them as part of my first and second degrees. The resulting paper (Chapman, Ward, Cooper, and Page, 1984) revealed I was not alone. It flushed out some related earlier papers, generated considerable discussion, and led to a stream of subsequent papers addressing the impact of inflation and free credit periods. However, for half a century most people who wrote about or used a very popular basic inventory model were not aware of key implicit assumptions, an important form of 'stealth assumption'. Many remain unaware. Yet the consequences in this chapter's tale are orders of magnitude more important than Nicola's pass 1 and pass 2 models, and they take the solution in a different direction. Using OPM (other people's money) is not a new idea – this was a published term in the US more than a century ago and used internationally as a core concept for many centuries in many industries, but its implications in EOQ models had been largely overlooked for a very long time.

The free credit period and inflation-driven appreciation modelling developed in this chapter's tale can be interpreted as both a useful illustration of the importance of stealth assumptions *and* the related importance of using framing assumptions which are as general (unrestricted) as we can make them. The way Nicola was potentially moving in the wrong direction in terms of order quantity size on pass 1 and pass 2 as identified by pass 3 illustrates the importance of both issues in a reasonably simple way, providing a basis for understanding the implications in more complex contexts.

Stealth assumptions are comparable to and can be usefully viewed as unknown unknowns in the sense that they are misconceptions associated with ambiguities beyond the scope of our framing assumptions. These unknown unknowns are very important aspects of ambiguity relative to the more obvious known unknown aspects of uncertainty – what we know is an issue even if we cannot size or shape it. The no free credit period or appreciation stealth assumptions implicit in all early EOQ models illustrate unknown framing assumptions which once recognised in this chapter's tale transformed the analysis and all follow-on planning.

Unknown unknowns are often associated with events which are not predictable, sometimes using the term 'black swans' (Taleb, 2007). However, stealth assumptions involving misconceptions can be even more important than unpredictable events, and they can be minimised by ensuring that we use the widest feasible set of framing assumptions as a basis for explicitly testing working assumptions. This is *much* easier said than done. However, the difficulty involved does not make it less important – it makes it more important to know how to approach the key issues.

Linking this to the discussion of Chapter 3, this kind of potential decision-making error is not usually considered 'bias', but its basis and implications are comparable – omitting to address important sources of underlying uncertainty. Furthermore, this important source of uncertainty and bias is an unknown unknown for everyone using the stealth assumptions underlying the basic EOQ model. It can be viewed as a 'risk' associated with a capability-culture source of uncertainty – leading to missed opportunities if those involved fail to recognise these important issues.

Returning to the tale, Nicola pointed out that direct use of this pass 3 model required prediction of *average* appreciation per month over the order interval T_o. In practice, the implications of general inflation for the cost of controls would not be a small amount of appreciation per month, but a significant amount linked to price changes every 6 to 12 months, recent and more distant past appreciation being no more than a guide. However, a large recent price increase for controls might suggest no further price increases for some time. Assuming they were aware of the inflation issue, one important residual risk (or mistake) was a relatively large order based on assumed appreciation when none took place or an economic slump led to price decreases. A much more important risk (or mistake) was a relatively small order based on assumed stable prices when large price increases took place regularly. But by far the biggest risk (or mistake) of all was simply ignoring inflation driven appreciation and associated gearing because of a free credit period – because the associated stealth assumptions had not been identified and tested. Using a simple expected value approach was not ideal, but it was much better than just ignoring the issue.

Nicola finished this part of her presentation by indicating that these results might be implemented directly with a safety stock = one days production rule. Relative to the current standard order quantity of 2,000, in terms of order, holding, and appreciation costs as captured by the revised economic order quantity model, Table 5.4 indicates that they could achieve a saving of about £64 per month with an order quantity of 7,000. And the safety stock implications (risk of stock-out every 3–4 months instead of every month) should save a further £16 per month relative to the three days production rule with $Q_o = 2,000$, about £80 per month in total.

Pass 3 – exploiting creativity to interpret an emerging plan 3

By this stage George was glowing with family pride. Nicola, who was beginning to enjoy herself, and to see why her mother's advice to join the family business was a lot better than she had previously thought, now built on the firm foundations had laid so far. She had already approached the boundaries of conventional textbook interpretation of traditional OR process use. She now drew on her innate creativity, crucial to really effective use of a UP, to begin a transition into more general UP territory.

Nicola observed that a working assumption underlying Table 5.4 and Figure 5.4 was inventory was paid for when it was used during the free credit period. Nicola then observed there would be no point in offering to pay for inventory when it was used (not the case now) unless this benefit for the firm supplying controls could be balanced by a reciprocal benefit for TLC. The obvious reciprocal TLC benefit in her current view was a longer free credit period. A longer free credit period would result in an even larger order quantity, delivering no inflation-driven price increases during an even longer period between orders. She had undertaken sensitivity analysis on the effect of paying for stock as it is used in conjunction with a longer free credit period which suggested that if an extra four months of free credit on *unused* stock was on offer, *paying for stock as it was used*, this justified TLC using an order of about 12,000 (rounded from a calculated value of 12,884), a six-month supply. This was coincidentally what Dave had suggested – but for rather different reasons. If 12,000 was the TLC order on offer, the control supplier might be persuaded to offer an inducement comparable to four months' free credit on unused stock. This would generate a further cost saving of about £80 per month. TLC might not be able to secure agreement to this much free credit from the controls firm, but it would be a good stretch target to negotiate towards. As a linked suggestion, Nicola observed that they did not need to see this target 'plan 3' as an optimal fixed order quantity Q_0^* of 12,000 controls roughly every six months. They might find it useful to see it as an optimal fixed order interval T_0^* of six months for the roughly 12,000 controls required every six months, using a Periodic Review interpretation of the EOQ model.

George immediately recognised this creative interpretation of her pass 3 results involved important insights which he and Nicola needed to share with Bob, TLC's buyer.

Pass 4 – Bob's crucial clarification of the plans/models distinction

After Bob was fully briefed by George and Nicola, taking him through the same learning process to reach Nicola's target plan 3, Bob spent some time thinking about the implications. During this period he had several discussions with Nicola to clarify his evolving ideas. He then approached the managing director of the firm supplying controls with what we will call 'Bob's plan 4', built on a transformation of 'Nicola's plan 3' by Bob and Nicola working together. Bob referred to his plan 4 when talking to Nicola and George as 'their TLC plan 4'.

Bob started his discussion with the managing director of the controls firm by indicating that TLC would be interested in replacing their current orders for 2,000 controls as needed by contracting for a six-month supply of about 12,000 controls *at a discounted price to be agreed*. The contract would involve TLC paying for controls without the need for invoices at a uniform rate over the six-month period at the end of each month, *roughly equivalent* to paying for them as they were used. The controls firm would deliver them *at the control firm's convenience without letting TLC run out of inventory*, with stock-level information available for the controls supplier as needed. He suggested this might be in the context of a one or two year rolling contract, rolled forward every six months, with the price for the next six months negotiated well in advance.

From a TLC perspective what was desirable about this transformation of Nicola's plan 3 was the discounted price for six months negotiated in advance, *plus* zero TLC investment in inventory, *plus* delivery of controls by the controls supplier, *plus* no stock-outs, *plus* not having to cope with a very large inventory every six months, *plus* no invoices to process monthly because automatic payment by the bank could be arranged, *plus* some longer price and relationship stability built into a rolling contract agreement, *plus* a new collaborative relationship with a supplier of a key component which increased TLC market power as a supply-side buyer.

From the control supplier's perspective what was desirable about this transformation of Nicola's plan 3 was regular payment monthly without invoices requiring generation, *plus* less free credit for TLC on average than the present case, *plus* the freedom to deliver when it suited the controls firm. The controls firm might or might not see freedom to deliver when it suited them as beneficial, but the other features of the collaboration with a customer proposed by Bob ought to be attractive.

Bob was clear before he approached the controls firm that there was no need to even mention the extended free credit or fixed order quantity aspects of Nicola's plan. Bob was also aware, before he visited the controls firm, that freedom to deliver when they wanted might not be highly valued, but it would be very valuable if the controls firm could exploit it by negotiating similar arrangements with other firms they supplied with the same component, and when he briefly explained why the managing director of the controls supplier became very interested.

A similar arrangement with the other firms supplied with controls would allow the controls firm to significantly reduce their finished goods inventories *and* use longer production runs. Producing an inventory of controls on equipment used to produce a wide variety of other components involved a 'set-up cost'. This setup cost was equivalent to TLC's order cost, and directly comparable holding costs were involved, with no free credit period possibilities. This implied an Economic Lot Size model approach might be employed, directly comparable to an EOQ approach. However, because the controls firm primarily supplied a small number of local firms that all purchased their controls when it suited them, demand for the controls firm was not smooth – unlike TLC's demand for controls, it was decidedly lumpy and unpredictable. This implied a relatively large safety stock for the controls firm, assuming orders were unpredictable and could not be kept waiting, in conjunction with short production runs. An arrangement with the other firms supplied with controls comparable to Bob's plan 4 would allow the controls firm to produce a large batch, deliver it to all its customers on planned routes to top up current stocks, and then repeat this cycle on a fairly stable basis. It could size its production runs based on its distribution plans, with most inventories being held by its customers.

Bob knew that the joint implications of a more flexible and cost-effective approach to production of controls and associated inventories plus the stable revenue based on pre-agreed prices should be worth a significant discount from the control firm's perspective if they could make effective use of TLC's plan 4 with other customers, in effect sharing the benefit with TLC of an improved operating position for both firms which the controls firm could exploit with its other customers. What was involved was a form of 'supply chain management', taking a partnership view of supply chain linkages to share the benefits of integrated practices to some extent but looking after TLC's interests as far as possible. Bob had limited interest in the deeper implications for TLC suppliers, but he understood very clearly why it would be useful to know about and be sensitive to their concerns.

Even if the controls firm could not negotiate similar arrangements with its other customers, it should be in their interests to undertake delivery for no more than the cost to TLC of using Dave, with some discounting of the current standard price to share a more limited set of other benefits.

Bob had recognised that Nicola's plan 3 based on her creative interpretation of the model developed during pass 3 provided crucial insights. However, he had used those insights and his understanding of Nicola's UP-based planning process to build a pass 4 plan which was *much better*. It replaced the fixed order quantity model or its fixed order interval equivalent with a negotiated contract for a fixed period, at discounted prices, with flexible deliveries by the supplier at the supplier's convenience, plus other suitable contract provisions, plus less formal but important understandings and agreements.

When Bob reported back to George, he started by indicating that the negotiated contract meant 12,000 would not have to be made available for collection by Dave every six months. All the controls would be delivered to TLC by the controls firm. It would do so as and when it wished, in whatever delivery size it wanted, but would guarantee TLC would not have a stock-out. Crucially, there would be a significant discount on the current standard price fixed for six months at a time on a rolling basis. Bob explained that he had bargained hard to negotiate what he believed was a fair discount, suitable arrangements to ensure both companies worked together to avoid stock-outs, and a rolling review process to ensure contract renewal was always timely. Letting the controls supplier make the deliveries when it suited them was a key step in generalising Nicola's invaluable plan 3 basis for their TLC plan 4 because TLC did not want the order costs or the physical inventory with its holding costs. TLC wanted a reliable supply at a low price which offered protection from rising prices and no capital tied up in inventories. Indeed, having a large physical inventory at the start of each cycle would be distinctly unhelpful and might require rethinking using an opportunity cost approach to storage costs.

When George, Bob and Nicola then got together to review the implications of Nicola's plan 3 and Bob's plan 4 they jointly agreed on a number of observations:

1   Nicola's concerns about seasonal swings in cost parameters driven by the upswing in demand for lawnmowers in the spring plus complications associated with stock-outs in the spring raised a very important set of concerns, but they would all be resolved without further effort, because Bob had arranged for delivery by the controls supplier. It was agreed that the resolution of these concerns was *very* important. Nicola had probably understated the impact during the spring rush of any component supply stock-outs, and the way Bob's plan reduced their problems during the spring rush would be very useful.

2   It had been worthwhile delaying exploring the complexities of this spring rush complication, because the effort would have been wasted at best, reducing the clarity efficiency of the overall analysis and synthesis process. It would also have risked diverting analysis into a complex mess which might have led to them missing the real opportunities. If Bob's plan 4 insights had not eliminated this concern, it would have deserved attention, perhaps warranting an approach like a once a year using an order of 6,000 or more controls just before the spring rush.

3   It had also been worthwhile delaying worrying about Nicola's factor of 100 assumption about the difference between stock-out costs and C_h, but suitable stock-out cost penalties could be built into Bob's plan 4 contract with the controls firm if this was appropriate.

4   In system monitoring terms, Pete would have to keep an eye on his stock of controls, but life should be easier for him.

5   Ajit and the accounting staff who paid the bills should be pleased with the outcome because their workload would be lower and smoother.

6   Dave would never have to visit the controls firm again, and he would have more time for delivering finished goods inventory or other tasks throughout the year.

7   TLC would no longer have to be a 'price taker' with respect to the price of controls because Bob had established a new negotiating position which pleased him and strengthened TLC's position.

8   Had they simply implement Nicola's pass 1 or pass 2 plans, they would have moved in the wrong direction, arguably making things worse, not better. This was an 'enlightened retrospective view' from the position of insight they had gained via Nicola's plan 3 plus Bob's plan 4. They did not have this insight when they started, or at the end of passes 1 and 2. They had acquired it on the journey during passes 3 and 4, a corporate learning process as well as a corporate planning process.

9   It would be appropriate and useful to acknowledge the value of the textbook OR process contribution in terms of the generic model and process ideas which Nicola had contributed to the overall TLC learning process, and the crucial impact of the free credit period and inflation model. However, the TLC corporate learning process also needed to recognise the importance of Nicola's insight and creativity, George's judgement, and

Bob's absolutely crucial role – transforming Nicola's plan 3 into a supply chain plan 4 which included a much more sophisticated approach to shared benefits from collaboration with the control supplier firm than Nicola's.

All three agreed there were remaining sources of uncertainty, risks, and potential problems which would need addressing. For example, if the controls firm suddenly went bankrupt, or tried to drive up prices unreasonably, TLC would need another supplier quickly. As a second example, lawnmower sales were reasonably stable but inherently uncertain, and if the demand for TLC lawnmowers suddenly slumped, TLC might find itself locked into a supply contract for more controls than they wanted. However, both of these issues needed separate management anyway, perhaps with more attention than they currently received.

From an EP perspective, Dave's grumpy reaction to no tea and biscuits provided an opportunity to put the new skills Nicola brought to TLC to use – pure serendipity in a sense – but arguably a minor problem which George responded to wisely, transforming a problem into an opportunity because of the way Nicola and Bob worked together as a very effective team.

TLC's primary concern from Nicola's initial perspective was dealing with the ambiguity uncertainty and underlying complexity associated with 2,000 being the right answer to the question, 'What should the order quantity be?' The underlying, long-standing assumption that an order quantity approach to supply-side management for input components like controls was appropriate was not questioned. Both the deterministic prescriptive EOQ models and the probabilistic descriptive safety stock models were tools for understanding this complexity and managing its implications, resolving the associated uncertainty. The EOQ models provided a deterministic model understanding with no associated stochastic model understanding. The safety stock models provided associated stochastic model understanding. The EOQ and safety stock models together with a creative interpretation of the implications provided the basis for qualitative and quantitative analysis for a supply chain plan which went well beyond both the initial models in terms of its scope and the opportunities addressed.

Bob's contribution in terms of planning a more general supply chain contracting approach, using his creativity and insight into their supplier's objectives as well as TLC's real concerns, was about further exploring the complexity and ambiguity uncertainty addressed by Nicola. Bob saw beyond the assumption that an optimal fixed order quantity or an optimal fixed order interval was appropriate. He addressed a higher-order level of uncertainty and underlying complexity. He envisaged and implemented plans which separated the strategy associated with the contracting period from the tactics of delivery. In this sense Bob's plan 4 involved a level of both strategic vision and strategic clarity which was completely missing in Nicola's more tactically focused plan 3 and the earlier TLC fixed order quantity plan, and it clearly distinguished between his plan 4 as a whole and the models underlying its shaping while Nicola was leading the analysis development.

Discussing his emerging approach at length with Nicola before his visit to the controls supplier was important for Bob, Nicola, and TLC. It was during these discussions that Nicola made the connection between her EOQ approach for TLC and an Economic Lot Size approach for the controls firm for its stock of controls. Her sharing of this connection with Bob triggered the insights behind a key aspect of Bob's plan 4. Bob discussed his approach at length with Nicola after his visit to the controls supplier, before he reported back to George, and at Nicola's suggestion they jointly labelled Bob's plan 4 approach 'My-Place-Your-Timing' – as a catchy variation on the currently fashionable 'Just-In-Time' label. One potential problem with this label, which Bob observed, was the perspective basis.

My-Place-Your-Timing from a TLC perspective was Your-Place-My-Timing from their supplier's perspective. However, Bob wanted Nicola to feel that she had an acknowledged ownership stake in 'their TLC plan 4 approach', and he did not see any need to quibble about a label which he thought some suppliers might find attractive, using 'their version' of the language of the label. These labels and their discussion with George triggered some of George's subsequent ideas.

The overall teamwork was crucial. Nicola had used a traditional OR process, with particularly effective robustness testing to pick up the free credit period and effects of inflation on the cost of capital, plus a particularly creative interpretation of her results. George wisely saw the need to involve Bob at this point. Bob then recognised the need to move from EOQ models or Periodic Review equivalents to a complete supply chain plan for controls with a negotiated rolling contract based on supplier delivery at the supplier's convenience plus other terms and conditions, supported by Nicola in terms of knowledge about generic inventory models for supply-side or demand-side analysis plus the role of a systematic approach to testing all of the assumptions associated with a plan.

Put slightly differently, Nicola had been testing assumptions systematically to resolve uncertainty by understanding complexity within the assumed question, 'What is the optimal order quantity?' George sensed the strategic implications of Nicola's answers. Bob then tested the assumption this was the right question and had the insight to see that it wasn't. Bob then initiated a higher-order exploration of uncertainty and underlying complexity, guided by what they had both learned from the lower-order analysis. In UP terms Nicola was looking at assumptions within the bounds of a fixed order quantity or interval model, but Bob addressed relevant 'create and enhance the plan' assumptions which could be relaxed.

To replicate the effectiveness of their joint efforts in other EP contexts, the UP's separation of create and enhance the plans to address all relevant concerns and 'shape plans by modelling core issues' which are a subset of the broader plans is a very helpful distinction. It facilitates understanding how to make the transition from Nicola's plan 3 to Bob's plan 4. It also stimulated George to go right back to the capture the context phase of the UP, the next issue in our tale. Bob built on Nicola's pass 3 models, but he couched his plans in spreadsheet terms with his altered assumptions, using price as a variable to be negotiated below current standard price based on the attractiveness of the other contract features to the controls firm. Bob's 'test the plans' involved testing all his assumptions, and he interpreted his plans creatively throughout the process of their development. Whether or not *Bob* thought of 'Bob's plan 4' as the result of using a UP pass 4 approach building on Nicola's passes 1 through 3 does not really matter in some ways, but ongoing joint planning does make corporate use of an explicit UP concept perspective useful for everyone involved.

Furthermore, it is the team use of the UP concept which needs a collective understanding. The UP front-end phase structure clarifies the difference between a model of some core issues, the plans as a whole, based on insights provided by models, the context the plans are set in, and the effective implementation of those plans. Different people may have different contributing roles to play in effective corporate use of a UP approach, but they need to work together, moving towards a common vision of where they want to go. They may not share this common vision of where they want to go at the outset, and finding an enlightened shared vision may be a particularly important part of the journey.

Some OR textbooks, and some courses based on them, present EOQ models as tools for direct use – once you understand the formula you can plug in your parameters and get the optimal answer. Some practice-focused OR experts are highly critical of their use in any way. Gene (Robert E. D.) Woolsey provides a good example of the latter school – see *Real World*

Operations Research: The Woolsey Papers (Woolsey, 2003, chapter 4.4) for example. The EP perspective advocated by this book assumes that EOQ models are an excellent conceptual framework for developing an *initial* understanding of what matters a lot, and what does not matter quite so much, *provided all the working assumptions that matter are tested very carefully, even when that leads to abandoning an order quantity concept altogether. This makes EOQ models particularly good examples for explaining how to use a UP concept.* But an EOQ initial model approach can demonstrably move suggested changes in plans in the wrong direction and provide seriously unhelpful advice if the robustness of the assumptions is not tested carefully. Initial and later models of all kinds always need very rigorous testing in the general UP sense.

To link this point to the anti-aircraft guns on merchant ships example of 1930s-40s OR discussed in Chapter 2, Nicola's pass 1 and pass 2 analysis is comparable to a statistical analysis of the relative ability of ship versus shore-based anti-aircraft guns to destroy enemy aircraft without looking at the extent to which anti-aircraft guns mounted on merchant ships increases the survival capability of the ships and the morale of their crew. Nicola's pass 3 followed by Bob's plan 4 were comparable to beginning to see the bigger picture more clearly in the sense that it was not losing the war that really mattered.

Nicola, Bob and George were all delighted with their new approach to controls, and all three appreciated there was clearly scope for extending this kind of joint bottom-up corporate planning process to other input components for the firm's lawnmowers. Some suppliers might not be interested in anything other than a conventional order quantity relationship, but some might welcome a variant of the controls supplier approach, and some might warrant very different approaches developed in a related manner. Bob's plan 4 soon became known as 'Bob's proposition', and the further propositions which it seeded, to be discussed in the next section, are a much smaller scale variant of the rapid spread of OR use throughout the Allied war effort. They each went well beyond the range of the initial TLC concerns, and collectively they embraced extensive use of a UP concept which went well beyond the scope of the UP variant Nicola had started with to address a bottom-up approach to corporate strategy development.

Further creative testing of capture the context assumptions

George, Bob and Nicola working together soon came up with a very different proposition. This time George provided the leadership, Bob and Nicola the support, and the result became known as 'George's proposition'. Surinder, the sales manager for TLC's lawnmowers, then led the development of 'Surinder's proposition'. Lunchtime TLC discussion of a proposition developed predominantly by Pete was then followed by a proposition from Ajit.

Consider George's proposition first, then the others. Bear in mind each 'proposition' was the result of very preliminary pass 1 through a UP equivalent without any formal use of models by a group of people focused on 'create and enhance plans to address all relevant concerns', in each case starting in a slightly different context but learning from Nicola's use of a UP and her resulting plan 3, plus Bob's use of the UP concept and his resulting plan 4, plus the immediately preceding propositions and the way they were generated.

George's proposition – an engine wholesaler

George began his first discussion of this proposition with Bob and Nicola by reminding Bob of the discussions they had about a year ago involving switching the TLC lawnmower engine supplier from a British based supplier used for decades to a Japanese supplier. TLC customers liked the new engines, and all relevant TLC staff liked the new arrangement. However, George felt TLC was vulnerable to the long supply route and possible price increases if a dominant supplier situation developed. He was also concerned about the space requirements for large order sizes because the engines were bulky. He observed that Bob had recently commented that buyers for several other local firms producing pumps, generators and other equipment had switched to using the same small engine supplier, and while they were equally pleased, they shared the same concerns. George then indicated the lease for the warehouse across the road from TLC was currently available.

Putting these issues together, George proposed a new company – a small engine wholesaler. He suggested calling the new company The Engine Company – contracted to TEC. He suggested TEC should be controlled and probably wholly owned by TLC, but some funding involving local users of TEC's services might be useful. TEC's initial core mandate would be contracting with TLC's Japanese engine supplier as a wholesale distributor for their small engines for the UK Midlands. TEC's initial core market would be TLC and all the other local users of these engines. The core service offered to TLC and other local users by TEC would be a Your-Place-My-Timing supply of engines on a rolling horizon contract arrangement to provide secure supply and stable prices without the current space concerns for TEC customers, with alternative contracts negotiable. This could approach a Just-In-Time position from a TEC customer perspective if a Your-Place-Your-Time variant was what the customer wanted, with the customer specifying delivery times. However, the TEC approach would be better conceived as daily or weekly deliveries to top up safety stocks with Just-In-Time special case (Your-Place-Your-Time) options TEC would not recommend. If a TEC customer had lots of storage space, a special case Your-Place-My-Timing variant might be offered with the customer storing engines well beyond their immediate needs, with discounts, to employ this space in a jointly useful manner, but this could be seen as an option to be recommended only when relevant.

These TEC customer arrangements would require coordination with TEC contracts and delivery arrangements with their Japanese supplier. A My-Place-Your-Timing contract could be offered to the engine supplier. This might facilitate quite large deliveries to TEC if this suited the Japanese supplier. Recognising the more complex demand forecasting now involved would be important. However, this issue could be addressed effectively, and a reduced risk of engine stock-outs should be feasible for TLC and all other TEC customers.

A number of important developments from this basic concept would need careful consideration. TEC might diversify its engine suppliers and provide a range of engine choices for TEC customers, perhaps with related design advice. TEC might expand its geographic remit. All these options would depend upon the market opportunities and threats.

The core concept driving the creation of TEC was making a successful business proposition out of a gap in the market for an organisation which would resolve difficulties for TLC plus comparable difficulties for other firms using the same engine supplier. It might also resolve difficulties for their engine supplier, but it could be viewed as creating difficulties for their engine supplier if their engine supplier attempted to exploit their market position, operating as 'a tasty carrot with big stick potential'. TEC's basis was a buffer between one or more small engine suppliers and users of those suppliers, ideally developing a scale of business which would provide market power plus a broader understanding of the small engine market for TLC.

With important stimulation, support, and help from Nicola and Bob, what George had created was a significant generalisation of the My-Place-Your-Timing approach to the controls supplier, creating a new intermediate engine supplier operation with a new profit stream in addition to other direct and indirect benefits for TLC.

George's proposition was eventually explained to all interested parties in an ordered fashion as outlined earlier, but it had not suddenly occurred to George in this orderly manner – it had emerged from iterations of his UP equivalent, building on what Nicola and Bob had demonstrated and interactive discussions with both of them.

The crucial lesson George had picked up was testing *all* his planning assumptions as he experimented with new planning ideas, *being especially sensitive to long-standing context assumptions*. In UP concept terms he had started to test 'capture the context' assumptions, asking even more fundamental questions than Bob or Nicola did. The key new idea was TLC did not need to stick to just manufacturing lawnmowers if an interesting upstream supply chain opportunity presented itself. George had tested and relaxed an assumption which he had inherited from his father which had become central to the nature of TLC's business and culture. Until now they had been assuming that TLC's *only* business was manufacturing lawnmowers. Now their eyes were opened to other opportunities.

George's proposition demonstrates a whole new level of creativity with strategic vision and strategic clarity implications for *any organisation* which might be triggered by the widespread use of a UP which targets the testing of context assumptions. In particular, once George understood the benefits to both TLC and their controls supplier of supply chain management based on Bob's plan 4, he could see a rich set of related contract variants as a basis for a new company which could make a profit out of a gap in the small engine supply market as well as resolving TLC engine supply problems. His starting place for TEC was trying to resolve the obvious difficulties associated with simply replicating Bob's approach to controls when the items purchased from a supplier were relatively large, relatively expensive, and shipped a long distance, by a company which was becoming very popular with a wide range of customers in the UK and worldwide.

Once George had the basis of his proposition clear in his own mind, he began shaping the plan and further testing of associated assumptions with Nicola and Bob. They did not take it as far as using formal models to shape the emerging plans, but they did test and develop some of the key planning assumptions necessary for a very preliminary business case model.

George was very keen to discuss his TEC proposition with Ajit as soon as possible. He knew he might be getting out of his depth with a whole new business model involving TLC and TEC. George relied on Ajit's council on all strategic choices. However, at this point Ajit was taking a well-deserved holiday.

Surinder's proposition – a machinery company

Surinder and George had always struggled with the very large inventories of lawnmowers which accumulated during the autumn and winter, prior to the spring rush and the reasonably steady summer demand rate. George had used local warehouses to provide space on an ad hoc basis, partially linked to comparable arrangements for large deliveries of engines, and on an ad hoc basis Surinder had negotiated some large winter period sales of TLC lawnmowers to large retailers with price reductions they passed on to customers, plus various other tactics of this kind. These ad hoc approaches had kept TLC finished goods lawnmower inventories within manageable bounds, but both felt a more systematic approach was overdue.

A related but separate issue was George and Surinder had always agreed 'standard prices' for TLC lawnmowers on a basis largely driven by costs and set with limited pricing expertise within the upper 'quality' end of prices charged by competitors. Surinder had always seen

TLC as a 'production driven' organisation, with her sales role as primarily an order processor for the retail outlets and garden machinery servicing companies selling the lawnmowers which TLC produced. She had always wondered if a stronger marketing lead from her might be better for TLC as well as more stimulating for her.

Once George was comfortable with the way his TEC discussions with Bob and Nicola were progressing, he began related discussions with Surinder. Surinder was particularly interested in Bob's increased market power in the controls supplier relationship, plus the broader market power issues raised by George's proposition for TEC. In addition to her conversations with George, Surinder started talking to Bob and Nicola, and the seeds of her own proposition began to take root.

The assumption that TLC was just in the lawnmower manufacturing business had been questioned and revoked by George's TEC concept, a change of working assumptions with some quite fundamental further corporate change implications. Surinder and George soon saw some of the implications in terms of a further new company which Surinder developed preliminary plans for, calling it The Machines Company – contracted to TMC.

TMC could share warehouse space with TEC. Its initial core business could be systematic marketing of TLC lawnmowers to current sales outlets, using Your-Place-My-Time options comparable to TLC and TEC. But these options could be generalised to include delivery of lawnmowers direct to customers when ordered in a shop which just kept a limited range of show models, or a garden machinery servicing company which just kept a range of brochures. It could be further extended to direct marketing to customers via a mail-order business prototype of post-millennium online web-based direct sales. Managing TLC's finished goods inventory would be a by-product of this TMC core business.

However, the really big growth in business which TMC might be set up to exploit could be using TMC direct retail and wholesale capability to market machinery manufactured by other companies as well as TLC lawnmowers. As Surinder saw it, this was revolutionary because it moved TCL's focus from producing lawnmowers to marketing machines.

Two very different and probably incompatible directions for a single new company might be pursued. One was selling generators, pumps, and other equipment, probably manufactured in the UK by companies with sales capabilities which were limited in a manner comparable to TLC, perhaps some of the initial partners in TEC, or other TEC customers. The other was selling machinery manufactured by other companies which was all garden machinery, possibly manufactured in other countries with lower costs, probably limited to high-quality up-market products like TLCs current mower range. Surinder proposed a focus on the second option.

Surinder's proposition was initiated by applying the supply-side (upstream) thinking behind TEC to the demand-side (downstream) management of lawnmower sales, initially transforming George's proposition into a generalised form of 'vertical integration'. However, the potential ramifications of a fully developed TMC concept were very much broader and more complex, taking the TLC/TEC/TMC group into a whole new corporate strategy.

George soon began to see the wider implications and started an ongoing conversation about some of the more important possible consequences with Pete. George greatly valued Surinder's new ideas and enthusiasm, but he had well-founded concerns about Surinder's limited experience base for managing a venture like TMC, and even more concerns about how he might manage the important implications involving Pete and TLC's manufacturing operations. George was now becoming very anxious about the need to talk to Ajit. But he was far too enthusiastic about the possibilities emerging to slow down his discussions with Surinder and Pete until Ajit's return.

Pete's proposition – formally testing design, production and product range assumptions

George's father had set up and nourished a long-standing TLC tradition of companywide morning coffee and afternoon tea breaks. They were usually completely informal. Football and similar topics or the latest gossip usually dominated discussion in small groups, but sometimes company business was discussed.

After extensive discussions between Pete and George, and considerable thinking about the issues by both, George used a longer than usual coffee break to outline 'Pete's proposition'. Pete was personable, thoughtful, and respected by all, but slightly shy, and he preferred George presenting his proposition. George was very pleased to do so. Pete's proposition raised some sensitive issues which George wanted addressed along the lines Pete proposed. However, George believed it would be useful if he was the one explaining Pete's proposition.

George began by first outlining Dave's suggestion, Nicola's plan 3, Bob's plan 4 or proposition, George's own TEC proposition, and Surinder's TMC proposition. He suggested most TLC employees had no doubt heard about these propositions via the usual gossip, but he wanted them all to hear the same story as he saw it in its current form. He nodded to Ajit, who had returned from holiday the previous evening, and indicated that now that Ajit was back, he and Ajit had a lot of further work to do, with Ajit taking the lead in some key areas, but he wanted to bring them all up to date now. He then explained that Pete had built on Surinder's TMC ideas to develop several suggestions, in effect dealing directly and explicitly with two sensitive issues which Surinder's proposition had exposed but avoided discussing.

The first was the advantages and disadvantages of their current product range relative to competitors. The second was the possible advantages and disadvantages of outsourcing some of their current production and design processes.

In effect, a questioning of long-standing working assumptions had been kicked off by Dave. The basis of a new approach to all supply-side issues had been triggered by Nicola. This development had been very ably transformed into a more general supply-side planning approach by Bob. George had then taken the supply side ideas further with his TEC proposition. Surinder had taken George's ideas further still, into demand side issues including sales of machines produced by other manufacturers. But Pete had started to integrate Surinder's concerns with some very fundamental core issues for TLC. George and Pete had spent some time developing some preliminary plans for an internal review of key working assumptions underlying their current manufacturing operations. There was a lot more work to do, but he and Pete had provisionally agreed to a four stage process, subject to discussions he now wanted to initiate with Ajit, and further ideas any TLC staff might like to suggest.

First, Pete and Surinder should test the quality of TLC's lawnmower designs in terms of purchaser preferences, benchmarking the TLC designs against all relevant competitors. Pete thought Surinder might lead, perhaps with support from Nicola, but he also thought buying in some marketing expertise would be wise. In the past George and Pete had evolved TLC designs based on feedback from TLC lawnmower owners and garden machinery servicing companies plus their use of the products in their own gardens. They had never undertaken a systematic direct investigation of all relevant competitive machines. TLC needed a step change increase in its marketing management and planning capabilities.

Second, Pete should test the quality of TLC's current and evolving lawnmower designs in terms of economic production in a more formal way than they had in the past. Pete thought he could probably manage this on his own, but they might consider outsourcing some aspects of design to get the best possible overall approach once he and George and Surinder were clear about what they thought mattered and wanted to test their preliminary plans.

Third, Pete should test the efficiency of TLC's production processes more formally than he had in the past, perhaps benchmarking it against outsourcing production to a more efficient supplier of complete or partially assembled lawnmowers with a view to ensuring all current TLC production processes remained competitive. Pete thought Bob could probably help with this, and possibly lead on some aspects. Pete suggested visits to carefully selected other production facilities would be a crucial aspect of this, and George might want to be involved before it progressed very far.

Fourth, George, Pete, Bob and Surinder, perhaps with help from Nicola, and certainly with the enhanced marketing capability noted above, should test the effectiveness and efficiency of TLC's range of products in portfolio terms at an overall corporate strategy level, with a view to a wider range of complementary equipment, some produced by them, some supplied by others. Their intention would be preserving a core of high-quality British products built in their current Birmingham facilities, perhaps as only part of a much wider set of complementary products bearing the TLC brand. Expansion of their current production with bigger premises and a wider range of products was George's aim, but this ambition would need to be tested against the obvious alternatives.

In terms of all four stages just carrying on as at present was an option, but assuming this was the best choice needed a systematic approach to assumption testing. A fixed order quantity for controls had needed testing – but it was pure serendipity that Dave had raised the issue and Nicola had been there to kick off a very enlightening chain of developments. Pete and George were now convinced that a systematic approach to well-considered change as and when appropriate throughout TLC was probably crucial to a healthy future for TLC, starting with core business assumptions.

George thanked Dave for raising the need to test the fixed order quantity assumption for controls, briefly but sincerely. He then thanked Nicola, Bob, Surinder and Pete for their subsequent efforts, much more fully as was clearly appropriate, with special emphasis on the crucial roles played by each. He suggested all TLC employees help to carry these propositions forward when opportunities to make suggestions occurred to them. TLC did not have a 'suggestions box', but the employees all knew that he was open to suggestions anytime. He now wanted to spend a significant amount of time discussing all these propositions with Ajit before they went any further.

George was a natural optimist, and he liked having other natural optimists around him. However, he was well aware that this sometimes left him exposed to misguided enthusiasms. George was also aware of two other relevant issues: he knew he was not as systematic as he might be, and he recognised he was not the natural top-down thinker Ajit was. Nicola had motivated him to start testing all key assumptions in a more systematic manner, as well as triggering creativity which led to the emergence of a number of potentially very important possible opportunities. But he relied on Ajit to keep his more dangerous ideas in check and to impose some systematic top-down strategic planning on TLC.

Ajit was a natural top-down strategic thinker, who liked to start with questions like 'Where do we think we are trying to get to?' and 'Why?' before getting into the details of 'How are we going to get there?'

In addition to insisting that George address these top-down concerns, Ajit played the insightful natural pessimist role in the context of discussing George's latest enthusiasm – he saw this as part of his job description. However, Ajit reverted to an optimist out of the office and in the office once he believed George had a reasonable grip on the threats as well as the opportunities associated with his current passions.

George and Ajit were a leadership partnership, and both understood the complementary nature of their roles.

Ajit's proposition – the TXC group mission, ownership and financing structure

After extensive discussions between Ajit and George, George asked Ajit to outline his proposition at a TLC coffee break.

Ajit started by indicating that George thinking of TEC as a separate company was useful in several ways, as was Surinder thinking of TMC as a separate company, but Pete's proposition made it very clear that TLC, TEC, and TMC had to be operated within a coherent overall corporate strategy, and further separate companies needing a collective strategy might be required over time.

Ajit suggested they use TXC with X = L + E + M + other company identifiers in the group which might emerge over time as a working label for the new group of companies. TXC might evolve in ways they could not foresee now, but an initial view of what direction they wanted TXC to move in and how it should decide its strategy was an urgent priority concern.

A particular component concern for Ajit was financing for the kind of expansion being discussed. He did not think simply going to the bank for further finance was viable, and he did not think doing so would be sensible even if it did prove viable.

This raised quite fundamental concerns – the desirable future of TXC in terms of its ownership structure and its basic mission as seen by its owners.

One option which he and George had discussed was George and other members of his family, Nicola's mother for example, taking big mortgages on their houses and pulling together other assets to transform TLC into TXC. One variant of this approach was TXC becoming listed on the stock exchange as a public limited company after five or ten years. This could keep the TXC cost of capital reasonably low in the crucial early years and provide a long-term return for George and his family when TXC was floated in a form they might find attractive. However, it would concentrate the risk on George and his family in the short-term and the medium-term, and the current TLC friendly and collaborative family company feel – very much enjoyed by all TLC employees including him – would probably be lost if and when TXC became a public limited company.

Ajit emphasised the obvious fact that shareholders in public or private companies of any kind wanted a return on their financial investment, and George was not an exception. George was very keen to make long-, medium-, and short-term profits. But George saw the corporate culture issues associated with his approach to collaboration and respect for all employees as an enlightened way to achieving lower costs and higher productivity as well as a matter of social responsibility and enjoying working with people who took pride in what they did and how they did it. George understood that the TLC employees he wanted to hire and retain wanted to work in an atmosphere where their contributions were valued and they could work with people they respected in a collaborative manner. This was a central aspect of the current TLC corporate culture. It had begun with George's father, and it could be lost when George retired if TLC had become a public limited company in the interim. For example, even if TXC thrived in all respects, if it were a public company a majority shareholding might be purchased by a non-UK manufacturing company which valued the

TLC brand plus TEC and TMC operations but not manufacturing in the UK, with massive implications.

George and his father had been long-time fans of the Cadbury family approach, the locally based (Bournville) world-famous chocolate company founders who began with 19th-century Quaker zeal to build an ethically driven form of capitalism. The Cadbury's approach was respected worldwide, inspiring Milton Hershey for example, America's 'chocolate king'.

It would be 25 years before Kraft buying Cadbury-Schweppes in 2010 seriously damaged Anglo–US relationships from the perspective of some people in the UK. The results received very hostile UK national press attention immediately and later because of the behaviour of Mondelez International, the company Cadbury was spun into by Kraft, and ongoing concerns show no current sign of going away. George and Ajit did not have the foresight to anticipate this outcome, but in general terms, both understood this kind of threat.

George knew TLC needed to raise more capital, but his current preference, which Ajit strongly supported, was an employee partnership form of corporate structure using features of the John Lewis Partnership and other similar approaches. Ajit was letting everybody know this now, with George's approval, because they both wanted to test this proposition in terms of everyone's reaction. If George decided to go this way, it did not mean that all TLC employees would be required to invest financially in TXC themselves. But it did mean that part of their income would be dividends on an 'employee partnership shares' basis, a form of bonus linked to profitability. Furthermore, they might opt to take all or some of this bonus in the form of 'investment partnership shares', which would earn a return on the capital they choose to invest. Further financial investment might be feasible for those who wished and encouraged for those with senior management responsibilities.

Ajit emphasised that making this kind of employee partnership organisation work effectively and efficiently over the long-term was *much* more complex than at first sight it might seem. The John Lewis Partnership had a long and highly respected history in the UK retail trade, with department stores and Waitrose supermarkets, but it had a carefully crafted structure suited to its particular context. To develop a variant suited to TXC, George would have to test all key assumptions very carefully, with reference to what worked well and what failed elsewhere, from all relevant perspectives.

Ajit did not think it was appropriate to share with all TLC employees his view that the most appropriate ownership structure for TXC needed careful consideration in the context of an assessment by George of the extent to which his ambitions for TXC were motivated by his relative priorities in terms of a balanced mix of a desire to:

1 provide a sustainable and secure income for himself and his family,
2 provide his employees with sustainable and rewarding jobs, and
3 provide his customers with high-quality products at a fair price,
4 plus being socially useful in other ways important to George.

However, he did share this view with George. Ajit knew the fourth item probably included continuing to support George's favourite football team as a corporate sponsor plus his TLC apprentice training programme, but he did not say so or elaborate further on any of the other issues. Indeed, he explicitly omitted even thinking about the considerable complexities involved, because doing so would not be productive.

Although Ajit did not think it relevant to take this further with George at this stage in their discussion, you may find it useful to briefly explore the basis of Ajit's understanding of what shapes corporate ethos in a very simple organisation like TLC, linking this discussion to the capability-culture concept and the underlying corporate structure and values concepts using one of many possible sets of simple common language. Doing so has immediate value, but it also allows comparisons in the contexts of the tales in Chapters 6 to 9.

Ajit included personal 'passions', 'responsibilities' and a wide range of 'issues in between' in his views of how he, George, and other people might approach all relevant corporate objectives. He used a common working definition of *passions* – 'what normally gets you up in the morning and keeps you going all day'. He used a compatible definition of *responsibilities* (that need to be met) – 'what normally keeps you fully engaged all day in an appropriate manner even if you are not really enjoying meeting the responsibilities involved'.

From Ajit's perspective everyone had their own individual views about what were preferred 'pleasurable passions', 'painful responsibilities' that needed to be met, and everything in between. He saw corporate motivation as a very complex set of issues not immediately relevant to his discussion with George, but he knew George's pleasurable passions included high-quality lawnmowers at a fair price and football, his painful responsibilities included paying all relevant taxes at a fair level, and his issues in between included providing a sustainable and secure income for himself and his family, providing his employees with sustainable and rewarding jobs, and training apprentices who might or might not stay on as TLC employees.

Pleasurable passions for Ajit included his family and doing his job as well as he could, and he was not much interested in either lawnmowers or football, but he strongly approved of George's underlying values defined in broad terms to include his generosity of spirit, his open approach to everyone, his ethical values, and their effect on the ethos of TLC.

Ajit greatly enjoyed working with George and the opportunity provided by his role in TLC, and he believed that most other TLC employees shared his appreciation of the opportunity provided by their role in TLC, with a wide mix of pleasurable passions and views on painful responsibilities. He believed that the TLC corporate ethos was shaped by George's own version or variant of Ajit's passion-responsibility concept and underlying values plus the reactions of others to George's actions, and the family firm feel about TLC was part of this. It was also shaped by the social and political culture which TLC operated in. Ajit thought corporate ethos was an important issue of considerable complexity, even in the context of this relatively simple family business. It mattered greatly, and it had an impact on corporate capability as well as corporate culture, although exactly how corporate ethos operated was ambiguous and not a matter of immediate concern. It would become a matter of great concern if George allowed the management of TLC to become controlled by an organisation which wanted the brand but not the manufacturing organisation.

Returning to Ajit's discussion with George, having raised the issue of ownership and financing structure options, Ajit then suggested that whatever approach TLC adopted, TXC corporate governance arrangements would have to be more formal than the structure currently used by George as TLC's 'general manager'. He assumed George would become Chief Executive Officer (CEO) and Chairman of the Board for TXC if and when it emerged as a separate company. He assumed Bob, Pete, Surinder and he would all become executive directors with 'operations director' roles. He assumed an employee partnership organisation would require at least one non-executive 'employee director' representative of all employees, if they went that route. He assumed at least one non-executive director representative of all investors who were not employees, like Nicola's mother. Furthermore, and crucially, he thought two new executive director positions were probably essential – defined by significant TXC roles which were currently less significant TLC roles.

One of these new executive director roles was leading corporate planning in top-down strategic terms, coordinating this with the bottom-up strategic implication of all the current propositions and those to come. For example, it seemed to him that Pete's proposition should be their first priority, then Surinder's, then George's, the reverse of the order in which they had emerged, because Pete's proposition was at the very core of TLC's current operations and Surinder's TMC was more closely coupled to this core than was George's TEC proposition. TXC needed a more ordered and experienced approach to this kind of top-down strategic thinking than he or George could currently provide, and in his view, early recruitment of someone who could bring the needed new capabilities but fit well with existing TLC capabilities and culture was an important consideration.

Ajit believed a wide range of backgrounds might be suitable for the new corporate planning director TXC needed, but someone with extensive marketing experience who could mentor Surinder and help shift the corporate culture towards marketing would be particularly attractive. TLC needed this culture shift, support for Surinder was needed, and meeting both via the new corporate planning director with marketing expertise seemed a useful possibility.

The other new executive director role was leading all the change-management 'project planning' – the portfolio of projects and programmes which would achieve the envisaged corporate changes. For example, Pete needed someone to help him lead the change programme he was suggesting they should embark on who could later help Surinder and George with the coordinated change-management programmes associated with TMC and TEC.

A relatively stable past had allowed George to deal with the top-down strategic corporate planning and the project (change-management) planning leadership roles plus the CEO and chairman roles, with support from Ajit. However, the proposed transition from the current TLC to TXC would need careful preparation and testing of emergent corporate structures. This ought to involve at least two more people with additional skill sets who could also help them to lead the ongoing changes.

Ajit's natural capabilities had been marginally strengthened by using some features of the UP demonstrated by Nicola and the resulting development by Bob plus the propositions by George, Surinder and Pete in a somewhat different manner. However, he was not a fluent user of process ideas, and he recognised that he and everyone else needed support if the degree of change envisaged was going to be pursued effectively and efficiently. He found it difficult to translate his colleagues' use of the UP concept in simple bottom-up analysis terms into the forms needed, as discussed in Chapters 6, 7, 8 and 9 of this book, because there was a big difference between bottom-up and top-down thinking, and he lacked the requisite experience base. Bottom-up thinking was not the focus of his normal approach to the issues just discussed. Indeed, his natural top-down thinking approach with a direct concern for strategy was crucial to balance the bottom-up creativity of the others.

Testing assumptions about how top-down and bottom-up thinking meshed was crucial. Ajit did not have formal training in this area, but his significant natural ability included the wisdom to see when more capability was needed because of his own limitations.

Ajit might have noted that Nicola was very lucky that her knowledge of inventory models and a UP concept fitted the controls context so well – with a corporate need for wider access to relevant generic models and specific processes as well as other variants of the universal process which Nicola could contribute to but not necessarily lead. Furthermore, he might have noted that Bob was clearly able and experienced and very insightful to have seen the advantages associated with transforming Nicola's plan 3 into Bob's plan 4, but he might benefit from more exposure to wider supply chain management experience via professional courses. Pete was a very capable operations manager, but some more exposure to formal concepts in this area would probably be useful. And as he indicated earlier, Surinder could definitely do with some additional marketing expertise and experienced support to exploit her obvious potential.

Creative testing of all the UP front-end working assumptions

If he had been familiar with the UP concept and the rest of this book, Ajit might have understood and mentioned several additional points.

First, the testing of working assumptions associated with models used to shape plans is the traditional focus of OR process explanations, but the importance of testing working assumptions is often overlooked by those who use models from other professional perspectives. It is crucially important to test underlying assumptions for all relevant models, including those borrowed from behavioural and physical sciences not always seen as cognate sciences, whatever the professional decision-making perspective involved.

Second, extending the testing of working assumptions to a view of plans which is much broader than just the models used to shape aspects of the plans is an important issue highlighted by adding the 'create and enhance the plans' phase to the UP concept. It significantly broadens the scope of the UP concept, as demonstrated by Bob's plan 4. It acts as a gateway concept which facilitates bottom-up strategic thinking instead of just tactical thinking.

Third, extending the testing of working assumptions to 'capture the context' assumptions is highlighted by adding this phase to the UP, and it further broadens the scope of the UP. This was demonstrated by Bob seeing the need to shift to a much broader supply chain perspective which triggered George thinking about a new business opportunity and then the successive propositions generated by Surinder, Pete, and Ajit. Creative testing of the assumptions associated with 'capture the context with appropriate clarity' ultimately had to address the implicit TLC assumption 'TLC is a family owned lawnmower manufacturing business'. George was the most appropriate person to lead on this, but Surinder, Pete, and Ajit built on George's leadership in the way good leaders encourage. The UP concept should encourage this kind of thinking and interaction. Understanding the relationship between assumptions and reality is the key to creative leaps. Creative leaps are central to opportunity efficiency. The higher the strategic level of the assumptions, the bigger the prizes for creative leaps. The early analysis by Nicola was, in effect, an investment in insight and understanding, a learning process with returns which could be leveraged by an understanding of all relevant issues in top-down terms. To fail to look for and make associated creative leaps is to waste this investment. Creative leaps are central to clarifying opportunity, complexity, uncertainty, and risk. Careful analysis without inspired synthesis can be a serious waste of opportunities. Creative leaps and inspired synthesis may be led by specific individuals, but corporate groups who enjoy the kind of teamwork-based capability-culture assets demonstrated by TLC are particularly well placed to make effective use of their opportunities.

Fourth, creative testing of 'select and focus the process for appropriate clarity' is also important, to complete the testing of UP front-end assumptions. Adding the 'select and focus the process' phase to the UP has yet to play a demonstrable role, but Chapter 6 starts to do so, and Chapter 7 does so more extensively. Chapter 7 also outlines a project planning process which Ajit's suggested project's director might bring to TXC, Chapter 8 outlines a corporate planning approach which Ajit's suggested corporate planning director might bring to TXC, and Chapter 9 extends the capabilities of the Chapter 8 framework.

Fifth, this chapter demonstrates the effective use of a simple basic form of the UP concept as understood by Nicola and built on by the others, but it does not even attempt to demonstrate how best to turn George's proposition and all subsequent propositions into operational plans as explored in following Part 2 chapters.

Ajit's crucial observations about the need for top-down thinking plus necessary additions to TXC competence before they go very far could be extended to include experience with unfamiliar UP and SP concepts as well as the knowledge and experience specific to wholesale operations and marketing which TLC did not currently have. Put a bit differently, if TLC wants to build on George's proposition and any of the other subsequent propositions in an effective manner, TLC would be well advised to acquire all the planning capabilities discussed later in this book. The UP concept employed by this chapter achieved a great deal for TLC, in part because the tale of this chapter was based upon working assumptions explicitly chosen to maximise what might be achieved. However, while Nicola's approach in passes 1, 2 and 3 generalises in a fairly obvious way to Bob's plan 4, and use of the front-end phases of a UP is clearly linked to the propositions generated, it is not obvious how the UP can be used to develop these propositions. The basic difficulty is that the very general (unrestricted) nature of the UP concept is valuable when starting with a simple and specific 'problem' like 'What order quantity is appropriate?' But the model focused interpretation of the UP Nicola understood is not broad enough or capable enough when we start with a much more complex context like the need to consider how to develop TXC as a whole or as specific new companies in its portfolio, issues addressed in Chapters 7 and 8. We need a more developed set of capabilities for the UP which recognises the need to address these issues, and seeing this need as a key capability-culture concept issue is useful.

Finally, it might seem that the capability-culture concept as elaborated in Chapter 2 has yet to play a demonstrably important role, but Nicola's arrival would arguably have had very little immediate impact if TLC did not have the capability-culture asset characteristics portrayed in this tale. TLC had a capability-culture with deeply embedded natural competence and teamwork, and when TLC acquired the modest UP concept process knowledge Nicola brought, it was used very effectively. This role for capability-culture assets was shaped by the underlying corporate structure and the way George interpreted and developed that structure. The capability-culture concept lies behind and reinforces Ajit's case for a significant strengthening of TLC capabilities before making radical changes in terms of TXC development. It should also help to clarify the 'learning process' ideas introduced in this chapter and later tales and the capability-culture interactions. This capability-culture assets and corporate structure relationship are also used in a range of quite different contexts in following chapters.

Looking wider or deeper at key strategic and tactical choices

The iterative process illustrated by this chapter's tale may suggest a smooth succession of iterations, gradually seeing a bigger picture emerge as 'layers of the onion' are peeled away, and gradually developing more definition detail of what really matters as what matters most gradually emerges from the initial fog of ambiguity. The TLC tale was designed to build understanding in layers which is bound to give this impression. However, in practice iterations do not usually proceed as smoothly as this chapter's tale suggests. Even if we have useful prior views about the scope for bigger picture or 'greater depth' perspectives, we may need to overcome some significant surprises and obstacles to get there.

Nicola's discussion of her three pass approach explicitly acknowledged that she simply ignored dead ends she had explored in her discussion with George. Bob's pass 4 discussion also indicated that the development of his proposition was not entirely straightforward. This was implicit in all the later proposition development discussion when not mentioned.

Successive testing of working assumptions and creative interpretation of results is the basis of the iterative nature of the UP. Sometimes the consideration of further possible iterations suggests that enough has been done and the process should stop. Sometimes it suggests a need to 'look deeper' – as when planned and unplanned stock-outs were addressed and a free credit period plus inflation-driven appreciation was identified as a key issue. Sometimes looking deeper suggests big opportunities may be available if the process changes direction to 'look wider' – as when the much bigger order suggested by the free credit period in conjunction with inflation identified by Nicola triggered Bob's move into a supply-side management strategy which meant delivery by the controls supplier when it suited the supplier based on a collaborative supply contract. George's proposition and the subsequent TXC generalisations kept looking wider, but each required later attention to more depth.

Iteration management involves some subtle issues which significantly benefit from craft and experience, associated judicious anticipation in particular. Effective and efficient iteration management also benefits from remaining flexible and open to surprises.

Any of the characters in this tale might have had less luck than they all enjoyed. The tale of this chapter involves an explicit assumption that good luck does not always happen, but good luck needs to be appreciated and exploited when it does happen, and bad luck needs to be overcome too.

It was convenient starting our series of chapter length tales with a story which illustrates an optimistic perspective by people who on this occasion are lucky. Later chapters give more emphasis to bad luck. Sometimes bad luck needs to be overcome when quite serious unanticipated outcomes occur. Sometimes bad luck needs to be avoided in advance. Often a combination of both is the best planning basis.

This is a very brief section. However, the subtle nature of iteration control is of crucial importance in terms of strategic vision and strategic clarity plus underlying tactical clarity. It involves a key capability-culture asset. That is why a separate section has been used. It is central to the significant discussion in all following chapters of this book, although drawing attention to its importance each and every time is avoided because doing so would soon get tedious.

Consolidating key concepts

To help you synthesise the strategic clarity roles of some of the ideas explored in this chapter, this section provides some consolidating comments.

Goals–plans relationships development

A lack of clarity about *all* relevant objectives is a fundamental problem for any kind of planning. The obvious follow-on problem is a failure to understand how plans should lead to achieving those objectives, including the use of appropriate contingency plans. This is what goals–plans relationships development is about, and clarity about the relationship between what is planned and the outcomes anticipated in terms of all relevant objectives is important.

What Nicola's pass 1 demonstrated was the development of a very simple starting point set of assumptions about goals–plans relationships for that part of Pete's current plan which had been questioned – the optimal order quantity. This starting point addressed the trade-off between the cost per order and the cost of holding inventory per item per unit of time in the simplest terms feasible given a competent level of clarity about the working assumptions employed. Uncertainty about the expected value of both these costs was addressed in terms of an interval estimate of the expected values, with an explicit focus on the wide range associated with C_o and the seasonal variations suggesting bigger orders in the spring period clearly flagged. A simple understanding of the relationship between stochastic (probabilistic) and deterministic (non-probabilistic) models to explore goals–plans relationships was evident from the outset. But the emphasis in pass 1 was a simple view of what both order costs and holding costs involved, initially used in a prescriptive deterministic model of a central causal relationship in the optimal order quantity concept. This model suggested plan revision from 2,000 controls per order to 1,500 controls.

Nicola's pass 2 identified and clarified a starting point set of assumptions about goals–plans relationships for the safety stock part of Pete's current plan which had not been questioned in pass 1. However, it was worth attention in an integrated way to review Pete's current plans for the supply of controls as a whole. Furthermore, the stochastic (probabilistic) modelling approach illustrates the way a statistically based understanding of uncertainty in a HAT framework can be integrated with a very different kind of model, tailoring a hybrid approach to what is needed.

Nicola's pass 3 and her creative plan 3 interpretation demonstrated the value of a deeper look at these relationships in terms of assumptions about free credit periods and related price inflation. In this case the aspects of uncertainty addressed, completely overlooked earlier, were rather different, and the plan revision from 1,500 to 7,000 involved a massive move in the opposite direction. This illustrated how important what we overlook can be, a way of looking at unknown unknowns driven by stealth assumptions.

Bob's pass 4 to create plan 4 broadened the scope of the plans, dropping the assumption of a fixed order quantity determined by TLC, but retaining the testing of all relevant assumptions to shape the plan. In this case understanding the value of going beyond the original plan assumption that an optimal order quantity was appropriate was very different again, and even more important in terms of cost savings. This further demonstrated how important testing this kind of assumption can be in relation to clarifying goals–plans relationships. We need to test all assumptions associated with plans, not just those associated with aspects which have been modelled.

The basis of the resulting plans and their relationship with associated objectives remained fairly clear for Bob's proposition. However, the plans necessary to implement the following propositions started to become relatively ambiguous.

All the subsequent proposition developments involved further questioning of earlier TLC corporate assumptions associated with goals–plans relationships, clearly a beneficial process. George's proposition was a key one for unlocking further creativity. It questioned the basis of the family business in a way Surinder could build on, which, in turn, exposed the need for Pete to develop his proposition.

Ajit introduced some basic top-down goal planning ideas. All organisations need a top-down approach which asks 'Where do we think we want to get to?' and 'Why?' Goals–plans relationships need top-down assessment. Ajit made it clear that this top-down approach should lead to a coordinated view of *all* corporate objectives, addressing how all aspects of operations management and project management contribute to overall performance, to plan how to get there. But Ajit did not address how to undertake any of this planning, even in outline what needs to be done terms. These issues are explored in Chapters 6, 7, 8 and 9.

One of this book's framing assumptions is *all* target readers need the broad understanding of the role of processes and models in helping planners to achieve clarity about goals–plans relationships. This chapter provides a foundation for this aspect of strategic clarity, exploring its tactical clarity basis in a relatively simple context.

Useful perspectives on the opportunities which underlie unexplored uncertainty

A starting point for several linked issues briefly explored in this subsection is a quotation often attributed to Sir Winston Churchill:

> *A pessimist sees the difficulty in every opportunity,*
> *an optimist sees the opportunity in every difficulty.*

Churchill may have borrowed the underlying idea from someone else, but whoever first captured this idea, Churchill's version is a very useful reminder to stay optimistic *when appropriate* even when confronted with great difficulties, interpreting *difficulties* in generalised terms as unwelcome constraints, problems, challenges, risks or threats.

During my involvement with the IBM UK Forum 2 culture change programme in the 1990s, an often-quoted mantra embedded in IBM culture, which can be seen as a variant of the Churchill quote, was:

> *There is no such thing as problems – only opportunities,*

with some of the older and wiser hands muttering under their breath the proviso:

> *although sometimes opportunities are insurmountable!*

This IBM mantra can be seen as a very useful reminder to focus on the opportunities *when appropriate*, remembering that exploiting some opportunities may not be feasible. In a worst-case scenario trying to capture 'insurmountable opportunities' can serve as a self-inflicted fatal wound.

It is obviously important to understand that not all opportunities present as unwelcome constraints, problems, challenges, risks or threats. Some opportunities present as 'gifts'. Gifts may be just variants of fate or good luck, and gifts may be the straightforward genuine benevolence of family or close friends, but especially in a commercial context, gifts may be conditioned by an expectation of reciprocation. An obvious and possibly relevant saying here is perhaps:

> *Never look a gift horse in the mouth,*

with constructive tension provided by the proviso,

> *but sometimes assumptions about 'gifts' need a*
> *'there is no such thing as a free lunch' test.*

Opportunities of many different kinds have been considered in this chapter's tale, without always using the term opportunity. The starting point was Dave attempting to find an opportunity to reduce the number of times he had to go to the control supplier by testing the current TLC order quantity assumption. George, Surinder, Pete and Ajit's propositions to test current TLC corporate boundaries were end points for this chapter but opportunities which are starting points for much bigger journeys to a TXC company group. The central part of the journey in this chapter involved Nicola looking for useful ways to test and relax key assumptions underlying her EOQ model, followed by Bob seeking a much better supply plan and supplier relationship with the benefits of Nicola's ideas plus the further benefits of generalisation of the assumptions underlying the EOQ concept.

When Nicola began developing the basic EOQ model in pass 1, the basic form of the TLC plan was predetermined – assumed to be a fixed order quantity. The uncertainty addressed was limited to 'What value should this fixed order quantity take, and why?' The underlying complexity first addressed was the relationship between holding cost and order cost per unit time for different order quantities. Both Nicola and George needed to understand how this relationship worked, and the asymmetry associated with rounding the order quantity for convenience and errors in their parameter estimates. The basic EOQ model should be seen as a way of educating people about this relationship, not a simple golden rule with a formula for inventory management to crank out optimal solutions.

When Nicola began pass 2 by demonstrating planned stock-outs altered the result so little that rounding produced exactly the same answer, she was illustrating the robustness of her pass 1 result to the implicit assumption that planned stock-outs would not be considered. This was complementary to demonstrating that unplanned stock-outs were important but arguably overplayed by Pete's three day (300 controls) safety stock. Reduction to one day (100 controls) plus an informal contingency plan involving enhanced communication between Pete and Dave might save significant sums. Resolution of additional uncertainty by exploring underlying complexity that might matter, with everyone understanding why it did or did not matter, was the purpose of the exercise, not just a more sophisticated model.

When Nicola began pass 3 by exploring the implications of a free credit period and simultaneous significant inflation, the optimal order quantity which pass 1 moved from 2,000 down to 1,500 shot up to 7,000, making it very clear that passes 1 and 2 were taking TLC in the wrong direction. The 7,000 figure in itself was not all that important. What was crucial was understanding that if you can enjoy the upside of inflation by buying large quantities of inputs with someone else's money, you are onto a winner – an opportunity which passes 1 and 2 had completely missed.

Bob's further developments in his pass 4 plan built upon Nicola's pass 3 to grasp what really mattered. They did not actually want to order a large amount every few months for immediate delivery. What they wanted was a fixed price for six months, orderly price increases within a rolling annual contract, and no stock-outs. It was better for TLC *and* for its controls supplier to let the controls supplier deliver smaller amounts when it suited the controls supplier so long as TLC did not run out, paying for the controls according to an assumed uniform rate of usage over the six-month period. Some of the benefits to the controls supplier could be leveraged into lower prices. This could produce a win–win situation, with Bob making sure that TLC got as much of the joint pot of winnings as he could.

Getting beyond the EOQ model to an understanding of the My-Place-Your-Timing approach, and an ability to sell it to its supplier, is a demonstration of clarity efficient resolution of uncertainty and underlying complexity to harvest an opportunity that was just waiting to be found. Nicola and Bob were on a treasure hunt, looking for opportunities amongst the uncertainty previously unexplored. Generally speaking, people do not find treasure if they do not know both what to look for and how to search for it in a systematic manner. The tale ensured that Nicola and Bob jointly had the toolset, skill set, mindset, and good luck to find treasure.

What they found, having understood its nature and implications, then inspired George, Surinder and Pete to undertake similar searches for comparable opportunities in other areas of the business. In each case there were associated risks which needed attention. But it was the opportunities that mattered most, and responses to uncertainties which jointly captured opportunities while limiting risks were central to all the propositions. Indeed, there is an important argument that the biggest single risk for TLC was failing to capture sufficient opportunities, leading to corporate failure because the competition was better at finding and capturing opportunities.

However, as Ajit pointed out, before they set out to make too many decisions they needed to enhance their capabilities without weakening their considerable current capability-culture assets. They had been very good at operating a stable business model which had changed very little over a long time. Radical change required some new toolsets and skill sets as well as the new mindsets already emerging.

Nicola had started with a very self-contained and limited amount of uncertainty – 'What should the order quantity for controls be, and why?' But TLC was now addressing very large and complex sets of uncertainty, needing tools beyond the collective capabilities of the current TLC team.

A common thread in the contributions of all this chapter's characters, starting with Dave, was:

> *Seek opportunities by testing all working assumptions,*
> *including those perceived as difficulties for current plans,*
> *by creative exploration of alternatives using a generalisation of those assumptions*
> *with a view to discovering possible new opportunities,*
> *and then testing working assumptions about these possible new opportunities*
> *in an iterative systematic process which keeps it simple throughout.*

The starting point for a generalised view of what opportunity efficiency is about is a synthesis of this common thread throughout this chapter, the Churchill quote, the IBM mantra, and the gift-horse sayings. You may look at this starting point in many ways, and choose to emphasise various features.

One aspect is the recognition that a well-managed unwelcome constraint, problem, challenge, risk or threat – or any other variant of these terms – can become a very big opportunity. Constraints, problems, challenges, risks or threats are usefully viewed as difficulties waiting to be transformed into opportunities. This involves testing all relevant current assumptions and resolving ambiguity and complexity in a clarity efficient manner with a view to opportunity efficiency in a general sense *whenever this is feasible*. Most of this chapter has this emphasis.

Another aspect is the recognition that a badly managed opportunity can become a very serious difficulty. All the TXC propositions have this possibility if they are not individually and collectively managed in an opportunity efficient manner, as Ajit observed.

A further aspect is the importance of starting with a systematic search for opportunities before getting too bogged down with the difficulties. This is, in part, linked to the commonly observed notion that most people cannot work effectively in 'optimist mode' and 'pessimist mode' at the same time – because we cannot multitask effectively in this way. Indeed, some people by nature work in one mode or the other virtually all the time. This implies ordering these two modes of operation when designing processes is essential, and having a well-balanced and mutually supportive team is crucial.

Further still, making sure that all the opportunities which present themselves as gifts are also identified and addressed effectively and efficiently is equally important, testing all assumptions. A top-down corporate planning view of this 'futures planning' issue which has to work alongside 'goals planning' is discussed in Chapter 8, along with long-term, medium-term and short-term planning frameworks, all separable but interconnected aspects of an enlightened approach to planning.

Ajit's recommended new corporate planning director would need to develop a top-down approach to both opportunities and threats which encouraged ongoing bottom-up development of strategy propositions, integrating all relevant bottom-up strategic corporate thinking with systematic top-down processes.

Achieving clarity efficiency by starting with simple plans and basic models

Simple plans and basic models are very valuable, as illustrated by the TLC fixed order quantity plan for controls and basic EOQ model used in Nicola's pass 1 analysis. The basic structure and guidance such simple models provide can be a crucial starting point for examining and understanding key features of a decision situation and guiding further analysis. In particular, they can identify basic goals–plans relationships which need to be understood to shape plans and suggest appropriate choices. The 'prescriptive' (yielding an optimum solution) and 'deterministic' (non-probabilistic) aspects of an EOQ model can be an asset, not a limitation or liability, because the deterministic aspect facilitates a clear focus on particular aspects of the ambiguity being addressed without the complexity of associated variability, and it facilitates a prescriptive modelling approach which yields a recommended optimum plan given the assumptions, sometimes the 'right kind' of initial simplification of a complex situation. As Stephen Ward (1989) observed when describing the 'constructive simplicity' concept which underlies both enlightened simplicity and clarity efficiency, constructive simplicity designated and described in various ways is not a new or revolutionary idea. For example, the EOQ or 'Wilson' rule has been around for about a century, and it has been widely used, with good reason. But it is not a tool to be used in a mechanistic manner to crank out 'optimal order quantities', as very vocal critics of simplistic EOQ use have argued from the outset.

An EOQ model is comparable to the minimum clarity estimate approach outlined earlier in Chapter 2 in the sense that both involve a minimum level of complexity to get started. But there are important relevant differences. The minimum clarity estimation approach of Chapter 3 was designed to be robust in relation to a very broad set of working assumptions and provided unbiased first pass estimation is all that is sought, and fairly conservative estimates of both the expected outcome and the associated range posed no concerns, deeper analysis may reasonably be assumed to be less likely to prove productive than more obvious sources of concern revealed by the first pass. The EOQ model was not developed with this kind of robustness in mind, and the underlying issues are different. It is worth constant reminders to start with a simple capture of the key features of a context, but it is equally important to appreciate that further complexity may need to be recognised and explored, and knowing when this is the case can be important. Nicola's pass 3 illustrates this.

Simple probabilistic models can also be very useful, even if they are descriptive in their basic form (not yielding a recommended optimum plan), as illustrated by the stochastic safety stock model introduced by Nicola's pass 2. Complexity is added, but in the spirit of clarity efficiency, it more than pays its way.

All passes through the UP of Figure 2.1 should involve keeping the models as simple as possible, preserving clarity efficiency but facilitating the introduction of further clarity as and when appropriate. This was illustrated by Nicola's pass 2, further illustrated by the consideration of inflation and free credit in Nicola's pass 3 and her plan 3. It was illustrated again in Bob's My-Place-Your-Timing plan 4. Yet more follow-on illustrations build on Bob's plan 4 in a series of TXC propositions. Central to this incremental addition of more clarity in an efficient manner was the transparency of assumptions, the rigorous testing of assumptions, the highly iterative nature of the process, and the concern for a form of synthesis which extends to 'interpret the results creatively'. Enlightened simplicity as a basis for clarity efficiency involves many features not yet touched on, which subsequent chapters will illustrate. However, this chapter's tale provides a useful starting point.

Developing a 'feel' for when deterministic models will be useful is an important capability, central to the EP skill sets which are needed for corporate clarity efficiency and corporate tactical clarity which corporate strategic clarity has to address. If you do not have this feel yourself, you should be aware of the need to work with those in your organisation who do when it could be useful – otherwise, you are going to lack strategic clarity and miss opportunities. If nobody in your organisation has these capabilities, this is a capability-culture liability worth attention by someone, even if you are not directly interested yourself.

When parameter values are uncertain it is always important to understand sensitivity issues, including asymmetries associated with the implications. Beginning with a clear understanding of plausible ranges to estimate expected values is always good practice, but sometimes the additional effort of a stochastic model is not clarity efficient. One reason, illustrated by this chapter's tale, is systemic uncertainty (such as seasonal variations) may be involved, and if this is the case, some aspects of it may need to be clearly understood and treated effectively. But this may not involve useful modelling. Furthermore, if the outcome of a modelling approach will be a very complex plan, it may be useful to consider an altogether different approach, a very different approach may be the consequence of other concerns, and it may be useful to delay any complex modelling and planning until it is clearly needed.

The example model this chapter is centred on is a prescriptive calculus-based model, a particularly powerful exceptionally simple model in terms of insight *provided the assumptions hold*. Such models predate the mathematical programming models which began their extensive development and use in the 1950s as computer capability increased, and they can be seen as a very simple special case of a mathematical optimisation approach which facilitates a very traditional prescriptive interpretation even when great complexity is involved. Some people who are particularly fond of 'optimising' things are very keen to use prescriptive models whenever feasible, but often it is wiser to settle for a less ambitious descriptive model, used within a less direct optimisation process framework. Sometimes it is useful to stick to a qualitative analysis 'exploratory model' of the soft OR variety, which simply helps with exploring the relevant issues. Sometimes a quantitative exploratory model based on simulation as explored by Pidd (1996) can be very useful. Decision trees in a HAT framework as used for safety stock modelling in this chapter are just a very simple example of a descriptive model approach. Prescriptive models are more useful if *suitable* models are available, but the assumptions required may not be tenable, and if the assumptions required are not obvious, these models can be extremely misleading.

When Nicola addressed safety stock sizing, uncertainty associated with stock-outs had to be addressed in stochastic terms to estimate the expected costs involved. Avoiding specific probability distribution assumptions led to a descriptive basis used within a tabular framework based on an underlying decision tree to seek optimality less formally – a simple HAT approach. This is an example of a descriptive model used within a less formal process-based approach to optimisation. Prescriptive safety stock models are available, but they make strong assumptions about the shape of the probability distribution defining uncertainty associated with demand – a Normal (Gaussian) distribution for example – in addition to assuming expected values for holding and stock-out costs. They provide no way of testing this kind of assumption, and they can also encourage less concern about approaches to testing other assumptions, including sensitivity analysis about all parameter assumptions.

Developing an understanding of when the complexity of stochastic modelling using an informal process-based approach to optimality is needed for even a basic level of clarity, and how to couple simple stochastic models plus linked deterministic modelling is part of the EP toolset and skill set craft which Nicola brought to the family firm. If you do not need to have these skills yourself, you may still need to know when they could be useful and how to get access to people who can apply them for you when this would be useful.

Appreciating trade-offs when seeking opportunity efficiency

An important aspect of shaping plans via models is the role of trade-offs between performance measures. In this chapter's tale trade-offs between order costs and holding costs was a central issue. Simple deterministic models can be particularly useful in clarifying the nature of appropriate trade-offs when different parties have different priorities.

Informal approaches are usually biased by the provider of the intuition. This can shape informal plans to a greater extent than related formal processes which make a point of minimising bias. For example, Pete's intuitive approach led to a slightly larger order quantity than the pass 1 analysis. This was marginally more expensive for TLC *if the pass 1 working assumptions were accepted as valid*, and marginally more convenient for Pete. This result should not have been a surprise. Pete did not need to be familiar with EOQ models to have an intuitive grasp of the trade-offs involved, for himself and for TLC. On a learning-by-doing basis, Pete would tend to settle on a reasonably appropriate solution in these terms. However, even a very simple formal model may provide the insight for a modest improvement, in terms of separating out what is in the best interests of the individuals and what is in the best interests of the organisation, as well as in terms of classifying what key trade-offs need attention, *provided the assumptions used are robust*. What pass 3 and 4 suggested was Pete was actually closer to the true optimum than Nicola's pass 1 plan, albeit perhaps for the wrong reasons. That is, if Pete had not thought about inflation and free credit period assumptions, bias might be the explanation.

Explicit treatment of uncertainty associated with Pete's safety stock was useful to capture further trade-offs, in this case between holding costs and stock-out costs. This provided much more fertile grounds for improvements in cost, despite the very low level of uncertainty involved, in terms of zero, one, or two days needed to replenish stock and the small size of the safety stock relative to the order quantity. Again the validity of Pete's intuitive solution was debatable, but in the context of Bob's plan 4 level of clarity, both bias issues no longer mattered.

Seeking opportunity efficiency including clarity efficiency in the most general sense feasible within the EOQ framework was clearly the thrust of pass 3, and the 'interpret the plans to exploit creativity' phase developments by Nicola for plan 3. Bob builds on this for plan 4 but moved beyond the EOQ formula. George, Surinder, Pete, and Ajit then each built their propositions on the basis of the clarity provided by the preceding stages of the planning process.

Risk efficiency in a basic expected value form as a basis for opportunity efficiency

A minimum level of expected cost without any direct concern for the level of associated cost risk was the objective pursued by Nicola on behalf of TLC in terms of her formal EOQ models. She recommended taking account of asymmetric penalty costs associated with departures from expectations when dealing with the cost of stock-outs, the basis of her rounding-up recommendation for Q_0^*. But she did not recommend any formal trade-off processes involving expected cost and associated cost risk in the sense associated with the decision diagrams of Figures 3.6 and 3.7 and the efficient frontier of Figure 3.8. This was appropriate because cost risk in these terms was not relevant. When the level of risk involved means that risk does not need attention in the sense of Figure 3.8, ignoring risk is sensible.

That said, to understand her working assumptions within broader framing assumptions, from a broader perspective on relevant costs each time a successive pass identified an expected cost reduction, this was an improvement in terms of risk efficiency, and it may be useful to see these improvements in terms of finding opportunities by working in the opportunity management area of Figure 3.8, moving from a point not on the efficient frontier towards point a without being concerned about either the absolute level of risk or risk–reward trade-offs at the boundary point being sought.

If you are familiar with modern decision analysis and use its concepts as part of your perspective on decision making, it is important to understand that the equivalent of 'risk neutrality' in modern decision analysis terms is a common and useful mode of seeking risk efficiency in EP terms, directly equivalent to aiming for point 'a' in Figure 3.8. However you prefer to look at this issue, a focus on point 'a' does not make the risk efficiency concept less useful. It simply demonstrates a common and very important special case. If risk, in the sense of downside departures from expectations, is not important in terms of objectives directly relevant to decisions being addressed, we can concentrate on the opportunity implications of uncertainty, and ignore expected reward trade-offs with the associated risk of downside departures from expectations. We can aim for point 'a' in Figure 3.8. Nine times out of ten this may be clarity efficient and effective in an opportunity efficient sense – the best way to proceed.

It is also important to understand that the opportunity/risk datum concept discussed earlier involves a degree of subjective convenience. Relative to George's starting position, Nicola uncovered enormous opportunities. Relative to where Nicola, Bob, George, Surinder, Pete and Ajit working together with other TLC staff could take TLC, prior to Nicola's arrival TLC was arguably risk and opportunity inefficient to a degree which could lead to bankruptcy if TLC competitors were to prove better at opportunity management.

Risk efficiency is always a basis for finding opportunities in the process of seeking opportunity efficiency, but when risk, as modelled directly in terms of downside variations from expected outcomes, is not a useful issue to talk about in terms of risk–reward trade-offs, a focus on all relevant uncertainty from an opportunity management perspective can be more useful. This does not mean we can or should forget about risk in a more general sense. Nicola was careful to consider some of this more general risk. Bob's plan did so too. George, Surinder, Pete and Ajit's propositions would require significant attention to risk.

Risk and risk appetite as a multiple attribute concern

Throughout this chapter, minimising expected cost has been the modelling focus, as pointed out in the last subsection and earlier. However, risk in a general sense has been recognised as important and addressed, sometimes without emphasising that risk was involved or using risk management language.

For example, George did not risk offending Dave by failing to take his suggestion seriously, and Nicola explicitly avoided the risk of offending Pete for negligible gain because that kind of risk often matters a great deal in practice.

Furthermore, Nicola suggested it might (or might not) be worth forgoing a change in the status quo with implied criticism if only £5 per month was saved, but a larger saving might make the trade-offs worthwhile, even if inconvenience for Pete and other staff were involved. A moderately aggressive approach to cost risk is not incompatible with a cautious approach to offending staff. A sizable cost improvement may make inconvenience as well as sensitivity to changes worth tolerating, but a diplomatic approach to managing this kind of change may be essential to avoid the risk of permanently damaged relationships. What some people call risk appetite is a multiple attribute concern, and some attributes which are important are not measurable.

Furthermore, there are some serious sources of supply chain risk which Nicola drew George's attention to. For example, if the firm producing controls went into liquidation, or suffered a major industrial dispute, or dramatically increased prices, and there were no alternative suppliers, TLC might be in significant difficulty. George's proposition could be seen as building on this in the engine supply context, when it mattered even more.

All the TXC propositions involved significant risk that was not even considered. These opportunities require significant further attention beyond the scope of this chapter.

Put slightly differently, a clear understanding of all the relevant issues can lead to a successful transformation of difficulties into opportunities, but requisite knowledge and skill are important, and a limited understanding of what matters most can be dangerous, transforming an opportunity pursued into a risk or a problem.

In some ways even more important is what might be called 'missed opportunity risk'. If the opportunities identified by TLC had been missed, much higher expected costs would be endured, perhaps ultimately leading to company failure. A broad view of what really matters is crucial. The risk our conceptual and operational models are missing relevant concerns and our creative interpretation of results does not address all important relevant concerns is the really difficult risk to manage and often the most important. Anyone who argues that it is always easy to keep it simple using simple methods usually does not have even the vaguest idea about what is involved. In my experience they often subscribe to the common initial interpretation of KISS – keep it simple, stupid. The point of the revised definition – keep it simple systematically – is the right kind of simplicity for any given context needs systematic attention to avoid being simplistic, and the wrong kind of simplicity is a basis for both serious risks and important lost opportunities.

A somewhat different example of the right and wrong kinds of simplicity with immediate and later direct relevance is worth brief consideration now. At a time when mathematical programming in general and linear programming in particular was generating a great deal of interest, Dasgupta and Dasgupta (1966) used crop yield and related market price data in a very interesting manner. They demonstrated that a linear programming approach to maximising income for typical farmers in India would *double* their income, as also demonstrated earlier by Indian agricultural economists who were urging the government to spend more money on 'educating' the farmers to change from current traditional crop patterns to the agricultural economists recommended crop patterns based on linear programming models. The Dasgupta paper then demonstrated that the same data employed in a Markowitz (1959) quadratic programming model, which used the same expected outcomes in addition to considering risk associated with income variability measured by variance, led to several very different inferences. The Dasgupta quadratic programming model made it clear that the farmers were already using an optimal solution which maximised expected income given a minimum level of risk. The farmers were intuitively using a Markowitz mean–variance portfolio management model. The farmers needed to minimise risk because given their lack of financial assets, without any form of government insurance scheme to protect them, they and their families could starve in a bad year. It was the agricultural experts who needed 'educating', not the farmers, because the agricultural experts were using crucial stealth assumptions with myopic models. The government also needed educating, but not by the agricultural 'experts' who believed linear programming was the way forward.

Over many generations the Indian farmers had developed a highly diversified crop pattern which protected them as far as possible from drought, crop diseases, and market price fluctuations, maximising expected income as a secondary objective within a minimum risk primary objective, an approach common to most subsistence farmers. The trend towards monoculture prevalent in Western economies was the result of a combination of wealth accumulation by farmers plus government price intervention and support when disease or other reasons for crop failure would otherwise devastate the industry. Governments in both developed and developing economies needed to understand the insurance role they could play. If they did so there were very beneficial behavioural implications, *provided* the farmers knew they had an explicit insurance contract with their governments.

One general point which follows from the Dasgupta paper, as well as this chapter's tale, is that following simplistic models when they fail to capture key issues can do more harm than good. If Nicola had not progressed beyond her pass 2 analysis, it might be reasonable to judge her in the same light as the Indian agricultural experts limited by a linear programming perspective. Later chapters will explore further examples linked in a fairly direct way to the Dasgupta paper.

A second general point is the importance of not underrating the intuitive expertise of someone like Pete or the Indian farmers, and the importance of being *very* careful before you suspect bias or enforce changes their intuition is suspicious about, testing the assumptions responsible for differences in views.

A third general point is that in top-down strategic corporate management terms, cost variations relative to unbiased expected outcomes were just noise, not risk worth the analysis effort, but seriously biased expected values and biased decision making more generally were risks. Furthermore, while the set of propositions considered could lead to some very useful TLC corporate risk reduction via diversification, a more general approach to the key risks which could put TLC out of business was needed, drawing on ideas developed in later chapters.

The most difficult risk to manage is failing to understand what really matters – what a management consultant friend of mine has called 'stupidity risk' in its most serious forms, although this is clearly not a label any sensible consultant would use with his or her clients unless the consultant was a very good judge of the client's sense of humour. 'Strategic myopia' might be a better label for discussions within organisations, whether or not consultants are involved, comparable to the use of strategic misrepresentation as a euphemism for lying, but my inclination is using the phrase 'lack of strategic clarity'. Whatever you chose to call your equivalent of strategic myopia or lack of strategic clarity, the EP approach attempts to manage it in various ways. The central unifying theme is trying to persuade all relevant decision makers to adopt a systematic approach to using identified and tested working assumptions within framing assumptions which are as general (unrestricted) as possible to achieve strategic clarity plus requisite linked tactical clarity in a clarity efficient manner.

The key role of the capability-culture concept and revisiting the tale's credibility

TLC seems to have had no basis for getting beyond a very simple optimal order size and safety stock approach, intuitively sized by those directly involved, until Nicola arrived. In stealth assumption terms, George and his colleagues seem to have used an implicit approach to planning which accommodated very limited capability in terms of testing inventory policy and broader supply chain assumptions. Nicola brought the capability needed to explore the sizing of order quantities and safety stocks. But much more important, she also prompted the development of a corporate curiosity to test assumptions and explore more sophisticated policies with implications for purchasing and marketing strategy, pushing back the ambiguity associated with many TLC working assumptions via the use of explicit UP variants, triggering an ambition to evolve the capability to do this more effectively.

This may seem implausibly flattering to Nicola and unreasonably unfair to all other TLC employees. But the tale is trying to demonstrate what adding the capabilities associated with a basic understanding of the UP concept and generic models can do, even if they are brought into an organisation by someone like Nicola with very limited experience.

What is crucial to add is with the apparent exception of prior skills with the formal process aspects of the UP concept and related generic models, TLC was a very capable organisation with a very sound corporate culture. If George, Bob, Surinder, Pete and Ajit had not played their roles as they did, as very effective members of an unusually capable team, no significant progress would have been made.

More generally, Nicola's management course material was important to the progress made by TLC – but so was her intelligence and skill. Furthermore, *even more important was the inherent planning skills of all this tale's characters*. In particular, their collective ability to synthesise what they learned from analysis using models with the complexities of the 'real world' was central to the inspiration behind the My-Place-Your-Timing strategy variants developed by Bob and George and then built on by all the others.

In terms of the Figure 2.1 portrayal of the UP concept, TLC had the right stuff in element 11 terms plus elements 1 through 10, with the exception of UP/SP process skills and associated generic models plus the EP tools to be developed in the rest of Part 2.

As an observation on the credibility of the tale, a crucial working assumption when drafting this chapter was that Nicola was bright enough and lucky enough to reach her plan 3 and not insightful enough to get beyond her plan 3, but Bob was insightful enough to transform her plan 3 into his plan 4. This implies the person in the organisation in the supply side operations director role has to be insightful enough to see the benefits of what was clearly a better approach, or a more experienced variant of Nicola is needed to help them. Furthermore, each of those in all the other operations management roles discussed have to have the insight to play their roles – otherwise, the organisation is clearly going to be opportunity inefficient. Finally, George in his CEO role, and Ajit in his supporting leadership role, clearly need to acquire further capability for TLC before proceeding with the propositions generated, perhaps in the form of two further directors as well as further training and support for all existing TLC staff. Your credibility may have been stretched by assuming all these people were enlightened enough to quickly pick up and employ Nicola's UP concepts after her arrival, without indirectly having come to similar conclusions informally on their own, but this stretch was in a good cause. What is particularly stretching is the importance of Nicola as a catalyst, especially given other TLC staff were so adept at communicating and working as a team as well as being creative on their own.

Despite their assumed lack of earlier exposure to generic models, UPs and SPs, in practice we could expect any organisation with this level of capability and cultural maturity to find some of the opportunities discussed in this tale on an ad hoc basis. Many small organisations like TLC make negligible use of UP concepts or generic models, but few have the capabilities attributed to TLC, and any that did would probably generate some of the improvements suggested by Bob, or the propositions suggested by the others, without the equivalent of a contribution from a Nicola.

Future relevance of this chapter's tale

My most recent involvement in the practice of managing a manufacturing business was in the early 2010s, providing in-house training on managing uncertainty in change management projects for Volvo staff in Sweden via Chalmers University of Technology in a series of courses over several years. The change management issues they had to deal with included Volvo trucks manufacturing MAC trucks (a US brand) and Renault trucks (a French brand) in addition to its own Volvo brands, Nova buses, and Terex construction equipment, while Volvo cars initially became part of Ford and then part of Geely. Geely, originally in the refrigerator business in India, also acquired the British manufacturer of London Taxi Cabs, and in late 2017 Geely bought an 8.3% stake in the Volvo Group, 'putting them in the driving seat' (Lea, 2017a) of a reunited version of the 100 year-old Swedish Volvo company with 90,000 employees. The Volvo Group's annual revenues as of 2017 were £27 billion, and Geely is China's most international automotive group, with a Hong Kong stock market value of £22 billion. Volvo had earlier bought a large minority shareholding in Dongfeng, China's largest lorry maker and a rival to Geely in the car market.

Simply being aware of the world around us makes it very clear that globalisation in the manufacturing industry has changed everything beyond recognition relative to the 1980s setting of this chapter's tale. The full implications of many other issues are still emerging, like the ongoing development of artificial intelligence. There is no reason not to expect new currently unpredictable fundamental changes. However, while current and future levels of complexity may be orders of magnitude greater than that faced by TLC, most of the basic concerns TCL faced as addressed in this chapter have not gone away. They remain a useful starting point for Part 2 of this book in terms of the basic broad questions addressed.

The pace of change is unlikely to slow for any organisation in the manufacturing business, and the same is true of most other businesses in most countries. Some widely acclaimed authors saw this coming some time ago. For example, Alvin Toffler (1970) in *Future Shock* famously said, 'The illiterate of the 21st century will not be those who cannot read and write, but those who cannot learn, unlearn and relearn'. This first book in a series of three by Toffler sold 17 million copies and became mandatory White House reading. Current eagerness to learn about what may be involved is illustrated by the popularity of books like *Beyond Competitive Advantage* (Zenger, 2016), a useful overview of what sustains corporate success in a rapidly changing world drawing upon a range of illustrative examples.

An interesting contemporary book looking at a 'new' basis for sustainability which accords with the ideas cherished by George and Ajit is *The Conscience Economy: How a Mass Movement for Good is Great for Business* (Overman, 2014). The basic ideas explored are not new in the sense that the Cadbury's approach to looking after its employees which George and his father admired has a very long history, which Steven Overman discusses. However, some aspects are new in the sense that Overman argues that the current new generation of young adults (millennials) have a basic inbuilt wish to do 'good' as a way of doing 'well' which he believes was not observable in the preceding generation, and they want to do so through their businesses as entrepreneurs, their work as employees, and their purchases as consumers. Overman argues that this is being driven by post-millennium technological, economic, social, and political forces which imply it is not a passing phase, and it is actually a threat to organisations which fail to see the opportunities associated with a significant mass movement. The threatened organisations may be in the private sector with any form of ownership or in the public sector.

This contention is controversial and what will actually happen is highly uncertain, but what is certain is this issue matters, and it is now receiving significant attention. I did not read Overman's book until August 2017, but within a few weeks I observed a lead article in a feature on franchising with the title 'When Doing Good Is Great for Business: Socially Responsible Franchising Is a Growing Trend Which Can Benefit Business and the Community' (Coleman, 2017), followed later by another titled 'Tech Kings Must Learn from Our Great Entrepreneurs' (Byrne, 2017), attacking organisations like Google and explaining the scope as well as extolling the efforts of George Cadbury, William Lever, and John Lewis. Coleman's article warns there are difficulties which need care, comparable to Ajit's warning about getting a model like the John Lewis Partnership approach to work effectively. Franchising is a controversial form of business operation for many people who are interested in the kinds of operations which 'doing good' implies, but franchising operations with closely coupled community and charitable goals which are consistently operated within good, sustained values are a development which is clearly a plausible and potentially optimistic possibility given the many other aspects of our post-2020 future.

The relevant and interesting short article 'Bosses Discover it Pays Dividends to Put Workers First' in Luke Johnson's regular Enterprise column in the *Times* (Johnson, 2018) argues there is a strong case for medium-sized family businesses using this strategy, based on the recommendations of highly successful entrepreneurs like Julian Richer and his book *The Ethical Capitalist*. He suggests the complexities involved in large public companies, or those owned by institutional private equity, will raise additional significant challenges, but he points to General Electric as a current example of why they need to move forward too.

Whatever the ultimate directions of the key aspects of change, the current pace of changes implies a growing need to understand how to make effective use of the most sophisticated UP concept equivalents available, avoiding the limitations of simplistic interpretations of models like Nicola's pass 1 and 2, and achieving the much more useful results of Nicola's plan 3 and Bob's plan 4, plus the follow-on TLC propositions. Furthermore, the role of capability-culture concepts in the UP concept matter. The current pace of changes and uncertainty about the direction of key aspects of these changes imply a growing need to generate propositions suited to a frequently disrupted future and then deal with them collectively in an opportunity efficient manner in all organisations. How to deal with them in an opportunity efficient manner for a very unpredictable future is directly relevant to all the tales to follow in Part 2, the basis of strategic clarity.

The specific example context used in this chapter is clearly dated, but not the messages, and most of the messages are relevant to all organisations. The same comment applies to all other Part 2 chapters, for different but related reasons.

The very simple context used in this chapter was a convenient starting point for Part 2, but much more complexity now needs addressing.

6   Building 'specific processes' – a bidding process example

The experience base which underlies this chapter's tale about 'Astro' includes a case study initially developed in the 1990s with an IBM UK senior executive for a culture change programme, its use with groups of IBM staff about 40 times, plus follow-on consulting which included helping IBM to develop and use related bidding processes. You may find it helpful to see Astro as an organisation comparable to IBM.

The scope of this chapter is much broader than bidding might suggest for several reasons worth understanding before beginning the tale which is central to this chapter.

First, bidding is a particular approach to selling which is an aspect of the much broader field of marketing which, in turn, is a central aspect of operations management with corporate strategic management roles. In this chapter, bidding and associated marketing are assumed to include underlying aspects of managing internal market structures plus strategic relationships with subcontractors, with important implications for approaches to both the outsourcing of currently internal corporate operations and the 'friendly takeover' purchases of valued subcontractors who might otherwise be bought by competitors. The implications are relevant to many aspects of demand chain management, supply chain management, interdependent product design, and broader operations and corporate management concerns.

Second, much of the tale of this chapter is also relevant to organisations concerned with managing purchases because to manage their side of what can be a complex relationship, 'customers' often need to understand their 'suppliers' concerns and perspective.

Third, some aspects of the approaches discussed in this chapter are of interest in all decision-making areas. As one example, this chapter's tale illustrates one key reason why organisations may spend 80% to 90% of their effort using formal planning approaches to clarifying aspects of a situation which they understand fairly well, only 10% to 20% of their effort using formal approaches to providing more clarity for aspects they do not understand as well as they need to, when reversing these effort allocations would be far more opportunity efficient. This switch in effort allocation may be difficult, but it may be crucial, and it may require new conceptual and operational tools to achieve a new and significantly enhanced level of clarity efficiency.

Fourth, even if you are not currently interested in any of these particular areas or aspects of decision making, the fundamental reason you need to understand the basic ideas explored in this chapter is because several of the conceptual and operational tools discussed will be used as basic building blocks in later chapters. A key example is the '*specific* planning uncertainty and complexity management *process*' concept, contracted to 'specific process' or 'SP'.

An SP is a 'process model' – a model which is itself a process involving a designed sequence for using one or more lower-order models in a specific corporate decision-making context.

The relationship between a UP and the generic models of Chapter 5 is extended – the UP is used to create, enhance, shape, test and implement an SP.

As in Chapter 5, some aspects of this chapter's tale may stretch your credibility, but this stretch is in a good cause, so please suspend your concerns about credibility until closing sections of this chapter with this 'good cause' in mind. The set of credibility issues involved are more usefully discussed later, in conjunction with the relevance of a 1990s tale to post-2020 contexts and the role of other real cases underlying the tale. The credibility issues are not the same as those of Chapter 5. In this case they maximise the scope to communicate what effective use of a UP to create SPs can achieve. The tales of following chapters also all delay the consideration of plausibility issues until the end, but the issues will be different in each case. By way of a reminder linked to these credibility issues, the language of EP will be used throughout, as in all Part 2 tales, translating from the context language usage you might expect within the tales.

Capturing some of the context information to get started

The tale of this chapter is set in the 1990s in the Astro Wales regional head office of Astro UK. Astro UK was part of Astro Inc, an international shareholder owned firm in the computer information systems business based in the US. The key characters were

> Martha, marketing manager for Astro Wales, recently appointed;
> Ben, bidding process facilitator reporting to Martha;
> Trevor, transport-sector lead sales representative for Astro Wales;
> Sian, Systems manager for Astro Wales;
> Sam, a Systems group member reporting to Sian;
> Rhys, regional manager for Astro Wales; and
> Steve, Service Bureau manager reporting directly to Rhys.

As with the last chapter's tale, it is not a problem if you identify with some of these characters more than the others, but seeing all of them as a team who worked together exceptionally well is important. The nature of the teams' working relationships was different from those in TLC, to be expected when moving from a small family owned business which was manufacturing driven to an international shareholder owned organisation which was market driven.

Martha was a central character in this tale. Martha studied philosophy at university because ideas about different ways of thinking particularly interested her at that stage in her education, and she was uncertain about what kind of ideas interested her most. Martha's first job was in computer sales for Astro Scotland, part of Astro UK. She made very rapid progress, in part, because a wide range of ideas associated with having a successful career seemed very interesting to Martha. She was still in her 20s when she was promoted to marketing manager (Head of Sales) for Astro Wales.

Ben was also a central character in this tale. Immediately after completing a BSc degree in economics and management science Ben started work as a Sales trainee at the Cardiff office of Astro Computer Systems, head office for Astro Wales, reporting to Martha.

Trevor was the third central character in this tale. He was the transportation industry lead sales representative Martha assigned to the bid which forms the basis of this chapter.

Sian was a further key character in this tale. Sian was Systems manager (Head of Systems) for Astro Wales – Martha's opposite number in the Sales–Systems silo structure used within Astro Wales. Sam, a Systems group member reporting to Sian, had a minor role.

Rhys was the regional manager for Astro Wales who Martha and Sian both reported to. Rhys was also responsible for the Astro Cardiff Service Bureau managed by Steve, operating outside the direct remits of Martha and Sian in a separate operations management silo.

Martha was in 'respond-to-crisis' mode the morning Ben started working for Astro. Astro Wales had just lost the third of three unsuccessful bids that month for major 'systems integration' projects. Systems integration was Astro jargon for a complete computer-based information system, including hardware, software, physical facilities, and training, normally incorporating the functionality of 'heritage systems' (existing hardware and software) in addition to providing new functionality, usually tendered for on a fixed-price basis with performance penalties. Martha knew that the failure of three major systems integration bids in a row was not just bad luck. There were other clear symptoms of underlying problems.

For example, sales representatives were complaining to Martha that the 'Systems people' were taking far too long to cost things, and their solutions to problems were often far too conservative (safe and expensive), resulting in lost sales that should have been won. In addition, the Systems personnel were complaining to Martha that the 'Sales people' were putting unreasonable pressure on them to provide quick responses to difficult questions and to cut corners, that most of their efforts were wasted because of lost bids, and that the bids that were won were usually the 'wrong ones'. Both groups were implying that the problems were serious, and it was up to Martha to resolve them. Neither group seemed to understand why their own approaches might be part of the reasons Astro Wales was so unsuccessful. The 'panic level' was rising. It was clearly up to Martha to clarify the situation and resolve the underlying problems.

Martha knew that Astro Inc was experiencing similar difficulties worldwide. She also knew that a common perception within and outside Astro was that 'Astro Inc had lost its way and was in danger of losing the plot altogether'. Martha's view was that 'the technology and the markets had changed, the competition had become a lot tougher, and Astro Inc had not yet adjusted in terms of organisational structures, products, processes and culture'.

Since her promotion Martha had focused on the 'strategic' or 'macro management' aspects of her new job, which were unfamiliar. She had deliberately avoided getting involved in the details of individual bids or bid processes. However, Martha was aware that she did not have sufficient clarity about Astro's many problems, and more specifically, she knew she needed to get a grip on the details of Astro Wales difficulties with bidding for systems integration projects.

The present systems integration sales crisis was viewed by Martha as a catalyst for sorting out bidding processes more generally in Astro Wales and starting to address the difficult organisational, process, and cultural issues within her remit. She subscribed to the notion 'never waste a good crisis'. If she could help to sort out Astro Wales, starting with systems integration bids, she might get the opportunity to help sort out Astro UK on her next step up the Astro corporate ladder.

The nature of Ben's degree was understood by Martha, and she had checked that he had the background to understand bidding models and processes, the insight to critically appraise and learn from the relevant literature, and the interpersonal skills to make a competent facilitator. Martha asked Ben to act as coordinator and facilitator for a new bidding process, an 'SP for bidding'. Martha and Ben would design this process drawing on other Astro expertise.

Martha had taken numerous advanced-level professional development short courses which gave her exposure to both general and specific process concepts, using variants of the EP, UP, and SP concepts discussed here. Martha's academic training, especially the way she saw philosophy as a kind of 'glue' among behavioural issues, politics, economics, and everything else that mattered, underlay a very structured approach to business issues, with a strong concern for the internal consistency of sets of assumptions, and clear logic.

An invitation to tender had been received from Transcon the day before. Transcon was a containerised freight road transport company recently formed from the merger of two successful firms, one based in Wales and one based in Hampshire, with a view to attracting an increased share of the growing Euro container freight market. Martha had decided to use a bid for Transcon as the basis for developing a new prototype SP for bidding for Astro Wales which they could then continue to develop for use with all similar future bids.

Astro had a tradition of 'throwing new staff into the deep end of the swimming pool', with a view to stretching them and rewarding them if they learned to swim the requisite strokes quickly. Martha made this clear to Ben, and she made it clear that she expected him to take the lead with the details of the bidding model and some of the related process design issues. However, she reassured him that she would provide leadership on the overall approach framework, all his ideas could be tried out on her first, she would contribute as required to their development, and her authority would be behind him when they had an agreed-on approach. Martha let it be known that she was marketing manager for Wales while she was still in her 20s because she had been given similar tests in Astro Scotland. Martha was now on a fast track, and if Ben succeeded, he could expect similar recognition.

It had been obvious to Martha that Trevor was the Astro sales representative to help with the development of the bidding process. This was not just because Trevor was the transport sector lead sales representative when the Transcon opportunity arose. He had particularly enlightened intuition based on extensive experience which Martha wanted to capture for all sales staff to learn from. In addition, Trevor was respected by all the other Sales staff – Martha fully appreciated that having Trevor help her to change local processes would make change easier. To a significant extent, Martha had seized the opportunity to use Transcon as the basis for developing an SP for bidding because of Trevor.

Martha introduced Ben to Trevor. Martha indicated that she wanted Trevor to help her and Ben develop a new systems integration bidding process for Astro Wales using the Astro bid for Transcon as a prototype development project. She emphasised that she believed Trevor's input could help to shape the process as a whole in a crucial manner. Furthermore, she wanted Trevor to take on some key leadership roles when the roll-out of the prototype became a follow-on project. She wanted Trevor to use Ben as a bid coordinator and facilitator for the Transcon bid. Trevor knew Martha well enough to know that responding as constructively as possible to a nuanced interpretation of her requests was the only sensible option.

Martha also introduced Ben to Sian. Sian was responsible for the Systems people who would cost the Transcon systems integration project and the Systems people who would implement some of it if the bid was won, other aspects being outsourced to subcontractors. Martha made Ben's and Trevor's role clear to Sian. She then emphasised the importance of Sian's input to shaping the process as a whole and making it work on an ongoing basis. In some ways Sian knew Martha even better than Trevor. Sian and Martha were technically on the same management level, both reporting to Rhys, regional manager for Astro Wales, but Martha had a significant edge because Astro was a market-driven organisation. Sian understood that Martha was inviting her to join in an Astro Wales Sales–led Sales/Systems process development project as a partner, and she was very happy to do so.

Martha indicated that she wanted Trevor, Sian, and Ben to prepare a document for her that summarised what this bid was about, in the sense that everyone involved could agree that the document they had prepared succinctly captured the current best practice starting point for formal analysis of the Transcon bid. In UP terminology this was a 'capture the context' phase document.

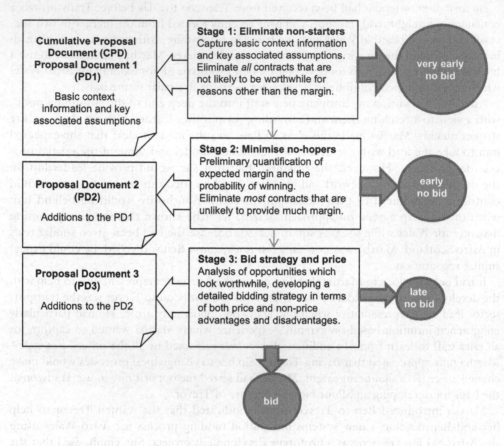

Figure 6.1 The overview plan of Astro's SP for bidding portrayed as a flow chart.

Ben was provided with a desk and Martha left him to it. It wasn't even time for lunch on his first day with Astro Wales.

To help you follow the way Martha and her colleagues developed a bidding process for Astro as outlined in this chapter, Figure 6.1 is provided now.

Although it was not formalised until later, Martha did anticipate some of the key characteristics of Figure 6.1 from the outset, and seeing it now in its final form will help you to better understand how the SP for bidding takes shape. The overall rationale for the structure portrayed by Figure 6.1, plus some immediately relevant aspects of its details, will now be explained in terms of the story of their development. Martha's initial vision of the Figure 6.1 overview plan at this stage in its evolution is referred to as the 'initial process overview'.

A preliminary proposal document

Trevor and Ben had a brief initial discussion right after Martha's briefing, and Trevor suggested they start by visiting Transcon together. Trevor would do most of the talking, but Ben could take notes. Extended and reshaped by Trevor, these notes would form the basis of the documentation which 'Sales' passed to 'Systems' to facilitate a technical specification and costing. Trevor was very happy to start this way. Ben would be making himself useful as Trevor's assistant, and Trevor could control the shape of the document Martha wanted. Ben was also pleased to start this way. By lunchtime Trevor had arranged an appointment that afternoon with key Transcon staff.

Following the meeting with Transcon, Ben edited his notes and passed them to Trevor. Trevor added detail, shaped the terminology as well as the structure, and appended the 'invitation to tender', which he always referred to as an 'ITT'.

Trevor loved acronyms and similar abbreviations. Although most Astro staff winced every time a new one was invented, they usually adopted it, for convenience as well as to humour Trevor, whom everybody liked. Trevor referred to Ben's reshaped document based on the meeting and other information as the sales draft of the 'PPD', a contraction of 'Preliminary Proposal Document'.

This draft PPD began with some general background information. For example, Transcon had been formed eight months earlier by the merger of Eurofleet Containers and Continental Haulage. The new company would be operating from 15 depots, all in the UK. The head office was in Cardiff. The managing director of Transcon had commissioned an assessment of Transcon's future information system's needs by a leading firm of consultants. The consultants had reported that about half the systems being used in the former companies would remain useful, but they should be converted for a single new-generation mainframe computer. The rest of the systems should be scrapped and replaced with proprietary software packages, and a major new distributed scheduling system would be required, with capability distributed to the 15 depots. The consultants went on to recommend that Transcon should go out to tender for a new computer system capable of taking over the existing work and providing additional capacity to cope with the new scheduling system. Their offer to develop the invitation to tender was duly accepted, executed, and sent to Martha at Astro Wales amongst others.

The PPD provided a brief summary of the technical details in terms of Trevor's views on what should be provided. This involved a simple five item breakdown of the work to be included in the bid. The PPD also provided a brief summary of the marketing issues in terms of information gleaned by Trevor, influenced to a very modest extent by Ben's input.

Following their meeting with Transcon, Ben had pushed Trevor to give him what he referred to as 'a preliminary maximum bid estimate' and Astro's chance of winning at this bid price level to size the uncertainty about winning at the upper end of the bid range. He was anticipating what he believed would be needed for the most basic bidding model he could envisage and thought this was a good time to elicit this information. Trevor's preliminary maximum bid estimate was £20 million, with a 10% chance of winning. Trevor reminded Ben that a senior manager in Transcon had let slip (probably deliberately) that Transcon's budget for this contact was a maximum of £20 million. He also observed that no information on competitive bids was available as yet. Ben had also pushed Trevor to give him what he called 'a preliminary minimum bid estimate' and Astro's chance of winning at this level to size the lower end of the bid range. Trevor's preliminary minimum bid was £15 million, with an 80% chance of winning. The preliminary maximum and minimum bid information was noted in Ben's first draft of the PPD.

As soon as Trevor had a draft PPD that he was happy with, he asked Ben to discuss it with Sian and indicate that it was clearly a preliminary document which did not require any commitments on Sian's part, but it needed completing by Systems at the level of detail set out in Trevor's input. Sian agreed that Sam, a member of her Systems staff, would do this.

Table 6.1 summarises core aspects of Ben's and Trevor's input in Trevor's five item breakdown structure, plus Sam's added elaborations, leaving out details which you do not need to see to get the flavour of what was involved.

Table 6.1 Preliminary Proposal Document (PPD)

Item 1, Central Site Equipment

One new mainframe computer was required to replace two existing mainframe computers. It would be located in Transcon's Cardiff head office. It must run the converted and new software. The proposed equipment should have spare memory capacity of at least 50% in terms of the converted and new software as installed, to allow for post-installation growth. Contractual guarantees on this were required. An Astro mainframe computer and peripherals were specified and the direct cost to Astro Wales for this equipment (from Astro Inc) was £3.6m. The usual selling price for this equipment was £5.0m.

Sam noted a high degree of confidence in the utilisation estimates for the proposed new equipment, based on extensive experience of similar bids. However, there was a source of risk for this component linked to item 4 implying a possible need for additional memory.

Item 2, Computer Suite Modifications

The new mainframe computer would be installed in a room adjacent to the existing mainframe computer room at Transcon's head office, to avoid disturbing existing operations. The existing mainframe computer rooms would be emptied and released for alternative use as soon as parallel operation was no longer required. Astro would design the new facility and provide a project manager to supervise the work. A subcontractor, Zenith Controls, could undertake the installation work for a fixed price.

Sam noted that an Astro direct cost estimate of £0.30m had been prepared based on the information provided by Trevor plus further enquiries. Zenith had been approached based on Trevor's information and further enquiries, and they provided a preliminary quote of £1.00m. Sam had a high degree of confidence in the Astro component estimate and suggested treating it as a fixed price. However, actual prices contracted with Zenith were usually between 10% and 30% higher than preliminary quotations.

Item 3, Initial Operation and Training

Operators would be provided to run the new systems in parallel with the old systems initially. Transcon's staff would then be trained to take over, and supported during the takeover process. The transition should be complete within 6 months from the installation of the new system. Trevor indicated two options were available.

(a) Zoro Computing could undertake this task on the Transcon site for a fixed fee.
(b) An existing Astro computer site, an Astro Service Bureau close to Transcon's head office, could be used for initial operation, with Service Bureau staff training the customer's operators on Astro premises.

Sam noted that Zoro had been approached based on Trevor's information and further enquires and a £1m provisional bid estimate obtained. However, experience with Zoro on previous contracts suggested that fixed prices actually contracted were between 20% and 40% higher than preliminary quotations. Zoro had a very good track record of success on Astro and other contracts. However, they were currently the subject of a hostile takeover bid.

Sam noted that Astro had two contracts in progress similar to option (b), both going reasonably to plan, but no other similar contract experience. In this case the Astro estimate of direct cost was £1.14m, based on estimated hours of effort by Astro Service Bureau staff at standard rates with backup from Astro's training staff. Both existing contracts were close to completion. One was currently 10% below budget, the other 40% over budget.

Sam recommended option (b).

Item 4, Convert Existing Programmes

A subset of Transcon's existing financial programmes would be converted and associated documentation would be updated. Run-time savings of 25% would be required. The 'invitation to tender' (ITT) stated that current documentation was 'believed to be reasonable – 95% accurate'. Trevor indicated two options here.

(a) Datapol Systems could use new generation languages to rewrite all the software.
(b) Sysdoc Autocode could use an automatic converter to translate about 90% of the code, manual patching to deal with the balance of about 10% which proved non-viable for automatic translation.

Sam noted that Datapol were a large well-established company. Using Trevor's information and further enquiries Datapol was willing to commit now to the required run-time savings and a 'firm fixed price' of £1.2m.

Sam noted that Sysdoc was a relatively new company, with only 100 employees, but a good record of success on smaller projects. Sysdoc would not commit to a fixed price but would commit to a measured day-rate contract. They had provided an initial estimate of £0.5m based on a fixed day-rate. Cost variability was associated with the proportion of the translation achieved automatically, programme documentation, house standards, and so on.

Sam also noted that either approach could give rise to a requirement for more memory than that assumed in relation to the central site equipment (item 1 above). Sam believed there was a 50% chance that additional memory would be needed to meet the capacity and performance guarantees. Sam estimated that if sufficient additional memory to meet this contingency was specified and installed at the outset, the additional cost would be £0.50m. If installed subsequently, Sam estimated the additional cost would be £1.0m.

Sam recommended the option (a) Datapol approach and pre-installing the additional memory.

Item 5, Distributed Scheduling System
A distributed scheduling system would have to be developed, to operate in each of the 15 depots, linked to the mainframe. Sub-second response time was required. Trevor indicated two options in this case as well. Both involved 15 Astro workstations with a direct cost of £3.00m (usual selling price £4.20m) However, the development and installation of the system involved a choice between

(a) using Astro Systems staff and
(b) a subcontract with Zoro.

Sam noted that information provided by Trevor plus further enquiries suggested the Astro approach would involve a day-rate cost of £1.10m plus a 20% contingency for a total of £1.32m. Astro had completed three successful projects very similar to option (a).

Sam noted a preliminary estimate from Zoro of £1.00m, and drew attention to the comments on Zoro associated with 'initial operation and training' (item 3 above), in terms of high-quality deliverables but a potential hostile takeover, and 20% to 40% uplifts from preliminary quotes to fixed prices.

Sam also noted that either approach might give rise to a need for more powerful distributed computing equipment. Sam believed there was a 50% chance that additional performance would be required to meet response time performance guarantees. Sam estimated that if higher performance equipment to meet this contingency was specified and installed at the outset, the additional cost would be £1.00m. If installed subsequently, Sam estimated that the additional cost would be between £1.5m and £2.5m.

Sam recommended the Astro Systems staff option (a) and pre-installing the additional performance.

Preliminary maximum and minimum bids estimates
Preliminary maximum bid estimate £20m, with a chance of winning of 10%.
Preliminary minimum bid estimate £15m, with a chance of winning of 80%.

Sian and Sam were both pleased with the form and content of the PPD. Sian had ensured that the quality of the drafting matched Trevor's, and she was confident that the level of the detail provided would be seen as useful. When Ben received the PPD with the Systems' contribution incorporated and edited, he was very impressed. He showed it to Trevor, who interpreted it as the best practice he expected of his Sales team plus the best practice he expected of Sian's Systems' staff. Ben then showed it to Martha, who said she would start to think about it that evening and discuss their next steps with Ben first thing the next morning. In the meantime, she would like him to start a systematic review of relevant bidding literature. He should be aware from the outset that she had a multiple stage process in mind, which she explained in terms of the 'initial process overview' which would evolve to become Figure 6.1.

The initial process overview – early development

Martha had at least two phases in mind for her process overview plan from the outset, with front-end filtering to ensure that the time wasted on bids which Astro did not want or could not win on a profitable basis was minimised. She was not surprised by the PPD information, but reflecting on it confirmed her preference for three stages, for reasons explained shortly.

When discussing her evolving thinking with Ben the next day, she asked him to test her three stage choice in his review of the literature, as well as a list of other concerns. This was an initial aspect of drawing Ben into the process of jointly evolving her initial process overview, the basis of Figure 6.1. Ben would test her strategic clarity primarily by helping to develop tactical clarity, ensuring that there were effective and efficient how to do it ways to achieve what Martha currently thought needed to be done.

As part of a process of familiarising Ben with Astro practice and terminology, Martha explained that current Astro UK policy was a 'normal' overhead recovery rate of 30% (for indirect costs) on all Astro direct costs. Direct costs included all internal Astro transfer costs plus subcontractor costs. Current Astro UK policy also specified a further 10% profit uplift on total (direct and indirect) cost for all contracts, implying a cumulative 'normal uplift' of 43% which was usually referred to as the 'margin'. *Margin* was the common usage Astro term for selling price less direct costs, a contribution to profit measure, profit being defined by margin less overhead costs.

Martha indicated that she had observed some people interpreting the 'normal' uplift or margin of 43% and its components as a corporate standard which should be achieved on every potential contract whenever that was a convenient interpretation for their current purposes, these same people being ambiguous about corporate norms whenever they did not suit their purposes, while other people were consistently ambiguous. Under her watch, using their new SP for bidding departures from 'normal' mark-ups would not just be routine; they would also be expected, but so would a clearly stated and documented case for departures from the norm, a formal tracking of margin achieved in relation to margin expected, and a formal tracking of cumulative achieved margin relative to cumulative normal margin. Her light touch approach to enlightened governance required everyone being clear about how all component aspects of Sales performance contributed to corporate judgement of their overall performance.

As part of her coaching on process development planning for Ben, Martha explained that at a later stage in the development of their bidding process a useful alternative to the 30% overhead uplift plus a further 10% profit uplift (43% cumulative uplift for both) might be a 'nominal 60% expected margin' uplift. This 60% might include the current 43% plus a 17% provision for errors and omissions in the traditional sense plus further a no quibbles provision, in part, to keep it simple and, in part, to remind everyone that errors and omissions *plus* a no quibbles provision would usually be involved. However, she did not want to combine these separate reasons for the uplifts embedded in margin estimates until later, primarily because she did not want to distract attention from the more basic changes she wanted addressed first. But she also suspected that 50% or 70% might be more appropriate than 60%, and she thought it would be useful to acquire some data before suggesting a starting point estimate which could evolve over time. She explained her reasoning to Ben, emphasising that they would have to plan which changes to implement in what order, informally and intuitively most of the time, but explicitly some of the time. She was just using a simple example to illustrate what was involved in early planning for the evolution of her initial process overview.

Martha and Ben spent some time working through what they anticipated would be the formal analysis structure within each of the stages in Martha's initial process overview, building on the PPD starting point plus Ben's literature review. They also discussed how they should set about prototype development and testing. Martha ensured that Ben's initial literature review was focused, and any interesting ideas were explored further and incorporated in their emerging plans when relevant. On the basis of this initial process overview development, Martha briefed Rhys on their progress, tested all her key ideas on him, and sought his support for any controversial issues. Martha and Ben then planned a workshop with Trevor and Sian which would take a full day and arranged a date.

Workshop presentation of the Astro SP for bidding overview

Martha opened the workshop by suggesting that bid preparation for systems integration contracts ought to involve a multiple stage process. Based on the PPD prepared for Transcon and her understanding of current Astro problems and processes, plus analysis of a literature review by Ben, she was proposing Astro Wales move to a bidding process with three stages.

Stage 1 should be concerned with eliminating from further consideration all contracts which were 'non-starters' in terms of issues other than expected margin as a basis for a very early no-bid decision. This would involve identifying all the important positive and negative issues over and above margin. Stage 1 would also ensure the residual 'starters' with important positive and negative issues had these issues flagged for attention during the decision making of later stages. Two related but different stage 1 concerns were implied.

One was making some no-bid decisions as early as possible before wasting time addressing margin concerns, whenever this was sensible. For example, the potential customer might involve significant credit risk or other potential payment difficulties, the potential customer might involve significant reputation risk, or the potential project might mean Astro effort investment in activities which did not involve synergies with ongoing Astro corporate goals.

The second was identifying all key non-margin issues which needed ongoing consideration if the process continued to stage 2. These might include positive issues like knock-on sales opportunities, a particularly good fit with new Astro sales expansion plans, and other positive corporate synergies. They might also include negative issues which were not serious enough to eliminate the possibility of a bid in stage 1, like an indifferent fit with sales expansion plans which would be tolerable if the profitability was good.

Direct cost, selling price and the margin defined by the difference would not be stage 1 issues, but an extensive set of other concerns would be.

Stage 2 should have the goal of eliminating most of the 'no-hopers' – contracts which pass the stage 1 hurdle but did not look promising enough to analyse any further because of the likely potential margin given ongoing considerations identified in stage 1. The assessment of likely margin would be preliminary and simple, with a balanced approach to likely cost if the contract was won and the likelihood of winning it.

Stage 3 should be concerned with developing a bidding strategy and tactics including deciding a bid price for the remaining candidates, with a flexibly controlled low level of late or very late no-bid decisions.

She thought the outline information provided by Trevor in the PPD was perfect as the basis for stage 2, aimed at identifying and minimising no-hopers, but it did not address the issues she had associated with stage 1. She thought the more detailed information provided by Sian and Sam in the PPD was perfect as the starting point for stage 3, aimed at developing a bidding strategy and deciding a bid price, given a potential contract had passed the stage 2 hurdle. However, she thought Sian's input was too good for stage 2. Furthermore, like Trevor's input it did not address the issues she had associated with stage 1. Two concerns needed addressing immediately.

First, there was a mismatch between the levels of effort provided by Trevor and Sian. She appreciated that Trevor may have expected the level of detail provided by Sian from the outset in the past, and Sian may have felt a professional approach required it, but Astro could not afford to invest this much effort in a bid proposal which might be revealed as a no-hoper with relatively simple input from Sian's staff.

Second, the PPD was missing a suitable basis for a stage 1 process, concerned with identifying and eliminating non-starters plus effective and efficient ongoing consideration of relevant non-margin issues.

She might have raised further concerns – like Trevor's input was good enough for stage 2 but only because he had provided answers to Ben's questions about preliminary minimum and maximum bids, and a much more sophisticated approach to match Sian and Sam's efforts was required for stage 3. However, she saw deferring these concerns until later and then dealing with them indirectly as a more useful approach.

Martha suggested that Transcon might not warrant any significant attention in this stage 1 context, so it was perhaps entirely reasonable that neither Trevor nor Sian had noted any relevant issues. Furthermore, she had not encouraged a direct conversation between Sian and Trevor or other Sales and Systems staff about balancing their efforts in a multiple stage process earlier, so it was not unreasonable this mismatch had arisen. However, *everyone* involved in Astro bidding would benefit from a simple non-starters test followed by a simple no-hopers test, as well as a more orderly ongoing treatment of non-margin issues, and *she* should have thought about this sooner.

Sian and Trevor were both pleased by the way Martha put these observations, a situation Martha had planned for to encourage acceptance of both criticisms and change. Trevor and Sian both realised that either might have been held at least partially accountable and appreciated Martha's deliberately accepting the oversight as hers, setting a tone which minimised recriminations and encouraged candid critiques of current practice.

Martha then suggested that the time Sales and Systems staff would save by filtering out the non-starters and no-hopers in stages 1 and 2 should be used to provide more clearly communicated depth of understanding in stage 3 than she had seen in past bids.

In summary, using EP language, Martha wanted a step change in opportunity efficiency to be achieved by everyone using their time and effort in a new formal planning framework which would be designed and then developed via prototype applications with clarity efficiency in mind, achieving different levels and kinds of clarity in each successive stage.

Martha indicated that the exercise to produce the current PPD as portrayed in summary form by Table 6.1 was in no sense a waste of time – it was a crucial first step. What Trevor and Sian had produced was of good quality, perfect in the right context. Also, it was important to begin with a clarification of the best of current practice before considering change. Martha regarded the PPD material of Table 6.1 as an approximation to the best of current practice which they could continue to use *when appropriately placed within a more clarity efficient overall process.* However, they now had to address change, starting with the basis for a suitable stage 1 and a plan to develop that basis in stages 2 and 3.

To preserve the spirit of Trevor's PPD concept – but clarify what was different – she would refer to the replacement for the PPD as the 'Cumulative Proposal Document' (CPD), with a Proposal Document 1 (PD1) portion of the CPD generated by stage 1, a Proposal Document 2 (PD2) portion of the CPD generated by stage 2, and a Proposal Document 3 (PD3) generated by stage 3. She then showed them an early version of Figure 6.1 using this notation.

When she was sure everyone was comfortable with the basis of Figure 6.1, Martha suggested they began consideration of stage 1. You should now see how the process portrayed by the overview plan of Figure 6.1 was starting to emerge.

Initial observations on Martha's rationale

Martha wanted to take all the relevant people with her through the 'capture the context' phase and into the 'create and enhance the plans' phase of what we can interpret as Martha's implicit UP. She was using her own intuitive approximation to the UP concept, but we can interpret what she was doing using the formal UP framework of Chapter 2. Creating the PPD had been a part of her 'capture the context' phase which explicitly involved Trevor and Sian. But all her Astro Wales involvement to date was also crucial, as was her wider Astro experience.

Martha had already concluded that the 'select and focus the process' phase of her UP required the development of an SP for bidding. She had an outline of the SP for bidding of Figure 6.1 in mind already, but she wanted her initial plan to evolve with all the relevant people playing a part in shaping it, so they would 'buy in' and 'own it jointly', the position eventually achieved with Figure 6.1 and the component processes for each stage.

In terms of her implicit UP, Martha was beginning with a top-down vision of what she wanted the SP to achieve. In terms of immediately obvious objectives within her emerging goals–plans relationships framework, stage 1 and stage 2 were designed to filter out the customers Astro did not want and the projects Astro did not want. This would allow Astro to use the time wasted by their current single stage process to much better effect in stage 3. But better focus on different issues which needed a different kind of treatment at different stages in the process was also part of the rationale, for greater clarity efficiency. New features in her approach within each stage would address root causes of her concerns with the current bidding process and underlying corporate problems.

The overall uncertainty which had to be addressed was visualised by Martha in terms of seven partially separable component sources of uncertainty about:

1   the desirability of doing business with the potential customer,
2   synergy between the potential project and Astro corporate goals,
3   what package of deliverables to commit to,
4   the cost of meeting these commitments if the bid was successful,
5   how the bid price and contractual terms should be influenced by uncertainty about the cost estimate and the desirability of winning the contract,
6   non-price advantages relative to different potential competitors which might be influenced by the package of deliverables committed to and other aspects of the approach taken to the bid, and
7   how best to approach the first six sources of uncertainty.

Martha had developed a structured appreciation of this complexity working in sales in Astro Scotland, ultimately in a role like Trevor's. She knew Trevor understood these issues intuitively, possibly better than she did, but probably without this clarity of structure. She was less certain about Sian's understanding.

It is fairly obvious that increasing a bid price increases the chance of making a profit if the bid is accepted, but it also reduces the chance of the bid being accepted. Conversely, decreasing a bid price increases the chance of winning work but also decreases the chance of the work being profitable. What is much less obvious is how to develop a clarity efficient approach to all seven of the components of uncertainty which Martha was aware of and achieve an opportunity efficient level of clarity for each.

What Martha was doing with her initial overview plan structure was suggesting that they focus stage 1 on sources of uncertainty 1 and 2 – the uncertainty about the desirability of doing business with the potential customer, if a contract were won, in terms of customer characteristics and project issues which were not contribution to profit related in a direct manner. Part of the rationale for this focus was filtering out undesirable customers and projects for non-margin reasons. But also important was making sure that they did not overlook any big opportunities in terms of non-margin issues, and they did not lose sight of ongoing positive issues as well as ongoing negative issues. Indeed, early attention to upside non-margin issues which might need ongoing attention was crucial before getting too immersed in downside concerns or costing and pricing detail.

Her stage 2 was focused on potential profitability in terms of margin if they won the bid and associated unconditional expected margin incorporating the probability of them winning the bid. She wanted stage 2 to be an effective minimum clarity approach to estimating both the probability of winning and the margin if they did win, without getting into the details of sources 3 to 7 of her seven sources of uncertainty decomposition. In terms of the cost of delivery if Astro got the job, to some extent this view of stage 2 is analogous to the minimum clarity approach provided for William in Chapter 3, but the probability of winning issue in the bidding context added some new and rather different forms of complexity.

Her stage 3 was focused on addressing sources 1 through 7 in more detail in a holistic manner, building on stage 1 and 2 information and making effective use of the time saved by eliminating wasted effort using stages 1 and 2.

Stage 1 – identifying non-starters plus ongoing concerns

When opening her discussion of stage 1, Martha reminded them that non-starters meant potential contracts that Astro did not want to get involved with for reasons which were not contribution to profit related in a simple or direct sense. One key role for stage 1 was providing a screening process designed to filter out non-starters because of negative concerns which are fairly obvious if the usual rush to look at direct cost and margin is put aside for the moment. But a second key role was documenting important positive synergies and any other non-margin issues needing ongoing attention in later stages. Indeed, this second role was arguably much more important than the filtering role because it was about effectiveness while filtering was indirectly about effectiveness but focused on efficiency.

There were a number of quite different kinds of uncertainty and complexity associated with capturing issues of ongoing concern and filtering out non-starters, but she wanted all the relevant stage 1 uncertainty and complexity issues addressed in a very simple *qualitative* form. In principle this might just involve qualified 'yes' or 'no' answers to a series of basic questions about key assumptions, but she believed they would find 'traffic light' models useful for communicating answers to an initial overview question, subsequent more detailed questions and a final summary overview question, developed in a manner which she would illustrate shortly. A final summary traffic light rating explained briefly by a verbal 'balanced view' would provide the opening executive summary for the PD1.

Visiting the customer should not be necessary most of the time, but exceptions could be made if the lead salesperson involved thought this was appropriate.

The starting point for preparing the PD1 would be the basic context information provided by the potential customer's invitation to tender (ITT) information plus a covering note which summarised relevant context facts and issues known to the person drafting the PD1 which were not included in the ITT. This would be followed by an initial overall traffic light response to the question, 'Can we assume this customer and this project bring no special opportunities or difficulties?' Her traffic light interpretation suggestions for this first traffic light were:

> red – unambiguous significant difficulties,
> amber – possibly important difficulties,
> green – a neutral situation with a clear balance of modest opportunities and difficulties,
> yellow – possibly important opportunities, and
> blue – unambiguous significant opportunities.

She had put the red light first, the blue light last because the sequence red–amber–green was the common practice 'traffic light' starting point, but in practice she would like them to use the reverse sequence and start by looking for the unambiguous significant opportunities. The blue light was associated with unambiguous significant opportunities. This might be interpreted in 'blue light emergency service' terms, giving crucial opportunities the priority treatment accorded to ambulances, fire engines, and police cars, even at junctions involving red lights, provided due care and attention was involved.

More than one traffic light colour could be used. For example, the joint use of red and blue lights would indicate significant difficulties *plus* significant opportunities which need much more detailed attention if on balance proceeding to stage 2 and then perhaps stage 3 was appropriate. Astro staff would need to discuss and jointly agree on interpretations like this, perhaps modifying them as experience was gained. The role of the traffic light model she was suggesting was simply a way of providing clear and concise qualitative communication in an agreed-on 'traffic light' format at a summary level.

An initial overall traffic light assessment resulting in a blue light plus an amber light might suggest a complex set of issues warranting decomposition immediately or in a later stage. But a green light with no other colours might indicate 'a minimum effort stage 1 was appropriate' which only required the need to address two further closely coupled questions of detail using a second traffic light:

1 Is this potential customer a good credit risk?
2 Does this customer have a track record for paying their bills in full without difficulty?

To answer both of these questions within stage 1, simple tests of creditworthiness and attitudes to valid payment demands should be tried first. If these simple tests proved inconclusive, more onerous tests should be used next. Very expensive tests might be left until stage 3, to ensure a bid looked promising enough to warrant the cost. If simple tests revealed a clear lack of creditworthiness or other serious payment difficulties, the proposal should be given a red light and dropped at the outset of stage 1, before any serious analysis effort was wasted. But if the position was ambiguous, progress to stage 2 or 3 noting the concerns and using an amber light might be sensible.

She would assume for present purposes that Transcon had an initial overall green light followed by a 'creditworthy customer who pays without difficulties' green light which implied a final summary green light and the end of stage 1 analysis. However, this assurance was important, and a simple 'triple green' stage 1 outcome should not be presumed to be the norm or assumed to apply to individual cases without asking the relevant questions. Trevor needed to confirm this position using the accounting department staff.

To give them a few illustrative examples of departures from this minimum effort triple green stage 1 outcome, a blue light might be associated with a customer who wanted a sporting events audience information system for international level events which would be central to television coverage and give Astro valuable public exposure, or a business system in a rapidly expanding new area Astro Inc wanted to break into or a system requiring special Astro skills which Astro was currently underusing and wanted to keep fully employed. A red light might be associated with a customer who was known to use exploitive labour, or dishonest customer relationship practices, or could seriously damage Astro's reputation for any other reasons.

The more important the ambiguity posed by blue–yellow plus amber–red combinations, the greater the need for more detailed questions to explore underlying issues, but in stage 1 the focus was stopping further effort if a bid did not look appropriate without trying to resolve ambiguity better left until stage 2 or 3.

Important ambiguity involving multiple issues should be clearly flagged by multiple traffic light ratings – a multiple light cluster with different colours visible as separate lights rather than a single 'white light blur'. A linked key issue was always using short and concise notes to explain the nature of each judgement, with no attempt to use simple scoring schemes which 'add apples, pears and oranges and equate the sum to bananas or banana equivalents'. That is, a red light plus a blue light is not equal to a green light, and there is no meaningful way to just average the implications of different colours within this framework.

One detailed question revealing a lack of synergy about the project or the customer might suggest an amber light but not define a non-starter, but two or more might make a non-starter designation likely. Questions which reveal very strong synergy would be useful for passing the stage 1 or 2 test and for opportunity management purposes in stage 3, but their immediate purpose would be counterbalancing negative answers when taking and explaining a balanced view, and it would be important to identify them as part of stage 1 for all these reasons.

To help clarify the boundaries when ethical judgements might be involved, and indicate the possible need to flag some stage 1 end-point ethical issues, Martha suggested they use a variant of a 'red face test' once suggested by her uncle Paul: if you would go even slightly red in the face explaining to a valued customer, your boss, or a close family member, why you did something because of the ethical/moral issues involved – give it a red light. If you would not go red but had to think about it carefully – use an amber light to communicate your concern.

It was important to understand clearly that such judgements were complex and debatable, but Astro needed a simple corporate system to ensure that the obvious was not overlooked and important concerns were treated consistently even if the issues involved were debatable.

Martha suggested it would clarify matters if she gave them a simple illustrative example of the overall approach which Astro needed in her view – a view endorsed by Rhys. If Astro had a potential customer who sold very high interest rate 'payday' loans – widely but not universally judged to be extortionate – she would personally be inclined to give a bid for them a red light because in her view there was a case for rejecting this kind of customer for very good business reasons as well as for important underlying moral reasons. However, she could clearly understand why Rhys or those further up the Astro corporate ladder might feel there was a case for charging the upper limit of Astro's mark-ups or perhaps not even trying to make a moral judgement of this kind. She had never encountered this particular kind of case and would not waste time attempting to make a judgement until she did, but when such a case arose, if she had any doubts, she would seek advice from Rhys and expect him to seek advice from his boss if need be. Furthermore, she thought all Astro Wales staff should see Rhys as their local gatekeeper for these issues, working up the corporate ladder to the Astro UK board as and when necessary.

The key message was she did not want individual Sales or Systems people feeling uncomfortable about making these ethical judgements on their own, and she did not want them making them inappropriately. If Astro Wales staff flagged this kind of issue to her and Sian via the formal bidding process traffic light approach as soon as possible, they would take advice when in doubt, and the necessary communication channels would be used effectively and efficiently. She wanted a consistent and open policy which the Astro UK board ultimately took full responsibility for when critical choices were involved, defined by potential issues as they arose, unless Rhys or the board or intermediate levels were alerted to issues they wanted to cascade down. She and everyone else would then be obliged to conform to an internally consistent board-led Astro position all staff understood or find other employment.

A reasonably obvious flip side generalisation of the red face test was a 'halo test'. For example, a blue or yellow light might be associated with a deserving charity with good business case reasons for a low margin (they could project a favourable public image and perhaps Astro could sell similar systems to other customers), as well as ethical reasons the whole office and the Astro UK board might support.

A less obvious generalisation of the red face test for ethical concerns was a 'frowns test' to deal with all non-ethical concerns associated with any other red or amber light issues, like key staff needed for a potential customer were already fully stretched on other highly profitable and sensitive work. She did not want to overdo the idea of carefully chosen labels for all tests associated with qualitative issues leading to traffic light colours other than green. However, raising the possibility of such labels emphasised the need for clear recognition of all relevant qualitative issues needing ongoing consideration. She did not want such issues addressed via bias of the strategic misrepresentation variety when it came to the estimates of quantitative measures in stages 2 and 3. For example, later in this tale Sian will be seen to want higher cost estimates than Trevor for what might be usefully treated as a frowns test amber light result, explained by the stage 1 documentation using a brief note from Sian which Trevor and Martha would find useful.

The flip side generalisation of a frowns test was a 'smiles test', associated with all yellow or blue light triggers which did not involve halo test ethical issues, like key staff needed for a potential customer were underused and needed this kind of opportunity, or Astro Inc was encouraging a move into this new business area.

The overall implication was four basic kinds of tests leading to all the coloured lights: a smiles test and a frowns test for positive or negative issues needing qualitative attention, with halo test and a red face test for special cases for ethical concerns.

As an aside, Martha suggested that Trevor or others might prefer alternative labels for the tests of their own choosing, and she was always open to this kind of modification.

Martha indicated that she wanted the completed PD1, however complex or simple, to involve a final overall summary traffic light assessment with a concise verbal statement of the recommendation. A triple green might not warrant anything more than a standard 'proceed to stage 2'. However, one or more other colours would warrant an 'executive summary' which argued a view for or against proceeding with a bid 'on balance'. If moving to stage 2 was recommended, preliminary guidance should be provided on any recommendations for higher or lower than normal margin, with the detailed questions and answers plus the rest of the PD1 serving as backup.

She would expect Sales to operate this stage 1 process, with support from Systems on issues like which Astro skills were currently underused or overstretched, the Accounting Department regarding credit checks, and other departments as appropriate. Stage 1 should be formal, focused, carefully designed, evolved and updated in the light of experience, and documented on each application. All aspects of it should be both efficient and effective. She would take responsibility for the nature of the process, but she wanted Rhys to take overall responsibility for the way it was implemented, which he had agreed to. This was because Rhys had to be the conduit for red face tests and halo tests, and he was best placed to take responsibility for ensuring that the more general frowns tests and smiles tests took place, with top-down input when relevant about key new red or blue light concerns. However, for most purposes oversight from both Rhys and Martha would involve very light touch audits. They would all need to work together to evolve the operational details, but neither Martha nor Rhys would expect to be consulted about individual bid PD1's unless asked.

As guidance to be used to develop early versions of the stage 1 analysis, Martha suggested Sales and others involved should aim to apply about 1% to 5% of the effort required for a complete three stage bid process. The 1% estimate was her current best guess of a plausible minimum to use as an aspirational stretch target if a triple green was involved. The 5% estimate was her current best guess of a plausible maximum to use as a target if a joint blue and red was involved. A 2% anticipated average outcome was her current best estimate – the skew implying most outcomes would be closer to 1% than 5%. These estimates were intended to illustrate roughly what she was anticipating, but the reality might prove quite different.

Furthermore, they should expect to reject about 10% to 50% of the potential contracts at this stage, with 50% as a stretch target when lots of work was available. She would be surprised if they found less than 10% or more than 50% appropriate, but a 30% midpoint of the 10% to 50% range was a very nominal rough guess at the expected outcome without ruling out surprises.

These anticipated ranges and associated expected outcomes should be subjected to careful review over time to see if adjusting their expectations would improve the efficiency and effectiveness of the bidding process as a whole.

Ben would coordinate the development of this stage 1 process, working with Trevor and his sales team plus Sian to start with, then other sales staff, and then other Astro staff, reporting to her and Rhys as appropriate.

Martha observed that the computer-based information systems nature of Astro's business might suggest to some Astro staff that 'the deliverable' documentation for stage 1 should be electronically based. If and when this development looked effective and efficient at a later date, she would obviously consider this possibility. That is, at some time in the future the questions could be presented to the sales staff responsible for each bid electronically, and their responses would trigger the follow-on questions. This would be convenient for staff executing stage 1 analysis. It would also ensure that she had a good database for Ben to use for post-outcome analysis of bids continuing past stage 1, bringing important special cases to her attention and consideration by Rhys when appropriate. However, it was premature to waste time even thinking about this possible later development now, and her personal view was the complexity involved and the flexibility needed implied that they should not rush a computer-based stage 1 process.

Martha emphasised she expected enlightened judgements reflecting the context and asymmetric penalties. For example, if winning new contracts was especially difficult, then risking early rejection of what could prove to be a big opportunity would not be worth a minor saving in effort. But if Astro sales were at a very healthy level, and Systems staff in a crucial area were already seriously overstretched, then a potentially difficult customer might warrant early rejection without too much probing of the opportunity potential.

She also emphasised that it was separability she wanted to see between the different stages, not independence. The objectives and the resulting processes and outputs were highly inter-connected in very important ways, despite important reasons for the separable structure. In particular, stage 1 would be qualitative in nature and quite different in character from most aspects of stage 2, but stage 2 would draw upon stage 1, stage 3 might add to the qualitative knowledge generated by stage 1 as well as drawing upon it, and the stage 2 process was a special case of the more general stage 3 process.

She would not expect to see most PD1s, Rhys would be involved only on an exception basis unless he wanted to feed down Astro UK concerns, and sales personnel would normally move directly to stage 2 if a potential contract survived stage 1. But a formal hurdle test administered by the responsible sales executive would be involved, and subsequent audits might include non-starters as well as those potential contracts which progressed to stages 2 and 3.

The focus of this monitoring would be the system and the players in the system rather than individual decisions, but seriously inappropriate individual decisions would receive attention, as part of an overall concern for learning from experience.

She wanted Ben to work with Trevor and Sian and other Astro staff as appropriate to develop a simple PD1 example for Transcon, in parallel with their follow-on development for stages 2 and 3. However, for that day's purposes they would just assume a prototype stage 1 process would lead to a final overall summary green light for Transcon with a 'pro-ceed to stage 2' recommendation, subject to confirmation from Trevor that Transcon had a triple green light. She would finish her presentation on stage 1 now, taking feedback after they had time for further reflection whenever issues occurred to them, unless they had immediate questions. There were no immediate questions, so Martha suggested a coffee break, to be followed by addressing stage 2.

Stage 2 – identifying no-hopers

Martha began the stage 2 discussion by indicating that the *preliminary* view of profitability required by the test for 'no-hopers' of stage 2 justified the working assumption that Astro could use a simple single-pass approach to unbiased estimation of:

1   the expected direct cost of meeting bid commitments,
2   the expected value of the probability of winning for a plausible set of margins on the expected cost just estimated.

The working assumptions employed to estimate the expected cost associated with the first part would be used to assess the probabilities in the second part. However, further inter-dependence between assumptions underlying expected cost estimates and assumptions underlying expected probability of winning estimates at any given level of margin would be deferred until stage 3.

After a single pass through sequential analysis of these two components, synthesis which also addressed stage 1 results would be needed to filter out the stage 2 no bid decisions – the no-hopers. As a rough guide, Martha was anticipating rejecting 10% to 50% of the potential bids which survived the non-starter tests, with 50% as an aspirational stretch target if a lot of work was available, 10% as a comparable lower bound, and 30% as a mid-range expected value. She was anticipating about 5% of the effort required for a complete three stage bid process would be needed in stage 2 for all potential customers, centrally located in a 1% to 10% range. The 5% was an expected outcome estimate which should be achievable on average, although she would not rule out surprises.

Stage 2 was similar to stage 1 in terms of the anticipated rejection rate, the use of a single pass process, and the need for ongoing review and evolution. But stage 2 would be very different from stage 1 in most other respects.

Martha indicated that PD2 would be produced by a five phase process. She then showed them an early draft version of Figure 6.2, emphasising that all the ideas and associated assumptions might evolve.

You should find it helpful to see the final form of Figure 6.2 now and use it to follow the way Martha and her colleagues developed it. The five phases imply five process

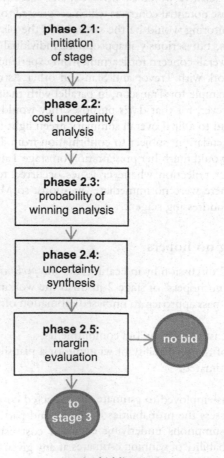

Figure 6.2 The stage 2 plan of Astro's SP for bidding.

components for stage 2, referred to as phases 2.1 to 2.5, producing five components for the PD2, referred to as the PD2.1 to PD2.5.

Phase 2.1 – stage 2 initiation to produce a PD2.1

Martha indicated that the information provided by Trevor in the draft PPD of Table 6.1 was a good basis for what she would call 'phase 2.1' – phase 1 of stage 2. If a member of Sales wanted to take a bid beyond a PD1, they should proceed as Trevor had, visit the customer, and make summary notes. The resulting document, a PD2.1, could then be sent by Sales to Systems for cost input. It should have the completed PD1 as an annex.

A triple green or a complex multiple colour rating would clearly be of direct interest for decision making in stage 2, but it should not significantly affect the effort required in stage 2. If stage 3 was reached, then a multiple colour rating would have an impact on the stage 3 effort required, especially if a blue light signalling an important opportunity was involved.

Martha might have added that preliminary draft preparation of part of the PD2.1 based on the PD1 prior to visiting the customer might provide a plan which would help to focus the discussion in a useful manner in areas of uncertainty flagged by stage 1. However, she knew Trevor and other sales staff would make good use of the PD1 in this way and did not want to labour the obvious.

Phase 2.2 – stage 2 cost uncertainty analysis to produce a PD2.2

Martha indicated that if a PD2.1 as just described was sent to Systems in the future, in her view Sian or a senior member of the Systems group ought to be able to suggest an unbiased expected direct cost estimate of about £12m associated with a preliminary range of actual outcomes of about £10m to £20m without expending the considerable effort Sam had put into the PPD. By 'unbiased' she meant 'an estimate which was not systematically too high or too low – about right on average'. The £10 million lower end of the range would be a 'nominal minimum' which was in the P1–P10 range, with allowable ambiguity about which percentile value was involved, although she would recommend targeting a P10. The £20 million upper end of the range would be a 'nominal maximum' which was in the P90–P99 range, with allowable ambiguity, although she would recommend targeting a P90, and consistent upper and lower nominal range boundaries were essential.

Crucially, it should be feasible to do this on the basis of about an hour's consideration at a simple overview level, without referring it to Sam or other staff for the development of the considerable level of detail which Sam had contributed to the PPD of Table 6.1. Whoever did it would need an overview perspective based on experience, like Sian, but it might be someone reporting to Sian trained for this task. This was the level and kind of input from Systems which Martha wanted for stage 2. Could Sian provide this sort of precision with that level of effort?

Sian had not actually read the draft PPD prepared by Trevor or the invitation to tender before passing it on to Sam, but her subsequent close reading of Sam's detailed estimates suggested an expected cost easily exceeding £13 million could have been estimated without all the detail Sam had provided. She did not want to seem too pessimistic relative to Martha, and the nominal range was wide, so she said she was happy to agree that an estimate of expected direct cost of £13 million associated with a £10 million to £20 million anticipated outcome range was the kind of '*preliminary*' estimate that she or one of her staff with wide experience could produce in an hour or so. Sian liked the way the discussion was going, and she believed that with suitable mentoring Sam could meet the requirements Martha was suggesting.

Martha smiled when Sian increased the expected outcome estimate from £12 million to £13 million but did not comment. She emphasised that they were now assuming £13 million was an expected outcome in a nominal uncertainty range of the order £10 million to £20 million and indicated that adding this preliminary cost estimate to the PD2.1 would make it a PD2.2, which could then be sent to Ben. She then asked Ben to explain what he would do for phase 2.3, phase 3 of stage 2.

Phase 2.3 – stage 2 probability of winning analysis to produce a PD2.3

Ben started by reminding everyone that Trevor had provided a preliminary maximum bid estimate and a preliminary minimum bid estimate with associated estimates of the chance of winning in the draft PPD. He indicated that in terms of future practice the working assumption was Trevor would produce these estimates for a PD2.3 in the light of the PD2.2, making use of the initial Systems view of expected cost in the PD2.2, in this case, the £13 million estimate just discussed. For today's purposes he would assume Trevor had guessed correctly that £13 million was the kind of estimate Systems would provide later. Trevor's estimates would be used to produce a 'preliminary probability of winning curve', illustrated in Figure 6.3.

Ben began explaining Figure 6.3 by pointing out that the version of the preliminary probability of winning curve he recommended for use today was the solid straight line between points 'a' and 'b', the simplest approach feasible. However, it would be useful to spend a few minutes discussing what using the straight line between points 'a' and 'b' in Figure 6.3 implied in terms of underlying assumptions and associated more complex possibilities. Trevor had provided a preliminary maximum bid estimate of £20 million, with a chance of winning at

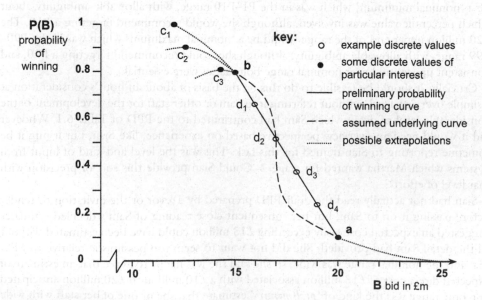

Figure 6.3 Preliminary probability of winning curve.

this level of about 10%. This information had been used to plot point a in Figure 6.3. Point 'a' was linked to the information slipped, deliberately or otherwise, by a Transcon senior manager, that £20 million was their budget figure. The £20 million figure was presumably based on a recommendation from the consultants who prepared the invitation to tender, and most of their competitors probably had the same information. It was sensible to use such a figure as a preliminary maximum bid estimate, with an associated probability of winning estimated approximately to the nearest 10%, as Trevor had done. Trevor had also provided a 'preliminary minimum bid estimate' of £15 million, with a chance of winning at this bid level of about 80%. This information had been used to plot point 'b' in Figure 6.3. Ben indicated it had not occurred to him at the time to ask Trevor what the basis of point 'b' was, and the rationale involved might be important. However, when drawing Figure 6.3 he assumed that Trevor had chosen £15 million because he had a Systems preliminary cost estimate of about £13 million in mind, he was unsure about the shape of the probability of winning curve below this value, *and* he did not think it was worth worrying about the curve below this value given the £13 million expected cost. By implication, he was reasonably confident about the shape of the curve for bids above £15 million.

Trevor indicated that Ben was quite right in assuming he was reasonably confident over the range £15 million to £20 million but not below £15 million, and he doubted that a bid below £15 million would be of interest, given the information available. Trevor had smiled approvingly at Ben's inferences on his behalf, particularly appreciated because he too had not thought this through earlier. He had certainly not *explicitly* thought about the role of the £13 million expected cost estimate in the way it was assumed he had in mind, but he liked the idea of formally doing so. He also liked the idea of avoiding considering a curve range that did not matter. Martha had carefully coached Ben to make sure he was aware of the need for this sort of facilitation skill, helping him to acquire this particular insight, and Ben was a fast learner.

Ben thanked Trevor for confirming his interpretation of point b. He then indicated that he had joined point 'a' and 'b' in Figure 6.3 with a solid straight line to define a preliminary probability of winning curve over the 'preliminary bid range' £15 million to £20 million, plotting intermediate points d_1 to d_4 at £16 million to £19 million.

Ben had added the curve shown by dashes between 'a' and 'b' to indicate the assumed nature of the underlying curve. He highly recommended using a 'best estimate' of this dashed curve in future stage 2 analysis if they found this option helpful, but he would avoid doing so today to 'keep it simple'. He had also added the dotted curve beyond the preliminary bid range at the top end, and he had added three dotted curves at the bottom end for bid values below £15 million to indicate some of the possible scenarios which might be involved. For example, the curve to c_1 implied a bid of about £12 million would win for sure. This might be interpreted in terms of three linked working assumptions: Transcon could be convinced that such a bid was the result of a decision by Astro 'to buy the work to keep Astro staff busy', Astro was the highest quality bidder in the contest, and a £12 million bid by Astro represented outstanding value for Transcon which no competitor could touch. As another example, the curve through c_3 implied a bid below about £14 million would lead to a decrease in the probability of winning. This might imply that a bid this low would suggest to Transcon that Astro lacked credibility, Astro was desperate for work because it was inferior to others in the marketplace, and Astro did not understand what the job was about. The curve through c_2 was an intermediate case, with a peak probability of winning of about 0.9 at a bid of about £13 million.

Ben encouraged a limited discussion about these dashed and dotted curves, to gain understanding of (and approval for) his simple linear probability of winning curve by exploring the potential alternative natures of the underlying 'true' curve it approximated, both within and beyond the presumed range of interest.

When Ben was pushed about the obvious lack of data associated with this preliminary curve, Martha immediately interjected that it should become clear shortly that such a curve was always used implicitly if it was not made explicit, and *crude but simple explicit use was much better than ambiguous implicit use* for a number of reasons. One of the key reasons of immediate relevance was the basis it provided for gathering appropriate data later, and ultimately building a data basis for probabilities which had to be purely subjective initially, but could be given an objective data-driven basis if they started on a purely subjective basis. Another immediately relevant key reason was testing for alternative views, by revealing the views to be used if testing for alternative views did not suggest changes.

Martha observed that Astro staff currently always made a note of the expected cost estimate used for bidding, £13 million in this case. They discussed any relevant differences of opinion which were generated by the process of committing to the figure generated. Furthermore, they compared each outcome with the estimate, testing for bias over sets of completed projects for bids won. From now on they were also going to make a note of the assumed probability of winning in stages 2 and 3, testing both these probability estimates for bias immediately when relevant differences of opinion surfaced, and later using outcomes to test over sets of bids won and lost. For example, if over ten projects which made stage 3 the average stage 3 probability of winning was 0.6, and bidding with an expectation of winning six, they actually won five, six, or seven of the ten potential contracts, it would look as if they were reasonably competent at estimating probabilities in stage 3. However, no wins or ten wins would indicate very serious stage 3 probability of winning estimation problems.

Martha then suggested they leave the question of how data might be accumulated and used for the moment, pressing on with the stage 2 analysis, assuming that the preliminary linear curve between a and b provided sufficient precision over a suitable range for the preliminary quantitative analysis involved in stage 2 to define the PD2.3. Trevor indicated he was happy with this, although he was not too sure where it was leading. Sian looked puzzled but intrigued. There were no more questions, so Ben pressed on with his presentation.

Phase 2.4 – stage 2 uncertainty syntheses to produce a PD2.4

Ben indicated that the preliminary cost estimate of £13m provided by the PD2.2, plus the preliminary probability of winning curve illustrated by Figure 6.3 which defined the PD2.3, needed integration. This integration would be provided by a 'preliminary margin evaluation table' illustrated by Table 6.2, which would define the PD2.4. He would now explain how this table was produced, and how they could interpret it, as a basis for using it in the next phase.

The first row in this table introduced the $E(C) = £13m$ notation for the expected cost estimate provided by Systems, which he had put into his spreadsheet as soon as Sian confirmed the £13 million estimate. His working assumption earlier had been £12 million, but a spreadsheet basis for Table 6.2 made this kind of real-time adjustment simple.

The second row headings for the columns defined further notation which clarified the calculations. The concepts used and the associated notation choices were all straightforward, but he would take them through each entry in the first option row, so they had a clear view of what was involved. He would then consider relationships between option rows.

The first three entries of the $B = £15m$ row of Table 6.2 indicated that the corresponding point in Figure 6.3 was 'b' and the associated probability of winning was $P(B) = 0.8$. The fourth entry indicated a corresponding conditional margin of $M = £15m - £13m = £2m$. This M value was the contribution to overhead and profit if the bid of £15 million was

Table 6.2 Preliminary margin evaluation table (the PD2.4 produced in stage 2 phase 4).

Expected direct cost E(C) = £13m working to the nearest £m with an outcome in the range of £10m to £20m anticipated

Bid values B (£m)	Points on curve used	Corresponding probabilities P(B)	Margin (conditional) M = B − E(C)	Expected margin E(M) = P(B) × M	Comments
15	b	0.8	15 − 13 = 2	2 × 0.8 = 1.60	Minimum bid
16	d_1	0.66	3	1.98	Buying work worth it?
17	**d_2**	**0.52**	**4**	**2.08**	**Maximum E(M)**
18	d_3	0.38	5	1.90	Approaching normal M
19	d_4	0.24	6	1.44	Normal
20	a	0.1	7	0.70	range for M

A decision tree with six options and row values indicated in bold for the maximum E(M) option

successful – it was conditional on winning. Multiplying M by P(B) yielded E(M) = £2m × 0.8 = £1.60m, the expected margin indicated by the fifth entry.

The B = 16, 17, 18, 19, and 20 rows of Table 6.2 completed the underlying the decision tree. There were six bid value choices in the first column, working to the nearest £m. About half a dozen alternative bid scenarios was a suitable level of detail for preliminary margin evaluation, but more detail could be provided if deemed useful. The second column indicated the corresponding points in Figure 6.3 and the third column indicated the corresponding probabilities of winning. The interpolated points d_1 to d_4 taken from the linear version of the curve of Figure 6.3 used a second decimal place to aid interpretation.

The final column provided a set of notes indicative of the discussion which needed to take place when exploring the basis for selecting a preliminary bid and using possible choices to assess whether Transcon was a no-hoper. For example, the 'maximum E(M) bid' of £17 million involved an M of £4 million, a 31% uplift on E(C) = £13 million, well below the 30% plus 10% 'normal M'. The £18 million bid increased the uplift to 38%, while the £19 million bid increased it to 46%, above the 'normal M'. These uplifts could be included in the table.

Table 6.2 used a HAT approach which is comparable to but marginally more complex than Nicola's safety stock model, a relationship illustrating the portability of HAT models you may find useful.

There were no questions about how Table 6.2 was generated or the basics of its interpretation, so Ben pressed on to discussing how they could use it.

Phase 2.5 – stage 2 margin evaluations to produce a PD2.5

Ben indicated that stage 2 phase 5 involved the use of the PD2.4 plus the PD1 to discuss possible bid choices and evaluate the key associated trade-offs given the information available to date. If Transcon had a stage 1 traffic light rating that was anything other than the triple green that they were assuming, the PD1 would need careful attention when interpreting the right-hand column of Table 6.2, synthesising the quantitative basis of Table 6.2 with the qualitative basis of the PD1 executive summary to prepare these notes. They did not need to determine a proposed bid value – they just needed to decide whether to make a no bid decision or move on to stage 3. The potential profitability of this contract given any PD1 issues was the core concern in stage 2, and a specific bid price was not required. The

PD1 information about the desirability of the customer and Astro's appetite for more work of this kind might be highly relevant, including complex circumstances like the need for a balanced view based on a mixture of blue, yellow, green, amber, and red lights.

A summary of this discussion added to the PD2.4 would define the PD2.5. Ben suggested they have such a discussion with an assumed triple green stage 1 result to illustrate what was involved in a simple basic case. For example, if the preliminary estimate of the expected direct cost was £13 million, and the simple linear 'curve' of Figure 6.3 was approximately correct, then a bid of £17 million maximised expected margin at a value of £2.08 million, with a conditional margin of £4 million and a chance of winning of about 0.52 (shown in bold in Table 6.2 to assist identification). They would have to increase their bid to £19m to achieve a bid above the 'normal M', which reduced the probability of winning to 0.24, but this might be acceptable if M was more important than P(B) on this occasion. The key was Table 6.2 gave them a basis for this kind of discussion, without any need to determine their bid at this stage. All they had to decide was whether to carry on to stage 3. Ben suggested that Table 6.2 clearly indicated to him that the Transcon bid was *not* a no-hoper. Transcon was a preliminary 'goer', requiring a more detailed stage 3.

At this point Sian suggested that the Transcon contract would be a useful one to win. However, in her view it was 'nice to have' rather than critical. She suggested that a bid of £19 million with an assumed margin of £5 million on a £14 million cost looked about right to her. She would be happy to get the work, but with her £13m cost estimate increased by a further £1m provision to allow for unknown unknowns and ensure they did not overrun on cost, playing by the rules on margin. She had been tempted to increase Martha's £12 million initial suggestion to £14 million earlier but did not want to look too pessimistic at that stage of their discussion.

Trevor's rejoinder was he thought a bid of £15 million with an assumed margin of £3 million on a £12 million cost looked about right to him. He believed that £13 million might be a reasonable estimate by Sian for the expected cost given her current assumptions, and a further £1 million provision for the reasons Sian suggested might seem sensible from a Systems perspective, but they could reduce the expected cost if both Systems and Sales worked at it. Furthermore, there was no point in risking the loss of this important contract in what was clearly a tough market. He did not say so, but he was not keen to chance four lost systems integration contracts in a row because it would seriously damage his credibility and the commission-based part of his income, and playing by the rules on margin was not a big concern for Trevor.

Martha then suggested that Sian and Trevor had both raised extremely important issues which needed addressing. However, before they were considered, along with a number of other concerns, like how do these issues relate to PD1 multiple coloured lights, it would be worth beginning a stage 3 analysis. It would be helpful to clarify both the expected direct cost and the shape of the probability of winning curve in the process of addressing Sian and Trevor's concerns, in addition to reasons possibly underlying Sian's comment about this contract being just a 'nice to have' with a much higher expected or commitment value cost than Trevor was suggesting. Sian and Sam had already done what was needed as a starting point basis for the stage 3 expected direct cost estimate, but some additional effort was needed by Systems, and much more needed to be done by Sales to underpin the probability of winning curve.

Martha did not raise the issues associated with Martha and Trevor having different incentives because Trevor was on commission and Sian was not, but this was part of the considerable complexity stage 3 had to deal with and part of the cost estimation process bias concerns (by no means the whole story).

Martha indicated that Rhys was fully briefed and happy with the stage 2 process as just outlined by Ben, and she would take ongoing responsibility for the stage 2 process, with important input and support from Trevor, Sian, and Ben.

To illustrate how she wanted the formal stage 2 process to work in the future, Martha suggested they finished stage 2 now by agreeing that Transcon was a 'preliminary goer', progressing to stage 3 was appropriate for the Transcon bid, and it would be reasonable for sales staff to make this judgement subject to later audit by her. Everyone readily complied. She then indicated that this decision noted on the PD2.5 should be taken to define the end of stage 2.

The rationale for separate stages – further comments now

Reflecting on the details of stages 1 and 2 as explored so far, one of Martha's reasons for separating stages 1 and 2 was using stage 2 to concentrate its focus on a minimum clarity *quantitative* approach while stage 1 provided a concentrated focus on a minimum clarity *qualitative* approach, both minimum clarity approaches, but very different in nature. Martha was aware that experience in many contexts over many years suggests that people can do a much better job of two different kinds of tasks at any given level of total effort if they do one at a time in a suitable sequence. In this case, stage 2 clearly had to follow stage 1 to avoid rejecting blue and yellow light projects with low contributions to profit in margin terms, the rationale for the ordering.

Assuming what needed to be done in stages 1 and 2 could be separated and ordered in this way, with greater efficiency and effectiveness as a result of exploiting the separability involved, this implied the effort saved by no bid decisions after stage 1 can be viewed as a bonus even if the proportion rejected was quite low – a clarity efficient bundled package of benefits was involved. Despite the obviously important value of screening out non-starters in stage 1, the more fundamental reason for separating stages 1 and 2 might actually be seen as more effective analysis in both stages with less effort. This was a clarity efficiency process design issue which is useful to understand, even if designing processes is not your direct responsibility or concern. For example, if you are a board level manager you might want to ask why other comparable processes do not have this kind of feature.

Separating stage 3 from stages 1 and 2 involves a further bundle of benefits. However, this time stage 3 builds on two earlier stages using a significant increase in sophistication relative to both, and you need a working understanding of what stage 3 involves before exploring these benefits. As a hint about what is involved, we can exploit the benefits of focusing on one task at a time in a suitable sequence, *and* deal with complex interdependencies, *if we plan on using an iterative approach*, the basis of key differences in stage 3.

Martha briefly summarised these observations for Sian and Trevor so they had some feel for her overall process design rationale and then finished the morning's discussion by suggesting they now enjoy a well-earned lunch, with a view to dealing with stage 3 suitably refreshed.

Stage 3 overview – bidding strategy and tactics development

After lunch Martha prefaced their workshop resumption by reminding Sian and Trevor that stage 3 was about developing a bidding strategy and tactics involving non-price features of their bid and then making a pricing decision to bid for potential contracts Astro wanted to win, with a small chance that a late no bid situation might emerge.

Her first key point of substance was introduced by indicating that she would maintain oversight of the form of the stage 3 process as well as an audit of outcomes, as for stage 2. However, with Ben's support and her assistance when needed, Trevor would be formally responsible for individual stage 3 execution exercises involving Transcon and all other transport sector bids, in conjunction with Sian whenever joint working was essential, *and* Trevor's role would go beyond just being responsible for the outputs of individual bid exercises as in stages 1 and 2. He would be leading bidding process development on behalf of Sales. Sian's role would also extend beyond her Systems Manager roles in stages 1 and 2 to joint leadership of bidding process development. Trevor's leadership in the shaping of stage 3 process developments in partnership with Sian would be a key feature of the way Astro Wales would address stage 3. Both Martha and Ben would be behind Trevor and Sian's development of the generalisation of the starting point prototype process outlined today, but Trevor and Sian would take leadership of bidding process development as far as possible, with Trevor leading the Sales aspect of what had to be viewed as a Sales/Systems partnership. Furthermore, once Trevor and Sian were comfortable with the evolution of a suitable version of today's prototype process, and she was also happy with it, she would expect Trevor to help other sales staff responsible for all other areas of Astro Wales business to develop variants suitable for their areas.

Martha then moved on to the specifics of the stage 3 process, emphasising that stage 3 was a multiple phase iterative process by design. Stages 1 and 2 were both single pass non-iterative processes by design. This multiple pass aspect of stage 3 was an important difference which would significantly affect the tasks facing the process developers as well as all the users of this stage 3 process.

She then showed them an early draft of Figure 6.4. Like Figures 6.1 and 6.2, the final form of Figure 6.4 has been provided now so you can use it to follow the way Martha and

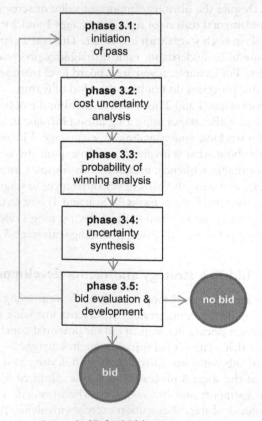

Figure 6.4 The stage 3 plan of Astro's SP for bidding.

her colleagues developed it. She indicated that after a few overview comments they would consider phases 3.1 to 3.5 in turn, producing PD3 components 1 to 5, referred to as PD3.1 to PD3.5.

Pass 1 of stage 3 would be centred on higher clarity quantitative analysis addressing uncertainty about the expected direct cost of meeting bid commitments, followed by higher clarity quantitative analysis of uncertainty about the probability of winning for an assumed margin, separating the analysis of these two components. But following this separate higher clarity analysis of these two components, an iterative approach which addressed interdependences would be needed to explore planning decisions about what the customer is being offered which affect both the expected cost and the expected probability of winning. Iteration was required because of these interdependencies. Eventually detailed bidding tactics within an evolving bidding strategy would become the focus.

In outline the stage 2 and stage 3 processes had exactly the same basic phase structure, but because a multiple pass approach was involved in stage 3, each stage 3 phase was more complex than the stage 2 equivalent. The stage 2 approach could be viewed as a special case of the more general stage 3 approach – a minimum clarity variant they might see as 'pass zero' version, not to be confused with 'pass 1' of stage 3, which would seek a much higher level of clarity than stage 2.

Phase 3.1 – initiation of stage 3 on pass 1

Martha indicated that initiation of stage 3 on pass 1 would begin in phase 3.1 by planning the remaining four phases for pass 1, bearing in mind what had been achieved in stages 1 and 2, and anticipating further stage 3 passes. This kind of planning the planning was not part of the stripped-down more basic phase 2.1 variant used in stage 2.

As part of these plans for the development of the Transcon bid, Sian and Ben would be asked to plan the production of an 'enhanced cost estimate' to form the PD3.2, the deliverable of phase 3.2. This would be an enhanced version of the PD2.2 preliminary cost estimate.

Trevor and Ben would be asked to plan the production of the PD3.3, the phase 3.3 deliverable. The PD3.3 involved an 'enhanced probability of winning curve', a more developed version of the simple Figure 6.3 approach used for the PD2.3.

The PD3.2 and PD3.3 would then be combined by Ben to produce an 'enhanced margin evaluation table', defining the PD3.4, an enhanced version of Table 6.2.

PD3.5 development would follow, analogous to but generalising phase 2.5 production of the PD2.5. The phase 3.5 process had to consider a possible no bid decision, but its focus would be refining earlier analysis in an iterative manner. Further analysis passes would address selected non-price aspects of their bidding approach, initially at a broad strategic level and then in terms of tactical detail within an emerging strategy.

Sian and Trevor both agreed that this outline made sense, but Martha had primed this reaction by suggesting that she was sure they would not yet be very clear about where the discussion was going and that they would have to explore what followed in some detail before they could really understand this initiation phase.

Martha now indicated that Sian and Sam had already provided a starting point basis for the stage 3 cost estimates, in terms of the details in the PPD of Table 6.1 discussed earlier, which she had excluded from the PD1 and PD2 documents. Ben had already used this material to complete a draft of the PD3.2 deliverable, with her support and input.

Ben would present this draft now. Martha observed that in practice Sian or her delegated Systems person and Ben should discuss Ben's contribution to this document before it was released to others, and Martha would become involved only when requested. Ben's current example was purely illustrative. Martha also observed that Sian or other Systems people and Ben or Trevor did not need to agree on all issues, but it would *very* be important to highlight any differences in view.

Phase 3.2 – enhanced cost uncertainty analysis on pass 1

Ben began his presentation of the PD3.2 by revealing Table 6.3.

Ben indicated that he would explain the Table 6.3 item entries based on the PPD information line by line, using backup diagrams to elaborate the summary provided by Table 6.3 in some cases, as soon as he had explained the four individual direct cost column headings. Table 6.3 would be spreadsheet based to facilitate evolution, and together with associated backup diagrams Table 6.3 would be his part of the PD3.2.

When explaining the four individual direct cost column headings, Ben indicated that:

1   the 'base' estimate was the starting point estimate provided by Sam,
2   he and Martha had agreed to use P10 to P90 ranges based on the information provided by Sam,
3   they also agreed to assume a uniform probability distribution model,
4   this meant that the nominal expected outcome would be a simple average of the nominal minimum and maximum, and
5   a more complex assumed underlying reality needed general understanding.

What each of these five points implied was then outlined, with a view to discussing alternatives later. Its basis was discussed with William in Chapter 3 in the context of minimum-clarity estimates, not repeated in this chapter.

Ben then made a series of observations for each of the five items listed in Table 6.3, starting with item 1.

Item 1 – central site equipment

The base cost for item 1 was the direct cost to Astro Wales of £3.6 million. This could be taken as the nominal minimum, maximum, and expected cost. There was no uncertainty of interest because determining Astro Inc to Astro Wales transfer costs was well beyond Martha's remit.

For Table 6.3 purposes direct cost was the issue, not selling price, and it was important to maintain this focus. Margin (overall overhead cost recovery and profit) would be determined later. After the bid price was decided, the bid presentation package for the customer would be drafted using standard list prices and suitable discounts.

There was no choice to be made for item 1, as noted in the right-hand column. This item provided the simplest possible example of the cost analysis required in the stage 3 cost estimate format of Table 6.3.

The issue of possible additional memory could be addressed as part of item 1, but he would deal with it as part of item 4, following the approach to the descriptive material taken by Sam.

Everyone nodded approval, so Ben moved on to item 2.

Table 6.3 Enhanced cost estimate summary table (the PD3.2 produced by pass 1 in phase 2 of stage 3).

Items	Item components and options	Direct costs (£m)				Choices and assumptions
		base	nominal minimum	nominal maximum	nominal expected	
1 Central site equipment	Astro main frame plus peripherals	3.6	3.6	3.6	3.6	No choice
2 Computer suite modifications	Astro	0.30	0.3	0.3	0.3	
	Zenith	1.00	1.1	1.3	1.2	
	Total	1.30	1.4	1.6	1.5	No choice
3 Initial operation and training	(a) Zoro	1.00	1.2	1.4	1.3	No hostile takeover effect
	(b) Astro 1	1.14	1.0	1.6	1.3	Sam's preferred option
	Astro 2	0.8	0.7	1.1	0.9	Martha's revised option
4 Convert existing programmes	(a) Datapol	1.2	1.2	1.2	1.2	Sam's preferred option No non-compliance effects
	(b) Sysdoc	0.5	0.5	1.5	1.0	Martha's preferred option assuming Sysdoc 2
Additional memory	(a) Pre-install	0.5	0.5	0.5	0.5	Sam's preferred option
	(b) Post-install if necessary	1.0	0	1.0	0.1	Martha's preferred option
5 Distributed scheduling system	Astro equipment	3.0	3.0	3.0	3.0	
	(a) Astro software	1.1	1.2	1.4	1.3	Sam's preferred option
	(b) Zoro software	1.0	1.2	1.4	1.3	No hostile takeover effect
	Total (a) or (b)		4.2	4.4	4.3	
Additional performance	Adjustment to (a)	+ 1				Clear switch of preference to (b) with no other impact
	(a) Pre-install	1.0	1.0	1.0	1.0	Sam's preferred option
	(b) Post-install if necessary	1.5–2.5	0	2.5	0.4	Martha's preferred option
Contract nominal direct cost		**10.4**	**10.4**	**15.7**	**11.8**	**Round to £12m in the range £10m to £16m**
Overhead at 30%					3.5	
Nominal total cost					14.3	
Profit at 10%					1.4	
Nominal price					**16.7**	**Round to £17m**
Nominal margin					**4.9**	**Round to £5m**

Item 2 – computer suite modification

The item 2 base cost estimate of £0.30 million for Astro's direct costs was the £0.30 million provided by Sam, as was the £0.3 million nominal maximum, minimum, and expected value, apart from rounding to the nearest tenth of a million. They could treat this as a fixed price estimate as suggested by Sam, with the P10 = P90. However, spurious precision wastes time and, more importantly, can be misleading. Working to the nearest £0.1 million (about 0.5% of total expected cost) would be useful for most purposes in the Transcon case, with a view to overall clarity efficiency.

The item 2 base cost of £1.00 million for Zenith was as provided by Sam, but in this case the nominal minimum, maximum, and expected values were different. The range of 10% to 30% uplift from preliminary quotes to actual prices for Zenith as reported by Sam had been used to determine a P10 nominal minimum value of £1.1 million (£1.0 million × (10 + 100)/100) and a P90 nominal maximum value of £1.3 million (£1.0 million × (30 + 100)/100). Ben suggested values outside this range were clearly possible, but in the present context it was not worth being too concerned about the chances of this.

The expected value of £1.2 million defined by (1.1 + 1.3)/2 could be associated with a uniform probability distribution density function defined by the P10 nominal minimum and P90 nominal maximum values, with an associated underlying assumed reality as discussed in terms of Figures 3.1 and 3.2 in Chapter 3. These Chapter 3 figures using an MoD context were not used here, but variants based on this item could have been employed to explain minimum clarity estimates using an Astro example.

Table 6.3 shows a single total for the two components of item 2. The no choice note in the right-hand column is applied to the total, and by implication both components. The highlighting (in bold) makes later interpretation of totals easier.

Ben's presentation on item 2 finished with a request for questions or comments, but none were forthcoming, so he moved on to item 3.

Item 3 – initial operation and training

Ben began his discussion of item 3 by indicating that when two or more choices involved probability distributions for a continuous variable, a useful conceptual and operational framework which was widely employed involved plotting cumulative probability distributions for both choices on the same graph, what he called a 'decision diagram'. He then showed them Figure 6.5, which used simple linear cumulative curves for three options.

All three curves in Figure 6.5 were plotted using the Table 6.3 item 3 nominal minimum and maximum values interpreted as P10 and P90 values.

The Zoro curve nominal minimum P10 = £1.2 million used the Zoro choice (a) base value of £1.0 million plus 20%. The corresponding Zoro curve nominal maximum P90 = £1.4 million used the same base value of £1.0 million plus 40%. The base value of £1.0 million was provided by Sam, as were the +20% and +40% estimates for the P10–P90 range. The expected value was the midpoint, £1.3 million. This Zoro curve ignored the possible implications of the hostile takeover bid, as noted in the right-hand column of Table 6.3.

The Astro 1 (before adjustment) curve nominal minimum P10 = £1.0 million used the Astro choice (b) base value of £1.14 million less 10%. The corresponding P90 = £1.6m used the same base value of £1.14m plus 40%. The base value of £1.14 million was provided by Sam, as were the –10% and +40% estimates for the P10–P90 range. The expected value was £1.3 million, the same expected value as the Zoro option.

In terms of 'risk' associated with direct cost variability as portrayed by Figure 6.5, Astro 1 (before adjustment) was clearly riskier than Zoro. Sam's preference for Astro, noted in the right-hand column of Table 6.3, could be assumed to be based on the hostile takeover threat, which Sam had associated with ambiguous implications and uncertain consequences. Ben indicated that Martha had taken the view that Sam's preference was both reasonable and representative of current best practice, but it raised three issues which she had discussed with him that they all needed to discuss now.

First, a hostile takeover of Zoro was a risk of strategic concern for Astro. Astro routinely used Zoro to good effect, and it was important to preserve the possibility of doing so in the future because Zoro was a key subcontractor for Astro. To facilitate this, Martha had approached Rhys about a possible friendly takeover approach by Astro Wales. Rhys had acted immediately. Zoro would shortly become a 'strategic partner', owned by Astro, but run by its existing management on terms that the Zoro management team were very pleased with.

Second, given the elimination of takeover risk, the Zoro option clearly became the preferred option if risk associated with direct cost variability was considered, no other objectives apart from expected direct cost were relevant, and the Astro 1 (before adjustment) option was the only alternative. However, Martha had approached Steve, the Service Bureau manager, and with approval from Rhys, they had agreed to a 30% discount on the charge rates relative to the standard rates assumed by Sam, the basis of the Astro 2 (after adjustment) curve. The reason Martha had taken this action was the Service Bureau was very short of work, with very low marginal costs and a risk of redundancies if their business did not turn around soon. Steve and Rhys both preferred a 30% discount on standard rates to the Astro Service Bureau option being dropped from item 3 in the Transcon bid – a smaller margin for the Service Bureau was better than no margin at all. Ben did not say that Martha achieved the 30% discount in a hard-nosed bargaining discussion, but this was understood without being explicit. This point raised a number of questions because it introduced the concept of different parts of Astro Wales bidding internally for work in a way not previously entertained. But these questions were not asked or addressed immediately.

The expected cost of the Astro 2 (after adjustment) option was lower than the Zoro option (£0.9 million compared to £1.3 million, a difference of £0.4 million), and the Figure 6.5 curves did not cross. This meant that the Astro 2 (after adjustment) choice was risk efficient

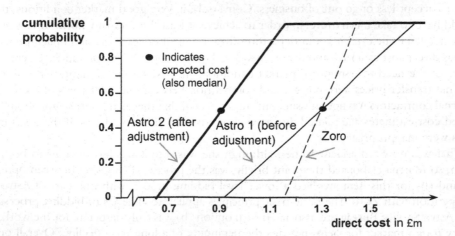

Figure 6.5 Decision diagram: item 3 (initial operation and training) example.

with a clear basis for clarified dominance. Sticking to cost for the moment, Astro 2 (after adjustment) had a lower expected cost, and the probability of exceeding any given cost was less. The Astro 2 (after adjustment) choice involved more variability, but it was less risky. Unless 'qualitative benefits' (non-quantified benefits) worth £0.4 million could be associated with the Zoro choice, Astro 2 (after adjustment) was Martha's preferred choice, as indicated in the right-hand column of Table 6.3.

Third, there was a difference between the Zoro approach and the Astro 2 (after adjustment) approach which Astro needed to sell to Transcon as an important non-price advantage for Astro relative to the competition. This was Transcon being able to use the Astro Service Bureau site before the new Transcon site was ready. The supporting case Astro should provide ought to argue that this Astro choice would allow the training to start well in advance of the Transcon facility being ready, spreading it out for the convenience of Transcon staff (and Astro staff), and it would decouple training from the risk of any delays with the new computer suite in addition to saving £0.4m. None of their competitors could offer this non-price advantage. There might be important linked ongoing non-price advantages which also needed effective marketing, like backup services in the event of a major fire in the Transcon office, because all Transcon software would be up and running on the Service Bureau hardware and Transcon staff would be familiar with its use at the nearby Service Bureau site. To win bids they needed to systematically search for non-price-advantage opportunities like this. They also needed to try to avoid letting their competitors convince Transcon that training they would provide on the Transcon site was better than off-site training by Astro. Furthermore, they needed to offer a Zoro option on the Transcon site for an extra £0.4 million if there was any risk that they might fail to convince Transcon that the off-site Astro training option was a good one, preferably linked to an approach to item 5 which demonstrated the value to Zoro of their new strategic partnership with Astro.

Trevor and Sian were both comfortable with the obvious implications of this part of the presentation. Neither had come across the risk efficiency or clarified dominance concepts, but both seemed clear enough in this context. At this point Sian asked Martha for clarification about the internal market issue.

Martha responded by first indicating that the Astro Inc 'normal' 30% and 10% mark-ups for overhead and profit were what she would call 'nominal', for use as a guideline to indicate what was needed as a minimum on average. In very tough market conditions, they would have to accept less or go out of business. Conversely, in very good market conditions, they would have to take much more, in order to achieve at least the company norms on average. They needed to be explicit about departures from nominal values, to avoid implicit pressure to bias direct cost estimates and distort associated option choices. Trevor and Sian were well aware of the need to respond to market conditions in these terms assuming that standard internal transfer prices were correct and competition between different parts of Astro and external contractors was not an issue, but she suspected that they had not thought about the biased cost estimates and related distorted choice issues which could arise if these assumptions were inappropriate.

What was now self-evident to her, although she was sure it was less obvious to both of them, so Martha elaborated the point briefly, was the process of choosing between options (a) and (b) for this item involved a lower level bidding process with one part of Astro in competition with Zoro. The same basic principles applied to all levels of bidding processes. The Astro Service Bureau site associated with option (b) was truly desperate for the work, in a very tough market for them, perhaps the beginning of a long-term decline. Overall optimisation of the Astro Wales position required the use of adjusted costs whenever this kind of consideration was relevant. Whether or not it was seen as a formal part of her brief in terms of her responsibilities to Rhys, Martha had agreed with Rhys and Steve that it was in the best interests of Astro Wales to ensure that underused capacity in the Astro Wales Service Bureau was pushed with the support of Sales and Systems. The Service Bureau Manager reported directly to Rhys, outside the Sales and Systems structure, but when she could Martha needed to push their sales as well as the sale of Systems peoples' time and Astro Inc hardware and software. This kind of adjustment was the instrument they all needed to use to help push the marketing of underused Astro capacity. Of course, Astro could not sustain consistent negative adjustments of this kind in any resource area and would look to the elimination of such areas in the medium term. However, in the short term it was important to make explicit negative adjustments which made direct cost as computed using internal accounting conventions more accurately reflect actual marginal cost to align short-term choices with longer-term corporate goals. The flip side of this, protecting high-demand resource areas from overuse via positive adjustments to reflect opportunity costs, would arise in item 5.

Trevor and Sian were a bit stunned by this revelation, but they were both smiling, and Sian could already anticipate part of what was coming in item 5.

Ben then indicated that the Figure 6.5 decision diagram format was a crucially important basic tool for considering choices. He would organise some computer software to make their production simple. But once Astro staff became comfortable with the operational use and implications of decision diagrams, Table 6.3 could be used on its own. That is, the risk efficiency and clarified dominance of the Astro 2 (after adjustment) option for item 3 were indicated by a lower expected value and a lower nominal maximum value on Table 6.3. Once everyone involved became familiar with the use of backup figures like Figure 6.5, there was no need to actually produce a Figure 6.5 equivalent each time. The Figure 6.5 decision diagram could become a background conceptual device which only required operational use when someone did not understand direct use of Table 6.3 to make risk efficient choices or it was a close call or controversial for other reasons. If it was a close call, they might use a higher clarity version which he would explain later.

Trevor and Sian both nodded again, and Sian smiled, indicating she appreciated the efficiency of the simple procedure which was emerging to justify clear-cut decisions by experienced team members.

Ben then moved on to item 4.

Item 4 – convert existing programmes

Ben began by showing them Figure 6.6.

The 'firm fixed price' of £1.2 million for the Datapol option implied a vertical cumulative probability curve in Figure 6.6, assuming P10 = P90 = £1.2 million as indicated in Table 6.3. If a failure to comply with contract conditions or successful additional cost claims by Datapol against Astro which could not be passed on to Transcon were a significant risk, the actual Datapol curve should have a tail moving to the right at the top before the cumulative probability reaches 1.0. The possibility of Datapol going broke could imply a very long tail for the underlying actual curve as it moved to right at the top, perhaps going off the page. Figure 6.6 assumed a P90 nominal maximum for Datapol of £1.2 million in the same spirit of ignored tails as earlier nominal values, although in this case the P100 equal to the P90 was a very extreme special case.

Ben indicated that Sysdoc's P10 nominal minimum of £0.5 million was derived from Sam's base value and discussion in a straightforward way. Although the chance of a lower

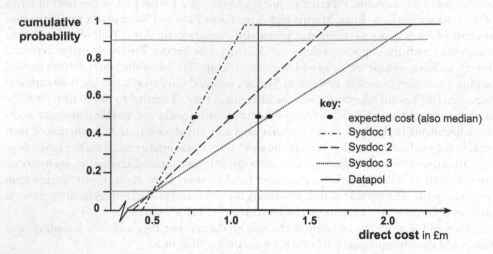

Figure 6.6 Decision diagram: item 4 (convert existing programmes) example.

cost than this P10 = £0.5 million might be negligible in practice, this did not matter. The obvious significant difficulty with Sysdoc was a basis for defining a complementary P90 nominal maximum. Sam had not made any suggestions, and the unknown nature of this nominal maximum cost was an understandable basis for Sam's suggested choice of Datapol. However, Martha had taken the view that although Sam's preference was reasonable, and it was probably typical of current Astro practice, it was not best practice. It was actually bad practice which highlighted several issues which she wanted everyone involved to understand, and he would explain them now.

First, the unknown nature of such a maximum cost should not induce automatic preference for a known cost alternative like Datapol. Whenever there was significant uncertainty about a nominal maximum cost, different 'scenarios' might be worth considering, without any immediate consideration of associated probabilities, to explore a plausible range of possible values. For example, to choose between Datapol and Sysdoc by considering a plausible range for possible P90 Sysdoc values, Figure 6.6 portrayed three illustrative alternative nominal maximum value scenarios which provided a useful basis for discussion:

Sysdoc 1, with a P90 maximum of £1.0m, 100% more than £0.5m (minimum × 2),
Sysdoc 2, with a P90 maximum of £1.5m, 200% more than £0.5m (minimum × 3),
Sysdoc 3, with a P90 maximum of £2.0m, 300% more than £0.5m (minimum × 4).

Putting aside 'non-price advantages' qualitative concerns for the moment, assuming that both Astro and the customer perceive no 'quality' difference in the two approaches, a Sysdoc choice in terms of each of these three scenarios could be compared with the Datapol choice in risk efficiency terms.

If the Sysdoc 1 curve applied, then Sysdoc was a clearly preferred choice in terms of risk efficiency and clarified dominance. Sysdoc cost was more variable, but it is always cheaper, and the expected cost saving was £0.45 million (1.2 − (0.5 + 1.0)/2), using a second decimal place at this stage to clarify comparisons.

If the Sysdoc 2 curve applied, the expected cost saving was £0.20 million. This was still a significant saving, but Sysdoc was not the only risk efficient choice, because the Sysdoc 2 curve involved a risk of costs in the range £1.2 million to £1.5 million not associated with Datapol. A trade-off was involved in terms of this particular decision, clarified by the Figure 6.6 portrayal.

At this point Ben made the point that Astro Wales had to make choices involving trade-offs like that portrayed for the Sysdoc 2 versus Datapol in terms of minimising expected cost, *accepting the risk involved to do so,* on a routine basis in many contexts. That is, *all decisions should always be made* on the basis of minimising expected cost *unless unacceptable risks were involved,* in order to aggressively minimise costs and maximise profits over time on average. Achieving risk efficiency in the Figure 6.5 sense was important, but so was taking acceptable risk in the sense of using Figure 6.6 assuming Sysdoc 2 was the relevant curve. If Sysdoc 2 was the appropriate curve, *there was a clear case for Sysdoc.* Put another way, the possibility of an additional cost up to that they might reasonably associate with the true curves underlying the Datapol and Sysdoc 2 curves in Figure 6.6 was an acceptable risk in the context of an expected saving of £0.20 million on this particular decision. In the context of a £15 million to £20 million contract, this was not really risk at all – it was just variability which was 'noise'. Hence, Astro should choose Sysdoc if the Sysdoc 2 curve was believed to be appropriate.

If the Sysdoc 3 curve applied, then Datapol became the only risk efficient choice, with an expected cost advantage of £0.05 million $((0.5+2.0)/2-1.2)$, and clarified dominance was portrayed in Figure 6.6.

In summary, if Sysdoc 2 was a 'best estimate', or a curve in the Sysdoc 1 to Sysdoc 2 range was thought to be appropriate, then Sysdoc should be the initial choice prior to considering qualitative benefits. If Datapol were to be selected without reference to qualitative benefits, then it would be important to verify that the Sysdoc 3 curve or a curve even further to the right was a best estimate of the reality, with a flip point between the Sysdoc 2 and Sysdoc 3 curves when the expected Sysdoc and Datapol costs coincide.

Ben then indicated that Martha had suggested using the Sysdoc 2 curve as an illustrative best estimate for illustrative purposes, with the Sysdoc 1 and 3 curves interpreted as 'nominal bounds', in a second-order probability model sense which could be explored further later.

As an aside, this three scenario approach has some of the characteristics of a 'parametric analysis': finding the value of an unknown parameter which 'flips' the decision, in this case, a 'nominal maximum' of £1.9 million or more. However, it places this flip value in the context of a best estimate. Even if you are not interested in techniques like this form of parametric analysis at a detailed how to do it level, you should have a what needs to be done level of strategic clarity which includes understanding the value of analysts who can implement this kind of technique whenever they become relevant.

You may find it useful to understand that this part of the analysis was dealing with a higher-order level of uncertainty which matters. It could be dealt with by parametric analysis or modelled directly, the choice depending upon a number of issues.

You should certainly be aware that more sophisticated curves for Sysdoc (tilted S shapes) and a tail for the Datapol distribution would enhance the case for Sysdoc, and a skilled modeller using an EP perspective should understand this in all comparable contexts. The simple modelling used here is robust, and simple follow-on testing for robustness would probably support the choice of Sysdoc if Sysdoc 2 looks appropriate using the simple model and the underlying judgements are reasonable.

Trevor and Sian were both impressed by this part of the presentation. They were both comfortable with the Sysdoc choice given the analysis while recognising that Datapol, as recommended by Sam, was typical of past Astro decision making. Everyone understood the new bidding process should lead to taking more risk to reduce expected costs and increase expected profits as demonstrated by choosing Sysdoc rather than Datapol. Sian did not feel threatened by Sam's Datapol recommendation being reversed or by the modification of Sam's other recommendations.

However, both Trevor and Sian wanted to talk about the Datapol approach in terms of what Trevor called 'non-price advantages' and Sian referred to as 'qualitative benefits for the customer'. This was, in essence, the same concept from two different perspectives, although there are nuanced distinctions in some cases, and *value added* or *added value* are further terms which Trevor and Sian both used for the same basic concept. Ben let them 'have the floor' to do so. In brief, the Datapol new generation language rewrite approach would be a much better basis for future changes, and as such from a Transcon perspective it would provide value added relative to a Sysdoc approach.

Martha then made the point that all these arguments were sound, and they should be documented as part of the PD3.2 in order to make them clear to the customer later, using clearly explained and consistent common language. However, it would be a serious mistake to add cost to the bid by making this kind of choice for the customer, behaving like a 'nanny contractor'. It was crucially important to bid on the basis of the lowest expected cost choices which are compliant with the customer's stated requirements *and offer options at extra cost in cases like this.* That is, if Sysdoc 2 is the accepted basis in terms of minimum expected cost, Transcon should be told that the Astro bid minimised the cost to Transcon by using Sysdoc, but for the difference in expected costs, currently estimated at £0.2 million, Transcon could have Datapol as a 'costed option', with a clear case for why Transcon should seriously consider this option.

Martha then made the additional point that costed options like this should be individually and collectively sold to customers as 'bonus opportunity options' – a set of opportunities for the customer to get a better system than that required for compliance with their contractual terms, in this case, a 'bonus opportunity option' associated with the deliverable provided by Datapol being better suited to future changes than the Sysdoc deliverable. Part of the rationale was the competitive advantage this could give them in both non-price and price terms. But also important was looking professional, guiding the customer towards better choices for a range of reasons without being critical of the customer's specification or pushy.

Trevor pointedly indicated he would normally expect to do this, but Sian's uncomfortable look suggested he was not always given the opportunity to do so. Martha picked up the message clearly, and without making Sian more uncomfortable than necessary made sure that Ben, Trevor, and Sian had understood and resolved to make good use of this insight – the new Astro bidding process would improve communication on this kind of issue – and better communication in this sense should be a built-in feature of the process, worth explicit emphasise when other Astro staff were later introduced to the SP for bidding.

Ben then suggested they move on to the 'possible additional memory' issue.

Item 4 – the possible additional memory issue

Ben began by showing them Figure 6.7, which used a simple conventional textbook decision tree format to portray the uncertainties associated with the two choices available to address this issue as initially specified by Sam (pre-install the additional memory or post-install if necessary). Figure 6.7 also included one key chance node and associated possible outcomes identified by Martha which Sam had overlooked (if the extra memory is needed

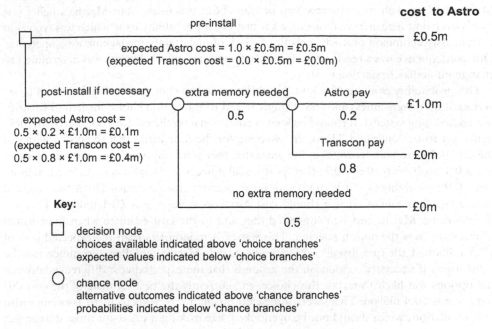

cost to Astro

pre-install — £0.5m

expected Astro cost = 1.0 × £0.5m = £0.5m
(expected Transcon cost = 0.0 × £0.5m = £0.0m)

post-install if necessary   extra memory needed   Astro pay — £1.0m
0.5   0.2

expected Astro cost =
0.5 × 0.2 × £1.0m = £0.1m
(expected Transcon cost =
0.5 × 0.8 × £1.0m = £0.4m)

Transcon pay — £0m
0.8

no extra memory needed — £0m
0.5

Key:

☐ decision node
choices available indicated above 'choice branches'
expected values indicated below 'choice branches'

○ chance node
alternative outcomes indicated above 'chance branches'
probabilities indicated below 'chance branches'

Figure 6.7 Decision tree: possible additional memory example.

Astro might have to pay for it, but this might not be the case, and Martha was assuming an 80% chance Transcon would have to pay for it). The version of Figure 6.7 which Ben was using at this point was without the text in brackets on the 'pre-install' or 'post-install if necessary' options. Ben did not want to show this text until he used it to discuss the basis of an option for Transcon which Martha had suggested, but you might like to see it now, and using just one version of Figure 6.7 is simpler for our purposes.

The top branch from the square decision node associated with choosing the 'pre-install' option shows the £0.5 million 'cost to Astro' outcome assumed by Sam. No chance nodes were associated with this branch, so the expected Astro cost outcome shown on this option branch was obviously £0.5 million without any need to formally compute it. When preparing Figure 6.7, Ben had assumed that Astro would pay this £0.5 million *if* the pre-install option was chosen, but Martha's bonus memory option for Transcon to be discussed shortly assumes a £0.4 million contribution from Transcon *if* Transcon decides to take the bonus memory option, an opportunity for Transcon *and* Astro not revealed at this point, with formal modelling of associated higher-order uncertainty not even considered for reasons which will be clarified shortly.

Two chance nodes were associated with the 'post-install if necessary' branch. The first addressed the probability extra memory would be needed or not. The second addressed the probability Astro would have to pay or not if additional memory was required. Ben indicated that Sam had estimated the cost to Astro if it paid at £1.0 million, used as shown. Sam had also estimated the 0.5 probability extra memory would be needed, as also shown. Sam had not addressed the possibility Astro might not have to pay for a post-installed memory, but Martha's reading of Sam's documentation in the PD3.2 suggested a probability that Astro would have to pay of the order of 0.2, not the 1.0 implicitly assumed by Sam. Sam's oversight of this issue might reveal a preference for pre-installing. Ben emphasised that Martha had no wish to embarrass Sam or Sian about this issue – but Martha's belief was Sam's oversight here involved missing a key first order probability issue which was typical of current Astro common practice, a result of a lack of uncertainty management competence. One consequence was a tendency to favour 'safe options', which Martha was determined to change immediately, starting today.

This probability estimate of 0.2 was clearly linked to the choice of option for item 4 (convert existing programmes) and less strongly linked to the option choice for item 5 (distributed scheduling system). It should be seen as conditional on the choice associated with these items, yet to be confirmed. However, assuming for the time being that the probabilities of 0.5 and 0.2 were both 'correct' in the sense that they were unbiased expected values, there was a 0.1 probability (0.5 × 0.2) that 'post-install if necessary' would cost Astro £1 million, but a 0.9 probability (1 – 0.1) of no additional memory cost for Astro. The Astro expected cost, a best estimate of what it should cost Astro on average, was £0.1 million. This was the provision Martha and Ben suggested they add to the cost estimate when 'post-install if necessary' was the option selected. This was £0.4 million less than the expected cost of £0.5 million if the 'pre-install' option was selected. Martha and Ben recommended the 'post-install if necessary' option on the grounds that the expected cost difference between the options was likely to favour this choice, and currently the best estimate of the cost difference was £0.4 million. There were some clear qualitative benefits to Astro associated with pre-installation, which should not be overlooked, like making it easier for those developing the new systems associated with items 4 and 5. But at present Martha took the view that the sum of all such benefits could not be assessed in terms of a value exceeding the £0.4 million difference in expected costs. There were also clear and important implications for Transcon which this analysis had ignored thus far.

Sian immediately indicated that she was not comfortable with this approach. Sian's challenge was that Ben and Martha's approach put only £0.1 million into the budget as a provision for an event which might cost £0 but might cost £1 million – and would *never* cost £0.1 million. Surely, she argued, the 'long-term average' cost might be £0.1 million if this was done time after time, but this was a 'one-off' project. Putting £0.5 million in the budget for the 'pre-install' option was a prudent (safe) policy for this project, while a provision of only £0.1 million with a one in ten chance of a £1 million 'hit' was a high risk gamble. Surely playing it safe was sensible in a situation like this.

Martha responded by saying that if extra memory was needed which Astro had to pay for, the Transcon project would have to take a £1 million 'hit' against a budget with a provision of only £0.1 million in it for this eventuality. But this should average out with other reasons for cost variations on this and other projects. *Her policy, approved by Rhys and as of that day Astro Wales policy in any comparable bidding context, was ALWAYS avoid increasing expected cost to reduce direct cost risk when making option choices like this.* Astro could afford to take the risk some projects would involve a direct cost outcome which was often more than expected, occasionally a lot more than estimated. It was not opportunity efficient to increase expected cost to avoid risk Astro could live with. She was determined that Astro would *ALWAYS* avoid increasing Astro expected direct cost by reducing risk which did not need reducing. Reducing risk which did not need reducing by increasing the expected direct cost involved what she would call 'unenlightened caution'. Taking risk which reduced expected direct cost and could be afforded involved what she would call 'enlightened gambles'. The post-install if necessary choice, putting a £0.1 million provision in the cost estimate assuming a one in ten chance £1 million will be needed, was a good example of an enlightened gamble.

As of that day enlightened gambles were mandatory, and unenlightened gambles involving unenlightened caution would not be tolerated. The pre-install choice was a good example of unenlightened caution because it involved an expected cost of £0.4 million more than post-install if necessary choice. A comparable issue had been central to their earlier discussions involving Figures 6.5 and 6.6.

Martha elaborated briefly, explaining why the need for change arose. She explained that for cultural reasons many Astro staff, not just Sian and Sam, currently took what they saw as 'low risk' decisions, like pre-installing the extra memory in this case, choosing Datapol in the first part of item 4 providing another example. These low risk choices increased expected costs. Such decisions were low risk from their current personal perspective because they anticipated hassle if they took the 'high risk' alternative of not adding extra memory or choosing a subcontractor with unknown costs, and they implicitly assumed that Astro preferred they avoided such decisions because of the hassle. But this low risk approach lowered the chances of Astro winning bids, and it lowered the expected margin if they did win. In terms of winning bids and making a profit from an overall Astro marketing perspective, decisions like adding extra memory were high risk choices, not low risk choices, in the sense that they led to a high risk of losing bids and less profit on average when bids were won. This lowered average profitability, increasing the risk that Astro as a whole would fail. Across all bids such decisions increased the chances of Astro 'going broke' (being 'broken up' in practice) because Astro did not have enough business, and what it had was not profitable enough, now a very serious threat. There was 'no such thing as a no-risk business', just as there was 'no such thing as a free lunch'. Astro could balance the risk of losing money on some contracts and the risk of going out of business as currently structured because it did not get enough contracts or make enough on those it got. But Astro was no longer in a position to avoid taking significant risk on individual contracts. Technology and market changes had transformed Astro's competitive position, and they all needed to adapt or face the implications of Astro going out of business.

Martha then made it clear that she saw the need for significant changes in operating policy linked to significant culture changes. One component key issue was taking more risk on each bid to maximise expected return for Astro Wales over all contracts over time. She did not want to labour this complex set of issues now. But she was grateful Sian had triggered the need to flag them – she would organise a separate session later to make sure everyone was comfortable with all her new policy directions, including the way enlightened governance would ensure that staff who took enlightened gambles which proved unlucky did not have problems as a result.

Sian was still not entirely convinced, but she realised Martha had anticipated this challenge. She didn't fully understand Martha's position but felt it was not sensible to prolong the discussion at this stage. You may also have reservations about Martha's position, sympathising with Sian and Sam. What is involved is important as is its contentious nature, and there was a case for Sian's position *if* Astro could not be trusted to reward people for taking enlightened gambles whether or not they were lucky. It is crucial for you to understand Martha's thinking on this issue, but prolonging discussion at this point would not be helpful.

Ben then eased Sian's discomfort slightly by indicating that the textbook decision tree format of Figure 6.7 did make discrete events (like a need to post-install additional memory at Astro's expense) seem risky, but the cumulative distribution decision diagram format of Figures 6.5 and 6.6 could be used for discrete as well as continuous variable outcomes, as indicated in Figure 6.8.

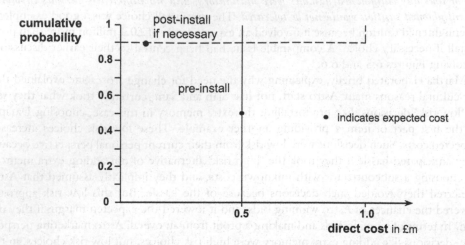

Figure 6.8 Decision diagram: possible additional memory example.

Ben suggested that in the format of Figure 6.8 the pre-install or post-install choice was clearly analogous to the Sysdoc 2 versus Datapol choice in Figure 6.6, and it might seem less threatening in this format. The expected value of £0.1m plotted on the 'post-install if necessary' curve of Figure 6.8 was on the horizontal part of the curve because £0m or £1m discrete values were assumed to be the only feasible outcomes and point estimates of probabilities were used (P10 = P90 in minimum-clarity terms, implying both equal the P0 and P100 values). This makes Figure 6.8 seem a bit odd. However, Figure 3.8 and the associated discussion in Chapter 3 in an IBM UK and BP context makes the implications of the assumed situation very clear, and it highlights the rather special nature of either-or outcomes involving both assumed certain outcome values and exactly known probabilities as conventionally used with decision trees.

These conventional textbook decision tree assumptions could be relaxed, and sometimes should be relaxed to aid understanding. For example, if the 0.9 probability Astro would not have to pay defined by 1 − 0.5 × 0.2 was assumed to be an expected value with an appropriate asymmetric and skewed probability distribution P0 to P100 uncertainty range from 0.5 to 1.0, and the £1 million post-installation cost was assumed to be an expected value with another appropriate asymmetric and skewed probability distribution P0 to P100 uncertainty range from £0.8 million to £5 million, then the 'post-install if necessary curve' will leave the y-axis at a probability of 0.5 and approach a probability of 1.0 at a direct cost value of £5 million. If Astro used a Monte Carlo simulation package to accommodate these asymmetric and skewed smooth curves for both component distributions, the resulting curve would be smoother. Some decision analysis textbooks refer to using simulation in this way as 'risk analysis', but in an EP framework it is more usefully seen as simply uncertainty analysis which goes beyond the basic textbook first order uncertainty modelling of Figures 6.7 and 6.8.

Item 4 – the ethical issue and a red face test amber light example

Martha then intervened, suggesting that Sian and Trevor might both have somewhat different reservations about assuming a 0.8 probability Transcon would have to pay if extra memory was needed *without telling Transcon* – was this ethical? In her view it was a red face test amber light issue – a source of concern on an ethical issue which caused her to pause and think about the implications. The ITT stated that current documentation was 'believed to be reasonable – 95% accurate'. This implied that the customer's consultants who prepared the ITT were well aware that one or more errors and omissions making Transcon responsible for extra memory could be expected, and Transcon should be prepared for most tenders to assume this, using some variant of Figure 6.7 implicitly if not explicitly. However, in her view there was an important potential ethical problem if the customer did not understand this. On reflection Martha thought there was a very good business policy case for being honest and helpful, with due concern for the prospective customer's best interests as well as protecting Astro's commercial position, assuming the customer might or might not understand the issues involved. As an illustrative example of how they might proceed, she suggested a three step plan for addressing a 'bonus opportunity option'. The bonus opportunity in question here was 'bonus additional memory', and she would explore further bonus options shortly.

The first step was exploring what proposition they might reveal to the customer *if* they got the job *after* they had developed a strategic implementation plan with the customer but *before* they made a final commitment to memory size *assuming* they would prepare the ground and perhaps avoid the issue arising with a suitable bonus memory option at the bid stage.

The second step was exploring how they would condition the customer for this proposition by offering a 'bonus additional memory option' as an add-on to the basic bid.

The third step was developing a strategy linking all related bonus opportunity options plus later post-bidding issues. She would outline her current thinking on steps 1 and 2 now and deal with step 3 later.

If they won the bid, then in the process of planning the job with the customer, before they were committed to the memory size the bid was based on but after they had undertaken a review of the current position and developed implementation plans at a strategic level, they should raise the issue directly and explicitly using an updated and generalised variant of Figure 6.7 showing expected cost for Transcon as well as for Astro – at this stage assuming no mark-up charges or potential legal costs involved. She then showed them a version of Figure 6.7 with the text in brackets included and suggested they consider it assuming for the moment that the Figure 6.7 probabilities were still their best estimates. Assuming they showed it to their customer and outlined its implications in terms of the basic bid assuming the customer had not taken their offered bonus additional memory option, their proposition now could be as follows.

Astro would re-offer the bigger memory for pre-instalment as a bonus additional memory option at a special cost of £0.4 million (the £0.5 million it would cost Astro less a £0.1 million discount with no mark-up, implying an Astro cost of £0.1 million). This would involve the same expected cost for both options for both parties, but it would eliminate the risk for both, it would eliminate the need for a possible argument, and it would give Transcon a 0.5 probability of significantly exceeding their minimum spare memory capacity requirement. From the perspective of Transcon and Astro as a collaborating partnership, it was a risk efficient choice which was best for both, with benefits and costs shared in a manner which was arguably fair to both.

To prepare the ground for this revelation, at the bid stage they would offer this same bonus additional memory option, described as 'pre-installation of additional memory for £0.4m, a very deep discount price (expressed as a discount of about 50% on the normal price defined by £0.5m plus overhead and profit), because it *might* be useful for Astro to meet compliance guarantees as well as for Transcon'. They would emphasise this extra memory would probably not be needed by Astro in the short run, probably significantly exceeding Transcon's requirements, but it might be needed in the short run by Astro, and in the long run it probably would prove useful to Transcon, an added-value feature of the Astro approach. They need not reveal their assumed probabilities or any other working assumptions, but they could if pushed admit a mix of 'looking after their customer's best interests' plus 'enlightened self-interest'. If they did so they should make it clear that other bidders could not be assumed to take a similar line of thinking – many other bidders would not have the integrity Astro prided itself on, an important non-price advantage of Astro which ought to be discreetly but firmly pushed in advance. Indeed, if they wanted to emphasise this issue, they might be explicit and completely open in the bid. The associated commercial risk was competitors copying their lead.

To put it a bit differently, Astro could do a bit of planning ahead, to allow them to offer a draft version of their anticipated proposition as an option, without revealing their probability estimates or upsetting or confusing a customer who did not understand the situation if that was the preferred route. They might revise their option if it was not taken to reflect new information. If their option was taken the risk associated with possibly needing more memory was eliminated for them and for Transcon and a useful early step towards a partnership approach to contracting taken, perhaps finding a subtle way of selling the benefits of this approach to their potential customers in advance, with or without being completely open. Numbers which were not as conveniently simple as this example would obviously complicate matters, but the basic ideas would generalise in reasonably clear ways.

Both Sian and Trevor looked very happy at this stage, so Martha indicated that Ben should now carry on with his presentation, moving on to item 5.

Item 5 – the distributed scheduling system

Ben suggested they began addressing item 5 as assessed on Table 6.3 by looking at the line dealing with estimates for option (b) Zoro software. The 20% to 40% uplift from preliminary quotes to the agreed prices for Zoro noted in the item 3 information implied the £1.2 million to £1.4 million range associated with a £1.0 million base value for Zoro, computed as in earlier examples. Then looking at the line dealing with option (a) Astro software, the Astro potential variability was unclear from Sam's note, but a base cost of £1.10 million and a 20% contingency for a total of £1.32 million suggested a £1.2 million to £1.4 million range and an expected value of £1.3 million, directly comparable to option (b) to the nearest £0.1 million. The line dealing with hardware cost took an approach directly comparable to that used for item 1, with £3.0 million for all estimates. As shown in the fourth line, the implication of these three preceding lines was the same expected cost and associated uncertainty ranges for both options. Diagrams like Figure 6.5 and 6.6 could be used, but they would probably not suggest a significant difference in terms of the quantified costs, and it would not be clarity efficient to attempt to discriminate between them for present purposes. Ben suggested Sam's preference for the all-Astro option seemed reasonable given the Zoro hostile takeover risk, and the presumed desirability of keeping the work in-house given the recent spate of lost contracts. However, he indicated Martha had three serious problems with the all-Astro option choice which she wanted him to explain.

First, Martha had discovered the hostile takeover bid for Zoro emanated from one of Astro's key competitors. If it went ahead, Zoro would probably become an effective instrument of the competition, no longer a considerable asset available to Astro. Astro's position would become seriously restricted in relation to work like that on item 5, competition on cost would become very difficult for this kind of work, and work like that associated with item 2 could become a further problem. This implied the need for a friendly takeover as discussed earlier, plus the need to add an opportunity cost to the all-Astro approach which should cause them to make a definitive switch to option (b) to reassure Zoro that their new strategic partnership with Astro would work in Zoro's interests.

Second, in this case they had another opportunity cost issue which was the flip side of the earlier item 2 adjustment. Some of Sian's staff who would have to execute the all-Astro option were currently very busy, with very important major contracts from Astro Inc to develop software for global markets. Delay on this work would be extremely serious. This implied a further opportunity cost associated with the all-Astro approach which should cause them to switch to option (b). Sian's preference for a £19 million bid and £13 million or £14 million cost estimate in the context of PD2.5 no doubt implicitly reflected this concern, and it was *very* important to provide Sian with a simple tool for explicitly feeding this kind of concern into bidding decisions to avoid ineffective choices from an overall corporate perspective. Sian and Sam might have used a red or amber light driven by a frowns test to flag the issue earlier, and in the future, that is what Martha wanted Systems to do. It would help communication and teamwork if Trevor understood this concern directly and explicitly, Trevor and Sian jointly adjusting the bid on an agreed-on basis to reflect it without Sian indirectly biasing cost estimates with unidentified opportunity costs.

Third, the application of a 30% overhead cost uplift on an efficient, well-managed subcontractor like Zoro and the same 30% overhead charge on an in-house development using staff already stretched with important work was biased against the use of efficient subcontractors and towards overloading internal staff already fully engaged with profitable work. Astro overheads on their own staff time were actually higher than the 30% nominally assumed, perhaps closer to 50%, and in this particular case, a much bigger opportunity cost rate was relevant. Astro overheads on a contractor like Zoro were actually lower than 30%, perhaps only 10%. If this kind of bias forced ineffective choices it was a *major* strategic problem for Astro. Even if it didn't force ineffective choices, it would adversely affect the level of bid price chosen, itself a *major* problem. *This implied that they should adjust the costs to reflect actual overhead cost differences whenever doing so mattered, and being aware of this issue ALWAYS mattered.*

In the goal programming framework outlined in Part 1, seeing the protection of the time of internal Systems staff involved in other very valuable contracts was a very important issue for Martha. So was the protection of valued subcontractors. Both implied objectives requiring opportunity costs driven by underlying shadow costs as an essential aspect of achieving corporate optimality. Normal overhead rates of 30% were too crude to address this aspect of the relevant big picture. Martha did not need to understand goal programming to see this, but she did need an intuitive grasp of opportunity costs of this kind, and you may find it helpful in the context of this book as a whole to take a goal programming perspective. Doing so involves an intermediate level link between the very simple and conventional opportunity cost issues addressed in Chapter 5 and the much more complex and controversial use of the same basic foundation level goal programming framework to come in Chapters 7, 8 and 9.

Martha intervened in Ben's presentation again at this point. She outlined her understanding of these opportunity cost issues and then indicated that she did not know what these opportunity cost effects together amounted to in terms of a total opportunity cost adjustment to option (a). However, £1 million seemed to her a very modest and robust 'best current guess', and the exact number did not matter. In summary, her concerns were protecting already busy Systems staff, ensuring trust was maintained with Zoro, and unequivocally overriding the 30% overhead mark-up norm as a clear precedent for future opportunity cost assessments and associated departures from standard mark-ups, the basis of the Table 6.3 adjustment line. This meant that the £1 million adjustment was usefully interpreted as a nominal opportunity cost adjustment associated with mandating a switch to option (b) to protect critical Systems staff and Astro's relationship with Zoro without worrying about the exact amount, clearly understanding that there was no actual change to the item cost for bid purposes or for monitoring estimated and actual outturn costs later if they won the contract. In future it would be helpful for everyone involved if this kind of frowns test opportunity cost adjustment issue and the Zoro friendly takeover opportunity (turning a frown into a smile) were flagged earlier, as red light and blue light issues in stage 1.

Martha emphasised that from her perspective the need for a friendly takeover of Zoro was a key strategic insight which came from her involvement in the details of the Transcon bid. She explained that she wanted to make this clear to Trevor and Sian as part of a general effort to ensure that they were comfortable with her ongoing involvement in the PD3, and would not see it as just 'looking over their shoulder all the time', especially as she had earlier suggested they ought to take responsibility for the details of specific stage 3 analysis choices plus leading on process development.

At this point Martha also made it clear that all the PD3s would be assessed by her on a case-by-case basis initially, but just a sample audit basis later, providing Trevor and Sian kept her fully informed of crucial new insights. The reason was the learning processes involved for her, as well as wishing to make ongoing contributions to the evolution of the SP for bidding. Even the PD1s and PD2s involved learning processes, like identifying strong synergies between a contract and Astro's objectives in the PD1. However, the insights provided by the PD3 process were much deeper and more general, and there was a much stronger and wider need to share the learning involved. She thought this issue would be crucial and ongoing, but particularly intense early on. It could be viewed as gaining strategic clarity, building on key aspects of tactical clarity.

Ben then picked up his presentation again by noting it was now very clear that the item 5 Zoro choice was preferred, because of the opportunity cost adjustment to protect busy Systems staff and the trust central to Astro's relationship with Zoro following on from the friendly takeover. However, had the two expected cost estimates been identical and these other concerns not been involved, as a process issue it was very important everybody understood that Astro did not usually need to commit to decisions where there was no direct cost benefit either way at the bid stage. All that mattered for bidding purposes in such cases was an unbiased estimate of the expected cost. That is, had the takeover and appropriate average overhead and other opportunity cost issues not been present, it might have been useful to keep their options open, assuming an expected direct cost of £4.3 million without making a commitment to option (a) or (b).

Item 5 – the additional performance issue

Ben then suggested they move on to the decision tree of Figure 6.9.

The format of Figure 6.9 was much like that of Figure 6.7, used to consider the possible additional memory issue. However, three differences were noteworthy. First, in this case Martha had suggested that if additional performance was needed the probability Astro would have to pay for it was 0.4, twice as likely. Second, he had not included the expected cost

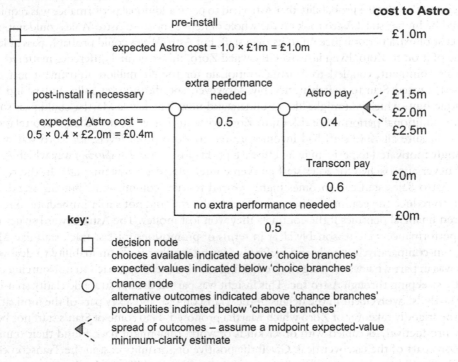

Figure 6.9 Decision tree: possible additional performance example.

estimate for Transcon or an 'additional performance bonus' calculation to keep their analysis simple in terms of this complication. And third, Sam had suggested a spread of costs, from £1.5 million to £2.5 million, which he had treated as a nominal range between P10 nominal minimum and P90 nominal maximum values as earlier, with a midpoint expected value of £2.0 million. The latter would slightly complicate the additional performance equivalent of Figure 6.8, suggesting the sort of Monte Carlo simulation approach he had hinted at earlier might be useful, but the only complication for Figure 6.9 was replacing the nominal range of £1.5 million to £2.5 million with its £2.0 million expected value prior to computing the expected value of the post-install if necessary option. Table 6.3 showed that Martha preferred the post-install if necessary option because of the £0.6 million (£1.0 million – £0.4 million) advantage relative to 'pre-install' given the assumed probabilities, although Sam had indicated a preference for 'pre-install'.

The nominal maximum of £2.5 million shown on Table 6.3 was not a simple P90 in the same sense as the other Table 6.3 nominal maximums, but the difference was not worth explaining immediately unless it was raised by Sian or Trevor. A similar comment applied to the nominal maximum entry for additional memory.

Martha then interjected to pointed out that the probability Astro would have to pay given extra performance was needed was higher (0.4) than in the additional memory case (0.2), by a factor of two. She wanted them to understand why. In the additional memory case, the invitation to tender statement about current documentation 'believed to be reasonable – 95% accurate' was 'an invitation to make claims'. Accepting this invitation could be based wholly on insisting that the customer pay for the additional memory in full if it became clear it would be needed post-installation because of inaccuracies in customer documentation. However, she suggested that the 0.4 probability that Astro had to pay if additional performance was required would be higher still if Astro took on the whole of item 5, because Astro Wales could not pass the cost of extra performance on to its own staff, but Astro Wales could probably pass at least some of it on to Zoro. Even if Astro UK owned Zoro, this structural difference mattered.

This comment, coupled to Martha's rationale for the £1 million adjustment just discussed, caused Sian to twitch noticeably. However, she did not yet fully understand the oblique hint, which you might like to understand now. The key is Martha could pass some of the additional performance risk on to Zoro without damaging the Astro–Zoro relationship. Because all Zoro staff had incomes geared to Zoro profit levels, *all* Zoro staff were strongly motivated to perform in an effective profit-driven *and loss sharing* way which Astro had never approached for Sales staff or even contemplated for Systems staff. In the recent past Astro Sales staff had incomes highly geared to sales commissions, but the trend had been to reduce the gearing for many years, and Sales staff did not suffer immediate, directly geared financial penalties if the contracts they won lost money. The Astro reward structures for performance were reasonably clear in terms of promotions for fast-track staff like Martha, but comparatively woolly and ineffective for most other staff. An inability to deal with this was in part what was driving the 'redefining core business' approach to outsourcing currently sweeping through Astro Inc. This insight was part of the key strategic clarity spin-offs of Martha's involvement in the details of the Transcon bid, and a key part of the motivation for the friendly takeover of Zoro which Martha proposed. Had some of Sian's staff not been very productively occupied with other kinds of work, they might have found their transfer to Zoro part of the takeover deal. Given the positive opportunity cost in the Transcon context it would have been inappropriate to even raise this possibility in the Transcon contract context, but it might need addressing soon.

Sian was aware that Martha was sending an oblique message, despite her inability to decipher this message. This took away her appetite for discussing the particular probabilities associated with Figures or 6.7 and 6.9. She would revisit them later.

A set of bonus performance options as a new feature of the Astro bidding strategy

Martha then indicated that a 'bonus performance option' offer as part of their basic bid should be developed, as discussed in the possible additional memory context. Furthermore, having done so they would then need to consider the third step of her three step plan for dealing with all bonus opportunity options – developing a strategy linking all related bonus options at a pre-bidding stage, and thinking about related post-bidding issues. She explained that what she had in mind was making customers 'strategic partners' to the maximum extent that this was feasible. They should pursue this 'strategic partnership' goal at all stages in the overall process of bidding and then executing the work, using whatever approaches seemed most appropriate in the particular circumstances.

Pre-bidding strategy development linking all bonus options identified earlier might be explained to the potential customer in terms of a further overall discount of say £0.5 million if they took the full set of three bonus opportunity options: a Datapol approach plus extra memory plus extra performance. This would provide assurance for both parties that their interests would be protected in a collaborative manner, sharing the benefits, and laying sound foundations for an ongoing relationship built on trust.

Briefly exploring the post-bid benefits and the robustness of the simple pre-bid models used so far, Martha began by reminding everyone that to be compliant with the Transcon invitation to tender, a 'fixed price' bid was required. However, there was a significant chance Transcon would have to pay the successful contractor's claims for additional costs in relation to additional memory and performance provisions, whether or not Transcon could see this coming and whether or not they selected Astro. In addition to the red face test, her uncle Paul had suggested that 'the moment the contracts come out of the drawers, everyone was in trouble', an adage which she thought worth remembering at this point. She strongly believed that as a matter of good business practice it was important to try to avoid all 'contracts out of the drawer' situations and to try to avoid arguments about fine print clauses and fault. More generally, Astro had to comply with contractual terms specified by potential customers, but sometimes it might be in a customer's best interests to vary these terms as well as in a contractor's best interests, and if this was the case an enlightened contractor would try to use this possibility as a competitive advantage so long as it did not weaken their bargaining position. More generally still, building a strong partnership-driven customer–contractor relationship had significant short-term benefits as well as crucial long-term benefits in some cases, with knock-on repeat business and reputational implications. Developing and maintaining trust was central.

When it came to negotiating post-contract, Astro and Transcon would obviously have different views about probabilities, claims could in practice arise and include very large contributions to profit, claims could be structured to cover Astro failures indirectly, and legal costs could be crucial. 'Claims engineering' was a highly developed skill set for some contractors, and Astro needed some of these skills. But a very simple trade-off deal like 'you pay for the extra performance and we will pay the extra for Datapol' might be the anticipated outcome of a complex negotiation, and avoiding the need for a situation requiring complex negotiation can be a crucial opportunity to focus on as part of the bidding process – a non-price advantage for the customer as well as the contractor, usefully marketed in these terms.

As soon as Martha was sure Sian was reasonably comfortable with this approach she suggested that Ben start to bring their PD3.2 discussion to a close.

Drawing the PD3.2 process discussion to a close

Ben now drew attention to the highlighted total direct cost of £11.8 million in the final portion of Table 6.3, rounded to £12 million to reflect the 'nominal precision' of this estimate as a whole. He indicated that it was important to use a nominal precision level like working to the nearest £0.1 million earlier for individual items to clarify choices, and some of these choices might benefit from slightly more precision, like the Sysdoc 1 to 3 choices. However, Astro staff would be misleading themselves if they believed the Transcon PD3.2 of Table 6.3 provided an accuracy level greater than the nearest £1 million for expected total cost, and it was particularly useful to formally acknowledge this now to simplify the example analysis to follow.

The associated nominal range of £10.4 million to £15.7 million for the anticipated actual outcome was rounded to £10 million to £16 million to reflect a comparable level of nominal precision for the overall project-level direct cost estimate.

The additional stage 3 pass 1 estimating effort had significantly refined the earlier information basis. The PP3.2 expected overall cost was lower than the PP2.2 expected overall cost (as anticipated by Trevor). The associated range was also reduced. However, *both the expected overall cost and the range might have increased*. A reduced range should be *expected* if the process is functioning properly, but the expected overall cost moving up or down with equal likelihood suggests a process functioning properly.

Ben then indicated they could associate the £10 million to £16 million range with a 10–90 percentile range consistent with the use of other 'nominal ranges' throughout the analysis.

He passed over the additional memory and performance minor complications. However, he did point out that internal consistency implied perfect positive correlation when defining the nominal range for total cost in terms of the nominal ranges for each of the five items, a coefficient of correlation of 1.0 assuming well-behaved dependence. Well-behaved dependence and less than perfect positive correlation implied that five 10–90 percentile ranges added in this way yield a percentile range like 5 to 95, with less chance of being outside the plausible minimum and maximum P values defining the range. An assumption of independence (a coefficient of correlation of zero) was the only other simple assumption, this was much further from the truth, and it was inappropriately wildly optimistic. Ben suggested that in this context it was important to use a simple assumption which *should* be conservative (pessimistic) most of the time to preserve some robustness for those occasions when dependence was not well behaved and not understood, and even perfect positive correlation proved seriously optimistic.

Despite the probable conservative nature of this correlation assumption, the nominal range of £10 million to £16 million revealed no significant threat to Astro Wales from cost variations as estimated, although an outcome of £16 million or more which could not be explained might be a threat to the careers of those involved in the Transcon bid and the execution of the project. Ben indicated the key reasons for assuming perfect positive correlation were keeping it simple and ensuring that Astro did not ignore the uncertainty range unless it could be tolerated, but another useful reason from Sian's perspective was it made it easier to explain departures from expectations. The last comment was to some extent designed to cheer up Sian, although Ben was making what he knew to be very important practical points. Sian managed a smile, although her unease remained. She resolved to see Martha after, which Martha anticipated.

Ben then drew attention to the 30% overhead and 10% profit margin calculations which finished off Table 6.3, indicating a highlighted nominal price of £17 million with a nominal margin of £5 million. He made the point that this nominal price was a *cost-based price* as a guide to what Astro Inc 'normally expected' in terms of anticipated average mark-ups on cost. It was not a *market-based price*, reflecting what the market would bear in terms of their competitors' behaviour.

Martha now intervened again, thanked Ben for his presentation to this point, and indicated that she hoped it was clear to Sian how her Systems input to the PD3.2 via the PPD was transformed in an efficient and effective way. She indicated that she needed to further pursue some important issues which the process highlighted, part of the purpose of the process. But she suggested that they all had a good basis to proceed with discussing the rest of pass 1 of the stage 3 Transcon bid process for that day's purposes.

Martha then indicated that six things should come out of the PD3.2 process, and their pursuit should be the clear and conscious goals of this phase:

1   An unbiased estimate of the expected overall direct cost, without being concerned about choices associated with project execution at this stage except insofar as such choices affected expected cost or contractual commitments or other concerns like their Zoro relationship and the system's commitment to Astro Inc work.
2   Contractual options offered to the customer when mutual benefit could provide non-price advantages as a competitive strategy in appropriate cases, with a range of approaches perhaps proving worth developing.
3   Insights about negative and positive adjustments to direct costs as normally assessed which were critical to reflect lower marginal costs or opportunity costs associated with

other uses of resources, distinguishing between transfer costs which actually change (like the Service Bureau costs) and nominal opportunity cost adjustments to protect overstretched resources without changing actual costs for accounting purposes (as in the item 4 distributed scheduling system case to protect critical Systems staff).

4 Insights about qualitative benefits of the options chosen which could be played up as non-price advantages in the bid, like those associated with starting to train Transcon staff earlier on a nearby Astro site, were also critical.

5 Insights about more general issues which go beyond the case in question, like the need to mount a friendly takeover for Zoro, and the need to consider differential overhead rates, were of strategic importance.

6 Comfort with the fairly wide nominal range for anticipated outcomes was important, in this case, £10 million to £16 million, in particular, recognising that some contracts are going to lose money, and this should not be a problem provided it is not a crippling unexplainable surprise because of incompetence.

In summary, the pass 1 stage 3 cost uncertainty analysis of phase 3.2 was not just a matter of refining estimates of the expected cost and anticipated range of actual outcomes. It was about an enhanced understanding of all the issues which drive such cost estimates, including associated non-price advantage and other qualitative benefit issues, along with other working assumptions which need explicit understanding. A core concern was using this understanding to add value to the proposition offered to their potential customer.

At this point Martha suggested they might all enjoy a tea break, to catch their breath before moving on to Trevor's role and phase 3.3. She said she appreciated this was going to be a long day, with a lot of new ideas to absorb.

You may feel you need the equivalent of a tea break at this point, and if you have a limited interest in tactical clarity concerns in a bidding context, you may be tempted to just skim-read the next few sections. However, while the next few sections may look specialised and technical, with no immediately obvious role in more general terms, they are important in terms of providing a foundation for some of the key strategic clarity insights to follow.

Phase 3.3 – enhanced probability of winning analysis on pass 1

After a tea break, while Sian was still trying to take in the full implications of the process underlying the PD3.2, Martha opened the session and turned her attention to Trevor's role. She moved on to what she had earlier designated the PD3.3, obtaining an enhanced probability of winning curve using the phase 3.3 process on pass 1.

Martha began by reminding Trevor and Sian that the preliminary probability of winning curve of Figure 6.3 was new to Astro as an explicit tool, although Trevor and other sales staff had obviously used such a curve intuitively. This was not unusual. Very few organisations made direct use of an explicit Figure 6.3 equivalent. Astro was going to obtain significant competitive advantage by using Figure 6.3 in phase 2.3. But Astro was going to obtain *much* more additional competitive advantage by using a refined version in phase 3.3. Ben and Trevor had not yet addressed this issue, but she had worked with Ben to develop and then illustrate the basis of what she wanted.

She reminded them that one of the key advantages of Figure 6.3 was that it enabled the use of Table 6.2, which explicitly brought together costing and pricing issues in a manner which clarified what was involved, including providing useful sensitivity analysis. For example, it clearly indicated the bid which maximised expected margin, and it also indicated the sensitivity of expected margin and the probability of winning to alternative bids, to allow explicit consideration of key trade-offs. Crucially, this made trade-offs very clear as the bid was changed, between the expected margin, the actual (conditional) margin if they won, and the probability of winning, letting them consider these trade-offs in relation to other key trade-offs involving qualitative issues identified in stage 1. The more refined version of Table 6.2 which pass 1 of phase 3.3 would enable was going to be a major competitive weapon for Astro because it would extend this kind of insight to specific competitors who mattered, including qualitative issues like non-price advantages specific to particular competitors which might be built into their bid, encouraging and facilitating a process of systematically seeking these advantages using their understanding of key competitors.

Among the advantages of Figure 6.3 or refined versions discussed earlier was the ability to record the estimated P(B) for whatever bids were chosen over time to also record how many bids were won over time and to compare these predictions and outcomes to provide feedback on the accuracy of the P(B) estimates. That is, only if P(B) values associated with bids were explicitly recorded could data be collected which would help to improve the estimation of P(B). Stage 3 would refine this capability in ways not considered earlier, to assess Astro's ability to estimate probabilities of beating the specific competitors who really mattered.

Martha stressed that as useful as Figure 6.3 was, it was very crude relative to the refined estimate for the PD3.2 provided by Table 6.3. It should be clear that significant benefit was attached to using the PD3.2 process just discussed relative to Sian's direct cost estimate in the PD2.2. A comparable increase in benefit from the PD3.3 process relative to the PD2.3 process was the goal.

One of the keys to the benefits provided by the PD3.2 was the decomposition of the contract cost into five component items, and different option choices within some items. This decomposition allowed a clearer view of what was involved, the use of different people with different expertise to work on different items, and the use of past experience with similar items and option choices to facilitate more effective use of data associated with past experience. The effective pursuit of non-price advantages was also triggered by this decomposition. A comparable decomposition was required for the third stage enhanced probability of winning curve for different but broadly comparable reasons.

Martha then asked Ben to illustrate the basis of how they might approach the Transcon case if they explicitly associated the Figure 6.3 preliminary probability of winning curve with a 'composite competitor' – and asked the question, 'How should we decompose this composite competitor?'

Ben took the floor and began by explaining that the theoretical basis for the decomposition Martha wanted had been published many years ago, and his critical review of the extensive literature had included a classic 1950s' paper (Friedman, 1956) which provided a useful basic generic bidding model starting point. If there were n competitors, $1, \ldots , n$, if they assumed that the lowest bid wins, and if they knew the probability each competitor would bid at or below any given bid level, they could use well-known statistical procedures to combine these probability distributions to derive a probability of winning (being below all competitors) for any given bid level. Several important practical difficulties were stopping most people using this basic theoretical model to build practical operational models for widespread routine use. But he and Martha now had the basis of a practical clarity efficient way of overcoming these difficulties, and with Trevor's help they believed Astro had an effective way forward.

The first difficulty he would comment on was in practice a significant number of competitors might be involved, not all these competitors might be worth formal analysis on an individual basis, and some might be unknown. To begin to deal with this issue he suggested ordering the competitors 1, . . . , n by their importance, and assuming that only the first one or two would receive individual attention *most* of the time, perhaps as many as half a dozen *some* of the time but *probably never* the complete set if n was larger than about half a dozen. Those not considered individually would need collective treatment as a residual 'composite competitor' which explicitly embraced 'all unknown competitors as well as all known competitors not worth decomposition' – a closure with completeness component.

The second difficulty was 'non-price advantages' – the extent to which Astro might command a premium relative to different competitors (possibly negative) because of Astro's 'quality' (non-price advantages) relative to competitors as perceived by Transcon.

To address both of these difficulties, Ben suggested they limited their discussion that day to working with clearly identified working assumptions which could be generalised later that were currently very strong in order to keep their initial illustrative analysis simple:

1 Separate assessment was worthwhile for only one competitor – designated 'competitor 1'. All other competitors could be treated as a closure with completeness residual not worth decomposition – designated 'competitor 2'.

2 Astro had a known constant £2m non-price advantage relative to competitor 1 and a known constant £1m non-price advantage relative to competitor 2, and both of these non-price advantages were constants in the sense that they were independent of what competitors 1 or 2 bid.

3 Competitors 1 and 2 could both be assumed to understand that Astro was the market leader, to be capable of using their expected cost estimate to estimate that Astro's cost-based nominal price had an expected value of about £17 million, and to plan to beat Astro by about £1 million in adjusted price terms, understanding Astro's non-price advantage relative to their own position.

To interpret the implications of these assumptions, if for example competitor 1 bid £13 million, then Astro would beat competitor 1 if Astro bid less than £15 million, and if competitor 2 bid £14 million, then Astro would also beat competitor 2 if Astro bid less than £15 million, with the same £2m million and £1 million non-price advantages applying whatever competitors 1 or 2 bid.

Ben indicated that they could use more sophisticated working assumptions in various ways, including associating non-price advantages with probability distributions and making these distributions dependent on what competitors bid. These were complications which Martha and Ben correctly anticipated would prove crucial later, deliberately avoided at this stage.

To start to make use of his assumptions and further interpret the implications, Ben suggested that Astro Sales staff might find it useful to consider direct estimation of the probability that competitor 1 would bid at a given level and the associated adjusted bid using the three scenario tabular format of Table 6.4. This table could then be used to generate Figure 6.10. He would explain the generation of Table 6.4 first, then the construction and meaning of the density and reverse cumulative portrayals of Figure 6.10.

You might find it helpful to observe that Table 6.4 involves a three scenario version of the HAT approach discussed in Chapter 3, with a corresponding rectangular density function portrayal illustrated by the first part of Figure 6.10. The Table 6.4 reverse cumulative probability distribution provided by the right-hand column was the basis of the second part of Figure 6.10, a curve defining the probability of Astro beating competitor 1 for the relevant range of Astro bids. Ben's explanation incorporated relevant Chapter 3 discussion.

Table 6.4 Tabular format for estimating the probability that competitor 1 will bid at three scenario values.

Actual bids (£m)	Scenario labels	Probability	Adjusted bids (£m)	Reverse Cumulative Probability
13	low bid	0.2	15	1.0
14	medium bid	0.6	16	0.8
15	high bid	0.2	17	0.2

Expected bid = £14 million, and adjusted expected bid = £16 million

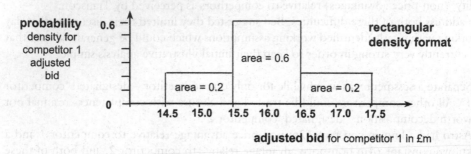

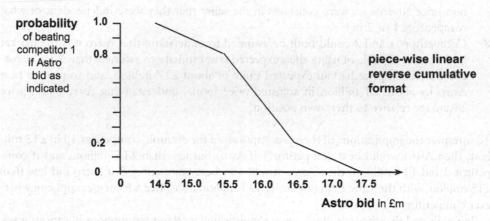

Figure 6.10 Three scenario representation of Astro's probability of beating competitor 1.

Ben suggested that preparation of Table 6.4 might start by estimating a 'plausible minimum' (P10) 'low bid' of £13 million, next estimating a 'plausible maximum' (P90) 'high bid' of £15 million, and then interpolating a single 'medium bid' of £14 million. These three scenarios implied corresponding adjusted bids of £15 million, £17 million, and £16 million. The £1 million constant interval basis of Table 6.4 could be interpreted to imply a range of +/–£0.5m associated with each central value in the rectangular density function intervals. This meant that a low bid scenario adjusted value of exactly £15 million interpreted as a P10 was consistent with a probability of 0.2 for the range 14.5 to 15.5, a similar logic made the high bid scenario probability 0.2 as well, with 1 – 0.2 – 0.2 = 0.6 being the probability residual for the medium bid scenario. In practice more than three scenarios could be used and asymmetry might be involved.

Ben emphasised that he had kept Table 6.4 and Figure 6.10 as simple as he could for illustrative convenience, but the approach easily generalised; he would provide seminars and coaching on the whole family of available associated approaches as required, and he would develop simple computer software which would help them to produce Table 6.4 and use the fourth and fifth columns to produce Figure 6.10.

Using the fifth column of Table 6.4 to produce the second part of Figure 6.10 involved recognising that the adjusted bid by competitor 1 probability density function in a reverse cumulative form defined the probability that Astro would win against competitor 1, clearly the case in this simple example. With a non-price advantage of £2 million, if Astro bid less than £14.5 million, the probability of Astro beating competitor 1 was one, because there was no chance that competitor 1 would bid less than £12.5 million, an adjusted bid less than £14.5 million. If Astro bid £15.5 million, there was a 0.8 probability of beating competitor 1, because there was a 0.2 probability competitor 1 would bid in the range £12.5 million to £13.5 million with an adjusted bid equivalent of £14.5 million to £15.5 million, and so on.

This Table 6.4 approach could also be applied to competitor 2, a composite of all other competitors, as illustrated by Table 6.5.

As indicated in Table 6.5, for illustrative purposes he had assumed competitor 2 would involve a smaller non-price advantage associated with a broader distribution of actual bids and probabilities. His rationale was based on its composite nature. Table 6.5 could be portrayed as a five scenario equivalent of Figure 6.10 if this was useful.

Ben had made the competitor 1 and 2 estimates of Tables 6.4 and 6.5 different in part to make the illustration easier to follow, but the differences also made the example more credible. Both were simple and symmetric, with a common expected value of £16 million for the adjusted bids, for convenience not credibility. This meant that he could provide a particularly simple but useful illustration and interpretation of the adjusted bid for composite competitor 1 + 2, the composite derived when competitors 1 and 2 were formally combined using the information in Tables 6.4 and 6.5. The symmetry and the same expected value for both competitors' adjusted bids implied that both competitors were equally likely to win.

He could extend the computer software handling the individual competitor Tables 6.4 and 6.5 to combine the associated two probability distributions using the HAT probability tree discrete probability computation scheme of Table 6.6.

A comparable Monte Carlo simulation approach was an option. However, he had used the Table 6.6 approach because this was the easiest framework for understanding how any two distributions could be combined, allowing for later generalisation as needed.

Table 6.5 Tabular format for estimating the probability that competitor 2 will bid at five scenario values.

Actual bids (£m)	Scenario labels	Probability	Adjusted bids (£m)
13	very low bid	0.1	14
14	low bid	0.2	15
15	medium bid	0.4	16
16	high bid	0.2	17
17	very high bid	0.1	18

Expected bid = £15m and adjusted expected bid = £16m

Table 6.6 The probability of adjusted bids from competitor $1+2$, a composite of competitors 1 and 2.

Competitor 1		Competitor 2		Competitor $1+2$ adjusted bid probability contributions			
Adjusted bid	Probability	Adjusted bid	Probability	14	15	16	17
15	0.2	14	0.1	0.02			
		15	0.2		0.04		
		16	0.4		0.08		
		17	0.2		0.04		
		18	0.1		0.02		
16	0.6	14	0.1	0.06			
		15	0.2		0.12		
		16	0.4			0.24	
		17	0.2			0.12	
		18	0.1			0.06	
17	0.2	14	0.1	0.02			
		15	0.2		0.04		
		16	0.4			0.08	
		17	0.2				0.04
		18	0.1				0.02
Composite competitor $1+2$ probabilities (column sums)				0.10	0.34	0.50	0.06
Reverse cumulative probabilities				1.0	0.90	0.56	0.06	0.00
for plotting Figure 6.11 at Astro bids of				13.5	14.5	15.5	16.5	17.5

A tabular form of probability tree was defined by the body of Table 6.6, with probability contributions to common result values associated with different probability tree branch end points collected on the right-hand side. Understanding the probability tree involved was facilitated by this sort of tabular form, especially important when dependence was a concern.

To clarify line 1 in the body of Table 6.6: a bid by competitor 1 of £13 million was associated with an adjusted bid of £15 million and a probability of 0.2 as indicated in Table 6.4, a bid of £13 million by competitor 2 was associated with an adjusted bid of £14 million and a probability of 0.1 as indicated in Table 6.5, and the Table 6.6 joint scenario with a probability of $0.2 \times 0.1 = 0.02$ was associated with the composite competitor $1+2$ adjusted bid of £14 million because competitor 2 would beat competitor 1.

All the other lines did the same, for each of the possible combinations of competitor 1 and 2 bids, giving $3 \times 5 = 15$ lines in all, associated with 15 probability tree branch end points.

If you are interested in the detail, the pattern of adjusted bid probabilities should make sense if you work down row by row. You do not need to follow *all* the how to do it detail if you are not mathematically inclined or you are not interested in the arithmetic details, but you do need to understand what needs to be done in terms of an overview appreciation of what is involved. This comment will apply to all future HAT portrayal tables of this kind, throughout the rest of this book, but it will not be repeated.

The competitor $1+2$ column sums collected these probability calculations together, to define a probability distribution for the adjusted bid for composite competitor $1+2$.

These probability contribution products were then used in the form provided by the last two lines to produce the basis for plotting a probability of winning curve for Astro (beating competitor $1+2$), interpreting discrete bid scenarios as £1 million ranges.

For example, in the 'composite competitor 1 + 2' (column sums) row the probability of 0.06 of a bid of 17 (bold entry on Table 6.6 to assist identification) was associated with a 0 probability of Astro winning with a bid of 17.5, rising to 0.06 by 16.5. In conjunction with a probability of 0.50 of a competitor adjusted bid of 16 (next to the bold entry), this implied a chance of Astro winning with a bid of 15.5 was 0.56. Similarly, Astro's chance of winning with a bid of 14.5 was 0.9, and Astro was certain to win with a bid of 13.5.

As soon as Trevor and Sian were comfortable with this aspect of Table 6.6, Ben showed them Figure 6.11.

The solid curve for composite competitor 1 + 2 in Figure 6.11 simply plotted the final row values of Table 6.6, a rectangular probability histogram assumption being used in its equivalent piecewise linear reverse cumulative probability distribution form to yield the probability of Astro winning.

Figure 6.11 also used a dashed curve to display the comparable distribution for competitor 1 on its own, based on Table 6.4 as portrayed in Figure 6.10, to indicate the contribution to composite competitor 1 + 2 provided by competitor 1. The gap between the two curves indicated the impact of competitor 2. There was no need to plot competitor 2 as well as 1 and 1 + 2, but competitor 2 could have been plotted instead of competitor 1 for a similar gap. Both competitors made a comparable contribution to the 1 + 2 total in this particular example to illustrate what equal contributions implied.

Adding a cumulative probability curve for one of the two components involved in this way made Figure 6.11 a form of 'sensitivity diagram' which is directly comparable to Figure 4.1 as discussed in Chapter 4. The same HAT computational process framework underlies both, albeit with a different mathematical operation. These features of a HAT approach, including the probability arithmetic option used for the tables, the sensitivity diagram options, related use of decision diagrams to judge risk efficiency, and the related framework to seek overall opportunity efficiency, are central to using the EP toolset to understand the way components of uncertainty from different sources accumulate and the implications for alternative

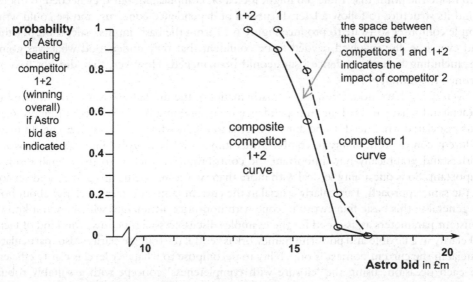

Figure 6.11 Sensitivity diagram format for a probability of winning curve for Astro using Table 6.6 plus Table 6.4 (Figure 6.10) for the competitor 1 curve.

planning options, as discussed in the somewhat different context of BP offshore projects in Chapters 3 and 4. In this Astro bidding context a sensitivity diagram provides a useful basis for building up an understanding of the impact of successive competitors, with the lowest adjusted bid of a complete set of n competitors' bids defining winning or losing for Astro. You may find it useful to recall the Chapters 3 and 4 discussion of BP's separately identified and analysed sources of uncertainty associated with an activity like offshore pipe-laying in a SCERT framework, instead of using a PERT model treating each activity as a single source of uncertainty, which has directly comparable features. *The way all these features of the HAT approach can be employed in a flexible toolset which adapts to very different contexts is an important overall characteristic of the EP toolset, also illustrated and exploited in Chapters 8 and 9.*

Ben explained these separately decomposed components plus a 'closure with completeness' component with minimal reference to the ideas illustrated by the earlier BP illustrations, but he did emphasise understanding the way the build-up of uncertainty occurred was of crucial importance in any context. In this bidding context he explained that the curve for any composite competitor 1 + 2 would always be to the left of the curve for one of its components, regardless of the ordering. But three different variants need distinction and anticipation in practice:

1   If competitors 1 and 2 were a fairly even match, approaching the equality assumed by Tables 6.4 and 6.5, a shift like that illustrated in Figure 6.11 would be observed.
2   If competitor 1 completely dominated competitor 2, the competitor 1 and competitor 1 + 2 curves would coincide, approaching this position as partial dominance increases.
3   If competitor 1 was dominated by competitor 2, a more significant shift to the left would be observed, and plotting the contribution of competitor 2 instead of 1 might be more instructive to show the difference made by the less important of the two competitors, perhaps also formally reordering competitors to amend the earlier assumption about which mattered most and clarify the assumption required revision.

Ben made the point that Table 6.6 might look a bit complicated, but they needed to understand its structure to follow a later discussion of dependence concerns, and he could write simple computer software to produce Figure 6.11 from the basic inputs. Sales staff, Martha, and everyone else involved needed to be confident that they understood what was going on, including how dependence issues could be managed. However, they did not have to 'crunch the numbers'.

Even if you have no interest in the mathematics of the modelling issues, you do need to understand what can be done in dependence terms building on Table 6.6 and Figure 6.11 plus associated what needs to be done concerns to follow where this book is going. In many different contexts our ability to combine the estimates for two probability distributions and understand graphically how important the contribution of each is to the overall result is important. So is our ability to deal with more than two components in a generalised version of the same approach. Particularly crucial in the current context is tactical clarity about how to generalise this basic framework to cope with non-price advantages which are not known constant parameters as assumed for the examples discussed so far, because this kind of tactical clarity in a flexible and powerful framework is central to strategic clarity. Also, particularly crucial in the current context is our ability to decompose to whatever level is clarity efficient on each occasion, using the 'closure with completeness' concept with a suitably robust understanding of the implications. Astro could usefully see the stage 2 approach of their new bidding process as a particularly simple special case of their stage 3 approach when a single composite competitor was addressed – no individually decomposed competitors. In a stage 3 context it would be crucial to develop the ability to make the decomposition level judgement skilfully as experience is gained, and it would be important to err on the side of too much decomposition initially to develop and test their understanding of how much decomposition provided extra insight that more than paid for the effort involved.

These were all issues that Trevor needed to understand as well as Ben and Martha. The reason you need to understand them at an overview level, whatever your perspective and management level and areas of interest, is comparable concerns may need to be addressed whenever multiple sources of uncertainty and their relationships need clarity in the possibly very different contexts of interest to you, a central strategic clarity concern.

Ben now suggested that they could relax all their earlier working assumptions, but the only one he wanted to explore that day was treating more than one competitor separately, and he would do so very briefly at an overview outline level. He would use a high clarity $n = 6$ illustrative example, involving five separately identified competitors plus a sixth closure with completeness composite competitor. Composite competitor 6 was, by definition, a residual of all those competitors not worth further decomposition. They could use an even bigger n, but in practice this was very unlikely to pay, even for early very high clarity learning process studies. He and Martha believed that usually one or two separate competitors would suffice after they had gone down the requisite learning curve and become used to the approach.

He then showed them Figure 6.12.

Ben's version of Figure 6.12 had named companies beside competitors 1 to 5, and composite competitor $n = 6$ involved an incomplete list of possible competitors with illustrative examples. The competitor 6 information explicitly recognised that some competitors might be unknown, and which of the known competitors would bid might be uncertain.

Ben explained that a pairwise approach to this grouping like that portrayed by Figure 6.12 was not essential, but it could be useful for reasons associated with 'common features or characteristics' of members of each pair plus dependence assumptions which they would explore later if and when they became relevant. One reason worth mentioning immediately was a pairwise build-up using a Figure 6.11 format sensitivity diagram was facilitated if a

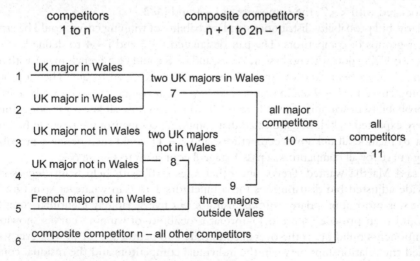

Figure 6.12 Competitor grouping structure example, n = 6.

structure like Figure 6.12 was used. One diagram could be used for competitors 1 plus 2 yielding composite competitor 7, followed by another for 3 + 4 = 8, followed by a third for 8 + 5 = 9, followed by a fourth for 7 + 9 = 10, followed by a fifth for 10 + 6 = 11. Separate sensitivity diagrams for each pair could be summarised using a single diagram (like Figure 4.1), and a simpler sequential pairing would facilitate a direct route to a single diagram generalisation of Figure 6.11 (like Figure 4.1).

Using any pairwise structuring meant that n competitors required n – 1 pairs, 6 – 1 = 5 pairs in this example. The pairing structure of this particular example assumed that competitors 1 and 2 were the most important at least in part because they were both UK majors with offices located in Wales, it was convenient to think about 3 and 4 as the next strongest pair with common features, and it was convenient for the trio 3 to 5 being paired with 1 and 2 before pairing 1 to 5 with the residual composite competitor n = 6. Any convenient structure could be used, but there were underlying separability working assumptions involved which he would explain later (a purely intuitive grasp of what pairwise composition approach involves will suffice at present for all target readers, and Ben did not want to explore these issues at this stage). Ben did suggest that if any variant of this kind of pairwise nested build-up structure was used, a recommended approach to keeping the notation as simple as possible was always dealing with competitor i and competitor j to form the composite competitor k, with k = n + 1 to 2n – 1 for n – 1 pairs. For any variant of Figure 6.12, he would ensure the computer software equivalent of Table 6.6 would allow the definition of Figure 6.11 equivalents for each pair of competitors so that it would be very clear which competitors mattered most within each pair.

At this point Ben showed them a version of Figure 4.1 to explain how BP used sensitivity diagrams as explored in Chapter 4, and how they might look for similar insights in terms of which competitors mattered most, and then direct more time and effort to exploring what seemed to matter most as more insight was gained.

Ben indicated that if the Figure 6.12 pairing structure was appropriate, they could start by estimating bid probabilities for competitors 1 and 2, their two closest and most obvious competitors, both international organisations with bases in Wales who could be expected to bid. This would define the probability of winning curves for i = 1 and j = 2, and allow a composite probability of winning curve associated with both competitors to be calculated and associated with k = 7, the composite of i = 1 and j = 2.

Similarly, bid probability distributions and probability of winning curves could be estimated for other groups of competitors. The pair designated i = 3 and j = 4 to define k = 8 could address two UK majors with no base in Wales, and j = 5 could be a French major with no base in Wales, all three being known competitors who were expected to bid. Then a probability of winning curve for k = 9 could compose known major competitors with no base in Wales, and a probability of winning curves for k = 10 would compose all known major competitors who were expected to bid. Ben indicated that composite competitor n = 6 would be a residual concept to include all unknown competitors, and k = 11 could then define a probability of winning curve for all competitors, a pass 1 stage 3 equivalent to Figure 6.3.

Ben said Martha wanted Trevor and other sales staff, with help from Ben as needed, to provide adjusted bid distributions for competitors 1 to 6 in whatever structure Trevor thought was most appropriate, *initially* using *about* five separately identified competitors. Ben would then provide Figure 6.11 format probability of winning curves showing how the components build up to the overall composite competitor k = 11 in whatever way best explained the relationships between the individual competitors and the residual composite competitor, with an overall summary in the Figure 4.1 format.

The simplest version of this approach assumed that the probability distributions for adjusted bid values for competitors i and j are independently distributed in terms of probability distribution shapes which can be estimated approximately by a rectangular histogram probability density function and combined using a discrete probability tree approximation. Rectangular histogram forms could approximate any distribution to whatever level of precision was required so that was not a restrictive assumption, simply a useful working assumption. Discrete probability arithmetic was approximate when continuous variables were involved, but the error was modest and it could be controlled or eliminated. Alternatively, standard Monte Carlo simulation software could be used to achieve the same ends. Statistical independence in this case seemed a reasonable assumption if collusion between competitors was not suspected, but statistical dependence could be modelled if appropriate to reflect possible collusion or other sources of dependence.

The key assumptions which this approach made included the ability of Astro Sales staff to estimate all the required input distributions, and the levels of decomposition used for each bid was clarity efficient. They could employ any variant of Figure 6.12 they were comfortable with. Once they had used about five separately assessed competitors a few times, they would probably find that just two or three separately identified key competitors was more than enough most of the time, and just one separately identified key competitor might eventually be enough much of the time.

Martha interjected here on cue. She suggested that sets of versions of Figure 6.11 with a summary like BP's Figure 4.1 based on variants of Figure 6.12 had to be estimated for as many separately identified competitors as experience with about five suggested was worthwhile. This was because she was determined to have a refined version of Table 6.2 to refine the bid price and the treatment of non-price advantages with a clear understanding of what a clarity efficient level of decomposition of their competitors looked like.

If Astro sales staff were uncomfortable estimating the non-price advantages and competitor bid distributions probabilities this required, they were just going to have to get over it. In her view, an inability to estimate the equivalent of Figure 6.11 for each pair of the overall composite of all competitors using an appropriately decomposed competitor structure was tantamount to not understanding the marketplace in a way which was directly useful to her and Astro more generally.

However, she could assure them that what she was asking for would not be as difficult to deliver as it might seem, and successive use of figures of the form of Figure 6.11 or versions with more than two components (like Figure 4.1) would help them to understand the implications of their assumptions. Furthermore, this kind of decomposition would yield benefits which were broadly analogous to those observed from the five item breakdown of costs. For example, Astro could start to acquire data on winning bids by individual major competitors relative to Astro's nominal price, to develop a database relevant to their probability distribution estimates. As this data grew, Astro could start to look for formal analysis explanations for changes in these distributions over time – systematic variations due to the state of the market, the state of the order book of particular competitors, and so on. These models would provide a framework to test hypotheses about the implications of strategy changes by competitors as well as helping to identify changes.

The curve for the final composite of all competitors, $k = 11$ in Figure 6.12, would be the bottom line, what Sales staff had to produce before any bid was considered. If they started with $n = 6$ they might soon find that $n = 2$ or 3 or 4 was actually adequate, but a plausible case for aggregate treatment of competitors who did not matter much would be needed.

How they produced it would be up to the sales team leaders like Trevor, with extensive support from Ben and Martha's help whenever she could be useful. How they proceeded would be audited initially by Martha on a case-by-case basis, to see if the approach adopted made sense at all levels, with constructive feedback.

Obviously, there was no guarantee that any Figure 6.11 format curve or n greater than two equivalents (like Figure 4.1) would be correct. However, Martha could apply two tests. First, did all the underlying assumptions seem to make sense? Second, as data accumulated, did it confirm the order of magnitude of the estimates used at the final 'all competitors' level and at the level of individual competitors they understood?

Martha stressed that it would be some time before significant data were available, but the first of these tests would be used with immediate effect, with some intensity, until she was convinced that everyone had a joint understanding of what they were doing. The technical details of this approach could clearly take a while to get used to, but Martha did not want to spend more time on technical details now. Ben would arrange for special seminars to take everyone through the basics, and workshops to develop the details, which she would support whenever this was useful. She wanted to finish off the current meeting with a formal presentation by Ben on the enhanced bid setting summary table and discussion based on that table.

Martha knew that Trevor would be struggling to visualise how to deal with her requirements at this stage, and if you are not struggling to see were this chapter is going at this point you are unusually perceptive. However, when we begin to discuss the way Trevor started to respond to his challenges a few sections on, you should begin to see the point of the framework established in this section, and its wider relevance.

To finish on an encouraging note, Martha reemphasised the message that once they got used to using about five individual competitors employing a structure like Figure 6.12, they should find competitor 1 defined as 'the key competitor' plus a composite competitor 2 embodying the residual was good enough much of the time, and Ben would assume that this was the case for the rest of their discussion that day.

Phase 3.4 – enhanced uncertainty syntheses on pass 1

Ben began his discussion of the first pass through the phase 3.4 process to produce an enhanced margin evaluation table by indicating that these enhanced tables could have the same basic structure as Table 6.2, but the illustrative version he would use that day was slightly complicated because it used both Figure 6.3 and Figure 6.11 information – two $P(B)$ curve information sets to facilitate useful comparisons. He then showed them Table 6.7.

Ben started to explain and explore the implications of Table 6.7 by noting that he wanted to use this table to clarify how crucial an unbiased and enlightened estimate of the $P(B)$ relationship was. That was why Table 6.7 made use of $P(B)$ curves from *both* Figure 6.3 *and* Figure 6.11, showing the different results for these two alternative $P(B)$ curve information sets. He would focus on the differences, assuming Figure 6.11 was 'correct' for illustrative purposes because these differences illustrated key points he wanted to make. In practice they could use a simplified variant of Table 6.7 with only one set of $P(B)$ values.

The Figure 6.3 curve through c_1 had been used to extend the bottom end of the range to match that of the Figure 6.11 curve range. He appreciated that this was not necessarily what Trevor had in mind. Its choice here was purely illustrative.

Furthermore, the Figure 6.11 estimate as a whole was not intended as a suggested revision to Trevor's Figure 6.3 estimate – its role in Table 6.7 was purely illustrative to show the extent to which differences of the scale illustrated by these two $P(B)$ curves matter.

Table 6.7 Enhanced margin evaluation table (the PD3.4 produced in stage 3 phase 4) with two P(B) curves.

Expected direct cost E(C) = £12m working to the nearest £m with an outcome in the range of £10m–£16m anticipated

Bid values B (£m)	P(B) Figure 6.3*	P(B) Figure 6.11	Margins (conditional) M = B – E(C)	Expected margins E(M) = P(B) × M		Comments
				Figure 6.3	Figure 6.11	
13	0.97	1.00	1	0.97	1.00	New minimum B
14	0.94	0.95	2	1.88	1.90	
15	0.80	**0.72**	3	2.40	**2.16**	New maximum E(M)
16	**0.66**	0.30	4	**2.64**	1.20	Figure 6.3 probability curve maximum E(M)
17	0.52	0.03	5	2.60	0.15	
18	0.38	0	6	2.28	0	No chance of winning
19	0.24	0	7	1.68	0	at a bid level of £18m
20	0.10	0	8	0.80	0	or more assuming the Figure 6.11 probability of winning curve is correct

* using the dotted line through point c_1 in Figure 6.3 for illustrative purposes.

As an initial comparison, for a bid B of £15 million as indicated in the first column of Table 6.7, the second column indicated a P(B) of 0.8 taken from Figure 6.3, while the third column indicated a P(B) = 0.72 taken from Figure 6.11, a difference of about 10%, which was within the range of acceptable variations they might expect between stage 2 and stage 3 estimates. There was no cause for concern here.

As the bid B was reduced from £15 million to £14 million and then £13 million, the probability of winning increased at a faster rate using the Figure 6.11 column than even the dotted line through point c_1 in Figure 6.3, but the two curves crossed and then remained close. That is, over the bid B range from £13 million to £15 million, the two curves roughly coincided if the extension through point c_1 of Figure 6.3 was assumed. There was no cause for concern here either, in terms of different P(B) curves implying significantly different implications.

But the difference started to show and its implications became significant as B values increased above £15 million. When the bid B increased to £16m, the Figure 6.3 P(B) dropped to 0.66 while the Figure 6.11 P(B) dropped to 0.30, a difference of more than 50% using the larger number for percentage comparisons, highly significant. When B increased to £17 million, the Figure 6.3 P(B) dropped to 0.52 while the Figure 6.11 P(B) dropped to 0.03, a difference of more than 90% using the larger number for percentage comparisons, a huge difference. At a B of £18 million or more the P(B) for Figure 6.11 is zero, massively different from the Figure 6.3 situation although not meaningfully associated with a percentage difference.

The E(M) column of Table 6.7 associated with the Figure 6.3 curve suggested a maximum expected margin of £2.64 million, with a bid of £16 million, and a 0.66 probability of winning. Ben used bold type for these P(B) and E(M) values to highlight the implications of a B = £16 million decision assuming Figure 6.3 was the basis for this decision. This looked quite attractive. It was an even more attractive scenario than the Table 3.2 E(M) maximising bid of £17 million with a probability of winning of 0.52 and a maximum expected margin of £2.08 million because of the lower E(C).

However, if the Figure 6.11 columns of Table 6.7 was the reality, the chance of winning with this bid of £16 million was only 0.30, and the expected margin was only £1.20 million, about half the P(B) and E(M) values assumed on Table 6.2.

Furthermore, if Figure 6.11 was the reality, a maximum margin was achieved with a bid of £15 million, and a lower bid like £14 million was suggested because a probability of winning rapidly approaching 1.0 can be obtained with very little loss of expected margin in the £14 million to £15 million range.

A key message Ben wanted to make using Table 6.7 *was it clearly mattered that they knew which probability of winning curve they were dealing with when differences of this order were involved. More generally, being capable of estimating the P(B) curve without bias and with a clarity efficient level of uncertainty about its location really mattered.*

Figures 6.3 and 6.11 might be roughly the same in the bid B = £13 million to £15 million range, but the differences outside this region were of crucial importance. Astro need to confirm (or revise) and refine Trevor's probability of winning estimates.

To get started, Ben recommended working with best estimates associated with close competitors in a structure comparable to Figure 6.12 to define a single best estimate P(B) set of Figure 6.11 equivalents for use in a simplified version of Table 6.7. They might always estimate the bounds first and then interpolate the best estimate P(B) curve to be used as a way of minimising bias and making themselves aware of their uncertainty about the location of a best estimate curve.

As a form of sensitivity analysis while they were in the early stages of acquiring experience with this new framework, they might find it useful to explore the implications of nominal optimistic and pessimistic bounds for each best estimate P(B) curve by showing the best estimate plus its bounds on a three P(B) curve variant of Table 6.7. However, he envisaged this kind of sensitivity analysis as a possible learning tool for the team preparing the estimates in the early stages, probably not necessary once they got used to the approach.

Phase 3.5 – bid evaluation and development on pass 1

Ben finished his final presentation of the workshop by indicating that the sort of bid 'pricing' level and underlying cost estimation discussion that Sian and Trevor started in the context of Table 6.2 and the PD2.5 would clearly be much better informed by a variant of Table 6.7 using one best estimate probability of winning curve they trusted as an unbiased estimate. The discussion would not just be working with more precise numerical estimates; it would be working with a quite different level of understanding of all the uncertainties involved.

He reminded Sian and Trevor that Martha believed stage 1 and 2 of their bidding process should jointly target the use of less than 10% of the effort required for the full bid preparation process (about 2% followed by about 5%). They should initially anticipate the elimination of about 50% of the potential bids in the first two stages (about 30% followed by 30% of the remaining 70%, midpoints in the 10%–50% ranges). This would leave a residual of about 50% of the bids for stage 3 consideration. Martha wanted them to try to do better than these crude expectations, with more aggressive stretch targets to maximise the time available for more effective analysis of 'the right contracts to win'. The aim was to spend about 80% of their time on the 20% of the bids that really mattered – a variant of the traditional 20:80

rule. However, Martha's initial estimates were just intuitively based initial guidelines to be refined over time as they gained experience.

Another variant of this rule would apply to their approach to successive passes through the stage 3 process of Figure 6.4. Ben indicated that Martha thought pass 1 through stage 3 should target using 10% to 20% of the effort required for the full bid preparation process *once they became familiar with the process.* However, initially they would be in learning mode and might take 10 to 20 times what they could expect after six months or a year of experience. Occasionally the first pass through stage 3 would prove enough to clarify a 'minimum effort' bid, or a late no bid decision.

Most of the time, an optimal bid preparation process would involve further effort building on the insights provided by pass 1, in subsequent passes and parallel bid management processes which exploited the insight gained earlier, to make bids that Astro wanted to win more attractive to the potential customers. It would not just be a matter of refining earlier estimates; it would be a matter of addressing different kinds of uncertainty and complexity in different ways as appropriate. Even the pass 1 form of the PD3.5 should address these kinds of issues as a basis for possible further stage 3 passes and other forms of analysis.

Sometimes a very late no bid decision would be an unplanned and unwelcomed outcome of later stage 3 passes – but it was important to keep an open mind.

Martha then interjected to remind Trevor and Sian that Ben would support the PD3 processes and make the provision of necessary information as easy as possible for Systems staff, Sales staff, and any other Astro staff involved. They did not have to understand the technical computational issues in detail, or the separability structure nuanced implications, just the basic principles. She knew that Trevor and all other Sales staff would find the new approach to explicit use of P(B) curves particularly challenging to get to grips with in the early stages, but they would find it very rewarding as well, and she was convinced that Trevor had crucially important expertise which he could share with other Sales staff, her included, via the new process, playing a leading role in the shaping of their stage 3 approach. She also knew that Sian and all other Systems staff would find knock-on implications of the new bidding process challenging, but she hoped she could help Sian deal with the underlying changes impacting them both which had triggered the need for a new approach to bidding.

Martha closed their workshop by emphasising that she was determined to make the Sales contribution to Astro Wales a success, and she would support Sian's wider role as well as Sian's relationship with Sales in any way she could. She would now let them to recover from the information overload of this very long and intense workshop.

Trevor's transformative insights

Martha needed time to reflect on how the workshop had gone, update and extend her plans for further development of the new bidding process, brief Rhys on her plans and get his feedback, and begin some conversations with Sian. However, she attended to these tasks in parallel with a top priority series of meetings with Trevor and Ben, beginning the next day.

Martha started the first of these meetings by indicating to Trevor that she thought the very basic known constant non-price advantage bid adjustment assumption which Ben had used to produce Figure 6.11 was a useful simplification for their workshop discussion. However, it lacked sophistication relative to the feel for non-price advantage issues which she believed Trevor had and Astro needed to capture. She knew the framework of the approach Ben had provided would easily accommodate the more insightful working assumption structure which she thought Trevor could help them to develop. She then outlined what she had in mind based on extensive prior discussions with Ben.

Trevor quickly responded to this opportunity, with a view to making his mark on the new bidding models and processes. He 'thought out loud' with a whiteboard and marker pen for several hours while Martha prompted him and Ben made notes and asked clarification questions. Trevor, Ben and Martha then started to put together an initial presentation for Trevor to make to his Transcon bid sales team. This was used to trigger further ideas, which eventually evolved into what Martha referred to as 'Trevor's plan'.

Before considering the detail necessary for strategic clarity about Trevor's plan at this stage in its development, you may find it useful to consider a brief outline of the transformative insights which created the basis for and then shaped Trevor's plan, ordered to provide a simple initial overview.

First, Trevor and his Transcon bid sales team needed to start by focusing considerable effort on the competitor which mattered the most – 'competitor 1' using Ben's labels. Trevor identified competitor 1 as Tauris. As Trevor would put it later, to compete effectively the Astro bid team 'needed to get to know the opposition', with a focus on what really mattered, initially in the context of their relationship with the competitor which mattered most.

Second, they needed to formally acknowledge that Tauris was 'the market leader', not Astro. This was a mindset change for Trevor and for Astro more generally. As Trevor would put it later, 'getting to know Tauris was a significant reality check result for him, and Tauris was by no means the only competitor they were behind in ways needing explicit and focused attention'.

Third, they needed to assume that Tauris used an approach to bidding which never led to a no bid decision, but always varied the effort expended in proportion to how much Tauris wanted to win any particular bid and how tough Tauris thought the competition was going to be. That is, Tauris would always bid for sure, but with significant and crucially important variability in the level of effort expended on their bidding effort.

Fourth, Astro adopting the working assumption that Tauris would never no bid but could produce a 'no bid equivalent' involving a very low effort but very high price bid made the Astro analysis framework much simpler. The primary purpose of this working assumption was making Astro analysis simpler, but it was a reasonable working assumption for a sophisticated competitor like Tauris which Astro could learn from for direct use.

Fifth, a no bid equivalent approach by Astro should be built into Astro's SP for bidding as a 'diplomatic option', for possible use whenever Astro wanted to maintain a market presence or not offend an organisation which they wanted to maintain good relationships with despite not wanting this particular contract.

Sixth, in stage 3 a no bid equivalent approach by Astro should be viewed as the extreme end of a spectrum of 'provisions for cost ambiguity uncertainty for a possible "nice to have" contracts which they would not mind getting at a high enough mark-up but did not believe were worth further analysis effort'. In effect, stage 3 iteration decisions have to consider a number of trade-offs, including a judgement about given other possible uses for the time of those involved in the bidding process, is it worth spending more time trying to better understand how to increase the expected margin and reduce the risk associated with not winning this particular potential contract, or would it be better to just add a bigger provision for what they still do not know and stop investing any more time on this bid now, proceeding with a fairly high bid and not being too worried if they lose it.

Seventh, they should assume that the systematic relationship between how much Tauris wanted to win and the price Tauris would bid could not be used to predict the Tauris bid at this stage by Astro. An attempt to penetrate the ambiguity associated with predicting what Tauris would bid might be contemplated later, if a particularly important contract Astro really wanted to win was involved. They might base this on approaches employed by oil majors when bidding for oilfield exploration sites which they really wanted. It was known that some oil majors sometimes assessed likely bids from other oil companies, but Trevor, Martha, and Ben were agreed that this level of sophistication was not a current Astro concern.

Eighth, the systematic relationship between the price which Tauris decided to bid for the Transcon contract and the non-price disadvantage which Astro would suffer could be assessed by Astro fairly simply using crucial working assumptions which were central to his transformative insights. *Given Tauris made a plausible minimum bid, a plausible working assumption was that Tauris really wanted to win this contract and had put a maximum level of effort into the bid; given Tauris made a plausible maximum bid, a plausible working assumption was Tauris were not too concerned about winning this contract and had put a minimum level of effort into the bid; given Tauris make a mid-range bid, a mid-range scenario in terms of Tauris effort could be inferred.* Astro's immediate priority was developing clarity about what this view of the relationship between Tauris bids and associated effort implied in terms of Astro's non-price disadvantage, and how this understanding could be used by Astro.

After Trevor had acquired strategic clarity about the what needs to be done implications of these eight components of his transformative insights, he became comfortable with tactical planning for their next steps, briefing his Transcon sales team to bring them up to date with progress so far, and beginning to seek input from his Transcon team for developing the new bidding process for Transcon.

The next section addresses the resulting first meeting with the Transcon sales team. But before moving on you might find it useful to understand that we might perceive Trevor's transformative insights as roughly comparable in terms of process and *some* aspects of the effects to Nicola's pass 3 *plus* Bob's plan 4 evolution in Chapter 5. The key difference is Trevor's transformative insights did not lead to putting aside the equivalent to Nicola's formal EOQ model – they led to tactical clarity which enhanced Ben's basic models within the bidding framework envisaged by Martha all along, making the overall evolving bidding process much easier to use as well as much richer and much more robust. Full understanding of the implications is central to the enhancement of your strategic clarity which this chapter provides.

An alternative analogy is the intended evolution of your thinking in Chapter 3 when moving from William's minimum clarity approach to unbiased estimation towards Peter's eventual understanding that unbiased estimates were just one useful spin-off from an opportunity efficient approach to all relevant aspects of contingency planning.

Trevor takes up the leadership role which Martha planned

Trevor began his first presentation to the Transcon bid sales team by outlining all their progress to date, using all the tables and diagrams discussed earlier in this chapter to ensure that his sales team understood the tools developed thus far, and the lessons learned. He finished his summary by confirming the importance of using a structure like Figure 6.12 to order competitors in terms of importance, with competitor $i = 1$ being 'the key competitor' by definition, competitor 2 the next most important, and so on.

Trevor then suggested they spend some time 'getting to know competitor $i = 1$', and they start exploring their relationship with this key competitor by explicitly asking the question

'Was the key competitor the market leader?' If the answer was 'no', then Astro was the market leader by definition. For the Transcon bid he was now assuming that Tauris was the key competitor, and Tauris was the market leader.

The core issue they needed to explore immediately was generalising Ben's non-price advantage adjustment approach. Ben's Table 6.4 for competitor i = 1 assumed a known constant £2 million adjustment between all actual and adjusted bids, with competitor j = 2 involving a known constant £1 million adjustment on Table 6.5. This working assumption was far too restrictive and unrealistic. It oversimplified in a counterproductive way, to such an extent that until he, Martha, and Ben had agreed on an effective practical way to accommodate a more sophisticated approach to non-competitive disadvantage assessment which was both probabilistic and conditional upon the bid made by Tauris, he had not been convinced there was any feasible way to get beyond his very basic Figure 6.3 direct estimation of a preliminary probability of winning curve.

Trevor's generalised variant of Ben's approach involved associating each competitor with formal modelling of systemic uncertainty about non-price advantage or disadvantage using what Trevor (with Ben's prompting) had labelled 'conditional probabilistic bid adjustment tables'. These tables would capture crucial uncertainty and associated dependence issues which Trevor had understood intuitively for some time. He was now convinced that he plus all his Sales team needed to develop significant additional clarity about these issues via formal analysis. Crucially, these 'conditional probabilistic bid adjustment tables' would allow Trevor to develop more clarity and then explain his understanding to others so that they could all develop and exploit comparable understanding. Trevor believed that all of Martha's sales teams ought to understand these relationships, although previously he had no tools to explain his understanding to anyone. Using the new tools which he, Ben, and Martha had evolved had greatly clarified his own understanding as a direct consequence of formalising what had previously been intuitive. Trevor now saw developing collective Sales team clarity about key aspects of systemic uncertainty as *very* important, and well worth thoughtful direct *formal* treatment. Clarity efficient formal treatment of key aspects of uncertainty was going to prove the *key* reason why the new Astro approach to bidding was going to revolutionise Astro's competitive capability.

Trevor indicated that they would initially concentrate on a 'conditional probabilistic bid adjustment table' for Taurus, their most important competitor for the Transcon bid. But all other important competitors plus a composite of the residual could also be assessed via the same tabular format, then combined via Table 6.6 format computations. In practice, they would develop and use computer software to keep the input requirements minimal and the computations as easy as possible, and they would later have to learn how to use these tools. The focus that day would be the principles behind what had to be done and why. Formally modelling the systemic uncertainty associated with the adjustment process would help to give them confidence that the expected values used for their analysis were unbiased, because they could express their lack of certainty about the adjustment process visibly and explicitly, and later use actual outcomes to monitor and control estimation error.

Trevor then showed his team Table 6.8.

Trevor began by indicating that Table 6.8 had been developed using a highly iterative process with considerable detailed help from Ben and crucial oversight help from Martha. While it had not been straightforward evolving Table 6.8, he was now confident that with suitable training and background understanding all Astro sales teams could construct similar tables for any key Astro competitor which was judged to be worth careful thought.

Table 6.8 Conditional probabilistic bid adjustment table: Taurus, assuming a £12m Astro cost estimate.

Probability tree estimates				Probability contributions for an adjusted Taurus bid of						
Actual bid	Probability	Adjusted bid	Probability	(0)	15	16	17	18	19	20
19	0.2	20	0.1							0.02
		19	0.2						0.04	
		18	0.5					0.10		
		17	0.2				0.04			
18	0.6	18	0.1					0.06		
		17	0.2				0.12			
		16	0.4			0.24				
		15	0.3		0.18					
17	0.2	16	0.1			0.02				
		15	0.3		0.06					
		(0)	0.6	0.12						
Adjusted bid probabilities (column sums)				0.12	0.24	0.26	0.16	0.16	0.04	0.02
Reverse cumulative probabilities for plotting Figure 6.13 at Astro bids of				1.0 (0)	0.88 14.5	0.64 15.5	0.38 16.5	0.22 17.5	0.06 18.5	0.02 19.5

(Reverse cumulative probabilities: 1.0, 0.88, 0.64, 0.38, 0.22, 0.06, 0.02, 0 at Astro bids of (0), 14.5, 15.5, 16.5, 17.5, 18.5, 19.5, 20.5)

He thought they needed a simplified acronym label for this table, but he had yet to take the time to think of one.

Trevor started to explore the thinking behind Table 6.8 by indicating that the first four columns defined a probability tree which Sales had to estimate. Constructing Table 6.8 had to be grounded on understanding this probability tree. They might begin by noting that the second level branches were conditional on the first level, a defining characteristic of the model they would be using.

The 'actual bid' probability distribution in the first two columns of Table 6.8 defined three bid scenarios which reflected the range of actual bids by Taurus anticipated by Trevor, with illustrative initial probabilities estimated by Trevor. The 'adjusted bid' distributions in the third and fourth columns were conditional on the actual bids, with illustrative uncertainty ranges and probabilities also estimated by Trevor. They could debate and perhaps modify these estimates later, and several approaches to more refined portrayals were feasible if they thought the effort was worthwhile.

To explain the rationale for the actual bid distribution in the first two columns, Trevor started by observing that Taurus had low costs relative to Astro's. That was *part* of the reason Tauris were the market leaders. Astro's current cost estimate of about £12 million would be high relative to a comparable cost estimate by Taurus for its direct cost, and Tauris would recognise that its approximate cost estimate equivalent was less than £12 million. But Tauris also had technology quality advantages in some areas, which were further sources of non-price advantage. In addition, Tauris was very capable of generating non-price advantages comparable to the set of 'opportunity options' which Martha had identified during the workshop he had outlined.

Trevor had assumed that even if Tauris had decided to put minimal effort into a bid for the Transcon contract, because they were very busy or not very interested in winning this particular contract for other reasons, and they used a 'high bid' of £19 million, they still had a low but plausible chance of winning. If Taurus wanted to win this contract very badly, for a range of possible reasons which Trevor assumed Astro could only guess at, Tauris might put in a 'low bid' of £17 million. Trevor assumed that the most likely Tauris bid was £18 million, given their cost base plus their non-price advantages and no obvious reasons for high or low bids *currently known to Trevor*. Trevor had used a 'plausible maximum' P(90) 'high bid' (and low Tauris effort) estimate followed by a 'plausible minimum' P10 'low bid' (and high Tauris effort) estimate with an 'intermediate bid' scenario on an integer scale to keep his example simple, and his current working assumption about Astro's inability to forecast the extent to which Tauris wanted to win a contract made assuming a simple symmetric probability distribution plausible.

The adjusted bid probability distributions in the third and fourth columns completed the probability tree which defined appropriate adjusted bids given the actual bids assumed. The probabilities in this case captured Trevor's best estimates of bid adjustment uncertainty associated with non-price advantage and disadvantage issues. For example, if Taurus bid £19 million, Trevor thought that appropriate adjusted bids might be £20 million, £19 million, £18 million or £17 million, with the probabilities indicated. His example stuck to the same integer value £ million scale and only four probability tree branch end point scenarios for simplicity, but demonstrated clearly that he believed an asymmetric conditional distribution should be expected.

Trevor suggested that they think of adjusted bids as 'the maximum bid Astro could make to beat the associated actual Taurus bid'. The adjustment for non-price advantage and disadvantage concept was usefully conceived and numerically estimated in these terms. For example, looking at the first line in the body of Table 6.8, if the Taurus actual bid was £19 million (assumed probability 0.2), and given this the Taurus adjusted bid was £20 million (assumed probability 0.1), this probability tree branch end point scenario implied that Astro should win with a bid of less than £20 million, lose with a bid of more than £20 million, £20 million being the flip point. This involved a non-price advantage for Astro of +£1 million, which he would refer to as a non-price disadvantage of –£1, because this would reduce the number of negative numbers they had to work with and clarify the new mindset they all needed. The associated unconditional probability of this probability tree branch end point scenario was $0.2 \times 0.1 = 0.02$.

They should see the right-hand columns of Table 6.8 as a way of recording the probability products associated with each actual bid and adjustment combination to facilitate later computation. For example, in the body of the table the probability product $0.2 \times 0.1 = 0.02$ in line 1 was associated with an adjusted bid of £20 million.

The rationale provided by Trevor for the bid adjustment range plus the probabilities for each value in the range for each actual bid value was then developed row by row.

Line 1 was a convenient starting point for exploring the assumptions underlying the estimates. It involved combining the highest plausible Taurus bid and the lowest plausible non-price disadvantage for Astro. This defined the most optimistic plausible scenario from an Astro perspective. It was worth further brief elaboration for several reasons.

Trevor had assumed that if Taurus bid at £19 million, Transcon might not recognise that Taurus was not particularly keen to get the job, but the minimal effort which Tauris expended on developing a package of non-price advantages would mean that Astro *might* be able to bid as high as £20 million and still win, implying a non-price disadvantage of –£1 million for Astro relative to Taurus as perceived by Transcon, an adjusted Taurus bid of £20 million. Trevor associated this scenario with Astro bidding in its 'premium end of the market' manner with the package of opportunity options and other non-price advantage features developed earlier in their bidding process, and Transcon being prepared to pay for Astro quality given the consequences of a lack of enthusiasm for developing non-price advantages on the part of Taurus. Trevor thought that the probability of this very optimistic outcome was only 0.1 *given* a Taurus bid of £19 million, implying an unconditional probability of only $0.2 \times 0.1 = 0.02$. Trevor emphasised that this was the *only* negative non-price disadvantage in Table 6.8. An obvious part of the rationale for his use in Table 6.8 of non-price 'disadvantage' instead of 'advantage' was minimising the negative numbers they had to deal with, but the implied mindset change was actually more important in his view.

Lines 2, 3 and 4 continued to assume a Taurus bid of £19 million, considering successively lower adjusted bid values together with the probabilities of associated probability tree scenarios until the successive conditional probability estimates summed to one. These scenarios explored a £19 million adjusted bid scenario followed by £18 million and £17 million adjusted bid possibilities. Together with line 1 this defined a probability distribution of adjusted bids (and associated non-price disadvantages) conditioned on Taurus bidding £19 million. With Taurus bidding at £19 million, Trevor was confident that Astro could win for sure with a bid of £16 million, assuming that a non-price disadvantage of £3 million or more being ascribed to Astro as perceived by Transcon was not possible using probabilities defined to the level of precision employed in his example. Working to the nearest £1 million, non-price disadvantages of –£1 million, £0 million, £1 million, and £2 million were possible but no values outside this set. Trevor thought that given a Taurus bid of £19 million, the most likely adjusted bid was £18 million, involving a non-price disadvantage to Astro of £1 million, with a 0.5 probability. He associated a 0.2 probability with the adjusted bid possibilities of £19 million and £17 million, both twice as likely as the £20 million possibility.

Line 5 of Table 3.8 associated a Taurus bid of £18 million with a maximum adjusted bid value of £18 million, because Trevor assumed that the most optimistic possible scenario was Transcon would see an £18 million bid from Taurus and the associated package of non-price advantages for Tauris as directly comparable to an Astro bid of £18 million, with no chance of Astro doing any better than parity in non-price advantage or disadvantage terms. Indeed, even a parity situation had only a 0.1 conditional probability in Trevor's view.

Lines 6, 7 and 8 continued assuming a Taurus bid of £18 million and considered decreasing adjusted bid values (increasing non-price disadvantages to Astro) until the conditional probabilities summed to one and a highest plausible non-price disadvantage was addressed. If Taurus bid £18 million, Trevor was confident that Astro could win for sure with a bid of £14 million, implying a non-price disadvantage for Astro of £4 million was not possible. Trevor believed that with Taurus bidding at £18 million, the most likely equivalent Astro bid as perceived by Transcon was £16 million, implying a non-price disadvantage of £2 million with a probability of 0.4.

Trevor observed that the conditional probability distribution shapes were different for the actual Taurus bids of £19 million and £18 million, in addition to the range shift, to emphasise the flexible approach to systemic dependence provided by Table 6.8 without trying to overstate the implications in this example. If the Table 6.8 structure was used to model exactly the same adjustment probability distribution for each actual bid value, this would imply a probabilistic approach which assumed that the non-price disadvantages were unconditional – independent of the actual bid. If in addition there was only one common possible outcome for each plausible Taurus actual bid, this would be a very simple special case directly comparable to Ben's earlier model.

Line 9 was associated with a Taurus bid of £17 million and a maximum adjusted bid of £16 million, a further conditional distribution shift. This was because Trevor assumed that

Transcon would see a £17 million bid and the associated package of non-price advantages for Taurus as very competitive, with no chance of Astro doing any better than a £1 million non-price disadvantage, and only a 0.1 probability of this occurring.

Line 10 continued the definition of a conditional probability distribution given a Taurus actual bid of £17 million, with a £15 million adjusted bid associated with a 0.3 probability.

With a big but noticeably sad smile on his face, Trevor indicated that when he initially addressed line 11, he had associated an actual Taurus bid of £17 million with an adjusted bid of £14 million, a non-price disadvantage for Astro of £3 million. He was sure many of them were puzzled about why Table 6.8 used (0). But in discussion with Ben, they had both come to the conclusion that in practice if Taurus bid £17 million and put the maximum effort into non-price advantages he was assuming, there was actually a zero probability Astro would win with a bid of £14 million and further Astro price reductions would not help – there was a 0.6 probability Astro could not win at any price. This could be interpreted as implying an adjusted bid of zero because the market leader Taurus wanted this job so much they had put together a package which was beyond Astro's reach.

A useful way to interpret this was Taurus had made Transcon an offer Transcon could not refuse, with a probability of winning of unity. Trevor suggested that this scenario should be called 'a zero bid equivalent' to signify that there was a probability of about 0.6 that 'Astro couldn't give it away in the face of a £17 million Taurus bid'.

The 0.6 adjusted bid probability entry defined by $(1 - (0.1 + 0.3))$ was associated with a zero-adjusted bid in brackets so that the adjusted bid probabilities associated with a Taurus bid of £17 million sum to one. The (0) notation signified that this was the zero-bid equivalent for Astro bids in the range 0 to 14, a simple way of dealing with the complete set of Astro bids which they had no chance of winning.

The columns collecting together the adjusted bid unconditional probability contributions incorporated the 'zero bid equivalent' under the (0) heading with a 0.12 entry (0.2×0.6).

The 'adjusted bids probability' row near the bottom of the table just collected the column sums, and the last two rows just converted the discrete outcome distribution of adjusted bids into a continuous distribution approximation for later use in Figure 6.13.

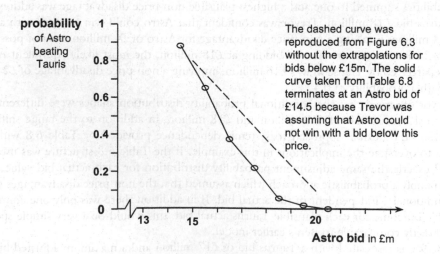

Figure 6.13 Probability of Astro beating Tauris curve from Table 6.8.

As soon as Trevor thought his Transcon Sales team understood how Table 6.8 worked, he showed them Figure 6.13.

Trevor then began his explanation of the relationship between Table 6.8 and Figure 6.13. He pointed out that the last two lines of Table 6.8 allowed the preparation of Figure 6.13 by transforming the discrete probability tree end point probabilities collected by the right-hand columns of Table 6.8 into a piecewise linear continuous variable distribution for the probability that Astro would beat Tauris. Working from the right-hand end: if Astro bid £20.5 million or more, the probability of beating Tauris was zero; if Astro bid £19.5 million, the probability of beating Tauris was 0.02; if Astro bid £18.5 million, the probability of beating Tauris was 0.06; and so on until the curve simply ends at an Astro bid of £14.5 million – if Astro bid at £14.5 million the probability of winning was 0.88. The probability of winning curve just stops at that point, in effect, dropping to zero for bids below £14.5 million.

Trevor then explained that as illustrated by Figure 6.11, any competitor i curve plus competitor j curve would yield a composite competitor k curve result which was to the left of i or j. Assuming that i = 1 and j = 2, if i dominated j the shift to the left would be negligible, but if j dominated, i then the shift to the left would be substantial. The curve for k would never shift to the right. This meant that as they consider other competitors, things could only get worse relative to the solid curve associated with Tauris in Figure 6.13. As they could see, this solid curve was already well below the dashed curve associated with his preliminary curve addressing all competitors in Figure 6.3, which he had overlaid for comparison.

The solid curve in Figure 6.13 showed only a 0.22 probability of winning with a bid of £17.5 million, only a 0.38 probability of winning with a bid of £16.5 million, rising to 0.64 for £15.5 million and 0.88 for £14.5 million. Trevor suggested that if this Figure 6.13 assessment based on Table 6.8 was reasonably robust, they need to work out how to attack the massive non-price and cost advantages Taurus had before worrying about other competitors.

Trevor indicated that this result had surprised him greatly. Relative to his preliminary assessment it was *very* pessimistic. But he believed addressing the specifics of their key competitor relationship in the way he had illustrated provided a much more realistic basis for understanding the competition as a whole than anything they had undertaken in the past, and they could build on it. Furthermore, when they built upon it they could use their time much more effectively than they had in the past. They would be able to better focus on what really mattered, which they had earlier lacked the tools to address systematically and effectively.

Trevor then suggested that they could use everything they had learned since Martha and Ben began the Transcon bidding exercise to stimulate what he called a 'further search for value added', building on the value added opportunities they had identified earlier. Using the Astro site for training illustrated what he was after. So did the three bonus opportunity options identified via Martha's and Ben's revisions to system input: the option of Datapol at a low extra price, the option of additional memory at a minimal extra price, and the option of a bonus level of performance at a very low extra price. More value added was needed to be competitive with the market leader Taurus, and other strong competitors, targeting potential Astro strengths and weaknesses in relation to identified specific strengths and weaknesses of their key competitors.

Trevor now showed his Transcon bid team Figure 6.14.

Trevor indicated that Ben could produce software to provide this rather different representation of Table 6.8 in addition to Figure 6.13, all three portraying the same basic

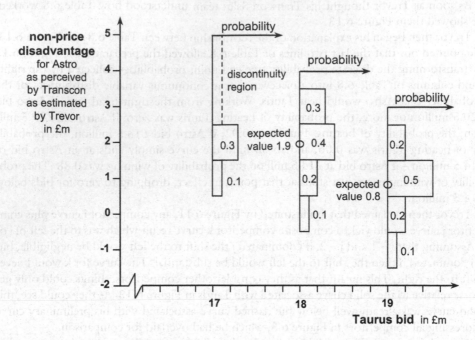

Figure 6.14 Non-price disadvantage probability distributions from Table 6.8.

information in different ways. The Figure 6.14 format could be used as a basis for estimating the Table 6.8 equivalents as well as a way of portraying those estimates, and he found the Figure 6.14 format a particularly useful basis for thinking about the information they needed to generate and fully understand for each of the important competitors.

To understand the relationship between Table 6.8 and Figure 6.14, given a Tauris bid of £19 million, the fourth column of Table 6.8 defines the adjusted bid conditional probabilities shown for the right-hand distribution in Figure 6.14. Similarly, given a Tauris bid of £17 million, the fourth column of Table 6.8 defines the adjusted bid conditional probabilities shown for the left-hand distribution in Figure 6.14. The middle case is directly comparable.

They could use the Figure 6.14 format to explore the implications of the less important competitors too, including the residual composite n = 6 in a structure like Figure 6.12. He thought some of them might prefer thinking about what they were doing by starting with the Figure 6.14 format and using it to generate all the Table 6.8 input estimates, and he was quite interested the possibility of developing the use of this option.

Trevor also indicated that once they were comfortable using Table 6.8 and Figure 6.14 formats for estimating curves in the Figure 6.13 format, they could revisit their estimates post bidding whenever they were able to acquire relevant information using the Figure 6.15 format.

For example, if they believed that Table 6.8 and Figures 6.13 and 6.14 were appropriate, made a bid of £19.3 million and won, and then discovered Tauris had bid £18.3 million, the Figure 6.15 data point a implied they had been plausible in their assessment of what Tauris would bid but excessively pessimistic about Astro non-price disadvantage. Their Figure 6.15

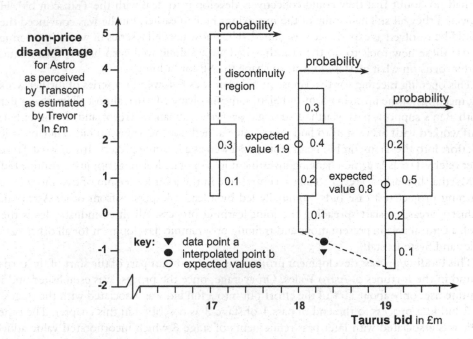

Figure 6.15 An example data point on the Figure 6.14 non-price disadvantage probability distributions.

distributions for Tauris bids of £18 million and £19 million interpolated to define point b for a Tauris bid of £18.3 million suggested winning with an Astro bid of £19.3 million was not plausible. Their win was an unanticipated outcome implying that they needed to shift the lower tail of these two conditional distributions downwards, or the whole of these distributions downwards, to take a more optimistic view of non-price disadvantage relative to Tauris in the future.

Winning given a key competitor's bid when this event had been assumed non-feasible would obviously be good news in part, but a bad news sting in the tail might be relevant if they had bid significantly lower than they needed to, a form of lost opportunity. Losing when this event had been assumed non-feasible given a key competitor's bid would be unambiguously unwelcome, implying points comparable to points a and b above the Figure 6.15 conditional distributions. Most of the time data points should fall within ranges assumed to be feasible, and assuming this was the case it would clearly take time to start to confirm the reasonableness of expectations and ranges and refine them appropriately. However, the conditional framework of Figures 6.14 and 6.15 and Table 6.8 clearly gave them the tools to model their subjective understanding of the issues and then start to acquire data to further develop their understanding.

When closing this meeting, Trevor reaffirmed that after the initial full-day workshop with Sian, Martha, and Ben, he had not understood how Martha's and Ben's stage 3 enhanced process for Sales was going to work, and he had significant concerns about it, as indicated at the beginning of this meeting. However, he now understood clearly how the Tauris example approach worked in the conditional probabilistic framework he had just outlined, and he had no doubt that they could collectively develop it to deal with the Transcon bid. He expected they all still had some of the misgivings he had earlier, but he was convinced they would be resolved as experience was gained. They now needed a series of working meetings to use these new tools to do the task they had always done well even better, with a much better focus on what mattered most, to shape the SP for bidding.

This opening meeting for the Transcon bid team was followed by a series of further working meetings, some involving Sam and Sian, some involving Martha, almost all involving Ben. With Ben's support, plus Martha's strategic overview guidance, Trevor and the other Sales staff worked with Sian's staff to find more 'value added' for the Transcon bid. They put a lot of effort into the Transcon bid because it was viewed as a learning project. It was what Trevor later referred to as 'a game-changing investment in corporate learning, not just a routine bid'.

Martha then asked Trevor to take a central role in the joint leadership of two more initial learning project test case bids, nominally led by a lead salesperson from other Astro sales industry areas, to start spreading the joint learning process. All three industry leads then took a central role in presentations and training programme development for all other Astro Sales and Systems staff.

This bidding process development project was an important part of the start of the turnaround in the fortunes of Astro Wales. On average, once the process was established and in routine use, only about 20% of the effort put into a full bid was associated with the stages 1 to 3 bidding process to the end of pass 1 of stage 3 as described in this chapter. The other 80% was associated with later pass refinements of stage 3 which incorporated value added searches to develop the bid in terms of non-price advantages for Astro, better-quality deliverables for their customers.

What emerged from the Transcon exercise as a general consensus and basis for building upon was summarised as follows:

1   Starting with an extensive analysis of Astro's key competitor in stage 3 was crucial. Furthermore, they had learned so much from this Tauris exercise that it was beginning to look like a simple approach to a key competitor curve with a following simple adjustment for a residual of all other competitors might be the best basis for the preliminary probability of winning curve used for the PD2.3 as well.

2   It was important to 'anchor' the development of Table 6.8 to an estimate of Astro's direct costs on the assumption that key competitors had a correlated comparable anchor reflecting their relative cost advantages or disadvantages. But it was also crucial to assume that each key competitor would vary their bid according to how much they wanted to win this particular contract, a low bid being assumed to reflect extensive effort putting together packages of non-price advantages, a systematic uncertainty assumption associated with key competitors. Relatively unimportant competitors incorporated in composite competitor n would not justify this assumption, part of the rationale for not expending effort decomposing composite competitor n.

3   The format of the conditional probabilistic bid adjustment portrayal of Table 6.8 provided a simple tabular framework for capturing the key issues which needed to be quantified, in particular the range and relative likelihood of actual bids by the key competitor, and the associated possible non-price advantage scenarios which defined adjusted bids conditional on the key competitor bid.

4   It was important to explicitly consider systemic uncertainty associated with non-price advantages and to assume this uncertainty was related to the bid levels of key competitors,

because this dependence and the associated conditional estimates of uncertainty were very important, and they required explicit and focused discussion by those with relevant knowledge.

5   Figures 6.13, 6.14 and 6.15 all provided useful frameworks for interpreting Table 6.8, and having a single key competitor underlie Figure 6.13 made the graph very credible. Everyone could accept that it approximated reality. The story it told was clear. The messages it sent were clear. Its basis was subjective but sound.

6   Once a way of improving the picture portrayed by Figure 6.13 had been identified and developed, it was relatively straightforward to consider an equivalent of Table 6.8 and Figures 6.13 through 6.15 for the next most important competitor. The approach employed in Table 6.6 and Figure 6.11 could then be applied to combine these two competitors. Again, the results were accepted as subjective but sound. A second wave of value added searches, perhaps in slightly different directions, could follow if needed. This process could continue as necessary, as the basis of a revised later pass version of the emerging PD3. However, the dominance of the first few competitors, because of the ordering approach, made everyone reasonably confident of a final composite competitor n approach to considering 'all other competitors', once the process and the model results became reasonably familiar.

7   There was a very clear need to use this basic approach to the PD3 even when no data was available to confirm or deny the validity of subjective estimates agreed on by relevant staff, but there was also a clear need to start thinking about data acquisition from the outset, making use of the Figure 6.15 starting point.

8   On the first pass through the stage 3 process early non-price advantage creation and analysis by Systems were separated from later comparable non-price advantage creation and analysis by Sales. But the iterative framework of the process meant that Sales and Systems could jointly understand and manage the interconnections, plus the way these interconnections were linked to particularly important individual competitors as well as the composite of all other competitors.

In summary, Martha initiated and provided strategic shape and direction for an overall set of changes within the Astro Wales Sales team approach with significant implications. With Martha's support, Ben facilitated and provided the basis for appropriate operational models and processes used to facilitate these changes. However, Trevor was also a clearly visible leader for Sales staff, using a generalisation of Ben's very basic non-price disadvantage model, and Martha was very shrewd to have engineered this, as well as lucky to have someone with Trevor's skill set and mindset. The models chosen and the processes evolved were simple but effective. The new ideas were an unqualified success.

Trevor and Ben, as well as Martha, established reputations which soon went well beyond Astro Wales. Sian shared some of the glory, and Rhys felt some of the benefits too, in both cases because of their direct contributions to the changes led by Martha, as well as further spin-offs not yet discussed. All their careers took a strong turn for the better because of these bidding process developments.

Key steps in Martha's approach to change management

Martha had synthesised six key steps from her analysis of the 'change management' literature which she believed were relevant to the approach she needed to adopt for changing the way her Astro Wales Sales team addressed bidding processes. They are a useful general checklist which you might build on, summarised as follows:

1   Make sure everyone involved understands that 'no change' is not an option.
2   Make sure that the strategic direction of the change and the key deliverables from the change are clear.
3   'If you cannot change the people, then change the people' – redeploy (transfer, retire, or fire) anyone who, given reasonable support, is not willing or able to make the change as soon as feasible to minimise the negative effects of unconstructive dissent on overall team morale, as well as the operational burden of people who are not pulling their weight. Crucially, make it *very* clear from the outset that this is your intention, with a view to motivating the willing parties to focus on meeting the challenges involved and encouraging the difficult parties to leave voluntarily as soon as possible with minimal aggravation before they go.
4   Manage the whole change process as a very high risk programme (portfolio of high risk projects), with an initial focus on flexibility and effectiveness rather than efficiency (initially doing the right things is usually *much* more important than doing things right, although later continuous improvement also matters).
5   Facilitate joint development of the new models and processes that the change requires by everyone involved so that they all have a strong sense of ownership.
6   Facilitate learning processes so that everyone involved can develop the skills necessary to develop and implement the new models and processes.

By the end of the developments discussed so far Martha had done what she could to minimise uncertainty with respect to the first three steps, and she had initiated the last three.

Martha had learned a lot from being involved directly in the bid process development project, as well as what she learned directly from Trevor, Ben, and the others involved. She knew that this would be the case. More generally, from the outset Martha knew roughly what she wanted all key Astro staff to learn and what she wanted the Transcon bid process development project to deliver. Any project requires as much of this kind of strategic clarity about all intended deliverables as the context and the capabilities available allow.

Wider impacts on Astro Wales

Martha could think top-down within her Astro Wales Sales responsibilities, a key capability. She could also think sideways to Sian's concerns, and upwards to the issues that mattered for Astro Wales, Astro UK, and Astro Inc.

Martha had been clear from the outset that she would have to proactively manage sideways and upwards as well as downwards within her Sales team. Her highest priority outside Sales was changes within Systems. She knew there were changes in Systems which Sian was going to have to deal with if they were going to jointly resolve the core problems for Astro Wales, and a coordinated joint effort was essential. Towards the end of her focus on the enhanced cost estimate process with Sian, Martha had deliberately provided Sian with some clear hints that they needed to get together on these joint concerns. She made it clear that not all Sian's staff would attract favourable cost adjustments, and all groups of staff within Systems had to be competitive to survive beyond the accommodation of short-run difficulties. Martha would try to ensure that Sian's underutilised groups had work generated for them in the short run if they could compete on price and quality in the medium-term.

But nobody in any group could be carried for long if Astro Wales as a whole was going to succeed.

The degree of difficulty inherent in adopting the new models which Sian and her staff had to make use of in Table 6.3 was trivial in comparison to those Trevor had to develop. Sian did not need Ben's support to a significant extent with the costing of bids. Table 6.3 and the supporting figures could be facilitated with software tools, and Ben helped with the specification and testing of these tools, but Ben's support for Sian was low key compared to his support for Trevor and other Sales staff in terms of developing formal models and processes to implement these models. However, the new internal bidding process which Table 6.3 cost adjustments made explicit involved a major culture change within Systems. Sian needed Martha's support to a significant extent to cope with this, and she got it. She also needed and got support from Rhys, with Martha playing the facilitator role here. More generally, Rhys, Martha, and Sian needed to work as a team, with flexible role changes when needed. How they did this is briefly elaborated now, starting with a focus on Sian.

Sian's Astro career had always been in Systems, and she had always seen the role of a head of Systems like herself in terms of a conventional matrix-based 'service' organisation: Sales people were responsible for getting the work and making a profit on the sales; Systems people were responsible for doing the work and ensuring that the quality generated a good reputation which would lead to future work. This built in a quality–profit tension management process with clear 'champions' for each. Sian had recognised the ambiguity about responsibility for Astro losses on contracts was a long-term Astro problem, and the growing use of subcontractors like Zoro involved a complication of the simpler historical situation, but she had never seen marketing her Systems people in competition with external suppliers of the same or similar skills as a key part of her job. Nor had she fully appreciated the conflicts of interests inherent in her current role as judge in a process which entailed her Systems staff bidding against external subcontractors. She now recognised these complications were crucial. Her job, as she now saw it, involved serious conflicts of interest, and it was not clear to her what ought to be done. Massive uncertainties and complexities she had not previously seen suddenly revealed themselves. Martha anticipated this because she had thought about and understood to some extent the coming changes. They had been forced on her thinking when she confronted the fact that as a salesperson in Astro Scotland she had done very well selling on commission, but she now had no commission, and she was responsible for profitability within her Sales silo with staff reporting to her paid commissions on sales (not profit) in addition to those responsible for delivery like Systems motivated very differently to those working for organisations like Zoro. In terms of the capability-culture concept discussed in Chapter 2, Martha could see some important liabilities needing effective immediate accommodations and important longer-term resolution, although she might use different language to explain them.

Rhys, the manager in charge of Astro Wales, had a systems background like Sian. He was a native of Wales, but most of his modestly successful career had been spent in various other locations in the UK and US. Martha and Sian were both keen to involve him in Sian's difficulties from the outset, and he was very keen to be involved. He had held his current post longer than Martha or Sian, but he had never been very comfortable telling either of them or their predecessors what to do. He kept himself busy acting as a front man for Astro Wales in ways which did not always seem as useful as he wanted to be. For some time he had been as uncertain about his proper role as Sian had suddenly become.

Martha, Sian and Rhys began a series of discussions about these issues, initially usually just two at a time in various combinations, but increasingly as a three person team working in a coordinated manner. Five significant changes emerged from these discussions:

1   With crucial support from Rhys, Sian should divide Systems into a number of groups, and ensure that each had a strong 'group head' who would take full responsibility for the quality and cost of work by that group, with requisite authority to hire, promote, and recommend redeployment in order to maintain a group size agreed on with Sian. Sian would be responsible for the performance of her group heads, but not the quality or cost of the work by groups so long as a group head was not in obvious trouble as a manager. In effect, important roles Sian currently played would be devolved to group heads, drawing lines around what was devolved and what Sian kept with a view to effective management of uncertainty and complexity without direct conflicts of interest for any of the players. Sian was 'subcontracting' part of her job to her group heads in order to enhance her performance with the residual responsibilities, analogous to Astro Wales subcontracting parts of systems integration projects in order to enhance overall performance. Martha was the one who guided their thinking in this direction and who suggested the subcontracting analogy, but the solution was obvious to all of them as soon as they understood what was involved and the rationale for the changes.

2   Each Systems group would be regarded as a profit centre, not just a cost centre. Each group head was responsible for cost and quality, but Sian would accept responsibility for the profit aspect of each group, in conjunction with group sizing decisions. The size of each group would be a focus of discussions between Sian and her group managers, with oversight by Rhys. Groups which made a sustainable profit would grow; groups which could not make a sustainable profit would shrink or 'relocate'.

3   Sian would see one key aspect of her job as an internal marketing manager for her Systems groups, to Martha's Astro Wales projects, to Astro UK, and to Astro Inc more generally. She would take a reasonably reactive role to the first, but a highly proactive role to the second and third. That is, she would trust and rely on Martha to take a proactive interest in generating local (Welsh) work for her people, given support and guidance, but she would proactively seek systems contracts with Astro UK and Astro Inc because Martha's remit did not include this kind of sales, and in the past such contracts did not really have a 'champion'. Sian had to take on some of this 'champion' role, working explicitly towards this end with Rhys.

4   Rhys would serve as Sian's 'front man' and 'chief salesman' for internal 'sales' to Astro UK and Astro Inc, making effective use of his extensive network of connections and his wide experience. Martha would also support Rhys and Sian's internal sales in the Astro UK and Astro Inc areas in terms of the marketing experience which Sian and Rhys lacked. Ben might provide backup analytical support as well. Sian would be 'in charge' of marketing in this internal markets for Systems sense, but she would be fully supported by all Astro Wales staff whenever they could contribute, whether they were technically a level above (Rhys), on the same level (Martha), or somewhere below in someone else's reporting structure (Ben). Martha's responsibility for Sales would have a local (Welsh) focus, explicitly restricted to non-Astro markets in terms of proactive leadership.

5   Rhys would take personal responsibility for developing and maintaining a suitable list of 'partnership external subcontractors', and for looking after their interests in any competition with Astro Wales Systems groups on Martha's contracts unless and until this

task warranted a separate manager. Rhys, Martha and Sian all agreed that an internal bidding process involving sealed bids, replicating what Martha faced with customers like Transcon, would not be helpful. However, an open process with a 'level playing field' was necessary. A 'strategic partnership' relationship with subcontractors was a productive way of levelling the playing field, working towards putting them on a par with internal Systems groups, rather than the other way around. It also had direct benefits, which business fashion was beginning to recognise. The concept of non-price advantage was central to these considerations. One of the key non-price advantages was trust that subcontractors and internal groups could deliver what they promised when they promised, without arguments and without close management. Another was confidence that 'partners' would be open and honest about uncertainties which could become sources of risk. Partners who could not be trusted should be rejected as partners, and all partners needed to understand this clearly from the outset.

Rhys, Sian and Martha did not attract the immediate attention with these developments that Trevor, Ben and Martha generated with their bidding models and processes. To some extent they were competing with other Astro UK and Astro Inc groups, so they did not want to shout about these changes and give away competitive advantage. However, within a few years Astro Wales became prominent for attracting many large systems development contracts from other parts of Astro, as well as for working effectively with a wide range of partner subcontractors in a growing volume of local business, and it was clear where the credit was due. Zoro was one of their partners, as were several Astro groups which were floated off as separate businesses, usually to everyone's benefit, although sometimes these float-offs failed, and sometimes very few people were surprised by such failures.

The uncertainties and complexities to be faced, the uncertainty and complexity associated with the best way to handle them, and the uncertainty generated by associated changes which Sian had to address, were all quite different from those Trevor and the other sales staff had to address. The support Sian needed was very different as a consequence. The 'softer', less clear-cut nature of the issues made formal models less useful, but the need for flexible formal processes and attention to organisational structure correspondingly more important. There was no need to redefine Sian's job and the organisational structure around her in formal terms for all to see, but there was a crucial need to redefine Sian's roles in agreement with those she worked with. Equally important was the flexibility implied in both Martha and Rhys 'working for Sian' in some contexts when this was useful. The senior staff of Astro Wales worked as a close team, with role changes according to context, to effectively manage the opportunities inherent in the complex uncertainty associated with redefining Sian's role in relation to their own roles. The experience was very positive for Martha and Rhys, as well as for Sian, and enlightening for everyone involved. It was an example of enlightened teamwork fully integrated with enlightened governance. Ben regarded his limited involvement in it as an important part of his apprenticeship, learning what management was all about beyond his immediate role as facilitator for the development and use of Astro's SP for bidding.

The example set by Rhys, Sian and Martha in terms of their approach to teamwork and governance was infectious. It was supported by Trevor and other Sales staff turning to Systems staff to help in the search for 'value added' in order to develop winning bids. It was reinforced by heads of Systems groups seeking a degree of marketing expertise from Trevor and other Sales staff as well as Martha. There was a visible flow of ideas and help from Sales to Systems and from Systems to Sales, which expanded to include the Service Bureau operation, Accounting and other support groups. To a lesser but significant extent it also embraced the partner external subcontractors. Apart from the direct benefits of the ideas and help, as silo boundaries softened and barriers went down, trust grew, and new synergy was identified and exploited.

'Managing upwards' and 'managing across' became operational aspects of the Astro office jargon – natural complements to 'managing downwards'. This collaborative style of management was recognised as the glue which closely bonded the Welch office as a team. Managing the uncertainty and complexity facing Astro Wales as a whole was very much a 'team sport'. Teamwork became the key driver of Astro capability-culture evolution.

Uncertainty and complexity management models and processes helped to 'shape the key and lubricate the lock'. Astro Wales as a whole prospered. Astro Wales was seen to be in the vanguard of the turnaround in Astro UK, and a very useful contributor to the turnaround in Astro Inc.

Effective and efficient external bidding processes were often held up as illustrative of the contribution Astro Wales made to Astro Inc. Those directly involved knew these bidding processes were a catalyst or a driver, in some ways only a very small part of the whole Astro recovery story, but arguably this kind of catalyst was crucial. All major corporate changes usually need a portfolio of catalysts and drivers.

The credibility of this tale and linked issues

The basis of this chapter's tale is a case study which I initially developed for an IBM UK culture change programme based on ideas and information provided by 'Edward', an executive at a very senior level in IBM UK. Edward provided most of the context information of Table 6.1 and its background. Bidding was the topic Edward chose because the market-driven nature of IBM meant that all IBM UK staff could relate to what was involved. This 'Transcon case study' was used about 40 times in its initial form with about 25 IBM staff each time from a wide range of roles. During this period IBM staff initiated a number of the ideas incorporated in this chapter, including the friendly takeover of Zoro. Subsequently, Stephen Ward and I have used this case study hundreds of times, on in-company short courses and on open short courses in the UK, the rest of Europe, North America and Africa, with participants from many companies and countries. We have also used it for university courses.

The three stage structure aspects of this chapter's approach were developed earlier when Stephen and I were working with Southern Gas and one of our MSc students on tendering for large service contracts with local authorities and housing trusts. It involves a particular form of sophistication not used for the IBM-related work but tested elsewhere.

Some of the contracting ideas derive from a Science and Engineering Research Council (SERC) research contract with Stephen Ward and Bernard Curtis plus follow-on work with Stephen and others, and some of the internal contracting and outsourcing ideas were triggered by my work with BP.

All the initial full-day workshop ideas were part of the framework IBM employees were exposed to, but the Table 6.8 conditional probabilistic bid adjustment approach plus the linked clarification of 'Trevor's transformative insights' were not developed in this particular form until this book was in its fourth draft. Some much more sophisticated ideas of a different kind were developed with IBM in the 1990s on a follow-on consultancy basis.

One aspect of this follow-on work with IBM considered a potential customer with a very large project (say, £200 million plus) who invites up to a dozen bids from different companies, perhaps paying them a fee to tender, with a view to eliminating all but three or four who then get a chance to bid in a second round. The key purpose of the multiple rounds approach from the potential customer's perspective is the second round specification is based on a synthesis of the best ideas on project strategy from the first round tenders. This means first round tendering has to include a portfolio of ideas which are good enough to get into the second round, but all tendering organisations have to preserve competitive advantage to win the second round by holding back some key ideas not to be shared with the potential customer during the first round. In the first round the potential customer is in effect buying relatively low cost or free consultancy on project strategy, with a view to a fairly crude form of partnering approach to contracting the project. An aspect arguably needing refinement from the customer's perspective is the gaming strategies of the first round players decrease the value to the customer of what could be learned. Having won the second round stage, third round partnership negotiations are anticipated, with some further negative implications of potential gaming. What this multiple rounds study illustrated to me, incorporated into Astro's approach when a single round is involved as far as possible, is the importance of the 'bonus opportunity' concept and other 'added value' ideas as a contractor's way into an efficient and effective form of 'strategic partnership' relationship with the client. Customer organisations need to understand these ideas as well as contractor organisations, as part of seeking 'strategic partner' relationships with their contractors. Furthermore, contractor organisations which use subcontractors need to understand they are simultaneously involved in both.

Using the Transcon case study for many years with people from a wide range of organisations it has become increasingly clear that customer organisations almost always need much more clarity about the significant difference in the nature, quality and performance of 'deliverables' provided by different contractors. They also need a very clear understanding of the need to avoid the significant foolishness of assuming that the lowest price is the best deal for the customer, unless they are *JUSTIFIABLY* very confident that they know *exactly* what they want and how to *unambiguously specify* what they want, all competing contractors are equally competent and honest, and all competing contractors are equally keen to win the contract. The probability of all these working assumptions holding at the same time is zero for most practical purposes. More generally, there are a number of reasons why the tale of this chapter is directly relevant to customer organisations, whatever they have to purchase, understanding how to seek best 'value for money' from purchases being one aspect. To some extent all organisations are both 'customers' and 'contractors'.

Astro is comparable to IBM, but Astro is not just a disguised version of IBM. Astro is a fictitious basis for a tale. However, all the Astro capability-culture assets assumed for the tale are consistent with those observed in IBM UK groups when I worked with them as a consultant in the 1990s and in IBM Canada colleagues when I worked for IBM in various roles in Toronto in the 1960s. IBM has a well-deserved long-standing international reputation for periodically reinventing itself with teams like Martha, Sian, Trevor, Rhys and Ben working together in the way described in this tale.

Martha's capabilities may pose a credibility issue for some people, but in my experience, what is needed to make Martha's success plausible includes a deep understanding of what is interconnected in the industry involved, a deep understanding of how processes can be designed around models to make decision making more effective, what is needed to lead teams making significant changes, and the personality to carry it off. Martha did not have a formal degree-based background in MS/OR, information technology or management. Suitable in-house or open course experience to fill in gaps can clearly be crucial, but a very general initial background like philosophy or history or physics or simple learning by doing on the job from an early age is not an issue, nor is youth, nor is a limited depth of knowledge of the industry. Martha's characterisation deliberately clarifies the need for requisite in-house or open course experience to fill in the gaps, technical input like that provided by Ben plus experience based input like that provided by Trevor, but their inputs plus those provided by Sian and Rhys need the synthesis plus the understanding of process design, strategic vision, and change management capabilities which the tale assumed Martha could provide. A technical background in an area like MS/OR would be a useful asset if it did not detract from Martha's abilities to think and plan top-down as well as synthesise sideways and upwards, and it might make her less dependent on Ben's capabilities. However, when drafting the tale it seemed worth making the point that the capability set provided collectively by Edward and myself plus the IBM sales teams we interacted with via the case study and follow-on consulting exercises could be provided by the Martha, Trevor, and Ben trio plus Sian and Rhys or some other combinations with the same overall capability-culture asset set. The implications if you associate yourself with Martha, Trevor, Ben, Sian, Rhys or higher levels of management could be particularly important.

Another credibility issue which you might reflect on is the way an absence of any of these key inputs or a capability-culture asset set which did not facilitate synthesis in the way achieved by Astro Wales would damage and perhaps destroy the ability of the team to succeed on this scale. The way Trevor, Sian, Rhys and Ben all supported Martha was crucial, as was the way she supported them. This teamwork issue could be particularly important if you associate yourself with comparable teams or have them working on your behalf.

The only really debatable credibility issue is whether someone just out of university like Ben would have the experience necessary to help Trevor be as creative in technical terms as the tale suggests, unless Trevor himself had skills he had been hiding for some reason, or Martha had chosen her professional development short courses *very* effectively, or some lucky combination of all these factors. Arguably someone with much more experience than Ben might be a safer proposition which was very worthwhile, and this is clearly an option you might prefer in practice. However, this aspect of the tail is arguably just a good way to challenge those who associate themselves with Ben, or managing the teaching of people like Ben at universities, and those who associate themselves with Trevor or Martha. Hopefully your credibility has been usefully stretched in a good cause and not permanently damaged.

As in Chapter 5, the UP and the EP perspective as a whole have been used throughout to bring the interpretation up to date. It should be clear that although the context of the tale was the 1990s, the substantive ideas are all relevant to the 2020s and beyond. Furthermore, a periodic need to reinvent successful organisations as well as dealing directly with comparable organisational difficulties in organisations yet to achieve significant success are perennial concerns.

A clear and explicit modelling framework for competitive bidding has been available for some time. The literature I drew on post Friedman (1956) includes Ruthkopf (1983), Samuelson (1986), King and Mercer (1985, 1991), and Tweedley (1995), to illustrate some of the relevant sources. However, in contexts directly comparable to Astro's, very few organisations I have experience of have even approached the effective implementation of these ideas in the way achieved by Astro in this tale, with notable exceptions like IBM UK. Use of the case study underlying this chapter on professional short courses for more than two decades provides considerable evidence of this. The perception of organisations which deliberately avoid such formalisations must be that such formalisations will not be helpful or that they do not want to change their ways and the competition will not force them to change. These perceptions are very risky, as is a failure to even consider the issues. The power of formalisations which can effectively separate the quantitative and the qualitative aspects of complex decisions are increasingly recognised as such formalisations become better developed. If one significant player in any given marketplace adopts the effective use of such approaches, their competitors will have to follow suit or pay a heavy price.

In somewhat different contexts some very sophisticated bidding processes and models are now common practice because others have had to follow where one successful pioneer led. For example, purchasing an airline ticket now usually involves a price set by a 'yield management' system, a bidding process and model allowing airlines to maximise revenue via separate price bids for each flight for each prospective passenger. My understanding is this approach was originally pioneered by an in-house American Airlines MS/OR group. Booking hotel rooms and many other services now involves widespread use of the same approach. The growth of Internet booking and other Internet-based online purchasing decisions can be expected to accelerate the use of simpler variants of the kind of marketing approach explored in this chapter, and more sophisticated variants could also find accelerating interest, both increasing the direct relevance of Astro's approach in post-2020 contexts.

This chapter's stage 2 approach to the probability of winning curves and the stage 3 approach to 'enhanced cost estimation' have been tested in practice as well as being published earlier (Chapman, Ward, and Bennell, 2000). Some aspects of the stage 3 formalisations of the probability of winning curve developed by Trevor and Ben were key new material provided by Chapman and Ward (2002, chapter 3), further evolved in this book, which has not yet been tested in practice. However, one of the reasons many organisations may have failed to adopt formal bidding processes might be resolved by the further new material associated with Table 6.8 and 'Trevor's transformative insights'. The lack of simple explicit ways of considering important individual competitors in the conditional non-price advantage framework of this chapter's tale, plus simple ways of accommodating the rest, may have been a key barrier in the past, a 'missing link' developed into an easier form for practical application during the drafting of this chapter.

This 'enhanced probability of winning' material may help to spread the development of approaches to bidding like that explored in the tale of this chapter, breaking new ground. But its real purpose in this book is illustrating ideas with wider implications. In particular, you might find it useful to understand that the Table 6.8 and Figures 6.14 and 6.15 approaches coupled to Trevor's transformative insights did not 'pop out' until I spent some time thinking about how to make this missing link as simple to use in practice as possible. This implies a key message from this tale is when any aspect of an overall approach does not seem to be working very well, taking the time to explore what alternative working assumptions might work better can be fruitful if you are both persistent and lucky.

A general point worth emphasis in this section is bidding processes are simply a special case of selling a product or service or combination of the two by a 'contractor' (vendor) to a 'client' (purchaser or customer), one way of approaching marketing or purchasing. From both vendor and purchaser perspectives value for money is or should be the crucial issue, not just price. And crucially, a strategic partner approach by both parties can be in the best interests of both parties. These two issues are central to this chapter's tale, and they are key linkages to all other Part 2 tales.

A related final general point worth emphasis in this section is 'marketing' as it is approached by the Astro team in this tale is not separable from 'product development' and 'corporate innovation' more generally, and breaking down the 'Sales' and 'Systems' silos is an obvious early step in dealing with crucial corporate interdependencies which also have to embrace outsourcing with residual strategic partnership linkages as well as forms of insourcing like the friendly takeover of Zoro.

Synthesis and reflections at an overview level

This final section summarises synthesis and reflections on a few aspects of the tale of this chapter at an overview level which you may find helpful for stimulating your clarification of the emerging messages about EP.

Formal analysis of uncertainty to take more risk on some decisions, not less risk

Astro's strategy of developing formal probabilistic based models to take enlightened gambles involving *more* cost risk on each bid, not *less* cost risk, was central to the tale of this chapter and a core component concern in the risk efficiency discussion of Chapter 3. It was also central to the IBM culture change programme that both draw upon. This strategy has general applicability in a very broad sense. Risk efficiency and its generalisation as a central part of opportunity efficiency always imply that it is important to take all risk which is bearable and worth taking, *to increase expected performance*, and this may be crucial to reduce the risk of higher order concerns, like avoiding bankruptcy.

However, taking enlightened gambles in terms of more *cost risk* in all bids does not imply anything about *reputation risk*, and this chapter's tale introduced a red face test to avoid any reputation risk the board did not explicitly condone. Martha explicitly assumed that the board would and should be risk averse in terms of reputation risk, and the board should take responsibility for leading on this issue. Furthermore, there was an unstated assumption that Astro needed to manage higher levels of decision making with due concern for relevant cost and revenue risk comparable to those to be addressed in Chapter 8 but not even mentioned so far in this chapter. For example, at board level Astro Inc needed to address what portfolio of products and services they should be targeting now to characterise where the organisation wanted to be at five or ten year strategic planning horizons. They would have to do this bearing in mind the need for enlightened caution in the context of diversifying efficiently because the information technology business is inherently unpredictable, ideas explored in Chapter 8 needing attention. They would also have to bear in mind the need for each development team to focus on what they believed was the best bet, taking enlightened gambles when appropriate.

A focus on using unbiased expected values when associated variability is 'noise'

If variability associated with expected values is 'noise', not significant 'risk' which needs to be reduced, then we can focus on maximising opportunities in terms of expected outcomes and forget about risk in terms of downside variability relative to unbiased estimates of expected outcomes. Biased estimates of expected values remain an important risk, be it biased estimates of expected outcomes, biased estimates of the probability of key events like winning a contract at a given bid price, or any other key parameter in any context. However, being able to focus on decision making using expected values which can be assumed unbiased is useful because it improves clarity efficiency, letting us focus on what really matters using simpler approaches.

Part 1 introduced this idea, the tale of Chapter 5 made use of it, and this chapter makes a central point of further demonstrating the rationale. Further illustrations are part of all following chapters. A key message in this book as a whole is do not worry about risk that does not matter. Focus your attention on being more effective and efficient at capturing the opportunities that really matter and avoiding the risks that really matter. Opportunities that really matter should be your top priority or first order concern, *almost always*. Risks that really matter should be your second order concern, *whenever relevant*. Persistent bias is usually a risk that matters. A follow-on issue is the almost inevitable need for explicit initial plans to minimise bias plus subsequent data gathering and analysis to monitor and control bias.

Simple strong assumptions which are robust but potentially counter-intuitive

Sometimes it is very useful to employ strong assumptions that are robust but require an appreciation of the underlying complexity to fully understand them because they go beyond natural intuitions, and they may also go beyond common practice. One example is using a perfect positive correlation assumption when adding up nominal minimum and maximum values of cost items to define the overall cost range, as in Table 6.3.

Over many years numerous seminar participants who clearly believed they had a good understanding of correlation have challenged this working assumption, arguing that it is far too pessimistic. They are almost always implicitly arguing that the common practice of assuming independence is preferable. Without making too much of it, my response always begins with the observation that their intuitive preference for assuming independence makes the analysis computations *much more* complex – not simpler. However, the more serious concern is an assumption of independence is almost always seriously and inappropriately optimistic because variability largely cancels out if independence is assumed, even for as few as five items as for this chapter's example. Empirical work with BP on correlation between cost items for refinery projects suggested 0.6 to 0.9 was a common range for the coefficient of correlation, and 0.7 or 0.8 are reasonable best guesses in other contexts if more careful consideration is not worthwhile. This is much closer to 1.0 (perfect positive correlation) than zero (statistical independence). If knock-on, cascade effect and other feedback loop effects are involved, but not fully appreciated and built into the 'unconditional' estimates of component distributions, a perfect positive correlation assumption can actually prove far too optimistic. If the simple procedure of just adding nominal maximum costs suggests a risk level which is tolerable, then a reasonable inference is 'what is *probably* a modestly pessimistic estimate of the range is acceptable and reasonably robust, but it could actually prove optimistic, and any well-founded suspicions about knock-on, cascade effect and other feedback loops concerns should be pursued'. If this estimate of the range suggests associated risk is not tolerable, then *much* more sophisticated estimation of the range is potentially important and well worth undertaking. A common practice default assumption of independence generally involves a failure to even consider these concerns. The seminar participants raising the question are almost always immediately convinced because the underlying complexity is appreciated in a way which adjusts their intuition. My surmise is those who are not convinced simply do not yet understand dependence at an acceptable level.

Managers at senior and intermediate levels in organisations are often dependent on advice being reliable. To be confident that their organisations are effective and efficient, board level managers need to ensure that all those designing and implementing all the decision-making processes used by their organisations fully understand the complexities underlying important simplifying assumptions. Those responsible for selecting or designing processes and training staff to use them need to meet the challenges this raises. Especially for specific processes which are core to an organisation's success, keeping it simple is very important, but doing so appropriately is crucial, a very general concern.

A key risk is organisations using stealth assumptions which matter – assumptions which simplify in the 'wrong way' to a significant extent.

More complex general models which are easier to use than 'simpler' models

The way Ben explained adjusting each competitor's bid for non-price advantage using a constant value which was assumed to be independent of the bid prices was a sensibly simple way to start, keeping it simple to build an initial understanding of the basic framework. That was why this approach was taken in the section dealing with the enhanced probability of winning aspect of the full-day workshop. However, when the generalisations which led to using the 'conditional probabilistic bid adjustment table' portrayed by Table 6.8 and the follow-on use of Figures 6.13–6.15 were explored, it soon became clear that this more complex conditional probability approach was actually *much* easier to use. It provided a *much* clearer understanding of what was involved than the 'simpler' and more restricted portrayals Ben had employed initially, the basis of 'Trevor's transformative insights'.

I was surprised, as I often am, by how a more complex general conceptual framework actually makes it simpler to see what is going on because the additional complexity captures important features of the reality. Assuming away important relevant features of reality is part of the conceptual difficulty people sometimes have with the 'simpler' model, because the gap between the simple model and a more complex reality becomes dysfunctional – the model is not a credible proposition. An ability to keep an open mind on when further generality is likely to prove useful with a nuanced understanding of the implications is a valuable capability-culture asset which all organisations need. It is closely coupled to making understanding easier for those who need new and deeper understanding in order to communicate effectively what they already understand at an intuitive level. Both are closely coupled to understanding when simplicity of particular kinds pays or does not pay. An overview understanding of all three is part of the strategic clarity you need to acquire which all Part 2 chapters build in a layered manner, whether or not you are also interested in associated further tactical clarity. They are also part of the generalisation of constructive simplicity to the aspirational enlightened simplicity target which EP needs to seek.

To be confident that their organisations are effective and efficient, board level managers need to ensure that all those designing or selecting or contracting for their corporate processes fully understand what is involved to a meet the challenges this raises, especially crucial when specific processes which are core to an organisation's success are involved. All those using corporate processes can also contribute to corporate progress in this area if they understand the issues.

Explicitly addressing 'traffic light' issues in qualitative terms

Martha's 'traffic light' approach to stage 1 addresses important concerns needing qualitative treatment via red and blue lights plus an intermediate spectrum. This facilitates giving *qualitative* concerns appropriate direct and explicit consideration when addressing related *quantitative* issues, avoiding inappropriate bias of cost estimates or judgements of appropriate prices as part of the associated process. Even ethical issues can be addressed using this framework. Biased cost and other parameter estimates leading to inappropriate decisions are endemic in many organisations. *Part* of the problem *may* be no formal provision for the separate *qualitative* consideration of important objectives and constraints which should not be addressed by the metrics being used but do need systematic and effective consideration by all relevant parties.

The general issue is making sure that all important concerns are properly addressed in a way everybody understands which is appropriate, effective, and efficient. If important concerns cannot be effectively addressed directly by the cost and margin metrics being used, then addressing them effectively by some variant of Martha's traffic light concept may be crucial. A spinoff will be the removal of bias in estimates of what does need measuring. These issues need attention in a very wide variety of contexts.

The red face test aspect was introduced to me fairly recently by Paul Thornton. But I have found the smiles test for blue light concerns conceptually and operationally useful for many years. Both the frowns test and the halo test concepts have clear complementary roles, completing the 'traffic light' concept expounded by Martha in a form you could build on and adapt to suit the needs of other kinds of organisations.

It is worth reiterating the crucial importance of avoiding a 'white light' averaging of multiple coloured lights – there is no numeric content or inference involved. The common practice use of probability-impact graphs (PIGs) with red to green colour coding addressed in Chapter 7 not only fails to deal with an equivalent 'white light' averaging concern; it fails also to deal with very different basic meanings for 'amber'. In a PIGs context these issues present in a slightly different form. 'Low impact', 'high probability' scenarios and 'high impact', 'low probability' scenarios which *may* both have comparable expected outcomes are both rated 'amber light' concerns in a PIG framework when they obviously have very different implications in an EP framework. Comparable confusion exists for other combinations given the same colour, explored in Chapter 7 in terms of shifting corporate cultures which favour this kind of dysfunctional simplicity towards a more enlightened approach.

A formal corporate approach to not doing 'bad' as well as doing 'good'

The notion that 'doing good is great for business' and associated underlying trends identified by Overman (2014) was discussed in Chapter 5, but some of the underlying issues and trends have different implications in this chapter, directly linked to the way Martha's red face test with board level approvals was managed upwards by Rhys for Astro Wales, as well as opening channels for downward communication by the board. Arguably all organisations need comparable qualitative communication channels *primarily for positive opportunity efficiency reasons which are an internal concern*. That was the way Martha dealt with the red face test in her generalised traffic light framework, with 'smiles' and 'frowns' playing the primary roles, 'halos' and 'red faces' treated as special cases of smiles and frowns. However, from an external perspective with a view to regulation and law enforcement, it is important to protect employees who are not happy with corporate ethics who feel a moral obligation to do more than just vote with their feet (leaving if they are not comfortable), and it is important to make boards accountable for effective processes to ensure that employees who do not uphold corporate standards are required to leave, also facing prosecution if appropriate. This is not an issue in any of this book's tales, but it is a general concern which needs to be addressed effectively.

Process stages, by design, to filter potential opportunities plus other process objectives

Martha developed a formal three stage process to clarify why Astro should not expect to bid in response to every invitation to tender, to begin to use a formal process to discriminate between the opportunities presented at an early stage before too much effort was wasted, and to begin to order the acquisition of knowledge appropriate to rejection or not in an efficient sequence.

An important further feature or benefit of this stage structure was the orderly acquisition of qualitative information which might get overlooked once quantification of a bid began, exploiting the focus on one kind of task at a time to do a better job of each task.

Arguably all potential corporate opportunities need this kind of multiple stage clarity efficient filtering process to exploit systematic acquisition of all relevant information, qualitative and quantitative, in a wide variety of contexts and forms. Seeing they get it should be part of an enlightened approach to all aspects of corporate decision making, at all levels.

The benefits of doing a better job with less effort if carefully planned separability is used are of general relevance – even if filtering is not an issue.

Also of general relevance is our ability to design processes which deliver complex sets of multiple objectives if we are clear about what we want from the processes and how oversimplification in the 'wrong way' can be avoided.

Process iterations within stages by design, to seek more clarity as needed

Astro developed a formal iterative process within stage 3 to mobilise efficient searches for value added and better understand competitors. It was crucial that Astro staff understood why they should not expect to finish pass 1 of stage 3 ready to bid.

A target of expending 10% to 20% of the effort available to achieve completion of the first pass of stage 3 to produce the first version of the PD3 would be reasonable for any variant of this tale, with 80% to 90% left to enhance the bid further using further passes or parallel complementary processes like Trevor's 'search for value added'. This was a simple application of the traditional 80:20 rule – a small proportion of the effort available should be used to identify where a large proportion of the effort should be expended. It is widely applicable and usually usefully approached by a multiple phase approach embedded in a multiple stage approach.

A broader implication is that iterative processes are not just about efficient knowledge acquisition. Iterative processes can be focused on shaping any 'project' being developed, and most sets of corporate opportunities and threats can be viewed as 'projects' which need explicit shaping. Making a bid more attractive in Trevor's competition focused 'value added' terms or Sian's more customer needs driven 'quality' terms are interdependent variants of developing a better business proposition. Arguably all potential corporate opportunities need this kind of clarity efficient shaping process, to add value to opportunities in whatever way this is most usefully understood by all relevant players. Seeing opportunities get this kind of development should be a central part of an enlightened approach to corporate decision-making processes which board level managers understand and insist upon, with corporate teams capable of delivering what is required.

Arguably all potential corporate threats can and should be approached in comparable terms, usually in a single coordinated process which addresses uncertainty and underlying complexity with respect to both opportunities and risks.

Spending more time on what is ill understood, less time on what is understood

Most people involved in bidding processes have rather different expectations to those developed by this chapter's tale. They usually expect to spend *much more* time on costing options using well-understood approaches. They usually expect to spend *much less* time on understanding what advantages competitors can offer, and the implications for pricing decisions if more added value cannot be developed. Astro staff should not have been expecting to spend 80% of the effort available to prepare a bid developing a specification and costing it, followed by 20% considering the competition and pricing the bid, the usual starting position. These ratios can and should be reversed.

A closely related issue is the crucial need for formal systems to help communication between those who currently understand the key complexities in intuitive terms and all other relevant players who also need this expertise in a formalised structure.

A very simple variant of these two related issues is often encountered in terms of a common preference for people in meetings spending a lot of time discussing what is well-understood and easily communicated, much less time on what is unfamiliar or ill understood in a structured sense. It is sometimes referred to as 'the car park syndrome' – because everybody understands and wants to talk about the difficulty involved in parking their car. It is related to a common preference for polishing well-worn tools instead of developing new tools and the new skills needed to use them when it is not clear what these new tools might do or how they might be used. A general implication worth emphasis is the need to focus on what *really* matters most, even if doing so is uncomfortable because it is difficult. We need to consciously avoid just spending our time on what we are most comfortable addressing. We need to be prepared to routinely 'go beyond our comfort zone', as part of aspiring to do better.

Spending more time (not less) on what is ill understood is not common practice for a complex set of behavioural reasons. The need to do so may include coming to terms with why the key to past organisational success is no longer working. Most organisations which have a long-term reputation for success have had to reinvent themselves several times as their history evolved. Astro is portrayed as an organisation needing reinvention, in this sense directly emulating IBM's many very different re-inventions. But addressing a deeper understanding of current success, to leverage it to achieve greater success, is relevant to all organisations which do not take a complacent approach to current success.

This chapter's tale is a story of corporate reinvention, but that is just an extreme variant of the general need to improve organisations on a scale from 'reinvention' to 'continuous improvement'. At any point on this scale what is crucial is the right mix of people, who are collectively able to identify what needs to change and capable of responding to an enlightened appreciation of what needs to be done. Central to corporate reinvention or more modest ongoing incremental change for continuous improvement is getting to grips with what is currently ill understood. Also central is strong corporate leadership which is not necessarily top-down. Nor is it likely to be bottom-up in a simple sense. Corporate change of this kind is often most successful when it is led by intermediate levels of management with crucial teamwork characteristics involving all levels of management, with receptive and supportive top levels of management being particularly crucial. Ensuring that an organisation has the 'right stuff' to deal with these issues is a broad general concern the tale of this chapter tries to address.

Understanding these ideas at board level is important. Even if the board does not lead on these issues, it needs to accept responsibility for encouraging and facilitating those who do, with a clear understanding of what needs to be done and whether it is being achieved.

Top-down use of the UP concept to develop the SP for bidding

Martha had always followed global Astro Inc concerns as well as national Astro UK issues as far as this was feasible given her current Astro roles so that she could understand 'the big picture'. She began her new sales manager job by deliberately avoiding becoming immersed in the details too soon so she could develop an understanding of the strategic level issues which were new to her new role. Her top-down UP approach to the development of an SP for bidding began with a 'capture the context' phase which reflected this perspective.

For example, changing the Astro Wales culture to put Astro Wales firmly on the trajectory she believed the rest of Astro Inc would have to follow sooner or later was part of her initial planning concerns. She did not have any colleagues to discuss this perspective and sense of direction with directly. But she was confident her Astro Wales colleagues would help her to shape her ideas as well as play their role in their development and implementation. The key was convincing them that the basis of her plans made sense from an Astro perspective and from their own perspectives. She was also confident that both Astro UK and Astro Inc would welcome successful bottom-up strategy development with a wider potential application if they could see the merit involved, even if they did not arrive at the same or similar conclusions before this became an issue.

Letting Trevor and Sian develop the PPD as a single stage basis for the three stages of her new approach was an effective starting point for developing the details of the SP for bidding. It captured a current best practice basis for part of her proposed stages 2 and 3, and it provided a clear basis for exposing the imbalance between Sales and Systems inputs in addition to highlighting what was missing in relation to stages 1 to 3.

These are example aspects of Martha's use of the capture the context phase of the UP in a top-down manner, but they also demonstrate some flavour of the select and focus the process, create and enhance plans, and shape the plans using models of key issues phases, as do some further aspects of Martha's approach. For example, encouraging Ben to develop and present the simple, constant non-price advantage version of the stage 3 approach, and then facilitating Trevor to lead development of the more complex but easier to use competitor bid price dependent variant, might have been just good luck of the kind that tends to follow starting with what looks like the simplest approach cast in a general framework with everyone encouraged to test the simplifying assumptions. However, the tale implies that Martha suspected Trevor would be more comfortable using his knowledge in the more general framework he was credited with but deliberately avoided suggesting this framework was a requirement or letting Ben push it at their initial full-day workshop. This was because everybody benefitted from the increase in motivation which cascaded through Sales when Trevor took on important aspects of the shared leadership roles, soon further shared with other industry leads. Encouraging everybody involved to contribute to the shaping of the new bidding process as far as possible was an explicit part of Martha's top-down strategy, a key aspect of her strategic clarity.

The three stage structure of the SP for bidding is itself usefully interpreted as a direct result of the top-down UP select and focus the process approach that Martha used. It facilitated a carefully sequenced series of related but different component processes addressing different sets of issues.

Stage 1 was a question and answer-based qualitative approach which was very simple and quick if only green lights were encountered. It was only moderately complicated by coloured lights. But Martha's red face test was an example of explicitly addressing potentially complex ethical issues which matter a great deal in practice. It used a simple approach which should lead to consistent decisions the board can take responsibility for, as they should. The frowns test, halo test, and smiles test generalisations are also illustrative ways to emphasise simple but effective processes for capturing and continuing to reflect important non-quantitative issues, avoiding some people embedding them in bias but nobody addressing them systematically and effectively. Finding a simple way to capture important corporate concerns in danger of being completely overlooked or ineffectively dealt with is an important opportunity, part of the opportunity efficiency of the approach as a whole.

Stage 2 was a separate minimum clarity quantitative approach, designed with considerable care to achieve clarity efficiency in conjunction with stage 1 in terms of terminating the SP for bidding as quickly as possible if the time saved was better spent in stage 3 for other potential contracts.

Stage 3 used the same phase structure pattern as the stage 2 process, but the stage 3 process added significant complexity in a clarity efficient manner. Understanding broadly what the stage 3 process involved was essential to designing the stage 2 process as a minimum clarity special case and stage 1 as a separate and somewhat different effective and efficient front-end qualitative approach. The three stages were separable by design for sequential use but designed as an integrated interdependent whole.

The create and enhance plans approach in top-down UP terms can also be interpreted as part of Martha's joint approach with Sian and Rhys. Martha was clear from the outset that 'her top-down plans' had to address concerns like dealing with competition between Astro internal groups, subcontractors that were strategic partners and other subcontractors, in addition to outsourcing some current in-house group functions when appropriate to reduce costs, and this had to be incorporated in Astro's SP for bidding to deal with it directly for each specific bid.

The shape the plans using models of some key issues phase was initially focused on models for the stage 2 and 3 processes rather than the wider plans so far as Sales and Systems staff were concerned. These models were important, but they were not a complete answer to the questions being addressed. Crucially, they facilitated both Sales and Systems staff working together to add value and improve Astro competitiveness in terms of all aspects of their bidding plans. The SP for bidding was not just about models. It was about creating and enhancing plans involving both qualitative and quantitative approaches in order to produce a winning bid. Shaping the quality and competitiveness of what Astro offered a customer was *much* more complex than just assessing the cost of a particular assumed approach plus an associated bid price, and formally planning to do so in a clarity efficient manner for all bids was a significant challenge.

The test the plans phase in top-down UP terms was crucial throughout, as was 'interpret the plans to exploit creativity'. 'Implement appropriate aspects of the plans' followed naturally, with Martha taking considerable care to avoid rushing into limiting the flexibility of any key aspects of the approach before testing was based on experience as well as critical thinking and reflection.

Aspects of a bottom-up UP embedded in the SP for bidding

In Chapter 5 the 'models of some key issues' addressed in the shape the plans phase of the UP were generic EOQ model variants in the first three passes. In the tale of this chapter, the models of some key issues from a UP perspective was the three stage SP for bidding – itself a process. Some but not all the features of a bottom-up UP approach are built into this SP for bidding. For example, phase 3.1 (initiation of a pass in stage 3) is directly based on the 'capture the context' and 'select and focus the process' phases of the UP, phase 3.5 (bid evaluation and development) is directly based on the 'test', 'interpret', and 'implement' phases of the UP, and there are some clear relationships in the middle phases of these two processes. However, the 'select and focus the process' aspects of the UP are very restricted within the SP for bidding because the SP for bidding has been carefully tailored in advance to a very specific context to gain efficiency and effectiveness within that context.

In the tale of Chapter 7 an SP for projects is explored which is much closer to an unrestricted UP variant. This chapter's SP for bidding illustrates a midway position.

Comparing top-down and bottom-up UP approaches

In UP terms, 'bottom-up' planning means starting at a fairly low level in terms of a tactical to strategic level of planning spectrum, decomposing in a 'reductionist' mode, and then using a broad synthesis process to reassemble what was decomposed and perhaps take creative leaps further upward. The 'analysis' part of the process is focused at a low level initially, with tentative movement upwards a significant possibility later.

For example, in Chapter 5 Nicola began with a focus on the two key components of the average cost per unit of time for the inventory of controls given the use of an optimal order quantity $Q_0{}^*$. Her pass 2 approach began by extending the EOQ model to address planned stock-outs and then shifted the starting point upwards (to a broader set of concerns) by considering Pete's safety stock for dealing with unplanned stock-outs as well as the order quantity, but it also decomposed the implications of safety stock using a different kind of model, the need for different model forms to address different issues being part of the insight necessary to deal with this higher level perspective. Her pass 3 further decomposed holding costs, recognising that whose money was tied up was crucial, as well as introducing price changes linked to inflation. Her creative leap at the end, further developed by Bob's pass 4 to the My-Place-Your-Timing approach, released TLC from the key limitations associated with the optimal order quantity assumption.

This quite subtle moving up and down was associated with both 'looking wider' and 'looking deeper', key alternative basic UP options as discussed in Chapter 5. This looking wider/up and looking deeper/down feature needed building into the SP for bidding, with the looking wider aspect including going beyond quantitative analysis to address quality and value for money competitiveness concerns, plus a level playing field for internal groups and key subcontractors.

In UP terms, 'top-down' planning means starting as close to the top as is feasible, predominantly working down, although sometimes moving back up beyond the starting point may be very important. The same looking wider, as well as looking deeper, concepts are involved in the UP test and evaluate phases, but the predominant direction of travel is down rather than up.

Ajit was the key top-down thinker in Chapter 5, Martha playing this role in this chapter's tale, as well as guiding the development of the SP for bidding in terms of bottom-up features.

In general, if it is not clear that we need to start low down as in Nicola's case, or as near to the top as we can as in Martha's case, we need to make a judgement and start at whatever level seems suitable for the introduction of UP-based EP approaches. However, working downwards in analysis decomposition terms and the follow-on synthesis putting components together again has to consider a broad approach to synthesis which questions starting point working assumptions to take the process into emergent strategy issues whenever this is appropriate.

Using a top-down UP approach to develop an SP with strategic concerns

When using any variant of the UP concept, the core issues to be modelled when shaping plans are often perceived as particular decisions. However, the core issues modelled can involve the design of appropriate processes for addressing a common set of decisions. In this chapter, the focus was the design of an appropriate SP for bidding to help Astro make systems integration bidding decisions. Figure 6.1 illustrates the stage structure of this SP for bidding, elaborated by Figures 6.2 and 6.4.

One useful way to interpret this SP for bidding is as a form of UP concept which has been made specific to a particular assumed context.

The stage 3 process of Figure 6.4 is itself a specialised variant of the UP concept, designed to develop a successful bid for potential customers when a bid is deemed worth spending time on. Martha's team needed to spend most of their time on the development and then the use of this stage 3 process model, part of the overview process model of Figure 6.1.

The stage 2 process of Figure 6.2 is a special case of the stage 3 process, simplified to a single pass using minimum clarity models to filter out potential bids which are unlikely to provide sufficient margin.

The stage 1 process is a further filter and context capture process designed to clarify whether any further bid development effort makes sense in terms of qualitative issues and, if so, help to clarify what level of margin might be appropriate.

The process model as a whole, as portrayed by Figure 6.1, draws on general purpose UP tools, and the stage 3 component process of Figure 6.4 involves a phase structure which can be directly compared to the UP portrayal of Figure 2.1. However, this stage process and the SP of Figure 6.1 as a whole are specific to bidding for systems integration projects by Astro; they are not 'universal processes'.

The 'specific' nature of this SP for bidding means that its loss of generality carries a price. Each time the Astro SP for bidding is used it may need some further shaping in the context of background ongoing use of the higher level UP. This further shaping may be of a minor kind, to reflect modestly different features of a specific bid. But it might be of a major kind to reflect very different features or unfamiliar characteristics of a novel kind of bidding context or significant lessons learned from bids just lost or won. A radically different type of bid or a significant change in the corporate context may require a major rethink. This price is significant but worth paying because it buys an increase in efficiency and effectiveness in the context the process was designed for.

If the SP for bidding of Figure 6.1 is viewed as a 'process model' created by using the UP of Figure 2.1 applied in top-down and bottom-up terms, it becomes clear that the team of people using the UP need all the associated requisite capabilities, but routine users of the SP for bidding do not require these skills. Martha, Ben, and Trevor working as team were the central contributors to the management of the development of this specific process, Martha largely on her own managing the higher order top-down use of a UP to define the SP for bidding, Ben leading some of the bottom-up UP based content of the SP for bidding. These capabilities in terms of effective use of the UP concept are in the background of this chapter's development because the chapter structure had to focus on the nature of the SP for bidding, but this does not mean these issues are not important. Most of the Sales, Systems, and other staff involved did not need the same UP concept user capability skills as the core team developing the basis of the SP for bidding, but it was very important everybody involved had a reasonable degree of understanding of what was going on, and Martha's leadership with a top-down UP perspective was crucial. Martha and Ben characterise those who need this kind of UP based understanding in depth, but Trevor also needed to develop some directly relevant capabilities, and it will help all those involved in using the SP for bidding if they have strategic clarity about what these capabilities involve at a level of sophistication appropriate to their role.

When the tale of this chapter began, Martha had strategic clarity in terms of a broadly defined game plan which evolved, shaped by her top-down UP approach. She knew that she had a change programme to manage from the outset, and bidding for systems integration projects was recognised as a useful vehicle for this broader ambition early in the tale. But Martha did not know how the story would evolve at the outset. The conceptual framework she used is usefully interpreted as a UP applied to building an SP for bidding, but mapping higher level formal processes onto successful practice is rarely simple or straightforward.

All these ideas can be applied in any area of an organisation's operations which needs change. If you want to apply them yourself, or have others apply them for you, the way forward may not be obvious or straightforward. However, developing new tools to deal with what your organisation does not understand very well can be much more fruitful than polishing existing tools.

7   Adapting 'generic processes' – a project planning example

Planning for 'projects' has received a lot of attention in the management literature. However, when drawing on this literature, it is often worth remembering that some common practices receiving a lot of attention adopt *MUCH* narrower interpretations of both 'projects' and associated 'project risk management' than the perspective adopted in this book.

In this book 'projects' are *VERY* broadly defined, and it is useful to understand the nature of this breadth in three separate senses:

1   embracing not only the creation of physical assets like buildings but also the management of change which may not involve a physical asset, as in a culture change programme or a decision-making process;
2   accommodating distinctions among projects, programmes, and portfolios of projects and programmes, when this is important, but for simplicity sticking to 'projects' terminology to cover all three most of the time;
3   addressing the whole project lifecycle, defined in terms of the lifecycle of the asset produced by the project, from concept initiation to termination of the asset's relevance.

Developing a '*specific* uncertainty and complexity management *process* for projects', an 'SP for projects' concept, is the central mission for this chapter. The SP for projects is an operational tool which also serves very broad background conceptual roles – it is a very high level gateway concept as well as an operational tool for direct application.

Chapter 1 introduced project planning at an overview level and developed a 'four Fs' concept in general framing assumption terms, a high level gateway concept involving four component frameworks which are each lower level gateway concepts: a project lifecycle framework, the seven Ws framework, a goals–plans relationships framework, and a process framework that builds on the other three frameworks. This process for project planning is given an operational form in this chapter, as the SP for projects, and it makes use of operational examples of the other three components of the four F, using working assumptions suitable for the example context of the tale. The resulting operational form for all four Fs is relevant to all the organisation's projects in the tale. It is specific to the context of the tale, but it is an illustrative example with a very general nature, and each of the four Fs operational frameworks discussed can have their working assumptions tested and adjusted as necessary for all contexts of interest to you and your organisation.

Most of the issues addressed in this chapter draw on a wide range of both successful and unsuccessful engagements with organisations in a wide range of industries. In the successful category relevant examples which stand out include BP International, National Power, Sir William Halcrow and Partners, Severn Trent Water Authority, British Maritime Technology,

Gulf Canada, Petro-Canada, Fluor Engineers and Contractors Inc, Statoil, NatWest Bank, Consorzio Venezia Nuova, IBM UK and the UK Highways Agency. In the mixture of success and failure category examples which stand out include the Alaska Power Authority, UK Nirex and the UK Ministry of Defence (MoD). Each of these engagements taught me important lessons and helped to shape the approaches discussed. The reasons will be indicated when directly relevant and generally useful.

Even if you have a limited interest in project planning at present, the basic ideas explored in this chapter are a core component of the overall EP framework, and there are several useful implications for all aspects of decision making in all organisations. For example, the SP for bidding developed in Chapter 6 can be usefully viewed as a special case of the SP for projects developed in this chapter. In addition, the approach which Martha took to developing the SP for bidding can be usefully viewed as a further higher order application of the SP for projects approach developed in this chapter. That is, Chapter 6 uses the SP for projects developed in this chapter in two different ways at two levels as part of its use of the UP concept at various levels. Deferring formal consideration of project management until now allows us to build on concepts explored in Chapters 5 and 6 as well as Part 1 at a convenient point in the development of EP as a whole.

Generic processes used for project planning

Project management as a separate management profession with its own professional societies has been growing at a significant rate since the 1950s. There has been a related growth in the associated professional knowledge base, including a wide range of models, 'techniques' and 'generic processes'. However, for what might be perceived as territorial reasons in part, some professional project management societies tend to promote a relatively narrow view of projects, with what might be seen as a natural tendency to overemphasise the current roles of the majority of the practicing project managers who belong to the societies, to some extent inhibiting evolution to broader roles for 'project management' as a central aspect of all management. Everyone interested in management decision-making needs to understand the techniques and generic processes involved in what needs to be done terms.

'Techniques' for project planning can be interpreted as simple SPs: generic models embedded in a simple associated process which have been generalised to accommodate comparable contexts in all organisations. For example, CPM (Critical Path Method) is often referred to as a 'technique', sometimes using the alternative label Critical Path Analysis (CPA). In its initial basic form CPM involves a finish-to-start activity-on-arrow precedent relationship network diagram model. This model is embedded in a simple iterative process for planning project activities. It was initially developed by a team of consultants for Westinghouse in the US in the 1950s, primarily for factory construction and refurbishment projects. It was very quickly adopted as a basic tool by most project planners and used across a very wide range of organisations and projects, along with PERT (Program Evaluation and Review Technique). PERT is a simple stochastic model variant of CPM, developed by another team of consultants for the US Navy and the Polaris Missile project. For an early but still useful introduction to both and subsequent generalisations see *Project Management with CPM and PERT* (Moder and Philips, 1970). CPM and PERT both exploited newly available computer support approaches and built on earlier models. For example, Henry Gantt's bar chart, widely used for project planning in the early 1900s, became the basis of the 'linked bar chart' concept, illustrated earlier in this book in Figure 4.4 and employed again later in this chapter.

Generic processes are a more recent development. A broad interpretation of generic processes is that they are SPs which have been generalised beyond the scope of specific techniques like CPM or PERT to accommodate much broader families of relevant models and processes, and they should help users to choose appropriately from the available families of options.

If this broad interpretation of generic processes is used, an important feature is some variant of the UP 'select and focus the process' phase being incorporation in the associated SP to *explicitly* facilitate the use of different variants of the generic process for different kinds of models for different projects in different contexts. For example, the Association for Project Management (APM) *PRAM Project Risk Analysis and Management Guide* (APM, 1997) involved a working party of about 20 people synthesising what they saw as best practice processes across all UK users of project risk management models, techniques, and processes. From my perspective, the inclusion of a 'focus the process' phase variant of the UP select and focus the process phase was a defining characteristic of the PRAM approach, making it unequivocally a generic process. I drafted the process chapter of the 1997 PRAM guide, and co-authored a 2004 version, having earlier served as the founding chair of the APM Specific Interest Group for Project Risk Management which produced the PRAM Guides as part of its evolving role (Hillson, 2012).

The initial trigger for including an explicit focus the process phase in PRAM, the first time I used this concept explicitly, was addressing the need to accommodate a wide range of views about what models and associated processes work best in different contexts, based on an implicit assumption that members of the working party producing the PRAM Guide held different views because we had worked in different contexts, and agreement on 'best' practice would be reached this way. Alternative views were strongly held and firmly advocated, sometimes with more heat than light, although we all remained civil, empathetic, and friendly. It is now clear that achieving a clear consensus amongst all those involved in PRAM and other guides about 'best', 'good', and 'bad' practice was a crucial goal at the time which we failed to achieve. It is still an ongoing issue in a PRAM context, with comparable differences of opinion across the project management profession, only partially reflected by differences between guides. The way PRAM as published uses the focus the process phase was agreed and remains an important evolutionary step in generic processes, but the PRAM focus the process phase did not resolve all the differences of opinion which triggered making it explicit.

The aspect of project management which I have been most closely associated with since the 1980s is commonly referred to as 'project risk management'. However, my interpretation of what needs to be done under this heading is more accurately referred to as 'project uncertainty and complexity management which addresses opportunity first, risk second, in a manner fully integrated with project management as a whole'. For example, *How to Manage Project Opportunity and Risk: Why Uncertainty Management can be a Much Better Approach than Risk Management* (Chapman and Ward, 2011) provides a generic process referred to as a 'performance uncertainty management process', contracted to 'PUMP'. This 2011 book is the third edition of *Project Risk Management: Processes, Techniques and Insights* (Chapman and Ward, 1997, 2003), retitled to make it clear that our interpretation of project risk management is not the conventional interpretation. All three editions were based on an evolving synthesis of SPs for projects and other closely coupled frameworks developed for a range of client organisations, plus my experience and Stephen Ward's experience contributing to the working parties producing several 'generic' project risk management guides, including PRAM (APM, 1997, 2004) and *Risk Analysis and Management for Projects – RAMP* (ICE and IFoA, 1998, 2005).

Project risk management generic processes are very widely deployed. The most widely used is probably the Project Management Institute (PMI) approach described in the PMBoK Guides (PMI, 2008, 2009, 2013, 2017a), but there are many others.

Both relatively simple techniques like CPM and PERT and relatively sophisticated generic processes like PRAM and PUMP are usefully seen as SPs which are relevant to project management. An important common feature of all SPs is they require initial development using a UP concept (or comparable general process – implicitly if not explicitly). Furthermore, their ongoing use in different contexts requires adaptation using a UP concept (or comparable general process) unless some variant of the UP concept is effectively built into the SP to make it 'universal' in the full set of contexts where it might be used. Making an SP for projects 'universal' in all project management contexts is a strategy explored in an initial manner towards the end of this chapter, but the focus is transforming a very broadly defined generic process into an even broader SP for projects within a particular organisation.

This chapter uses the UP concept plus other relevant concepts to generate an SP for projects which is suitable for all aspects of project planning within an illustrative specific organisation. In doing so, the SP for projects developed in this chapter makes extensive use of the performance uncertainty management process, or PUMP, developed more fully by Chapman and Ward (2011) – PUMP is a central component of the overall approach taken. However, there are two very fundamental and crucial differences in perspective.

First, PUMP uses what is referred to as a 'performance lens'. The purpose of this performance lens concept is emphasising a focus on project performance when PUMP is used to *shape* project plans. What is crucial in the context of this chapter is appreciating that the PUMP approach *assumes that the plans were probably initially created and developed prior to 'project risk management' shaping of project plans using separate processes involving separate people if PUMP is replacing widespread common practice.* The rationale was accommodating the common perspective that project risk management should contribute to project management but maintain a separable role executed by separate people. PUMP as developed by Chapman and Ward (2011) introduces, but does not fully develop or exploit, a linked 'knowledge lens' associated with 'What else do we need to know to get to the next stage of the overall project planning process?' Although Chapman and Ward (2011) argue that full integration with the rest of project management is essential, using both lenses, the case for doing so is made from a perspective that those familiar with common practice project risk management approaches can identify with and feel comfortable with. This chapter uses an explicit 'planning lens' which operates as a performance lens plus a knowledge lens. The intention is fully embedding the PUMP concepts in an SP for projects concept which addresses all relevant aspects of project planning in a direct manner from an EP perspective. The starting position is a fully integrated approach which addresses creating and enhancing all relevant plans as well as shaping them using PUMP concepts. The embedding of PUMPs in a holistic approach to project planning argued for by Chapman and Ward (2011) is implemented directly in the tale of this chapter.

Second, the 'basic' PUMP discussion that Chapman and Ward (2011) start with is focused on the execution and delivery strategy stage of the project lifecycle. In part this was because the origins of PUMP in terms of my early work with BP were focused on this stage of the project lifecycle, and I had a much wider range of experience with this stage than other stages. A more important second reason was most members of the PRAM working party (which significantly influenced PUMP in terms of mid-1990s developments) were more concerned with this stage or the later detailed planning, execution, and delivery stages, as were most APM members. An underlying third reason was the project management profession as a whole tends to have minimal involvement or interest in the early portion of project lifecycles, with notable exceptions like RAMP (ICE and IFoA, 1998, 2005). This chapter explicitly addresses the implications of the third reason. It starts with a focus on the concept strategy stage of the project lifecycle. The use of PUMPs from the outset of the project lifecycle, which is argued for by both Chapman and Ward (2011) and the RAMP guides, is implemented directly in the tale of this chapter.

The SP for projects approach developed in this chapter might be interpreted by some advocates of project risk management as a takeover of project planning which is likely to offend project managers. On this basis they might judge it as 'a bridge too far' (a World War II analogy involving a strategic failure because a stretch target proved too ambitious). Some people concerned with project management as a whole who have a limited interest in project risk management may share this view.

Furthermore, the SP for projects approach developed in this chapter might be interpreted by some advocates of project management as a significant unwarranted extension of project planning and management, likely to offend many people project managers report to or work alongside, a second bridge too far. However, the intended and much more fruitful interpretation is a long overdue takeover of project risk management, including PUMP and all other generic processes like PRAM and RAMP, by a more enlightened approach to planning projects which incorporates coordinated involvement of operations and corporate management with a much broader and more effective form of project management.

This book promotes the perspective that enlightened planning of projects should start with project concept creation, involving all relevant players, addressing all relevant uncertainty in a systematic manner. It then has to build on this foundation throughout the whole lifecycle of the asset created by the project. Sometimes the conventional 'from the cradle to the grave' expression may be apt, but usually a much more appropriate phrase is 'from conception to "legacy" – for however long the legacy implications need considering'. Net Present Value (NPV) issues become particularly crucial when long time horizons need effective treatment, and legacy issues can involve relevant time horizon issues which are infinite for all practical purposes.

This EP starting position conflicts with the traditional position of some project management professionals. An example is those who take a contractors' perspective and see their role in terms of the project execution and delivery aspects of project lifecycles, assuming that project owners know what they want and that after delivery of the asset is achieved the project is complete – the rest of the asset lifecycle is somebody else's problem.

This EP starting position also conflicts with the idea that project risk management can be treated as a separable silo within the project management profession, and the project management profession can be treated as a silo separable from operations and corporate management.

Key implications of eliminating this nested silo approach need to be seen as important by everyone who is interested in any areas and aspects of management in all organisations. The concerns addressed in this chapter are not just project management concerns – they are central to *all* planning.

The need to clarify ambiguity

One useful aspect of using multiple stages in a project lifecycle framework is a framework for explicitly cultivating an enlightened view of ambiguity which involves seeking 'clarified ambiguity'. This involves recognising that *some* ambiguity needs early resolution, but leaving 'the right kind of ambiguity' in plans may provide very important benefits, and we have no choice about other kinds of ambiguity. Put slightly differently – not all ambiguity is equally bad. Some ambiguity may not matter, some may be irritating but relatively harmless, some may be serious and resolvable but only at considerable cost, and some is inevitable even if it is a problem. This implies a sound case for formally planning a roughly optimised sequence and timing for addressing all the different kinds of ambiguity, with a view to clarifying it in an opportunity efficient manner as part of our clarity efficiency concept.

Five basic reasons for developing this clarified ambiguity perspective are the following:

1   Some aspects of both strategy and tactics are usefully given priority because of inherent precedence relationships – it is simply not possible to do everything at one time, and some things are better done earlier, leaving other things until later.

2   Telling people what you want done, and why, is usually much more effective and efficient than telling them what to do in detail, *PROVIDED they are competent and imaginative, and you can trust them to pursue aligned interests.* The basis of this idea can be linked to a useful quotation attributed to General George Patton (Ambrose, 1994): 'Tell people what you want done, not how to do it, and you will be amazed by their ingenuity'. But it also involves *very important provisos*.

3   It is always cost-effective to clarify strategic choices before spending a lot of time on detailed planning for implementation purposes, *although we do need to be aware that sometimes 'the devil is in the detail'.* This idea can be usefully generalised to include 'angels in the detail'. Strategic clarity includes clarity about how to capture the opportunities which different kinds of 'angels' offer, as well as how to deal with the 'devils', and this aspect of strategic clarity is a very important corporate capability.

4   At the outset of a substantial project all plans are necessarily very ambiguous. The people who are being asked, 'What will it cost?' and 'How long will it take?' to deliver objectives which those formulating the project have yet to fully define face ambiguity which is so large, and so uncomfortable, that most organisations have some degree of 'a culture of denial' about this kind and level of uncertainty. This is understandable, but it can be seriously dysfunctional. The first step to avoid the problems which usually flow from this 'uncertainty denial' is recognising the size and shape of the ambiguity involved, its implications, how best to confront it explicitly and directly, and how best to exploit potential positive aspects as well as avoiding potential negative aspects. Using interval (range-based) estimates, with any key 'conditions' (associated assumptions) clearly stated and understood, are essential aspects of this. So are the ABCs of targets, with clear distinctions drawn between all three target types and expected values whenever this is appropriate – most of the time in practice.

5   Usually, as soon as any single-value 'point estimates' of a project's profit, cost, duration or quality measures are agreed on, opportunity efficient decision making starts to become increasingly handicapped until it becomes obvious that the point estimates adopted have become inappropriate and need to be changed. This is because the focus soon becomes staying within bounds on key performance measures when these bounds have become inappropriate. Frequently, cycles of successive changes which are inherently opportunity inefficient to an obvious extent become 'the norm'. Along the way, opportunities are lost and threats are dealt with ineffectively. Furthermore, usually the process of successively changing point estimates results in an inevitable loss of trust and permanently damaged relationships. All these effects are dysfunctional for some key parties, although other parties may prosper from dysfunctional relationships, and may

be motivated to encourage them. The biggest cost may be the opportunity inefficiency associated with failing to pursue aggressive stretch targets to manage good luck, failing to respond effectively and efficiently to bad luck, taking inappropriate amounts of risk (too much or too little), and generally failing to even understand the opportunities or risks involved.

To respond to reasons four and five an enlightened approach to ambiguity *always* avoids point estimates unless appropriate aspirational targets and commitment targets are identical (zero provision plus zero contingency is appropriate). This is because point estimates fail to address any kind of uncertainty, never mind facilitating monitoring and managing ambiguity with clarity efficiency. If significant ranges are a feature of early estimates, this clarifies the need to systematically reduce associated uncertainty, *making VERY clear distinctions between uncertainty and risk*. Reasons one, two and three underlie reasons four and five, and collectively all five reasons may help to clarify why the very general notion

we always need to be clear about the nature, size and shape of all the ambiguity involved

is not the paradox it may sound. It is the basis of a useful 'clarified ambiguity' concept. You may even find a version of this notion a useful mantra.

Some aspects of clarified ambiguity underlie the discussion of Chapters 3 and 4. In addition, some features were developed in the three stage SP for bidding of Chapter 6. This chapter makes the clarified ambiguity concept explicit as a useful way to visualise the management of knowledge as a project evolves in a more traditional project context than 'forerunner to a traditional project' operations management 'bidding project' context of Chapter 6. There are closely coupled implications for all operations and strategic management processes.

The context and characters of this chapter's tale

The context used for the tale of this chapter draws upon my experience as a non-executive director of Southern Water, for six years beginning in 1997. This was a period of significant changes in the UK water and sewage utility sector. It also draws on important positive features of Southern Water approaches, including capability-culture assets of their executive directors throughout my involvement, but a disguised version of Southern Water is not involved.

The water and sewage utility context of this chapter is useful because the key features of project planning 'best', 'good' and 'bad' practice which this particular example context helps to clarify have general implications for most decision making in all organisations, including the importance of dealing appropriately with the cost of capital and other relevant factors when determining the discount rates used to shape what projects deliver and how their execution is approached as well as the decisions about which projects should be undertaken.

The main characters in the tale of this chapter are seven of the directors on the board of Water and Sewage Limited (WSL):

Paul, Projects Director, recently appointed;
Ollie, Operations Director;
Frank, Finance Director;
Richard, Regulation Director;

> Curt, Customer Relations Director;
> Michael, Managing Director;
> Charles, Chairman of the Board.

When he was appointed Projects Director of WSL in 2012, Paul had 30 years of project experience, mainly with design and construction contractors. His initial training was civil engineering, and if asked what he did in casual conversation he replied, 'civil engineering'. But he had always been a serious student of all aspects of management relevant to his job.

WSL had been privatised in the early 1990s, along with all other UK water and sewage providers. Like many of the other UK water and sewage companies, WSL used bond funding for about 80% of its capital value to gear up the return on shareholder equity capital in the face of multiple regulator pressures on profits from two directions: constraining prices to look after water and sewage customer interests in terms of cost and constraining water supply and wastewater quality to look after health and environmental interests.

Paul's most recent job was programme manager for a major sewage scheme constructed by a civil engineering contractor for WSL. This project was completed on time and under budget, part of the reason Paul was head-hunted for his new post, his first in a 'client-side' organisation. Paul had limited earlier experience in the water and sewage industry but significant relevant earlier experience in the UK oil and gas industry and some road and rail construction industry experience in other European countries and in the US. Crucially, he had introduced significant changes in the practices and processes of his previous employer which were highly relevant to WSL needs.

Paul had attended a 2011 IPMA (International Project Management Association) advanced training programme in Milan based on Chapman and Ward (2011) and understood its concepts. He had attended an earlier version of the same course in Copenhagen a decade earlier, and he became an experienced user of early variants of most EP concepts soon after.

After taking up his WSL appointment, one of Paul's first actions was to hold an initial workshop for his 'Projects Group' staff to explain:

1   the role of 'project management' within WSL as he saw it,
2   the role of the Projects Group within WSL and his role as he saw it,
3   a new Projects Group structure they would target as of that day,
4   some very basic problems the new Projects Group structure would address, and
5   four frameworks which all WSL projects under his control would use, the four Fs.

The role of project management within WSL

Paul began his initial workshop by suggesting that from the perspective of all those seeking overall corporate opportunity efficiency, project management had to be seen as an integral part of three related perspectives on management: corporate management, operations management, and project management. He used his variants of the EP language developed earlier in this book to a significant extent, always explaining it to his colleagues when appropriate in language they were comfortable with. The concepts involved in terms like 'opportunity efficiency' will not be considered again in this chapter unless specific aspects need emphasis, but the terms 'corporate management', 'operations management', and 'project management' are worth brief reconsideration now, with a focus on the concerns which Paul emphasised.

Operations management involved a creative top-down approach to business as usual, integrated downwards with all appropriate bottom-up planning of business as usual, integrated sideways with all projects concerned with new relevant assets and other related corporate changes, and integrated sideways and upwards with corporate management.

Corporate management involved a creative top-down approach to corporate strategy formation, fully integrated with all relevant bottom-up approaches. It also involved overall corporate responsibility for governance and all corporate resources and competencies. Not all corporate management was at a 'higher' level – a simple example at a 'lower' level was human resource management involving operations management roles like water metre reading.

One key role of project management was the change management component which interfaced corporate and operations management. However, many of the ongoing operations and corporate management activities within an organisation could also be given a project management perspective, including decision making and change management. 'Projects' in this very broad sense included programmes and portfolios of projects.

The role of the Projects Group within WSL

All WSL staff in the Projects Group reported to Paul. The remit of the WSL Projects Group was projects involving the construction of physical plant and facilities – engineering projects like new water mains and sewage collection pipes, new water treatment plants and sewage treatment works. The Projects Group's remit did not extend to projects undertaken under the auspices of other directors. For example, information systems projects were the responsibility of the information technology director plus the directors whose systems were being addressed, like Finance. Nor did the Projects Group have any responsibility for project management in the very broad sense which included decision making and change management in operations or corporate planning contexts. In the longer term, Paul wanted to *influence* all WSL project management practice, by examples of Projects Group best practice and by helping other groups to embed compatible project management practices in their groups to facilitate joint working. His long-term overall ambitions included full integration of best practice project management with corporate management and operations management. However, Paul had no wish to redefine the current boundaries of responsibilities for the Projects Group, and he saw it as very important that all Projects Group staff understood both the wider possible implications of the changes Paul would be making and the considerable sensitivities associated with group and departmental boundaries that might be triggered by some of the changes he would stimulate. All members of his group needed to understand and support his concerted efforts to ensure that nobody outside the Projects Group felt inappropriately threatened by the significant changes Paul was planning to make.

Paul explained that he saw his WSL board membership role in terms of contributing to overall WSL governance and some aspects of overall WSL strategy shaping in addition to reporting on his responsibilities as head of the Projects Group. He indicated that Ollie, the operations director and head of the Operations Group, had a directly comparable role for operations in the physical plant and facilities sense. However, Frank, the finance director; Richard, the regulation director; Curt, the customer relations director; Ian, the information technology director; and Hannah, the human resources director, all had responsibilities at board and group or department levels which were somewhat different in terms of interactions. All these interfaces had to be managed by Charles, the chairman of the board (a non-executive chair appointed by the company which owned WSL), Michael, the managing director (the chief executive officer or CEO), plus all other board members working as an integrated group.

The new structure of the WSL Projects Group

Paul then indicated that his view of the role of the Projects Group meant that as of that day they needed to start working together as a single 'Projects Group planning team' – the 'PG planners' or the 'PG team' when these contractions were useful.

By PG 'planners' he meant PG 'EP planners' using an '*enhanced* planning' label for the '*enlightened* planning' concept developed earlier in this book they would all adopt as their basic planning framework, which he would outline that day and continue to clarify in a project planning context. He made it clear that there was a need to distinguish current WSL 'planning' from a very different EP approach they would all adopt starting that day, but it was important to avoid any hint of pretention and possible associated empire building which might threaten other groups and reduce their willingness to collaborate, his rationale for interpreting EP as 'enhanced planning' for WSL purposes.

A key feature of this new PG team was eliminating the existing departmental boundaries which currently placed everybody into one of three departments: the estimating department, the planning department, or the risk management department. Currently staff in these three departments initially became involved in projects separately, in a sequence which began with estimating, put risk management in the middle, and put planning supported by further estimating and risk management at the end.

From the outset the PG team was going to provide cost estimates as a part of a revised fully integrated planning remit. The new remit involved uncertainty and complexity management which included risk management plus opportunity management built into all planning and costing involving the PG team from the concept stage initiation of projects. All existing skills and experience would need integration with new concepts and capabilities in a new framework. In the short run, the existing management support functions would remain in place, but as of that day they would start working together in teams which cut across departmental boundaries, developing new processes which helped to integrate their toolsets, skill sets and mindsets.

The new PG team structure would involve the current Projects Group heads of estimating, planning and risk management being *promoted* to senior PG planning managers, with significantly broader and more flexible remits than at present. He had spoken to all three departmental heads earlier and had their support. All other PG staff – previously in one of these three groups – would be given comparable PG team positions. He had not spoken to any of them individually yet, because he thought it best to let them all know at the same time as soon as possible, but he would have individual meetings with everyone as soon as this could be arranged.

The basic idea in terms of staff structure was breaking down the current departmental silos, moving to a much more flexible multi-skilled team approach, initially with larger teams than would be the case later, to facilitate learning from each other and joint 'learning by doing' while they were transforming the way the Projects Group operated. There would be scope for 'promoting' a number of people because most people would need a wider and more flexible skill set in relation to new roles, but some people with specialist expertise would be less affected than others. Meeting mutually agreed-on personal capability development goals, with sustained WSL support from him and all senior PG managers, was the general idea.

Paul made it clear that he would work with everyone involved to ensure that the new more flexible structure worked as smoothly as possible from the outset. He would always welcome one-to-one confidential discussions about problems of any kind, and he was looking forward to ensuring that tensions created by the changes were constructively and creatively resolved. He emphasised that in private conversations open and candid constructive criticism of his approaches would always be welcomed, but the direction and degree of change being pursued would have to be embraced positively to remain a member of the PG team.

Paul indicated that more workshops and some training exercises would be an early priority, but to some extent they would all have to learn by doing, initially working with larger teams than usual to ensure cross-fertilisation of ideas from the currently different perspectives of planning, costing, and risk specialists. Their first few exercises should be seen as development projects initially and then demonstration projects. These early projects would be investments in the development of their new working practices, which could then be used to demonstrate what was involved. The initial focus would be on effectiveness, with later refinement also concerned with achieving efficiency.

Paul explained that he had outlined his proposed approach to restructuring the Projects Group and the way it would operate to Michael, their managing director, prior to accepting his appointment. He now had Michael's approval for a reasonably detailed change management programme, which included changing the current PG departmental structure and that day's workshop. Charles, chairman of their board, was fully informed and supportive. But Paul had not yet discussed his approach with other directors.

Basic problems the new structure would address

Paul indicated that the new PG team structure was just part of the move to a new PG approach to projects involving a wide range of changes with advantages and implications he would gradually explain in detail. He would start by indicating some basic aspects of the underlying 'mess' which the new PG team structure would help the new PG approach address. By 'mess' he meant a set of important basic 'problems' which were fundamental and not easily separated or decomposed because of complex interconnections, but they could also use a plain English interpretation of 'mess'.

Currently, when a new project was being conceived, early PG team involvement was limited to the estimating department providing a point (single-value) estimate of construction cost. Later the risk management department used event-based common-practice project risk management techniques to provide a cost estimate 'risk adjustment', also a point estimate, derived via the expected value of a probability distribution defined by 'risk' probabilities and their impact probability distributions. Later still, following on from considerable expenditure on project development in terms of operating and design features, the Planning Department became involved, with further follow-on involvement from the Estimating Department and the Risk Management Department. About this time serious cost escalation usually set in, building on some earlier cost escalation while design issues were addressed. By the time a contract was signed for execution and delivery, the original 'risk adjusted estimate' had almost always been increased, by an average of about 50% with a range of about 20% to 150%. Even then most projects still came in over budget and late, sometimes badly over budget and seriously late.

The recent WSL sewage plant project which he had been involved in as the contractor's programme manager came in under budget and on time, but this was an exception to the norm, and the contracted budget was 60% more than the original board-approved 'risk adjusted cost estimate'. Some of this 60% increase arose because the head of planning in the Projects Group had become involved after the initial budget was approved, and Planning Department input plus follow-on input from the other two Projects Group departments had consolidated a cost escalation process triggered by Planning Department input which should have preceded setting the initial budget. But Paul had been forced to make a convincing case for a significant further increase, his ability to justify doing so, and then deliver the project within budget and on time, being part of the reason for his appointment to his current post.

These large cost increases after initial project approval based on a 'risk adjusted estimate' were not just a minor common problem to be accommodated. They were significant symptoms of a large set of serious underlying concerns. Paul understood why (in terms which build on your understanding of all previous chapters), but he needed to transfer this understanding to his team members gradually, layer by layer, building on their current base point.

One of the concerns this systematic cost growth revealed was a lack of WSL planning which fully integrated the management of opportunity, risk, uncertainty and complexity from the outset. This, in turn, required fully integrating not just the skill sets and toolsets of the PG team but also the skill sets and toolsets of other WSL groups and departments and WSL contractors. What was involved was not a single 'problem' with a simple solution – it was a very large mess of interconnected sets of problems which needed holistic resolution.

The PG team would have to undertake a portfolio of programmes to resolve this mess in conjunction with other WSL groups. Paul had clear ideas about the resolution of the mess in terms of the overall shape of his strategy and targets, but the details were unclear, the strategy was still fluid, and some of the WSL staff they were going to have to work with closely were not yet involved.

Paul indicated that this mess was the result of *some* common corporate practices which he saw as problems to be resolved or dissolved from a systems analysis perspective, not solved individually. He made it very clear that *some* common practices were very good practice, but *some* common practices were not good practices, and *some* of the common practices adopted by WSL were so bad they had to be changed as soon as possible.

In his view, endorsed by the WSL board, 'the current WSL overall approach to Planning Group projects was not fit for purpose, and its transformation needed immediate attention, beginning with the WSL approach to the concept strategy stage of the project lifecycle for all projects within the remit of the Projects Group'. Paul made it clear that Projects Group were not fully responsible for this situation, but he had been hired to sort it out, he was directly accountable for sorting it out, and he was determined to see to it that all the needed changes were made within a reasonable timeframe.

The first step to resolve the aspects of this mess which he had direct control over was starting to move to a new PG team structure. The next step was everybody in WSL starting to understand four crucial frameworks which he would refer to as the 'four Fs'. The four Fs were the basis of the new PG team approach to project planning they would be working with. Each of the four component frameworks was usefully seen as a 'tool' in the conceptual model sense, with some crucial operational toolset implications. *Everybody* within WSL – including all board members – would need to make direct use of the first two of these new frameworks. The PG team would need to make direct use of all four Fs in a fully integrated manner.

Each of the four Fs would now be considered, in turn, in some detail: a project lifecycle framework, the seven Ws framework, a goals–plans relationships framework, and a specific planning process framework for projects (SP for projects) with an initial focus on the front-end strategy development stages of the project lifecycle.

A project lifecycle framework

Paul indicated that a project lifecycle was the first framework which WSL as a whole needed to understand in terms of a common portrayal for all WSL projects involving the Projects Group because the rest of the four Fs built upon this foundation. He would refer to a *'project'* lifecycle to follow convention, but it was the *'asset'* lifecycle he was talking about – the lifecycle of the asset created by the project from its conception until its disposal or in some cases until the end of its 'legacy'. In their case, physical assets like water mains and sewage works were the immediate focus. However, corporate change management projects also produced an 'asset' which warranted design and execution and utilisation planning within the same project lifecycle concept.

The basic role a project lifecycle concept serves is providing a time-based framework for staged evolution of 'the project' so that different parties can play different roles in an effective and efficient sequence as inherent ambiguity in a project is systematically clarified.

A traditional four stage project lifecycle structure

To clarify what was involved, Paul explained that he would initially consider a traditional four stage view of a project's lifecycle from a client organisation's perspective, incorporating stated assumptions about the dominant management aspects of each stage. Because they would have to consider several project lifecycle structure definitions, he would refer to his initial example as 'stage structure one', contracted to 'SS1'. This SS1 version of a traditional four-stage project lifecycle from a client perspective used an *asset* lifecycle basis, because from a client perspective the utilisation stage was central to the rationale for the project. He then showed his team the SS1 lifecycle portrayal of Table 7.1.

His first observation was that a common practice variant often used by project management professionals working for contractors involved dropping the 'utilisation' stage and separating 'execution' and 'delivery', with delivery of the asset ending the project lifecycle. From a contractor perspective this could make a lot of sense, but the utilisation stage was crucial for a client organisation like WSL, as part of a full asset lifecycle view of the project lifecycle. One inference of this observation of general importance was that contractors often had different concerns driving different conceptual frameworks. Enlightened clients should ensure that their contractors used the same project lifecycle and employ incentives

Table 7.1 SS1 – the dominant management aspects defining a traditional client's four stage project lifecycle.

Basic lifecycle stages	Dominant management aspect
Conceptualisation	Operations or corporate management initially, then corporate management
Planning	Corporate management initially, then operations and project management
Execution and delivery	Project management initially, then project and operations management
Utilisation	Operations management and corporate management

to motivate their contractors to concern themselves with the project's performance over the whole lifecycle as effectively as possible. For example, a client might use explicit rewards for providing quality which ensured low operating costs.

In his view SS1 was a reasonable portrayal of the way most WSL staff currently thought about project lifecycles at this very basic level of decomposition, but various more detailed decomposition structures were also employed within WSL, for various purposes.

This kind of four stage structure plus versions with five or more stages were very widely used beyond WSL, with many different variants of the stage labels, the assumed dominant management aspects, and the assumed approach to those management aspects. A feature of the SS1 portrayal was emphasising the relationship among the four generic project lifecycle stages employed and the corporate, operations and project perspectives on management discussed at the outset of this workshop. The role of these three perspectives and the best way to manage their interactions were crucial to the elaborations of SS1 which WSL needed.

The 'conceptualisation' stage included initial concept development and the development of an early version of the business case for investing in the asset produced by the project – be it a physical asset like a water main or a less tangible asset like a new process or corporate culture. This stage might be initiated from the bottom up to meet operations needs or from the top down to meet corporate level strategic needs, but corporate management considerations usually dominated by the end of the conceptualisation stage, with a focus on business case issues.

The 'planning' stage involved a complex and potentially lengthy process that began at a strategic level and progressively refined the design of the asset, an understanding of intended benefits from the asset, how it would be used, how it would be created, what resources would be needed, and when and how it would be delivered. The focus by the end was detailed tactical plans for execution and delivery, but the starting point was an initial version of the concept and business case plans which needed refining from a corporate perspective. There was a great deal of ground in between, with a central role for planning associated with design development based on operations plans for the utilisation stage.

The 'execution and delivery' stage involved implementation of the plans for creation and then delivery of the asset to its users. The 'planning' focus became a 'doing' focus, although important ongoing detailed planning and control incorporating possible replanning of strategic issues were also involved.

The 'utilisation' stage involved the operation of the asset throughout its operating life to eventual termination of use. The doing and planning focus was very different, and while operations management now dominated both tactical and strategic planning, corporate planners had to maintain an interest for their strategic planning purposes.

The way the dominant management aspect pattern portrayed in Table 7.1 changed over time, the lack of real separability between these management aspects, the very broad scope of the planning stage, and the complexities introduced by divisions of responsibilities, all encouraged a wide range of different more detailed project lifecycle structures in different project contexts to ensure clear definition of who does what, when and how in an orderly manner. WSL needed one common way to deal with these issues.

Looking at Table 7.1 from an EP perspective, one important issue was which group led the effort carried out in each stage in the lifecycle. A second was which other groups supported their efforts in what ways. A third was ensuring that *all* uncertainty and complexity associated with different stages of the lifecycle received appropriate attention by the right people at the most appropriate time, bearing in mind the clarified ambiguity concept mentioned earlier. Maximising the opportunities presented by the creation of proposed assets warranted careful attention to all stages of the project lifecycle, individually and in terms of integrated teamwork by all the appropriate people. Furthermore, maximisation of opportunities required careful attention to what role the asset created by the project would play in the context of WSL's other investments and operations.

Characterisation of the project lifecycle as four sequential stages in Table 7.1 started to indicate the scope of the tasks involved from corporate, operations and project management perspectives, and the scope of the uncertainty and complexity that warranted attention. However, a significantly more detailed decomposition of these four basic stages could provide much deeper insight into the scope of the decisions involved in different parts of the lifecycle, the goals being addressed, who were the main players, and the extent and nature of the uncertainty involved. To deal with these issues effectively WSL badly needed this additional insight in a framework common to all associated WSL decision making.

Distinguishing progress stages and gateway stages

Paul indicated that one aspect of this additional detail was a clear distinction between what he would call '*progress* stages' and '*gateway* stages'. In broad terms:

1   'progress stages' would progress the planning process by getting the planning work done and achieving the execution of the plans,

2   'gateway stages' would provide independent scrutiny of the quality of progress stage efforts with a view to corporate governance considerations before moving on to the next progress stage, plus 'lessons learned' reviews to address corporate learning concerns as and when appropriate.

Each progress stage should be followed by a closely coupled gateway stage. Most of their discussion today would focus on progress stages at a strategic level. He would start by explaining his recommended use of nine progress stages which cover the whole lifecycle. He would briefly outline the nature of associated gateway stages later.

The nine progress stages Paul was proposing for WSL

In Paul's view WSL needed to change immediately to 'stage structure 2' (SS2), and he began his explanation of SS2 by showing his group Table 7.2, which relates the nine SS2 progress stages to the four SS1 stages.

Table 7.2 SS2 – Nine nominal progress stages for the WSL project lifecycle.

Basic lifecycle stages	Nine nominal progress stages
Conceptualisation	**Concept strategy**
Planning	Design, operation and termination strategy (**DOT strategy**)
	Execution and delivery strategy (**E&D strategy**)
	Concept, DOT and E&D 'devils and angels' in the detail tactics testing to confirm the overall strategy (**D&A strategy**)
	Concept, DOT and E&D implementation tactics (**Implementation tactics**)
Execution and delivery	**Execution**
	Delivery
Utilisation	**Operation**
	Termination

Table 7.2 used terms like *devils and angels*, which he would clarify shortly, and useful contractions (like D&A for 'devils and angels') serving as labels in bold. It portrayed stage alignments with the four basic lifecycle stages of Table 7.1 which were a convenient starting point for understanding SS2 stage roles and their relationships with SS1 but approximate for reasons worth understanding which he would explain in a few moments.

SS2 was a convenient contraction, following SS1 and anticipating an SS3 possibility which other directors might require. He knew that some of his fellow directors might want to argue for modifications, and because the whole of WSL needed a common and agreed-on project lifecycle definition, he clearly had to be flexible about capturing complexities which others thought important. He would use SS3 as a contraction of stage structure three to represent what his fellow directors might later agree. The nine stages of SS2 were 'nominal' in the sense that variations could and should be adopted as appropriate by WSL and any other organisation using an SS2 variant.

In some organisations simplifications of SS2 might be sensible. However, in his view simplification was not a viable option for WSL, so SS3 would need to be more detailed than SS2 if changes were made. He would assume SS2 was accepted by the board as a working assumption for present purposes.

Paul began a more detailed explanation of the SS1 transformation into the SS2 structure by indicating that the central change driving much of the other changes was the single 'planning' stage of the Table 7.1 SS1 structure being decomposed into four separate components for SS2:

1   'DOT strategy' (DOT was a useful contraction for design, operation and termination),
2   'E&D strategy' (E&D was a useful contraction for execution and delivery),
3   'D&A strategy' (D&A strategy was a useful contraction for finding and dealing with all 'devils in the detail' of tactics plus any 'angels in the detail' in the context of addressing *strategic planning*),
4   'implementation tactics' (to deal with tactical planning for implementation purposes).

This four components SS2 decomposition of SS1 planning was directly linked to decomposing the single SS1 'conceptualisation' stage of Table 7.1 into five SS2 components, embedding all but the first in the four components of SS2 planning listed earlier:

1   an opening 'concept strategy' progress stage – the first of four SS2 strategy stages,
2   a concept strategy development component in the DOT strategy progress stage,
3   a concept strategy development component in the E&D strategy progress stage,
4   a concept strategy development component focused on crucial tactical concerns in the 'D&A strategy' progress stage, and
5   a residual 'concept tactics' component in the 'implementation tactics' progress stage.

The resulting first five SS2 stages in Table 7.2 were followed by the SS1 'execution and delivery' stage decomposed into the SS2 'execution' and 'delivery' stages, then the SS1 'utilisation' stage decomposed into SS2 'operation' and 'termination' stages, with some aspects of the strategic planning for utilisation and termination being embedded in earlier stages.

There were several reasons for treating the first five progress stages of SS2 in this way which required understanding by all relevant WSL staff.

First, clarity efficiency suggested that all strategic planning should precede all tactical planning apart from a form of planning intended to test tactics with respect to the 'devils in the detail', plus equivalent 'angel in the details', in terms of the robustness of strategic choices. This was because planning costs escalate when detailed tactical planning begins, the effort involved in detailed tactical planning may be largely wasted if strategy changes, and late changes in strategy can have hugely expensive knock-on cost implications because of interdependent commitments. The 'D&A strategy' stage facilitated a strategy-oriented focus on tactical planning to find and test key tactical aspects of earlier strategic planning for 'the devils or the angels in the detail'. The 'implementation tactics' stage could make very good use of D&A strategy stage tactical plans, but it addressed tactical planning for implementation purposes, a very different task in terms of objectives, concerns, the time required and the effort involved. Usually it was not worth starting detailed planning for implementation purposes until a rigorously tested appropriate strategy had been agreed on. An inability to distinguish which areas of the plans needed devil or angel in the detail testing and which did not, plus time pressures which made it worthwhile risking wasted effort by overlapping lifecycle stages, were both examples of potential complications which he would consider later but wanted to avoid now.

Second, it was important to distinguish between planning for concept, design, operations and project execution purposes, because although they were closely related, they involved different purposes and different people in different WSL groups. Design and operations issues plus key termination concerns like the design life of an asset were particularly closely coupled concerns and by tradition reasonably well integrated within WSL. However, much better integration was needed for some key aspects of concept strategy currently given early consideration by an inappropriately limited set of people, with directly related aspects of execution strategy currently given later separate consideration by people who should have been involved earlier.

Third, it was important to distinguish between strategic planning and tactical planning for all purposes because they involved different goals as well as different people who might be in different organisations. For all WSL purposes, strategic planning would be in-house with support from consultants. Some of these consultants might later become contractors. All detailed planning for asset design, execution and delivery would be a contractor responsibility with WSL support. The WSL Projects Group did not have the capability to undertake detailed planning for major projects. Part of the historical reason was his predecessor had taken the policy decision 'it is best to let contractors do their own detailed planning within a WSL approved strategy' – and he supported this policy with the modest revision of more emphasis on WSL support and early dialogue when late strategy changes looked advisable. For related reasons, the WSL Operations Group did not have in-house detailed design capability.

The rationale for decomposing the last four SS2 progress stages as portrayed by Table 7.2 was relatively straightforward. The execution and delivery stage in Table 7.1 needed decomposition because the Projects Group would be the lead WSL group interfacing with the contractors while they were undertaking execution, but the Operations Group would become the lead WSL group during delivery, by tradition for very good reasons. The utilisation stage in Table 7.1 needed decomposition to separate termination because the Operations Group was the responsible WSL group during operation, but although the Operations Group usually took the lead on design life issues, the initially planned timing and later implementation of termination usually gave rise to wider WSL involvement.

The same decomposition structure would be needed for all nine of the gateway stages corresponding to each of the progress stages. Each of these gateway stages was very different from the associated progress stages, requiring very different processes, because different people and different objectives with different kinds of outcomes were involved.

Paul explained that the four strategic level gateway stages after the first four Table 7.2 strategic level progress stages were primarily board led governance exercises to control projects proceeding to the next stage while WSL was addressing strategy directly. Each should build on all earlier stages, testing strategic decisions made in earlier stages, making full use of all information arising from interim planning progress and other updating where appropriate.

The fourth of these strategic level gateway stages was the last gateway stage addressing strategic planning before detailed tactical planning for implementation began. This meant the D&A strategy gateway stage was a particularly crucial stage – an important 'watershed' – the last chance to amend the strategy without serious cost implications. Part of this stage was usually setting a budget which was linked to granting permission to let contracts which would start detailed tactical planning for implementation purposes. 'Overall strategy gateway stage' and 'contracting strategy gateway stage' were probably more useful alternative labels for the D&A strategy gateway stage, a suggestion he would be making to the board.

The fifth gateway stage, the implementation tactics gateway stage, would also be a crucial lifecycle stage if all the tactical planning had to be completed before board level approval for detailed plans and the beginning of implementation. However, he was assuming this was not the case, and he would explain why in detail later. In outline, he was assuming that implementation tactics gateways would be partial as tactical planning rolled forward during execution, and these gateways plus the gateway stages after the next four progress stages were primarily ongoing project control exercises plus lessons learned exercises for WSL as a whole, with governance oversight to ensure that no important lessons were overlooked and no inappropriate actions were condoned. Sometimes agreeing to major plan revisions could become crucial, abandoning a project after detailed tactical planning or during execution or delivery remained an option, and in all gateway stages the transfer of responsibility involved important issues.

Paul finished his introduction to this SS2 lifecycle structure with four observations that he particularly wanted his team to bear in mind.

First, as they all knew, currently the Projects Group initially became involved in projects when someone in other WSL groups asked them for an initial cost estimate for the execution and delivery of a project which was still early in its concept strategy stage, often defined in terms best described as a 'preliminary statement of intent by project initiators'. The Projects Group were not invited to assist with 'planning' within the current equivalent of the SS2 concept strategy stage – they were asked to base their estimate on someone else's 'plan', This initial estimate was currently referred to as a 'best estimate', but in his view this was a euphemism for what in practice was a 'best guess' based on an unacceptably informal and ambiguous understanding of the DOT strategy to be created and shaped later, plus the E&D strategy to be created and shaped later still. D&A strategy was not part of the current agenda, which was an important oversight. Despite this unacceptably ambiguous best guess nature, point estimates were used, with a failure to secure clarity about the range of uncertainty or the nature of the point estimate. Point estimates might be a very ambitious aspirational stretch target, a commitment, an expected value, or something else that might mean different things to different people. This point estimate approach had to be scrapped immediately, and effective and efficient formal linkages between the four strategic planning stages had to be established as rapidly as possible.

Second, as they all knew, currently the WSL Projects Group was asked for a 'risk adjustment' estimate towards the end of the current equivalent of the SS2 concept strategy progress stage. This practice also had to be scrapped immediately, with effective opportunity and risk management input to the concept stage provided by the Projects Group from the outset as part of the required formal linkages between strategic planning stages.

Third, the Projects Group contribution to the new concept strategy progress stage needed to be a balanced and integrated package providing opportunity, risk, uncertainty and underlying complexity management input. This input needed to include estimating expertise driven by and empowered by holistic planning input of a kind which was currently completely missing without WSL even understanding the nature of the implications.

Fourth, if any WSL project did not pass the concept strategy gateway test when it should pass, or if it passed when it should fail, or if it passed in a form which is not appropriate with an initial budget which is not sensible, serious corporate inefficiencies would be involved. As the first gateway following the first progress stage, the concept strategy gateway had to address *all* key objectives for *all* relevant parties, allowing for *all* the inherent uncertainty and complexity underlying *all* the 'best guesses'. Following gateways had to further test the validity of the earlier gateway decisions in the light of further plan development. A lack of well-defined plans and the lack of objective data in all concept strategy stage estimates involved inherent difficulties which required effective treatment. They needed systematically derived subjective range estimates using the best available judgements in the most appropriate structures. A core issue in the concept strategy stages (both progress and governance) was appropriate WSL understanding of the size and shape of the ambiguity involved, and the implications of clarifying it in an enlightened manner. As head of Projects Group a very early concern was addressing the most appropriate form of Project Group input into WSL concept strategy progress stage estimates, a topic he would return to shortly.

However, he would first look at the other three frameworks WSL needed as part of their four Fs concept. The 'seven Ws' framework, which builds on the project lifecycle, was next, followed by a goals–plans relationships framework, building on the first two. Fourth was a 'specific process for projects' framework (sometimes usefully contracted to SP for projects framework or SPP framework), building on and embedding the first three.

The seven Ws framework

Paul started discussing the seven Ws framework by observing that the motivation for introducing and developing formal risk management in a project planning context since PERT approaches were first introduced in the 1950s had varied widely. In part this variability was driven by a range of very different understandings of how opportunity, risk, uncertainty and complexity were related. In part this variability was also driven by particular concerns which needed systematic consideration for each project in each organisation, like:

1   sources of risk in design and logistics issues which involved the large-scale use of new and untried technology;
2   sources of risk associated with shortages of key resources, including finance;
3   contractual issues;
4   communication and trust issues; and
5   conservation, pollution potential or political imperatives.

However, it was now very clear to Paul that WSL and most other organisations had to embrace the view that whatever the areas of concern:

1   opportunities in a general EP sense should always be a key issue,
2   clarity about the relationship between opportunity and risk in terms of underlying uncertainty and complexity was always crucial, and

3   uncertainty about *the full set* of performance objectives and associated relationships between *the full set* of stakeholders and other key interested project parties was always central.

For example, a common and ongoing issue was 'Did everyone involved in a project know what they were trying to achieve in agreed and clearly defined terms that linked the corporate objectives of the project's owners and those of other key parties to project plans?' WSL as a whole needed a clear corporate understanding of why such concerns arise, and WSL had to respond effectively in a coherent manner in *any* project context at *any* stage in the lifecycle, starting with the concept strategy stage. This was not just a PG team issue.

Paul then showed his group Table 7.3.

Paul's first observation was this seven Ws structure had evolved from the notion of 'six honest serving men' used by Rudyard Kipling for a comparable purpose at a personal planning level, and Kipling did not claim it was a new idea. Table 7.3 had provenance, a basic practical idea which had been tried and tested in well-known earlier variants.

His next observation was the key questions in the middle column provided a starting point for thinking about issues which were crucial for all WSL staff, not just the PG team.

For convenience, WSL staff could refer to key questions in the middle column of Table 7.3 as 'the seven Ws', using the seven 'W labels' in bold in the left-hand column as a short form when appropriate. But in practice the 'further clarification labels' in italics in the right-hand column would usually be more useful than the 'W labels'.

Paul acknowledged that there was clearly an artificial flavour about some of the W labels, especially 'wherewithal' and 'whichway' – he had smiled when he observed several of his group wincing noticeably when the 'seven Ws' designation was first revealed. He suggested that the seven Ws terminology for this conceptual model might irritate some sensibilities, but it was just a handy reminder that an operational form of this framework would help them to consider all seven of these aspects of a project, their multiple components in some

Table 7.3 The seven Ws – key questions needing answers in the basic project definition process.

W labels	Associated key questions	Further clarification labels
1. who	Who are the parties involved?	*parties*
2. why	What do the parties want to achieve?	*motives*
3. what	What is the deliverable product (asset) that the parties are interested in?	*design (plans for design purposes)*
4. whichway	How will all relevant plans in each life-cycle stage deliver what is needed?	*plans for relationships and contracts, business case purposes, operations processes, project execution activities*
5. wherewithal	What resources need prior planning to achieve the execution of these plans?	*resource plans for operations, project activities, other plans?*
6. when	When do all relevant activities and events have to take place?	*integration of all plan-based timetables*
7. where	Where is the project in its lifecycle? Where will the project take place physically, and where will its deliverables be located if different? Any other relevant context issues?	*context where*

cases, their inherent interdependence, the comprehensive set of 'plans' involved as clarified in the third column, and the basis for the link between these plans and the life-cycle stages in Table 7.2.

He then introduced Figure 7.1, an influence diagram which builds on Table 7.3 to begin to clarify the operational implications of the seven Ws framework plus the project lifecycle framework. Table 7.3 and Figure 7.1 were taken directly from Chapman and Ward (2011).

Figure 7.1 employs Table 7.3 'further clarification label' designations as well as W labels to show a set of relationships which elaborate how Table 7.3 purposes can be linked to plans as the project lifecycle evolves. Paul used Figure 7.1 to explore the nature of these relationships with his group.

He began by observing that in the concept strategy stage the plans for business case purposes usually became a central concern fairly quickly. An NPV cash flow model at the heart of the business case might act as the axle, the plans for business case purposes as the hub of a wheel. However, *from the outset* it was crucial to avoid too much inward focus on the cash flow model aspects of the business case. As soon as possible, the 'plans for business case purposes' should reflect all the key objectives of all the key players. Some people were inclined to limit the business case concept to cost and revenue concerns, but it was misleading to

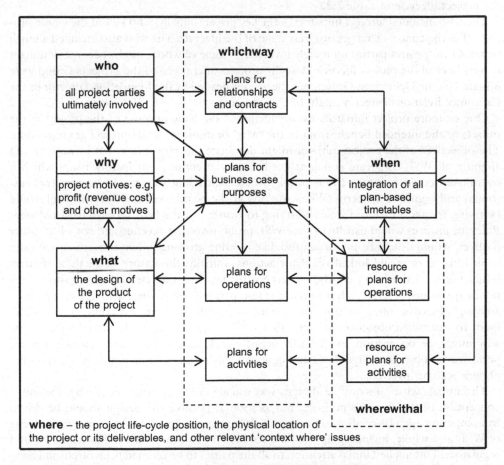

Figure 7.1 The basic project definition process – the clarified seven Ws structure.

define a business case in such narrow terms. Who 'owned' or controlled a business case could be crucial to the scope of that business case, and the breadth of vision that a project planning team as a whole brought to the interpretation of a business case was critical.

Paul observed that the 'hub' status of 'plans for business case purposes' was modestly emphasised by slightly bolder lines for its box. The comparably bold lines of the overall box signified the wheel rim. The other boxes were analogous to spokes. He suggested those worried about square wheels and hubs (and square pegs in round holes) might prefer using circles instead of boxes – he had stuck to boxes, in part, because they were a more convenient shape for most purposes of interest to him, in part to remind him that all analogies of this kind can produce problems if taken too far. The 'spokes' and 'wheel' notions centred on the plans for business case purposes were useful but by no means perfect analogies. An alternative hub, associated with an alternative axis, was often a useful focus for different people for different purposes. For example, the Operations Group might view plans for operations as their focus sometimes, but the design of the product of the project their focus at other times. The Projects Group might see plans for activities as the focus sometimes, but plans for relationships and contracts as the focus at other times.

The 'who' was a good place to begin considering the spokes of the wheel which circled the business case hub and the way the clarified seven Ws structure of Figure 7.1 related to the project lifecycle of Table 7.2.

The who included 'project initiators' – the key players initially, who kicked the whole project off in the concept strategy progress stage of the lifecycle. The who also included a much wider set of 'project parties ultimately involved' – some of whom might become dominant players later in the project lifecycle. Usually projects of concern to the Projects Group were initiated by the Operations Group, but the groups headed by the Regulation Director or the Customer Relations Director might be the initiators.

One or more project initiators usually identified the basic purpose of the project at the outset, or the intended benefit from it, the 'why' or motives for the project at conception. The objectives of the project initiator might dominate the why at first, but identifying and aligning all WSL corporate concerns needed early attention, anticipating issues which if overlooked could become serious problems later, including shareholder, contractor, customer, and regulator concerns. When working at the board level as a director, Paul would be trying to take a balanced view and trying to ensure that the board took a balanced view. Relevant motives would usually include WSL profit, involving revenue and cost. But 'other motives' would usually be important too, like meeting growing public concern about water main leakage rates and linked regulator actions. Initially, the nature of all these motives might not be defined very clearly, and even when motives were clearly defined they might not be quantified objectives. In terms of the four part mission–goals–attributes–criteria hierarchy of objectives often used to move from an overall corporate mission or vision statement to quantified objectives at a criteria level like expected cost, the initial focus of the why might be on mission and broadly defined goals rather than more detailed, specific performance objectives. Significant ambiguity initially might be coupled to changes as other players become involved.

The initial 'what', an outline design, was usually driven by the initial why, the initial conception of the project's purpose. But as soon as possible the design should be driven by competing agendas of all who parties which have been aligned in the corporate interests of WSL as a whole, including appropriate concessions to other parties like customers and regulators. This implied initial attention to all the parties to be ultimately involved, and associated relationship plans and contracts, *before* getting too deeply into design. WSL needed to give *effective* early attention to the who–why–what trio, plus the 'plans for relationships and contracts', plus the 'plans for design purposes', as an integrated set. For example, if WSL wanted to put a new sewage works in a sensitive location for the residents of that area, it might be important to minimise intrusive characteristics of all the new facilities, as well as providing recreational facilities for local residents if some of the land involved could be used as a public park. All these features might be designed into the facility and the project management process from the start to plan to manage resistance by local residents in a constructive and transparent manner. Some aspects might be addressed before the local residents were even aware of the possibility of such a project, although very early consultation with residents might be crucial in establishing trust and generating ideas. Some of these features might be anticipated concessions to demonstrate a willingness to listen to concerns and respond, if needed, later in the process. Some might be seen as worth clear presentation from the outset. And some might be tentative suggestions which local residents could usefully shape as part of a joint approach.

Useful ways of addressing clarified ambiguity might take a variety of forms, evolving as the project lifecycle progressed, with some clear views of where and how to look for opportunities from the outset.

The initial and evolving 'design' concept was part of an interdependent set of plans of interest. What was realised during delivery might not be what was intended earlier, and managing the implications of design changes was often an important part of the wider planning process.

Especially during the concept strategy progress stage, it could be very useful to see the initial outline 'plans for design purposes' as central in a different way to 'plans for business case purposes' – a separate and different hub on a different axis for everyone involved to focus on and think creatively about. 'Plans for design purposes' were arguably central to the creativity which ought the drive the overall creation and shaping of the complete set of plans – in this sense usurping the role of 'plans for business case purposes'. At the very least, there was often value in some constructive tension between creative and imaginative approaches to meeting the ambitions of other interested parties and the purely financial aspects of the business case plans when producing an outline design in the concept strategy progress stage.

This outline design, be it of a physical facility like those of interest to the Projects Group, a less tangible asset like a service, or a relatively intangible organisational change, should drive and be driven by the initial outline 'plans for operation'. These outline plans for operation needed consideration in conjunction with the outline plans for design from the start, as did initial outline 'resource plans for operation', both of which might involve important feedback into design. The timing of all these aspects also needed consideration.

The who–why–what trio plus the 'plans for activities' and the 'resource plans for activities' were also interdependent, with linked timing implications. But in the concept strategy progress stage the plans for activities and associated resources might be driven by business case considerations from both ends – capital cost and delivery time for a very high level design concept might be all that was required by the owners of the plans for business case purposes. If the business case was the focus, how the asset produced by the project would be delivered by the Projects Group was often seen as relevant only insofar as cost, duration and 'quality' assumptions made for the business case might prove non-feasible. Paul indicated that the current minor and subordinate role played by the Projects Group in the concept strategy stage of projects was causing difficulties for WSL projects which needed clarity of understanding in the framework portrayed by Figure 7.1, and effective resolution at the board level. Furthermore, the board also needed to understand the need for corporate process changes linked to problems arising because of the minor and subordinate role often played by the Operations Group at the concept stage of projects. With support from other WSL directors, he needed to achieve this understanding by the board as a whole as quickly as possible. Charles and Michael had already approved the basic ideas, but he now needed to involve other directors like Ollie and Frank as a matter of urgency.

The initial development of the who–why–what plus 'plans for relationships and contracts' might be driven later by the 'when' and the business case as a whole. The initial pass around the hub might be largely clockwise, feeding the business case through the spokes, with feedback shaping in reverse directions.

If producing or implementing 'plans for relationships and contracts' had critical resource implications, they might need picking up as 'other plans?' in Table 7.3, omitted for simplicity in Figure 7.1. A similar comment applied to all 'other plans' needing direct attention within the Figure 7.1 'wherewithal' box. For example, it might be important to recognise that WSL did not currently have all the in-house expertise to ensure that early concept planning involved local residents as effectively as possible.

In the DOT strategy progress stage the focus shifted to the way the plans for operations and associated resources drove the design and the business case instead of the other way around, with feedback as appropriate. The purpose of the exercise and the team of people involved usually changed significantly. Involving operations staff or other ultimate users and linked stakeholders as well as design staff at this point in the project definition process usually had significant benefits, particularly in terms of building in 'operability' and 'user-friendly' opportunities via feed-forward and feedback between the 'plans for design purposes' and the 'plans for operation'. This might lead to feedback to modify the why or who. This stage usually provided a refined quantification of operating cost, possibly linked to refined revenue feedback. It often also provided a more refined view of why in terms of a more developed understanding of performance objectives.

One of the first allies Paul would seek at the board level was the Operations Director Ollie, by helping to ensure that the Operations Group was not just the lead player in a clearly defined DOT strategy stage, but also the contributor of a prototype version of the DOT strategy in the concept stage – even if some other group initiated the project. He would like the Projects Group to start seeing the Operations Group as very important members of a joint team from the outset.

In the E&D strategy progress stage the purpose of the exercise and the team of people involved usually changed significantly. In the WSL context the Projects Group now became the lead group. The focus shifted to the way the who–why–what trio drives execution and delivery strategy, shaping the project from an execution perspective, with feedback as appropriate. When execution stage strategic plans were fully developed, delivery stage strategic plans could receive similar consideration. The design developed earlier drove the execution plans, associated resource use plans followed on in a natural manner, and the delivery timetable might just follow on again. But as execution and delivery strategic plans were developed from a Projects Group perspective there might be significant feed-forward and feedback between which-way plans for activities, wherewithal resource plans for activities and when. Some 'build-ability' opportunity for feedback to the plans for design and operations may also prove useful, and the Projects Group needed to involve the Operations Group directly if this was the case. It was important the Projects Group understood all these internal loops and interactions. It was also important some prototype variant of all these concerns was built into the concept strategy stage, at the very least in terms of suitable provisions for initial business case purposes.

In the D&A strategy progress stage *all* the parties involved earlier, plus some who might not have been involved so far, needed to address the potential opportunities, problems and risks which later detailed tactical planning and subsequent implementation and use might reveal. The focus was key areas of tactical planning for project execution and asset use which might give rise to this kind of issue. It was the potential for involving new players who perhaps should have been involved earlier that made the overall strategy testing aspect of this stage complete, within both the progress and the governance components. For example, if local authority planning application issues including actions by potential objectors to plans were not considered earlier in terms of talking to the people directly involved, it might be crucial to rectify this omission.

From a corporate strategy perspective, as the four strategic planning progress stages unfolded, it might be appropriate and important to bring in key stakeholders not initially involved in a carefully pre-planned manner. For example, when the business case had reached a suitable stage of development the who might be extended to banks or bond funders via the Finance Group for financial resource reasons. As another example, enlarging the who to regulators via the Regulation Director for relationship development purposes at a point when useful advice might be sought could be invaluable. Whether or not this pre-planning takes place, the D&A strategy progress stage needed to ensure that any residual 'devils and angels in the detail' were identified and managed effectively.

Paul picked this point to indicate that for some purposes it might be useful to see 'angels' as 'agents of opportunities'. Such angels might include local residents living near a new sewage works site who could make WSL aware of important opportunities if they were appropriately approached – or local planning authority officers who might be helpful if approached with this possibility in mind. Both were examples of parties usually associated with problems and threats, potential 'devils', and the way they were approached might condition their response.

In the 'implementation tactics' progress stage detailed planning for implementation began, and for WSL projects involving the PG team this meant contractors became the lead party, a major transfer of responsibility with big implications for the PG team role. The letting of contracts might introduce a significant lag between the overall strategy gateway stage and the actual start of detailed planning, which he would embed in the plans for the following stage.

It would not be useful to consider the seven Ws in terms of other lifecycle stages at this point in their discussion, but later the role of the seven Ws would need exploring in all lifecycle stages through to termination.

The 'context where' involved potentially important location issues that might be overlooked without this focus. For example, the physical location of the project execution activities and delivered assets might be important if 'ground conditions' proved troublesome during construction and should have been anticipated much earlier.

Paul concluded his discussion of the seven Ws by suggesting that the interactions among Ws were key aspects of any project which needed to be explicitly recognised and appropriately managed. The clarified seven Ws framework portrayed by Figure 7.1 which he had just explained in outline would help the PG team to see their role within WSL projects as a key part of the bigger picture, helping them to integrate their work with other WSL staff and other players. The seven Ws were central to each stage of the project lifecycle, although the emphasis and focus would vary as the lifecycle unfolded. All seven Ws should be addressed by WSL in an orchestrated manner, initially in the context of project definition during the concept strategy progress stage, with further development as appropriate in all subsequent stages.

A goals–plans relationships framework

Paul emphasised that every project needed an explicit and carefully defined goals–plans relationships framework built on the project lifecycle and seven Ws frameworks to develop clarity about the relationships between the very broad goals being pursued by WSL at a corporate strategy level and the project plans being used to contribute to the achievement of some aspects of those goals. These relationships had to address goals directly concerned with project execution and delivery plans which the Projects Group were directly responsible for. They also had to address all other plans within the seven Ws structure over the whole of the lifecycle – in some cases an indirect responsibility of Projects Group which other WSL groups might feel was their territory. At its simplest this meant the WSL project team as a whole had to address concerns like through-life costs for the assets and associated revenue issues. But a complex related concern he thought important was return on equity issues for shareholders which had to reflect the cost of borrowed capital to gear up returns on equity capital.

For most purposes the Projects Group would be focused on criteria like expected project execution cost and associated cost risk driven by possible significant delays or materials cost overruns. However, they needed to be very aware of the broader goals of interest to WSL, and formally consider associated intermediate level objectives whenever they were relevant, involving other WSL groups when appropriate.

Furthermore, WSL had corporate goals which included building well-founded trust with their customers in a reliable and safe source of water at low cost plus reliable and efficient wastewater removal at low cost, without smells, local flooding, pollution of streams, rivers, or beaches. WSL also had to maintain good relationships with their regulators and with local councils in relation to planning permissions and issues like approvals when they needed to dig up roads to install new water mains or sewers.

A goals–plans relationships framework was not easily characterised in a seven Ws framework like Figure 7.1 or a lifecycle framework like Table 7.2. Its nature was very specific to each context. However, it had to become a WSL corporate tool, used along with the project lifecycle framework and the seven Ws framework that it built on, plus the specific process for projects framework to be considered next.

A specific process for the strategy progress stages

Paul indicated that *all* WSL staff also needed to understand a fourth framework in broad overview terms, some getting directly involved in part of it. This fourth framework was an integrated set of specific process framework components which accommodated each of the progress stages of the project lifecycle plus each of the gateway stages. The PG team had to make the whole of this fourth framework a central part of their mindset as well as their toolset.

He would concentrate his attention on the specific process framework components for the progress stages that day, in particular the four strategy progress stages.

The specific process the PG team was going to use in the four strategy progress stages was the 'basic *specific* planning uncertainty and complexity management *process* for *projects*', contracted to the 'basic *specific process* for *projects*' or 'basic SPP'. In the context of discussing the 'basic SPP' the further contraction of 'SP for projects' kept the terminology simple and easy to interpret.

It was useful to see this basic SPP as a composite of three contributing components making interdependent contributions:

1   one 'framing process',
2   one 'named contributing specific process',
3   plus an open set of 'all further contributing processes' which might prove useful.

The framing process was the '*universal* planning uncertainty and complexity management *process*', contracted to 'UP'. The named contributing specific process was the 'basic *performance uncertainty management process*', contracted to the 'basic PUMP'. The basic PUMP was associated with the strategy progress stages in Chapman and Ward (2011). The further contributing processes included *all* other processes relevant to WSL project planning, another EP usage of the closure with completeness concept.

Paul explained the nature of the UP concept using a few examples and a summary of some of the key relevant features explored in Part 1 and Chapter 5, with special attention to the generality of the framing assumptions and the value of clarity about working assumptions.

He next provided a brief background introduction to the PUMP concept. His explanation included earlier comments in this chapter. He explained that the basic PUMP was developed for the E&D strategy progress stage, but used in its basic form for all earlier project lifecycle progress stages and adapted for all later progress stages. The basic SPP was developed for the concept strategy progress stage, to be used in its basic form for all later strategy progress stages and adapted for all following progress stages. He indicated that the focus of his discussion that day would be using the basic SPP in the concept strategy progress stage, but he would also consider using the same basic SPP structure for all three of the following strategy progress stages. Using the same strategy gateway stage PUMP after all four SPP strategy progress stages would also be addressed briefly. Adaptations to the remaining five progress stages and their gateway processes would be deferred until later meetings.

The nature of other relevant '*specific* planning uncertainty and complexity management *processes*', contracted to SPs, was then briefly explored using a summary of Chapter 6 ideas plus an overview of the broad scope of all aspects of project planning beyond PUMP – building on a brief overview of all CPM and PERT based approaches as discussed in Chapter 3.

Paul then showed his group Table 7.4.

At an overview level the basic SPP phase structure largely follows the UP phase structure, with some features drawing from related PUMP phases. The 'create and enhance plans for all relevant concerns phase was not part of the basic PUMP, nor was the following shape base plans phase. These two phases of the SPP have to draw on a wide range of other project planning model and process concepts, working within a UP perspective. The joint role of these two phases is a central aspect of the SPP not provided by the PUMP because it was assumed that other people had provided this aspect of planning separately. The integration of the UP shape, test, interpret, and implement phases followed by a different decomposition structure involved relatively complex SPP/PUMP relationships, which he would outline shortly.

This overview portrayal of UP/SPP/PUMP relationships was a useful starting point for the more detailed understanding which was needed. Paul indicated that he would use the second column to structure his discussion, outlining the basic SPP one phase at a time, but

Table 7.4 Key phase alignments for the basic SPP with the UP and the basic PUMP.

UP phases	Basic SPP phases	Basic PUMP phases
Capture the context with appropriate clarity	**Capture** the context with appropriate clarity	**Define** the project
Select and focus the process for appropriate clarity	**Select and focus** the process for appropriate clarity	**Focus** the process
Create and enhance plans for all relevant concerns	**Create and enhance** plans for all relevant concerns	
Shape the plans using models of some key issues,	**Shape base plans** using models of some key base plan issues	
test the plans to ensure robustness,	**Identify** *all* relevant sources, responses and conditions	**Identify** *all* relevant sources, responses and conditions
interpret the plans to exploit creativity,	**Structure** *all* uncertainty	**Structure** *all* uncertainty
and	Clarify **ownership**	Clarify **ownership**
implement appropriate	**Quantify** *some* uncertainty	**Quantify** *some* uncertainty
aspects of the plans	**Evaluate** *all* the implications	**Evaluate** *all* the implications

he would link his comments to the other two columns. Table 7.4 showed the key phase alignments, but all alignments would need clarifying.

Paul then showed his group Figure 7.2. He used this flow chart portrayal to help everyone to focus on the basic SPP phases one at a time within a UP-based framing assumption perspective, as outlined in the following subsections.

The basic SPP 'capture' phase – capture the context with appropriate clarity

Paul indicated that the first pass through the first phase in the first stage of a project was about using the four Fs to capture an initial corporate understanding of the context which gave rise to the project – all the relevant immediately obvious aspects of the 'project context', portrayed in a systematic structure which was designed for clarity efficient use as it evolved throughout the project lifecycle.

The basic SPP 'capture' phase involved seeing the context of a project in terms of the project lifecycle, the seven Ws, and the goals–plans relationships as currently understood, with a view to the requirements of all following process phases. This initial use of the four Fs concept as an integrated toolset provided usefully structured focus from the outset, increasing the clarity efficiency of the process relative to the completely general capture the context phase of a UP. However, the capture phase of the basic SPP and the capture phase of the unrestricted UP as discussed in Part 1 and Chapter 5 were otherwise directly comparable.

Comparing the capture phase of the basic SPP to the define phase used to initiate the basic PUMP, the fundamental difference was the basic PUMP assumed that responsibility for creating base plans lay with others who had already executed this responsibility, but the basic SPP assumed that responsibility for creating the base plan lay with those using the basic SPP. This meant that the capture the context phase of the basic SPP had further scope.

Making use of the four Fs in this way was not difficult in principle for well-trained and experienced planners, and they would soon get used to capturing initial project information

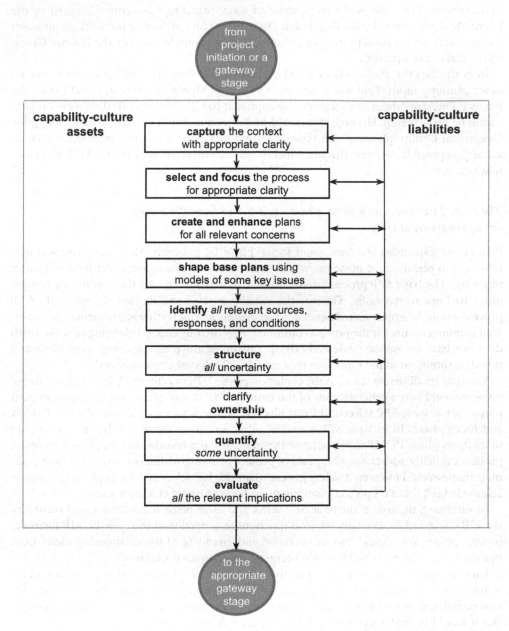

Figure 7.2 The basic SPP (specific process for projects).

and updating that information as the project evolved in this structure. However, working in the concept stage would be a new experience for the PG team, with some important new toolset, skill set, and mindset implications.

Two projects of current interest would serve as illustrative initial test and demonstration case studies, to be added to as further proposals arose. One was a new sewage works – with a concept strategy progress stage study initiated by the Operations Group still in early development. The other was a programme of water mains replacements – initiated by the board after prompting by the Regulation Director because of adverse publicity about water leakage rates, with a concept strategy progress stage study undertaken by the Finance Group still in early development.

In both cases the Projects Group had been asked for early cost estimation input but no other planning input. Paul would approach Ollie, the Operations Director, and Frank, the Finance Director, about both studies. An approach to Ollie about both these new projects would be his first step. His objective would be Projects Group 'planners' working alongside Operations Group 'planners' and Finance Group 'planners', to jointly capture the context as early as possible in a new manner which was much more appropriate for WSL than current practice.

The basic SPP 'select and focus' phase – select and focus the process for appropriate clarity

Paul began explaining the 'select and focus' phase by indicating that this phase was usefully seen as planning the planning, what might be viewed as a higher order form of project planning. The basic SPP process needed to be adjusted to whatever the capture the context phase had uncovered so far. The way the initially selected and focused version of the SPP process would be implemented needed initial planning, with further adjustments and associated planning control as the process continued. Any broadly defined planning process which does not have an *explicit* phase embodying a planning the planning component involves a stealth assumption of the form 'one process suits all relevant circumstances'.

You may recall that in terms of the evolution of the UP concept, the UP 'select and focus' phase concept was a generalisation of the basic PUMP 'focus' phase. However, for present purposes the basic SPP select and focus phase is best seen as a special case of the UP select and focus phase. In its basic SPP form the select and focus phase is richer in nature than in its focus phase PUMP form, because the basic SPP is a broadly defined project planning process explicitly addressing all aspects of project planning within one overall project planning framework. However, it is less general than the UP select and focus phase because an acknowledged focus on project planning provides very useful efficiency gains.

In summary, the role of the basic SPP select and focus phase is a more focused version of the UP select and focus phase, which is much more general than the basic PUMP focus the process phase. You should find an overview understanding of this relationship useful now, but the full implications will have to emerge as this chapter progresses.

Paul suggested that understanding this planning the planning concept in any detail required a comprehensive understanding of the options available, which he would not discuss until later, so it would not be helpful to dwell on the select and focus phase at present. But it would be useful to briefly consider Figure 7.3 now.

In the bar chart (Gantt chart) format of Figure 7.3, the capture (the context) phase is the first phase, followed by the select and focus (the process) phase, and then the create and enhance (plans) phase – an obvious basic precedence ordering. However, these three phases are portrayed as proceeding in parallel during the first complete pass, with linked start-to-start precedence relationships plus common finish-to-start precedence links to the shape base plans phase. Paul explained that this portrayal of the formal plan by Figure 7.3 allowed for extensive unplanned iterations within the first pass throughout these three phases – it made an explicit provision for informal use of multiple iterations which it would be fruitless to try to plan in advance. All other phases could then follow using finish-to-start precedence

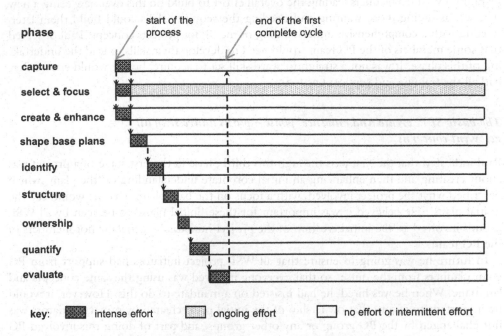

Figure 7.3 An example basic SPP bar chart (Gantt chart) for the first pass.

relationships to complete the first full pass, iterating back to the capture phase after the evaluate phase. Sometimes partial passes through some of the later phases might prove useful, provided for in Figure 7.2 by the multiple loop-back options shown using pairs of arrows in both directions, but Figure 7.3 'kept it simple systematically' in a useful manner.

You may find it helpful to note that the Figure 4.4 portrayal of the UP concept is similar, with comparable implications, although Paul did not explore this relationship with his group.

Paul did emphasise that a highly iterative process should be planned for, completing the first complete pass in 10% to 20% of the time available.

He also explained there was no point in detailed planning in the Figure 7.3 framework beyond the first pass until the evaluate phase was completed at the end of the first pass, but an 80 to 90% time provision for later iterations needed planning from the outset. This was comparable to the idea that there was no point in attempting to even portray the iterations needed within the first three phases because in capable hands these three phases seem to proceed in parallel, nor was there a need to portray the occasional use of incomplete iterations later. Figure 7.3 was a guide, not a prescription, and it provided strategic clarity, not detailed specific tactical advice.

The 'ongoing effort' aspect of the select and focus phase (as distinct from the initial 'intense effort' aspect and the intermittent intense effort nature of all the other phases) portrayed by Figure 7.3 involved adjusting the initial planning the planning plans as they were implemented in two senses: dealing in real-time terms with unexpected outcomes and learning from experience about what to do differently later.

This overview pushed the 'formal' planning aspects of planning the planning about as far as it was useful for Paul to go in his presentation. In practice he would be relying on informal planning by skilled planners leading the overall effort to build on this overview using a new skill set, assuming those wanting and needing the requisite skills could build them later, starting with a comprehensive understanding of the SP for projects concept. Paul observed that some members of the PG team would need to develop their skills to lead the undertaking of this phase. It was not a straightforward skill set to acquire, but he would ensure they had all the training and support needed.

The basic SPP 'create and enhance' phase – plans addressing all relevant concerns

Paul indicated that the first pass through this third phase in the first stage of a project was about creating and then enhancing an initial corporate understanding of 'the plans' which described what the project involved, with a focus on the base plans, what he would call the 'initial plans'. He believed it was important for these 'initial plans' to be seen by all WSL groups involved as 'the initial creation of the project initiators' – generally not members of the PG team.

In future he was going to ensure that all WSL project initiators had support from PG team planners from the outset so that everyone involved was using the same concepts and language. When he was hired, he had insisted on a mandate to do this. However, it would be important to ensure that ownership of the initial plans created by project initiators was not challenged by the PG group or any other groups, and part of doing this involved PG planners being seen by project initiators as 'working for the project initiators', helping them with 'their' ideas, not 'taking over their creation'. 'Ownership' of plans (being in control) was usually an extremely sensitive issue, which the PG team would have to manage with care and diplomacy.

The basic SPP 'shape base plans' phase – using models of some key base plan issues

Paul wanted to couple this ownership of 'initial plans' by the project initiators, with support by the PG team which reinforced their ownership, to moving as soon as possible towards a broader ownership of what he would call 'grounded plans'. He would associate the initiation of 'grounding the plans' with beginning the first pass through the 'shape base plans' phase using models of some key base plan issues. This, too, might be led by the project initiators, but in some areas joint ownership involving a broader project team might start to develop, as part of a gradual evolution of ownership to the comprehensive integrated team basis which he wanted to encourage.

To begin with a minimum clarity position for the aspects of initial plans based on activities, Paul suggested project initiators might model the construction portion of project duration using just one activity. A directly related minimum clarity position for estimating construction cost might use two construction cost components associated with the cost of the construction contract: a fixed direct cost component linked to contractor costs like materials and a variable direct plus indirect cost component linked to the joint effects of resources committed and project duration. For example, he knew Finance Group planners were currently assuming one contract undertaken by one national contractor for all the new water mains, so in principle a one activity structure could be used for a PG team–supported initial estimate of project construction duration. Overall project duration would involve additional pre-construction activities like getting permissions, plus post-construction activities like the testing of completed facilities. Furthermore, partial delivery of the new water mains network would need attention in practice. But maximum simplicity could be maintained for project initiators if that is what they wanted for their initial plans.

Paul made it clear that he wanted to encourage project initiators to start with a minimum clarity position on the project construction period duration and associated construction cost estimates if that was what the project initiators really seemed to want. However, as soon as possible he wanted the PG team to diplomatically move them towards a 'grounded version' of their initial plans which ensured that the uncertainty associated with duration and cost estimates was clearly and explicitly articulated and linked. All the components would have to be interval (range-based) estimates portraying *very* significant associated uncertainty, and *all* underlying uncertainty would need identification. He would insist that the PG team supporting initial plans should refuse to reduce their view of uncertainty if they did not have a clear basis for doing so. He indicated that project initiators creating 'initial plans' might very reasonably concentrate on their areas of expertise, but they should be encouraged to collaborate with others in order to address all other relevant concerns even if some concerns were not modelled.

One of Paul's basic premises, backed by a mandate when he was hired, was that by the end of the concept strategy progress stage, the business case focus of 'the plans' had to be supported by plans for all other aspects of the seven Ws which were in effect relatively low clarity prototype variants of the plans the Operations Group would produce in the DOT strategy stage, the Projects Group would produce in the E&D strategy stage, and the Operations Group plus the Projects Group plus all other relevant WSL groups would produce in the D&A-strategy stage. Furthermore, these concept strategy progress stage plans had to reflect effective treatment in a coordinated manner of generally understood and tested goals–plans relationships.

A terminology which he thought WSL as a whole might find useful was the 'initial plans' had to be 'grounded' – developed and documented by *all* relevant WSL planners. PG planners would take the lead in their traditional activity-based planning roles, but these efforts would be coordinated with cost estimating and uncertainty management roles, and PG planners would also work as facilitators alongside all other WSL planners to ensure that all of the seven Ws plus the goals–plans relationships received balanced and integrated treatment within the lifecycle framework before the concept strategy stage was completed. Helping project initiators to develop their initial plans to achieve a grounded form would be the focus of the PG planners' role as facilitators. Operations Group planners, Finance Group planners, and others with planning input roles, would have to join this 'grounding the initial plans' effort, working as an integrated team, with some of the coordination provided by PG planners in this shape base plans phase.

This shape base plans phase (using models of some key base planning areas) and the preceding create and enhance plans (for all relevant concerns) phase were both central parts of the UP concept, but they were not part of the PUMP structure, and the way they were approached would be new to all WSL groups.

Paul wanted the project initiators to lead the create and enhance plans phase with PG team support initially, recognising that many important aspects of plans are clear to project initiators but not expressed explicitly in models of any kind. He then wanted the PG team to unobtrusively lead the coordination of the grounding aspect in a facilitating role with an EP agenda and the seven Ws structure plus the goals–plans relationships as an operational framework. They would begin with a model-based approach to shaping base plans drawing upon all relevant project planning models and processes in the shape base plans phase, like

CPM. They would then move on to a PUMP based approach to the concept strategy progress stage as a whole. The concept strategy gateway stage was often highly focused on the plans for business case purposes, and some people expected this business case focus for the whole of the preceding concept strategy progress stage, with very little background planning in a full seven Ws plus a complete goals–plans relationships structure sense. Paul would focus on the development of grounded plans underlying the concept stage business case strategic plans today, with an immediate focus on the activity-based plans.

Most projects would need more than one main activity plus some secondary activities to provide a credible estimate of project construction period duration and construction cost for concept strategy gateway purposes. But a low level of detail relative to later planning would be a defining feature of appropriate concept strategy stage planning. Paul wanted a clarity efficient approach to this PG team responsibility which would serve as a demonstrator for all other WSL groups.

He started by observing that most of the current Planning Department activity modelling he had seen used finish-to-start activity-on-arrow diagram CPM modelling. This was simple, it was widespread common practice, and it worked well for detailed planning. However, sometimes it did not work well for E&D strategic planning stages because the low level of detail involved made precedence relationships ambiguous, and it was certainly not suitable for the prototype preliminary forms of planning needed in the concept strategy stage. Planning Department staff had not been involved in concept strategy planning before, which was particularly demanding if opportunity efficiency was the goal.

A generalised and much more flexible approach than activity-on-arrow CPM models was activity-on-node models (precedence diagrams), sometimes synthesised with Gantt charts (making activity nodes time-scaled) to form 'linked bar charts', as illustrated by the basic SPP diagram of Figure 7.3. Figure 7.3 illustrated start-to-start precedence relationships (one activity cannot start until another activity starts), plus finish-to-finish precedence relationships (one activity cannot finish until another activity finishes), as well as the finish-to-start precedence relationships assumed by activity-on-arrow CPM models. Also feasible if the activity-on-node format was adopted were either–or precedence relationships (one activity must follow the other but with the order unrestricted), and other flexible choices like overlaps of an uncertain size. The activity-on-arrow CPM format was popular because it was very simple if finish-to-start precedence relationships were the only precedence relationships involved. But this kind and level of simplicity carried a serious cost in terms of generality, and PG planners needed more generality to cope with their new roles.

Paul then observed that even the basic CPM model was always employed using an iterative 'method', this method included steps which addressed timetable constraints and resource constraints, sometimes generalised to deal with timetable and resource optimisation, and these issues were all relevant to all WSL project planning in the shape base plans phase. Books like *Project Planning with CPM and PERT* (Moder and Philips, 1970) provided a useful guide to the models and associated processes available and used by most professional planners in a large number of countries for many years. He believed WSL planners needed to be *fully* capable of drawing on *all* these models at a conceptual level, operationally employing particular practical examples when relevant, to make effective contributions to the initial plan create and enhance phase and the following shape base plans phase. He wanted to start with very simple variants. He would then illustrate the range of complications which could be addressed.

He began by observing that there was a significant project planning literature on models which looked at optimising the balance between direct and indirect costs as project expected duration is shortened or lengthened.

In their simplest form these models assumed that any project had 'direct costs' associated with executing each activity plus 'indirect costs' (overhead costs) which were a simple linear function of overall project duration. These models assumed that each activity had a 'normal' duration which involved a 'normal' direct cost, and most 'normal' activity durations could be shortened to a minimum ('crash') duration if the direct cost of execution was increased. Furthermore, they assumed that the activity direct cost increase from the normal cost to the crash cost involved a linear intermediate relationship. They used an iterative search procedure to achieve 'crash cost efficiency' – identifying an efficient frontier defined by the minimum direct cost for all project activities for a feasible range of project duration compressions, from a 'normal project duration' (minimum direct cost) to a 'crash project duration' (all activities on the critical path at crash duration). The results could then be portrayed using Figure 7.4.

As shown in Figure 7.4, the minimum project cost level which defined the optimal project duration point was the point on the joint cost curve when it departed from a zero slope. This was determined by the point where the rising direct cost curve had the same rate of increase as the falling indirect cost curve as project duration declined.

This simple model was a useful conceptual model as a starting place to consider trade-offs between project duration and cost, but in practice it was far too simplistic to use for operational purposes in most contexts. One simple generalisation of this model recognised that indirect cost was never just a simple linear function. If the cost of capital invested in a project (not yet productive) was considered, then project direct cost rises at an increasing rate. Opportunity costs (forgone pay-offs from a completed project) can also be very important. However, an obvious and reasonably robust implication of this basic model was most critical path activities would need some compression from their normal duration, most paths would become critical as compression took place, and the optimal project duration was often closer to crash project duration than normal project duration. More sophisticated inferences could be drawn from more complex generalisations of this basic model.

These issues were of direct relevance for all projects in all stages of their lifecycle. They were especially important during the first and third strategy progress stages – when a key

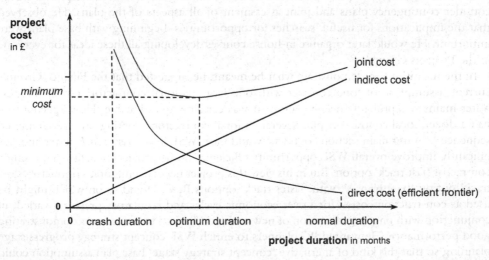

Figure 7.4 Joint cost relationship graph for the basic project duration-cost trade-off model.

strategic concern was project duration–cost trade-offs. The inferences involved needed sophisticated consideration by skilled planners within the iterative process framework even if formal models were not used directly. This meant PG planners needed to understand what all these models could and could not do, even if they did not use them directly in formal planning terms to a significant extent.

The underlying more sophisticated models he was talking about included project planning models addressing resource allocation and resource usage smoothing, which in their most sophisticated forms looked at optimal resource use, generalising the simple linear crash cost and duration models.

One of the most general deterministic project planning models of this kind in some respects, referred to as 'Decision CPM', recognised that activity definitions could be changed as well as activity durations, at a cost, by changing construction technology choices and design choices, and activity sequence choices involved important working assumptions which could also be changed. This implied project planners had to enhance the deterministic modelling basis of their plans by considering all these degrees of freedom in a creative fashion, using iterative processes to test initial working assumptions in a flexible manner. This involved a form of ambiguity uncertainty inherent in base plan creation which needed systematic attention. It needed consideration over and above uncertainty in the event, variability, systemic, and other ambiguity uncertainty senses. Managing uncertainty driven by ambiguity in this particular sense, plus all associated systemic uncertainty, was a demanding craft which all PG planners needed to acquire and share with other WSL planners because it was central to an EP view of uncertainty and complexity. In practice Paul recommended largely informal comparisons of options addressing the full range of generalisations available. Informal planning of this kind would require understanding the nature of the options, facilitated by an understanding of models that could be used but using them directly if at all only on selected occasions when this looked likely to pay in opportunity efficiency terms. He observed this was not project risk management as commonly conceived, nor was it addressed in a direct way by the PUMP approach – it was basic project management addressing an aspect of base plan option choice uncertainty and underlying complexity with a view to achieving overall opportunity efficiency. In this phase they were starting with a focus on shaping base plans prior to addressing contingency plans. Later phases would consider contingency plans and joint assessment of all aspects of the plans. He observed that the implications for useful 'searches for opportunities' beginning with base plans were important. He would later organise in-house courses developing all these ideas for everyone in the Projects Group.

In the meantime, to demonstrate what he meant, he suggested that the Finance Group's current assumption of 'one contract with one large national contractor' for all the new water mains was probably deeply flawed. It was certainly questionable. He suspected that half a dozen local contractors plus several national contractors working on a programmed sequence of water main section contracts would meet WSL needs *very much* better and significantly improve overall WSL opportunity efficiency. Some projects benefit from a single contractor 'fast track' option. But in his view this project needed a multiple contractor 'slow track' option 'base plan A', with 'faster track' options B, C, D and so on which might be used as construction costs varied over economic cycles and regulatory pressures varied, in conjunction with ongoing allocation of new contracts limited to contractors demonstrating good performance. He wanted PG planners to enrich WSL concept strategy progress stage planning so that this kind of alternative 'concept strategy stage' base plan assumption could be tested. This particular base plan option set required a project work package structure which accommodated a multiple contractor programme view of the project. They needed to convince Finance Group planners this was a good idea fairly soon, but a more urgent need was persuading Operations Group planners to explore 100 year design life technology, because the Finance Group's current assumption of a 50 year design life was also deeply flawed in his view, for reasons driven by discount rate assumptions in the business case concept strategy plans.

To further demonstrate what was implied by the scope of this approach, Paul indicated that Operations Group planners addressing the new sewage plant were currently assuming that WSL would replicate the last sewage plant built, and they were currently considering urban site A as the preferred choice, with urban site B as an option. He suspected that a very different layout would improve overall WSL opportunity efficiency. In his view, this preferred layout would involve a bigger footprint but a lower profile, landscaped into a rural setting at locations like site C, with surrounding landscaped grounds made available to the public. He thought this would be better than squeezing a new sewage plant into an urban location like A or B for a number of reasons. He wanted to persuade Operations Group planners to explore this approach to a site like C.

In the near future, he wanted all PG planners to get used to, and become skilled at, developing these kinds of opportunity, and stimulating other WSL planners to do the same, at a 'grounded base plan' level, later building on this with 'grounded contingency plans'.

If the PG team had been familiar with Chapter 5 of this book, Figure 7.3 might have been compared to Figure 5.2, discussing the comparable need for subsequent generalisation of associated analysis. Paul might have pointed out that WSL had to get beyond the equivalent of a basic EOQ model to explore Nicola's equivalent of a My-Place-Your-Timing approach in the basic SPP create and enhance plans phase. You may find these relationships useful at a conceptual level. The direct cost (efficient frontier) curve of Figure 7.3 is a piecewise linear curve obtained iteratively in this case, a more complex basis than Nicola had to deal with, but otherwise comparable trade-off issues are involved in similarly simple base plan models of complex associated realities.

The 'identify' phase – identify all *relevant sources, responses, and conditions*

Paul indicated that the 'identify' phase of the basic SPP could be viewed as the next step of the UP shape phase. It addressed a further aspect of 'shaping the plans using models of some key issues', moving on from those aspects of ambiguity uncertainty addressed by traditional planning approaches for base plans in the previous phase to the full treatment of *all* aspects of uncertainty using a PUMP framework. Any serious potential misconceptions in the base plans were sources of uncertainty, along with many other sources of uncertainty not addressed by current WSL project risk management.

The base plan issues which he had just explored were so complex PG planners had to not only understand underlying models which can in principle be applied, but also understand that in practice they had to depend to a significant extent upon informal planning craft skills and relatively simple formal models. They had to use the potential models as a way of understanding what was involved – usually employing them as conceptual tools as opposed to operational tools. The contingency planning issues were also very complex, but well-chosen simple operational models plus a well-developed understanding of the more complex models underlying them would be invaluable.

The 'sources, responses and conditions' modelling initiated in the identify phase embodied the PUMP equivalent of the phase of common practice project risk management processes which involved producing a 'risk list' or 'risk log' plus a later phase which addressed responses to the risks. The 'source' concept was a 'source of uncertainty' concept which generalised the traditional project risk management 'risks' concept. The rationale for closely coupled joint treatment of sources and responses included dealing with the inevitable ambiguity uncertainty associated with a source of uncertainty which as yet had no assumed proactive or reactive treatment, but encouraging a much richer overall approach, including facilitating later specific and general response distinctions, was actually more important. There were other very important departures from common practice involved, but for present purposes the key thing the PG group needed to understand was the identify phase was about beginning a clarity efficient approach to structuring the grounded initial plans in a form suitable for managing contingency plans including base plan adjustments to deal with uncertainty associated with key plan components, with a view to shaping the project concept to achieve opportunity efficiency as outlined in Chapters 3 and 4. This involved decomposing key sources of uncertainty within each of the key concept strategy stage plan components, associating that uncertainty with responses to the extent this was currently relevant, and identifying important underlying assumptions to be treated as conditions.

As a very simple example, if a single cost component approach was taken to construction cost for the new water mains or sewage plant projects, a single source of uncertainty prior to decomposition would have to include everything that Estimating Department staff traditionally thought about when they produced an initial point estimate, everything that Risk Management Department staff traditionally thought about when they produced a 'risk adjustment', everything that the Planning Department then thought about with further Project Group support, *plus everything else that was relevant but traditionally got left out, the basis of current duration and cost overruns plus less visible but equally important lost opportunities.*

He would later hold a series of workshops, which would address how best to decompose a complex single source of uncertainty like this, and particularly for the benefit of PG planners with mainstream project risk management expertise, he would explain the differences between SPP approaches based on the PUMP approach which they would be using and common practice project risk management equivalents.

In practice, WSL would have to address a programme-based decomposition of the water main construction period and all the additional activities involving setting up contracts, getting planning permission, and so on, well before the four strategy progress stages were completed, and well before a reliable project cost estimate could be developed. This would raise important practical issues to address in the concept strategy progress stage. For example, if there was uncertainty about how long it might take to get planning permission for the new sewage works currently being considered by the Operations Group, this might drive related uncertainty about where to locate it and how to design it, a systemically related set of concerns associated with his suggested site C option needing attention in the concept strategy stage.

The basic SPP 'structure' phase – structure all uncertainty

Paul indicated that the 'structure' phase of the basic SPP was another elaboration of the UP shape phase which also incorporated some aspects of the UP test phase. The basic SPP structure phase embodied the PUMP structure phase. The model structuring concerns included identifying any important dependencies between components of the plans across all seven Ws. One particularly crucial aspect of the structuring was identifying 'general responses' to sets of identified sources – a key basis for building robustness to deal with significant sets of both identified sources *and* unidentified sources (the unknown unknowns). The SPP structure phase was also concerned with testing *all* the earlier working assumptions involving the structuring of plans.

An illustrative example was a failure to get planning permission for a new sewage works at a stage when knock-on delays would be very expensive. This might be avoided by much earlier exploration of alternative sites where the local population might be quite receptive if significant recreational facilities as part of the site development plans were on offer, and concerns about current local flooding risks or other linked issues were also addressed. As part of the planning of activities following on from obtaining planning permission, they would not only have to address what responses might be used to respond to delays, but they would also have to deal with what might be done to reduce the risk of this problem arising – both proactive and reactive responses.

A closing aspect of the structure phase was addressing a preliminary ordering of WSL preferences for all relevant options available, within the specific and general response sets which clarified which responses would only deal with specific reasons for delay and which responses would deal with sets of reasons for delay.

The basic SPP 'ownership' phase – clarify ownership

Paul indicated that the 'ownership' phase of the basic SPP was yet another elaboration of the UP shape phase plus some aspects of the UP test phase. The basic SPP ownership phase embodied the PUMP ownership phase. Basic questions addressed included the most appropriate forms of contract for all aspects of the project, plus being clear about which party was responsible for managing which aspects of all opportunity and risk, and who benefited or suffered if opportunities and risks were realised.

To illustrate the role of this phase, applying the thinking which it involved was in part what lay behind Paul's suggestion that a single contractor for the water mains contract which the Finance Group had recommended should be avoided. Assuming a multiple contractor approach, if *any* of the set of contractors Paul envisioned working on the water mains contracts failed in *any* significant respect, they could *immediately* be excluded from further work, perhaps after terminating their current contract, and they would understand this was the position from the outset. In conjunction with trusting all contractors to use their initiative and sharing the benefits this provided when they performed well, this form of 'partnership contracting' approach would give WSL a robust, low-cost approach to a wide range of sources of uncertainty not even worth identification given this kind of contracting concept. If a single contract with a single contractor was the approach adopted, this kind of simple robustness was not available. The ownership phase should be looking for this kind of built-in robustness if any useful options were not identified earlier, and the sooner this concern was addressed in the concept strategy stage of the project the better. You might interpret this advice coming from Paul as the words of 'a poacher turned gamekeeper', but all enlightened clients should understand the issues involved.

Paul emphasised building and sustaining trust was a central aspect of EP approaches, usually a complex matter. The ownership phase facilitated a careful context specific focus on these issues. All aspects of ownership concerns would need attention in the ownership phase, and the robustness of all associated thinking would need rigorous testing. Some aspects might not be immediately obvious. For example, could WSL use the same contractor for consulting advice in the strategic planning stages and in the later implementation tactics and execution and delivery stages, and if so, how would WSL deal with the associated potential conflict-of-interest problems? Paul thought the multiple contractor approach might make this issue reasonably easy to deal with, but there were some obvious difficulties needing resolution.

This kind of testing of the contracting strategy and more general relationships strategy included some particularly important aspects of the UP test phase in PUMP form within the SPP structure. This phase provided a separate point of focus for ownership, contracting and other relationship issues because associated opportunity and risk concerns were somewhat different in nature and particularly difficult to deal with in some circumstances. Most common practice project risk management processes, including those currently used by WSL, did not have a similar process component, nor was it provided as a formal aspect of any other contributor to the concept strategy stage of project planning.

The basic SPP 'quantify' phase – quantify some of the uncertainty

Paul indicated that the 'quantify' phase of the basic SPP was a further elaboration of the UP shape phase, and it embodied the PUMP quantify phase. Like the PUMP quantify phase, this SPP phase started to address 'quantitative' modelling concerns, normally incorporating an explicit probabilistic (stochastic) component, building on the earlier 'qualitative' (non-numeric) modelling framework. He emphasised the importance of understanding that probabilistic quantification was not just a matter of addressing risk in the event uncertainty sense associated with common practice risk management approaches – it was about addressing *all* relevant sources of uncertainty.

A minimum clarity approach to all sources of uncertainty deemed worth quantification on a first pass might be appropriate. Paul showed them a simple variant of Figures 3.1 and 3.2 and explained briefly in outline using Chapter 3 material what minimum clarity involved and how modest clarity efficient enrichment of this kind of model could be used. He also indicated much more sophisticated approaches might be relevant, and he provided a very brief overview of immediately relevant aspects of the rest of Chapter 3. He assured them the planned workshops and demonstration projects would allow them to quickly acquire the capability to develop a clarity efficient approach tailored to the context of each project they had to deal with which would build on all the insights revealed by the process thus far. He also emphasised that he had experience to base this assurance on.

At this point Paul emphatically emphasised a key issue – the process was not mechanical. For example, at this point in the basic SPP each PG team would have to choose what to quantify and what to treat as unquantified uncertainty associated with working assumptions which implied 'conditions' for the quantified analysis. The choices made should depend upon whether or not the PG team members making the choices thought quantification would be useful. This need for careful and enlightened judgement was true of earlier process decisions too, and many of the earlier choices were even more important and much subtler. For example, back in the identify phase they needed to decide whether to further decompose each source of uncertainty of significant interest, depending on whether doing so looked useful. He linked this need for insightful thinking to the creative nature of the process. The need for both thoughtful analysis and creative synthesis was the reason most EP planners were stimulated by the work, which, in turn, was why the quality of their work usually rose to meet the challenges which an ambitious EP process involved.

The basic SPP 'evaluate' phase – evaluate all the relevant implications

Paul began discussing the 'evaluate' phase by recommending that they avoid putting any faith in simple analogies with other 'evaluate' concepts they might be familiar with. It was crucial to see the basic SPP evaluate phase as a pivotal phase with a very rich set of roles.

The evaluate phase of the basic SPP began as yet another elaboration of the UP shape phase, by finishing off the process of 'shaping the plans by modelling the core issues' concerns, like combining quantified sources of uncertainty and modelling all associated dependence. It then moved on to residual aspects of 'test the plans to ensure resilience and robustness'. After that it moved on to the whole of 'interpret the plans to exploit creativity' plus 'implement appropriate aspects of the plans'. The basic SPP evaluate phase was based upon the PUMP evaluate phase.

In the context of combining sources of uncertainty, it was important to understand that *some* common practice project risk management approaches involved using Monte Carlo simulation packages to combine all probabilistically quantified risks at the same time, with a statistical independence default assumption and limited departures from this default position. The PG team would proceed in a *very* different manner. Key differences would include:

1   starting with the two or three most important sources of uncertainty,
2   gradually adding further sources as a growing set of sources was understood,
3   avoiding statistical independence assumptions unless they were clearly robust,
4   using whatever approach to dependence best suited each particular context,
5   modelling all important dependencies with increasing clarity as they progressed,
6   testing all working assumptions as they went,
7   gradually building a layered understanding of overall quantified uncertainty using sensitivity diagrams when appropriate,
8   making provisional decisions as they went using decision diagrams when appropriate to seek opportunity efficiency for the project concept as a whole, and
9   always being clear about the role and implications of important assumptions which condition the quantitative analysis and underlying qualitative analysis.

Paul emphasised the workshops he would organise would develop all the necessary skills for those facilitating this aspect of the quantitative and underlying qualitative modelling. They would build a significant skill set on the Chapters 3 and 4 discussions you have already been exposed to plus Chapman and Ward (2011). However, what all PG group staff needed to understand immediately was everybody involved in WSL projects would need to become familiar with the use of 'sensitivity diagrams'. He then showed his group the Figure 7.5 example, identical to Figure 4.1 example used in Chapter 4.

Paul began by explaining the Figure 7.5 example in its original BP offshore North Sea context, as discussed in Chapter 4. Repeating some of this discussion here as a reminder for clarity, Figure 7.5 portrayed six sources of uncertainty addressed in quantitative terms in relation to a jacket fabrication activity during the E&D strategy stage of an offshore North Sea project. The jacket was the steel structure fabricated in a dry dock referred to as a 'yard', floated out to the oil production site, upended and pinned to the ocean floor, and then fitted with modules for producing the oil and sending it via an oil pipeline to the shore. The six sources of uncertainty were ordered during the structure phase to facilitate a planned senior management discussion, noting that causal dependency relationships could also influence the ordering of sources. The notes addressed sources of uncertainty treated as conditions – the quantification was conditional on no major fires for example.

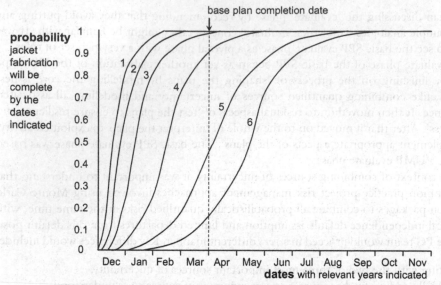

probability curves show the cumulative effect of the following sources of uncertainty:

1. yard not available or mobilisation delays
2. construction problems/adverse weather
3. subcontracted nodes delivery delays
4. material delivery delays
5. industrial disputes
6. delayed award of fabrication contract

notes:
1. the curves assume a minimum fabrication period of 20 months
2. no work is transferred offsite to improve progress
3. no major fire, explosion, or other damage

Figure 7.5 Sensitivity diagram: North Sea oil project platform jacket fabrication example.

Outlining what was involved usually started with the curve for source 1 – in this case starting with a composite of two mutually exclusive reasons for a delayed start to the activity (the yard was not available because another jacket in the yard was behind schedule and had to be finished before work on BP's jacket could start, or mobilisation delays because the yard was free but had not been used for some time, so a labour force with all the requisite skills had to be built up again). The curve for source 2 portrayed the joint effect of 1 + 2, adding to source 1 the impact of construction and weather problems relevant for the whole activity duration. The closeness of curve 2 to curve 1 indicated a very limited contribution by source 2 to the total 1 + 2. The curves for sources 3 to 6 indicated successive further additions to the total uncertainty. The significant size of the contributions made by sources 5 and 6 reduced a 0.9 probability of completing by the base plan end of March date to 0.15. The ordering of sources 5 and 6 facilitated a discussion focused on the elimination of sources 5 and 6, starting with source 6.

Source 6 could be eliminated if commitment to a fabrication contract for the jacket involved was made as soon as possible – a key role for the diagram was stimulating early award of the fabrication contract so that uncertainty associated with source 6 was eliminated and overall total uncertainty was now portrayed by curve 5. This was followed by discussion about the possibility of also eliminating source 5.

Having introduced Figure 7.5 in the original BP context, Paul then linked this discussion to the way the PG team might use this approach in the concept strategy stage to address the new sewage works project. The WSL new sewage works equivalent to source 6 might be possible local planning permission delays leading to additional costs which could be avoided by committing to a preliminary design strategy contract on a consultancy basis with one of the potential DOT strategy phase contractors for the project before the end of the concept strategy progress stage with instructions to liaise with the local authority planners to ensure that all their concerns were addressed to speed all associated regulatory processes. The WSL sewage works equivalent of source 5 might be further possible local planning approval delay driven by local residents' objections, leading to additional costs which could also be avoided by somewhat different responses. In this case, the best way to avoid delays might be incorporating significant consultation with *and carefully listening to* local residents during the DOT strategy stage, *prior* to letting the preliminary design strategy contract. The WSL equivalent of source 4 might involve possible delays and additional costs driven by ground condition and associated design uncertainty. This might be eliminated if ground conditions for several possible sites were considered and perhaps tested if this seemed advisable before engaging local populations and then letting preliminary strategic design stage contracts. This might all be part of the Projects Group and Operations Group saying to the WSL board when the board were asked to approve the concept strategy stage plans 'we do not yet have a clear recommendation for site A, B or C, and they all involve very different design and construction scenarios, but we believe it would be worth approving the concept strategy plans and associated cost estimates now, and getting on with ground condition surveys followed by preliminary consultations with local residents followed by a design strategy contract'.

If a diagram like Figure 7.5 was used to develop this kind of dialogue with the board, the board would want to revisit concept strategy stage approval at the gateway stage following the DOT strategy progress stage, and again after the E&D and D&A strategy progress stages. But it would not be helpful to overlook important ambiguity at the concept strategy stage which could be resolved in various ways depending upon how WSL chose to shape *all* relevant plans. This kind of thinking involved the PG team providing duration planning with built-in contingency planning. This went well beyond the construction cost concerns usually addressed by PG group estimators, because explicitly considering design uncertainty and linked planning permission uncertainty had significant knock-on implications which Project Group planners could address with Operations Group planners.

Paul explained that everybody involved with WSL projects should have a shared understanding of the implications of all quantified sources of uncertainty using 'sensitivity diagrams' in the Figure 7.5 format or simpler linear versions *beginning in the concept strategy stage*. Sensitivity diagrams of this kind were a key EP tool. More than half a dozen sources on any one diagram usually made reading them too complex, but sensitivity diagrams could be used in a nested form, employing from two to ten sources per diagram to cope with any required number of sources in any framework structure which suited the context. For offshore North Sea projects in the E&D strategy stage, BP targeted 20 activities (with a nominal upper limit of 50), and the number of quantified sources per activity was usually in the range 5 to 15, each associated with one to five responses specific to that source, plus general responses. WSL activity and source-response structures would be *much* simpler in *all* lifecycle stages, at their simplest in the concept strategy stage, and they would seek simplicity in a systematic manner. He would later organise workshops which would help them to develop an initial feel for judging what level and kind of complexity would work best in

WSL contexts. They could build on this basis employing a learn-by-doing approach like all other organisations which had adopted EP approaches.

These sensitivity diagrams would be used in conjunction with 'decision diagrams', which Paul now explained using Figures 3.5 through 3.8 to develop a summary of the Chapter 3 discussion of clarity efficiency, risk efficiency and opportunity efficiency, followed by WSL concept strategy progress stage reinterpretations.

The purpose of the evaluate phase as a whole was evaluating all the relevant implications of a creative planning process. This had to be done in a way which allowed all the important insights to be communicated effectively to everyone who needed to understand them *after* the PG team had used these insights to shape, test, and creatively interpret the plans. Combining the uncertainty sources which were quantified in the previous phase using standard commercially available Monte Carlo–based simulation software would be a part of the evaluate phase effort, essential to beginning the evaluation required. But it was a relatively minor part of the evaluation phase as a whole. Of crucial importance was clearly communicated collective understanding of the implications of assumptions about statistical and causal dependence when combining sources, assumptions about what combinations of responses were the preferred options, and assumptions about the significance of sources not quantified – treated as conditions. Furthermore, early passes through the evaluate phase had to attempt to clarify *for the analysts* which areas need further work to let them plan further passes in a clarity efficient manner. More generally, PG planners and Operations Group planners, plus the relevant project initiators, needed to develop a joint understanding of why they needed to iterate the process and revisit areas identified by the evaluate phase until they were satisfied that their plans were fit for the purpose *before* they recommended moving on to gaining approval for their plans.

Paul reminded his team that Figure 7.3 suggested that the first pass might take 20% of the time available, leaving 80% to focus on the now identified 20% of the issues needing 80% of the effort. This was an application of the widely cited 80:20 rule, often called the Pareto rule, although a more ambitious 90:10 rule might be a stretch target aspiration. Sensitivity diagrams like Figure 7.5 were a key tool for deciding whether or not further iterations were likely to be useful, and if so, which sources of uncertainty looked worth further decomposition, *before* as well as after the kind of management discussion just considered. They currently did not use sensitivity diagrams of this kind, or decision diagrams, clear symptoms of a lack of understanding of what an effective and efficient evaluate phase ought to involve.

Paul then completed his phase-by-phase discussion of Figure 7.2 by linking each phase of the basic SPP back to their alignment with the UP phases and PUMP phases in Table 7.4. He first noted that the UP interpret the results-creatively phase was central to the basic SPP evaluate phase. That is, the 'combining probability distributions' aspect of the evaluate phase was a necessary component part of the modelling, but doing so incrementally using sensitivity diagrams to interpret the results plus decision diagrams to build up an integrated set of provisional decisions (contingency plans) was the central concern.

Paul pointed out that the UP test the process rigorously phase was embedded in earlier phases to a significant extent, but a final summary 'test' in the evaluate phase had to address both 'the project' plans and 'the process' plans. That is, iteration control as envisaged in the basic PUMP concept meant considering the possibility of revising both the project plans and the process plans on each successive potential loop back until moving on to the following gateway stage could be judged appropriate. Planning the project and a higher order planning the planning were both involved, and they should not be confused. The final aspect of the UP phase 'implement the results' was moving on to the next stage when iteration was completed, in this case moving on to the concept strategy gateway stage when the concept strategy progress stage conclusions and recommendations were judged fit for the purpose.

The flexible iteration structure of the Figure 7.2 format and the underlying Figure 2.1 format generalised the simpler iterative structure of the Figure 7.3 linked bar chart portrayal, with implications which Paul would explore at a later date.

The role of the capability-culture assets and liability concepts which Figure 7.2 included within the outer box would also need exploring at a later date (building on all the ideas developed in previous chapters).

An interim overview for the PG team

At this point Paul used the PG team's initial understanding of the project lifecycle, seven Ws, goals–plans relationships and basic SPP frameworks as an integrated toolset to give an overview of changes in the WSL approach which would impact the PG team.

One key set of changes was working together in a fully integrated manner, dissolving the current departmental boundaries within the PG group, and softening boundaries with other groups, especially their boundary with the Operations Group. Other closely coupled changes included beginning intensive PG input in the concept strategy stage, working directly on all of the activity-based plans, but also helping to coordinate development of all the other plans associated with the seven Ws, including helping to develop common corporate understanding of key goals–plans relationships concerns.

The linked set of all changes driven by their new EP approach had a number of very broad implications which were important. For example:

1   The risks which current Risk Management Department staff looked for in earlier concept stage estimates would be more broadly framed as 'sources', a convenient contraction of 'sources of uncertainty'. These sources could include issues like 'Should a different design for a sewage plant in a different location be addressed?' The use of the word *risks* in the current Risk Management Department sense would be dropped. It was essential to do so because the 'baggage' which a common practice view of risks carried had implications which needed to be left behind by everyone involved in WSL planning.
2   The 'responses' to sources interpreted in this general way might have to include concept strategy progress stage planning associated with consulting customers, organising planning permissions processes, and relating both these activities to the timing of property purchases and ground-condition tests. This planning activity might not be undertaken with a view to resolving detailed planning concerns. Its aim might be tentative planning with a view to developing a better understanding all the ambiguity involved, and sizing all relevant uncertainty in approximate but unbiased terms, before deciding whether several possible variants of the project concept were the basis of the best way forward. It required the use of prototype variants of the DOT, E&D and D&A strategy progress stage approaches to be employed later in more developed forms.
3   The generalisation of traditional project risk management this involved meant that current Planning Department, Estimating Department and Risk Management Department staff needed direct and coordinated joint involvement from the outset.
4   Operations Group staff should be involved to a significant extent in a coordinated manner as soon as possible, and facilitating closer integration of effort across all groups involved in projects within and outside the WSL corporate structure would be an important feature of the new PG team approach.

5   The basic SPP framework provided a practical overall process framework to facilitate this integration of both process ideas and input to particular projects.

6   Thinking about all plans from the outset in terms of shaping ambiguity in an enlightened manner, and ensuring WSL avoided their current misleading rush towards inappropriate certainty, would be a fundamental change in mindset for everyone involved.

An extended overview not provided by Paul for his first workshop

Paul did not want to overload his first workshop more than he had to, and you probably feel more than ready to move on too, but you may find a brief treatment of further observations on the Figure 7.2 links to earlier discussion useful now.

Everyone involved in the use of a process like the basic SPP needs to remain aware of the important difference between useful models and much more complex realities. The basic SPP is a concept model to be used operationally as a map or plan – like the UP as outlined in Chapter 2 and demonstrated in Chapter 5 and the SP for bidding of Chapter 6. It is always important to avoid confusing a model with the more complex reality the model represents. Anyone familiar with going for a walk or driving a car or sailing a boat with a plan based on a map will understand the possibility of important differences between reasonable plans and what actually happens if best use is made of the plans, with effective departures as intruding realities are encountered along the way. However, process models used for management decision making have a tendency to lead those using well-worn processes to lose sight of the limitations of familiar process portrayals. This is especially true if the processes being used are presented in simple and highly prescriptive terms as mandated corporate processes, perhaps based on professional guidelines.

This limitation of process models is crucial, but equally crucial is the need to employ the best maps we can get based on empirical observation, simplified to a level which is convenient for current usage. The basic SPP and its embedded four Fs are based on a synthesis of what works in practice in three integrated base and contingency planning spheres: general unspecified planning contexts, project planning contexts, and project risk management contexts when a broad uncertainty and complexity management interpretation is used. If the basic SPP is not used, then something demonstrably better needs to replace it. If this is not done *explicitly*, something which is probably inferior will replace it implicitly.

Like Figures 2.1 and 4.4, Figures 7.2 and 7.3 are process models which help to shape creative thinking, to be used to guide what people actually do – not to constrain their thinking. They indicate 'what needs to be done' to make effective and efficient decisions at an overview level, not 'how to do it'. They provide guidance on the most appropriate sequence for doing things, but their iterative nature means a very flexible approach to sequencing issues is crucially important in practice. The capability-culture assets and liabilities of those involved in implementing this approach will determine 'how it is done' and the overall effectiveness and efficiency of the planning.

The role of the basic PUMP in the basic SPP is the provision of a generic process model for addressing opportunity and risk in terms of underlying uncertainty and complexity in a project planning context which is the most general I am aware of. It has been used successfully in practice by a range of organisations in various prototype forms for more than 30 years, and the prototypes themselves rest on earlier successful toolsets. Your organisation can add other approaches which prove useful in the context of 'further contributing processes'. But keep testing what you use for clarity efficiency.

The primary role for 'further contributing processes' is up-front integration of useful processes for creating and enhancing initial plans and then developing shaped base plans, drawn from all literature and practice relevant to projects, including everything relevant which you and your colleagues currently know how to use, and all relevant future learning.

The role of the UP is expanding the scope of PUMP and all the other embedded project management process approaches so the basic SPP looks at *all* relevant aspects of creating, enhancing, shaping, and implementing project plans in an integrated manner.

The capability-culture assets and liability concepts can make important contributions to this generalisation role for the UP. For example, 'effective and efficient monitoring and review within the PG team' might be defined as a key capability-culture asset. This asset might address issues like ensuring all estimates are unbiased and everyone involved learns from experience (in the manner outlined in the Astro tale of Chapter 6) under the overall supervision of a PG management team which understand what this means and what it requires in the way of aptitudes, skills, training, and on-the-job support. A facilitating role for PG staff when other WSL planners were the central players was a crucial component of Paul's need, as a board member, to deliver unbiased estimates to the board for opportunity efficient plans, and to demonstrate that he had done so. A failure in any of the plans covered by any of the seven Ws undertaken by other WSL groups would mean a project failure which Paul would bear some responsibility for, even if the plans involved were not within his direct remit. Persistent bias was a guaranteed source of failure. Any guaranteed source of failure implies a form of 'premeditated failure'.

A specific process for the strategy gateway stages

Paul reminded his group that the basic SPP portrayed by Figure 7.2 was designed to facilitate WSL planners making progress until all the project plans embraced by the seven Ws and associated goals–plans relationships were judged 'fit for the purpose' at the end of the concept strategy progress stage. At this point independent governance was needed by the WSL board, treated as a separate concept strategy gateway stage. Different people were involved, the *gateway* and its preceding *progress* stage process purposes were very different, and an appropriate gateway process was not iterative by design.

He then showed them the gateway stage process of Figure 7.6, which he would refer to as the 'gateway SPP', and began his explanation by indicating that it was simply the PUMP gateway process discussed by Chapman and Ward (2011) embedded in the UP framework of Figure 2.1. It was a gateway SPP which would serve all the WSL strategy gateway stages in conjunction with the basic SPP of Figure 7.2 serving all four of the WSL strategy progress stages. Later progress and gateway stages would require modest modifications, discussed by Chapman and Ward (2011), which would not be considered that day.

The 'consolidate and explain earlier progress stage deliverables' part of the gateway SPP involved producing an executive summary for the board of all relevant base plans, contingency plans, and commitment plans, with backup detail as needed. What was presented to the board should be judged 'fit for purpose' if it allowed the board to decide whether:

1   the project should be passed to the next progress stage as recommended,
2   the project should be terminated now for identified reasons as recommended, or
3   the project should be sent back to an earlier progress stage for identified reasons as recommended.

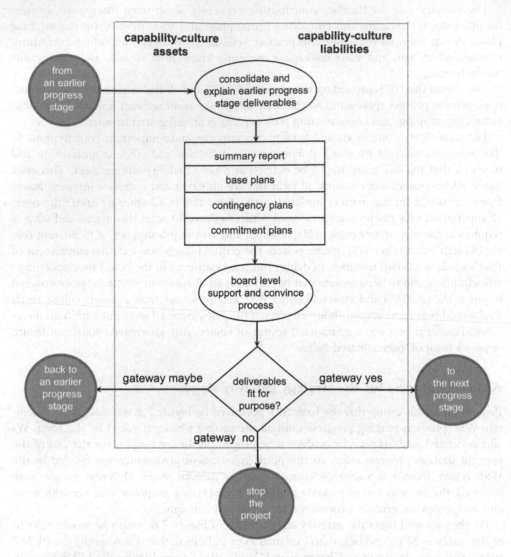

Figure 7.6 A gateway SPP to follow the basic SPP of Figure 7.2.

If these deliverables were judged 'not *fully* fit for purpose', the project plans might be sent back for modest revision or clarification or both – a form of 'gateway maybe' outcome which required the resolution of unacceptable aspects of the plans or unacceptable ambiguity in the basis for current recommendations. This outcome might imply a degree of incompetence during the progress stage without making too much of an issue about it. This was quite different from a form of gateway maybe which accepted the validity of the progress stage but acknowledged that further ambiguity resolution or potential new opportunities identified by the board during the gateway stage was worth the investment. Crucially, it was also very different from a form of gateway maybe which rejected the validity of the progress stage explicitly, explicitly calling into question the competence of those making the recommendations. Important complexity in a maybe might be left ambiguous or spelt out very clearly, at the board's discretion, and spelling it out very clearly might be a precursor to somebody being subjected to explicit personal criticism plus proportionate action.

No *planned* iterations were involved in this gateway SPP. Usually recommended options for further ambiguity resolution would only be offered because current timetable, scope, or financial constraints did not allow a clear recommendation to proceed to the next stage by the planning team. Usually new opportunities or risks identified at the board level would be surprises which might have been anticipated and explored earlier.

What the PG team needed to understand that day was when the PG planners and all the other WSL planners involved thought they were ready to move from a strategy progress stage using Figure 7.2 to a strategy gateway stage using Figure 7.6, a very different process began, usefully associated with an entirely different project lifecycle stage. Unlike preceding strategy progress stage SPPs, a following strategy gateway SPP was not iterative by design, and the decision makers were the board, not the PG planners and other WSL planners.

The PG planners would be directly involved in the first part of this gateway SPP, working with other WSL planners to produce a summary report. This report would be based on documentation developed during the progress stage basic SPP. It would incorporate expected outcomes and associated ranges for all key parameters. It would include associated base plans (based on balanced targets or on aspirational targets equivalent to P10 plans in duration, cost, and other performance measurement terms). It would include basic contingency plans (indicating fall-back options to cope with targets not being achieved plus 'fall-forward' options to capitalise on good luck not incorporated in the target values used for base plans). It would include commitment plans (indicating the equivalent of P90 or P80 plans in duration, cost, and other performance measurement terms). It might also include further contingency plans to deal with failing to meet commitments which need prior planning.

Paul would take a direct interest in helping Project Group and Operations Group team members and other WSL planners meet the board's expectations, coordinating all their input to the board, and presenting their plans to the board. But the decision making based on that input in the gateway SPP of Figure 7.6 would be a boardroom exercise.

Paul would later explain to the board that embedding the PUMP gateway in the UP concept to define the gateway SPP of Figure 7.6 emphasised several key features:

1   The full UP process in its basic SPP adaptation had been used by PG planners and other WSL planners to prepare the basis for a board decision, but the board members could now use all relevant UP concepts to add their own judgement to any aspect, they should do so wherever and whenever they had knowledge not available earlier, and they should expect to play an important role in these terms.
2   The board members should also add their own creativity when appropriate, asking the question 'Do the plans as a whole, given all the assumptions underlying them as just considered, offer any further scope for creative improvements in opportunity efficiency, perhaps involving a redefined wider scope or more financial flexibility?'
3   Even if the board members did not add knowledge or creativity which might lead to revised plan suggestions, they needed to ask the question 'Do the plans *as a whole, as understood by the board*, make sense, making full use of all board level expertise?'
4   Robustness testing in very broad terms within a UP framework was a key board responsibility which could not be delegated.

All the capability-culture asset concepts discussed in Chapter 2 were relevant, not just the governance role capabilities. So were the associated capability-culture liabilities and accommodations. Paul understood these issues should not be laboured with the board, but as a responsible board member he had to confront them when and where appropriate.

The board might, of course, reject a concept strategy stage recommendation that a project should proceed to the next stage or be stopped now and send it back for reconsideration with a very different line of thinking. The board might even reject a recommendation to return to an earlier stage, because the grounds were held to be inappropriate, and insist that different considerations were addressed in a different manner. However, this kind of iteration suggests earlier errors of judgement. It explicitly finds *the recommendations* are not fit for purpose. This ought to be avoided if possible, and it should be unusual, possibly career-limiting.

The *planned iteration* which Paul argued must be built into the *progress stage* basic SPP evaluate phase involved using insight generated by the evaluate phase to decide whether a further pass of the whole SPP or part of the SPP would be useful. In this context, sensitivity diagrams like Figure 7.5 played a central role which was very different from their communication role for the board. For example, if a large contributor to overall uncertainty like source 5 in Figure 7.5 was not well understood, and it looked as if this mattered, further effort to understand what was involved and how it might be managed needed careful consideration as a *process management decision before going to the board*.

However, given the effective communication provided for the presumed one pass gateway SPP, board members might well draw different inferences based on wider experience or different perspectives, a central aspect of governance interpreted in positive terms, and this might lead to further unplanned iterations.

Wrapping up his first workshop

Paul brought his first workshop to a close with a brief review session. He made sure that all the main messages had been absorbed, and there was a positive perspective on the changes ahead. He knew that he had just started a change management project of considerable complexity which would raise many challenges, for many practical purposes usefully seen as a programme or portfolio of change management programmes and projects. As soon as possible he wanted to start to build an appetite for change, confronting the associated challenges working with individuals and small groups. He made this very clear and emphasised that this first workshop was about a very high level summary overview of where they were going which they could all share at the outset to help them get started. Paul wanted to move each member of his group forward at a pace they could cope with, and he wanted to ensure that capability development and culture changes kept pace with the tasks they addressed.

Paul's overall change management strategy – initial goals

Paul had a much more developed overall strategic change management plan than Martha in Chapter 6. In part this was because he had extensive project planning experience using PUMP-based approaches which provided a sound foundation for his current understanding of the basic SPP, the associated gateway SPP, and the 'SPP pack' of all progress and gateway SPP concepts for all lifecycle stages. In part, it was also because he could use a variant of all these SPP concepts to address the management of change within WSL – a higher level use of the same basic conceptual framework. But he was open to changes in his strategy and the operational form of his underlying concepts as he learned during the initial implementation and ongoing development of his strategy, and he took a very flexible approach to his rate of progress. He wanted to avoid rushing key developments that had to bed down to provide firm foundations for later developments.

While his group was adapting to their new approach via a programme of technical workshops to be discussed shortly, trying out the ideas using some basic aspects of current projects in progress as simple test beds, and having one-to-one conversations about their own roles, Paul started parallel detailed discussions with Ollie. As soon as he could, Paul developed a close working relationship with Ollie at a personal level, working towards a strong partnership between the Operations Group and the Projects Group.

When Paul was confident that he and Ollie had a rich set of planning options which would integrate Operations Group and Projects Group input to the business case for the proposed new sewage plant project, Paul did some joint strategic change management planning with Ollie. They then jointly briefed Michael. As part of briefing Michael, they outlined the purpose of a proposed meeting with Frank and ensured that they had Michael's support for this next stage. They then approached Frank with a view to a joint presentation about their progress so far on the sewage plant and some related issues involving the water mains project. When Frank agreed, and a date was set, Paul had several rehearsals with Ollie, before a meeting designed to lead Frank to the conclusion that he had to significantly redefine his role in WSL business plan modelling. For all projects within the PG remit, near the outset of the concept strategy stage WSL needed much more focus on plans for design purposes created by the Operations Group to identify options which would drive early versions of all the other plans, including dependent business case plans. Crucially, the business case plans were not the primary driver for the sewage works, nor should they be viewed as the primary driver for the new water mains programme. Furthermore, the discount rate applied to future cash flow was not a parameter WSL could treat as a technical judgement within a straightforward NPV process approach best left to Frank without board level scrutiny. Board level responsibility for testing the robustness of *all* underlying assumptions needed a very different approach. At their heart was the implications of assumptions underlying the discount rate and the decision-making process it was embedded in for business case purposes which had important interdependencies with central concerns for Ollie and Paul.

The discount rate used to shape and select projects

Paul started the meeting with Frank with an outline of the proposed agenda. Paul did not hide the importance of a discussion about the discount rate which he would soon come to. However, in addition to the usual opening pleasantries, Paul wanted to begin by indirectly selling Frank the benefits of an EP approach in broad terms. He particularly wanted to sell the proposition that an EP approach for all aspects of WSL decision making would give Frank's role as custodian of WSL finances more opportunities. He also wanted to ensure that Frank understood why uncertainty and complexity associated with their sewage plant case – like no choice of site as yet with all the follow-on uncertainties – was an opportunity to be embraced by the board, not risk to be avoided.

Paul began his discussion of the appropriate discount rate to use for NPV calculations by acknowledging that this was usually seen as the Finance Director's responsibility in companies like WSL. As an immediately relevant comparison, it was usually seen as the responsibility of bodies like HM Treasury for UK government decisions. Furthermore, those responsible for choosing the discount rate to be used usually drew on financial economics as outlined by standard texts which were based on well-established schools of thought.

However, HM Treasury had recently acknowledged earlier misconceptions of a very serious and fundamental nature, which had important, direct implications for the private sector as well as the public sector, especially private sector companies like WSL which used bond funding to leverage return on shares. *A fundamental underlying flaw in most* (not quite all) *NPV modelling was a failure to recognise the need for more than one hurdle rate test if more than one objective or any constraints on investment were involved, keeping most of these tests OUTSIDE the discount rate.* This was essential to avoid bias associated with a discount rate set too high in an attempt to get away with a single-hurdle rate test of the form 'Is the NPV positive?' Paul emphasised that HM Treasury (2003a) recognised this fundamental problem and mandated a multiple test approach for all UK public sector decision making, *explicitly* removing the 'risk premium' and 'the opportunity cost of other forgone investments' from the discount rate mandated by HM Treasury prior to 2003, acknowledging a long history of previously getting this important issue wrong.

Paul said he had undertaken considerable background reading – enough to verify that the question of choosing an appropriate discount rate had a very long and confusing history, with no stable generally accepted 'received wisdom' as yet, although many people would disagree and argue that their perspective was '*the* received wisdom *which was correct*'. This was the case 50 years ago, and central underlying issues were still unresolved. His position would be seen as highly contentious by many people, and he acknowledged he was not a financial economist. But anyone disagreeing with him would have to acknowledge a particular school of thought and demonstrate a clear understanding of the nature of disagreements with other schools of thought if they had any real clarity about the issues. There was a very old 'joke' that could be stated in the form 'If you ask 10 economists a serious question you should be prepared for at least 11 answers'. It was not very funny if the serious question urgently needed an answer, but it was relevant to understanding what was going on here. So was the EP position on this controversy, and the concept of stealth assumptions from an EP perspective.

The starting point for understanding an EP position, which Paul made direct use of, was the paper 'An Optimized Multiple Test Framework for Project Selection in the Public Sector with a Nuclear Waste Disposal Case-based Example' (Chapman, Ward, and Klein, 2006). This paper argued that in public sector projects the government's expected future bond rate was the only consideration which should be embedded in the discount rate – all other considerations needed separate tests, building on the HM Treasury (2003a) multiple-tests approach. A positive NPV using the expected future bond rate for discounting purposes involves passing a 'bond test'. Passing this bond test confirms that if expectations about the bond rate and the cash flows were correct, then the cost of borrowing could be covered. *No other objectives or constraints were addressed by this test, and its validity depended on unbiased estimates of all expected outcomes being used – not just the discount rate.*

A separate 'return test' was needed to address the question, 'Does the surplus return after borrowing costs compare favourably with other available options given constraints on public sector investment *in this particular sector*, like education, defence or transport?' This was a generalised variant of the opportunity cost considerations often embedded in the discount rate for all possible government investments, *but it was specific to expenditure categories as well as being outside the discount rate*. A high priority expenditure category implied a relatively low return requirement and vice versa – priorities were reflected by the shadow prices associated with constraints defining how much investment to make in each expenditure area. As government priorities changed for political reasons, different priorities could be reflected by different return tests in different expenditure areas, with significant negative returns allowed in very high priority cases. As an extreme example, military expenditure would not be tightly constrained in the middle of a war of survival, but it would be in a time of peace with no obvious prospects of war on the horizon. From an EP perspective, embedding these return tests in opportunity cost contributions to the discount rate was an extremely serious conceptual mistake, with crucial operational bias implications, because it muddled different return requirements for different sectors in a discounting process which should not address considerations other than the expected cost of capital raised via government bonds.

Further necessary tests included 'risk' tests – to address *all* relevant sources of uncertainty giving rise to important risks. Many of the most important risks were not financial or financial markets related – like the possibility of contaminating groundwater with nuclear waste if disposal of nuclear waste using deep mines was allowed to proceed or the risk of failing to preserve a UK capability to develop nuclear power if disposal was deferred and this had an impact on political pressure to stop producing more nuclear waste and the demise of national nuclear engineering capability. From an EP perspective, 'risk premiums' in a discount rate were another extremely serious conceptual mistake, with crucial operational error implications. Even if the risks involved were purely financial in nature, which often they clearly were not, the market-based assumptions, plus any other assumptions needed, require effective robustness testing. Any aspects of projects which may change fundamental market perceptions of an organisation needed *very* special care and attention, even if the organisation involved is a national government.

In a national government context, important further tests were needed to address intergenerational transfer issues – was this generation having economic advantages paid for by future generations, or vice versa, to an extent that either generation would find unacceptable? This 'heritage' test was a good example of a test which had to be addressed at a portfolio level (not a specific project level or a particular sector level) because it was the overall balance across all new projects which mattered, one of several ongoing flaws in the 2003 HM Treasury position from an EP perspective. Furthermore, this heritage test was also a good example of a test with ethical content – simply observing past revealed preferences (as the 2003 HM Treasury approach does) involved working assumptions which needed to be questioned and tested effectively.

The Chapman, Ward, and Klein (2006) paper showed why a 1990s decision by the UK Department of the Environment (DoE) to postpone nuclear waste disposal in order to save £100 million using the HM Treasury mandated real discount rate of 6% real (DoE, 1994) at that time was seriously ill informed. It was actually a £2 billion mistake, 'other things being equal', in terms of the less than 3% real discount rate mandated by HM Treasury a decade later (HM Treasury, 2003a). On its own figures, given its own assumptions, what might be reasonably interpreted as a £2 billion error was involved because of mandated HM Treasury advice. It was very obvious that 'other things were by no means equal', but it was also very obvious these 'other things' had been ignored in terms of the single test NPV approach mandated by the Treasury before 2003, and not effectively considered within the rest of the decision-making framework. In effect, the 1994 decision using a discount rate which was far too high gave excess weight to the money saved by putting off doing anything new and too little weight to the future implications, bearing in mind sooner or later something different had to be done, with no direct consideration of the risks and opportunities which really mattered.

Paul emphasised that it was the implications of immediate relevance to WSL which mattered to WSL, not the nuclear waste issue or the more general debate about 'best' practice decision making in a discounted cash flow framework. As explained by Chapman and Ward (2011) when using a private sector water mains investment example directly comparable to the WSL context, in the simplest case this boiled down to two WSL discount rates for two portfolios, one associated with bond funding and the other associated with corporate working capital funding, and separate tests for all relevant objectives other than covering the cost of capital for associated planning.

For example, Paul, Ollie, and Michael were all agreed that the new sewage works project should be part of WSL's 'bond funded portfolio', and he was sure Frank would also agree. This meant Frank ought to make the best estimate he could of the expected cost of bond funding over the life of the asset and use this bond rate in his NPV calculation. He should also take a view on the best timing for this funding, which might or might not coincide with the currently planned timing for the execution stage of the project. The board should use Frank's views on bond market rates and funding availability when considering trade-offs between alternatives like the proposed new sewage works and the water mains replacement programme and the timing for both because bond funding could be used for both and relative returns after the cost of bond funded capital investment as well as other benefits and risks had to be addressed explicitly and directly by the board. Issues beyond return on investment, including regulator and public pressure, might be crucial. Most important, in the case of both these projects the low bond rate relative to the much higher rate of return on shares expected by shareholders meant that WSL would avoid the well-understood problems of bias associated with using discount rates which were too high – a bias towards 'quick buck' high risk projects, away from long payback period low risk projects. Current WSL practice meant that the discount rates used were too high because they incorporated a risk premium as well as other factors which should be outside the discounting process.

At this point Ollie led the conversation for a while, as prearranged. He began by emphasising that it was not just a question of which projects were selected when choosing between projects. The discount rate also had a dramatic effect on the way projects were shaped prior to the project selection process. He used current planning for the new sewage works to explain that WSL traditionally used a high discount rate which was driven by shareholder rate of return expectations. This led to what might be termed 'low quality' choices, in the sense that they involved relatively low capital cost estimates coupled to relatively high operating cost estimates. He was now exploring the use of a relatively low discount rate which was largely driven by bond funding rates. This was leading to what might be termed 'high quality' choices, involving relatively high capital costs coupled to relatively low operating costs. It was also leading to a very rich set of new kinds of options because of new levels of creativity triggered by the new perspective. He emphasised the obvious direct importance of the lower discount rate in justifying much higher quality plant with much lower maintenance cost expectations as well as a much longer life expectancy. He also emphasised the importance of the new insight he now had, which he hoped would become a mindset shift associated with EP thinking in WSL: *quality now matters much more to WSL than it did previously because a lower discount rate means the future now matters much more – chasing a 'quick buck' is now much less attractive, despite a very aggressive sustained focus on a high expected rate of return for WSL shareholders.*

This can be seen as simply recognising the implications of the well-established benefits of using other people's money (extending a key aspect of the Chapter 5 tale).

Paul then suggested that they briefly discuss the 'working capital funded portfolio'. This second portfolio would involve NPV calculations using a discount rate based on Frank's best estimate of WSL shareholder rate of return expectations. This was the working capital funded portfolio for investments which clearly should not be viewed as bond funded. A relevant current example was a project to encourage customers to use less water initiated and managed by Curt, the Customer Relations Director. It involved significant investment in advertising, advertising having an impact half-life measured in months, as well as subsidised sales of water butts for storing rainwater by customers and other devices which would impact consumption for some time. A shareholder expected rate of return was clearly more appropriate than a bond rate as the basis of the discount rate for some aspects of this kind of investment.

There might be some projects which involved the middle ground, especially if funding issues linked to project lifecycle concerns were highly uncertain. In such cases generalising a two portfolio approach to three or more portfolios might be useful.

Paul then observed that the arguments used to support received wisdom approaches which always used the shareholder expectation rate or a weighted average of this rate and the bond rate were using stealth assumptions which did not withstand scrutiny from an EP perspective. If WSL discounting used an expected rate of return on shares or an 80/20 weighting of the bond and shareholder expectation rates for all business cases as their central test, they were implicitly assuming there was no distinction between investing in new water mains designed to last 100 years exclusively funded at bond rates and advertising to reduce water consumption with a half-life impact measured in months funded via working capital.

Frank quickly understood in intuitive terms the stealth assumption implications of the 'at least two separate portfolios and a multiple tests approach to discounting' EP perspective. He had always been slightly uneasy about the received wisdom used in WSL's current approach, but unwilling to say so and depart from his textbook basis without a clear rationale for an alternative. Paul anticipated this understanding and pressed on, but in case it was needed he had prepared additional explanation, explored with Michael earlier. You might find a brief exploration of Paul's contingency plan explanation useful now.

The EP perspective on discount rates underlying Paul's two or more portfolios, and a multiple tests discount rate approach, can be explored in terms of four steps.

The first step involves understanding that the most general (unrestrictive) basis for adding monetary values in time period t and time period t + 1 for any relevant t is a decision maker preference (or revealed preference) function which effectively asks, 'How much money in time period t + 1 is equivalent to £1 in period t, as a basis for "adding apples to apple equivalents" to get a total in terms of apple equivalents?' If the answer is £1.04 the implication is a 4% discount rate equates to the implied indifference needed in order to work with 'apple equivalents' instead of 'apples, pears, bananas and so on'.

The second step involves recognising that a 4% discount rate is a reasonable working assumption if the options being considered can be funded at 4% real (net of inflation) on average over the horizon being considered, and all cash flows are in today's (un-inflated) money values. However, a positive NPV using this discount rate simply indicates a 'borrowing rate test' has been passed, which means the decision maker can expect to get their money back after borrowing costs.

The third step involves appreciating that putting any other considerations into the discount rate to facilitate a single test approach produces bias, distorting the role of discounting. Future cash flows (positive or negative) will be excessively discounted. For example, adding an opportunity cost premium to impose capital rationing through a higher hurdle rate means the decision maker will reject low risk projects involving a long payback period which should be accepted, replacing them with high risk quick-buck projects which should be rejected. Opportunity cost considerations should be considered separately, using appropriate shadow prices outside the discount rate, even if this is the only additional consideration and its nature is very simple. Many economists made this very clear in the 1960s and 1970s, in the different context of discussing IRR (Internal Rate of Return, the discount rate that produces a zero NPV). The key concern then was arguing the case for never choosing between projects based on relative IRR, although using a cash flow defined by the difference in alternative projects was a very useful parametric analysis approach in an IRR framework if decision makers were unsure what interest rate should be used, *and all relevant working assumptions were understood.*

The final step, as outlined in Chapman, Ward and Klein (2006) and Chapman and Ward (2011), is recognising that a multiple criteria mathematical programming framework is the most general conceptual framework to deal with all relevant objectives and constraints other than the cost of borrowing embedded in the discount rate, but simple and visible working assumptions can be used to provide simple practical approaches which do not require direct use of mathematical programming. For example, capital rationing in particular bond funded portfolio areas (water mains versus sewage plants for example) could be imposed by guessing at the shadow price associated with an annual capital spending budget constraint in each spending area, testing each new possible investment with this shadow price in terms of rate of return over and above borrowing cost, passing clear winners immediately and rejecting clear losers immediately, but ordering all the 'maybe' outcome projects towards the end of the financial period used for planning to spend whatever remains of the available funding.

WSL operation of some variant of a two-portfolio approach means Frank has to ensure WSL does not invest more at any given time than the bond market can take (with bank bridging funding if appropriate). Frank also needs to ensure that this bond funding is not used in ways the bond market would not endorse. But Frank is not a gatekeeper for projects operating a single hurdle rate test. The board as a whole will have to take a view on the monetary expected return and associated risk after borrowing costs *plus all* the other expected benefits and risks of options like new sewage works, water main replacement and conservation measures. Other benefits and risks include customer perceptions of WSL and regulator relationship concerns.

Furthermore, Frank, Ollie and Paul needed to work together to manage other constraints and factors, like the limitations of local contractor availability, and the implications of traffic disruption caused by WSL construction activities or WSL operations disruption issues. Many of these issues need qualitative judgements at the board level, and some implied ongoing planning to deal with complexity needing attention outside the basic business case metrics embedded in common hurdle rate tests.

Having omitted this aside, which Paul had ready to go in the form outlined earlier, Paul went on to clarify his other concerns by suggesting that he had two lines of input he would like to pursue later with Frank. One was the use of a bond rate discount factor made higher capital cost but longer life and lower maintenance water mains a preferred option – as for *all* bond funded WSL capital assets. The other was replacing the one national contractor approach currently proposed with a portfolio of contracts for tranches of new water mains installation. They could use several local contractors as well as several national major players. This would yield significantly lower costs. They could ensure a degree of ongoing competition between multiple contractors to keep delivered quality high and costs achieved low. Frank, Ollie and he could work together with other directors to speed up or slow down the programme depending on both bond rates and construction cost rates, as well as regulator and customer views on leakage rates from old water mains, and local resident and council (local government) views on traffic disruption due to mains replacement projects.

Low interest rates coupled to low economic activity driving low construction cost expectations was the time to press ahead with the maximum rate of progress they could manage. The issues they would have to address in this maximum rate of progress scenario would include avoiding traffic and WSL operations disruption that was unacceptable, involving close coordination with Ollie and local government road traffic planners. He indicated that Michael was *very* enthusiastic about this possibility, as was their board chairman Charles. If *Frank* were to present a business case to the board based on this approach, Paul was sure the support for *Frank* would be unanimous.

Paul did everything he could to ensure that Frank felt he was a key player in the new thinking that was going to implement an EP perspective across the whole of WSL's planning, and in no way remiss in not being aware of the flaws in conventional wisdom about NPV discount rates from an EP perspective. Paul had been clear from the start that he needed to treat Frank as an equal but senior partner, and Paul could not afford to offend Frank, unless his very best efforts failed, and both Michael and Charles were on his side of an argument that was best avoided.

The basis of the critique of conventional NPV analysis using a single hurdle rate test just outlined is conceptually sound and the suggested alternative approach using multiple tests in a goal programming conceptual framework is operationally feasible. But it is important to acknowledge that accepted wisdom does not yet reflect these views, and *all* views in this context are highly contentious. This book is not the place for a technical debate about this controversy. However, consider the following paragraph, and reflect on its relevance to your organisation when you review this book's implications as a whole.

The view ANY organisation takes on the correct discount rates to use in all investment appraisals matters greatly, and distinguishing between different kinds of investments may be an important factor. These issues may matter more than avoiding inappropriate time scale and cost estimates. They do not just affect all project selection choices. They also affect the way projects are shaped, and they may affect underlying corporate culture. Any organisation which risks continuing with discount rate policies which may be inappropriate is taking a risk which really matters. Taking this 'discount rate risk' is both wholly inappropriate and totally unnecessary – a particularly dysfunctional form of opportunity inefficiency.

Regulation risk – privatisation and nationalisation risk concerns

Frank had no difficulty understanding the rationale or the very significant implications of the two or more portfolios and multiple test approach as explained by Paul and Ollie. He also saw some possible further implications of importance. He reciprocated Paul's cooperative spirit by suggesting they both needed a conversation as soon as possible with Richard, WSL's Regulation Director, to explore these further implications.

'Regulation risk' was a WSL category of 'enterprise risk' which Richard had to lead on. Ofwat, the regulator concerned with customer prices, was currently advocating privatisation of primary water supply sources like rivers and reservoirs on a basis which would be separate from earlier privatisation of water and sewage companies – purportedly to lower prices for consumers, although some read these privatisation proposals as playing silly political games motivated by seriously unsound economic beliefs. The water industry as a whole was resisting as strongly as it could, with some success, arguing that this form of privatisation would not lower customer costs – it would increase customer costs.

Frank thought that Paul's multiple tests and multiple portfolios approach might help to clarify the way bond price destabilisation driving share price destabilisation would work to increase the cost of capital underlying water and sewage costs for consumers if this form of privatisation was pursued – but it also suggested a further possible opportunity.

WSL had major reservoirs used for leisure and recreation purposes. WSL might counter Ofwat by more explicitly linking WSL bond funding to assets like reservoirs, as well as water mains built to last 100 years, and sewage works built to very high standards for long life, low operating costs, and reliability. They might use this link to encourage their water and sewage customers to buy bonds to preserve local control of their reservoirs and keep their water rates low and encourage their customers to attack the Ofwat plans to devalue its bonds and drive up water rates, interfere with their local amenities, and 'steal their local natural resources', perhaps providing financial support for a lobby which also addressed government views in a direct manner.

When he met with Frank and Paul, Richard was very interested in Frank's line of thinking. Richard warmly endorsed Paul's multiple portfolios and tests approach as well as the broader EP approach, but he suggested they also involve Curt, the Customer Relations Director. His reasoning was Frank's strategy might decrease the risk of privatisation of this kind, but increase the risk of nationalisation of all primary water sources, plus all the currently privatised closely coupled assets like reservoirs, plus perhaps the water and sewage industry as a whole, a risk which was very much in the background but a concern Curt had raised.

Curt was very pleased that Richard had suggested a meeting, enthusiastic about Frank's involvement, and delighted that Paul had triggered consideration of this aspect of his EP approach. As Curt put it when he elaborated on Richard's introduction, most customer groups had raised some significant objections when all the UK water and sewage companies were first privatised via a nationwide restructuring, but they had not been very militant about their objections because of what seemed like a plausible government sales pitch and ambiguity about the implications. Big profits by early investors had attracted some early complaints. What was now making customer groups increasingly hostile and potentially very militant was a growth of ownership of water and sewage companies by banks, sovereign wealth funds and other investors clearly in it for short horizon profitability reasons. This was leading to high profit rates because of bond gearing. It was also leading to an increasingly strident view by consumer groups that 'their rivers and groundwater and reservoirs being used to make people rich who were not part of or interested in the local community'. Indeed, some of the water and sewage industry 'bond' funding was now offshore, making relatively high rates of return which was exempt from UK taxation. Sooner or later customer backlash might catch up with the water and sewage industry. Although complete re-nationalisation was currently unlikely, it was possible, and there was a growing consensus that the original privatisation had been misjudged and the politics which underlay current regulation was being mishandled.

In Curt's view, the current Ofwat privatisation proposals were just plain silly, but what made a lot more sense was nationalisation of all these resources, plus national control of new ways to shift water from areas in surplus to areas in deficit (water pipelines and canals for example), a nationally determined set of undistributed water costs, and much more effective competition among existing water companies to distribute water at the least cost. A plausible nationalisation variant was forgetting about more effective competition amongst existing water companies and nationalisation of the whole of the water supply and sewage disposal industry. With his WSL 'customer hat' on Curt privately thought that both these nationalisation variants were quite attractive, but with his WSL 'executive director hat' on he viewed either as a very serious problem.

Paul encouraged Frank, Richard and Curt to embrace the EP perspective which gave rise to seeing the links between these concerns, and he contributed to their ongoing pursuit of these issues, but he avoided direct personal involvement in board level controversy involving emotive issues like privatisation versus nationalisation when he did not need to be a part of it at this stage. He had more than enough controversy to cope with within the Projects Group, and it needed his undivided attention.

We will return to these issues in Part 3. They are important in the context of the full set of this book's messages. However, for the moment their pursuit would be a distraction from the central thrust of this chapter which is best avoided, and both Chapters 8 and 9 shed further light on linked underlying issues, a further reason for delaying the discussion.

Technical workshops plus other parallel activities

Immediately after his first workshop, in parallel with the meetings with Ollie, Frank, Richard and Curt just discussed, Paul began one-to-one meetings with everyone in his group. He saw direct discussions on a personal basis as a crucial and immediate need, with careful prior planning of each meeting to ensure that all topics needing this personal private treatment were covered.

Paul also initiated small group working on a carefully selected and planned series of 'demonstration tasks' within carefully chosen 'demonstration projects'. He wanted everyone to learn by doing, with mentoring provided by himself and supporting consultants he could depend on, starting with relatively straightforward tasks his team was prepared for via a series of 'technical workshops'.

The series of technical workshops were mandatory for the PG team and optional for other selected WSL staff. In particular, through Ollie, he invited Operations Group participation from the start. The workshops were technical in the sense that they provided conceptual and operational tools to support the learning by doing, but they had other objectives too, like building teamwork and morale.

This section addresses the topics of *some* of these technical workshops which are immediately relevant to most target readers. It omits those discussing reasonably straightforward but essential background issues covered in earlier chapters of this book, and Chapman and Ward (2011) topics you might explore later. It begins with probability-impact grids as clarity inefficient tools and ambiguity uncertainty and underlying complexity as key aspects of estimates. The use of the same basic SPP strategy progress stage process by the OG and PG teams in all four strategy progress stages is then considered in three subsections, followed by three more subsections addressing plans for relationships and contracts, teamwork, and an overview of the progress stages which follow on after strategy has been agreed on.

PIGs (probability-impact grids or graphs) as clarity inefficient tools

One of Paul's early priorities was eliminating from 'the WSL toolset' any tools which were clarity inefficient in all relevant circumstances. He wanted to make it easier for everyone to learn how to select and use tools which were clarity efficient in the right context. He was particularly concerned about one very simple and much loved but seriously dysfunctional operational tool which carried 'conceptual baggage' with surprisingly broad implications.

Paul began one of his early technical workshops by explaining that he knew many of the PG team used and liked what he would refer to as PIGs (probability-impact grids or graphs), also known as probability-impact matrices (contracted to PIMs), probability-impact diagrams (PIDs), and other comparable labels. He indicated their origins lay in pre-1960 safety management, a context in which they made sense for reasons outlined later, but they were now used very widely in many operations and corporate management contexts in a dysfunctional manner for reasons about to be explored. For example, Operations Group staff might be regular users, and he knew that Enterprise Risk Management (ERM) was one of Frank's current interests, some ERM also using PIGs. He planned to discuss PIGs and ERM later with Frank and Ollie. PIGs were part of current WSL practice within and beyond the PG team, needing attention in all decision-making areas using them, but his focus that day would be PG team usage.

Paul observed that many of the risk management experts he had met over the last two decades defended PIGs vigorously – even though they all understood their shortcomings to some extent, usually arguing that PIGs may have important defects but that they were easy to explain and a good place to start. He observed that PIGs were advocated in PMI PMBoK guides as the basis of what was referred to as 'qualitative analysis' which preceded directly linked 'quantitative analysis', reflecting what he had observed as widespread international common practice (e.g. see PMI, 2008). He also observed that PIGs were tolerated in some APM PRAM chapters (e.g. see APM, 1997) and used in many other guides. Furthermore, he acknowledged that no project risk management guides he was aware of clearly stated 'under no circumstances use PIGs'.

Paul then put on a deliberately rather forced but broad smile and said, 'But under no circumstances are PIGs to be used by PG planners from now on,' and he would be 'arguing for PIGs being dropped from usage by all WSL management decision making'.

He then said *all* members of the PG team needed to understand why, *that day*, and reboot their thinking using a much broader conceptual framework, and a much more powerful associated set of tools. Given the support for PIGs by many guides, and the lack of direct condemnation by other guides, it was not surprising that WSL staff might be confused on this issue, but they now needed clarity without delay. In particular, he was depending upon some of the former Risk Management Department members to provide technical EP support to PG team led planning addressing all stages in the project lifecycle using their modelling and facilitation skills, and they could not do that effectively if the PG team as a whole did not understand why PIGs were a symptom of restricted and limiting thinking within a framework which had to be abandoned. Complete and unequivocal rejection of any framework which made use of PIGs was mandatory for anyone who wanted to continue reporting to him.

Paul made a point of saying he believed he was not dogmatic in most circumstances, and he generally took a very flexible approach to issues like this, but he believed a determination to keep using PIGs despite their clear defects was a clear and endemic symptom of a failure to fully understand the underlying basis of an EP for projects toolset, skill set, and objectives. He then showed them Figure 7.7, indicating that it was a simple example of a preferable alternative to *any* PIG variant in *any* context from an EP perspective.

He explained that Figure 7.7, taken from Chapman and Ward (2011), had been designed to help those who value PIGs as basic tools understand why it is clarity efficient to abandon the use of PIGs in all contexts – *provided those they have to work with can also be convinced*. He observed that many others in the project management community were opposed to the use of PIGs, for a wide variety of at least partially related reasons. Debates on this issue were common but often confusing because different basic framing assumptions and very different objectives were involved – stealth assumptions which really mattered were rife. They needed an overview understanding of the issues to deal with this.

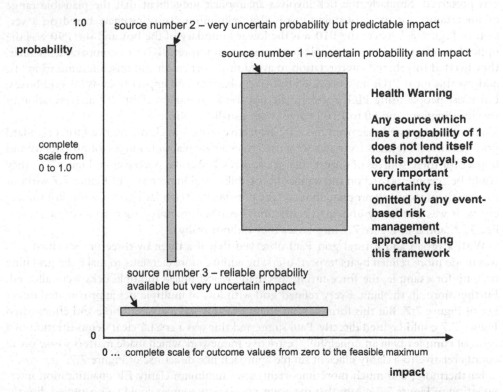

Figure 7.7 A more powerful portrayal of the information on any PIG.

Paul briefly elaborated his first workshop description of the clarity efficiency concept in terms of its Figure 3.5 efficient frontier portrayal plus the 'stealth assumption' concept introduced in Part 1. In earlier technical workshops he had covered an introduction to the stealth assumption concept along with an overview of all the Chapter 3 estimation and opportunity efficiency concepts. He then made several points related to Figure 7.7 which needed clear understanding.

To begin he suggested that those familiar with PIGs could visualise any PIG structure they preferred superimposed in Figure 7.7, but three probability classes and three impact classes would be a convenient default assumption for present purposes. He indicated that if he was explaining Figure 7.7 to someone who was not familiar with PIGs, he would suggest they should imagine three rows and three columns of equal width defining nine boxes (elements), with the outer (top-right) box associated with 'high probability' and 'high impact' coloured red, the inner (bottom-left) box associated with 'low probability' and 'low impact' coloured green, with amber or yellow intermediate boxes.

Paul then suggested they picture ticking a box to represent a particular risk – a source of event uncertainty from the perspective of the more general EP framework. From an EP perspective, placing this tick in a box involved an implicit judgement that the plausible range of uncertainty for the impact involved a minimum clarity estimate based on a version of Figure 3.1 he had used earlier, where the P10 is the left-hand boundary of the box and the P90 was the right-hand boundary, unless some alternative quantitative interpretation was preferred. Similarly, the tick involves an implicit judgement that the plausible range of uncertainty for the probability involved a minimum clarity estimate based on a version of Figure 3.1 where the P10 was the lower boundary of the box and the P90 was the upper boundary. If different people were going to interpret PIGs in a comparable manner, they needed this shared interpretation to avoid misinformation and miscommunication. To address this most PIGs now provided formal probability and impact bounds for grid boxes, but most people using PIGs regularly did not use a minimum clarity EP interpretation of this information, and P0 to P100 ranges were usually *implicit*.

He next suggested that from this EP perspective there was clearly no need for a standard grid, because if Figure 3.1 variants were used to estimate plausible ranges for probability and impact for three sources of uncertainty like sources 1, 2 and 3 portrayed in Figure 7.7, they could be accommodated on the standard probability and impact axes of Figure 7.7 without forcing them to fit inappropriate boxes – the pre-specified standard grid was not just unnecessary, it was a seriously unhelpful restriction, because it required users to force-fit sources like 1, 2, and 3 in Figure 7.7 into boxes they did not really fit.

With a broad and natural grin Paul observed that if a three-by-three pre-specified grid was made more refined by its 'expert' users, by adding more elements to make the grid nine by nine for example, the force-fitting was made worse unless multiple ticks were allowed. Furthermore, in the limit a very refined grid with lots of multiple tics approximated direct use of Figure 7.7. But this form of refinement of PIGs was a waste of time and effort when Figure 7.7 could be used directly. Paul suggested this was a crystal-clear demonstration of a form of complexity in an unhelpfully restrictive framework which made matters worse on all counts relative to a clarity efficient simple approach like direct use of Figure 7.7.

Furthermore, and much more important, any minimum clarity EP quantification interpretation of Figure 7.7 meant that the event uncertainty sources could be quantified directly, using a clarity efficient minimum clarity approach or preferred alternatives, to be combined later in a simple but effective quantitative analysis, without the confusing qualitative analysis followed by quantitative analysis transformation process distinctions made by common practice. Furthermore, if appropriate, sources like the three portrayed could be decomposed first, and they could be associated with responses, decision diagrams and sensitivity diagrams. This opened a portal into a wide range of possible qualitative analysis approaches to be followed by probabilistic quantitative approaches to analysis and synthesis which were simply not available to those using a traditional 'qualitative analysis' interpretation of PIGs which was treated as a separable precursor to common practice follow-on quantitative analysis approaches. This portal into EP qualitative and closely coupled quantitative approaches also provided a much richer understanding of a holistic approach to all analysis concerns. It provided a 'gateway concept' in the Biggs and Tang (2011) sense into a much deeper understanding of what might be involved in any context of interest, which could be used in a clarity efficient way.

From an EP perspective, PIGs were not a sensible basis for initial qualitative analysis to be followed by optional quantitative analysis using the traditional common practice approach previously adopted by WSL. From an EP perspective, PIGs were not a *qualitative* approach at all – they were a weak approach to quantification in a very poorly structured and highly inflexible, pre-specified qualitative analysis structure. PIGs were clarity inefficient to a wholly unacceptable extent, *even when dealing with event uncertainty in the absence of any other kinds of uncertainty.*

Further still, and most important of all, the biggest flaw of PIGs was that they lead people to ignore, or attempt to treat separately, any sources of uncertainty which are not events. Indeed, many PIG users formally defined 'issues' as 'sources of uncertainty with a probability of one', to be treated separately from risk management as they defined 'risk management', arguably a dysfunctional approach of Mad Hatter proportions in the Alice in Wonderland league as defined by the Chapter 1 discussion of terminology.

Paul emphasised that all relevant inherent variability uncertainty, systemic uncertainty, ambiguity uncertainty, and capability-culture uncertainty, needed clear and effective integrated treatment with event uncertainty, building on his earlier use of Part 1 material to explain what these five portrayals of uncertainty involve. This was why PIGs were not just a badly designed tool for thinking about event risks and a waste of time which failed to make effective use of the information obtained, they were a dangerous distraction. They had to be banned by any organisation adopting an EP approach because they ignored four of the five kinds of relevant uncertainty, and they misconceived the relationships between qualitative and quantitative analysis.

Paul also emphasised that the sensitivity diagram example of Figure 7.5, used in a layered manner for any number of sources, could portray any information contained by common practice PIGs plus subsequent common practice quantitative analysis in addition to dealing with all relevant sources of uncertainty. If the way Figure 7.5 portrays dependencies between sources of uncertainty which involve variability and systemic uncertainty plus ambiguity uncertainty is used to assess common practice examples focused on independent event uncertainty risks, the associated stealth assumptions became clear. Furthermore, the EP toolset he would equip them with, involving sensitivity diagrams, decision diagrams and source-response diagrams, could replace PIG-based analysis with simple clarity efficient qualitative and quantitative analysis which was totally 'off the radar' of a PIG-based approach.

In part to ease the pain for those particularly attached to PIGs, and minimise related withdrawal symptoms, in part to acknowledge aspects of the PIG framework which could be useful provided the underlying basic assumptions were generalised, in part just to further demonstrate the limitations, Paul briefly explored using variants of Figure 7.7 within an EP perspective.

For example, PG planners could start with the Figure 7.7 probability and impact axes, and use rectangles or rounded equivalents representing two or more sources of event uncertainty on one diagram as a form of 'heat graph'. A heat graph (or diagram) was a commonly used portrayal of complete sets of event uncertainty risks on one page, using the same axes as Figure 7.7, with a 'hot' zone coloured red at the top right, a 'cool' zone coloured green or blue at the bottom left, and graduation bands in between.

If important variability, ambiguity, or capability-culture sources of uncertainty involving a probability of one needed inclusion, they could be ordered in terms of impact and included on the top of the same diagram, straddling the probability of one line normally treated as an upper bound, to ensure they were not overlooked.

If systemic uncertainty linking any two or more of these sources of uncertainty needed attention, the nature of simple one-way dependencies plus positive and negative feedback loops could be explored on the same figure in graphical terms using influence diagrams or other related soft systems tools for mapping relationships.

Whether or not influence diagrams or other comparable tools were used as a preliminary to modelling systemic uncertainty, probability trees could be used to model well-behaved dependence and more complex knock-on relationships involving inherent variability uncertainty and ambiguity uncertainty portrayals in variability terms. Causal decision analysis models to explain and manage response relationships could also be developed.

Furthermore, alternative approaches to dependence which were not addressed or even mentioned by Chapman and Ward (2011), like using sets of 'dependence drivers' to capture key aspects of systemic dependence (Cooper et al, 2014), could be addressed in this kind of framework, as they could in a more conventional EP framework.

All these possible generalisations were relevant to WSL contexts, as they are elsewhere, even if event uncertainty is the starting place. But what is always crucially important is being clear from the outset that sources of uncertainty need not be events. Indeed, events might be of minor importance relative to inherent variability uncertainty, ambiguity uncertainty, capability-culture uncertainty and systemic uncertainty. *Capturing ALL relevant uncertainty at a suitable level of detail within a holistic framework is always what really matters.*

At any suitable level of detail in this structured understanding of uncertainty sources, decision trees and associated decision diagrams could be used to address risk efficient choices. Paul emphasised this was where the clarity efficiency concept really started to pay dividends, in terms of delivering risk efficiency and opportunity efficiency. He then spent some time elaborating the decision-making power of the EP framework, developing this book's Part 1 examples and further Chapman and Ward (2011) examples. Unbiased estimating was a necessary basic condition for good decision making, but there was a lot more to good decision-making practice which they also needed to understand to help WSL achieve an EP approach.

Along the way he made it very clear that the absence of PIGs did not mean 'risk lists' (logs or registers) would simply disappear – they would be transformed into 'source of uncertainty lists', referred to using the contraction 'source lists', and extended to 'source and response lists'. These source lists would normally be much shorter than current risk lists because decomposition of sources would only be encouraged where it paid off in clarity efficiency terms. But source and response lists would be much broader in scope, much more sophisticated in terms of their structure, and much more useful because of specific and general response linkages between sources and responses. Some responses would be specific to particular sources. But general responses to sets of sources would prove very important. Some responses might involve significant secondary sources and responses – first choice responses might not work. Diagrams to assist when the complexity involved was worth exploring would also be important. Some sources would receive quantitative treatment, but some would be treated as conditions.

In summary, Paul's technical workshop on PIGs made it clear to *all* PG team members that the Projects Group were starting in a different place than *some* (not all) common-practice project risk management, certainly very different from the variant of common practice used by the old WSL Risk Management Department. Everything they used to do would now be done within a broader framework. This would provide them with much greater power when needed, but with the flexibility to keep it simple in a rich range of ways appropriate to the context. Most important, their ambitions would be very much higher, and their jobs would be much more interesting because they would be addressing a much broader role within WSL.

Paul indicated that current members of the Risk Management Department might feel that they had been especially targeted on this occasion, and to some extent this was intentional. However, all members of the PG team needed a clear understanding of the rationale for 'no more PIGs'.

Paul then suggested that all members of the old Risk Management Department had one of two key roles to play in the new restructured PG team.

In some cases, their current role as facilitator and modeller might simply broaden to not only providing a lead on model structuring for all relevant plans and all associated uncertainty and complexity in a clarity efficient manner, including the elicitation of probabilities, execution of quantitative analysis, and interpreting the synthesis of both quantitative and qualitative analysis, but also to addressing the range of deterministic models underlying project base plan development. They would have to broaden their skills base, but they would be given all the help they needed. He emphasised there was an ongoing role for people with modelling skills, both deterministic and probabilistic models, and there was a lot of scope for helping everybody involved to use them on their own as well as assisting with formal modelling of novel or complex issues. Former Planning Department staff who were experienced users of project base plan models might be interested in moving into probabilistic modelling of all planning and playing a similar role.

In other cases, along with former members of the two other PG departments, some of the former Risk Management Department staff might move towards a team leader role as PG group members learned to work together in flexible teams. Team leaders would need good interpersonal skill sets as well as relevant technical skill sets and a good understanding of EP in holistic terms. Team leaders might have a background in project risk management, but they could have a background in traditional project planning or estimating, and they might have a background outside of all three.

Paul emphasised that he wanted *all* PG team members to clearly understand that fundamental change was not an option if they wanted to remain in his team, but he also wanted to be as positive and supportive as he could for those willing to make the change.

Ambiguity uncertainty and underlying complexity as a key aspect of estimates

Paul began a follow-on technical workshop by acknowledging that former Risk Management Department members might have felt some discomfort in his last workshop, and the current workshop might continue their discomfort. However, it would also prove uncomfortable for former Estimating Department members. Furthermore, former members of the Planning Department need not feel smug because their complete absence from concept strategy stage participation was arguably an even greater cause for concern, and he would pick up related issues in later workshops.

Having made the overall nature of his critical position clear, to ensure everyone understood they all had to embrace change, he added that none of the PG team should feel personally or professionally responsible for the problems explored last time or in the current and later workshops, and he hoped the current workshop would start to explain why.

He reminded everyone that WSL concept strategy stage cost estimates were currently based on a point estimate provided by the Estimating Department plus a 'risk adjustment' produced at a later date by the Risk Management Department.

The risk list used for this risk adjustment was generated by a common practice approach based on PIGs, often running to 50 or more risks, with risks being 'event uncertainty sources' from an EP perspective – sources of uncertainty associated with events. Each risk had a point estimate of its probability of occurring, plus an estimated probability distribution for its impact in terms of cost. The risk adjustment was the expected value of the complete list, obtained via Monte Carlo simulation, usually assuming independence between events.

To understand why this was an inappropriate place to start, and how much better estimates could be provided with a lot less effort, it would be useful for the PG team and the Operations Group planners present to understand how the UK Highways Agency (HA) started from a directly comparable position in 2007 and made its first move towards the position WSL would adopt.

The first step in the HA journey began when the secretary of state for transport responded to a very critical House of Lords review of HA estimating performance by commissioning a report by Mike Nichols (Nichols, 2007).

The second step began when the HA accepted the Nichols Report conclusions and commissioned Nichols Group support for a re-estimation study. Some of the implications of the re-estimation study were published in the Association for Project Management guide *Prioritising Project Risks – A Short Guide to Useful Techniques* (Hopkinson, Close, Hillson, and Ward, 2008). They were discussed further by Chapman and Ward (2011).

Prior to the re-estimation study, HA estimators were expected to provide a point estimate early in the concept strategy stage for new major road projects, and later a risk adjustment was provided – a situation directly comparable to the current WSL approach. Indeed, the pre-2007 HA approach was directly comparable to the current WSL approach apart from one notable difference. Mandated UK government 'advice' required the HA to implement HM Treasury rules on the adjustment of all estimates for 'optimism bias' (HM Treasury, 2003a, 2003b) *unless* a formal risk management approach approved by HM Treasury was used to adjust for risk, in which case no 'optimism bias' uplift adjustment was required. The HA used a risk management approach comparable to WSL's current approach to remove this adjustment as soon as possible or avoid it at the outset. Adjusting for optimism bias would amount to an uplift of about 65% for most major new road projects. Optimism bias uplift factors were dependent on the category of project, based on a table of factors produced by leading consultants derived from average cost overruns for a set of projects which had not used 'approved' project risk management.

Key stealth assumptions which were implicit in the Treasury approved pre-2007 HA approach were *all* approved project risk management processes were equivalent to an optimism bias uplift on average (untrue for several reasons explored shortly) and approved risk management adjustments were preferable because they reflected the particular context being addressed instead of the average (true, in part, with important reservations). From an EP perspective it was obvious that this pre-2007 HM Treasury approach was not a good idea – as clearly demonstrated by the ongoing bias in pre-2007 HA estimates. The exact nature of reasons it was not a good idea was less obvious and worth understanding.

Related stealth assumptions implicit in the current WSL approach included: there was no need to even think about an optimism bias adjustment, despite the clear ongoing evidence of unacceptably large optimism bias, and there was no need to fix an obvious problem or explore what might turn out to be an underlying mess.

Prior to the 2007 Nichols report, HA estimators created a starting point 'outline initial plan' based on their understanding of intentions associated with the business case, and used this plan to produce a 'base estimate' of the construction cost, but there was no significant planning input from the equivalent of a Projects Group, and no linked significant design or operations input from the equivalent of an Operations Group. For example, a new motorway project might have a type specified and a route indicated on a map but no further design or construction planning input. This was directly comparable to the current WSL position unless the Operations Group initiated a project, and even then, comparable concerns remained.

To demonstrate why the estimate plus a risk adjustment approach as used by the HA produced a biased estimate, and indicate a way forward, the Nichols led re-estimation study started by identifying a sample of projects which had recently completed the equivalent of the concept strategy stage and passed the associated gateway as a representative subset of all projects from the £20 billion portfolio of HA projects currently in progress. Some WSL projects could be sampled in the same way to explore a similar learning curve.

HA estimators revisited the outline initial plans used to represent their understanding of intentions associated with the business case, and the associated 'base estimate' of the construction cost was used as a starting point for the sample projects.

Nichols facilitators then used the following minimum clarity approach to *all* relevant uncertainty *given* the original estimation and risk adjustment process, explicitly working within a prototype EP framework.

The equivalent of a pre-planned version of the identify phase of a basic SPP designed by Nichols staff employed five sources of uncertainty for the 'construction cost' estimate for a new motorway. The construction cost of a new motorway was the costs paid to a contractor to provide a detailed design and plan and deliver an operational road, comparable to what WSL paid Paul's firm for the sewage project he had recently delivered. The HA's cost of land acquisition and traffic management during construction were examples of costs excluded from construction cost. The five sources of uncertainty in the decomposition of the 'construction cost' estimate used by Nichols were:

1   all sources explicitly considered by the estimator originally,
2   all sources explicitly considered at least in part by the risk adjustment,
3   all other sources best considered at the project level,
4   all other sources best owned by the HA at portfolio level, and
5   all other sources best owned by the UK government.

Nichols staff clarified this structure for HA estimators who had provided the original estimates in the sample as follows.

Source 1 was everything estimators had in mind at the time the estimate was made, explicitly or implicitly, as best they could recall, referring to notes made at the time plus any other relevant documents if they wished.

Source 2 was everything covered by the risk adjustment process, referring to the list of risks and the component expected values, plus associated systemic uncertainty (dependence) they were aware of.

Source 3 was anything else which they might reasonably be held accountable for thinking about and including in future estimates – bearing in mind the exclusions associated with sources 4 and 5, but assuming zero tolerance of *any* persistent bias in future estimates.

Source 4 was sources of uncertainty best owned at portfolio level by the HA, like European Union (EU) safety regulation changes which would affect crash barrier designs for all motorways, and HA design rules associated with the 'quality' of delivered road projects, including quality issues driven by maintenance cost expectations.

Source 5 was sources of uncertainty the HA should refuse to accept responsibility for unless and until a contractor was prepared to accept them, like inflation. Inflation was best owned by the UK government, with all HA cost estimates in the money of the day, unless it was cost-effective to give inflation risk (and opportunity) to a contractor.

There was no equivalent to the basic SPP structure phase beyond what was built into the identify phase in the sense that there was no formal testing of the robustness of the assumptions used for qualitative analysis thus far in the process and no formal consideration of restructuring. The focus phase equivalent explicitly selected a robust approach which included all relevant uncertainty, and the explicit working assumption was that the use of source 3 in the context of the other four sources would deliver sufficient robustness because it was defined to do so, and facilitators would do their very best to make sure this robustness was delivered.

The ownership phase was also built into the focus phase in the sense that the UK government was allocated to source 5, the HA at portfolio level took responsibility for source 4, the estimator's original assumed responsibility was allocated to source 1, the risk management group to the basis of source 2, and a residual of everything else of relevance was allocated to source 3.

Having made sure HA estimators understood the nature of all five sources, Nichols facilitators made direct use of the Figure 7.8 format for a minimum clarity estimation process, initially showing estimators a variant of Figure 7.8 without probability curves 1 to 3 and the associated notes. For confidentially reasons, as well as expository convenience, Figure 7.8 uses a normalised scale to portray the sample average in approximate terms instead of individual project cost values. For Paul's purposes, and ours, it is simpler just to work directly with Figure 7.8 with this in mind.

For each estimate in the sample, the Nichols facilitator first asked estimators to think about the uncertainty they had in mind when producing their base value estimate, source 1. They were then asked to estimate a P90 value in money of the day used for that estimate. On average this was about 25% more than their base estimate, as indicated by Figure 7.8. Next, they were asked to estimate a P10. On average this was slightly less than their base estimate, as also indicated in Figure 7.8. Curve 1 was then plotted and explained in terms of the estimates the estimator had provided and the expected value implications. Estimators soon understood that they should have used something like a P50, which was about 15% more than their base estimate, to provide an unbiased estimate of what they thought they had considered. However, they were comfortable with the results of the re-estimation process, once the observed bias was explained in terms of an underlying 'anchoring effect', which is

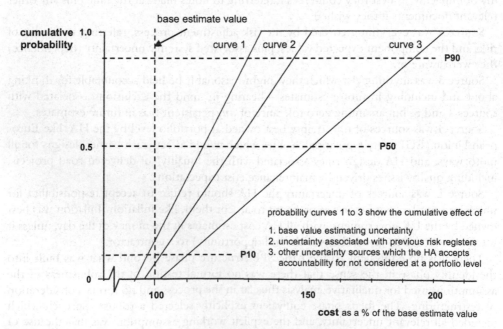

Figure 7.8 Sensitivity diagram: Highways Agency (HA) example.

common whenever estimators address a point estimate by starting with an optimistic estimate and then adjust upwards, instead of looking at the P90 first. The sequence in which estimation processes proceed affects bias, which was understood when it was explained. In future, estimators would be comfortable with a minimum clarity approach or a more sophisticated EP variant as explored in Chapter 3.

When estimators were comfortable with the location of the source 1 line on their equivalent of Figure 7.8, they were asked by the Nichols facilitator to think about all the uncertainty associated with source 2 in terms of 1 + 2 and identify a P90 on the same sensitivity diagram. On average this was about 40% more than the base estimate, as indicated in Figure 7.8. Next, they were asked to estimate a P10. On average this was slightly more than their base estimate. Curve 2 was then plotted and explained. The resulting P50 was about 25% more than their base estimate on average, a further 10% uplift on their base estimate.

When estimators were comfortable with the location of the source 2 line portraying 1 + 2 on their equivalent of Figure 7.8, they were asked by the Nichols facilitator to think about all the uncertainty associated with source 3 and identify a 1 + 2 + 3 line P90 on the same diagram. On average this was about 90% more than the base estimate, as indicated in Figure 7.8. Next, they were asked to estimate a P10. On average this was about 10% more than their base estimate. Curve 3 was then plotted and explained. The resulting P50 was about 50% more than their base estimate on average, source 3 providing a further 25% uplift on their base estimate.

The way Figure 7.8 linear cumulative distribution lines were added during the estimation process could be associated with the minimum clarity process of Chapter 3 and Figure 3.1 assuming 100% dependence (perfect positive correlation) between sources 1 to 3, but direct estimation in cumulative form could also be associated with indirect estimation of dependence levels other than 100% – see Chapman and Ward (2011) for an explanation.

Everybody involved in the re-estimation study soon understood what Figure 7.8 portrayed and the implications. Figure 7.8 was a sensitivity diagram portraying sources of uncertainty given currently assumed response choices – a key EP tool, introduced in this chapter in Figure 7.5, used here to clarify what was missing from an HA approach because of previously unidentified stealth assumptions, also used in a somewhat different manner in Chapters 4 and 6.

The final right-hand curve – the line for source 3 in this case – portrayed the overall total quantified uncertainty of interest in this example – the composite source 1 + 2 + 3. The gap between curves 2 and 3 showed the contribution of source 3, and the gap between curves 1 and 2 showed the contribution of source 2. The contribution of source 1 was directly portrayed. Overall, an uplift of about 50% to the base value would produce an unbiased expected outcome estimate given the current understanding of sources 1, 2 and 3 and ignoring sources 4 and 5, with an expectation that the 10% to 90% uplift confidence band would be exceeded about 10% of the time. Source 3 was the biggest contributor to the uplift and associated uncertainty of composite source 1 + 2 + 3. Source 2 was the smallest. Sources 4 and 5 were additional issues, not quantified for current purposes, and at this stage in the lifecycle quantification of source 5 would not be appropriate. The earlier risk adjustment approach was capturing source 2 but ignoring sources 1, 3, 4 and 5. Source 2 was about 20% of the composite source 1 + 2 + 3, perhaps 10% of the composite source 1 + 2 + 3 + 4 + 5.

The uncertainty indicated by curve 3 in Figure 7.8 and its contribution to an expected value uplift was clearly huge compared with the variability embodied in source 2 and the earlier common practice risk management approach. However, the variability aspect associated with the 10% to 90% confidence band portrayed by curve 3 in Figure 7.8 was not risk – it was just uncertainty *until commitments were made. The risk involved that really mattered was continuing with a biased estimation approach which failed to capture information and knowledge which was readily available providing the right questions were asked.*

Paul indicated that the basic SPP evaluate phase equivalent for the HA re-estimation study was about wider dissemination of the implications of Figure 7.8 and encouraging a corporate-level revisiting of approaches to estimation by the HA. The HA and HM Treasury responded very positively to the re-estimation study report (see HM Treasury [2014] for example). Paul was determined WSL would learn the same lessons. WSL could take the same approach if they undertook a comparable re-estimation exercise, an option that was available. But he suggested they should just learn the same lessons as the HA from the HA study as discussed in their current workshop and move on directly to a revised estimation approach.

One obvious conclusion was they needed to base WSL estimates at a project level on a comprehensive view of *all* the relevant uncertainty – to estimate the equivalent of line 3 in Figure 7.8, considering sources 4 and 5 later when appropriate.

A second obvious conclusion was source 2 was the least important of the three sources of uncertainty needing immediate project level consideration by the HA – and clearly not worth the extensive level of decomposition effort currently used and wasted by WSL. This was consistent with general EP advice to use fewer 'sources' than common practice 'risks', with a much wider scope, plus a closure with completeness approach explicitly employed for the final component, coupled to a clear understanding of specific and general responses.

A third obvious conclusion was WSL needed to develop a form of decomposition of sources of uncertainty that distinguished sources which would resolve themselves as the lifecycle evolved (like uncertainty about what kind of design approach would be used) and sources which needed direct management, or they would still be there when execution and delivery began (like uncertainty about the most appropriate contracting structure). The need to distinguish sources in this way was a key aspect of clarified ambiguity. Paul observed that the Nichols Report addressed this for the HA, and WSL could take a comparable approach. Paul also observed that WSL could use this kind of decomposition of uncertainty to produce a very useful 'control chart' projection of how the concept strategy stage uncertainty *ought* to contract as the lifecycle continued to evolve assuming that their current assessments of uncertainty were unbiased. To explain in outline what this involved and how it could be addressed he used Figure 7.9.

Paul explained that he had used the term 'cost uncertainty-time profile graph' in the title for Figure 7.9 because diagrams employing this format would not be used by WSL in a simple classic control chart manner. This particular very simple illustrative example used a number of assumptions which he needed to explain in outline shortly, in detail later. At an overview level, Figure 7.9 portrayed how quantified uncertainty at the concept strategy gateway stage might decline gradually until a fixed price contract was agreed, when a significant step change reduction was obtained, followed by further uncertainty reductions as the project proceeded.

The Figure 7.9 example assumed a single contractor would undertake a fixed price contract for the construction of a new sewage work with an unbiased expected cost estimate of £100 million at the concept strategy gateway stage, an estimate which remained stable over the whole of the timeframe portrayed. At the concept strategy gateway stage uncertainty was at its maximum, with a P90 of about £250 million. The DOT strategy progress stage was assumed to have a big impact on uncertainty, with the P90 decreasing to about £185 million at the DOT strategy gateway stage. The E&D strategy progress stage was associated with

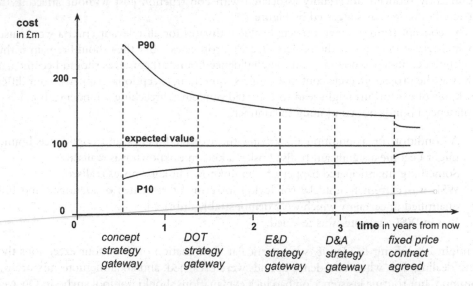

Figure 7.9 Cost uncertainty–time profile graph for the construction cost of a sewage works based on the four WSL gateways followed by a fixed price contract.

a more modest impact on uncertainty, with the P90 further decreasing to about £170 million by the E&D strategy gateway stage. The D&A strategy progress stage further reduced the P90 to about £160 million. D&A strategy gateway approval meant an overall WSL strategy for this project was sanctioned by the board with a budget approved by the board but obtaining all necessary local government planning department permissions and contract negotiations then took another eight months or so. Following the contract being agreed on, there would be further modest uncertainty reductions. But uncertainty would not be eliminated until the contract was completed at a future point off the graph.

Paul suggested that if all these assumptions proved sound, actual outcomes could be plotted on the initial version of this chart as the lifecycle evolved in a simple, classic control-chart manner. But in practice, revised charts would also be needed to reflect revisions to corporate understanding of both expected outcomes and associated further future uncertainty. He anticipated both plotting outcomes on earlier graphs and revising graphs would be useful at all gateways. Furthermore, he was convinced that this approach would be crucial whenever significant unanticipated risks were realised. The mechanics of constructing these charts was just a matter of clarifying when in the project lifecycle each identified source of uncertainty should be resolved, with reference to the lifecycle projection used along with the seven Ws structure to identify sources of uncertainty.

In practice, contracting assumptions other than a fixed price contract with one contractor might be used, and criteria other than cost might also be measured. And in practice, they might want to look at full lifecycle costs, including maintenance costs over the life of the assets. If they did this, important sources of uncertainty would persist until the termination stage was complete, and the importance of operating stage uncertainty would become visible. This visibility of uncertainty over the whole anticipated project lifecycle stage structure could prove very important, even if a single contractor were used and a fixed price significantly reduced uncertainty associated with construction cost without affecting the expected outcome, as suggested by Figure 7.9.

The concept strategy stage expected value estimates for all relevant criteria would usually increase or decrease as the project lifecycle progresses – but they should remain within predefined confidence bounds, and the confidence bounds themselves should become narrower as the project lifecycle continues, unless something exceptional happens. Four different kinds of exceptions might lead to expected outcomes breaching confidence bounds or confidence bounds not continuing to contract:

1   A condition or assumption underlying the expected values and confidence bounds might become a significant realised risk – a known unknown was realised.
2   Something unanticipated happened – an unknown unknown was realised.
3   WSL was extremely unlucky (or lucky) in terms of estimates of identified and fully quantified uncertainty which were demonstrably unbiased.
4   Bias in WSL estimates was revealed.

It might be difficult to identify what particular combination of these four exceptions they were dealing with when confidence bounds were breached, and an ambiguous mixture was common, but routine insistence on bad luck explanations should not fool anybody. On average all project criteria expected value and range estimates should prove unbiased in a demonstrable manner, and all associated confidence bounds should contract fairly smoothly over time, *provided* identified conditions or assumptions were not realised, unknown unknowns were not realised, or unusually good or bad luck was not involved.

Figure 7.9 confidence bound revisions might involve the spread increasing or decreasing as the lifecycle progressed, but on average all confidence bound estimates should decrease in a reasonably stable manner over the lifecycle, without unpleasant surprises that would call PG team competence into question. Ongoing statistical analysis and control of bias which ensured that this was the case would be important.

Plotting actual outcomes on a graph with a Figure 7.9 format, with a contracting projection of remaining uncertainty, could be a very useful EP tool, the reason for elaborating what is involved in this chapter, and refinements like those just outlined could be crucial.

Paul was determined to use several variants of this kind of approach for all projects, and he thought the uncertainty–time profile graph was an important conceptual tool, usefully understood by all members of the PG team in broad terms at this point.

Paul finished this workshop by stimulating discussion about why WSL's current problems were comparable to HA problems and those of all other organisations which did not take an enlightened view of ambiguity with clarified ambiguity in mind. He wanted the very important practical problems resulting from biased initial estimates based on point values and common practice risk management risk adjustments to be clear – without implying he associated blame or incompetence with his group. The WSL Projects Group had been following widespread common practice, although *a lot of much better* practice had been used by many organisations for many years, some linked to authors drawing on Chapman and Ward (1997, 2003, 2011) and some drawing on many other authors taking a wide variety of approaches. Paul wanted his group to understand why a new conceptual framework based on EP was essential before discussing how they would use a new EP framework. He wanted his group and the Operations Group staff present to think about this discussion and then return fresh and ready to go for the next workshop.

Use of the same basic SPP by the Operations Group and PG teams in all four strategy progress stages

By the time Paul was preparing the technical workshop discussed in this subsection, Ollie and some senior members of Ollie's staff who had attended all the earlier workshops were convinced that working with Paul and the PG team was a good idea. They were also convinced they should start thinking about the Operations Group as the OG team with some implications similar to those for the PG team. In addition, Paul had been invited to run special workshops for the OG team as a whole on its own to cover the material dealt with in his initial workshop for the PG team plus all the technical workshops so far. This led to Paul's persuading the OG team to treat this subsection's workshop for the PG team as a joint OG/PG team workshop, initiating joint OG/PG team working, an outcome Paul had hoped for from the outset.

Paul started this joint OG/PG team workshop by emphasising the importance to WSL of a particularly close working relationship for the OG and PG teams. He believed they needed to work together as a joint OG/PG team in the concept-strategy progress stage. They then needed to continue to work in a closely coordinated manner through the rest of the project lifecycle.

To facilitate this there would be both immediate and long-term benefits if the OG team agreed to use the same Figure 7.2 basic SPP concept tool for their management of the DOT strategy progress stage as the PG team would use for the E&D strategy progress stage, both groups also using their variants in simplified prototype forms during the concept strategy progress stage, with ongoing implications in the fourth strategy progress stage addressing angels and devils in the detail on a joint basis. There would be important differences in the way these progress stage SPP frameworks were used by the two groups in all four stages, and the language employed might be very different, but the use by both teams of a shared common conceptual framework structure was crucial. In particular, once they got used to using the same basic SPP in the DOT and E&D strategy progress stages, it would be much easier to work as a joint OG/PG team in the concept strategy progress stage.

As an example of differences in use, the OG team would approach the basic SPP create and identify phases by drawing on the design and operations management literature, not the project planning literature. As a sewage works example of the different language involved, the OG team would see key plan components and sources of uncertainty during the operations phase of the project in terms of key sewage works component availability and reliability concerns, not key activity cost or time concerns in the project planning sense.

Paul then emphasised that neither OG planners nor PG planners were involved in the current concept strategy stage business case preparation process for the new water mains project in the way he thought they should be. After the concept strategy gateway was passed, the OG team would use the DOT strategy progress stage to develop their part of the overall WSL strategy for this project. After the DOT strategy gateway was passed, the PG team would use the E&D strategy progress stage to develop their part of the overall WSL strategy for this project. However, all important interdependencies between these strategies and the other seven Ws plans need addressing in a preliminary manner during the concept strategy stage in grounded plan terms, prior to the concept strategy gateway stage. This was not current WSL practice. In his view, their joint involvement in the concept strategy progress stage was usefully viewed as collaborative development of prototypes of the DOT strategy and E&D strategy they would each need later, with a focus on the key relationships between their concerns and the rest of the seven Ws plans plus associated goals–plans relationship concerns.

To illustrate what this involved, Paul reminded them that Frank had started the Finance Group led concept strategy progress stage study of the water mains project by assuming one large contract would be let to one national contractor. Paul was convinced that much smaller work packages let to a number of medium sized local contractors as well as several of the larger national contractors would be a much better strategy, making use of component separable projects within a programme portfolio of projects structure. He was determined to get a board level resolution of this issue *before* the concept strategy gateway approval. Part of his rationale was lower construction costs, part was more flexibility in terms of finance costs, part was more flexibility in terms of dealing with traffic disruptions, and part was ensuring ongoing competitive market discipline for water mains contractors. An aspect which he believed the OG team needed to stress as part of their concept strategy stage contribution was more flexibility in terms of design considerations related to operations issues, which might evolve over time. There were several other important issues needing OG team input in the concept strategy stage. For example, a 100 year planned life for water mains instead of 50 years not only involved technical specification issues they would need to address, but it also involved longer term water demand forecasting and capacity planning issues. This might involve different water main patterns as well as different water main pipe sizing options – a network built on six primary feeders instead of the current four, for example.

Paul did not want to labour what an EP approach adopted by the OG team which was coordinated with a compatible PG team approach, or bore them with technical details. He just wanted to make them receptive to starting to work with the PG team on a joint basis to ensure consistent and coherent concept strategy stage input plus fully coordinated follow-on work for both groups. But it would be useful if the OG team saw this as a joint development project with the PG team, involving one joint OG/PG simplified prototype basic SPP process for the concept strategy progress stage, plus two common higher clarity basic SPP processes: one for the DOT strategy progress stage for use by the OG team, a second for the E&D strategy progress stage for use by the PG team. He thought the OG team might like to start this kind of prototype basic SPP development working on the new sewage project, where the OG team were currently leading the early concept strategy progress stage.

Taking this argument a bit further, he believed a significant investment in effort now in their joint OG/PG prototype planning for the sewage works in the concept strategy progress stage would help them learn how to use simple variants for the key issues that mattered most in future concept stage studies, followed by directly dependent DOT and E&D strategy progress stage studies. At present it was not entirely clear where their efforts would best pay off, but he did have some ideas where they might start.

For example, he knew the OG team were already looking at urban sites A and B as options for the proposed new sewage works, assuming a design based on the last sewage works built. He had already suggested rural site C might be better in an earlier discussion with Ollie, based on a different design approach. But elaborating now, he thought the OG team might be able to identify options that were even better – designated D, E, or F. Design features which were of immediate and obvious concern in terms of ongoing operation of the sewage works, which he believed the OG team would obviously address, included its 'quality' in reliability and maintainability terms (crudely measured by expected operating costs), its ability to cope with low probability flooding events and the impact of such events on people living in the vicinity, issues associated with smells, the everyday visual impact of the proposed design, and WSL's ability to get planning permission to build the sewage works given the earlier considerations. However, the PG team was also directly concerned with what might be termed 'traditional build-ability' issues, which included ground conditions, access for contractors' heavy equipment and so on, and he appreciated the OG team might not think of all these concerns if the PG team did not raise them. Furthermore, the OG/ PG team might usefully go well beyond the usual concerns of the OG or PG teams and offer local residents compensation for undesirable features – in the form of amenity parks or river fishing provision on what had been private land with no public access for example. This might have implications for objectives relevant to other WSL groups. In the concept strategy project lifecycle stage there was room for creativity which needed to be exploited – it could become an opportunity lost completely if not exploited in this stage. In Paul's view, leadership seeking this creativity was up to the OG/PG teams, seeking allies from within WSL like the Customer Relations Director, and allies from outside WSL which included local customer organisations.

Paul suggested the OG team might be already thinking along these lines for the proposed new sewage works, but he thought they should also be involved in the proposed water mains replacement programme in similarly broad design option studies as soon as possible, and all other projects to follow.

The rest of this workshop was spent developing these ideas and beginning to use them in terms of WSL illustrative examples.

Use of the same basic SPP in the next two strategy progress stages

Later workshops developed DOT strategy progress stage use of the basic SPP by the OG team and comparable E&D strategy progress stage use of the basic SPP by the PG team, plus associated collaboration, to support earlier use as prototypes in the concept strategy progress stage as well as preparing for following stages.

Actual DOT strategy progress stage use of the process in Figure 7.2 would clearly start with the prototype used to seek concept strategy gateway approval. It would focus on the ambiguity uncertainty which needed reduction before DOT strategy approval. For example, if concept strategy gateway approval for the new sewage works was based on urban sites A and B being rejected but rural sites C, D, E, and F all being possible options, depending on further design work, site tests, and consultation, the OG/PG team might need to pursue the consultation jointly while the OG team pursued further design work and the PG team pursued site ground-condition tests.

Actual E&D strategy progress stage use of the Figure 7.2 process would also start with the prototype used to seek concept strategy gateway approval, updated as necessary by all the progress made prior to DOT strategy gateway approval. It would focus on the ambiguity uncertainty which needed reduction before E&D strategy approval. For example, if DOT strategy gateway approval for the new sewage works confirmed rural site E, the PG team would now need an E&D strategy which was refined enough to use the results for tendering purposes once overall E&D strategy testing was complete, assuming the successful contractor would undertake detailed DOT design plus detailed E&D planning within the strategies approved by the board.

Paul made it clear that the reason the DOT strategy progress stage preceded the E&D strategy progress stage was the obvious need for PG planners to be clear what they were planning to build before starting, but the reason prototypes of both had to be used jointly in the concept strategy stage was to identify and address key interdependencies before committing to a concept strategy, and some aspects of these key interdependences might be ongoing.

Another way to visualise and deal with this was a whole series of partial DOT strategy progress stages followed by partial E&D strategy progress stages, gradually evolving towards both being jointly optimised. But in practice a period of close OG/PG joint working during the concept strategy stage, followed by a period of more independent focus during the next two stages, ought to be more clarity efficient. This was a working assumption which Paul had made that could be tested, with a view to making revisions if doing so was deemed worthwhile.

Use of the same basic SPP in the final strategy progress stage and linked earlier use

Separate later workshops addressed why there was a need to anticipate any areas where 'devils or angels in the detail' needed OG/PG consideration in prototype terms within the concept strategy stages of WSL projects, linked to discussion about how these issues should be addressed later in the actual D&A strategy progress stage.

To initiate this discussion Paul explained that the Chapman and Ward (2011) approach he was building on did not use a separate D&A strategy progress or gateway stage, but there were clues about why a D&A strategy progress stage might be useful when PUMP concepts were fully integrated with the whole planning process starting in the concept strategy progress stage as recommended. He had thought about these clues and turned them into what he now saw as a definitive case for a D&A strategy progress stage plus a following gateway stage, plus earlier use in prototype form in the opening concept strategy progress stage.

An example used by Chapman and Ward (2011) to illustrate both the D&A stage concept and DOT strategy progress stage planning using a prototype basic SPP involved Petro-Canada considering a 'pilot LNG (liquified natural gas) project', explored in more detail by Chapman, Cooper, and Cammaert (1984). Paul explained that this example study explored the possibility of producing liquefied natural gas on Melville Island in the high Arctic, transporting it via icebreaking tankers to US markets. Because of the speculative nature of this venture, a single compression chain LNG production plant had been specified by Petro-Canada. An Acres study was commissioned to look at LNG plant reliability in the context of LNG storage and tanker arrival patterns using E&D strategy stage prototype PUMP methodology and software developed by BP in a DOT strategy stage context. This study demonstrated clearly that a single compression chain design plan was a false economy, a kind of 'devil in the detail'.

A second example used by Chapman and Ward (2011) with a more detailed discussion in another paper (Chapman, Cooper, Debelius and Pecora, 1985) involved a study for Fluor on behalf of the Northwest Alaska Pipeline Company. This study explored the possibility of taking a 48 inch gas pipeline across the Yukon River on a bridge, using spare pipe-racks provided by the bridge's builder when it was constructed to carry a 48 inch oil pipeline across the river several years earlier. An Acres study was commissioned to explore this option in comparison with a separate pipe-rack or a separate suspension crossing. It used an E&D strategy stage prototype PUMP methodology and software developed by BP in a significantly modified form in a DOT strategy stage context. This study demonstrated that serious drawbacks for all three of the options initially identified were very effectively overcome by a previously unconsidered fourth option involving a separate submarine crossing, a kind of 'angel in the detail'.

A third example involved a 'demonstration project' used by National Power. This study addressed developing and implementing a simplified variant of the SCERT methodology developed by BP in the E&D strategy stage of a National Power project. This example was outlined earlier in Part 1 of this book, and it is not worth repeating that outline here, but Paul explained it in detail treating the whole chain of improvements in opportunity efficiency discussed earlier as 'angels in the detail'. He emphasised that it was this whole series of 'angels' which sold everyone in National Power on the value of a simplified prototype PUMP approach which could be replicated at least in part in a comparable D&A strategy stage by WSL. Finding these 'angels' was attributable to a systematic search for 'general responses' involving all relevant perspectives and effectively capturing all the key interdependencies between issues.

The WSL equivalents were illustrated by ideas already touched on earlier. One example was early preliminary exploration with local residents of issues concerning them which were relevant to choosing a location and design. Features that might make a particular sewage works site attractive to local residents, an asset rather than a liability, included local amenity value if the site provided a park, fishing access, or flood protection. WSL could then consider these potential assets as well as the liability aspects in conjunction with other issues, like ground-condition variations with construction implications.

Another example was exploring why a single contract and single contractor approach to water main construction revised to a multiple contract and multiple contractor partnerships approach might yield significant opportunities.

Paul suggested that all these examples were reasonably obvious possibilities for someone relatively unfamiliar with the water and sewage industry – like Paul. He then made it clear that these were his initial suggestions to clarify what was involved. But Paul wanted the OG/PG team to use their deep fund of experience and that of all other relevant WSL staff to ensure that the plans which went to the board in the D&A strategy gateway stage were 'free of devils and full of angels', and the earlier prototype version of the D&A stage analyses were used effectively in the concept strategy progress stage.

They might also find it useful to draw on any experience relevant to the water and sewage industry available from outside of WSL – perhaps using consultants, perhaps stimulating dialogue with other comparable organisations.

Plans for relationships and contracts

Paul held a separate technical workshop on plans for relationships and contracts. He saw plans for relationships and contracts as an important special case of planning areas where 'devils and angels in the detail were abundant'. He wanted to explain to the OG and PG teams why this aspect of the seven Ws and associated goals–plans relationship linkages were crucial. He wanted to enlist their support for well-developed prototype plans for relationships and contracts which he could use to demonstrate why his concept strategy approach to contracting for the new water mains project was opportunity efficient relative to current Finance Group assumptions. He also wanted comparable prototype contracting plans for the new sewage works, but this had a lower priority, and they should be relatively straightforward.

He began by explaining that formal contracts could be seen as necessary legal documents to protect the rights of all parties, but some contract specialists were inclined to focus on looking after the particular party who paid their invoices, with an overemphasis on legal protection issues. He argued that preserving the spirit of a positive relationship was crucial to any successful contract. Because the PG team would interface with WSL construction contractors during the execution stage, and the OG team would become the interface with these same contractors during the delivery stage, the OG/PG team needed lead roles during a period of relationship design starting in the concept strategy stage, followed by a period of contract design which reflected the intended long-term relationships.

His starting point for relationship design was the need for a win–win philosophy. A clear requirement was flexibility to cope with *all* uncertainty, and resilience to cope with significant surprises. Resilience was a core aspect of his general view of 'robustness'. He believed they needed to develop a 'big team' approach with local and national contractors which kept all WSL contractors honest, competitive, and very keen to reliably deliver quality work for WSL. The latter condition meant they had to be well paid for their efforts if they were effective and efficient. Some of these relationships would involve using potential future contractors as appropriately funded supporting consultants while WSL strategy was developed, perhaps using WSL as supporting consultants in an appropriate manner once contracts were signed. A series of fixed price contracts might be a reasonable expectation, and using fixed price contracts in this way to keep it simple was highly desirable, but a wide range of other 'partnering' and 'risk sharing' approaches might be preferable.

Paul made it clear that he did not want to overburden them with contentious theories and details. But he wanted their input to a prototype set of plans for the water mains project which made sense from an OG/PG perspective, which he could then use with Frank to attempt overall agreement within WSL before they started to explore their approach with potential contractors. The new sewage plant's contracting and relationship plans could follow later.

The full OG/PG group approached this workshop as an initial brainstorming session, with numerous follow-up meetings involving smaller groups to develop and test the earlier ideas.

Later detailed planning of implementation tactics and further follow-on stages

Paul had a further separate workshop to discuss in outline what would be involved in all later project lifecycle stages while they were still engaged with the concept strategy stage so they could see what was coming without getting into the detail until they needed to.

He started by pointing out that detailed design and detailed planning for execution and delivery would usually be a contractor responsibility in the 'implementation tactics' progress stage. This progress stage would start immediately after contract signing, but some aspects would continue after execution started. Detailed planning for WSL operations during the operation lifecycle stage would be an OG responsibility, at a time to suit the OG prior to the operation stage beginning. Furthermore, detailed planning for termination would involve OG and PG responsibilities plus further new contractor responsibilities, starting just prior to termination. Further still, detailed planning associated concept tactics including ongoing updating of the business case would begin as soon as the concept strategy was approved and continue until termination was complete.

He wanted all the OG/PG team members to understand how the whole lifecycle of each project would unfold, and their roles in each stage. He dealt with progress stages first and then related gateways.

Paul explained how the basic SPP of Figure 7.2 and the gateway SPP of Figure 7.6 would need adaptation to detailed planning in the 'implementation tactics' stage, with further modification to deal with the execution and delivery stages. For example, during the execution stage, the efforts of most people would have to focus on getting things done, but monitoring progress against plans was important, rolling detailed planning forward building in lessons learned from monitoring was important, and dealing with any surprises was crucial, as discussed in part 3 of Chapman and Ward (2011) and the wider project management literature.

He did not labour the details of what would be involved, but he did emphasise that all their current skills and experience would be made full use of in their new OG/PG team structures, collaborative effort and learning from each other being the major changes. What he wanted to do was shape the overall process and coordination structure they used.

Crucially, he would not be telling them what to do – but he would be telling them what he wanted done within broad frameworks. They would be teaching him some important aspects of how to do it and teaching each other.

They all needed strategic clarity within a common corporate basis from the outset. They also needed tactical clarity in their own areas of responsibility, balancing the need to minimise late unanticipated surprises without wasting time 'crossing bridges before they got to them'.

Paul's 'Quartet' illustrations of enlightened planning teamwork

Before he began his series of technical workshops, Paul explained his strategy for the workshops and their role in his more general strategy to his father during a family Sunday walk. Part of the feedback from his father was a suggestion that he read a current magazine review of the film *Quartet*, recently released, about opera singers in a retirement home for gifted musicians, of interest to his father because the film's director and almost all of the cast were in his father's post-retirement age group. Paul decided directly citing *Quartet* in his presentations was not compatible with his style, but several ideas in the review struck him as important things he needed to emulate.

First, Dustin Hoffman, directing his first film aged 75, observed that he had never liked directors who worked out all the scenes in their heads in advance. Despite his reputation as a perfectionist, Hoffman insisted he wanted everybody involved 'to surprise him' – pleasantly if possible, of course. Paul took this as an enlightened view of the need for creativity and avoiding over planning which he needed to explicitly facilitate and encourage in the OG/PG team and wider WSL teams.

Second, Hoffman significantly changed the tone of *Quartet* with a simple early decision to use real musicians and opera singers who were retired in supporting roles because they brought enormous enthusiasm and passion onto the set. Paul overlooked the fact that this might be a consequence of nobody having offered them work for several years and took it as an enlightened view of the need to ensure passion and commitment, bearing in mind the mature members of the current Planning and Estimating Departments might prove more important advocates of an EP transformation than some of the relative youngsters in the current Risk Management Department, if their enthusiasm could be stimulated.

Third, an important part of sustaining the passion and teamwork was everybody enjoying themselves and making generous allowances for the limitations and capabilities of others. Paul took this as an enlightened view of part of what made strong teams – particularly important when people were being asked to change their conceptual frameworks and mindsets as well as their toolsets and skill sets.

Fourth, Hoffman made a point of freely admitting when he was wrong and taking the blame himself when things did not turn out right. Paul took this as part of what an enlightened view of risk taking leadership involved – particularly important to remember when his underestimation of other peoples' reluctance to change was the underlying problem.

Further technical workshops

Paul never stopped what evolved into a tradition of weekly workshops, some involving other groups, some involving a focus on OG or PG issues with attendance by others optional. Making the learning processes and team-building exercises an enjoyable part of the overall WSL capability-culture evolution development project, which he had initiated as part of his broader change management project, became central to developing specific areas of competence and broader capability-culture assets as well as eliminating capability-culture liabilities.

Beyond the technical workshops – key corporate clarity concerns

A significant very specific concern for Paul was corporate clarity about provision and contingency ownership issues associated with aspirational targets, balanced targets which might or might not be expected outcomes, and commitment targets. So was his concern for a sound corporate understanding of the ideas discussed in Chapters 3 and 4 with what needs to be done corporate implications as well as how to do it implications. He made extensive use of material borrowed from Chapman and Ward (2011) to emphasise what was involved at board level as well as within the PG and OG teams.

For example, when BP adopted the SCERT prototype PUMP approach they developed a new 'uncertainty management group' over a period of several years which was eventually empowered to get involved in leading project planning and estimating, not just build on earlier planning. BP then merged their estimating, planning, and uncertainty management groups within a new group with uncertainty management leadership.

From the outset, BP made use of expected cost estimates approved in the governance (gateway) stage following strategy shaping for execution and delivery for corporate budget management purposes, and plan revisions at this stage sometimes went back to DOT strategy stage and even concept strategy stage decisions approved by earlier gateways. These expected values were defined in terms of underlying aspirational targets plus associated provisions for expected levels of difficulty. But project budgets were defined in terms of expected values plus a contingency sum defined by estimated potential upside cost variability at an estimated 80% confidence level. At board level, it was clearly understood that this gave ownership of a reasonable contingency to the project manager (which would not be spent on average if known unknowns and unknown unknowns did not occur), as well as suitable provisions (which would be spent on average). BP project managers found the implications of this change in practice a major transformation. They no longer had 'a date' and 'a cost' to meet which was repeatedly adjusted as achievement became demonstrably impossible. They had ambitious aspirational targets, usually referred to as 'stretch' targets, but credible completion date commitments and cost commitment targets defined by their budget and intermediate expected duration and cost estimates, with all these values understood by everyone involved. Provided they used their provisions and contingencies effectively and efficiently, they could deliver most projects within budget and timetable commitment targets. Paul had insisted on a comparable starting position for his successful WSL sewage plant project when he re-negotiated the budget before the contract was agreed. Paul was convinced that the contract re-negotiation he had insisted upon should be avoided by WSL now that he was Projects Director, using this form of EP approach from the concept strategy shaping stage onwards. Furthermore, when he was approached to become Projects Director for WSL, he had insisted on the transformation of his departmental structure to the new WSL structure, following BP's example immediately.

One offshore North Sea project which BP was involved with in the early 1980s required a new subsea oil pipeline that had to cross three existing pipelines. The risk of damaging an existing pipeline was a serious concern, and for obvious reasons this risk was given considerable attention. The probability that such an incident might happen was estimated in order of magnitude terms. The range of possible impacts was also estimated, in terms of additional expenditure to repair the damage, to pay for opportunity costs experienced by the owners of the damaged pipeline, to cover all pollution recovery and related compensation costs, and to reflect reputational damage with widespread implications.

A key insight was the need for a board level financial provision for appropriate aspects of the expected cost of such an incident, as was ensuring that the board was comfortable with the associated contingency sum which might be required, and the reputational concerns, keeping this issue outside of the project's budget. This insight can be decomposed into three component aspects:

1 Including any part of this possible incident's impact costs in the project's budget was a clear lose–lose proposition from the board's perspective. If this incident happened the project manager would have to come back to the board for more money anyway because it was a low probability high impact event which would not average out. If this incident did not happen the board did not want the project manager to have an associated provision to spend on other problems.
2 The project manager had to take full managerial responsibility for making sure this incident did not happen on BP's behalf – he knew his career was riding on it.
3 The board had to own this risk financially, making a suitable provision and being prepared to deal with the contingent implications if it happened, including implications which are not just financial.

It soon became clear that the project manager could cascade a variant of this idea downwards within his project team, using lower level variants of his relationship with the board to control all his project staff in terms of stretch targets, maintaining ownership of most of his contingencies and provisions for low probability issues. He could release more time and money without argument whenever the project was unlucky but the member of staff involved had clearly done his or her best to meet a difficult stretch target. He could prerelease some provision and contingencies to limit the dialogue necessary for normal variations – to avoid excessive micromanagement. Why a difficult stretch target was not achieved would always be questioned, but the expectation on both sides would be a reasonable explanation with no blame which was not clearly deserved. The project manager was cascading the comparable treatment of his position by the board.

Paul wanted all these ideas implemented from the concept strategy stage onwards, with a common corporate understanding of what this implied, at board level as well as within his PG team and the OG team. In the early days of a project lifecycle, this meant significant provisions and contingencies would be based on unresolved ambiguity uncertainty. For example, if a new sewage works might be at possible locations C, D, E, or F and the decision would not be made for some time, provision and contingency sums would have to reflect this uncertainty. An enlightened approach to clarified ambiguity meant recognising the importance of making provisions for extra cost and time which would be needed on average from the outset, in addition addressing appropriate contingencies so that commitments had a reasonable chance of being met, gradually refining the definition and ownership of provisions and contingencies as time progressed. *Before a contract was let, this uncertainty should never be confused with risk*, and its ownership was not a budget issue in the post–contract letting sense. It was just ambiguity as currently assessed which needed identification and approximate sizing with a view to accommodating it, and avoiding inappropriate decisions because of bias until better information for making a commitment was available.

Paul pointed out that BP initiated formal statistical analysis of project outcomes about five years after adopting an SPP prototype approach. This analysis confirmed that BP was now bringing in projects on budget and on schedule most of the time – better than just 'on average' because of the role of provisions. However, this analysis suggested that it was easy to lose sight of the importance of working assumptions which might not hold (known unknowns) and implicit assumptions (unknown unknowns) which might provide unpleasant surprises, eventually suggesting a no quibbles provision to meet some aspects of these ongoing concerns.

Paul also pointed out that BP clearly had a corporate memory loss in terms of some of these concepts in the planning process for their 2010 Gulf of Mexico projects, or perhaps they had just never made the important distinction between making a project manager fully responsible for managing all risks and the implications of a board level policy of contracting that exposed BP to contractor failures, or perhaps something else had gone wrong. WSL had to ensure they learned lessons from this too. WSL had to acquire, continue to develop, *and maintain*, all the key corporate capability-culture assets needed *at all relevant corporate levels.*

Enlightened approaches to governance, teams and contracts

Martha's goal of an enlightened approach to governance, teams and contracts as explored in Chapter 6 can be both reinforced and further clarified in Paul's context.

One basic feature is a need for everyone involved in 'a team' to work with a shared understanding of three very different values: optimistic stretch targets, unbiased expected outcome estimates, and plausible worst-case outcome scenarios. If you clearly understand the value and the satisfaction of working in this way and you find yourself working for a person or an organisation which insists on a single number point estimate of cost, duration, and other performance measures, only reveal a commitment figure with a high probability of achievement, and be prepared to look for another job if this strategy does not look like succeeding. This is empirically tested advice which many people with confirm. The corollary is that if you are trying to manage a team without understanding this point, you should expect your team members to try their best to build enough fat into all estimates to facilitate an easy life. Sometimes they will still fail to deliver even if significant fat is built into estimates, and leave just before it all goes horribly wrong if they are able to do so.

Another key feature is a need for everyone involved to understand that 'team commitments' should reflect the possible cost to the team of failing to meet the commitments and the likely reward for the team of exceeding expectations. If these costs and rewards do not align with costs and rewards for the organisations involved, this implies incentive and broader motivation problems needing immediate attention. Capability-culture liability risks with serious implications are involved.

Furthermore, if team members individually fail to meet team targets for good reasons beyond their control, any 'punishment' is usually completely inappropriate and counterproductive, and if they exceed expectations for reasons beyond their control, 'reward' is usually equally inappropriate and counterproductive. The net effect will be driving away competent team members and promoting incompetent team members.

Enlightened governance is in part about a nuanced understanding between team members, plus those ultimately responsible for the team's performance, which involves everyone doing their best to pull in the same direction, accommodating delays, cost escalation and other performance failures which may not have been anticipated if there were good reasons for not anticipating them. Unconscious reciprocation of favours and tolerance of shortcomings across contractual boundaries as well as within organisational boundaries can be a crucial part of associated trust, and it is trust which makes the whole thing work smoothly.

Enlightened governance in this sense involves a 'covenant' between all members of the team and those the team works for. It may have some very important legal contract components, but large parts of it will be informal and perhaps implicit. Trust is a crucial aspect, and a loss of trust or misplaced trust can be cataclysmic.

'Teams' in this enlightened sense may be just small components of a much larger project team within one organisation or a department in one organisation. However, they may embrace a whole organisation or several organisations united by one project. Some very small teams are narrow and dysfunctional. But some very large and extremely broad teams work very effectively. How we choose to define the key team structures and their interfaces matters a great deal. How we ensure each group which should work as a team does work as a team also matters. Multiple team relationship structures may be multilayered and complex.

'Enlightened contracts' are frameworks for relationships which facilitate enlightened governance. How we choose to define contracts clearly matters a great deal. The legal aspects obviously matter. But all the informal aspects and trust issues also matter. Incentives are part of this, especially the use of incentives to ensure the alignment of goals. Crude financial incentives are often seriously dysfunctional, not simply ineffective. 'Enlightened incentives' may be highly dependent on the context and geared to behavioural issues like group pride.

A key risk that really matters is failing to fully understand these issues and their implications. A failure to act effectively based on appropriate understanding is a follow-on risk, a part of this being a failure to understand all the options available. *If realised, these risks are also usefully viewed as important lost opportunities, and seeking opportunity efficiency needs to include a focus on avoiding this kind of lost opportunity.*

Paul's overall change management strategy – target 1

The WSL board as a whole had very good reason to support Paul's EP approach to the concept strategy stage and rolling out its implications for all following stages. Furthermore, Paul had done what was crucial to secure the full support of his PG team and most of the OG team. Paul had already achieved most of what he needed to do to reach his first overall change management strategy goal – target 1. However, as we bring this tale to an end, Paul still had a lot of work to do to achieve his ambitions.

Target 1 loosely defined the end of the first lifecycle stage in his overall change management project for WSL. Target 1 was ambitious, but it involved a coherent set of goals which needed coordinated early achievement.

In summary, for all projects which ultimately involved the Projects Group, achieving Paul's target 1 involved WSL adopting:

1   the Table 7.2 lifecycle structure or a more complex SS3 variant;
2   the seven Ws structure of Table 7.3 and Figure 7.1 building on point 1;
3   a goals–plans relationships framework building on points 1 and 2;

4   the basic SPP of Figure 7.2 and the gateway SPP of Figure 7.6;

5   initiation of enlightened planning in the concept strategy stage of all projects involving the PG group, with companywide involvement coordinated by a PG team;

6   planning input in the concept strategy stage led by the OG/PG team using approaches which were closely coupled prototype forms of later DOT strategy, E&D strategy and D&A strategy development approaches;

7   planning input associated with financial resources and business case planning led by the Finance Group using a two (or more) portfolios approach to discounting;

8   corporate understanding of the need for clarity about provision and contingency ownership issues and underlying aspirational targets, unbiased expected outcome values and commitment targets (the basic ABCs of targets using expected values as balanced targets); and

9   growing understanding of the role and importance of enlightened governance and enlightened contracts, the importance of significant mutual support, and the crucial role of enhanced team-working companywide.

Fundamental differences which would be noticeable when target 1 was fully embedded as established practice included:

1   all point estimates of cost, duration, and other performance measures were replaced by interval estimates;

2   uncertainty associated with interval estimate ranges was generally very wide but not confused with risk;

3   an initial working understanding of ambiguity uncertainty which needed shaping and sizing was acquired;

4   unbiased estimates were expected, with formal ongoing testing for bias an inbuilt part of the overall SP for projects approach, and serious questions were anticipated if bias persisted;

5   a wider range of design options with follow-on implications for other plans were addressed at the outset of the concept strategy stage, keeping options open until it was clear that the big opportunity strategic options which could be identified had been identified, and as far as possible the big threat strategic options had been avoided;

6   a dynamic portrayal of how uncertainty would resolve over time in a Figure 7.9 framework was understood by everyone involved, helping to clarify the difference between risk associated with commitments and high levels of uncertainty early in a project lifecycle which was not risk because commitments had not been made;

7   a companywide understanding of the nature of risk in terms of lost opportunities and the role of this understanding as a capability-culture asset;

8   an overall WSL capability-culture change which all WSL staff embraced and were proud of.

In summary, uncertainty, risk, and opportunity were clearly distinguished and related to complexity, understanding the overlaps and interdependencies, using framing concepts and operational tools which were clarity efficient to the extent that current capability-culture assets allowed; aggressive further development of capability-culture assets was underway; and ongoing 'lessons learned' reviews ensured relentless elimination of any capability-culture liabilities which were exposed by reviews of what might initially look like bad luck.

Paul's overall change management strategy – target 2 and beyond

Paul's goals for target 2 were loosely defined as the goals to be achieved by the end of the second lifecycle stage in his WSL change management strategy. In overview terms, they were supporting OG implementation of an EP approach to the DOT strategy stage and leading his PG team through successful implementation of an EP approach to the E&D-strategy stage for an initial set of projects to consolidate the target 1 achievements. His basic guide was Chapman and Ward (2011), embedding the PUMP in the much broader SPP as outlined in this chapter, but he also needed to add significant base plan creativity, informal planning and formal planning process content. Paul needed his broad experience base and his familiarity with complementary ideas to achieve his target 2 goals. Furthermore, Paul needed the rich WSL capability-culture asset set he started with, as well as building on it and eliminating identified capability-culture liabilities.

As additional goals and targets became the focus, concerns like companywide use of these concepts for projects not directly involving Paul's Project Group might become part of the agenda – new customer-driven information systems led by Ian, Curt, and Frank for example, which raised new issues touched on in the next chapter.

If you are interested in trying to follow Paul's example as a Projects Director yourself, or if you have someone like Paul reporting to you, or if you are reporting to someone like Paul, you will need to consider these first two targets plus follow-on targets in the context of your personal potential contributions to your own organisation's needs, your own organisation's capability-culture asset and liability sets, discussion in the rest of this book, and significant further thinking. Given the starting position this chapter associates with achieving target 1, you should be able to work out approximately how the broadly defined EP concepts and tools interface with the needs of projects and their partial resolution via PUMP concepts and tools for all later targets.

The focus of Chapman and Ward (2011) is the E&D strategy stage, but earlier stages are explored using case study examples, and how later stages flow on from the E&D strategy stage is covered in some detail. This book, plus Chapman and Ward (2011), is a reasonable starting point. However, this chapter is about how you might set about the kind of very broad change programme discussed and the corporate advantages doing so might bring – it is clearly not a definitive plan. To make its recommendations operational will require considerable further effort tailored to the context of interest.

If you are not directly interested in project planning yourself, the purpose of this chapter is clarifying the role project planning from an EP perspective could play in relation to other aspects of organisations that are of interest to you in a preliminary way which following chapters and later reflection can build on. For example, if you are a board level equivalent of Charles or Michael, you might ask whether your organisation's equivalent to Paul is currently making comparable contributions to your organisation, and if not, how you should respond. Furthermore, you might ask related questions about your organisation's equivalent to Frank, or Ollie, or any other relevant directors.

Key credibility issues for this chapter

Interpreting WSL as a typical company which just happens to be in the UK water and sewage industry (specifically not a disguised variant of Southern Water), I believe all the key features of the tale discussed in this chapter are highly plausible.

First, consider the discount rate issue. I developed my initial understanding of discounting beyond attending undergraduate and MSc university courses discussing a mutual interest in IRR controversies with Chris Hawkins and David Pearce when they were working on an economics textbook addressing this topic (Hawkins and Pearce, 1971). David Pearce later became a very distinguished professor of economics, and some of his later work underlies HM Treasury (2003a) approaches to the discount rate. My first published assessments of discounting issues were Chapman and Cooper (1983, 1985), based on work under the direction of Gavin Warnock of Acres for the Alaska Power Authority, trying to support the case for proceeding with the Susitna Falls hydroelectric project, still not built. The approach in the first of these papers was extended in Chapman and Howden (1997), based on its use in the Nirex argument for proceeding with their plans to test the viability of disposing of nuclear waste using a deep mine in Cumbria in their battle with HM Treasury rules during the preparation of DoE (1994), a battle lost. It was not until after reflecting on HM Treasury's 2003 groundbreaking shift to a multiple tests approach outside the discount rate for the public sector and publishing Chapman, Ward, and Klein (2006), that my understanding of the implications for a private sector organisation discussed in this chapter started to emerge. They were first published in Chapman and Ward (2011). Hopkinson (2016) develops some aspects of these concerns in a project management context, coupled to a directly related concern for more project management with an uncertainty management focus at the front end of the project lifecycle. The financial economics community has not yet been directly confronted by these ideas on their own turf so far as I am aware. However, any private sector organisation which uses bond funding or could use bond funding might find this issue directly relevant, and 'risk premiums' in a discount rate are inappropriate with serious implications whether or not bond funding is involved. All organisations need to review their position on discounting. When doing so they will find the issues are highly contentious and very complex. But they matter so much that it would be well worth attempting to properly understand all the relevant implications and test all the key assumptions. Some people may disagree strongly with these assertions and prefer sticking to a conventional received wisdom position without really understanding the issues. But my contention is this aspect of the tale is both very plausible and extremely important for a wide range of organisations in a wide range of industry sectors. When the implications for a water and sewage industry organisation emerged, prior to publishing Chapman and Ward (2011), a draft paper was sent to the Southern Water finance director. He responded positively and encouraged publication, although I had been off the board for some time. It clearly has implications significantly wider than project management or the water industry. It is certainly contentious. But there can be no doubt that it matters greatly and needs careful attention by all organisations affected by inappropriate choices.

Second, consider the problems associated with a common practice event-based approach to project risk management. The event uncertainty based pre-2007 HA approach to estimating attributed to WSL was not an issue for Southern Water, a point I would like to emphasise. While I was a non-executive director of Southern Water, the Projects Director had previous experience which included offshore BP projects, and I was not aware of any evidence of unusual estimation bias or other project management concerns. However, an approach based on event uncertainty may be a significant issue for other players in the UK water and sewage industry. In my experience it is certainly a central issue for a large proportion of the UK organisations beyond the water and sewage industry, and it is a general issue in Europe, North America, and many other parts of the world. The UK water and sewage industry provides a useful illustrative context, but plausibility issues addressed here are not specifically UK or water and sewage industry concerns – they are global concerns for all organisations. My contention is this aspect of the tale is also very plausible and important in this general context. Many colleagues share my views, and a well-established literature supports these views, but there are also wide groupings of 'experts' and 'professional guidelines' strenuously defending an opposing view. This, too, is a highly contentious issue with wide implications.

Third, consider the problems associated with three separate departments in the WSL Planning Group dealing with estimating, planning and risk management. Link this to a Projects Group which does not work closely with an Operations Group during the concept strategy stage of projects when the focus is the business case. My contention is yet again that this aspect of the tale is both very plausible and extremely important. In some respects, Paul's approach to merging his three departments simply follows what BP did a few years after adopting SCERT, which proved highly successful. The tale draws directly on this BP example, and this helps to illustrate why the implications are in no way restricted to the UK water industry.

Fourth, consider the problems associated with simplistic views of any aspects of any of the four Fs – the four crucial frameworks developed in this chapter: the project (asset) lifecycle, the seven Ws, the goals–plans relationships and the SP for projects in progress and gateway forms. Link the implications to simplistic views of projects and all the other related concerns addressed by the SPP concepts explored in this chapter. Yet again my contention is these aspects of the tale are very plausible, and extremely important, with widespread implications.

The reasons for choosing the water and sewage industry in the UK as an illustrative context for this chapter are various. One is it illustrates all these concerns when projects may be one-off construction projects like a new sewage works, ongoing construction projects like a water main replacement programme, or complex mixtures including water consumption reduction programmes or change management portfolios. Another is it clearly demonstrates that employing discount rates which are inappropriate involves crucial impacts that go well beyond choosing the wrong projects. They imply shaping projects inappropriately, as in a 50 year designed life for water mains instead of 100 years, with too little concern for the future (because it is discounted into insignificance), too much focus on a quick return as a result. In some cases, this may drive or be driven by a culture which is inappropriate. High quality assets with a long life, high reliability, and low operating costs in an organisation with a long-term vision and a high quality service/products ethos can be fundamental to a very strong capability-culture asset set. This can both support and enhance very strong concern for maximum rates of return for shareholders, with a clear understanding of both long-term and short-term issues. This strategic clarity and supporting ethos can be a missed opportunity for organisations which suffer from short-term vision and quick-buck goals driven by inappropriate discount rates leading to low quality assets which have a short life, low reliability, and high operating costs.

Apart from the specific capability-culture liabilities addressed by Paul in the tale, WSL enjoyed a very limited capability-culture liability set, and a formidable capability-culture asset set. Paul had a very strong background and the knowledge plus the skill set and the mindset needed to lead the changes involved. He also had a very supportive set of very capable colleagues. Charles, Michael, Ollie, Frank, Richard, and Curt were all unusually collaborative and very skilled, with a shared corporate vision and an appetite for effective team working, as well as achieving the goals of immediate and direct interest. If either Charles or Michael had been interested in preventing Paul from achieving any of his key goals, Paul's task would probably have been non-feasible. Opposition from Frank or Ollie would pose a very serious threat. Two or more directors Paul needed support from who were simply not up to the task would also pose a serious threat. It might be argued that such a strong team is unlikely. As with earlier chapters, this is a reasonable view, but this aspect of the working assumptions used to develop the tale serves to demonstrate what can be achieved if capability-culture concerns are addressed effectively as part of the EP approach.

I have frequently encountered 'models' for Paul during in-house and public courses based on Chapman and Ward (2011) and earlier versions of its approaches, in many different countries. But the world could certainly do with many more of them, as well as many more other board level managers like those WSL enjoyed.

Some further implications of clarity inefficient toolsets

One of the important roles of EP is using an EP perspective to explain why some common practice tools are clarity inefficient and should be eliminated from everyone's toolset if they want to embrace an EP perspective. This section begins by consolidating why this is the case for reasons addressed earlier, as a basis for then briefly considering some further implications of crucial importance.

Clarity inefficient tools which should not be used

Figure 7.7 was used by Paul to explain why he would not tolerate further use of PIGs within his Projects Group, and Figure 7.9 was used in the HA Nichols study discussion to drive home one of the results of a PIG-based approach to risk adjustment estimates which are widely employed. Some risk management experts within and beyond the project risk management community may be seriously offended by this view. Professional bodies which advocate PIGs (under various labels) may feel this is an unwarranted attack on their professional standards. It is a clear attack on some professional standards and many people's preferred perspective. But in my view, it is an attack which is long overdue, very badly needed, well founded, and fully justified. It is important *everybody* understands why PIGs once made sense and what has changed, *especially* those involved in employing people who persist with using PIGs or supporting organisations which persist with promoting PIGs.

When PIGs were first employed in a pre-1960 safety context the only risks being addressed were events (specific failures and accidents) happening or not. Appropriate data for conventional objective data-based statistical methods were not available, subjective probabilities were generally held to be inappropriate for any formal decision-making procedures, and a 'decisions under uncertainty' mode of classic decision analysis was the obvious conceptual and operational framework. Safety managers needed a simple, rational means of prioritising the list of threat events they were able to identify so that they could allocate resources to risk minimisation in a defensible manner. In these circumstances PIGs were a very reasonable basic or starting point tool. Fault trees and event trees used within an expected outcome framework were richer tools, employing a generalisation of classical decision analysis in 'decisions under risk mode'. But they were very demanding in terms of data and analysis effort, and they had some common or comparable weaknesses in practice, like largely ignoring ambiguity uncertainty, systemic uncertainty and risk associated with overall variability.

Since the 1960s, authors like Raiffa (1968) have made the framing assumptions for the view 'proper probabilities require data' redundant, along with classical decision analysis. Modern decision analysis is founded on framing assumptions about subjective probabilities shared with EP. This shared view of probabilities is a crucial issue, and it means that for

EP purposes, all well-founded probabilities should reflect data and their objective analysis insofar as this is both feasible and useful, but probabilities should be statements of belief which reflect a synthesis of all relevant decision-maker knowledge of the implications of data and analysis shortcomings. This includes addressing all relevant reasons why the future may be different from the past, with effective treatment of valid and important differences of opinion.

Furthermore, since the 1960s, all effective approaches to risk management have recognised the importance of dependence and systemic risk, especially approaches building on a Markowitz (1959) approach to portfolio management and the role of risk efficiency.

From this perspective PIGs are simply weak quantitative tools in a qualitative framework which is not sufficiently general. From this perspective PIGs should be made redundant as a starting point for all analysis in all contexts – including ERM. ERM in many different forms has blossomed in the last couple of decades. The forms discussed in Chapters 8 and 9 are generalisations of a well-established portfolio management framework which ought to be central to ERM but often is not. Safety and security risk management as addressed in Chapter 9 is a special case within the Chapter 8 approach.

Even if events are the only sources of risk of interest, Figure 7.7 or some of the variants discussed earlier using subjective probabilities are a superior tool in all respects. There is a growing body of other people sharing this view, but the rate of enlightenment needs to accelerate.

However, there are important further reasons for rejecting the conceptual framework underlying PIGs – reasons which go beyond operational tool concerns illustrated directly by Figure 7.7. For example, PIGS and related 'risk list' event-based approaches do not lend themselves to dealing with sources of uncertainty which are not events, central to the issues explored using Figure 7.8, and they do not facilitate effective assessment of alternative responses, some of which may be specific to particular sources of uncertainty, some of which may be a deal with sets of sources of uncertainty. The full implications of these reasons are complex and not immediately obvious to many people who do not adopt an EP perspective, but this does not make them unimportant.

Paul's use of Figure 7.8 plus his use of the HA examples illustrates how estimation based on *some* conventional event-based project risk management ignores information readily available which results in persistent bias. Persistent bias as displayed by the HA pre-2007 and WSL is unacceptable. Some people see it as so widespread it is inevitable, not an avoidable dysfunctional risk, but a fact of life people have to live with. Just 'get over it' sometimes seems to be the attitude. But I am not alone in seeing it as both dysfunctional and preventable, and many share my view that it ought to be seen as incompetent in the very near future, ultimately as professionally negligent.

Persistent bias associated with estimates is not by any means the only driver of clarity inefficiency associated with PIGs, but it does stem from related underlying assumptions. Furthermore, it can be exposed and avoided by adopting low clarity but clarity efficient EP tools to capture all relevant uncertainty. As skill and understanding are gained, higher clarity approaches will provide big dividends. The biggest benefits associated with dropping PIGs may be driven by risk efficiency and further higher order opportunity efficiency gains.

Paul's approach to discounting further widens the focus of *some* received wisdom to be explicitly avoided. Embedding issues other than an appropriate cost of capital in NPV discount rates is an example of a source of persistent bias with a somewhat different underlying assumption basis. Before we had a multiple criteria mathematical programming framework available, single hurdle rate discount factor tests for projects seemed plausible, if not the only way to go. It is not surprising that finance texts rationalised single-hurdle rate-test approaches with working assumptions which became invisible framing assumptions – stealth assumptions in EP terms. HM Treasury's 2003 advice (HM Treasury, 2003a) on discounting uses a multiple test framework, the first published recognition of this issue that I am aware of and a notable breakthrough. My belief is HM Treasury reducing the real discount rate required in 2003 from 6% to 3% was about right, but the basis of its 3% choice was not appropriate. The published argument (Chapman, Ward and Klein, 2006) that the 2003 Treasury approach correctly uses a multiple tests approach grounded on an underlying multiple criteria framework, but it couples this to an inappropriate conceptual basis for the choice of discount rate, which has not been accepted yet so far as I am aware. Most public and private sector approaches have yet to even recognise the need for multiple tests to deal with multiple objectives in a general manner.

The idea that unbiased estimates of a discount rate ought to be driven by the expected cost of capital, *and nothing else*, is a very important aspect of the arguments about privatisation and nationalisation of a wide range of assets. This chapter only touches on an exploration of the implications, but they are clearly significant. Private sector funding rate of return expectations are usually very much higher than public sector bond funding rates. This very important difference will drive very different asset investment strategies. This will not just affect which projects are selected. It will affect the way the basic nature of the projects is shaped. It may also affect underlying culture and ethos issues in important ways.

Nobody should believe that public sector organisations funded by government bonds will have the same investment strategies if they are transformed into private sector equivalents with 100% equity funding of capital investment, organisations like WSL occupying a middle ground. But also very important, *nobody* should believe that nationalisation of private sector organisations is a simple transformative change with impacts centred on discount rate considerations, whether or not a reversal of previous decisions is involved. The implications of this kind of change are extremely complex, and context specific assumptions need careful attention, with some examples explored in Chapters 8, and 10.

One of the most fundamental concerns this book addresses is stimulating an understanding of the need to establish a widely accepted set of general framing assumptions which can be used to identify and overcome stealth assumptions which cripple capabilities in many planning and decision-making contexts. Project planning is a particularly good context to illustrate what this might involve. But the evaluation of conceptual and operational tools addressed in this chapter just scratch the surface.

Some organisational structure and professional body implications

EP for projects as explored in this chapter not only builds on the central ideas in *How to Manage Project Opportunity and Risk* (Chapman and Ward, 2011), but it also builds on a vast project planning literature, with many important influences not even referenced.

There are particularly important implications associated with managing the creation and enhancement of plans as well as shaping plans in all stages of a project from the concept strategy stage onwards. Using the SPP approach implies that risk management in the broad opportunity plus risk and underlying uncertainty management sense should *never* be pursued in a separate silo, separated from associated planning and estimation, which should themselves never be in separate silos. The focus is a project planning context, but the SPP approach links project planning to operations and corporate planning directly, crossing silo boundaries in the process. Furthermore, this perspective is also clearly relevant in any planning context when a project planning perspective may be appropriate, including the management of change. It also implies that all aspects of planning covered by the seven Ws plus associated goals–plans relationships need fully integrated treatment across operations, project, and corporate planning functions. Paul's OG/PG team concept jointly using a WSL basic SPP is a sound starting point, but Frank's Finance Group and those directly concerned with the legal aspects of contracts also need effective integration. This, in turn, has implications for *all* the professional bodies involved, especially those associated with the project management profession.

Like most professions, the project management profession wants to carve out a territory, define professional standards, and protect the reputations and incomes of both the members of the professional bodies and those involved in running the professional bodies. Over the past decade this has created understandable pressures to resist many of the ideas advocated in this chapter, in part because they imply changes to a status quo with important costs for those committed to the status quo.

I believe it is important to support the stimulation of a growing understanding of the need to recast 'the project management profession' in the broadest possible terms, as advocated by Morris (2009) and others in *Making Essential Choices with Scant Information – Front End Decision Making in Major Projects* (Williams, Samset and Suannevag, 2009).

There are many linked lobbies which also need support in my view, like advocating the softening, if not the deconstruction, of counterproductive silos within the project management profession (like those separating project risk management from planning and estimation); seeing all professional technical guidelines and standards dealing with best practice management decision making as supportive but not prescriptive; and insisting that a mandatory supportive role involves identifying and eliminating tools like PIGs which are clarity inefficient.

Perhaps less obvious, but arguably central, is using some variant of the UP concept as a unifying framework. The use of the SPP framework concepts proposed in this chapter involves a view of project management professionals working with all other related professionals in a directly interactive manner. This is a wider view than the current common practice of how all management professionals ought to work together, with greater mutual understanding than is usually the case at present. But it is certainly not a new idea. It is just an eternal truth which tends to get overlooked, possibly to an increasing extent because of the politics of increasing use of experts and professionals who are focused on specialty areas.

The SPP concept as a position in the very basic SP to UP concept spectrum

With Stephen Ward and many other colleagues, I have been working towards the SPP concepts developed in this chapter for several decades via specific processes for particular organisations like the SCERT approach for BP and variants for other organisations, generic processes for a range of guidelines, and generic processes like PUMP and its precursors. We have not yet even considered the use of a very broad SP concept like the SPP beyond a project management context, but there is obvious potential. Indeed, there is a case for suggesting most SPs should be designed thinking about embedding the UP in the way this chapter does for a specific organisation to some extent, the only other option being the routine use of a UP concept to manage changes, implicitly if not explicitly.

To keep it simple, this book distinguishes just two fundamental process types: a UP and SPs. But a wide range of SPs is illustrated. Perhaps the simplest is the minimum clarity estimation approach outlined at the beginning of Chapter 3. The most complex is the SP for projects approach illustrated in this chapter. The SP for bidding of Chapter 6 illustrates a mid-range position. If the 'select and focus the process' phase of the SPP used by any organisation does not accommodate what is known about useful processes for *all* the contexts to be addressed by that SPP, then *someone* directly involved needs to use a UP equivalent to assess how to modify the SPP to accommodate new contexts beyond the current scope whenever this may be appropriate. This is true of all SPs.

Common 'techniques' of all kinds can be seen as SPs in this sense and assessed for critical stealth assumptions using an EP perspective. A key EP capability is testing common practice techniques for stealth assumptions which make them inappropriate for some contexts, suitable for other contexts, to facilitate enlightened choices.

8 Corporate strategy formulation – an electricity utility example

The questions raised by the brief discussion of Ajit's corporate strategy formulation concerns towards the end of Chapter 5 need responses now. Building on Ajit's observations, one set of issues which needs to be addressed involves developing a clear top-down view of the full scope of corporate goals, starting with key ownership issues. A second set of issues involves formulating a top-down view of appropriate corporate strategy directions given corporate goals. A third set of issues involves deciding which bottom-up propositions for corporate changes with strategic implications need further attention.

The focus of this chapter is structuring top-down formulation of corporate strategy in a way which facilitates integrating bottom-up strategy formation and collectively testing the resulting overall corporate strategic plans. Bottom-up corporate strategy formation triggered by the strategic needs of specific operations has already been addressed in several ways in all preceding Part 2 chapters, and the role of enlightened project planning in the integration of some corporate-wide issues was considered in Chapter 7. However, top-down corporate strategy formulation and testing have so far been discussed to a very limited extent.

'Strategy' is used in the usual plain English sense of 'choices involving decisions with important, broad or long-term implications'. 'Corporate strategy formulation' assumes a broad plain English interpretation of 'formulation' in the 'setting forth in a systematic manner' sense. This 'setting forth in a systematic manner' is interpreted in terms of creating, enhancing, shaping, testing, and interpreting prior to implementation, in a manner consistent with the UP of Figure 2.1. A narrow interpretation of 'formulation', like 'reducing to or expressing in a formula', is explicitly avoided. The key underlying framing assumptions are 'corporate strategy formulation' should involve a formal corporate top-down overview from the strategic end of a strategy-to-tactics scale, but integrating bottom-up strategy formulation is an essential part of the holistic approach required. This is consistent with earlier usage of these words and common practice.

Most organisations distinguish between short-term and long-term corporate planning, and many use a variety of additional categories. The enlightened approach to corporate planning advocated in this book adopts a formal separation of the approaches taken to short-term, medium-term and long-term corporate planning horizons as a basic default position. It also assumes that all three of these 'categories' of corporate planning are focused on 'feasible' options, where 'feasible' is assumed to mean 'known to be technical feasible', explicitly excluding 'currently technically non-feasible' options. For reasons clarified later, it may be important to include some technically feasible options which are not economically feasible at present, and it may also be crucial to include some options which are currently non-feasible in terms of the organisation's capability-culture assets and liabilities. The complex set of underlying issues clarified by this interpretation of 'feasible' in technical terms, with economic feasibility and capability-culturally feasible nuances, are important in practice. They are handled as simply as possible by restricting the long-term, medium-term, and short-term planning concepts to feasible options in this nuanced sense plus the use of two further separate 'categories' of corporate planning, referred to as 'futures planning' and 'goals planning'.

'Futures planning' provides a focus for addressing what might be feasible but is not currently feasible for technical, economic or capability-culture reasons. Futures planning may look beyond the long-term planning horizon to a very distant 'futures horizon', but it may also work within the range of the long-term, medium-term and short-term planning horizons. 'Futures planning' includes a number of different common practice approaches, many with labels which indicate their nature – like 'horizon scanning', 'futures research', and 'technological forecasting'. But a core component which is less well-known is Ackoff's 'designing desirable futures' perspective. 'Futures planning' in an EP sense uses a 'designing desirable futures' perspective to get beyond a 'predict and prepare' mindset when addressing the gap between currently feasible options and options which are currently judged or implicitly deemed non-feasible but might be made feasible, identifying what is involved, where attempting to close the gap may or may not be a valuable option, and how to pursue the chosen options. The 'gap' may be a technical, economic, or capability-culture issue.

'Goals planning' is about a fully integrated formal view of corporate goals in an operational goals–plans relationships structure. Corporate goals may be initially expressed in a wide variety of ways, using words like 'vision', 'core values', 'mission', 'aspirations', 'aims', and 'objectives'. But however corporate goals are expressed, they need to be formally structured for operational purposes within and between four nominal planning horizons: the short-term, medium-term, long-term and futures planning horizons. Goals planning is about addressing where an organisation wants to be at any point in the future in terms of basic corporate goals relevant to all planning horizons, giving the vision which shapes goals operational content. Some goals may be associated with measurable criteria, but some crucial goals may not be measurable in any meaningful sense. The achievement of some goals may not be feasible currently, but trying to make their achievement feasible via futures planning may be crucial.

'Long-term planning' addresses where the organisation should aim to be in terms of key capability-culture assets and liabilities plus all other relevant assets and liabilities at a suitable long-term planning horizon. This form of planning is based on the organisation's corporate goals and what is currently known to be feasible, acknowledging all relevant uncertainty, including opportunities associated with the possible transformation of currently non-feasible options into feasible options via futures planning.

'Medium-term planning' is about given where the organisation is now and where it is aiming to be at the long-term horizon, what is the best way to plan to get there over a medium-term horizon, making commitments when appropriate. Medium-term planning has to address commitment and lead-time issues in terms of both expectations and associated uncertainty. It also has to address changes in objectives which might reasonably be expected in the process of getting to the long-term horizon, including those driven by possible successes with attempts to transform currently non-feasible options into feasible options via futures planning.

'Short-term planning' is about making the best use of current resources in the usual short-term-planning sense, responding to new feasible options as they arise if appropriate.

Assuming separable treatment of these five different categories of approach in four different planning horizons does not imply assuming independence. Addressing all relevant decision-making interdependencies is a central concern. However, formally acknowledging separable categories of approach facilitates using different operational frameworks within each of the five categories of planning, a practical concern of central importance.

It can be useful to associate different categories of approach and their associated horizons with different 'levels' of planning, putting goals at the top level, followed by futures, long-term, medium-term, and short-term. Using this view there are obvious 'downward dependencies': goals planning decisions shape futures planning decisions, futures planning decisions shape dependent long-term decisions, and so on. These downward dependencies are clearly important. But there can also be very important 'upward dependencies', which are often overlooked. Examples illustrating 'upward' as well as 'downward' dependencies are developed in this chapter.

Strategy formulation and testing also involves 'management levels' and associated 'management structures' to deal with the integration of top-down and bottom-up strategy formulation and testing processes. Boards of directors and supporting strategic planning staff have to shape strategy from the top down, but effective strategy management also requires 'emergent' strategy processes driven from the bottom up or 'sideways' within corporate management structures which have to serve a number of functions. This chapter emphasises the structure provided by an effective top-down approach, but it also recognises and addresses the importance of integrating bottom-up and sideways approaches in whatever management structures an organisation adopts.

Within the EP corporate strategy formulation and testing framework developed in this chapter, all aspects of corporate capability-culture and other relevant asset/liability issues need explicit attention. The capability-culture aspects are given limited attention, and they are not addressed until later, but they are much more important than suggested by the ordering used and the extent of the discussion.

At a corporate strategy formulation and testing level, it is crucial to remember that ultimately everything is *potentially* connected to everything else – and key interdependencies are a major source of both opportunities and risks. This makes keeping strategy formulation and testing simple and focused for everyone involved particularly difficult but particularly rewarding. And it means that not doing so effectively is particularly damaging. The notion of enlightened simplicity in process terms will receive very limited direct consideration, mostly deferred until towards the end of the chapter, but this seriously understates its crucial role.

Within the overall formal corporate planning framework developed in this chapter, it is useful to routinely remind ourselves that the form and interpretation of formal corporate planning by all participants is always heavily influenced by the context details. Furthermore, 'context' includes all other planning activity, both formal and informal. In an implementation context, background informal planning enhances and shapes plans as well as filling in necessary detail. Prior to implementation, context assumptions raise important questions about communication and motivation. For example, will all the parties involved interpret plans in the same way, and are they all motivated to pursue aligned objectives?

This chapter's tale involves a Canadian electricity utility owned by its provincial government, labelled 'Canpower'. In some respects an electricity utility has strategy formulation and testing concerns which are particularly difficult. This gives the tale useful richness. In other respects strategy formulation and testing for an electricity utility is particularly straightforward to structure, which helps to make the tale effective.

The basis of the tale is a consulting contract undertaken over the period from 1991 to 1993 for the Independent Power Producers Society of Ontario (IPPSO). IPPSO was an official 'intervener' in an Ontario government formal enquiry process set up because

Ontario Hydro (now OPC, Ontario Power Corporation) wanted approval for the construction of ten nuclear power stations over a 25 year planning period. IPPSO was opposed to these plans, and because it was an official intervenor, it obtained funding from Ontario Hydro for my contract. I acted as a consultant and expert witness for IPPSO, producing *Predicting and Dealing with an Uncertain Future* (Chapman, 1992), a report published by the government commission. My report was a highly critical assessment of Ontario Hydro's overall approach to corporate strategic planning for the next 25 years, including underlying forecasting. The Ontario Hydro corporate plans assessed were built around the proposed ten new nuclear power stations, justified using just two planning horizons – short-term, plus what Ontario Hydro called 'long-term', referred to in this chapter as 'medium/long-term'. Ontario Hydro used a largely deterministic approach to medium/long-term planning, employing demand and cost forecasts which were seriously optimistically biased but associated with a wholly unwarranted degree of confidence.

My report argued that the deterministic treatment of medium/long-term planning within a two horizon approach involved a serious set of flaws; the forecasting approaches which Ontario Hydro's medium/long-term strategic planning approach was based on, including cost estimation approaches in a broad view of 'forecasting', were seriously unreliable and would probably fail in an empirically demonstrated manner before long, a second serious set of flaws which underlay the first; Ontario Hydro's whole approach to strategic planning and associated forecasting should be scrapped, and its recommended strategy should be rejected, as a consequence of the combined effect of these two serious sets of flaws; a very much better approach to strategic planning based on separate medium-term and long-term planning approaches should be developed, built on a revised interpretation of current forecasting and a much better approach to all cost estimation aspects of forecasting.

To avoid criticising current practice without explaining the nature of better alternatives my report outlined what an appropriate approach ought to look like in 'what needs to be done terms', the starting point for drafting this chapter.

Ontario Hydro's forecasting failed as I had predicted, and this failure was picked up by the Canadian press, shortly before I was due to appear in person as an expert witness. Ontario Hydro then withdrew its 25 year corporate plan.

Three key sets of flaws are attributed to Canpower in the tale of this chapter. The basis of the two sets of flaws identified near the outset of this chapter and the nature of the proposed treatment of them draw on my Ontario Hydro report with enhanced illustrative examples enabled by EP developments over the last 25 years. Some of Canpower's characteristics underlying the third key set of Canpower flaws are based on my understanding of hearsay evidence about Ontario Hydro capability-culture liabilities in the early 1990s. In brief, this third set of flaws involves capability-culture liabilities driven by assumptions about how a public sector utility might reasonably address feasible options which were arguably flawed in a way which put the organisation's public-sector status at risk. Dealing with the issues associated with this third set of flaws was not part of my IPPSO contract, and the approach to this third set of flaws adopted in this tale would not have occurred to me 25 years ago.

The story told by the tale of this chapter is grounded in a very real situation. However, the plot of this chapter's tale and all the characters in the tale are fictions. I have no wish to embarrass Ontario Hydro (OPC) beyond the public critique in my 1992 report.

That said, I would urge *all* the citizens of Ontario to ensure that flaw sets one, two, *and three* have *all* been dealt with effectively if the current momentum behind OPC privatisation does not make it too late to do so, in which case a more complex but directly related set of problems will have to be addressed or endured. Furthermore, my plea to anyone with electric power supplied by a government utility is to see resolving the third Canpower flaw set, or comparable issues, as the key to avoiding the very serious damage to a national treasure caused by the 1980s privatisation of the UK Central Electricity Generating Board (CEGB) and the politics of subsequent regulation of energy utilities in the UK. Further still, my plea to all those who prefer having their electricity provided by private sector utilities is to make sure that there are no features of the approach to this chapter's tale and the linked discussions in later chapters which might improve private sector performance from a consumer perspective.

You may regard my view that privatisation of electricity generation in the UK was a serious mistake as contentious and misguided and perhaps as irrelevant to a book on planning in general terms. However, if you currently support private sector ownership as a political preference in all contexts, I hope you might wish to reconsider your position on the basis of the approach developed in this chapter plus the next three chapters. Furthermore, if you currently support a more conventional approach to public ownership of utilities than that proposed for Canpower by the end of this chapter, I hope you might also reconsider your position.

The position on public versus private sector ownership choices argued by this book is there is no such thing as a 'good' or 'bad' choice in all contexts – the overall merits of the options involved depend on the context and how the selected choice is likely to be implemented. Chapter 7 touched on this issue but avoided dealing with it directly. Chapter 9 develops further related issues, and Chapter 10 provides a synthesis of the earlier discussions, briefly added to in Chapter 11.

The capability-culture issues underlying the third key flaw set in Canpower's approach were not addressed until the third draft of this book. The insight needed to identify and address this third flaw set is attributed to the joint use of the capability-culture concept and the revised front end of the UP when using the UP concept in top-down planning mode. The basis of this additional insight had a related impact on my third draft treatment of TLC's approach to EOQ (Economic Order Quantity) models in Chapter 5. However, in this chapter the UP concept functions in the background. There are brief clarifying comments about top-down UP use at the end of the chapter, but directly illustrating the role of the UP in the development of this chapter's position as the chapter progressed did not seem feasible. A very simple process to make use of the top-down structuring is described, which should be interpreted as a sketched outline of an SP which needs further development and tailoring by any organisation adopting a variant of the approach advocated in this chapter. This further development will require the use of some variant of the UP concept.

The critique of Canpower's approach in terms of flaw sets one and two starts with a simple explanation of what the pre-1992 approach adopted by Canpower was doing instead of the more technical treatment in my 1992 report on Ontario Hydro. This is closer to what I would have liked to have said in a private conversation with the board of Ontario Hydro, had I been asked for such a confidential discussion instead of the formal public report.

Most of the key concepts developed in this chapter are relevant in all corporate strategy formation contexts, but some important details may need significant adaptation in other contexts because context is so central to the shaping of strategy formulation processes. As with the context of preceding tales, you may have a limited interest in electricity utilities, but to fully understand how to adapt the key ideas which this chapter explores, you will need to engage with the electricity utility context and examples.

An EP mantra particularly relevant to this chapter is a generalised and holistic interpretation of the common saying

If it ain't broke don't fix it.

This is a very widely used saying, but the generalised and holistic interpretation intended is not the usual emphasis. It is attributed to Paul Henderson, because he introduced me to both the basic mantra and its holistic interpretation in the 1950s. I was learning to race small sailing boats on Toronto Harbour in my early teens, and Paul was the senior instructor at the junior club that I was very lucky to attend every weekday over two months for four summers. Paul represented Canada in three Olympics in the 1960s and 1970s, sailing as helmsman in the Flying Dutchman class, just one of his many contributions to Canadian sailing. Paul's take on 'if it ain't broke don't fix it' in terms of racing dinghies was 'understand what lies behind your boat speed and that of your competitors in terms of a holistic systems view, and only make changes which make you more likely to win overall. Furthermore, don't fiddle with the tuning of your boat (e.g. adjusting mast rake) unless there are good reasons to make you think that you know what you are doing and may currently have it wrong'.

I remember the mantra and Paul's broad interpretation because when I was about 14 he used the mantra with characteristic sarcasm to admonish me when I was guilty of fiddling (inappropriate fine-tuning). Having grabbed my full attention he then explained, with trademark kindness and clarity, a systems theory view of winning sailing races which a 14 year old could understand and implement. Several years later when I was an undergraduate engineering student, a professor at the University of Toronto explained the importance of safety factors as provisions for uncertainty to deal with complexity we do not fully understand which should not be fiddled with because engineers had a habit of reducing safety factors until bridges and buildings started to fall down more often than expected, a notion which when generalised intersects with Paul's mantra. Many years later, Stephen Ward suggested I read an article with the memorable title 'Beware Fine-Tuning', the same basic idea from a further perspective, exploring issues like making organisations more fragile by removing 'organisational slack'.

This seems a particularly apt mantra for EP in this chapter, reinterpreted in terms of the achievement of corporate aims and objectives in holistic terms, recognising that everything is potentially interconnected, much of the complexity is difficult or impossible to really understand, and the difference between unhelpful fiddling and continuous improvement is very subtle but absolutely crucial. It can be interpreted as a top-down take on 'keep it simple systematically' aspects of enlightened simplicity, linked to but not quite the same as the bottom-up take on enlightened simplicity developed in earlier chapters.

Constructive tension between the mantras 'keep it simple systematically' and 'always "go the second mile" when appropriate' is useful, as argued earlier. Comparable constructive tension between the mantras 'if it ain't broke don't fix it' and 'if it's worth doing it's worth doing right' is important in a top-down strategic planning context, as is understanding the subtle but important differences between *inappropriate* fine-tuning or 'fiddling' and robust development and implementation of a continuous improvement policy.

All these concerns and their interdependencies are arguably central to developing strategic clarity in terms of your personal perspective and strategic clarity for organisations of interest.

As in previous Part 2 chapters, the credibility of the tale raises issues discussed towards the end of this chapter, the issues are different from those addressed in earlier chapters, and EP language is used throughout. Like Chapter 7, the emphasis is not quantitative models, but a few illustrative numerical examples are employed to illustrate key issues.

Carl's situation and all the key characters in this tale

The key characters in this chapter's tale are

Clive, the recently appointed chairman of the board of Canpower;

Ivor, the Canpower director made responsible for innovative thinking by Clive;

Carl, a consultant hired by Canpower for a study initiated by Ivor;

Larry, the director responsible for Canpower's long-term planning and forecasting;

Dick, the director responsible for Canpower's 'day-to-day' operations and associated short-term planning and forecasting; and

Pat, the director responsible for Canpower's project planning.

In the early 1990s, Carl was a corporate strategy consultant in the UK. He was contracted to advise 'Canpower', a Canadian electric utility owned by its provincial government, with a remit summarised by Ivor as 'How should Canpower embed all key management issues associated with uncertainty, risk, opportunity and underlying complexity into the formal corporate strategy formulation processes employed, revising current approaches as necessary?'

Carl believed he had the background needed for this assignment, but he knew from the outset that Ivor, the director who had insisted on his appointment and created the study brief which he had to address, was not fully supported by Canpower's board. Three executive directors were openly hostile: Larry, Dick, and Pat – led by Larry.

Larry was responsible for what he viewed as long-term strategic planning. Larry was also responsible for what he viewed as Canpower's long-term corporate forecasting, including electricity demand and all relevant costs. His title was Corporate Planning Director. He used a framework for long-term strategic planning involving a deterministic approach with a mathematical programming optimisation basis, which was unusual. He used conventional approaches to long-term forecasting which formally acknowledged uncertainty in probabilistic terms, but his understanding of the implications was seriously flawed. Carl will refer to *Larry's long-term* as 'medium/long-term'. Carl's terminology is this chapter's default interpretation of 'long-term' and 'medium-term' from here on.

Dick was responsible for day-to-day operations management of electricity production and distribution. He was also responsible for associated short-term forecasting, plus all generation and distribution plant maintenance, repairs, and minor refurbishment projects. He viewed his remit as short-term corporate planning and short-term plan execution. His title was Operations Director. His role was comparable to Ollie's role in Chapter 7.

Pat was responsible for the planning and delivery of all new electricity power station and distribution grid projects plus major refurbishment projects – a Projects Director with a role comparable to the Projects Director Paul replaced in Chapter 7.

This trio had oversight of three largely independent empires, whose senior management liked it that way, and wanted to keep it that way. They saw no reason to change what, in their view, they had done successfully for some time. Larry was incensed that anyone should even suggest that significant change to his approach to corporate planning might be necessary.

Ivor, the Canpower director who initiated Carl's study, was 'the board's innovator and catalyst for new thinking', as he described his role. Ivor had just been appointed as an executive director on the insistence of Clive.

Clive was a recently appointed new chairman of the board. Clive had insisted on Ivor's appointment, to test the status quo by challenging it where there might be room for improvement. He was convinced there was room for improvement, but he wanted clarity about where, and what needed to be done. Clive sometimes referred to Ivor as 'the board's devil's advocate'.

Ivor had yet to prove that he was not just 'a devil of a nuisance', as Larry referred to him in private conversations with Dick and Pat.

Luke Johnson provides a contemporary summary of what Ivor's role might imply in the short article 'Every Board Needs a Member of the Awkward Squad' (Johnson, 2017), using the 'devil's advocate' term. However, it is useful to see Clive, Ivor, and Carl as a team who are focused on designing a desirable future for Canpower, with Ivor's responsibility for innovation involving a much wider and deeper interpretation than 'devil's advocate' might suggest.

The hunch which motivated Ivor to pick on corporate strategy formulation in relation to uncertainty, risk, opportunity, and underlying complexity management was aspects of the Canpower culture driven by the way Larry, Pat and Dick managed their groups, as portrayed by a number of 'cultural clues' which Ivor had observed. Several relevant strong 'revealed preferences' were observed by Ivor:

1 'Big was beautiful' in terms of plant sizes and developments. Larry and all his managers seemed to favour big developments. Dick and all his managers liked big plants. Pat and all his managers seemed to favour big projects.
2 'Deterministic detail was desirable' in terms of all plans. They all liked detailed deterministic plans for many years ahead which assumed things would go as planned.
3 'Control was crucial' in terms of keeping operations in-house.
4 'Collaboration with others and projecting influence to other organisations which mattered, but Canpower could not control, was not a priority'.

Revealed preference 4 was a particularly perverse preference in Ivor's view, in the sense that it amplified the difficulties generated by the first three preferences.

In terms of some obvious consequences and knock-on implications, when things didn't go as planned it was never anybody's fault within Canpower – it was always external events or organisations beyond Canpower's control – and sometimes it wasn't clear who was responsible for sorting it out.

In terms of a sample of some specific recent developments, Ivor observed the following:

1 Several small output (and low hydraulic pressure) hydroelectric plants owned by the utility for many years had been sold because they were 'unprofitable', but the new owners were making money with them, in addition to achieving a high-profile 'green' reputation, and Canpower badly needed a greener image for a number of reasons.
2 The current medium/long-term plan was built around a proposal to build a series of six new nuclear power stations over a 20 year period, but the business case ignored uncertainties about full lifecycle costs which Ivor thought needed much more attention.
3 There was a degree of Canpower resistance to private power producers within the province which seemed both counterproductive and politically dangerous.
4 There were political movements afoot to break up the public sector monopoly position currently enjoyed by Canpower, with an international history of similar pressure on other publicly owned utilities, but nothing had been done within Canpower to even think about how to react effectively to such a development.

Ivor explained to Carl that he had not indicated to anyone other than Clive what his hunch was based on. He saw no point in challenging what he called 'the terrible trio' on such issues directly at this stage. These issues were simply symptoms of an underlying culture and inter-dependent capability problems which Ivor wanted to diagnose and cure.

Ivor wanted Carl to test Canpower's current frameworks and models for strategy formulation with respect to corporate uncertainty, risk, opportunity, and underlying complexity management. He wanted Carl to address all relevant concerns and suggest enhancements or alternatives which would provide immediate improvements in corporate performance and help Canpower to address the associated culture problems. Ivor wanted Carl to proceed with as much tact as possible but with clarity and frankness. Carl would report to Ivor in the first instance, but subject to Ivor's approval, Carl would then brief Clive. Subject to Clive's approval he would then report directly to the board.

Carl began by talking to Larry, Dick, Pat, and their staff. He reviewed a sizeable collection of documents they provided to illustrate the way their groups operated. He then prepared a presentation for the board to outline his preliminary findings and a recommended way forward. He tested his presentation for the board on Ivor, section by section as it was developed. He then reported to Clive and incorporated Clive's feedback over a cycle of meetings. What follows outlines the form Carl's presentation to the board took, over a full day at a suitably isolated and comfortable location. It does not include the preliminaries or the comfort building or the explanations of issues discussed earlier in this book – just a distillation of the day's proceeding which concentrate on what you might find interesting. It complements earlier tools and insights, building on them to provide further new tools and insights. The discussion assumes you are interested in how boards need to deal with these issues, whether or not you currently have or aspire to this kind of role.

Interjections link the discussion to earlier tales and broaden the discussion to other kinds of organisations when this seems useful, primarily towards the end of the chapter.

Corporate planning horizons and associated planning categories

Carl began his presentation by indicating that all Canpower staff should find it useful to think in terms of four 'nominal planning horizons' for formal corporate planning, each linked directly to an associated 'category' of corporate planning which is focused on different sorts of decisions using different kinds of planning tools within each of the four categories of planning. They would also find it useful to understand a fifth category of formal corporate planning which addresses the 'goals' of all of the other four planning categories in a fully integrated operational manner. He then outlined what each category involved as discussed in this chapter's opening section, using Figure 8.1 to provide a specific operational form.

Carl suggested that in some contexts some organisations might find fewer than five categories appropriate as special cases, and some organisations might want more categories. Different nominal horizons might be appropriate in some cases. However, Figure 8.1 provided a suitable framework for Canpower in terms of their current discussion.

By 'short-term planning' in a 'short-term planning horizon' he meant what he believed all Canpower staff currently meant by both these terms, and everyone involved could agree without controversy or discussion to put an outer bound on the short-term at about a year for most formal short-term planning purposes. The exact boundary was flexible, and different approaches could use variations.

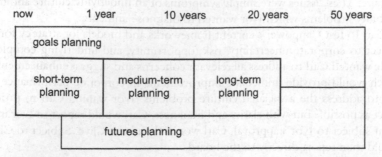

context – including all other planning which significantly influences the way participants interpret formal corporate planning plus other relevant capability-culture concerns

Figure 8.1 Formal corporate planning portrayed in terms of five different planning categories using four nominal planning horizons plus a comprehensive view of all the relevant issues.

By both 'medium-term planning' and 'long-term planning' he meant new approaches to corporate planning for Canpower which he would start to explain shortly, the first associated with a 10 year planning horizon, the second associated with a 20 year planning horizon.

By 'medium/long-term planning' he meant medium and long-term planning addressed jointly as a single category over a 20 year medium/long-term planning horizon without any separability, Canpower's current approach, referred to as just 'long-term planning' by Larry.

Carl made it clear that he appreciated Larry would not like this terminology change, but Carl and Larry meant very different concepts when they used the term 'long-term planning', and it was essential for Canpower to use one agreed-on definition for one agreed concept which was clearly understood by all relevant people. In Carl's view Larry's definition of 'long-term planning' had to be scrapped to make way for a better interpretation of this very important term and its underlying defining component concepts, linking a new and very different Canpower definition of 'long-term planning' to a separate 'medium-term' planning concept.

Elaborating on this observation, Carl said he appreciated this meeting was going to be a very uncomfortable experience for Larry, and some other directors would also feel some discomfort. However, he had reviewed his messages carefully with Clive as well as with Ivor, and they all believed there was no point in him not being completely open about all the key changes he believed Canpower had to make, starting with some of the more straightforward fundamental concerns.

Both goals planning and futures planning were implicit in Larry's corporate planning approach, in terms Carl would explain. Initially he would use Larry's implicit assumptions as he understood them – stealth assumptions in EP language.

He would now develop a brief overview of Canpower's current practice in the form of an outline of a first pass approach to top-down planning in the Figure 8.1 framework using current Canpower corporate planning assumptions. He would start with goals planning, followed by futures planning, medium/long-term planning, and short-term planning. He would then consider underlying short-term and medium/long-term forecasting, offering a critique of the latter and a summary explanation of what it was doing and why this meant that neither the current medium/long-term planning approach nor its underlying forecasting could be trusted. He would finish this part of his presentation by briefly outlining the implications of separating medium-term and long-term planning. This will take us to the end of this section.

He would then start to address how to replace the key features of the current approach in some detail – the following sections which are central to this chapter.

Goals planning

To address Canpower planning in an effective and efficient manner, they had to start with initial goals planning, and then systematically link this initial goals planning to futures, long-term, medium-term, and short-term planning in operational terms. To address the underlying complexity associated with Canpower's goals in a clarity efficient manner, they had to begin with a clear and comprehensive understanding of the basic nature of Canpower's 'goals'. These 'goals' might be described using words like vision, core values, aspirations, mission, key aims and objectives. Underpinning their approach, they needed robust assumptions, a sound appreciation of critical corporate strengths to be preserved, and clarity about important weaknesses to be overcome. This category of planning was crucial, but Carl indicated it would get limited attention initially that day, only modest attention later, for convenience in terms of ordering their discussion. In practice, goals planning provided the foundations for all four of the other categories, so it should always be given extensive attention before moving on. However, starting to probe what was involved would raise significant complexities better left until later that day, so they would begin with a very simple minimum clarity view of what was currently being assumed.

He would interpret this minimum clarity starting point as his current inference about the 'primary criteria' which underlay Canpower's current approach to corporate planning plus several 'secondary criteria', recognising that Canpower had many other criteria which were also very important to the overall set of criteria defining their goals.

He thought a non-controversial and simple initial understanding of Canpower's primary criteria over the planning period of interest was a minimum expected value for the standard tariff (price) per kWh (kilowatt-hour) for electricity, based on a minimum average expected cost per kilowatt-hour in each of the 20 years between now and the long-term horizon, with a reasonably smooth expected tariff profile over time. Canpower's current approach to corporate planning clearly implied that this was the central concern because expected cost over the medium/long-term horizon of 20 years was the *only* criterion used in their current linear programming medium/long-term corporate planning model.

He thought a non-controversial and simple initial understanding of Canpower's most important secondary criteria over the planning period of interest was an acceptable level of associated risk of higher costs and tariffs than the expected outcomes, plus acceptable levels of risk associated with availability and reliability. Canpower's current corporate planning approach did not measure the risk associated with expected cost and tariffs, or address it effectively even in qualitative terms, so their currently recommended strategy implicitly assumed that an acceptable level of cost risk was involved, and he was assuming that Larry and the Canpower board recognised the importance of this assumption.

This minimum clarity perspective meant that they could start their discussion today by looking at medium/long-term planning in terms of expected cents/kWh costs associated with all through-life costs, including depreciation of capital expenditure, the cost of capital, fuel costs, other costs like maintenance and repair, checking on associated uncertainty implications including risk. After they had developed an initial first pass understanding of futures, medium/long-term and short-term planning given this minimum clarity perspective of initial goals planning, plus underlying forecasting concerns, they could start to consider some of the key implications of the changes he would propose. Addressing further goals could follow later.

Futures planning

Carl indicated that it was important to limit what he meant by short-term, medium-term, and long-term planning to *feasible* options in a 'technically feasible' sense. However, it was also important to look beyond proven technology which was currently economically viable to decide where investment in technology development and close scrutiny of developments by others might pay. One way to look at this was testing current context assumptions about feasible technology.

A useful generalisation of the testing of current technology assumptions in both technical and economic terms was the testing of all other current corporate context assumptions for new approaches better suiting corporate goals. He had in mind some key capability-culture liabilities, the third key flaw in Canpower's approach he wanted to address later in the meeting, not elaborated at this stage.

He did not want to spend too much time on futures planning at this point in his presentation, but he wanted to introduce the idea of a comprehensive set of formal planning approaches addressing a mix of planning horizons ranging up to about 50 years, in all cases looking beyond existing technology and beyond existing approaches in all other respects. In particular, he wanted to explicitly avoid framing assumptions which locked Canpower into an approach which was passive, in the sense that it began by predicting a future which must be accepted, like it or not, what some people call a 'predict and prepare' paradigm. He wanted Canpower to attempt 'the design of desirable futures' (Ackoff, 1974) – to adopt a proactive approach to shaping the future as well as accommodating aspects beyond Canpower's control.

Carl emphasised the importance of comprehensive uncertainty and complexity management processes that can be used to help organisations plan and then achieve desired futures, as well as to help foresee and then avoid undesirable futures. Uncertainty and underlying complexity involved very serious problems and risks, but they also involved very important opportunities. Opportunities must be identified and then seized to exercise control over Canpower's destiny to the extent this was feasible, and ensuring this happened was an important role for the board.

In terms of his overview of current practice, they could just adopt what he inferred was Canpower's current corporate attitude to futures planning – Canpower should keep an eye on possible developments but focus on medium/long-term and short-term planning in relation to feasible options they were comfortable with in current corporate culture terms.

Canpower's current medium/long-term planning approach

Carl expressed the view that the central formal long-term corporate planning issue for any electricity utility anywhere in the world should be 'What mix of hydro, nuclear and thermal power units of different kinds (gas, oil, coal) by type (large high-head hydro, small low-head hydro, and so on) plus "other" sources (renewables for example) should be aimed for at a nominal long-term planning horizon like Canpower's 20 years?' The *separate* companion medium-term planning issue which needed addressing was 'How should we plan to get there in terms of "action plans" we can make commitments to as necessary in the near-term with associated longer-term provisional plans plus contingency plans to deal with reality departing from predictions?'

His interpretation of Canpower's current medium/long-term planning approach was they did not actually ask either question, which meant they had no *explicit* sense of long-term direction for their variant of medium/long-term planning, and no *explicit* sense of commitment timing. Instead, they derived a mix of unit types at the 20 year horizon indirectly, by assuming they could use a deterministic detailed planning process over the 20 year medium/long-term planning horizon employing:

1   point estimates of the expected supply available from current existing power stations in each year over the medium/long-term planning horizon until they were retired because they were no longer economically competitive or other reasons, plus
2   point estimates of how long it would take to get new power stations operational from the point when permission to build was given, plus
3   point estimates of the expected costs per kilowatt-hour for all existing and possible new sources in each year over the medium/long-term planning horizon, plus
4   point estimates of the expected demand for electricity in each year over the medium/long-term planning horizon, plus
5   a linear programming computer software system to minimise the expected overall cost over the medium/long-term planning horizon, with
6   no integrated contingency planning for the medium/long-term.

This linear programming model approach optimised medium/long-term planning assuming that the measure of expected cost employed was their primary criteria and uncertainty associated with all the point estimates plus the indirectly derived outcome at the long-term and futures horizons was not an issue. It produced a 20 year schedule of current power station retirements and new power station first availability dates.

The current Canpower approach to medium/long-term (and short-term) planning distinguished between 'base-load' requirements associated with electricity demand 24 hours per day 365 days per year and 'peak-load' requirements. Peak-load requirements involved demand over and above the 'base load', very important distinctions in practice because no significant energy storage was currently available. Turning power stations on and off involved different degrees of difficulty and cost – nuclear being the most difficult and small hydro and gas-powered stations being amongst the easiest. However, current medium/long-term planning did so assuming predictable base-load and peak-load variations within predictable overall load growth patterns over the 20 year horizon.

This current Canpower approach to the medium/long-term assumed forecasting electricity demand, current power station availability, and all the relevant costs involved so little uncertainty a simple deterministic corporate planning model could be used for their joint medium-term and long-term planning approach. In Carl's view this was an unusual and wholly unacceptable approach which needed replacing immediately. He was aware of no other electricity utility explicitly adopting such an inappropriately simplistic 'optimised' approach.

That said, *it was crucial to understand that in practice any utility which used a largely deterministic rule-based or heuristic approach to medium/long-term planning which focused on point value estimates without explicitly addressing associated uncertainty in effective for-mal terms would have directly comparable performance problems.* This was because they were actually just doing the same thing without trying to optimise in a formal manner. Many other utilities used largely deterministic approaches which were comparable in terms of per-formance problems, so Canpower's problems were more visible and demonstrable because they used linear programming, but they were by no means unique. It was important the board understood that the fundamental underlying flaw in the Canpower approach was not the use of linear programming per se – it was the deterministic approach based on point estimates which failed to address relevant uncertainty in an effective and efficient formal planning framework.

Relevant uncertainty had to be addressed in terms of two very different concerns. One was the need for a portfolio theory approach to define their direction of travel for long-term planning purposes. The second was their need for a separate medium-term plan-ning approach to address commitment timing decisions including associated contingency planning.

Linear programming was just a way to optimise given seriously flawed underlying assump-tions about the relevance of uncertainty. The use of linear programming might have been a 'good thing' because it indicated a desire to achieve a 'best solution', if a deterministic approach based on point estimates had been appropriate. However, in the Canpower con-text the use of linear programming was an unequivocal symptom of a 'very bad thing' because it implied (and highlighted) a failure to grasp the implications of significant uncer-tainty which rendered *any* deterministic approach which did not address uncertainty effec-tively inappropriate. An appropriate set of effective and efficient formal planning approaches for dealing with all relevant uncertainty and underlying complexity was essential, simplifying in the right way.

Canpower's current short-term planning approach

Canpower's current short-term planning was conventional in approach and well executed, needing no further attention from Carl other than modest clarification of what it involved when explaining forecasting issues for those directors who were not familiar with the details of what was involved.

Dick was obviously pleased to hear this, as was everybody else apart from Larry, who could see the potential for one of his usual allies deserting him.

Short-term forecasting of costs, power station availability and electricity demand

Short-term planning for Canpower depended on four very different kinds of short-term forecasting, approached in four very different ways.

One kind of forecasting addressed power station generation availability, interpreted by Dick in traditional availability and reliability terms. Models used for forecasting short-term availability and reliability of individual power station units were well developed and estab-lished, drawing on conventional state-of-the-art approaches. The short-term action plans Dick used were deterministic and assumed no power station failures, but contingency plans were in place, and the spinning reserve and standby reserve which Dick's plans included should provide the cushions Dick needed to implement these contingency plans when needed in most circumstances.

The second kind of forecasting involved estimating the costs associated with electricity generation to make short-term planning decisions about which power stations to operate. The dominant issue was fuel costs. In the short-term fuel cost estimates were based on known contracted prices or reasonably predictable forecasts just days or weeks ahead. Start-up and shutdown costs were also relevant to managing peak demand satisfaction, but they were reasonably straightforward to estimate using well-established accounting practices.

The third kind of forecasting addressed estimating the electricity tariffs needed for forecasting demand for electricity plus all other key explanatory variables used to drive their electricity demand forecasts. All demand forecasting had to accommodate the effect of the cents/kWh tariffs on demand, incorporating the underlying effect of all relevant Canpower costs. However, in a short-term planning context tariffs could be treated as known or reasonably predictable. Other key explanatory variables (like temperature) could also be forecast a short time ahead.

The fourth kind of forecasting considered the demand for electric power on a time-of-day, day-of-week, and week-of-year basis. This captured daily, weekly, and monthly (seasonal) cycles. Models used for short-term demand forecasting typically included exponential smoothing (adaptive expectation) models which track a variable, predicting future values based upon past observed values and their related forecasts; time-series models, which identify systematic variations relating to trends and cycles; and econometric regression models, which also use external or exogenous explanatory variables identifying causal relationships, like the effect on the demand for electric power of temperature, the current level of economic activity, the current price of electricity, the current price of substitute energy, and so on. All these approaches were well-developed and established within Canpower, drawing on a widely used and well-established literature. The most effective short-term demand forecasting models were typically hybrid regression models incorporating all useful features of the preceding models. Effective use required intelligent manual adjustments when factors not in the model were recognised, such as industrial action against major industrial consumers. Such models provided expected value point estimates and associated fit (forecasting) error probability distributions which could be used to define confidence bands. For short-term use, such models were well understood and reasonably straightforward to use effectively. Canpower made effective and efficient use of state-of-the-art approaches to these models.

Short-term planning built on these four different kinds of forecasting to match demand and supply at minimal expected operating cost – planning decisions involving minute-by-minute implementation, in terms of which electric power generation units to run within each station and how much spinning reserve was appropriate to cope with unexpected surges in demand and unplanned outages, plus planning decisions with slightly longer-term concerns about next week or next month in terms of planned maintenance and putting units on or off standby status. The basis was a 'merit ordering' of all power stations available by operating cost per kilowatt-hour, selecting the cheapest first and then working up towards the most expensive to meet expected demand with spinning reserve and standby reserve to cope with unexpected surges in demand or plant failures.

In Carl's view Canpower's approach to short-term forecasting and associated planning was exemplary with just one key proviso – short-term power station outages which proved to be longer-term failures relevant to medium/long-term planning were not addressed with the degree of formality he would argue for later. A more general view of 'availability' was needed to accommodate this concern because it was not currently addressed as part of the medium/long-term planning agenda either. It involved what might seem to be a short-term incident initially which turned into a medium-term or long-term concern.

To illustrate what he was getting at, a worst-case scenario was a nuclear power station failure which investigation showed was caused by a fundamental design problem which would require shutting down all their nuclear power stations with comparable designs permanently.

Larry knew this possibility was not addressed by his approach because he had in effect deemed the probability of it happening 'too small to worry about' for formal planning purposes. He could see Carl saw it as his problem, not Dick's, and he correctly suspected Carl was going to return to this issue later, but neither said anything more at this stage.

Medium/long-term forecasting of costs, availability and electricity demand

Medium/long-term planning for Canpower depended on the same four kinds of forecasting as short-term planning, but each of these four kinds of forecasting had to be approached in very different ways relative to their short-term equivalents, with a clear understanding of some crucial differences.

One kind of forecasting addressed power station availability on a year-by-year basis given current supply capability, provisional medium/long-term plans to release current supply sources by taking them out of service, and a provisional view of the implementation of the medium/long-term plans to make new power stations available. This meant the reliability of new power stations and their technology was of concern as well as existing power stations, and the reliability of the estimated time between deciding to build a new station and having it operational was also an issue. Carl indicated these issues were all very important, but they were not at the top of his agenda for the moment.

The second kind of forecasting considered cost estimates to make medium/long-term planning decisions. An obvious central concern was fuel costs – easy to predict a week ahead but sometimes getting difficult to predict a year ahead, becoming virtually impossible 5, 10, or 20 years ahead. A less obvious but also central concern was the full capital cost of all new power stations, expressed in an amortised form so that the capital costs for proposed new power stations could be combined with operating costs to derive the estimated full lifecycle overall costs estimates per kilowatt-hours delivered to the grid for new power stations to make capital investment choices. These costs depended upon usage assumptions. Assuming a new power station would run for 90% of the time it was available for medium/long-term planning purposes, but then only using it for 45% of the time for any combination of reasons, doubled the amortised capital cost per kilowatt-hour, a crucial source of uncertainty and risk currently ignored.

The third kind of forecasting addressed the electricity tariffs and other key explanatory variables used to drive their electricity demand forecasts. All demand forecasting had to accommodate the effect of the cents/kWh tariffs on demand, and the effect of all relevant Canpower costs on the cents/kWh tariffs. Larry's approach involved two key unrealistic assumptions with effects which became visible at this point. First, the expected capital cost of new nuclear power stations was optimistically biased to the extent that it needed uplifting by a significant amount in Carl's view, for reasons he would explain shortly. Second, all fossil fuel costs were assumed to rise at a steady rate of climb from current levels, with gas maintaining its current cost advantage relative to oil and coal. These two assumptions confirmed Larry's current revealed preference for building new nuclear power stations for base-load as soon as current base-load power stations reached the end of their planned life or became relatively uneconomic, plus Larry's current revealed preference to build large new gas-fired power stations as soon as current peak-load stations reached the end of their planned life or became relatively uneconomic. Without looking any further, the board could assume these revealed preferences meant that Larry's linear programming framework would drive Canpower to preserve current big hydropower stations, but otherwise move Canpower towards an all nuclear base load plus all gas-fired peak-load position. They could get *exactly* the same result using a simple variant of Dick's 'merit-ordering' approach, achieving this position by the 50 year futures horizon if all aspects of the plan held.

Carl assumed Larry was probably aware of this, but most other members of the board probably were not. He did not want to linger on or labour this issue at present, but he wanted to start to trigger a crystal-clear understanding by all board members by the end of this meeting that the sophisticated linear programming basis for Canpower's corporate planning was in practice just a simplistic device for delivering Larry's revealed preferences – his 'desirable future' in Ackoff's terms. Larry's 'desirable future' was an existing large hydro plus nuclear base-load future, plus gas-powered peak-load stations. The use of linear programming simply produced a variant of Dick's merit-order approach, without Dick's associated recognition of uncertainty and the need for effective contingency planning.

The fourth kind of forecasting addressed the demand for electric power on a year-by-year basis 1, 2, 3, . . . , 20 years ahead. Forecasting demand for electric power for the short term as undertaken by Dick was exemplary in Carl's view, as observed earlier, and adaptations of the same forecasting model approaches could serve as a starting point for medium/long-term forecasting. Hybrid regression models incorporating smoothing effects, causal factors like population growth and economic variables like price tend to fit annual past data reasonably well, although not as well as short-term forecasting models, and this kind of long-term forecasting models were generally well understood by electricity utilities and other experienced users. Relative to their short-term forecasting use, such models required reformulation for the peaks associated with different time period structures, and re-estimating, with significant changes in some of the individual variables involved. For example, seasonal temperature variations would cease to be relevant, but population growth might become a key explanatory variable, and economic variables like price would become crucial. Such changes might seem to pose no immediately obvious difficulties in terms of the econometrics involved in estimating the models used. Given stable relationships and appropriate data, these top-down forecasting models can work quite well over the data period used to estimate the models in the sense that they fit the past data set. However, they cannot cope with a future involving significant new issues or structural changes. Furthermore, the error terms associated with their 'fit' to past data ignores errors associated with predicting explanatory 'exogenous' variables used to drive the forecasts of interest beyond the data period into the future – fuel prices, capital costs in amortised form, population growth, underlying industrial demand, technical changes, the load levels new power stations achieve, and so on. A failure to deal with the implications was seriously negligent.

A very important complement to these top-down demand forecasting models, widely used by Canpower and other electric utilities, was bottom-up or 'end-use' models, which looked at how much electricity refrigerators or air conditioning or other consumer and industrial uses involve, together with trends and cycles in associated use levels and efficiency levels. These bottom-up models provided significant insight into the nature of some changes in the structure of the market and the instruments available for 'active demand management' (encouraging consumers to use less electricity). However, they did little to help forecast when structural changes might take place.

A residual significant difficulty posed by both top-down and bottom-up demand forecasting models used in combination for medium/long-term planning purposes was predicting the values of all the explanatory economic variables used to drive the forecasting process and underlying structural changes not addressed by the models.

Carl emphasised that it was crucial everybody understood now, with complete clarity, several reasons why medium/long-term forecasting was not the same as short-term forecasting.

First, matching supply and demand at the heart of medium-term planning had to focus on peak demand within months or years over the medium/long-term planning horizon rather than hourly or daily demand in the immediate future. Larry's forecasting team worked with Dick's forecasting team, and both teams understood these differences and adapted their approaches accordingly. This issue was not a problem, unlike all the others.

Second, forecasting up to one year ahead using the confidence bounds associated with goodness of fit over the data period assuming known values of all the exogenous explanatory variable values was optimistic but with a modest bias adjustment could be reasonable. However, forecasts 2, 3, 4 or 5 years ahead were problematic, and forecasting 10 or 20 years ahead was just wishful thinking because of structural shifts not addressed by the models even if correct values of all the explanatory variables were known. Canpower's projected confidence bounds 5, 10 or 20 years hence were just fantasy because of underlying structural changes not modelled top-down econometrically or via bottom-up models *even if explanatory variables could be correctly predicted – which they could not.* For example, a social change towards greener consumption patterns might have profound effects on electricity demand, but predicting the nature of all relevant shifts and whether or not such shifts would happen was not feasible.

Third, while the cents/kWh tariffs could be assumed to be known in the short-term, tariffs needed forecasting in the medium/long-term, along with the direct effect of changes in tariffs on demand. This meant amortised capital costs and operating costs including fuel needed medium/long-term forecasting, along with the costs of buying power instead of generating it. These forecasts had to be translated into standard tariff levels which would drive demand, a further source of electricity demand unpredictability associated with a key explanatory variable. Canpower's current medium/long-term planning models assumed all new base-load power stations would be nuclear because extremely optimistically biased estimates of the cost of nuclear power stations had been used, driving up the assumed demand for electricity in a very optimistically biased manner which became increasingly unrealistic as time went on. The assumed dominance of gas-fired peak power at higher but still modest prices reinforced this growing bias as forecasts approached the 20-year planning horizon.

Fourth, further explanatory variables of importance also need forecasting, like population growth. Population growth had been rapid in the near past, and Canpower's medium/long-term forecasts assumed this would continue, probably too optimistically, further biasing the forecast for electricity demand on the high side.

The net result was a corporate planning model seriously overestimating rapid growth in demand which Canpower was planning to meet at the very low tariffs helping to generate this demand. The reality was Canpower's actual costs would be very much higher, and the tariffs needed to cover these higher costs would lower demand relative to forecasts, causing second order cost increases and third order demand decreases which continue to have further higher order effects. Canpower would build a lot of new nuclear power stations to meet base load, plus new, big gas-fired stations to meet peak loads, and then find that the actual costs of both were much higher than anticipated and demand was much lower than anticipated.

In Carl's view they would be setting out on this disastrous journey with no properly grounded sense of direction, no understanding of the serious risks associated with a planned future dominated by nuclear power stations for base-load and big gas-fired stations for peak load, and no effective contingency planning in place when their 'plan A' started to unravel.

The linear programming approach Larry was using was capable of going well beyond the simple model currently used by Canpower in terms of additional detail, following established practice by oil majors running refineries and other sophisticated deterministic planning users. For example, they could use the linear programming model to decide when to take on potentially useful non-utility generation (electric power purchased from outside the province or private sources within the province), when to negotiate the sale of power to other provinces or utilities in adjacent US states, and when to start and expect results from new conservation programmes (selling low energy consumption light bulbs for example). But the focus would still be all relevant costs in a deterministic framework, with no feedback to corrective action when forecasts did not hold, and nothing to stop the current momentum towards a seriously disastrous situation until it became blindingly obvious to some more insightful observers that they were heading for serious trouble.

Carl's overview of what separating medium-term and long-term planning involved

Carl repeated the view expressed earlier that the central issue for formal long-term corporate planning for any electricity utility anywhere in the world should be the addressing the question, 'What mix of hydro, nuclear, thermal of different kinds (gas, oil, coal) and "other" units by type should be aimed for at a nominal long-term planning horizon like Canpower's 20 years?' This question needed addressing explicitly, with considerable care and attention, deferring until later the companion closely coupled medium-term planning issues. Only after Canpower was clear about their intended long-term planning direction should they consider 'how should we plan to get there'. This would involve 'action plans' requiring commitments, with associated provisional plans to deal with *any aspects* of reality departing from base plans and parameter predictions like demand for electricity.

To keep the long-term planning approach as simple as possible, the mix of unit types targeted at the horizon could be addressed in proportionate terms first. This initial proportionate approach could be used for an initial assessment of the average cost per kilowatt-hour at the 20 year horizon. This could be used to predict tariffs. These predicted tariffs could, in turn, be used to predict the demand for electricity. At this point they could start to move beyond a mix to aim for in proportionate terms, addressing issues like the need to retire some specific current power stations but retain others. Specific choices would require revised tariff estimates. However, they should be able to converge to a planned set of specific new power stations to meet demand the forecast 20 years ahead with minimal iteration.

Looking at the long-term planning issue in proportionate terms first, Carl suggested it was important to acknowledge that many organisations in a wide variety of industries had done a great deal of pioneering work on the use of what he called 'robustness-driven scenario' approaches to long-term planning to cope with significant uncertainty. These scenario approaches involved 'qualitative' or 'semi-quantitative' scenario approaches to planning which used forecasts but focused on planning a *robust* approach which can cope with any plausible future. Such approaches were particularly relevant for organisations with a strategy largely driven by uncertainty about one parameter, like the cost of oil. Marsh (1991) provided a current synopsis of Shell International practice, Shell being an early pioneer of this kind of scenario approach. This kind of scenario approach abandons the notion of point estimates with an associated error or confidence band. The focus is two scenarios which represent in a consistent way the credible extremes of an infinite number of possible futures, plus a middle of the range possibility to formulate base plans for some form of 'central forecast' future.

This kind of robustness-driven scenario approach and its concern for robust planning were a significant positive step which Canpower had yet to exploit, unlike some other electricity utilities. However, such approaches did not on their own resolve the difficulties facing electricity utilities in a 'risk efficient' manner. He believed Canpower needed a 'portfolio-driven' framework with a focus on *both robustness and risk efficiency* via explicit pragmatic use of robustness-driven scenario approaches *plus* portfolio theory ideas, effectively linked to an understanding of all relevant systemic uncertainty as well as ambiguity. He would explain what this involved shortly, but the basis of his generalisation of the Marsh/Shell scenario approach was recognising that the key driver was not the uncertain price of one key factor like oil, but the uncertain cost per kilowatt-hour of electricity produced by a portfolio of possible choices. This portfolio included hydro, nuclear, gas, oil, and coal, buying power from non-utility sources (any provider outside Canpower); conservation (persuading customers to use less); and any other options thought relevant. Canpower should develop a *formal planning* approach to long-term planning which would produce a target mix of sources to aim for in portfolio terms with requisite robustness. They might usefully see the needed approach as directly comparable to a financial investor picking a risk efficient portfolio of stocks and shares which would maximise return for an acceptable level of clearly understood risk.

It was also very important to acknowledge that many electricity utilities had done a great deal of pioneering work on the use of informal portfolio planning approaches to seeking a reasonable approximation to both risk efficiency and robustness. For example, before its recent privatisation the UK's CEGB had a formal policy of seeking efficient diversification of power sources, including a very clear formal policy to avoid only one approach to nuclear power station technology, pursued, as far as he knew, by informal planning means.

Looking at the separate medium-term planning issue, once Canpower had a clear idea of their approximate target mix of power stations 20 years hence, they could look at the difference between that target and where they would be if they built no new plant, use the gap to draw up priority lists of new power stations, and then start building commitments to begin construction and further commitments to get ready to begin construction as well as other provisional plans up to 20 years ahead, using a very different but compatible formal planning approach.

With nuclear power station construction high on Canpower's current agenda, and a minimum construction period for nuclear power stations of about ten years, this defined the ten year potential commitment horizon in terms of the maximum lead time they needed to consider for medium-term planning commitments. Other organisations would, of course, define their horizons on a basis appropriate to their context, and might use different horizons for different kinds of planning. Within this ten year horizon, medium-term planning decisions might be based on estimated dates to the nearest month. More tentative provisional plans might be to the nearest year for years 11 through 20, to profile plans to move towards the target mix of generation types by year 20 for the demand expected by the time they reached the long-term horizon.

Contingency plans could be developed to look at medium-term departures from expectations, with costs linked to prior option choices when relevant, as they often were. Every year Canpower would have to review their long-term plans and underlying forecasts, updating their target mix at the 20 year horizon and medium-term plans.

An important feature of Canpower's current corporate culture was the mantra 'we must keep the lights on', and meeting this objective was clearly very important. But simply relying on significant surplus capacity, which seemed to be the current corporate strategy to achieve this goal, was both an expensive approach and a potentially unreliable approach.

When closing his introductory overview discussion of corporate planning horizons and associated formal approaches to planning categories as a whole, Carl emphasised that Canpower's current approach to short-term planning was very good, and not in need of any changes. However, they had to confront their inability to forecast with any certainty beyond the short-term, and the quite profound difficulties associated with long-term forecasting of cost per kilowatt-hour for different sources of electric power. He suggested long-term planning had to focus on uncertainty relevant to targeting the mix of supply sources they needed in 20 years given what they knew was feasible now, and medium-term planning needed to focus on uncertainty relevant to timing movements towards the 20 year horizon targets, emphasising commitments within the first 10 years of the medium-term planning horizon. Futures planning needed to start on a sound basis provided by goals planning, addressing aims and objectives over the whole of the 50 year planning period of interest.

When he had made sure everyone understood this overview in broad terms, Carl moved on to more detailed consideration of what was involved, starting with long-term planning.

Long-term planning

Long-term planning in the Figure 8.1 framework started by asking the question, 'Given what was currently known, where did Canpower want to aim to be in 20 years, in terms of an appropriate mix of hydro, nuclear, thermal, and "other" units by type, assuming the use of feasible technology options and other robust working assumptions?' Canpower should be aiming for a target mix of sources of electricity at a planning horizon of 20 years, recognising that within 5 years the target would probably have moved, and annual reviews with adjustments whenever needed would be necessary. For example, 'working to the nearest 10%, should the current base-load contribution of nuclear power of 50% be increased to 70%, as currently implied by Larry's plans, or should it be decreased to 40% (which he was inclined to believe might make more sense although he did not say so at this point), and what did this imply for other target proportions?'

When Canpower had the approximate target proportions assessed, they could forecast their cents/kWh tariffs at the 20 year target horizon, and use a 20 year electric power demand forecast to convert target proportions into target gigawatt (GW) capacities.

Each year both long-term and medium-term plans would have to be reviewed in the light of emerging information about economic, political, and social issues and in the light of futures planning. Significant changes in long-term plans might occur, and some knock-on changes in medium-term plans might become essential. However, medium-term plans involving action plan commitments ought to be fairly stable, and this ought to be an explicit objective of the overall approach. For example, it should now be very clear to all Canpower directors that it was crucially important to *never* delay new nuclear power station projects already under construction because demand had fallen, but how much it was worth spending to avoid doing so, and how best to address both proactive and reactive contingency plans to implement this insight, had not yet been assessed. This was a deliberately unsubtle reference by Carl to a current nuclear power station project which had recently revealed that factor of ten cost increases were now anticipated, largely attributable to such delays by Pat and Larry. Carl knew that other important factors were also in play, but Pat and Larry blamed the whole of the increases on changes in safety regulations which occurred during a deliberate pause in construction following a downturn in the demand for electricity. In Pat and Larry's view, neither the demand downturn nor the change in safety regulations could have been anticipated. The consequences included a need to redesign core aspects of the power station halfway through construction, with obvious serious knock-on implications. Ivor and Carl saw the safety regulation changes as a development which should have been anticipated, along with the downturn in the forecast demand, and the resulting debacle as the result of a particularly glaring example of incompetent medium-term planning in conjunction with incompetent long-term planning. Carl wanted to indicate to all the directors what they were addressing without dwelling on it at this stage. Pat and Larry flushed when most of the other directors looked at them for a reaction, but they remained silent.

Keeping their attention to the long-term for the moment, Carl suggested that a number of ingredients were needed before they could evaluate where they currently thought Canpower should aim to be in 20 years. These ingredients were a full set of feasible options, unbiased full lifecycle cost estimates for each option addressing all relevant uncertainty, and unbiased estimates of the key interdependencies between all relevant uncertainties in an appropriate form. He would deal with these ingredients one step at a time.

A full set of feasible options

A full set of possible new power stations was an obvious place to start. The currently proposed series of six new nuclear power stations to begin construction over the next 20 years were obvious examples. In addition to hydro, coal, oil, and gas alternatives, proposed 'new supply' which provided equivalent power without construction cost investment by Canpower also needed attention – like buying power from other utilities. Furthermore, renewable sources like wind power and solar power should be included as possible options in their best currently feasible technology forms, even if their inclusion was believed to be inappropriate at this stage of their development because of current costs. Canpower needed to be able to explain why they were not going down any potentially useful technically feasible routes if that was the choice, and they needed to understand the exact nature of the gap between exclusion and inclusion in the portfolio of priority new supply which would emerge. Put slightly differently, the feasible/non-feasible boundary in economic terms was uncertain. This uncertain boundary needed explicit formal recognition in terms of including all potentially feasible options and measuring cost gaps associated with exclusions for cost-based reasons. The size of these gaps was important input to futures planning, and a good example of one way interdependencies between the five categories of planning portrayed by Figure 8.1 could be approached.

To compare different types of power stations and their equivalents, and to build trial portfolios of options, Canpower would find it useful to work in terms of 1 GW 'new units' of additional nuclear power and 1 GW 'new units' of all other 'new supply' types, initially addressing base-load and peak-load portfolios separately.

For those not familiar with electricity power station planning, planning assumptions used at that time meant that 1 GW '*planning* units' would provide power for about a million homes, with a significant proportion of total demand servicing industry and commerce (non-domestic demand). Carl chose 1 GW 'new units' in a 'planning unit' sense to facilitate a simple discrete value illustrative HAT (histogram and tree) approach which avoided excessively detailed planning without excluding low-output possibilities dealt with on a collective basis. Large nuclear power stations normally use multiple 'physical generation units' in addition to involving multiple new units in our planning-unit sense. For illustrative simplicity this tale assumes that Canpower's current plans for six new nuclear power stations involved 1 GW *physical and planning* units, with three of these units per power station, 6 × 3 = 18 new units of nuclear power in total. Conventional thermal power stations might be significantly less than 1 GW, and very low output sources dealt with on a collective basis might involve several dozen physical generation units to provide a 1 GW new unit of power in these planning terms.

Carl suggested they defer consideration of new hydro, gas, oil, coal, and a range of other further technically feasible options that day, and focus on simple illustrative numerical examples for just three base-load portfolio possibilities to explore simple portfolio models:

1   a 1 GW new unit of nuclear power,
2   a 1 GW new unit of 'conservation' (using 'active demand management' to reduce demand), and
3   a 1 GW new unit of 'non-utility power' (buying electric power from other organisations, including the currently very limited number of privately owned electricity utilities within the province plus electricity utilities in other adjacent Canadian provinces or US states).

Nuclear needed consideration that day because it was Canpower's currently preferred option for their base-load portfolio and he wanted to illustrate key asymmetric distribution concerns.

Canpower was under significant political pressure to consider conservation. Simple forms of active demand management which they might adopt included the 'supported sale' of low energy consumption light bulbs, implying 'subsidised sale' in the sense that full retail marketing levels of profit would certainly not be required, and a further subsidy might be considered. But a rich set of further options could be considered. Carl knew that Larry was considering some options, but a much more proactive stance was an immediate requirement in his view, *one* reason Carl had included conservation in his illustrative set of three options.

Canpower also needed to give very close consideration to non-utility power options in Carl's view. He believed an increase in the attention paid to privately owned utilities within Canpower's province was essential, as was a much more collaborative approach to utilities in other adjacent provinces and US states, *one* reason Carl included 'non-utility power' in his illustrative set of three options.

A further key reason Carl included both non-utility power and conservation examples was the plausibility of simple symmetric probability distribution examples plus associated simple dependence issues facilitating a usefully straightforward initial discussion of portfolio modelling to address risk efficiency concerns, as you will see shortly.

Unbiased cost estimates for each option as a starting point

Carl began by indicating they needed to use a full lifecycle approach for each option of interest, spreading the capital cost over the asset lifecycle on a 'levelised' cents/kWh basis. This would involve annualised average cost using a variant of the discounted net present value approach outlined in Chapter 7 to amortise the capital cost component.

He would focus on assessing 'direct' costs initially. For the moment, he would explicitly exclude 'indirect' costs like reserve backup units in case of unit failures, electricity transmission lines, overhead management costs, and further potentially complex and contentious items, deferring consideration of these concerns until later. He would use 1992 Canadian cents/kWh 'money of the day', prior to adjusting for general inflation and further 'escalation' (differential inflation) of items like non-renewable fuel costs. They could later consider adding provisions for all relevant indirect costs and all relevant inflation and escalation, including economic, political, and social effects on markets and prices. Initially they could assume specific sites were not being considered. Ignoring site-specific issues introduced some uncertainty requiring a provision, and they would have to make the initial estimate unbiased given what was known about the sources of ambiguity in these provisions.

In the context of nuclear units, the resulting initial cost estimates would include amortised capital costs, fuel, all further operating costs, decommissioning costs, and any federal government levies or incentives specific to nuclear power. In the context of non-utility generation, this would involve market costs reflecting electricity supply and demand balance as well as underlying fuel supply and demand balance plus amortised capital costs, other operating costs, and government subsidies or levies for the supplier. In the context of conservation, the cost structure was less conventional, but consistency would be important.

One key aspect of these estimates was an unbiased view of the expected cost. A directly related concern was an unbiased view of the potential for variability associated with this expected cost. A further directly related concern was an unbiased view of the interdependence of variability when individual units were combined into a portfolio of units. Pursuit of risk efficiency, a core uncertainty and complexity management concept from an EP perspective, required clarity about all three of these component concerns and unbiased estimates of all three components. Pursuit of clarity efficiency in conjunction with risk efficiency plus related aspects of opportunity efficiency required a reasonably simple practical approach to addressing the complexity underlying uncertainty in this context, and this demanded a carefully judged approach to keeping it simple systematically.

Carl said he assumed most members of the board were convinced that they had a very good grasp of expected values and their relationships with associated probability distribution spread and shape, including the role of interdependence when portfolios were involved, but he wanted to explore some very simple illustrative numerical examples with them to ensure they all had a shared understanding of the key concerns in the Canpower context. He would use a HAT approach which was designed to help them all to understand both simple and complex forms of statistical dependence in a way which would facilitate agreeing to a collective board level Canpower understanding of key issues which could be communicated effectively to others.

Constructively simple models of asymmetric nuclear power cost distributions

They would focus their initial attention that day on what he would refer to as the 'example A' estimate of Table 8.1 and the related Figure 8.2, which he showed them.

Carl began by suggesting that Larry might see some aspects of this example A estimate as pessimistic, but he believed all aspects were actually *very* optimistic and roughly consistent with the numbers currently used by Larry. However, his focus for that day was constructively simple numerical examples to illustrate key concepts, not reliable estimates. They should defer the issue of reliable estimates until a later date.

They would use the Table 8.1 and Figure 8.2 example to consider the levelised full lifecycle cost of delivered power at the 20 year long-term horizon in 1992 Canadian cents/kWh for 1 GW of nuclear power. They should see this example as an illustration employing just three scenarios for simplicity of interpretation using a HAT approach which he would explain.

Table 8.1 Example A cost distribution for one GW of nuclear power, tabular form.

Scenario value in 1992 cents/kWh (range)	Scenario probability (probability density per unit over the range)	Product	Cumulative probability
4 (3–5)	0.5 (0.25)	2	0.5
10 (5–15)	0.3 (0.03)	3	0.8
25 (15–35)	0.2 (0.01)	5	1.0
Expected cost ('product' column sum)		10	
Most likely (most probable or modal) cost 4 cents/kWh, and median (P50 or fifty percentile) cost 5 cents/kWh			

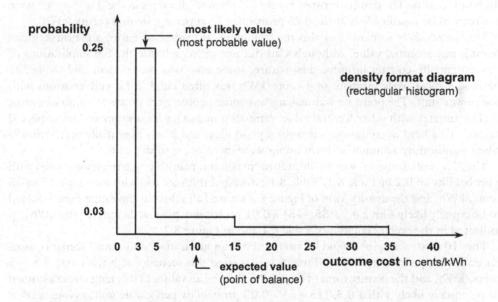

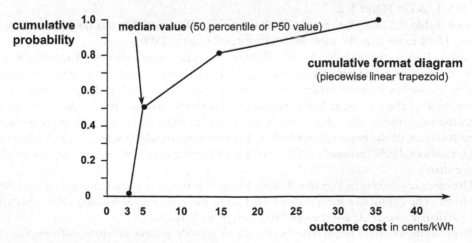

Figure 8.2 Density and cumulative probability format diagrams for the Table 8.1 probability distribution.

To relate the Table 8.1 approach to earlier HAT based approaches you might like to see it as an example of enlightened simplicity which used just three scenarios to capture the important implications of asymmetry with the minimum level of complexity needed for the initial messages which Carl wanted to communicate in this particular presentation context, a form of 'enlightened' simplicity in a context when reverting to Stephen Ward's initial 'constructive' simplicity terminology (Ward, 1989) is arguably useful to illustrate the basis or starting point.

The '4 cents scenario' was the 'most likely' scenario, associated with a probability of 0.5 in Table 8.1, bigger than the probability associated with any other scenario. The first column of Table 8.1 associated the central scenario value of 4 cents/kWh with the range 3 to 5 cents/kWh, putting the range in brackets. The second column of Table 8.1 indicated that a probability of $0.5/(5 - 3) = 0.25$ was associated with both 3 to 4 and 4 to 5, putting the 0.25 in brackets. The density form of Figure 8.2 showed all values in the 3 to 5 range were assumed to be equally likely at the 0.25 probability level per x-scale unit (cents/kWh).

This most likely scenario was also the 'minimum plausible' scenario, a plausible lower bound, not a central value. Although Carl did not overemphasise the full implications of this potentially counter-intuitive dual nature, some emphasis was evident and deliberate because a most likely estimate of 4 cents/kWh was often cited in his conversations with Canpower staff. The point he was making was some people were prone to confusing most likely estimates with other 'central value' estimates, including 'best estimates' or 'expected values'. This kind of confusion was *never* a good idea, and it was potentially very seriously when significantly asymmetric distributions were involved, as in this case.

The '25 cents scenario' was an illustrative 'maximum plausible' scenario, associated with a probability of 0.2 in Table 8.1. Table 8.1 associated this scenario with the range 15 to 35 cents/kWh, and the density form of Figure 8.2 showed all values in this range were assumed to be equally likely with a $0.2/(35 - 15) = 0.01$ probability per x scale unit (cents/kWh), as indicated in the second column of Table 8.1 and in Figure 8.2.

The '10 cents scenario' should be interpreted as an illustrative 'mid-range' scenario, associated with a probability of 0.3. Table 8.1 associated this scenario with the range 5 to 15 cents/kWh, and the density form of Figure 8.2 showed all values in this range were assumed to be equally likely with a $0.3/(15 - 5) = 0.03$ probability per x scale unit, as indicated in Table 8.1 and in Figure 8.2.

Both Table 8.1 and Figure 8.2 also showed that 10 cents/kWh was the expected outcome, 150% more than the most likely estimate of 4 cents/kWh.

Carl had portrayed what he saw as a deliberately crudely structured but defensible initial view of the relevant uncertainty at this stage. He had chosen the three scenario structure and his example's numeric values carefully to illustrate, in simple but dramatic terms, the importance of the long right-hand tail associated with the density format. The 150% uplift from the most likely value of 4 to the to the expected value of 10 was a clear preliminary demonstration of the implications of this level of asymmetry, which some people might prefer to read as a 250% 'increase' ($100\% \times 10/4 = 250\%$ instead of $100\% \times (10 - 4)/4 = 150\%$) 'more than'.

The cumulative form in Figure 8.2 followed directly from the rectangular histogram density form. The cumulative form showed the P50 or median value of 5 cents/kWh, which in this particular case could also be observed directly in Table 8.1.

More scenario values could have been used to provide greater precision with associated smoother curves in both the Figure 8.2 formats. This could have been based on probability values in Table 8.1 estimated to the nearest 0.01 instead of the nearest 0.1, using 30 or more scenarios instead of three if a high level of precision was worthwhile. But a limited level of precision and a simple structure were useful places to start to maximise clarity by keeping it as simple as possible, adding precision when this became useful later. Carl emphasised the role of Table 8.1 and Figure 8.2 was illustrative, different probabilities could have been argued for, and he did not wish to defend the values used. However, both the 4 cents/kWh most likely value and the approximate factor of ten range between 3 and 35 cents/kWh was consistent with the shape and spread of Canpower's current planning values as he interpreted them.

The low most likely (modal or most probable) value of 4 cents/kWh, a 25% higher P50 (median) value of 5 cents/kWh, and a 150% higher expected value of 10 cents/kWh, were a consequence of the overall spread combined with the long right-hand tail in Figure 8.2. There was a 0.25 probability of a value below 4, but very limited scope for costs very much below the most likely value of 4. There was a 0.75 probability of a value above 4, and considerable scope for much higher costs, albeit with a relatively low likelihood of such costs being realised as the right-hand tail is approached. There was a very wide range of potential reasons for these higher costs, some of which they could explore later. The simple model nature of this portrayal relative to a more complex reality could be explored later using Chapter 3 ideas.

The expected value was a best estimate of what should happen on average. Because of this and because of its additive properties, expected values should be the basis of all estimation processes at a portfolio component level as well as at a total portfolio estimate level. Most likely values were of interest at a component level, especially because they tend to be the implicit basis of deterministic estimation processes but also because they sometimes approximated to reasonable aspirational targets (such as an initial 'no major problems' budget given to the manager of a project component). Median values were of less interest. With skew to the right as indicated, median values always lie between most likely and expected values, and the probability of an outcome less than the expected value was always greater than 0.5, as illustrated in Figure 8.2.

A key aspect of quantitative evaluation of uncertainty was the identification of an *unbiased* estimate of the overall expected value. If uncertainty was only partially considered, the spread of the probability distribution would be less, especially to the right in terms of Figure 8.2. As indicated by this numerical example, reasonably full consideration of uncertainty involving a significant skew leads to dramatic differences among most likely, median, and expected values. Underlying conditions and dependence can be part of and amplify these effects. Carl knew this illustrated one reason why Larry and Pat's cost estimates for nuclear power were generally out by a factor of two or more, a factor of ten having been recently experienced with respect to construction cost estimates – Larry was not addressing all relevant sources of uncertainty.

Carl was not looking at low or medium levels of bias here. Relative to the levels of bias which Paul had to confront in the Chapter 7 context, or BP had to address in the Chapter 3 context, in a cost of nuclear power context Carl was addressing *very* high levels of bias because of the combined effect of asymmetry (skew) and omitted sources of uncertainty.

Carl then drove home the basis of this preliminary demonstration. The 150% uplift from nuclear power's most likely cost of 4 cents/kWh to an expected cost of 10 cents/kWh was large, this difference was generated by the long right-hand tail of Figure 8.2, the 'product' column of Table 8.1 showed the way extreme values influence expected values, and the simple three scenario approach facilitated sensitivity analysis he would now pursue.

He had deliberately used an illustrative example A which he believed was very optimistic to avoid being accused of being alarmist. He would now consider further examples B and C.

As a simple illustrative example B, if the 25 cents/kWh scenario really ought to be a '35 cents/kWh scenario' associated with a range from 15 to 55 cents/kWh, with no changes to the other two scenarios, then a 200% uplift from the most likely 4 cent/kWh to an expected value of 12 cents/kWh was involved ($0.2 \times 35 = 7$ instead of $0.2 \times 25 = 5$).

As an illustrative example C, if the 25 cents/kWh scenario of example A really ought to be a '65 cents/kWh scenario' associated with a range from 15 to 115 cents/kWh, with no changes to the other two scenarios, then a 350% uplift from the most likely 4 cent/kWh to an expected value of 18 cents/kWh was involved ($0.2 \times 65 = 13$ instead of $0.2 \times 25 = 5$).

Examples B and C involved the same most likely and median values as example A, but the expected values were clearly very sensitive to the length of the distribution tail.

The implications associated with the long right-hand probability distribution tail were also of crucial importance for reasons which go beyond biased expectations of expected outcomes, taking us into enlightened prudence concerns associated with the risk of higher cost outcomes.

You may feel you already understand why long tails associated with highly asymmetric distributions are crucial in terms of both expected outcomes and risk, perhaps drawing on your understanding of some of the ideas discussed in Chapter 3. However, what Carl did not explain here – which you may find useful to think about briefly now – is that 'experts' involved in estimating these tails may be very poor at it because they may suffer from both conscious and unconscious bias at serious levels, some aspects involving highly contentious issues. Carl would later suggest a number of reasons, not discussed earlier in this book, which you may not be familiar with which clarify why an even more pessimistic view of the impact of this tail than example C might be appropriate. As fairly simple extreme examples, there is a case for including 'indirect costs' which incorporate the possible costs of a nuclear accident like that at Chernobyl, plus other concerns like failing to find a cost-effective way of dealing with nuclear waste. There is no provision in Table 8.1 for the possible indirect cost implications of concerns of this kind. Many people who are pro-nuclear would be very concerned if there were, but many people who are anti-nuclear would argue that is just one very good reason why 'experts' employed by the nuclear industry should not be trusted. Chapter 9 will touch on these issues, and later discussion in this chapter will suggest examples B or C might be more appropriate than example A for much less contentious reasons.

Constructively simple models of non-utility and conservation cost distributions

Carl suggested that Table 8.2 provided a useful example A estimate for 1 GW of either non-utility power or conservation, comparable to the example A estimate of Table 8.1.

Table 8.2 would let them begin to explore building portfolios without suggesting any preferential ordering of nuclear, non-utility, and conservation in terms of expected cost. A figure based on Table 8.2 comparable to Figure 8.2 could have been provided, but its form was fairly obvious, and the cumulative format would be used in a comparative diagram to follow shortly.

Again, a finer definition with more scenarios could have been used, but the immediate concern was constructive simplicity to illustrate key issues, this time with a focus on dependence relationships. The numbers were for illustrative purposes and could be argued with, but the shape and spread of the distribution illustrated in Table 8.2 were reasonable. There was scope for sizeable departures from the expected value in both directions, but a reasonably symmetric distribution shape without extremely long tails either side, for reasons he

Table 8.2 Example A cost distribution for one GW of non-utility power or conservation, tabular form.

Scenario value in 1992 cents/kWh (range)	Scenario probability (probability density per unit over range)	Product	Cumulative probability
6 (4–8)	0.2 (0.05)	1.2	0.2
10 (8–12)	0.6 (0.15)	6.0	0.8
14 (12–16)	0.2 (0.05)	2.8	1.0
Expected cost (column sum)		10.0	
Most likely (most probable) cost 10 cents/kWh, also equal to the P50 (median) values			

would develop shortly. For illustrative purposes when considering dependence concerns in a discussion focused on diversification, assuming complete symmetry was a helpful simplification, recognising that in practice modest asymmetry would be likely. As a result of this assumed symmetry the most likely, median, and expected values were all the same.

Carl then emphasised that estimation of distributions like those of Tables 8.1 and 8.2 in practice would require considerable effort. The uncertainty involved should include a very wide range of technical and economic issues. In practice it would be important to use a carefully structured approach to building these distributions from component factors and provisions. It would also be important to use this uncertainty composition process to develop an understanding of the relationships between different sources of uncertainty associated with the overall probability distribution for each potential type of electric power, or its equivalent in the case of conservation. He had in mind the use of nested sensitivity curves like those discussed in Chapters 4, and 7 as well as the full range of approaches discussed in Chapters 3, 6 and 7, but he did not develop examples at this point.

Building a portfolio of two units – with a focus on the importance of dependence

Carl began exploring portfolio concepts by arguing that all members of the board needed a shared conceptual framework for building and testing their joint understanding of the implications of different kinds of causal dependence between distributions plus different forms and levels of statistical dependence.

'Causal' dependence implied systemic uncertainty relationships which were understood and modelled in cause–effect terms, while 'statistical' dependence implied underlying causal relationships which were not fully understood or not worth modelling. An absence of both causal dependence and statistical dependence implied 'independence'.

He would start with a focus on statistical dependence between probability distributions like those portrayed by Tables 8.1 and 8.2 for different types of electric power or its conservation equivalent. For example, the extent to which the unit costs of non-utility power and conservation might depart from current expectations in opposite directions would require careful study by Canpower, with all directors understanding the implications. The HAT approach he would use was a very simple conceptual framework in its basic forms which could be generalised to visualise and model complex causal and statistical dependences associated with very important practical issues – like economies of scale, common-mode failures, and cascade effects. He would use it initially at a relatively simple illustrative level to portray a limited number of complexity issues, but practical adaptations they did not need to consider until later could cope with any complexities worth analysis.

What follows makes basic causal and statistical dependence issues as simple as possible in a framework which is as general as possible. It is relevant to EP as discussed in this book as a whole, not just portfolio modelling. It builds on earlier use of the HAT framework, and it is also directly relevant to implementing some of the approaches discussed in earlier chapters.

To begin to illustrate what was involved, and provide a basis for numerical models used later, the board were asked to assume that the immediate concern was restricted to the provision of 2 GW of power from the three options identified earlier, as the starting point for developing a portfolio of proposed new units to meet anticipated load growth and current unit retirements at a 20 year long-term planning horizon. For illustrative convenience, this provision would involve two choices from the three options listed earlier – both of one kind or any mix.

They would look at the independence and dependence issues in illustrative terms by first considering independence, using a 1 GW unit of conservation plus a second 1 GW unit of conservation to provide 2 GW of conservation in total. They would work with the discrete scenario values and a probability tree framework, assuming that these two units of conservation involved very different types of conservation approaches, with reasons for potential cost variations which might be assumed to be independent.

Figure 8.3 portrayed the nature of the independence assumption and the calculation of the joint cost distribution in a standard probability tree format, which Carl explained and then related to Table 8.3.

The first number on each branch of the Figure 8.3 probability tree portrayal was the assumed scenario value, the second the probability of that branch occurring. The Figure 8.3 joint cost column entries were averages and the probabilities were products.

Table 8.3 used a tabular format to convey the same information, but it also combined the probabilities for common outcome values, and it included the implied cumulative distribution which was useful for the graphical portrayals to follow.

'Independence' required the probability distributions for the second unit to be exactly the same whatever the outcome of the first, all first unit probability tree branches leading to identical sets of second unit branches in Figure 8.3. Sometimes it would be convenient to refer to independence as portrayed in Figure 8.3 and Table 8.3 as '0% dependence', equivalent to a 'coefficient of correlation' of zero. A working assumption of independence in this case was reasonable if the two units involved very different uncertainties, perhaps because very different approaches and technologies were involved, as assumed in this case.

The next step was considering the +100% dependence case (perfect positive dependence equivalent to a coefficient of correlation of +1) by considering a 1 GW unit of non-utility generation plus a second 1 GW unit of non-utility generation, with prices set in the same marketplace to provide 2 GW of non-utility generation in total, working with the same discrete scenario values and the same probability tree framework. Figure 8.4 portrayed the implications of assuming +100% dependence and the calculation of the joint cost distribution using the same probability tree format as Figure 8.3. The joint cost calculations were dropped for simplicity, but probability calculations were maintained.

In this case the +100% dependence assumption implied that the second distribution outcome was known given any outcome for the first, and directly positively correlated, interpreting 'directly positively correlated' to mean that all percentile values correspond. If both units involved prices set in the same marketplace, it was reasonable to use this working assumption. It corresponded to a coefficient of correlation of +1.

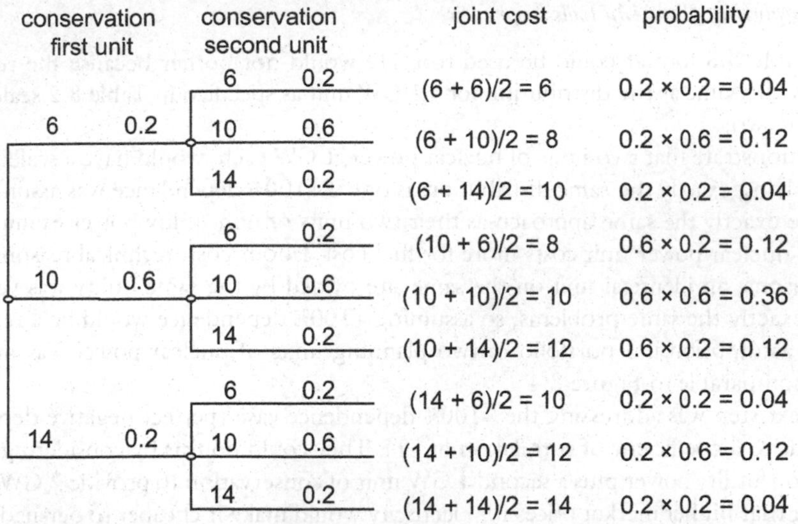

conservation first unit | **conservation second unit** | **joint cost** | **probability**

6 0.2	6 0.2	(6 + 6)/2 = 6	0.2 × 0.2 = 0.04
	10 0.6	(6 + 10)/2 = 8	0.2 × 0.6 = 0.12
	14 0.2	(6 + 14)/2 = 10	0.2 × 0.2 = 0.04
10 0.6	6 0.2	(10 + 6)/2 = 8	0.6 × 0.2 = 0.12
	10 0.6	(10 + 10)/2 = 10	0.6 × 0.6 = 0.36
	14 0.2	(10 + 14)/2 = 12	0.6 × 0.2 = 0.12
14 0.2	6 0.2	(14 + 6)/2 = 10	0.2 × 0.2 = 0.04
	10 0.6	(14 + 10)/2 = 12	0.2 × 0.6 = 0.12
	14 0.2	(14 + 14)/2 = 14	0.2 × 0.2 = 0.04

Figure 8.3 Example probability tree specification for two units of conservation, assuming independence.

Table 8.3 Cost distribution for 2 GW of conservation assuming independence as in Figure 8.3.

Average of scenario values	Probability calculation components			Probability (density)	Cumulative probability
6	0.04			0.04	0.04
8	0.12	0.12		0.24	0.28
10	0.04	0.36	0.04	0.44	0.72
12		0.12	0.12	0.24	0.96
14			0.04	0.04	1.00

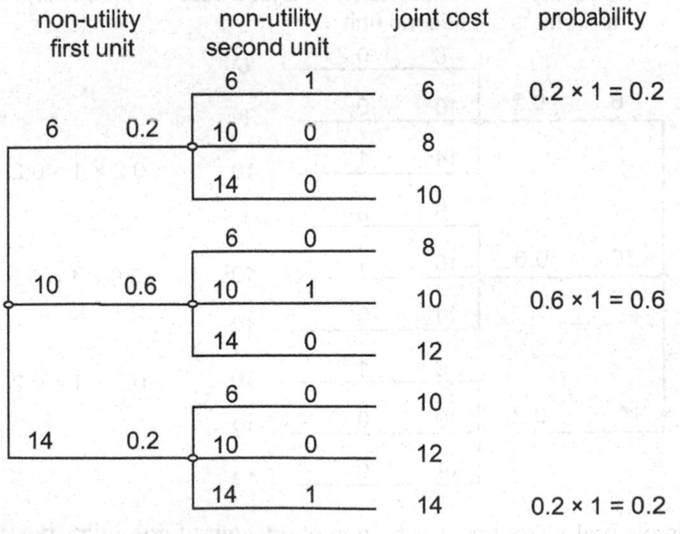

non-utility first unit | **non-utility second unit** | **joint cost** | **probability**

6 0.2	6 1	6	0.2 × 1 = 0.2
	10 0	8	
	14 0	10	
10 0.6	6 0	8	
	10 1	10	0.6 × 1 = 0.6
	14 0	12	
14 0.2	6 0	10	
	10 0	12	
	14 1	14	0.2 × 1 = 0.2

Figure 8.4 Example probability tree specification for two units of non-utility power assuming +100% dependence (all percentile values coincide).

The Table 8.3 format could be used too. He would not bother because the result was obviously the same as the distribution for a 1 GW unit as specified in Table 8.2 scaled up by a factor of two.

To demonstrate that two units of nuclear power, 1 GW each, would have a scaled-up version involving exactly the same distribution as one if +100% dependence was assumed, they could use exactly the same approach as their two units of non-utility power example. That is, if one nuclear power unit costs more for fuel cost, labour cost, technical reasons, or any other reasons, an identical unit on the same site owned by the same utility was very likely to have exactly the same problems, so assuming +100% dependence would be a reasonable working assumption if a portfolio of two planning units of nuclear power was modelled, directly comparable to Figure 8.4.

The next step was addressing the –100% dependence case (perfect negative dependence equivalent to a coefficient of correlation of –1). They could do this by considering a 1 GW unit of non-utility power plus a second 1 GW unit of conservation to provide 2 GW in total, assuming that higher market prices for electricity would make it cheaper to persuade people to reduce demand via low energy consumption light bulbs and similar devices. Figure 8.5 portrayed the nature of the –100% dependence case and the calculation of the joint cost distribution in the same probability tree format as Figures 8.3 and 8.4.

Again a Table 8.3 format could also be used. In this case the –100% assumption implied a P0 outcome for one unit meant a P100 outcome for the other, a P1 for one unit meant a P99 for the other, and so on, with the result being a 10-cents scenario with certainty – conservation was assumed to work as a perfect hedge for non-utility power.

In practice –90% or –80% might be involved rather than –100%, and Canpower might want to model this departure from the obviously overly optimistic –100% assumption. Indeed, the 0% assumed earlier might be better estimated as +20%, and the +100% assumed earlier might be better estimated as +90%, to correct for optimistic bias in the first case and pessimistic bias in the second case.

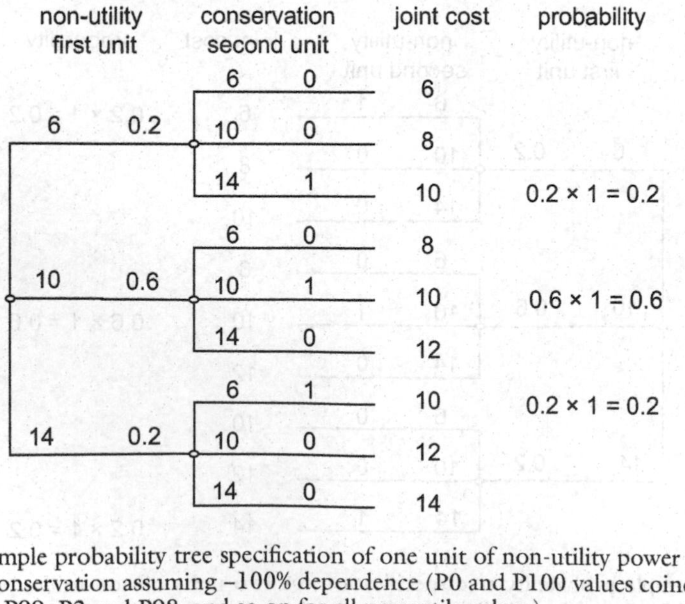

Figure 8.5 Example probability tree specification of one unit of non-utility power plus one unit of conservation assuming –100% dependence (P0 and P100 values coincide, as do P1 and P99, P2 and P98, and so on for all percentile values).

More generally, negative or positive dependence need not be perfect, and interpolations need not be simple. A key reason for using a HAT portrayal of uncertainty framework was the generality it provided for alternative forms of dependence and alternative levels of sophistication in the modelling used to facilitate clarity efficiency. To demonstrate the basis of this generality using a simple initial example Carl employed Figure 8.6.

This example illustrated a situation when there was a variable degree of dependence. If the market price for non-utility electricity increased above the expected value, this might stimulate stronger negative dependence than would be the case if the price decreased below the expected value, illustrated by the example probabilities. That is, if electricity consumers were more sensitive to price rises than they were to price falls, the level of dependence experienced would be different for variability above and below expected outcomes. Again the Table 8.3 format could also be used.

Carl explained that they could model much more complex relationships in practice, but he was deliberately keeping his examples as simple as he could for the moment.

He then indicated that Canpower had to address the portfolio management implications of the issues raised by dependence using a generalisation of Markowitz's mean–variance approach within the HAT framework he had just illustrated. The basic ideas which EP portfolio models can capture which the board needed clarity about were:

1 'don't put all your eggs in one basket',
2 'diversify using a risk efficiency concept',
3 'use an opportunity efficient approach which includes the right risk–reward trade-off', and
4 'use a clarity efficient approach which includes the right trade-offs between clarity of various kinds and the cost of further clarity in terms of analysis effort'.

Choosing the mix of sources of electric power by an electric utility was a classic portfolio analysis problem, whether or not the board appreciated this was the case. Many electricity

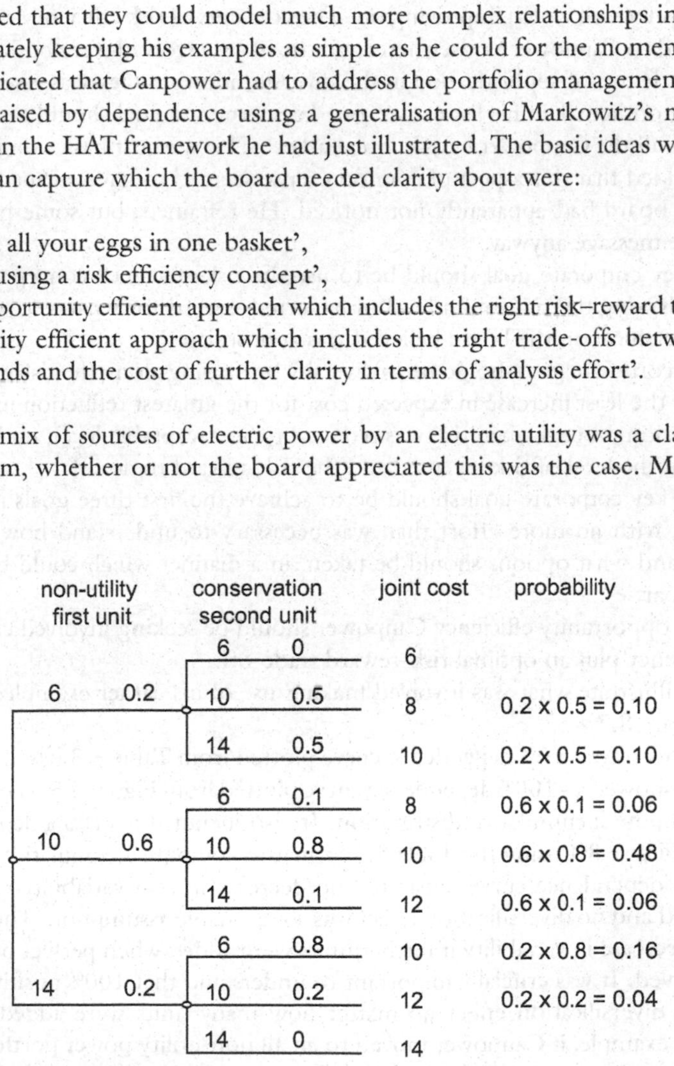

Figure 8.6 Example probability tree specification of one unit of non-utility power plus one unit of conservation assuming variable dependence.

utilities recognised this explicitly and formally, even if they did not model the issues formally. For example, as noted earlier, prior to the privatisation of electric power in the UK, the CEGB policy of building a limited number of nuclear power stations, and doing so based on several different technologies, was explained to the public as a deliberate attempt to spread the risk to ensure that if nuclear power was required in the future, at least one successful UK-developed technology would be available.

One very simple diversification policy to achieve a robust balance of generation types was just using equal proportions of all available options. Some early investment advisors (well before the 1929 stock market crash) recommended 'keep a third of your assets in property, a third in fixed interest vehicles (bonds) and a third in stocks (shares)'. These early investment advisors had much more wisdom than those who put everything into stocks. However, a very simple diversification policy like this would probably decrease expected reward in an inefficient manner well worth improving on. The concepts of risk efficiency and risk/reward balance applied to Canpower as elsewhere, and the issues involved were both important and complex, so a degree of sophistication in the diversification strategy was essential.

Elaborating on item 1 in his list earlier, one key corporate goal should be to diversify, to avoid 'putting all the Canpower eggs in one basket'. This was just basic common sense. He might have added that this aspect of common sense seemed to have escaped Larry's attention, and the board had apparently not noticed. He refrained, but some board members clearly got the message anyway.

A second key corporate goal should be to use the risk efficiency concept to ensure that they were delivering the maximum level of expected reward for whatever level of risk and associated diversification the board believed was appropriate.

A third key corporate goal should be to diversify by moving along the risk efficient boundary to achieve the least increase in expected cost for the greatest reduction in risk, stopping this diversification process when risk was reduced to an acceptable level, understanding the implications of the level of risk accepted and the risk–reward trade-off.

The fourth key corporate goal should be to achieve the first three goals in a clarity efficient manner, with no more effort than was necessary to understand how diversification was working and what options should be taken, in a manner which could be explained to all interested parties.

The overall opportunity efficiency Canpower should be seeking involved clarity efficiency plus risk efficiency plus an optimal risk–reward trade-off.

To start to illustrate what was involved making use of his earlier examples, Carl showed the board Figure 8.7.

Figure 8.7 portrayed a 0% dependence curve plotted from Table 8.3 based on Figure 8.3. In addition, it showed a –100% dependence curve plotted from Figure 8.5 using the Table 8.3 format to compute a cumulative distribution. It also included a +100% dependence curve plotted from Figure 8.4 using the Table 8.3 format to compute a cumulative distribution.

The +100% dependence curve illustrated no decrease in cost variability when two units were combined and no diversification effect was a reasonable assumption. The clear implication was no decrease in variability if further units were added when perfect positive correlation was involved. It was crucially important to understand that 100% positive dependence meant a zero diversification effect no matter how many units were added together in a portfolio. For example, if Canpower moved to an all non-utility power portfolio, buying all its power in a perfect marketplace involving producers of electricity within their province, neighbouring provinces, and US states, it had a zero-diversification policy. Simply relying on the market to provide the electricity required by its province involved a zero-diversification

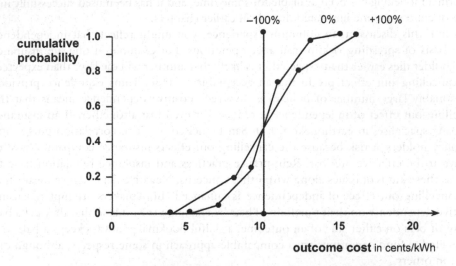

Figure 8.7 Cumulative probability diagrams for the +100%, 0% and −100% dependence examples.

policy in terms of this model. Also, if Canpower had a policy that decreed all new base-load power would be Canpower-owned nuclear, it was adopting a zero-diversification policy for all new base-load power.

The 0% dependence curve illustrated a significant decrease in variability when two units were combined and zero correlation was a reasonable assumption. This clearly implied further significant decreases in variability if further units were added and independence was involved. The 0% dependence curve in conjunction with the +100% dependence curve illustrated what interpolating at something like +60% or +90% dependence might yield.

The −100% dependence curve illustrated the huge impact of negative correlation, in the limit just two units with perfect negative correlation eliminating uncertainty completely. Furthermore, what −80% dependence might imply was indicated by the −100% curve taken together with the 0% dependence curve. Even very modest levels of negative dependence could be extremely useful, a very important feature of conservation which was clearly a considerable asset.

As indicated when discussing Figure 8.6, analysis of partial dependence was not restricted to interpolation, and results based on various forms of variable dependence modelling could be compared using an approach like Figure 8.7. He had not plotted the Figure 8.6 example in Figure 8.7, but if they wanted a clear understanding of what Figure 8.6 implied and they wanted to communicate that understanding to others, then showing the cumulative curve defined in Figure 8.6 between bounds portrayed by the 0% and −100% curves of Figure 8.7 might be very helpful.

Carl did not want to develop these ideas further for the board at this point, but you might find it useful to understand now that the HAT approach and the Figure 8.7 portrayal of results also provided a basis for generalisation to portray the implications of more detailed and sophisticated modelling, including those discussed in Chapters 3, 4, 6, 7, and 9. BP software developed in the late 1970s provided support for all these forms of dependence modelling, and they were employed in the Canadian and US studies discussed briefly in Chapter 7. The toolset for a rich set of alternative approaches to understanding dependence via formal modelling has been available for some time, and it has been used successfully in a range of contexts, some illustrated directly in earlier chapters.

To link this discussion to common experience, you might reflect that independence is the basis of spreading risk in insurance operations. For example, if one life insurance policyholder dies earlier than expected, it is likely that another will die later than expected, this cancelling out effect producing an acceptable average claims experience provided a reasonably large number of policies is involved. Positive dependence means that the cancelling-out effect of independence is reduced or even lost altogether. If an insurance company specialises in earthquake risk in San Francisco, positive correlation puts it and its policy holders at risk because the cancelling-out effects insurance companies have to achieve to be effective are lost. Reinsurance practices and insurance regulation have to address these kinds of issues along with other concerns. Negative dependence means that the cancelling-out effect of independence is enhanced. Bookmakers attempt to ensure negative dependence on their portfolio of bets by changing the odds so that they get a balancing of bets on either side of an outcome: a skilful bookmaker always keeps a balanced book. Hedge fund operations try a comparable approach in some respects, although different in others.

Understanding how all these concepts operate in terms of one very general framework with a rich set of implementation approaches which can be tailored to the context is not easy, but this understanding is central to the aspects of corporate strategy formulation addressed by Carl via portfolio-driven long-term planning. Larry's approach to medium/long-term planning simply ignored all these considerations, implicitly assuming they did not matter. Comparable deterministic merit-order approaches also ignore these considerations. There is a reasonable case for suggesting that ignoring issues as important as this in Larry's context involved very serious incompetence, on his part, and with respect to the board as a whole because they did not understand what Larry was doing, but Carl was careful not to say so in a direct manner. Nor did he bother to develop the implications for any organisations adopting a simple robustness-driven scenario approaches which focus on a single source of uncertainty like the price of oil when some aspects of diversification might be important and warrant explicit formal attention, an issue you may find relevant in other contexts of interest.

Building a portfolio of different unit types to define the long-term target proportions

Carl began building on this Figure 8.7 discussion by making it very clear that developing suitably robust operational portfolio models in any context was difficult, for a number of technical reasons. Even in the context of managing a portfolio of financial securities, the simplest classic portfolio problem, simplifying the complications involved in a clarity efficient manner was a demanding task. However, Canpower could address a portfolio-driven long-term planning approach using practical tools in a manner he would outline.

The illustrative numerical example distributions used so far all assumed a common expected cost of 10 cents per kilowatt-hour. This was in part for expository convenience, in part, to avoid seeming prejudiced in relation to any particular option.

Canpower's current medium/long-term plans assumed nuclear power units had the lowest expected cost per kWh. Carl did not believe this was true, but assuming for the moment that it was, it should be clear that six new nuclear power stations would involve very significant risk of costs well above the expected cost. The board needed to understand and deal with this risk in an effective and efficient manner.

If Canpower wanted to make a case for this kind of significant nuclear power increase at the 20 year horizon, they might start by refining Table 8.1 and Figure 8.2 and understanding the importance of components of the uncertainty which drove different degrees of dependence. They might then use a generalisation of the HAT based approach of Figure 8.6 and interpolation structures like Figure 8.7 to consider likely actual locations for nuclear power stations, the grouping of multiple units within power stations, economies of scale, and related dependence concerns as more units of nuclear of the same or different designs were added to a portfolio. They could add to these basic approaches a range of additional tools to build a clear understanding of the expected cost trajectory, and the associated cost variability risk trajectory, as the proposed nuclear portfolio grew.

In terms of new sources of electric power, there was nothing wrong with the Canpower board starting where their instincts suggested they should concentrate, but they needed an unbiased first-cut estimate of *all* key sources of uncertainty, including an unbiased estimate of associated variability about expected outcomes, plus how these sources of uncertainty were related. They needed a robust understanding of the effects of these sources of uncertainty on both expected costs and spread, including the dependence issues involved when units were combined, acquired in a clarity efficient manner.

All other technically proven sources of electric power which were relevant then needed comparable treatment – conservation and non-utility power as just discussed, plus the obvious hydro and thermal options, plus currently technically feasible renewables options they ought to consider, even if they did not expect to include them on economic grounds, so they could be clear about the current cost gap preventing their inclusion. These gaps would be relevant to all futures planning, and any discussions about government sponsored subsidies.

They could use this starting point to take a view on the lowest expected cost 'initial core' of new power stations for their target overall portfolio at the planning horizon. It might be all nuclear, it might be all gas-fired power, or it might be something else.

Instead of an initial focus on new power stations, they might start with all the existing power stations which they expect to still have at the 20 year horizon, adding currently preferred minimum expected cost new power stations to work towards the total capability needed at the horizon. This would let them start by dealing with dependence between new and existing power station cost variability.

They could then use their initial starting point portfolio to start replacing some of their initial core with alternative options which offered negative dependence or a minimum degree of positive dependence together with a minimum increase in expected cost. Their initial focus on lowest expected cost could be used as a basis for starting to explore risk efficient ways of reducing risk.

Whichever route they took, there was nothing wrong with starting with simple models like those illustrated by Figures 8.3 to 8.7, but to develop a more complex understanding of dependence relationships between identified components of uncertainty, they might draw on a wide range of more sophisticated models. All the contingency planning models developed by BP for offshore projects as discussed in Part 1 and Chapter 7 used exactly the same HAT approach, so all the associated modelling capabilities could be brought to bear on this kind of analysis, plus further alternatives, including those discussed in Chapter 9 and a range of approaches making use of quite general Monte Carlo simulation techniques.

The first order objective would be seeking risk efficiency. In this context, one obvious view of risk efficiency involves minimising cost risk defined in terms of cost which exceeds expectations for any given level of expected cost. A more convenient view was minimising reward risk in terms of a reward which fails to meet expectations for any given level of expected reward. Carl preferred this less obvious alternative because it links the current discussion to the Part 1 discussion, and he provided a background explanation of the reason he preferred a reward-based approach to risk efficiency, drawing on the ideas discussed in Part 1 as a preliminary to explaining that if the board viewed Canpower's basic corporate strategy goal as providing provincial electricity needs at a minimum cents per kWh tariff, then 'reward' and risk efficiency in reward terms might be assumed to involve expected cost savings relative to just buying power from other utilities in the province or in adjacent provinces or US states.

He then showed the board Figure 8.8, a variant of Figure 3.8.

If an all nuclear base-load portfolio provided the lowest expected cost option, *and if* cost was deemed to be the only relevant objective so an all nuclear base-load portfolio equated to highest expected reward option, *then* point 'a' in Figure 8.8 could be associated with an all nuclear base-load portfolio. However, even if this was the case, *and* it made sense to limit the scope of 'reward' to cents/kWh cost, an all nuclear base-load portfolio would be extremely risky, because of the very long tails associated with distributions like that illustrated by Table 8.1 and Figure 8.2, or more extreme possibilities, plus the positive dependence relationships between the units in a portfolio of nuclear power units. Canpower needed a corporate understanding of how this level and kind of cost risk could be reduced efficiently, so it could move around the risk efficient boundary towards a point like b_1 or b_2, accepting a risk efficient decrease in expected reward (increase in expected cost) and choosing an appropriate level of risk given the cost of reducing risk. As they progressed around the risk efficient boundary, they would be using the insight developed earlier, plus new insight about the dependence between types of units already in their provisional core and new candidates for inclusion.

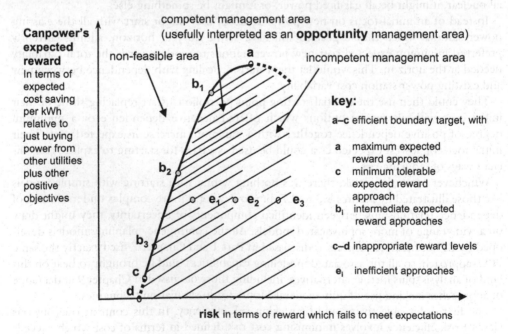

Figure 8.8 Canpower's expected reward and associated risk in an efficient frontier portrayal.

If nuclear power *did not* provide the highest expected reward (lowest expected cost) option, which Carl believed was highly probable, *then* an all nuclear new plant core might be a risk inefficient point like e_1, e_2, or e_3. In this case their first task might be viewed as getting to a point like b_2 to get on the risk efficient boundary, or they might reconsider the starting-point core.

> *It was crucial that Canpower had a clear idea where point 'a' was in expected reward and associated risk terms, and what point 'a' involved in terms of the proportions of different unit types in its proposed portfolio.*
> *Furthermore, Canpower could not afford to miss the opportunity to reduce risk to some extent, whatever type of unit had the lowest expected cost.*
> *Further still, Canpower could not afford to fail to understand its options in terms of an unbiased view of expected outcomes plus all associated variability, including the crucial role of relevant interdependencies.*

Canpower needed risk efficiency, generalised to opportunity efficiency, and it needed to explore what this meant in practice.

Carl did not labour the 'competent management area' associated with 'opportunity management' or the 'incompetent management area' where they currently resided to the extent he was tempted to, but he used BP, IBM and other examples comparable to this book's Part 1 discussion to make sure they understood what was needed, in the language of electricity generation in the 1990s.

He did emphasise that if Canpower continued to reduce risk by moving around the risk efficient boundary from point 'a' to b_1 and then b_2 in the way just described, the expected reward would decrease (expected cost would rise), and the value of further diversification would decrease, so Canpower must select a point of balance when the diminishing returns from further diversification made further risk reduction inappropriate. Those who were unwilling or unable to undertake any more than a minimum level of risk might wish to continue to reduce risk until risk was very low, but this could involve a significant decrease in expected reward (increase in expected cost). Electricity utilities like Canpower should not take an extreme position on either minimising risk or maximising expected reward (minimising expected cost), and Canpower needed to understand clearly what this meant in practice.

Carl also emphasised that the portfolio-driven long-term planning modelling he was advocating would not itself yield a precise prescriptive 'optimal' solution. It would provide the insight required to make a reasoned set of robust judgements which achieved risk efficiency in approximate terms with an appropriate trade-off between expected reward and associated risk, plus an appropriate trade-off between effort expended on analysis and clarity achieved via this analysis – opportunity efficiency. It would help Canpower to get approximately correct answers to the right questions. He was tempted to suggest that a precisely correct answer to the wrong question was an accurate characterisation of Larry's approach, but resisted the temptation. Larry understood the unstated message, as did several other directors.

At this point Carl did point out that a high nuclear base-load future exposed Canpower to risks he had yet to address, like the identification of a design failure that might necessitate shutting down all nuclear power stations with the same or similar design features.

An introjection to clarify your interpretation of Figure 8.8

Carl was convinced that Canpower was currently at a point like e_3 in Figure 8.8, with plans to move farther to the right in terms of their six new nuclear power stations core strategy. He thought starting to lead the board towards this view from the outset was important, but he did not think it would be helpful to say so in a direct manner at this stage in the meeting. The reasons Carl believed this will become clearer as this chapter's tale progresses, but the basis was Carl's view that Canpower's current levels of bias in favour of nuclear power relative to other sources, plus its total failure to address all relevant risk or the concept of risk efficiency, meant that moving from the current 50% of base-load nuclear power towards 40% rather than 70% was a much better bet given his current understanding of the issues. In Carl's view, the case for nuclear was a degree of diversification away from an overly fossil fuel dependent approach in the economic climate of the early 1990s, not minimum expected cost per unit of electricity. This was a position many energy experts would have agreed with unless they were anti-nuclear for reasons which went beyond cost as portrayed by Carl's example A. Issues associated with examples B and C are addressed later in this chapter, and Chapter 9 develops further related concerns.

The importance of size and variety to risk reduction

While 3 GW was a practical size for a nuclear power station, many hydro, thermal, and other power stations would be smaller. In particular, most renewable sources, conservation measures, and many sources of non-utility generation available within province would involve '*operating* units' which were much smaller than 1 GW '*planning* units'.

This meant that 1 GW *planning* units of sources of new electric power like conservation or within province non-utility power would usually themselves be a portfolio of components with dependence/independence characteristics. This would tend to reduce cost variability and centralise the expected value of the distribution, as assumed for the Table 8.2 illustration.

More generally, a large number of relatively small operating units with a variety of technologies were inherently very much less exposed to cost variation uncertainty and associated risk than a limited number of relatively large operating units involving similar technology. Put the other way around, any new very large power stations with a common technology would significantly increase the overall cents/kWh risk relative to diversified smaller units, be they nuclear, gas-powered thermal units, or anything else.

Alternative portfolio modelling approaches to risk efficiency and separability

Carl explained that the formal modelling approach developed by Markowitz (1959) for any number of possible allocations (securities in a financial portfolio context, electricity generation units in the present context) used quadratic programming (a form of mathematical programming) to consider all possible allocations simultaneously. Quadratic programming algorithms were, in fact, first developed to provide solutions to this model. Such models involved technical complications which his presentation did not need to address. However, the simple approach to considering a portfolio of two allocations he had used could be generalised to any number by building up a nested structure, a pairwise approach to nesting being particularly useful. He had in mind a framework described at that time (Chapman and Ward, 1992), but more relevant and recent treatments are now available (e.g. Chapman and Ward, 2002, chapter 10).

This framework could be used to provide a basis for overlaying a 'softer' (more intuitive) approach to portfolio risk management which addressed issues not measured numerically in a direct manner. The consideration of these softer concerns might manifest itself in terms of constraints on the proportions of a portfolio which could be associated with any single allocation or any set of allocations. For example, this framework could be used to assess regulatory or planning constraints of the form 'no *less* than X_1% of the supply capability of an electricity utility should be nuclear, no *more* than Y_1% an electricity utility should be nuclear, no *less* than X_2% of the supply capability of an electricity utility should be non-utility power from sources within the province, and so on, for all possible sources of electric power'.

These constraints could reflect the board's intuitive view of the portfolio risks as well as external views of this risk. These constraints could also reflect political or regulatory views based on quite different considerations which were superimposed on the cost-driven risk efficiency basis for a portfolio approach. For example, if the Canadian federal government was offering 'support' for Canpower's nuclear programme in terms of subsidies for Canadian Candu nuclear technology used by Canadian utilities, the political price might be an agreement that no less than X_1% of Canpower's supply capability must be Candu nuclear power stations. Other constraints might be driven by security of supply concerns, including concerns like a common fault in nuclear power stations of the same kind leading to a major loss of supply, as viewed by a regulator.

Considerable development of the interface between intuition-driven approaches based on constraints on proportions of the X_i minimum and Y_i maximum form and more direct modelling frameworks might be useful, and this development was a practical proposition, but it might not be needed. Whether or not it was used, translating the results of various direct forms of portfolio-driven modelling into a policy result in the form of proportion minimum and maximums should be very attractive to a board which wanted to understand what really mattered in a long-term planning context. Carl suggested this would be the form of output from the long-term planning process which most board members would probably find particularly useful.

Using decision diagrams and sensitivity diagrams

Carl might have spent some time explaining that the nested composition structure he had in mind lent itself to using decision diagrams for making choices and sensitivity diagrams to understand the composition of the uncertainty portrayed by decision diagrams. He did not have time, and we will leave even overview discussion these issues until later in this chapter.

Decisions involving timing considerations

Carl made the point that this portfolio modelling approach could, in principle, be extended to a multiple period model which explicitly looked at the timing of all new plant decisions at the same time, in a manner comparable to Canpower's current linear programming models for long-term planning. Indeed, doing so on a year-by-year basis using a Markowitz mean–variance portfolio model with zero concern for risk was a special case which equated to Larry's approach. However, he would not recommend this approach.

Most timing issues should be deferred to the proposed separate medium-term planning approach for clarity efficiency reasons. However, any potential source of power at the horizon which involved important timing considerations could be treated as a set of options which allowed consideration of key timing relationships. For example, there were important cost savings and associated simplifications in approvals processes if new thermal or nuclear power stations were built on the sites of retired power stations. If an existing plant was due for retirement, starting to replace it on the planned retirement date was an obvious choice, with related options involving early retirement, postponed retirement, or retirement followed by site preparation for new plant at a later date.

Concluding summary for long-term planning

Carl finished his discussion of long-term planning by emphasising four basic deliverables *must* be provided by the Canpower approach to long-term planning:

1   Estimates of maximum and minimum proportions of each type of currently feasible electric power generation capability which Canpower should be aiming for at its 20 year long-term planning horizon – an interval or range-based set of target proportions.
2   An estimate of electricity demand at the 20 year horizon used to convert the proportions provided by point 1 into generation capacities for each type of power station and associated demand driven uncertainty.
3   Clarity about the risk of possible variations from the expected cents/kWh cost of electricity associated with the target portfolios defined by points 1 and 2.
4   Clarity about the robustness of all key assumptions underlying points 1 through 3.

From an EP perspective, all four of these deliverables were essential and would be provided by a practical operational form of his recommended approach.

Medium-term planning and integration upwards

Carl began his treatment of medium-term planning by reminding everyone that medium-term planning must deliver Canpower commitments to agreed plans over the next ten years. But it had to relate these commitments to other tentative plans for the rest of the 20 year horizon so that the commitments plus the tentative plans fully bridged the gap between the current situation and the long-term planning targets. He would begin with the basis of this complete set of bridging plans – what he would refer to as the 'provisional overall plans'.

Generating provisional overall plans in approximate time-based profiles

Overall corporate strategic plans had to clarify current assumptions about the total portfolio of existing sources of electric power which would still be operational at the 20 year planning horizon, when any current sources would retire in the interim, plus when all new units would become operational. When developing plans defined in these overall terms they would have to be decomposed into different types of units, and all associated uncertainty would need clarification. For example, all new units would need provisional 'start construction' and 'start operation' time-based profiles to meet anticipated load growth plus retirements. As a specific illustration, the board would want to know that if 18 GW of new nuclear power units for base load were planned to be in service at the 20 year horizon, this meant something like 'all new base-load units would be 3 GW Candu power stations with construction starts for the six new power stations planned at one year intervals beginning in about four years, starting operation about ten years after beginning construction'. If this information had not been created to clarify the long-term planning target for the board, it would need to be created as the first step in the medium-term planning process. He thought the development of this kind of component of the 'provisional overall plan' was usefully seen as part of the medium-term planning process for that day's discussion purposes, but the board could see it as part of the long-term planning process to help interpret the long-term plan if they preferred.

He indicated this kind of approximate time-based profile for each type of new unit, plus associated plans for retiring units linked to load growth assumptions, should match expected demand and supply at the 20 year horizon and for interim years and clearly portray obvious priorities if a currently imbalanced portfolio needed rebalancing as soon as possible.

Actions plans and associated medium-term provisional plans

The rest of medium-term planning was about transforming part of the first ten years of this provisional overall plan into 'action plans' which reflected agreed commitments set within the context of the provisional overall plans. The commitments aspect of the medium-term plan as a whole would have to include immediate commitments to nuclear power stations required within the decade if Canpower wanted to be clear about when commitments to build nuclear power stations should translate into realised capacity.

'Action plans' and 'action horizons' would be associated with each commitment to action. An action horizon was the period requiring commitments to implement associated action plans because of the need for lead times and the 'irreversible' or 'reversible at a considerable cost' nature of associated decisions. Long lead times required long action horizons.

The medium-term planning horizon would not be equated to an action horizon in a general sense. For example, it was now clearly recognised that giving the 'go-ahead' to build a nuclear power station was a decision which ought to be seen as irreversible in the sense that it was not sensible to plan a significant slowdown, and a construction period of the order of ten years was involved, the reason that a ten year action horizon for nuclear power stations was needed plus a ten year medium-term planning horizon overall. However, a project involving building a gas-turbine power plant with all permissions in place and the site prepared might be deferred for six months without comparable risks, and once the go-ahead to begin construction was given, action horizons might be reasonably long for key components like the turbines and generators but fairly short for the civil construction building materials and virtually zero for the landscaping supplies.

This implied a need for action plans which involved commitments appropriate to each part of the plans, embedded in provisional medium-term plans using a nominal planning horizon of ten years to cope with the longest lead times needed. Canpower needed to plan commitments as far ahead as necessary to optimise the action plans, but no further, recognising that it could later alter aspects of the other provisional medium-term plans if unfolding events suggested this was advisable. Indeed, it might have to alter action horizon plans, but this should be avoided to the extent that the costs warranted doing so.

Detailed planning for implementation of an action plan was appropriate, but other parts of the medium-term plans which did not involve commitments might not receive any detailed planning effort until it was needed.

It was in this medium-term planning context that Canpower had to address when to start the construction of new units, when to implement a new conservation programme, when to retire or mothball existing units, and so on.

This was part of the interface between corporate planning in top-down terms and project planning, as discussed in Chapter 7, which Carl would have to return to later.

Modelling load growth uncertainty

What Carl wanted to focus on next was how modelling load growth uncertainty could help medium-term planners to begin to understand and deal with some of the important issues they needed to address. Figure 8.9 could be used to start exploring some of the features of interest.

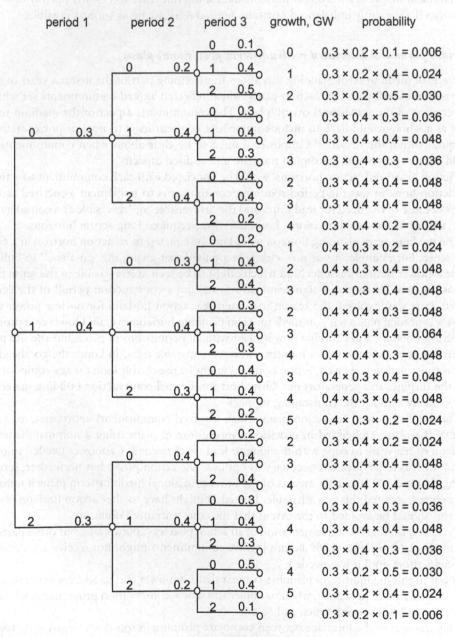

Figure 8.9 Example load growth probability tree for three three-year periods, nine years in total.

Figure 8.9 employed the same basic HAT framework introduced earlier. It portrayed load growth in three sequential periods, each period three years long, for nine years total. Each period employed three probability tree branches associated with load growths of 0, 1, and 2 GW. Some correlation was assumed over the nine years. For example, on the top branch a load growth of zero in the first period was assumed to have a 0.3 probability, but if it was zero in the first period the chance that it would also be zero in the second period was assumed to be 0.2, lower than it was in the first period. This interdependence extended to third period relationships in a similar manner. For example, on the top branch the chance that it would be zero in the third period if it was zero in the first two dropped to 0.1.

Figure 8.9 reflected random shocks which might or might not be sustained over time, as Canpower should expect in practice. That is, over time there was a general tendency to return to underlying trends, although such returns might not occur, and trends might alter. More generally, Figure 8.9 illustrated a probability tree approach for uncertain load growth which allowed the portrayal of statistical dependence structures which might take any plausible form. This included the tendency to return to a long-term growth pattern after random shocks, sometimes referred to as 'regression to the mean', but a possibility that this would not happen and that sustained changes in the trend would occur. A very general modelling approach to explore understanding what was involved could be used by Canpower. The net effect over nine years of the three levels of branches in terms of outcomes was computed by summing the growth over the branches. For example, zero growth in all three years yielded zero growth over the nine years. The probability of each outcome was the product of the associated branch probabilities. For example, the probability of zero growth was $0.3 \times 0.2 \times 0.1 = 0.006$ over nine years, obtained following the top branch to its end point.

This three level tree could be collapsed to an equivalent single level tree, as shown in a tabular form in Table 8.4, a generalisation of Table 8.3.

Each of the probabilities associated with an end point of the Figure 8.9 probability tree was allocated to its GW value in the 'probability calculation components' column. Summing across rows yielded the density form of the distribution. What was involved was the repetitive addition of conditionally specified dependent probability distributions, a slight generalisation of the treatment of adding conditionally dependent distributions in Figure 8.6. The symmetry of the dependence pattern resulted in an expected growth in each of the three three year periods of 1 GW, equating an expected growth of 3 GW over the nine years, as indicated in the final row of Table 8.4. In practice asymmetric dependence patterns might be extremely important, a complication avoided for this example.

Table 8.4 Load growth probability distribution for nine years.

Load growth GW	Probability calculation components								Probability (density)	Cumulative probability
0	.006								0.006	0.006
1	.024	.036		0.24					0.084	0.090
2	.030	.048	.048	.048	.048		.024		0.246	0.335
3		.036	.048	.048	.064	.048	.048	0.36	0.328	0.664
4		.024		.048	.048	.048	.048	.030	0.246	0.910
5			.024			.036	.024		0.084	0.994
6							.006		0.006	1.000

Expected growth 3 GW, 1 GW every three years

One message that Carl wanted to begin to convey to the board, using the example portrayed by Figure 8.9 and Table 8.4, was load growth (demand) uncertainty was an important component of the overall uncertainty associated with matching demand and supply for medium-term planning. For some purposes, load growth could be treated simply via a single level tree like Table 8.4, but load growth for a new power station was intended to meet also needed understanding using context specific decomposed models underlying the very general model of Figure 8.9. They needed to link econometric demand model approaches with presumed future possible price changes and other market and political changes beyond the end of the construction period. For example, if a demand growth of 3 GW over nine years was expected, but 0 GW was the outcome, an ongoing zero or low growth outcome might have a very high probability. To have confidence in a Table 8.4 summary, with likely ongoing trends part of that understanding, it would be important to understand some fairly complex underlying relationships.

A second message was the possible relevance of asymmetric penalty cost functions associated with the direct use of Table 8.4 together with inferences about longer-term trends. This was a concern which could be addressed using approaches he would illustrate using a numerical example in a moment.

A third message, to be further developed later, was large power stations with long construction lead times and high capital costs involved a significant contribution to the system's cost per kilowatt-hour of electricity which was associated with Canpower's inability to forecast precisely when its power would be needed, and this cost was not normally attributed to it. A set of small power stations with short lead times and proportionately lower capital costs involved much less system cost per kilowatt-hour of this kind for the same total amount of power because the uncertainty associated with load growth during construction was very much less. In decision analysis (decision theory) terms, this cost was known as 'the value of information'. In the present context, it was more appropriately termed 'the cost of uncertainty about load growth', a cost which was a function of the size of the power stations being considered and the lead times involved. For present purposes, Carl was not considering uncertainty about lead times between a commitment to build and power being available – a further complication considered later.

Modelling the cost of uncertainty about demand with an asymmetric penalty function

As the basis for a simple illustrative example, Carl suggested the board assume that nine years was the minimum construction period for a 3 GW nuclear power station, given design had been completed, permissions were in place, and so on; construction would take the nine year minimum duration; they wanted to model the implications of committing now to the construction of this nuclear power station with the probability tree of Figure 8.9 as summarised by Table 8.4 representing their current view of load growth over the next nine years, with trends established over these nine years probably carrying on; and contingency plans to cope with a departure from the expected load growth of 3 GW were reflected in the costs per kilowatt-hour associated with the possible load growth outcomes over the GW range shown in Table 8.5.

The second column of Table 8.5 associated a load growth of 3 GW over the nine year period with 10 cents/kWh, consistent with the expected cost discussed earlier.

Working outwards from this 3 GW expected load growth outcome in an upwards direction, gigawatt load growths of 2, 1 or 0 were associated with cents/kWh costs of 12, 15

Table 8.5 Cost outcomes linked to load growth outcomes.

Load growth, GW	Cost, cents/kWh	Probability (density) from Table 8.4	Product
0	20	0.006	0.120
1	15	0.084	1.260
2	12	0.246	2.952
3	10	0.328	3.280
4	11	0.246	2.706
5	12	0.084	1.008
6	13	0.006	0.078
Expected cost, cents/kWh (column total)			11.404

and 20 respectively. The 12 cents/kWh reflected an assumption that if a load growth of 2 GW occurred, the most effective contingency plans were expensive, but not hugely so. However, if a load growth of only 1 or 0 occurred, the whole lifecycle cost per kilowatt-hour increased in a non-linear manner. The zero load growth scenario assumed a new nuclear power station or other existing stations intended for base-load generation (24 hours per day) being used for shoulder periods and peaks (perhaps 10 hours per day) for many years, perhaps shutting down the lower merit order plant completely, only recovering from this position when existing plant retired if the zero growth continued. There was a less extreme variant on this theme if 1 GW of growth occurred. All three of these scenarios assumed the full cost was attributed to the new nuclear power station in question because it gave rise to a cost which alternatives might avoid.

Similarly, working outwards from the 3 GW expected load growth outcome in a downwards direction, gigawatt load growths of 4, 5 or 6 were associated with cents/kWh costs of 11, 12 and 13, respectively. The 13 cents/kWh reflected an assumption that if the 6 GW growth case occurred, the most effective contingency plans were expensive but much less expensive than the zero load growth case, and the intermediate 11 and 12 cents/kWh assumptions reflected a simple linearity assumption. In the 6 GW growth case, he assumed Canpower would have to use a source like outdated base-load plant due to retire or new peak-load gas turbines to meet the unexpected load until the nuclear power station under consideration was on stream, the additional cost during this period being attributed to the nuclear power station cost per kilowatt-hour. However, a second nuclear power station or some other new base-load equivalent would be initiated part way through the nine year period if load growth looked as if 3 GW might be exceeded, reducing the impact. There were less extreme variants on this theme if 4 or 5 GW growth scenarios occurred.

As with earlier examples, more precision could be used, different numbers could be argued for, and Carl indicated that he would not wish to defend the numbers used for illustrative purposes. But the importance of the asymmetry of the penalty costs associated with being early or late with a nuclear power station reflected in Table 8.5 was worth understanding, as was the increase in expected cost even if symmetry was assumed for the penalty costs. Indeed, whatever the nature of the penalty cost distribution, in practice Canpower medium-term planners would need to undertake extensive contingency planning exercises to both estimate penalty costs without undue bias and prepare robust plans to deal with the implementation of their plans, a Canpower capability not currently in evidence.

The 14% increase in expected cost per kilowatt hour portrayed in Table 8.5, from 10 to 11.4 cents/kWh, was clearly relevant. It implied a 14% increase in expected cost per kilowatt hour associated with imperfect knowledge of demand growth in conjunction with a nine year lead time for a nuclear power station, given a policy of building nuclear power stations in line with expected load growth.

The asymmetry of the penalty costs was also important because it suggested that a policy for the medium-term planning process which involved never attempting to meet the whole of anticipated base-load growth with nuclear power stations was the optimal approach. The expected cost was lower, meeting such anticipated load growth at least, in part, with non-nuclear, and then bringing in nuclear stations to take over established base load. That is, deliberately lag the introduction of the new nuclear plant because if being late is less expensive compared to being early, it pays to be late, although there are still costs involved. The extent to which it pays to be late is a function of the relative penalties associated with being early or late.

Furthermore, whether or not asymmetry of the penalty costs was involved, this example made it clear that if there was a way of meeting commitments which did not involve large units and lags, it would be worth paying a premium to use it.

Table 8.6 illustrated what the modelling of a policy using alternative lags might imply.

The 0 years (0 GW) 'target capacity lag' column corresponded to planning to meet the expected load growth of 3 GW over the assumed nine years of construction with zero planned lag in terms of years or gigawatts. In this case the Table 8.5 results were repeated, including the expected cost of 11.404 cents/kWh.

The 3 year (1 GW) target capacity lag column corresponded to starting three years later with a planned lag of 1 GW. In this case an 'on target' 2 GW load growth implied a cost of 10 cents/kWh, consistent with Table 8.4. The rising costs if load growth was 0, 1, 3, 4, 5 or 6 GW (2 or 1 under target or 1, 2, 3 or 4 over target) were consistent with Table 8.4, with a slight extrapolation. The expected value of 11.294 involved a decrease in expected cost relative to the 11.404 of Table 8.4 and the 0 years (0 GW) case of Table 8.6. Planning as if 2 GW of growth will take place over nine years was an improvement on assuming a mean growth rate of 3 GW, as might be expected given the assumed asymmetry of the penalty costs.

The 6 year (2 GW) target capacity lag column corresponded to starting six years later with a planned lag of 2 GW. In this case the rising cost if load growth was 6 GW (5 over target) was also consistent with Table 8.4, with a longer extrapolation. In this case the same approach had been used. However, comparable treatment of planning as if only 1 GW of growth would take place was not an improvement, and it was worse than planning for 3 GW.

Table 8.6 Cost outcomes linked to alternative levels of 'target capacity lag'.

Load growth, GW	Probability (density) from Table 8.4	Cost, cents/kWh, given a target capacity lag in years (GWs) as indicated		
		6 years (2 GW)	3 years (1 GW)	0 years (0 GW)
0	0.006	12	15	20
1	0.084	10	12	15
2	0.246	11	10	12
3	0.328	12	11	10
4	0.246	13	12	11
5	0.084	14	13	12
6	0.006	15	14	13
Expected cost, cents/kWh		12.018	11.294	11.404

These results suggested an optimal strategy involved a deliberate lagging of load growth in terms of new nuclear capacity for about three years, assuming a nine year construction lead time and an expected increase in demand of 3 GW over these nine years, 1 GW every three years. This lag would involve an expected cost saving per kilowatt hour of about 1% (the difference between 11.404 and 11.294) relative to scheduling construction of a 3 GW capacity to meet to expected demand at the end of year nine. A 1% cost saving was clearly not of great importance, but even with this optimised lag policy, the nine year construction lead time involved, in conjunction with demand uncertainty, added about 13% (the difference between 11.294 and 10) to the expected cost of 10 cents/kWh. A 13% bias favourable to nuclear power might be significant. In particular, if a short lead time option with a lower expected cost than nuclear was available, it should be seen as preferable.

The load growth distribution used for this example was assumed to be symmetric, to focus attention on the asymmetric penalty costs. If the load growth distribution was not symmetric, this would complicate the situation, and two sources of asymmetry reinforcing each other might become much more significant. The same principles would apply, but the 1% improvement via the lag optimisation might become a more significant 3% or 4%. Carl made the point that asymmetric functions, such as the one for cost illustrated here, were quite common. Sometimes they could be dealt with effectively on an intuitive basis, but sometimes it was worth modelling them to test intuition. It was not intuitively obvious that planning to bring nuclear power stations in later than needed was sensible. Indeed, it conflicted with Canpower's traditional bias in favour of trying to bring them in early 'to ensure the lights never went out'.

Integration upwards

Even the preferred option indicated by Table 8.6 involved a significant increase in the expected cost and some increase in risk. Carl suggested that the lag optimisation effect as portrayed so far was not of huge importance. However, what was very important was embedding this optimised expected cost and risk increase in Table 8.1. It was crucial to consider these optimised increases in expected cost and cost risk in the long-term planning process discussed earlier. Current Canpower practice would not involve attributing the additional costs associated with temporary use of gas-fired units to a nuclear power station as assumed for Tables 8.5 and 8.6. Nor would current practice attribute the full costs at the margin to the system of completing a nuclear power station prematurely as assumed for Tables 8.5 and 8.6. But if such costs must be borne by the system and they stem from the particular nuclear power station decision, they needed to be considered in the context of long-term planning if alternative sources of electricity did not involve comparable costs.

Small hydro units or small gas-fired units that could be constructed very quickly did not involve such large additional expected costs and risk of this kind. In the latter case, relatively low capital cost and savings in fuel costs if the gas-fired units were not operated contribute to a reduction in penalty costs (over and above the shorter construction period). What this implied was the need for an 'integration upwards' process which adjusted the long-term strategy formulation process to reflect medium-term strategy formulation impacts. This, in turn, implied a need for a second pass through the long-term strategy formulation process to incorporate what was learned in the medium-term planning process.

Linking this to the approach outlined earlier based on Table 8.1 for nuclear power, with comparable distributions for all other power sources considered, suggested that this earlier modelling ought to be extended to consider these additional system costs and risks associated with new supply implementation lags. This might or might not involve embedding them directly in the cost per kilowatt hour distributions of individual sources. The effect would have to be the same: a shift in the preferred mix, away from sources involving large power stations with high capital costs and long lead times, towards sources involving smaller power stations with proportionately lower capital costs and shorter lead times.

In practice, models of this kind to assist an electricity utility with medium-term system planning would have to examine reasonably complex decision rules associated with contingency responses, to develop appropriate rules to manage the medium-term planning decisions involved, and to provide a basis for capturing the dependence upward illustrated by the numbers of Tables 8.4 to 8.6. And in practice, as further medium-term planning complications were addressed, the use of commercial Monte Carlo simulation software might become a clarity efficient replacement, to generalise the computational aspects of the simple illustrative models used here. However, for some exploratory and presentational purposes, at a conceptual level it would be very worthwhile avoiding simulation, exploring trees and tables using HAT models in the forms employed by these examples. They clarified the structure of the models required and the key working assumptions which the board needed to understand.

Modelling other medium-term planning uncertainty concerns

Medium-term planning also needed to consider other sources of uncertainty which had important implications for the timing of commitments to action plans plus linked provisional plans, and some could involve further dependencies upwards. For example, supply uncertainty driven by construction period uncertainty was particularly important for nuclear power stations, because significant uncertainty over long construction periods clearly exacerbated the demand uncertainty issues of the last section. Canpower had significant difficulty with completing all big projects on time. This situation would need dramatic improvement, which was feasible. However, even assuming this was done, the risk of significant departures from expected dates would remain an important source of uncertainty in terms of matching supply and demand, perhaps increasing the 13% just observed to 15% to 20% or more.

Supply uncertainty driven by reliability concerns also needed attention, perhaps further increasing the 13% to 20% to 30% or more. For example, Carl suggested the board contemplate the implications of an expected load growth of 3 GW becoming a realised growth of 6 GW *plus* the planned 9 year construction period becoming 12 years *plus* an extended unplanned outage period for a base load power station currently delivering 3 GW.

He would not further develop medium-term uncertainty models today, but he hoped that it was now *very* clear that *all relevant uncertainty* needed explicit attention when making commitments to the full range of medium-term decisions involved in matching supply and demand. The examples he had used illustrated the use of a HAT framework in a very different manner to its earlier use for long-term planning, to address a very different set of questions. Canpower currently lacked the capability to address medium-term uncertainty issues effectively, in addition to its long-term planning failures.

Carl finished his discussion of medium-term planning by emphasising the usefulness of explicit uncertainty modelling in a framework focused on timing, the bias associated with currently omitted 'upward integration' adjustments to expected costs and associated risk, and the very different nature of the issues addressed and the models required for medium-term planning relative to a portfolio-driven approach to long-term planning. He made a particular point of emphasising that the long-term planning process had to focus on 'portfolio issues' in the sense of trade-offs between cents/kWh expected costs and risk exposure associated with different proportions of hydro, nuclear, thermal and so on, leaving the medium-term planning process to focus on timing issues and minimising the expected cost of implementing the long-term strategy. However, links and interdependencies between them needed addressing via multiple pass approaches, and a HAT-based framework with Monte Carlo simulation options was a flexible toolset for addressing all the relevant issues.

Short-term planning and integration upwards

Carl began his treatment of short-term planning by reminding everyone that short-term planning was about 'keeping the lights on at the lowest feasible cost *given the generation capability currently available*'. This involved short-term demand forecasting plus short-term supply availability issues which had to include reliability concerns.

Canpower's approach to demand forecasting for short-term planning purposes was 'at the top of the class' in terms of industry standards, and posed no concerns. Canpower's approach to availability planning was generally good by industry standards so far as he was aware, but there were two closely coupled serious problems which had an impact on medium-term and long-term planning needing attention. The availability of generation capability was assessed for the whole system in a way which needed revision, and the way the cost for reserve generation capability was attributed needed revision. His next step was to illustrate how modelling could illuminate the nature of these issues, and help Canpower to resolve them using simple models.

One important message was large power stations units, and large numbers of units of a common type exposed to common-mode failure, both involved a greater need for system spare capacity than small units of different types. A closely coupled message was this increase in spare capacity involved an increase in system cost which ought to be attributed to the large units, or large numbers of units of a common type, in terms of an increase in their expected lifecycle cost when choosing the desired mix of units. Another related message was large power station units, and large numbers of common units, also increased the risk of major losses of availability which have to be borne by the consumers. Unlike smaller capacity losses, it would not be economic to provide spare capacity to eliminate the risk of failures which affected a large proportion of a system. This risk might be fully borne by customers rather than Canpower, in the form of unreliable service, but it might be partially borne by Canpower using compensation payments. But in either case it ought to be reflected in the long-term portfolio modelling discussed earlier, because it was an important additional type of risk, unless it could be effectively mitigated by mutual backup arrangements with other utilities within the province or in other adjacent provinces or US states. For example, a constraint of the form 'no more than X_1 percentage of the supply capacity of Canpower should be of nuclear power station type A1' might be appropriate, entirely driven by this kind of reliability/availability risk considerations, perhaps within an overall restriction of nuclear power as a whole being driven primarily by the cents/kWh cost-risk issues discussed earlier, perhaps with other background secondary constraints.

Modelling unplanned outage within one multi-unit nuclear power station

For illustrative purposes, Carl asked the board to consider one of the 3 GW nuclear power stations used earlier, for simplicity, assuming it consisted of three 1 GW units, all to the same specification, the probability of a 1 GW unit becoming unavailable in any month for unplanned reasons which were independent across units (such as damage caused by operator error restricted to a single unit) was 0.01, and the probability of a unit becoming unavailable in any month for unplanned reasons which involve common-mode failures across units within the power station was 0.005. If one unit was unavailable they would all be unavailable in a common-mode failure context, as would be the case if common systems failed. In practice, both these probabilities would be functions of time since operation of the units began, so for illustrative purposes, he was assuming that these probabilities were both averages over time. Intermediate levels of dependence might also require modelling in practice. Carl acknowledged that both these probabilities might not be correct, but revisions would not alter the substance of what these numbers would illustrate, and he had deliberately chosen very simple round numbers.

Figure 8.10 portrayed a three level probability tree associated with these assumptions, and Figure 8.11 illustrated the equivalent single level collapsed tree.

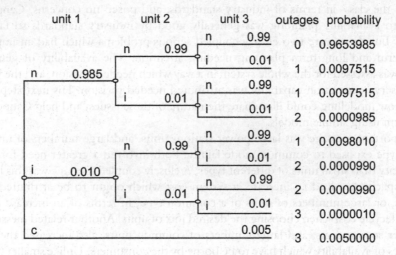

unit 1
unit 2
unit 3
outages
probability
n
0.99
n
0.99
0
0.9653985
i
0.01
1
0.0097515
n
0.985
n
0.99
1
0.0097515
i
0.01
i
0.01
2
0.0000985
n
0.99
1
0.0098010
n
0.99
i
0.01
2
0.0000990
i
0.010
n
0.99
2
0.0000990
i
0.01
i
0.01
3
0.0000010
c
0.005
3
0.0050000
Key: n = no outage, i = independent outage, c = common-mode outage

Figure 8.10 Example outage probability tree for a 3 GW nuclear power station-with three 1 GW units.

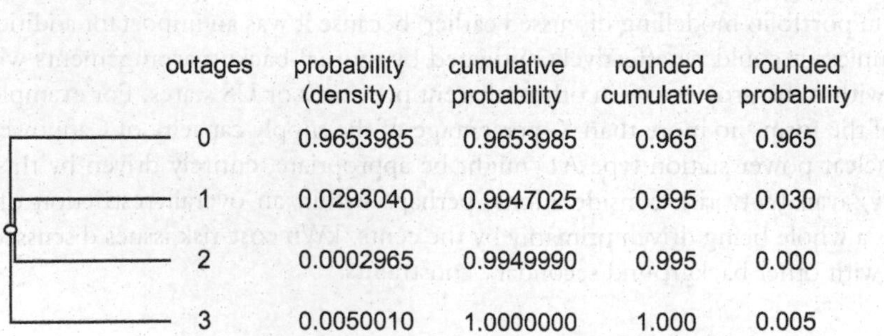

outages
probability (density)
cumulative probability
rounded cumulative
rounded probability
0
0.9653985
0.9653985
0.965
0.965
1
0.0293040
0.9947025
0.995
0.030
2
0.0002965
0.9949990
0.995
0.000
3
0.0050010
1.0000000
1.000
0.005
expected number of outages
0.0449000 rounded to 0.045
contribution of common mode
0.0150000 rounded to 0.015 (33%)

Figure 8.11 Collapsed single level probability tree associated with Figure 8.10.

These two probability trees and the associated rounded values indicated a high probability of no outage (0.965), a significant probability of one outage (0.030), and virtually no chance of two or three outages because of independent outage sources (rounded to 0.000), but a probability of three outages due to common-mode failures of 0.005. The probability of three outages due to common-mode failure of 0.005 was small, but large enough to be of serious concern given the consequences. The bimodal nature of this distribution might be counter-intuitive, and it was worth trying to understand why it arose, as a general feature of all common-mode failures, using *mode* in the sense of a 'mechanism' or 'set of causes'. Earlier in this chapter *mode* was used in the sense of a 'most likely' value associated with a single 'peak' value, a somewhat different meaning which can be confusing.

In addition to the risk associated with losing all three units at the same time, Figure 8.11 showed that these common-mode failures contributed about a third of the expected number of outages in any month, a perhaps surprisingly high proportion.

Carl then assumed that any of these outages might be associated with the duration of outage probability tree associated with Table 8.7, to illustrate the overall impact.

Table 8.7 used a HAT approach which made explicit use of continuous variable ranges plus a non-linear scale for outage duration. At this point Carl indicated that he could explain the rationale and implications explored in Part 1 for this kind of modelling at a later date if they were interested, linked to but slightly different from that used for Table 8.1 and Figure 8.2.

The expected values from Figure 8.11 and Table 8.7 could be used to compute the expected unit months of outage per month of operation on start-up, $0.045 \times 4.4 = 0.198$. This approximated the expected unit months of outage per month of operation once the system's operation reached a steady state (which could be computed using a semi-Markov process). It was slightly higher than the result a steady state calculation would provide, because when units were not available the probability of additional units becoming unavailable falls. Availability per unit using this result was 93.4% (obtained by $100 \times (3 - 0.198)/3$), about 95% if a steady state calculation was used. This implied an increase in expected cost per kilowatt-hour of just over 5% to meet the expected level of outage. This increase was normally associated with the units in question through the standard treatment of availability.

The risk of losing large units required a further increase in expected cost associated with additional reserve capacity provision to that required if smaller units were used, which was not normally associated with the units in question. Furthermore, it required another increase in cost associated with the risk of this increased reserve proving inadequate and requiring contingency demand management or other responses with significant costs borne by electricity consumers, also not normally associated with the unit in question. The risk of being unable to meet demand was inevitably increased if larger units were used because it would be uneconomic to scale up reserve capacity in direct proportion.

Table 8.7 Example outage duration probability distribution.

Outage duration (months)	Associated range	Probability	Product
0.5	(0 to 1)	0.4	0.2
2	(1 to 3)	0.3	0.6
6	(3 to 12)	0.2	1.2
24	(12 or more)	0.1	2.4
Expected value			4.4

*Modelling unplanned outage for a set of nuclear power stations
of a common type*

Carl then turned his attention to the situation if this 3 GW nuclear power station was one of
four similar stations, each of 3 units, making a total of 12 units. He assumed that the same
probabilities of independent and common-mode outage within a single station applied.
He also assumed that one in ten of the within-station common-mode outages involved a
common-mode outage across all four stations. Such common-mode outages would include
the discovery of design defects with safety implications requiring immediate shutdown of
all stations using the same design, for example. One in ten is a monthly probability of only
0.0005, which is very low. However, the impact would be substantial.

The implications of these across-station common-mode outages included a direct contribution to the expected cost of outages already costed in relation to station availability and
normally included in the cost attributed to a nuclear power station, plus all the additional
costs considered in the last subsection. The implications also included a very much larger
system reserve to keep the consequences of such an outage acceptable, and the cost of this
reserve was directly attributable to the use of a number of nuclear power stations of the same
type, although it was not usually associated with them in this way. More important was the
large increase in expected cost associated with such common-mode failures which would
be borne by customers which should be considered when choosing the mix of sources of
power, although this was not usually done. More important still, if the consequences of
such a very large loss of availability were unacceptable for any reasonable increase in reserve
capacity, from a regulator's perspective it might be critical to restrain a utility from undertaking any developments which implied a plausible possibility of common-mode failure on this
scale. That is, externally imposed constraints of the form 'no more than X_1 percentage of
the available supply of a utility should be from nuclear power stations of type A1' may arise
because of availability risk rather than the cost risk considered earlier. Such constraints might
be imposed after a major incident, if the regulator was not aware of the possible implications
in advance.

The additional reserve costs, and the high costs of responses borne by consumers, clearly
needed to be considered by Canpower, and both the expected cost implications and the risk
implications needed to be considered and attributed to the nuclear power stations in the
context of long-term system planning. In practice, the 'consumers' who suffer most may be
electricity-dependent industries. Their boards ought to be aware of the issue and be politically vocal and proactive if appropriate, as should their employees and customers.

Modelling unplanned outage for small hydro units

Carl then considered the situation if a 3 GW nuclear power station was replaced by 300
relatively small units of hydropower. For simplicity he assumed the same probabilities of
independent and common-mode outage applied, and the same outage duration distribution. In this case common-mode outage would include a drought affecting all 300 units,
for example.

The impact of the large number of units in relation to independent sources of outage was
a marked increase in the predictability of outage, but the common-mode outage issue was
not changed. Using the 95% availability figure, they could expect about 15 of the 300 units
to be out at any one time, with very little variation relative to the nuclear power station risk
of having one or more units out at any one time for reasons not involving common-mode

outage. This meant that Canpower did not have to provide as much reserve for individual unit failures, with lower expected cost per kilowatt hour implications. However, Canpower would still have to worry about the risk of common-mode outage and its expected cost implications.

To consider the impact of the larger number of units in relation to the common-mode outages Carl assumed the same 0.005 probability of losing all 3 GW, with the risk that reserve capacity provision would prove inadequate, requiring contingency demand management responses with costs borne by electricity consumers. If Canpower reduced reserve provision because of the larger number of units and the more stable outage pattern, then the cost implications of common-mode failure in terms of costs borne by electricity customers become even more serious than in the nuclear power station case. The costs associated with restoring hydropower are likely to be rather less than those associated with common-mode failures within a nuclear power station, and very long outage periods are less probable, but the short-term impact on the consumer is similar. This strengthened the case for inter-utility collaboration across provincial and national boundaries.

As with nuclear power stations, to some extent common-mode outages needed to be considered in relation to all existing units, as well as all proposed new units. That is, a serious nuclear incident could lead to the recognition of design defects which resulted in all nuclear power stations being shut down, and a long-term drought might seriously affect most of an electricity utility's hydro facilities. In practice the probability of common-mode outages on this scale, and on a smaller scale, might be very different for different sources of power. If, for example, nuclear power was very exposed to this kind of common-mode outage relative to hydro (or vice versa), then failing to address these issues biases the case for one option and against the other.

Modelling unplanned outage for a portfolio of electricity power sources

Carl next considered the situation if the four 3 GW nuclear power stations considered earlier were replaced by one 3 GW nuclear power station, the 3 GW of small hydro as just discussed, 3 GW of gas-fired power, and 3 GW of conservation. What were the implications?

If the gas units were midway between the nuclear and small hydro units in terms of size, and the same probabilities applied, the situation with respect to the 3 GW of gas power will be intermediate in terms of the characteristics described earlier in relation to 3 GW of nuclear and 3 GW of small hydro. In this case, common-mode failure might involve loss of gas supply, for example. On the other hand, the 3 GW of conservation raises quite different issues. It might be argued that if conservation was unpredictable it should contribute to reserve requirements, but most demand management concerned with conservation was aimed at smoothing demand variations as well as reducing average consumption. This implied an expected cost reduction as well as a risk reduction in terms of the contribution of conservation to the portfolio considered by the long-term system planning process comparable to a hedging effect.

A key difference in the situation for the 12 GW as a whole was the absence of common-mode failures outside the nuclear, gas, and hydro subsets. It was for this reason that regulators might wish to constrain the proportion of electricity produced from any single source which was subject to the possibility of common-mode failures.

Again, this realisation might follow a major outage. However, it would clearly be preferable for everybody if it was anticipated before a major outage.

Explicit risk sharing with customers and other utilities

Carl now made the point that outage costs borne by customers should be considered by Canpower when determining strategy. However, sometimes it might be in the customers' interests to share outage costs as part of an efficient approach to risk sharing. When this was the case it might be important to make it clear to both customers and regulators that to do otherwise would involve increasing the cost per kilowatt hour charge to an extent which most customers would not support – they would prefer the outage risk.

Developing this a bit further, if customers wanted Canpower to insure them against the consequences of major outages by paying compensation, Canpower would have to charge a premium for that insurance which would involve expected costs plus administrative costs. Canpower might argue that this would not be good value for money for customers.

Alternatively, if customers wanted Canpower to avoid the risk of outage by increasing spare capacity, Canpower might have to charge even more. Canpower might argue this would be even worse value for money for customers.

One way to mitigate this effect would be explicit risk sharing arrangements with other major utilities in other adjacent provinces or US states. Such arrangements might help to cope with shortages for combinations of reasons – outages in conjunction with delayed project completions and unexpected load increases – a form of general response to build in robustness which includes 'any other unspecified problem'. However, common-mode failures and common reasons for other problems would still need consideration.

Explicit costing of regulatory constraints

Carl also made the point that costs associated with regulator/government constraints on the make-up of Canpower's portfolio imposed for reliability/availability reasons would be passed on to the customers. Such costs could be identified and measured in a shadow cost framework, to test the appropriateness of the constraints as well as providing a simple systematic basis for embedding them in the long-term planning process.

An overview of integrated short/medium/long-term planning

Modelling short-term availability issues as addressed in the last section was clearly a useful basis for considering short-term corporate planning issues. However, in the context of an overview of what integrating short-term, medium-term and long-term planning involved for Canpower, the implications for long-term planning were also extremely important – the primary reason for raising these issues that day. The need for reserve capacity was a function of the size of the units involved and the extent to which common-mode outage could occur, plus the availability and effectiveness of general responses based on collaboration across provincial and national boundaries. As a consequence, all reserve capacity costs should be attributed to types of unit, as should the risk of costs borne by electricity consumers as a consequence of involuntary demand management (or other responses), in terms of both expected costs and associated risks. Outage risk might also require limits on the proportion of power provided by any single source in the overall system. As an extreme example, if one kind of nuclear power station had the lowest expected cost in cents/kWh, and it was the most reliable of all available sources, diversification might still be absolutely essential just to avoid the risk of a design fault being found after the system was 100% this source. A shutdown of the whole system because of a design fault affecting 100% of the system would clearly be catastrophic.

A portfolio view of the system in reliability terms was as important as a portfolio view of the system in cents/kWh cost terms or a national security perspective based on fuel availability if potential hostilities threatened fuel supplies or technical dependence if the country of origin of a supplier of part of the generation portfolio became belligerent. These issues should be considered explicitly by Canpower within its long-term planning framework. If they were not, it would fall to a perceptive regulator or government to take appropriate action, if either was aware of the issues and motivated to act effectively.

Carl's portfolio-driven approach to long-term planning accommodating more than one attribute plus more than one criterion per attribute facilitated this. Although the analysis needed was clearly made much more complicated as additional attributes were addressed, whatever really mattered could and should be considered.

It is always crucial to be able to both recognise and deal with everything that really matters, a central feature of Carl's recommended EP approach. Carl might have observed that people who do not know how to deal with difficult issues tend to avoid looking for them, and sometimes they do not recognise them even when they are blindingly obvious or they bump into them. Carl did not do so to avoid antagonising the board. But I will, because you should find it useful to remember this observation in a wide range of contexts. To see this tendency in ourselves as well as others, and deal with it as effectively as possible, is arguably a core aspect 'enlightenment'.

Futures planning of all kinds and its integration at all levels

Goals planning plus futures planning jointly inform long-term, medium-term and short-term planning. Carl suggested that once a mature approach to goals planning was in place, futures planning was usefully seen as a layer of planning primarily driven directly by goals planning, but making use of cost-gap information feedback involving shadow costs from long-term, medium-term and short-term planning.

Futures planning could itself be associated with a top-level to bottom-level internal structure which was comparable in some respects to the long-term, medium-term and short-term horizons of planning currently feasible options but very different in others. It could also be associated with project lifecycle stage structures with features comparable to the bidding stages of the Astro tale in Chapter 6. For example, 'horizon scanning' could be seen as a largely passive process of assessing technology developments by others with a view to possible Canpower usage or research and development for usage; 'futures research' could be seen as a higher level of resource commitment for selected areas needing clarification research prior to possible 'futures development', which, in turn involved significant development expenditure to make new technology feasible or economically viable. Gateway stages between 'scanning', 'research' and 'development' futures planning process stages could ensure unbiased assessment of the options to progress propositions to a following stage or not.

However, there were a number of reasons why a much more complex interdependent perspective might be relevant in any context. In a Canpower context, Carl was convinced that an approach addressing Canpower's capability-culture assets and liabilities, as well as related external concerns, was crucial, with an overall emphasise on 'designing a desirable future' and exploring the feasibility of delivering it with an in-house variant of entrepreneurship some people call 'intrapreneurship' driving Canpower's innovation agenda. One feature of this kind of futures planning he believed especially important was a concern for developing awareness of threats to Canpower's public ownership status. Carl believed these threats might be transformed into Canpower opportunities.

What Carl believed was crucially important for the Canpower board to begin to understand immediately was the need for a proactive top-down approach to 'designing desirable
futures' based on the premise that all organisations needed a clear understanding of the
opportunities and risks associated with their 'business model' which summarised their most
important goals, in particular, their core values, in terms of their key operating rules and
policies. This 'business model' needed robust assumptions and clarity about key corporate strengths and weaknesses. Understanding Canpower's key strengths and weaknesses
required corporate self-knowledge. It also required a well-founded appreciation of their
potential political allies and similar knowledge of crucial political opponents, fully understanding that potential allies could prove indifferent bystanders or enemies if not treated
appropriately.

What Carl had in mind was starting to address Canpower's key fault set number three – a
serious capability-culture liability which he believed needed fixing immediately. He did not
put it quite so bluntly, but he made no effort to hide his concerns. To briefly illustrate what
he had in mind he suggested they started by looking at some of the key criticisms of Canpower currently receiving public attention and media focus.

Influential international 'green' movements like Greenpeace were strongly opposed to
nuclear power. In Canpower's province, these groups were also strongly opposed to public
sector ownership of Canpower, although they did not state this opposition explicitly. Their
opposition to a public sector ownership position arose, in part, because the low cost of capital associated with provincial government bond funding of Canpower assets made electricity
cheaper than it would be if Canpower used private sector funding, which made consumers
relatively wasteful. This effect was amplified by the implicit national government subsidy of
nuclear power associated with further hidden indirect costs linked to nuclear waste disposal
and potential nuclear accidents. Green movement supporters would not openly criticise
Canpower for its low costs because they did not want to draw attention to the benefits of
public sector ownership in terms of low electricity costs, but they were indirectly supporting calls for the privatisation of Canpower as a route to removing all subsidies for electricity
costs and openly attacking Canpower for lack of leadership on green concerns. Some of
Canpower's owners/customers (the citizens of its province) were beginning to sympathise
with the Greenpeace position.

Vocal private sector power producers and potential members of this group wanted less
nuclear power and higher electricity prices for straightforward commercial reasons. They
would not openly attack Canpower for its low costs, but they were indirectly attacking
the public sector status of Canpower and openly attacking Canpower for its restrictive and
obstructive approach to private power (within province non-utility power) because Canpower were visibly unhelpful when small rural communities might benefit from small scale
local private power projects. When renewable sources were involved, this exacerbated Canpower's current lack of 'green credibility'.

Many economics, finance, and political media commentators who were critical of Canpower were convinced that public ownership of utilities was not a good idea for purely
ideological reasons, and they tended to see the low capital cost of public ownership as a
threat to private enterprise, with scope for potential application in many other industry sectors, not as an opportunity for private enterprise which needed electric power to produce
their services and products, arguably much more relevant. These critics of Canpower usually
did not even mention the low cost of capital benefits, seeing this as an argument put by its
ideological opposition which needed ignoring or discrediting, a variant of the strategic-
misrepresentation euphemism discussed earlier. Some of these critical media commentators

actually believed economic theories which suggested public and private sector cost of capital should be seen as the same, a reasonably clear indication of the effectiveness of the misrepresentations involved. Many of Canpower's owners/customers were either misinformed or confused by the media or the textbook treatment of the cost of capital discussions they were exposed to in their earlier education.

Some of Canpower's owners/customers who worked as non-union tradespeople saw the people doing similar jobs employed by Canpower as overpaid and overprotected from the marketplace due to overly powerful union pressures as a direct result of its public sector status. Some of Canpower's owners/customers who worked as private sector managers or entrepreneurs saw both the unionised employees of Canpower and their managers as overpaid and overprotected from the marketplace as a result of its public sector status.

Most of Canpower's owners/customers were ambivalent about the strengths and weaknesses of public versus private sector status for Canpower, but a combination of adverse pressure group rhetoric, misinformation, political opportunism, and growing public concern about green issues was building a groundswell of hostility to Canpower in general, and its public sector status in particular.

Canpower's obstructive approach to private power producers, its weakly grounded plan for six new nuclear power stations, and growing evidence of its lack of competence when costing and planning other new developments were crucial issues the board needed to address. They were key components of Canpower's dangerous reinforcement of a complex set of factors making privatisation a serious and growing threat. Carl believed privatising Canpower would be a needless social disaster, a catastrophe easily avoided provided Canpower could effectively meet all genuine criticisms and disarm all unfounded prejudices. He had no strong personal prejudices or feelings about private sector versus public sector ownership in general terms, but he was convinced that in most respects Canpower was a national treasure – an excellent example of what a good public sector utility ought to be, and the recent privatisation of the CEGB in the UK provided a directly comparable example of a fundamentally flawed approach which Canpower's province should avoid. He believed Canpower needed to design a future which would eliminate all the genuine criticisms of Canpower which contributed to the case for its privatisation by its enemies, make allies of some of those currently hostile or indifferent, and plan the realisation of this future.

Goals planning as a starting point for all planning

Carl reminded the board that at the outset of this meeting he had suggested goals planning should be the starting place for all planning. The rationale was quite simple – whenever goals planning was not the explicit starting point, by default it was the implicit starting point, with an implied failure to test the implicit planning assumptions.

Goals planning should be followed by futures planning in designing a desirable future mode, followed by other aspects of futures planning. Again, implicitly doing so was the implication of not doing so explicitly, with an implied failure to test all associated assumptions.

Futures planning should be followed by long-term, medium-term, and short-term planning. Goals planning also had to drive long-term, medium-term and short-term planning directly. Complete downwards passes should then be followed by ongoing iteration in a planned and orderly manner, integrating bottom-up dependencies, along with other adjustments and elaborations which testing the robustness of the analysis as a whole suggested were needed. He would return to the idea of orderly cycles later. His immediate concern was starting to revisit the minimum clarity position on goals planning which he had used earlier. He had delayed beginning to address more sophisticated goals planning because the changes implied were radical and likely to generate significant controversy. He thought the changes discussed earlier needed clarity first because they were relatively straightforward and unequivocal.

He believed the board now needed to begin addressing goals planning for Canpower from the perspective of its owners, explicitly asking what Canpower's key goals and core values ought to be from this perspective, and what crucial operating rules and policies might flow from this perspective. Before long it would be crucial to ensure that there was board level agreement to a formal summary of the results of an effective development of this exercise which they could agree with the government and their regulator and then publish, with a view to responding positively to any constructive public criticism by Canpower's 'owners'.

Canpower's 'owners' were 'the citizens of the province'. For the most part, their 'owners' were also their 'customers', although some 'owners' produced electricity for their own use and sale to others and some 'customers' who operated businesses within the province were not citizens of the province. He suggested they use the term 'owners/customers' to start talking about key goals and core values that day, treating owners and customers as the same for most practical purposes, but testing the assumption that there might be differences between owners and customers that matter when relevant.

It seemed reasonable to Carl to assume that their owners/customers wanted Canpower's key goals and core values to be 'serving the needs of owners/customers in terms of a low cost, reliable and secure electricity supply provided in a responsible manner and charged for in a fair and transparent manner – today and for the foreseeable future'. They might debate and refine this statement – but it was not worth doing so that day.

He suggested they started from this position and ask the question 'What are the crucial operating policies and rules this suggested?' These crucial policies and rules would in effect define the basis of 'Canpower's desirable future' at a corporate strategy level.

They might begin with the crucial policy understanding that Canpower had to *provide a low cost, reliable and secure electricity supply, but Canpower did not have to generate all that supply.*

They might then link this to the crucial rule that Canpower had to maintain responsibility for planning and implementing an ongoing coordination of the portfolio of electric power sources of all kinds for their province, operating in close cooperation with their provincial regulator under the supervision of the provincial government and working closely with the federal government and relevant national regulators (on nuclear safety for example).

He thought that an equally crucial set of rules should be based on the assumptions that Canpower needed to maintain responsibility for owning and operating all electricity transmission capability and connections to the grid, as well as all customer-facing operations, including dealing with billing, relationship management during outages, and all aspects of safety and security. He pointed out that all these rules were broken by the privatisation of the CEGB, so all the assumptions involved were clearly debatable, but he believed they were crucial working assumptions underlying the value of public sector status for Canpower to its owners/customers.

However, private sector companies might take over some aspects of the operation of power transmission assets and some aspects of customer-facing operations – Canpower's employees and their trade unions did not own Canpower as a consequence of their jobs, although employees were also citizens of the province, and as employees they were interested parties who needed very careful consideration for a number of reasons. Although outsourcing in any Canpower context would need considerable care and caution, and there was a good case for avoiding even raising the issue as a possibility in the immediate future, outsourcing was an important option which needed thorough exploration in the longer term. When it was discussed they should start from a clear acknowledgement of the ethos of service to the public which all Canpower employees were justly proud of which should be preserved and enhanced – treating it as an important capability-culture asset. But they might embrace a possible 'friendly float-off' variant of the Astro 'friendly takeover' which Martha discussed in Chapter 6, and float-off strategic partners that might be owned by their employees, along the lines Ajit suggested TLC ought to consider, as well as accepting that direct market competition in some areas made sense for its owners.

For example, Canpower did not need to own and operate all power stations. In simple 'traffic light' terms there was a blue–green–red light spectrum with intermediate shades in terms of private sector generation of power they should vigorously encourage (assign a blue light), welcomed (assign a green light), or firmly resist (assign a red light).

The extreme deep-red light end of the spectrum might be characterised by the ownership of existing large hydropower stations which usually involved exploiting important geographic assets of the province which the citizens of the province should continue to own for the benefit of their children and grandchildren as well as current generations. As with transmission assets, private sector companies might take over some aspects of the operation of these assets, but he believed outsourcing these jobs would be on the light-red end of a red–green spectrum of job outsourcing priorities.

Equally deep-red was the case for Canpower maintaining full responsibility for both owning and operating all existing nuclear power stations. It could make an equally strong case for building and operating all new nuclear power stations, given a working assumption that Canpower would want to maintain some nuclear power and Canada's Candu reactors and associated nuclear technology would remain internationally competitive. However, if the Canadian federal government did not ensure that the Candu technology remained competitive, the international market for nuclear technology would need consideration. Furthermore, if the federal government made nuclear power too expensive for reasons explored towards the end of Carl's presentation, other futures involving less or possibly no nuclear power would need exploring.

The blue light to deep-green end of the spectrum was small scale local cogeneration facilities. For example, the board might begin *immediately* by mandating efforts to foster, not hinder, the kind of cogeneration facilities which were currently the basis of private power in their province, like combined heat and light facilities in timber processing towns which might produce more electric power than normal local needs by burning wood waste. It might be crucial to formally and explicitly adopt Martha's Chapter 6 'blue light' for this kind of option to emphasise much stronger support than a 'green light' might imply.

A jointly optimal blue light approach might go *well* beyond Canpower just buying surplus electricity to coordinated concentration of the surplus to reduce peak-load requirements for new Canpower stations, with contracts explicitly facilitating this focus. Canpower could effectively advertise explicit 'support' by visibly erring on the generous side with their contractual arrangements. For example, they could provide free consultancy based on pooling the experience of other private power producers, treating private power producers as valuable members of an extended Canpower team – not competitors with a high nuisance value.

Canpower could extend this supportive approach to local low-head hydropower and combined cycle gas-burning facilities which might become economically attractive given Canpower technical support, supportive joint finance, and risk sharing on prices for fuel as well as electricity purchase prices.

Furthermore, they could fund research into and prototype developments of wind and solar and small scale low-head hydropower. This could be followed by assisting those interested in developing them in a locally accepted manner when cost-effective contributions to meeting provincial base-load and peak-load power demands were feasible. The objectives could include minimising provincial and national expenditure on subsidies for renewables but helping to ensure their province was at the leading edge of cost-effective use of these emerging technologies as their cost-effectiveness was established.

Further still, they might encourage, not discourage, appropriate private power producers to build and operate some significant new facilities they believed the system needed. Canpower ownership and funding could be preserved, using contracts which reflect enlightened risk sharing. For example, the globally used traditional BOOT contract approach (the contractor Builds and Owns, Operates, and then Transfers at a fixed horizon like 20 years) should be seen as a form of contract which was wholly unsuited to *any* public sector organisation, because it means relatively expensive private sector ownership of the capital needed, also true of the UK Private Finance Initiative (PFI) approach and related Private–Public Partner (PPP) variants. However, if the BOOT approach was adjusted to reflect the lower cost of public sector capital which could be used by Canpower, an adjusted version might be highly suitable. He suggested what was needed might be reflected in the modestly modified acronym BOLT (the contractor Builds and Operates a new power station using a Loan from Canpower secured on the asset, and then Transfers the operating contract to Canpower or another competitor contractor at a review gateway if Canpower is not fully satisfied with the contractor's performance, with an agreed-on routine and exceptional gateway structure built into the initial contract). Candidates might be non-Canadian or out-of-province utilities with new technologies, perhaps working in concert with gas-turbine manufacturers or gas producers or wind-turbine manufacturers. Appropriate risk sharing contracts would be crucial, even though private sector capital was not used for the assets themselves because issues like gas price rises in conjunction with electricity price decreases would remain a crucial risk issue for private sector participants in public sector managed electric power generation. There was no point in making private sector partners carry risks they would have to charge for if those risks were better carried as part of the Canpower portfolio of risks. Managing all relevant risks for their owners in opportunity efficient terms at a portfolio level should be a core Canpower role which should not be weakened or threatened by any changes Canpower supported.

And further still, Canpower might use federal government support and the support of all the agencies behind the Candu technology to develop Canpower's nuclear power programme but be open to approaches from competing non-Canadian sources if this provided better value for Canpower's owners/customers in the long-term.

Wherever new approaches might benefit its owners/customers, Canpower should be proactively seeking opportunities, recognising that its owners and customers had interests beyond electricity which might involve useful synergies. To illustrate the scope for such synergies, Canpower might help the city authorities responsible for rubbish removal from a city to find a suitable technology and site for incineration facilities which would also produce community heating plus electric power for the grid, perhaps to be loan funded in part by Canpower but owned and operated by the city, as a service to Canpower owners in this city in terms of waste management as well as a benefit to Canpower customers buying electricity in this city and elsewhere, but perhaps owned by Canpower if the cities involved preferred this route. A degree of 'support' for this kind of activity which had elements of 'subsidy' could be socially beneficial for Canpower's owners in terms which were directly comparable to low cost low energy consumption light bulbs, more efficient heating and cooling systems, and better building insulation. All these changes would involve opening Canpower up to significant competition plus a degree of diversification, but only where competition and diversification made sense for Canpower's owners/customers. Terms which were attractive to private sector 'big team' collaborators would have to be designed – but leadership of the design of the system and its incentives should remain firmly in the hands of a Canpower board which protected the best interests of Canpower's owners/customers.

One way to look at what Carl was suggesting was avoiding the risk of a complete privatisation breakup like that visited on the CEGB and its owners/customers in the UK by transforming a possible threat into a realised opportunity. Canpower's board members could do this effectively if they recognised that their core concern was a reliable supply of electricity at low cost for the private and corporate consumers of electricity in their province for the foreseeable future, produced in a socially responsible manner, overcoming as far as possible all the relevant weaknesses of public sector monopolies in general, and Canpower in particular, and capitalising as far as possible on Canpower's relevant strengths.

The move to supporting some power stations operated by other organisations, in place of blanket resistance, and outsourcing work on Canpower assets and functions which was previously not even contemplated, should be seen as part of an associated culture change. It was crucial to unobtrusively eliminate any evidence that Canpower was managed for the benefit of its employees. He did not emphasise the obvious fact that 'employees' included Canpower's board and other managers, but this was clearly implied. They could start by trying to develop a 'big team' approach to the sharp end as soon as possible. For example, the next time storms brought down power lines and caused local outages, they might give high public visibility to local contractors working alongside Canpower employees, drawing on experience gained assisting with routine construction, replacement, and maintenance work, and they might start planning for this now, involving local contractors much more on suitable routine maintenance work with immediate effect and scaling back internal teams as this capability was developed. This kind of approach could be central to the broader aim of breaking down 'them and us' attitudes and union-driven wage differentials. However, Canpower could also demonstrate the same kind of culture change in terms of some highly visible board level decisions as soon as possible. He did not elaborate using any of 'cultural clues' Ivor had discussed earlier, but his message was clear.

In summary, Canpower could disarm all their pro-privatisation critics by doing a much better job of opening themselves to appropriate competition and new environmentally friendly technology than any fully privatised utility or set of utilities could, saving the government the risk of trying to create and then regulate private sector generation of electricity to do better. They would have to work with their regulators and both provincial and national governments, but a collaborative approach to all these players should be best for all relevant parties if Canpower could formulate an appropriate approach. Canpower could continue to do what it could do well, getting better at it where needed, but it could collaborate effectively with those who could help it do even better in some areas.

Goals planning with a capability-culture focus

Carl indicated that he had used criticisms of Canpower as a basis for discussing goals planning in terms of a redesign of Canpower's 'business model' and all other planning which flowed from this. All ongoing strategy formulation and testing for any organisation had to flow from a broadly stated 'business model' which defined the organisation's key goals and core values in terms of implied crucial operating rules and policies from the perspective of its owners *bearing in mind the interests of other parties*. 'Bearing in mind the interests of other parties' implied a broad view of the implications of actions by and pressures from all relevant players needed careful attention, not just the direct and obvious interests of their owner/customers. A key issue this broad view raised was 'privatisation risk'.

Privatisation risk was a fundamental threat to Canpower's business model, but it was only a threat because Canpower had allowed the way its business model was interpreted to become distorted by managerial preferences and employee practices which lost sight of its core purpose to a significant extent. Canpower did not need a radically different set of values, but Canpower did need to readjust corporate focus and emphasis. To this end, the board members needed to be very clear about all the key assumptions underpinning their business model, testing them for robustness, and changing them to more appropriate, robust, and resilient forms when appropriate.

In terms of a holistic take on the mantra 'if it ain't broke don't fix it', three things were badly broken and needed fixing immediately. *The public sector status of Canpower was decidedly not broken and did not need fixing. However, Canpower's capability-culture was broken in the sense that capability-culture liabilities were a direct reason for current attacks on Canpower's public sector status, the third of the three crucial flaws which he was dealing with directly that day.*

Somewhat different capability-culture liabilities also underlay Canpower's other two key flaws, *and all three of these capability-culture flaws required immediate attention, dealing directly and explicitly with interdependencies that mattered.*

Current practice compared to Carl's proposed approach so far

After discussing goals planning with a capability-culture focus, Carl indicated this was an appropriate time to compare his outlined proposed approach with current practice in Canpower and other utilities. The following subsections provide outlines of the key points which he developed in more detailed summaries for the board.

Underestimation of variability in long and medium-term forecasts and cost estimates

Canpower had well-developed top-down and bottom-up demand forecasting models, as Carl had noted earlier. Canpower used these models to make 'long-term demand forecasts' in Larry's current Canpower terminology, 'medium/long-term demand forecasts' in Carl's terminology. Carl believed these forecasts needed reframing in separate medium-term and long-term categories of planning and associated planning horizons.

Canpower currently associated these demand forecasts with confidence bands which were too narrow. They were misleadingly narrow because of the framing assumptions underlying the statistical models plus the seriously misleading assumption that exogenous explanatory variables in these models could be predicted without errors. In Carl's view, these confidence bands needed massive adjustment to make them much wider, with rapidly growing ranges the farther they extrapolated from the data period. Cost estimates associated with forecasts of energy prices and capital cost estimates had similarly narrow and unrealistic confidence bands, requiring massive increases, and important interdependencies were involved.

Rejection of robustness-driven scenario approaches

Most other electricity utilities had demand forecasting models which were comparable to but not as well developed as Canpower's. Most other electricity utilities supplemented these models by robustness-driven scenario building approaches, an approach explicitly rejected by Canpower.

The reason given by Canpower staff for rejecting robustness-driven scenario approaches was their lack of precision. One option was to believe Canpower staff and draw the conclusion that they were confusing precision and accuracy. Another option was to reject the Canpower staff explanation as a deliberate cover-up and assume that what actually motivated Canpower staff to reject of this kind of scenario approach was a misguided attempt to cling to a largely deterministic view of a very uncertain situation that they were not equipped to deal with.

There might be other explanations, but whatever the rationale, Canpower's whole approach to long-term planning was premised on the validity of narrow confidence bands for their associated demand forecast, and similarly narrow confidence bands for cost estimates and duration estimates, and neither of these premises was realistic.

Carl chose his language very carefully but made it crystal clear that Canpower staff demonstrated an unacceptably low level of competence in terms of managing uncertainty and underlying complexity in what they currently called the long-term, usefully reframed as the medium-term plus the long-term.

Estimation bias for expected values and associated error bands

Canpower's excessively narrow error bands for demand forecasts over the medium-term and long-term, similarly narrow error bands for the cost per kilowatt hour estimates for a preferred set of options, and similarly narrow error bands for project duration estimates, should be interpreted as direct evidence of optimism bias associated with potential variability. This kind of bias implied that expected value estimates were also seriously biased on the optimistic side. Interdependencies would scale up this bias, long durations and high costs for projects driving up electricity prices which would depress demand. Demand estimate expected values were much too high, while cost and duration expected value estimates were much too low. That is, excessively narrow confidence bands implied both expected outcome and associated variability estimates were consistently biased on the optimistic side, and interdependencies significantly magnified this effect.

Given these biased expected outcome estimates and biased error bands, Canpower used elaborate linear programming models to minimise the expected cost of meeting demand over the medium-term and the long-term. These models simultaneously ordered the choices in Carl's long-term planning sense and timed their start of construction in Carl's medium-term planning sense. They provided an optimal solution which involved massive new plant commitments, exclusively large nuclear power stations for base load. However, the assumptions used involved a massive expected cost estimation bias in favour of nuclear. Carl's presentation had suggested this bias mattered. He was not in a position to measure it immediately, but he would be deeply surprised if future work on estimates, which he would recommend, did not confirm it was significant.

Simply looking at realistic probability distributions for direct costs, as he had illustrated by Table 8.1 example A plus the example B and C variants, might uplift currently assumed nuclear costs per kilowatt-hour by 100% or more. Other sources of bias might make an appropriate uplift of the expected cost of nuclear power 200% or more.

Canpower's linear programming models would give an entirely different solution if expected cost estimate bias was corrected. Carl believed nuclear power stations might play no part at all in such a revised solution, although he personally believed there was an important role for nuclear power in Canpower's portfolio.

Cost risk ignored

Bias associated with expected cost estimates and associated variability at the level of individual units was just the 'tip of the iceberg' of the problems associated with the Canpower approach as a whole. Even if the biased expected costs issue was put on one side, and it was assumed that large nuclear power stations really did provide the lowest expected cost per kilowatt-hour over the long term as perceived now, if correlated cost variability and other interdependences were addressed effectively it would be obvious that to move Canpower to a predominantly nuclear portfolio of electric power sources was very risky.

The conceptual basis provided by the linear programming framework completely ignored risk in the risk efficiency sense portrayed in Figure 8.8, limiting itself to always looking for the point on the risk–reward boundary defined by point 'a' because risk–reward (risk-expected cost) trade-offs are ignored. Implicitly the Canpower approach assumed that nuclear power would remain the lowest actual cost solution over the long term *and that there was no need to worry about ANY risk associated with a Canpower portfolio of base-load power sources which was 100% nuclear, perhaps 100% one particular kind and design of large nuclear power station.*

There was no need to take such an extreme position. Most utilities used a robustness-driven scenario analysis basis to test a range of demand and cost growth scenarios, and test proposed plans for robustness against the range of 'optimal' solutions which different assumptions produce. This could be a reasonably effective approach to managing risk. However, it was not always effective and it was rarely efficient, because it does not address risk efficiency or opportunity efficiency in a direct clarity efficient manner.

Some utilities used informal portfolio analysis based approaches, which could be a considerable improvement. But in his view formally addressing all risk in a framework based on risk efficiency was crucial. It was also crucial to seek associated clarity efficiency and opportunity efficiency.

No effective integration of dependence upward concerns

Carl suggested that full consideration of uncertainty within the short-term, medium-term and long-term planning frameworks had to address important dependence upward issues currently ignored. The contribution to significant biases was part of this, but so was the exposure of Canpower to serious potential supply shortfalls. A simple iterative approach would allow them to adjust their overall plans for these upward dependence concerns.

No formal futures planning or goals planning

Formal futures planning with underlying formal goals planning omitted in Canpower's current approach in the privatisation risk sense just developed was arguably as serious as any of the other concerns addressed above. Carl left this set of issues until last and gave it less space and emphasis than it deserved simply because it was much more complex, difficult to discuss, and controversial, and he did not want to get bogged down in controversial issues until the two flaws with much clearer implications and potential fixes were discussed. In practice, Canpower should address these formal futures and goals planning issues first, as its top priority.

A summary of Canpower's current position and proposed changes discussed so far

In summary, Carl suggested that his approach would allow Canpower to start by clarifying its goals. It could then plan how to shape a desirable future and deal with hoped for possibilities as well as currently feasible options. This would provide a basis for an enhanced and very different approach to long-term planning. Having established a set of current targets at its long-term planning horizon, it could develop detailed action plans within a medium-term planning framework using quite different processes to address timing concerns in a clarity efficient manner.

Taken as a whole, this approach would allow Canpower to identify where it ought to be going first, and how best to get there second. This could be viewed as a very complex portfolio of corporate change management projects in a practical framework for addressing what was involved. A risk efficient set of feasible solutions for a range of potential demand growth patterns would be central, assessing in approximate terms a preferred mix of sources of power to aim for at the long-term horizon. Also central would be a closely coupled medium-term planning approach to minimising the cost of meeting medium-term demand fluctuations while moving in the direction of the desired balance of sources at the long-term planning horizon.

If Canpower adopted Carl's approach, it could move 'from the bottom of the class to the top of the class' in terms of industry standards in one step. What would flow from a full implementation of Carl's approach was not just a different process for making decisions. Nor was it just a different solution. It was a different kind of process and a different kind of solution. Most of the differences should be self-evident already, but some further profound differences had yet to be discussed.

Organisational separability for integrating corporate planning

Carl indicated that the board had been extremely patient through a very long initial presentation with minimal breaks, and he was conscious that minimal discussion beyond simple clarification concerns had been involved. But before he concluded, he believed it would be useful to provide a very brief introduction to how Canpower's corporate planning might be structured in operational terms to achieve full integration of all Canpower planning, introducing the simplest structure which he believed would work effectively in practice.

He began by suggesting that he had significant concerns about important features of the approach to project planning and costing taken by Pat, but he believed that he and Pat should try to resolve these concerns without radical changes to Pat's role or to his Project Planning Group approaches and structure before more significant changes were contemplated. He had in mind the kinds of changes discussed in Chapter 7. He believed it was highly likely that Pat would need replacing by somebody like Paul in a 1990s prototype form, but he did not want to be distracted by these issues that day.

He suggested that relatively minor changes associated with Dick's role and his Operations Group approaches and structure were implicit in his earlier comments, and other directors would also feel very minor less obvious effects of the overall change required.

He then indicated what he wanted to focus on briefly was the massive changes to the current role, approaches, and structure of the group reporting to Larry as Canpower's Corporate Planning Director. Without having said so directly to this point, he was sure Larry would need immediate replacing. He now wanted to lead up to saying so unequivocally, having first addressed the implications in terms of what Canpower should expect of their new Corporate Planning Director, assuming for the moment minimal changes elsewhere, and reassuring everyone but Larry to avoid them feeling threatened.

Larry currently assumed his role as Corporate Planning Director equated to what Larry called long-term planning and associated long-term forecasting. Viewed from Carl's perspective, this amounted to a focus on medium-term plus long-term planning in terms of a framework which was not fit for the purpose, based on forecasting which was interpreted in an inappropriate manner, without addressing goals planning or futures planning in the explicit way required. In addition to executing these roles differently, Larry's current role needed expansion and more than one person to deal with its oversight management in a closely integrated team, and that team needed much better integration with the areas of responsibility of all other board members.

In Carl's view it would be useful to start discussing all the necessary changes to the role of Larry's current Corporate Planning (CP) group by visualising its decomposition into four subgroups – CP1, CP2, CP3 and CP4 for that day's purposes – these subgroups could be given more appropriate labels later. Each of these subgroups would require leadership by one of four new 'Corporate Planning Managers' reporting to the person holding the new Corporate Planning Director post, with separable roles for each of these four new managers and the groups reporting them outlined in the following. This separability would not imply independence – it would serve the same kind of role as separability between the five different categories of planning portrayed by Figure 8.1.

It would then be useful to discuss the roles of two new additional Canpower executive directors with their own small supporting groups to address some of the wider implications.

CP1: Goal alignment with owners using an enhanced regional customer focus

Addressing the goals which Canpower owners were concerned about at a regional level using a customer focus in a coordinated manner seemed a sensible place to begin. For example, say they looked at one particular region involving a dozen small towns plus the surrounding rural region in a far northern part of the province. Each town might be based on producing timber or mining, with significant industrial electricity demand driven by these industries as well as some manufacturing, retail, other business and domestic demand. Some of the timber producers might use wood waste to generate some of their electricity, but this might be a minor issue. A key local concern might be the long transmission lines to this region which were vulnerable to winter storm failures, with particularly concerning implications for the regional hospital, schools, and other key services. If a Canpower planning advisor looked at Canpower customer goals for this particular region in terms of a generalised and enhanced service from Canpower, what might emerge if the opening question to a panel of local people was, 'What would local Canpower customers like from a locally focused electric power company prepared to go beyond just supplying electricity in a supportive partnership relationship?'

A local multiple-unit combined-cycle gas-fired electricity generation station whose waste heat could be used for the regional hospital and schools plus other nearby users of a community heating service might be a central proposition, reducing the impact of possible winter transmission line losses being a core aspect of the rationale. The community heating idea might be a way of making local gas-fired electricity generation cheaper as well as serving heating needs more effectively. If it made economic sense, the community heating idea might be extended to waste wood and other joint purposes like waste disposal. This electricity generation station might be owned and operated by a company owned by the community with Canpower loan funding, a third party which also provided similar facilities elsewhere, or Canpower. If Canpower did not own the station, it might still export power to the grid as and when this was optimal for the Canpower system, at cents/kWh rates tied to the cost of gas but reflecting dual use, so it was part of Canpower's gas-fired portfolio for long-term planning purposes, and its owners would not be squeezed by rising gas prices coupled to falling electricity prices or peak/base-load distinctions. Its owners might in effect be subcontracting with Canpower to operate a small scale local gas-fired power station with linked other service facilities on behalf of Canpower. But the CP1 approach to the contract could be designed to look after the best interests of the regional Canpower customers, so long as this did not disadvantage Canpower customers in other regions without acceptable trade-offs.

If a key local customer benefitting from these arrangements was a company not owned by local citizens, but this company provided local jobs, associated complications could be accommodated explicitly as simply and effectively as possible.

Other rural regions might be encouraged and assisted to develop local low-head hydropower facilities, with complementary seasonal variation in demand and supply balance implications. Major urban area regions might be very different again, with a possible focus on converting rubbish into electricity or electric powered public transportation for example.

The CP1 manager responsible for this subgroup would see his or her group's goal as serving the best interests of Canpower customers in terms of an enhanced service in each of the regions Canpower had to serve, recognising that each region might have a unique combination of issues in addition to important areas of common interest. The CP1 focus would be the best interests of those the company were serving in each region, not the details of how the other groups within the CP group as a whole might meet those needs. However, explicitly starting with goals planning followed by futures planning followed by long-term planning, this group might generate specific project propositions in conjunction with the proposed collaborators.

This is a form of bottom-up strategy formation process driven by regional 'owners as customers' concerns. Because CP1 was focused on each region's individual concerns in terms of an enhanced service for customers, satisfaction with Canpower's service to customers should be maximised by creating this new subgroup – provided this subgroup's manager held an appropriate balance of power within the CP group as a whole, and provided the CP group as a whole was competent, suitably empowered and managed in an enlightened manner.

CG2: Goal alignment with owners focused on new collaborative non-utility generation

New collaborative non-utility generation of power like that associated with specific regions identified by CP1 might be championed and prospective players encouraged and facilitated on a province wide basis by CP2, a second subgroup who might see the focus of their role as serving the needs of local community owned or third party owned electricity generation companies. CP2 might also work with third party companies who do not have specific regions in mind and might be based outside the province. These third party organisations might have specific technologies in mind, like low-head hydropower or solar or wind power, which Canpower did not currently have the expertise for. In part, the role of CP2 might be seen as looking after the best interests of citizens of the province who wanted to produce electricity. But a broader interpretation would be ensuring a level playing field for all potential providers of non-utility generation in terms of their competitive relationship with electric power generation provided directly by Canpower. And the underlying role was ensuring the best deal for Canpower owners who are electricity purchasing customers, explicitly eliminating any bias towards keeping electricity generation in-house when this was not in the best interests of owners/consumers. Explicitly starting with goals planning followed by futures planning followed by long-term planning, this group might explicitly address a portfolio approach to generic types of non-utility power, to ensure that a balanced portfolio approach to non-utility sources and power generated by Canpower. It might also generate specific projects to develop new collaborations, in conjunction with the proposed collaborators.

Because CP2 was focused on the interests of potential providers of non-utility electricity in all regions, satisfaction with Canpower's treatment of non-utility providers should be lifted to an appropriate level by creating CP2 – provided the CP2 manager held sufficient power within the CP group as a whole, and provided the CP group as a whole was competent, suitably empowered and managed in an enlightened manner.

CP3: Long-term and medium-term planning of all feasible options

CP3 would be the subgroup within the overall CP group responsible for long-term planning in portfolio terms of all feasible options as addressed earlier in this chapter, incorporating generic consideration of non-utility and conservation options as well as Canpower owned and operated electricity generation stations, plus follow-on medium-term planning incorporating new proposals generated by CP1 and CP2 and agreed by the Canpower board. CP3 would have to reflect the interactions with short-term and medium-term planning discussed earlier, the reliability/availability concerns also associated with short-term planning, and any other relevant links. Goals and futures planning would be directly relevant in terms of a strategic view of appropriate trade-offs between cost per kilowatt hour tariffs driven by a policy of minimising expected cost and associated cost risk, risks associated with security of supply for economic, political or military reasons, and concerns like sustainability or environmental implications with or without government taxation or subsidy implications.

Because CP3 was focused on the best interests of owners/customers of all regions, balancing the overall and regional concerns of the CP1 and CP2 subgroups, satisfaction with Canpower's treatment of the overall planning of all currently technically feasible options should be maximised by creating CP3 – provided the manager of CP3 held sufficient power within the CP group as a whole, and the CP group as a whole was competent, suitably empowered and managed in an enlightened manner.

CP3 should not assume that its plans or those of CP1 and CP2 would be approved by Canpower's board, but jointly sought approvals following negotiation coordinated by CP3 would be the focus of their effort.

CP4: Potentially feasible opportunity realisation and related threat neutralisation

CP4 would be responsible for goals planning and futures planning plus follow-on project proposal planning and delivery in terms of addressing the gap between what is currently feasible and economic and what might become feasible and economic given the implementation of plans for direct investment or subsidies. For example, if solar power was not currently economic, plans to help make it an economically viable future proposition might involve collaboration with a company interested in developing a manufacturing capability for the ultimate products, and it might also involve provincial or national government direct investments and subsidies.

CP4 plans would require board level testing, and funded projects would feed-back into the other three group's plans in a lagged manner, with provisions and contingency plans associated with possible outcomes when appropriate.

Goal and gateway integration and testing processes with a new director responsible

Routine corporate planning updates from CP3, plus specific project proposals from CP1, CP2 or CP4, plus any bottom-up project proposals from Dick, plus more general current Operations Group plans, all needed effective and efficient integration involving Pat and his Projects Group as appropriate. Furthermore, this coordinated portfolio of propositions needed integrated testing in preparation for oversight by the board, using a suitably developed variant of the kind of gateway structure discussed in Chapter 7.

In Carl's view, this kind of integration and testing needed a small team with suitable expertise led by a new board level director with a title indicating a 'Gateway Director' role. This integration and testing in preparation for oversight by the board should probably be extended to include proposals from other directors with comparable implications, like a new information system proposal from Canpower's Information Systems Director. Whether or not its remit included all significant Canpower changes, such a group needed to use an approach to overall goals planning and overall futures planning, plus all other forms of corporate planning reflecting the preceding discussion, to provide an operational gateway structure designed for use by the board to approve any significant changes. This was a key role which should be separated from the Corporate Planning Director's role. The person fulfilling this role would be reporting to the board with a proposed balanced portfolio of recommendations for what would amount to all change management decision making associated with Canpower electricity generation assets plus other comparable assets. They needed a degree of distance between themselves and those generating all the proposals to ensure freedom from bias. Advocates of particular proposals are usually inherently biased in favour of those proposals. The balance of power between this Gateway Director and all other directors, including the Corporate Planning Director, would be very important.

A board level manager for this gateway group, separating this function from the groups preparing proposals, would be very useful in Carl's view. He did not say so directly, but helping to avoid the acceptance of a lack of competence in *any* proposals from *any* directors was a central role for this new Gateway Director in Carl's view, with Canpower's recent approvals of proposals from Larry clearly illustrating why this was needed.

A corporate processes group with a new director responsible

The four Corporate Planning Director's subgroups plus the new Gateway Director's group discussed earlier were all focused on planning the operation, renewal and extension of electricity generation and transmission assets, other comparable assets, and associated plan testing processes.

To achieve their goals these groups all needed appropriate people with the right skills and knowledge, and these people needed to be provided with all the appropriate processes if they do not bring them with them as part of their toolset.

Canpower and most other organisations did not have a Corporate Processes Director. Carl suggested that Canpower needed one, with an initial mandate to redesign the processes needed to implement the revised approach to corporate planning this chapter has outlined, working with Canpower's Human Resources Director to recruit the people needed to help develop and implement all the new processes. External consultants should be used whenever this was the most effective and efficient way forward, but in-house expertise needed well-planned personnel selection, development and retention, and overall management in a coordinated manner by a suitably capable and empowered board level manager seemed a sensible working assumption from Carl's perspective.

Concluding comments about the Corporate Planning Group

In Carl's view, none of Larry's current staff group should be replaced until it became clear that specific replacements would be necessary, but he anticipated a major transformation, and he did not see how any of his proposed changes could proceed with Larry still in post.

Carl finished his presentation on this note, put as tactfully but clearly as he could, apart from a brief closing summary.

Limited inferences instead of further developments for this tale

A plausible Canpower board reaction to Carl's presentation is highly debatable, and for a number of reasons attempting to conclude this tale with an outcome relevant to the 2020s and beyond in a wide range of contexts did not seem a useful strategy. However, briefly consider some of the additional advice that I would be inclined to offer Clive, the Canpower board chairman, if he had your understanding of EP as discussed so far in this book. Assume that you and Carl might be a part of this conversation, and both you and Clive might be interested in how the ideas discussed so far in this chapter relate to organisations other than Canpower.

A useful starting point might be interpreting the UP of Figure 2.1 as the overall guide to the analysis structure adopted by Carl, the basic SPP of Figure 7.2 and the rest of the SP for projects as an additional supporting more focused operational and conceptual framework for managing change. From this perspective, with the 'context – including all other plans' in mind, the impact of the 'capture the context' opening phase of the UP is clearly visible in Figure 8.1.

For any organisation, a top-down view of the role of the Corporate Planning Director in the Figure 8.1 framework might reasonably start with clarification of the owners' goals and then planning a desirable future from the perspective of the organisation's owners, drawing on the seven Ws framework of Figure 7.1, and using a suitable variant of the overall four Fs concept. This implies taking into account the relevant views and concerns of customers for the basic service currently provided whether or not they are also 'owners'. It also implies taking into account competitors, suppliers, employees, regulators, and other relevant interested parties and working with a separability structure which suits the nature of the different interests involved.

With his identification of a separable CP1 group with a manager given appropriate power, Carl was suggesting that goals planning ought to start with Canpower owners – citizens of the province – with a focus on their closely coupled role as electricity customers, decomposed region by region to ensure that a local perspective is given due weight, including an important potential creative influence. Carl was suggesting that the past Canpower failure to effectively respond to the best interests of their owners as customers with needs which were specific to where they lived was a crucial *board level* failure. It was arguably directly attributable to Larry, but it had been inappropriately tolerated by the board as a whole. Canpower needed a much more effective way to address its owners' best interests as domestic supply customers, employees of local firms using electric power, and users of local services requiring electric power, recognising that there may be important differences in different geographical regions as well as important commonalities.

There was no need for Canpower to get directly involved in running small gas-fired local electricity stations providing linked heating and other related local services if this was not economic for all Canpower owners/customers, but facilitating a better overall solution at no extra cost to other Canpower owners/customers should be part of Canpower's agenda if regions wanted this additional dimension to the role played by Canpower. It might not be convenient for Larry or some other Canpower employees to bother, and Larry might prefer to interpret private power producers as unwelcome competition rather than as part of a big team. But that was one of the key reasons for replacing Larry immediately, and for making the CP1 manager part of his replacement package.

To link this CP1 rationale to a private sector example using the Astro tale of Chapter 6, the sensitivity of Sian's Systems group to outsourcing some of their roles was directly comparable to outsourcing some electric power generation. Furthermore, the roles of Trevor and Martha within Astro were comparable in 'customer-facing dialogue' terms in some respects. However, Astro did not need to link this to Astro owners (shareholders) in the same way, and the comparison cannot be pushed too far.

What Carl was doing with his identification of a partially separable CP2 group with a manager given appropriate power was suggesting competitors might be a nuisance for Larry and some other Canpower employees, just as external providers in competition with Systems within Astro Wales were a concern for Sian and her Systems staff. However, if they provided better value for Canpower owners/customers than Canpower, they needed to be encouraged and protected by a suitably empowered Canpower manager, a role Rhys took on in the Astro context. A level playing field was essential, but not enough in itself. Astro's friendly takeover of a supplier faced by a hostile takeover illustrated the kind of enlightened self-interest the manager of CP2 might advocate. This might raise important concerns for Canpower employees, who might see outsourcing their jobs as a direct threat requiring union action. However, this concern needed management in the context of the overriding need to serve Canpower owners/customers. The unions should be respected, but they should not be allowed to wield inappropriate power. When I observed the outsourcing in IBM UK which inspired the Astro approach which Martha took, IBM colleagues were very concerned, as should be expected for the employees of any large and successful organisation which needed to restructure to cope with a changing environment, be it in the private sector or the public sector. It is not an issue specific to public sector organisations, unless they have excessively powerful trade unions which need better management by the organisation's board. Supervision of board appointments by a government which understands the nuances of these kinds of issues is a closely coupled concern.

What Carl was doing with his identification of a partially separable CP3 group with a manager given appropriate power was suggesting that the new options generated by CP1 and CP2 which were approved jointly or separately within overall Canpower goals planning, futures planning, long-term planning plus medium-term planning, needed effective integrated treatment by a group capable of the kind of approaches he had outlined earlier. This kind of planning was not discussed in an Astro context. However, a very different but comparable variant clearly had a role in a broader view of Astro operations and corporate planning at Astro UK and Astro Inc board level.

What he was doing with his identification of a partially separable CP4 group with a manager given appropriate power was suggesting that new technology developments leading to expenditure related to currently non-feasible options required separate encouragement and facilitation, avoiding distracting or confusing those concerned with planning in the CP1–3 sense. However, when appropriate, the long-term, medium-term and short-term planning processes for feasible options needed contingency plans in place to capitalise on successful new technology developments. Part of the focus of the CP4 group might be new business model developments in collaboration with other parties, like working with urban centres on waste incineration to produce electric power and using the power for local transport to reduce emissions, as well as costs and congestion.

What he was doing with his identification of two additional board level directors – a Gateway Director and a Corporate Processes Director – was arguing that implementing the overall changes that Canpower needed to make required two further roles which did not simply replace tasks Larry arguably should have been doing. These roles were outside the current Corporate Planning Director's role, and they should remain outside the future Corporate Planning Director's role.

What he was doing with his identification of the partially separable CP1–4 groupings plus the two additional directors and their supporting groups was suggesting that the Canpower overall corporate planning process needed separability (not independence) for these different roles, facilitating the separate 'creation of plans' to address all the relevant concerns and their integration, because different kinds of issues are involved. The same rationale underlay the separation of goals planning, futures planning, long-term planning, medium-term planning, and short-term planning.

These assumptions of separability did not mean these considerations were truly separable and could be treated independently. It did mean they needed separate pre-integration treatment which adopted different framework structures and goals to achieve an effective and efficient understanding of different issues before they were considered jointly. For example, long-term planning which addressed an optimal mix of currently feasible sources of electric power at the 20 year horizon needed an analytical framework which was very different from the framework required by medium-term planning to construct new electricity generation stations and then bringing them on-stream in conjunction with maintaining and retiring existing plants. Using the same framework for considering both at the same time might be feasible in principle, but it was not clarity efficient in practice, requiring more effort for less clarity at best. Producing seriously misleading results if inappropriate framing or working assumptions were adopted was a serious threat, as illustrated by Larry's approach, which was inappropriate for both long-term and medium-term planning. Short-term planning was different again, as were futures planning and goals planning. The CP1–4 structure plus two new directors with supporting groups just extends the use of this 'operational separability' concept *without* assuming independence, explicitly addressing coordination via iterative approaches to full integration.

Building on this initial discussion of the role of separability, the need for separate SPs plus the separate use of UP concept features leading to processes not developed in this book might be useful. For example, the application of Soft Systems and other soft OR approaches in a strategic planning context has enjoyed considerable success, and a wide range of other very different approaches to top-down organisational planning contexts might be integrated into a common broad framework.

Building on this further, a more general conversation about the role of the Corporate Process Director and the Gateway Director plus their groups might be useful. Without these two additional directors plus their groups, directors like Larry can attempt to build walls around separate empires which can prove seriously dysfunctional. One of the many very useful roles these two new groups might serve is effectively testing the clarity efficiency and the associated risk–reward trade-offs plus other goal trade-offs for all corporate processes, not just those associated with Corporate Planning. Helping to build the bridges needed to reach across the gaps created by separability working assumptions and avoid separate silo effects is a crucial role which both these new groups might help to fulfil in any organisation's context, whatever the nature of the business being pursued, regardless of its public or private sector status.

The need to effectively and efficiently test all proposed corporate changes via gateway process structures might be another useful area for focused general discussion. The need for an explicit focus on bias as part of this could be very important. This is about required features of specific decisions, not processes in general terms, although specific gateway processes would need development and ongoing testing with feedback. This is where the goal programming framework associated with multiple test approaches to discounted cash flow analysis discussed in Chapter 7 intersect with the goals planning framework discussed in this chapter, further intersecting with the discussion to follow in Chapter 9.

Goals planning and futures planning each need leadership and coordination, with specific people given coordinator roles but a wide range of Canpower staff involved. What the Gateway Director and supporting group needed to do is distil what might be thought of as 'the current corporate business model' as approved by the board, operating gateway processes to test all proposed changes to Canpower's current operations and explain the implications to the board. Apart from approving some of the recommendations and rejecting others, the board needs to consider adjusting the corporate business model when appropriate.

At a more specific level, if I were advising Clive in the 1990s or now, I would start by stressing that Clive was very clever suspecting the need for change as soon as he arrived as the new Canpower chairman of the board, praise the way he insisted on Ivor exploring what needed doing as an opening move, and support everything Carl had said. But I would then suggest that Clive and the rest of the board were going to have to be both seriously clever and exceptionally brave to make the significant changes outlined by Carl without serious mishaps, despite the very clear need to fix what was obviously broken.

I would emphatically acknowledge the importance of the 'if it ain't broke don't fix it' line of holistic thinking, but suggest that I fully agreed with Carl that Larry has to go with immediate effect, and Pat needed to be put on notice that keeping his job depended on rapid changes as advised by Carl. There was a very good case for suggesting that Pat should go immediately too, an important issue. Everybody else did need clear assurance their jobs should be safe assuming they could rise to the overall changes necessary.

Carl could be offered the new Corporate Processes Director role, at least on an acting basis as a short-term plan. Getting his agreement to take on this role before he made the presentation just outlined, or making sure someone else who could take on this job could be recruited, would seem prudent if not essential.

Clive might want to take on the role of Gateway Director on an initial interim basis, with immediate effort given to finding a suitable person to initially help him, develop and shape the role, and then take over the role.

Carl and the Canpower board were going to need the direct assistance of an additional director in charge of the corporate change process – preferably someone like Paul from

Chapter 7 with additional relevant change management experience. Their long-term role could be seen as comparable to a long-term role Paul might aspired to within WSL, with a Corporate Projects Director label. Pat or the individual taking Pat's place might then become one of several programmes directors reporting to the Corporate Projects Director with responsibilities in specific areas, like electricity generation and distribution assets, information system assets, and so on.

The Corporate Processes Director could use a UP concept plus SP for projects concepts plus a wide range of further SP concepts, plus any other compatible approaches or the equivalents, as a basis for developing the processes needed within each of the corporate planning groups. Each of these groups might need very different approaches, but one overall supporting process development group with a rich mix of different talents and skills would clearly be valuable.

The person replacing Larry as Corporate Planning Director obviously needed extensive knowledge and experience relevant to this post. I make no pretence of being competent to judge what this should include. However, they and a new Gateway Director and Corporate Processes Director plus Clive clearly need to be aligned in their views.

Carl's advice might not be taken in the sense that Clive might not prepared to agree to with Carl's presentation in the first place and then argue that the board needed to act on it and ensure that he won the argument. It is certainly easy to see why someone in Clive's position might feel the propositions put by Carl were too radical, or the board as a whole might not be convinced. For a start, Carl's propositions imply that Canpower's staff numbers might shrink significantly if outsourcing some electric power generation and other current in-house roles took off without compensating growth in other activities, implying the risk that all directors and senior managers might face salaries shrinking in real and relative terms if not in actual terms.

However, my working assumption when drafting this chapter was that a government in charge of a publicly owned company like Canpower *should* be capable of appointing a new chairman of its board who *would* want to act in the best interests of the citizens he or she serves, they *should* have the required competence and passion, and suitable incentives for all key staff *could* be engineered by a competent senior management team. Given these assumptions, all the changes suggested were a reasonable basis for discussion, without assuming that you or anyone else is going to be 100% convinced about all aspects now or later, including the likelihood that current and near future political realities make these assumptions as robust as most of us would wish them to be.

A brief exploration of the implications of context differences

The implications for Canpower of grasping all the feasible opportunities available and neutralising all the relevant threats could be quite profound. For example, Canpower might transition from a traditional public sector electricity generator and distributor which was heavily criticised for a range of reasons and at risk of privatisation into a reinvigorated national treasure involved in the operation of a portfolio of businesses which included waste disposal via incineration, community heating and electrically powered public urban transportation in addition to providing low cost electricity for provincial businesses and consumers. Doing so might involve a range of collaborative arrangements and a variety of new ventures. It might also involve outsourcing some current in-house operations. The overall approach might ensure that provincial ownership was a matter of ongoing pride and satisfaction for all its citizens, with no serious legitimate complaints about its operations which did not get resolved.

One obvious issue is the extent to which this kind of significant potential transformation might be feasible for other organisations in very different contexts if they used appropriate variants of some of the approaches considered in this chapter. But a more general question is, 'To what extent are the conceptual and operational tools explored in the very special Canpower context portable?'

If we start with the framework provided by Figure 8.1 and its five categories of planning (goals, futures, long-term, medium-term, and short-term) in four planning horizons, some variant of this approach would seem essential for all organisations operating in the private or public sector, and all of the key features look essential in most contexts. For example, failing to be very clear about how the goals of an organisation's owners relate to those of other relevant parties and the goals–plans structure for all four other categories of top-down corporate planning including a 'designing a desirable future' aspect of futures planning could cripple any organisation if associated risks were realised and important opportunities missed. Any aspect of this framework which was broken would seem to be in need of fixing. All associated capability-culture liabilities needing attention would seem to be an issue for any organisation, and most organisations might find scope for improvements in performance using this starting point for a reflective analysis review.

If we relate this to the need for separability to facilitate different people working in different groups in order to use some different conceptual and operational tools with a clear understanding that independence is not involved, and an iterative approach is needed to accommodate upwards, downwards, and sideways dependencies, again this seems universally applicable. Silos need avoiding, as everything is interdependent to some extent, but suitable working assumptions about separability need to be made and the operational implications tested to ensure effective and efficient functioning.

Also very general is the need for everyone involved understanding the role of diversification to reduce some forms of risk in a risk efficient manner and select risk–reward trade-offs which are suitable. This may not relate to major long-life capital investments like the portfolio of hydro, nuclear, thermal, and other sources of electric power decisions faced by Canpower. But diversification may be an issue in futures planning contexts involving research and development, or in terms of product ranges, product types, geographical markets, and input component sources, for example. Different contexts may require very different use of the formal operational tools provided by a flexible HAT framework, or just conceptual use of these frameworks for informal planning. However, ignoring issues of this kind may be risky, and not being capable of considering them effectively may be incompetent. Furthermore, this diversification concern usually needs to be balanced with the benefits of a clear focus on doing what an organisation does best, 'sticking to the knitting' in some people's jargon when the fashion for diversification via conglomerates ran out of steam – as many fashions do.

The role of 'balanced targets' which are not expected outcomes because of asymmetric penalty functions is a core component of the very basic ABCs of targets concept, conveniently explored with an illustrative numerical example in this chapter, but potentially relevant in all organisations in all contexts.

The scope for very high levels of optimistic bias driven by asymmetric probability distributions with very long tails if all relevant uncertainty is not considered appropriately is also relevant in most organisations in many different aspects of their operations. The need to illustrate its importance using numerical illustrations will come up again in the safety context of the next chapter, but it also underlies many other operations management contexts and many project management contexts.

9 Building well-founded trust about complex concerns – a railway safety example

This chapter addresses complex concerns deliberately avoided in Chapters 5 to 8 which need to be confronted before completing Part 2. The central concern considered is the conceptual and operational toolset and mindset needed to develop well-founded trust between different parties with different perspectives on complex concerns needing formal planning. The trust issues addressed in this chapter are particularly demanding in terms of the need to avoid the wrong kind of simplicity but leverage the benefits delivered by the right kind of simplicity.

A central feature of the tale used in this chapter is addressing potential catastrophes in an enlightened manner at a high level of clarity. 'Catastrophe' is used in the plain English sense of a very high negative impact incident which *may* have a very low probability and *may* have implications which go well beyond financial concerns. From an EP perspective, *all* potential catastrophes need to be approached using plausible worst-case scenarios defined with a particularly carefully considered systematic approach to achieving simplicity. Being especially careful to achieve the right kind of simplicity in a potential catastrophic context is enlightened because the wrong kind of simplicity matters much more than usual. However, the approach to developing well-founded trust used in this chapter's tale requires conceptual and operational tools which can be useful even if the kind of very high negative impact catastrophic outcomes initially addressed are not an issue – they have important implications and areas of application that are much wider than starting to read this chapter may initially suggest.

A defining feature of this chapter's approach to potential catastrophes is using a scenario-based approach to explicitly confronting both the extreme events associated with catastrophes and a full range of related but less serious intermediate events. The difficult trade-off concerns all these scenarios may give rise to is addressed using a practical holistic top-down framing assumption perspective which avoids common practice restrictive assumptions. The rationale for the approach as a whole includes avoiding inappropriate optimistic bias and eliminating serious blind spots, coping with very complex interdependencies, facilitating a 'big team' approach led by board members with strategic clarity who are supported effectively by all other relevant players, and the need to earn and maintain well-founded trust from different parties with very different perspectives working within a formal planning framework everyone involved can understand with appropriate clarity.

Defining features of the context are always crucial. Safety concerns in a railway system require planning approaches which confront a usefully rich set of complexities that need attention by a range of different people with different concerns. It is also a usefully simple context in some respects, which helps to keep the discussion as simple as possible before attempting to generalise to other contexts where different kinds of complexity are important.

Additional significant analysis complexity associated with concerns like extensive oil pollution or nuclear contamination is addressed briefly in the last section of this chapter. Quite different security issues which involve comparable concerns in some respects are also considered briefly in the last section, using cybersecurity as an example. Exceedingly complex political or military goals may be relevant if complete generalisation is considered.

A central part of the experience base for the tale of this chapter was a strategic level review of Railtrack's approach to safety for the UK railway system undertaken in the late 1990s. Views about relevant approaches were significantly updated and revised using a much more general conceptual and operational framework initially developed over the period 2010–13 for the UK MoD. The MoD work involved consulting support for the development of an operational procedure for the MoD to justify high levels of expenditure on a portfolio of approaches to preventing and mitigating the implications of low probability but potentially very high-impact non-conventional weapon attacks on British troops, given broader NATO airing subsequently. A number of other relevant background studies shaped some of the ideas, mentioned when directly relevant. What proved crucial was being forced to look for practical and robust new simplifications in order to cope with new complexities associated with the MoD context, followed by a period of reflection supported by feedback from colleagues.

A key feature of this chapter's approach is a formal acknowledgement that the nature of the relevant decisions and objectives means that the issues being addressed cannot be considered as separable 'add-ons' to operations or project plans at a tactical level. The nature of relevant objectives and the scale of potential impacts mean that both safety and security *must* be seen as a fully integrated 'designed-in' feature of corporate planning for operations and project planning concerns at a corporate strategy level. One implication is that this chapter's approach has to build on the framework developed in the last chapter, following instead of preceding it for expository reasons. We are dealing with a form of '*enterprise* opportunity, risk, uncertainty and underlying complexity management', but the approach advocated should not be confused with ERM as this term is usually interpreted.

The central role for fatalities as a core metric in the railway safety context of this chapter means that the number of people killed in railway incidents is one key basic metric which is unambiguously of central importance. However, injuries with a wide range of degrees of severity are also extremely important, and trade-offs between all key metrics, including cost and revenue measures, have implications which are inherently ambiguous.

One significant aspect of railway system accidents is the very wide range of numbers of people who might be killed or injured in a single incident. Small numbers of people are frequently killed or injured, perhaps several hundred per annum; 30 or 40 fatalities in a single incident is not a rare event, perhaps every other decade on average; and very large numbers of people might be killed or injured in very low probability incidents of a kind not yet experienced, perhaps not yet even contemplated, with a return period expectation like once every 1,000 years. The railway system examples which are central to this chapter address 'incidents' which include both accidents and malicious attacks.

Deciding whether to make strategic changes to a railway system with safety and security implications in the framework developed in this chapter requires board level leadership. It involves operational decision making which needs attention in the gateway processes discussed in Chapters 7 and 8. This means key strategic decisions must be part of the top-down strategic management processes addressing all issues relevant to corporate strategy, building on the frameworks developed in all earlier chapters.

The nature of the competing objectives involved means that attribute value trade-offs central to this chapter involve very different attributes (like fatalities, injuries, and financial costs), and very different perspectives on values associated with these trade-offs (like those of railway passengers and those of private sector railway company shareholders). This, in turn, means that trust is a core issue. An organisation's owners, employees, customers, and regulators need a robustly grounded basis for well-founded trust in the decisions made. Trust which can be assumed to be well founded invariably depends on corporate ethics as well as corporate competence. It may also depend on many other factors, like media responses to incidents and the way information is managed by regulators.

This book argues that all the relevant parties have a particularly strong need for a shared common basis for dialogue because their perspectives are so different and trust is so important. This makes designing a formal planning framework and using it for associated management decision making inherently very difficult, but that does not excuse not addressing the really difficult central issues with an enlightened level of competence. It simply makes finding an appropriate framework for effective dialogue about answers to the right questions more important, arguably essential. Furthermore, *any* relevant party that does not have well-founded trust needs to take decisive and effective remedial steps, reinforcing the need for widespread understanding of the central issues. In the context of a railway company, its contractors and subcontractors, this includes *all* relevant company board members, plus other employees associated with safety and security concerns, passengers, railway company shareholders, regulators, and governments.

When seeking simplicity, avoiding becoming confused by the wrong kind of simplicity is always important – clarity inefficiency involving seriously inappropriate assumptions can be very costly. Clarity efficiency concerns explored in Chapter 5 were at their simplest. This chapter's clarity efficiency concerns are unavoidably complex – the most complex addressed in this book. This is a central part of the rationale for deferring addressing them until the final chapter of Part 2.

This chapter has been written to provide those who are not safety and security experts with an accessible basis for deciding what really matters in terms of the overall approaches to complex trust concerns appropriate for their organisations. If safety and security are not part of your current responsibilities, much of this chapter's more technical discussion can be read without too much attention to the detail, so long as you develop a reasonable feel for 'what needs to be done'. However, selected specific technical issues which are contentious, and the reasons why associated differences in opinion matter, are discussed in this chapter because strategic clarity matters to all those who are not experts but have to live with the consequences of expert judgements. That includes *all* target readers for this book in terms of their roles as citizens and consumers, as well as their current or potential roles in terms of contributing to management decision making.

The primary readership target for this chapter is board level managers in private and public sector organisations, plus the regulators and politicians who influence their approaches, plus those aspiring to these roles. It is not aimed directly at safety or security experts or ERM experts. Nevertheless, the material of this chapter should be of direct interest to the professional safety and security community and the ERM community, and I certainly hope it will be.

Anyone even considering aspiring to board levels of responsibility, plus those involved in direct supporting and regulating roles, should find it useful to understand *all* the issues explored in this chapter at an overview what needs to be done level. This includes the very complex nature of the interconnected set of controversial issues which no doubt will continue to surround safety and other contexts associated with potentially catastrophic incidents for the foreseeable future.

Some of the key issues are *relatively* straightforward to deal with – like how should an organisation approach the framing of safety and security as a top-down strategic consideration fully integrated with the top-down and bottom-up treatment of all other strategic concerns. This is addressed in reasonably straightforward terms near the outset. However, other issues of central importance are relatively complex. Of particular importance, these more complex concerns include what *should* we mean by 'risk efficiency', 'enlightened caution', 'enlightened gambles' and 'enlightened prudence' which embraces a safety and security context when ethics and well-founded trust are crucial and 'revealed preferences' are central concerns, and how do we make these concepts operational in a robust but tolerably simple practical manner. Although these issues are of central importance, they are not addressed in a direct manner until towards the end of the chapter because providing requisite clarity involves building on earlier illustrative numerical examples and discussion in a layered manner.

Significant departures from conventional approaches to safety management include:

1   a holistic top-down approach to extreme and low-level and related intermediate-level incidents, with an initial focus on the extreme end of the range;
2   addressing 'risk' in terms of the full implications of departures from expectations in addition to expected outcomes, using a risk efficiency framework as for all other management decision making in an EP framework;
3   understanding the full implications of an opportunity efficiency view of concerns like clarifying the difference between good luck and good management, bad luck and bad management, and requisite enlightened prudence when very large numbers of people might be killed or injured with very low probabilities of this occurring;
4   employing an 'avoided fatality' concept with shadow price and revealed preference implications which are of crucial importance and need widespread understanding, including understanding why a common value independent of the number of people involved may appropriate in some contexts but not in other contexts;
5   a major clarity efficiency improvement which can deliver *much more* clarity at a *much lower* level of cost and effort, driven by the insight that considering potential fatalities in conjunction with correlated injuries plus physical damage to the system plus all other correlated impacts whenever scenarios involving fatalities are addressed delivers a game-changing increase in clarity efficiency; and
6   using the approach to point 5 to clarify what the process of earning and maintaining trust between all relevant parties in very complex contexts must involve.

Context and main characters

Only two named characters play a central role in this chapter's tale:

Oscar, the operations director of a railway company;
Sophie, a corporate safety manager hired by Oscar.

Sophie was an experienced management consultant who worked throughout Europe from her base in Copenhagen when she accepted an assignment to help Oscar rescue Northern European Railways (NER) from a crisis triggered by a major railway accident in 2013.

NER is a fictitious private sector organisation which owns and manages all aspects of a national railway network. NER is *not* a real company, and the country NER is located in is *not* Denmark. Both these points are explicitly emphasised because all the fictions involved in this tale are grounded on real cases which it would be inappropriate to discuss without unambiguous changes in context. This chapter will use US dollar monetary units in a European country throughout, in part to emphasise the maintenance of a deliberately fictionalised status for NER in a simple and convenient manner.

Sophie had 20 years of experience over a broad range of topics and contexts. Strategic change leadership on safety and security management was Sophie's current passion. The connecting thread in her career development was the routine use of her variant of the UP of Figure 2.1 to develop specific models and interpret the results creatively in the tradition illustrated by the tale of Chapter 5. Sometimes the creative interpretations led to an SP in the tradition illustrated by the tale of Chapter 6. Sophie used project management approaches including generic processes as discussed in Chapter 7, and she had attended the 2012 IPMA (International Project Management Association) Copenhagen advanced training workshop *Managing project risk, uncertainty and value in new ways* based on Chapman and Ward (2011). However, Sophie had never seen herself as a project management professional. She regarded project management as just one of the many toolsets needed for all her consulting roles. She had attended other courses provided by a wide range of other organisations on a comprehensive range of operations and corporate management topics, including corporate strategic planning, with a current focus on safety and security.

Oscar was an experienced and senior member of the Operations Group of NER when an accident in 2013 killed 40 people and injured several times that number. Two years earlier 30 people had been killed and more than 100 injured in another incident. The second accident triggered a corporate crisis, in part because most of the population of NER's country believed that two serious accidents in two years were unlikely to be just bad luck. The initiating fault for the first incident was a signalling malfunction, leading to a front-to-rear collision between one train travelling at the lower end of a 'medium speed range' and a stationary train on the same track. The initiating fault for the second incident was a track maintenance failure, leading to a higher end of medium speed derailment with the train falling down an embankment. Any maintenance failure was a matter of negligence for some people. For about a month after the second incident, the Operations Director of NER struggled to contain the fallout from these two incidents, with support from his board. However, knock-on operations problems and media pressure eventually led to both the Operations Director and the Head of Safety 'resigning'. Oscar became the new Operations Director on the same day. Oscar immediately asked Sophie to become his new Head of Safety. She had started work the following week on a short-term contract for a trial period.

Oscar had attended the same 2012 IPMA Copenhagen advanced training workshop as Sophie. Like Sophie, he regarded project management as just one of the many toolsets he needed. He had been seriously impressed by Sophie's approach to a case study (Transcon, based on the tale in Chapter 6 in this book), but the reason for appointing Sophie Head of Safety was a conversation in the bar after the case study session. Sophie had asked Oscar about his role within NER. As part of his response Oscar had explained his frustration with the NER board because they had turned down his proposal for a new generation signalling system before the first incident, caused by a signalling malfunction, and there had been ongoing procrastination about a new signalling system despite the incident. Oscar had then asked about Sophie's current work as a simple matter of reciprocating interest in a convivial conversation. He had been deeply impressed when she described recently completed work for the defence research section of Oscar's country's armed forces. Sophie had explained why her defence work was directly relevant to railway safety decisions like Oscar's signalling system example, and he saw the connection immediately. He hired Sophie to help him transform the safety aspects of his role as Operations Director of NER.

Oscar had initially assumed that Sophie would start with the track maintenance issues underlying the second accident and the ongoing signalling system issues. However, she quickly persuaded him that they had to start with much more fundamental concerns.

A few weeks after Sophie joined NER, Oscar held an extended workshop for the NER board. He used this workshop to introduce Sophie, ask her to explain how she would set about transforming the NER approach to safety, generate initial feedback, and make sure that he had board support for the radical programme of changes which he and Sophie now envisaged.

Generalised foundations for NER safety and security

Oscar began his workshop by indicating that the basic foundations of NER approaches to safety and security had to change radically. This would have to include board level corporate decision-making process changes and linked corporate culture changes. The board had a key leadership role in this transformation. The workshop that day had to communicate why, and an overview of what was involved.

Oscar said he had hired Sophie as Head of Safety for NER because he was convinced that she was the best person available. He observed that Sophie had accepted this post for a trial period on a short-term contract. He might have added that the trial period was a condition of Sophie's. From Sophie's perspective, the NER board were on trial, not Sophie. But he thought it best to let the board come to this realisation themselves. Oscar did stress that both he and Sophie were convinced that radical changes, starting at the board level, were essential, and if he and Sophie were going to resolve NER's current crisis board, feedback from today's workshop which was positive 'on balance' was also essential.

Oscar then outlined Sophie's credentials to the board before turning the meeting over to her. He emphasised the broad nature and importance of her current work for the defence research section of their country's armed forces, but also indicated her limited experience with railways.

'As low as reasonably practicable' (ALARP) as a starting point

Sophie began by reminding the board that the generally accepted starting point for the management of safety in their country was the risk of death or injury should be 'as low as reasonably practicable' (ALARP), and broadly comparable approaches were widely employed in the rest of the world. She asserted there was nothing contentious about this until you asked 'What *exactly* does "*reasonably practicable*" mean?'

Many safety professionals saw this issue in a legal framework, and some might begin with the practicability comments in what she believed was the original court judgement using this term by Lord Justice Asquith in the UK case of Edwards v National Coal Board 1949:

> 'Reasonably practicable' is a narrower term than 'physically possible' and seems to me to imply that a computation must be made by the owner, in which the quantum of risk is placed on one scale and the sacrifice involved in the measures necessary for averting the risk (whether in money, time or trouble) is placed in the other; and that if it be shown that there is a gross disproportion between them – the risk being insignificant in relation to the sacrifice – the defendants discharge the onus on them. Moreover, this computation falls to be made by the owner at a point of time anterior to the accident.

A large international body of safety experts had developed a rich body of relevant knowledge over many years. This knowledge base had to be applied in a coherent and comprehensive way to address this question effectively. Some of this body of knowledge addressed broader issues than NER had to face, including environmental risk and associated health risk.

Reports on the widely reported 2010 BP Macondo oil well blowout accident in the Gulf of Mexico by the US-based Centre for Catastrophic Risk Management (CCRM, 2011) outlined key lessons learned which echo many earlier reports in many different countries, as explained in more recent reviews. Viewing these reports and the wider global literature collectively, it was crystal clear that many of the crucial underlying issues had been understood, at least, in part, for many years, but they had not yet been fully grasped in a holistic manner by all those directly responsible for practice. This raised some very complex issues, including the necessary corporate strategy aspects of addressing potential catastrophic risks in conjunction with what were increasingly referred to as 'corporate culture' issues.

A central issue which NER had to address could be linked directly to a quote from the final CCRM (2011) report – 'It has been observed that "*BP forgot to be afraid*"'. In her view, *NER had never learned to be afraid*, and addressing this had to be a starting point. They needed to use their initial meeting to start to explore what needed to be done to deal with a plausible maximum level catastrophic risk incident, *plus* all related incidents involving relatively low and intermediate levels of related risk, using a systematic framework for asking the right questions in a practical way which was creative and optimistic in a realistic manner.

Her recent work addressing the safety of soldiers in terms of non-conventional weapon attacks, including large scale attacks on their bases, suggested that understanding the implications of a coherent and enlightened approach to all the stealth assumptions associated with key aspects of common practice provided new insights which NER needed, starting at the board level. She would first outline, in just a matter of minutes, some of the key NER concerns involved at a *very* high overview level (the remaining few subsections in this section).

To demonstrate the level of impact implied by her proposed changes in approach, she would then (in the following section) briefly outline one example of the very different NER strategy which might result from this approach. She would next (in another section) address a relatively simple context, using her proposed approach in a simple form, to provide an example of catastrophically bad management of safety issues in conjunction with conventional good practice management of directly related concerns, both interpreted in the best practice EP framework she was proposing. This would illustrate the basis of some key aspects of her approach in fairly simple terms. These two brief discussions (the next two sections) would be followed by filling in some of the key aspects of the detail of her proposed approach (an extensive series of sections), using a more sophisticated version of her basic initial framework and illustrative numerical examples so they could gradually build a layered understanding of how she believed they ought to proceed at a what needs to be done level, the main body of her presentation (and this chapter). She would finish by making a number of observations on what she believed should be the next steps.

A holistic base-case model set using a carefully structured top-down perspective

The starting point for an NER approach to ALARP had to be a '*holistic* base-case model set' which captured their railway system's current safety and security status with strategic clarity. In Sophie's view there was no alternative. This was a central aspect of replacing their current 'add-on' approach to safety by a fully integrated 'designed-in' approach to safety in terms of both accidents in the usual safety management sense and security in terms of malicious incidents comparable to accidents. She made this point forcefully and emphasised that this foundation level framing assumption change implied a mindset shift and a culture shift which she believed they would soon understand clearly and respond to positively, with follow-on toolset changes which were complex and would take longer to digest.

The purpose of this base-case model set would be to inform the assessment of *all* planned or imposed changes to the NER system with potential safety or security implications. Some potential changes to the NER system might be initiated by the safety team, to improve safety and security. However, the majority of the changes needing assessment would be suggested by others, to improve operational efficiency and profitability, like bigger or faster trains. Furthermore, some changes would be externally imposed, like new evidence that a key subcontractor could no longer be trusted or new information about increased terrorist activity threat levels.

The effect of Sophie's approach would be full integration of safety and security concerns with all other relevant issues at a corporate strategy level whenever this was relevant. Additionally, the proposed approach would provide a framework for integrated top-down and bottom-up safety and security planning for NER. She would emphasise the top-down perspective today, but full integration with bottom-up planning was crucial.

This holistic base-case model set would use a set of 'incident' scenarios which had to be addressed. She would use the word *incident* instead of *accident* for two reasons. The primary reason was NER needed to consider malicious acts and accidents *simultaneously in the same framework* because the effects of malicious acts may be directly comparable to the effects of accidents and the most effective preventative or mitigating responses may involve common issues. The importance of understanding *any* differences in causation could also be crucial when relevant, but this did not diminish the need for joint consideration of *some* responses to comparable incidents caused accidentally or maliciously. A secondary reason was that for some purposes it was convenient to consider 'near misses' as incidents using a very general interpretation. Near misses were an example of a form of highly relevant information which clearly needed consideration and sophisticated subjective probability perspectives.

For assessment to be complete, the set of incident scenarios addressed had to be exhaustive, with no blind spots. Furthermore, when addressing these scenarios, it was crucial to address all sources of uncertainty, including systemic uncertainty, making effective provisions for all relevant 'partially and wholly unknown unknowns'.

The NER Safety Department she was now responsible for need not change its name, but including a remit for security in her department's role in the sense that she was proposing was crucial. It was not clarity efficient to treat safety and security separately in terms of malicious acts leading to incidents in terms of her department's role. The existing NER Security Department responsible for security in the policing sense would need to contribute to her Safety Department analysis, and she anticipated much more coordinated effort between the two departments, but no really new issues of significance now. She would refer to 'her safety and security team' today, assuming that there was no need to even consider changing any departmental labels for the time being.

Before NER began any detailed safety and security analysis, it was essential to ensure that their potential incident set was structured so that they could address the most serious NER incident scenarios first, with the greatest level of effort. This was, in part, a clarity efficiency concern, but it was also linked to complex corporate bias and blind spot concerns.

This top-down strategic focus would involve significant corporate process changes and linked culture shifts for the board as well as for her safety and security team and other groups within NER. These corporate process changes and linked culture changes were badly needed. The 30 fatalities incident two years ago, followed by the 40 fatalities incident a month ago, had caught them all by surprise. At board level they needed to completely abandon their usual focus on small numbers of fatalities at any given time in an accident, which was what happened most years. They also needed to abandon an occasional crisis focus on one or two major incidents in the recent past, the current situation. They needed to start thinking clearly and systematically *all the time every year* about 'what-if' scenarios involving levels of fatalities which they had never experienced, and hopefully never would experience, possibly caused by wilful acts of terrorism, plus all intermediate-level incidences. For example, they should start thinking about scenarios like 350 fatalities in one incident, perhaps with several times that number of people seriously injured, as a 'plausible catastrophic incident' scenario which she would elaborate shortly. They could then address a representative set of relevant lower level incidents.

This revised perspective suggested a top-down decomposition of NER safety and security concerns into four '*types* of incident', associated with four '*grades* of incident', defined in a hierarchical nested end-event type-grade structure.

The four '*types* of incident' were

1   'collisions' – when two or more trains are involved,
2   'derailments' – when a train leaves the track but a collision is not involved,
3   'level-crossings' – a level-crossing incident without derailment or collision, and
4   'other incidents' – *any other* relevant kind of incident.

The four '*grades* of incident' were

1   'fatal incidents' – when one or more people are killed,
2   'injury incidents' – there are no fatalities but one or more people are injured,
3   'property incidents' – no fatalities or injuries but property is damaged, and
4   'other reportable incidents' – *any other* relevant observations including near misses.

For this initial meeting she would focus on what she would call the 'collision with fatalities' scenarios, 1–1 incident scenarios in her type–grade structure because the 1–1 scenarios were *potentially* the most serious and the board needed to start with what *might* matter most.

Sophie said she was very aware that 'derailment caused by maintenance failure with fatalities' was a subset of her 2–1 type–grade combination of special interest to the NER board. However, at their initial meeting she wanted the board to treat 'collisions with fatalities' as the first priority for a board level top-down view, with direct links to derailments and other types and grades of incidents which she would start to develop in a few moments.

She appreciated that her overall top-down approach using types and grades of incidents might look baffling for the moment. All the models and data and other knowledge associated with types of incident 2, 3 and 4 and grades of incident 2, 3 and 4 would have to be addressed as underlying components of NER consideration of 1–1 incidents, providing a foundation for understanding 1–1 incidents. However, in their first meeting she wanted them to 'see the wood' (the forest as a whole) 'without being distracted by the trees' (at an individual tree level). She would start to develop the underlying thinking now, and she believed they would begin to see the overall rationale as the day progressed.

She thought it might be helpful to observe now that the models used to understand all 'level-crossings' incidents had to underlie some of the models used to understand 'derailments' to explain why a level-crossing incident might turn into a derailment which might turn into a collision if another train became involved. In practice, analysis undertaken by the safety and security team would have to start at the bottom and build a pyramid of understanding from the bottom up. The reason they were starting their discussion that day at the top was that 1–1 scenarios were the most serious potential end-event scenarios, exposing to danger in the limit all the passengers on two or more trains, plus any other people who were not on the trains but could be killed by the consequences of a collision.

The top-down perspective the board needed had to see the pyramid built by the safety and security team from the top. The bottom-up building of that pyramid by the safety and security team needed to understand the architecture of the whole structure needed by the board. In this framework, a 2–1 scenario was a derailment involving fatalities which did not progress to a collision, and a 3–1 scenario was a level-crossing incident involving fatalities which did not progress to a derailment and then a collision.

Building on this comment, the collision with 30 fatalities two years ago might seem much less important than the derailment with 40 fatalities a month ago. In some respects, this was the case. In particular, the maintenance failure triggering the derailment had NER incompetence and possible negligence implications which were crucial, requiring immediate attention.

However, it was important to avoid too much focus on the specifics of recent major events. The low end of medium speed nature of the front-to-rear collision involving 30 fatalities two years ago might be viewed as a 'very lucky' type of incident relative to a head-on collision with both trains moving at very high speed in opposite directions, when many hundreds of fatalities might be involved. The derailment a month ago involving 40 fatalities might be viewed as a 'moderately lucky' type of incident relative to a train leaving the rails at even higher speed and colliding head-on with another train. They might observe that level-crossing incidents when a train strikes a vehicle are common and often cause the train to leave the track.

Finally, and crucially, they might *formally and explicitly acknowledge* that a very obvious and relatively easy 'soft target' for terrorists was a level crossing when two very high speed trains moving in opposite directions were due. Terrorists might smash a heavy vehicle through the level-crossing traffic gates just before the first train arrives, in a way calculated to send the first train into the path of the second train, perhaps using an articulated tanker full of fuel fitted with impact explosives, with a wide range of possible variants.

In summary, NER needed to 'learn to be afraid' and develop the capability and culture to use all relevant information and knowledge to develop a robust approach to managing *all* relevant uncertainty, not just focus on trying to making sure specific types of failures in the recent past were not repeated.

Building this line of thinking further, she had been unable to uncover any evidence that anyone within NER had ever considered the sort of terrorist threat she had just used as an example, or a head-on collision involving very high speed trains caused by defective track maintenance directly attributable to the kind of track maintenance outsourcing currently in place as recently approved by the board. If incidents of this nature occurred in the context of no fully documented effective prior analysis, the board would probably face negligence claims which could permanently destroy the credibility of each and every director as well as bankrupting NER. She assumed that the board would like her to eliminate this possibility, using a well-balanced approach which looked after the interests of *all* stakeholders in a *robust and reasonable* manner, including shareholders, passengers, staff, and everyone else with related interests.

Sophie indicated serving the NER board in this way was central to her role as she saw it, and it required 'opportunity efficiency', including underlying 'risk efficiency' and 'clarity efficiency' in respect of associated analysis, which she would explore that day. One aspect of this was an understanding of 'sources of uncertainty' of a composite nature viewed from the top down, making due provisions for all relevant 'partially and wholly unknown unknowns', to avoid bias associated with what is particularly difficult and ambiguous.

Many of these concepts have been discussed in rather different terms earlier in this book. When this is the case, they will not be discussed again here, apart from revisiting some particularly useful graphical tools later in this chapter. But let's assume that Sophie would find the most appropriate way to convey all the relevant ideas to the NER board without unnecessarily repeating material discussed in earlier chapters in the tale of this chapter, without worrying you about the details of how she achieved this.

Two basic probability distribution components of the proposed stochastic model

The holistic base-case model set which NER needed involved stochastic (probability based) models with two key component probability distributions. Sophie said she would assume for the moment that both were defined in terms of fatalities associated with collisions, but later generalisation would address all other types and grades of incidents.

One was a Poisson probability distribution defining P_i, the unconditional probability of i *incidents* per annum, with i = 0, . . . , n, and n defining the maximum number of incidents per annum. NER would use this Poisson probability distribution directly to calculate P_0, the unconditional probability of zero incidents (i = 0) in a given year, and NER would use P_0 to compute $(1 - P_0)$, the probability of one or more *incidents* in a given year. This Poisson process working assumption would be their starting point for modelling the implications of the incidents addressed.

The second component probability distribution would define CP_S, the conditional probability of S *fatalities*, given the occurrence of one or more incidents, for S = 1, . . . , m, with m defining the maximum number of *fatalities* per annum. This second component would use a HAT-based probability distribution approach which would not require any specific probability distribution assumptions.

For S = 1, . . . , m, the unconditional probabilities of S fatalities per annum would be calculated using the relationship $P_S = (1 - P_0) \times CP_S$ and the $(1 - P_0)$ value obtained via P_0. P_0 defines the unconditional probability of zero fatalities per annum (P_S for S = 0) as well as zero incidents per annum (P_i for i = 0). The only use made of the P_i for values of i other than zero that day would be background understanding for the P_S estimation process (for those interested indirect use of the Poisson process for P_i with i = 1, . . . , n). For all direct modelling purposes P_1 or P_5 or P_{350} implied an S value subscript, not i.

These two component probability distributions would be associated with two key metrics, L and S.

The metric L determined the value of P_0. Underlying the P_0 value was the single parameter which defined a Poisson probability distribution and process, a metric with an expected value they would have to estimate. She would define this metric as 'L', the '*level* of incident occurrence', more formally 'the expected number of incidents involving fatalities per annum', interpreted as an unbiased estimate of the average number of incidents involving fatalities to be expected per annum. Remember 'L for *level*', measured as an expected value for the number of incidents per annum.

The metric S was a '*size* of incident measure', formally defined as 'the number of fatalities per annum given one or more incidents involving fatalities occurs in any given year' for values of S = 1, . . . , m. Remember 'S for *size*', with S = 0 if no fatalities occur.

For illustrative purposes that day she would use a 'five size scenarios' portrayal of the S value range given fatalities occur, with S = 1, 5, 20, 70, and 350. This involved simplifying working assumptions to avoid working directly with the general size metric S = 1, 2, 3, . . . , m, where m was the maximum number of fatalities which was feasible.

She was treating the S = 350 scenario as a maximum plausible number of fatalities in any given year. This scenario covered, in conditional outcome terms, a range from 200 fatalities to the maximum number of fatalities physically possible in one or more incidents within a year, primarily associated with one catastrophic incident, with working assumptions and implications which she would have to explain in more detail later.

If a 1–1 scenario occurred, the conditional probability that this incident was an S = 350 scenario, CP_S for S = 350, would be a particularly important conditional probability in terms of defining the high S value conditional probability distribution tail. In overview terms the key probabilities include the P_0 value and the P_S value for S = 1 as well as S = 350. The P_S for intermediate S = 5, 20, and 70 values were relevant but constrained by the S = 1 and 350 values.

For all other types of incidents involving fatalities (2–1, 3–1 and 4–1 scenarios), she would assume the use of the same illustrative example size scenario values, although zero probabilities might be assigned to the higher S value scenarios. A credible narrative involving all the incident types and grades would have to underlie a credible set of P_S for collision incidents involving fatalities.

For ongoing operational purposes, she would assume that the probability an incident might occur was constant over time. This implied a stable Poisson process – a random process described by a Poisson probability distribution function with L constant over time. This in turn implied that the occurrence of one incident would not change the probability of another incident, a working assumption that in practice could be modified as soon as circumstances were deemed to have changed.

A stable Poisson process assumption was common for this kind of modelling, because it provided a very powerful and robust model based on realistic assumptions, *provided the constant probability of an incident assumption, with a mean as currently estimated, was routinely tested*. This needed to be coupled to ongoing testing for a stable set of CP_S values.

The probability of i incidents per annum using a Poisson distribution was defined by the function

$$P_i = e^{-L} L^{-i} / \, i! \, ,$$

for i = 1 . . . n, where e was the exponential number.

L defined both the mean and the variance of this single parameter probability distribution, a useful characteristic of the Poisson distribution. Tables provided in textbooks could be used to look up P_i values for particular values of L. In most textbooks, her L (for 'level') was replaced by a Greek letter *lambda* (or lambda × t with t = the number of time intervals). The Roman L given an average 'level' (frequency of incidents) per annum definition was more convenient for NER purposes.

A two part transformation of the fatalities metric S into a cost metric C_S

A transformation which converted fatalities as portrayed by S into an appropriate assumed monetary equivalent could be associated with all management decision making with safety and security implications by any organisation which wanted to minimise fatalities and minimise associated cost, whether or not all relevant parties chose to recognise this was the case.

Sophie emphasised the existence of such a transformation was not an option – it was an unavoidable fact of life.

What was an option was those involved recognising this reality explicitly and using associated insights effectively and efficiently. In her view, it was essential that the NER board explicitly and formally acknowledged a leadership role in the definition, use, and interpretation by others of this transformation. Furthermore, the board had to require explicit and formal acknowledgement of two inherent and inescapable properties of this transformation by all parties involved in NER safety and security decision making or concerned about the decisions made.

First, this transformation was a shadow cost concept, because NER wanted to minimise fatalities *and* minimise the cost of achieving an appropriate minimum number of fatalities, which implied an inescapable trade-off between fatalities and cost. NER had to explicitly recognise and use this trade-off consistently for all decisions which influenced safety and security to avoid wasting lives, as well as to avoid wasting money. This could be viewed as being 'fatality efficient', with a minimum level of fatalities for any given level of expenditure on avoiding fatalities. A shadow *price* (instead of shadow *cost*) alternative interpretation would useful if minimising fatalities and maximising profit was the preferred conceptual framework, but she recommended avoiding this perspective, for a number of reasons, some fairly obvious.

Second, this shadow cost transformation was also inescapably a 'revealed preference' concept. A trade-off rate between avoided fatalities and cost revealed by NER decisions revealed board approved trade-offs. These trade-offs *ought* to reflect *actual* preferences for *all* parties with a legitimate interest in the implications of the value being used, for ethical reasons with legal implications in ALARP terms. The ultimate decision makers responsible for the use of this transformation were dealing with the lives and money of other people, with inescapable ethical and legal implications in terms of articulating the different interests of different parties and taking all relevant legitimate concerns into account. An explicit requirement for all relevant parties to have an appropriate level of understanding of what this implied was an implication.

The transformation employed had to involve some form of 'value of an avoided fatality' concept. The 'value of an avoided fatality' was a widely used concept with a range of interpretations which she would discuss in terms of current practice within NER and elsewhere. This discussion would include her interpretation of key areas of contention associated with different approaches to decision-making practice which were relevant to NER.

At a basic working assumption level within these framing assumptions, she advocated using a two part transformation involving the option of further decomposition of the second part. She would begin with the basic two part transformation now and explain the further decomposition option for the second part shortly.

The notation she would use for a 'cost associated with fatalities' measure C_S and a 'two part transformation factor' T_S was:

$C_S = S \times T_S$, with

$T_S = V_1 \times E_S$,

V_1 defined as 'an appropriate benchmark value for one avoided fatality',

E_S defined as 'the everything else factor when S fatalities were involved'.

Her starting position was that NER needed a carefully selected benchmark value for V_1 associated with a trusted organisation independent of NER which would be generally accepted as a reasonable basis. She had in mind V_1 = \$2,000,000, the value of an avoided fatality currently used by the National Highways Agency (NHA) in NER's country to make all road planning decisions when safety issues were involved. This provisional choice assumed verification by the NER safety and security team that this was a sound benchmark choice and approval by the board. Assessment of other country's comparable values and alternative benchmark possibilities would be part of the verification process.

She assumed that when only one fatality was involved, $E_S = E_1$ was a factor for transforming the V_1 benchmark value chosen by NHA into a suitable value of one avoided fatality in an NER context, reflecting *all relevant views* about the implications of one fatality in this different context. One obvious key difference if NER used the NHA \$2 million for V_1 was the NER association with railway travel rather road travel. Another was that NER was a private sector organisation while the NHA was a public sector organisation. E_1 had to reflect these two differences plus all other relevant differences.

She assumed that when S was greater than one, E_S was a factor which reflected E_1 plus an appropriate increase to embody *all relevant views* about the implications of more than one person being killed in the same NER incident. In her view, NER had to acknowledge that most people believed that 1,000 people killed at the same time in one incident was much more serious than 1,000 people killed one at a time in 1,000 separate incidents, with intermediate valuations of 100 or 10 fatalities in one or multiple incidents. This was reflected in the observable differences in approaches to safety by highways agencies and air travel industries and public acceptance of those approaches. It was widely accepted that risk of death or injury when travelling by road, rail, and air was not the same, nor should it be assumed to be seen as the same by the travelling public, for a very complex set of reasons. One reason was how many people tend to be killed or injured in any given incident. Other concerns included the level of trust in the organisation and the nature of the death involved.

The starting point for defining $T_S = V_1 \times E_S$ equivalents in all contexts *ought to be* clarity about what she would refer to as 'revealed preferences' associated with:

1 preferences expressed by each of the parties with a legitimate interest other than the NER board, as interpreted by the NER safety and security team for use by the board;
2 a synthesis of all the components of the set of revealed preferences associated with point 1, as interpreted and reflected in revealed preferences *defined by NER board level decision making.*

The board was responsible for prudent decisions involving the lives and welfare of other people as well as other peoples' money. This implied that gathering and interpreting the implications of revealed preferences associated with all the parties directly involved other than the NER board ought to be a crucial aspect of the board's decision-making process, effectively supported by the NER safety and security team, and tested by other involved parties. *To fail to take proper account of the preferences of all relevant parties was arguably negligent, even if members of the board did not appreciate this was the case, and not all other relevant parties appreciated this was the case.*

The choices the board members approved would reveal the board's preferences, and *each individual board member* was accountable for those revealed preferences, both legally and in a more general ethical sense. In the EP framework that she would explain, this was the case whether or not they chose to understand that this was the case, and an important feature of the EP framework was making this clear. In her view every member of the board needed to understand why this was the situation and all the key implications by the end of their initial meeting. Subsequently, everyone else with an interest in NER decisions would also have to understand this was the situation, and the implications, at a level of clarity appropriate to their interests.

'All the parties directly involved other than the NER board' clearly included rail passengers plus on-board NER staff and the families of both these groups. It also included those paying for the railway travel, which included most rail passengers plus all citizens of NER's country because of significant government railway travel subsidies. Furthermore, it included NER shareholders. However, many approaches to estimating T_S values began with cost–benefit analysis, and some organisations never really got beyond this starting point. In practice, the values of $T_S = V_1 \times E_S$ employed by board level decision making should also pay close attention to interpreting the revealed preferences of other *indirectly* interested parties not yet mentioned. For example, the direct cost implications of compensation awards by the courts, plus the amounts involved in 'out of court' settlements, should be important practical concerns. The board also needed to consider the direct and indirect knock-on implications of hostile media attention and the consequences of commuters switching to the use of cars instead of trains, with immediate revenue effects, plus knock-on political and regulator implications.

NER had to recognise that small numbers of fatalities in frequent NER incidents might be seen as comparable to road traffic accidents in some respects, but very large numbers of fatalities in one incident would be seen by many people as comparable to airplane accidents, whether or not NER safety experts and other safety experts currently shared this view. To be more specific, plausible NER incidents could span a range of fatalities which was so wide that NER could not expect to get away with their current assumption of a single constant 'value of an avoided fatality' relevant to any feasible S value. There was a good case for highways agencies using a single value appropriate to the limited number of fatalities usually needing consideration in road traffic accidents, viewed as a relevant average. There was a somewhat different but reasonable case for aircraft travel organisations using a single value associated with average numbers of fatalities in major airplane crashes, despite the larger range involved than that associated with road traffic accidents. But NER had to explicitly confront an unusually wide range, with most incidents clustered at the bottom end, some very low probability but very high impact incidents at the top end, plus infrequent but moderate probability intermediate level incidents like the 30 and 40 fatality incidents in the last two years. In her view, moving to an S dependent E_S was an essential generalisation of NER current practice, with very important implications the board needed to understand.

To understand the implications of her $T_S = V_1 \times E_S$ framework when used by NHA or any other highways agency, a simplified $T = V_1 \times E$ form could be assumed, assuming E was not dependent on S. When any highways agency first used an avoided fatality transformation, V_1 might have been based on a cost–benefit analysis approach to a single fatality, and E might have been a constant uplift which was implicit and set to unity. But later on, the E value might have included an uplift to reflect feedback from road users, road funders, and other interested parties, plus inflation since V_1 was first disclosed, and possibly plus a further uplift to reflect more than one person being killed in the average incident involving fatalities. The highways agency might have never actually used T, V_1, E_S, and E parameter equivalents explicitly, simply employing a subscript-free $T = V$ equivalent for the average number of fatalities when incidents occur which was updated and redefined in the updating process on a regular basis, with a subscript t which was implicit to indicate the period, perhaps made explicit when relevant. Her current working assumption was that this was the case.

This notation for this kind of approach would be useful for their discussion shortly, and she wanted to emphasise now that she thought most highways agencies took a reasonable approach on the whole, viewed within her $T_S = V_1 \times E_S$ basic framework, recognising that they probably actually used another framework.

She thought aircraft industry use of related approaches, insofar as she understood them, were also very reasonable, and it was worth saying so now, although the plausible range of fatalities which might be involved was clearly very different.

Furthermore, there were a number of reasons why she thought aircraft industry safety and security approaches might offer NER some very useful ideas not usually found in approaches to road traffic safety or railway safety, but that was a matter for future discussions.

A key board level strategic issue needing clarity

Before getting into building the requisite 'how to do it' detail needed for strategic clarity by the board, Sophie thought an overview of the nature of the strategic issues which she was convinced needed attention might be useful. She suggested a very brief discussion of one example of a *potential* new strategic view of 'where NER should be going', to motivate the board's interest in understanding 'what needed to be done' in terms of 'how it might be done' and why the degree of complexity being advocated was necessary.

She began by indicating that the current NER strategy in terms of high speed intercity services 20 to 30 years into the future, as she understood it, was trains of about the same passenger capacity as current trains operating on modestly modified track layouts with comparable timetables with top speeds about 50% faster than the current trains. She believed that the approach she was advocating *might* lead them to the view that even current high speed trains involved a level of risk NER should not be taking, and enlightened prudence required much smaller trains in the future to reduce the scale of a potential catastrophic high speed collision incident. If no other changes were made, the additional costs might seem unacceptably high. However, if more frequent trains as a result of smaller trains were seen as a way of improving the service as well as reducing journey times, this was done in conjunction with a coordinated approach to improving service levels for other connecting train services, and an approach to all ticket pricing which significantly reduced crowding at current peak times, they might increase passenger satisfaction and NER profitability while increasing safety and security at the same time. This might or might not involve significant increases in passenger numbers and changes in their plans in terms of track layouts and other relevant interdependent issues.

One key reason for suggesting this *possible* change in strategic direction was NER's need to embrace 'enlightened prudence'. Enlightened prudence for NER might involve being prepared to reduce the size of all high speed trains in order to reduce the chance of catastrophic incidents involving deviations from expected costs which might put NER out of business. The concern might be reducing 'risk' as risk is viewed in both plain English and EP terms, by altering the risk–reward trade-off while achieving and maintaining risk efficiency. Currently NER used a definition of 'risk' for formal safety risk management planning purposes which did not facilitate NER addressing enlightened prudence because it did not address risk in the generalised Markowitz based risk efficiency plus opportunity efficiency EP sense. The NER current definition of 'risk' in a safety context for corporate, operations and project planning purposes limited what they formally addressed to expected outcomes, which was unacceptably myopic from an EP perspective. In all relevant contexts when safety was considered, NER needed to address risk efficiency in a general sense. NER also needed to address risk–reward trade-offs and clarity efficiency in an opportunity efficiency framework.

A second key reason was NER's need to understand that a failure to address enlightened prudence in a risk efficiency plus opportunity efficiency framework was aggravated by their failure to address an S dependent E_s concept or understand the implications of these interdependent framing assumption failures.

A third key reason was NER's need to understand why the distortions associated with her first two points earlier were aggravated and amplified by biases associated with the way they approached long tailed probability distributions.

A fourth key reason was a further compounding of these concerns associated with NER's need to understand the importance of ensuring that *all* negative aspects of catastrophic incidents correlated with high numbers of fatalities needed joint consideration *at the same time* to avoid underestimating the importance of such incidents and to capture clarity efficiency benefits.

The fifth reason she would mention was NER's failure to consider passengers' preferences for safer travel on all NER train services *in conjunction with* passenger's preferences for more frequent trains with crowding at peak periods reduced, even if they had to pay more. In some cases, these preferences might be linked to a willingness to travel more at different times if travel was more comfortable, as well as safer, on more frequent trains, allowing convenient transfers from high speed to local stopping services, as just one example of complex interdependencies which matter.

Sophie emphasised this particular *possible* change in strategy example was based on her EP perspective leading to immediate recognition of fundamental flaws in the current NER approach to conceptual and operational tools for strategic planning involving safety, and the nature of some reasonably likely implications. However, her currently limited understanding of railways in general, and NER in particular, meant that she could not yet be definitive about the exact nature of any needed NER changes in this kind of passenger service strategy. What she could be sure about was the need for all relevant NER staff to reframe NER understanding of their railway business using the EP approach she would provide, and then use this enhanced perspective in a creative way based on their extensive railway industry expertise.

It would take NER some time and effort to achieve this full integration of expertise. She would focus the initial board level discussion on gradually building a layered understanding of the key framing and working assumptions underlying the operational form the new NER approach would take. The board would then be able to see in more detail where they were going, how they could get there, and why a new approach was necessary.

The 1970s Ford Pinto controversy in the US

At this point Sophie indicated the board would find it useful to explore a context which was much simpler than the NER situation. They would consider using the simplified $T = V_1 \times E$ version of the basic $T_S = V_1 \times E_S$ framework in the context of road travel safety. This would clarify some basic issues without being distracted by the complications associated with an S dependent E_S.

To begin to explore the implications of her T_S framework at a $T = V_1 \times E$ level of complexity, the Ford Pinto 'controversy' as set out in *The Gift* (Hyde, 2006) provided Sophie with a useful example which could be linked to the NHA basis of her $V_1 = \$2$ million proposal.

Most North Americans who were adults in the 1970s knew about the Ford Pinto controversy, which severely damaged the reputation of Ford as well as cost–benefit analysis as used in this context. NER board members might not have heard about it, but it was an internationally renowned example of how not to approach safety which still attracted comment, and it provided a useful example for them to consider briefly.

'Controversy' was Sophie's choice of word to keep the discussion neutral and avoid emotive language. However, some people called the Ford Pinto 'controversy' a 'catastrophe', 'disaster', 'debacle', 'travesty' or 'outrage', and she had some sympathy with all these views. It was a catastrophe for those who lost loved ones in Pinto accidents involving fires resulting from low speed rear-end collisions which could and should have been avoided. It was also a catastrophe from the perspective of Ford Motor Company shareholders and the Ford board when the US press got involved. From a current perspective, she believed the Ford board was lucky to have escaped very serious charges.

Hyde, in *The Gift*, started his discussion of the Pinto controversy by observing that it was 'a classic example of both cost–benefit analysis and the confusion between "value" (as calculated by economists) and "worth" (as understood in broader frameworks which recognise the importance of "gifts" and other non-market-based concepts)'. Hyde's basic concerns about important limitations of cost–benefit analysis and Ford's use of it were well-founded and still current issues. NER did not want to replicate 'the Ford Pinto experience'.

Hyde noted that when Ford introduced the Pinto in 1971 (a relatively small 'compact' car of a kind not previously produced by Ford in the US), they were aware that the designs involved a fuel tank prone to rupture in rear-end collisions, even at low speed, with consequent avoidable fire risk. Ford had several tested options to reduce the risk, the most expensive (presumably the most effective) costing $11 per vehicle.

According to Hyde, an internal Ford memo estimated that if the Pinto was sold without the $11 safety feature, 2,100 cars would burn every year, 180 people would be hurt but survive, 180 people would burn to death. To assess the option of installing this safety feature Ford used a US National Highway Traffic Safety Administration (NHTSA) value of an avoided fatality of $200,000. In Sophie's terms, $200,000 was a $T = V_1 \times E$ value, an average value for all relevant S, because NHTSA was aware that 2 or more people might be killed in the same accident, and it was using a common value for all of them. For simplicity she would assume that E was equal to unity, all V_1 components were in the money of the day, and $T = V_1 = \$200,000$.

Hyde itemised the NHTSA components of T to show that it included $10,000 for 'victim's pain and suffering', along with $900 for 'funeral', and $173,000 for 'future productivity losses'. Ford used $67,000 for the average T equivalent for people injured (presumably related to a comparable NHTSA figure), $700 for each lost vehicle. Ford used a market estimate of 12.5 million vehicles per year. The resulting 'benefit' (money saved by a safer car) was $49.5 million. The corresponding 'cost' (money spent on safety devices) was $137.5 million. Based on these figures Ford decided not to install any safety devices. It would seem that the obvious option of reconsidering the whole design concept was not addressed.

What brought these internal Ford memos into the public domain was in part the reliability of the Ford forecasts of fatalities. Hyde noted that according to a *Mother Jones* magazine article by Mark Dowie, by 1977 at least 500 people had burned to death in Pinto crashes.

It was important for the NER board to understand that from her current perspective, she would be very comfortable defending the NHTSA approach *if it had formally recognised*, in a way that Ford in the 1970s and Hyde in 2006 plus everyone else involved would have subsequently been aware of, that *this kind of T value was a plausible minimum to be used as a starting point for a discussion about the role of shadow costs, revealed preferences and all ethical issues appropriate to the NHTSA context; but it should never be used in other contexts, like the*

Ford Pinto decisions, without a very carefully considered set of changes, including an E factor much greater than unity.

It was even more important for the NER board to appreciate that *Ford's decisions could not be defended from any perspective, at any point in time, by anyone who had a moral compass and modicum of common sense.* The reasons were very obvious in her $T_s = V_1 \times E_s$ framework, and they should have been obvious enough to Ford even without her EP framework.

To ensure that the board understood the EP perspective which NER had to adopt, she would use her $T_s = V_1 \times E_s$ framework to review all the key issues which NHTSA got absolutely right, plus those where improved practice would have been helpful. She would then comment on the Ford position and finish by linking this discussion to the NER position.

The key point to begin this discussion was that the NHTSA needed some way to shape the allocation of public funds to public road safety improvements, and they needed some basis for a benchmark starting point, a V_1 in her terminology. If they simply gave up on T_s concepts, they would have no way of influencing the level of fatalities for whatever safety budgets those spending the money on public roads in the US could make available. In the absence of other organisations that took over the public's concern about road safety in the USA, the NHTSA needed a V_1 value or it was doomed to wasting lives as well as money. The NHTSA was an important pioneer in this area and deserved full credit for formally and explicitly embracing a pioneering version of her T_s based approach and publishing its methodology and value estimates. A cost–benefit analysis basis for a V_1 concept was arguably the only obvious option at that time, and the NHTSA did implicitly allow it to acquire a shadow cost status via adjustments incorporating feedback on public exposure of its initial approach and value estimates.

Her second point was assuming that an S dependent approach was not necessary was a very reasonable NHTSA assumption, because their focus was small numbers of people being killed in each of a very large number of road traffic accidents. Although high speed bus collisions or major pile-up accidents would make S dependent generalisation worth considering if motorway crash barriers were being addressed, this was not an obvious initial concern. So, using an initial simplified framework with $T = V_1 \times E$ and $V_1 = \$200,000$ with $E = 1$ was very reasonable. This T or V_1 value needed to be interpreted as a per fatality transformation based on the average number of fatalities in road traffic accidents in the US around 1970, using a cost–benefit basis which was assumed to be suitable for the average person killed in typical road traffic accidents.

Her third point was that injuries and physical damage had been treated separately by the NHTSA, with injuries treated via a transformation linked to V_1 like the Ford $\$67,000$. In the 1970s NHTSA context was reasonable. It was still global common practice.

Her fourth point was the NHTSA explicitly adopted a full disclosure approach and implicitly moved towards a revealed preference interpretation of their shadow cost concept. They published the details of their approach to V_1 as well as the $\$200,000$ value. This full disclosure approach allowed road users and road funders (largely but not exactly the same set of people) who thought $\$200,000$ was too low, or too high, to provide an argument for change which allowed a very crude revealed preference adjustment to the initial value selected. Implicitly, the NHTSA associated a revealed preference status with its T value and embedded an ethical content in E by responding to feedback.

Her fifth point was that NHTSA contributed to the Pinto controversy and failed to escape criticism itself by four omissions, with closely coupled implications:

1   failing to *formally* treat T as a shadow cost concept,
2   failing to *formally* acknowledge a revealed preference status for a T concept,

3   failing to *formally* acknowledge that the relevant revealed preferences were always inherently ambiguous and difficult to capture in a fair and unbiased manner, and

4   failing to *formally* acknowledge a need for an E parameter adjustment to V_1 which had an ethical content which those determining T had considered and addressed in conjunction with the shadow cost and revealed preference issues.

Elaborating on the fourth omission, which addresses embedded responses to the other three, if the need for ethical content in a T value, which was both a shadow cost concept and an effectively managed revealed preference concept, had been formally addressed, then an E = 1 assumption would have clearly implied that T = V_1 = \$200,000 calculated in this way was usefully interpreted as a 'plausible starting point' for NHTSA use. It would have been clear that this value was based on a *particular* economic analysis approach in a *particular* context, *not* an evaluation which organisations like Ford should ever use directly and not a value NHTSA could expect others to trust until feedback had been considered. This particular economic approach could have no real ethical validity until the values involved were reviewed by those affected by associated decisions. It did not reflect what any of the people involved thought about the approach used, or the numbers produced, and its nature was totally unsuitable for direct use by Ford.

If used directly by NHTSA, with no acknowledgement of the need for an operational shadow cost trade-off or of a balanced and fair way of identifying relevant revealed preference concerns and then embodying related ethical concerns, it was not likely to receive a majority vote or engender trust. It was not a revealed preference concept *unless and until* all relevant parties agreed that its use in this way was appropriate. However, if it had been made clear that lives and money would be wasted unless a shadow cost was agreed on and applied consistently by the NHTSA and a formal approach for receiving and balancing feedback from all involved parties in a fair way had been put in place to move towards a robust revealed preference E value, arguably the NHTSA would have escaped all serious criticism, and Ford might not have initiated the Pinto controversy in the first place.

In a 1970s context, all these NHTSA shortcomings from an EP perspective were regrettable but understandable. The NER board might note that adjusted for inflation, and other relevant factors, the T value used by the NHTSA of \$200,000 was of the same order of magnitude as the \$2 million currently used by NHA, and both values seemed plausible sums in the intended context as far as she could currently judge, given suitable caveats about their interpretation.

Ford should have approached the role of trust and ethics with a clear recognition that their position was *entirely* different from that of NHTSA, *despite* NHTSA not making the need to do so explicit in formal terms. People could buy other cars if they felt Pintos were not safe. Ford had no intention of full disclosure. Ford's use of *any* T = V trade-off suitable for NHTSA use without significant E factor uplifts with a clear ethical basis and other careful revisions to the approach was unacceptable for very obvious reasons from an EP perspective. If Ford employees did not have the moral compass to see this difference in ethical terms, they should have had the insight to recognise the trust aspects in legal terms, and the inescapable fact that all the other interested parties involved would see their behaviour as inept, immoral, or criminal. Even a hardened cynic ought to have seen the chances of Ford not getting caught and being accused of being stupid at best, arguably criminal, was negligible. If Ford had added \$11 to the cost of a car (implying an E value of about 3 or more), they would perhaps have sold marginally fewer Pintos and possibly made less money, but there would have been no public sector trade-offs between expenditure on roads and expenditure on other public services. The ethical issues were *very* different. Somebody within Ford should have understood this, and there was a good case for arguing 'the buck stops with the board'.

As an interjected aside, we might observe that from an EP perspective it is obvious that Ford should have spent the $11 per Pinto as a minimum. But a redesign would have been much better, and getting the design right at the outset would be better still. Martha's Chapter 6 approach could provide the foundations of a basis, treating safety as a feature of cars which purchasers want, along with reliability, fuel economy, acceleration, and so on, the non-price value added or quality features which Trevor and Sian were concerned about in Chapter 6 which need building into products offered to potential purchasers. There was a clear need for Martha's 'red face test' built into Ford's design and engineering processes, along with suitable 'halo tests', 'smiles tests' and 'frowns tests'. On top of this basis, some features of a simplified and significantly revised variant of Sophie's NER approach as developed in this chapter might be used.

Returning to the tale, linking the NHTSA and Ford cases to NER, Sophie suggested that the way forward was a variant of the NHTSA approach. The shortcomings she had identified needed to be fully rectified. Furthermore, an S dependent E_S concept incorporating a four part decomposition generalisation was needed. They had to embrace what was common as well as what was different when comparing the NHTSA, NHA, and NER. For example, despite the private sector nature of NER, they needed an approach moving towards full disclosure with their regulator, as well as other parties, which she would comment on later.

As she had suggested earlier, given adjustments for inflation and other relevant factors, the $200,000 figure used by NHTSA in the 1970s was roughly comparable to the $2 million currently used by NHA, the highways agency responsible for road traffic safety in NER's country. She was not an expert in the road safety area, but she understood that the road traffic authorities in most countries had started with T values significantly below the NHTSA figure, experienced T value inflation which might be attributed to 'revealed preferences' of road users and other citizens, coupled to growing concerns about safety plus growth in real incomes as well as inflation. This had led to a revised T which could now be treated as a reasonable approximation to the kind of $T = V_1 \times E$ she would recommend.

She wanted the NER safety and security team to look very closely at the provenance and robustness of the $2 million NHA value, but it was clearly relevant, and she would assume an NHA based $V_1 = $2 million working assumption for NER to use that day.

Using numerical examples to clarify the board's understanding

Sophie started the next section of her presentation by explaining that some of the key concepts the board needed to understand were not going to be considered until near the end of her presentation – 'enlightened prudence' for example. This was because she believed the easiest way for board members to understand such concepts was via illustrative numerical examples demonstrating the use of decision diagrams plus underlying sensitivity diagrams to consider trade-offs when increasing the expected cost to reduce risk in terms of departures from expectations was worthwhile. *But before she* could demonstrate this, she needed to explain how all NER decisions involving safety and security concerns needed to address making risk efficient choices using decision diagrams and sensitivity diagrams. *Before she* could do this, she needed to build example numerical models which provided plausible portrayals of expected outcomes and associated variability in terms of all the costs relevant to choices between the current system and alternative proposed new systems. *Before she* could do that, she needed to build underlying plausible illustrative numerical models which transposed fatalities into 'cost related to fatalities'. *And before that*, underlying models which represented a plausible illustrative portrayal of the probability of any given number of fatalities per annum needed consideration. So, they were going to start at the bottom of an analysis structure using illustrative numerical examples, and gradually build towards a full understanding of 'what needed to be done' and 'why an EP approach made sense', deferring discussion of key considerations like enlightened prudence until they were reaching the top. Sophie had developed her layered approach to keep the discussion in this initial meeting as simple as possible in a systematic manner. But the issues were very complex, and she had not been able to make her presentation as short and simple as they might all wish had been feasible.

As an interjection, this is going to be the first of several significant sections in a long chapter, and in practice Sophie would have had to provide breaks, which will not be mentioned, and explain EP concepts which we will gloss over when the issues have already been covered. Your patience will be stretched as well as the NER board's endurance. But we are addressing the most complex interdependent concepts this book considers, the route taken is the most painless I could evolve, and I believe that you will begin to understand the rationale and find the journey worth the effort before the chapter's end.

Estimating key parameter values with an initial focus on L, P_0 and $(1 - P_0)$, then CP_S

Sophie indicated that the first step was addressing an estimate of the incident 'level' L – the metric for collisions with fatalities in terms of the expected frequency level of incidents per annum. L defined the P_0 and $(1 - P_0)$ associated with a Poisson process of incident occurrence, the probability of no incidents and the probability of one or more incidents per annum.

Associated CP_S defined the conditional probabilities of S fatalities given an incident occurs. They could use P_0, $(1 - P_0)$ and CP_S estimates to define P_S for S = 0, 1, 5, 20, 70, or 350, the unconditional probability of no fatalities or one of five 'size' scenarios she would use to illustrate a general EP approach. $P_S = (1 - P_0) \times CP_S$ is the relationship they would use to convert conditional probability estimates into unconditional probability estimates.

Any estimated values of L and the CP_S used to compute the associated P_S were defined given current physical systems (equipment), procedural systems (including information systems, maintenance regimes and associated contract structures), culture (including staff morale) and external factors (including terrorist threat levels). L, CP_S, and associated P_S would need estimation in terms of unbiased expected values. Variability in the number of fatalities each year, given these expected values, needed direct modelling which she would consider shortly. Variability associated with errors in the expected values for L and the CP_S required explicit consideration, but formal modelling of this higher order uncertainty beyond stating ranges and listing component issues of sources of associated uncertainty would be deferred.

To clarify their initial discussion, she had reviewed NER estimates related to L provided by Oscar. She had concluded that 0.05 was a plausible estimate of L for illustrative purposes. She would associate this estimate of an expected value of L with a plausible uncertainty range of approximately one order of magnitude, from 0.01 to 0.10.

She made it clear that this uncertainty range might be a good deal wider than some board members anticipated, but she believed it was realistic until a lot more analysis had been undertaken. Furthermore, L = 0.05 might be higher or lower than anticipated by board members, depending on the extent to which they believed the recent collision incident was bad luck or as yet unresolved bad management. She might want to make significant adjustments to this illustrative expected value for L, up or down, after further analysis. However, for illustrative purposes L = 0.05 would serve their current needs.

In practice, it would be crucial to decompose uncertainty associated with estimating the expected value of L and associated CP_S into at least five components when they did pursue further formal analysis:

1   uncertainty associated with data-based estimates using NER past experience;
2   uncertainty associated with data-based adjustments using relevant experience from other railway systems, plus a clear understanding of all related competency levels;
3   uncertainty associated with adjustments based on judgements of NER system change effects;
4   uncertainty associated with adjustments based on judgements of malicious incident threats; and
5   all other uncertainty which might be relevant.

Her current views on the expected value of L = 0.05 were dominated by item 1 and discussions with Oscar because she had no basis for items 2 to 5. But her current views on the uncertainty range were dominated by her uncertainty about items 2 to 5.

The fourth component, associated with malicious acts, should not be too significant in expected value terms for L. Even if they took a pessimistic view, a reasonable estimate might be of the order of 5% of the assumed L = 0.05, perhaps less. However, this fourth component needed estimation with great care, and it raised causal dependence issues with the CP_S expected values which might prove important. If malicious attacks took place, the conditional probabilities of large S values might be *much* bigger than they were for ordinary accidents because that would probably be the intent.

Some directors might intuitively associate her illustrative example L = 0.05 with a binomial process, which could be interpreted as a special case of the Poisson process when only zero or one incident was possible. She thought those inclined to this binomial model interpretation might like to know that in terms of her P_i notation, an example textbook table of Poisson distribution values (Yamane, 1973, page 1106) would show that for L = 0.05:

$P_0 = 0.9512$, which might be rounded to 0.95,

$P_1 = 0.0476$, which could be rounded to 0.05,

$P_2 = 0.0012$, which could be rounded to 0.00,

$P_3 = 0.0000$.

This clearly implied no chance of three or more incidents in any given year working to four places of decimal, a binomial approximation being reasonable for this fairly small L value if two places of decimal were used.

However, NER could use the Poisson model as their basic model without requiring binomial distribution approximations, and the 0.0012 probability of two incidents in a single year could be captured by the CP_S. This generality would be important if much bigger L values were relevant in other contexts and they did not want to use shorter time periods.

To keep her illustrative numerical examples reasonably simple, she would use the assumption $P_0 = 0.9500$, working to four significant figures, implying $(1 - P_0) = 0.0500$ but a slightly smaller L than 0.0500, still 0.05 to two places of decimal. This would be convenient because P_0 and $(1 - P_0)$ were the probabilities NER need to work with, L underlying the definition of both, and it was useful to distinguish $L = 0.05$ and $(1 - P_0) = 0.0500$.

The value of $L = 0.05$ and $(1 - P_0) = 0.0500$ was uncomfortably large, and plausible values in the uncertainty range were larger still – collisions involving fatalities in the sense being addressed were reasonably low probability events, but they were not rare events.

A useful feature of the Poisson model was $1/L$ defined the average time between incidents. Instead of thinking about L as an estimate of 'the average number of incidents per year', it was often useful to think in terms of $1/L$ as 'the average interval between incidents in years', commonly referred to as 'the return period'. Assuming $L = 0.05$ implied a $1/L$ return period of $1/0.05 = 20$ years. Many people found it easier to think about a context involving an $L = 0.05$, $(1 - P_0) = 0.0500$ and $P_0 = 0.9500$ as for their current example in terms of a return period of 20 years using the $1/L$ interpretation.

It was important to understand that the '20 year return period' perspective implied one incident involving a collision with fatalities every 20 years *on average*, but for all practical purposes any realistic notion of the average would rarely happen. Even with the usual 'random process means Poisson Process' assumption that the probability of an incident remains constant over time, bunching was likely to be observed – in popular parlance 'buses often come in threes'. Two incidents in two years did not mean no more for a while. Tomorrow could be the day their third bus arrived, and the day after might be the fourth.

Different board members might prefer different ways of thinking about what was involved, but several related issues needed clarity for everyone:

1 The uncertainty associated with an expected value estimate of L or P_0 was currently significant, and it would be both disingenuous and dysfunctional to suggest otherwise.

2 The subjectivity associated with estimates of L or P_0 and associated uncertainty required visibility, to clarify all working assumptions, and to avoid the dysfunctional stealth assumptions inherent in any pretence of 'objectivity' in a simplistic textbook 'objective probability' sense. If 'objectivity' was interpreted as 'reasonableness', in the sense that equally well-informed and enlightened people could agree proposed decisions without necessarily agreeing on the grounds for those decisions, then the only way to achieve 'objective decisions' was via 'subjective probabilities', with high clarity about *all* relevant assumptions. This applied to L and $(1 - P_0)$, their current concerns, but it also applied to the CP_S, and it applied to both the V_1 and the E_S values underlying T_S transformations.

3 The NER 'safety and security team', in the narrow sense of 'the set of experts she managed directly', needed to discuss the models and analysis underlying the range and expected value and agree they were 'reasonable' before this expected value and range became the basis of a board approved 'NER estimate'. The board would have to understand in broad terms the basis of these recommendations.

4 It was important that everyone involved understood that more effort could reduce the uncertainty range but not eliminate it, and the implications of the cost of using scarce resources to reduce uncertainty. Uncertainty about all relevant probabilities and all relevant transformations needed consistent clarity efficient treatment.

5 The board members needed to confirm that they understood what the safety and security team was doing well enough to confirm the NER estimate was 'reasonable' before

the associated conclusions became 'the NER policy'. The board were directly responsible for NER policy, including, in broad terms, the approach adopted by the NER safety and security team, the level of effort involved, and the competence of those undertaking the analysis.

6   All NER staff and contractors plus subcontractors whose work had an impact on NER safety and security had to be part of the NER 'safety and security team' in the broad sense of 'working together to deliver NER safety and security'. Crucially, they all needed an appropriate level of understanding of the way everyone had to work together to achieve shared goals.

7   It was also important to understand that if L or P_0 were viewed in a Bayesian framework, integrating 'prior' views with 'posterior' views based on recent data, many people would see $P_0 = 0.9500$ for all collision with fatalities scenarios as far too optimistic in the light of the last two years. Whether or not a formal Bayesian perspective was evoked, a very pessimistic view of NER safety by the public and relevant government agencies should be understandable.

8   It was important not to panic. There were very serious issues which needed addressing, but to some extent 'bad luck' might underlie the two NER incidents in two years. To most people, 'too much bad luck' was the same thing as 'careless', or even 'negligent', a reality they had to deal with. But they had to keep their nerve and focus on achievable changes which made matters better.

Her discussion that day would focus on NER collisions with fatalities, but all type–grade scenarios involving fatalities plus those involving injuries but no fatalities and those just involving damage needed an NER unbiased expected value estimates of L in this top-down framework as soon as possible. Initial first-cut estimates would be a high priority for her group, to be refined on an ongoing basis.

Estimating the CP$_S$ for a suitable set of incident size scenarios

The next step in their discussion was estimating the expected values of the conditional probabilities of a suitable set of incident size scenarios and then using these conditional probabilities to compute the unconditional probabilities.

A parametrically defined probability distribution approach was one option, and given the power and simplicity of the Poisson probability distribution just discussed, using a comparable parametrically defined probability distribution approach to estimating a full set of incident size scenarios was a very common and very tempting option. For example, a negative exponential distribution was a popular choice in some circumstances, like estimating the size of a seismic event (earthquake) given a seismic event occurs or estimating the depth of an ice scour in the ocean floor given a scour occurs, or estimating the duration of a telephone call, given one begins. The first two examples I have relevant direct consultancy experience with. The third involves an early application area for 'queueing theory' a century ago which most people familiar with traditional basic OR will have been exposed to.

There were two good reasons behind choosing to use a parametrically defined probability distribution like the negative exponential in the NER context, and Sophie believed that both were worth understanding by the board and everyone else involved in interpreting the analysis required.

First, a parametric approach allowed the estimation of the defining parameters using limited data. For example, the single parameter defining a negative exponential distribution could be estimated in terms of the average size of the incidents observed, which meant that even if only limited observations of small to medium sized seismic events over a 100 year history were available, assuming a negative exponential distribution provided a feasible approach to estimating the 10,000 year return period seismic event incident which might define the design approach to a nuclear power station. The 'price' for this 'power' was an extreme extrapolation. But the need to extrapolate was not going to go away, and 'tests for robustness' associated with the extreme extrapolations could be pursued by looking at history prior to seismic event data in addition to the usual tests for 'goodness of fit' using interpolation data. A key issue was *any available evidence* that there was a maximum plausible event size *or the complete lack of such evidence.*

Second, if some data were missing and systematic bias was involved, analysts could revise the estimation process to correct for systematic bias associated with any patterns in the missing data. For example, Chapman (1988) demonstrated how this kind of missing data adjustment process used in conjunction with a Poisson arrival process and a negative exponential depth distribution was employed to estimate the depth of ice scouring on the floor of the Beaufort Sea when the gradual silting-in of scours over time beginning immediately after a scour occurred meant that observations of very small scours were always missing, and all the scours observed using sonar had been partially filled in to various degrees. This approach allowed Gulf to assess oil pipeline bury depths when ice scours down to depths of the order of 10 metres with return periods in excess of 100 years were the concern and limited sonar scour depth data over about 5 years was all that was available.

Despite the advantages in terms of 'power' provided by using a member of the exponential family of distributions or a related distribution like the log-Normal, in the NER context the 'cost of that power' led her to believe they should not take this route. NER needed generality and a related ability to test a complex set of assumptions which meant that it was *much easier* for *all relevant parties* to follow what was involved using about five 'size scenarios' which were not defined using a specific distribution function. Alternative specific parametrically defined probability distribution functions could be tested within the framework this approach provided, and one or more specific parametrically defined examples could be used as a starting point, but they did not need to start with a commitment to a specific parametrically defined probability distribution function. She believed the additional generality allowed by this flexible scenario based approach was of crucial importance to NER. In broad terms the board should understand why in terms of the implications of testing and discussing assumptions about:

1 extreme distribution tails (maximum plausible values in particular),
2 security assessment information,
3 any missing data when other relevant information was available,
4 the two-part transformation they needed to consider in order to relate fatalities to expenditure on reducing fatalities, and
5 the four-part decomposition of E_S they needed to consider other correlated issues like injuries.

She did not think it would help the board to delve into the technical details, but she did think that an outline of some of the key working assumptions involved in her first cut at five suitable scenarios for her presentation that day might help them to understand the complex issues which NER needed to address, using some variant of these five size scenarios after they had been further developed.

Her starting position was the need for two 'benchmark scenarios' which facilitated talking about the transformations over the whole range and the extreme distribution tails, especially the high S value tail.

Her choice of 'lower benchmark' was simple. What she would call the 'S = 1 scenario' was unequivocally one fatality. This was simply the minimum feasible number of fatalities given fatalities occur. For transformation benchmarking purposes, it was comparable to a road traffic accident involving only one fatality in some respects, although it was different in other respects, for reasons she would touch on shortly.

Her choice of 'upper benchmark' was more complex. She had briefly experimented with several approximations to logarithmic fatality scales, to cope effectively and efficiently with the highly asymmetric probability distributions with very small probabilities of very large numbers of fatalities they had to address. She had decided that successive intervals or class marks increasing by a factor of about five for each successive increase led to an upper benchmark scenario which was appropriate given the physical upper limit on fatalities defined by the number of people on the trains colliding or otherwise directly involved who might be killed plus data available on relevant past incidents which went beyond NER experience.

A quick web search had revealed a French railway derailment accident 100 years ago involving 800 to 1,000 fatalities (there was uncertainty about the number). A physical upper limit for all fatalities resulting from a very high speed head-on collision involving two of NER's current trains might be in the range 1,000 to 2,000. But these were very extreme possibilities, with very low probabilities, and outcomes much closer to 200 fatalities were much more probable. She had concluded that a reasonable first-cut approach for illustrative purposes that day would use an 'S = 350 scenario' as the 'catastrophe scenario' which represented the 'maximum plausible number of fatalities incident', formally interpreted as 'a conditional expectation of 350 fatalities associated with a scenario when more than 200 fatalities occurred in a single year, for most purposes associated with a single incident'.

Strictly speaking, the $P_0 = 0.0500$ and $(1 - P_0) = 0.9500$ assumption implied a very small probability of a second incident in the same year (0.0012 as noted earlier, about 1 in a 1,000), but there were several ways of accommodating the implications in practice, and for present purposes the board need not worry about these technicalities when thinking about an S = 350 scenario in terms of a single incident.

Both the 350 conditional expectation and the 200 lower bound on the associated range were illustrative values that she would adjust after the safety and security team better understood the full range of potential catastrophic incidents and their probabilities defining this 'upper benchmark'. For benchmarking purposes this 'catastrophe' scenario was comparable to an airplane crash in some respects, different in others. NER had never experienced any incidents in this category, and there were very few worldwide. It would be reasonable to hope that for NER an S = 350 scenario would *never* happen, *ever*. But one could happen tomorrow, and to simply ignore this possibility would be negligent.

One way the board might find it useful to think about an S = 350 scenario involved assuming 300, 500, 700, 900, or 1,100 fatalities associated with 0.800, 0.160, 0.032, 0.006, and 0.001 conditional probabilities, a discrete S value probability tree with five equal interval S values representing a range of from 200 to 1,200 fatalities, with decreases for each successive probability which were about a factor of five. This implied a conditional expected outcome of 350. A simple continuous variable equivalent in the HAT framework involved assuming the discrete values of 300, 500, . . . , 1,100 are class mark values for a rectangular histogram conditional probability distribution. In continuous variable terms, 200 to 400 fatalities are portrayed by a mid-range class mark of 300. Similarly, 400 to 600 fatalities were portrayed by a class mark of 500 and so on (in practice, 200 to 399, 400 to 590, and so on).

The 350 needed rounding down to reflect the bias on the high side imparted by assuming a rectangular histogram distribution and then rounding up again to reflect the effect of possible values above 1,200. However, if this continuous variable distribution portrayal was assumed, it was useful to recognise the need to deal with a monetary unit later anyway, and the uncertainty levels associated with the T_S transformations.

Of *much* more importance, the S = 350 scenario needed linking to a set of contributing 'sub-scenarios' which the safety and security team could put together when they explored specific train layouts and the physical implications of what might happen in various kinds of incidents. These sub-scenarios could range from worst to best case examples within the catastrophe scenario range, with relative likelihoods, the shape of the curve as a whole, and the understanding the safety and security team had already in different frameworks. This would lead to adjusting the conditional distribution shape as well as the probability a collision involves 200 or more fatalities and the current nominal 200 and 350 values.

Her intermediate interpolation scenarios, S = 5, 20, and 70, used incremental increases from 5 to 20 and from 20 to 70 which were not a consistent exact factor of five change. This was to keep interpretation simple and credible, for reasons she would explain shortly.

The 'S = 70 scenario' was a 'disaster' scenario, nominally a conditional expected value of 70 in the 40–199 fatalities range, embracing their recent 40 fatalities derailment example. Although NER had never experienced as many as 70 fatalities in a single collision, they had experienced an S = 70 scenario in her 'disaster' scenario sense in a derailment context.

The 'S = 20 scenario' was a 'very serious incident' scenario, nominally a conditional expected value of 20 in the 10–39 fatalities range, embracing their recent 30 fatalities collision.

The 'S = 5 scenario' was a 'serious incident' scenario, nominally a conditional expected value of 5 in the 2–9 fatalities range, removing the 'very' from the S = 20 scenario, but avoiding any language which played down the situation.

For illustrative purposes, to put the definitions of these five scenarios together and provide some example P_S values for S = 0, . . . , 350 in a deliberately simple tabular framework for their 'collision with fatalities' example, they would use Table 9.1.

Table 9.1 was a plausible approximation to the assumptions needed by NER as a starting point for safety and security decisions centred on collisions with fatalities. In addition to the P_0 and some of the CP_S being contentious for reasons she did not want to discuss until they had more developed unbiased expected value estimates, this table as a whole would need revision and refinement by the safety and security team before it was used by the board to make real decisions.

Table 9.1 Example five scenario portrayal of 'collisions with fatalities' incidents for L = 0.05, $P_0 = 0.9500$ so $(1 - P_0) = 0.0500$, and the assumed illustrative values for CP_S shown.

Size scenarios	*CP_S for S greater than 0 and P_S for scenarios S = 0 to 350*			*Contributions to F, the annual expected number of fatalities*	
S (nominal range)	*CP_S*	*$(1 - P_0) \times CP_S$*	*P_S*	*$S \times P_S$*	*(as a %)*
0			0.9500	$0 \times 0.9500 = 0.0000$	(0%)
1	0.05	$0.0500 \times 0.05 = 0.0025$		$1 \times 0.0025 = 0.0025$	(0%)
5 (2–9)	0.50	$0.0500 \times 0.50 = 0.0250$		$5 \times 0.0250 = 0.1250$	(15%)
20 (10–39)	0.40	$0.0500 \times 0.40 = 0.0200$		$20 \times 0.0200 = 0.4000$	(47%)
70 (40–199)	0.04	$0.0500 \times 0.04 = 0.0020$		$70 \times 0.0020 = 0.1400$	(17%)
350 (200–1,200+)	0.01	$0.0500 \times 0.01 = 0.0005$		$350 \times 0.0005 = 0.1750$	(21%)
				F = 0.8425	(100%)

She needed to explain Table 9.1 to board members in some detail to ensure that they were all comfortable with what it said, *assuming that the numbers were reasonable for the illustrative purposes intended at this initial meeting.* All board members needed to be comfortable with what Table 9.1 implied in this sense. She would build an example analysis on the implications of Table 9.1 to explore the implications of her approach as a whole, so understanding its foundations clearly mattered.

On a column by column basis, starting with the left-hand column, the 'size of incident' was portrayed by S = 0 plus the five 'size scenarios' S = 1, 5, 20, 70, and 350. As already explained, S = 1 was the 'lower benchmark' scenario, S = 350 was the 'upper benchmark' scenario interpreted as a 'catastrophe scenario', and S = 5, 20, and 70 were the intermediate scenarios.

The 'nominal range' for each S in brackets was a convenient working assumption to assist interpretation for scenarios other than S = 0 and 1. The crucial choice was the nominal range for S = 350 of 200 to 1,200+ as already discussed. She had assumed that more than 200 fatalities involved a conditional probability of any particular S value in the region of 1,000 fatalities approaching zero fast enough to pull the expected value down to about 350 whatever the actual maximum number of fatalities involved might be. Her safety and security team would have to explore the robustness of this assumption, and perhaps adjust the 350 currently defining the conditional expectation or the 200 currently defining the bottom end of the range or the illustrative 1,200+ upper end. It was important that the S = 350 scenario, revised as appropriate, provided an unbiased estimate of a catastrophe scenario defined by a nominal range like '200 up to the physical maximum defined by the system accommodating the possibility of more than one incident in any given year'. The exact shape of the curve associated with this scenario range was important. How it linked to the rest of the curve for all scenarios was also important. But a coherent and robust understanding of the 'catastrophe scenario incident' based on the knowledge of the physical systems involved and what happened during an incident was essential, a deeper kind of understanding which she and her team would have to ensure was robust. They would have to be able to convince the board they had done this effectively for the board to do their job effectively, which is why the board needed to start to understand what needed to be done that day.

Five size scenarios were judged to be a reasonable compromise between the unhelpful simplicity of a smaller number and the unenlightening complexity of a larger number, but four or six might prove to be preferable alternatives.

The example scenario S values she had used increased on a scale which was approximately logarithmic – an exact factor of 5 increases from the lower benchmark value (from 1 to 5) and to the upper benchmark value (from 70 to 350), slightly compressed in the middle ranges (from 5 to 20 to 70). The size scenario ranges and spans also increase by approximately a factor of 5 each time. Approximate factor of five increases each time yielded the overall range needed, given five size scenarios. A logarithmic approach provided a simple way to capture the implications of the distribution's extreme asymmetry (skew) which was often used. In this case, Sophie thought from 1 to 5 was a useful start, but 5 to 25 followed by 125 and then 625 made both the 'catastrophe' scenario of 625 and the 'disaster' scenario of 125 too extreme, with a smaller probability for the 625 scenario than she wanted for her example purposes.

Generalisation within this framework to S = 1, . . . , m could be based on fitting a convenient non-linear curve to the five scenario S values and an assumed zero probability upper limit, then interpolating for all integer values of S.

The CP_S represented conditional probabilities associated with the five S = 1, . . . , 350 size scenarios. She was assuming they would estimate these five values directly. They would, of course, have to ensure that their CP_S estimates sum to unity, as for her example values. The Table 9.1 CP_S values were plausible, but estimated for illustrative purposes only, to two places of decimal.

For S = 0 the P_0 = 0.9500 in the second of the two P_S value columns was based on the Poisson distribution L = 0.05 assumption as discussed earlier. But for S = 1 to 350 the assumed illustrative CP_S values and the $P_S = (1 - P_0) \times CP_S$ relationship was used to calculate the P_S.

Examining past NER collisions with fatalities, and then other railway system collisions with fatalities, was obviously one starting place to build a story, if not a database in a direct sense, to underlie Table 9.1. However, the 'complete story' associated with incidents involving fatalities had to look at all NER near misses, plus all the ways incidents might happen which were suggested by a range of circumstances, from changes in operating practices to changes in maintenance contract structures. Furthermore, some of the 'missing data' were related to malicious incidents which did not involve railways.

For example, the 9/11 terrorist attacks in the US, and the 7/7 London bombings in the UK, were two examples with important implications for NER. A heavy vehicle left on a level crossing when two high speed trains were approaching from opposite directions was one possibility, but there were many others. Such attacks would specifically target S = 350 and 70 scenarios, also increasing the chances of an S = 20 scenario. Depending on assumptions about terrorist capability and intensions, the CP_S increases would favour the higher S-value scenarios to varying degrees.

All these P_S values were contentious, but she was convinced that they were appropriate for illustrative purposes, and NER would need to demonstrate *why* it was reasonable to use more favourable P_S values if that was what the NER board believed. NER could not afford to use any approach which implicitly assumed an optimistically biased variant of the implications of the S = 350, 70, 20, 5 and 1 scenarios portrayed by Table 9.1. She indicated she had actually estimated the 0.01 probability associated with an S = 350 scenario first, having adjusted her catastrophic scenario to get an answer of about 0.01 for illustrative convenience, and in practice a comparable approach based on suitable data could be useful.

The final columns showed contributions to F, with F defined as 'the annual expected number of fatalities', equal to the sum of the S × P_S. The sum yielded F = 0.8425, with the relative size of each contribution expressed as a percentage in brackets. F = 0.8425 rounded up to one implies that if these probabilities were of the right order of magnitude, NER should expect about one fatality per annum from collisions 'on average'.

The S × CP_S might have been shown, and then summed to compute the expected number of fatalities if a collision occurred, 16.85. In rounded terms this meant NER could expect about 17 fatalities on average when incidents involving fatalities occurred, about 20 fatalities rounded in a manner consistent with both one fatality per year on average and one incident every 20 years on average.

She then emphatically emphasised a point of crucial importance, central to understanding all safety and security analysis approaches and their implications – *the 'average' was not even remotely representative of what was actually going to happen most of the time, and all the 'averages' involved were only meaningful concepts over a VERY long period.*

For all practical purposes an 'average year' involving one fatality caused by a collision was exceedingly unlikely – the return period for this scenario was about 400 years. Furthermore, an 'average incident' was also very unlikely – assuming an 'average collision incident' meant 17 fatalities or 20 if rounding was used. Even if 20 fatalities were interpreted in the S = 20 scenario sense, meaning 10 to 39 fatalities, this view of 'an average collision incident' had only a 0.0200 probability, implying a 50 year return period, one every 50 years on average.

What was never going to happen was a regular pattern of collision incidents every 20 years, including one S = 350 every 2,000 years, and one S = 1 every 400 years. No collision incident was the most likely outcome, with an assumed 0.9500 probability per annum.

Furthermore, when all incidents involving fatalities were considered later in her analysis, they would have to formally recognise that most years involve no collisions and no derailments but very large numbers of suicides (people taking their own lives using trains) and small numbers of people killed accidentally in level-crossing incidents.

Random processes were notoriously difficult to visualise, even for people with extensive relevant theoretical and practical background. Highly asymmetric distributions with one very long tail made the implications of random processes even more difficult to visualise. The portrayal of an asymmetric distribution with one long tail provided by Table 9.1 helped to clarify some of the key issues driven by these very long tails in ways which were worth a brief pause for reflection before building on the basis it provided.

The S = 350 scenario had only 1% of the conditional probability, a $CP_S = 0.01$. But 21% of the value of F was contributed by this scenario, as indicated by the percentage contributions shown in brackets in the last column. This was because the leverage applied by the long distribution tail was crucial. The expected value was the point of balance of the probability distribution in density form – technically defined as the first moment about the origin. It was very important to understand that very small probabilities associated with very big numbers of fatalities mattered greatly in expected value terms. This was in addition to obviously mattering a very great deal if they occurred. In expected value terms, they mattered much more than the very small probabilities might suggest – a counter-intuitive implication for most people, including some experts.

The S = 70 scenario had 4% of the conditional probability, a CP_S four times more than the 0.01 of the S = 350 scenario. However, 17% of F was contributed by the S = 70 scenario, marginally less than the 21% contribution of the S = 350 scenario. This was because of the way the logarithmic S value scale highlights the inherent implications of very long distribution tails.

The S = 20 scenario had 40% of the conditional probability, with a CP_S ten times more than the S = 70 scenario, 40 times more than the S = 350 scenario. But it contributed 47% of F, only about three times as much as the S = 70 scenario, about twice as much as the S = 350 scenario.

The S = 5 scenario had 50% of the conditional probability, but it contributed only 15% of F, yet again because of the way the logarithmic scale highlights the importance of the long tailed distribution effect.

The S = 1 scenario contribution to F was 0%, working to the nearest percentage, despite the fact that it contributes 5% of the conditional probability.

The board needed to remember that NER had never had a 'collision with fatalities' incident greater than 30 before, their 40 fatalities 'derailment' was just into the S = 70 scenario range of 40 to 199, and NER had never had an S = 350 size of incident of any kind before. However, incidents involving more than 200 fatalities were clearly feasible, and if they happened the board would be directly accountable.

Table 9.1 indicates incidents involving 40 or more fatalities make a 17% + 21% = 38% contribution to the expected number of fatalities per annum, despite being associated with only 5% of the conditional probability, so the probability of 40 or more fatalities mattered greatly in expected outcome terms. Although the individual illustrative parameter estimates were contentious, Table 9.1 was a plausible overall portrayal, and in broad terms her inferences based on this table's values were robust for that day's discussion purposes.

If NER used a biased approach to estimating P_S and F values because of a lack of due atten-tion to what was possible but had not yet occurred, or there was a cultural tendency to ignore very low probability possibilities, NER was missing what really mattered. If this was the case, arguably serious negligence would be involved because NER experts should know what really mattered and the NER board members should know whether or not they could trust their NER experts to know what really mattered.

The board needed to remember that train carriages were much safer than they used to be, and many significant improvements in other safety features for the system as a whole had been achieved. NER had done a lot of very positive things to make rail travel safer. However, trains were faster than they used to be, with still faster very high speed trains on the agenda.

The board also needed to reflect that recent terrorist concerns around the world, coupled to a near-miss interpretation of the two major accidents in the past two years (both could have been very much worse), suggested *diligently maintaining a very healthy level of ongoing concern for 'long tail incidents' – learning to be afraid of potential extreme events.*

Table 9.1 suggested they were unlucky to have had an S = 20 collision with fatalities inci-dent (with 30 fatalities) in the last two years plus an S = 70 (with 40 fatalities) derailment, but they were also lucky that neither was *much* worse. A further very serious incident in the near future would be widely interpreted as negligence if they could not convincingly dem-onstrate why this was not the case, and at present they could not do so.

However, while this kind of inference was useful to familiarise the board with some basic implications of long tailed distributions associated with low probability but high impact incidents, the real purpose of Table 9.1 was starting to build a numerical model from the bottom in a series of layers, which the board could use to understand the top-down perspec-tive the board needed to make strategic decisions. As she had explained earlier, they had a series of steps to take, and a broad top-down understanding of Table 9.1 was the first of these steps.

There was an obvious need for the safety and security team to look at the conditional probability values and their links back to L in terms of all relevant underlying models and data. It would be crucial for her team and the board to preserve the clarity of the kind of top-down view illustrated by Table 9.1, maintaining a focus on what seemed to matter most.

The evidence basis for the base-case model probabilities they would use in practice needed to be as sound as possible, using all the lessons learned by an international community of safety experts over many years, plus the accessible databases of all other relevant railways as well as in-house NER data and expertise. However, synthesis of this evidence basis in an NER context also had to rely on inherently subjective expert judgement, guided by a range of models with inherent approximations built into their assumptions. One key issue was 'To what extent, and for what reasons, would near future and longer term future possible incident probabilities be different from those in the past?' Another was 'How should *all* relevant near-miss information and interpretations, including new security alerts, be linked to a coherent overview which made full use of all available information in a robust manner?' Sophie suggested that the Poisson model perspective was particularly useful when doing this from a top-down perspective, and it would help them to integrate these concerns with an approach to size scenarios which allowed them to avoid specific distribution assumptions and make use of physical characteristics, like 'the maximum number of passengers on the trains currently in use or proposed'.

The interpretation of Table 9.1 which she had just explored in considerable detail empha-sised that NER were dealing with a very simple basic model associated with a very complex underlying reality, and it was important to understand in broad terms what the underlying complexities involved and implied. Table 9.1 could be given an even simpler format, using a probability tree presentation without the range information, if this was useful, but the underlying complexities always need to be understood and remembered.

While keeping the modelled portrayals simple for board level presentations, a rich interpretation of significant underlying analysis would be their aim in practice. If useful as part of this, a different scale or more size scenarios or more sophisticated underlying curve assumptions could be used for additional clarity. NER could design an efficient approach to increasing clarity with no bounds imposed by specific distribution assumptions or any other assumptions that could not be tested for robustness, a defining characteristic of the EP approach she was using.

A two part transformation from fatalities to fatality related cost, $T_S = V_1 \times E_S$

Sophie emphasised that most organisations involved in operations which could lead to fatalities now used some variant of a 'value of an avoided fatality' concept to transform fatalities into a cost equivalent. The avoided fatality concept was by no means new – she was aware of one publication dating back to 1930, *The Money Value of a Man* (Dublin and Lotka, 1930). However, the exact nature of the concept was still evolving, ambiguous, and highly contentious.

There were a number of very different ways people currently viewed the nature of 'value of avoided fatality' concepts. They might be viewed on a spectrum, ranging from the 1970s bad practice Ford Pinto misinterpretation of the NHTSA cost–benefit analysis approach which she had just explained to a shadow price and revealed preference interpretation using the kind of T_S based approach she had used to interpret both the 1970s' NHTSA approach and Ford's inappropriate use of the $T = V = \$200,000$ NHTSA value. NER needed to adopt an S dependent variant of this T_S approach. It was important for NER to adopt the most general (unrestricted) perspective available, make use of a shadow cost and revealed preference interpretation with acknowledged ethical content, and chose numerical values appropriate to the NER context which could be linked to other current practice in terms of a grounded argument which all relevant parties could trust.

She observed that avoiding stealth assumptions was particularly difficult in a context involving trust between multiple parties and the possible loss of lives. But this made it especially important. A failure to address an effective shared understanding of all important assumptions which clarified important differences in opinion, as well as what did not matter, was arguably negligent in particularly serious terms.

As she had explained earlier, the simplest basic operational framework that NER could adopt to meet the crucial generality and clarity concerns involved a two part value transformation of the form $T_S = V_1 \times E_S$.

V_1 was a *benchmark* value of an avoided fatality at scenario level S = 1 relevant to NER, a suitable starting point or datum. E_S was an *everything else factor*. $T_S = V_1 \times E_S$ was the shadow cost and revealed preference transformation concept for all S = 1, . . . , m values, assuming that 'everything else' (over and above the V_1 value) which was relevant in terms of 'costs related to fatalities' was fully addressed by the E_S. By 'costs related to fatalities' what she meant in terms of the basic approach used earlier was 'all relevant costs *directly related* to fatalities'. She now wanted to start to explore a generalisation which interpreted 'costs related to fatalities' as 'all relevant costs *correlated with the number of fatalities* occurring'. The five size scenarios were a working assumption approximation which would let them focus on S = 1 and S = 350 scenarios initially and then interpolate for all relevant S values.

When using either the basic or the generalised form of this conceptual framework in the NER context, a $T = V_1 \times E$ special case was a gross oversimplification to a degree which was not acceptable in her view. But the board should know that the NER approach *being used at present* involved basic form approach with a $4 million value of an avoided fatality for all S values, so the NER current policy, implicitly if not explicitly approved by the board, was equivalent to approving her $V_1 = \$2$ million suggestion plus $E_S = 2$ for all S, a $T_S = \$4$ million for all S.

This current $T = \$4$ million value could be interpreted as 'an NER board approved revealed preference statement about the value of NER avoided fatalities for $S = 1, \ldots, m$'. $T = \$4$ million was currently being used for *all NER safety and security decisions with board approval. She appreciated that board members had probably not thought about it in these terms before. She believed they needed to start thinking about it this way immediately. Doing so was part of the process of beginning to understand why NER needed to remember to be afraid. It was also part of the process of beginning to understand what needed to be done about it and how they could develop a position which was defensible even if further serious incidents occurred.*

The five scenarios approach would allow NER to treat fatalities associated with the $S = 350$ scenario as more important *per fatality* than fatalities associated with the $S = 1$ scenario fatalities, with three intermediate levels of relative importance. This analysis could then be used as a basis for a non-linear curve generalisation.

The controversial nature of the appropriate T_S shadow prices and their revealed preference basis would not go away, but being able to accommodate increasing E_S values as S increased would allow NER to alter the trade-offs deemed appropriate between expenditure on making the system safer and tolerating fatalities as the value of S increased. *Crucially, it would allow NER to explore and test all related working and framing assumptions to better understand what they were doing, facilitating trust which would be seen as well founded by all relevant parties, even if very serious incidents took place in the near future.*

E_S had to reflect NER board views about an appropriate uplift from V_1 for $S = 350$ as well as $S = 1$, addressing the common view that large numbers of people killed in one incident was relatively more serious than the same number killed one at a time in separate incidents, as noted earlier. But while S dependence was important for NER, overall ethical and related trust concerns, including related tests for overall robustness, were *much* more important. E_S values used to make NER safety and security decisions were a board level decision that really mattered. *Directly confronting the full implications of E_S choices would help everyone to understand both what really mattered and why it really mattered.*

Using $E_S = A_S + I_S + D_S + R_S$ decomposition to make analysis simpler and more effective

Given the need to address E_S dependence on S to deal with fatalities, they could usefully employ this S dependent framework to make the overall analysis simpler in several key respects, as well as a more effective – achieving a higher level of clarity efficiency. They could do this by decomposing her generalised interpretation E_S involving cost related to fatalities which included the implications of injuries plus other relevant concerns usually correlated with fatalities into four component factors, each associated with three plausible options in terms of approach. They could use different options for different purposes at different stages in the analysis process. At first sight this might look even more complicated to a disturbing extent, but each aspect of the complexity involved was constructive – designed to pay significant dividends in terms of keeping it simple systematically at an overall analysis level.

As an initial overview, it involved decomposing E_S into four components in order to embed within E_S:

1   the treatment of fatalities, *plus*
2   injuries which were correlated with fatalities, *plus*
3   physical damage to the system and directly related knock-on implications which were correlated with fatalities, *plus*
4   any other issues which were correlated with the number of fatalities and not fully captured by the first three separate components, for 'closure with completeness'.

While this might initially look unnecessarily complicated, in practice it actually involved a form of *local complication which greatly simplified overall management decision making in an enlightened manner*, an important feature of the enlightened simplicity aspects of the EP approach she advocated.

Fully exploiting this multiple part decomposition of E_S as a potential approach option for all organisations would now be part of a generalisation and broadening of her interpretation of what all organisations could and should mean by E_S and the complete range of roles which E_S could perform.

A central issue for the NER board that day was why this particular four part decomposition was not really an option for NER and why the board had to mandate the use of a four component S dependent E_S concept. The board needed to understand what had to be done, which required an overview understanding of how to do it and why this complexity was necessary.

The first component was the 'avoided fatalities factor' A_S – a factor associated with adjusting V_1 for all the revealed preference implications of avoided fatalities on the NER railway system as distinct from road traffic accident avoided fatalities. A_S was focused on all NER revealed preference aspects of fatalities which were not captured by V_1.

'Option A' for this first component was further focused on the expected cost of legal settlements imposed by the courts, out-of-court settlements, legal fees and fines for the S level involved – the actual NER expected cash flow costs directly related to fatalities. Option A would not attempt to assess common practice shadow cost or ethical and trust related concerns which might go beyond these cash flow costs. This was her 'minimum plausible' option for the first component, which she believed was useful for some sensitivity analysis purposes at a later stage in the analysis but not initially. They had to formally acknowledge that A_S was an uncertain parameter even for a given S value, and the associated option A value was a useful plausible minimum for some purposes.

'Option B' would increase this plausible minimum to incorporate a fair and reasonable interpretation of common practice shadow cost values of avoided fatality concerns for the S level involved without going beyond a reasonable interpretation of 'good practice'. This was her 'mid-range' option, which she suggested they start with for initial analysis purposes. She believed that a good practice option was a convenient starting position working assumption and it was also a useful part of the basis for later discussion of best practice choices.

'Option C' would further increase this mid-range value by adding a maximum plausible ethics and trust provision to A_S. This was her 'maximum plausible' upper bound option, relevant to discussions of NER best practice A_S choices.

She believed the board should eventually agree an A_S estimate value in the option B to option C range, using carefully considered and delivered advice and guidance from the NER safety and security team, but without firm, specific recommendations from her team, *because the choice involved was a board level judgement with crucial ethical dimensions.*

As a summary for A_S, her option A was a 'plausible minimum', option B added a good practice uplift, option C added a further NER best practice driven 'maximum plausible' uplift, and she was suggesting starting initial analysis with the option B good practice uplift with a view to the board eventually making a choice in the range between options B and C.

The second component was the 'injuries factor' I_S – a factor associated with further adjusting V_1 in order to make a provision for injuries on a per fatality basis. At present, NER were assessing the number of people injured to various levels of severity in each relevant potential incident separately from their fatality estimates, making use of a number of categories of injury seriousness. They then used a proportion of the T = $4 million value of an avoided fatality for each of these categories of injury seriousness, plus the numbers of people injured in incidents. This was a variant of the NHTSA and Ford approach, which was still widespread common practice. She suggested NER could greatly simplify this approach in a manner consistent with common practice norms and make it much more effective and efficient at the same time. They could do so by looking at the expected number of injuries in all relevant injury categories on a per fatality basis as S changed and focus NER attention on the *overall* importance of these injuries relative to the associated number of fatalities because it was the joint importance of these correlated outcomes which really mattered. They would obviously have to test the robustness of this correlation working assumption, but she believed it would prove viable, given their focus on what really mattered.

She suggested they start with a mid-range option B working assumption for this I_S component. This was linked to the A_S component option B choice, bearing in mind that estimated option A and C alternatives for I_S linked to the A_S component could also be used for the I_S component. That is, for initial use they should estimate the expected value of avoiding all the injuries which occurred in conjunction with S fatalities as an expected cost function of S, using an approach consistent with the mid-range option B choice for A_S and comparable common-practice norms for different injury categories. Linked option A and C estimates would also be available.

The third component was the 'damage factor' D_S – a factor associated with further adjusting V_1 in order to make a provision for physical damage to the system plus all the associated knock-on operating cost and lost revenue effects assumed to be correlated with fatalities. Instead of estimating these direct and opportunity costs separately, NER should treat them as an expected value function of S within the E_S approach. In terms of the overall analysis and its interpretation, this would be much simpler, a further useful improvement in clarity efficiency. It was based on a strong and arguably crude assumption, which would need testing for robustness and might involve significant variability about the expected outcomes assumed, but she had no doubt that it would prove a viable working assumption given their focus on what really mattered. She suggested NER begin with a mid-range option B approach as for the first two components, but this time NER should recognise that the minimum plausible option A approach would be a plausible minimum cost estimate of actual direct costs and lost revenue, the maximum plausible option C was a plausible maximum cost estimate of actual direct costs and lost revenue, and the NER mid-range estimate ought to be an unbiased estimate of the expected outcome.

The fourth component was the 'residual factor' R_S – a factor associated with a 'residual provision' for any concerns not fully captured by the other three component factors of E_S. At its simplest this 'residual provision' would include a very simple rounding up to acknowledge the importance of all relevant unresolved ambiguity. But more specifically, it would also include a crucial 'prudence provision', to be discussed later in the context of enlightened prudence. In addition, R_S as a whole should round up the T_S relationship appropriately to validate an NER board view that *all* relevant concerns had been addressed appropriately and grounded trust which was well founded was assured. This would ensure 'closure with completeness'. R_S should explicitly address a residual to deal with *any* relevant issues not *fully* covered by the first three components, including *all* relevant trust contribution concerns not fully built into good practice approaches already embedded in the first three components. In the R_S case, the issues involved in the options A, B, and C approach would have to reflect plausible minimum, maximum, and mid-range views about trust contribution concerns given the option choices for the first three components. She suggested a mid-range option B working assumption as a starting position, consistent with three earlier option B choices, although the nature of the range involved was clearly much more complex, needing elaboration best deferred until later.

At this stage she wanted board members to understand in broad overview terms how the four components of E_S played their collective roles, not the details, but as summary they might find useful later, she was suggesting NER adopt her four option B assumptions and use

$$E_S = A_S + I_S + D_S + R_S,$$

where:

1   A_S was the 'avoided fatalities factor' associated with adjusting V_1 for all the revealed preference implications of avoided fatalities on the NER railway system as distinct from the road traffic accident avoided fatalities addressed by the NHA. Assuming option B would mean including a provision for all the S dependent implications of court judgements, out-of-court settlements, legal costs, and fines, and it would also reflect good practice approaches based on a shadow cost interpretation linked to earlier cost–benefit analysis practices, but it would not go beyond current good practice norms for an approach based on shadow cost and revealed-preference interpretation.

2   I_S was the 'injuries factor' associated with further adjusting V_1 in order to make a provision for avoided injuries on a per fatality basis. Injuries were assumed to be correlated with fatalities. I_S had to address revealed preference concerns comparable to those associated with fatalities. But a range of degree of injury categories needed to be addressed, and any other relevant differences between fatalities and injuries also needed consideration, like how did the numbers and distribution of different types of injury change as S changed. The approach to I_S in terms of options A, B, or C obviously had to be consistent with the approach to A_S.

3   D_S was the 'damage factor' associated with further adjusting V_1 in order to make a provision for physical damage to the system plus all associated knock-on direct cost and an opportunity cost portrayal of lost revenue effects assumed to be correlated with fatalities. D_S needed to reflect how all these costs on a per fatality basis changed as a function of S, using an expected value estimate of actual cash flow costs and the opportunity cost equivalent of lost revenues.

4   R_S was the 'residual factor' associated with a 'residual provision' for any concerns not fully captured by the other three E_S component factors which rounded up the T_S relationship appropriately to capture an NER board view of *all* the issues relevant to well-founded trust, including enlightened prudence, fully reflecting a board level test that all relevant concerns had been addressed appropriately.

Trust in NER board level decisions involving safety and security should be seen as directly dependent upon the R_S values *given* the other three E_S factor values and the V_1 value. *But trust in board level decisions was also conditional on the rest of the NER approach to safety and security, including implementation as well as planning.*

The choices of numerical values for A_S, I_S, D_S, and R_S which were preferred by each board member might be very different. All board members needed a reasonable degree of collective agreement about plausible working assumptions for external discussion purposes. But what really mattered was collective agreement about the board's preferred overall T_S values because it was the overall T_S values which defined the revealed preferences of the board implied by decisions taken.

All board members needed T_S values they could live with. T_S values were a board approved revealed preference statement by NER of how much NER was prepared to spend to reduce by one the number of fatalities associated with each possible S value associated directly with A_S, together with all the correlated issues addressed via I_S, D_S and R_S values. T_S values were shadow costs given ethical content based on a revealed-preference interpretation. R_S was a useful focal point for board level agreement about T_S, given assumed values of V_1, A_S, I_S, and D_S subjected to earlier scrutiny. *But different board members could have different views about R_S values and other T_S components, so long as they agreed to T_S values, and the broad nature of the case for the underlying four component values.*

The additive E_S components relationship was 'nominal' for two reasons, both worth understanding. One reason was that a multiplicative alternative to the additive form used earlier might be preferred, and this choice was a matter open to debate. The major reason, of *much* more importance, was the relationship defining T_S in terms of any four parameter structure was a 'nominal' relationship because if somebody believed the T_S values were about right overall, but one of these component factors should be much bigger, while any of the other components should be much smaller, with no net overall change in T_S, *it was crucial that they and everyone else understood this would make no overall difference to NER decision outcomes.* The NER board's revealed preferences were defined by the choices the board made as a collective group of people acting as a group, with no direct relationship to the underlying preferences of individual board members. This second reason meant that it might not be worth arguing about the details of different component values, although discussing the rationale of the component structure and the nature of the values used was, in general, very important, and crucial presentation issues would also need attention.

Trust depended on understanding in broad terms the practical implications of the T_S values used to make choices, plus the nature and motives of alternative perspectives and values, which need not be common, but have to be judged reasonable or not reasonable, given due accommodations for other peoples' different concerns and perspectives.

Crucially, the board needed to agree on the net effect of the E_S given V_1 without any *compulsory* need for agreement about the details of the component contributions within this E_S structure. *Agreement about the component values was highly desirable and should be addressed in an effective manner, but it was NOT compulsory.* Furthermore, and perhaps even more crucially, *NER needed to make it clear to all other interested parties why it could take a comparable view.*

Some substantive differences in component values might suggest differences in perspectives which do need extensive clarifying discussion and reconciliation, and where these differences of opinion really mattered they might need resolution. But when differences of opinion did not matter, or did not matter very much, everybody needed clarity about why this was the case. Discussion needed to take place within a commonly understood and accepted framework so that reaching an agreement could focus on what mattered, using shared framing assumptions to clearly articulate alternative perspectives on what mattered most. *Without shared framing assumptions effective dialogue would not be feasible.*

A key aspect of the rationale for the use of the $T_S = V_1 \times E_S$ structure defined in terms of four components of E_S was recognising the value of separate treatment of industry benchmarks, other relevant good practice approaches based on shadow cost and revealed-preference interpretations, and common practice values which were relevant over a bad or debatable practice to best practice range, plus the underlying role of legal settlements, out-of-court settlements, and fines.

Also key was board level judgements about each of these categories of concern in an integrated framework without the need for any more parameters or any more effort or any more agreement about components than necessary.

The structure itself was designed to make the first three of the four E_S components free of *direct* ethical and trust-based adjustments beyond good practice norms if a mid-range option B was used for the first two components. The option A approach to A_S and I_S meant that if the good practice increases used to define option B were moved to R_S, the first three components would all be direct cash cost measures, and separate decomposition of R_S components could be a focus for sensitivity analysis in a useful manner that she would discuss later.

She believed that the four components approach just outlined was sound in overall terms, and its particular four option B choice form was a good place to start for initial presentation purposes. However, a key EP tool was a rich range of *alternative presentation strategies* to clarify the analysis interpretation from different perspectives, briefly explored later. As an overview now, option A (minimum plausible) approaches to the first two components could be useful for comparative purposes, *provided* that the shadow price based good practice uplifts to the A_S and I_S, which were removed when dropping option B in favour of option A for these two components, were reinserted in the R_S in a clearly identified manner. This would mean that all the first three components were strictly limited to cash flow measures, allowing discussion of a decomposed R_S structure to focus on concerns going beyond issues which could be measured in cash flow terms. Having both these two *alternative presentation strategy choices* available was important, but starting with four option B choices was useful for several reasons. One reason was the need to make it very clear that even with four option B choices, a positive R_S was essential for enlightened prudence reasons.

In her initial four option B form, the R_S component was focused on trust contribution issues which the board believed were important and go beyond what is addressed by the first three components given option B choices. This approach reflected the recognition that good practices involved in defining V_1 and the A_S and I_S components of E_S would involve some trust-driven provisions. It was important to avoid missing out key trust contributions, but it was also important to avoid double counting when assessing good practice option B values for A_S and I_S. V_1 might be assumed to embody implicit ethics content basis even if NHA was not explicit about this issue.

The R_S component also formally addressed a 'rounding-up option', having required formal testing for completeness without double counting. As part of this it was useful to formally recognise the very ambiguous nature of revealed preferences, the further complexity introduced by a 'prudence provision', *plus the futility of excessively detailed calculations based on less important issues when the really big issues that really mattered were not amenable to precise numerical evaluation.* If estimating R_S beyond any given level of precision was not feasible, spending a lot of effort and money estimating A_S, I_S, or D_S to a significantly higher level of precision was a serious waste of time and money – clarity inefficient. This was wasted time and money which could be spent making the system safer. Put slightly differently, wasted effort on unproductive precision was a serious distraction when other activities would be much more useful, and the opportunity inefficiency which was implied needed to be avoided.

Part of the rationale for using an S dependent E_S instead of a $T = V_1 \times E$ approach was to allow incidents involving large numbers of fatalities to be weighted more heavily than incidents involving small numbers of fatalities via the A_S uplift. This issue might have been pursued via an $E_S = A_S$ concept which did not address the other three component factors. However, *overall* clarity efficiency was enhanced by the simpler four component E_S approach, considering S dependence only once, and allowing the board and other key interested parties to focus on agreed T_S values without necessarily reaching full agreement on component uplifts.

As an illustrative example, one director might see NER corporate reputation concerns as the really central issue, a second director might see the ethics of fatalities as the key, a third might see the full implications of life-changing injuries as the key – but it was the combined effect that actually mattered and required their collective agreement. They could agree to differ on their individual views about component parameter values, and even the nature of an appropriate V_1 and some of the underlying relationships, but if they disagreed about the total implied by T_S they were going to have to confront the implications and resolve their differences in a way they could all live with in the face of scrutiny by other interested parties.

Furthermore, passengers, staff, regulators, the courts, and the public needed to judge the board's decisions at a T_S level, no doubt with significant interest in exactly how they arrived at whatever numbers they used, but recognising the nominal nature of the components.

Different terminology and alternative views could be used, and comparisons which might become crucial in terms of disputes involving differences of opinion were complex. For example, an internal NER document about the $4 million value cited a report to the UK Rail Safety and Standards Board, *T430: The Definition of VPF and the Impact of Societal Concerns* by Oxford Risk Research and Analysis (Rail Safety and Standards Board, 2006). This report used the term *value of a prevented fatality* (VPF), a very limited view of 'revealed preference' approaches that explicitly rejected an S dependent approach to the A_S component, did not address an I_S or D_S component, did not explicitly address ethics and trust concerns, and omitted all other aspects of an R_S component. This approach was consistent with current NER practice and most common practice, the reason it was cited. In effect, Sophie being as highly critical of the Oxford Risk Research and Analysis approach as she was of the current NER approach, with concerns that went beyond the constant $T = \$4$ million value. She suspected the Oxford Risk Research and Analysis authors and many others might disagree with her approach. She believed that the enhanced and enlightened perspective that her overall approach provided could be defended against all critics who preferred alternatives by examining the stealth assumptions implicit in those alternatives from the general perspective which her EP approach provided. She accepted that a good case might be made for her simpler $T = V_1 \times E$ special case in many contexts which did not involve the very wide range of fatalities which railways had to cope with, but these would be special cases, not exemplars for a general rule which railways ought to use.

At an overview summary level, replacing the common practice S independent value of an avoided fatality approach with the more general S dependent $T_S = V_1 \times E_S$ approach using four component factors for E_S might not always be useful in direct operational terms with all four component factors S dependent in all contexts beyond NER. But the associated robustness tests were important in all contexts, and in her view the very wide range of potential fatalities involved in a single railway incident made it essential for NER. Furthermore, even if S dependence for A_S was not useful in some contexts (when only a very narrow range of fatalities was feasible for example), distinguishing T_S, V_1, and E_S concepts together with the four component factors for E_S was important *in all contexts* for several reasons. Acknowledging trust and underlying ethical concerns was particularly crucial, linked to the shadow cost and revealed preference basis for the T_S transformation, and these trust concerns involved complex issues like enlightened prudence which she would explore later, as repeatedly indicated.

Within this four component E_S framework, NER directors had currently approved R_S = 0 for all S, A_S = \$4 million for all S, and an approach which dealt with all I_S and D_S issues separately at a higher level of decision-making cost but a lower level of clarity. These choices involved stealth assumptions needing immediate attention.

The next stage in that day's overview of why this was the case would involve developing plausible illustrative numerical values for all four of the T_S components.

The avoided fatalities component $V_1 \times A_S$ for S = 1 and 350

To develop more clarity via illustrative numerical values for all four $V_1 \times E_S$ components of T_S prior to a detailed analysis of the issues and available data, a suitable starting point was A_S values for S = 1 and 350. Sophie had some feel for plausible ranges, and using these ranges she would suggest purely illustrative mid-range example values to outline her recommended approach. She was convinced that numerical examples would make it much easier for the board to understand what was involved, but she was also very concerned that they avoid wasting time on discussions about the validity of her particular illustrative example values for their initial meeting discussion, or even her assumed plausible ranges of values.

She would use A_1 = 1.1 and A_{350} = 5 so that the avoided fatalities component of T_S was

$$V_1 \times A_S = \$2m \times 1.1 = \$2.2m \text{ for S = 1,}$$
$$= \$2m \times 5 = \$10m \text{ for S = 350.}$$

This implied that a $V_1 \times A_S$ component of T_S varying over the range \$2.2 million to \$10 million as S went from S = 1 to S = 350 would replace the current T = \$4 million value for all S.

She suggested that A_1 = 1.1 might have a plausible range like –50% to +100%, but an uplift of 10% on the NHA value of V_1 = \$2 million to \$2.2 million provided what she thought was an appropriate illustrative initial stance when one NER fatality was involved. It implied a higher NER value than the NHA value even when only one fatality was involved because a lower value might be construed as unnecessarily controversial. But it was not much higher because she did not want to overstate the A_S values needed.

Her rationale for A_{350} = 5 was that no further uplift on A_1 = 1.1 did not seem plausible, and an uplift by a factor bigger than 10 seemed equally implausible. The approximate midpoint of these two equally implausible extremes was 5, a round number which would serve to illustrate what a number in the middle of what she saw as the plausible range did to the analysis results.

It was not worth trying to be precise about either of these example estimates for A_S or any of the other T_S components that day. She would later explain the basis of her views on ranges and outline the kind of research and operational development of parameters they would have to undertake.

For S = 1 and for S = 350 the essential core of this avoided fatalities uplift component of T_S was an adjustment to reflect the difference between road travel on public highways and rail travel on NER trains in measurable revealed preference terms, presented and explained as clearly as possible, which all parties could trust.

She thought it would not be useful to attempt to embed trust or ethically driven adjustments directly in A_S today in terms of a possible option C approach or address option A approaches and associated numerical differences.

The A_S fatalities uplift factor component of E_S had to reflect context specific concerns about both the underlying legal liability concerns associated with option A, plus the other revealed preference issues, measured using an option B approach in a plausibly neutral 'objective' manner. At this option B level, experts could argue about both values and methodological issues without addressing the ethical implications directly, but they did have to understand that 'common', 'good' and 'best practice' were not the same, and each meant different things to different people.

As an example of relevant context specific concerns, she suggested most people expected railway travel to be safer than road travel for a range of reasons. One reason was the loss of any semblance of control over personal safety by the traveller – people travelling in their own cars had a perception of control which they clearly lost when travelling by rail. She thought being sued by the families of those killed was generally not an issue for highways agencies, but NER might be sued even if only one fatality were involved, and action against NER in the courts would be almost inevitable following an S = 350 scenario, especially if any possibility of negligence was suspected. She did not think the private sector status of NER was very significant *at present* because NER was providing the only rail travel service available in the country, they operated like a public sector railway in most respects, including regulation, they were widely seen as a 'national treasure', and they had never been seen as an exploitive profit-maximising organisation. However, private/public sector status could become an issue, and she would return to this later. Even if only one fatality was involved in a collision, likely to be a train driver because of their position at the front of the train, in her view both staff and passengers would expect a private sector railway company to try to be safer than their country's road system and to be as safe or safer than other comparable private and public sector railways.

She thought that when S = 1 was involved, an A_S avoided fatality factor component of E_1 as low as 1.1 was appropriate because the highways agency T = \$2 million which she was proposing as V_1 presumably assumed two or more fatalities in a single road traffic accident was common, while the $V_1 \times A_1$ = \$2.2 million explicitly applied to only one fatality in a railway incident, linked to explicit provision for S dependent increases. This line of thinking could lead to plausible suggestions of a factor like 0.9 or less, involving an A_1 value lower than the benchmark, but she thought this would not be helpful in terms of approval by all relevant parties. There was a case for higher values than 1.1, but she believed they should link the current NER-assumed value of T = \$4 million to 'an average S level railway incident scenario' involving significantly more than one fatality for comparability purposes, part of her rational for settling on A_1 = 1.1 for illustrative purposes. Although she did not want to debate specific values today, it was worth observing that when she had the rest of her numbers and underlying models in order, this would be a key focal point for board level discussion.

When S = 350 was involved, the A_{350} = 5 and $V_1 \times A_{350}$ = \$10 million values had to reflect the difference between travel on public roads and rail travel on NER trains when very serious airplane crash levels of fatalities were involved. The public probably saw 1 to 3 fatalities as the usual outcome of car accidents involving fatalities, but 100 to 300 fatalities as the usual outcome of commercial airliner accidents involving fatalities, so an S = 350 scenario was a major catastrophe even by air crash standards.

NER might start by thinking about a V_{350} alternative to V_1 associated with its national airline instead of its national highways agency. The country's national airline had safety standards comparable to international airline safety standards which might suggest a V_{350} as much as ten times that of the V_1 for road traffic incidents. However, this ratio was highly controversial for a range of reasons, including the nature of the relationship between safety levels and levels of spending to avoid fatalities, what was measured, and the rationality of people expecting air travel to be safer than road and rail travel per passenger kilometre or mile.

She did not want to court controversy that day by overstating the case for an A_{350} which was bigger than A_1 to a questionable extent. However, in her view, the role of the courts and other aspects of revealed preference information available suggested that using an A_{350} = 5 value so that $V_1 \times A_{350}$ = $10 million provided a plausible round number illustration. The range for the value of $V_1 \times A_S$ from $2.2 million to $10 million as S went from 0 to 350 involved an average uplift by a factor of $10 million/$2.2 million = 4.5, which seemed plausible to her. Furthermore, this range was big enough to allow her to demonstrate what S dependence could imply but modest enough to avoid seriously overstating its importance.

The current V = $4 million used by NER was closer to the bottom-end $V_1 \times A_1$ = $2.2 million value than it was to the top-end $V_1 \times A_{350}$ = $10 million value and below the arithmetic mean of $6.1 million, but that was consistent with her understanding of the thinking behind the T = $4 million in current use.

Sophie reminded the board that they were talking about a catastrophic incident when they discussed the S = 350 scenario, involving from 200 to 1,200+ fatalities. NER had never experienced a catastrophe like this, and her working assumption was catastrophes at this level had a 2,000 year return period. But the S = 350 scenario clearly could happen, and the NER board had both a moral duty and a legal obligation to address how both the assumed impact and the assumed probability could be reduced, treating an S = 350 scenario with concern proportionate to its importance.

Assuming A_{350} = 5 was clearly debatable, over a very wide plausible range (like 1–10), but she did not want to engage in this debate today. The key issue here was she did not think that NER would be trusted, *nor should NER be trusted*, if they did not associate serious airplane crash levels of fatalities with air travel levels of safety as expressed through court judgements and all other relevant forms of revealed preference information. She had simply used what she saw as a plausible uplift from a road traffic situation basis to reflect this for illustrative purposes. When she had the rest of her numbers and underlying models in order, this would be another key focal point for board level dialogue.

The injuries component $V_1 \times I_S$ for S = 1 and 350

Sophie explained that she had outlined the rationale for her A_S illustrative numbers with some care because she believed the credibility of her approach with the board demanded this care, but it was not worth a comparable level of detail about her other example T_S component illustrative values for that day's presentation. Available data could be used in a relatively straightforward manner to develop initial estimate suggestions about appropriate operational values for I_S for S = 1 or 350 based on injuries at various levels of S, but she had not attempted anything more than purely illustrative numbers to illustrate her recommended approach for this initial meeting.

She would use $I_1 = 0.6$ and $I_{350} = 1.8$, so the injuries component of T_S was

$$V_1 \times I_S = \$2m \times 0.6 = \$1.2m \text{ for } S = 1,$$
$$= \$2m \times 1.8 = \$3.6m \text{ for } S = 350.$$

This implied that an I_S component of T_S varying over the range \$1.6 million to \$3.6 million would replace the current values derived from separate relatively complex computations.

She indicated that $I_1 = 0.6$ meant she was assuming that when $S = 1$ the total number of people injured in all categories of injury levels required slightly more than half of the weighting given to one fatality ($0.6/1.1 = 0.55$). She thought this was an appropriate illustrative initial stance when one NER fatality was involved in the absence of appropriate data analysis, to avoid playing down the importance of injuries without understating the importance of fatalities. A plausible range might be –50% to +100%, and both data and current NER equivalent fatality assessments for injuries would be used later.

NER currently used a proportion of their $T = \$4$ million for injuries in a number of different injury categories, comparable to common practice since the 1970s NHTSA and Ford Pinto approaches. In this way NER currently converted estimates of the numbers injured into 'equivalent fatalities', treating a small number of seriously injured people as equivalent to one fatality, a larger number of moderately injured people as equivalent to one fatality, and so on, separately estimating numbers of people in each of these categories. She was recommending they avoided this kind of detail, saving effort as well as increasing clarity. They would be basing their injuries component of T_S on an assumed expected number of injuries in different categories of seriousness for each fatality plus an average $V_1 \times A_S$ equivalence, linked to scenario examples to clarify the weighting behind these averages. Estimates of expected numbers of people injured to different degrees and associated ranges could be provided whenever injuries were an issue, and the kind of 'equivalent fatalities' metric currently used by NER might provide particularly useful initial guidance, drawing on their approach when modelling incidents involving injuries but no fatalities (grade 2). However, in her view modelling injuries within the E_S factor via I_S would save time currently spent on detail which was not very productive. It would also ensure that the correlation between the numbers of people killed and injured in incidents was dealt with effectively. And crucially, it would contribute to integrating all cost related to fatalities in a useful manner which allowed different people to weight injuries relative to fatalities in different ways within an agreed overall T_S value.

In her view, $V_1 \times I_1 = £2$ million $\times 0.6 = \$1.2$ million was a plausible order of magnitude until they had done more work on available data, but the numbers were purely illustrative, not intended to suggest recommendations. She suspected the board might want a very careful and detailed discussion of these issues after she and her team had done a significant background preparation. Testing the relationship between this greatly simplified I_S factor approach and current practice would be an essential part of initially estimating appropriate I_S values.

Her $I_{350} = 1.8$ rationale was simply a factor of three increase on the $I_1 = 0.6$ value, to reflect a lower level S effect than for fatalities, assuming the number of people injured in various categories for every fatality did not change too massively as S increased. She currently had no real understanding of how the scale and nature of injuries could be expected to change as S increased, so her purely illustrative example numbers for the I_S involved a particularly wide uncertainty range associated with her very simple factor of three assumption. Some directors might hold very different views about the relative importance of injuries versus fatalities, making discussion crucial when effective prior data analysis could support it properly.

The damage component $V_1 \times D_S$ for $S = 1$ and 350

It was obviously important to consider directly associated knock-on operating costs and opportunity costs associated with lost revenue in addition to any physical material damage costs as part of the costs NER had to meet given an incident involving fatalities. In her view a further T_S component factor defined by $V_1 \times D_S$ for the cost of damage to rolling stock and tracks plus *all* associated knock-on costs, including an opportunity cost portrayal of lost revenues, was both convenient and useful, instead of treating these costs separately, the current norm. For clarity efficiency reasons, it was important to simultaneously address fatalities plus correlated injuries, plus correlated cost implications of physical material damage to the system, plus all costs associated with this damage. The rationale was directly linked to the rationale for her separate I_S approach, ensuring effective internally consistent decision making with minimal effort and associated decision-making cost.

The board would no doubt want to see direct material damage expected cost estimates and associated knock-on expected cost estimates for a range of sub-scenarios associated with each of their five S value scenarios, and future practice would require modelling the relationship between fatalities and material damage plus direct knock-on costs in fairly complex terms.

For illustrative purposes she would just use $D_1 = 0.2$ and $D_{350} = 0.4$ so the damage component of T_S was

$$V_1 \times D_S = \$2m \times 0.2 = \$0.4m \text{ for } S = 1,$$
$$= \$2m \times 0.4 = \$0.8m \text{ for } S = 350.$$

This implied that a D_S component of T_S varying over the range \$0.4 million to \$0.8 million would replace the current values derived from separate relatively complex computations.

Her $D_1 = 0.2$ meant that when $S = 1$ she was assuming the average total material damage plus knock-on cost was \$400,000. She thought this was an appropriate illustrative initial stance when one NER fatality was involved in the absence of appropriate data analysis to avoid playing down the importance of injuries and fatalities while acknowledging the role of more direct material damage and knock-on costs. A plausible range might be –50% to +300%, and she suspected knock-on cost issues addressing lost revenues fully explored might prove much more important than her illustrative values would suggest.

Her $D_{350} = 0.4$ meant that when $S = 350$ the scale of the physical damage and knock-on implications involved per fatality might increase by a factor of two, as an illustration of possible scale changes, but again this was purely for illustrative purposes.

The residual component $V_1 \times R_S$ for $S = 1$ and 350

It was crucially important to address the dependence between the number of fatalities and a residual component to reflect *anything* not fully embedded in the other three T_S components. In her view it was useful to see the role of R_S as a very broadly defined 'residual provision' in a 'closure with completeness' sense which explicitly included a full synthesis of all three other T_S components, plus the 'prudence provision' with a nature and role still outstanding on their initial meeting agenda, plus an overall 'rounding up when in doubt'.

For illustrative purposes, $R_1 = 0.1$ and $R_{350} = 2.8$ would be used so that the 'residual provision' component of T_S was

$$V_1 \times R_S = \$2m \times 0.1 = \$0.2m \text{ for } S = 1,$$
$$= \$2m \times 2.8 = \$5.6m \text{ for } S = 350.$$

This implied that an R_S component of T_S varying over the range $0.2 million to $5.6 million would replace the current implicit NER values of zero for all S values.

She suggested they start to interpret these purely illustrative values in terms of the overall role of the 'residual provision' over the S = 1 to S = 350 range.

If $R_S = 0$ for all S was assumed, the implication was that expected costs as measured by the other three E_S component factors needed no further uplifts. In her view this *would not* be seen by all relevant parties as an appropriate position for the NER board to take, and there was a reasonable case for saying that it *should not* be seen as an appropriate position. The obvious and basic reason was $R_S = 0$ did not reflect a trust contribution based on the full range of ethical considerations which most people would hold to be relevant. She did not want to labour discussion of issues involved that day, but did want to emphasise the need to accommodate all relevant trust-based considerations. It was also crucial to accommodate a range of underlying technical concerns which she would touch on when they became relevant.

The T_S residual component $R_1 = $0.2 million implied that in an S = 1 context, NER was prepared to spend this sum in addition to the £3.8 million associated with the other three components of T_S, a total of $4 million.

This would round up the $3.8 million illustrative value to $4 million. Relative to using $T_1 = 3.8$, it implied a marginally reduced expected number of fatalities in an S = 1 context via additional spending on safety and security, attributing 5% of the total T_S value to an increased effort to reduce the probability of S = 1 scenario incidents because of NER revealed preferences associated with seeking trust for their overall approach. But it would also preserve consistency with the current NER use of T = $4 million, and it would avoid suggesting that NER would reduce their concern for single fatality incidents, which she thought was important.

What the T_S residual component of $R_{350} = $5.6 million implied was in an S = 350 context NER was prepared to spend this sum in addition to the $14.4 million associated with the sum of the other three components of T_S for S = 350, a total of $20 million.

This would round up the $14.4 million illustrative value to $20 million, a significantly bigger adjustment in proportionate terms than for S = 1. It should lead to increased focus on reducing the expected number of fatalities in an S = 350 context relative to T_S = $14.4 million, attributing 23% of the total T_S value to an increased effort to reduce the probability of S = 350 scenarios occurring because of NER board approved revealed preferences associated with a desire for trust by all relevant parties which went beyond the implications of the $A_S + I_S + D_S$ components and R_1 as S increased. Part of the rationale for this bigger uplift as S increases was based on the role of enlightened prudence provision, to be considered shortly.

Taking these two S value R_S scenarios together, the numerical example had simply rounded the $3.8 million up to $4 million and the £14.4 million up to £20 million. This provided a simple factor of five illustration for the increase in T_S over the range S = 1 to 350. It assumed that a very modest residual provision was appropriate for S = 1, in conjunction with a more significant residual provision for S = 350.

The absolute values would obviously matter in practice when a developed version of her approach was implemented. But it was the implications of NER explicitly showing more concern about the implications of very big S value incidents that she particularly wanted to communicate at their initial meeting, with medium range increases in T_S illustrating the effects of an overall S dependent relationship.

In summary terms the implication of her example was that NER was prepared to make only a nominal 5% uplift to go beyond the shadow cost of $3.8 million for the S = 1 scenario to avoid a reduction relative to the current use of $4 million purely for fatalities. However, when S = 350 was involved, the NER residual provision was midway between fatalities and injuries in importance, and much more important than physical damage to the system.

What she wanted to demonstrate to the board at their initial meeting was the implications if NER had a significant revealed preference for avoiding high S value scenarios which it was prepared to demonstrate to their passengers, their staff, their regulator, the courts, and the public at large, in terms of their willingness to spend additional money to reduce the risk of very low probability but very high impact incidents, going well beyond current 'good practice'.

Why this might be reasonable would be explored in more detail later that day, but some immediate indications of 'anything else' concerns associated with R_S included a need to regain the trust lost by two serious accidents in the last two years. This issue could become crucial if these two incidents triggered a campaign to nationalise NER. It was certainly very important to avoid complacency after long periods of no serious accidents, but significant additional weight given to preventing serious accidents in the present circumstances might be presented and interpreted as a prudent act of contrition, undertaken with a view to regaining lost trust, an acknowledgement that they had to demonstrate a willingness to try harder, and they had to back up their promises to try harder with cash expenditure.

There was also a case for the board making a generous S = 350 uplift via this fourth T_S component based on the grounds that for high S values it was better to err on the cautious side given the uncertainty involved, a variant of the 'precautionary principle', and of 'going the second mile'. That is, in terms of seeking an *optimal* T_S value, which is by nature very ambiguous and contentious, the 'penalty function' associated with getting it wrong was not symmetric, so erring on the high side when catastrophes were involved was a sound strategy. Formal and explicit acknowledgement of the need to round upwards to deal with ambiguity to cope with what the board acknowledged NER did not know, in addition to the role of asymmetric penalty costs, would not go amiss.

As a further somewhat separate issue, if the board wanted to develop its 'national treasure' status, as 'a gift to the nation' the NER board might want to go beyond the minimum needed to regain and then preserve trust. They might interpret this further uplift as an explicit 'gift adjustment'. Their intentions here could be sincere philanthropy or a bid for more passengers as a variant of Trevor's 'non-price advantages' (as discussed in Chapter 6). A 'bid for more passengers' interpretation was comparable to Volvo promoting their reputation for cars designed and built for safety starting many decades ago, when other car makers seemed less concerned about safety. The board should consider this component very carefully at a later date for all S values, and very significant uplifts might be appropriate for S = 350.

The NER board would have to address all relevant T_S residual component issues associated with R_S very carefully in the near future, including the role of enlightened prudence, still on their 'to do' list. But for current purposes they might just assume that NER was scaling up the A_S, I_S, and D_S components so that an overall factor of five for increase for T_S as S went from 1 to 350 could be used for numerical illustration simplicity.

Sophie's further reflections on the overall transformation factor T_S for S = 1 and 350

Sophie began a reflective review by suggesting that the illustrative example values selected meant that for S = 1 the overall value of T_S was $4 million, while for S = 350 the overall value of T_S was $20 million, a simple factor of five increase which could be linked to the pattern of component changes with a view to comparable illustrative simplicity.

With S = 1, the fatalities contribution defined by A_S dominated, providing 55% of the total, followed by injuries defined by I_S contributing 30%, followed by damage defined by D_S adding 10%, with the residual defined by R_S contributing just 5%.

With S = 350, fatalities still contributed 50% of the total, with injuries contributing 18%, damage adding only 4%, and the residual now a significant 28%.

She was sure they would find the implications and the full role of the residual provision puzzling until they saw how it worked in practice. But she would explain the rationale of the prudence provision shortly, and she believed they would soon begin to see the rationale for her illustrative example numbers for the first three components, even if they thought bigger or smaller numbers more appropriate for these components. Furthermore, she believed they would soon begin to see that what the R_S value was doing was providing them with the ability to increase the relative importance of R_S as S increased towards 350 for reasons related to the NER board's revealed preferences which could go beyond current industry good practice safety and security concerns *if the board believed that was appropriate*. $R_S = 0$ for all S values was a feasible choice within her framework – but she would strongly advise against this choice, and she believed they would see why shortly.

What was crucially important in her view was the development of a properly grounded T_S concept for operational NER use in the very near future which the board understood and took responsibility for. She believed this would prove a key aspect of NER building and retaining grounded trust by all relevant parties, even if tested by further serious incidents. The acid test of trust which was well founded was the maintenance of trust when things went wrong.

Their initial meeting was about the framework NER needed to build and maintain grounded trust, and the component concepts needed, in broad what needs to be done terms. The board should not get distracted by the example numbers used.

What the board had to do to when assessing the complete set of four components in the light of analysis her team would have to complete as soon as possible was ask the question, 'Were the T_S values fair and reasonable, deserving the trust of our passengers, our staff, and other interested parties, including shareholders, regulators and courts, given the way they were defined, and given the NER overall approach to safety and security?' If the board accepted V_1 but believed any T_S was too low or too high, they should mandate NER staff to adjust E_S up or down by revising appropriate components until the board were comfortable. Being comfortable with the basis of V_1 was the obvious starting point.

Furthermore, when they were confident that their approach was the basis of well-founded trust, NER needed to make the whole process public and transparent, in the same 'full disclosure' manner which should be expected of any public sector organisation in order to maintain NER 'national treasure' status. And NER needed to be ready to respond to reasonable representations to increase or decrease E_S or V_1 or adjust other aspects of its approach.

Individual board members need not fully agree on individual components – a higher A_S with a compensating lower I_S would not affect decisions. However, this flexibility did not justify bias, especially wilful and amoral bias like deliberately underestimating D_S in order to inflate A_S for public relations purposes. Legitimate differences of opinion should be anticipated but tested for legitimacy during the process of reaching agreement on overall T_S values.

Selecting a four factor E_S component set given V_1 and an overall approach to safety and security involved ethical aspects which should be related to trust concerns by all relevant parties. The T_S values selected could and should be judged as 'reasonable' or 'not reasonable' by all relevant parties given all the assumptions used to determine those values.

'Relevant parties' had to include courts of law, and satisfying the legal interpretation of ALARP in an NER context was clearly a very important issue. However, the overall judgement by the board on behalf of NER was much broader. The board's view had to accommodate differences in personal opinions within the board, but even bigger differences between shareholders, train drivers plus other 'on-board' NER staff, passengers, and the public. A key role for the board was setting the tone for the NER approach to the ambiguity implied by all these differences as judged by the board.

If boards of private sector organisations, *or* their public sector equivalents, were deemed untrustworthy in this role, some people would argue that governments had a clear duty to punish the directors for any failures to meet reasonable standards and relieve them of their responsibilities, in addition to punishing shareholders if a private sector organisation was involved. Most people would agree that it was crucial to avoid punishing passengers via crude fines which were simply passed on via ticket price increases.

Governments had a clear duty to regulate both private and public sector organisations in an effective and efficient manner, and they should not wait for a series of catastrophic accidents to happen – they should be proactive. If governments failed in this respect, railway user associations and other comparable bodies might need to raise funds to use the courts to sue relevant parts of the government, as well as NER, and apply other forms of leverage, seeking support from the press.

Sophie acknowledged that some board members might see these statements as controversial, and perhaps too boldly confrontational, but she thought the NER board should see all of them as issues worth addressing before others decided to do so.

Defining T_S for S = 5, 20 and 70

Moving on to E_S for S = 5, 20, and 70, Sophie now assumed

$$E_5 = 3, \quad \text{so that} \quad T_5 = 2 \times 3 = 6,$$
$$E_{20} = 5, \quad \text{so that} \quad T_{20} = 2 \times 5 = 10,$$
$$E_{70} = 8, \quad \text{so that} \quad T_{70} = 2 \times 8 = 16.$$

She suggested that in practice they would have to use the same four components decomposition pattern to clarify what they were doing in detail for each relevant S value, but for that day's purposes she would simply use an illustrative interpolation approach without even attempting to explore a rationale for the numbers. Her example assumed that the S = 5 context was closer to the S = 1 context than the S = 20 context. Furthermore, she had assumed that the S = 20 context was closer to the S = 1 context than the S = 350 context. But the S = 70 context was assumed to be closer to S = 350 context than the S = 20 context.

Overall these three intermediate scenario values defined an asymmetric 'S curve' with an asymptotic approach to both E_1 and an E_{350} upper limit defined by the physical capacity of the system. There was clearly room for a lot of debate about the best shape for the S curve used, but much more work was required before this debate would be productive.

Any other non-linear relationship which the NER board wanted to use could be portrayed with a five scenarios approach, and more or fewer than five scenarios could be used. One of the reasons five scenarios were used was the need to capture this level of flexibility to provide a plausible basis for discussion.

In Sophie's view an E_S which could not be given a non-linear asymmetric S curve as the parameter S increased was inappropriate, and the current NER use of $T = V_1 \times E = \$4$ million for all $S = 1, \ldots, m$ was an extremely limited special case which could not be defended. She believed testing its implications in the more general framework she was proposing would clearly demonstrate why it was not defensible. To fail to even consider such a test was unacceptable from an EP perspective. What they had to avoid at this point was locking NER into any particular restrictive approach.

The fatalities metric S transformed by T_S to define 'cost related to fatalities'

Sophie presented Table 9.2 next, building on Table 9.1 and the intermediate discussion plus the earlier relationship definitions $C_S = S \times T_S = S \times V_1 \times E_S$. She was now formally defining C_S as 'the expected cost (\$m) related to fatalities if scenario S occurred' and C as 'the expected cost related to fatalities for all S'.

Interpreting Table 9.2 involved understanding the notation definitions for C_S and C just provided plus the nature of the concepts and the underlying relationships.

$C_S = S \times T_S$ was 'the expected cost (\$m) related to fatalities if scenario S occurred', a conditional expectation associated with the complete set of S values in the range portrayed by the scenario. The T_S transformed fatalities as measured by S into \$m, using the two component transformations factors defined by $T_S = V_1 \times E_S$ to obtain the C_S values.

C was 'the expected cost (\$m) related to fatalities for all scenarios per annum', an unconditional expectation computed using the C_S and the associated P_S. The P_S weighted the C_S values to compute the unconditional expected value C.

The first column of Table 9.2 replicated Table 9.1 apart from dropping the size scenario ranges in brackets to keep Table 9.2 as simple as possible.

The second column simply repeated the P_S values of Table 9.1.

The third column showed the computation of the C_S values using $S \times V_1 \times E_S$ for each S value. The first row's entry accommodated the $S = 0$ special case. The second showed the calculations for $S = 1$ assuming $V_1 = 2$ and $E_S = 2$ to produce $T_S = 4$ (\$m). The third and subsequent entries showed $E_S = 3$ for $S = 5$ rising to $E_S = 10$ for $S = 350$, using the illustrative non-linear interpolation suggested in the last subsection. In addition to wanting to be able to deal with non-linear asymmetric 'S curves', Sophie wanted to provide a plausible range of variations in her set of everything else factors to illustrate how this transformation fed through to C.

Table 9.2 Cost related to fatalities table, based on Table 9.1.

Size scenario	Unconditional probability	C_S, expected cost (\$m) related to fatalities if scenario S occurred	Contributions to C, expected cost (\$m) related to fatalities for all S per annum	
S	P_S	$S \times V_1 \times E_S = C_S$	$P_S \times C_S$	(as a %)
0	0.9500	0	0	(0%)
1	0.0025	$1 \times 2 \times 2 = 4$	$0.0025 \times \quad 4 = \quad 0.010$	(0%)
5	0.0250	$5 \times 2 \times 3 = 30$	$0.0250 \times \quad 30 = \quad 0.750$	(8%)
20	0.0200	$20 \times 2 \times 5 = 200$	$0.0200 \times \quad 200 = \quad 4.000$	(38%)
70	0.0020	$70 \times 2 \times 8 = 1{,}120$	$0.0020 \times 1120 = \quad 2.240$	(21%)
350	0.0005	$350 \times 2 \times 10 = 7{,}000$	$0.0005 \times 7000 = \quad 3.500$	(33%)
			$C = 10.500$	(100%)

C was the expected cost related to fatalities for all S scenarios per annum, an expected value defined by the sum over S = 1, . . . , 350 of the $P_S \times C_S$ products, a key summary parameter.

The fourth column showed the contributions to C for each S value. C was the $m cost of annual expected number of fatalities (F in Table 9.1) transformed into a $m equivalent.

The percentage contribution to C made by each size scenario was shown in brackets, indicating that the significant proportionate contribution to F made by the higher S values in Table 9.1 was further increased here, as might be expected given the S dependent T_S effect. However, it was crucial to understand that the further increases driven by the S dependent T_S were not as big as some people might expect, perhaps counter-intuitive, and of considerable importance in terms of understanding what really mattered in broad overview terms.

To begin to elaborate the relative importance of the key drivers and their overall effect, the F and C percentage contributions for each S size scenario were

S equal to	1	5	20	70	350
F % contributions from Table 9.1	0	15	47	17	21
C % contributions from Table 9.2	0	8	38	21	33

What a simple starting point interpretation of C = 10.500 suggested was about $10 million per annum was the annual expected value of costs related to fatalities using all the underlying illustrative example parameters.

Linking this to the basic parameters L and F, in annual expected value terms using these example values, NER were dealing with

$$L = 0.05,$$
$$F = 0.84,$$
$$C = \$10m,$$

working to comparable levels of precision to emphasise these were order-of-magnitude example numbers.

The earlier breakdowns suggested that at least half of this C value was associated with fatalities, but some of it was associated with related injuries, physical damage to the system, associated knock-on costs, and a residual provision.

The Tables 9.1 and 9.2 contribution percentages implied that the S = 20 scenario contributed the most to both F and C, but the S = 70 and 350 scenarios played an even more significant role in C than they do in F.

On average less than one fatality per annum was expected, but Table 9.1 suggested that 85% (47 + 17 + 21) of this expected value was associated with S scenario values of 20 or more, and Table 9.2 suggested that 92% (38 + 21 + 33) of the expected transformed value of $10.5 million per annum was associated with S scenario values of 20 or more. *What mattered crucially in terms of the average outcome happened relatively infrequently, primarily because of the effect of the very long distribution tail. However, a factor of five increase in T_S as S increased from S = 1 to S = 350 did amplify the highly asymmetric distribution effect driven by one very long tail.*

The weighted mean value of T_S was $10.5 million/0.8425 = $12.5 million, approximately the same as the simple mean of ($4 million + $20 million)/2 = $12 million, with about $6 million of this associated with fatalities. A mean of about $6 million associated with the fatalities component of T_S equated to a 50% increase on the T = \$4 million currently used, weighting the increase by relevant P_S. In effect, *when* an incident happened, S = 1 and S = 5 scenarios were not very important in either F or C terms. It was the S = 20 or more scenarios which really mattered. Furthermore, the S dependence in the T_S amplified the long tail distribution effect portrayed by Table 9.1 in terms of F, *but the long tail distribution effect on F was crucial, arguably at least as important overall as the S dependence of E_S issue.*

Sophie emphasised that she had deliberately erred on the modest side for the illustrative effects of S dependent E_S changes as S increases from 1 to 350, and she had similarly erred on the low side when estimating CP_S values for high S values. She wanted everyone to concentrate on points of principle without feeling unduly threatened by the illustrative numbers. She suspected that the full implications of using real numbers would be much more concerning than her illustrative numbers, but she had deliberately avoided unnecessarily overstating any of the suspicions she had about possible concerns with big impacts, in case these suspicions proved incorrect.

The key thing she wanted the board to begin to understand from these two tables and their use so far was *the need for NER, operating as a 'big team', led by their board, to learn to be very afraid of very big S value scenarios, and never forget this fear.* The low probability of big S value scenarios occurring was *never* a valid excuse for complacency.

The key follow-on issue was the need to vigorously pursue opportunity efficiency in a very optimistic and positive spirit, always striving for zero injuries and fatalities.

This combination of well-founded fear and an enterprising and creative approach to remaining optimistic, grounded on a clear understanding of ambitious targets and opportunity efficiency, should be the key overall NER goal, and it could not be achieved without board leadership.

Building and using the rest of the base-case model set

Sophie indicated that practical use of the holistic base-case model set would require an extension of Tables 9.1 and 9.2 in terms of the incident sets addressed. These tables just addressed collisions with fatalities, and they would have to extend the range of incidents covered by such tables before they could use them directly to make decisions.

To address all aspects of collisions they would have to add consideration of collision incidents limited to injuries or just material damage and knock-on costs. Furthermore, they would have to consider 'derailment' incidents (not leading to collision), 'level-crossing' incidents (not leading to derailment), and 'any other incident' component models. Further still, they would have to use the level-crossing models to build a component of the derailment models which dealt with the subset of these incidents initiated by level-crossing incidents, and a component of the collisions models which dealt with the subset of these incidents initiated by derailments. Still further, they would have to decompose all these models to provide greater granularity for the NER safety and security team to understand failure modes and effects in the various ways which safety engineers have found useful for addressing the root causes of accidents for many decades. This might include, as an example, detailed studies into the implications of alternative particular designs for the new generation of very high-speed trains recently suggested.

The board did not need to explore what this involved until it was accomplished, but it was important to understand the need for a critical review of all current NER safety models, fitting them into the top-down structure just outlined. This review would have to modify the existing models as needed for compatibility and consistency, generalise their capabilities, and fill in any important gaps. The board should now assume this would be done as soon as possible and consider in outline how this extended base-case model set with its more comprehensive F and C values could be used to help NER make opportunity efficient choices.

For numerical example purposes in this first meeting she would just build on Table 9.2 and all the underlying parameter assumptions, assuming they incorporated all relevant incident sets, to keep her presentation simple. This implied a degree of optimism which she and her team would strive to achieve, but it might be useful to see her example results today as an aspirational stretch target. That is, she would, in practice, try to ensure that the numerical equivalent for NER addressing all types and categories of incidents was no more pessimistic than Table 9.2, but they should not be surprised if later estimates for the complete model set were *significantly* less optimistic. They should certainly not see her current numerical examples as pessimistic illustrations designed to frighten them. She wanted the board to have realistic expectations, but stay optimistic about what could be achieved by a well-grounded opportunity management approach. She would now begin to give them some hints about what fully developed opportunity management instead of traditional safety management could mean in a NER safety and security planning context.

A new generation signalling system as a simple 'physical system' example

Sophie suggested they start with a very simple analysis of a relatively simple 'physical system' example. Say they were considering investing in a new generation signalling system, and say they made the very strong working assumption that the new signalling system would reduce the $(1 - P_0) = 0.0500$ underlying Tables 9.1 and 9.2 by 10% without affecting the relative size of the conditional probabilities or anything else. The mechanics of the Table 9.1 and 9.2 calculations meant a 10% reduction in C, $10.500 million $\times$ 10/100 = $1.05 million.

If the 'new system cost' per annum as measured by the amortised annual cost of the new system was less than $1.05 million, and all associated working assumptions were reasonable, the new generation signalling system looked worthwhile, in the sense that the 'flip-point' value for the new system cost was $1.05 million per annum. For example, if the new system cost per annum estimate was of the order of $0.5 million, there would seem to be a strong case for agreeing to the new system in terms of an annual expected value reduction. However, if the new system cost per annum estimate was of the order of $2 million, there would seem to be a strong case for rejecting the new system in terms of an annual expected value cost increase.

Furthermore, if the new system cost per annum estimate was of the order of $1 million, the analysis would suggest 'no clear advantage either way in terms of C plus the new system cost'. This would be very useful guidance because all other considerations not measured by C or the new system cost can now be the focus of attention. Indeed, once it was clear how useful it could be, it became obvious that what was not measured directly *always* needed careful consideration.

Valuing the marginal changes in expected outcomes using the assumed costs defined by a benchmark avoided fatality parameter V_1 and an 'everything else factor E_S', the board had clear guidance whatever the outcome, *provided all the working assumptions were deemed reasonable, the board was clear about what T_S did not measure as well as what T_S did measure, and annual expected cost values could be used without considering departures from these expectations – a particularly big assumption which enlightened prudence would address.*

Apart from board level inferences, Sophie's team could use this kind of framework for developing proposals, in conjunction with any NER group which wanted to develop proposals with safety and security implications.

Of critical importance, leaving aside working assumptions about the T_S parameters for the moment, the board and all NER groups bringing proposals to the board have a clear basis for testing and exploring the implications of *all working assumptions within an expected outcomes framework, addressing qualitative assumptions as well as quantitative assumptions. Furthermore, we can later systematically generalise this framework, including addressing enlightened prudence in a much better framework for understanding what 'risk' ought to mean in a safety and security context.*

One of several crucial inferences which can be made building on this very simple example which Sophie wanted to emphasise was that safety and security planning needed to pay special attention to reducing the conditional probabilities associated with the high S values, and the implications of departures from expectations involving these scenarios. For example, if the assumed S = 350 scenario unconditional probability of = 0.0005 could be driven down by 30%, the reduction in C implied by Table 9.2 of $3.500 million × 30/100 = $1.05 million implied it would be worth about $1.05m per annum in expected value terms before considering any of the knock-on changes to other parameters, of the same order of magnitude as a 10% reduction in $(1 - P_0)$. The reason was the S = 350 scenario contributed about a third of the value of C in Table 9.2. In addition, it made the S = 350 scenario much less threatening in terms of potential departures from expectations, a risk issue going beyond expected outcomes which needed exploration later.

More generally, reducing the seriousness of incidents if they happen may be much more effective and efficient than reducing the probability of incidents happening. The base-case model set provided a comprehensive and coherent basis for exploring these central trade-off issues. Trade-offs between prevention and mitigation were a crucial issue to understand and deal with effectively.

In part this was why 'staying *very* afraid of *high S value* incidents' was a key part of the corporate culture NER needed, bearing in mind that the very low probability of such incidents made it exceedingly difficult for people to sustain focus on safety when immediate pressures on profit or cost were difficult to resist, and the practical difficulties associated with estimating very small probability values.

Sophie then very briefly considered some of the complications which would need addressing in practice.

A new generation signalling system might reduce some of the conditional probabilities more than other considerations. NER would need to model the underlying failure mechanisms to understand this, as well as linked impacts on L via P_0. Furthermore, the new-generation signalling system might have operational benefits which had significant value beyond safety, like allowing a higher traffic volume with higher revenue implications. They would need to ensure that this benefit was deducted from the new system cost or considered in conjunction with the new system benefits in relation to the total system cost changes. The latter approach would usually be simpler in practice. Sophie noted that there was no need to separate new system costs and benefits for different S values, and it was important to understand that in practice additional costs for decreasing expected fatalities could be difficult to separate from additional costs for other benefits. Benefits might come as bundles, roughly comparable to a generalisation of the marketing concept 'buy one, get one free', but potentially much more complex in a variety of important ways which needed context specific understanding.

Indeed, separating signalling from other aspects of the 'operations information system' might be very unwise if they wanted to develop the kind of redundancy, resilience, and robustness generally advised. For example, if a signalling system failure meant that a train driver was not advised that there was a stationary train on the track two kilometres ahead, a key question was, 'What other ways could a train driver get this information?' Sophie indicated she was not a railways expert, but on the train to their meeting that morning, she wondered if large screen TVs in train driver's cabs linked to a telescopic lens night-vision capability CCTV camera on the front of each train, perhaps computer adjusted for track curvature with driver override, might serve as backup to signal failures. But the point she really wanted to make was this kind of capability might also help to avoid or reduce the impact of full speed collisions with derailed trains and vehicles on level crossings – including vehicles maliciously placed there just before a train was due. If train drivers plus all other experts who understood the issues and the technology possibilities worked together, they might come up with a concept like that illustrated by her camera speculation that was novel, effective, and efficient. Furthermore, in conjunction with good controller-to-driver radio communication systems, adding this kind of feature to the system might be better value for money than new signalling system hardware, but neither or both may be worthwhile. Sophie emphasised that she had no idea whether CCTV cameras on the front of trains made any sense, but she was trying to illustrate the kind of creative thinking required of all those within NER, or available to NER, who might contribute to a creative search for safety and security improvements.

Furthermore, an even wider view of the physical system was important. As an example, the recent derailment interpreted as a collision near miss, not to mention recent terrorist tactics, meant that NER had to think about how to lower the fatalities and injuries implications of high impact incidents via creative design and operations changes which might be radical. The new very high-speed railway lines they were planning at present might benefit significantly from much greater separation of the tracks than currently envisaged, especially at vulnerable locations, perhaps also using a deflection barrier comparable in function if not in appearance to those used on separated motorway lanes. A related alternative which might be worth considering was a three or four track norm for all high speed lines, with only the outer tracks normally used unless maintenance was required. Driverless trains might be considered, with a view to large trains being replaced by sets of small trains, decreasing the time interval between trains for the convenience of passengers in terms of more frequent service as well as addressing catastrophe scenario safety concerns, just to illustrate the scope for flexible creative thinking.

Further still, a very effective approach not requiring driverless train technology might be just reducing train sizes by 25% but running more services at peak times, using safer carriages which were also more comfortable, and charging more for tickets for a better service, phasing in these components of a new overall strategy as soon as each component was feasible. This might let NER increase total passenger numbers, revenue, and profit simultaneously while also significantly increasing safety and security as measured by C.

What the board needed was a top-down view of potential physical system improvement options, with their safety and all other operational benefits fully integrated with their costs and revenues. What NER as a whole needed was extensive use of this perspective by the NER safety and security team, *plus all other relevant NER players*, to develop well-polished sets of options to recommend to the board. The board would need confidence that the safety and security team, plus all other NER staff with contributions to make, had explored a much wider set of combinations and permutations of changes in an internally consistent manner to eliminate dominated options.

The recommended proposals for board consideration would involve important trade-offs, leaving the board, with suitable support, to consider the trade-offs that were the board's responsibility.

The recommended changes might have been initiated by the perception that a new generation of signalling technology was now available, and the working assumption that it was worth a good look by NER. However, NER needed to ensure that everyone with useful input and creative ideas was able to contribute to the ideas ultimately tested before proposals came forward to the board. Train drivers who had experienced near misses or observed features of the current system which could lead to problems had knowledge which needed systematic gathering and integration. Other on-board NER staff, signalling staff, passenger associations, and railway safety consultants also had knowledge which might be useful.

Track maintenance contracting as a 'procedural systems' example

Sophie suggested they now consider looking at system changes which were initiated from a somewhat different perspective, using track maintenance contracting as a 'procedural systems' example. She did not wish to get into recriminations about what made the 40 fatality incident recently experienced 'an accident waiting to happen', as reported in the press. What she did want to explore briefly was a framework for considering procedural systems from a 'designing desirable futures' perspective.

What she meant by this was starting with the procedural system features and associated implications which they wanted, a luxury they could not afford in terms of most aspects of NER *physical* systems because of the 'heritage' issues. In the context of a *procedural* system they could afford to scrape the existing framework completely, after designing and appropriately testing a completely new procedural system to achieve as much of their 'desirable future' as they could. They could begin the design process by focusing on effectiveness in a 'creative thinking mode', without too much concern for efficiency issues. This could be followed by testing and shaping the proposed procedural systems for efficiency to get a practical and robust approach. When they were confident that the new approach could work in practice, they could implement it, perhaps initially in a prototype form in selected regions, gradually developing efficiency as well as effectiveness via practice focused on continuous improvement.

For example:

1   The current use of a very small number of big contractors might be convenient for some NER staff, in particular, those responsible for letting the contracts. However, a much larger number of contractors, some relatively small organisations, might allow much better response rates when urgent unscheduled maintenance work was needed. This approach might also help to keep cost rates more competitive for all scheduled and unscheduled maintenance work. It might also increase opportunities for new and creative responses, including new technologies. It would require more sophisticated NER inspection and management approaches, and it would be more challenging for all of Oscar's operations staff (Sophie was looking at Oscar when she said this, but he was smiling because he knew this comment was coming). She believed there was a very strong case for a more sophisticated approach which provided both less safety and security risk and lower overall cost, and she was determined to explore the possibilities effectively.

2   The current budgeting constraints and operations constraints on work deemed urgent by inspectors had to be eliminated, as soon as possible. Maintenance should be planned and associated budgets controlled as far as possible, closely integrated with operational needs. But a much enhanced and empowered safety and security inspection team who were always fully informed about the state of the system and empowered to act immediately without inappropriate financial constraints was a clear necessity in her view (she was looking at Oscar and the Finance Director alternately when she said this, but Oscar

had primed the Finance Director, and he was comfortable with the implications as he understood them thus far).

3   The kind of safety and security inspection team Sophie had in mind would have to work closely with the scheduled maintenance planners. But in Sophie's view they also needed to work closely with all their maintenance contractors and associated subcontractors, in 'coaching mode' as well as 'critic or examiner mode'. Furthermore, they needed to act as a conduit for feedback from staff working for NER contractors and their subcontractors on all relevant concerns. People working for contractors and subcontractors should feel they were an important part of the 'NER big team', responding as good team members in a carefully designed partnership relationship. If they could not be trusted to act as trusted partners in a big team they should be sacked as quickly as possible. If the NER staff managing them or designing the partnership arrangements could not be trusted to do so effectively, they too should be sacked or transferred to other jobs as soon as possible.

4   Having developed what Sophie and the NER 'core team' thought was the most effective contracting approach, more efficient regimes, in terms of reduced overall expected cost and possible departures from expectations, could be tested. They could try to ensure both fatality efficiency and appropriate trade-offs between the overall expected cost, the expected level of fatalities, and the risk of very high levels of fatalities like an incident portrayed by the S = 350 scenario.

A change in culture or ethos

Sophie was convinced that at a more general level, common to both physical and procedural examples, NER needed a significant culture change *led by the board*. This culture change had to be coupled to and facilitated by the other safety and security planning changes she was proposing. All the changes involved might be characterised as starting with a 'fail-safe culture', both driving and driven by a 'fail-safe planning' approach. She made these points as a starting position for a relatively 'soft issues' insertion in her otherwise predominantly numerical model focused presentation.

She had a personal preference for the word *ethos* instead of culture, to signal the trust and underlying ethical issues involved, but she would stick to the more common 'culture' word that day. They could debate terminology later.

They could discuss and change the labels and revise the features she was suggesting, but what she had in mind in broad terms was building on the idea that the Westinghouse fail-safe braking system for trains first introduced in the US many years ago was one of the biggest transformational steps forward in railway safety history. The basic idea behind 'fail-safe' brakes was a train would not be able to move if the brakes were not functioning properly.

She did not want to suggest NER should not be able to move if the NER approach to safety and security was not functioning properly, but enlightened use of the fail-safe principle might have significant useful implications which went well beyond the physical and procedural systems and needed careful development.

Building on this starting point, 'an enlightened culture' for NER in terms of safety and security might be encouraged if the overall strategy mandated by the board adopted policies like:

1   all changes to the system which demonstrated a reduction in the value of C were always implemented as soon as possible unless there was a *very* clear case against for other cost or further reasons,

2 all changes to the system which demonstrated an increase in the value of C would always be rejected unless there was an *extremely* clear case in favour of other cost or further reasons,
3 NER at all levels acknowledged that changes in C should *always* be an issue,
4 the search for reductions in C and improvements in other aspects of operations planning were always fully integrated, and
5 NER remained open to the value of any further 'culture' improvements which could be engineered.

To achieve the implementation of these policies in terms of some illustrative example features for engineering an enlightened culture:

1 All choices with safety and security implications would be assessed using an approach based on the set of V_1 and E_S values developed for and approved by the board. These parameter choices would drive safety and security related spending, not the other way around, *as soon as NER had a set of values for these parameters the board members believed were appropriate*. Initially significant iteration should be anticipated, testing assumed values of R_S and other E_S values until the safety and security team and the board were confident about the values used, with effective plans to manage the initial iterative process in place before iteration started. In the longer term, further iteration would be needed to revise the process as circumstances changed, new issues were identified, and they 'learned by experience'. A key aspect of learning by experience would be the 'enlightened prudence' role of R_S, to be clarified shortly.
2 The benefit of the doubt when making choices would always favour the safer and more secure approach, at the board level, at the level of a member of the safety and security inspection team asking for urgent unscheduled maintenance, at the level of adding or deleting approved contractors or changing the terms of contracts, at the level of managing staff culture and morale issues with safety implications, and at the level of decisions by individuals like train drivers or controllers.
3 The small 'core team' of safety and security staff managed by Sophie would be 'safety *planners*'. They would be responsible for developing safety and security plans and involved in integrating those plans with all other plans. They would emphatically *not* be 'safety *managers*'.
4 Responsibility for managing safety would rest with the 'NER big team' in terms of all relevant operations decisions. So far as possible, an inclusive and flexible 'NER big team' approach to safety planning and management would be adopted. Contractors' staff and subcontractors' staff, as well as NER staff, would be seen as contributors to corporate knowledge relevant to safety and security planning and responsible for managing their contribution to the system's safety and security.
5 A team of safety and security inspectors would audit all safety and security related performance, approaching this task with a supportive perspective, 'helping everyone to do better' rather than 'imposing rules which interfere with performance'. They would focus on 'enhancement' instead of 'compliance', 'enabling' rather than 'blocking'.
6 So far as possible, all the desirable features of the current approaches to safety and security would be preserved. But all the undesirable features of the current 'box-ticking' and 'back-side protection' health and safety management culture would be designed out, linking these mindset changes to toolset and skill set changes in some areas.
7 The wider culture change implications would focus on identifying 'bad behaviours' and replacing them with 'good behaviours'.

8   Staff morale and its role in a healthy 'fail-safe culture' would receive direct and focused attention. Formal recognition that best estimates of P_S values were always a function of morale and forms of contract, as well as physical systems, would be central to this. Eliminating resistance to acknowledging this dependence, driven by unenlightened prejudices about the role of subjective probabilities, would need early attention.

9   Current NER staff who were unwilling to change quickly enough, especially those who made it difficult for others to change, would be removed as quickly as possible, whatever their function and level in the management hierarchy.

10 NER could rely on Sophie to lead the planning of a culture change programme for NER, but all NER staff had to work collaboratively across all corporate boundaries as well as within their own areas. They would have to collectively 'engineer' a culture change, seeking to creatively synthesise ends and means in the sense Sophie understood was the driving culture of the engineering profession. She suggested there was a large literature on culture which was relevant but little meaningful agreement on what corporate 'culture' was, never mind what to do about it. In her view, *culture* could be given a simple working definition like 'the way we do things around here'. This was a perspective widely adopted and useful as a starting point. However, once NER started to approach how to change culture, the issues would become very complex very quickly. Changing culture takes all organisations firmly into the realm of values, leadership, teamwork, trust, and many other relevant bodies of knowledge which are not easy to disentangle. It also takes organisations into what Hyde (2006) referred to as 'mysteries' when addressing what makes people creative. In Sophie's view the safety-first enlightened culture which NER needed included a team spirit that was creative, supportive of others, optimistic in a constructive sense without forgetting what to be frightened about, professional in the vocation sense, ethically sound, and unambiguously intolerant of a lack of integrity in others. There was no room for 'faking concern' or using a public relations approach to selling a sense of values that was not genuine. Leadership had to be 'from the front', but that might mean 'from the side' or 'from the bottom' as well as 'from the top', and all the leaders involved needed to be open to constructive criticism and willing to learn from all relevant sources.

Sophie urged the board to be cautious about how quickly they could move with NER culture changes, but not at all cautious when estimating how wide and how crucially important the implications of an approach driven by this kind of opportunity management might be.

Using risk efficiency as a basis for option choices

For the NER board to understand the use of risk efficiency incorporating fatality efficiency, including the use of decision diagrams with underlying sensitivity diagrams and risk–reward trade-off concerns, Sophie needed to explain some of the material in earlier chapters of this book. This chapter simply assumes that she did so now, if not at an earlier point in the presentation.

Sophie had discussed the role of C as an expected value measure of the cost related to fatalities including correlated injuries and other consequences associated with $S = 1, \ldots,$ m, transformed via T_S in scenario terms into a monetary metric. This extended the reach of the analysis beyond fatalities to other concerns which were correlated in her scenario framework, but it was consistent with conventional safety practice thinking within a generalised EP framework, in the sense that it limited its consideration of risk to the expected value of C. That is, the safety management common practice employed by NER used an expected value metric for risk based on a definition of *risk* of the form 'risk = probability × impact', with 'impact' measured in 'value of avoided fatality' terms calculated for each 'risk', and summed over all risks.

What she had delayed considering until now was further generalising this approach to an extended view of risk which fully embraced the implications of potential departures from expectations associated with all relevant costs, the role of risk efficiency, the need to address risk–reward trade-offs on a risk efficient frontier, plus uncertainty about all modelling assumptions which did not involve quantification – the 'conditions' any probabilistic analysis rested on. She had often hinted at the need to do so, frequently mentioned enlightened prudence and a prudence provision, and sometimes linked this to R_S, but she had not developed any of the underlying concepts. The reason for this delay was she believed the illustrative numerical examples she had developed so far, plus the softer culture change issues just explored, would help them to better understand the key aspects of the complexity involved in what needs to be done terms.

Sophie now wanted the board to begin to understand why risk in terms of potential departures from expectations *always* needed to be addressed when considering options involving *all* possible changes to the railway system with strategic implications.

This would involve thinking about risk in terms of a much broader perspective than the common practice way of thinking about risk in a safety context. Although the much broader view of risk embracing departures from expectations was directly comparable to common practice approaches which had been used in security investment contexts for a very long time, with a growing role in best practice in many other contexts, common practice safety analysis had not yet adapted a direct and explicit formal planning role for risk metrics concerned with departures from expectations. In her view this was a very serious and fundamental flaw. Risk efficiency and all the more sophisticated ideas based on risk efficiency explored earlier in this book were simply 'off the radar' for common practice safety analysis approaches, and changing this position was long overdue.

NER had to take an approach to safety and security which avoided this significant common practice shortcoming. Doing so involved thinking about risk–reward trade-offs between expected outcomes and risk in a risk efficiency framework, working towards making decisions at the board level about which strategic changes should or should not be made in a manner directly comparable to BP board use of decision diagrams, but extended to address a generalisation of the enlightened prudence concept discussed earlier in this book.

To illustrate what was involved, Sophie suggested they start by associating Table 9.2 with the annual 'cost related to fatalities' for the current system – a 'no change' situation she would refer to as the 'old' system option.

An associated 'new' system option might be the best overall set of physical and procedural changes for the old system that the safety and security team could devise, working with all relevant NER employees, consultants, and contractors, developed after eliminating all dominated alternatives, incorporating systems changes proposed for reasons other than safety by all relevant NER players, incorporating current views about corporate capability-culture issues. This new system might involve an extensive portfolio of changes, like new signalling plus new communications equipment, coupled to new operations procedures and supportive training programmes, as well as new contracting approaches. Alternatively, this new system might just involve smaller trains run more frequently, any of the other approaches suggested earlier on its own, or a very different new one.

Sophie then suggested they use Table 9.3 to compare this proposed new system option with the old system option.

Table 9.3 Table of cost related to fatalities for two options, based on Table 9.2 for the old system.

Size scenario	Old and new system P_S and percentage change			Expected cost ($m) if scenario S occurred	Contributions to old and new C ($m)		Cumulative old and new P_S	
S	old P_S	new P_S	%	C_S	old	new	old	new
0	0.9500	0.96230	+1.3	0	0	0	0.9500	0.96230
1	0.0025	0.00225	−10	4	0.010	0.009	0.9525	0.96455
5	0.0250	0.02000	−20	30	0.750	0.600	0.9775	0.98455
20	0.0200	0.01400	−30	200	4.000	2.800	0.9975	0.99855
70	0.0020	0.00120	−40	1120	2.240	1.344	0.9995	0.99975
350	0.0005	0.00025	−50	7000	3.500	1.750	1.0000	1.00000
				old & new C	10.500	6.503		

The first and second column S values and P_S values were taken directly from Table 9.2. She would now explain the other columns from left to right, beginning with the third column 'new system' P_S values.

Sophie's discussion of the P_S for the new system began with her explaining that she wanted a numerical example involving just two options which portrayed the key messages the board needed clarity about and was as easy to understand as possible. For simplicity, the old system P_S values for S = 1, . . . , 350 scenarios had been reduced by 10%, 20%, 30%, 40%, and 50%, as shown in the third column. The rationale for her use of these percentages was simply illustrating the effect of prioritising high S value P_S reductions – the focus which she believed was essential for NER. The associated percentage changes were noted in the fourth column.

The sum of these new P_S values subtracted from unity defined the new system P_0 value, with an entry of 1 − 0.03770 = 0.96230 for the new system. This implied a 1.3% increase in the probability of no incidents in any given year, as indicated. It also implied an associated decrease in the value of $(1 − P_0)$ of 0.0500 − 0.03770 = 0.0123, a 25% decrease, arguably a more useful way to look at the same change.

This 25% decrease in $(1 − P_0)$ was a weighted average of the assumed set of five P_S reductions for S = 1, . . . , 350. It was smaller than a simple arithmetic mean of $(10 + 20 + 30 + 40 + 50)/5 = 30\%$ because high S value P_S were relatively small and the P_S weighting mattered.

To start to explore some immediate implications, Sophie observed that in practice her team would have to start with the CP_S *conditional* probabilities for S = 1, . . . , 350, and compute the unconditional probabilities, proceeding as illustrated in Table 9.1. The more technically minded directors might be interested in the implicit Table 9.3 CP_S values as well as the P_S, and the implied CP_S could be inferred from the P_S and $(1 − P_0)$ values provided. To demonstrate how this worked for those interested, the assumed *conditional* probability of an S = 350 scenario for the old system as indicated directly in Table 9.1 could be computed using the unconditional P_{350} value of 0.0005 and $(1 − P_0)$ of 0.0500. In a sense this involved working backwards to obtain $CP_{350} = 0.0005/0.0500 = 0.01$. Using an identical approach for Table 9.3 and the new system, the conditional probability $CP_{350} = 0.00025/0.0377 = 0.006631$ was significantly lower than the 0.01 value for the old system, a 34% reduction. Using this same approach again, the conditional probability $CP_1 = 0.00225/0.0377 = 0.059682$ for the new system was slightly higher than the 0.05 for the old system, a 19% increase. In other words, for the new system there was a 25% reduction in the probability of any kind of incident, and if an incident did happen, it was slightly more likely to be an S = 1, significantly less likely to be an S = 350, as might be expected given the unconditional probability changes.

The fifth column transformed fatalities metric C_S value entries are the same as Table 9.2.

The sixth column old system C contributions were the same as those of Table 9.2, and the seventh column new system C contributions were obtained via column products in the same way. The old system C = $10.5 million was reduced to $6.5 million for the new system, a $4 million or 38% decrease.

The final two columns cumulative probability entries just accumulated the second and third column's P_S values for the old and new systems as a basis for Figure 9.1. Figure 9.1 used these cumulative probabilities to plot the basis for several operational 'decision diagram' examples. She would consider these examples in terms of their implications for decision making as soon as she had explained how Figure 9.1 was related to Table 9.3, and what Figure 9.1 implied.

The y-scale for Figure 9.1 measured cumulative probability, as for all earlier decision diagrams in this book. The only difference was the use of a 'squiggle' below the cumulative probability of 0.95 to allow a focus on the region that mattered, from 0.95 to 1.00.

The first of two x-scales measured fatalities on the scale 1, . . . , m, using S size scenario values taken from the first column of Table 9.3. The second x-scale measured cost related to fatalities. It used the size scenario values taken from the C_S values in the fifth column of Table 9.3.

Both the S scale and the C_S based cost related to fatalities scale were approximately logarithmic (base five). They were directly linked via the T_S transformation.

The Figure 9.1 piecewise linear curves involved working assumptions linked to Table 9.3 which needed a high level of clarity for everyone involved, including the board. The board needed to be well aware of the approximations involved, but entirely comfortable with the robustness of what this kind of diagram was saying. Sophie wanted board members to begin by considering the general statement made by Figure 9.1 in terms of the situation being

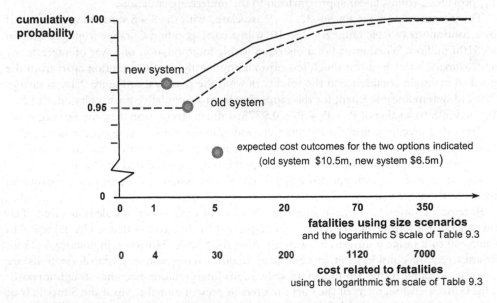

Figure 9.1 The basis for operational decision diagram examples provided by Table 9.3.

addressed, then the implications in terms of the old system option, and then the implications in terms of the new system option.

Figure 9.1 and its relationship with Table 9.3 used a variant of the rectangular histogram HAT based approach illustrated earlier, but this time the discrete value probability distribution for S being portrayed by a continuous variable distribution involved an approximation, because S really was a discrete value variable. This could be slightly confusing at the bottom end of the S value range if the approximation involved was not understood. The S = 0 value was not a problem, but S = 1 involved a particularly awkward approximation in presentational terms in Figure 9.1. In discrete value terms, S = 1 interpreted in terms of discrete numbers of fatalities had to involve a zero range, but in terms of a continuous variable HAT approach the linear curve segment had to associate S = 1 with a uniform probability distribution range from 0 to 2 fatalities, with a conditional mean of 1. In discrete value terms, S = 5 was nominally associated with 2, 3, . . . 9 fatalities, but in terms of a continuous variable HAT approach the linear curve segment associated S = 5 with the continuous variable range from 2 to 10 fatalities. There were similar interpretations associated with the S = 20, 70 and 350 scenarios, to make the piecewise linear curve as a whole continuous.

Considering the implications of these observations in relation to the old system option, if the S scale of Figure 9.1 was used to interpret the curve, the integer value S = 1 was associated with the midpoint class mark value of a continuous variable in the range 0–2 fatalities, so the approximation was particularly obvious in visual terms, but no errors were involved in terms of expected value calculations or other aspects of the portrayals.

If the cost related to fatalities scale from $0 million to about $10 million is used to interpret the 0–2 fatalities segment of the curve, the presentational implications of the approximation ceases to be a problem, because the I_S transformation factor component of T_S actually operates in terms of 'equivalent fatalities', transforming S into a continuous variable, and the uncertainty about all four T_S transformation components also mean cost related to fatalities is a continuous variable. In either case, the old system linear segment for this range rising from a cumulative probability of 0.9500 (defined by P_0) to 0.9525 (defined by P_0 + P_1) provides a robust linear approximation to the underlying situation.

The integer value range for S = 2, . . . , 9 associated with the S = 5 scenario was portrayed by a continuous variable range S = 2 to 10, with a corresponding C_S range from $10 million to $100 million. Whether or not a discrete variable interpretation of S was of interest, any approximation involved was much less obvious and hardly worth a mention apart from the need to maintain confidence in the validity of what the portrayal of Figure 9.1 was saying. The old system linear segment for this range rises from a cumulative probability value of P_0 + P_1 = 0.9525 to a value of P_0 + P_1 + P_5 = 0.9775, a much steeper rise than the first segment.

The other piecewise linear segments were added in the same way, using the same HAT-based approach employed earlier in a form which accommodates both a discrete value interpretation for S or a continuous variable interpretation for cost related to fatalities.

The same working assumptions applied to the new system curve, and its construction followed the same pattern.

Because a continuous variable approximation to a discrete fatalities scale is involved, if an integer value interpretation of S is used, interpreting the two curves defined by Table 9.3 in the S = 0 to 2 range is intuitively awkward using the S scale. However, in practice, because injuries require consideration in equivalent fatalities terms and cost transformations are essential, sticking to the $m monetary scale means interpretation becomes straightforward. This bottom-end segment of the curve matters in presentational terms if the S metric is of direct interest, accentuated by the expected value being located in this region, but it was purely a visual presentation issue, avoided in practice by working with just the $m monetary scale, the only x-scale used for the operational examples to follow.

Comparing the two curves in Figure 9.1 using either scale, the new system was clearly the only risk efficient choice. Stochastic dominance was involved. The probability of exceeding any given level of fatalities or cost was lower for the new system than for the old system, and in cost terms the expected outcome was $4 million less if the new system option is taken.

On Figure 9.1 the $7,000 million segment of the new system curve almost overlaid the old system curve because both cumulative curves were so close to a cumulative probability of 1.0000. However, Table 9.3 made it clear that the new system probability of an outcome value in this range was only half that of the old system, the differences for the P_{70} and P_{20} values were also important, and it was *very* important to understand this in order to appreciate the full picture portrayed by Figure 9.1 plus the underlying Table 9.3 values. Indeed, this difference in the curves at the top end was a matter of substance and importance. It must not be overshadowed by the bottom-end presentational issues, and it was part of the case for preserving a table *plus* curve approach based on a HAT framework in operational practice. The more commonly used Monte Carlo simulation approach could provide a comparable table but rarely did. This, in turn, was part of the broader case for ensuring that someone involved in implementing practical approaches clearly understood what really mattered, and what was relatively superficial. Sophie had risked boring the board with the bottom end of the curve explanation to make sure they appreciated the approximations involved did not matter because she wanted the board to be confident about all the expert advice they used in terms of what *really* mattered and what did not matter enough to need ongoing attention.

The expected cost values were plotted on the cumulative probability distribution curves, with expected cost values also noted in the text, to help the board deal with the combined effect of the piecewise linear histogram approximation and the logarithmic scale. The expected value of $10.5 million for the old system was plotted on the cumulative probability curve near the beginning of the second segment, while the $6.5 million value for the new system was plotted on the first segment, as illustrated.

Smoother curves could be used in practice, and board members would probably prefer smooth curves with good reason, but they needed to understand what underlay smooth curves in terms of all key working assumption. Indeed, more scenarios would obviously refine the precision in the definition of the probability distributions. But always basing interpretation on cost related to fatalities with a non-linear smooth curve fitted to $S = 0$ and the other five scenario values would probably be much more clarity efficient, and using m scenarios with a very large m would definitely not be clarity efficient.

As soon as Sophie was sure that board members were happy with the relationship between Figure 9.1 and Table 9.3, she explained that if the annual cost related to fatalities as measured and portrayed both in expected value (C) and associated C_S variability terms in Table 9.3 and Figure 9.1 was their only concern, then the new system was clearly better than the old system.

However, to make decisions of strategic importance in any realistic operational context, NER had to consider *all* cost, revenue, and other non-measurable issues which were relevant to making decision choices *in a fully integrated manner*. She now wanted to use Figure 9.1 as the basis for operational forms of decision diagrams with examples which involved considering a fully comprehensive annual 'cost relevant to system choices', defined as the sum of two items:

1   the 'cost related to fatalities' which they had just addressed and
2   the 'cost not related to fatalities'.

'Cost not related to fatalities' was defined to include the amortised (annual) capital costs for the new system (net of any scrap value associated with the old system) *plus* any associated differences in annual operating costs for both systems (net of any revenue benefits in the case of the new system).

Instead of subtracting increased revenue associated with the new system from the new system costs, in some cases it might be more convenient to treat increased revenue for the new system as an opportunity cost for the old system or address profit directly. But this was a technical detail they could address later.

For 'new system A1', the first of two 'new system' examples she would use, Sophie suggested they assume that the new system's 'cost relevant to system choices' which was cost not related to fatalities was estimated at $50 million per annum, and the corresponding old system 'cost relevant to system choices' which was cost not related to fatalities, was also estimated at $50 million per annum, in both cases with too little uncertainty to matter. This meant that Figure 9.1 could be transformed into Figure 9.2 by just changing what the second x-scale measures to the cost relevant to system choices and adding $50 million to the scale, as indicated. Dropping the S value x-scale was a convenient option which she had adopted, so they could consider fatalities in the broader context of cost relevant to system choices.

The x-scale $0m in Figure 9.1 had become $50 million in Figure 9.2, with other class mark values also increasing by $50 million: $4 million became $54 million, $30 million became $80 million, and so on.

Assuming that board members were all comfortable with an EP perspective on risk efficiency, the Figure 9.2 decision diagram clearly indicates that:

1   for new system A1 the risk of any outcome greater than $50 million was significantly less than it was for the old system, and
2   new system A1 had a $60.5 million – $56.5 million = $4 million expected cost advantage.

The expected cost of the old system was $60.5 million ($50 million + $10.5 million) in comparison to $56.5 million for the new system ($50 million + $6.5 million), and the new

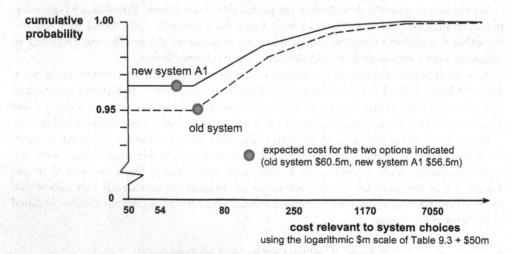

Figure 9.2 Decision diagram for the new system A1 option.

system curve was higher over the whole $m x-scale range of both curves, as indicated in Figure 9.2. Stochastic dominance was involved. *New system A1 was the only risk efficient choice.* Assuming the analysis underlying Figure 9.2 was complete and unbiased, the new system was clearly preferable to the old system in terms of both expected cost and risk.

Sophie ensured all board members were comfortable with this interpretation of Figure 9.2. She explained that some uncertainty associated with relevant system costs other than costs associated with fatalities as considered in Table 9.3 would imply that the rise in the cumulative probability curves to the 0.95000 and 0.96230 levels would be less than vertical. However, this uncertainty could be associated with bearable risk which was just 'noise' relative to the hugely significant uncertainty and associated risk which Figure 9.2 captured.

For those board members who might be focused on what usually happens, she emphasised that it might seem important that there would be no observable outcome change 95% of the time. That is, 95% of the time the old system would enjoy a $50 million 'all relevant systems costs' outcome associated with no incidents, while the new system would involve a $50 million cost associated with no incidents 96.23% of the time, a very modest looking change, the +1.3% change noted in Table 9.3.

For those board members who might be particularly concerned about how her EP approach related to common practice risk management based on expected values, she emphasised that the $4 million expected value cost advantage would be picked up by a common practice approach if the same numbers were used, but the associated variability issues would not be part of the analysis framework, because associated variability was not part of the risk concept.

The numerical values underlying this illustrative example had been developed with a focus on 1–1 scenarios – collision incidents involving fatalities. If the limited 1–1 incident nature of Tables 9.1 through 9.3 was extended to cover all type–grade scenarios involving relevant incidents, the sharp transition from mere noise to crucial distribution tails would be softened, but overall expected values and the very long probability distribution tails would still be the central concerns, and most of the softening of the sharp changes in the curves around the $50 million point would be in the $50 million to $60 million range. Changes in this region might matter in terms of expected outcomes, but they would not matter very much in terms of risk associated with departures from expectations.

Sophie emphasised that the NER current view of risk for safety and security decision-making purposes was limited to expected outcomes, completely ignoring risk in terms of departures from expectations, and this had to change immediately.

All board members now needed to begin to understand the implications as her examples became more sophisticated, beginning with the next example.

For 'new system A2', the second of two examples she would use, Sophie suggested that they assume that new system A2 'cost relevant to system choices' which was 'cost not related to fatalities' was estimated at $55 million per annum, and the comparable old-system cost relevant to system choices which was cost not related to fatalities was still estimated at $50 million per annum, in both cases with too little uncertainty to matter.

Then Figure 9.2 could be transformed into Figure 9.3.

The old system curves of Figures 9.2 and 9.3 were the same, with the same $50 million added to the x-scale. The difference between the new system A1 and A2 curves of Figures 9.2 and 9.3 was of crucial importance, as were the implications.

The new system A2 curve of Figure 9.3 involved accommodating the same x-scale by shifting the new system A2 curve to the right by $5 million, with a vertical segment at $55 million rising from zero cumulative probability to 0.96230 as a result of the $5 million

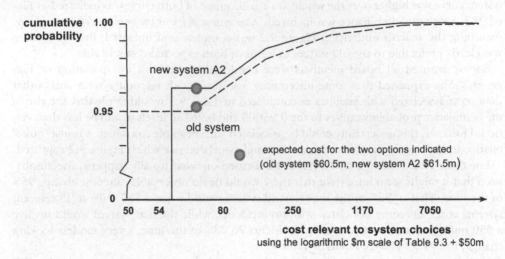

Figure 9.3 Decision diagram for the new system A2 option.

shift and the expected value becoming $61.5 million. There was a very noticeable shift in the new system A2 curve on the left-hand side. But the logarithmic nature of the x-scale meant that the visible differences in the relative positions of the curves rapidly diminished as the curves moved towards the right-hand side, with no real change in the region of the $7,050 million scenario.

What the Figure 9.3 decision diagram portrayed was 95% of the time the old system would involve the $50 million cost outcome, and the new system A2 would be $5 million more expensive, at $55 million. However, the risk of *any* outcome more than $55 million would be less for new system A2, with a massive 50% reduction in the chance of a $7,050 million scenario, a 40% reduction in the chance of an $1,170 million scenario, and so on down to a 10% reduction in the chance of a $54 million scenario.

Furthermore, new system A2 would cost $5 million more 95% of the time, but the *expected* cost disadvantage of new system A2 was only $61.5 million – $60.5 million = $1 million.

In this new system example, new system A2 did not dominate the old system in risk-efficiency terms because it increased the expected cost by $1 million. Risk–reward trade-offs were involved.

But new system A2 did *significantly* reduce risk in the general EP sense which considers potential departures from expectations as well as expected outcomes. For a relatively small $1 million increase in expected cost, there was a massive decrease in risk in the departures from an expectations sense, including a 50% decrease in the S = 350 scenario context, and *risk in the departures from expectations sense was actually the aspect of risk that really mattered here, arguably of MUCH more importance than a $1 million difference in expected outcomes.*

Furthermore, for anyone who understood risk efficiency and used it as a basic conceptual tool, restricting the interpretation of risk to expected outcomes in the context of this example was clearly seriously myopic. What was of crucial importance in practice was the risk–reward trade-offs involved when making choices, with risk FOCUSED on departures from expectations, not defined to EXCLUDE departures from expectations.

New system A2 delivered a massive reduction in risk for an expected annual cost increase of only $1 million, and rail passengers might be very pleased to pay marginally increased fares to enjoy this increase in safety, so even a $1 million decrease in reward might not be necessary for NER. *It was actually crucially important to understand that safety and revenue driven by ticket prices were not independent, and the interdependencies should NEVER be ignored.*

Some uncertainty associated with relevant system cost components other than cost related to fatalities would imply the rise in the cumulative probability curves to the 0.95000 and 0.96230 levels would be less than vertical. As in the Figure 9.2 context, this uncertainty could be associated with bearable risk – mere noise relative to the uncertainty and associated risk which Figure 9.3 captures. *But in practice it could confuse decision makers if they were not very focused on what really mattered, so it was important somebody kept everybody focused on what really mattered.*

Furthermore, in the Figure 9.3 context, even modest uncertainty of this kind poses the question, 'Could this kind of uncertainty flip the $1m expected cost disadvantage for the new system into an advantage of $1m or more?' There might be a significant chance that new system A2 could have both a lower expected cost *and* less risk, an aspect of higher-order uncertainty not considered directly by Figure 9.3, but important to understand when interpreting Figure 9.3 and more complex operational equivalents.

At this point Sophie believed that it was worth pointing out that the conditional nature of these curves and associated uncertainty mattered a great deal. For example, the P_0 and CP_S estimates might be biased, and even if they were not, associated variability uncertainty might matter. Possibly even more important, the T_S values might be too low or too high. Uncertain parameters central to the analysis inferences involved a higher order of uncertainty and risk which the decision diagrams could not capture, but which might really matter in a context like this.

The $1m expected cost advantage of the old system was not a sure thing – and it was ambiguous for an extremely complex set of reasons. In terms of a simple example, comparatively speaking the massive 50% reduction in S = 350 risk which was assumed might well be a sure thing, even if the associated unconditional probabilities were uncertain, with the same comment applying to the other high S value risk reductions. That is, NER might be able to estimate the probable reduction in fatalities given an incident of known physical characteristics occurred quite accurately relative to estimating the probability of that incident happening. *Ambiguity was involved for both concerns, but not comparable ambiguity. The difference might matter a very great deal, the reason clarification of ambiguity can matter a great deal in practice.*

In practice, the limited incident nature (1–1 type–grade) of Tables 9.1 through 9.3 had to be extended by NER to cover all relevant incidents. This meant that the issue of possible errors and bias in the estimates had a direct bearing on the question, 'Could uncertainty about costs which did not involve risk in a direct sense flip a computed expected "cost relevant to system choices" disadvantage for a new system into an advantage?'

Addressing this question together with the closely coupled issues associated with the new system risk reduction associated with high S scenarios took the discussion into enlightened prudence territory in a safety and security context, which was next on Sophie's agenda.

To start to consider the remaining aspects of the conceptual framework needed to explain enlightened prudence at a board level, Sophie posed a broad and fundamental question in an initial form: 'Assuming for the moment that the analysis underlying Figure 9.3 was complete and unbiased, but it incorporated sizable non-systematic errors, and there were no options available other the new system A2 or the old system, what choice should NER make?'

She said the board should find it useful to use Figure 9.4 to visualise how they might start to answer the initial form of this question and its generalisation.

You might begin to understand Figure 9.4 by observing that it is a variant of Figure 8.8 used in Chapter 8 and Figure 3.8 used in Chapter 3. The key modification is risk measured on the x-axis is focused on risk related to fatalities, ignoring other corporate risk because it was not immediately relevant to the NER board – it was 'noise', or it was associated with other kinds of strategic choices beyond current concerns.

Sophie used Figure 9.4 to provide the NER board with a thorough briefing on the role of risk efficiency and associated risk–reward trade-offs in the NER context, building on her earlier introduction to these concepts as addressed earlier in this book. You might like to recall the discussions in Chapters 3, 6 and 8, and assume that the NER board acquired a comparable understanding to yours in BP, IBM, Astro, Canpower, NER, and related contexts as a result of this discussion, so we do not need to revisit earlier material.

Building on this broad overview understanding, Sophie then explained that currently NER used an approach to safety based on minimising the expected cost associated with fatalities using a 'risk = probability × impact' perspective. This perspective implied that NER would currently choose the old system option, declining the new system A2 option because it increased risk as currently measured in expected value terms by $1 million. This perspective implied that the old system choice portrayed in Figure 9.3, which minimised expected cost, might be visualised as point 'a' in Figure 9.4, assuming that it was risk efficient and that risk associated with cost related to fatalities was the concern that really mattered for NER in terms of the current discussion. Prior to Sophie's arrival, NER moving away from point 'a' towards points b_1 or b_2 *would not be addressed for reasons associated with safety and security*

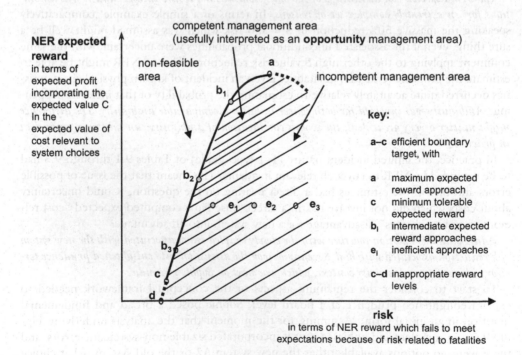

Figure 9.4 NER expected reward and risk immediately relevant in an efficient-frontier portrayal.

because *formal* assessment of safety was currently addressed in expected value terms without considering departures from expectations.

In current NER formal planning terms, risk associated with departures from expectations was entirely 'off the radar'. This was a fundamental and wholly unacceptable failing which needed immediate resolution, a huge blind spot in NER planning. It was a blind spot which was not unique to NER, but that did not make it tolerable.

Assuming that new system A2 was also risk efficient, choosing new system A2 implied a movement towards point b_1, with a very modest decline in expected reward (a $1 million increase in expected cost) but a very significant decrease in risk (measured in terms of the relative likelihood of high $m-value size scenarios). Indeed, if train passengers were prepared to pay higher fares for a much safer service, reward might actually increase. Even if this opportunity to shift the boundary is ignored, assuming rail fare ticket prices could not change, the efficient frontier curve in the region of point 'a' was very flat, and NER could *and should* take advantage of this massive decrease in risk for a modest increase in expected cost to meet their ALARP concerns. To have simply ignored this trade-off in the past was a symptom of a deeply flawed approach. *There should be no argument about the need to consider it. The only debatable issues were how to do so, and how far to go when moving towards b_1 and then b_2 and perhaps b_3.*

To address the trade-offs involved the board might start by looking at the S = 350 scenario as the $7,050 million scenario, perhaps usefully rounded to a $7,000 million scenario. The old system had a 2,000 year return period, compared to the 4,000 year return period for new system A2. That is, halving P_{350} for the new system S = 350 entry on Table 9.3 implied doubling the return period.

The board might observe that the S = 70 scenario, viewed as a $1,170 million scenario, perhaps rounded to a $1,200 million scenario, needed joint consideration too. The S = 20 scenario, viewed as a $250 million scenario was also important, and even the S = 5 and 1 scenarios had related relevance.

But before they took this exploration too far, it would be crucially important to examine some underlying assumptions about NER risk-taking *capability* as well as NER risk–reward preferences. *'Risk-taking capability' as a supplement to 'risk appetite' defined in terms of preferences was crucially important.*

As soon as the risk-taking capability issue was raised the board might observe that NER would be bankrupted if it had to pay out a figure of the order of $7,000 million, or $1,200 million, which immediately raised five key questions:

1 How much of the C_S would NER be legally required to pay in cash terms?
2 Who would bear the C_S costs in cash terms which NER was legally required to pay but not capable of paying?
3 What parties would share the further implications, and to what extent?
4 What about insurance?
5 What about ALARP from the perspective of the regulator and the courts?

The answer to the first question was NER would have to pay the A_S and I_S components associated with their option A approaches (full compensation costs for fatalities and injuries set out by the courts or associated out-of-court settlements, plus associated fines), plus actual outcomes associated with the D_S component. NER would not have to pay the full option B or C amounts associated with the A_S and I_S component amounts (assuming that these option B or C figures were higher, which was a reasonable working assumption if their estimates were unbiased). If R_S made an accurate provision for knock-on implications of loss-of-reputation issues and all other associated effects not covered by the other components, these opportunity costs and more direct cash costs would also have to be paid by NER.

The answer to the second question was the passengers and on-board NER staff involved in the incident, plus their dependents, would have to bear the consequences beyond the compensation amounts actually paid. Shortfalls in compensation payments might well be the least of the concerns of those who lost loved ones, but they would 'add insult to injury'. The government might share some of these losses if the government stepped in as an insurer of last resort in terms of fatality and injury compensations which were awarded by the courts but beyond NER resources. But this might not happen, and it was particularly unlikely given the private sector status of NER.

The answer to the third question was passengers and on-board NER staff involved in the incident, plus their dependents, would inevitably share the major portion of a failure to pay full compensation for fatalities and injuries as measured by good practice or best practice shadow price value of an avoided fatality concepts. The government could in principle share some of these losses if the government stepped in as an insurer of last resort in terms of fatalities and injuries and did not limit itself to court-based decisions if shadow costs were higher. But Sophie had never heard of any governments even thinking about doing this. The government would also share the loss in terms of all the other costs involved in rescuing a bankrupt railway which had a catastrophic incident to deal with, whether or not the government saw this in 'insurer of last resort' terms. Many further parties might also suffer knock-on effects, as for any bankruptcy, including all the shareholders and creditors of NER. Some of the creditors may be small local businesses which become bankrupt as a direct consequence.

The answer to the fourth question was complex. However, any commercial third party insurer with access to Table 9.3 and Figure 9.3 would probably want a good deal more than $1 million extra per annum in premiums to provide full cover for the old system instead of the new system, unless NER was planning to go bankrupt if a major claim arose and full compensation at shadow cost levels was unlikely to even be considered. At present NER did not have full insurance cover and bankruptcy was probably inevitable. This presumably implied that passengers and NER staff were taking a significant uninsured risk, as were other parties, and the government as an insurer of last resort was a possibility which could not be relied on.

The answer to the fifth question was more complex still, and perhaps even more contentious. At a very high overview level, if the regulator acting on behalf of the passengers, employees, and the government was given access to Table 9.3 and Figure 9.3, he or she *should* argue that the ALARP principle required NER to opt for new system A2, *even if the expected cost difference was MUCH more than the $1m assumed for* Figure 9.3. Furthermore, if NER did not disclose this information, and it was revealed post-incident, arguably NER would *and should* face a variant of the Ford Pinto controversy, intensified by a number of factors, with knock-on implications for the regulator and the government.

More generally, simply assuming that point 'a' in Figure 9.4 was acceptable without explicit and careful consideration of the risk of possible very high S and $m value scenarios was not acceptable from an EP perspective – but this could be inferred to be the current NER position, *without its regulator or the government being aware of this situation*. The current NER revealed preference was a definition of *risk* which did not address any of the risk efficiency concerns associated with Figures 9.1 through 9.4, and the current situation seemed to involve their regulator and the government not recognising that this approach posed any serious problems.

Current NER practice meant they were not explicitly thinking through the implications of high S value scenarios arising in a risk efficiency framework. *Sophie believed that the NER board members needed to fully understand the implications and make decisions accordingly, beginning that day, with a view to eventually sharing their new insights with all other interested parties.*

A key limitation of the current NER framework was that NER did not address risk–reward trade-offs on an efficient frontier in the Figure 9.4 sense. As a direct consequence, NER failed to address the trade-offs between risk measured in terms of expected outcomes and risk portrayed in terms of possible downside departures from expectations in the way she had illustrated with Figure 9.3.

Sophie indicated that NER was by no means the only organisation doing this, but in her view the very widespread nature of this common practice was no longer a viable defence for NER or any other comparable organisation. She believed she had a professional duty to act on this view, and she would be doing so, *whether or not she continued with NER.*

That is, any organisation which limits its definition of risk to 'impact × probability' was defining risk in 'expected outcome value' terms. If this was done, what she would call enlightened prudence was always ignored by the formal planning framework because the enlightened prudence concept along with its risk–reward trade-offs based on a risk efficiency perspective were outside the conceptual framework being used. Those organisations which did not use risk efficiency and enlightened prudence concepts were using a crucial 'stealth assumption' – that 'enlightened prudence did not matter', nor did the difference between enlightened prudence and enlightened gambles or enlightened caution. *What mattered a great deal was beyond the framing assumptions being used.*

It was vital for the NER board to understand *that day* why the search for a point like b_1 was important, why b_2 or b_3 might be more appropriate, why all relevant risk needed to be addressed, and why full consideration of risk generated by the significant uncertainty associated with high S and $m size scenarios might lead them to a *very* different overall corporate strategy.

Her view was it would not be helpful to try to take formal analysis of these issues further that day in terms of more sophisticated numerical examples and decision choices. They needed feasible real options requiring actual decisions, with realistic estimates which separated out the components of her transformed values via the T_S so that the board members could understand the complex nature of the expected values and the associated risk of downside departures in a specific real context. They also needed to deal with uncertainty and associated risk which she had not attempted to embed in Figures 9.3 and 9.4 which might also matter.

However, she would now try to clarify enlightened prudence in relation to enlightened gambles when 'clarified trade-offs' were involved, in addition to explaining 'clarified dominance' including enlightened caution, using simple variants of her Figure 9.3 example. She would also link these concepts to the 'fail-safe culture' which she believed NER needed. That is, she would look at 'what has to be done' in overview outline terms at a strategic level, without getting into the tactical level details of 'what has to be done', never mind the how to do it concerns, further drawing on our Chapters 3 and 6 discussion in an NER context.

Again, the next section focuses on the new issues for you, avoiding repetition of earlier material not essential for the new context.

Enlightened prudence and the board's leadership role

Sophie suggested the board reconsider Figure 9.3 in terms of a series of adjustments to the location of the new system curve, initially moving it to the left. These shifts might be associated with further revisions of the new system A2, designated A3, A4 and so on.

If new system A3's 'cost relevant to system choices' which was 'cost not related to fatalities' was $53 million, $2 million less than assumed for Figure 9.3, new system A3 would be more expensive 95% of the time, but $1 million cheaper on average. New system A3 would be the only risk efficient choice. In this case choosing the new system would involve an enlightened caution form of 'clarified dominance', in the sense demonstrated by BP's use of decision diagrams as discussed in Chapter 3 and Astro's use of decision diagrams as discussed in Chapter 6.

If the new system's cost relevant to system choices, which was cost not related to fatalities was less than $50 million, enlightened caution was not needed because the new system's cumulative probability curve was entirely to the left of the old system curve. Stochastic dominance made the new system the only obvious choice – clarified dominance in the sense discussed in terms of Astro's use of decision diagrams in Chapter 6. The decision diagram made the stochastic dominance involved clear and easy to explain so that enlightened caution was not needed, and sophisticated non-linear cumulative distribution curves were not needed. They were beyond the point illustrated by Figure 9.2 in terms of the new system curve moving to the left.

In summary, so long as the new system's cost relevant to system choices which was cost not related to fatalities was less than $54 million, the new system was the only risk efficient choice. Enlightened caution could be associated with choices involving a new system in the $50–$54 million cost not related to fatalities range because most of the time the new system would cost a small amount more but the expected cost was lower. Below $50 million, the new system was always cheaper, which was obvious in terms of clarified dominance without complex curves being required.

Sophie then asked the board to consider moving the new system curve to the right to define new system A4. Its position in Figure 9.3 associated with A2 had already taken it through the $54 million flip point, so further movement to the right meant that the $1 million *expected* cost relevant to system choices disadvantage would further increase. However, the risk reduction obtained for the *expected* $1 million cost relevant to system choices disadvantage was so huge it should be clear that an enlightened gamble in the sense discussed in relation to IBM in Chapter 3 and Astro in Chapter 6 was not involved if the old system was chosen. Making this expected cost disadvantage for new system A4 rise to $2 million or $5 million or even $10 million was not going to change this. Enlightened prudence, in the sense developed in Chapters 3 and 6, was involved if the NER preference remained the new system as the cost relevant to system choices disadvantage increased over the range $0 million to $5 million or $10 million and beyond.

The very long probability distribution tails involved implied that the risk in terms of departures from expectations was a very serious concern, and the importance of this concern made the new system the preferred choice even if the expected cost was significantly higher. The enlightened prudence this involves was based on the very rational preference for a small expected cost increase to achieve a massive risk decrease. The 50% reduction in the risk of a $7,000 million scenario was particularly attractive, but the smaller reductions in the risk of smaller $m value scenarios were also important.

In classic insurance terminology, in return for a very nominal insurance premium, a very big risk was avoided – comparable to a private individual insuring his or her house against fire and comparable risks for a premium larger than the expected cost per annum of fire damage to the house. The new system's failure to completely eliminate catastrophe risk was comparable to house insurance which covered fire or flood but not riots or warfare.

If new system A4's cost relevant to system choices, which was cost not related to fatalities was $150 million, it might be rational to argue that an additional $100 million was too much to add to the expected cost. This would certainly be a credible position if passengers were explicitly asked on a well-informed basis if they would pay for the extra $100 million through ticket price increases and a significant majority declined. Then NER would have a variant of the enlightened gamble situation discussed in Chapters 3 and 6 contexts, which Sophie explained. Certainly, an extra $1000 million suggested this. But the flip point was not $0 difference in the expected costs, and it was probably much more than $10 million given the risk differences portrayed by Table 9.3 and Figure 9.3.

Sophie then asked a question: 'Say the board had to choose between the old system and new system A4, the additional expected cost was significantly in excess of $10 million, and the board believed the expected additional cost was worthwhile. Was there anything else the board should do before deciding?'

She then suggested the EP response was 'the board should mandate Sophie's safety and security team to study a pattern of R_S adjustments over the $S = 1$ to 350 range which would allow the expected cost C to increase for further reductions in risk by moving from new system A4 to new system B1, B2, B3, and so on, increasing the relative importance of R_S via "prudence provisions", because it was important that NER explore the opportunity for doing better than new system A4 using an operational approach to "enlightened prudence" which she would now just outline in overview terms'.

In brief, what she had in mind was starting the development of a further full analysis of a new system B1 using a starting position set of T_S values comparable to her examples as discussed so far. She would have her team increase the R_S component for $S = 1$ to 350 so that it was bigger by a systematic set of increments, adding a prudence provision to R_S which would lead to new systems B1, B2, B3, and so on. What she would be doing is looking for points like b_1, b_2 and b_3 on the risk efficient boundary portrayed by Figure 9.4, assuming that the only operational way to do this was finding an optimal profile of prudence provisions to embed in R_S for $S = 1$ to 350 for points b_1, b_2, b_3, and so on.

It should be reasonably clear from the earlier discussion that if NER attached additional shadow cost weight to higher S value outcomes using a larger prudence provision in R_S in a systematic manner, expected cost increases should result in decreases in risk in the EP sense associated with Figure 9.4. It should also be reasonably clear that ultimately what really mattered was the complete set of R_S values over $S = 1$ to 350 given everything else, and the framing assumptions being used allow the R_S values to depend on all relevant considerations. Furthermore, this approach was also required if new system A1, A2, or A3 was the alternative to the old system, and the old system needed evaluation for comparative purposes using the same set of R_S values.

Sophie suggested that she and her team would have to begin using extensive sensitivity analysis associated with a systematic identification of points b_1, b_2, b_3, and so on for a real context, then share what was learned with the board, and then help the board to choose a target R_S profile for future analysis. If this was comparable to point b_2, it could be associated with plausible minimum and maximum prudence provision bounds. Future analysis of real system decisions could use this target profile and associated bounds, gradually refining the approach as experience was gained.

The crucial issues which the board needed to confront when deciding how big the R_S should be for $S = 1$ to 350 included an ethical approach to the interests of the other parties involved in a way which reflected the validity of the case made for the new and old systems in quantitative terms, bearing in mind the limitations of the numbers used. These limitations obviously included NER competence in estimating probabilities like the P_S. But they also included NER competence in estimating parameters like the T_S, *arguably MUCH MORE demanding because of the inherent ambiguity and subjectivity.*

For example, as NER Operations Director, Oscar had to judge the extent to which the estimates used to make decisions were fair and frank views of all the issues involved, with any suspected bias on the optimistic side requiring a pessimist adjustment to the appropriate boundary between enlightened prudence and enlightened gambles. If other directors did not have Oscar's grasp of the details, they still needed to satisfy themselves that sound decisions were being made in a competent manner in terms of a sufficient understanding of what really mattered.

In Sophie's view, the board's leadership of an enlightened culture which included a 'fail-safe culture' transformation had to start with a robust choice for V_1. This had to be followed by a robust and ethically sound set of choices for the E_S values conditioned by the V_1 choice. This had to include a prudence provision contribution built into the 'residual provision' associated with R_S. In addition, this had to be followed by a competent and ethically sound choice for the boundary between enlightened prudence and enlightened gambles in the context of decision diagrams and full background information for specific real cases, understanding the relationship between a prudence provision built into the residual provision and the boundary between enlightened prudence and enlightened gambles addressed in terms of decision diagrams plus underlying sensitivity diagrams.

An aspirational target for some directors might be to eventually fully embed the needed enlightened prudence into the T_S transformation as part of the prudence provision R_S component so that there was no need to keep judging a suitable $m value boundary between enlightened prudence and enlightened gambles using decision diagrams. But fully building all these ethically based concerns into the quantitative analysis was not an immediate prospect in her view. For the time being, they should limit themselves to R_S residual provisions including a prudence provision which the board saw as a clearly required target over and above current industry norms, adjusting this target prudence provision R_S if it remained clear that all the decisions they were making required a further implicit modification to reflect the preferred flip point from enlightened prudence to enlightened gambles. An R_S which was clearly 'too small' or 'too big' would damage the credibility of the approach in her view, and they did not want to rush towards simplifications which obscured the significant and difficult complexities they had to address. Her current perception was NER should make a significant movement towards a position where R_S embodied a board approved prudence provision which reflected NER willingness to reduce the probability of high S value size scenarios in any current NER context. But they should commit to continuing to test all key decisions for enlightened prudence to enlightened gamble flip points via decision diagrams plus supporting sensitivity analysis, communicating board preferences to all other relevant parties in terms of specific key choices with a comprehensive explanation of their overall rationale as well as provisions embedded in R_S and the other T_S assumptions. And they should anticipate R_S changes over time for a range of reasons.

All other NER staff could build on this board led initiative, but in Sophie's view, building a new enlightened culture had to start at the top. In her view any attempt to minimise the ethical issues by the board would compromise the NER culture as a whole. Sophie did not say so for obvious reasons, but she saw the board's view of this as a key determinant of her wish to stay with NER or not. She took the view that the necessary culture change was not going to happen if the board members could not be convinced they needed to lead from the front on this issue.

The initial operational value of the prudence provision component of the residual provision defined by R_S was a target value – an initial best guess which needed to be revised via extensive consideration of enlightened prudence based on the use of decision diagrams plus sensitivity analysis to test the implications. Testing the implications could include comparing the decision diagram implications of different levels of prudence provision via R_S in real contexts.

The use of decision diagrams like Figure 9.3 with extensive sensitivity analysis backup including clarification of actual cash costs as well as shadow costs could then be seen as a robustness test, a confirmation that the NER point of transition from enlightened prudence to enlightened gambles was ethically sound. All interested parties should see the basis of the decision-making process being used *before as well as after catastrophes occur.*

Alternative ways of presenting choices which Sophie thought most directors might find informative included reducing the A_S and I_S components of T_S to the minimum plausible 'option A' values and adding what was taken out back to R_S in various ways so that cost relevant to system choices was actual cash costs in terms of the first three component factors. This might provide a useful basis for alternative good and best practice provision testing, using sensitivity analysis in a way which would help them to understand what was involved.

Despite the complexity the board would have to engage with, if board members had decision diagrams for real choices they had to make with carefully designed example T_S values and appropriate underlying sensitivity diagrams to clarify what was involved, the board could begin to make appropriate choices in a practical context. They could start to develop a feel for ethical and defensible decisions if R_S took on various possible values given suitable working assumptions for the other T_S component values, gradually working towards values of R_S they would generally be comfortable with.

This implied a set of real decisions with trade-offs requiring extended discussions looking at complete C_S and F_S distributions as well as C and F values under a range of assumptions involving debatable parameters. In the early stages this would be a deep learning process for everyone involved, a non-trivial investment in corporate learning. But once they had acquired the mindsets and skill sets needed, decision making could become efficient as well as effective, with multiple order-of-magnitude reductions in the effort expended.

As a roughly comparable example, in the late 1970s BP spent about a year working on a prototype SCERT methodology design study, then six months on their first SCERT analysis, but within a year of making this approach mandatory worldwide, comparable analysis was taking about six weeks. It was worth bearing in mind BP invested this effort to reduce overall cost and increase overall profit via risk efficiency – to manage opportunity, and they were convinced they made a very large rate of return on this investment. Some aspects of NER's issues were much more complex, and in some respects much more new transformative learning was involved, implying an even bigger need to progress slowly and carefully with a focus on effectiveness first, later seeking massive efficiency improvements once they understood what really mattered. But the pay-off for NER was not just a better understanding of its safety and security concerns. It was an improvement in very broadly defined opportunity efficiency terms. It ought to deliver a wide range of improvements in corporate performance, not just improvements associated with safety and security.

Sensitivity diagram portrayal of option costs

Sophie suggested that whenever the board wanted to choose between two options, like no new system or a new generation signalling system coupled to other fully integrated changes, it would be crucial to understand the roles of expected values and associated variability for all key components of cost relevant to system choices plus underlying cost related to fatalities components. She indicated that sensitivity diagrams were the best way to portray this kind of information which she was aware of, and she believed that NER would find sensitivity diagrams indispensable aspects of sensitivity analysis exercises at the board level, as well as essential for her team plus all other NER staff involved in related bottom-up analysis and decision making. She did not have a developed example directly geared to their safety and security concerns, but she could show them a project planning example used by BP drawing on Chapman and Ward (2011), and she could explain how NER safety and security concerns could be addressed in this framework. She then showed the board Figure 9.5.

Sophie started by explaining how BP used this kind of sensitivity diagram as discussed in Chapter 4 using Figure 4.1, the basis of Figure 9.5. You might recall this explanation

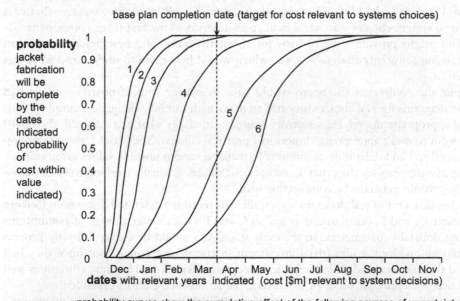

base plan completion date (target for cost relevant to systems choices)

dates with relevant years indicated (cost [$m] relevant to system decisions)

probability curves show the cumulative effect of the following sources of uncertainty:
1. yard not available, or mobilisation delays (annualised capital cost of new system)
2. construction problems/adverse weather (adjusted operating costs of new system)
3. subcontracted nodes delivery delays (physical system damage cost)
4. material delivery delays (compensation for fatalities)
5. industrial disputes (compensation for injuries)
6. delayed award of fabrication contract (residual provision – decomposed on a lower-level sensitivity diagram)

notes:
1. the curves assume a minimum fabrication period of 20 months (current legal climate)
2. no work is transferred offsite to improve progress (trial residual provision approach)
3. no major fire, explosion, or other damage (no incident sources not currently assessed)

Figure 9.5 Sensitivity diagram: North Sea oil project platform jacket fabrication example (with NER new system reinterpretations in brackets assuming no curve shifts).

looking at Figure 9.5, perhaps revisiting Chapter 4 if you do not remember the basic ideas. The use of sensitivity diagrams was also discussed in Chapter 6 in relation to Figure 6.11, and again in Chapter 7 in relation to Figure 7.5, which you might revisit later for a fuller understanding if necessary. This kind of sensitivity diagram was first used by BP in the 1970s, and in the following decades it was widely adopted by many other organisations for many other purposes. In the NER context of current interest Sophie suggested the board might re-interpret it as indicated using brackets, and she would take them through this now.

Beginning with the Figure 9.5 title in brackets – the NER 'new system' reinterpretations in brackets assumed no curve shifts to keep this example explanation simple, but in practice the curve shapes would change, radically in some cases. She would comment on this issue as she discussed each curve, after considering the axes.

Reinterpreting the x-scale as 'cost ($m) relevant to system decisions' meant that curve 6 in Figure 9.5 might be interpreted as the new system curve in Figure 9.3 in a smooth curve form, with the gaps between the six curves reinterpreted as a six component breakdown which used the minimum plausible option A approach to A_S and I_S, embedding the uplifts to option B good practice plus the option C maximum plausible best practice approaches in R_S. This might imply three versions of Figure 9.5 being required for considering three alternative approaches to R_S: a zero R_S version considering only cash flow costs, a mid-range good practice version, and a 'maximum plausible NER best practice' version based on carefully identified working assumptions about uplifts added to the good practice version. The key working assumptions involved would be specified in 'note 2 – trial residual provision approach'. The other two notes were self-explanatory. The board would presumably be seeking agreement to a position between the second two and might also want trial versions of working hypotheses about this.

The 'base plan completion date' might be reinterpreted as the 'target for cost relevant to systems choices' (as indicated in brackets) for the new system, with a cumulative probability of being within any cost value on the x-scale being indicated on the y-axis. The 'target' used might be a stretch target equated to the expected cost of the old system which the new system would replace. If this were the case, a chance of achieving it of about 15% for the assumed 'maximum plausible best practice' residual provision choice might be deemed reasonable in a context like Figure 9.3, with some expected cost increase being tolerated for a massive reduction in risk.

Each of the uncertainty sources might then be reinterpreted as indicated in brackets, and Sophie explained them as follows.

Source 1 plotted on the revised NER version of Figure 9.5 might be the annualised (amortised) capital cost of the new system per annum, net of any relevant scrap value adjustments associated with the old system. If relevant NER estimates were used, curve 1 would leave the x-axis at a plausible minimum value defining the left-hand end of the x-scale, and it might rise with the same overall 'S' shape as the curve shown in Figure 9.5 but a significantly steeper climb rate throughout.

Source 2 might be the annual operating cost of the new system adjusted for increases in revenue. Again, if relevant NER estimates were used, curve 2 would leave the x-axis at a plausible minimum for the first two components, it might rise reasonably parallel to curve 1 if little anticipated additional uncertainty was added, and it might have the same shape as the curve shown in Figure 9.5 but a steeper rate of climb throughout.

Source 3 might be the cost of physical damage to the system in terms of damaged trains and tracks as a consequence of all incidents relevant to the system changes being considered, plus direct knock-on operating costs and an opportunity cost view of lost revenues. Curve 3 might overlay curve 2 near the bottom and over the mid-range, with a significant chance of no cost in this range, and then move sharply to the right close to the top, with a long tail reflecting the very low probability of a catastrophic incident. Expected values plotted on all the curves (as in Figures 6.11 and 9.1–9.3) would probably be very useful to help to clarify how both the cumulative expected values and the ranges changed as more sources were considered.

Source 4 might be the cost of compensation for fatalities, including legal fees, fines, and payments to relatives in out-of-court settlements, as well as court-imposed settlements, separating out the components of the cost of an avoided fatality which would have to be actually paid by NER in cash terms from the good practice uplift incorporated in the residual provision of source 6. Curve 4 might overlay curve 3 for its lower and mid-range portion, plus its early dramatic movement to the right. But it would then move farther to the right very sharply to a massive extent, with an overall increase in importance which was significantly bigger than that shown in Figure 9.5.

Source 5 might be the cost of compensation for injuries. Like source 4, this might include legal fees, fines, and payments to relatives as well as payments to the injured parties themselves, separating this from good and best practice provisions incorporated in the residual provision of source 6. The overall shape might be similar to curve 4, almost overlying curve 4 over the lower portions, then moving off dramatically to the right. As for source 4, the relative increase in expected value and variability might be huge, very much bigger than that associated with Figure 9.5.

The shapes of curves 3, 4 and 5 would all be very different from that shown, with a significant bulge out to the right near the tops of the curves to reflect serious to catastrophic incidents.

Source 6 might be the residual provision, initially using the three alternative approaches already noted: a cash flow costs only minimum plausible approach (curves 5 and 6 are the same), a good practice approach (shifting curve 6 to the right), and a NER maximum plausible best practice approach (further shifting curve 6 to the right). A breakdown of the components of this sixth component could obviously be provided using the same Figure 9.5 sensitivity diagram framework, to clarify the relative importance and absolute size of all the key components of R_S, further discussed in a moment. Later tentative board choices which interpolated between the initial bounds could be explored in the same framework.

Separating source 6 from sources 4 and 5 in this way in effect separated the actual cash flow costs from the other revealed preference contributions to sources 4 and 5 in a way the board would probably find informative. All the relevant *actual* cost estimates could be portrayed using five components via sources 1 to 5 using this approach. Sophie was convinced that the board would want to see these components separated.

It would also be helpful to see good practice residual provisions, maximum plausible best practice residual provisions, and later proposed intermediate positions compared, in whatever structure the board preferred. This might include perhaps putting the good practice provisions back in A_S and I_S components and experimenting with associated best practice provisions in A_S and I_S, as well as a separate focus on enlightened prudence in R_S.

The overall structuring being suggested was slightly different from the structuring used to arrive at the T_S values at the outset of the analysis. However, it used the presentation options A, B, and C identified earlier, and NER was free to use whatever structure was most appropriate to the case being made and the story being told. This might change as the analysis progressed and NER learned what really mattered.

At a much later date, regulators, courts, and passenger representative groups might also find this kind of decomposition useful, with structures tailored to their interests.

Curves 1 to 5 as well as 6 could be decomposed in a nested structure with as many levels as the board or other users wanted, built from the bottom up by the safety and security team, explained from the top down to the level of decomposition currently available according to board concerns, or the concerns of other parties. Further diagrams portraying the composition of curve 6 would clearly be needed, but because any of the other curves would have to be built from the bottom up by her team, they could be explained from the top down using the initial structure or alternatives which the board or other users preferred.

As in their use in the contexts of Chapters 4, 6 and 7, the safety and security team could use nested sensitivity curves to develop their understanding of all relevant decisions, including process decisions about the need to do more analysis before making recommendations to the board. They could then use final forms to explain their recommendations after feedback on proposed formats.

In some cases which might arise in practice, the curve 2 sources for the new system might involve significant revenue benefits as well as reduced operating costs relative to the old system. This might be of special interest, perhaps actually driving the decision to change to the new system. Extensive decomposition of revenue benefits, as well as cost savings, might be of great interest to the board, and it might require careful attention to the effective portrayal.

BP's concerns in a North Sea project context were clearly very different from those NER had to address, but the opportunity efficiency approach Sophie was advocating shared more than just the use of decision diagrams plus underlying sensitivity diagrams, and its use in a wide range of contexts beyond BP was very extensive. One important common aspect was the extensive use of a nested analysis structure. The NER safety and security team could use this toolset with other NER staff to seek opportunity efficiency while building a bottom-up understanding of complex interdependent uncertainties with appropriate specific and general responses which the board could view from the top down when approving important recommendations in the NER gateway processes. Their goal would be opportunity efficiency in very broad terms, not just a safer and more secure railway system.

A process for clarifying NER revealed preferences

Sophie indicated that the T_S values adopted would define the basis of NER revealed preferences for decision-making purposes, with the R_S playing a pivotal role. At present NER implicitly set the R_S to zero and did not acknowledge the role of an S dependent T_S concept, but that was only part of the differences between current practice and required new approaches.

She emphasised that it would not be easy to develop and agree on initial R_S and other T_S operational values, because they would have to define NER revealed preferences for decision-making purposes in a way which reflected an ethical approach to interpreting the revealed preferences of their passengers and staff plus their dependents, plus other parties like their shareholders. Views about all these issues might not be shared by different groups, and opinions could vary significantly within groups.

She suggested trade-offs like those involved in R_S, if they assumed that treatment of enlightened prudence ought to be as fully embedded as possible, would be more difficult than those associated with A_S and I_S, and even D_S would not be straightforward. However, they could leave some of the particularly difficult issues until they needed to confront them in particular cases, dealing with all the issues involved on a case-by-case basis.

To address all these issues they could develop a process for clarifying NER revealed preferences. This process would be designed to make it as easy as possible to use the T_S approach in practice. She thought the following steps might serve as an outline of this process:

1   Safety and security staff could undertake background research on V_1 values, related potentially relevant V_{350} values, and T_S equivalent values used by other organisations, especially those used by relevant road traffic authorities, air safety authorities, and railway safety authorities. They would need to pay special attention to the explicit and implicit assumptions used by these other organisations which were relevant to the set of V_1 and E_S to be adopted by NER.
2   Safety and security staff could undertake related research to clarify the relationship between numbers of fatalities in railway incidents, correlated numbers of people injured in various categories, and the $m costs to be embedded in the D_S associated with related physical damage to facilities plus knock-on cost and lost revenue implications.
3   Safety and security staff could propose initial sets of V_1 and E_S values for NER based on the two sets of research outlined in the first two steps and both 'good practice' and 'maximum plausible best practice' proposed bounds, as well as an estimated 'cash costs only' lower bound.
4   Safety and security staff and other relevant NER staff could build on the first three steps using an extensive exercise applying these values tentatively to a range of relevant real decisions, picking a rich mix of decision types, including any currently contentious choices.
5   An extensive set of tentative decision recommendations and associated assumptions from step 4 could be used for board level discussions about appropriate modifications to the sets of V_1 and E_S values suggested by the safety and security team when the budget, F and C implications became clear. The budget, F, and C implications would all be driven by the V_1 and E_S choices, along with the probability estimates plus NER creativity in terms of the best possible ways to approach all planning.
6   Extensive and open debate at the board level about NER creativity in terms of the best way to approach safety and security planning, and its integration with all other planning, could then consolidate what was learned from the first five steps.
7   Formal implementation could begin, initially using the tentative approaches developed in the first six steps to make definitive specific decisions, with constant review to develop better approaches as experience was gained.
8   Using these initial definitive decisions in particular contexts to start to explore NER revealed preferences in more general terms could be a further level of purely internal NER learning.
9   When NER had developed a feel for what was involved, which was understood and trusted at an appropriate level by all the NER staff involved, a process of opening the discussion to the regulator and passenger representatives could begin. The goal would be a completely open relationship with a view to establishing and maintaining trust, even if a serious incident occurred.

The core revealed preference issues for NER

Sophie suggested that what the board ultimately agreed about the operational form of NER revealed preferences for decision-making purposes had to be seen as reasonable by the regulator to gain the regulator's approval and reasonable by passengers to achieve customer trust, in addition to being acceptable to NER staff and shareholders, unless NER chose to hide this information or deny that it was relevant.

NER revealed preferences had to be defined in terms of an NER view of what constituted a reasonable and fair compromise between the potentially conflicting views of these different parties, given all the ambiguity involved.

Current NER practices meant that none of the choices in her examples would be taken to the board level. Choices were currently being made on technical grounds without the carefully structured board input needed – equivalent to assuming $T = V_1 \times E = \$4$ million for all S with no concern for risk efficiency and related concepts like enlightened prudence plus a range of other stealth assumptions, with the board not even understanding that this was the case. She argued that the basis of V_1 should be of interest to the board, and the role in T_S of an S dependent E_S factor bigger than unity ought to be a very big concern for the board because *all associated issues were unequivocally a board responsibility.*

The new framework they would use to avoid ignoring the enlightened caution and enlightened prudence issues, which she had raised in relation to Figure 9.3 and the residual provision captured by R_S, was ultimately going to be of huge importance. Although she could not effectively demonstrate the full implications of all these issues at this initial meeting, she hoped they now had some feel for what was involved.

Sophie suggested that part of the reason NER had been taken by surprise by the public reaction to their 40 fatality derailment was that they had failed to understand the need to discriminate between expected fatalities associated with small numbers of people killed on a regular basis (as on the roads) and large numbers of people killed on an infrequent basis (as in serious airplane crashes). They had failed to see how elements of both had to be confronted by NER, and they had failed to undertake effective contingency planning associated with both prior preventative measures, and post-event mitigation measures, for high S level incidents. This could be linked to the use of a T_S concept which did not recognise the S dependency. It could also be linked to a failure to use any effective form of 'everything else' factor and a failure to understand both risk efficiency and enlightened caution. Furthermore, it could be linked to a failure by NER safety experts to understand that risk could not be measured *just* in terms of expected outcomes, *and addressing possible departures from expected outcomes was crucial to recognising the role of enlightened prudence within an effective framework for managing risk and opportunity. Any formal risk analysis framework which ignored possible departures from expected outcomes was untenable in her view.*

The unconditional *and conditional* expected implications of catastrophes mattered, but so did the full range of potential departures from expected outcomes if an incident occurred, and the implications of any associated ambiguity. From an EP perspective, it was wholly unacceptable to argue otherwise.

These were all technical safety and security management shortcomings which needed to be addressed. They were also clear evidence of why NER had not yet learned why they needed to be afraid. NER needed to develop and then use this fear productively to creatively address the issues associated with very low probability but very high impact incidents, plus all related intermediate level incidents. Exactly how they would address these concerns was still an open question, but the basic issues associated with the need to do so, and what had to be done, were clear to her, and she hoped they were now becoming clear to board members.

Communication and capability issues for NER

Sophie suggested that underlying what might be seen as *technical problems* associated with core revealed preference issues for NER, there was a set of *communication problems* and linked capability concerns which had to be addressed. NER needed an approach to these communication problems in terms of appropriate forms of dialogue or narrative fully embedded in the NER approach to corporate capability. Requisite capability included understanding how to synthesis goals for safety and security which were focused on effectively managing a zero fatalities aspirational target coupled to a sophisticated understanding of the difference between aspirational targets and other targets. An associated nuanced understanding of what should happen on average over an extended period also needed to be coupled to commitments which accommodated low probability but high impact incidents over a very wide range of possibilities. For example, the board might approve publication of a statement like

> NER is dedicated to always seeking a target of no injuries and no fatalities, and all NER staff will be ceaseless in their efforts to achieve this goal. But everyone involved has to live with the fact that even 'catastrophic' incidents are possible. Although a catastrophe like 350 fatalities in one incident is possible, NER believe that the current estimate of a return period of more than 4000 years for incidents of this severity involves a level of risk that is both prudent and acceptable in terms of a compromise between the interests of all the parties involved, having consulted with and listened to those parties, including railway passenger groups and the railway industry regulator.

The board might prefer a very different form of words, but they needed a tactful way of explaining clearly what was involved to everyone who was interested.

There was a technical aspect to this communication issue, associated with the need to explicitly and formally distinguish between aspirational targets, what usually happened, expected outcomes, and commitment targets defined in terms of target low probabilities for large S value scenarios. NER needed to generalise the 'ABCs of targets' initially discussed in Chapter 3, illustrated in later chapters. NER needed an 'XYZ of targets' addressing a much more sophisticated view of commitments and balanced target concepts. But there were also deep communication and linked cultural implications in terms of what they were trying to achieve, as well as what needed to be done, how they ought to set about doing it and how they ought to explain their position in terms of variations from both aspirational targets and expected outcomes associated with probability distributions with very long tails for possible injuries and fatalities which the industry had to live with.

Arguably a still deeper set of issues NER had to address was the current lack of an enlightened culture driven by an enlightened generalisation of a fail-safe culture which always balanced the need to remain optimistic about NER ability to improve risk efficiency related concerns while remaining alert to all possible adverse incidents, avoiding any complacency. Part of the solution to these concerns was first understanding and then managing some of the complex insurance and risk sharing issues which were involved. This needed further attention immediately.

An S = 350 scenario would bankrupt NER given current insurance arrangements as Sophie understood them, and much smaller S value incidents would risk NER bankruptcy, unless new insurance arrangements could be put in place. She understood that the majority of NER shareholders were domestic pension funds. She suspected that they were unaware of this risk, and would probably be very unhappy about it when they were made aware of it. She suspected that both the regulator and the government were also unaware of the scope and nature of NER bankruptcy risk, not to mention passengers and passenger associations. She believed that the NER board and their shareholders should seek insurance to avoid this risk, and by being open about the need for it with the regulator, they might be able to encourage the regulator to provide appropriate insurance via the government in a cost-effective way that would be a collaborative win–win for everyone.

She would now briefly consider what might be involved.

Enlightened regulation and risk sharing

Sophie emphasised that NER very clearly needed to develop a good working understanding of the approach she was proposing *before* approaching the regulator, but it might be useful if she now briefly sketched out what she called a 'new deal' scenario which the board might develop to take to the regulator, once they had some specific practical propositions to negotiate with.

They might start thinking about the issues from the perspective of an enlightened regulator. If she was planning the kind of meeting she thought NER needed with an enlightened regulator, there were a series of questions she might ask the regulator, with related observations. She would discuss these questions and observations in detail with the board well in advance of such a meeting, based on what they had learned in the meantime. But she would now outline her current view of some of the key questions to give the board a flavour of what might be involved.

The first question, after explaining NER's position, was, 'If NER chooses b_3 or b_1 instead of b_2 in Figure 9.4, would you like to be consulted and see the trade-offs involved linked to other aspects of your role as regulator, including rail fare levels and the structure and level of subsidies?' Sophie observed that choosing b_1 or b_2 or b_3, plus the V_1 and E_s choices made by NER, would seem to be core issues for regulator discussion with NER. NER proposing this degree of open sharing could be the basis of a 'new deal'. This new deal would have to fully acknowledge the need to preserve the independent stance the regulator needed to protect passenger, employee, and government interests. However, it could be based on assuming that transparency and trust were important for both NER and the regulator to a degree not fully appreciated or effectively developed earlier. The reason was neither NER nor the regulator previously understood the issues in a framework which made an open relationship an obvious win–win possibility for all parties involved – which *all parties ought to insist upon*.

The second question was, 'The government has made it an offence to drive motorised vehicles on public roads without liability insurance, for very obvious good reasons, so why do you not insist that NER had liability insurance in place to cover the liability aspects of $7000m incidents or smaller incidents which could lead to NER bankruptcy?' This question highlighted an obvious weakness in the regulator's current role if NER had another serious accident and became bankrupt – and someone might raise this question, even if no further accidents happened. The spirit of the question was revealing an uncomfortable truth for both NER *and the regulator* which they needed to deal with jointly. At this point in the dialogue it would be important to make it clear that NER profitability was so modest in general and so damaged by the two recent major accidents that there was no scope for further reducing it without forcing NER into bankruptcy.

The third question was, 'Private sector commercially provided liability insurance would clearly be very expensive, and its cost would have to be added to either the current fares passengers pay or current government subsidies for rail travel, so why not consider making this mandatory liability insurance part of your rail regulation remit, providing it as a government underwritten cost-effective part of your oversight role and extending the role of this insurance to ensure that massive physical damage to the system leading to NER bankruptcy was also avoided?' This would save money for passengers and the government by avoiding private sector commercial insurance companies duplicating work which the regulator arguably needed to do anyway. If it included prescribed payment guidelines for fatalities and injuries, it might be a popular way of avoiding much of the legal costs surrounding the ongoing disputes following the recent NER accidents. It would allow the regulator much closer supervision of NER safety and security practice. It would also facilitate incentives for safety and security which were directly linked to insurance premium levels.

The fourth question was, 'would the regulator like to take a proactive pioneering role as a partner with NER in the development of a "new deal" approach to regulation which both parties are fully comfortable with?' If so, the railway regulator might generate a model for much wider use, beyond the railway industry, and take the credit for doing so.

The fifth question was, 'Would the regulator like to involve passenger association representatives, and perhaps even government minister's representatives, in early discussions, as part of showing regulator leadership when fashioning a "new deal" for all involved parties?'

Sophie did not want to oversell the insurance issues, or any other particular aspect of the 'new deal' approach which she thought might be necessary, or take more board time that day. However, she did want to make it clear to the board that complex issues like self-insurance, partial insurance and risk sharing, in addition to economic efficiency, needed consideration. In addition, very important ethical issues and 'social efficiency' issues were also involved, because the trade-offs that needed making involved the interests of all other relevant parties. Furthermore, if NER wanted to rebuild trust with all these relevant parties, NER should show these parties enlightened plans which clarified who was taking what risks for what rewards and how an open and collaborative approach could prove a winner for all relevant parties, with the possible exception of some lawyers.

NER needed to show initiative and leadership but let the regulator, as well as rail passengers and NER staff on the trains, share the benefits from the change process with NER shareholders, provided the regulator was sufficiently enlightened to be open to this kind of approach. A hostile or uncooperative regulator would require a different plan.

Ambiguity which may be resolvable at least in part

Sophie indicated that she was about to draw her contribution to their current meeting to a close, but it was important to stress that the need for ethically grounded cost transformations associated with fatalities and correlated levels of injuries which would generate trust was beyond dispute. Furthermore, the need for appropriate risk efficient trade-offs involving prudence provisions was also beyond dispute. Despite the ambiguity about the relative merits and drawbacks of common practice T_S values and associated analysis frameworks versus her proposed approach, the basic ideas behind risk efficiency, cost related to fatalities transformations, and associated revealed preferences, had been implemented in practice across the world in a variety of forms at various levels of sophistication, and they would make intuitive sense to everyone interested in NER safety and security. For example, people did not have to understand multiple criteria mathematical programming and associated goal programming concepts to intuitively understand the idea that if you wanted to minimise expected fatalities *and* you also wanted to minimise associated cost, there must be trade-offs involved. When key decision makers commit to a course of action, they obviously reveal their preferences about appropriate trade-offs, and these trade-offs have ethical implications, whether or not the decision makers understand and accept this is the case. The NHTSA understood most of these issues in terms of its $T_S = T$ or V concept variant many decades ago, as did most other bodies responsible for trade-offs of this kind. In addition, there were important trade-offs between expected outcomes and possible downside departures from expectations which most areas of risk management had confronted to some extent. The existence of trade-offs always implied shadow costs if optimality was a concern. To some extent these ideas had always been implicit in the ALARP concept, although significant ambiguity of interpretation was also involved.

The ambiguity about common practice $T_S = T$ or V based approaches versus Sophie's framework was resolvable, as was ambiguity about how best to adjust and develop the operational form of her proposed approach, including the risk efficiency and enlightened prudence discussion associated with Figures 9.1 through 9.5. What was not resolvable was the ambiguity inherent in revealed preference interpretations of the preferences of other people or the inherent ambiguity in the ethical aspects of the residual provision in R_S or the inherent ambiguity associated with the boundary between enlightened prudence and enlightened gambles in the context of specific decision-making choices. NER had to confront all this ambiguity as best they could or admit defeat – and admitting defeat was not a tenable position for members of the board of NER.

More generally, difficult problems we are not sure how to solve are never resolved or dissolved by pretending that they do not exist. Difficult problems that are ignored simply become invisible off the radar sources of lost opportunity risk. In the NER context, this really mattered because hundreds of people might lose their lives or be critically injured when relatively small increases in expected cost spent in the most effective way could avoid or significantly reduce the chance of this possibility, perhaps simultaneously also improving the quality of service provided in other ways. *Everyone* involved *should* prefer an operational form of enlightened prudence, embedded in opportunity efficiency, to failing to even consider resolvable ambiguity because resolvable ambiguity was off their radar and beyond NER competence.

It was imperative that NER seek approximately correct answers to the right questions, avoiding wasting effort and misleading everyone by answering the wrong questions.

Sophie did not say so for obvious reasons, but in her view if the NER board failed to rise to this challenge, *all other interested parties needed to understand why this was not acceptable and do something effective about it.*

Sophie's closing remarks

Sophie said she appreciated that her presentation was technical, intense, and lengthy, but the problems addressed were difficult, complex, and extremely important. She apologised for not explaining any points as clearly as members of the board might have expected, but promised to spend more time whenever this was requested. She also apologised for any candour they might have found offensive, but suggested that the topic was much too important to risk failing to make the need for key changes clear. She finished by saying she hoped that the board understood the flavour of what she had been saying in broad terms, sufficient to see whether or not further dialogue would be fruitful.

She might have addressed the issues considered in the next section by way of a summary. She refrained, but they are a useful summary of some core aspects of what this chapter has been about from your perspective.

Biases, blind spots and bounds on formal analysis

From the board level down, all organisations can benefit from an inherently optimistic opportunity management perspective on safety and security, looking for creative ways to reduce expected fatalities or comparable issues in positive terms. 'Accentuate the positive' is a good general rule. However, 'eliminate the negative' is a relevant related goal providing constructive tension. At a 100% level of achievement, eliminating the negative is usually not feasible, no matter how positive the approach.

It is important to maintain a clear view of both the expected cost of failure and a plausible maximum realised cost if failure occurs, as well as a spectrum of intermediate scenarios. Always being aware of the full implications of catastrophic scenarios if they occur, and the full range of reasons they might occur, is part of avoiding complacency, and part of not allowing short-term financial considerations undue weight.

For example, NER board members and some other NER staff members needed routine reminders that the S = 350 scenario – if it happened – carried a $C_S = S \times V_1 \times E_{350}$ 'price tag' of the order of $7,000 million. When appropriate, they also needed to be reminded that the return period associated with this level of catastrophe would be directly influenced by a wide variety of procedural systems and cultural changes which only a 'fail-safe' culture could address in an effective and efficient way. They needed to set the cultural tone based on this understanding and help to ensure that it reached 'the big team' as a whole. An effective and efficient approach to safety and security risk, driven by an optimistic search for less risk in conjunction with lower costs for better service, might transform a 2,000 year return period estimate into a 4,000 or 8,000 year return period estimate, but eliminating any possibility of the maximum plausible number of fatalities was rarely an option. Staying vigilant was crucial.

A complacent approach to outsourcing some safety critical issues might change a 2,000 year return period to 200 years or even 20 years, especially if the way their contractors made use of subcontractors was not *very* carefully controlled. NER had to remain fully responsible for all outsourced components of their operations.

Enlightened optimism tempered by enlightened pessimism might be the way to present a well-balanced approach to 'do not forget to be afraid' with a view to everyone playing their role in responding to this key message.

A number of issues underlie the importance of this message and the overall approach of this chapter, briefly reviewed now under the headings 'biases', 'blind spots', and 'bounds on formal analysis'.

Biases

Bias is an endemic estimation problem. At its simplest, if we ask how long an activity will take or how much it will cost, assuming that conscious bias is not a concern, unconscious biases like 'anchoring' need addressing. During the discussion of a minimum clarity approach to estimation in Chapter 3 it was pointed out that asking for a P90 maximum plausible estimate first, a P10 minimum plausible estimate second, tends to reduce unconscious anchoring bias and offset some of the usual inherent bias associated with failing to understand the full scope of uncertainty. Identifying implicit conditions like 'this expected outcome estimate assumes the project will not be cancelled' pushed the sophistication of low clarity approaches to unconscious bias a little further. The extensive decomposition of sources of uncertainty prior to deciding what to quantify and what to treat as a condition, illustrated by the BP SCERT approach discussed later in Chapter 3, pushed the sophistication of higher clarity approaches further still. The sensitivity diagram discussion a few sections ago, and other links between best practice project planning and operations planning, should make it clear that this level of sophistication can be embedded in safety and security planning. There is a strong case for arguing it should be formally required as part of seeking an ALARP position.

One purpose served by emphasising the need for an early focus on a maximum plausible impact scenario like Sophie's S = 350 was minimising bias in this sense, using all available expertise from safety and security experts, as well as the more general literature on unconscious bias.

A closely coupled further purpose was providing a basis for explicitly addressing conscious bias. We know from widely reported 1960s PERT experience that forcing people to estimate ranges as a basis for providing expected value estimates reduces conscious as well as unconscious bias. It follows that forcing people to start with a plausible upper bound on the size and probability of a maximum plausible catastrophe scenario makes it relatively difficult to conceal the scale and likelihood of both potential catastrophic outcomes and less serious related outcomes. Making understanding the full implications mandatory at the board level, followed by regulatory approvals processes exposed to passenger, on-board staff, and more public scrutiny, can be seen as part of this attack on bias. Current common practice does not frame concerns about bias in this way, and doing so has important advantages.

Blind spots – expected outcomes, what usually happens, and the XYZ of targets

Safety and security planning, and managing the implementation of plans, needs clarity about expected outcomes, what usually happens, and the XYZ of targets. For example, NER needs staff and passengers to focus on zero fatalities and injuries as the aspirational target, understanding that zero fatalities and injuries are only going to happen if they are *all* both diligent *and* lucky. *Each and every* incident involving fatalities and injuries needs a proportionate assessment to ascertain whether bad luck or bad management was involved, dealing appropriately with root causes and responsible parties. This is part of managing safety and security in relation to aspirational targets.

However, targets which safety and security regulators control to, publish, and reward performance or punish in relation to should not be confused with aspirational targets, expected values used to make decisions, other balanced targets, or what usually happens. Targets used by safety and security regulators should be commitment targets with identified probabilities of exceeding a range of incident scenario values like the S = 5, 20, 70, and 350 values used here for specified categories of incidents like collisions with fatalities, derailments with fatalities, and level-crossing incidents with fatalities, with issues like terrorist incidents kept separate for some purposes, and suicides involving trains kept separate for most purposes. Commitment targets based on aggregate numbers of fatalities per annum, interpreted as a number not to be exceeded, are not appropriate. Any high S value incident should necessitate in-depth but proportionate independent audit of root causes and responsible parties which will be made public. This is part of managing safety and security in relation to commitment targets defined in probability of exceedance terms, comparable to using 100, 1,000, or 10,000 year return period specifications for the risk of structural failure for buildings and other facilities due to earthquakes, which traditionally distinguish between very different structures with different failure implications, like houses, high-rise apartments, large dams, and nuclear power stations.

There is a strong case for arguing that the XYZ of targets in this context must include full disclosure and effective dialogue between all interested parties. From an EP perspective, there is no plausible case for not making it legally required practice, and treating a failure to meet this required practice as a very serious matter involving custodial sentences for the senior level decision makers who should have understood the issues.

Blind spots – the ethical interpretation of shadow cost and revealed preference aspects of transformations from a fatalities metric S to a cost metric C_S via T_S

Safety and security planning and associated management by both public and private sector organisations, plus associated regulation, and ALARP discussions in a legal context, need clarity about the nature of the transformation from a fatality metric S to a C_S cost concept involving the value of avoided fatalities.

One aspect is the shadow cost nature of the transformation which dictates an explicit value for consistent decision making. If T_S values are not made explicit, both lives and money will be wasted, because different values will be used implicitly in different contexts in an inconsistent manner, sometimes spending too little, sometimes spending too much. Explicit values used consistently are required for fatality efficiency to minimise the number of fatalities for any given level of expenditure with safety and security implications.

A second aspect is the revealed preference nature of the shadow cost employed, dictating an interpretation which requires consideration of ethical issues. Whether or not the money being spent and the lives and health at stake are associated with the same set of people, all of them ought to have a say in the process of determining appropriate trade-offs, and there will be a range of views which cannot be averaged without ethical implications. Addressing these implications requires ethical judgements consistent with the ALARP principle, plus notions of fairness with respect to winners and losers. There are important implications which need considerable care.

In my experience, common practice is neither unambiguous nor consistent about these issues. From an EP perspective, there is no plausible case for not making a consistently high level of clarity associated with all relevant practice both an acknowledged ethical duty for all relevant decision makers, and a legal requirement enforceable at the level of suitable accountable individuals, with no acceptable avenues for organisations to avoid having appropriate accountable individuals.

Blind spots – the ethical interpretation of T_S values which are not S dependent

If the ethical nature of any T_S concept is clear, then making T_S independent of S in a context like road travel or aircraft travel may be a reasonable judgement if all those involved see no advantages in the added complexity of S dependent analysis that override the simplicity advantages of a $T_S = T$ approach. But being able to choose may be important. It is always an asset to have the ability to test the implications of possible simplification, and arguably it is essential to use framing assumptions which allow testing *any* simplifying assumptions which may really matter. The risk of seriously inappropriate simplifying assumptions is important.

In a railway travel context, insisting that 1,000, 100, or 10 fatalities in the same incident all have the same implications per fatality as single fatality incidents seems an inappropriate framing assumption at present, for a range of reasons, the need to consider enlightened prudence associated with departures from expected outcomes perhaps being the most fundamental. Although enlightened prudence was considered very late in this chapter for expository reasons, it matters greatly. If government insurance paid full compensation for fatalities and injuries at standard rates, and all the parties involved understood all the issues, then all parties might agree that $T_S = T$ was appropriate. However, at present it seems plausible to assume that most people involved would prefer additional concern for high S value incidents relative to low S value incidents for a very complex but entirely rational set of reasons. This should include NER shareholders and NER board members. It should also include rail regulators and governments.

In my experience $T_S = T$ is a common practice working assumption given framing assumption status, with closely coupled implications directly dependent on ignoring risk associated with departures from expectations. From an EP perspective, there is no plausible case for not making S dependence an option to be tested and used whenever appropriate.

Blind spots – the ethical interpretation of enlightened prudence in a C_S context

When a C_S concept is involved, enlightened prudence has an ethical aspect which goes beyond financial prudence. An NER S = 350 implying a C_S of the order of $7,000 million should frighten everyone involved enough to think very seriously about what can be done to reduce the probability and mitigate the impact as far as possible, however they chose to weight the relative importance of the fatalities, the injuries, and all the knock-on consequences.

In my experience, common practice does not address enlightened prudence in a safety context because risk efficiency and associated risk–reward trade-offs are not addressed explicitly. In effect, there is no framework for considering enlightened caution, enlightened gambles or enlightened prudence. This means there is no framework for thinking about distinguishing between good management and good luck, bad management and bad luck. This, in turn, means that motivating all staff to behave appropriately, including board members, is severely handicapped. Furthermore, an organisation's ability to retain good managers and dispense with bad managers is handicapped. From an EP perspective, this is inappropriate and unnecessary, and it is a board level failure, along with most of the other blind spots, especially the next.

Blind spots – the need for 'add-in' strategic consideration

If all the earlier blind spots are understood and dealt with, the need for board level top-down strategic management in a holistic framework addressing all related bottom-up planning becomes obvious, arguably 'blindingly obvious'. Boards clearly cannot get directly involved in tactical planning issues, but it is a board's responsibility to guide and deal with the strategic implications of lower level tactical choices. The implications of possible large numbers of fatalities and injuries require consideration of crucial issues that need to be explicitly *built into* board level strategic choices via a clear formal recognition of the role of revealed preferences about trade-offs among profit, fatalities, and injuries.

In my experience this is currently not common practice.

Blind spots – the clarity efficiency of an E_S which goes beyond fatalities

Whether or not an S dependent T_S concept is employed, being able to treat injuries and cost associated with damage to the system at the same time as fatalities within the E_S concept is an important clarity efficiency issue. It means that injuries and physical damage to the system plus knock-on cost and lost revenue concerns which are assumed to be correlated with fatalities can be addressed by the use of one common overall shadow cost and revealed preference transformation factor. This, in turn, means that agreement involving different directors with different views is facilitated. More important, different parties with different perspectives, like passengers and NER shareholders and regulators, can focus on what really matters.

This is an opportunity to improve the clarity efficiency of a general approach which was identified as a consequence of the need to consider the added complexity of an S dependent A_S in a particular context. It can be widely exploited, even if an S dependent A_S concept is not required. If it can also be made use of in other contexts which do not need the complexity triggering the insight, then it may provide further added value in a manner that needs exploration and exploitation. For example, it might prove useful in a road safety context, an air transport safety and security context, or many other very different contexts which have nothing to do with transportation.

Bounds on formal analysis

The generalisation of risk, clarity and opportunity efficiency as explored by Sophie for NER takes us to the limits of sophistication for EP which I am currently comfortable with. You may need to take things much further or in very different directions. But there are bounds on the levels of complexity which formal analysis can cope with, and it may not be straightforward to deal effectively with what we do not really understand or areas where we collectively understand the issues but do not agree about their relative importance.

'Understanding the scope of relevant ignorance is the beginning of wisdom', stated in numerous variants, is often quoted common wisdom which might be seen as a crucial component of 'remembering to be afraid'. It is also worth remembering in more general terms in the context of this chapter. More generally still, it is a useful mantra for the enlightened planning approach as a whole, which can be worth remembering even in comparatively simple contexts.

Earlier examples of related safety and security analysis

Sophie's approach to safety and security is directly grounded on 2010–2013 experience working in a military context. The central importance to the tale of this experience means that it is not feasible to further develop the tale of this chapter in a way that is grounded in empirical tests which can be discussed. However, the framework of Sophie's overall approach, and variants of the specifics of her approach to implementation, seemed to be making progress in a military context when feedback was last provided.

An earlier real case involving Railtrack, which Sophie's tale is also directly based on, tried in a different way to implement a somewhat different structuring of some of the basic ideas, including a prototype S dependent T_S shadow cost concept. My recommended approach failed to convince the key decision makers, no doubt at least in part because the four component E_S concept was missing, and at least in part because the implications of high S values and risk in terms of departures from expectations could not be explained with sufficient clarity to motivate a desire to 'learn to be afraid' in the sense this chapter addresses. Other relevant issues may have included a natural desire by Railtrack to keep the approach used simple in a manner which was in line with conventional expert thinking, unless there was overwhelming evidence of a need for change, and the lack of a clear case for specific reasonably simple defined changes.

Two subsequent very serious rail crashes were instrumental in Railtrack becoming bankrupt as much of the press interpreted it at the time, although some later explanations offer other reasons for Railtrack's bankruptcy. As a result, Railtrack was replaced by Network Rail and the current associated structure. This might be interpreted as evidence of the need for change in any organisation in a context comparable to NER, using approaches comparable to those attributed to NER which have yet to experience a crisis, in the sense that they may have been lucky so far, but sooner or later their luck may run out. I would strongly encourage this view for any organisation currently using a $T_S = T$ or V concept with no S dependence capability, no multiple part E_S concept, and no enlightened prudence concept linked to risk efficiency plus a more general opportunity-efficiency concept. This view may irritate some safety experts, but relevant board members may need to confront their experts. Additionally, passengers, on-board railway staff, regulators, and their political masters may need to take effective action contrary to relevant current expert advice.

An even earlier real case, that triggered the MoD study and provided some insights you may find useful, was undertaken for a public sector water authority. It involved addressing the risk of terrorist bomb attacks on water mains, when working with Sir William Halcrow and Partners over the period from 1986 to 1988 for the Severn Trent Water Authority on an overall review of their water supply systems. The analysis of a potential terrorist attack on a major water main supplying the city of Birmingham was highly successful at the board level. It resulted in a decision not to spend money on protecting the water main from potential terrorist attacks, so far justified empirically by good luck and political background changes, but it was explicitly designed to protect the board should bad luck occur in addition to making an appropriate decision. It triggered the military study initiated in 2010 by a very senior MoD manager who remembered my using the Halcrow example decades earlier for an MoD in-house course which he had been responsible for running.

The Halcrow potential terrorist attack approach adopted was very simple in comparison to the relatively high clarity approaches demanded by the MoD and NER contexts, but this makes it a useful example to explore briefly now.

The Severn Trent Water Authority board's concern was initiated by an unsuccessful attempt to blow up this particular water main by a Welsh extremist who objected to Welsh water going to England. This unsuccessful attack made the board aware that all significant water mains were exposed to possible successful sabotage attempts using explosives to destroy them and that the board would be exposed to reasonable charges of negligence if it did not formally analyse an appropriate response to this clearly demonstrated threat.

The starting point for analysis was the client's knowledge that the pipeline had been in place for a very long time with no successful attacks, a subsequent quick review which suggested that there was no other relevant data to assess the probability of a successful attack in terms of its expected value or an associated plausible range, and the resulting working assumption that a parametric approach centred on this probability expected value and its plausible range might be a good place to begin.

A review of the nature of the pipeline over its full length revealed that the obviously vulnerable points for terrorist attacks involving explosives were river crossings where the pipeline came out of the ground and crossed the river on its own trestle or bridge. The expected cost C_1 and a plausible associated cost range to bury the pipeline at all river crossings was assessed. This expenditure would not eliminate the risk of successful terrorist attacks, but it was the obvious cost-effective first step, and it involved reasonably straightforward civil engineering project cost estimates.

The expected cost C_2 and a plausible associated cost range to deal with all the direct and indirect cost implications of a successful attack was then assessed. Part of this was concerned with repairing physical damage, but the impact on domestic water consumers and industry was crucial, and there was particular concern for the complex economic implications of having to shut down water-dependent industrial operations.

The prior view when choosing a parametric approach was that if the C_1/C_2 ratio was of the order of $1/10,000$ or less, it would probably be prudent to spend the money burying the pipeline without further analysis because even very small probabilities of a successful attack made this a risk efficient choice, and nobody could make a convincing case for a probability lower than this parametric analysis 'flip point'. However, if the C_1/C_2 ratio was of the order of $1/10$ or more, most customers of what was then a publicly owned water company would probably support the view that it was not worth spending the money required to bury the pipeline or pursue further analysis because a successful attack every ten years on average was implausibly pessimistic. A C_1/C_2 flip point in the $1/10$ to $1/10,000$ range would require a more carefully considered decision, considering the ranges associated with C_1 and C_2 expected values, as well as any important issues not measured by these costs, like reputational concerns. A flip point in the middle might suggest that the choice was reasonably neutral in measured cost terms, and the choice could perhaps be made with an explicit focus on what had not been measured. The flip point measured, and the explanation of its implications for the board, let them make decisions they were comfortable with and could defend whether or not a successful attack took place, which they saw as based on very sound and effective clarity efficient analysis.

A key general message to take away from this example is that massive uncertainty about only one key parameter, like the probability of a successful attack on the water main, can be addressed using a parametric approach, a special kind of sensitivity analysis, linked to an iterative multiple pass approach. More than one key parameter involving massive uncertainty means sensitivity analysis remains crucial, but we have to simplify the key parameter relationships in a systematic manner, and test sensitivities in a systematic, multiple pass manner. That is at the core of the EP approach to the NER context.

The starting point for the differences between this Halcrow study and the MoD and NER contexts was the need for an explicit shadow price concept related to fatalities, and the value of a two component $T = V_1 \times E$ structure to link the transformation of a 'fatalities' metric to a 'cost' metric. Making $T_S = V_1 \times E_S$ dependent on the value of S was a further key new complexity, but getting all relevant parties to understand the way the four component E_S factor kept the number of parameters which drove decisions to a minimum was a key new simplification, by embedding multiple 'injuries' metrics, plus the cost of physical damage, plus a residual anything else factor which also addressed enlightened prudence to help capture concerns about departures from expected outcomes.

You might find it useful to see this as a demonstration of an elaboration of 'keep it simple systematically' to 'keep it simple systematically employing carefully considered complexity composition'. The pay-off from finding an appropriate structure for decomposing the T_S concerns is this chapter's illustration of why seeking carefully considered decomposition and composition, whenever it really matters, is worth the effort, building on simpler illustrations in earlier chapters.

In summary, Sophie's approach is flexible, sound, and robust. Significant relevant experience is the basis of this judgement. However, I emphatically do not wish to overstate the empirical basis of some details of its features or underplay the contentious nature of the very difficult and complex issues involved.

The credibility issues associated with this chapter's tale are again somewhat different from those associated with earlier chapters, but there are some common aspects, including public/private sector issues with regulator implications.

Sophie's views on politics and personal ethics

Sophie was politically neutral, in that she was not ideological in a political party or political movement sense to a degree which mattered for current purposes, and she resisted doctrinaire views on all related topics. She saw serious flaws as well as useful strengths in most of the approaches to politics and issues like public or private sector status for industries like railway travel which she was familiar with, acknowledging that the scope of her knowledge was limited. She had what most people would see as a clear moral compass, in terms of treating other peoples' interests and concerns empathetically, and taking full responsibility for her own actions.

Sophie had developed an approach for NER based on what she thought were reasonable beliefs. She was reasonably sure the NER board would be open to accepting leadership in the cultural and ethical terms she proposed, and while her hope that the regulator would also prove enlightened was more tentative, she thought it worthwhile starting with an optimistic premise and an ambitious stretch target. She saw these two working assumptions as a fundamental aspect of applying a UP with minimal constraints to 'design a desirable future' – to be as creative as possible in the time available. Part of her associated robustness testing was testing her working assumptions about the regulator and the board.

For example, the board would have to approve any position which she and Oscar negotiated with the regulator, and an approach which was as open as that proposed would need clear board approval in advance. If the board was convinced that the regulator would never be able to provide insurance, and nobody working for NER should explicitly encourage speculation about large S value incidents in the way that using an $S = 350$ scenario in her illustrative analysis did, she would have to respect that judgement to continue working for NER. It would marginally compromise her ethics to suggest an approach like reducing her five size scenarios just four defined by $S = 0, 5, 25,$ and 125, merging the earlier $S = 70$ and 325 into a single, less frightening $S = 125$ scenario which still covered fatality levels up to the feasible maximum with the same underlying probability distribution, increasing the $S = 20$ to 25. But apart from presentational issues, these four size scenarios now use a simpler strict log-base five scale, which would on the surface look like a benefit. The associated downside was the numbers she had used suggested that the $S = 125$ scenario would now be hugely important, with no framework for reassurance about what might be seen as an $S = 625$ scenario not addressed. She understood what she referred to with close associates as 'frightening the horses' risk. 'Frightening the horses' was a euphemism she frequently encountered for revealing unwelcome truths in a way which upset those you did not want to upset. In her first meeting with the board she wanted the discussion to reveal that she would compromise in this way without any problems if that was the board's wish because she had no wish to frighten the horses.

However, a crucial implication of this kind of compromise was the potential creation of an associated risk of what she and many other people referred to as 'an elephant in the room'. She and all other relevant players would have to manage this elephant in the room risk in a way which did not compromise her moral compass too far by obscuring what really mattered, including issues like a possible $S = 625$ scenario needing attention. Making sure that revealed preferences displayed by NER reflected any key NER risks, and appropriate enlightened prudence, would be crucially important to Sophie.

As a practical illustration of the way forward, if these issues came up and her numbers were realistic, she might propose $S = 1, 10, 100,$ and $1,000$ size scenarios, based on the hypothesis the 100 fatalities scenario would prove the dominant concern, the 1,000 fatalities scenario demonstrably improbable. In terms of working assumptions and issues like what S scenario size structure would work best, Sophie was flexible and creative.

In terms of ethical issues, Sophie's 'bottom line' was that she needed to trust that the board would engage with her basic T_S structure ideas and risk efficiency based conceptual framework and accept the need to work towards an ethically sound position to make *much better* the NER organisation which she believed was a genuine 'national treasure'. If that did not seem feasible, she would prefer working elsewhere, perhaps for a regulator, perhaps eventually becoming the head of a regulator organisation, as a different route to meeting her professional goals.

Public/private sector issues with regulator implications

Sophie assumed that NER directors would want to take an ethical approach to T_S determination and dealing with enlightened prudence, including addressing liability insurance for large S value incidents with the regulator in an open manner. She based these assumptions on the 'national treasure' nature of NER, driven by shareholders and board directors whose ethos included the belief that shareholders and employees of NER should all be fairly rewarded for providing the best service feasible, but there was no place for sharp practice or unfair exploitation of their monopoly position. Given these assumptions, Sophie was convinced that the current private sector ownership of NER was 'socially optimal'.

One of Sophie's central concerns, which she linked to her personal variant of the UP of Figure 2.1, and an EP perspective in general, was the concept 'the good must be promoted and protected, the bad contested and constrained'; otherwise, 'the bad will drive out the good'. She fully appreciated that an important corollary was 'recognise that different parties will have different views about what is "bad" and what is "good", and some parties will be driven by views entirely focused on what is good for them, including a wish for power or material benefit'. She had come across the basis of this idea in market behaviour contexts, discussed earlier in several chapters. For example, the winner in a bidding context is sometimes the lowest price bidder who least understands the problem or is the most prepared to engage in 'claims engineering' to drive up the actual cost, which makes life very difficult for more competent and honest bidders, as well as for all the customers/clients involved.

Sophie's current working assumption was that the regulator would probably have concerns about NER competence but would understand and want to preserve the ethos underlying the widespread 'national treasure' perception of NER. She hoped the regulator would share her view that NER's private sector status was socially optimal and assumed this was the case when proposing her approach to insurance.

Sophie was aware that the modest profits earned by NER shareholders, damaged by the two recent incidents along with the reputation of NER directors, put NER at risk of a hostile takeover by international players of several different kinds – for example, a private equity firm or a utility based outside NER's country. She took the view this was an obvious risk for NER directors, shareholders, and staff, but it was particularly important to her because it was also a critical risk for passengers and the government, and it needed attention by the regulator and possibly by other government agencies.

A predatory takeover by an organisation with a focus on profits remitted to another country would be a social catastrophe in Sophie's view. This kind of organisation might pass ownership of NER assets to low tax rate countries to evade taxes and avoid loss of ownership of the assets if NER went bankrupt, and having minimised the impact of bankruptcy, they might minimise their concerns about service as well as safety and security, disguising their short-term profit-driven stance with wholly unethical Machiavellian guile and cunning.

Sophie knew this issue was beyond her terms of reference, but finding the right way to make it a concern for the regulator could be an important part of the NER dialogue with the regulator. She wanted the regulator to see the need to make public a deal with NER which would make a predatory takeover of NER very unattractive for any organisation which would be prepared to exploit its position – to discourage any potential badness before any bad parties gave serious thought to driving out the good as a carefully planned pre-emptive strike. In Sophie's view, if this was not done, and an organisation which the regulator and everybody else could not trust took over NER assets, the situation would be exceedingly difficult to retrieve. A disastrous accident taking place against a background of other concerns, followed by nationalisation handled by a competent government with equally Machiavellian cunning, might be the only feasible way forward. This would clearly raise a number of immediate and ongoing political difficulties and other complications best avoided. To use another one of Sophie's favourite mantras – 'an ounce of prevention is worth a pound of cure'. In Sophie's view a 'safety-first' culture was needed by an enlightened regulator as well as NER. Waiting for a massive train accident before dealing with the preventable loss of a national treasure would be highly unenlightened.

The private sector status of NER should sharpen the focus of a regulator on safety and security relative to the position if NER were state owned and intensify the need for clarity about risk sharing and insurance issues. However, state ownership of a railway system instead of a private sector organisation operated in a holistic manner like NER should not change the nature of an enlightened approach to safety and security management in any fundamental ways.

Public/private sector issues as very briefly explored in this section for NER are complex. But they are very simple relative to other contexts. If a government has more than one organisation to deal with, competition between these organisations is involved, and some collusion may be a concern, the issues can become much more difficult.

Integration of safety planning and other corporate planning

The need to integrate safety planning with security planning and corporate planning as a whole at a strategic level has been central to the EP perspective developed in this chapter. This implies that integrating the approaches discussed in this chapter with the approaches explored in Chapter 8 is essential.

A starting point for achieving this integration involves working within an agreed NER version of the five categories of corporate planning framework summarised in Figure 8.1:

1   goals planning,
2   futures planning,
3   long-term planning,
4   medium-term planning, and
5   short-term planning.

Safety and security planning for NER also needs integration with some other aspects of planning, worth brief consideration now.

Oscar and Sophie both viewed safety and security planning as a special case of using an EP approach to dealing with uncertainty and complexity. This meant Sophie could use the

EP perspective developed in Chapters 1 through 8 plus all the ideas explored in this chapter, but also draw on all useful aspects of the considerable literature and experience behind safety and security management in general, and that related to railways in particular. It meant that Oscar could use the same EP perspective, but in addition he could draw on all useful aspects of the considerable literature and experience behind operations management in general, and that related to railways in particular. Furthermore, it meant they could both use these compatible frameworks to effectively integrate safety and security planning with other aspects of planning within Oscar's remit if the board approved Sophie's proposed approach.

An effective common perspective is important for full integration. It is also important to appreciate that this full integration means that whatever both Oscar and Sophie add to their EP frameworks needs internal coherence – any internal inconsistencies need resolution.

Oscar also needed a relationship with the NER Projects Director comparable to that between Ollie and Paul in Chapter 7. This in turn meant that Oscar, the NER Projects Director, and everybody else with NER interfacing with projects, needed to work within a common NER version of the four Fs:

1　a project (asset) lifecycle framework,
2　a seven Ws framework,
3　a goals–plans relationships framework, and
4　a planning process framework.

Both an operations planning perspective and a project planning perspective can and should use a common lifecycle structure and a common seven Ws structure to integrate their roles in any organisation, as discussed in Chapter 7.

A goals–plans relationships framework for all planning purposes needs to be built on these two frameworks, within the five categories of corporate planning discussed in Chapter 8. The rationale is comparable to that discussed earlier, in corporate planning, project planning and operations planning contexts.

Finally, a coherent approach to using processes in all contexts needs clarification for NER to make full use of an EP perspective.

Applications in other contexts when well-founded trust matters

Sophie's overview of what needed to be done to address safety and security planning in a railway context clearly needs generalising to accommodate other industries with different but comparable issues. This section briefly explores some of the issues which may need attention, assuming that well-founded trust needing explicit formal planning when dealing with important complexities remains a key concern. 'Catastrophes' in the low probability and high impact sense may or may not be an issue, but a level of clarity which is proportionate to what is at stake is always a clarity efficiency concern, and if a lot is at stake, some of this chapter's approaches may have useful formal roles in many different contexts.

The Shell HSSE (Health, Safety, Security and Environment) Award of the Association of Project Managers illustrates one broader perspective – generalising safety and security to also embrace environmental concerns plus associated long-term health implications. Adopting this perspective, by way of a specific example, what should Sophie say to an organisation involved in offshore drilling for oil or gas if they asked for her advice about preventing the kinds of problems BP ran into over the Deepwater Horizon incident in 2010, or a government concerned with regulating this kind of activity? Assume Sophie began by explaining in outline the ideas developed in this book thus far, as a starting point. How could she build on this?

The 11 fatalities involved in the Deepwater Horizon incident (people working on the oil well rig when the blowout occurred) clearly mattered a great deal, and any injuries associated with this kind of incident clearly matter too. Fatalities and injuries plus damage and knock-on implications comparable to those discussed by Sophie could be addressed using the framework outlined earlier in this chapter. But it was the scale of the oil spill triggered by the Macondo well blowout, and its ongoing pollution implications, which triggered US government and other reactions, and it was the net effect of all reactions which crippled BP. As of 2017, the *direct* cash flow cost estimate for BP exceeded $60 billion. Environmental damage with long-term as well as short-term implications, including ongoing health hazard concerns, raises some further very different and exceedingly complex issues relative to those addressed for NER.

This suggests a need to replace the NER fatalities metric with a generalised size of incident scale which is certainly more complex and might be multi-dimensional. A two dimensional scale might use $S_1 = 1, \ldots, m_1$ and $S_2 = 1, \ldots, m_2$, where S_1 measures incident fatalities in a manner directly comparable to Sophie's S, and S_2 measures oil spill volume. S_2 would be associated with non-financial environmental implications, as well as long-term health implications and economic losses associated with concerns like fishing, plus both short-term and long-term clean-up costs. But three or more dimensions might be needed in some cases. Assuming two dimensions for the moment, the $E_{S1\,S2}$ needed to transform S_1-S_2 combinations into a T measure generalisation of T_S would have to be a two dimensional matrix instead of a one dimensional vector.

Strong correlation or the dominance of one dimension might make it clarity efficient to collapse this multiple dimension approach into a single dimension S concept which uses composite scenario portrayals directly. For example, the S = 1 scenario might involve a minimum plausible oil spill volume blowout, with no fatalities or serious injuries, no ongoing health issues, and no fire or explosion. The S = m scenario might define the maximum plausible oil spill blowout oil volume in conjunction with the maximum plausible number of fatalities in total, the maximum plausible number of immediate injuries plus ongoing health impairments, and all other relevant maximum plausible negative outcomes. The S = 2 scenario might represent a much bigger plausible oil spill blowout than S = 1, involving one fatality and several injury cases. Fatalities and injuries plus a much bigger oil spill than S = 2 might be associated with S = 3, . . . , m − 1, portraying escalating disaster levels in terms of levels of severity measured on several scales, with scale alignments based on assumed levels of correlation. By S = m/2 everybody on the drill rig might be assumed to be killed, further scenarios reflecting bigger and bigger oil spills, perhaps with fatalities associated with those trying to contain it or living nearby. The S = m scenario might involve implications significantly exceeding all the BP Deepwater Horizon consequences, with direct cash flow costs of $100 billion or more, just in terms of fines and court settlements and out-of-court settlements.

The cost–benefit approach discussed earlier, plus a legal liability approach, could be used to estimate plausible V_1 and E_1 values, then the first T_S involving both fatalities and oil spills, and so on, with T_S values over the S = 1, . . . , n range addressing oil spill environmental damage issues and knock-on health concerns, as well as incident fatalities and injuries. Some variant of this kind of approach would seem to be an obvious and appropriate early step in an analysis which needs to take quantification of what really matters to its limits, but *it would be crucial to remain very clear about the limitations of all aspects of this kind of valuation.*

Issues of trust and their ethical basis clearly need direct and very careful treatment over the full range of relevant S values. No V_1 or V_m or intermediate interpretations addressing oil spill environmental damage issues and knock-on health concerns comparable to a 'revealed preference' interpretation of the value of avoided fatalities used for decades by government bodies responsible for travel safety are available which I am aware of. Although possible starting places include a traditional cost–benefit analysis approach or implicit revealed preference values assessed via reviews of past incidents, these are very different starting places, and both involve serious difficulties.

As part of processes associated with granting permissions to drill and operate by all directly involved governments, the use of some variant of Sophie's approach to T_S values as a starting point for an enlightened approach to planning might be required. Or it could be volunteered by the oil companies. This might provide a useful basis for the regulation of such development, and a useful way for oil companies to build trust with their regulators. However, to be effective, it would probably need auditing by external bodies who could be trusted by all parties, and auditing the procedural system and culture concerns, as well as the physical systems, would be crucial.

Whether or not governments get directly involved in this kind of enlightened planning, to be effective the risk of blowout addressed in this way has to be linked to all other threats which might share related initiating events or outcomes plus preventative, reactive, or mitigating responses. For example, if blowout during oil well development, and blowout as a consequence of an operating well being hit by a ship or an iceberg or a terrorist attack have comparable implications and ways of preventing or mitigating such events have any underlying commonality, a clear understanding of these relationships has to be a central part of the analysis. A prototype EP approach to this kind of situation is the basis of a paper which you might find useful (Chapman, Cooper, Debelius, and Pecora, 1985), but significant development of its approach would be essential.

Some organisations may take very large risks, like that of a blowout, and go bankrupt if these risks are realised because internal performance reward systems promote this. The shareholders and boards may not appreciate this risk, but some may explicitly set themselves up to profit from taking risks they cannot cover. In extreme situations they may operate like the organisation Sophie associated with 'hostile takeover risk', setting themselves up in carefully planned structures to minimise taxes as well as other liabilities. If governments are concerned about having to pay for the costs of clean-up because the responsible party has gone bankrupt or has all its assets offshore protected by governments they cannot confront (or will not prevail over if it do confront the responsible party), one obvious response is using license fees and taxation systems to charge an insurance premium appropriate to the risk born by the government and its citizens, or simply refuse permission in some cases. On-board ongoing inspection to ensure that insurance conditions are fully observed might be required by law. Clearly stated jail sentences might be the penalty for any compliance failures, with all appropriate directors in the frame as well as their operators. If up-front 'insurance' payments to cover the expected cost of all incidents of this kind are used explicitly, governments will clearly need to audit all aspects of safety and security. To set appropriate 'premiums', this will have to include physical and procedural systems, plus other capability-culture concerns, conditioned by all other relevant issues. The implicit 'uninsured risk' involved becomes more manageable because it is made visible when transforming it into an explicitly insured risk with this insurance mandatory. In turn, the 'dysfunctional incentives' driving organisations to take inappropriate risks become much easier to confront – mandatory insurance involving prohibitive insurance premiums might stop organisations taking risks which can be reduced effectively and efficiently, or stop them attempting this kind of project, providing wilful dishonesty by any key players is viewed as a criminal offence, law enforcement is viewed as non-negotiable, and the legal system is free of undue political influences. These provisos may be non-feasible. They are obvious sources of risk if this is the case.

An issue of considerable importance is that socially responsible organisations need to avoid a position of competitive disadvantage by promoting the kind of explicit government insurance approach just discussed, flushing out and removing from the market all those competitors who are not prepared or not able to work on these terms, to establish 'a level playing field' for ethical organisations and to exclude organisations society should not allow into the game.

Acting on a clear understanding that 'the bad drives out the good unless the good is promoted and protected, and the bad is contested and constrained', should be seen as central in a market regulation context. If bad behaviour organisations are allowed to get away with it, this will put those who do not copy their bad behaviour out of business. All regulators need to ensure this does not happen. Regulators need to take a very aggressive and proactive approach to contesting and constraining any behaviour which the regulators have reasonable grounds to suspect is bad behaviour, including pre-emptive strikes to design out this kind of behaviour. Regulators also need to take a well-founded and strong proactive approach to the promotion and protection of good behaviour.

If regulators wait until bad behaviours dominate good behaviours, and guilt can be proved, it may be far too late – the organisations which stick to high ethical standards may be out of business, and if catastrophic or disaster incidents have not already happened, they may now be inevitable.

In some cases, the best way forward may be a variant of Sophie's 'new deal' approach to the regulation of markets involving single players like NER, or many players like a mixture of national and international energy companies seeking to develop a county's energy sources. The key may be organisations being required to develop enlightened plans which demonstrate that they can be trusted whenever developments of very sensitive nature are involved.

One set of motives for using an explicit insurance premium approach to environmental risk is making the premiums a function of government assessments of the risk involved, to punish inappropriate safety and security planning, and to reward good safety and security planning. Another is making sure that appropriate parties pay for the insurance of last resort provided by governments. A third is making sure the market price of the energy or other natural resources involved reflects the full cost of its production, net of any separate and explicit subsidy or penalty adjustment. Governments often choose to subsidise some forms of energy and apply penal taxes to others for sound reasons, to encourage renewable or low carbon sources for example. But transparency about all aspects of these subsidies including implicit insurer of last resort costs is arguably essential in an open economy.

If any country is interested in an EP approach of this kind to their own natural resource areas, they may also need to protect their country from the implications of other countries being abused by organisations no country should be prepared to tolerate. To protect their own country, they may find it essential to spread the message that it is in everyone's collective interest to spread this kind of practice internationally to collaboratively put the 'bad' international organisations out of business.

Nuclear power raises some special and important concerns in this area. In principle, it should be feasible to further extend the kind of thinking just discussed in terms of railway incidents, and then oil well blowouts, but the multidimensional framing implied by the context may become exceedingly complex. The multiple-generation impacts, making future generations the losers in relation to present generation gains, and the huge uncertainty about very complex sets of assumptions addressing human factor errors, computer system failures and hostile cybersecurity attacks, low probability events like earthquakes with epicentres close to nuclear power stations, and so on may put well-founded trust beyond the bounds of viable approaches directly linked to those of this book. Well-founded trust about the use of potentially very dangerous technologies clearly needs a related form of thought. *It is crucial to remember that any issues which escape formal planning will require informal treatment – they will not go away.* Very difficult issues associated with greater uncertainty and underlying complexity are involved, but not confronting them is not acceptable.

My personal concerns about nuclear power issues began with work in 1974 for Acres related to Canadian and US nuclear power station seismic risk issues, when exploring the framing assumptions associated with seismic events having an epicentre under or near a nuclear power station. They grew during 1990s work for UK Nirex on nuclear waste storage concerns, touched on in Chapter 7. The 1990s report on Ontario Hydro's approach to strategic planning underlying Chapter 8 and the drafting of Chapter 8 reinforced these concerns. In the Canpower electricity utility context of Chapter 8, four points which need thinking about in the light of this chapter's approach are as follows.

One, both *opportunities* and *risks* associated with the nuclear generation of electricity are crucial. Leaving the long-term planning and futures planning which shapes a nation's approach to these concerns to market-driven private sector organisations offers no obvious robust advantages and many obvious disadvantages. If nuclear power is a viable part of the portfolio of sources of energy which a country needs, goals planning, futures planning, and long-term planning ought to be a public sector decision-making domain as a default choice unless there is a very convincing case otherwise.

Two, the Canpower framework developed in Chapter 8, extended to deal with Chapter 9 concerns, seems the ideal default framework for all related planning, in my view. The portfolio decision making required for long-term planning needs to address operational constraints on both downside risk aspects and upside opportunity aspects. The risks have to include nuclear contamination associated with both accidental and malicious attacks and very broad political and military concerns, including risks associated with possible cyberwarfare and more conventional warfare scenarios. Crucial intergenerational concerns need direct and explicit attention. The opportunities are also important, and the balancing of different kinds of risks and opportunities affecting different generations is a public issue which markets cannot possibly deal with.

Three, some aspects of operating nuclear power stations via private sector organisations may offer cost–benefit advantages, but allowing incentives linked to profitability which is not defined to reflect full costs including nuclear waste disposal and the risk of catastrophic nuclear accidents does not look like a sensible proposition from an EP perspective.

Four, from an EP perspective what has happened to the UK energy supply industry since privatisation is a national tragedy, with no viable case for arguing otherwise. UK press discussion broadly agrees with this view but for a range of very different reasons, driven by political and economic theory assumptions which are highly variable. It is tempting to blame the politicians and the party-political dogmas driving the politicians, but there is a reasonable argument for suggesting that it is the political system which is broken and needs fixing. Assuming that the system was ever up to the very long-term planning and associated decision making required for this kind of issue, including unbiased full disclosure of the information a well-informed public need, is clearly a contentious assumption. The operational features of the democratic systems which we currently depend upon may need adapting. Fixing the very complex interconnected sets of problems which define current political messes ought to be a key priority. We need to target *all* the best features of *all* alternative political perspectives, avoiding the worst. We need to exploit modern communication technology but avoid simplistic assumptions about the wisdom of majority public opinions which may not be well founded and may prove transitory. In contexts like the UK energy market, UK citizens seem to be getting most of the worst features with very few of the best, although some organisations clearly prosper from this muddle, as should be expected. 'It was ever thus' some people will argue, but change for the better is not impossible, and improvements are unlikely to be found unless systematic searches are undertaken.

Some organisations may have comparable but different issues which do not involve catastrophic incidents in the same sense which are worth looking at in this chapter's framework. Some *may* be simpler than those confronted by NER. For example, cybersecurity for banks or other financial institutions might address a scenario range where S is a single metric related to the severity of the problems which may arise, and T_S is a transformation to yield a \$m equivalent, recognising the non-financial implications of what is involved. Lives lost and serious physical injuries may not be involved, but customers may suffer in very important non-financial ways which are very difficult to assess using a monetary metric. Explicitly confronting some of the trade-offs using a variant of Sophie's NER approach might prove useful as part of addressing what are usually seen as reputational concerns. However, if the non-financial implications are very diverse in nature, a single metric may not be effective, and the complications may be comparable to those associated with oil well blowouts, perhaps involving a need for even more separate metrics. The EP framework of this chapter may prove a useful starting place, but important new concerns may need a lot of attention.

A striking feature of the *Final Report on the Investigation of the Macondo Well Blowout* by the Deepwater Horizon Study Group (CCRM, 2011), reviews of this report, and other related literature, is that many of the same messages were clearly communicated earlier in the context of a wide range of both similar and different but comparable contexts, and they are still being communicated. For example, a 1990 report by Lord Cullen on the 1988 Piper Alpha disaster in the North Sea which killed 167 workers was highly critical of management's training and safety culture – search the web using 'Piper Alpha' for access to copies of this report and many other related and comparable reports. There are similar observations in reports on Australia's 2010 Montara platform blowout, the 2003 *Columbia* space shuttle failure, the 1986 *Challenger* space shuttle explosion, and the 2011 Fukushima nuclear power station catastrophe. These kinds of incidents are not new. But collectively we keep making the same kinds of mistakes, again and again. Any organisations directly involved with this kind of issue needs to work out why and make a convincing case that they will not contribute to maintaining this tradition of failure.

As a contemporary example of somewhat different issues, linked to the Ford Pinto discussion earlier in this chapter in terms of an automobile context, the development of the Volkswagen diesel emissions controversy discussed in a *Der Spiegel* article involving collusion among VW, BMW and Daimler, which has been widely reported in the British press (e.g. see Crossland, 2017), clearly demonstrates that too many people are still unaware of basic aspects of the Ford Pinto controversy. In the German motor industry context, a misjudgement about the size of the tank needed for effective emission treatment seems to have triggered wilful deceptions about emissions. This is clearly comparable to the misjudged fuel tank design for the US Ford Pinto, as was the attempt to ignore the fatalities which would result from software which cheated the emissions test procedures. The fatalities involved in the emissions context are orders of magnitude larger than in the Ford Pinto case but not linked directly to the car purchaser, delayed, and not directly identifiable, raising significant new kinds of complexity. There are also international regulation failures involved which are very complex to address but arguably at the root of the problem because regulations which encourage cheating by facilitating it are obviously incompetent. In addition, European governments which encouraged the use of diesel failed to effectively address the trade-offs between CO_2 emissions, other noxious emissions, and fuel-efficiency concerns. The current acceleration of plans to eliminate all automobile diesel use as part of a movement towards electric and hybrid cars adds to the scope of what is becoming involved. Further still, at a government level, all these issues are clearly interdependent with energy market concerns, including electricity generation portfolio policy. As a consequence, it ought to be very clear that no government can leave the markets to take care of all of this in the best interests of their country's citizens.

As an example of a very different kind, in 2017 the British press widely reported very favourably on a Samaritan's suicide prevention course taken by 15,000 Network Rail staff and Transport Police, which was part of the reason for reducing the annual number of suicides involving trains to 237, the lowest level since 2010 (e.g. see Purves, 2017). Particularly interesting was the response of Network Rail staff who stated they had been sceptical prior to the training but became strong advocates after the training because they had put it into effect and were convinced that it had transformed their ability to prevent a needless tragedy. As of November 2018, the suicide levels are still failing, railway passengers have been involved as well as railway staff and Transport Police, and both the press and television coverage is encouraging broader use of the basic ideas, beyond railways. This is a very good example of the kind of imaginative bottom-up thinking which an EP approach ought to encourage, within the coherent top-down framework discussed in this chapter. Early in my 1990s strategic review of Railtrack's approach to safety, a feature which struck me as worth special attention was the very large number of suicides involving trains every year. Suicides were clearly very different from accidental fatalities in a number of respects, but apart from the tragedy for the person killed and their family, they are extremely distressing for the train driver involved, the emergency services who have to deal with the consequences may be traumatised too, and there are serious knock-on delay impacts which may affect thousands of railway passengers. The top-down focus of my review meant that the special nature of this issue got no further attention, other than noting that a single T value independent of S clearly had to deal with a very wide range of different kinds of circumstances, as well as the numbers of fatalities involved. The idea of a Samaritan's led course to address this specific kind of incident would not have occurred to me given the focus of my concerns when initially drafting this chapter. But while this chapter arguably should have given greater emphasis to the power of a 'big team' approach which encourages people to contribute ideas like this Samaritan's training course, it is a very useful example to mention at this point, as a late but hopefully useful attempt to adjust the balance of emphasis needed in practice. Within a coherent top-down approach led by the board, *all* staff at *all* levels need to think creatively in bottom-up approach terms, with a focus on opportunities to make the system they are collectively interested in safer and more secure, including directly involving customers and the wider public. This is the case whatever the context – it is not just true of railway safety contexts.

Part 3

Further synthesising and reflecting

Chapters 10 and 11 contents indicating sections within chapters

10 Immediate and longer term 'what needs to be done' priorities

All organisations seeking a significantly more enlightened approach to planning need to plan the first few steps with a reasonable degree of strategic clarity about what the rest of the journey might involve, including a broad understanding of both the opportunities and the obstacles likely to be encountered along the way. It is important to begin by developing change management plans which adopt an enlightened approach to clarifying ambiguity at strategic and tactical levels. As part of this, everybody directly involved needs to become comfortable with significant levels of the 'right kind' of ambiguity as quickly as possible, with an enlightened intolerance of the 'wrong kind' of ambiguity, and a mindset which embraces the need for significant ongoing change plus significant 'learning by doing' as progress is made. Some crucial early changes may be quite radical and fundamental.

In Parts 1 and 2 'what needs to be done' concerns were considered using a layered approach to gradually building understanding which employed a sequence of topics and areas of focus designed to explain what was involved as simply as possible. 'What needs to be done' concerns are considered in this chapter in terms of an overview of key priorities when an EP approach is initially introduced – precedence concerns ignored earlier are addressed with an explicit focus on what needs to be done early on if there are no obvious crises needing urgent attention. Longer term priorities are addressed when they are relevant to immediate plans.

The next section addresses starting with a comprehensive view of corporate goals with all inappropriate stealth assumptions exposed and revised to provide a dependable framing assumption perspective. Following sections then build towards an overview of enlightened plans for the management of change at a strategic level. Along the way inserted asides may seem to depart from this book's focus on planning for commercial organisations, to consider some wider inferences about regulation and associated politics. However, there are important implications from the perspective of most of the commercial organisations involved in the tales of Part 2 and all comparable organisations you may have an interest in. There are further important implications from the perspective of customers and employees of these organisations plus other citizens who may be directly affected positively or adversely. In terms of your overall understanding of an EP perspective, the interdependence of all these perspectives is a fundamental aspect of what everyone needs to consider.

Starting with a comprehensive view of corporate goals

From the corporate planning perspective discussed in Chapter 8 and portrayed by Figure 8.1, clarity about all relevant corporate goals is the obvious place to start. All aspects of all planning by an organisation involve a set of top-down flows of dependencies within the goals–plans relationships structure as well as bottom-up interdependencies.

A systematically developed comprehensive view of corporate goals from a top-down perspective ought to be an early high priority, because it is the logical place to start in terms of key decision-making precedence relationships. The opening set of concerns is 'Who owns the organisation, and from the perspective of the organisation's owners, what are the key goals which clarify the vision or mission statement that the organisation should be focused on achieving?'

The scope of this question means that those acting on behalf of the owners of the organisation need to address complexities raised by all relevant interests of the organisation's owners, plus the interests of all other parties which need attention by the owners in an effective manner. This includes accommodating the direct and indirect implications of other parties impacting the pursuit of the owner's goals in both positive and negative ways. Customers and employees obviously need attention, but regulators and further interested parties like bond funders may also prove crucial. Transforming potential adversaries into allies is part of this, as explored in most of the Part 2 tales, Chapter 8, in particular.

To provide examples of what a comprehensive view of corporate goals might involve from an EP perspective, consider the NER railway safety context of Chapter 9, then the other Part 2 example contexts, in a reverse ordering.

A comprehensive view of corporate goals for NER

A fair return on their financial investment in NER for shareholders was the obvious starting point for an NER board level overall top-down view of corporate goals if the board adopted the EP perspective developed in Parts 1 and 2. This observation was not made in Chapter 9, because the focus was well-founded trust associated with safety, but the financial return goal for shareholders had to be treated as inseparable for operational safety and security management purposes, fully integrated with minimising fatalities in a very general manner via a 'fatality efficiency' concept. The need to perceive return for shareholders and safety and security for those travelling on trains as inseparable was treated as a key framing assumption, demanding a carefully structured approach to associated working assumptions, making use of an S dependent T_S concept. However, for the purposes of Chapter 10 and all overall corporate planning purposes which go beyond safety and security, it is clearly important to separate the shareholder return financial goal for NER, recognising *all* key interdependencies with *all* corporate goals, not just those associated with safety and security.

As an initial set of illustrative examples, preserving NER private sector status and avoiding a hostile takeover might be seen as a component part of a decomposition structure for return on shareholder investment goals, but it would be very important to view these kinds of issues as separate interdependent goals with important additional nuances and interdependencies. For comparable reasons, well-founded trust associated with good employee, customer, and regulator relationships should be seen as directly related to both safety and the return on shareholder investment goals, but for many practical purposes it would be important to treat them as further separate interdependent goals, because of particular nuances needing focused attention.

As a more specific example, a collapse in industrial relations leading to on-board railway staff strikes might be linked to safety issues but strongly driven by other very different issues, and responses designed to address all relevant issues might be very important. These other issues might drive a collapse in passenger confidence in NER, also linked to service failures like lack of punctuality, overcrowding, and excessive fare rises, which may all go well beyond the strikes and the safety concerns, triggering hostile regulator reactions. Put slightly differently, complex sets of closely interrelated goals may require treatment as if they were separable in an iterative framework to ensure a comprehensive and balanced overall treatment. That is what clarity efficient decomposition of goals and objectives is about when very complex interdependencies are crucial – making effective use of separability to deal with different relevant nuances of closely coupled issues in an effective and efficient manner. This is an important underlying concern in the context of the tales about NER, Canpower, WSL, Astro, and TLC, and it is a concern needing careful attention in all other commercial organisations which may be of interest to you.

As an example, to put these issues in a realistic contemporary context, since privatisation in the 1990s, the UK railway system as a whole has demonstrably failed to look after the best interests of the railway travelling public. As of 2018, some of the companies operating trains are experiencing serious levels of adverse public reactions to these kinds of interconnected issues, with further interdependent issues involving Network Rail, the UK public sector operator of the track and stations. The extent of associated concerns about the system as a whole is reopening discussion of the 1990s privatisation of British Rail, the UK public sector operator of the whole system until its breakup – initially into private sector components. As of 2018, two-thirds of the UK railway system is back in public sector ownership, some of it involving Network Rail's UK public sector ownership of tracks and stations because of the bankruptcy of the private sector Railtrack organisation it replaced, some of it involving non-UK state owned train operators who are replacing UK private sector competitors in a very complex franchise-based marketplace. One of the contributing drivers of current change is that UK private sector train operators have a higher cost of capital than non-UK public sector competitors, but some of the non-UK public sector operators are themselves about to be privatised according to press reports. Another driver of current change is the role of preferred risk–return trade-offs for train operators which are in part driven by ambiguous regulation. According to the CEO of Network Rail (Carne, 2017), the recent switch from off-balance sheet to on-balance sheet government funding for Network Rail will now lead to third party funding of public sector assets and selling off public sector assets for reasons not stated. This will obviously lead to further change with a direction of travel and implications which are debatable to say the least. The muddled intersection of party-politics and market-driven commercial interests involved is a case study mess well beyond the scope of this book, but it was worth one paragraph in this subsection, in part for reasons developed in linked asides in the next two subsections, in addition to clarifying the nature of the complexity which may be involved in formalising goals planning and then moving towards futures planning.

In the absence of a safety crisis driven by two recent accidents, NER *ought* to begin the management of major changes in overall planning within their variant of an EP framework like that outlined for Canpower in Chapter 8 by thinking about safety and security planning goals at a strategic level *within* a comprehensive view of *all* the relevant interdependent corporate goals. NER might start with a mission statement like 'The best railway travelling experience in Europe, delivered to our passengers by railway staff who understand and care about what good service means, including comfort, safety, punctuality and convenience at a cost which is good value'. NER might then view 'goals planning' in terms of the development of a suitable operational structure for formalising this mission statement in terms of profits for shareholders linked to a service for travellers which is economical, punctual, comfortable, *and* safe, weighted to reflect long-term railway passenger priorities as well as long-term regulatory and shareholder concerns, then move on towards a closely coupled formal approach to 'futures planning', then move on to all other aspects of planning. But in the Chapter 9 situation, given a crisis induced by a second accident was pressing, putting many aspects of this starting point on hold for the moment, and picking them up as soon as possible, was a reasonable approach. In the short-term, priorities have to adjust to immediate crisis events, although avoiding being deflected too much from longer term concerns is very important.

Sophie's recommended EP approach for NER was designed to address all these issues in an integrated manner, but they were not discussed to avoid being distracted from the main messages of Chapter 9. How this might be done could draw on both Canpower and WSL goals planning ideas discussed earlier and in the next two subsections, without any interest in 'privatisation risk' but a concern for 'nationalisation risk' comparable in some ways to that faced by WSL, very different in others because of their national coverage as an integrated monopoly like British Rail prior to privatisation.

A comprehensive view of corporate goals for Canpower

In Chapter 8, the need for a comprehensive treatment of corporate goals for Canpower in the Figure 8.1 framework triggered the identification of a need to significantly shift the focus for the way Canpower ought to serve its owners, who were owners/customers for most purposes, as discussed towards the end of the chapter. Arguably, the need to address the wishes of Canpower's owners/customers in this way should have been obvious to the board from the outset – without any need to be worried about privatisation risk, and without any need to explore incompetent medium-term and long-term planning first. Indeed, from the perspective of the citizens of the province owning Canpower, the provincial government officers representing their interests by determining who was on the Canpower board ought to have insisted that those appointed to the board would look after the best interests of Canpower's owners in the way Chapter 8 suggested, explicitly holding the chairman of the board directly accountable for doing so effectively.

Furthermore, in the context of a clear strategy to move Canpower to a portfolio of power sources which was predominantly nuclear in terms of new base-load generation, the nuclear power safety and security issues addressed using the Chapter 9 NER framework *ought* to have been a further explicit focal point in the Chapter 8 tale – *for both the Canpower board and the provincial government.* The complete absence of a board level advocate of the kind of EP approach to nuclear safety and security touched on in Chapter 9 was arguably an important shortcoming in the composition of the Canpower board as portrayed in Chapter 8. If Clive did not identify and respond to this problem fairly quickly, Canpower's failure to address it could have been viewed as an ongoing serious failure on his part. Ultimately, this shortcoming was arguably attributable to the board chairman and the government officers responsible for appointing him or her. But in principle, and in practice, all the other board members were arguably also culpable for not being fully aware of the issue or doing anything effective about it. To keep the Chapter 8 tale as simple as possible it was convenient to avoid in-depth treatment of the Chapter 9 concerns, to maintain focus on what was already a broad agenda. But in practice, overlooking well-founded trust about nuclear safety and security when contemplating a portfolio of base-load electricity generation sources dominated by nuclear power stations would not involve enlightened planning on the part of any of those either on the board or responsible for who was on the board.

As an elaboration of this point which also serves as a brief aside linked to the last and next subsection's asides, consider a broadening of the current discussion to address a consistent treatment of nuclear power safety and security issues by all utilities in all countries in order to serve the best interests of the all citizens of all the countries involved.

France is the only country I am aware of which has adopted an explicit national government preference, over an extended period, for a portfolio of electric power sources involving a largely nuclear base-load capability. This is in the context of a long history of significant public sector involvement in electricity generation and distribution plus the design and construction of nuclear power stations. Base-load generation is about 75% nuclear as I understand it. In the past, the French approach has been viewed as a significant success by many French people and others. However, a growing range of recent concerns suggest opinions may be changing radically. In the US, the Three Mile Island incident early in the development of nuclear power, and a sustained national preference for minimal public sector involvement in all utilities, has led to a much more cautious approach to expanding nuclear power generation of electricity. Arguably Ontario Hydro was looking to the French model in the 1990s, with a very different policy after its plan for ten new nuclear power stations was rejected. Prior to privatisation of the CEGB, the UK had a reasoned and balanced mid-range preference exposed to public scrutiny. It is unclear what the UK policy has been since privatisation, and its rationale is equally ambiguous.

In the context of the possible use of nuclear power, for all the countries and all the associated electricity generation and distribution utilities plus their customers, whatever the party-political preference issues, developing a clear understanding of what really matters seems long overdue.

The international interactions are numerous. As one example, the Chernobyl incident was catastrophic locally and a disaster in the broader geographic region, but there was also a wide range of international repercussions, as diverse and distant as making Welsh lamb unsafe to eat for a while. As another interrelated set of examples, current French nuclear power station component safety problems are now linked to a large number of US nuclear power stations built some time ago, as well as French, UK, and other European power stations currently operating, under construction, or proposed. The Hinkley Point power station in the UK, which started construction in 2017 with an estimated cost of £19.6 billion, has planned French technology with significant Chinese involvement, potentially implying that if the French technology fails, Chinese technology might be a fall-back option. My earlier understanding was that the present thrust of Chinese nuclear power technology development was smaller modular nuclear power units than the current norm, the focus of effort of Siemens in Germany when it asked me to provide advice on project risk management concerns in the 1990s, an interesting option. But my current understanding is a Chinese ambition to part ownership of existing UK power stations of all kinds has finally raised the obvious concerns about significant involvement in UK electricity supply of other countries with potential geopolitical security implications, which arguably needed systematic and effective attention a long time ago. Germany's decision to shut down all nuclear power following the Fukushima disaster in 2011 and switch to burning coal, which is available from domestic mines but particularly polluting, was seen by many at the time as an obvious overreaction without thinking through the implications properly. However, there is a growing perception (e.g. see Pagnamenta, 2017), that current cost overruns and other problems could effectively shut down the international nuclear industry, apart from clean-up contracts. Pagnamenta cites the US example of a half-built VC Summer plant at Jenkinsville, SC, which already had $4.7 billion spent on it, cancelled because revised estimates involved a completion date now slipped five years and cost estimates requiring a further $7 billion, more than double the original $5.1 billion budget. He links this to Hinkley Point in the UK, French, and Finnish projects overrunning and uses the article heading *Fukushima disaster is still radiating fallout nuclear industry wishes to avoid*, opening the article by discussing the current $188 billion estimate for clean-up costs which could be interpreted as a very optimistic plausible minimum – no one knows what the final bill will be.

A positive case for nuclear power may still be tenable. However, the issues which really matter are extremely complex. They go well beyond the scope of this book's focus, but they are far too important to carry on failing to address them in a comprehensive manner which every citizen with a stake in the implications can understand at an appropriate level.

A comprehensive view of corporate goals for WSL

In the WSL tale of Chapter 7, focused on project planning, Paul did not want to be diverted from his primary concerns by involvement in the exploration of public versus private sector issues which his EP approach triggered. In Chapter 7 exploring the contentious nature of public sector ownership versus private sector ownership and related issues for WSL would have been a serious distraction in terms of the central messages and focus of the tale of that chapter. However, these issues were far too important to just ignore, and this subsection provides some comments directly linked to the tale of Chapter 7 which build on both the main messages and the asides in the last two subsections which should be useful for most target readers in terms of consolidating an EP perspective on public and private ownership issues.

In addition to illustrating a broadly defined EP approach to goals planning for any organisation using WSL as a specific example, this subsection clarifies some of the issues which ought to drive private sector versus public sector choices for any organisation. It uses what might be seen as further asides focused on private versus public sector concerns which have been integrated with the primary messages about the need for a *comprehensive* view of *all* corporate goals of *all* kinds in *all* organisations that has *no blind spots in terms of components or interdependencies*.

To put the WSL discussion of this subsection in context, in Chapter 8 it was argued that privatisation of the nationalised UK electricity industry was a serious mistake, and provincial government ownership of a comparable Canadian electricity utility should have been proactively defended as a central part of the Canpower corporate plan because public ownership was economically and socially desirable for the citizens of Canpower's province. However, in Chapter 9 a case was made for preserving the private sector status of a national railway system operated as a coherent fully integrated system, because the operational decision-making problems could be resolved effectively and the capability-culture liabilities could be transformed into appropriate assets without altering the current private sector nature of NER. The tale's working assumption was public sector ownership of NER was not worth even considering if the 'national treasure' nature of the organisation could be preserved.

The positions taken in Chapters 8 and 9 may have seemed inconsistent before reading both chapters. The tales should make it reasonably clear why this is not the case, but there is a need for a set of further key clarifications considered now.

In the Canpower context, the starting position for goals planning was ownership of Canpower by the citizens of the province, but in the NER context the starting position for goals planning was ownership by NER shareholders. This difference in perspective matters, with political implications which are complex but inescapable, and it involves crucial working assumptions within a framing assumption that allows for any form of ownership so long as its implications are clarified. One key set of issues is driven by citizens having a vote to determine the nature of the government setting the regulators' agendas, the need for the government and the regulators to show enlightenment, and the need for both private and public sector organisations to heed the implications.

To build on this perspective, and explore how to exploit it by a private sector organisation, consider in outline aspects of a 'desirable future' which might have been developed by WSL. The basic purpose of this exploration is further illustrating the nature of a comprehensive view of goals planning which is a suitable basis for moving into formal futures planning, but there are wider implications.

Following his discussions with Paul, Richard, and Curt as outlined in Chapter 7, Frank might have begun a dialogue with Richard, Curt, Michael, and Charles with a view to helping WSL to secure lower cost bond funding in addition to a broader WSL agenda. This might have led to further discussions triggering three closely coupled propositions.

The first proposition might have been a Local Assets Company (LAC), set up by WSL as a separate company. The purpose of this LAC might be to manage bonds used to fund water treatment and pipeline distribution networks, sewage collection and treatment systems, and all other bond funded WSL assets. These bond funded assets might include reservoirs used for recreational purposes by local residents, plus recreational areas and parks made available to local residents which are an integral part of the property used to accommodate water storage, treatment, or extraction works or sewage works. This LAC concept might be viewed as a 'WSL localisation' concept to link WSL to the local public who were also their customers. The LAC board might include local people with a reputation for good local citizenship. It might provide bond rate long-term loan funding secured by LAC ownership of the assets if WSL becomes bankrupt, directly comparable to a mortgage for these long-life 'local assets' which local investors might see as safe and secure locally beneficial investments that they would like to have a financial stake in for sound financial reasons as well as possible 'feel good' reasons. Genuine altruism might or might not be involved, and fostering local ownership of local assets in this form need not be concerned about enlightened self-interest serving the same goals as genuine altruism. The corporate design, including board membership structure, might be very carefully planned at the design stage and subsequently controlled by WSL, but this corporate design, and the associated broader approach taken by WSL to the LAC concept as a whole, might aim to make local people feel that they had a measure of ownership and control over a set of local assets which was on balance 'as good as or better than more conventional public ownership'. It would certainly not be 'public ownership' in the 'nationalisation' sense, but from a local population perspective it could provide better focus on local concerns.

One key objective might have been to secure funding for WSL long-term assets at the lowest feasible cost, not only Frank's central concern but also a local population concern, because it would help to keep water and sewage charges low. Frank might have been adamant that bond funding from outside the region should be part of the LAC proposition if the market made that significantly cheaper and no serious adverse effect for local people was involved, not only consistent with the central focus of his role as Finance Director as well as his general governance role, but also a concern for local people in terms of their interest in low cost water and sewage.

A second key objective might have been protection against nationalisation and privatisation threats plus exploitive non-UK ownership of local assets by providing the population served by WSL with a better alternative, not only Richard's central concern but also a local population concern. Richard might have been adamant that they should not just impress the regulators by their LAC proposition. WSL should aim to make their regulators firm allies in terms of a constructive long-term relationship, without losing sight of the constructive tensions to be managed, consistent with the central focus of his role as Regulation Director as well as his general governance role.

A third key objective might have been enhancing customer relationships by giving the local population a new form of direct input to the management of assets like reservoirs and parks used for public recreational purposes, Curt's central concern, and a local population concern. Curt might have been adamant that a 'big team' approach to WSL customers via the LAC proposition had to be based on a genuine concern for collaborative relationships clearly demonstrated by a willingness to spend money and effort making sure the LAC worked effectively from the perspective of the best interests of all local people, consistent with the central focus of his WSL board role as Customer Relations Director as well as his general governance role.

Michael and Charles might have both been adamant that the overall best interests of WSL and all its shareholder owners should be effectively served, consistent with their central and general governance WSL board roles.

However, meeting reasonable demands from all five directors and aligning all five sets of concerns, plus those raised earlier by Paul and Ollie, ought to have been feasible. They ought to have been able to reach agreement on a collective 'revealed preference' which balanced their concerns in a way the WSL board as a whole could support. Reducing the risk of nationalisation in the usual sense, or separate privatisation of some of the assets they owned (like reservoirs), or used (like rivers), ought to have been a welcome and very important spinoff, but these spin-offs could have been seen as simply the results of enlightened collaborative top-down planning at the board level by a set of directors with interrelated concerns and a willingness to work towards corporate revealed preferences which balanced all relevant concerns. Some negotiated version of this first proposition ought to have been a win–win package.

The second proposition might have been a National Asset Company (NAC), a further separate company set up and led by WSL. This NAC concept might have been a 'WSL nationalisation' concept, designed to link WSL to the public in the rest of the country to the extent that doing so might prove mutually useful. Its central purpose might have been developing a water distribution system and wholesale water supply market between different adjacent regions served by different water companies, starting with WSL's immediate neighbours but perhaps growing to complete national coverage. The corporate design including board membership structure might have been carefully planned and controlled by WSL, but mutual benefits for different regions might have been an explicit goal so that directors of collaborating water supply utilities in other regions might have been asked to serve on the board. Some regions are relatively rich in low cost water sources but have a limited customer base, while other regions are relatively poor in terms of low cost water supply with excessive demand. This implies that a degree of collaboration with other water companies ought to be 'socially optimal' from a UK national perspective, and 'commercially optimal' from the perspective of the private sector water suppliers. The goal for WSL might have been WSL advantage in cost or revenue or water-quality terms, to improve all aspects of WSL performance, plus further protection against nationalisation in the usual sense. To achieve these goals the benefits of collaboration would have to be shared with water suppliers in other regions, potentially benefiting the populations of these other regions as well, perhaps the whole country benefiting on a regional basis.

The third proposition might have been a quiet and unobtrusive lobby initiative that was aimed at making Ofwat and the other water regulators indirect SWL allies in terms of persuading them to impose regulatory rules which would stop all of WSL's water and sewage industry competitors using practices which were profitable for those competitors but unhelpful for their customers or other citizens of the UK. This might be based upon WSL adopting a quiet but effectively managed strategy characterised by:

> The good ought to be able to drive out the bad if the good is managed effectively and creatively. WSL needed to ensure that they were good enough to drive out or takeover all competitors who might negatively affect successful service provision for all WSL customers, ensuring that this objective was closely coupled to a good return for WSL shareholders. Being 'good enough' to achieve these goals *must* include a constructive relationship with their regulators, who must be motivated to provide an appropriate level playing field.

As part of this strategy, WSL might have indirectly tried to persuade the regulators to use the WSL business model as a regulatory aspirational target for the water and sewage industry, with a view to WSL making sure that WSL had 'a level playing field' that it could perform on better than their competitors. That is, WSL might have taken a strong and overt partnership approach to its own customers and to adjacent water companies, making their water and sewage services cost as little as possible as part of an approach based on short-term profit rates which were modest but fair for exemplary service, with a view to appropriate long-term profits driven by outstanding service provision provided in a cost-effective manner. They might have made this business model so attractive the regulators would look bad or even negligent if they did not actively encourage its use by other water and sewage companies, actively contest and constrain WSL competitors which tried to exploit their customers. This would protect WSL's own market position and long-term profitability, and it might allow expansion of WSL territory where appropriate in the longer term. It would not be sensible for WSL to advertise or promote this strategy to other water and sewage companies or make it obvious to anyone else that it was adopting this approach. But it might be very important to get regulator support, with a carefully prepared case and demonstrable benefits exposed to its regulators in a carefully planned manner.

For example, WSL might begin by explaining to Ofwat why its LAC approach was good for WSL customers in terms of lower costs but also make sure the regulator clearly understood that the LAC approach generated UK taxes on income paid to UK LAC bond investors, while some water and sewage companies not using this model were getting lower capital costs by just avoiding UK tax. WSL might then argue 'surely the regulator could see the political advantages of stopping a practice that would let "the bad drive out the good" in a classic market failure sense *before* the press got hold of the idea and *before* some of the good companies were driven out by the bad, never mind waiting until all the good companies had been eliminated'. WSL might carefully avoid any sense of direct threats but make sure the regulators understood that if they did not act on these ideas WSL would have to ensure that the government and the public understood the implications in terms of the lack of competence of the regulators as WSL saw it. This might be underscored by very publicly seeking tax exemption for LAC investors involving or comparable to ISA (zero income tax) status for UK taxpayers on the grounds that both the regulator and the government would otherwise be condoning a very unbalanced and unfair tax treatment for UK-based LAC investors relative to foreign investors.

This particular version of a desirable future for WSL might not attract favourable attention from post-2020 UK water and sewage companies, UK governments, or UK regulators, and its development in this book is not aimed at the water and sewage industry in particular. However, it provides an example which illustrates how a private sector organisation with a local natural monopoly *might*, with appropriate regulator encouragement and a broad view of goals planning, look after its own commercial interests in an enlightened manner. The intention is illustrating an overall approach capable of delivering outcomes which approximate to a 'social optimum' comparable to or better than a more conventional public sector approach or an inappropriately regulated private sector approach. The details are purely illustrative.

An EP framing assumption is that a 'social optimum' may exist in a clear and well-defined form in the judgement of each member of the relevant set of citizens, but even if this is the case, it may be different for each citizen, so any operational overall 'social optimum' concept involves appropriate working assumptions about aggregated revealed preferences, like an overall consensus given appropriate information and consultation processes. Ambiguity in some peoples' minds just adds to the ambiguity associated with revealed preferences for any aggregate of different peoples' views.

Assuming a 'social optimum' exists in this WSL context means assuming that 'the revealed preferences of the local population and other local users of WSL services would favour this choice, relative to all alternative feasible options, provided they were informed about the issues and then consulted in an effective manner, and provided there were no compelling reasons not to serve their wishes in favour of other commercial or political interests'.

There is a good case for arguing that this kind of desirable future for WSL would certainly have been achievable for all UK water and sewage utilities pre-privatisation of the UK water and sewage industry, if the UK government had considered the best interests of consumers as the government's primary objective in an enlightened manner when structuring the outcomes and mandating the regulators. This would have required treating the interests of commercial lobbies and political dogma as secondary concerns, to be managed and constrained, perhaps a non-feasible expectation for current governments. However, future governments might consider this kind of approach if a large enough group of people understood the issues and took effective political action.

To finish the WSL discussion on a contemporary note, an October 2017 article with the headline 'Water Firms Risking their own Demise' (Lee, 2017b) by the *Times* Industrial Editor reporting on 'a withering attack on the sector' by the industry's regulator ends with 'Asked afterwards whether she had made the comments because she was leaving the sector for a job with BT, Ms Ross replied "I said it because it needed saying and the sector needs to hear it. The sector is treating (the threat of nationalisation) as if it was an exogenous risk, as if there is nothing they can do about it"'.

Both private and public sector organisations can be 'national treasures', 'national tragedies', or anything in between. Taking the NER, WSL, and Canpower approaches together arguably illustrates how both private and public sectors *could* deliver a balanced approach to a 'socially optimal' choice which is very different from the common practice private versus public sector choices portrayed as the only choices by those with narrow political beliefs which push for either a 'free market with minimal regulation' option or a 'full lock-stock and barrel traditional nationalisation' option. From an EP perspective, one key working assumption is that relevant regulators, fully backed by their controlling governments as necessary, will act in a competent manner in the best interests of the customers for the services and other citizens involved. This will be the case for private sector industries and public sector industries in the traditional sense, including NER. It will also be the case for novel private and public sector organisations, to accommodate organisations like the LAC and NAC which WSL might set, and the form Canpower might transform itself into plus its associated novel partnership ventures. A public or private sector ownership starting position matters. The competence of those responsible for goals and futures planning within the organisations directly involved is also crucial. But the citizens who are customers of all local, provincial, national, and international organisations should press their governments for a social optimum defined by their interests in a suitable revealed preference form. Unyielding resistance from those determined to limit discussion to traditional extremes might be interpreted as evidence of stealth assumptions driven by goals not shared by the majority. It is the majority whose interests ought to prevail in an open democracy, given visible working and framing assumptions most people would support.

This book is not about definitive answers to very complex social optimisation issues with highly emotive political, ethical, and economic dimensions. It is about the conceptual and operational tools that might be used by private and public sector commercial organisations to seek better decision making within their planning frameworks. But there are wider implications which could be pursued elsewhere, and encouraging those with an interest in doing so might prove useful for all of us. For example, a novel framework developed in this spirit might provide a more desirable future for the UK rail system, addressing it from the perspective of rail travelling customers plus other UK citizens. This approach might use a nationalised organisation structure which was a variant of Canpower plus British Rail as the model or a privatised organisation which was a variant of NER plus WSL or a very different-looking hybrid based on features of an EP approach plus other relevant ideas. Whatever the approach adopted, it would have to be tailored to the context, including recent history.

When considering these broader implications, a saying attributed to Winston Churchill is

> *Some people regard enterprise as a predatory tiger to be shot.*
> *Others look on it as a cow they can milk.*
> *Not enough people see it as a healthy horse, pulling a sturdy wagon.*

Elaborating Churchill's notions in terms of public enterprise as well as private enterprise in a post-2020 context, the key issues are 'Whose wagons are we talking about?' and 'What is the best way to look after the horses pulling all the "good" wagons, while appropriately ensuring that the horses pulling all the "bad" wagons put their efforts to better purpose?' This seems to be a key opportunity and an important challenge worth taking very seriously.

Doing so successfully would obviously not be a simple matter. It would need to embrace complex long-term cultural issues and shifts in people's value systems, as well as enlightened approaches to short-term 'carrots and sticks' which go well beyond crude financial incentives or prison sentences for serious misdemeanours. Failing to try to do so, or failing to even understand why trying to do so might be a good idea, can be seen as fundamental social risks which involve lost opportunities that really matter. Lost opportunities present particular difficulties because their perception is never easy, with different people inevitably seeing them very differently. But a focus on avoiding lost opportunities provides a usefully positive perspective.

A comprehensive view of corporate goals for Astro

In Chapter 6 Martha was operating at the level of a marketing manager for a regional office of Astro UK, part of the US-based Astro Inc, an international organisation comparable to IBM. Martha was sensitive to the national and international competition issues as well as their local implications, but it was convenient for the purposes of the tale to limit the focus to the regional situation. Encouraging other regional offices of Astro to move in the same direction that Martha was advocating with coordinated variants of comparable approaches is one obvious potential component of the overall corporate goal sets needed by Astro Inc and Astro UK corporate goals planning. However, viewed from the top down in overall corporate goals planning terms, Astro Inc and Astro UK face tasks which have to visualise Martha's concerns as relatively low-level issues. The high level issues at international and national levels are very different from those just discussed for WSL, Canpower, and NER, but the basic concerns are comparable and some of the EP conceptual and operational tools are clearly relevant. It would not be helpful to speculate here on how an organisation like Astro Inc might set about structuring its goals planning, as a basis for futures planning in the Chapter 8 sense. However, successful reinvention of itself by IBM on more than one occasion since the 1950s is a good illustration of what can be done in practice. The complexities IBM has faced were obviously very different from those associated with NER, Canpower, and WSL, but the degree of difficulty was arguably comparable or greater, the required creativity was arguably significantly greater, and the scope for using all the EP toolset along with many other toolsets should be reasonably clear.

A comprehensive view of corporate goals for TLC

In Chapter 5 the need for a comprehensive view of corporate goals was triggered by Nicola's low level tactical analysis of an optimal order quantity for lawnmower engine speed controls. Nicola's efforts initiated a sequence of propositions with some features common to those just discussed for WSL. Ajit's contribution provided a fairly comprehensive starting point for TLC goals planning, and the propositions generated by the others provided a fairly comprehensive starting point for related futures planning. However, even a very small family-owned organisation like TLC really ought to begin with the kind of nuanced initial goals planning associated with Ajit at the tale's conclusion and have in mind the generation and shaping of a comprehensive portfolio of possible propositions prior to moving fully into futures planning along some of the lines explored for Canpower in Chapter 8.

A comprehensive view of corporate goals for all organisations of interest to you

The defining characteristics of most organisations of interest to you are unlikely to directly match any of those explored in Part 2, and specific aspects of each context will significantly drive the most effective and efficient approach for any given specific organisation. General advice at a detailed level for all contexts is not a viable proposition, and even overview advice is a very difficult proposition, because a 'one size suits all' approach is seriously inappropriate. But a top-down UP perspective making use of some variant of a Figure 8.1 perspective and many of the interdependent EP conceptual and operational tools does seem universally useful. Specific process variants of the soft OR variety designed to explore and help structure the 'mess' of interconnected 'problems' associated with strategic issues may be helpful, viewed as particular tools within a UP approach. Testing the robustness of early portrayals as rigorously as possible is clearly essential, as a core part of the process adopted. The way the Chapter 8 tale identified Canpower's need to reinvent its approach to avoid privatisation but missed the full implications of the Chapter 9 nuclear power issues as explored in this section may be a helpful reminder of the need to keep pushing the scope of what is addressed, avoiding crucial blind spots. The way this section addressed the privatisation and nationalisation concerns for WSL may also serve as an illustration of one way to push the scope of what is addressed, bearing in mind that organisations which are more closely related to Astro or TLC will have very different issues needing this kind of creativity in a form relevant to their specific contexts.

Moving on to a comprehensive view of futures planning

Effectively linking goals to plans in operational terms needs an operational form for all five of the categories of planning within the four planning horizons discussed in Chapter 8 and portrayed by Figure 8.1, adapted to the context of the organisation involved. This operational framework will have to include a gateway structure for approving corporate changes to link bottom-up and top-down proposition generation and overall management of change decision making. This, in turn, needs intersecting operations planning and project planning as outlined in Chapters 5, 6, 7, and 9. Testing the robustness of what has been achieved during goals planning, and then moving on to a comprehensive view of futures planning, with all other aspects of planning to follow, is the obvious next step.

The boundary between futures planning and long-term, medium-term, and short-term planning was defined in Chapter 8 in terms of currently feasible and non-feasible options. There is a particularly important need to avoid approaches which fail to distinguish futures planning from the long-term planning of currently feasible options. Considerable clarity enhancement is provided by using explicit contingency plans to embrace opportunities that might arise if futures planning provides new opportunities by offering new feasible options in the long-term planning framework, with follow-on medium-term and short-term contingency plans. Futures planning focused on designing desirable futures to aim for, given a comprehensive view of corporate goals, then planning to make feasible any key potential opportunities that were both desirable and open to cost-effective research and development or other transition mechanisms, needs explicit separate consideration. The realisation of a transformation to feasibility can feed into long-term planning using prior contingency plans when relevant. Successful realisation of a feasibility transformation might also have an impact on medium-term or short-term planning, and awareness of this possibility could be important follow-on concerns.

Arguably a crucial and central aspect of early 'futures planning' for all organisations is ensuring that all the key corporate capability-culture assets needed to translate corporate goals into futures plans are in place, and any key liabilities are dealt with. The questions raised are not really separable from those associated with the last section, and the interdependencies are complex. For example, in Chapter 8, Carl's recommendations to replace Larry *and* his corporate planning director role with several board level posts and a new associated management structure was a crucial first step towards a radically different approach to corporate planning. It was directly linked to a broadened view of corporate goals planning and a broadened view of futures planning, with toolset, skill set, and mindset implications for all the key players involved. As another example, in the much simpler TLC context of Chapter 5, Ajit indicated the need for new people with appropriate skill sets in addition to new skill sets for existing staff. But even in this relatively simple context there were complexities of importance. As an illustration, picking up on the inherent interdependencies between marketing and product innovation, TLC needed to move away from a highly production-led perspective towards a more market-led perspective which embraced this interdependence.

Because the nature of the frameworks needed for extensive formal futures planning is highly dependent on the context, a detailed exploration of futures planning in Chapter 8 would not have been very instructive for other contexts, in addition to being a distraction in terms of the main messages of the Canpower tale. In this section it was assumed that the most appropriate approach to get you started in the contexts of interest to you was a very limited list of observations, as follows.

First, in the rapidly changing environment that most organisations now have to live with, effective futures planning needs to be seen as central to corporate survival as well as corporate prosperity.

Second, it is crucial not to muddle futures planning with long-term planning or follow-on medium-term and short-term planning. Exploring what is not currently feasible but might be made feasible makes futures planning very different from follow-on long-term, medium-term, and short-term planning.

Third, the span of issues futures planning could usefully address might be very wide, with considerable depth needed in many areas. Technology based and driven organisations like Astro need to confront an enormous span and depth of complexity. Manufacturing based and driven organisations like TLC might anticipate relatively simple issues, even if the scale of their operation is quite large.

Fourth, there is a sizable relevant literature, but it needs synthesis in the specific contexts of interest to you with considerable care taken to clarify the framing assumptions and working assumptions made by the authors of the approaches being discussed.

Developing and testing other planning capability areas

A number of other planning areas need clear separation from goals and futures planning in conceptual and operational terms, plus careful early attention in terms of requisite capabilities. Going beyond emphasising a few key issues in this section would not be very productive, but you may find the following points worth reflecting on if they have not received your attention already.

Long-term, medium-term and short-term corporate planning capability

The ability to translate the results of goals and futures planning into long-term, medium-term and short-term plans in terms of top-down and integrative corporate planning capability is clearly an early essential. In particular, having people with the requisite toolsets, skill sets, and mindsets to begin developing and testing appropriate long-term and medium-term planning within the corporate planning function is an early priority, perhaps just behind the need for people to revise goals and futures planning approaches, but probably best thought about at the same time. Short-term planning is usually less of a concern.

Developing and testing project planning capability

As soon as any organisation starts to address the management of change, project planning in the broad Chapter 7 frameworks becomes directly relevant. The related capability-culture issues are core concerns. Project planning capability is obviously essential in terms of detailed change management plans as and when tactical concerns start to emerge in all different specific areas of an organisation. But it is particularly relevant at an overall strategic level from the outset. All change management is usefully perceived as a breed of project management dealing with very high levels of ambiguity as well as very high levels of other aspects of uncertainty, which implies some very big potential opportunities and risks. Ensuring those involved have the requisite toolsets, skill sets and mindsets is obviously a crucial issue.

This point was made in an initial low-key way by Ajit in Chapter 5, and it was developed significantly by Paul in Chapter 7. It suggests a very early focus on hiring someone with Paul's capabilities if an organisation does not already have a seasoned Paul equivalent or finding a suitable 'prototype Paul' and ensuring well-informed access to appropriate training along with appropriate mentoring.

Developing and testing operations planning capability

Even if no immediate changes in operations management areas is the initial working assumption, ongoing operations need planning in the sense of a generalisation of the areas addressed in Chapters 5, 6, and 9, and integrative operations planning concerns as addressed in Chapters 7 and 8 are also important. Again, the availability and quality of directly related toolsets, skill sets, and mindsets should be the central initial focus. For example, are the inherent interdependencies between demand side marketing, product design, production technology, and supply chain concerns being addressed effectively, including all relevant safety and environmental concerns, and the way operations management concerns in particular areas feed into corporate planning and management of change project planning?

Developing specific planning capability aspects

A number of specific planning capability aspects may need early focused effort. As for the last section, going beyond emphasising a few key issues in this section would not be very productive, but observations in the following subsections should be worth you thinking about in your own context as a starting point.

Development of key corporate tools and initial use in a coordinated manner

The priority ordering of corporate, operations, and project planning concerns will vary with the context, and any one of these three areas might be judged the most important in terms of the need for immediate change. However, all these areas of planning need integration, and a coherent approach to *all* new frameworks, processes, and other tools need early attention in terms of overall coordination to achieve compatibility and coherence.

Project planning as discussed in Chapter 7 uses four frameworks, the four Fs for project planning:

1   a lifecycle framework,
2   a seven Ws framework,
3   a goals–plans relationships framework, and
4   an SP for projects framework.

It is useful to see these four frameworks plus the embedded models as the project planning versions of a four Fs 'corporate tools' concept which has related variants in operations and corporate planning contexts.

For example, the project lifecycle stage structure equivalent for corporate planning is the goals, futures, long-term, medium-term and short-term planning structure. In an operations planning framework like that of Chapter 6, Martha's three bidding stages are the equivalent of project lifecycle stages until the bid is won or lost, but other equivalents may be involved in different operations management contexts.

As another example, the way the seven Ws framework was adapted to mesh with the lifecycle framework in Chapter 7 needs an equivalent treatment in the Chapter 8 corporate strategy formation structure of Figure 8.1 for goals, futures, long-term, medium-term and short-term planning. There will not only be important commonalities but also important differences with a nature dependent upon the context details. In the operations planning framework of Chapter 6, the seven Ws needs adapting to Martha's three bidding stages in a reasonably obvious way, but other adaptations will be required in different contexts, and the differences will be highly context dependent.

As a further example, the way the SP for projects concept was adapted to mesh with the goals–plans relationships via the seven Ws frameworks plus the lifecycle framework in Chapter 7 also needs equivalent adaptations in a corporate planning context, and the notion of a common overall framework for project planning and operations planning explored briefly in Chapter 7 needs further generalisation.

Chapter 8 suggested a 'Processes Director' for Canpower, who might be responsible for these kinds of issues at the board level. However, a generalised version might be someone with appropriate skills and authority having 'corporate EP tools' responsibility, covering the coordinated development and initial use of all the new conceptual and operational tools required by the organisation, with a job title suitable for the specific organisation and its history of related positions. An internal consulting group with EP implementation planning and supporting roles might be one useful way to see this role.

Some organisations may need help from external consultants, as well as appointing new staff to new roles and helping existing staff to understand the direction of change plus acquiring new toolsets, skill sets and mindsets. It is important to avoid letting action on this front get delayed because new territory is involved and the uncertainty associated with difficult choices is very high. But it is also important to avoid expensive false starts which take the organisation in the wrong direction. Furthermore, there is a need for ongoing vigilant attention to a constructive tension between taking externally provided advice and developing internal capability.

As with all early management of change, effectiveness rather than efficiency needs to be the early emphasis. Initially doing the right things is more important than doing them right. Getting approximately correct answers to the right questions in an appropriate timeframe is another way of looking at the same concern.

Addressing trade-offs between precedence relationships and pressing priorities

The ordering of concerns addressed in terms of the trade-offs between priorities associated with major or intermediate crises (like a second serious railway accident), and important precedence relationships (like being clear about *all* key objectives before investing heavily in dependent plans), needs coordination by someone, or a small team, with significant insight and authority from the outset. This is arguably as crucial at the outset as any other urgent concerns. This aspect of managing change was implicit in Part 2 chapters. The implications of key choices may be very uncertain for complex reasons. Predominantly informal planning by people with the requisite insight and sound instincts may be what is needed in many contexts. Formal planning approaches may not be appropriate, and directly related experience may not be relevant even if it is available, depending on the circumstances.

Developing and implementing change incrementally

In the Astro tale of Chapter 6, Martha's approach to involving Trevor has a number of features worth testing for relevance in your organisation's context. For example, using one particular development case example, with a carefully selected player like Trevor contributing to development, testing, demonstration, and roll-out into other areas, illustrated the effective capture of opportunities and knowledge in a number of areas which Trevor was particularly well placed to contribute to. His role in the incremental roll-out planned by Martha might be particularly relevant in your organisation.

In the 1990s, I developed a consultancy relationship with NatWest Bank which lasted several years, helping two of their staff develop what they referred to as a 'benefits risk management' approach for a very large information system development programme involving the computerisation of all NatWest branch banking in the UK. The benefits management framework NatWest used had been developed with consultants based at Cranfield University advocating a 'balanced scorecard' view of business cases for change, driven by a portfolio of benefits. The Cranfield consultants, in turn, had drawn on the Harvard-based authors Kaplan and Norton (1992, 1993a and b, 1996). The two NatWest staff I worked with used the balanced scorecard starting point to overlay a prototype of the Chapter 7 approach then available to develop their prototype specific process for managing uncertainty. One of the key contributing factors to the significant overall success of their efforts was rolling out the initial branch implementation with a very small number of carefully selected branches, then using the branch staff involved to refine the approach before rolling out a revised approach to a slightly bigger set of branches, only moving on to a general roll-out when all the early concerns had been resolved effectively.

This illustrates a practical example of a way to focus on being effective first, then moving on to efficiency concerns as experience was gained. It also illustrates one way to move from a focus on a limited number of metrics like cost or profit, and associated uncertainty, to a broader set of objectives portrayed as 'benefits' which may not have simple metrics.

A specific interest group of the APM (Association for Project Management) and many others have developed these ideas since. From an EP perspective, it is clear that trade-offs between benefits have implicit if not explicit shadow price interpretations linked to the T_S concept explored in Chapter 9, possibly an area worth further exploration.

This was long before NatWest became part of the Royal Bank of Scotland (RBS), part of a series of developments which ended in UK government rescue to prevent UK financial market meltdown during the 2007–2008 crisis. As part of the run-up to these problems, both of the NatWest people I worked with moved to other employers. RBS might have been well advised to have retained and made effective use of them, employing a generalised variant of their own 1990s NatWest benefit risk management approach at the RBS board level.

Testing actual outcomes and learning from experience, recognising limitations

Testing actual outcomes against expectations and learning how to do better next time was clearly part of the strategy adopted by Astro's Martha as discussed in Chapter 6 and NatWest's benefit risk management developers as discussed in the last subsection, but there are wider implications which also need addressing. For example, the way BP used formal assessment of how cost and duration outcomes compared with plans in the early 1980s was a robustness test and a learning process at a corporate level, and it was both useful and effective in terms of what it addressed. But what it did not address, which with hindsight might have been extremely useful, is the extent to which using simpler approaches once lessons have been learned may lead to overconfidence, and the extent to which ongoing robustness testing ought to be wide enough and deep enough to test for potential issues which are 'off the radar' because they have not yet been encountered.

The Chapter 9 discussion made a point of avoiding bias and blind spots associated with too much focus on what happened in the past and not enough attention to very different things that might happen in the future. The very long return periods of catastrophic incidents make it particularly obvious that the relevant future may not resemble the past. But in a very different context, the early parts of Chapter 3 made similar points about the need to treat the past as a very limited lens for thinking about the future. All intermediate chapters involved related thinking because this issue is a very general concern. The management of change needs leaders who are very clear about the importance of learning from experience and the pressures imposed by understandable concerns about evidence-based decision making but who are also very comfortable about creative planning for uncertain issues of importance which have not been encountered in the past. This kind of competence is not as common as it needs to be.

Key opportunities and risks associating with outsourcing

In Chapter 5, TLC's in-house manufacturing operation used lawnmower engines and other components which were outsourced, but the possible option of outsourcing the manufacture of complete lawnmowers or other garden machinery was new territory. In Chapter 6, outsourcing some of the current roles of Sian's Systems group, including moving existing Astro employees into new companies and current strategic partners, was also new territory. In Chapter 7 Paul suggested WSL keep strategic design in-house but continue a policy of outsourcing detailed design to their contractors, with no radical changes. But a much more flexible approach to construction outsourcing was proposed. In Chapter 8, outsourcing a range of current in-house activities was a central aspect of the broadened approach to goals and futures planning developed by Carl. In Chapter 9, continuing to rely on external maintenance contractors and moving to a larger number of possibly smaller organisations to reduce costs for NER was recommended by Sophie, comparable in part to some aspects of the Chapter 7 approach. In all these cases important opportunities were being identified, and exploiting these opportunities was recommended, despite a lack of earlier experience of this kind in some particularly important cases.

It is obvious that outsourcing can involve strategic levels of risk as well as tactical risk concerns. The sources of these strategic level risks need early identification and treatment in the goals and futures planning stages, as well as ongoing treatment at long, medium and short-term levels.

Outsourcing first raised concerns for me in the context of BP outsourcing significant aspects of design associated with offshore North Sea projects in the 1980s. Earlier outsourcing of *some aspects* of cost uncertainty and associated risk for activities like pipe-laying by seeking fixed price contracts, which outsourced detailed plan management including cost–duration trade-offs, did not worry me at the time, but perhaps it should have. A linked issue in the 1970s and 1980s was separate risk management in a safety sense by BP, which was

simply well beyond my remit and off my radar. Arguably, the 2010 Deepwater Horizon incident was a direct result of a mix of many things, including inappropriate outsourcing of cost
risk, and inappropriate management of other sources of risk in separate silos. Outsourcing
risk and uncertainty via contractual arrangements is a much broader interpretation of outsourcing than may be common, but it is a useful perspective, for reasons clearly illustrated by
many misguided organisations with a cultural bias towards outsourcing risks to contractors
which the contractors would take to get the job but prove unwilling or unable to meet if it
was realised.

All enlightened planning needs an effective uncertainty management process which deals
with outsourcing opportunities and risks in a very broad sense, fully integrated with all
related contract planning. Decisions to outsource or keep key functions or issues or sources
of risk and opportunity in-house are central to the public versus private sector status of
organisations and a wide range of hybrid approaches. But they are also central to organisations like TLC and Astro, plus all other private sector organisations, when possible public
sector status is nowhere near the agenda.

Investing in future learning

Early investment in corporate learning, via development and demonstration projects for example, can be exceedingly valuable central aspects of moving an organisation towards fully implemented EP based approaches to planning. Examples associated with BP, National Power and
IBM UK were mentioned earlier. Each illustrate some of the tactical options available, but a
broad strategy also needs consideration as part of change-management planning.

Future learning strategy has to address a very wide range of issues in a systematic and
coherent manner. For example, the different learning needs of different groups of people
within an organisation need addressing, as well as common needs.

Approaches to learning which address this, like the Biggs and Tang (2011) 'constructive
alignment' approach, contain ideas which might be adopted by organisations other than
universities and issues as diverse as apprenticeships for early development of technical skills
and mentoring of new board members, or those being prepared for new senior management
roles at other organisational levels, are all part of the big picture needing attention.

Much of the associated planning has to be informal, but enlightened formal planning
based on a rich understanding of a wide range of alternative approaches can shape what happens informally in crucial ways.

Overall strategic level change management planning

To introduce any significant changes in any organisation, there is an obvious need to evolve
an overall strategic level change management plan. If the significant changes include a shift
to a variant of an EP perspective which is substantially different from current approaches,
the plans will have to cope with an emerging sense of direction and priorities, with flexible
and robust provisional plans, anticipating a wide range of significant surprises, some entirely
unpredictable. The plans will have to ensure that the organisation responds effectively
to all surprises. This is a very demanding kind of project planning, which needs effective
integration with corporate and operations planning needs, and addressing it is particularly
challenging.

The frameworks provided by Chapter 7 are a useful basis, and this chapter has emphasised
some key issues, but there is a vast literature on the management of change which also needs

to be drawn on. What needs to be done has to include making effective use of a compatible and coherent version of what an organisation currently knows, plus what it can usefully learn from all other sources, testing all aspects for robustness.

Someone within the organisation needs to take or be given responsibility for coordinating the acquisition and the ongoing coherent application of corporate management of change capability. It may be very important for this person to be at the board level. What other roles they might play and what they are called will clearly have to depend on the context. Widespread capability-culture asset and liability changes may be integral aspects of what is involved, touching all parts of the organisation. Making these kinds of significant changes to an organisation in a successful manner obviously requires competent management of change leadership with appropriate support from everyone else. Associated formal planning can and should be approached as a supporting framework, a vehicle for testing and communicating ideas, not just a prescription for action.

11 Ongoing enhancement of strategic clarity and tactical clarity

The next three sections of this chapter consider broad aspects of EP which need ongoing attention by all participants in an EP approach. These sections address important aspects of strategic and tactical clarity which are recurrent themes in all earlier chapters: teamwork and wider collaboration, biased decision making, and contingency planning aspects of EP which may underlie some aspects of biased decision making but have much wider implications. Enhancement of strategic clarity and tactical clarity at personal and corporate levels depends on ongoing attention to these three broad concerns.

Further sections then consider broad planning areas, perspectives, frameworks or approaches which most readers ought to have some interest in which may be a particular focus of interest for subsets of readers: overall corporate planning, operations planning, project planning, process planning, safety and security planning, risk management, lean and agile approaches, the histogram and tree (HAT) framework and Monte Carlo simulation approaches. The primary purpose of these sections is exploring tactical clarity issues which underpin ongoing strategic clarity enhancement for all readers. But an important secondary purpose is helping readers with interests in specific areas to take their personal tactical clarity enhancement further.

A section addresses regulation which many organisations may have to deal with and the relevance of EP concepts to regulation. A following section very briefly addresses politics and associated public pressure as part of the environment which all organisations have to consider when planning and all of us as citizens have ultimate responsibility for.

The final section provides an overview summary which uses 'smiles' as an indicator of EP effectiveness in terms of corporate progress with capability-culture concerns. It employs an influence diagram structure evolved over many years which has been updated in this book to incorporate 'frowns', a 'red face' special case of 'frowns', and a 'halo' special case of 'smiles'.

Teamwork and collaboration as key capability-culture issues

Teamwork plus wider collaboration is a central feature of all five Part 2 tales. You may have always regarded teamwork and wider collaboration as crucial, but formally recognising their value as key capability-culture assets, with direct implications for both formal and informal approaches to planning, seemed a very useful feature to embody in an EP approach via the UP concept. Some approaches to planning do not exploit the importance of teamwork and wider collaboration enough, and some seem to make inappropriate stealth assumptions about teamwork and collaboration which need systematic identification and testing. A lack of effective teamwork and insufficient attention to broader collaboration are capability-culture liabilities which often require effective resolution and at the very least need effective accommodation. At worst, a lack of effective teamwork and collaboration may prove a fatal flaw for an organisation, and realisation of associated risk can be catastrophic.

The need to make effective use of an organisation's capability-culture assets in terms of big and little team working in an explicit manner, as well as either eliminating or accommodating all relevant associated liabilities, is always crucial in the context of deciding how an organisation should approach formal and interrelated informal planning. Put the other way around, assumptions about what teamwork and collaboration are needed in a planning context should depend on the nature of the plans in terms of their informal planning implications as well as their formal content, and the competence of everyone involved is always crucial. These aspects of EP are operationally inseparable, and they need nuanced and well-grounded operational attention, recognising all relevant interdependencies.

One illustrative key implication is the need for careful and enlightened consideration of an organisation's approach to formal contractual relationships and the closely coupled central role of the operational interpretation of formal contractual relationships. Work with Stephen Ward in this area, stimulated by a Science and Engineering Research Council (SERC) grant which funded two years of research undertaken by Bernard Curtis, led to a report published as a book in 1991 which Stephen and I have built on. Curtis, Ward, and Chapman (1991); Ward, Chapman and Curtis (1991); Ward and Chapman (1994, 1995, 2008); and Chapman and Ward (1994, 2008) might usefully supplement other relevant literature to help you develop your views of the formal and associated informal concerns which need to be addressed. A core theme of this cited work is that contracts are not just legal constructs designed to protect particular players. They are frameworks for a collaborative approach to sharing risk and reward which require interpretation by people who have a nuanced understanding of 'reciprocation' concepts, a practical aspect of successful collaboration. All the parties and people involved need to be prepared to 'give' as well as 'take' in relationships founded on reciprocation of generosity and well-founded trust. As one of our particularly enlightened experienced practitioner SERC grant contributors put it, 'as soon as "the contracts are out of the drawers", everybody is in trouble'. This is a comment Martha attributed to her uncle Paul in Chapter 7 and used to clarify her approach to clients on associated issues. Contracts which are confrontational may be common, and they may suit the style of many organisations, but avoiding confrontation when feasible is usually a more enlightened approach for most parties. Simply refusing to work with parties who are confrontational whenever possible is usually a sound strategy for a complex set of reasons, including attracting and retaining staff with the 'right stuff'. Most really good staff with the right stuff will not put up with routinely working with people who cannot be trusted to be collaborative if they have alternative job opportunities.

Other key implications include the need to very carefully assess the extent to which *formal* relationship planning beyond contractual planning is currently needed and effective in an organisation. This assessment should consider the nature of all associated *informal* planning, the way related positive and negative feedback loops work, and the way these issues interact with corporate policies designed to address attracting new staff plus the ongoing retaining, training, and motivating of all staff. Well-motivated people who can work together as effective members of a team with all the other requisite capabilities may be drawn into an organisation and retained if that organisation fosters those characteristics by light-touch formal planning systems and associated governance with strong and consistent informal planning approaches both encouraged and facilitated. Inappropriate formal planning approaches which inhibit skilled and creative informal planning may attract people with seriously inappropriate attitudes, and drive out the people who really matter. The interdependencies which need thoughtful attention are very complex.

Both the opportunities and the challenges involved are significant, and a focus on these issues using the capability-culture asset and liability concepts relationship to both the UP and all dependent SPs may be useful.

Being open to approaches to collaborate for mutual benefit and proactive in seeking out new possibilities for cooperation has been a core feature of the Part 2 tales. Generating and sustaining a successful collaboration track record within and beyond a generalised form of 'big team' approach is a capability-asset worth investing in. It may not happen without explicit facilitation.

I found *The Road to Co-operation: Escaping the Bottom Line* (Pearson, 2012) useful background reading when writing this book, and you might find it useful as part of your further reading in this area. Although Pearson's approach and mine are very different, because the context and concerns are different, you are likely to find a wide range of perspectives and approaches relevant, and this is just one illustrative example. *The Gift* (Hyde, 2006) also addresses 'reciprocation' from a perspective you may find useful, and there is a developing literature addressing related 'reciprocal altruism' concepts as well as genuine altruism plus other related and relevant approaches – see *Altruism: The Science and Psychology of Kindness* (Ricard, 2018) for a very interesting synthesis. What is particularly relevant about Matthieu Ricard's book is its well-argued modern science–based critique of all approaches to philosophy and psychology which are grounded on egocentric selfish behaviour, including that of Ayn Rand, Sigmund Freud and Machiavelli, coupled to well-argued endorsement of writers like Charles Darwin, with direct implications for economic and environmental concerns as well as greater life satisfaction for those who embrace Ricard's ideas.

There is a very rich literature on teamwork, collaboration, and associated culture concerns. Most of it is more specifically focused than the very broad references provided when introducing the capability-culture concept in Chapter 2, and quite different from the very specific references to my work on contracting with Curtis and Ward and the other references just discussed. For example, in a website paper Matthew Leitch looks at the nature of 'risk culture' and how to change it (Leitch, 2013), building on ideas in his book *Intelligent Internal Control and Risk Management* (Leitch, 2008). You may find it useful to explore a quite wide range of how to do it literature relevant to your specific concerns to deepen your strategic clarity and build tactical clarity.

As with many other aspects of the proposed EP approach, the teamwork and collaboration opportunities and challenges relevant to the organisations of interest to you may be somewhat different from those explored in this book. However, making these issues an explicit part of the basic frameworks used for thinking about planning via the capability-culture concept seems a useful step forward. Responding effectively to all the complex questions raised by the capability-culture concept is a significant how to do it challenge, and the role of teamwork and wider collaboration for you and your organisation may be a good place to start to get to grips with how to do it concerns. If nothing else, it is a reminder to ask some useful questions which need thinking about in most organisations.

Biased decision making as a ubiquitous concern

Unbiased estimation of key parameters for decision-making purposes is a ubiquitous concern in Parts 1 and 2 – because biased parameter estimation is an obvious basic reason for biased decision making, and biased decision making in a general sense has a very broad range of forms and causes which all need attention.

For reasons outlined in Chapter 3, and illustrated by later chapters, parameter estimation approaches based on a point estimate *framing* assumption ought to be scrapped in all contexts. Point estimates are simplistic, in the sense that they are usually too simple in the 'wrong way', and keeping it simple in the 'right way' is important. A 'minimum clarity' approach can be a useful place to start, and there is a rich range of ways available to add more clarity in an efficient manner whenever more clarity is worthwhile.

There is a rich literature on controlling unconscious bias in parameter estimates which some readers may need detailed knowledge of. For example, a classic reference which I first used with university students in the 1980s is *Judgement Under Uncertainty: Heuristics and Biases* (Kahneman, Slovic, and Tversky, 1982, especially chapters 21 [Alpert and Raiffa] and 23 [Fischoff]). Recently reading *Thinking, Fast and Slow* (Kahneman, 2012), and then *The Undoing Project* (Lewis, 2017) about the Kahneman and Tversky partnership, greatly enhanced my understanding of these issues, and working backwards with these three references might play a useful part in your exploration of the literature in this area.

There is a growing literature on conscious (deliberate) bias which all readers should at least be aware of, and some may need to engage with. *Megaprojects and Risk: An Anatomy of Ambition* (Flyvbjerg, Bruzelius, and Rothengatter, 2003) is a good starting point, but be aware that the way much of this literature is often used is highly controversial.

Even those who do not need to understand the conscious or unconscious bias literature in detail do need a clear understanding of how to deal with the broader issues underlying 'a conspiracy of optimism' and 'strategic misrepresentation'. They also need to understand that biased decision making viewed in general terms involves issues which go well beyond conventional interpretations of biased estimation of component parameters, for a range of reasons touched on in Part 1 and addressed throughout Part 2.

As an opening example, Nicola's Chapter 5 pass three treatment of the cost of capital associated with a credit period when an order quantity arrives but has not yet been paid for can be seen as an approach to eliminating bias in the economic order quantity model overlooked for many decades, with significant implications. Nicola's pass two plans, based on an over-estimated cost of capital, reduced an initial order quantity of 2,000 to 1,500. But her pass 3 plans, which recognised the value of using other people's money to avoid her pass 2 biased estimate of the cost of capital, increased the order quantity to 7,000. This triggered Bob's very different pass 4 approach, which then triggered a whole string of bottom-up strategic-change proposals. You may prefer to see this as a biased approach to decision making which goes beyond biased parameter estimates used in models, addressing biases in the models themselves, and the processes used to construct or select and adapt the generic models.

Martha's Chapter 6 approach to avoiding biased estimation of costs and probabilities via explicit qualitative analysis using a traffic light approach is also an illustration of a biased decision-making issue with implications of importance which go well beyond the usual unbiased parameter estimates concerns. This kind of concern is not usually thought of as a biased parameter estimation concern, or addressed effectively in any other way. You may prefer to see it as an illustration of biased decision making driven by the need for qualitative analysis of important issues which quantitative analysis cannot deal with, a very basic decision-making process concern.

Biased discount rates for NPV calculations, as addressed by Paul in Chapter 7, provides another example of important bias inherent in the framing assumptions of the decision-making approach itself, not just a matter of biased estimation of parameters. Bias associated with approaches to NPV calculations is somewhat buried in Chapter 7. However, the disposal of nuclear waste example, discussed in more detail by Chapman, Ward and Klein (2006), suggests a very serious bias in NPV calculations, of the order of billions of pounds in a context when a hundred million pounds was the determining feature of a crucial choice. Ignoring objectives which arguably mattered more than those addressed probably further increased the implications of the biased decision making involved, and may have led to a national strategic mistake with 1990s 'present value' consequences involving many billions of pounds and ongoing consequences which will matter even more this century and the next. There are directly equivalent concerns for private sector organisations, demonstrated as clearly as possible by the Chapter 7 discussion, in terms of shaping the nature of projects as well as influencing which projects get selected. And this is just part of the biased decision making which can be driven by an inappropriate approach to project planning and interdependent operations planning, the primary focus of Chapter 7.

Biased estimates of nuclear power expected costs and ranges, as explored by Carl in the context of corporate planning for Canpower in Chapter 8, was a relatively minor part of the biased corporate strategic planning approach adopted by Canpower. Biased management decision making in relation to goals planning, futures planning, long-term planning, and medium-term planning was the real issue in Chapter 8.

Bias associated with estimating 'value of an avoided fatality' concepts as the number of fatalities in a single incident varies as addressed by Sophie is the focus of Chapter 9, and bias in this sense also matters greatly, especially if we broaden the set of relevant objectives to embrace ongoing health and environmental concerns in a wide range of relevant contexts. These concerns might include very low probability major international events, like nuclear catastrophes, but they may also include issues we have to face for certain, like the implications of toxic hydrocarbon combustion emissions and the full and very complex implications of the current international movement towards electric motive power.

These Part 2 biased decision-making issues involving framing assumption approaches as well as parameter values are all ongoing concerns, some with complex political and ethical dimensions requiring pragmatic resolution strategies which are inherently very difficult to address. What is needed is testable working assumptions that facilitate properly grounded management decision making at all levels, avoiding the wrong kind of simplicity, and facilitating well-informed debate whenever this is appropriate. Early and ongoing how to do it attention by your organisation which addresses *all* sources of biased decision making is very important, and you may be able to make key contributions. Plans built upon seriously biased parameters are inherently unsound. But if the basic frameworks which underlie peoples' understanding of the way decision making should be approached are biased, the implications can be orders of magnitude more serious. There are huge opportunities to make *much better* management decisions associated with overcoming these bias issues.

A particularly difficult challenge is finding effective ways to confront wilful bias, whatever its form, whatever its motivation, whatever its justification, and whatever the power and influence of those perpetrating it.

Contingency planning as a constant background concern

In Chapters 3, 4, and 7 contingency planning ideas based on the SCERT (Synergistic Contingency Planning Evaluation and Review Technique) approach were discussed directly. A generalisation of this approach underlies EP as a whole, and you may find it helpful to see the EP approach to contingency planning as a synthesis of seven central ideas.

First, it can be important to address sources of uncertainty in terms of one or more of five different partially overlapping portrayals of uncertainty: event uncertainty, variability uncertainty, ambiguity uncertainty, capability-culture uncertainty, and systemic uncertainty. The way we frame our contingency planning is affected by the uncertainty portrayals we employ, so we need to choose appropriate portrayals carefully with this in mind.

Second, it is often important to consider *proactive* responses which involve changing the current base plan A1 to a better base plan A2 or A3 *plus* developing pre-planned *reactive* responses in the form of a plan B, C, or D and so on to be used if the base plan does not work out *or new opportunities are identified*. These contingency plans may need their own higher order contingency plans with obvious practical limits on this kind of complexity.

Third, it is generally important to consider the use of responses which are *specific* to individual sources of uncertainty *plus* further broadly defined *general* responses which deal with combinations of sources net of the residual implications of a specific response, including a widely defined view of the 'unknown unknowns'.

Fourth, it is crucial to understand that general responses are essential to deal with the unknown unknowns which are 'unknowable', but general responses are also very useful for dealing with any unknowns which are simply not worth the effort or cost involved in identification and follow-on planning.

Fifth, as soon as we start planning with options in mind, risk efficiency should be a central concern, and contingency planning is one route into addressing planning options.

Sixth, it is always important to see opportunity efficiency as the motivation for all aspects of planning in a very general sense, including identifying and capturing the important opportunities associated with simplifications of the right kind and avoiding serious risks associated with simplifications of the wrong kind. Put a little differently, there are uncertainties associated with the way we choose to plan which require their own particular kind of contingency planning.

Seventh, managing the extent to which we have yet to unravel ambiguity uncertainty associated with contingency planning because we have not yet addressed it, although we might now address some aspects of it if doing so looked worthwhile, is always essential.

Eighth, understanding that 'strategic clarity' involves a good grasp of how all these ideas can be made operational in any given context without losing any key opportunities or realising any key risks is the essence of an EP approach to contingency planning.

A key working assumption when we use these central ideas explicitly in a high clarity approach, or implicitly in a low clarity approach, is that the assumed general responses are effective and efficient enough to cope with all relevant sources of uncertainty net of the effect of the specific responses. Anything general responses cannot cope with appropriately needs effective and efficient specific responses, and vice versa. Both specific and general responses can incorporate higher order responses if primary responses fail, but this kind of higher order contingency planning has practical limitations and costs which must be addressed effectively and efficiently. It is *always important* to have sufficient understanding of what is involved in order to make a judgement about the validity of this key working assumption.

This generalised high and low clarity view of contingency planning is central to EP as a whole in all contexts. In the early stages of decision-making processes only a modest degree of contingency planning may be desirable to reduce potential bias associated with expected outcome estimates and associated variability estimates, so those involved know what they are doing in strategic clarity terms *before* making commitments. Sometimes organisations should wait until strategy has some stability and commitments become necessary before investing in detailed contingency planning. This involves a 'clarified ambiguity' approach to complexity which project management has to address via carefully planned and controlled lifecycle stage structures, and *all* planning needs to draw on this aspect of project planning within comparable structures appropriate to the context. In the very early stages, sometimes a very simple minimum clarity approach may be suitable, completely ignoring any explicit formal contingency planning. But when this approach is adopted, someone who understands the implied assumptions should ensure that the simplicity currently assumed remains robust overall, and effective and efficient in terms of each component of the planning.

Depending on the specific concerns that you and your organisation have to address, exploring suitable corporate perspectives on contingency planning, plus associated robustness and resilience concerns, may pay significant dividends. I cannot offer any useful general advice on where best to start, but each of the very different tales of Part 2 may offer some clues relevant to the contexts of interest to you and your organisation.

Corporate planning

Several interrelated key messages for readers interested in top-down, bottom-up, and integrative corporate planning as part of a more general corporate management perspective were central to Chapter 8. However, some important messages were introduced late in Chapter 8 without a lot of emphasis or were left until Chapters 9 and 10.

In Chapter 8, Canpower's need for formal corporate planning involved a very much bigger set of concerns than those embodied in the role Larry had been given as the 'Corporate Planning Director'. An implication was central aspects of the formal corporate planning concerns which Canpower had to address probably needed at least two separate directors, with a carefully defined form of separability in their relationships so that the board was presented with a balanced perspective when making decisions about the portfolio of change projects defining the organisation's future evolution. A 'balanced perspective' in this context implies an unbiased portrayal. A degree of separation between plan creation and enhancement initially and the follow-on integration of plans plus governance are central bias control concerns at an overall corporate decision-making process level.

Assuming these roles are executed along the lines suggested in Chapter 8 by capable directors, formulating corporate strategy also involves a capable board led by a capable managing director and chairman in terms of managing creative bottom-up option generation as well as some direct top-down thinking and overall governance. It may be useful to explicitly associate the label 'corporate management' with the board as a whole, supported by the crucial overall leadership roles of the CEO and board chair but also jointly led by a number of directors with explicit formal corporate management roles, fully integrating relevant emergent strategy roles for all the 'operations' directors plus interrelated change-management roles for one or more 'projects' directors.

More generally, from an EP perspective corporate planning involves central roles for the director or directors responsible for 'corporate planning' in a traditional direct sense, but other members of the board also need to take a very close interest, perhaps with clearly defined and formally identified corporate management roles. This flows from seeing corporate planning as part of a holistic corporate, operations and project planning trio which embraces all planning within an organisation. Chapter 8 is a fairly rich example, but the treatment is necessarily very context dependent, so other contexts may require significant differences in approach.

The tale of Chapter 9 suggested the possible need for a board level 'Director of Safety and Security' to carry forward Sophie's ideas, with sufficient power to play a full role in top-down corporate strategy formulation as well as bottom-up planning in this area, with related implications for Chapter 8. For organisations facing any significant safety and security issues, this is an area of complexity which must be addressed effectively. If the potential catastrophic nuclear incident issues associated with the electricity utility context of Chapter 8 are replaced by a possible set of 'nuclear catastrophe equivalents' for other organisations when relevant, there may be important analogous implications. Nuclear catastrophe equivalents might include cybersecurity attacks with safety, reputational and financial implications or disruptive new technologies or disruptive political changes driven by social and economic changes, for example.

The way all these directors and associated senior managers need to work together as a team clearly needs understanding and acting upon by everyone involved. Opportunity efficiency for the organisation as a whole depends on how well this is done. The tales of Part 2 all contribute some ideas relevant to the contexts of each chapter, but putting all these ideas together with adaptation to other contexts is clearly a significant challenge.

Key aspects of any organisation's capability-culture asset and liability set will be driven by these considerations and will interact with the planning processes needed. To take a very simple example, even after Nicola's arrival, TLC as discussed in Chapter 5 had very limited formal planning process capability, but under George's leadership with Ajit's guidance TLC functioned very effectively. This effectiveness included responding to the opportunities Dave triggered recognition of, using strategies created, enhanced, shaped, and tested by Nicola initially, and then by all the other relevant players. However, as Ajit advised, if they were going to effectively grasp the opportunities associated with all the identified propositions, they needed to build on their current capability-culture assets and add more requisite skills, especially in a corporate planning context from a marketing perspective.

There is an extensive literature on corporate and associated strategic planning which anyone who is an effective reflective manager in this area clearly needs to draw on. Some of it has MS/OR aspects. For example, the UK Strategic Planning Society was originally started as a study group of the OR Society, soft OR authors have been active in the strategic planning area, and forecasting as discussed in Chapter 8 is MS/OR territory as well as that of economics and econometrics. However, mainstream corporate and associated strategic planning is very much wider, and a coherent, broad and internally consistent view of the whole field is well beyond the scope of my grasp of this area. I have acquired some familiarity over the years with a few of the well-known mainstream standard texts, like *Implanting Strategic Management* (Ansoff, 1984), *The Rise and Fall of Strategic Planning* (Mintzberg, 1994) and *Strategic Safari* (Mintzberg, Ahlstrand and Lampel, 1998), but I do not have an up-to-date knowledge of strategic planning or broader corporate management and associated governance in sufficient depth to offer useful advice about how to approach it here. I do know enough about it to suggest that a *very* serious challenge is integrating all the relevant aspects of it into an internally consistent set of approaches which can be used in a coherent manner with all the enlightened planning ideas explored in this book.

Within every organisation this is a challenge which needs addressing in an effective manner. If it is not directly relevant to your interests, some of the key 'big picture' concerns addressed in Chapter 8 are still worth thinking about in the context of your organisation because of the interdependencies with your concerns. If it is relevant to your interests, Chapter 8 should provide some useful frameworks and ideas for integrating with other frameworks and ideas, but they will need adapting to the contexts of interest to you along with careful linking to consistent frameworks and ideas from the significant relevant literature. If you are a director with expertise in this area, you will already have a much richer background in this area than I have, and testing your framing assumptions with a view to developing a more general set of framing assumptions embracing EP concepts will be a challenge, with difficulties dependent on the scope of the desirable changes. If you are a student at an early stage in your career, in a sense your challenge is easier, because you can use the EP frameworks as a starting point, and test both your reading and your experience against that framework as your views mature.

Wherever you are in terms of the director, expert and student categories of target readers it would not be helpful for me to try to provide more detailed guidance focused on corporate planning here. However, it may be useful to end this section by encouraging you to see an interest in corporate planning as closely connected with both operations planning and project planning – for some purposes they need to be treated as separable in working assumption terms, but the interdependencies are crucial because they are not really separable, and your framing assumptions need to explicitly acknowledge the importance of this lack of separability.

Operations planning

In Chapter 5, the operations planner who Nicola saw herself supporting initially was Pete, TLC's production manager. However, as the tale evolved, the buyer Bob became involved and supply chain management in general became an issue, then TLC's sales manager Surinder and demand chain management in even broader terms became relevant. George and Pete then had to confront complex interdependencies between operations concerns involving product design driven by marketing as well as supply chain and production concerns, with broad overall corporate strategy implications. Finally, corporate strategy requiring top-down corporate planning of operations management issues starting from basic goals for TLC's owners became an obvious concern which Ajit picked up when addressing finance. The opportunities for all those involved in operations planning were wide in range and rich in possibilities.

In Chapter 6, the operations planner involved directly was Martha, the Astro Marketing Manager for Wales. However, as the tale evolved Martha was clearly going to be a key player in reshaping the approach Astro Wales took to strategic partners and related internal market structure concerns as part of a much bigger national and international redefinition of the Astro business model. There was a lot of scope for more effective and efficient operations planning, including a much greater depth of understanding about quite basic issues like 'adding value' to requirements specified by customers to increase profitability with possible international portability of key insights and processes.

In Chapter 7, Ollie was an operations planner with a more traditional Operations Manager role and an Operations Director title. He was only involved in the tale indirectly because the focus of the tale was Paul's approach to project management. However, Ollie's supporting role was crucial because he was a key player in terms of initiating projects to invest in some of the new facilities WSL corporate planning had to consider and Paul had to deliver as Projects Director, and even more important was their joint role at the front-end of all project lifecycles. As Operations Director, Ollie needed a much closer relationship with Paul than was the case with Paul's predecessor to provide more effective input to corporate planning, an opportunity of strategic importance to WSL as well as to Ollie and Paul.

In Chapter 8, Dick was in a traditional Operations Director role, but Larry seemed to pre-empt his bottom-up strategy formation role. Carl's approach to corporate planning meant that operations planning of all kinds should be seen as a source of emergent strategy formulation, a bottom-up approach to corporate planning needing effective integration with top-down corporate planning. This implies a collective opportunity for all bottom-up corporate planners addressed individually in terms of specific operations management examples earlier. It also suggests other operations directors need integrated treatment, like 'finance directors' and 'human resources directors'.

In Chapter 9, Oscar was concerned with all operations planning as part of his Operations Director responsibilities for NER. Oscar needed support from Sophie, a new Head of Safety whose responsibilities were extended to security. As an operations planner Sophie might need direct board level representation to influence corporate strategy appropriately.

The opportunities for operations planning and associated operations management are clearly immense in terms of the range of possibilities and the richness and depth of what might be done. Seeing operations management in these very broad terms should not be an issue – the labels 'operations planning' and 'operations management' can mean different things in different contexts, as long as everyone is clear about how key terms are used.

The key challenges are everyone in the organisations involved having a common understanding of what can be done, what should be done, and how to do it effectively and efficiently, working together as both small teams and big teams, with broader collaboration when appropriate. These are non-trivial challenges, but overcoming them is worth a lot of thought and effort, perhaps starting with the easy bits unless a difficult bit is 'mission critical' for your organisation.

The literature on the range of areas operations planners and operations managers have to address is several orders of magnitude bigger than the corporate planning literature as I understand both. As in the context of the last section on corporate planning, I do not have an up-to-date knowledge of enough of it to provide useful detailed guidance on how to approach it, and you will have to be selective according to the contexts of interest and where you are in the director, expert, and student space. But all relevant aspects of interest to you and your organisation need internally consistent integration with the enlightened planning ideas if joint use is going to work, part of the overall challenge to be faced which is well worth rising to. If you are not directly interested in rising to it, you still may need to take advice from those who are doing so because the impacts have very wide implications.

Project planning

The tale of Chapter 7 suggested that Paul's predecessor was lacking competence in some areas which Paul provided. Paul's approach outlines the portfolio of key conceptual and operational tools all project planning teams need, using his WSL projects in the water and sewage industry as an example context. The broad 'management of change' interpretation of project management which this book adopts made Paul's approach directly relevant to the tales of Chapters 8 and 9. It was also relevant to Chapters 5 and 6. This broad interpretation also makes it a basis for your management of change planning if you and your colleagues want to introduce an enlightened planning approach into your organisation.

There is much literature to draw on in the project planning and associated project management area. I do know this literature better than those considered in the last two sections. The perspective outlined in *How to Manage Project Opportunity and Risk* (Chapman and Ward, 2011), updated and broadened by this book's Chapter 7 approach as developed by Paul, is a good starting point. Work outwards in a way reflecting your interests and priorities, reviewing your earlier understanding of issues as well as addressing unfamiliar territory within the framework this provides. This approach should avoid a good deal of potential confusion when trying to develop internal consistency across the whole spectrum of issues that project planning in a very broad management-of-change sense has to address.

The scope for potential confusion is high because different people use very different framing assumptions without identifying them – never mind clearly testing the robustness of crucial assumptions – like what they mean by 'opportunity', 'risk', and 'uncertainty'. But if you can learn how to deal with the sources of this kind of confusion in a project planning context, there will be immediate and wider pay-offs.

As you work outwards, make sure you take an early look at influential project management thinkers who from a practical perspective argue complimentary positions to those adopted by this book, about the need to embed project management from the concept stage for example, as in Morris (2009, 2013) and Williams, Samset, and Suannevag (2009). It is particularly important to resist arguments directed at keeping the focus of 'project management' narrow because a broad management of change perspective is crucially important. Even in a traditional area like that confronting Paul in Chapter 7, a broad set of conceptual and operational tools is essential. It is also essential to maintain a very broad view of 'opportunity management' grounded on 'uncertainty management'.

You might then move on to more general project management literature like Muller and Turner (2010), Turner (1992, 2014) and Pinto (2016).

You might both extend and test your understanding by reading books with many particularly useful ideas worth reading about in a primary source but with some underlying premises which differ from mine in ways which matter to various degrees, like Lichtenberg (2000); Hillson (2004, 2009); Cooper, Grey, Geoffrey, and Walker (2005, 2014); and Hopkinson (2011, 2016). These examples involve some authors who I view as good friends as well as colleagues with original ideas and approaches that should be cherished, but key framing or working assumptions include terminology choices where we sometimes take a different path.

You may also find it very useful to take a critical look at the wide range of key guides and standards – for example APM (1997, 2004), ICE and IFoA (1998, 2005), PMI (2008, 2009, 2013, 2017a) and ISO 31000 (International Standard, 2009). Even if like me you do not agree with important aspects of what these guides say, you are likely to find it useful and perhaps very important to understand what they are saying and the perspective portrayed.

Process planning

Chapter 8 suggested a 'Process Planning Director' was needed, to give board level leadership to the corporate use of UP variants and their application to the development and testing all SPs that were needed, including a set of specific processes for projects like those developed by Paul in Chapter 7. Chapter 10 raised this issue again, considering generalisation to cover all relevant toolsets and skill sets. The conceptual basis of the Process Planning Director's group, if a very general approach is taken, could be an internal consultancy service which includes all kinds of planning process facilitation plus problem solving and mess resolution services, drawing on external consultants as an 'enlightened customer' whenever this is worthwhile, perhaps also providing external consulting to other organisations for a range of reasons.

My inaugural address as President of the Operational Research Society (ORS), published as 'My Two Cents Worth on How OR Should Develop' (Chapman, 1992b), urged the MS/OR profession to see themselves as 'process planners' who could play key roles in this kind of group. They are not a new idea, and there have been some very successful examples in many contexts and countries. In the 1990s there was no discernible rush of ORS members to respond to my inaugural address, and from a current perspective this might have been anticipated, because ORS members have a wide range of different agendas and many of them do not align with this process planning role in any obvious ways. However, I know some are very interested, and if even a few members of the 'broad church' of MS/OR in all countries, plus everyone else interested in process planning from a perspective comparable to EP, took an interest and began a collaborative conversation about what they were doing, I believe this could become a useful area to develop in a more coherent manner. As long as a viable proportion of those involved share a moderately aligned set of goals and some common language, there is no need for concern if different people have different perspectives and priorities.

We don't even need common labels, like 'Planning Process Director', except for particular applications and discussions. But *somebody* has to be responsible for getting board level agreement about a coherent and effective approach to all corporate planning and component decision-making processes and then delivering what is needed in an opportunity efficient manner, and an EP approach can clarify aspects of their overall aspirational goals.

Safety and security planning

Safety planning has a long history and a rich literature which I first engaged with in a serious manner looking at US nuclear power stations (NUREG, 1975) with a view to the need to draft very specific aspects of design standards related to seismic risk associated with Canadian nuclear power stations. It seemed to me then that key players had a deep understanding of the importance of assumptions like excluding common-mode failures via inappropriate independence assumptions. However, there were important areas where new generalisations would provide new insights. One example was building effective contingency planning capability using decision trees into otherwise well-developed fault and event tree concepts. My thinking has been influenced by following some of the many useful contributions by authors like Perrow (1984, 1994), Reason (1990, 1997), Wynne (1992) and Woods et al (2010), but I am not up to date on this literature.

One big opportunity in this area from an EP perspective flows from initiating analysis with a top-down corporate strategy concern for all very high impact incidents, starting with a maximum plausible impact scenario perspective to avoid a complex set of bias and blind spot concerns. Another is seeing a key aspect of risk as departures from expectations with all the conceptual and operational tools which flow from the clarity, risk, and overall opportunity-efficiency aspects of an EP approach, including enlightened prudence concerns. The relevant incidents may be accidental or malicious. Using this perspective we can decompose and structure all associated safety and security concerns, working from the most important towards the least important. *All* relevant stealth assumptions and other unknown unknowns need to be accommodated in the analysis at all relevant levels. Particularly crucial is ensuring that the unknown unknowns are addressed in terms of robust and resilient plans which include appropriate provisions and prudence considerations. This is the approach Chapter 9 outlines, using a railway safety and security context with a top-down focus on catastrophic scenarios to avoid bias and blind spots as well as ensuring full integration at a strategic level. But it is relevant in many other contexts, and in all these contexts contributing bottom-up analysis has to play a very important role. For example, the application of contingency planning in the SCERT driven approach to estimation discussed in Chapter 3, and its elaboration in Chapman and Ward (2011), can deal with unknown unknowns of various kinds at all levels.

This perspective and the implied scope of the relevant underlying literature separates it from a mainstream ERM (Enterprise Risk Management) approach like that suggested by Duckert (2010) or AIRMIC/ALARM/IRM (2010), and much other mainstream 'risk management' as discussed next. However, there is no reason all the *compatible* ideas from all sources cannot be synthesised. Adopting the Chapter 9 perspective opens a rich set of opportunities for further development, but it can also embrace all the useful features of current approaches.

Risk management

From an EP perspective, anyone using the term 'risk management' in their current job or departmental label or professional affiliations needs to address several key issues, and everyone else needs an overview understanding of these issues.

One is the toolset and associated skill set plus mindset implications driven by the definitions adopted for 'risk', 'opportunity', 'uncertainty' and 'complexity'. The broadly defined 'risk management community' uses the term 'risk' to mean radically different things to different people in different contexts, with nuances associated with these interpretations changing over time, and complex associated implications for what is meant by 'opportunity', 'uncertainty' and 'complexity'. This is a source of serious confusion with crucially important and very complex implications in many different areas and contexts.

Another is the mindset implications of using the terms 'risk *management*' and 'risk *manager*' when 'risk management *planning*' or 'risk management *coordination*' or 'risk management *enabling*' might be a better term because clarifying the need for others to actually manage the decision making directly involved would more accurately reflect the collaborative teamwork required. Although 'risk managers' in some contexts may have crucial duty of care and legal compliance concerns to manage, the most effective ways to achieve organisation-wide compliance with a best practice approach may be best seen as 'enabling' in a 'team coach' sense, not 'blocking' in a 'compliance enforcement' sense, with requisite compliance concerns addressed in a deliberately unobtrusive manner. The spirit of 'promoting and protecting the good as well as contesting and constraining the bad' is a useful general perspective.

These key issues raise interdependent problematic concerns which are overdue for effective consideration and resolution by all the key players in 'the risk management community' broadly defined.

If we start with the meaning of 'risk', it may be worth emphasising that this is by no means a new problem, nor am I the only one concerned. Arguments about appropriate boundaries for 'risk' concepts have been going on for at least a century. Some attack very specific issues, like Cox (2008). Some people are so fed up with the whole business they have suggested, not entirely in jest, that the basic word *risk* is itself not really necessary (Dowie, 1999). The EP position is that 'risk' is a crucially important word, and a plain English basic interpretation linked to compatible interpretations of 'opportunity', 'uncertainty', 'complexity' and other associated terms plus clear working assumptions within very broad framing assumptions is the only plausible way forward, as discussed in detail in Chapter 1. This view is unlikely to attract unanimous support. You will have to make your own judgement and act accordingly based on your own circumstances.

Parts 1 and 2 explored the implications of the overall EP toolset in some detail at a strategic clarity level. You will need more tactical clarity to fully understand how to do it in specific areas where that is your direct responsibility, but a suitable set of conceptual and operational tools to address 'what needs to be done' is a key aspect of what this book as a whole is about. Skill set and mindset issues build on the toolset issues in an interdependent manner. They are very complex, but important, and the focus of capability-culture aspects of the EP perspective.

Chapter 7 was explicitly critical of a current mainstream project risk management perspective which sees project risk management as an 'add-on' to the rest of project planning and project management more generally. The tale of Chapter 7 built directly on an 'add-in' perspective developed in more detail by Chapman and Ward (2011) to provide a 'designed-in' approach. What the additional development of Chapter 7 involved in terms of important details had not been fully developed and thought through until writing Chapter 7 of this book, although the strategy adopted was explicitly recommended in the 2011 book plus its earlier 2003 and 1997 editions. Indeed, it was actually implicit in my 1970s and 1980s work with BP and other clients. In more implicit terms this critique applies to operations and corporate planning and management contexts, especially the latter if an event-based approach is involved. Furthermore, safety and security as addressed in Chapter 9 involve some related themes.

The key opportunity for those directly interested in risk management as a discipline or as a professional label is embracing the full implications of responding to a general need for a much broader scope for their agenda to appropriate aspects of opportunity as well as risk, plus underlying uncertainty and complexity, working with others more collaboratively to address this much broader scope of work. In many contexts this includes abandoning the idea that risk *managers* manage the risk so others in the organisation can leave risk to the risk managers and recognising that *everybody* has to take direct appropriate responsibility for the full interplay of opportunity, risk, uncertainty and complexity associated with their role.

Risk Management Organisation and Context (Ward, 2005) is an Institute of Risk Management (IRM) textbook which, unlike most professional society guides and standards, discusses the controversial nature of definitions of risk and uncertainty with clarity in a comprehensive manner. But all professional organisations with risk management concerns need clear statements about their particular approaches in relation to the wide range of alternative views taken by all relevant players.

The key challenge for *all readers* and *everyone* affected is dealing with the implications if risk managers and their supporting professional societies do not see these toolset, skill set, and mindset changes as an opportunity and resist them as a challenge. If the risk management community does not rise to the challenge of dealing with these issues, the risk managers in some organisation may themselves become identifiable risks which you and your colleagues might have to deal with effectively.

Lean and agile approaches

'Agile' approaches using operational tools derived from 'lean' enterprise approaches were not discussed earlier, but if we adopt plain English interpretations of 'agile' and 'lean', arguably being agile and employing a lean perspective are central characteristics of much of EP. A section addressing lean and agile approaches in this final chapter is relevant, in part, because there is a current very widespread resurgence in interest in these approaches; in part, because they overlap with a wide range of issues which an EP perspective has to address; and, in part because they provide one useful example of a wide range of alternative perspectives which need embracing by any approach to planning which is general by design in the EP sense.

'Lean enterprises' as explored in books like *When Lean Enterprises Collide: Competing Through Confrontation* (Cooper, 1995) have their origins in fundamental changes in the way organisations operate, initially developed by Toyota and a number of other leading Japanese corporations that transformed Japanese industry in the 1950s and 1960s. Lean enterprise conceptual and operational tools have since become embraced worldwide. For example, most managers will have heard of, and perhaps used, aspects of 'Total Quality Management'.

Some of these lean tools are specific techniques or models, like 'Just-In-Time' approaches to supply chain inventories, mentioned in Chapter 5, and treated as a special case of the 'Your-Place-My-Time' variants discussed for TLC.

Other lean tools are very general conceptual models, like 'the survival triplet', which involves cost price plus functionality plus quality, assuming carefully defined distinctions between cost and price and a decomposition of functionality, as discussed in the book by Cooper (1995) cited earlier. This approach is consistent with the Chapter 6 approach to bidding when Astro addresses a search for value added.

Futures planning, as portrayed by Figure 8.1 and discussed in Chapters 8 and 10, is one area where being agile is particularly important. A central EP concern is being 'agile' when considering the way futures planning needs to be driven by goals planning, and the way futures planning needs to then interface with short-term planning, as well as medium- and long-term planning, with direct implications for overall corporate planning, operations planning, and project planning. In Chapter 8 a key working assumption was long-term, medium-term, and short-term *base* plans should focus on what was assumed to be feasible, but associated *contingency* plans should address possible new opportunities that futures planning plus projects driven by making currently non-feasible options feasible might deliver. This is about highly proactive and ambitious 'agile planning' in a plain English sense, maintaining a robust feasible solution fall-back position while systematically trying to do better. It is an approach which should generalise, bearing in mind different contexts may involve much shorter time horizons than those relevant to an electricity utility. But it is not an explicit focus for agile planning or related lean approaches in the technical senses used by the many authors addressing these topics in the literature.

Early in 2017 I became interested in better understanding the relationship between agile planning tools directly linked to lean organisations and EP tools. Several developments then fostered this interest, and a few related comments here may relevant to your concerns.

The initial trigger was my younger son Andy asking me to read *Lean Enterprise: How High Performance Organisations Innovate at Scale* (Humble, Molesky, and O'Reilly, 2015), and let him know what I thought about the efficacy of agile approaches to project planning. He was encouraging several key players managing a software programme to adopt a more formal approach to planning, and they were resisting, one of them citing this book as the rationale for what could be interpreted as an absence of the useful discipline which the programme's owner wanted Andy to instil. The agile approach in question seemed to promote less focus on clearly defined project deliverables and associated cost and duration outcomes. Comparing an EP approach and an agile perspective in the lean approach sense looks like an interesting area for further work from both perspectives, and it is near the top of my 'to do' list.

Associated agile approaches to project planning have a wide range of both promoters and detractors. Their current growth has significant and widespread implications. As one immediately useful illustrative example of what is involved, from an agile perspective all project management methodologies are often put on a spectrum from 'plan-driven' to

'Scrum' interpretations of 'agile', the latter using a series of 'sprints' in place of more conventional detailed tactical plans which elaborate strategic plans on a rolling basis. A simple characterisation of a plan-driven approach to project planning is a traditional 'waterfall' approach. PMI (2017b) explores linking this end of the plan-driven to Scrum spectrum to agile approaches. The most recent edition of the PMBOK project management guide (PMI, 2017a) also addresses these issues, as does a 2017 APM publication. Scrum approaches (Rubin, 2013) can vary significantly, but a simple example is a software development project which explicitly avoids predefined criteria for outcome goals, assuming that incremental evolution in a very flexible planning framework is more effective than attempting to eliminate what some writers on agile approaches call 'end uncertainty'. Some advocates of agile approaches claim that risk and opportunity, as well as agility and discipline, can be balanced to make agile approaches highly resilient, issues explored by Boehm and Turner (2003, 2004) for example. However, a broad study of agile project risk management literature by Gold and Vassell (2015) suggests that there are serious ongoing problems which can only be overcome by risk management approaches which are more compatible philosophically and practically than current common project risk management practice. It seems reasonably clear from an EP perspective that SP for projects adaptations could address these agile perspective concerns, but it is not immediately obvious to me what the best way forward might be.

One possible approach would involve exploiting the advantages of the 'uncertainty management' aspects of an EP approach which Black (2017) attributes to my uncertainty management work with Stephen Ward over several decades. In Black's words, 'What makes Chapman & Ward "Risk Originals" is they have developed a risk control approach that focuses on maturing controls in order to reduce the uncertainty that creates risk, rather than attempting to actually predict the risks'. That is, deal with the 'end uncertainty' by replacing a plan-driven concern for end-point clarity with a more flexible 'maturing controls' approach.

However, the opportunity efficiency driven framing assumptions underlying an EP approach suggests acknowledging an enlightened view about the ambiguous nature of end of project goals at a detailed tactical planning level within a sprint framework, but sustaining a focus on 'clarified ambiguity' during the strategic planning stages. From an EP perspective, a sustained search for clarity about what will be delivered and associated cost and duration outcomes ought to remain a concern in the sense that strategic goals need articulation and systematic ongoing attention to maintain a clear sense of direction, even if the details of what the goals are remain unclear, and how they might be achieved also remains unclear.

Just how this might be done, whether or not an intermediate D&A strategy progress stage tailored to agile planning would be needed, and whether or not some of the portfolio analysis ideas discussed in Chapter 8 might be relevant to hedge bets about what the achievement of end goals might involve, are not clear to me. What is clear is the interface between futures planning and other planning in the Chapter 8 sense may be central, context specific issues would inevitably be particularly crucial, and thinking through how best to adjust the SP for projects as discussed for WSL in Chapter 7 would require considerable care. Indeed, synthesising 'agile', 'Scrum', and related non-conventional methodological perspectives with a sound overall EP approach driven by strategic clarity is a good example of the challenges facing any attempt to develop a fully comprehensive 'universal SP for projects'.

Linking agile approaches to project planning to the SP for projects of Chapter 7 and the broader issue of linking EP as a whole to lean approaches to organisations remains a work in progress for me. If this area is of special interest to you, it may be useful to begin by seeing different people's definitions of 'lean' and 'agile' and related terms as raising problems which are directly comparable to different people using very different technical definitions for 'risk', 'opportunity', 'uncertain' and 'complexity'. The exponential acceleration of the rate of change over the past few decades is a key reason for considering the use of an EP framework for carefully integrating our collective wisdom about agility in a lean sense plus agility defined in more general terms from all relevant perspectives.

The HAT framework and Monte Carlo simulation approaches

The basic question addressed in this section is:

> *If an analysis involves multiple sources of uncertainty which require probabilistic modelling, what is the best way to estimate probability distributions for each source and then compute and display the combinations required, given an extensive range of possible assumptions about both probability distribution specifications for each source and interdependency patterns between sources?*

This section briefly consolidates what most readers need to understand for strategic clarity, and it also provides some initial information for those readers with further tactical clarity concerns. It links the HAT framework used throughout this book to the Monte Carlo simulation approaches many readers will be familiar with and addresses computer software choice concerns of importance in all practice contexts.

Prior to about 1960, many practitioners and academics assumed methods of moments was the best general answer to the question this section addresses, usually using a mean–variance approach. For example, Markowitz (1959) used a mean–variance model for financial investment portfolio planning purposes, and quadratic programming was developed to exploit this model. Initial 1950s' approaches to PERT used a different very simple mean–variance approach, assuming independence between activities on the critical path, with no subcritical paths becoming critical. A mean–variance approach can be clarity efficient if the key working assumptions required hold, but they rarely do.

A somewhat separate school of thought, which was well developed prior to 1960, used discrete probability tree approaches, sometimes with specific forms like fault trees and event trees for safety analysis purposes, sometimes with a focus on decision trees for 'decision analysis' or 'decision theory' purposes. This school of thought continues to command a lot of interest, unlike approaches based on moments.

After about 1980, most practitioners assumed stochastic models of any size required computer software based on Monte Carlo simulation or some other variant of sampling to assess the combined effect of several sources of uncertainty. For example, by this time most people using PERT models employed PERT software which used Monte Carlo simulation to address 'criticality' in stochastic model terms, and many decision analysis texts recommended Monte Carlo simulation for complex probability tree structures, referring to this option as 'risk analysis'. Some people had used these Monte Carlo simulation methods manually before computers, there are some 'non-reducible' combinations which cannot be solved by sequential discrete probability distribution methods, and some people interested in simulation modelling simply did not worry about reducibility issues. However, it was the power and speed of modern computers plus the availability of reasonably inexpensive off-the-shelf simulation packages which changed common practice and made approaches to stochastic (probabilistic) modelling using simulation the norm.

In the 1970s, when the SCERT model and its prototypes were being developed, my modelling preference was a prototype HAT framework because interdependences between sources had to be modelled effectively and efficiently, and causal dependence structures driven by decision tree structures were central to my concerns and those of my clients. I still believe that a HAT approach conceptual basis is by far the best way to understand these issues. That is the rationale for the HAT based approach taken in Parts 1 and 2 of this book.

In the early 1980s, I still believed that the kind of HAT software developed by BP, and used by Acres for several Canadian and US studies, was the best way forward in operational terms, because apart from the conceptual power of the HAT framework it was about 1,000 times faster than a sampling equivalent for a comparable level of computational precision/ error. That is why the BP/Acres collaboration which facilitated Acre's use of BP software was very important to me. Sampling approaches involve sampling error, normally reduced by larger samples, although sampling stratification approaches are also possible. Discrete probability arithmetic HAT approaches involve a computational error associated with using a discrete representation of variables which are actually continuous, discussed in Chapter 3 in terms of just adding two sources of uncertainty defined by uniform distributions. When rectangular histograms involving n histogram classes are involved and n = 10 or more this computational error is reduced dramatically, but it can be further reduced by a correction based on one-eighth the difference between adjacent class probabilities being moved from the higher probability class to the adjacent lower probability class, as discussed in Cooper and Chapman (1987) and other earlier publications. That is, functional integration techniques can be used to size and correct the computational error. Furthermore, this software approach is not limited to addition operations. It can deal with multiplication, division and 'greatest' operations, the latter necessary for merge events in a network model.

By the late 1980s I had given up the idea of discrete probability arithmetic HAT based computer software becoming readily available on a commercial basis, and advised all users of HAT based approaches to employ commercially available Monte Carlo simulation software appropriate to their application areas, with several key provisos.

First, they needed to understand and model all relevant interdependencies, avoiding a common tendency to assume independence, usefully stated as a 0% dependence assumption.

Second, usually perfect positive correlation was a better default assumption than independence if a low clarity analysis was appropriate, usefully stated as a 100% positive dependence assumption.

Third, sometimes a 70% or 80% positive dependence assumption was a reasonable and very useful improvement on 0% or 100% assumptions, defined by interpolation, an approach tested empirically by studies for BP concerned with the cost of refineries.

Fourth, it was crucial to have the capability to use much more complex dependence structures whenever this was clarity efficient, drawing on a range of approaches illustrated in the Part 2 tales.

Fifth, it was crucial to provide a full set of relevant sensitivity diagrams, like Figure 4.1 or simpler variants, using whatever nested structure best suited the working assumptions about interdependences. Pairwise separability was a particularly useful basis for thinking about specifying estimates of uncertainty incorporating interdependence, computing results incorporating interdependence, and then portraying of the way uncertainty accumulates net of all responses of both specific and general forms.

Put slightly differently, it doesn't really matter what computational basis drives the software employed, *provided* the capabilities discussed in Parts 1 and 2 of this book are feasible. Simulation capabilities when non-reducible computational sequences need confronting may prove an invaluable further capability in some particularly complex contexts. An understanding of clarity efficient software choices if and when a lot of modelling and computation is involved may also prove very useful. However, if your organisation does a limited amount of this kind of modelling, then clarity efficiency will dictate the initial use of off the shelf software. You can later consider alternatives more fully when you are clear what you need.

Just be very careful that the initial software choice does not constrain your organisation's understanding of what really matters. You may have to work at ensuring that sensitivity diagrams and decision diagrams are produced as required, and dependence is modelled as required. Bear in mind the simulation structure has to reflect any pairwise separability assumed for sensitivity diagram purposes, more general separability assumptions may be important in some contexts, and some simulation packages may make separate packages necessary for a flexible approach to sensitivity diagrams and decision diagrams.

If you are particularly interested in software, it might be useful to start with the most flexible Monte Carlo simulation software package available. As a first step, build input modules which facilitate direct and easy specification of sensitivity diagram structures within a pairwise separable structure when non-reducible structures are not involved. Then add a hybrid approach to computation which exploits reducible combinations using computation error corrected probability arithmetic when this is feasible, if this capability looks cost-effective. The most important issue is the flexibility to facilitate employing the most effective forms of modelling in the contexts of interest. Almost as important is making it easy to obtain the form of output needed so that everyone involved can understand what the analysis is saying, as it evolves during the iterative analysis process, and later when it is used by senior decision makers. Modern computers make computational efficiency issues a relatively unimportant tertiary concern in most contexts.

Regulation and related issues

Most of the private and public sector commercial organisations which are the focus of this book need to consider taking a proactive approach to the regulation of their sector, for a variety of reasons. Some reasons are obvious, some perhaps less obvious. One reason worth emphasising here is the need for 'good' organisations to collaborate to ensure that regulators do their best to maintain a level playing field for good organisations, proactively promoting and protecting all good organisations, contesting and constraining, if not pre-emptively driving out, all 'bad' organisations.

Some regulators might make use of some of the ideas explored in this book and work in a collaborative manner with the organisations they regulate where and when this is in the best interests of the citizens they serve. They might also work with other regulators to make 'enlightened regulation' using 'systematic simplicity' an area of serious development, feeding into and leading linked political developments – not just waiting for politicians to direct them.

Crucially, politicians and the layers of government between them and regulators need to actively promote and protect 'good' regulators who act in this way, contest and constrain 'bad' regulators who manage ineffectively or collude with those they are supposed to regulate, showing enlightened governance of the regulation system.

In his first public address as a recently appointed chairman of the UK Health and Safety Executive (HSE), Martin Temple made several points of relevance to this book's perspective on all aspects of regulation, some very directly and highly relevant to the EP perspective developed in this book (Temple, 2016).

First, people working at all levels in a regulatory organisation can and should start with a passion for looking after the best interests of those they serve – employees in UK organisations and the general public in the HSE case.

Second, looking after the best interests of those they serve successfully is most effectively achieved via an 'enabling' approach rather than a 'blocking' approach to those they need to regulate – primarily industry in the HSE case. Enlightened industry leaders will see the value of aligned objectives. However, if any industry leaders do not demonstrate requisite enlightenment, firm enforcement is also required.

Third, embedding core values at a board level which are communicated to and embraced by all an organisation's employees and contractors is crucial.

Fourth, some of the challenges take society into very new territory which needs great care and insight – like the impact of growing cybersecurity concerns in relation to chemical industry facilities and other potentially dangerous contexts in the HSE case.

Fifth, *very* difficult issues to deal with, like long-term health effects, are not being addressed as effectively as more obvious issues like fatalities, but even cursory use of what data is available suggests they are several orders of magnitude more important than the current focus of attention of the HSE, industry, and society more generally.

My invitation to attend Martin Temple's address arose because I had been an invited speaker (Chapman, 2002) for an earlier session in the same series of annual lectures, and I went because the summary of Temple's paper provided with the invitation suggested it might be relevant to this book, which it certainly was. There is a very good case for arguing that variants of all the ideas he outlined as summarised above need addressing by all regulators, with strong support from all relevant layers of the governments responsible for their governance. There is also a strong case for linking this perspective to the growing use across the world of very big fines by a wide variety of regulators for a wide variety of behaviours deemed unacceptable. And there is a good case for arguing that regulators need to be agile and enlightened users of sound goals planning, futures planning, and long-term planning which anticipates and avoids regulatory problems before they become serious crises, with the powers, attitude, courage, and resilience needed to take on big international corporations which abuse their power. The whole business of regulation can and should embrace massive change to confront a wide range of challenges, with important international implications.

'Regulation' can be defined and addressed in very broad terms, going well beyond traditional government directed regulation. It can include forms of self-regulation which those who favour minimal government interference will clearly want to encourage. However, the limitations as well as the strengths of all approaches to regulation clearly need addressing, scrutiny by a proactive investigative press and other investigative media is crucial, and policing the overall effectiveness and efficiency of all regulation is ultimately a government responsibility.

A particular current concern which illustrates one aspect of the complexities involved is the need for a generalised view of 'level playing fields' which involves national government responses to the taxation of multinational companies which ensure that no honest and competent businesses operating in that nation are disadvantaged by any businesses indulging in aggressive tax avoidance, regardless of the physical or nominal domicile locations of these organisations. Related legal system responses may also be essential. National governments have to look after the interests of *all* that nation's businesses as well as *all* that nation's consumers in a balanced manner, as part of looking after *all* that nation's citizens. Due regard to international collaboration at a range of levels, some not necessarily involving governments directly, has to be a part of this approach.

A famous quote from the Melian dialogue by Thucydides (a Greek historian who lived about 460–400 BC) is 'the strong do what they can and the weak suffer what they must'. Regulators and their sponsoring governments might do well to also consider a quote from

Thucydides's *History of the Peloponnesian War* – 'when one is deprived of one's liberty, one is right blaming not so much the man who put the shackles on as the one who had the power to prevent him, but did not use it'. In the present context 'liberty' needs interpretation to cover the interests which regulators might address of all the citizens they serve, as both 'buyers' of services or products in a private consumer or corporate context, and as 'sellers' of labour, skills, capital, services, or products in a private citizen or corporate context. Being at liberty to unfairly exploit markets will always be a clear goal for some people and some organisations, and some will try to protect this liberty by promoting a minimal government involvement in regulation or public sector provision of services. Good regulators, with the support of good governments, will successfully 'promote and protect "good" citizens and organisations and contest and constrain "bad" citizens and organisations'.

Regulation which embraces in an effective and efficient manner what is fair and reasonable, as well as what is economically efficient, is essential to make a capitalist system desirable for the majority as well as acceptable for everyone else. What is 'fair' and 'reasonable' is debatable, and managing associated ambiguity is an inherent part of the planning problems which have to be confronted. But there is growing evidence that a very complex set of drivers of change in public expectations about regulation and associated governance by their controlling governments is swinging public opinion and political agendas radically in directions which are quite new and fundamentally different in the UK, in Europe generally, in the US and Canada, and in many other parts of the world.

For example, in September 2017 a Populus poll of UK citizens showed massive support for the nationalisation of various industries, from 83% for water through 50% for banks to 23% for travel agents. As Hugo Rifkind commented in an article citing these results with the title 'For Generation Rent, Owning Things Is History' (Rifkind, 2017), 'what on earth is going on?' Rifkind, like me, was particularly surprised by 23% wanting travel agents nationalised. He offered some very interesting suggestions, but several other interesting articles in the same edition addressed directly related concerns, and the wide range of views being expressed in the UK media as a whole suggests we clearly need a much more coherent understanding of the questions which need to be addressed before attempting coherent answers for any given country of interest.

One thought which may interest some regulators and other readers interested in regulation is that emergent government policy on regulation led by bold and innovative regulators seems to be gaining ground, and provided it is led by good regulators who are both competent and motivated to serve 'the right social interests', this looks like a very promising development. In particular, it suggests a nuanced separation of the leadership and governance of regulation from some aspects of direct political pressures which may be very helpful. However, regulators are watchdogs that need to be empowered by governments, and they need effective teeth as well as fearsome growls and tails that wag which are not feasible without coherent long-term government support.

It would be naïve to think that appropriate government support might be achieved without having to overcome exceedingly difficult obstacles in some areas, and even if governments are determined to resolve the issues, reaching a consensus on key concerns is going to prove very difficult in many areas of regulation that really matter. As an example, in his 2016 book *The End of Alchemy: Money, Banking and the Future of the Global Economy*, Mervyn King, governor of the Bank of England from 2003 until 2013, a distinguished economist with international credentials, makes a number of important and practical suggestions about the need for financial regulation which less concerned about the best interests of those who are part of the finance industry they are supposed to regulate and more concerned about non-financial industry organisations and most of their country's citizens. At the heart of King's recommendations is public sector ownership of the money supply, private sector ownership of all financial industry organisations, including banks and organisations operating like banks. Crucially, the government and its central bank would refuse to continue to play the role of 'lender of last resort' (or 'insurer of last resort') with respect to any financial industry organisations. There would be much simpler regulation of the financial industry, which addresses all the 'right questions', with a view to what is in the best interests of the county as a whole. The government's central bank would provide a 'pawnbroker for all seasons' role. Related regulation would require finance industry organisations to pre-position collateral which would become government central bank property if liquidity loans provided by the central bank were not repaid. The pre-positioning agreements would involve 'haircuts' to ensure that the realisable value of the assets used as collateral exceeded the loans, as required by pawnbrokers (or prudent mortgage providers including banks). This looks eminently sensible and practical in an enlightened planning sense as far as I can judge, although I do not profess expertise in this area. This kind of thinking is certainly worth very careful consideration in the context of a clear need for a new approach to financial regulation which is effective from the point of view of the population as a whole. But King is not optimistic about the rate at which progress might be made because it would be firmly resisted by a powerful set of people with influential allies. In effect, there is a widely understood argument that the financial sector is currently being subsidised by everyone else, a less well-understood argument that regulation is overcomplicated in the 'wrong way' because it is addressing the 'wrong questions'. King has useful ideas about avoiding the current subsidy situation which would be less expensive for the banks than the more extreme capitalisation requirements which have earlier been assumed to be the only solution available, but King's suggestions, as well as the more expensive alternatives, will be resisted by a financial sector which wants to preserve its current advantageous position.

The underlying economics driving bank runs that led to the 2008 financial crisis are even more complicated and difficult to deal with. The nature of some of this complexity is also explored by King, from a perspective which has an EP flavour in some very interesting respects. However, convincing evidence of effective solutions likely to be forthcoming from current macroeconomic thinking was not provided from my perspective. The macroeconomic problems involved are not going to go away, and resolving them matters greatly to everyone, but the first priority is a consensus on regulation which is effective even if there is no consensus on a coherent understanding of the underlying economic issues.

A review by Gerard Baker (Baker, 2018) of *Capitalism in America: A History* (Greenspan and Wooldridge, 2018) begins by noting that an August 2018 Fox News survey reported 36% of US citizens said it would be a good thing to "move away from capitalism to more socialism". Alan Greenspan has played a central banking role in the US which has perhaps been even more prominent than Mervyn King's comparable role in the UK, and the review approaches its conclusion noting that Greenspan and Wooldridge argue that a robustly free-market approach with minimal government involvement is the American tradition, with a long history of success despite some bumps along the way, and betting against this argument might be unwise.

I suspect Greenspan and most minimal government advocates living in the US or any other country would not be keen on strong and effective regulation of the financial sector or any other sector in what an EP perspective might judge a 'socially optimal' manner. However, *significant* direct involvement of governments in *simple* but *effective* regulation, and encouraging *some* use of novel public sector organisations comparable to the recommended

Canpower approach of Chapter 8 to provide government leadership of issues like energy market management, *addressing the right questions*, has to be part of any enlightened government approach in my view. Encouraging novel private sector organisations like the WSL local and national asset companies discussed in Chapter 10, building on the Chapter 7 discussion of a UK private sector water and sewage utility, may also be useful. A completely unconstrained free-market approach with no coherent, centralised government decision-making input into issues like financial markets and energy markets does not seem viable for a host of reasonably obvious reasons, and however limited the regulation level you believe to be appropriate, an EP perspective should be useful.

Chapter 10 addresses effective ways a private sector organisation like a water and sewage utility in the UK might set up novel private sector organisations to help serve local and national citizens in ways which are beneficial for the local and national private and corporate customers they serve. The issues involved are certainly not simple, but an enlightened approach based on a consensus view of what really matters seems viable. The Canpower discussion of Chapter 8 explores how an organisation in the electricity utility industry in Canada which was owned by the citizens it served but was prepared to transform itself from a traditional public sector organisation into something very different might operate. Again, the issues involved are certainly not simple, but an enlightened approach based on a consensus view of what really matters seems viable.

The final section in Chapter 9 builds on a railway safety and security context discussion to explore a number of important private and public sector contexts where a consensus view on the best way forward seems much more difficult. All these contexts require well-founded trust supported by high clarity analysis of exceedingly complex issues. They all also involve pressures from interested parties with conflicting narratives tailored to the messages they want to sell which will tend to ensure ongoing controversy and confusion.

All these contexts require enlightened regulators with strong and effective government backing, and relatively simple regulatory rules addressing the right questions, instead of relatively complex rules addressing the wrong questions. In all these contexts we need effective regulatory and other direct government action which is not dependent on achieving a consensus on a full detailed understanding of underlying factors. Key issues include the effective regulation of organisations which might be directly responsible for large numbers of fatalities or ongoing health difficulties because of pollution of many kinds, including nuclear contamination. Example concerns include the very complex issues associated with the current movement towards electric and hydrogen motive power and linked reduced use of fossil fuels for other purposes, for a range of health and environmental reasons, in conjunction with the need to address coherent and coordinated plans for supplying the resulting increased demand for electricity. A common central argument is current approaches are clearly unenlightened when they involve leaving key aspects of decision making to private sector organisations in contexts which very clearly need a holistic national perspective and an integrated overall approach to achieve outcomes in the best interests of the majority of the population. The basic problems arising from a lack of requisite government controlled direct management are often aggravated by a lack of effectively coordinated regulation, and in some cases by an absence of requisite international cooperation. This seems to me an inescapable fact of life, whatever the nature of government you prefer. Even in these very difficult cases, effective coordinated decision making and regulation is clearly essential, and some variants of the novel public and private sector approaches just mentioned in conjunction with other EP concepts might provide a contribution to an enlightened way forward. Assuming that doing nothing new is appropriate is certainly not a viable option.

Politics and associated public pressure

Politics, and the public pressure that drives political decision making, is an inescapable aspect of reality which all commercial organisations have to deal with. This includes, but is not limited to, the way governments approach regulation.

All organisations adopting any plausible variant of an EP approach have to accommodate the implications of their political environment, and associated public pressure, as effectively and efficiently as possible. Several of the Part 2 tales illustrate what might be involved. The key is making working assumptions which are realistic, systematically testing the robustness of all associated assumptions, looking for opportunities as well as threats, and adopting a proactive 'designing desirable futures' approach whenever this may be useful. A traditional 'predict and prepare' mindset is not opportunity efficient. Proactively seeking opportunities as well as looking for and avoiding threats is crucial, and collaboration essential.

Individual citizens addressing broad social concerns, not organisations or pressure groups, arguably ought to determine government policy. However, collaboration via single issue or multiple issue pressure groups is undoubtedly more effective than exercising lone voices, and wider collaboration via political parties which successfully align a coherent set of objectives is undoubtedly the most sensible approach for most purposes.

Some hypotheses for putting together and managing coherent political groups might be inferred from this book's EP approach. However, the context is very different, with important implications. For example, if we begin with the working assumption 'the majority' ought to define the 'central ground' in a way which may incorporate most political parties but not their extremes, one obvious complexity is the complications associated with adversarial approaches by key political parties or factions within them having a dysfunctional effect on majority best interests, including the viability of this working assumption. An even more fundamental example complication is political views are founded on framing assumptions we might debate in stealth assumption terms, but they are also based on personal context and cultural values which are not usually debatable in any direct or objective manner.

These issues are well beyond my areas of experience, and it would not be useful for me to speculate on them in this book, but in the context of all broad social concerns as well as all commercial organisations of interest to you they should not just be put in a 'too difficult' box, because they matter greatly.

Using 'smiles' as an indicator of EP effectiveness

When I was giving public seminars and short courses on project risk management processes in the 1980s, building on work with BP and linked work with other clients, a challenge which had to be addressed was people who were acclimatised to very informal and unstructured approaches to planning feeling that the structured and formalised processes I was advocating, like SCERT, would restrict their ability to be creative, reducing job satisfaction.

Part of the response was developing and explaining a 'smiles test', which has gradually evolved into Figure 11.1. You might like to study the form and content of Figure 11.1 very briefly before its background and interpretation are explored.

When I went into an organisation where those involved in planning didn't smile very much, one possible working assumption, soon viewed as a hypothesis worth testing, was that they were unhappy with their work or working environment for reasons which might involve important capability-culture liabilities needing exploration. A linked working assumption which seemed to hold true was that if they became familiar with formal

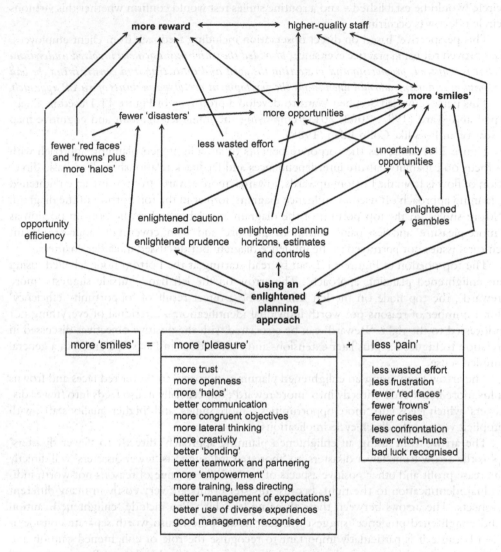

Figure 11.1 Corporate benefits of using an enlightened planning approach with a focus on smiles and associated capability-culture concerns, including the way these concerns drive 'reward' (profit and other positive objectives).

processes of the prototype EP kind being advocated and used them effectively, they would not be constrained and bored by the kind of discipline involved – quite the opposite. They would be set free, enabled, and encouraged to ask the right questions and then answer the right questions in the most effective manner feasible within the time available. They could do so by being innovative when generating the most appropriate responses, greatly increasing their creativity and job satisfaction. This would tend to mean good people were attracted to and stayed with the planning groups in these organisations, and because their roles became more demanding as the scope of the jobs increased, people who were not so good at it would tend to leave and be replaced by people who were better at it. A 'virtuous circle' would be established – and a routine smiles test would confirm whether this virtuous circle effect was occurring.

This perspective, based on direct observation including feedback from client employees, has proved robust in practice ever since, *provided the senior management involved understand what is required, promoting and protecting the good and contesting and constraining the bad as part of endorsing a broad agenda for the development prototype variants of an EP approach.*

This perspective led Stephen Ward to develop a prototype of Figure 11.1 used in Chapman and Ward (1997, 2002, 2011) employing the influence diagram and cognitive map ideas of authors like Colin Eden (1988).

Figure 11.1 addresses the corporate benefits of an enlightened planning approach with a focus on capability-culture interdependences and feedback relationships. The basic direction of flow is from the bottom upwards, towards 'more reward' from 'using an enlightened planning approach'. It uses an 'influence diagram' format in the top portion of the diagram. 'More smiles' in the top portion of the diagram are elaborated in the bottom portion as 'more pleasure' and 'less pain', with both 'pleasure' and 'pain' covering a range of relevant cultural issues not portrayed in the influence diagram but discussed in earlier chapters.

The top portion of Figure 11.1 can be read starting at the bottom node labelled 'using an enlightened planning approach'. The arrow on the left-hand outside suggests 'more reward', the top node on the left side, will be a direct result of 'opportunity efficiency' for a number of reasons not worth individual identification – a residual of everything not addressed to the right. 'Reward' can be associated with the positive objectives discussed in relation to Figure 3.8 plus later extensions and clarifications in Parts 1, 2 and 3 in a general unified sense.

The arrow from 'using an enlightened planning approach' to 'fewer red faces and frowns plus more halos' feeds directly into 'more reward', but crucially it also feeds into 'fewer disasters' which feeds into 'more opportunities', 'more smiles' and 'higher-quality staff', with implicit virtuous feedback cycle implications.

The arrow from 'using an enlightened planning approach' directly to 'fewer disasters' plus the arrow from 'fewer disasters' to 'more reward' suggests 'fewer disasters' will directly increase profit and other positive aspects of 'reward' for a range of reasons not worth individual identification to the right, because disaster events are very costly in many different respects. The arrows between these three nodes which also include 'enlightened caution and enlightened prudence' suggest this four-node route is also worth separate consideration because it is particularly important to recognise the role of enlightened caution and prudence even if the concern for avoided disasters is not directly relevant. Both routes send arrows to 'more smiles', which sends an arrow to 'higher-quality staff'.

'Higher-quality staff' is at the same top level as 'more reward' because an important top-level two way relationship is involved, again with implicit virtuous feedback cycle implications.

All the other arrows tell the same sort of story. 'Fewer disasters', 'more opportunities' and 'more smiles are all at roughly the same level, just below the top level, but moving to the right involves even more dependencies, including some important two way dependencies. 'Less wasted effort' and 'uncertainty as opportunities' are at the next level down, both feeding upwards. 'Enlightened gambles' are at the same level as enlightened caution and enlightened prudence', with slight differences in implications. 'Enlightened planning horizons, estimates, and controls' have different implications again. The two way arrows involve feedback as well as feedforward, the basis of explicit virtuous circles in this case.

The summary boxes associated with 'more smiles = more pleasure + less pain' draws together associated messages scattered through this book.

You might like to regard the 'soft' or systematic approach to qualitative concerns portrayed by Figure 11.1 as an illustration of the need to go well beyond quantitative analysis, understanding all the key qualitative analysis features in a framework which encourages and facilitates thinking about non-separable qualitative issues, before you even consider starting a quantitative analysis.

You might wish to revise the top portion of this diagram, and the linked lists below, and see Figure 11.1 as just a starting point for exploring your own interpretation of what using an enlightened planning approach can achieve if the capability-culture concerns are comprehensively addressed along with all other aspects of an EP approach. More generally, you need to see my variant of EP as a starting point for your own framework for considering capability-culture interdependencies in a 'systematic simplicity' framework relevant to you and your organisation, taking from this book whatever is most relevant to your organisation and integrating everything else of relevance in a coherent framework.

There are many ways you might use Figure 11.1. But the key intention is providing you with one possible basis for thinking about an overall conceptual framework for applying all the ideas in this book to help you and those you work with to smile in the sense that Figure 11.1 portrays and keep on smiling.

References

Ackoff, R.L. (1974) *Redesigning the Future*. John Wiley and Sons, Chichester.

Ackoff, R.L. and Sasieni, M.W. (1968) *Fundamentals of Operations Research*. John Wiley and Sons, New York.

AIRMIC/ALARM/IRM (2010) *A Structured Approach to Enterprise Risk Management (ERM) and the Requirements of ISO 31000*. Association of Insurance and Risk Managers (AIRMIC), Association of Local Authority Risk Managers (ALARM) and Institute of Risk Managers (IRM), London.

Ambrose, S.E. (1994) *D-Day, June 6, 1944: The Climatic Battle of World War II*. Touchstone, New York.

Ansoff, H.I. (1984) *Implanting Strategic Management*. Prentice-Hall International, Englewood Cliffs, NJ.

APM (1997) *PRAM Project Risk Analysis and Management Guide*. Association for Project Management (APM), Norwich.

APM (2004) *PRAM Project Risk Analysis and Management Guide*, second edition. Association for Project Management (APM), Norwich.

Baker, G. (2018) US capitalism: not dead yet. *The Times*, 27 October, Saturday review, 14.

Becker, H.S. (1983) Scenarios: a tool of growing importance to policy analysts in government and industry. *Technological Forecasting and Social Change*, 23, 95–120.

Biggs, J. and Tang, C. (2011) *Teaching for Quality Learning at University: What the Student Does*. Society for Research into Higher Education & Open University Press, McGraw Hill, Maidenhead.

Black, W. (2017) *Originals: How Non-Conformists Will Ultimately Disrupt the World of Risk Management*. Downloaded from www.linkedin.com/pulse/orginals-how-non-conformists-ultimately-disrupt-world-warren-black, 12 May 2017.

Boehm, B. and Turner, R. (2003) Using risk to balance agile and plan-driven methods. *Computer*, 36(6), 57–66.

Boehm, B. and Turner, R. (2004) Balancing agility and discipline: evaluating and integrating agile and plan-driven methods. *Proceedings of the 26th International Conference on Software Engineering*.

Byrne, L. (2017) Tech Kings must learn from our great entrepreneurs. *The Times*, 10 October, 26.

Carne, M. (2017) The state of rail. *Letters to the Editor, The Times*, 14 January, 26.

Carroll, L. (1865) *Alice's Adventures in Wonderland*, commonly contracted to *Alice in Wonderland*, Lewis Carroll being the pseudonym of Charles Lutwidge Dodgson. Use the web for a range of current publishers.

CCRM (2011) *Final Report on the Investigation of the Macondo Well Blowout*. Deepwater Horizon Study Group (DHSG) of the Centre for Catastrophic Risk Management (CCRM), The University of California at Berkeley, available online as a pdf.

Chapman, C.B. (1974) Modular portfolio selection: an introduction, in Dickinson, J.P. (editor), *Portfolio Analysis: Book of Readings*. Saxon House/Lexington Books, Farnborough.

Chapman, C.B. (1975) *Modular Demand Analysis: An Introduction in the Context of a Theoretical Basis for Consumer Demand Analysis*. Saxon House/Lexington Books, Farnborough.

Chapman, C.B. (1979) Large engineering project risk analysis. *IEEE Transactions on Engineering Management*, EM-26, 78–86.

Chapman, C.B. (1988) Science, engineering and economics: OR at the interface. *Journal of the Operational Research Society*, 39(1), 1–6.

Chapman, C.B. (1992a) *Risk Management: Predicting and Dealing with an Uncertain Future*. Exhibit #748, Province of Ontario Environmental Assessment Board Hearings on Ontario Hydro's Demand/Supply Plan, submitted by the Independent Power Producers Society of Ontario, 30 September.

Chapman, C.B. (1992b) My two cents worth on how OR should develop. *Journal of the Operational Research Society*, 43(7), 647–664.

Chapman, C.B. (2002) *Constructively Simple Probabilities: Taking the Guesswork out of Risk Management*. Eleventh Annual Symonds Lecture in Association with the Health and Safety Board of the Institution of Civil Engineers (ICE), London.

Chapman, C.B. and Cooper, D.F. (1983) Parametric discounting. *Omega – International Journal of Management Science*, 11(3), 303–310.

Chapman, C.B. and Cooper, D.F. (1985) A programmed equity redemption approach to the finance of public projects. *Managerial and Decision Economics*, 6(2), 112–118.

Chapman, C.B., Cooper, D.F. and Cammaert, A.B. (1984) Model and situation specific OR methods: risk engineering reliability analysis of an L.N.G. facility. *Journal of the Operational Research Society*, 35, 27–35.

Chapman, C.B., Cooper, D.F., Debelius, C.A. and Pecora, A.G. (1985) Problem solving methodology design on the run. *Journal of the Operational Research Society*, 36(9), 769–778.

Chapman, C.B., Cooper, D.F. and Page, M.J. (1987) *Management for Engineers*. John Wiley and Sons, Chichester.

Chapman, C.B. and Harwood, I. (2011) Optimal risk taking and risk mitigation, in Cochran, J.J. (editor in chief), *Wiley Encyclopaedia of Operations Research and Management Science*. John Wiley and Sons, New York.

Chapman, C.B. and Howden, M. (1997) Two phase parametric and probabilistic NPV calculations, with possible deferral of disposal of UK Nuclear Waste as an example. *Omega, International Journal of Management Science*, 25(6), 707–714.

Chapman, C.B. and Ward, S.C. (1992) Financial control of portfolio management decisions, in Ezzamel, M. and Heathfield, D. (editors), *Perspectives on Financial Control: Essays in Memory of Kenneth Hilton*. Chapman and Hall, London.

Chapman, C.B. and Ward, S.C. (1994) The efficient allocation of risk in contracts. *Omega – The International Journal of Management Science*, 22(6), 537–552.

Chapman, C.B. and Ward, S.C. (1996) Valuing the flexibility of alternative sources of power generation. *Energy Policy*, 24(2), 129–136.

Chapman, C.B. and Ward, S.C. (1997) *Project Risk Management: Processes, Techniques and Insights*. John Wiley and Sons, Chichester.

Chapman, C.B. and Ward, S.C. (2002) *Managing Project Risk and Uncertainty: A Constructively Simple Approach to Decision Making*. John Wiley and Sons, Chichester.

Chapman, C.B. and Ward, S.C. (2003) *Project Risk Management: Processes, Techniques and Insights*, second edition. John Wiley and Sons, Chichester.

Chapman, C.B. and Ward, S.C. (2008) Developing and implementing a balanced incentive and risk sharing contracts. *Construction Management and Economics*, 26(6), 659–669.

Chapman, C.B., Ward, S.C. and Bennell, J.A. (2000) Incorporating uncertainty in competitive bidding. *International Journal of Project Management*, 18(5), 337–347.

Chapman, C.B., Ward, S.C., Cooper, D.F. and Page, M.J. (1984) Credit policy and inventory control. *Journal of the Operational Research Society*, 8(12), 1055–1065.

Chapman, C.B., Ward, S.C. and Klein, J.H. (2006) An optimized multiple test framework for project selection in the public sector, with a nuclear waste disposal case-based example. *International Journal of Project Management*, 24, 373–384.

Chapman, C.B. and Ward, S.C. (2011) *How to Manage Project Opportunity and Risk: Why Uncertainty Management Can Be a Much Better Approach than Risk Management*. John Wiley and Sons, Chichester.

Checkland, P.B. (1981) *Systems Thinking, Systems Practice*. John Wiley and Sons, Chichester.

Checkland, P.B. and Scholes, J. (1990) *Soft Systems Methodology in Action*. John Wiley and Sons, Chichester.

Churchman, C.W., Ackoff, R.L. and Arnoff, E.L. (1957) *Introduction to Operations Research*. John Wiley and Sons, New York.

Coleman, A. (2017) When doing good is great for business: socially responsible franchising is a growing trend which can benefit business and the community. *Raconteur Insert in The Times*, 5 September.

Cooper, R. (1995) *When Lean Enterprises Collide: Competing Through Confrontation*. Harvard Business School Press, Boston.

Cooper, D.F., Bosnich, P.M., Grey, S.J., Purdy, G., Raymond, G.A., Walker, P. and Wood, M.J. (2014) *Project Risk Guidelines: Managing Risk with ISO 31000 and IEC 62198*. John Wiley and Sons, Chichester.

Cooper, D.F. and Chapman, C.B. (1987) *Risk Analysis for Large Projects: Models, Methods and Cases*. John Wiley and Sons, Chichester.

Cooper, D.F., Grey, S., Geoffrey, R. and Walker, P. (2005) *Project Risk Guidelines: Managing Risk in Large Projects and Complex Procurements*. John Wiley and Sons, Chichester.

Cox, L.A. (2008) What's wrong with risk matrices? *Risk Analysis*, 28(2), 497–512.

Crossland, D. (2017) Carmakers 'colluded on technology for years'. *The Times*, 22 July, 53.

Curtis, B., Ward, S.C. and Chapman, C.B. (1991) *Roles, Responsibilities and Risks in Management Contracting (Special Publication 81)*. Construction Industry Research and Information Association (CIRIA), London.

Dasgupta, A. and Dasgupta, S. (1966) *Crop-Planning in a Risky Environment*. Read to the European Meeting of the Econometric Society, Warsaw.

DoE (1994) *Review of Radioactive Waste Management Policy Preliminary Conclusions: A Consultative Document, Radioactive Substances Division*. Department of the Environment (DoE), London.

Dowie, J. (1999) Against risk. *Risk Decision and Policy*, 4(1), 57–73.

Dublin, C.I. and Lotka, A.J. (1930) *The Money Value of a Man*. Ronald Press, New York.

Duckert, G.H. (2010) *Practical Enterprise Risk Management: A Business Process Approach*. John Wiley and Sons, Chichester.

Eden, C. (1988) Cognative mapping, a review. *European Journal of Operational Research*, 4, 1–13.

Fischoff, B. (1982) For those condemned to study the past: heuristics and biases in hindsight, Chapter 23, in Kahneman, D., Slovic, P. and Tversky, A. (editors), *Judgment Under Uncertainty: Heuristics and Biases*. Cambridge University Press, New York.

Flood, R.L. (1999) *Rethinking the Fifth Discipline: Learning Within the Unknowable*. Routledge, London and New York.

Flyvbjerg, B., Bruzelius, N. and Rothengatter, W. (2003) *Megaprojects and Risk: An Anatomy of Ambition*. Cambridge University Press, Cambridge.

Friedman, L. (1956) A competitive bidding strategy. *Operations Research*, 4, 104–112.

Gawande, A. (2011) *The Checklist Manifesto: How to Get Things Right*. Profile Books Ltd, London.

Gold, B. and Vassell, C. (2015) Using risk management to balance agile methods: a study of the Scrum process. *2015 2nd International Conference on Knowledge-Based Engineering and Innovation (KBEI)*.

Goodwin, P. and Wright, G. (2014) *Decision Analysis for Management Judgement*, fifth edition. John Wiley and Sons, Chichester.

Greenspan, A. and Wooldridge, A. (2018) *Capitalism in America: A History*. Allen Lane, London.

Grey, S. (1995) *Practical Risk Assessment for Project Management*. John Wiley and Sons, Chichester.

Harari, Y.N. (2014) *Sapiens: A Brief History of Humankind*. Harvill Secker, London.

Hardy, C. and Macquire, S. (2016) Organising risk: discourse, power and "riskification". *Academy of Management Review*, 41(1), 80–108.

Hawkins, C.J. and Pearce, D.W. (1971) *Capital Investment Appraisal*. Macmillan Studies in Economics, Macmillan, London.

Hertz, D.B. (1964) Risk analysis in capital investment. *Harvard Business Review*, 42(1), 95–106.

Hillson, D. (2004) *Effective Opportunity Management for Projects: Exploiting Positive Risk*. Marcel Dekker, Inc, New York.

Hillson, D. (2009) *Managing Risk in Projects*. Gower, Abingdon, Oxon.

Hillson, D. (2012) *History of the Special Interest Group on Project Risk Management of the Association for Project Management*. APM Press Limited, High Wycombe.

HM Treasury (2003a) *The Green Book: Appraisal and Evaluation in Central Government*. HM Treasury, 1 Horse Guards Road, London SW1A 2HQ.

HM Treasury (2003b) *The Green Book Supplementary Guidance – Optimism Bias*. Downloaded from www.hm-treasury.gov.uk, November 2010.

HM Treasury (2014) *Improving Infrastructure Delivery: Project Initiation Route Map Handbook*. Downloaded from www.gov.uk/government/organisations/infrastucture-uk, February 2015.

Hopkinson, M. (2011) *The Project Risk Maturity Model: Measuring and Improving Risk Management Capability*. Gower, Farnham, Surrey.

Hopkinson, M. (2016) *Net Present Value and Risk Modelling for Projects*. Gower, Farnham, Surrey.

Hopkinson, M., Close, P., Hillson, D. and Ward, S. (2008) *Prioritising Project Risks: A Short Guide to Useful Techniques*. Association for Project Management (APM), Princes Risborough, Bucks.

Humble, J., Molesky, J. and O'Reilly, B. (2015) *Lean Enterprise: How High Performance Organisations Innovate at Scale*. O'Reilly Media, Sebastopol, CA.

Hyde, L. (2006) *The Gift: How the Creative Spirit Transforms the World*. First published in the US and Canada in 1983 by Random House, Cannongate, Edinburgh.

ICE and IFoA (1998) *RAMP Risk Analysis and Management for Projects*. Institution of Civil Engineers (ICE) and the Institute and Faculty of Actuaries (IFoA). Thomas Telford, London.

ICE and IFoA (2005) *RAMP Risk Analysis and Management for Projects – A Strategic Framework for Managing Project Risk and its Financial Implications*, second edition. Institution of Civil Engineers (ICE) and the Institute and Faculty of Actuaries (IFoA). Thomas Telford, London.

International Standard (2009) *ISO 31000 Risk Management – Principles and Guidelines*. ISO, Switzerland.

Johnson, L. (2017) Every board needs a member of the awkward squad. *The Sunday Times*, 7 May, 12.

Johnson, L. (2018) Bosses discover it pays dividends to put workers first. *The Sunday Times*, 24 June, 9.

Kahneman, D. (2012) *Thinking, Fast and Slow*. Penguin Books, London.

Kahneman, D., Slovic, P. and Tversky, A. (1982) *Judgment Under Uncertainty: Heuristics and Biases*. Cambridge University Press, New York.

Kaplan, R.S. and Norton, D.P. (1992) The balanced scorecard – Measures that drive performance. *Harvard Business Review*, 70(1), 71–79.

Kaplan, R.S. and Norton, D.P. (1993a) Putting the balanced scorecard to work. *Harvard Business Review*, 71(5), 134–147.

Kaplan, R.S. and Norton, D.P. (1993b) Using the balanced scorecard as a strategic management system. *Harvard Business Review*, 71(1), 75–85.

Kaplan, R.S. and Norton, D.P. (1996) *The Balanced Scorecard: Translating Strategy into Action*. Harvard Business School Press, Boston.

Kennedy, P. (2014) *Engineers of Victory: The Problem Solvers Who Turned the Tide in the Second World War*. Penguin Books, London.

Keeney, R.L. and Raiffa, H. (1976) *Decisions with Multiple Objectives*. John Wiley and Sons, New York.

King, M. (2016) *The End of Alchemy: Money, Banking and the Future of the Global Economy*. Little, Brown Book Group, London.

King, M. and Mercer, A. (1985) Problems in determining bidding strategies. *Journal of the Operational Research Society*, 36, 915–923.

King, M. and Mercer, A. (1991) Distributions in competitive bidding. *Journal of the Operational Research Society*, 42(2), 151.

Knight, F. (1921) *Risk, Uncertainty and Profit*. Houghton Mifflin, Boston.

Lea, R. (2017a) Chinese in the driving seat with deal for Volvo Lorries. *The Times*, 28 December, 43.

Lea, R. (2017b) Water firms risking their own demise. *The Times*, 18 October, 37.

Leitch, M. (2008) *Intelligent Internal Control and Risk Management*. Gower, Aldershot, Hants.

Leitch, M. (2013) *Working in uncertainty: What is 'risk culture' and how can 'risk culture' be Changed*. Downloaded from www.workinginuncertainty.co.uk/risk_culture.shtml, 14 November 2013.

Lewis, M. (2017) *The Undoing Project: A Friendship that Changed the World*. Penguin Random House, London.

Lichtenberg, S. (2000) *Proactive Management of Uncertainty using the Successive Principle*. Polyteknisk Press, Copenhagen.

MacNulty, A.A.R. (1977) Scenario development for corporate planning. *Futures*, 9(2), 128–138.

Markowitz, H. (1959) *Portfolio Selection: Efficient Diversification of Investments*. John Wiley and Sons, New York.

Marsh, B. (1991) *Coping with uncertainty: rational investment*. Paper presented at 'Chaos Forecasting and Risk Assessment', Join Strategic and Operational Research Society Conference. London, February.

Marshall, T. (2015) *Prisoners of Geography: Ten Maps That Tell You Everything You Need to Know About Global Politics*. Elliot and Thompson Limited, London.

Mintzberg, H. (1994) *The Rise and Fall of Strategic Planning*. Prentice Hall, New York.

Mintzberg, H., Ahlstrand, B. and Lampel, J. (1998) *Strategy Safari*. Prentice Hall Europe, Hemel Hempstead.

Moder, J.J. and Philips, C.R. (1970) *Project Management with CPM and PERT*. Van Nostrand, New York.

Morris, P.W.G. (2009) Implementing strategy through project management: the importance of managing the project front end. Chapter 2, in Williams, T.M., Samset, K. and Suannevag, K.J. (editors), *Making Essential Choices with Scant Information: Front End Decision Making in Major Projects*. Palgrave Macmillan, Basingstoke.

Morris, P.W.G. (2013) *Reconstructing Project Management*. John Wiley and Sons, Chichester.

Muller, R. and Turner, J.R. (2010) *Project-Oriented Leadership*. Gower, Abingdon, Oxon.

Nichols, M. (2007) *Review of Highways Agency's Major Roads Programmer: Report to the Secretary of State for Transport*. Nichols Group London. Available on the Department for Transport (UK) website at www.dft.gov.uk/pgr/roads/nicholsreport/NUREG (1975) *US Nuclear Regulatory Commission Reactor Safety Study – An Assessment of Accident Risk in US Commercial Power Plants*. WASH-1400, NUREG-75/014.

Overman, S. (2014) *The Conscience Economy: How a Mass Movement for Good is Great for Business*. Bibliomotion, Brookline, MA 02445.

Pagnamenta, R. (2017) Fukushima disaster is still radiating fallout nuclear industry wishes to avoid. *The Times*, 3 August, 41.

Pearce, I.F. (1964) *A Contribution to Demand Analysis*. Oxford University Press, Oxford.

Pearson, G. (2012) *The Road to Co-operation: Escaping the Bottom Line*. Gower, Farnham Surrey and Ashgate Publishing Company, Burlington Vermont USA.

Perrow, C. (1984) *Normal Accidents: Living with High Risk Systems*. Basic Books, New York.

Perrow, C. (1994) Accidents in high risk systems. *Technology Studies*, 1(1).

Pidd, M. (1996) *Tools for Thinking: Modelling in Management Science*. John Wiley and Sons, Chichester.

Pinto, J.K. (2016) *Project Management: Achieving Competitive Advantage*, fourth edition. Pearson, USA.

PMI (2008) Project risk management, Chapter 11, in *A Guide to the Project Management Body of Knowledge (PMBOK® Guide)*, fourth edition. Project Management Institute (PMI) Inc, Newtown Square, Pennsylvania.

PMI (2009) *Practice Standard for Project Risk Management*. Project Management Institute (PMI) Inc, Newtown Square, Pennsylvania.

PMI (2013) Project risk management, Chapter 11, in *A guide to the Project Management Body of Knowledge (PMBOK® Guide)*, fifth edition. Project Management Institute (PMI) Inc, Newtown Square, Pennsylvania.

PMI (2017a) Project risk management, Chapter 11, in *A guide to the Project Management Body of Knowledge (PMBOK® Guide)*, sixth edition. Project Management Institute (PMI) Inc, Newtown Square, Pennsylvania.

PMI (2017b) *Waterfall Methodology Agile Approach*. Downloaded from www.pmi.org/learning/library/waterfall-methodology-agile-approach-5821, 17 April 2017.

Purves, L. (2017) Small acts of kindness that can save a life. *The Times*, 3 July, 27.

Rail Safety and Standards Board (2006) *RSSB T430 – Definition of VPF & the Impact of Societal Concerns – Final 30/1/2006*. Oxford Risk Research and Analysis, Clarendon Enterprise Centre, Oxford.

Raiffa, H. (1968) *Decision Analysis: Introductory Lectures on Choices Under Uncertainty*. Addison Wesley, Reading, MA.

Reason, J. (1990) *Human Error*. Cambridge University Press, Cambridge.

Reason, J. (1997) *Managing the Risks of Organizational Accidents*. Ashgate, Farnham Surrey.

Ricard, M. (2018) *Altruism: The Science and Psychology of Kindness*. Atlantic Books, London. Earlier hardback edition 2015, French edition 2013.

Rifkind, H. (2017) For generation rent, owning things is history. *The Times*, 3 October, 31.

Rivett, P. (1994) *The Craft of Decision Modelling*. John Wiley and Sons, Chichester.

Rivett, B.H.P. and Ackoff, R.L. (1967) *A Manager's Guide to Operational Research*. John Wiley and Sons, Chichester.

Rosenhead, J. (1989) *Rational Analysis for a Problematic World: Problem Structuring Methods for Complexity, Uncertainty and Conflict*. John Wiley and Sons, Chichester.

Rosenhead, J. and Mingers, J. (2001) *Rational Analysis for a Problematic World Revisited: Problem Structuring Methods for Complexity, Uncertainty and Conflict*, second edition. John Wiley and Sons, Chichester.

Rubin, K. (2013) *Essential Scrum*. Addison-Wesley, Upper Saddle River, NJ.

Ruthkopf, M.H. (1983) *Auctions, Bidding and Contracting: Uses and Theory*. New York University Press, New York.

Samuelson, W. (1986) Bidding for contracts. *Management Science*, 32(12), 1533–1550.

Sasieni, M.W., Yaspan, A. and Friedman, L. (1959) *Operations Research: Methods and Problems*. John Wiley and Sons, New York.

Schoemaker, P.J.H. (1992) How to link strategic vision to core capabilities. *Sloan Management Review*, 34(1), 67–72.

Schoemaker, P.J.H. (1995) Scenario planning: a tool for strategic thinking. *Sloan Management Review*, 36(2), 25–40.

Senge, P.M. (1990) *The Fifth Discipline: The Art and Practice of the Learning Organization.* Doubleday, New York.

Taleb, N.N. (2007) *The Black Swan: The Impact of the Highly Improbable.* Allen Lane and Penguin Books Ltd, London.

Tamiz, M., Jones, D. and Romero, C. (1998) Goal programming for decision making: an overview of the current state-of-the-art. *European Journal of Operational Research,* 111, 569–581.

Taylor, F.W. (1911) *The Principles of Scientific Management.* Harper and Brothers, New York and London.

Temple, M. (2016) *First Public Address as Chair of the Health and Safety Executive: Twenty Fifth Capita Health and Safety Lecture.* The Royal College of Surgeons, London.

Toffler, A. (1970) *Future Shock.* Random House, London.

Turner, J.R. (1992) *The Handbook of Project Based Management: Improving Processes for Achieving Your Strategic Objectives.* McGraw-Hill, New York.

Turner, J.R. (2014) *Gower Handbook of Project Management,* fifth edition. Gower Press Aldershot.

Tweedley, N. (1995) *Winning the Bid: A Manager's Guide to Competitive Bidding.* Financial Times Pitman, London.

van der Heijden, K. (1996) *Scenarios: The Art of Strategic Conversations.* John Wiley and Sons, Chichester.

Ward, S.C. (1989) Arguments for constructively simple models. *Journal of the Operational Research Society,* 40(2), 141–153.

Ward, S.C. (2005) *Risk Management Organisation and Management.* Institute of Risk Management (IRM) Series. Witherby & Co. Ltd, London.

Ward, S.C. and Chapman, C.B. (1994) Choosing contractor payment terms. *International Journal of Project Management,* 12(4), 216–221.

Ward, S.C. and Chapman, C.B. (1995) Evaluating fixed price incentive contracts. *Omega – The International Journal of Management Science,* 23(1), 49–62.

Ward, S.C. and Chapman, C.B. (2008) Stakeholders and uncertainty management in projects. *Construction Management and Economics,* 26(6), 563–578.

Ward, S.C., Chapman, C.B. and Curtis, B. (1991) On the allocation of risk in construction projects. *International Journal of Project Management,* 9(3), 140–147.

Williams, T.M. (2002) *Modelling Complex Projects.* John Wiley and Sons, Chichester.

Williams, T.M., Samset, K. and Suannevag, K.J. (2009) *Making Essential Choices with Scant Information: Front End Decision Making in Major Projects.* Palgrave Macmillan, Basingstoke.

Williams, T.M. and Samset, K.J. (2012) *Project Governance: Getting Investments Right.* Palgrave Macmillan, Basingstoke.

Woods, D.D., Dekker, S., Cook, R., Johannesen, L. and Starter, N. (2010) *Beyond Human Error,* second edition. Ashgate Publishing Ltd, Farnham Surrey.

Woolsey, R.E.D. (2003) *Real World Operations Research: The Woolsey Papers.* Abe Books, USA.

Wynne, B. (1992) Uncertainty and environmental learning – Reconceiving science and policy in the preventative paradigm. *Global Environmental Change,* June, 111–127.

Yamane, T. (1973) *Statistics: An Introductory Analysis,* third edition. Harper & Row, New York.

Zenger, T. (2016) *Beyond Competitive Advantage.* Harvard Business Review Press, Cambridge, MA.

Website information

The website associated with this book may be accessed using www.enlightenedplanning.uk website address.

The short-term plan is to launch this website shortly after the book's publication, using it to support those who want to use aspects of this book when leading professional courses and workshops for practitioners and their managers, including board-level managers, or teaching university courses. Initial support focuses on perspectives and areas of application where I have relevant experience to share in terms of slides, case studies, and other material which might be useful. I plan to provide papers on a few particular aspects of enlightened planning and more general systematic simplicity concerns.

I also plan to indicate websites with relevant papers and other material created by others that I am aware of with a view to contributing to a wider discussion of systematic simplicity approaches. As one example, my colleague Matthew Leitch, who provided a contribution to the 'Comments by other colleagues' section in the front of this book, has included his website address, and one paper available on it has been cited and included in this book's references, illustrating one website address with papers directly relevant to enlightened planning which I plan to list on the book's website. As another example, Stephen Cresswell, who also provided a contribution to the 'Comments by other colleagues' section and included his website address, has papers plus other material you may find helpful available on his website, illustrating further kinds of material which others might make available in a similar manner via their website addresses on this book's website.

Suggestions for further material directly relevant to enlightened planning or systematic simplicity and an address to access it will be sought via this book's website. The long-term plan is this book's website evolving to provide access to material provided by myself and others which I am aware of and can help to make others aware of in a manner which is as balanced and non-judgemental as possible on a simple website.

Index

Note: page numbers in *italic* indicate a figure and page numbers in **bold** indicate a table on the corresponding page.